CCIE Routing and Switching v5.1 Foundations

Bridging the Gap Between CCNP and CCIE

Narbik Kocharians, CCIE No. 12410 (R&S, Security, SP)

Cisco Press

800 East 96th Street

Indianapolis, Indiana 46240 USA

CCIE Routing and Switching v5.1 Foundations

Narbik Kocharians

Copyright © 2017 Pearson Education, Inc

Published by:
Cisco Press
800 East 96th Street
Indianapolis, IN 46240 USA

Printed in the United States of America

1 17

Library of Congress Control Number: 2017935919

ISBN-13: 978-1-58714-472-1

ISBN-10: 1-58714-472-7

Warning and Disclaimer

This book is designed to provide information about the skills necessary to bridge the skills gap between the CCNP Routing and Switching Exams and the CCIE Routing and Switching Exam. Every effort has been made to make this book as complete and as accurate as possible, but no warranty or fitness is implied.

The information is provided on an "as is" basis. The authors, Cisco Press, and Cisco Systems, Inc., shall have neither liability nor responsibility to any person or entity with respect to any loss or damages arising from the information contained in this book or from the use of the discs or programs that may accompany it.

The opinions expressed in this book belong to the author and are not necessarily those of Cisco Systems, Inc.

Trademark Acknowledgments

All terms mentioned in this book that are known to be trademarks or service marks have been appropriately capitalized. Cisco Press or Cisco Systems, Inc., cannot attest to the accuracy of this information. Use of a term in this book should not be regarded as affecting the validity of any trademark or service mark.

Special Sales

For information about buying this title in bulk quantities, or for special sales opportunities (which may include electronic versions; custom cover designs; and content particular to your business, training goals, marketing focus, or branding interests), please contact our corporate sales department at corpsales@pearsoned.com or (800) 382-3419.

For government sales inquiries, please contact governmentsales@pearsoned.com.

For questions about sales outside the U.S., please contact intlcs@pearson.com.

Feedback Information

At Cisco Press, our goal is to create in-depth technical books of the highest quality and value. Each book is crafted with care and precision, undergoing rigorous development that involves the unique expertise of members from the professional technical community.

Readers' feedback is a natural continuation of this process. If you have any comments regarding how we could improve the quality of this book, or otherwise alter it to better suit your needs, you can contact us through email at feedback@ciscopress.com. Please make sure to include the book title and ISBN in your message.

We greatly appreciate your assistance.

Editor-in-Chief: Mark Taub

Product Line Manager: Brett Bartow

Business Operation Manager, Cisco Press: Ronald Fligge

Managing Editor: Sandra Schroeder

Development Editor: Eleanor Bru

Project Editor: Mandie Frank

Copy Editor: Bart Reed

Technical Editors: Terry Vinson, Jeff Denton

Editorial Assistant: Vanessa Evans

Cover Designer: Chuti Prasertsith

Composition: codeMantra

Indexer: Erika Millen

Proofreader: Larry Sulky

CISCO.

Americas Headquarters
Cisco Systems, Inc.
San Jose, CA

Asia Pacific Headquarters
Cisco Systems (USA) Pte. Ltd.
Singapore

Europe Headquarters
Cisco Systems International BV Amsterdam,
The Netherlands

Cisco has more than 200 offices worldwide. Addresses, phone numbers, and fax numbers are listed on the Cisco Website at **www.cisco.com/go/offices**.

About the Author

Narbik Kocharians, CCIE No. 12410 (Routing and Switching, Service Provider, and Security) is a triple CCIE with more than 40 years of experience in this industry. He has designed, implemented, and supported numerous enterprise networks.

Narbik is the president of Micronics Networking and Training, Inc. (www.micronicstraining.com), where almost all Cisco authorized and custom courses are conducted, including CCIE-DC, CCIE-SP, CCIE-RS, CCIE-Security, and CCDE classes.

About the Technical Reviewers

Terry Vinson, CCIE No. 35347 (Routing and Switching, Data Center), is a seasoned instructor with nearly 25 years of experience teaching and writing technical courses and training materials. Terry has taught and developed training content as well as provided technical consulting for high-end firms in the Northern Virginia/Washington, D.C. area. His technical expertise lies in the Cisco arena, with a focus on all routing and switching technologies as well as the latest data center technologies, including Nexus switching, unified computing, and storage-area networking (SAN) technologies. Terry currently teaches CCIE R&S and Data Center Bootcamps for Micronics Training, Inc., and enjoys sailing and game design in his "free time."

Jeffrey A. Denton is a network engineer leading the protection of secure enterprise network systems. Offering more than 12 years of experience designing, deploying, and supporting comprehensive networks for classified, defense-related systems integral to national security, he is an expert at leading complex projects and managing all phases of network installation, administration, and monitoring. Jeff is currently the network team lead for General Dynamics in Kabul, Afghanistan.

Dedication

I like to dedicate this book to my wife Janet, my children (Christopher, Patrick, Alexandra, and Daniel), and my students, colleagues, and friends.

Acknowledgments

I am thankful to God for giving me the opportunity to teach and write labs, which I truly love. I'd like to thank Janet, my wife of 31 years, for her encouragement and hard work in dealing with the day-to-day management of our training and consulting company. I'd like to thank both Terry Vinson and Jeff Denton for tech-editing this book in such a meticulous manner—thank you for an excellent job. Finally, I'd like to thank Brett Bartow and Eleanor Bru for their patience and constant changing of the deadline.

Contents at a Glance

Online element: Appendix A Configuration Files

Contents

Reader Services

Register your copy at www.ciscopress.com/title/9781587144721 for convenient access to downloads, updates, and corrections as they become available. To start the registration process, go to www.ciscopress.com/register and log in or create an account*. Enter the product ISBN 9781587144721 and click Submit. Once the process is complete, you will find any available bonus content under Registered Products.

*Be sure to check the box that you would like to hear from us to receive exclusive discounts on future editions of this product.

Icons Used in This Book

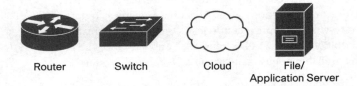

Router   Switch   Cloud   File/
                                               Application Server

Command Syntax Conventions

The conventions used to present command syntax in this book are the same conventions used in the IOS Command Reference. The Command Reference describes these conventions as follows:

- **Boldface** indicates commands and keywords that are entered literally as shown. In actual configuration examples and output (not general command syntax), boldface indicates commands that are manually input by the user (such as a **show** command).

- *Italic* indicates arguments for which you supply actual values.

- Vertical bars (|) separate alternative, mutually exclusive elements.

- Square brackets ([ ]) indicate an optional element.

- Braces ({ }) indicate a required choice.

- Braces within brackets ([{ }]) indicate a required choice within an optional element.

Introduction

This book is designed to bridge the knowledge gap for those who are functional and well prepared in CCNP-level technologies. One of the biggest issues in preparing for the CCIE Routing and Switching exam is the significant gap between being a functional, well-trained network professional and the level of knowledge and experience needed to be a well-prepared CCIE candidate. This book is intended to provide significant hands-on exercises in all the critical domains of knowledge needed to prepare for the extensive demands of the CCIE examination. Industry leaders were consulted for technical accuracy throughout this book.

Who Should Read This Book?

This book is designed for those Routing and Switching Engineers and technologists who want to prepare for the CCIE Routing and Switching exam, or those looking for the equivalent knowledge. The reader is expected to have a network professional-level certification or the equivalent field experience.

How to Access the Lab Configuration Files

This book comes complete with the lab configuration files, which we have made available to you online. To access these files, simply register this book (ISBN: 9781587144721) at www.ciscopress.com/register. You will be asked to answer a security question based on the content of the book to verify your purchase. Once you have registered your book, you can access the lab files by going to your account page, clicking on the Registered Products tab, and then clicking the Access Bonus Content link under your registered book.

How This Book Is Organized

Chapter 1, "Physical Topology": In this chapter, we explore the topology that will be used in subsequent chapters. The hope is to provide a clear and detailed explanation of the physical interconnection between devices that will be used to explore the technologies and features contained in this book.

Chapter 2, "Physical and Logical Topologies": After decades of working with CCIE Candidates I have learned that there are some fundamental levels of knowledge that most students are missing. Among them is the ability to differentiate between physical and logical topologies. A well-prepared candidate should have an absolute mastery of the syntax and processes needed to discover the physical topology for any network deployment. Chapter 2 of this book focuses on that specific skill set.

Chapter 3, "Spanning Tree Protocol": We explore all things Layer 2 in this chapter. In the Routing and Switching exam, the key focus seems to be on the Layer 3 components of routing; however, without a seamless Layer 2 infrastructure, routing protocols will not work. In fact, not even the most basic of IP communications can take place. We will focus on this very critical network element that prevents the formation of bridging loops.

Chapter 4, "Point-to-Point Protocol": PPP in all its various flavors has been a long-time "go-to" technology to support wide area networking (WAN) infrastructures. However, in recent years, with the advent of Ethernet-based WAN deployments, we have found ourselves needing the traditional serial-based functionality in the context of Ethernet interconnectivity. This makes understanding how to deploy Point-to-Point Protocol over Ethernet a very important skill. This chapter explores its deployment, optimization, and capabilities.

Chapter 5, "DMVPN": Dynamic Multipoint Virtual Private Networks are the replacement for Frame Relay technologies in the context of the CCIE Routing and Switching exam. I personally feel that knowledge of DMVPN is a critical skill for anyone working in a modern network enterprise, but I have also observed that it is one of least understood domains in the CCIE exam. As a direct result of this observation, I first deal with the fundamental technologies that enable DMVPN and its operation. Once these have been highlighted, I provide very clear delineations between the DMVPN operational phases and behaviors, recognizing that there absolutely has to be a concrete understanding of these elements before you can even hope to understand how a routing protocol behaves when running on top of a DMVPN.

Chapter 6, "IP Prefix-List": IP Prefix-List has applications in almost every aspect of prefix filtering and packet filtering. IP prefix lists offer capabilities to match traffic based on variable ranges of networks and mask lengths. This tool, unlike other pattern-matching tools such as access lists, allows us to match multiple aspects of a network simultaneously. This chapter explores all aspects of prefix lists as independent tools.

Chapter 7, "EIGRP": Enhanced Interior Gateway Protocol figures significantly into the makeup of the CCIE RS Lab exam. This demands a concrete understanding of both classical and named operations. This book looks at the operation of both these modes from a command-line perspective as well as covers how the two modes can and do interoperate between enabled devices. But whether you are running named or classic mode, as a candidate you need to master how to manipulate the protocol. This chapter covers both basic and advanced EIGRP operations. EIGRP is the first protocol that provides granular traffic engineering and prefix filtering, as well as various methods for injecting default routes. All these capabilities are covered in the hands-on labs in this chapter.

Chapter 8, "OSPF": Single handedly, OSPF is responsible for more failed CCIE attempts than any other protocol (including BGP). I have observed that most candidates do not have a firm understanding of what actually takes place behind the scenes with OSPF. OSPF has many varying modes and enhancements that make it difficult to master. Route filtering, LSA operation, various stub configurations, and update filtering are just a handful of the protocol's operational aspects that need to be managed. The labs in this chapter illustrate the function and configuration of each of these topics. We focus on how OSPF operates in single- and multi-area configurations as well as on how to manipulate its behavior in every way possible.

Chapter 9, "Redistribution": When you talk to students that are preparing for the CCIE Lab Exam, most will tell you that they are terrified of redistribution. This is a direct result of Grey Market Trainers flooding the Internet with horrendously complex and error-fraught redistribution labs. The average student sees this and is immediately intimidated by what should be a straightforward routing mechanism. What are missing are the foundational basics associated with how to perform redistribution, and what happens when you do. My approach to the topic is to discuss the methodology and situations where redistribution can be problematic. Again this will be illustrated in labs that focus on the types of loops that can be generated, how to mitigate loops that have occurred, and procedures that will insure they never occur.

Chapter 10, "Border Gateway Protocol": Border Gateway Protocol introduces complexity based on its overall scope and capability to "tune" or engineer control plane exchange based on attributes. These attributes far exceed the capabilities of protocols such as RIPv2, EIGRP, and even OSPF. This brings with it an ordered approach to how to conduct configuration and some interesting configuration syntax based on the desired manner of deployment. First, this chapter focuses on a concrete understanding of BGP's complex Adjacency State Machine capabilities. After the introduction of both the internal and external peering mechanisms employed by the protocol, we explore how and what next-hop information is exchanged, plus we explore how to manipulate these basic operations. From there, we explore how to manipulate attributes or decisions based on attributes via ACLs, prefix lists, route maps, and regular expressions. Lastly, we focus on mechanisms designed to simplify BGP configuration by providing reduced command sets, behavior optimizations, and streamlined configuration syntax.

Chapter 11, "IPv6": Gone are the days of being able to focus just on IPv4 addressing and routing protocols. IPv6 figures significantly into the CCIE Routing and Switching exam in that the exam requires a full understanding of the variants of protocols that support IPv6. Additionally, this chapter explores the operation of IPv6 in non-broadcast multi-access (NBMA) topologies such as DMVPN.

Chapter 12, "Quality of Service": Given that the majority of QOS mechanisms that involve hardware-optimized operation have been removed from the exam, it is important to focus intently on what remains. This chapter explores the key fundamentals of QOS in the IOS-driven enterprise. This includes all aspects of marking and classification of traffic via enhanced and traditional mechanisms. Lastly, the chapter deals with the manipulations of such traffic after it has been marked. Emphasis is given to both policing and shaping of traffic. This focuses on both classical serial WAN connections and high-speed Ethernet WAN connections.

Chapter 13, "IPSec VPN": The focus of the CCIE Routing and Switching Lab has expanded significantly in its last iterations. This expansion has included the incorporation of site-to-site solutions such as GRE/IPSec Tunnel mode as well as multisite VPN technologies and their protection/encryption. This chapter covers the application of encryption on these tunnels and VPNs from a command-line level. At this point, you should be able to apply encryption to DMVPNs. By waiting until this point in the lab exploration, you are able to better separate the DMVPN configuration task requirements from the necessary encryption and security configurations.

Chapter 14, "Multicast": This chapter explores solutions that require end-to-end IPv4 and IPv6 transport between all devices. This includes protocol-independent routing optimizations such as policy-based routing, First Hop Redundancy Protocols and network address translation.

Chapter 15, "MPLS and L3VPNs": MPLS and L3VPNs are tested heavily in the CCIE Routing and Switching Lab exam. This chapter takes a step-by-step approach to demonstrating the operational capabilities and deployment concerns involved in VPNv4 tunnels. Specific focus is given to the protocols running between the customer edge and premises edge equipment.

Chapter 1

Physical Topology

This book focuses on the commands and methodologies necessary to deploy technologies in a Cisco Routing and Switching environment. This means that if you want to follow along on a task-by-task basis, you will need a lab environment that supports the commands and verification mechanisms this book provides. I consider this an invaluable part of the learning process. All procedural tasks in this book are performed against a specific arrangement of equipment. This chapter illustrates exactly how this equipment will be connected (using both Ethernet and serial interconnections) so that you can create your own training environment.

It should be noted that the CCIE Lab Exam employs two variations of Cisco IOS. Those two versions are relative to routers and switches. In the actual lab, the routers run the 15.3T Universal Software release; this version can be supported on the ISR 2900 Series routers. If you have the ability to acquire access to physical devices, this version of the IOS will support all possible technologies and features that can be seen in the lab. Additionally, the switching environment runs IOS 15.0SE Universal (IP Services). This is supported on the Catalyst 3560X Series switches. It is understood and expected that the majority of readers will not have access to these physical devices. If this is the case for you, it is suggested that you do as much as possible via emulation/virtualization (which may or may not support the IOS versions just listed) using the tools mentioned in this chapter. This leaves you with just a small subset of protocols and features that require rack rental or access to physical equipment.

Physical Layout of Switching Devices

In keeping with how most networks are designed, we will turn our attention to the Layer 2 switching environment we will use to perform all labs found in this book. We begin with a specific arrangement of four Cisco switches. The switches used in this book have Fast Ethernet ports, although switches with Gigabit Ethernet ports can also be used.

If you use switches with Gigabit Ethernet ports, you have to keep in mind that when the book asks you to configure interface **fastethernet0/1**, you will have to configure interface **gigabitethernet0/1** instead. These switches will be connected by a series of Ethernet connections, as illustrated in Figure 1-1.

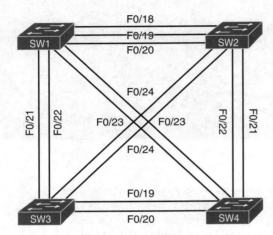

Figure 1-1   *Physical Topology—Switches*

This arrangement of devices provides a full mesh of redundant connects that support both basic and advanced switching features such as trunks and Ether-channels, while simultaneously providing serviceable links that can be employed to create a wide range of logical topologies. We explore logical topologies verses physical topologies in Chapter 2, "Physical and Logical Topologies."

Whereas Figure 1-1 outlines the core switching infrastructure used in this book, Figure 1-2 illustrates how the routing—or Layer 3 components—will be connected to this Layer 2 core.

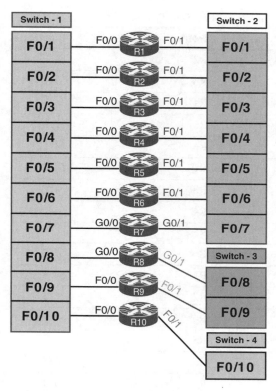

Figure 1-2 *Physical Topology—Router Connections to Switches*

As you can see in Figure 1-2, we have 10 routers that will be physically connected via Ethernet cables to each of the four switches illustrated in Figure 1-1. All routers will be connected to Switch-1 via their FastEthernet0/0 interfaces. However, to facilitate the creation of more diverse Layer 3 topologies, the FastEthernet0/1 interfaces of each router will connect to different switches. Figure 1-2 illustrates how these connections are dispersed between the remaining physical switches.

Serial Interconnections Between Routers

Serial interfaces are slow by comparison to the various types of Ethernet connections available. As a direct result of this, many organizations are moving away from them. However, many technologies and features specific to serial interconnections are still part of the CCIE Routing and Switching blueprint. In order for you to see and experiment with these technologies, I have specified that several groups of routers be linked by individual connections and some multiple connections. Table 1-1 illustrates what devices share these connections and how many.

Table 1-1   *Physical Topology—Serial Connections Between Routers*

Router	Interface	Router	Interface
R1	S1/2	R2	S1/1
R1	S1/3	R3	S1/1
R1	S1/4	R4	S1/1
R1	S1/5	R5	S1/1
R1	S1/6	R6	S1/1
R2	S1/1	R1	S1/2
R2	S1/3	R3	S1/2
R2	S1/4	R4	S1/2
R2	S1/5	R5	S1/2
R2	S1/6	R6	S1/2
R3	S1/1	R1	S1/3
R3	S1/2	R2	S1/3
R3	S1/4	R4	S1/3
R3	S1/5	R5	S1/3
R3	S1/6	R6	S1/3
R4	S1/1	R1	S1/4
R4	S1/2	R2	S1/4
R4	S1/3	R3	S1/4
R4	S1/5	R5	S1/4
R4	S1/6	R6	S1/4
R5	S1/1	R1	S1/5
R5	S1/2	R2	S1/5
R5	S1/3	R3	S1/5
R5	S1/4	R4	S1/5
R5	S1/6	R6	S1/5
R6	S1/1	R1	S1/6
R6	S1/2	R2	S1/6
R6	S1/3	R3	S1/6
R6	S1/4	R4	S1/6
R6	S1/5	R5	S1/6

Router	Interface	Router	Interface
R9	S0/0/0	R10	S0/0/0
R9	S0/1/0	R10	S0/1/0
R10	S0/0/0	R9	S0/0/0
R10	S0/1/0	R9	S0/1/0

Lab Options

It is important to note that this book was written using a rack of actual Cisco switches and routers; however, I recognize that many readers might not have access to this type of lab environment. Therefore, this book contains labs that can be run on many different software emulators. Whether you opt to use live equipment, Cisco Virtual Internet Routing Lab (VIRL), or some other emulation package, my intent is to provide you with as much directed hands-on experience as possible. Whereas actual hardware supports every lab included in this book, many emulators do not support features such as serial connections. In these situations, I suggest that you leverage an emulator (such as VIRL) to practice as many labs as possible, and then it may be necessary to get access to live equipment. Another suggestion would be to use Cisco's Lab Builder offering, which will support all the labs included in this book.

Summary

Hands-on experience working with technologies is the best way to learn and to demonstrate your learning. I cannot emphasis enough how important practical exercises, like those included in this book, will be to your success. So whether you have a lab of real equipment or use an emulator platform, I suggest you practice these labs many times. This will help you learn new things as well as help you retain what you learn longer as you progress through your studies.

Chapter 2

Physical and Logical Topologies

The ability of CCIE candidates to read physical and logical topologies and perform a transition from one to the other is a crucial skill to be mastered because it is an everyday task in a networker's life. Unfortunately, the common CCENT–CCNA–CCNP progression does not focus on sharpening this skill, and even CCNP holders often struggle with it. This chapter strives to cover this particular gap.

Topology Types

Often, the difficulty lies in a vague understanding of what constitutes a *physical* topology versus a *logical* topology. Therefore, let's spend some time clarifying these two terms, including the rationale behind them.

The term *physical topology* denotes all the *physical devices* (repeaters, transceivers, media converters, hubs, bridges, switches, wireless access points, routers, firewalls, servers, end hosts, and so on) and *their interconnections* that make up a particular network. A physical topology diagram contains all physical devices contained in a network that operate on OSI Layer 1 and higher, including all their interconnections. A diagram of a physical topology describes a network in detail.

The TCP/IP protocol architecture does not care much about the physical topology, though. In RFC 1122, the TCP/IP architecture is loosely described in four layers: Application (roughly covering OSI Layers 5–7), Transport (roughly equivalent to OSI Layer 4), Internet (roughly equivalent to OSI Layer 3), and Link Layer (roughly covering OSI Layers 1 and 2), which is sometimes suitably renamed the Network Access Layer. TCP/IP does not exactly specify how the Link Layer should operate; instead, it only imposes a set of requirements and restrictions on its operation, and for the most part, the operation of the Link Layer is transparent to the TCP/IP stack. In particular, hosts in the same Link Layer domain (that is, interconnected only by OSI Layer 1 and Layer 2 devices) are considered to be in the same IPv4 or IPv6 network, and they can communicate directly and instantly. Exactly how the Link Layer allows these hosts to mutually exchange frames with IP packets inside is irrelevant to IP as long as it gets done.

Therefore, when focusing on IP networking in particular, it often makes sense to abstract from the step-by-step operation of the TCP/IP Link Layer (OSI Layer 1 + Layer 2) and instead assume that this functionality is simply present and working. Every Link Layer domain is also a broadcast domain, because a broadcast frame sent from one host in a Link Layer domain will be delivered to all other hosts in the same domain. In IP networking, a single broadcast domain is treated as a single IP network. Therefore, if we ignore the details of every Link Layer domain and simply assume it is present and working, the physical topology collapses into a set of IP networks and their attachment to individual devices operating at OSI Layer 3 and above (routers, firewalls, and end hosts, to name a few). This is what we call a *logical topology*. A logical topology keeps all routers, firewalls, end hosts, servers, load balancers, and other devices that operate at OSI Layer 3 and above, and replaces all switches and other Layer 1 and Layer 2 devices with IP networks that run over them.

Transitioning from a physical topology to its logical counterpart is relatively straightforward—simply remove all OSI Layer 1 and Layer 2 devices from the topology and replace them with proper IP networks that have been spanned over individual broadcast (that is, Link Layer) domains. Naturally, every technology that virtualizes a physical broadcast domain into multiple virtual broadcast domains, such as VLANs, must be taken into account.

Transitioning from a logical topology to its physical counterpart, on the other hand, is a much more difficult task. Precisely because every Link Layer domain is transparent to IP, based on IP information alone, it is not possible to know how many switches comprise a single IP network, how they are interconnected, whether VLANs are in use, and so on. These details can be obtained by OSI Layer 2 management protocols such as CDP and LLDP, and sometimes inferred from various diagnostic outputs on Layer 2 devices. An unmanaged Ethernet switch, however, is completely transparent, and without knowing about this switch through other means, it is not possible to detect it reliably.

The ability to quickly move from a physical to a logical topology and back is an acquired skill and needs practice. The most important parts of transitioning from a physical to a logical topology are the ability to properly identify broadcast domains and their boundaries and the ability to properly replace them with corresponding IP networks. The reverse process, moving from a logical to a physical topology, is often detective work, requiring piecing together various shreds of information from different OSI Layer 2 and Layer 3 sources. Here, hands-on experience is a great asset.

Lab 2-1: Introductory Lab

Let's say we come across the topology shown in Figure 2-1 and the trouble ticket states that R1 cannot ping R2.

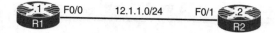

Figure 2-1   *Simple Topology with a Trouble Ticket*

Notice that I intentionally do not comment on whether Figure 2-1 contains a physical or a logical topology. If we read the topology in Figure 2-1 literally, it is tempting to quickly conclude that the two routers are connected back-to-back with an Ethernet crossover cable. However, there is a significant chance, both in the CCIE Lab Exam and in real-life scenarios, that their interconnection is more complex than initially thought.

Let's troubleshoot this problem. As the first step, let's verify the ticket by pinging R2 from R1:

```
R1# ping 12.1.1.2
Type escape sequence to abort.
Sending 5, 100-byte ICMP Echos to 12.1.1.2, timeout is 2 seconds:
.....
Success rate is 0 percent (0/5)
```

Because the ping is not successful, we should check the ARP table to see if R1 is at least able to learn the MAC address of R2:

```
R1# show arp
Protocol   Address           Age (min)   Hardware Addr   Type   Interface
Internet   12.1.1.1              -        0000.1111.1111  ARPA   FastEthernet0/0
Internet   12.1.1.2              0        Incomplete      ARPA
```

Obviously, ARP has failed. Because this potentially can be caused by a Layer 2 problem, let's verify the interface configuration by inspecting the F0/0 configuration on R1:

```
R1# show run interface FastEthernet0/0
interface FastEthernet0/0
 ip address 12.1.1.1 255.255.255.0
 mac-address 0000.1111.1111
 duplex auto
 speed auto
end
```

Nothing suspicious shows up here. Let's verify whether there is an access control list configured on R1, which could be blocking the communication in some not-so-obvious way—perhaps in a local Policy Base Routing configuration or a class map:

```
R1# show access-lists
```

No ACLs on R1, either. Let's see if R1 is connected directly to R2:

```
R2# show cdp neighbors
Capability Codes: R - Router, T - Trans Bridge, B - Source Route Bridge
                  S - Switch, H - Host, I - IGMP, r - Repeater, P - Phone,
                  D - Remote, C - CVTA, M - Two-port Mac Relay


Device ID        Local Intrfce     Holdtme    Capability  Platform  Port ID
SW1              Fas 0/0             154            S I    WS-C3560- Fas 0/2
```

As it turns out, R1 is *not* connected to R2; rather, it connects to SW1's F0/1 interface. Obviously, there is at least one switch between R1 and R2 that was not depicted in Figure 2-1, and as a consequence, we immediately know that Figure 2-1 is not a physical topology diagram. Let's therefore check the configuration of the F0/1 interface on SW1:

```
SW1# show run interface Fastethernet0/1
interface FastEthernet0/1
 switchport access vlan 12
 switchport mode access
 spanning-tree portfast
end
```

We can see that the F0/1, and R1 along with it, is placed into VLAN 12. Let's check for access control lists (ACLs) or virtual LAN (VLAN) access maps on SW1 that could be blocking the communication:

```
SW1# show access-lists

SW1# show vlan access-map
```

No ACLs, no VLAN access maps. Let's view the topology from the perspective of the Spanning Tree Protocol (STP):

```
SW1# show spanning-tree vlan 12
VLAN0012
  Spanning tree enabled protocol ieee
  Root ID    Priority    32780
             Address     0012.7f40.9380
             This bridge is the root
             Hello Time   2 sec  Max Age 20 sec  Forward Delay 15 sec

  Bridge ID  Priority    32780  (priority 32768 sys-id-ext 12)
             Address     0012.7f40.9380
```

```
              Hello Time   2 sec  Max Age 20 sec  Forward Delay 15 sec
              Aging Time 300


Interface        Role Sts Cost      Prio.Nbr Type
---------------- ---- --- --------- -------- ------------------------
Fa0/1            Desg FWD 19        128.3    P2p Edge
Fa0/21           Desg FWD 19        128.23   P2p
```

We know already that the F0/1 interface of SW1 is connected to R1, and it looks like SW1 is connected to another device via its F0/21 interface. Cisco Discovery Protocol (CDP) can hopefully tell us more about the neighboring device:

```
SW1# show cdp neighbors
Capability Codes: R - Router, T - Trans Bridge, B - Source Route Bridge
                  S - Switch, H - Host, I - IGMP, r - Repeater, P - Phone

Device ID        Local Intrfce     Holdtme    Capability  Platform  Port ID
SW3              Fas 0/21          172            S I     WS-C3550- Fas 0/21
R1               Fas 0/1           142          R S I     2811       Fas 0/0
```

In this output, we can see that F0/21 on SW1 connects to another switch whose name is SW3. Let's move on to SW3 and verify its ACLs, VLAN access maps, and STP:

```
SW3# show access-lists



SW3# show vlan access-map



SW3# show spanning-tree vlan 12

Spanning tree instance(s) for vlan 12 does not exist.
```

SW3 reports that there is no STP instance for VLAN 12. That either means that the VLAN does not exist on this switch or that there are no ports in VLAN 12 that are currently in the up/up state. Let's verify the VLAN database first:

```
SW3# show vlan brief
VLAN Name                             Status    Ports
---- -------------------------------- --------- -------------------------------
1    default                          active    Fa0/1, Fa0/2, Fa0/3, Fa0/4
                                                Fa0/5, Fa0/6, Fa0/7, Fa0/8
                                                Fa0/9, Fa0/10, Fa0/11, Fa0/12
                                                Fa0/13, Fa0/14, Fa0/15, Fa0/16
                                                Fa0/17, Fa0/18, Fa0/20, Fa0/22
                                                Fa0/23, Fa0/24, Gi0/1, Gi0/2
```

```
1002 fddi-default                     act/unsup
1003 token-ring-default               act/unsup
1004 fddinet-default                  act/unsup
1005 trnet-default                    act/unsup
```

Clearly, VLAN 12 is missing. Let's create it:

Note   When configuring a VLAN in the global configuration mode, you must exit the VLAN submode in order for the changes to apply.

```
SW3(config)# vlan 12
SW3(config-vlan)# exit
```

While we are on SW3, let's verify the topology from the perspective of STP:

```
SW3# show spanning-tree vlan 12
VLAN0012
  Spanning tree enabled protocol ieee
  Root ID    Priority    32780
             Address     000c.858b.7a00
             This bridge is the root
             Hello Time   2 sec  Max Age 20 sec  Forward Delay 15 sec

  Bridge ID  Priority    32780   (priority 32768 sys-id-ext 12)
             Address     000c.858b.7a00
             Hello Time   2 sec  Max Age 20 sec  Forward Delay 15 sec
             Aging Time 300


Interface        Role Sts Cost      Prio.Nbr Type
---------------- ---- --- --------- -------- --------------------------
Fa0/21           Desg FWD 19        128.21   P2p
```

Although there is no obvious problem in this output, it is slightly suspicious that the only port participating in VLAN 12 should be F0/21, which goes back to SW1. In order for R1 and R2 to communicate, R2 must be connected to a port—either on this switch or on some other switch—that participates in VLAN 12, and so far, neither SW1 nor SW3 shows such a port. Next, let's verify the trunk interfaces configured on SW3:

```
SW3# show interface trunk
Port       Mode      Encapsulation  Status     Native vlan
Fa0/19     on        802.1q         trunking   1
Fa0/21     on        802.1q         trunking   1
```

```
Port          Vlans allowed on trunk
Fa0/19        1-11,13-4094
Fa0/21        1-4094


Port          Vlans allowed and active in management domain
Fa0/19        1
Fa0/21        1,12


Port          Vlans in spanning tree forwarding state and not pruned
Fa0/19        1
Fa0/21        1,12
```

We can see that VLAN 12 is not allowed on the F0/19 interface, even though F0/19 is a trunk port leading to some yet-unknown device. Why is that?

```
SW3# show run interface Fasterethernet0/19
interface FastEthernet0/19
 switchport trunk encapsulation dot1q
 switchport trunk allowed vlan 1-11,13-4094
 switchport mode trunk
end
```

We can clearly see the problem: VLAN 12 is not in the list of allowed VLANs on this trunk. Let's add it:

```
SW3(config)# interface FastEthernet0/19
SW3(config-if)# switchport trunk allowed vlan add 12
```

We can now verify the modification, like so:

```
SW3# show interface trunk
Port      Mode          Encapsulation  Status      Native vlan
Fa0/19    on            802.1q         trunking    1
Fa0/21    on            802.1q         trunking    1


Port          Vlans allowed on trunk
Fa0/19        1-4094
Fa0/21        1-4094


Port          Vlans allowed and active in management domain
Fa0/19        1,12
Fa0/21        1,12


Port          Vlans in spanning tree forwarding state and not pruned
Fa0/19        1,12
Fa0/21        1,12
```

This looks much better. What does the STP say now?

```
SW3# show spanning-tree vlan 12
VLAN0012
  Spanning tree enabled protocol ieee
  Root ID     Priority    32780
              Address     000c.858b.7a00
              This bridge is the root
              Hello Time   2 sec  Max Age 20 sec   Forward Delay 15 sec

  Bridge ID   Priority    32780   (priority 32768 sys-id-ext 12)
              Address     000c.858b.7a00
              Hello Time   2 sec  Max Age 20 sec   Forward Delay 15 sec
              Aging Time 300


Interface        Role Sts Cost      Prio.Nbr Type
---------------- ---- --- --------- -------- --------------------------------
Fa0/19           Desg FWD 19        128.19   P2p
Fa0/21           Desg FWD 19        128.21   P2p
```

Using CDP, we should now see the device that is connected to the F0/19 interface of SW3:

```
SW3# show cdp neighbors
Capability Codes: R - Router, T - Trans Bridge, B - Source Route Bridge
                  S - Switch, H - Host, I - IGMP, r - Repeater, P - Phone

Device ID        Local Intrfce    Holdtme    Capability  Platform  Port ID
SW4              Fas 0/19         162            S I      WS-C3550- Fas 0/19
SW1              Fas 0/21         123            S I      WS-C3560- Fas 0/21
```

According to this output, F0/19 on SW3 leads to SW4. Let's move to SW4, then, and verify the VLAN database on SW4 right away:

```
SW4# show vlan brief
VLAN Name                             Status    Ports
---- -------------------------------- --------- -------------------------------
1    default                          active    Fa0/1, Fa0/2, Fa0/3, Fa0/4
                                                Fa0/5, Fa0/6, Fa0/7, Fa0/8
                                                Fa0/9, Fa0/10, Fa0/11, Fa0/12
                                                Fa0/13, Fa0/14, Fa0/15, Fa0/16
                                                Fa0/17, Fa0/18, Fa0/20, Fa0/22
                                                Fa0/23, Fa0/24, Gi0/1, Gi0/2
1002 fddi-default                     act/unsup
1003 token-ring-default               act/unsup
1004 fddinet-default                  act/unsup
1005 trnet-default                    act/unsup
```

VLAN 12 is not configured on this switch. Let's add it and verify the topology from the perspective of STP:

```
SW4(config)# vlan 12
SW4(config-vlan)# exit
SW4(config)# end

SW4# show interface trunk
Port          Mode          Encapsulation  Status       Native vlan
Fa0/19        on            802.1q         trunking     1
Fa0/21        on            802.1q         trunking     1


Port          Vlans allowed on trunk
Fa0/19        1-4094
Fa0/21        1-4094


Port          Vlans allowed and active in management domain
Fa0/19        1,12
Fa0/21        1,12


Port          Vlans in spanning tree forwarding state and not pruned
Fa0/19        1,12
Fa0/21        1,12

SW4# show spanning-tree vlan 12
VLAN0012
  Spanning tree enabled protocol ieee
  Root ID    Priority    32780
             Address     000c.302d.9980
             This bridge is the root
             Hello Time   2 sec  Max Age 20 sec  Forward Delay 15 sec

  Bridge ID  Priority    32780  (priority 32768 sys-id-ext 12)
             Address     000c.302d.9980
             Hello Time   2 sec  Max Age 20 sec  Forward Delay 15 sec
             Aging Time 15

Interface         Role Sts Cost      Prio.Nbr Type
----------------- ---- --- --------- -------- --------------------------------
Fa0/19            Desg FWD 19        128.19   P2p
Fa0/21            Desg FWD 19        128.21   P2p
```

SW4 is connected to a device through its F0/21 interface. Let's verify this information with CDP:

```
SW4# show cdp neighbors
Capability Codes: R - Router, T - Trans Bridge, B - Source Route Bridge
                  S - Switch, H - Host, I - IGMP, r - Repeater, P - Phone


Device ID        Local Intrfce    Holdtme    Capability  Platform  Port ID
SW2              Fas 0/21         149           S I      WS-C3560- Fas 0/21
SW3              Fas 0/19         136           S I      WS-C3550- Fas 0/19
```

SW4 is connected to SW2 via its F0/21 interface, so let's move on to SW2:

```
SW2# show vlan brief
VLAN Name                            Status    Ports
---- -------------------------------- --------- -------------------------------
1    default                         active    Fa0/1, Fa0/3, Fa0/4, Fa0/5
                                               Fa0/6, Fa0/7, Fa0/8, Fa0/9
                                               Fa0/10, Fa0/11, Fa0/12, Fa0/13
                                               Fa0/14, Fa0/15, Fa0/16, Fa0/17
                                               Fa0/18, Fa0/19, Fa0/20, Fa0/22
                                               Fa0/23, Fa0/24, Gi0/1, Gi0/2
12   VLAN0012                        active    Fa0/2
1002 fddi-default                    act/unsup
1003 token-ring-default              act/unsup
1004 fddinet-default                 act/unsup
1005 trnet-default                   act/unsup
```

VLAN 12 does exist on SW2, and the only access port in this VLAN is F0/2. Before we verify reachability, let's see the STP status:

```
SW2# show spanning-tree vlan 12
VLAN0012
  Spanning tree enabled protocol ieee
  Root ID    Priority    32780
             Address     000c.302d.9980
             Cost        19
             Port        23 (FastEthernet0/21)
             Hello Time   2 sec  Max Age 20 sec  Forward Delay 15 sec

  Bridge ID  Priority    32780  (priority 32768 sys-id-ext 12)
             Address     001d.e5d6.0000
             Hello Time   2 sec  Max Age 20 sec  Forward Delay 15 sec
             Aging Time 300
```

```
Interface          Role Sts Cost     Prio.Nbr Type
---------------- ---- --- --------- -------- -------------------------
Fa0/2              Desg FWD 19       128.4    P2p Edge
Fa0/21             Root FWD 19       128.23   P2p
```

All looks good here. Let's see which device is connected to the F0/2 interface of SW2:

```
SW2# show cdp neighbors
Capability Codes: R - Router, T - Trans Bridge, B - Source Route Bridge
                  S - Switch, H - Host, I - IGMP, r - Repeater, P - Phone

Device ID          Local Intrfce     Holdtme   Capability  Platform  Port ID
SW4                Fas 0/21          144           S I     WS-C3550- Fas 0/21
R2                 Fas 0/2           126         R S I     2811      Fas 0/1
```

The output of the preceding **show** command reveals that the Fa0/2 interface of SW2 is connected to R2's Fa0/1 interface. Let's go to R2 and verify reachability with R1:

```
R2# ping 12.1.1.1
Type escape sequence to abort.
Sending 5, 100-byte ICMP Echos to 12.1.1.1, timeout is 2 seconds:
.!!!!
Success rate is 80 percent (4/5), round-trip min/avg/max = 1/1/4 ms
```

The problem is fixed, and we can see how a simple logical diagram can translate into the physical diagram shown in Figure 2-2.

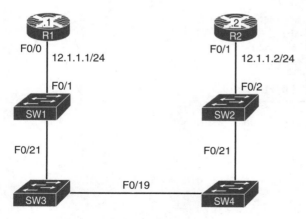

Figure 2-2 *Physical Topology of the Network*

Lab 2-2: Physical-to-Logical Topology

By this point, it should be obvious how important it is to know the physical topology of a given logical topology. This next lab demonstrates the configuration of physical topology in order to achieve a particular logical topology, and it will give you a better understanding of what to expect in the actual CCIE lab.

Figures 2-3 and 2-4 describe the physical connections of routers and switches. Figure 2-5 shows the desired logical topology that will be created as a result of accomplishing the tasks in this lab.

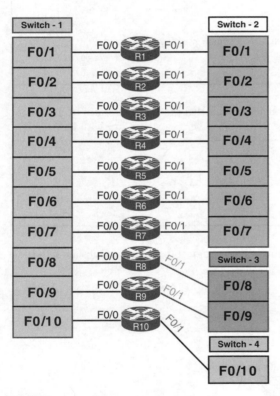

Figure 2-3   *Physical Topology—Router Connections to Switches*

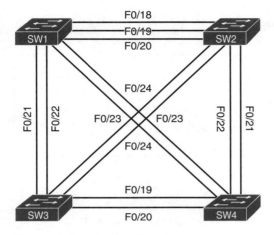

Figure 2-4   *Physical Topology—Switches*

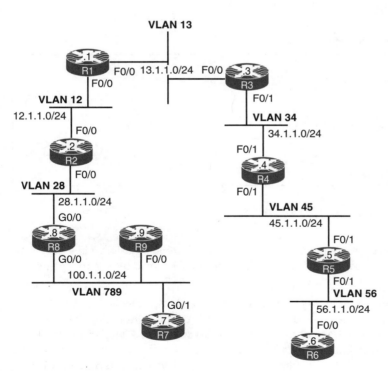

Figure 2-5   *Desired Logical Topology*

Task 1

Shut down all ports on all switches:

```
! On all switches:

SWx(config)# interface range fastethernet0/1 - 24
SWx(config-if-range)# shutdown
SWx(config-if-range)# interface range gigabitethernet0/1 - 2
SWx(config-if-range)# shutdown
```

Task 2

Configure the hostnames of the switches based on the following assignment:

- Switch 1: SW1
- Switch 2: SW2
- Switch 3: SW3

To perform this task, do the following:

```
! On Switch 1:
Switch(config)# hostname SW1

! On Switch 2:
Switch(config)# hostname SW2

! On Switch 3:
Switch(config)# hostname SW3
```

Task 3

Configure the physical topology to implement the logical topology shown in Figure 2-3. If this configuration is completed successfully, every router should be able to ping its neighboring routers in the same subnet.

Let's do a top-down configuration starting from VLAN 13. As shown in Figure 2-5, the F0/0 interfaces of R1 and R3 should be placed into VLAN 13. However, the R1 F0/0 interface also appears in VLAN 12 toward R2. In other words, R1 F0/0 participates in two distinct VLANs, and this requires creating two subinterfaces under this interface, one for each VLAN. Additionally, according to Figure 2-3, R1 F0/0 connects to the SW1 F0/1 interface, which can also be confirmed by using the command **show cdp neighbors** after both interfaces are started. Consequently, the SW1 F0/1 interface must carry multiple VLANs, so it must be configured as a trunk.

> **Note**   Although the subinterface number (the *X* in F0/0.*X*) does not need to match the VLAN ID of the subinterface, looking at the full name makes it much easier to know the VLAN of the subinterface.

```
! On SW1:

SW1(config)# interface fastethernet0/1
SW1(config-if)# switchport trunk encapsulation dot1q
SW1(config-if)# switchport mode trunk
SW1(config-if)# no shutdown

! On R1:

Router(config)# hostname R1
R1(config)# interface fastethernet0/0
R1(config-if)# no shutdown
R1(config-if)# exit
R1(config)# interface fastethernet0/0.12
R1(config-subif)# encapsulation dot1q 12
R1(config-subif)# ip address 12.1.1.1 255.255.255.0
R1(config-subif)# exit
R1(config)# interface fastethernet0/0.13
R1(config-subif)# encapsulation dot1q 13
R1(config-subif)# ip address 13.1.1.1 255.255.255.0
R1(config-subif)# do show cdp neighbors
Capability Codes: R - Router, T - Trans Bridge, B - Source Route Bridge
                  S - Switch, H - Host, I - IGMP, r - Repeater, P - Phone,
                  D - Remote, C - CVTA, M - Two-port Mac Relay

Device ID       Local Intrfce     Holdtme     Capability  Platform   Port ID
SW1             Fas 0/0           143              S I    WS-C3560- Fas 0/1
```

Note that we have not created VLAN 13 on the switch yet.

Next, we focus on R3 F0/0. Figure 2-5 shows that this interface participates only in VLAN 13, and according to Figure 2-3, R3 F0/0 connects to SW1 F0/3. Although we could solve this task by using subinterfaces on R3 and trunking on SW1, it would make the configuration needlessly complex. In this particular topology, R3 F0/0 is never going to participate in multiple VLANs, so it is perfectly fine to directly configure F0/0 on R3 without subinterfaces and to make F0/3 on SW1 a simple access port in VLAN 13. Note that SW1 creates an access VLAN automatically if that VLAN does not exist at the moment of adding an access port to it.

```
! On SW1:


SW1(config)# interface fastethernet0/3
SW1(config-if)# switchport mode access
SW1(config-if)# switchport access vlan 13
% Access VLAN does not exist. Creating vlan 13
SW1(config-if)# no shutdown


! On R3:


R3(config)# interface fastethernet0/0
R3(config-if)# ip address 13.1.1.3 255.255.255.0
R3(config-if)# no shutdown
```

Now verify the configuration:

```
! On SW1 - VLAN 13 should exist

SW1# show vlan brief

VLAN Name                             Status    Ports
---- -------------------------------- --------- -------------------------------
1    default                          active    Fa0/2, Fa0/4, Fa0/5, Fa0/6
                                                Fa0/7, Fa0/8, Fa0/9, Fa0/10
                                                Fa0/11, Fa0/12, Fa0/13, Fa0/14
                                                Fa0/15, Fa0/16, Fa0/17, Fa0/18
                                                Fa0/19, Fa0/20, Fa0/23, Fa0/24
                                                Gi0/1, Gi0/2
13   VLAN0013                         active    Fa0/3
1002 fddi-default                     act/unsup
1003 token-ring-default               act/unsup
1004 fddinet-default                  act/unsup
1005 trnet-default                    act/unsup


! On R1: Pinging between R1 and R3 should work


R1# ping 13.1.1.3

Type escape sequence to abort.
Sending 5, 100-byte ICMP Echos to 13.1.1.3, timeout is 2 seconds:
.!!!!
Success rate is 80 percent (4/5), round-trip min/avg/max = 1/1/1 ms
```

Let's move on to VLAN 12. In VLAN 12, we have the R1 F0/0 and R2 F0/0 interfaces. The R1 F0/0 interface is already configured with a subinterface for this VLAN (VLAN 12). Figure 2-5 shows that the R2 F0/0 interface is again placed into two VLANs: 12 and 28. Therefore, we will configure R2 F0/0 with two subinterfaces—one for VLAN 12 and the second one for VLAN 28. Also, according to Figure 2-3, R2 F0/0 connects to SW1 F0/2. This switchport is again required to carry multiple VLANs, so it must be configured as a trunk.

```
! On SW1:

SW1(config)# interface fastethernet0/2
SW1(config-if)# switchport trunk encapsulation dot1q
SW1(config-if)# switchport mode trunk
SW1(config-if)# no shutdown

! On R2:

R2(config)# interface fastethernet0/0
R2(config-if)# no shutdown
R2(config-if)# exit
R2(config-if)# interface fastethernet0/0.12
R2(config-subif)# encapsulation dot1q 12
R2(config-subif)# ip address 12.1.1.2 255.255.255.0
R2(config-subif)# exit
R2(config)# interface fastethernet0/0.28
R2(config-subif)# encapsulation dot1q 28
R2(config-subif)# ip address 28.1.1.2 255.255.255.0
```

Now verify the VLANs on SW1, like so:

```
SW1# show vlan brief
VLAN Name                             Status    Ports
---- -------------------------------- --------- -------------------------------
1    default                          active    Fa0/2, Fa0/4, Fa0/5, Fa0/6
                                                Fa0/7, Fa0/8, Fa0/9, Fa0/10
                                                Fa0/11, Fa0/12, Fa0/13, Fa0/14
                                                Fa0/15, Fa0/16, Fa0/17, Fa0/18
                                                Fa0/19, Fa0/20, Fa0/23, Fa0/24
                                                Gi0/1, Gi0/2
13   VLAN0013                         active    Fa0/3
1002 fddi-default                     act/unsup
1003 token-ring-default               act/unsup
1004 fddinet-default                  act/unsup
1005 trnet-default                    act/unsup
```

As you can see, VLAN 12 is not created yet because it wasn't configured explicitly and an access port wasn't configured in VLAN 12. Therefore, we need to add VLAN 12 to SW1 explicitly:

Note   Creating or modifying VLANs in global configuration mode is one of the very few commands in Cisco IOS that is not applied immediately after you enter it. With VLANs, all changes are applied only after you exit the VLAN configuration submode.

```
SW1(config)# vlan 12
SW1(config-vlan)# exit
```

Now, test the reachability between R1 and R2:

```
R1# ping 12.1.1.2

Type escape sequence to abort.
Sending 5, 100-byte ICMP Echos to 12.1.1.2, timeout is 2 seconds:
.!!!!
Success rate is 80 percent (4/5), round-trip min/avg/max = 1/2/4 ms
```

Let's move on to VLAN 28.

R2 has been already configured with a proper subinterface for VLAN 28. To complete the configuration on R8, first note that in Figure 2-5, G0/0 on R8 is shown to participate in two VLANs: 28 and 789. Therefore, R8 will need to be configured with two subinterfaces—one for each of these VLANs. The configuration steps on R8 and SW1 are as follows:

1. Configure the SW1 F0/8 interface toward R8 G0/0 as a trunk port.

2. Create VLAN 28 on SW1.

3. Configure the R8 G0/0 interface with two subinterfaces—one for VLAN 28 and the other one for VLAN 789.

4. Configure the R8 subinterface in VLAN 28 with an IP address of 28.1.1.8/24.

5. Configure the R8 subinterface in VLAN 789 with an IP address of 100.1.1.8/24.

```
! On SW1:

SW1(config)# interface fastethernet0/8
SW1(config-if)# switchport trunk encapsulation dot1q
SW1(config-if)# switchport mode trunk
SW1(config-if)# no shutdown
SW1(config-if)# exit
```

```
SW1(config)# vlan 28
SW1(config-vlan)# exit


! On R8:


R8(config)# interface gigabitethernet0/0
R8(config-if)# no shutdown
R8(config-if)# exit
R8(config)# interface gigabitethernet0/0.28
R8(config-subif)# encapsulation dot1q 28
R8(config-subif)# ip address 28.1.1.8 255.255.255.0
R8(config-subif)# exit
R8(config)# interface gigabitethernet0/0.789
R8(config-subif)# encapsulation dot1q 789
R8(config-subif)# ip address 100.1.1.8 255.255.255.0
```

Now verify and test the configuration:

```
! On SW1:


SW1# show vlan brief


VLAN Name                             Status    Ports
---- -------------------------------- --------- ------------------------------
1    default                          active    Fa0/4, Fa0/5, Fa0/6, Fa0/7
                                                Fa0/9, Fa0/10, Fa0/11, Fa0/12
                                                Fa0/13, Fa0/14, Fa0/15, Fa0/16
                                                Fa0/17, Fa0/18, Fa0/19, Fa0/20
                                                Fa0/23, Fa0/24, Gi0/1, Gi0/2
12   VLAN0012                         active
13   VLAN0013                         active    Fa0/3
28   VLAN0028                         active
1002 fddi-default                     act/unsup
1003 token-ring-default               act/unsup
1004 fddinet-default                  act/unsup
1005 trnet-default                    act/unsup

! On R2:


R2# ping 28.1.1.8
Type escape sequence to abort.
Sending 5, 100-byte ICMP Echos to 28.1.1.8, timeout is 2 seconds:
.!!!!
Success rate is 80 percent (4/5), round-trip min/avg/max = 1/1/4 ms
```

Having this done, let's proceed to VLAN 789.

VLAN 789 consists of the R8 G0/0, R9 F0/0, and R7 G0/1 interfaces. Looking at the physical topology diagram in Figure 2-3, you can see that the R8 G0/0 and R9 F0/0 interfaces are connected to SW1 but the R7 G0/1 interface is connected to SW2. In other words, VLAN 789 members are spread across two switches. To have VLAN 789 span two switches, we need to configure a trunk between SW1 and SW2 to pass the VLAN 789 traffic between them. Any of the direct links between SW1 and SW2 shown in Figure 2-4 can be used for this purpose.

Furthermore, Figure 2-5 shows that the R7 G0/1 and R9 F0/0 interfaces participate only in VLAN 789; therefore, we do not need to configure them with subinterfaces. R8 has already been configured for VLAN 789 connectivity, so we don't need to focus on it at this point.

The steps to configure this part of the topology are as follows:

1. Configure the SW1 F0/9 interface toward R9 F0/0 as an access port in VLAN 789.

2. Configure a trunk between SW1 and SW2. We'll choose F0/19 for this purpose.

3. Configure the SW2 F0/7 interface toward R7 G0/1 as an access port in VLAN 789.

4. Configure the R7 G0/1 interface with an IP address of 100.1.1.7/24.

5. Configure the R9 F0/0 interface with an IP address of 100.1.1.9/24.

```
! On SW1:

SW1(config)# interface fastethernet0/9
SW1(config-if)# switchport mode access
SW1(config-if)# switchport access vlan 789
% Access VLAN does not exist. Creating vlan 789
SW1(config-if)# no shutdown
SW1(config-if)# exit
SW1(config)# interface fastethernet0/19
SW1(config-if)# switchport trunk encapsulation dot1q
SW1(config-if)# switchport mode trunk
SW1(config-if)# no shutdown


! On SW2:

SW2(config)# interface fastethernet0/19
SW2(config-if)# switchport trunk encapsulation dot1q
SW2(config-if)# switchport mode trunk
SW2(config-if)# no shutdown
SW2(config-if)# exit
SW2(config)# interface fastethernet0/7
SW2(config-if)# switchport mode access
```

```
SW2(config-if)# switchport access vlan 789
% Access VLAN does not exist. Creating vlan 789
SW2(config-if)# no shutdown

! On R7:

R7(config)# interface gigabitethernet0/1
R7(config-if)# ip address 100.1.1.7 255.255.255.0
R7(config-if)# no shutdown

! On R9:

R9(config)# interface fastethernet0/0
R9(config-if)# ip address 100.1.1.9 255.255.255.0
R9(config-if)# no shutdown
```

Now let's test the connectivity:

```
R8# ping 100.1.1.7
Type escape sequence to abort.
Sending 5, 100-byte ICMP Echos to 100.1.1.7, timeout is 2 seconds:
.!!!!
Success rate is 80 percent (4/5), round-trip min/avg/max = 1/1/1 ms

R8# ping 100.1.1.9
Type escape sequence to abort.
Sending 5, 100-byte ICMP Echos to 100.1.1.9, timeout is 2 seconds:
.!!!!
Success rate is 80 percent (4/5), round-trip min/avg/max = 1/1/4 ms
```

Now we can move to VLAN 34 and work down all the way to VLAN 56.

VLAN 34 interconnects the F0/1 interfaces of R3 and R4, but in Figure 2-5, the R4 F0/1 interface appears in two different VLANs. This translates into the following sequence of steps:

1. Configure the SW2 F0/3 interface toward R3 F0/1 as an access port in VLAN 34.

2. Configure the SW2 F0/4 interface toward R4 F0/1 as a trunk port.

3. Configure the R3 F0/1 interface with an IP address of 34.1.1.3/24.

4. Configure the R4 F0/1 interface with two subinterfaces—one in VLAN 34 and the second in VLAN 45.

5. Configure the R4 subinterface in VLAN 34 with an IP address of 34.1.1.4/24.

6. Configure the R4 subinterface in VLAN 45 with an IP address of 45.1.1.4/24.

```
! On SW2:

SW2(config)# interface fastethernet0/3
SW2(config-if)# switchport mode access
SW2(config-if)# switchport access vlan 34
% Access VLAN does not exist. Creating vlan 34
SW2(config-if)# no shutdown
SW2(config-if)# exit
SW2(config)# interface fastethernet0/4
SW2(config-if)# switchport trunk encapsulation dot1q
SW2(config-if)# switchport mode trunk
SW2(config-if)# no shutdown


! On R3:

R3(config)# interface fastethernet0/1
R3(config-if)# ip address 34.1.1.3 255.255.255.0
R3(config-if)# no shutdown
! On R4:

R4(config)# interface fastethernet0/1
R4(config-if)# no shutdown
R4(config-if)# exit
R4(config)# interface fastethernet0/1.34
R4(config-subif)# encapsulation dot1q 34
R4(config-subif)# ip address 34.1.1.4 255.255.255.0
R4(config-subif)# exit
R4(config)# interface fastethernet0/1.45
R4(config-subif)# encapsulation dot1q 45
R4(config-subif)# ip address 45.1.1.4 255.255.255.0
```

Let's now test the configuration:

```
! On SW2:

SW2# show vlan brief

VLAN Name                             Status    Ports
---- -------------------------------- --------- -------------------------------
1    default                          active    Fa0/1, Fa0/2, Fa0/5, Fa0/6
                                                Fa0/8, Fa0/9, Fa0/10, Fa0/11
                                                Fa0/12, Fa0/13, Fa0/14, Fa0/15
                                                Fa0/16, Fa0/17, Fa0/18, Fa0/20
                                                Fa0/21, Fa0/22, Gi0/1, Gi0/2
```

```
34    VLAN0034                          active     Fa0/3
789   VLAN0789                          active     Fa0/7
1002  fddi-default                      act/unsup
1003  token-ring-default                act/unsup
1004  fddinet-default                   act/unsup
1005  trnet-default                     act/unsup

! On R3:

R3# ping 34.1.1.4
Type escape sequence to abort.
Sending 5, 100-byte ICMP Echos to 34.1.1.4, timeout is 2 seconds:
.!!!!
Success rate is 80 percent (4/5), round-trip min/avg/max = 1/1/1 ms
```

Let's move on to VLAN 45. This VLAN should connect together the F0/1 interfaces of R4 and R5, but once again the R5 F0/1 interface is also in another VLAN (VLAN 56). Note that R4 has already been configured with the necessary settings for VLAN 45.

Hence, the steps for configuring the VLAN 45 segment are as follows:

- Configure the SW2 F0/5 interface toward R5 F0/1 as a trunk port.

- Create VLAN 45 on SW2.

- Configure the R5 F0/1 interface with two subinterfaces—one in VLAN 56 and the second in VLAN 45.

- Configure the R5 subinterface in VLAN 45 with an IP address of 45.1.1.5/24.

- Configure the R5 subinterface in VLAN 56 with an IP address of 56.1.1.5/24.

```
! On SW2:

SW2(config)# interface fastethernet0/5
SW2(config-if)# switchport trunk encapsulation dot1q
SW2(config-if)# switchport mode trunk
SW2(config-if)# no shutdown
SW2(config-if)# exit
SW2(config)# vlan 45
SW2(config-vlan)# exit

! On R5:

R5(config)# interface fastethernet0/1
R5(config-if)# no shutdown
R5(config-if)# exit
```

```
R5(config)# interface fastethernet0/1.45
R5(config-subif)# encapsulation dot1q 45
R5(config-subif)# ip address 45.1.1.5 255.255.255.0
R5(config-subif)# exit
R5(config)# interface fastethernet0/1.56
R5(config-subif)# encapsulation dot1q 56
R5(config-subif)# ip address 56.1.1.5 255.255.255.0
```

Now let's verify the connectivity between R4 and R5:

```
R5# ping 45.1.1.4
Type escape sequence to abort.
Sending 5, 100-byte ICMP Echos to 45.1.1.4, timeout is 2 seconds:
.!!!!
Success rate is 80 percent (4/5), round-trip min/avg/max = 1/2/4 ms
```

The last segment of this topology is VLAN 56. Following Figure 2-5, routers R5 and R6 are connected together in this VLAN using the R5 F0/1 and R6 F0/0 interfaces. On R5, we have already created the proper subinterface under its F0/1 interface. R6 does not use its F0/0 for any other connection, so R6 does not need to use subinterfaces. However, because R5 F0/1 is connected to SW2 F0/5 whereas R6 F0/0 is connected to SW1 F0/6, VLAN 56 needs to span both switches, which means we need a working trunk between SW1 and SW2.

We first verify whether there is a trunk configured between the two switches:

```
SW2# show interface trunk

Port        Mode          Encapsulation  Status       Native vlan
Fa0/4       on            802.1q         trunking     1
Fa0/5       on            802.1q         trunking     1
Fa0/19      on            802.1q         trunking     1

Port        Vlans allowed on trunk
Fa0/4       1-4094
Fa0/5       1-4094
Fa0/19      1-4094

Port        Vlans allowed and active in management domain
Fa0/4       1,34,45,789
Fa0/5       1,34,45,789
Fa0/19      1,34,45,789

Port        Vlans in spanning tree forwarding state and not pruned
Fa0/4       1,34,45,789
Fa0/5       1,34,45,789
Fa0/19      1,34,45,789
```

F0/19 is the trunk link between the switches we set up earlier, and it is shown correctly in the output.

Next, verify whether VLAN 56 is created on both SW1 and SW2, and if it isn't, create it:

```
! On SW1:

SW1(config)# do show vlan brief
VLAN Name                              Status     Ports
---- ------------------------------    --------   ------------------------------
1    default                           active     Fa0/4, Fa0/5, Fa0/6, Fa0/7
                                                  Fa0/10, Fa0/11, Fa0/12, Fa0/13
                                                  Fa0/14, Fa0/15, Fa0/16, Fa0/17
                                                  Fa0/18, Fa0/20, Fa0/21, Fa0/22
                                                  Fa0/23, Fa0/24, Gi0/1, Gi0/2
12   VLAN0012                          active
13   VLAN0013                          active     Fa0/3
28   VLAN0028                          active
789  VLAN0789                          active     Fa0/9
1002 fddi-default                      act/unsup
1003 token-ring-default                act/unsup
1004 fddinet-default                   act/unsup
1005 trnet-default                     act/unsup

! VLAN 56 is missing; create it manually.

SW1(config)# vlan 56
SW1(config-vlan)# exit

! On SW2:

SW2(config)# do show vlan brief | e unsup
VLAN Name                              Status     Ports
---- ------------------------------    --------   ------------------------------
1    default                           active     Fa0/1, Fa0/2, Fa0/6, Fa0/8
                                                  Fa0/9, Fa0/10, Fa0/11, Fa0/12
                                                  Fa0/13, Fa0/14, Fa0/15, Fa0/16
                                                  Fa0/17, Fa0/18, Fa0/20, Fa0/21
                                                  Fa0/22, Fa0/23, Fa0/24, Gi0/1
                                                  Gi0/2
34   VLAN0034                          active     Fa0/3
45   VLAN0045                          active
789  VLAN0789                          active     Fa0/7

! VLAN 56 is missing; create it manually.

SW2(config)# vlan 56
SW2(config-vlan)# exit
```

At this point, you might wonder why VLAN 56 was not propagated automatically by the VLAN Trunking Protocol (VTP) from SW1 to SW2. In order for VLANs to be propagated to another switch over VTP, the following must be true:

■ A trunk link must be connecting the two switches. (This is already configured.)

■ The switches must operate in VTP Server or Client mode. By default, switches run in the VTP Server mode.

■ If VTPv3 is in use, the primary server must be elected. By default, switches run VTPv1.

■ The VTP domain name must match and be non-NULL. Because we have not touched VTP settings, both switches default to the NULL (empty) VTP domain name, and so the VLAN database contents are not propagated.

Let's finish the necessary configurations:

```
! On SW1:

SW1(config)# interface fastethernet0/6
SW1(config-if)# switchport mode access
SW1(config-if)# switchport access vlan 56
SW1(config-if)# no shut

! On R6:

R6(config)# interface fastethernet0/0
R6(config-if)# ip address 56.1.1.6 255.255.255.0
R6(config-if)# no shutdown
```

Now let's verify and test the configuration:

```
! On SW1:

SW1# show vlan brief | exclude unsup
VLAN Name                             Status     Ports
---- -------------------------------- ---------  -------------------------------
1    default                          active     Fa0/4, Fa0/5, Fa0/7, Fa0/10
                                                 Fa0/11, Fa0/12, Fa0/13, Fa0/14
                                                 Fa0/15, Fa0/16, Fa0/17, Fa0/18
                                                 Fa0/20, Fa0/21, Fa0/22, Fa0/23
                                                  Fa0/24, Gi0/1, Gi0/2

12   VLAN0012                         active
13   VLAN0013                         active     Fa0/3
28   VLAN0028                         active
56   VLAN0056                         active     Fa0/6
789  VLAN0789                         active     Fa0/9
```

```
SW1# show interface fastethernet0/19 trunk

Port          Mode            Encapsulation  Status        Native vlan
Fa0/19        on              802.1q         trunking      1

Port          Vlans allowed on trunk
Fa0/19        1-4094

Port          Vlans allowed and active in management domain
Fa0/19        1,12-13,28,56,789

Port          Vlans in spanning tree forwarding state and not pruned
Fa0/19        1,12-13,28,56,789

! On R6:

 R6# ping 56.1.1.5
Type escape sequence to abort.
Sending 5, 100-byte ICMP Echos to 56.1.1.5, timeout is 2 seconds:
.!!!!
Success rate is 80 percent (4/5), round-trip min/avg/max = 1/2/4 ms
```

With this test, Task 3 has been fully completed. Erase the startup configurations and reload the routers and switches before proceeding to the next lab.

Summary

In this chapter, we have explored the steps required to translate from a logical topology to a physical topology. This skillset is essential in order to extrapolate any information not provided by a drawing given to you in the exam. I will go a step further by stating that this is one of the most critical skills needed to function as a consultant who is exposed to many new and different network environments. It is widely considered the most useful troubleshooting skill there is.

Chapter 3

Spanning Tree Protocol

Lab 3-1: Basic Spanning Tree Protocol (802.1D)

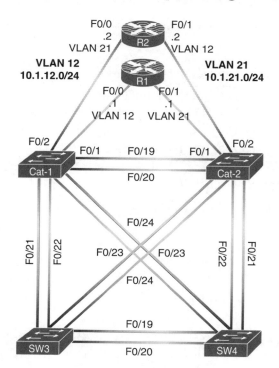

Figure 3-1 *Spanning Tree Protocol (802.1D)*

Figure 3-1 illustrates the topology that will be used in the following tasks.

Task 1

- Name the first switch CAT-1 and shut down interfaces F0/3 through F0/18.

- Name the second switch CAT-2 and shut down interfaces F0/3 through F0/18.

- Name the third switch SW-3 and shut down interfaces F0/1 through F0/18.

- Name the fourth switch SW-4 and shut down interfaces F0/1 through F0/18.

- Create VLANs 12 and 21 on all four switches.

- Place R1 F0/0 and R2 F0/1 interfaces in VLAN 12.

- Place R1 F0/1 and R2 F0/0 interfaces in VLAN 21.

- All switch-to-switch links should be 802.1Q trunks.

- Permit only VLANs 12 and 21 on the switch-to-switch links.

- Assign IP and MAC addresses as shown in Table 3-1.

- Verify that R1 can ping R2 on both subnets.

You can also use the initial configuration file from the Boot-Camp-Init directory.

Table 3-1 *IP and MAC Addressing*

Router	Interface	IP address	Mac-address
R1	F0/0	10.1.12.1/24	0000.**1111**.0000 → identifies **R1**'s **F0/0**
	F0/1	10.1.21.1/24	0000.**1111.1111** → identifies **R1**'s **F0/1**
R2	F0/0	10.1.21.2/24	0000.**2222**.0000 → identifies **R2**'s **F0/0**
	F0/1	10.1.12.2/24	0000.**2222.1111** → identifies **R2**'s **F0/1**

Once the configuration is compete, you can proceed with the following task.

Make sure that traffic on VLAN 12 between R1 and R2 uses only the following switch-to-switch links:

- F0/21 between CAT-1 and SW-3

- F0/23 between SW-3 and CAT-2

Use only the command **spanning-tree vlan vlan-id priority priority**, use it only on one switch, and make the minimum changes possible from the default value.

The spanning-tree algorithm creates loop-free paths connecting all active switched ports. For each broadcast domain, it chooses one root bridge. Each non-root bridge then chooses one root port, and each link chooses one designated port. Ports not chosen as either root or designated ports go into the blocking state. Task 1 requires you to affect the path that traffic will take by setting which switch will be the root bridge. This is accomplished by changing the bridge priority on one switch.

First, let's determine the existing topology:

```
On CAT-1:


CAT-1# show spanning-tree vlan 12


VLAN0012
  Spanning tree enabled protocol ieee
  Root ID    Priority    32780
             Address     000c.ce44.7d80
             Cost        19
             Port        25 (FastEthernet0/23)
             Hello Time   2 sec  Max Age 20 sec  Forward Delay 15 sec

  Bridge ID  Priority    32780   (priority 32768 sys-id-ext 12)
             Address     001a.a174.1f00
             Hello Time   2 sec  Max Age 20 sec  Forward Delay 15 sec
             Aging Time 300


Interface        Role Sts Cost      Prio.Nbr Type
---------------- ---- --- --------- -------- -------------------------
Fa0/1            Desg FWD 19        128.3    P2p
Fa0/19           Altn BLK 19        128.21   P2p
Fa0/20           Altn BLK 19        128.22   P2p
Fa0/21           Altn BLK 19        128.23   P2p
Fa0/22           Altn BLK 19        128.24   P2p
Fa0/23           Root FWD 19        128.25   P2p
Fa0/24           Altn BLK 19        128.26   P2p
```

The required path uses port F0/21 on CAT-1. But as you can see in this topology, that port is in the blocking state. F0/23 is the root port, the one closest to the root bridge, and it is forwarding. The root bridge has a cost of 19 out of interface F0/23 from CAT-1's perspective, so the root bridge in this topology is SW-4.

SW-4 is chosen as the root bridge because it has the lowest bridge ID of all four switches in VLAN 12. The original 802.1D protocol specification defined the bridge ID as a 16-bit priority field and a 48-bit MAC address. The default priority value is the midpoint of the range (32768 in decimal or 8000 in hexadecimal). So by default, the root bridge will be the one with the lowest built-in MAC address. You can see this MAC address by using a **sh version | inc Base** command or by noting the output of **sh spanning-tree**.

In the preceding output, you see the MAC address for the root bridge is 000C. CE44.7d80 and the MAC address of CAT-1 is 001A.A174.1F00. Note that the root bridge MAC address is lower in the third hexadecimal place from the left. These results will be different on your equipment. You may have a different root bridge at this point in the lab.

To achieve the required path between R1 and R2, you need to make SW-3 the root bridge for VLAN 12. This will cause CAT-1 to choose F0/21 as its root port and move it to the forwarding state (it has a lower port ID). Similarly, CAT-2 will change its root port from F0/21 to the required F0/23. You cannot change the MAC address portion of the bridge ID.

To change the root bridge, you change the bridge priority portion of the bridge ID for that VLAN. Let's change the priority to 100 for VLAN 12 on SW-3.

```
On SW-3:

SW-3(config)# spanning-tree vlan 12 priority 100

% Bridge Priority must be in increments of 4096.
% Allowed values are:
  0     4096  8192  12288 16384 20480 24576 28672
  32768 36864 40960 45056 49152 53248 57344 61440
```

Catalyst 3550 and 3560 switches implement the extended system ID feature, so you can only set the bridge priority to one of the 16 different values shown. This feature divides the original bridge priority field into a 4-bit priority and 12-bit system ID. The system ID codes the VLAN ID. It allows for 4096 values (the number of VLANs permitted in the 802.1Q trunking protocol). In the following output, you can see that the bridge priority field for SW-3 has a value of 32780. This is the sum of the default priority and the extended system ID fields.

```
On SW-3:

SW-3# show spanning-tree vlan 12 bridge

                                          Hello  Max  Fwd
Vlan                     Bridge ID        Time   Age  Dly
---------------- -------------------------------- ----- --- ---
VLAN0012          32780 (32768,  12) 000d.2870.fe00   2    20   15
```

Let's lower the SW-3 VLAN 12 bridge priority to 28672:

```
On SW-3:

SW-3(config)# spanning-tree vlan 12 priority 28672
```

Let's verify the configuration:

```
CAT-1# show spanning-tree vlan 12


VLAN0012
  Spanning tree enabled protocol ieee
  Root ID    Priority    28684
             Address     000d.2870.fe00
             Cost        19
             Port        23 (FastEthernet0/21)
             Hello Time  2 sec  Max Age 20 sec  Forward Delay 15 sec

  Bridge ID  Priority    32780  (priority 32768 sys-id-ext 12)
             Address     001a.a174.1f00

             Hello Time  2 sec  Max Age 20 sec  Forward Delay 15 sec
             Aging Time 300


Interface         Role Sts Cost      Prio.Nbr Type
----------------- ---- --- --------- -------- ------------------------
Fa0/1             Desg FWD 19        128.3    P2p
Fa0/19            Altn BLK 19        128.21   P2p
Fa0/20            Altn BLK 19        128.22   P2p
Fa0/21            Root FWD 19        128.23   P2p
Fa0/22            Altn BLK 19        128.24   P2p
Fa0/23            Altn BLK 19        128.25   P2p
Fa0/24            Altn BLK 19        128.26   P2p
```

CAT-1 shows the root bridge with a priority of 28684. This is the sum of the configured bridge priority on SW-3 (28672) and the VLAN ID (12). The root bridge address is the base MAC address on SW-3. Only interfaces F0/1 and F0/21 are forwarding for VLAN 12, so traffic arriving from R1 on F0/1 will be forwarded out F0/21 as required.

```
On CAT-2:


CAT-2# show spanning-tree vlan 12


VLAN0012
  Spanning tree enabled protocol ieee
  Root ID    Priority    28684
             Address     000d.2870.fe00
             Cost        19
             Port        25 (FastEthernet0/23)
             Hello Time  2 sec  Max Age 20 sec  Forward Delay 15 sec

  Bridge ID  Priority    32780  (priority 32768 sys-id-ext 12)
             Address     0019.e780.6d80
```

```
                   Hello Time    2 sec  Max Age 20 sec  Forward Delay 15 sec
                   Aging Time 300


Interface          Role Sts Cost        Prio.Nbr Type
----------------   ---- --- ---------   -------- --------------------
Fa0/2              Desg FWD 19           128.4    P2p
Fa0/19             Desg FWD 19           128.21   P2p
Fa0/20             Desg FWD 19           128.22   P2p
Fa0/21             Altn BLK 19           128.23   P2p
Fa0/22             Altn BLK 19           128.24   P2p
Fa0/23             Root FWD 19           128.25   P2p
Fa0/24             Altn BLK 19           128.26   P2p
```

On CAT-2, the root bridge is shown with the priority and address from SW-3. Traffic arriving on root port F0/23 can be forwarded toward R2 on F0/2, as required by the task. For these switches, ports F0/19 and F0/20 are also forwarding. These links are blocked on the CAT-1 side, so traffic cannot flow between the routers on these links. We will come back to this issue in a later task.

```
On SW-3:


SW-3# show spanning-tree vlan 12


VLAN0012
  Spanning tree enabled protocol ieee
  Root ID    Priority    28684
             Address     000d.2870.fe00
             This bridge is the root
             Hello Time    2 sec  Max Age 20 sec  Forward Delay 15 sec

  Bridge ID  Priority    28684  (priority 28672 sys-id-ext 12)
             Address     000d.2870.fe00
             Hello Time    2 sec  Max Age 20 sec  Forward Delay 15 sec
             Aging Time 300


Interface          Role Sts Cost        Prio.Nbr Type
----------------   ---- --- ---------   -------- --------------------
Fa0/19             Desg FWD 19           128.19   P2p
Fa0/20             Desg FWD 19           128.20   P2p
Fa0/21             Desg FWD 19           128.21   P2p
Fa0/22             Desg FWD 19           128.22   P2p
Fa0/23             Desg FWD 19           128.23   P2p
Fa0/24             Desg FWD 19           128.24   P2p
```

Because SW3 is the root bridge, all ports on SW-3 are in the forwarding state. You will find blocked ports on a root bridge only when it is looped to itself.

If you do not get any output in the following verification steps, you should generate a ping from the hosts within VLAN 12. As an example you can ping 10.1.12.2.

```
On SW-3:




SW-3# show mac address-table dynamic vlan 12
          Mac Address Table
-------------------------------------------

Vlan    Mac Address      Type       Ports
----    -----------      --------   -----
 12     0000.1111.0000   DYNAMIC    Fa0/21 →
 12     0000.2222.1111   DYNAMIC    Fa0/23 →
Total Mac Addresses for this criterion: 2
```

Using **sh interface** on the routers and **sh mac-address-table** on the switches, you can further verify that traffic is taking the required path. In the output of the preceding **show** command, you see that traffic to the MAC address 0000.1111.0000 is sent out of the F0/21 interface. The traffic to the MAC address 0000.2222.1111 is sent out SW-3's F0/23 interface toward R2's F0/1.

Task 2

Raise the spanning-tree cost on a port in VLAN 12 so that CAT-1 chooses F0/22 as its root port instead of F0/21.

A non-root bridge chooses one root port based on the following criteria:

- Choose the port with the lowest root path cost.

- If the root path costs are equal, choose the port connected to the upstream neighbor with the lowest bridge ID.

- If the bridge IDs of the upstream neighbors are the same (parallel links between two switches), choose the port that receives the lowest port ID.

The parallel links connecting CAT-1 and SW-3 have an equal cost. You are asked to raise the cost on a port for VLAN 12 so that CAT-1 chooses F0/22 as its root port. You will need to raise the cost of the F0/21 link, but which port on this link needs to be adjusted? The root port on CAT-1 or the designated port on SW-3?

The root path cost is incremented as Bridge Protocol Data Units arrive on designated ports. Changing the spanning-tree cost on the root bridge has no effect.

On CAT-1, enable debugging and raise the cost on F0/21:

```
On CAT-1:


CAT-1# debug spanning events
Spanning Tree event debugging is on


CAT-1(config)# int f0/21
CAT-1(config-if)# spanning vlan 12 cost 20


23:57:18: STP: VLAN0012 new root port Fa0/22, cost 19
23:57:18: STP: VLAN0012 Fa0/22 -> listening
23:57:18: STP: VLAN0012 sent Topology Change Notice on Fa0/22
23:57:18: STP: VLAN0012 Fa0/21 -> blocking
23:57:33: STP: VLAN0012 Fa0/22 -> learning
23:57:48: STP: VLAN0012 sent Topology Change Notice on Fa0/22
23:57:48: STP: VLAN0012 Fa0/22 -> forwarding
```

As soon as the cost of F0/21 is raised above the default value of 19 for a 100Mbps link, CAT-1 chooses F0/22 as its root port and the port transitions from the blocking state to the listening state. The old root port, F0/21, immediately goes into the blocking state.

F0/22 spends 15 seconds in the listening state (the default value of the forward delay timer) and then transitions to the learning state. While in the learning state, F0/22 spends another 15 seconds building its MAC address table before it transitions to the forwarding state. Traffic between R1 and R2 would have been disrupted for a total of 30 seconds, which is twice the forward delay timer.

Let's verify the configuration:

```
On CAT-1:


CAT-1# show spanning-tree vlan 12 | b Interface


Interface         Role Sts Cost      Prio.Nbr Type
----------------- ---- --- --------- -------- -------------------------
Fa0/1             Desg FWD 19        128.3    P2p
Fa0/19            Altn BLK 19        128.21   P2p
Fa0/20            Altn BLK 19        128.22   P2p
Fa0/21            Altn BLK 20        128.23   P2p
Fa0/22            Root FWD 19        128.24   P2p
Fa0/23            Altn BLK 19        128.25   P2p
Fa0/24            Altn BLK 19        128.26   P2p
```

Task 3

Links F0/19 and F0/20 connecting CAT-1 and CAT-2 are in the blocking state on one side for VLAN 12. Use the command **spanning-tree vlan-id priority priority** to move the VLAN 12 designated ports on these links from one switch to the other. Do not change the root bridge for VLAN 12.

For VLAN 12, there is a physical loop connecting CAT-1, SW-3, and CAT-2. The spanning-tree algorithm broke this loop at OSI Layer 2 by placing ports in STP blocking state. Because all of the forwarding link costs are equal (19), the blocked ports will be on the parallel links connecting CAT-1 and CAT-2. But which side will block and which side will have the designated port? With equal path costs to the root, the algorithm chooses the port on the link that is connected to the switch that has the lowest bridge ID. As you saw earlier, this will be the switch with the lowest MAC address by default, and this is purely a matter of chance.

Let's determine which switch has the designated ports:

```
On CAT-1:


CAT-1# show spanning-tree vlan 12 bridge


                                               Hello  Max  Fwd
Vlan                          Bridge ID        Time   Age  Dly
---------------- -------------------------------- ----- --- ---
VLAN0012           32780 (32768,  12) 001a.a174.1f00   2    20   15

CAT-1# show spanning-tree vlan 12 interface FastEthernet0/19 detail

 Port 21 (FastEthernet0/19) of VLAN0012 is blocking
   Port path cost 19, Port priority 128, Port Identifier 128.21.
   Designated root has priority 28684, address 000d.2870.fe00
   Designated bridge has priority 32780, address 0019.e780.6d80
   Designated port id is 128.21, designated path cost 19
   Timers: message age 3, forward delay 0, hold 0
   Number of transitions to forwarding state: 1
   Link type is point-to-point by default
   BPDU: sent 27, received 41329
```

```
On CAT-2:

CAT-2# show spanning-tree vlan 12 bridge


                                               Hello  Max  Fwd
Vlan                          Bridge ID        Time   Age  Dly
---------------- -------------------------------- ----- --- ---
VLAN0012           32780 (32768,  12) 0019.e780.6d80   2    20   15
```

```
CAT-2# show spanning-tree vlan 12 interface FastEthernet0/19 detail

Port 21 (FastEthernet0/19) of VLAN0012 is forwarding
  Port path cost 19, Port priority 128, Port Identifier 128.21.
  Designated root has priority 28684, address 000d.2870.fe00
  Designated bridge has priority 32780, address 0019.e780.6d80
  Designated port id is 128.21, designated path cost 19
  Timers: message age 0, forward delay 0, hold 0
  Number of transitions to forwarding state: 1
  Link type is point-to-point by default
  BPDU: sent 41380, received 7
```

On our pod, CAT-2 happens to have the lowest base MAC address and thus the lowest default bridge ID. Link F0/19 is therefore forwarding on the CAT-2 side and blocking on the CAT-1 side.

Note that this result may be reversed on your pod, depending on your switch base MAC addresses.

The command **sh spanning-tree vlan 12 interface f0/19 detail** indicates the bridge ID of the switch that has the link's designated port. Note the BPDU counts. Designated ports source BPDUs. Root ports and blocking ports receive BPDUs. In our case, you need to move the blocked ports from CAT-1 to CAT-2.

Let's raise the bridge ID for VLAN 12 on CAT-2:

```
CAT-2# debug spanning-tree events
Spanning Tree event debugging is on

CAT-2(config)# spanning-tree vlan 12 priority 100

% Bridge Priority must be in increments of 4096.
% Allowed values are:
  0     4096  8192  12288 16384 20480 24576 28672
  32768 36864 40960 45056 49152 53248 57344 61440

CAT-2(config)# spanning-tree vlan 12 priority 36864

1d01h: setting bridge id (which=1) prio 36876 prio cfg 36864 sysid 12 (on) id
  900C.0019.e780.6d80

1d01h: STP: VLAN0012 sent Topology Change Notice on Fa0/23
1d01h: STP: VLAN0012 Fa0/19 -> blocking
1d01h: STP: VLAN0012 Fa0/20 -> blocking
```

Instead of raising the bridge priority of CAT-2, you might have been able to lower the bridge ID of CAT-1. But this might have made CAT-1 the root bridge for VLAN 12 rather than SW-3, as required. It would depend on the switch base MAC addresses.

Let's verify the configuration:

```
On CAT-1:


CAT-1# show spanning-tree vlan 12


Interface          Role Sts Cost        Prio.Nbr Type
---------------- ---- --- ---------- -------- --------------------

Fa0/1              Desg FWD 19         128.3    P2p
Fa0/19             Desg FWD 19         128.21   P2p
Fa0/20             Desg FWD 19         128.22   P2p
Fa0/21             Altn BLK 20         128.23   P2p
Fa0/22             Root FWD 19         128.24   P2p
Fa0/23             Altn BLK 19         128.25   P2p
Fa0/24             Altn BLK 19         128.26   P2p
```

Note   The output of the previous **show** command reveals that F0/19 and F0/20 are in the forwarding state on CAT-1. The output of the following **show** command reveals that ports F0/19 and F0/20 are in blocking state on CAT-2.

```
On CAT-2:


CAT-2# show spanning-tree vlan 12 | begin Interface


Interface          Role Sts Cost        Prio.Nbr Type
---------------- ---- --- ---------- -------- ----------------------

Fa0/2              Desg FWD 19         128.4    P2p
Fa0/19             Altn BLK 19         128.21   P2p
Fa0/20             Altn BLK 19         128.22   P2p
Fa0/21             Altn BLK 19         128.23   P2p
Fa0/22             Altn BLK 19         128.24   P2p
Fa0/23             Root FWD 19         128.25   P2p
Fa0/24             Altn BLK 19         128.26   P2p
```

Task 4

Make sure that traffic on VLAN 21 between R1 and R2 uses only the following switch-to-switch links:

- F0/21 between CAT-2 and SW-4
- F0/23 between SW-4 and CAT-1

Use only the command **spanning-tree vlan vlan-id root**, and use it only on one switch. Set the appropriate diameter value.

Similar to Task 1, you must configure a root bridge so that traffic takes the required path. In this case, you must set the bridge priority indirectly by using the **root primary** macro. This macro determines the bridge priority of the current root bridge and sets the local bridge priority to a lower value. To achieve the required path, you need to make SW-4 the root bridge for VLAN 21.

But what is diameter and how should it be set? The **diameter** option for the **root primary** macro will calculate the optimum maximum delay and forwarding delay timer values, based on the size of the switched network. The smaller the network, the lower the timer values and the faster the topology will converge. For this calculation, the diameter of the switched network is the maximum number of switches that could possibly be in the path between two end stations. In our case, the correct diameter is 4. The default and maximum value is 7.

Use the following command to configure the **root primary** macro on SW-4 for VLAN 21:

```
SW-4(config)# spanning vlan 21 root primary diameter 4
```

Let's verify the configuration:

```
On SW-4:

SW-4# show spanning-tree vlan 21

VLAN0021
  Spanning tree enabled protocol ieee

  Root ID    Priority    24597
             Address     000c.ce44.7d80
             This bridge is the root
             Hello Time   2 sec  Max Age 14 sec  Forward Delay 10 sec


  Bridge ID  Priority    24597   (priority 24576 sys-id-ext 21)

             Address     000c.ce44.7d80
             Hello Time   2 sec  Max Age 14 sec  Forward Delay 10 sec
             Aging Time 300
[output is omitted for brevity]
```

Note   The bridge priority on SW-4 was lowered to 24576, making SW-4 the root bridge. The Max Age timer has been reduced from the default 20 seconds to 14 seconds, and the Forward Delay timer has been reduced from the default 15 seconds to 10 seconds. However, you will not see the **root primary** or the **diameter** command in the running configuration of the switch. Instead, you will see the following commands configured:

```
On SW-4:

SW-4# show running-config | include vlan 21

spanning-tree vlan 21 priority 24576
spanning-tree vlan 21 forward-time 10
spanning-tree vlan 21 max-age 14
```

Here is the output on CAT-1:

```
On CAT-1:

CAT-1# show spanning-tree vlan 21

VLAN0021
  Spanning tree enabled protocol ieee

  Root ID    Priority    24597
             Address     000c.ce44.7d80
             Cost        19
             Port        25 (FastEthernet0/23)
             Hello Time   2 sec  Max Age 14 sec  Forward Delay 10 sec

  Bridge ID  Priority    32789  (priority 32768 sys-id-ext 21)
             Address     001a.a174.1f00
             Hello Time   2 sec  Max Age 20 sec  Forward Delay 15 sec
             Aging Time 300
```

Note   CAT-1 has learned the Max Age and Forward Delay timers configured on SW-4. These values are advertised in configuration BPDUs sourced by the root bridge and are forwarded from switch to switch. It is these timers that all switches on VLAN 21 will actually use. The locally configured timers are only used if that switch happens to be the root bridge.

To verify the required path between R1 and R2 for VLAN 21, you could issue the commands **sh interface** and **sh mac address-table dynamic vlan 21** as you did in Task 1 for VLAN 12.

Task 5

Raise the spanning-tree port ID on a port in VLAN 21 so that CAT-2 chooses F0/22 as its root port instead of F0/21.

Here is the spanning tree topology for VLAN 21 on CAT-2 for our pod. Note that CAT-2 chose F0/21 as its root port rather than F0/22. Both ports have a local cost of 19, and BPDUs received on each port report the same value for sender bridge ID. The ports differ in their local port IDs. The port ID for F0/21 is 128.23 and the local port ID for F0/22 is 128.24.

```
CAT-2# show spanning-tree vlan 21 | begin Interface


Interface        Role Sts Cost      Prio.Nbr Type
---------------- ---- --- --------- -------- -----
Fa0/1            Desg FWD 19        128.3    P2p
Fa0/19           Desg FWD 19        128.21   P2p
Fa0/20           Desg FWD 19        128.22   P2p
Fa0/21           Root FWD 19        128.23   P2p
Fa0/22           Altn BLK 19        128.24   P2p
Fa0/23           Altn BLK 19        128.25   P2p
Fa0/24           Altn BLK 19        128.26   P2p
```

The port ID is sent in BPDUs sourced by that interface. It is a 16-bit field. Originally, the first 8 bits were priority and the last 8 bits were an interface number. This limited the number of ports on a switch to 255. To increase the number of potential ports on a switch, this field is now divided so that only the first 4 bits can be used for priority, and the last 12 bits can be used for interface number. The priority value is still evaluated as if it were a full 8-bit number, with the four lowest bits set to zero. Here you see the resulting configuration options:

```
CAT-2(config-if)# spanning-tree vlan 21 port-priority ?

 <0-240>  port priority in increments of 16
```

To change CAT-2's root port from F0/21 to f0/22, you will need to raise the port priority on the F0/21 link for VLAN 21. But should you do this on CAT-2 or SW-4?

Let's raise the port priority for f0/21 on SW-4:

```
SW-4(config)# int FastEthernet0/21
SW-4(config-if)# spanning-tree vlan 21 port-priority 144
```

Non-root bridges choose their root port based on *received* port IDs, not the locally configured port IDs. Change the port ID on the upstream switch, the switch on the designated port for the link. This is the opposite of the cost configuration, where the local, downstream cost is effective.

Let's verify the configuration:

```
On SW-4:


SW-4# show spanning-tree vlan 21 interface FastEthernet0/21


Vlan              Role Sts Cost      Prio.Nbr Type
----------------  ---- --- --------- -------- -----
VLAN0021          Desg FWD 19        144.21   P2p
```

```
On Cat-2:


CAT-2# show spanning-tree vlan 21 | begin Interface


Interface         Role Sts Cost      Prio.Nbr Type
----------------  ---- --- --------- -------- --------------------------
Fa0/1             Desg FWD 19        128.3    P2p
Fa0/19            Desg FWD 19        128.21   P2p
Fa0/20            Desg FWD 19        128.22   P2p
Fa0/21            Altn BLK 19        128.23   P2p
Fa0/22            Root FWD 19        128.24   P2p
Fa0/23            Altn BLK 19        128.25   P2p
Fa0/24            Altn BLK 19        128.26   P2p
```

Notice that CAT-2, a 3560 switch, shows F0/21 as link number 23. SW-4, a 3550 switch, shows F0/21 as link number 21. This difference is irrelevant to the spanning-tree algorithm, because port IDs are only compared when the sending bridge IDs are equal. In other words, spanning-tree never compares a port ID from one switch to a port ID on another switch.

When dealing with parallel links, you change local cost to change the local root port, and you change the local port ID to influence a neighbor's choice of root port.

Erase the config.text and vlan.dat files on all four switches and reload before proceeding to the next lab.

Lab 3-2: Advanced Spanning Tree Protocol (802.1D)

Figure 3-2 illustrates the topology that will be used in the following tasks.

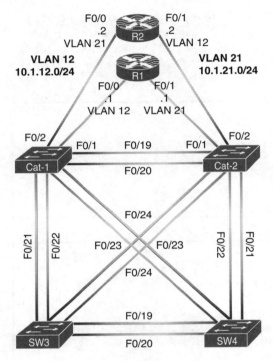

Figure 3-2   *Complete 802.1D Lab Topology*

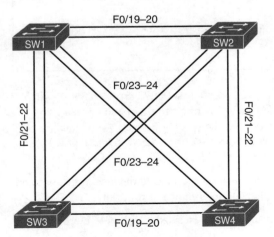

Figure 3-3   *Advanced Spanning Tree Protocol (802.1D)*

Task 1

Shut down all ports on all switches and configure the hostnames of these switches based on Figure 3-3.

```
On All Switches:


SWx(config)# interface range FastEthernet0/1 - 24
SWx(config-if-range)# shut
```

Let's verify the configuration:

```
On All Switches:


SWx# show interface status


Port         Name            Status        Vlan     Duplex  Speed Type
Fa0/1                        disabled      1        auto    auto 10/100BaseTX
Fa0/2                        disabled      1        auto    auto 10/100BaseTX
Fa0/3                        disabled      1        auto    auto 10/100BaseTX
Fa0/4                        disabled      1        auto    auto 10/100BaseTX
Fa0/5                        disabled      1        auto    auto 10/100BaseTX
Fa0/6                        disabled      1        auto    auto 10/100BaseTX
Fa0/7                        disabled      1        auto    auto 10/100BaseTX
Fa0/8                        disabled      1        auto    auto 10/100BaseTX
Fa0/9                        disabled      1        auto    auto 10/100BaseTX
Fa0/10                       disabled      1        auto    auto 10/100BaseTX
Fa0/11                       disabled      1        auto    auto 10/100BaseTX
Fa0/12                       disabled      1        auto    auto 10/100BaseTX
Fa0/13                       disabled      1        auto    auto 10/100BaseTX
Fa0/14                       disabled      1        auto    auto 10/100BaseTX
Fa0/15                       disabled      1        auto    auto 10/100BaseTX
Fa0/16                       disabled      1        auto    auto 10/100BaseTX
Fa0/17                       disabled      1        auto    auto 10/100BaseTX
Fa0/18                       disabled      1        auto    auto 10/100BaseTX
Fa0/19                       disabled      1        auto    auto 10/100BaseTX
Fa0/20                       disabled      1        auto    auto 10/100BaseTX
Fa0/21                       disabled      1        auto    auto 10/100BaseTX
Fa0/22                       disabled      1        auto    auto 10/100BaseTX
Fa0/23                       disabled      1        auto    auto 10/100BaseTX
Fa0/24                       disabled      1        auto    auto 10/100BaseTX
```

```
On SW1:


SW1(config)# hostname SW1
```

```
On SW2:

SW2(config)# hostname SW2
```

```
On SW3:

SW3(config)# hostname SW3
```

```
On SW4:

SW4(config)# hostname SW4
```

Task 2

Configure ports F0/19–20 connecting SW1 to SW2 and SW3 to SW4 as trunk ports. You should use an industry-standard protocol to accomplish this task. These ports should never become an access port through negotiation.

```
On SW1, SW2, SW3 and SW4:

SWx(config)# interface range FastEthernet0/19-20
SWx(config-if-range)# switchport trunk encapsulation dot1q
SWx(config-if-range)# switchport mode trunk
SWx(config-if-range)# no shut
```

Let's verify the configuration:

```
On SW1:

SW1# show interface trunk | include trunking

Fa0/19        on              802.1q        trunking      1
Fa0/20        on              802.1q        trunking      1
```

```
On SW2:

SW2# show interface trunk | include trunking

Fa0/19        on              802.1q        trunking      1
Fa0/20        on              802.1q        trunking      1
```

```
On SW3:


SW3# show interface trunk | inc trunking


Fa0/19        on           802.1q          trunking      1
Fa0/20        on           802.1q          trunking      1
```

```
On SW4:


SW4# show interface trunk | include trunking


Fa0/19        on           802.1q          trunking      1
Fa0/20        on           802.1q          trunking      1
```

Task 3

Configure ports F0/21–22 connecting SW2 to SW4 and SW1 to SW3 as trunk ports. You should use an industry-standard protocol to accomplish this task. These ports should never become an access port through negotiation.

```
On SW1, SW2, SW3 and SW4:

SWx(config)# interface range FastEthernet0/21-22
SWx(config-if-range)# switchport trunk encapsulation dot1q
SWx(config-if-range)# switchport mode trunk
SWx(config-if-range)# no shut
```

Let's verify the configuration:

```
On SW1:


SW1# show interface trunk | include trunking


Fa0/19        on           802.1q          trunking      1
Fa0/20        on           802.1q          trunking      1
Fa0/21        on           802.1q          trunking      1
Fa0/22        on           802.1q          trunking      1
```

```
On SW2:

SW2# show interface trunk | include trunking

Fa0/19        on             802.1q           trunking        1
Fa0/20        on             802.1q           trunking        1

Fa0/21        on             802.1q           trunking        1
Fa0/22        on             802.1q           trunking        1
```

```
On SW3

SW3# show interface trunk | include trunking

Fa0/19        on             802.1q           trunking        1
Fa0/20        on             802.1q           trunking        1
Fa0/21        on             802.1q           trunking        1
Fa0/22        on             802.1q           trunking        1
```

```
On SW4

SW4# show interface trunk | include trunking

Fa0/19        on             802.1q           trunking        1
Fa0/20        on             802.1q           trunking        1
Fa0/21        on             802.1q           trunking        1
Fa0/22        on             802.1q           trunking        1
```

Task 4

These switches should be configured in a VLAN Trunking Protocol (VTP) domain called "CCIE":

```
On SW1:

SW1(config)# vtp domain CCIE
```

This configuration will be propagated via VTP to the other switches.

Let's verify the configuration:

```
On All Switches:

SWx# show vtp status | include VTP Domain Name

VTP Domain Name                    : CCIE
```

> **Note**   The domain name is propagated by VTP messages when the trunk is established between the switches.

Task 5

Create the VLANs 100, 200, 300, and 400 and ensure they are propagated to all four switches:

```
On SW1:

SW1(config)# vlan 100,200,300,400
SW1(config-vlan)# exit                 You must "exit" for the VLANs to be
  propagated.
```

Let's verify the configuration:

```
On SW1:

SW1# show vlan brief | include VLAN

VLAN Name                     Status     Ports
100  VLAN0100                 active
200  VLAN0200                 active
300  VLAN0300                 active
400  VLAN0400                 active
```

```
On SW2:

SW2# show vlan brief | include VLAN

VLAN Name                     Status     Ports
100  VLAN0100                 active
200  VLAN0200                 active
300  VLAN0300                 active
400  VLAN0400                 active
```

```
On SW3:

SW3# show vlan brief | include VLAN

VLAN Name                          Status    Ports

100  VLAN0100                      active
200  VLAN0200                      active
300  VLAN0300                      active
400  VLAN0400                      active
```

```
On SW4:

SW4# show vlan brief | include VLAN

VLAN Name                          Status    Ports
100  VLAN0100                      active
200  VLAN0200                      active
300  VLAN0300                      active
400  VLAN0400                      active
```

Task 6

Ensure that SW1 is the root bridge for VLAN 100, SW2 is the root bridge for VLAN 200, SW3 is the root bridge for VLAN 300, and SW4 is the root bridge for VLAN 400. You should use a macro to accomplish this task.

```
On SW1:

SW1(config)# spanning-tree vlan 100 root primary
```

```
On SW2:

SW2(config)# spanning-tree vlan 200 root primary
```

```
On SW3:

SW3(config)# spanning-tree vlan 300 root primary
```

```
On SW4:

SW4(config)# spanning-tree vlan 400 root primary
```

Let's verify the configuration:

```
On SW1:


SW1# show spanning-tree vlan 100


VLAN0100
  Spanning tree enabled protocol ieee
  Root ID    Priority    24676
             Address     0012.7f40.9380
             This bridge is the root
             Hello Time   2 sec  Max Age 20 sec  Forward Delay 15 sec

  Bridge ID  Priority    24676  (priority 24576 sys-id-ext 100)
             Address     0012.7f40.9380
             Hello Time   2 sec  Max Age 20 sec  Forward Delay 15 sec
             Aging Time 15


Interface          Role Sts Cost      Prio.Nbr Type
------------------ ---- --- --------- -------- ----------------------
Fa0/19             Desg FWD 19        128.21   P2p
Fa0/20             Desg FWD 19        128.22   P2p
Fa0/21             Desg FWD 19        128.23   P2p
Fa0/22             Desg FWD 19        128.24   P2p
```

Note   Because SW1 is the root bridge for VLAN 100, all of the trunk interfaces are designated ports.

```
SW1# show version | include Base

Base ethernet MAC Address       : 00:12:7F:40:93:80
```

```
On SW2:


SW2# show spanning-tree vlan 200


VLAN0200
  Spanning tree enabled protocol ieee
  Root ID    Priority    24776
             Address     001d.e5d6.0000
             This bridge is the root
             Hello Time   2 sec  Max Age 20 sec  Forward Delay 15 sec
```

```
   Bridge ID  Priority    24776   (priority 24576 sys-id-ext 200)
              Address     001d.e5d6.0000
              Hello Time   2 sec  Max Age 20 sec  Forward Delay 15 sec
              Aging Time 300


Interface          Role Sts Cost      Prio.Nbr Type
------------------ ---- --- --------- -------- ---------------
Fa0/19             Desg FWD 19         128.21   P2p

Fa0/20             Desg FWD 19         128.22   P2p
Fa0/21             Desg FWD 19         128.23   P2p
Fa0/22             Desg FWD 19         128.24   P2p


SW2# show version | include Base
```

```
Base ethernet MAC Address        : 00:1D:E5:D6:00:00
```

```
On SW3:

SW3# show spanning-tree vlan 300


VLAN0300
  Spanning tree enabled protocol ieee
  Root ID    Priority    24876
             Address     000c.858b.7a00
             This bridge is the root
             Hello Time   2 sec  Max Age 20 sec  Forward Delay 15 sec

  Bridge ID  Priority    24876   (priority 24576 sys-id-ext 300)
             Address     000c.858b.7a00
             Hello Time   2 sec  Max Age 20 sec  Forward Delay 15 sec
             Aging Time 15


Interface         Role Sts Cost      Prio.Nbr Type
---------------- ---- --- --------- -------- -------------------------
Fa0/19            Desg FWD 19         128.19   P2p
Fa0/20            Desg FWD 19         128.20   P2p
Fa0/21            Desg FWD 19         128.21   P2p
Fa0/22            Desg FWD 19         128.22   P2p


SW3# show version | include Base
```

```
Base ethernet MAC Address: 00:0C:85:8B:7A:00
```

```
On SW4:


SW4# show spanning-tree vlan 400


VLAN0400
  Spanning tree enabled protocol ieee
  Root ID     Priority    24976
              Address     000c.302d.9980
              This bridge is the root
              Hello Time   2 sec  Max Age 20 sec  Forward Delay 15 sec



  Bridge ID  Priority    24976   (priority 24576 sys-id-ext 400)
             Address     000c.302d.9980
             Hello Time   2 sec  Max Age 20 sec  Forward Delay 15 sec
             Aging Time 300


Interface        Role Sts Cost      Prio.Nbr Type
---------------- ---- --- --------- -------- ----------------
Fa0/19           Desg FWD 19        128.19   P2p
Fa0/20           Desg FWD 19        128.20   P2p
Fa0/21           Desg FWD 19        128.21   P2p
Fa0/22           Desg FWD 19        128.22   P2p

SW4# show version | include Base


Base ethernet MAC Address: 00:0C:30:2D:99:80
```

Task 7

Implement the following policies:

- VLAN 100 should never traverse SW4. This switch should *not* receive/send traffic for this VLAN.

- VLAN 200 should never traverse SW3. This switch should *not* receive/send traffic for this VLAN.

- VLAN 300 should never traverse SW2. This switch should *not* receive/send traffic for this VLAN.

- VLAN 400 should never traverse SW1. This switch should *not* receive/send traffic for this VLAN.

Let's configure the first policy:

```
On SW2:

SW2(config)# interface range FastEthernet0/21-22
SW2(config-if-range)# switchport trunk allowed vlan except 100
```

```
On SW3:

SW3(config)# interface range FastEthernet0/19-20

SW3(config-if-range)# switchport trunk allowed vlan except 100
```

```
On SW4:

SW4(config)# interface range FastEthernet0/19-20 , FastEthernet0/21-22
SW4(config-if-range)# switchport trunk allowed vlan except 100
```

Now let's verify the configuration:

```
On SW2:

SW2# show interface trunk | exclude trunking|200|300|domain|pruned|Enc


Port       Vlans allowed on trunk
Fa0/19     1-4094
Fa0/20     1-4094
Fa0/21     1-99,101-4094      The traffic for VLAN 100 is NOT
Fa0/22     1-99,101-4094      allowed on these trunk links.
```

```
On SW3:

SW3# show interface trunk | exclude trunking|200|300|domain|pruned|Enc


Port       Vlans allowed on trunk
Fa0/19     1-99,101-4094          The traffic for VLAN 100 is NOT
Fa0/20     1-99,101-4094          allowed on these trunk links.
Fa0/21     1-4094
Fa0/22     1-4094
```

```
On SW4:


SW4# show interface trunk | exclude trunking|200|300|pruned|domain|Enc


Port       Vlans allowed on trunk
Fa0/19     1-99,101-4094
Fa0/20     1-99,101-4094          The traffic for VLAN 100 is NOT
Fa0/21     1-99,101-4094          allowed on these trunk links.
Fa0/22     1-99,101-4094
```

Now let's configure the second policy:

> **Note**   Make sure the first policy in this task is *not* overridden by the next policy.

```
On SW1:


SW1(config)# interface range FastEthernet0/21-22
SW1(config-if-range)# switchport trunk allowed vlan except 200
```

```
On SW4:


SW4(config)# interface range FastEthernet0/19-20
SW4(config-if-range)# switchport trunk allowed vlan except 100,200
```

```
On SW3:


SW3(config)# interface range FastEthernet0/19-20
SW3(config-if-range)# switchport trunk allowed vlan except 100,200

SW3(config)# interface range FastEthernet0/21-22
SW3(config-if-range)# switchport trunk allowed vlan except 200
```

Let's verify the configuration:

```
On SW1:
SW1# show interface trunk | exclude trunking|200|300|100|pruned|domain|Enc


Port       Vlans allowed on trunk
Fa0/19     1-4094
Fa0/20     1-4094                 The traffic for VLAN 200 is NOT
Fa0/21     1-199,201-4094         allowed on these trunk links.
Fa0/22     1-199,201-4094
```

```
On SW4:

SW4# show interface trunk | exclude trunking|200|300|400|pruned|domain|Enc

Port        Vlans allowed on trunk
Fa0/19      1-99,101-199,201-4094      The traffic for VLANs 100 or 200
Fa0/20      1-99,101-199,201-4094      is NOT allowed on these trunk links.
Fa0/21      1-99,101-4094          .    The traffic for VLAN 100 is NOT
Fa0/22      1-99,101-4094               allowed on these trunk links.
```

```
On SW3:

SW3# show interface trunk | exclude trunking|200|300|pruned|domain|Enc

Port        Vlans allowed on trunk
Fa0/19      1-99,101-199,201-4094       The traffic for VLANs 100 and 200
Fa0/20      1-99,101-199,201-4094       is NOT allowed on these trunk links.
Fa0/21      1-199,201-4094              The traffic for VLAN 200 is
Fa0/22      1-199,201-4094              NOT allowed on these trunk links.
```

Now let's configure the third policy:

```
On SW2:

SW2(config-if-range)# interface range FastEthernet0/21-22
SW2(config-if-range)# switchport trunk allowed vlan except 100,300

SW2(config-if-range)# interface range FastEthernet0/19-20
SW2(config-if-range)# switchport trunk allowed vlan except 300
```

```
On SW4:

SW4(config)# interface range FastEthernet0/21-22
SW4(config-if-range)# switchport trunk allowed vlan except 100,300
```

```
On SW1:

SW1(config)# interface range FastEthernet0/19-20
SW1(config-if-range)# switchport trunk allowed vlan except 300
```

Now you need to verify the configuration:

```
On SW2:


SW2# show interface trunk | exclude trunking|200|400|pruned|domain|Enc


Port          Vlans allowed on trunk
Fa0/19        1-299,301-4094              The traffic for VLAN 300 is NOT
Fa0/20        1-299,301-4094              allowed on these trunk links.
Fa0/21        1-99,101-299,301-4094       The traffic for VLANs 100 or 300 is
Fa0/22        1-99,101-299,301-4094       NOT allowed on these trunk links.
```

```
On SW4:


SW4# show interface trunk | exclude trunking|200|300|400|pruned|domain|Enc


Port          Vlans allowed on trunk
Fa0/19        1-99,101-199,201-4094       The traffic for VLANs 100 or 200 is
Fa0/20        1-99,101-199,201-4094       NOT allowed on these trunk links.
Fa0/21        1-99,101-299,301-4094        The traffic for VLANs 100 or 300
Fa0/22        1-99,101-299,301-4094       is NOT allowed on these trunk links.
```

```
On SW1:


SW1# show interface trunk | exclude trunking|200|300|100|pruned|domain|Enc


Port          Vlans allowed on trunk
Fa0/19        1-299,301-4094               The traffic for VLAN 300 is NOT
Fa0/20        1-299,301-4094               allowed on this trunk link.
Fa0/21        1-199,201-4094              The traffic for VLAN 200 is NOT
Fa0/22        1-199,201-4094              allowed on this trunk link.
```

Finally, let's configure the fourth policy:

```
On SW1:

SW1(config)# interface range FastEthernet0/19-20
SW1(config-if-range)# switchport trunk allowed vlan except 300,400

SW1(config)# interface range FastEthernet0/21-22
SW1(config-if-range)# switchport trunk allowed vlan except 200,400
```

```
On SW2:

SW2(config)# interface range FastEthernet0/19-20
SW2(config-if-range)# switchport trunk allowed vlan except 300,400
```

```
On SW3:

SW3(config)# interface range FastEthernet0/21-22
SW3(config-if-range)# switchport trunk allowed vlan except 200,400
```

Let's verify the configuration:

```
On SW1:

SW1# show interface trunk | exclude trunking|200|300|100|pruned|domain|Enc

Port        Vlans allowed on trunk
Fa0/19      1-299,301-399,401-4094      The traffic for VLANs 300 or 400
Fa0/20      1-299,301-399,401-4094    is NOT allowed on these trunk links
Fa0/21      1-199,201-399,401-4094    The traffic for VLANs 200 or 400
Fa0/22      1-199,201-399,401-4094    is NOT allowed on these trunk links.
```

```
On SW2:

SW2# show interface trunk | exclude trunking|100|200|300|pruned|domain|Enc

Port        Vlans allowed on trunk
Fa0/19      1-299,301-399,401-4094    The traffic for VLANs 300 or 400
Fa0/20      1-299,301-399,401-4094    is NOT allowed on these trunk links.

Fa0/21      1-99,101-299,301-4094     The traffic for VLANs 100 or 300 is
Fa0/22      1-99,101-299,301-4094     NOT allowed on these trunk links.
```

```
On SW3:

SW3# show interface trunk | exclude trunking|200|300|pruned|domain|Enc

Port        Vlans allowed on trunk
Fa0/19      1-99,101-199,201-4094     The traffic for VLANs 100 or 200 is
Fa0/20      1-99,101-199,201-4094     NOT allowed on these trunk links.
Fa0/21      1-199,201-399,401-4094    The traffic for VLANs 200 or 400 is
Fa0/22      1-199,201-399,401-4094    NOT allowed on these trunk links.
```

Task 8

Configure SW1 such that it's the root bridge for VLAN 500. If this switch goes down, SW2 should become the root bridge for this VLAN. Do *not* override any of the previous tasks to accomplish this one.

```
On SW1:


SW1(config)# spanning-tree vlan 500 root primary


SW1# debug spanning-tree events
Spanning Tree event debugging is on


SW1(config)# vlan 500
```

Note   When you're creating a VLAN in global config mode, the VLAN is *not* created and propagated unless you exit out of VLAN configuration mode:

```
SW1(config-vlan)# exit
```

Once you have exited out of VLAN configuration mode, you should see the following console messages:

```
setting bridge id (which=3) prio 25076 prio cfg 24576 sysid 500 (on) id

 61F4.0012.7f40.9380
set portid: VLAN0500 Fa0/19: new port id 8015
STP: VLAN0500 Fa0/19 -> listening
set portid: VLAN0500 Fa0/20: new port id 8016
STP: VLAN0500 Fa0/20 -> listening
set portid: VLAN0500 Fa0/21: new port id 8017
STP: VLAN0500 Fa0/21 -> listening

STP: VLAN0500 heard root 33268-000c.858b.7a00 on Fa0/21
STP: VLAN0500 heard root 33268-000c.858b.7a00 on Fa0/22
STP: VLAN0500 heard root 33268-001d.e5d6.0000 on Fa0/19
STP: VLAN0500 heard root 33268-001d.e5d6.0000 on Fa0/20

STP: VLAN0500 Fa0/19 -> learning

STP: VLAN0500 Fa0/20 -> learning
```

```
STP: VLAN0500 Fa0/21 -> learning
STP: VLAN0500 Fa0/22 -> learning

STP: VLAN0500 Fa0/19 -> forwarding
STP: VLAN0500 Fa0/20 -> forwarding
STP: VLAN0500 Fa0/21 -> forwarding
STP: VLAN0500 Fa0/22 -> forwarding
```

Let's disable the debug:

```
On SW1:

SW1# undebug all
```

```
On SW2:

SW2(config)# spanning-tree vlan 500 root secondary
```

Now let's verify the configuration:

```
On SW2:

SW2# show spanning-tree vlan 500 | exclude Interface|Fa0


VLAN0500
  Spanning tree enabled protocol ieee
  Root ID    Priority    25076
             Address     0012.7f40.9380
             Cost        19
             Port        21 (FastEthernet0/19)
             Hello Time   2 sec  Max Age 20 sec  Forward Delay 15 sec

  Bridge ID  Priority    29172  (priority 28672 sys-id-ext 500)
             Address     001d.e5d6.0000
             Hello Time   2 sec  Max Age 20 sec  Forward Delay 15 sec
             Aging Time 300


-------------------- ---- --- --------- -------- ---------------------------------


Note: SW1 is the root.
On SW1:


SW1# show version | include Base

Base ethernet MAC Address       : 00:12:7F:40:93:80
```

Task 9

Create VLAN 500 and ensure the traffic from SW2 for VLAN 500 takes the following path:

SW2 → SW4 → SW3 → SW1

SW2 should use port F0/19 or F0/20 *only* if the path through SW4 → SW3 → SW1 is *not* possible due to a link failure.

```
On SW2:

SW2# show spanning-tree vlan 500

VLAN0500

  Spanning tree enabled protocol ieee
  Root ID    Priority    25076
             Address     0012.7f40.9380
             Cost        19
             Port        21 (FastEthernet0/19)
             Hello Time   2 sec  Max Age 20 sec  Forward Delay 15 sec

  Bridge ID  Priority    29172  (priority 28672 sys-id-ext 500)
             Address     001d.e5d6.0000
             Hello Time   2 sec  Max Age 20 sec  Forward Delay 15 sec
             Aging Time 300

Interface          Role Sts Cost      Prio.Nbr Type
------------------ ---- --- --------- -------- --------------------
Fa0/19             Root FWD 19         128.21   P2p
Fa0/20             Altn BLK 19         128.22   P2p
Fa0/21             Desg FWD 19         128.23   P2p
Fa0/22             Desg FWD 19         128.24   P2p
```

Note   SW2 is taking port F0/19 to get to the root bridge for VLAN 500, and its root cost is 19, which is the cost of a 100-Mbps link. If these ports (F0/19 and F0/20) are shut down, you should see the cost of the local switch (SW2) to the root bridge, which should be 57. The following reveals the cumulative cost of the local switch to the root bridge for VLAN 500.

Let's add the total cost:

The cost of the link from SW2 → SW4 is 19.

The cost of the link from SW4 → SW3 is 19.

The cost of the link from SW3 → SW1 is 19.

The total cost should therefore be 57.

Let's verify this information:

```
On SW2:


SW2(config)# interface range FastEthernet0/19-20
SW2(config-if-range)# shut
```

Let's verify the new cost:

```
SW2# show spanning-tree vlan 500


VLAN0500

  Spanning tree enabled protocol ieee
  Root ID    Priority    25076
             Address     0012.7f40.9380
             Cost        57
             Port        23 (FastEthernet0/21)
             Hello Time   2 sec  Max Age 20 sec  Forward Delay 15 sec

  Bridge ID  Priority    29172   (priority 28672 sys-id-ext 500)
             Address     001d.e5d6.0000
             Hello Time   2 sec  Max Age 20 sec  Forward Delay 15 sec
             Aging Time 300


Interface          Role Sts Cost      Prio.Nbr Type
------------------ ---- --- --------- -------- --------------------
Fa0/21             Root FWD 19        128.23   P2p
Fa0/22             Altn BLK 19        128.24   P2p
```

Note   VLAN 500 is taking port F0/21 toward the root bridge through SW4. If this is traced all the way back to SW1, you will see the path from SW2's perspective.

SW2 → SW4 → SW3 → SW1

To configure this task, you should issue **no shutdown** on ports F0/19–20 first:

```
On SW2:


SW2(config)# interface range FastEthernet0/19-20
SW2(config-if-range)# no shut

SW2(config-if-range)# spanning-tree vlan 500 cost 58
```

> **Note**   The preceding command sets the cost through ports F0/19–20 higher than 57. Therefore, traffic from SW2 for VLAN 500 will have two paths:
>
> ■ **Primary:** SW2 → SW4 → SW3 → SW1
>
> ■ **Backup:** SW2 → SW1

Let's verify the configuration:

```
On SW2:


SW2# show spanning-tree vlan 500


VLAN0500


  Spanning tree enabled protocol ieee
  Root ID    Priority    25076
             Address     0012.7f40.9380
             Cost        57
             Port        23 (FastEthernet0/21)
             Hello Time   2 sec  Max Age 20 sec  Forward Delay 15 sec


  Bridge ID  Priority    29172  (priority 28672 sys-id-ext 500)
             Address     001d.e5d6.0000
             Hello Time   2 sec  Max Age 20 sec  Forward Delay 15 sec
             Aging Time 300


Interface          Role Sts Cost      Prio.Nbr Type
------------------ ---- --- --------- -------- ----------------------
Fa0/19             Altn BLK 58         128.21  P2p
Fa0/20             Altn BLK 58         128.22  P2p
Fa0/21             Root FWD 19         128.23  P2p
Fa0/22             Altn BLK 19         128.24  P2p
```

```
On SW2:

SW2(config)# interface range FastEthernet0/21-22
SW2(config-if-range)# shut
```

You should wait 30 seconds before performing the following **show** command:

```
SW2# show spanning-tree vlan 500


VLAN0500
  Spanning tree enabled protocol ieee
  Root ID    Priority    25076
             Address     0012.7f40.9380
             Cost        58
             Port        21 (FastEthernet0/19)
             Hello Time   2 sec  Max Age 20 sec  Forward Delay 15 sec

  Bridge ID  Priority    29172  (priority 28672 sys-id-ext 500)
             Address     001d.e5d6.0000
             Hello Time   2 sec  Max Age 20 sec  Forward Delay 15 sec
             Aging Time 300


Interface          Role Sts Cost      Prio.Nbr Type
------------------ ---- --- --------- -------- ----------------
Fa0/19             Root FWD 58        128.21   P2p
Fa0/20             Altn BLK 58        128.22   P2p
```

```
On SW2:

SW2(config)# interface range FastEthernet0/21-22
SW2(config-if-range)# no shut
```

Task 10

Create VLAN 600 and configure SW3 as the root bridge for this VLAN. This switch should be configured such that traffic for VLAN 600 uses the following ports:

- F0/22 from SW1
- F0/20 from SW4

```
On SW-3:

SW3(config)# vlan 600
SW3(config-vlan)# exit
SW3(config)# spanning-tree vlan 600 root primary
```

Let's look at the existing path from SW1 and SW4:

```
On SW1:


SW1# show spanning-tree vlan 600


VLAN0600
  Spanning tree enabled protocol ieee
  Root ID    Priority    25176
             Address     000c.858b.7a00
             Cost        19
             Port        23 (FastEthernet0/21)
             Hello Time   2 sec  Max Age 20 sec  Forward Delay 15 sec

  Bridge ID  Priority    33368  (priority 32768 sys-id-ext 600)
             Address     0012.7f40.9380
             Hello Time   2 sec  Max Age 20 sec  Forward Delay 15 sec
             Aging Time 15


Interface           Role Sts Cost      Prio.Nbr Type
------------------- ---- --- --------- -------- --------------------


Fa0/19              Desg FWD 19        128.21   P2p
Fa0/20              Desg FWD 19        128.22   P2p
Fa0/21              Root FWD 19        128.23   P2p
Fa0/22              Altn BLK 19        128.24   P2p
```

```
On SW4:


SW4# show spanning-tree vlan 600


VLAN0600
  Spanning tree enabled protocol ieee
  Root ID    Priority    25176
             Address     000c.858b.7a00
             Cost        19
             Port        19 (FastEthernet0/19)
             Hello Time   2 sec  Max Age 20 sec  Forward Delay 15 sec

  Bridge ID  Priority    33368  (priority 32768 sys-id-ext 600)
             Address     000c.302d.9980
             Hello Time   2 sec  Max Age 20 sec  Forward Delay 15 sec
             Aging Time 300
```

```
Interface          Role Sts Cost       Prio.Nbr Type
---------------- ---- --- ---------- -------- --------------------
Fa0/19             Root FWD 19         128.19   P2p
Fa0/20             Altn BLK 19         128.20   P2p
Fa0/21             Desg FWD 19         128.21   P2p
Fa0/22             Desg FWD 19         128.22   P2p
```

Now we can configure the task:

```
On SW3:

SW-3(config)# interface range FastEthernet0/20 , FastEthernet0/22
SW-3(config-if)# spanning-tree vlan 600 port-priority 0
```

By default, the port priority of all interfaces for all VLANs is set to 128. Remember, the lower cost has higher preference. If the port priority of the ports connecting this switch to SW1 and SW4 (F0/20 and F0/22 for SW4 and SW1, respectively) is reduced, these ports will be the preferred ports for connecting to the root bridge, which in this case is SW4.

Let's verify the configuration:

```
On SW3:

SW3# show spanning-tree vlan 600 | begin Fa0

Fa0/19             Desg FWD 19         128.19   P2p
Fa0/20             Desg FWD 19           0.20   P2p
Fa0/21             Desg FWD 19         128.21   P2p
Fa0/22             Desg FWD 19           0.22   P2p
```

```
On SW1:

SW1# show spanning-tree vlan 600 | begin Interface

Interface          Role Sts Cost       Prio.Nbr Type
---------------- ---- --- ---------- -------- ----------------
Fa0/19             Desg FWD 19         128.21   P2p
Fa0/20             Desg FWD 19         128.22   P2p
Fa0/21             Altn BLK 19         128.23   P2p
Fa0/22             Root FWD 19         128.24   P2p
```

```
On SW4:

SW4# show spanning-tree vlan 600 | begin Interface

Interface          Role Sts Cost      Prio.Nbr Type
---------------    ---- --- ---------  -------- -------------------
Fa0/19             Altn BLK 19         128.19   P2p
Fa0/20             Root FWD 19         128.20   P2p
Fa0/21             Desg FWD 19         128.21   P2p
Fa0/22             Desg FWD 19         128.22   P2p
```

Erase the config.text and vlan.dat files and reload the switches before proceeding to the next lab.

Lab 3-3: Rapid Spanning Tree Protocol (802.1w)

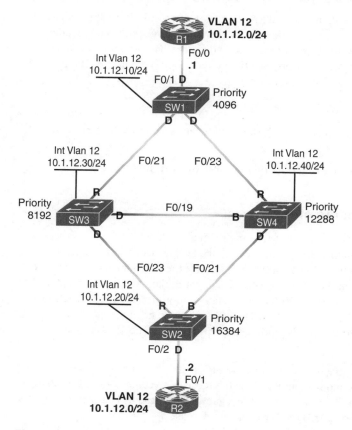

Figure 3-4 *Rapid Spanning Tree Protocol (802.1D)*

802.1w Port States

On a non-root bridge running 802.1w (Rapid STP), there are fewer port states than those found in 802.1d. 802.1w makes things much easier but only has two states:

- **Discarding:** This state encompasses the disabled, blocking, and listening states used in 802.1d.

- **Forwarding:** This state is unchanged from its 802.1d counterpart.

802.1w Port Roles

The major advantage of the Rapid Spanning Tree Protocol (RSTP) is that switches use BPDU frames differently than before. Ports, when they first come up or when a topology change occurs, exchange BPDUs with something called "proposal/agreement flags" set. This is done to achieve faster transition times to the appropriate state for a given port. These flags are used as part of the negotiation of whether a port should fall into the designated, nondesignated, or root port role.

If a given port should suddenly be elected as a root port as a result of a failure, all other ports will immediately begin renegotiations by exchanging more "proposal/agreement BPDUs" since the path toward the root bridge is no different. This one process is what gives 802.1w its extremely fast reconvergence time after a topology change. The port roles described in this protocol are as follows:

- **Designated:** The same role as that in 802.1d

- **Alternate:** A port that is in a blocking state and receives superior (better) BPDU frames from another switch

- **Backup:** A port in the blocking state that receives superior BPDU frames

Operational Enhancements of 802.1w

All switches exchange BPDUs instead of relaying them after they have received them from the root bridge. In 802.1w BPDUs are treated like keepalives. 802.1w-enabled switches do not have to wait for the root bridge to notify them about topology changes that occurred somewhere in the network. The switch that initially detects a change is the device that is responsible for notifying its neighbors about it. And those neighbors, in turn, notify their neighbors immediately. This eliminates the need for the root bridge to manage this process. However, this modification brings up the need to embrace the older BPDU format.

RSTP is backward-compatible with traditional 802.1d speaking switches. This is accomplished because the moment an RSTP switch receives a version 1 (802.1d) BPDU, that switch will transition that port back to the legacy STP protocol. This means the timers we studied as part of 802.1D STP will again be in use.

802.1w Rapid Convergence Mechanisms

All the alterations made to this version of STP have a single purpose: They help accelerate convergence when a new connection or a topology change is detected. With RSTP, fast convergence is accomplished as an industry-standard mechanism that is part of the 802.1w standard. So keep in mind that RSTP not a proprietary solution, but the Cisco deployment of RSTP supports Per-VLAN Spanning Tree, and as such it is referred to as Rapid Per-VLAN Spanning Tree and supports the mandated convergence mechanisms listed here:

- **Edge port:** A port that is a candidate for a quick transition to the forwarding state because it is connected to devices that cannot create a loop (this means that no BPDUs are received on this port). Cisco IOS enables edge port capability via the **spanning-tree PortFast** command. The ports must be a point-to-point link type that supports full duplex. PortFast will be discussed later in this chapter.

- **Link type:** Link type is derived from the duplex state of the port:

  - **Point-to-Point Link:** Full duplex

  - **Shared Link:** Half duplex

Now let's explore the aspect behind 802.1w via the following labs and tasks.

Lab Setup

- Shut down all interfaces that are not shown in Figure 3-4.

- Configure all the interfaces shown in Figure 3-4 as access links in VLAN 12.

- On each switch, configure the bridge priority for VLAN 12 as shown in Figure 3-4.

- Switch ports should be root (R), designated (D), or blocking (B), as shown in Figure 3-4.

- Assign IP addresses as shown in Table 3-2.

- Configure **ntp server 10.1.12.1** on all devices, except R1.

- On R1, configure **ntp master 4**.

- Configure the following commands on each switch:

  - **service timestamps debug datetime msec**

  - **service timestamps log datetime msec**

  - **logging buffered 100000 debugging**

- Verify that all IP addresses are reachable and that all switches have learned the time from R1.

Table 3-2 outlines the IP addresses necessary to implement this lab.

Table 3-2 *IP Addressing*

Router	Interface	IP address
R1	F0/0	10.1.12.1/24
R2	F0/1	10.1.12.2/24
SW1	Interface VLAN 12	10.1.12.10/24
SW2	Interface VLAN 12	10.1.12.20/24
SW3	Interface VLAN 12	10.1.12.30/24
SW4	Interface VLAN 12	10.1.12.40/24

Task 1

Configure *only* the following switches to operate in **rapid-pvst** mode:

- SW1

- SW3

- SW4

Examine the output of the **sh spanning-tree vlan 12** command for any changes.

The Catalyst 3550 and 3560 can operate in one of three spanning-tree modes:

- **PVST:** Per-VLAN Spanning Tree (the default 802.1D mode)

- **Rapid-PVST:** Rapid Per-VLAN Spanning Tree, based on IEEE standard 802.1w

- **MST:** Multiple Spanning-Tree, based on IEEE standard 802.1s

Note   The switch can only be configured for one mode.

```
Enable Rapid Spanning-tree on SW1, SW3 and SW4:

SWx(config)# spanning-tree mode rapid-pvst
```

Let's verify the configuration:

```
On SW1:

SW1# show spanning-tree summary | include mode

Switch is in rapid-pvst mode
```

```
On SW3:

SW3# show spanning-tree summary | include mode

Switch is in rapid-pvst mode
```

```
On SW4:

SW4# show spanning-tree summary | include mode

Switch is in rapid-pvst mode
```

```
On SW2:

SW2# show spanning-tree summary | include mode

Switch is in pvst mode
```

When you examine the output of the **show spanning-tree vlan 12** command, you will see *no* difference between SW1 and SW2. There is only a minor difference on SW3 and SW4. The bridge priorities, timer values, port costs, and port IDs are identical. RSTP and 802.1D use the same algorithm and the same criteria to determine the active topology. On SW3 and SW4, you should notice the following differences:

```
SW3# show spanning-tree vlan 12 | begin Interface

Interface        Role Sts Cost      Prio.Nbr Type

---------------- ---- --- --------- -------- -------------

Fa0/19           Desg FWD 19        128.19   P2p
Fa0/21           Root FWD 19        128.21   P2p
Fa0/23           Desg FWD 19        128.23   P2p Peer(STP)
```

```
SW4# show spanning-tree vlan 12 | begin Interface

Interface        Role Sts Cost      Prio.Nbr Type
---------------- ---- --- --------- -------- -------------
Fa0/19           Altn BLK 19        128.19   P2p
Fa0/21           Desg FWD 19        128.21   P2p Peer(STP)
Fa0/23           Root FWD 19        128.23   P2p
```

SW3 and SW4 are both in the RSTP mode, but they detected a PVST-mode switch on the indicated ports. SW3 and SW4 will send standard 802.1D BPDUs on these border ports.

Task 2

Use debug output to explain how RSTP achieves rapid convergence when SW3 loses its root port.

- Shut down SW3's F0/23 port and SW4's F0/21 port to simplify the problem.

- Verify that SW3's F0/21 and SW4's F0/23 are root ports.

- Verify that SW3's F0/19 is a designated port and SW4's F0/19 is in discarding (blocking) state.

- On SW3 and SW4, enter the following commands:

  - **clear logging**

  - **debug spanning-tree events**

  - **debug spanning-tree synchronization**

- Shut down SW3's F0/21 port and observe the logs on these three switches.

To begin, let's shut down the ports connected to the PVST switch:

```
On SW3:

SW3(config)# interface FastEthernet0/23
SW3(config-if)# shut
```

```
On SW4:

SW4(config)# interface FastEthernet0/21
SW4(config-if)# shut
```

Let's verify the starting STP topology:

```
On SW3:

SW3# show spanning-tree vlan 12

[output omitted for brevity]

Interface        Role Sts Cost      Prio.Nbr Type
---------------- ---- --- --------- -------- -----
Fa0/19           Desg FWD 19        128.19   P2p
Fa0/21           Root FWD 19        128.21   P2p
```

```
SW4# show spanning-tree vlan 12

[output omitted for brevity]

Interface         Role Sts Cost      Prio.Nbr Type
---------------- ---- --- ---------- -------- -----
Fa0/19            Altn BLK 19         128.19   P2p
Fa0/23            Root FWD 19         128.23   P2p
```

When SW3 loses its root port, F0/19 on SW4 will need to transition to the forwarding state. Standard 802.1D would require up to 50 seconds (20 seconds Max Age plus twice the Forward Delay timer, 15 seconds).

Let's clear the logs and start debugs on SW1, SW3, and SW4:

```
SWx# clear log
clear logging buffer [confirm]

SWx# debug spanning events
Spanning Tree event debugging is on

SWx# debug spanning-tree synchronization
Spanning Tree state sync support debugging is on
```

Now let's shut down SW3 F0/21 and analyze the results:

```
SW3(config)# interface FastEthernet0/21
SW3(config-if)# shut

RSTP(12): updt roles, root port Fa0/21 going down
RSTP(12): we become the root bridge

RSTP(12): updt roles, received superior bpdu on Fa0/19
RSTP(12): Fa0/19 is now root port
RSTP(12): synced Fa0/19
RSTP(12): transmitting an agreement on Fa0/19 as a response to a proposal
```

According to this debug output, RSTP was able to determine the proper role for F0/21 and move F0/19 to the forwarding state in less than 20 milliseconds. Port F0/19 became active and immediately sent a BPDU claiming to be the root bridge. Eight milliseconds later, it received a BPDU with the proposal bit set from SW4. SW3 synchronized all of its ports (only F0/19 is active) and replied to the proposal with an agreement to complete the transition. Here, you see the final state on SW3:

```
SW3# show spanning-tree vlan 12

VLAN0012
[output removed for brevity]

Interface          Role Sts Cost        Prio.Nbr Type
---------------- ---- --- --------- -------- -----
Fa0/19             Root FWD 19          128.19   P2p
```

Next, you see the debug output on SW4. (NTP has synchronized clocks to the second, but not to the millisecond. The sequence may not always be precisely comparable to SW3.) From this output, you can see RSTP took less than 10 milliseconds to determine its role and move to the forwarding state.

```
SW4# show logging

[output omitted for brevity]

18:45:31.076: RSTP(12): updt roles, received superior bpdu on Fa0/19
18:45:31.076: RSTP(12): Fa0/19 is now designated
18:45:31.080: RSTP(12): transmitting a proposal on Fa0/19
18:45:31.084: RSTP(12): received an agreement on Fa0/19
```

As soon as F0/19 received the first BPDU from SW3, it changed its role from discarding to designated. SW4 sent a proposal to SW3 and went to the forwarding state as soon as it received an agreement. Here, you see the final state for SW4:

```
SW4# show spanning-tree vlan 12 | begin Inter

Interface          Role Sts Cost        Prio.Nbr Type
---------------- ---- --- --------- -------- -----
Fa0/19             Desg FWD 19          128.19   P2p
Fa0/23             Root FWD 19          128.23   P2p
```

In 802.1D, this would be a scenario where Cisco's Backbone Fast feature could be used to time out the Max Age as well as speed up the convergence from 50 seconds to *only* 30 seconds. The point-to-point link type and the explicit proposal agreement process of RSTP permit convergence in less than 1 second.

Task 3

Use debug output to demonstrate the RSTP convergence process as SW3's F0/21 returns to its role as root port, SW3 F0/19 transitions from root port back to designated port, and SW4's F0/19 transitions from designated port back to discarding.

■ Clear the logs on SW1, SW3, and SW4 and verify spanning-tree debugging is enabled on these switches.

■ **no shut** (activate) SW3 F0/21 and analyze the results.

This task builds on Task 2 and restores the original RSTP topology.

Let's clear logs and verify spanning-tree debugging on SW1, SW3, and SW4:

```
SWx# clear log
clear logging buffer [confirm]


SWx# show debug


Spanning Tree:
  Spanning Tree event debugging is on
  Spanning Tree state sync support debugging is on
```

Activate SW3 F0/21 and analyze the results:

```
On SW3:


SW3(config)# interface FastEthernet0/21
SW3(config-if)# no shut
```

As you see here, SW3's F0/21 took from 07.955 to 07.971 (about 16 milliseconds) to determine it should be the root port and transition to the forwarding state. As part of the synchronization process, SW3 temporarily blocks all other non-edge ports, including F0/19 in this example.

```
20:01:07.955: RSTP(12): initializing port Fa0/21
20:01:07.955: RSTP(12): Fa0/21 is now designated
20:01:07.959: RSTP(12): transmitting a proposal on Fa0/21


20:01:07.967: RSTP(12): updt roles, received superior bpdu on Fa0/21
20:01:07.967: RSTP(12): Fa0/21 is now root port
20:01:07.967: RSTP(12): Fa0/19 blocked by re-root
20:01:07.967: RSTP(12): synced Fa0/21
20:01:07.967: RSTP(12): Fa0/19 is now designated
20:01:07.971: RSTP(12): transmitting an agreement on Fa0/21 as a response to a
  proposal
20:01:07.971: RSTP(12): transmitting a proposal on Fa0/19
20:01:07.975: RSTP(12): transmitting a proposal on Fa0/19
20:01:08.099: RSTP(12): transmitting a proposal on Fa0/19
20:01:08.439: %LINK-3-UPDOWN: Interface FastEthernet0/21, changed state to up
20:01:09.439: %LINEPROTO-5-UPDOWN: Line protocol on Interface FastEthernet0/21,
  changed state to up
```

```
20:01:10.099: RSTP(12): transmitting a proposal on Fa0/19
20:01:12.099: RSTP(12): transmitting a proposal on Fa0/19
20:01:14.099: RSTP(12): transmitting a proposal on Fa0/19
20:01:16.100: RSTP(12): transmitting a proposal on Fa0/19
20:01:18.100: RSTP(12): transmitting a proposal on Fa0/19
20:01:20.100: RSTP(12): transmitting a proposal on Fa0/19
20:01:22.100: RSTP(12): transmitting a proposal on Fa0/19
20:01:22.968: RSTP(12): Fa0/19 fdwhile Expired
20:01:24.100: RSTP(12): transmitting a proposal on Fa0/19
20:01:26.100: RSTP(12): transmitting a proposal on Fa0/19
20:01:28.100: RSTP(12): transmitting a proposal on Fa0/19
20:01:30.100: RSTP(12): transmitting a proposal on Fa0/19
20:01:32.100: RSTP(12): transmitting a proposal on Fa0/19
20:01:34.100: RSTP(12): transmitting a proposal on Fa0/19
20:01:36.100: RSTP(12): transmitting a proposal on Fa0/19
20:01:37.968: RSTP(12): Fa0/19 fdwhile Expired
```

F0/19 sends a proposal every hello time (2 seconds). Because SW4 F0/19 will go to the discarding state, it does not reply with an agreement. Without an explicit agreement, SW3's F0/19 must go through 15 seconds of listening state and 15 seconds of learning state before it can move to the forwarding state.

The output on SW4 is quite brief. It received the superior BPDU from SW3 on F0/19, immediately transitioned the port from designated to discarding (alternate), and ignored the incoming proposals.

```
On SW4:

SW4# show logging

[output removed for brevity]

20:01:07.970: RSTP(12): updt roles, received superior bpdu on Fa0/19
20:01:07.970: RSTP(12): Fa0/19 is now alternate
```

Here, you see part of the resulting log entries for SW1 as SW4 activated its port. In just a few milliseconds, it sent a proposal toward SW4, received an agreement, and moved the port to the forwarding state:

```
On SW1:

20:01:07.960: RSTP(12): initializing port Fa0/21
20:01:07.960: RSTP(12): Fa0/21 is now designated
20:01:07.969: RSTP(12): transmitting a proposal on Fa0/21
```

```
20:01:07.969: RSTP(12): received an agreement on Fa0/21
20:01:09.965: %LINK-3-UPDOWN: Interface FastEthernet0/21, changed state to up
20:01:10.972: %LINEPROTO-5-UPDOWN: Line protocol on Interface FastEthernet0/21,
  changed state to up
```

In this task, you saw that RSTP rapid convergence depends on the explicit proposal/agreement process. Links could still take 30 seconds to become active.

Task 4

Use debug output to demonstrate the importance of link type in RSTP convergence.

- On *both* SW3 and SW4:
    - Clear the logs.
    - Verify spanning-tree debugging is enabled.
    - Configure the shared link type for F0/19.
- Shut down SW3 F0/21 and observe the result.

In Task 2, you saw the blocking port F0/19 on SW4 went to the forwarding state almost immediately when SW3 lost its root port. In Task 3, you saw that rapid convergence depends on the explicit proposal/agreement process.

The proposal/agreement process can only be used on point-to-point links, where switches can be certain of having only one possible neighboring switch. By default, switches associate the point-to-point link type with full-duplex links and the shared link type with half-duplex links. However, the link type can be manually configured.

On SW3 and SW4, issue **clear log** and change the F0/19 link type to shared:

```
SWx# clear log
clear logging buffer [confirm]

Switch# show debug

Spanning Tree:
  Spanning Tree event debugging is on

  Spanning Tree state sync support debugging is on

SWx(config-if)# interface FastEthernet0/19
SWx(config-if)# spanning-tree link-type shared
```

Let's verify the configuration:

```
SW3# show spanning-tree vlan 12 | begin Interface

Interface        Role Sts Cost      Prio.Nbr Type
---------------- ---- --- --------- -------- ----
Fa0/19           Desg FWD 19        128.19   Shr
Fa0/21           Root FWD 19        128.21   P2p


SW4# show spanning-tree vlan 12 | begin Interface

Interface        Role Sts Cost      Prio.Nbr Type
---------------- ---- --- --------- -------- -----
Fa0/19           Altn BLK 19        128.19   Shr
Fa0/23           Root FWD 19        128.23   P2p
```

Shut down SW3 F0/21 and observe the results:

```
SW3(config)# interface FastEthernet0/21
SW3(config-if)# shut

SW3# show logging
[output omitted for brevity]

21:00:41.578: RSTP(12): updt roles, root port Fa0/21 going down
21:00:41.578: RSTP(12): we become the root bridge
21:00:41.594: RSTP(12): updt roles, received superior bpdu on Fa0/19
21:00:41.594: RSTP(12): Fa0/19 is now root port

SW3# show spanning vlan 12 | begin Inter

Interface        Role Sts Cost      Prio.Nbr Type
---------------- ---- --- --------- -------- -----
Fa0/19           Root FWD 19        128.19   Shr
```

As you can see in this output, SW3 rapidly changed the role of its F0/19 port from designated to root port. But you will recall that in Task 2, SW3 responded to SW4's proposals with an agreement. With a shared link instead of a point-to-point link, SW3 ignores the proposals. Here you can see that SW4's F0/19 did eventually transition from blocked to designated. Without an explicit agreement from SW3, SW4 has to wait 30 seconds before it can move the port to the forwarding state.

```
SW4# show logging
[output removed for brevity]

21:00:41.589: RSTP(12): updt roles, received superior bpdu on Fa0/19
21:00:41.589: RSTP(12): Fa0/19 is now designated

21:00:41.593: RSTP(12): transmitting a proposal on Fa0/19
21:00:43.161: RSTP(12): transmitting a proposal on Fa0/19
21:00:45.161: RSTP(12): transmitting a proposal on Fa0/19
21:00:47.162: RSTP(12): transmitting a proposal on Fa0/19
21:00:49.162: RSTP(12): transmitting a proposal on Fa0/19
21:00:51.162: RSTP(12): transmitting a proposal on Fa0/19
21:00:53.162: RSTP(12): transmitting a proposal on Fa0/19
21:00:55.162: RSTP(12): transmitting a proposal on Fa0/19
21:00:56.590: RSTP(12): Fa0/19 fdwhile Expired
21:00:57.162: RSTP(12): transmitting a proposal on Fa0/19
21:00:59.162: RSTP(12): transmitting a proposal on Fa0/19
21:01:01.162: RSTP(12): transmitting a proposal on Fa0/19
21:01:03.162: RSTP(12): transmitting a proposal on Fa0/19
21:01:05.162: RSTP(12): transmitting a proposal on Fa0/19
21:01:07.162: RSTP(12): transmitting a proposal on Fa0/19
21:01:09.162: RSTP(12): transmitting a proposal on Fa0/19
21:01:11.163: RSTP(12): transmitting a proposal on Fa0/19
21:01:11.591: RSTP(12): Fa0/19 fdwhile Expired

SW4# show spanning-tree vlan 12 | begin Inter

Interface       Role Sts Cost     Prio.Nbr Type
--------------- ---- --- --------- -------- ------------------------
Fa0/19          Desg FWD 19        128.19   Shr
Fa0/23          Root FWD 19        128.23   P2p
```

Task 5

Using debug output, explain how RSTP switches interoperate with switches in legacy, 802.1D mode.

- Reactivate F0/21 on SW3 and remove the **link-type** commands from F0/19 on SW3 and SW4.

- Clear the logs on SW3 and SW4 and verify spanning-tree debugging.

- Enter the following commands on SW2:

  - **clear logging**

  - **debug spanning-tree events**

  - **debug spanning-tree synchronization**

- Reactivate SW3's interface F0/23 and observe the result.

- Clear the logs on SW2, reactivate SW4's interface F0/21, and observe the result.

Recall that SW2 is in the default PVST mode.

Let's configure SW3, SW4, and SW2:

```
SW3(config)# interface FastEthernet0/21
SW3(config-if)# no shut

SW3(config)# interface FastEthernet0/19
SW3(config-if)# no spanning-tree link-type shared

SW3# clear log
clear logging buffer [confirm]
```

```
SW4# clear log
clear logging buffer [confirm]

SW4(config)# interface FastEthernet0/19
SW4(config-if)# no spanning-tree link-type shared
```

```
SW2# clear log
clear logging buffer [confirm]


SW2# debug spanning-tree events
Spanning Tree event debugging is on

SW2# debug spanning-tree synchronization
Spanning Tree state sync support debugging is on
```

Now we need to reactivate SW3's F0/23 and observe the result:

```
SW3(config)# interface FastEthernet0/23
SW3(config-if)# no shut

22:08:04.457: %LINK-3-UPDOWN: Interface FastEthernet0/23, changed state to down
22:08:04.789: RSTP(12): initializing port Fa0/23
```

```
22:08:04.789: RSTP(12): Fa0/23 is now designated
22:08:04.793: RSTP(12): transmitting a proposal on Fa0/23
22:08:05.445: RSTP(12): transmitting a proposal on Fa0/23


22:08:06.789: %LINK-3-UPDOWN: Interface FastEthernet0/23, changed state to up


22:08:07.445: RSTP(12): transmitting a proposal on Fa0/23
22:08:07.789: %LINEPROTO-5-UPDOWN: Line protocol on Interface FastEthernet0/23,
  changed state to up
22:08:19.790: RSTP(12): Fa0/23 fdwhile Expired
22:08:34.790: RSTP(12): Fa0/23 fdwhile Expired
```

Note   SW3 did send a few proposals on the link, but it received no replies and had to wait
30 seconds for the listening and learning states to expire before it could transition F0/23 to
the forwarding state. Here, you see the final state:

```
SW3# show spanning-tree vlan 12 | begin Inter

Interface         Role Sts Cost      Prio.Nbr Type
---------------- ---- --- --------- -------- -----
Fa0/19            Desg FWD 19        128.19   P2p
Fa0/21            Root FWD 19        128.21   P2p
Fa0/23            Desg FWD 19        128.23   P2p Peer(STP)
```

Here is what the process looked like from SW2's perspective. SW2 ignores the proposals sent by SW3 and goes through the normal 802.1D process for activating a root port,
which takes 30 seconds.

```
SW2# show logging
[output omitted for brevity]

22:08:04.735: set portid: VLAN0012 Fa0/23: new port id 8019
22:08:04.735: STP: VLAN0012 Fa0/23 -> listening

22:08:06.739: %LINK-3-UPDOWN: Interface FastEthernet0/23, changed state to up
22:08:07.746: %LINEPROTO-5-UPDOWN: Line protocol on Interface FastEthernet0/23,
  changed state to up

.Apr 22 22:08:09.432: STP: VLAN0012 heard root  4108-001a.a174.1f00 on Fa0/23
22:08:09.432:      supersedes 16396-0019.e780.6d80
22:08:09.432: STP: VLAN0012 new root is 4108, 001a.a174.1f00 on port Fa0/23, cost 38
22:08:19.742: STP: VLAN0012 Fa0/23 -> learning

22:08:34.750: STP: VLAN0012 sent Topology Change Notice on Fa0/23
22:08:34.750: STP: VLAN0012 Fa0/23 -> forwarding
```

Reactivate SW4 F0/21 and observe the result:

```
SW2# clear logging
clear logging buffer [confirm]
```

```
SW4(config)# interface FastEthernet0/21
SW4(config-if)# no shut

22:26:20.284: %LINK-3-UPDOWN: Interface FastEthernet0/21, changed state to down
22:26:20.737: RSTP(12): initializing port Fa0/21
22:26:20.737: RSTP(12): Fa0/21 is now designated
22:26:20.741: RSTP(12): transmitting a proposal on Fa0/21
22:26:21.389: RSTP(12): transmitting a proposal on Fa0/21
22:26:22.737: %LINK-3-UPDOWN: Interface FastEthernet0/21, changed state to up
22:26:23.389: RSTP(12): transmitting a proposal on Fa0/21
22:26:23.737: %LINEPROTO-5-UPDOWN: Line protocol on Interface FastEthernet0/21,


changed state to up
22:26:25.389: RSTP(12): transmitting a proposal on Fa0/21
22:26:35.737: RSTP(12): Fa0/21 fdwhile Expired
22:26:50.738: RSTP(12): Fa0/21 fdwhile Expired
```

SW4's interface f0/21 sent a few proposals, but waited the full 30 seconds before going to the forwarding state. Here, you see its final state:

```
SW4# show spanning-tree vlan 12 | begin Inter

Interface        Role Sts Cost      Prio.Nbr Type
---------------- ---- --- --------- -------- -----
Fa0/19           Altn BLK 19        128.19   P2p
Fa0/21           Desg FWD 19        128.21   P2p Peer(STP)
Fa0/23           Root FWD 19        128.23   P2p
```

And, finally, you can see the spanning-tree operations on SW2 as its F0/21 interface becomes active in its final state:

```
SW2# show logging

[output removed for brevity]

22:26:20.747: set portid: VLAN0012 Fa0/21: new port id 8017
22:26:20.747: Found no corresponding dummy port for instance 12, port_id 128.25
22:26:20.747: STP: VLAN0012 Fa0/21 -> listening
```

```
22:26:22.752: %LINK-3-UPDOWN: Interface FastEthernet0/21, changed state to up
22:26:23.758: %LINEPROTO-5-UPDOWN: Line protocol on Interface FastEthernet0/21,
  changed state to up
22:26:27.382: STP: VLAN0012 Fa0/21 -> blocking


SW2# show spanning-tree vlan 12 | be Inter


Interface         Role Sts Cost        Prio.Nbr Type
---------------- ---- --- ---------- -------- -----
Fa0/2             Desg FWD 19          128.4    P2p
Fa0/21            Altn BLK 19          128.23   P2p
Fa0/23            Root FWD 19          128.25   P2p
```

In this task, you saw that the RSTP and PVST mode switches do interoperate and provide convergence similar to that in a purely PVST environment.

Task 6

In your final RSTP lab task, enable SW2 for RSTP mode. Make sure that none of the edge ports flap when the switched infrastructure reconverges. Use debugging output on SW2 to explain your results.

- Shut down SW2 interfaces F0/21 and F0/23.
- Enable the required RSTP configurations.
- Clear the logs on SW2.
- Reactivate SW2 interfaces F0/21 and F0/23 at the same time and observe the results.

To begin, we need to shut down SW2 F0/21 and F0/23:

```
SW2(config)# interface range FastEthernet0/21 , FastEthernet0/23
SW2(config-if-range)# shut
```

Let's enable RSTP mode on SW2 and clear the logs:

```
SW2(config)# spanning-tree mode rapid-pvst

SW2# clear logging
clear logging buffer [confirm]
```

Now we need to reactivate SW2's F0/21 and F0/23 at the same time and observe the result:

```
SW2(config)# interface range FastEthernet0/21 , FastEthernet0/23
SW2(config-if-range)# no shut

SW2# sh log
[output removed for brevity]

22:52:11.005: RSTP(12): initializing port Fa0/21

22:52:11.005: RSTP(12): Fa0/21 is now designated
22:52:11.013: RSTP(12): transmitting a proposal on Fa0/21
22:52:11.047: RSTP(12): initializing port Fa0/23
22:52:11.047: RSTP(12): Fa0/23 is now designated
22:52:11.055: RSTP(12): transmitting a proposal on Fa0/23
22:52:11.449: RSTP(12): updt roles, received superior bpdu on Fa0/21
22:52:11.449: RSTP(12): Fa0/21 is now root port
22:52:11.449: RSTP(12): syncing port Fa0/2
22:52:11.449: RSTP(12): syncing port Fa0/23
22:52:11.449: RSTP(12): synced Fa0/21
22:52:11.458: RSTP(12): transmitting an agreement on Fa0/21 as a response to a
  proposal
22:52:11.458: RSTP(12): transmitting a proposal on Fa0/2
22:52:11.458: RSTP(12): transmitting a proposal on Fa0/23

22:52:11.466: RSTP(12): updt roles, received superior bpdu on Fa0/23
22:52:11.466: RSTP(12): Fa0/23 is now root port
22:52:11.466: RSTP(12): Fa0/21 blocked by re-root
```

At this point, everything looks as it should. Within less than half a second, RSTP started forwarding on root port F0/23 and blocked port F0/21. The problem can be seen in the very next message:

```
Apr 22 22:52:11.466: RSTP(12): syncing port Fa0/2

Apr 22 22:52:11.466: RSTP(12): synced Fa0/23
Apr 22 22:52:11.475: RSTP(12): transmitting an agreement on Fa0/23 as a response to
  a proposal
Apr 22 22:52:11.483: RSTP(12): transmitting a proposal on Fa0/2
Apr 22 22:52:11.550: RSTP(12): transmitting a proposal on Fa0/2
Apr 22 22:52:13.010: %LINK-3-UPDOWN: Interface FastEthernet0/21, changed state to up
Apr 22 22:52:13.052: %LINK-3-UPDOWN: Interface FastEthernet0/23, changed state to up
```

```
Apr 22 22:52:13.563: RSTP(12): transmitting a proposal on Fa0/2
Apr 22 22:52:19.603: RSTP(12): transmitting a proposal on Fa0/2
Apr 22 22:52:21.617: RSTP(12): transmitting a proposal on Fa0/2
Apr 22 22:52:23.630: RSTP(12): transmitting a proposal on Fa0/2
Apr 22 22:52:25.643: RSTP(12): transmitting a proposal on Fa0/2
Apr 22 22:52:26.457: RSTP(12): Fa0/2 fdwhile Expired
Apr 22 22:52:27.656: RSTP(12): transmitting a proposal on Fa0/2
Apr 22 22:52:29.670: RSTP(12): transmitting a proposal on Fa0/2
Apr 22 22:52:31.683: RSTP(12): transmitting a proposal on Fa0/2
Apr 22 22:52:33.696: RSTP(12): transmitting a proposal on Fa0/2
Apr 22 22:52:35.710: RSTP(12): transmitting a proposal on Fa0/2
Apr 22 22:52:37.723: RSTP(12): transmitting a proposal on Fa0/2
Apr 22 22:52:39.736: RSTP(12): transmitting a proposal on Fa0/2
Apr 22 22:52:41.464: RSTP(12): Fa0/2 fdwhile Expired
```

Before F0/23 can send an agreement, it must sync all non-edge ports. RSTP disabled F0/2, which connects to R2, for 30 seconds. To avoid this, you need to enable PortFast on all edge ports.

Therefore, let's enable PortFast on SW1 F0/1 and SW2 F0/1:

```
SW1(config)# interface FastEthernet0/1
SW1(config-if)# spanning-tree PortFast
```

```
SW2(config)# interface FastEthernet0/2
SW2(config-if)# spanning PortFast
```

Now let's verify:

```
On SW1:

SW1# show spanning-tree vlan 12 | begin Inter



Interface        Role Sts Cost      Prio.Nbr Type
---------------- ---- --- --------- -------- -----
Fa0/1            Desg FWD 19        128.3    P2p Edge
Fa0/21           Desg FWD 19        128.23   P2p
Fa0/23           Desg FWD 19        128.25   P2p
```

```
On SW2:
SW2# show spanning-tree vlan 12 | begin Inter


Interface          Role Sts Cost      Prio.Nbr Type
---------------- ---- --- --------- -------- --------
Fa0/2              Desg FWD 19        128.4    P2p Edge
Fa0/21             Altn BLK 19        128.23   P2p
Fa0/23             Root FWD 19        128.25   P2p
```

If you now shut down and then reactivate SW2's F0/21 and F0/23, you will see that F0/2 no longer synchronizes and remains active:

```
SW2(config)# interface range FastEthernet0/21 , FastEthernet0/23
SW2(config-if-range)# shut

SW2(config)# interface range FastEthernet0/21 , FastEthernet0/23
SW2(config-if-range)# no shut

23:18:27.671: RSTP(12): initializing port Fa0/23
23:18:27.671: RSTP(12): Fa0/23 is now designated
23:18:27.679: RSTP(12): transmitting a proposal on Fa0/23
23:18:27.696: RSTP(12): updt roles, received superior bpdu on Fa0/23
23:18:27.696: RSTP(12): Fa0/23 is now root port
23:18:27.696: RSTP(12): synced Fa0/23
23:18:27.704: RSTP(12): transmitting an agreement on Fa0/23 as a response to a
  proposal
23:18:27.754: RSTP(12): initializing port Fa0/21
23:18:27.754: RSTP(12): Fa0/21 is now designated
23:18:27.763: RSTP(12): transmitting a proposal on Fa0/21

23:18:27.771: RSTP(12): updt roles, received superior bpdu on Fa0/21
23:18:27.771: RSTP(12): Fa0/21 is now alternate

23:18:29.675: %LINK-3-UPDOWN: Interface FastEthernet0/23, changed state to up
23:18:29.759: %LINK-3-UPDOWN: Interface FastEthernet0/21, changed state to up
23:18:30.682: %LINEPROTO-5-UPDOWN: Line protocol on Interface FastEthernet0/23,
  changed state to up

23:18:30.766: %LINEPROTO-5-UPDOWN: Line protocol on Interface FastEthernet0/21,
  changed state to up
```

Erase the config.text and vlan.dat files and reload the switches before proceeding to the next lab.

Lab 3-4: Multiple Spanning Tree Protocol (802.1s)

Figure 3-5 illustrates the topology that will be used in the following tasks.

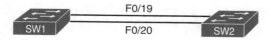

Figure 3-5 *Multiple Spanning Tree Protocol (802.1s)*

Multiple Spanning Tree (MST) applies the 802.1w Rapid Spanning Tree algorithm we just discussed to multiple-instance spanning trees. For the longest time the industry was resistant to adopting the concept of PVST; instead, it accepted the notion that there was a definitive need for multiple instances of spanning tree for a number of reasons. However, the concept of supporting 4096 instances was considered unreasonable. The compromise was MST, or 802.1s.

The main purpose of MST is to reduce the overall number of spanning tree instances to match the physical topology of the network. The goal was to minimize the CPU cycles needed by the spanning tree process using traditional methods. As a result, MST converges faster than Cisco's Rapid PVST+ and is backward-compatible with 802.1D (C-STP), 802.1w (RSTP), and Cisco's proprietary PVST+ implementation of STP.

MST supports the creation of multiple spanning tree topologies over trunks by grouping and associating VLANs into spanning tree instances. Each of these instances can support a separate topology that can be independent of the other spanning tree instances. This design approach allows us to create multiple forwarding paths for data traffic and still have concepts like load balancing. A single forwarding path failure will not affect other instances that take separate forwarding paths. The direct benefit of this is that the design is more fault tolerant than, say, common-instance spanning tree. Configuring a group of switches with matching MST configurations allows them to interoperate via a shared set of spanning tree instances. The term *MST region* is used to refer to a set of interconnected switches with the same MST configuration. MST allows us to do the following:

- Load-balance traffic by putting some VLANs in one MST instance and others in one or more different instances.

- Conserve switch resources because we will no longer have a separate STP instance per VLAN (PVST+).

MST supports multiple spanning trees over trunks by grouping VLANs and associating them with spanning tree instances. Each instance can have a topology separate from other spanning tree instances in the domain. In a nutshell, MST means that there can be multiple active forwarding paths for data traffic as well as an administratively managed load-balancing mechanism.

Fault tolerance in a network is improved with MST over other versions of STP, meaning that a failure in one forwarding path does not necessarily affect other paths. This is accomplished by grouping specific VLANs into specific MST instances. This VLAN-to-MST grouping must be consistent across all switches in the MST region. As mentioned previously, each switch must share the same MST configuration information; this will allow them to participate in a specific set of spanning tree instances. As pointed out earlier, these interconnected switches that have the same MST configuration uniformly applied are said to be in the same MST region. Switches with different MST configurations or legacy bridges running 802.1D are considered separate MST regions. Now that you know what a region is, we will explore the concept more closely.

MST Regions

An MST region defines a boundary where a single instance of STP operates. MST employs the use of regions because there could be situations where not all switches in the network run or even support MST; this means that these situations will break the network up into STP regions. In the case of the 802.1D standard, all instances will map to a unique and common instance, thus making these deployments far less complex. However, in the case of PVST+, each VLAN will carry the specific BPDUs for its respective instance. This will result in one BPDU per VLAN per trunk.

A collection of interconnected switches that have the same MST configuration makes up an MST region. As mentioned previously, the MST configuration must match on all switches in the same MST region; this includes the following user-defined parameters:

- The MST region name (up to 32 bytes)

- Configuration revision number (0 to 65535)

- VLAN-to-instance mapping (up to 4,096 entries)

In order for two or more switches to be in the same MST region, they must have the same VLAN-to-instance mapping, configuration revision number, and MST region name. If these configurations do not match, the switches will belong to two independent regions as a result. To ensure uniform VLAN-to-instance mapping, the protocol must exactly identify the boundaries of the regions.

To ensure this takes place, the region characteristics are always included in each 801.1's BPDU. The switches, however, do not propagate the actual VLAN-to-instance mapping in the BPDUs because adjacent switches only need to know if they are in the same region as their neighbors. Switches will simply communicate a digest of the VLAN-to-instance mapping table, along with the revision number and the region name. If these digests do not match, the port that received the BPDU is seen as a boundary between regions.

MST Region Components

An MST region consists of two different components:

- **Edge port:** A port that connects to a non-bridging device, such as a network host. Additionally, a port that connects to a hub is also considered an edge port.

- **Boundary port:** Connects an MST region to a single STP region running RSTP, 802.1D, or to another MST region with a different MST configuration. Also, an MST boundary port may also connect to a LAN, or to the designated switch that belongs to a single STP instance or another MST instance.

MST Spanning Tree Instances

Unlike PVST+, in which all STP instances are independent, or Common Spanning Tree (CST), where only a single STP instance exists, MST establishes and maintains two types of STP instances.

Internal Spanning Tree (IST)

The MST region sees the outside world via its Internal Spanning Tree (IST) interaction only; the IST will present the MST region as one single virtual bridge to the outside world. This leads to only one BPDU being shared over the native VLAN of the trunks, as it would do if it were running in CST mode. IST is the only instance that sends and receives BPDUs. Other STP instances that are running are contained in the M-record, which is encapsulated within the BPDU. Because the information for multiple instances can be found within a BPDU, this helps to reduce the processing a switch needs to perform.

At the boundary of the MST region, the Root Path Cost and Message Age values are incremented as though the BPDU had traversed only a single switch.

IST Master

The IST connects all the MST switches within a region. When the IST converges, the root of the IST becomes the IST master. IST master election takes the same process as STP root bridge election (lowest BID wins the election). Switches within the region then exchange BPDUs, and eventually the switch within the region with the lowest BID (bridge ID) and lowest path cost to the CST root is elected IST master. If there is only a single region, the IST master will also be the CST root. In the event the CST root is outside of the region, one of the MST switches at the boundary of the region is selected as the IST master. In such cases, at the boundary, the MST switch adds the IST master ID as well as the IST master path cost to the BPDU, which is then propagated throughout the MST region.

Hop Count

IST and MIST do not use the message age and maximum age information in the configuration BPDU to compute the STP topology. Instead, they use the path cost to the root and a hop-count mechanism, which is similar to the IP TTL mechanism. The hop-count mechanism gives us the same results as message age information would in determining when to trigger a reconfiguration. The root bridge of the instance always sends a BPDU (or M-record) with a cost of 0 and the hop count set to the maximum value (20 by default). When a switch receives this BPDU, it removes one of the hop counts before sending it on to the next downstream switch. When the count reaches zero, the switch discards the BPDU and ages the information it holds for the port. The message age and maximum age information in the BPDU remain the same throughout the region; also, these same values are propagated by the region's designated ports at the boundary.

Multiple-Instance Spanning Tree Protocol (MSTP)

Multiple-Instance Spanning Tree Protocol (MSTP) represents STP instances that exist only *within* the region. The IST presents the entire region as a single virtual bridge to the CST outside. MSTP, however, does not interact directly with the CST outside of the region.

MSTP 0 is mandatory and is always present; however, all other instances are optional. Each MSTP typically maps to a VLAN or set of VLANs. By default, all VLANs are assigned to the IST, which is MSTP 0. Cisco switches support up to 16 MSTPs on a single switch. These are identified by the numbers 0 through 15.

MSTP exists on all ports within the MST region, and only the IST has timer-related parameters. Also, unlike in the traditional Spanning Tree Protocol, MSTP BPDUs are sent out of every port by all switches—versus being sent out only by the designated bridge. However, MSTP does not send BPDUs out of boundary ports because only the IST interacts with external instances of STP.

We will explore using MST in the following tasks.

Task 1

The first Catalyst switch should be configured with a hostname of SW1, and the second Catalyst switch should have a hostname of SW2. The third and the fourth switches should have all their ports in administratively down state.

```
On the first switch:


Switch(config)# hostname SW1
```

```
On the second switch:


Switch(config)# hostname SW2
```

```
On the third and the fourth switch:


Switch(config)# interface range FastEthernet0/1-24
Switch(config-if-range)# shut
```

Task 2

Configure all the ports, except F0/19 and F0/20, in shutdown mode:

```
On Both Switches:


SWx(config)# interface range FastEthernet0/1-18 , FastEthernet0/21-24
SWx(config-if-range)# shut
```

Task 3

Ports F0/19–20 on both switches should be in trunking mode. These ports should use an industry-standard protocol to establish the trunk.

```
On Both Switches:


(config)# interface range FastEthernet0/19-20
(config-if-range)# switchport trunk encapsulation dot1q
(config-if-range)# switchport mode trunk
```

Task 4

Create VLANs 12, 34, 56, and 90 on SW1 and ensure these VLANs are propagated to SW2 via VTP messages. Use any name to accomplish this task.

```
On SW1:


SW1(config)# vlan 12,34,56,90
SW1(config-vlan)# exit
```

Let's verify the configuration:

```
On SW1:


SW1# show vlan brief | exclude unsup

VLAN Name                             Status    Ports
---- -------------------------------- --------- ---------------------------
1    default                          active    Fa0/1, Fa0/2, Fa0/3, Fa0/4
                                                Fa0/5, Fa0/6, Fa0/7, Fa0/8
                                                Fa0/9, Fa0/10, Fa0/11, Fa0/12
                                                Fa0/13, Fa0/14, Fa0/15, Fa0/16
                                                Fa0/17, Fa0/18, Fa0/21, Fa0/22
                                                Fa0/23, Fa0/24, Gi0/1, Gi0/2
12   VLAN0012                         active
34   VLAN0034                         active
56   VLAN0056                         active
90   VLAN0090                         active
```

```
On SW2:

SW2# show vlan brief | exclude unsup

VLAN Name                             Status    Ports
---- -------------------------------- --------- -------------------------------
1    default                          active    Fa0/1, Fa0/2, Fa0/3, Fa0/4
                                                Fa0/5, Fa0/6, Fa0/7, Fa0/8
                                                Fa0/9, Fa0/10, Fa0/11, Fa0/12
                                                Fa0/13, Fa0/14, Fa0/15, Fa0/16
                                                Fa0/17, Fa0/18, Fa0/21, Fa0/22
                                                Fa0/23, Fa0/24, Gi0/1, Gi0/2
```

Note   None of the switches are in VTP transparent mode, yet the VLANs are not getting propagated from SW1 to SW2. This is because the VTP domain name is not configured. If the VTP domain name is not configured, the switches will *not* propagate their VLAN information across the trunk links. Because the task states that you can use any name, a VTP domain name of "TST" is configured here:

```
On SW1:

SW1(config)# vtp domain TST
```

Note   The preceding command configures a VTP domain name. If the other switch does not have a domain name configured and a trunk has been established between the two switches, SW1 will convey the domain name via VTP messages. The two switches will then synch up their VLAN information based on the highest VTP rev number. In this task, a domain name of "TST" has been configured.

Let's verify the configuration:

```
On SW2:

SW2# show vlan brief | exclude unsup



VLAN Name                             Status    Ports
---- -------------------------------- --------- -------------------------------
1    default                          active    Fa0/1, Fa0/2, Fa0/3, Fa0/4
                                                Fa0/5, Fa0/6, Fa0/7, Fa0/8
```

```
                                                  Fa0/9, Fa0/10, Fa0/11, Fa0/12
                                                  Fa0/13, Fa0/14, Fa0/15, Fa0/16
                                                  Fa0/17, Fa0/18, Fa0/21, Fa0/22
                                                  Fa0/23, Fa0/24, Gi0/1, Gi0/2
   12    VLAN0012                      active
   34    VLAN0034                      active
   56    VLAN0056                      active
   90    VLAN0090                      active
```

You can see the VLANs are now propagated.

Task 5

Configure Multiple-Instance Spanning Tree on these two switches using the following policies:

- There should be two instances of STP: instance 1 and 2.
- The revision number should be 1.
- The MST region name should be CCIE.
- Instance 1 should handle VLANs 12 and 34.
- Instance 2 should handle VLANs 56 and 90.
- All future VLANs should use instance 0.
- Instance 1 should use F0/19.
- Instance 2 should use F0/20.
- SW1 should be the root bridge for the first instance.
- SW2 should be the root bridge for the second instance.

The default mode for spanning tree is PVST. The output of the following **show** command verifies this information:

```
On Both Switches:

SWx# show spanning-tree summary | include mode

Switch is in pvst mode                  The default mode of Spanning-tree.
```

Now you need to change the spanning tree mode to MST:

```
On Both Switches:

SWx(config)# spanning-tree mode mst
```

Let's verify the configuration:

```
On Both Switches:


SWx# show spanning-tree summary | include mode

Switch is in mst mode (IEEE Standard)
```

Let's configure MST on the switches. The following command enters the MST configuration mode:

```
On Both Switches:

SWx(config)# spanning-tree mst configuration
```

The following command sets the MST configuration revision number to 1 (the range for this number is 1–65535):

```
SWx (config-mst)# revision 1
```

The following command configures the name of the region to be "CCIE":

```
SWx (config-mst)# name CCIE
```

MST supports 16 instances. Once the spanning tree mode is changed to MST and the MST configuration mode is entered, instance 0 is created automatically and all VLANs are mapped to that instance.

The following commands map the requested VLAN(s) to the specified instances. By default, all the future VLANs or any VLAN(s) not statically mapped to a given instance will be assigned to instance 0. Instance 0 is the catchall instance.

```
SWx (config-mst)# instance 1 vlan 12,34
SWx (config-mst)# instance 2 vlan 56,90
SWx (config-mst)# exit
```

Let's verify this configuration:

```
On Both Switches:


SWx # show spanning-tree mst configuration

Name       [CCIE]
Revision  1        Instances configured 3
```

```
Instance  Vlans mapped
--------  -----------------------------------
0         1-11,13-33,35-55,57-89,91-4094
1         12,34
2         56,90
--------  -----------------------------------
```

Note   VLANs 12 and 34 are mapped to instance 1, VLANs 56 and 90 are mapped to instance 2, and the rest of the VLANs are mapped to instance 0.

Let's verify the configuration before configuring the next portion of the task:

```
On SW1:

SW1# show spanning-tree bridge

                                      Hello  Max  Fwd
MST Instance            Bridge ID     Time   Age  Dly  Protocol
---------------  ----------------------------  -----  ---  ---  --------
MST0             32768 (32768,   0) 0012.7f40.9380    2    20   15   mstp
MST1             32769 (32768,   1) 0012.7f40.9380    2    20   15   mstp
MST2             32770 (32768,   2) 0012.7f40.9380    2    20   15   mstp
```

Note   The preceding command displays the bridge ID (BID) for your switch (this is *not* the BID of the root bridge). The BID is a combination of the bridge priority and the MAC address. Instead of a BID being assigned to each VLAN, there is a BID for each instance. The priority is incremented based on the instance number. A lower bridge priority has preference.

Here are some examples:

> For instance 0, 0 is added to the default priority of 32768, for a bridge priority of 32768.

> For instance 1, 1 is added to the default priority of 32768, for a bridge priority of 32769.

> For instance 2, 2 is added to the default priority of 32768, for a bridge priority of 32770.

Here's how you would see the root bridge for a given instance:

```
On SW1:


SW1# show spanning-tree root

                                   Root    Hello Max Fwd
MST Instance          Root ID      Cost    Time  Age Dly  Root Port
----------------   ----------------------  --------- ----- --- ---   -----
MST0               32768 0012.7f40.9380          0     2   20  15
MST1               32769 0012.7f40.9380          0     2   20  15
MST2               32770 0012.7f40.9380          0     2   20  15
```

```
On SW1:


SW1# show version | include Base

Base ethernet MAC Address       : 00:12:7F:40:93:80
```

```
On SW2:


SW2# show spanning-tree root

                                   Root    Hello Max Fwd
MST Instance          Root ID      Cost    Time  Age Dly  Root Port
----------------   ----------------------  --------- ----- --- ---   ------------
MST0               32768 0012.7f40.9380          0     2   20  15  Fa0/19
MST1               32769 0012.7f40.9380     200000     2   20  15  Fa0/19
MST2               32770 0012.7f40.9380     200000     2   20  15  Fa0/19
```

The preceding command displays the BID of the root bridge for different instances. The output may vary based on the switch's BID, but in this case everything is pointing to SW1.

By default, the **spanning-tree extend system-id** is configured as part of your startup configuration. Because the extended system ID is set, the priority must be configured in increments of 4096. Remember, the lower value has higher preference.

The following commands will change the switch priority so that SW1 will be chosen as the root switch for instance 1 and SW2 will be chosen as the root bridge for instance 2.

Let's configure the root bridge for instance 1 and 2:

```
On SW1:


SW1(config)# spanning-tree mst 1 priority 0
SW1(config)# spanning-tree mst 2 priority 4096
```

```
On SW2:

SW2(config)# spanning-tree mst 1 priority 4096
SW2(config)# spanning-tree mst 2 priority 0
```

Now let's verify the configuration:

```
On SW1:

SW1# show spanning-tree root

                                     Root   Hello Max Fwd
MST Instance            Root ID      Cost   Time  Age Dly Root Port
---------------  --------------------  ---------  ----- --- --- ------------

MST0            32768 0012.7f40.9380       0     2   20  15
MST1                1 0012.7f40.9380       0     2   20  15
MST2                2 001d.e5d6.0000  200000     2   20  15  Fa0/19
```

The local switch (SW1) is the root bridge for instances 0 and 1. The column that specifies the root ID shows the priority for MST1 and MST2 as 1 and 2, respectively, because the priority is the sum of the instance number plus the priority. Remember that this switch's priority is set to zero.

Note   This switch is not the root for MST2. An indication that this switch is *not* the root for instance 2 is the root port. The root bridge does not have any ports set as the root port for the VLANs for PVST and Rapid-PVST. For MST, the root bridge does not have any ports set as the root port for the instances.

```
On SW2:

SW2# show spanning-tree root

                                     Root   Hello Max Fwd
MST Instance            Root ID      Cost   Time  Age Dly Root Port
---------------  --------------------  ---------  ----- --- --- ------------

MST0            32768 0012.7f40.9380       0     2   20  15  Fa0/19
MST1                1 0012.7f40.9380  200000     2   20  15  Fa0/19
MST2                2 001d.e5d6.0000       0     2   20  15
```

Note   SW2 is the root bridge for instance 2, whereas SW1 is the root for the MST instances of 0 and 1.

To configure the last portion of this task, we display the existing state in the output of the following **show** command:

```
On SW1:

SW1# show spanning-tree interface FastEthernet0/19


Mst Instance      Role Sts Cost        Prio.Nbr Type
---------------- ---- --- --------- -------- -----
MST0              Desg FWD 200000     128.21   P2p
MST1              Desg FWD 200000     128.21   P2p
MST2              Root FWD 200000     128.21   P2p


SW1# show spanning-tree interface FastEthernet0/20

Mst Instance      Role Sts Cost        Prio.Nbr Type
---------------- ---- --- --------- -------- -----
MST0              Desg FWD 200000     128.22   P2p
MST1              Desg FWD 200000     128.22   P2p
MST2              Altn BLK 200000     128.22   P2p
```

```
On SW2:

SW2# show spanning-tree interface FastEthernet0/19

Mst Instance      Role Sts Cost        Prio.Nbr Type
---------------- ---- --- --------- -------- -----
MST0              Root FWD 200000     128.21   P2p
MST1              Root FWD 200000     128.21   P2p
MST2              Desg FWD 200000     128.21   P2p

SW2# show spanning-tree interface FastEthernet0/20

Mst Instance      Role Sts Cost        Prio.Nbr Type
---------------- ---- --- --------- -------- -----
MST0              Altn BLK 200000     128.22   P2p
MST1              Altn BLK 200000     128.22   P2p
MST2              Desg FWD 200000     128.22   P2p
```

Note   Based on the output of the preceding **show** commands, traffic for all MST instances take port F0/19 and none of the instances are using port F0/20.

To configure items 7 and 8, we use the **port-priority** command:

```
On Both Switches:


SWx(config)# interface FastEthernet0/19
SWx(config-if)# spanning-tree mst 1 port-priority 0
SWx(config-if)# spanning-tree mst 2 port-priority 128


SWx(config)# interface FastEthernet0/20

SWx(config-if)# spanning-tree mst 1 port-priority 128
SWx(config-if)# spanning-tree mst 2 port-priority 0
```

In this task, **port-priority** is used to select an interface to put into the forwarding state for a given instance. A lower value has a higher priority.

In this case, port F0/19 will be used by all the VLANs that are assigned to instances 0 and 1, because it has a higher priority (lower value). Instance 2 will use port F0/20, because it has been configured with a higher priority (lower value).

```
To verify the configuration:


On SW1:


SW1# show spanning-tree interface FastEthernet0/19


Mst Instance      Role Sts Cost      Prio.Nbr Type
----------------  ---- --- --------- -------- --------------------
MST0              Desg FWD 200000    128.21   P2p


MST1              Desg FWD 200000      0.21   P2p
MST2              Altn BLK 200000    128.21   P2p


SW1# show spanning interface FastEthernet0/20


Mst Instance      Role Sts Cost      Prio.Nbr Type
----------------  ---- --- --------- -------- -----
MST0              Desg FWD 200000    128.22   P2p
MST1              Desg FWD 200000    128.22   P2p
MST2              Root FWD 200000      0.22   P2p
```

```
On SW2:

SW2# show spanning-tree interface FastEthernet0/19

Mst Instance       Role Sts Cost      Prio.Nbr Type
----------------   ---- --- --------- -------- -----
MST0               Root FWD 200000    128.21   P2p
MST1               Root FWD 200000      0.21   P2p
MST2               Desg FWD 200000    128.21   P2p

SW2# show spanning-tree interface FastEthernet0/20

Mst Instance       Role Sts Cost      Prio.Nbr Type

----------------   ---- --- --------- -------- -----
MST0               Altn BLK 200000    128.22   P2p
MST1               Altn BLK 200000    128.22   P2p
MST2               Desg FWD 200000      0.22   P2p
```

Note   Instances 0 and 1 use port F0/19, whereas instance 2 uses port F0/20.

Lab 3-5: Spanning Tree PortFast

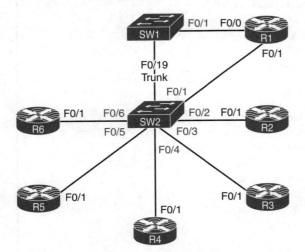

Figure 3-6   *Spanning Tree PortFast*

Figure 3-6 illustrates the topology that will be used in the following tasks.

Task 1

Shut down all ports on SW1 and SW2. Configure an industry-standard trunk between the two switches using port F0/19. *Only* the F0/19 interface should be in **no shutdown** state.

```
On SW1:

SW1(config)# interface range FastEthernet0/1-24
SW1(config-if-range)# shut

SW1(config)# interface FastEthernet0/19
SW1(config-if)# switchport trunk encapsulation dot1q
SW1(config-if)# switchport mode trunk
SW1(config-if)# no shut
```

```
On SW2:

SW2(config)# interface range FastEthernet0/1-24
SW2(config-if-range)# shut

SW2(config)# interface FastEthernet0/19
SW2(config-if)# switchport trunk encapsulation dot1q
SW2(config-if)# switchport mode trunk
SW2(config-if)# no shut
```

Let's verify the configuration:

```
On SW2:

SW2# show interface trunk

Port         Mode          Encapsulation  Status        Native vlan
Fa0/19       on            802.1q         trunking      1

Port         Vlans allowed on trunk
Fa0/19       1-4094

Port         Vlans allowed and active in management domain
Fa0/19       1

Port         Vlans in spanning tree forwarding state and not pruned
Fa0/19       none


SW2# show interface status | exclude disable

Port       Name            Status       Vlan      Duplex  Speed Type
Fa0/19                     connected    trunk     a-full  a-100 10/100BaseTX
```

```
On SW1:

SW1# show interface status | exclude disable

Port      Name            Status      Vlan     Duplex  Speed Type
Fa0/19                    connected   trunk    a-full  a-100 10/100BaseTX
```

Task 2

Configure the appropriate switch to implement the following policies:

- Configure the F0/0 interface of R1 for VLAN 100.

- The F0/0 interface of R1 should immediately transition into the forwarding state, bypassing the spanning tree listening and learning states.

- Test this configuration to ensure the correct feature is enabled.

- You should use an interface configuration command to accomplish this task.

```
On SW1:

SW1(config)# interface FastEthernet0/1
SW1(config-if)# switchport mode access
SW1(config-if)# switchport access vlan 100
SW1(config-if)# no shut
```

In order to accomplish this task, you need to enable PortFast on SW1's F0/1 interface:

```
On SW1:

SW1(config)# interface FastEthernet0/1
SW1(config-if)# spanning PortFast
```

You should see the following console message:

```
%Warning: PortFast should only be enabled on ports connected to a single
 host. Connecting hubs, concentrators, switches, bridges, etc... to this
 interface  when PortFast is enabled, can cause temporary bridging loops.

Use with CAUTION

%PortFast will be configured on FastEthernet0/1 but will only  have effect when the
   interface is in a non-trunking mode.
```

Let's verify the configuration:

```
On SW1:


SW1# show spanning-tree interface FastEthernet0/1 PortFast


no spanning tree info available for FastEthernet0/1
```

Because the F0/0 interface of R1 is *not* enabled (it's in the shutdown state), you should get the following console message:

```
On R1:


R1(config)# interface FastEthernet0/0
R1(config-if)# no shut
```

```
On SW1:


SW1# show spanning-tree interface FastEthernet0/1 PortFast

VLAN0100          enabled
```

Now we need to test the configuration. To test the spanning tree PortFast feature, **debug spanning-tree events** is enabled on SW1. R1's F0/0 interface is **shutdown** and then **no shutdown**. This can emulate a brand-new connection to the switch port.

Once the port on R1 is enabled using the **no shutdown** command, the spanning tree states can be verified in the output of the **debug** command:

```
On SW1:


SW1# debug spanning events
Spanning Tree event debugging is on
```

```
On R1:


R1(config)# interface FastEthernet0/0
R1(config-if)# shut
R1(config-if)# no shut
```

```
On SW1:


00:58:53: set portid: VLAN0100 Fa0/1: new port id 8003

00:58:53: STP: VLAN0100 Fa0/1 ->jump to forwarding from blocking
```

```
00:58:55: %LINK-3-UPDOWN: Interface FastEthernet0/1, changed state to up
00:58:56: %LINEPROTO-5-UPDOWN: Line protocol on Interface FastEthernet0/1, changed
  state to up
```

Spanning tree changes a mesh topology into a loop-free star topology. When a host is connected to a port, the link on the switch comes up and spanning tree starts its calculation on that port. The result of the calculation is the transition of the port into the forwarding state. This calculation can take between 30 and 50 seconds.

The **spanning-tree PortFast** command can be enabled to allow immediate transition of a given port into the forwarding state. Once this feature is enabled, the port transitions into the forwarding state immediately.

Task 3

Enable the F0/1 interfaces of R1–R6 and configure SW2 such that all ports, except the trunk port(s), bypass the spanning tree listening and learning states. Do *not* use an interface configuration mode command on SW2 to accomplish this task.

```
On R1 - R6:

Rx(config)# interface FastEthernet0/1
Rx(config-if)# shut
Rx(config-if)# no shut
```

```
On SW2:

SW2(config)# spanning-tree PortFast default
```

You should see the following console message:

```
%Warning: this command enables PortFast by default on all interfaces. You
  should now disable PortFast explicitly on switched ports leading to hubs,
  switches and bridges as they may create temporary bridging loops.
```

Let's verify the configuration:

```
On SW2:

SW2# show spanning-tree interface FastEthernet0/6 PortFast

no spanning tree info available for FastEthernet0/6
```

Let's enable ports F0/1–6 on SW2 and try the **show** command again:

```
On SW2:


SW2(config)# interface range FastEthernet0/1-6
SW2(config-if-range)# no shut


SW2# show spanning-tree interface FastEthernet0/6 PortFast

VLAN0001            enabled
```

Now let's test the configuration:

```
On SW2:


SW2# debug spanning events
Spanning Tree event debugging is on
```

```
On R6:


R6(config)# interface FastEthernet0/1
R6(config-if)# shut
R6(config-if)# no shut
```

```
On SW2:


01:24:08: set portid: VLAN0001 Fa0/6: new port id 8008
01:24:08: STP: VLAN0001 Fa0/6 ->jump to forwarding from blocking

01:24:10: %LINK-3-UPDOWN: Interface FastEthernet0/6, changed state to up
01:24:12: %LINEPROTO-5-UPDOWN: Line protocol on Interface FastEthernet0/6, changed
  state to up
```

Spanning tree PortFast can be enabled on an interface basis or it can be enabled globally. When spanning tree PortFast is enabled globally, the IOS will apply the spanning tree PortFast configuration to all interfaces that are in access mode. Let's verify this information:

```
On SW2:


SW2# show interface trunk


Port          Mode          Encapsulation  Status       Native vlan
Fa0/19        on            802.1q         trunking     1
```

```
Port            Vlans allowed on trunk
Fa0/19          1-4094


Port            Vlans allowed and active in management domain
Fa0/19          1


Port            Vlans in spanning tree forwarding state and not pruned
Fa0/19          1


SW2# show spanning-tree interface FastEthernet0/19 PortFast


VLAN0001            disabled
```

Note   Spanning tree PortFast is disabled on interfaces that are configured as trunks.

Task 4

Configure VLANs 100 and 200 on SW2. Configure SW2's F0/5 as a trunk and *only* allow VLANs 100 and 200 to traverse through this trunk.

R5's F0/1 interface should be configured to provide inter-VLAN routing using 100.1.1.100/24 and 200.1.1.100/24 as the gateway for the hosts in VLANs 100 and 200, respectively. This configuration should *not* modify the PortFast feature implemented in the previous task.

```
On SW2:


SW2(config)# vlan 100,200
SW2(config-vlan)# exit


SW2(config)# interface FastEthernet0/5
SW2(config-if)# switchport trunk encapsulation dot1q
SW2(config-if)# switchport mode trunk
SW2(config-if)# switchport trunk allowed vlan 100,200
```

Let's verify the configuration:

```
On SW2:


SW2# show interface FastEthernet0/5 trunk


Port       Mode        Encapsulation  Status       Native vlan
Fa0/5      on          802.1q         trunking     1


Port       Vlans allowed on trunk
Fa0/5      100,200
```

```
Port          Vlans allowed and active in management domain
Fa0/5         100,200

Port          Vlans in spanning tree forwarding state and not pruned
Fa0/5         100,200
```

Now let's configure R5:

```
On R5:

R5(config)# interface FastEthernet0/1.100
R5(config-subif)# encapsulation dot1q 100
R5(config-subif)# ip address 100.1.1.100 255.255.255.0

R5(config-subif)# interface FastEthernet0/1.200
R5(config-subif)# encapsulation dot1q 200
R5(config-subif)# ip address 200.1.1.100 255.255.255.0
```

Note   The last item of this task states that the configuration should *not* modify the PortFast feature implemented in the previous task. Because **spanning-tree PortFast** was enabled on all interfaces except the trunks in the last task, you must ensure that **spanning-tree PortFast** is still enabled after this configuration.

Let's verify PortFast on the F0/5 interface of SW2:

```
SW2# show spanning-tree interface Fastethernet0/5 PortFast

VLAN0100          disabled
VLAN0200          disabled
```

Note   PortFast is disabled on the F0/5 interface of SW2. This is because the F0/5 interface is configured as a trunk. The global **spanning-tree PortFast default** command does *not* affect the ports that are configured as the trunk.

Configure the following to enable the PortFast feature on the F0/5 interface of SW2, even though it's configured as a trunk:

```
On SW2:

SW2(config)# interface FastEthernet0/5
SW2(config-if)# spanning-tree PortFast trunk
```

You should see the following console message:

```
%Warning: PortFast should only be enabled on ports connected to a single host.
  Connecting hubs, concentrators, switches, bridges, etc... to this interface
  when PortFast is enabled, can cause temporary bridging loops.
Use with CAUTION
```

Let's verify the configuration:

```
On SW2:

SW2# show spanning-tree interface FastEthernet 0/5 PortFast

VLAN0100          enabled
VLAN0200          enabled
```

Now let's test the configuration:

```
On R5:

R5(config)# interface FastEthernet0/1
R5(config-if)# shut
R5(config-if)# no shut
```

```
On SW2:

set portid: VLAN0100 Fa0/5: new port id 8007
STP: VLAN0100 Fa0/5 ->jump to forwarding from blocking

set portid: VLAN0200 Fa0/5: new port id 8007

STP: VLAN0200 Fa0/5 ->jump to forwarding from blocking

%LINEPROTO-5-UPDOWN: Line protocol on Interface FastEthernet0/5, changed state to up
```

Task 5

Disable spanning tree PortFast on the F0/1 interface of SW2. Do *not* remove the
spanning-tree PortFast default command to accomplish this task.

Let's verify the PortFast state on the F0/1 interface of SW2:

```
On SW2:

SW2# show spanning-tree interface FastEthernet0/1 PortFast

VLAN0001          enabled
```

Here's how to disable PortFast on a given port:

```
On SW2:

SW2(config)# interface FastEthernet0/1
SW2(config-if)# spanning-tree PortFast disable
```

Let's verify the configuration:

```
On SW2:

SW2# show spanning-tree interface FastEthernet0/1 PortFast

VLAN0001        disabled
```

Lab 3-6: UplinkFast

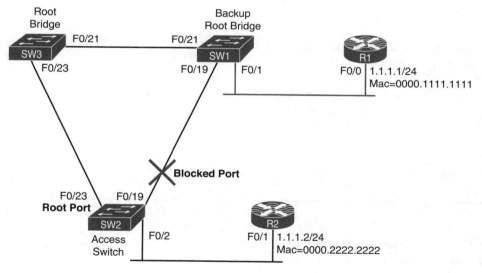

Figure 3-7 *UplinkFast*

Task 1

Configure the topology shown in Figure 3-7 using the interfaces that are identified. The unused interfaces should be in shutdown state.

```
On R1:

R1(config-if)# interface FastEthernet0/0
R1(config-if)# ip address 1.1.1.1 255.255.255.0
R1(config-if)# mac-address 0000.1111.1111
R1(config-if)# no shut
```

```
On R2:

R2(config)# interface FastEthernet0/1
R2(config-if)# ip address 1.1.1.2 255.255.255.0
R2(config-if)# mac-address 0000.2222.2222
R2(config-if)# no shut
```

```
On SW1:

SW1(config)# interface range FastEthernet0/1-24
SW1(config-if-range)# shut

SW1(config)# interface FastEthernet0/1
SW1(config-if)# no shut

SW1(config)# interface range FastEthernet0/19 , FastEthernet0/21
SW1(config-if-range)# switchport trunk encapsulation dot1q
SW1(config-if-range)# switchport mode trunk
SW1(config-if-range)# no shut

SW1(config)# spanning-tree vlan 1 root secondary
```

```
On SW2:

SW2(config)# interface range FastEthernet0/1-24
SW2(config-if-range)# shut

SW2(config)# interface FastEthernet0/2
SW2(config-if)# no shut

SW2(config)# interface range FastEthernet0/19, FastEthernet0/23
SW2(config-if-range)# switchport trunk encapsulation dot1q
SW2(config-if-range)# switchport mode trunk
SW2(config-if-range)# no shut
```

```
On SW3:

SW3(config)# interface range FastEthernet0/1-24
SW3(config-if-range)# shut

SW3(config)# interface range FastEthernet0/21, FastEthernet0/23
SW3(config-if-range)# switchport trunk encapsulation dot1q
SW3(config-if-range)# switchport mode trunk
SW3(config-if-range)# no shut

SW3(config)# spanning-tree vlan 1 root primary
```

Let's verify the configuration:

```
On SW1:

SW1# show spanning-tree vlan 1

VLAN0001
  Spanning tree enabled protocol ieee
  Root ID    Priority    24577
             Address     0011.928e.9c00
             Cost        19
             Port        23 (FastEthernet0/21)
             Hello Time   2 sec  Max Age 20 sec  Forward Delay 15 sec

  Bridge ID  Priority    28673  (priority 28672 sys-id-ext 1)
             Address     0014.6a8d.2280
             Hello Time   2 sec  Max Age 20 sec  Forward Delay 15 sec
             Aging Time 300

Interface           Role Sts Cost      Prio.Nbr Type
------------------- ---- --- --------- -------- -----
Fa0/1               Desg FWD 19          128.3   P2p
Fa0/19              Desg FWD 19          128.21  P2p
Fa0/21              Root FWD 19          128.23  P2p
```

```
On SW2:

SW2# show spanning-tree vlan 1

VLAN0001
  Spanning tree enabled protocol ieee
  Root ID    Priority    24577
             Address     0011.928e.9c00
```

```
                 Cost        19
                 Port        25 (FastEthernet0/23)
                 Hello Time    2 sec  Max Age 20 sec  Forward Delay 15 sec

    Bridge ID  Priority    32769  (priority 32768 sys-id-ext 1)
                 Address     0015.c621.f980
                 Hello Time    2 sec  Max Age 20 sec  Forward Delay 15 sec
                 Aging Time 300

Interface             Role Sts Cost      Prio.Nbr Type
------------------- ---- --- --------- -------- -----
Fa0/2                 Desg FWD 19         128.4    P2p Edge
Fa0/19                Altn BLK 19         128.21   P2p
Fa0/23                Root FWD 19         128.25   P2p
```

```
On SW3:

SW3# show spanning-tree vlan 1

VLAN0001
  Spanning tree enabled protocol ieee
  Root ID    Priority   24577
             Address    0011.928e.9c00
             This bridge is the root
             Hello Time    2 sec  Max Age 20 sec  Forward Delay 15 sec

  Bridge ID  Priority   24577  (priority 24576 sys-id-ext 1)
             Address    0011.928e.9c00
             Hello Time    2 sec  Max Age 20 sec  Forward Delay 15 sec
             Aging Time 300

Interface             Role Sts Cost      Prio.Nbr Type
------------------- ---- --- --------- -------- -----
Fa0/21                Desg FWD 19         128.21   P2p
Fa0/23                Desg FWD 19         128.23   P2p
```

Task 2

Configure SW2 such that if its root port (F0/23) goes down, the alternate port (F0/19) transitions into the forwarding state immediately:

```
On SW2:

SW2(config)# spanning-tree uplinkfast
```

UplinkFast is a Cisco proprietary feature that improves convergence time when there is an uplink failure. This feature is designed to run when the local switch has at least one alternate root port. The alternate port is in the blocking state.

UplinkFast is an access layer solution, and it works based on an uplink group. An uplink group consists of the root port, which is in the forwarding state, and one or more backup connections to the root bridge, which are in blocking state.

If the root port fails, a port with the next lowest cost in the uplink group will transition into the forwarding state and will become the root port.

If UplinkFast is *not* enabled and the primary port on the access switch fails, spanning tree must recalculate and eventually unblock the backup uplink port. This can take up to 30 seconds. With UplinkFast enabled, the recovery can occur in 1 second.

The following events occur when the UplinkFast is *not* enabled (see Figure 3-8):

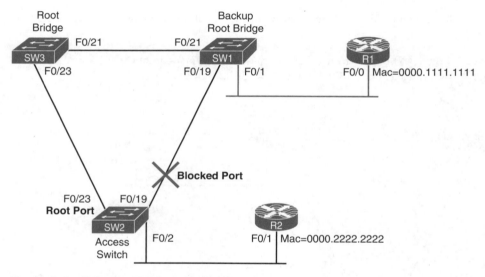

Figure 3-8   *Behavior Without UplinkFast*

- Port F0/23 on the access switch (SW2) goes down.

- The access switch declares its uplink to SW1 as down.

- The access switch looks at its F0/19 interface, which is still receiving BPDUs from the root bridge through SW1.

- The access switch needs to transition its F0/19 interface into the forwarding state. This process means the port has to go through the listening and learning states. Each state takes 15 seconds by default, unless the **forward-delay** command or the **diagram** option has been configured.

The UplinkFast feature is based on the definition of an uplink group. The uplink group consists of the root port and all the ports that provide an alternate/backup connection to the root bridge (blocked ports). If the root port fails, a port with the next lowest cost from the group is placed immediately into the forwarding state. The uplink group of the access switch consists of the F0/19 and F0/23 interfaces.

The following outlines the events that occur when the UplinkFast is configured:

- The F0/23 interface of the access switch fails.

- The access switch detects a link down on its port F0/23.

- The access switch immediately knows the link to the root bridge is lost and the other path in the uplink group is in a blocked state.

- The access switch places the F0/19 interface in the forwarding state. This is done immediately.

- The content addressable memory (CAM) tables of the other switches are updated.

Note   If the CAM tables of the other switches are *not* updated, they will be invalid for a short period of time. Figure 3-9 outlines the reason for this behavior.

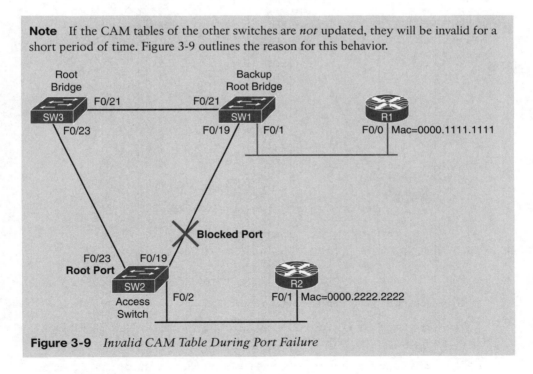

Figure 3-9   *Invalid CAM Table During Port Failure*

In order for R1 to reach R2, it has to take the following path:

SW1 → SW3 → SW2 → R2

The CAM table of the switches before the failure is as follows:

On SW3, the F0/23 interface is associated to R2, and the F0/21 interface is associated to R1.

To generate some traffic, R1 is configured to ping R2 with a high **repeat** count:

```
On R1:


R1# ping 1.1.1.2 repeat 1000000
```

```
On SW3:


SW3# show mac address-table dynamic

          Mac Address Table

-------------------------------------------


Vlan    Mac Address      Type       Ports
----    -----------      --------   -----
   1    0000.1111.1111   DYNAMIC    Fa0/21 → R1
   1    0000.2222.2222   DYNAMIC    Fa0/23 → R2
   1    0014.6a8d.2297   DYNAMIC    Fa0/21 → SW1's F0/21 interface
   1    0015.c621.f999   DYNAMIC    Fa0/23 → SW2's F0/23 interface

Total Mac Addresses for this criterion: 4
```

On SW1, the F0/1 interface is associated to R1 and the F0/21 interface is associated to R2:

```
On SW1:


SW1# show mac address-table dynamic

          Mac Address Table

-------------------------------------------


Vlan    Mac Address      Type       Ports
----    -----------      --------   -----
   1    0000.1111.1111   DYNAMIC    Fa0/1 → R1
   1    0000.2222.2222   DYNAMIC    Fa0/21 → R2
   1    0011.928e.9c15   DYNAMIC    Fa0/21 → SW3's F0/21 interface
   1    0015.c621.f995   DYNAMIC    Fa0/19 → SW2's F0/19 interface
Total Mac Addresses for this criterion: 4
```

On SW2 (the access switch), R1 is associated to interface F0/23 and R2 is associated to interface F0/2:

```
On SW2:

SW2# show mac address-table dynamic
        Mac Address Table
-------------------------------------------

Vlan    Mac Address      Type      Ports
----    -----------      --------  -----
  1     0000.1111.1111   DYNAMIC   Fa0/23 → R1
  1     0000.2222.2222   DYNAMIC   Fa0/2 → R2
  1     0011.928e.9c17   DYNAMIC   Fa0/23 → SW3's F0/23 interface
Total Mac Addresses for this criterion: 3
```

But once spanning tree converges, the actual topology looks like that shown in Figure 3-10.

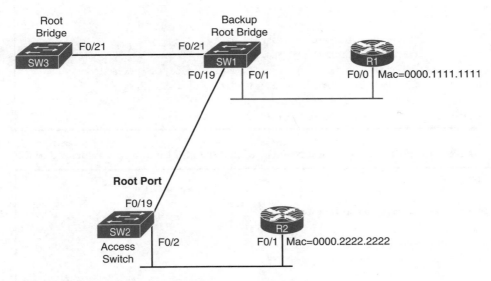

Figure 3-10 *L2 Environment After Reconvergence*

The backup link is brought up quickly, but from the CAM's perspective, things have not changed yet. Therefore, it will be inaccurate.

In order to solve this problem, the access switch (SW2) begins to flood dummy packets with the MAC addresses that it has in its CAM. It uses those MAC addresses as the source and Cisco's proprietary multicast MAC address as the destination.

This method will ensure the dummy packets are flooded on the entire network and the CAMs of all switches are updated.

Figure 3-11 illustrates how this information is flooded on a link-by-link basis.

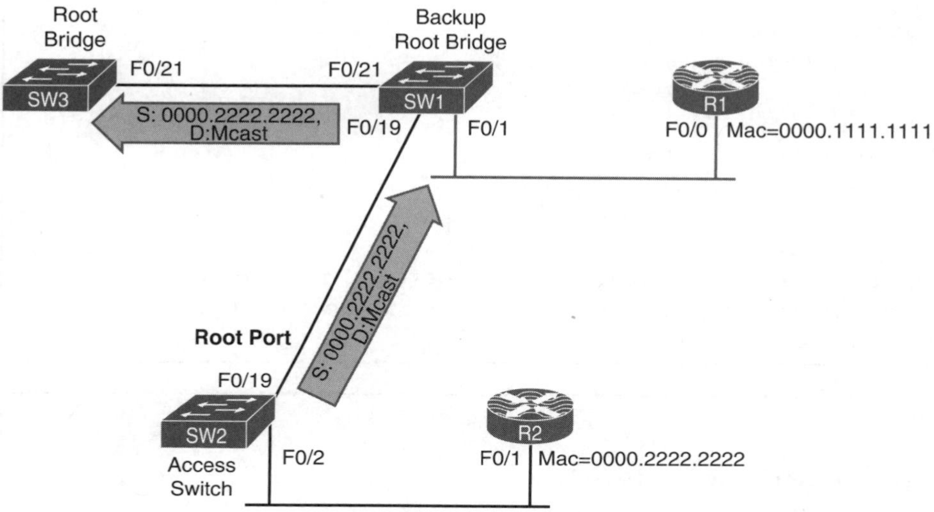

Figure 3-11 *MAC Flooding Toward the New Root Bridge*

The CAM table of the switches will look like the following after the flooding. However, before we see the MAC address table of the switches, let's shut down the F0/23 interface of SW2:

```
On SW2:


SW2(config)# interface FastEthernet0/23
SW2(config-if)# shut
```

Let's verify the configuration:

```
On SW3:


SW3# show mac address-table dynamic


        Mac Address Table
-------------------------------------------


Vlan    Mac Address      Type       Ports
----    -----------      --------   -----
   1    0000.1111.1111   DYNAMIC    Fa0/21 → R1
   1    0014.6a8d.2297   DYNAMIC    Fa0/21 → SW1's F0/21 interface


Total Mac Addresses for this criterion: 2
```

```
On SW1:


SW1# show mac address-table dynamic
          Mac Address Table
---------------------------------------------

Vlan    Mac Address      Type        Ports
----    -----------      --------    -----
   1    0000.1111.1111   DYNAMIC     Fa0/1   → R1
   1    0000.2222.2222   DYNAMIC     Fa0/19  → R2
   1    0011.928e.9c15   DYNAMIC     Fa0/21  → SW3's F0/21 interface
   1    0015.c621.f995   DYNAMIC     Fa0/19  → SW2's F0/19 interface
Total Mac Addresses for this criterion: 4
```

```
On SW2:


SW2# show mac address-table dynamic
          Mac Address Table
---------------------------------------------

Vlan    Mac Address      Type        Ports
----    -----------      --------    -----
   1    0000.1111.1111   DYNAMIC     Fa0/19  → R1
   1    0000.2222.2222   DYNAMIC     Fa0/2   → R2
   1    0014.6a8d.2295   DYNAMIC     Fa0/19  → SW1's F0/19 interface
Total Mac Addresses for this criterion: 3
```

To verify the operation of spanning tree before the configuration of UplinkFast, the UplinkFast feature is disabled and the **debug spanning-tree events** is enabled.

Let's see if the UplinkFast feature is enabled:

```
On SW2:


SW2# show spanning summary | include Uplink

UplinkFast                      is enabled
UplinkFast statistics
```

Let's disable the UplinkFast feature:

```
SW2(config)# no spanning-tree uplinkfast
```

Let's see if the UplinkFast feature is disabled:

```
SW2# show spanning-tree summary | include Uplink

UplinkFast                      is disabled

SW2# debug spanning events
Spanning Tree event debugging is on
```

Let's shut down the root port on SW2.

```
SW2(config)# interface FastEthernet0/23
SW2(config-if)# no shut
SW2(config-if)# shut
```

You should see the following debug output:

```
00:43:57: STP: VLAN0001 new root port Fa0/19, cost 38
00:43:57: STP: VLAN0001 Fa0/19 -> listening

*Mar  1 00:43:59.173: %LINK-5-CHANGED: Interface FastEthernet0/23, changed state to
  administratively down

00:43:59: STP: VLAN0001 sent Topology Change Notice on Fa0/19

*Mar  1 00:44:00.180: %LINEPROTO-5-UPDOWN: Line protocol on Interface FastEther-
  net0/23, changed state to down

00:44:12: STP: VLAN0001 Fa0/19 -> learning

00:44:27: STP: VLAN0001 sent Topology Change Notice on Fa0/19
00:44:27: STP: VLAN0001 Fa0/19 -> forwarding
```

Note   It took 30 seconds for STP to converge. Enable **spanning-tree uplinkfast** and test the same scenario again.

```
On SW2:

SW2(config)# interface FastEthernet0/23
SW2(config-if)# no shut
```

Let's configure UplinkFast:

```
On SW2:

SW2(config)# spanning-tree uplinkfast
```

> **Note**   The spanning tree UplinkFast can *only* be configured in the global configuration mode. As a result, it affects the entire switch.

Let's verify the primary and alternate uplink ports:

```
SW2# show spanning-tree vlan 1 | include Fa0

Fa0/2              Desg FWD 3019      128.4    P2p
Fa0/19             Altn BLK 3019      128.21   P2p
Fa0/23             Root FWD 3019      128.25   P2p
```

With the **debug spanning-tree events** command still configured, the F0/23 interface of SW2 is shut down and the convergence time can be verified:

```
SW2(config)# interface FastEthernet0/23
SW2(config-if)# shut
```

You should see the following debug output:

```
01:07:37: STP: VLAN0001 new root port Fa0/19, cost 3038

01:07:37.418: %SPANTREE_FAST-7-PORT_FWD_UPLINK: VLAN0001 FastEthernet0/19 moved to
  Forwarding (UplinkFast).

01:07:39.406: %LINK-5-CHANGED: Interface FastEthernet0/23, changed state to
  administratively down

01:07:39: STP: VLAN0001 sent Topology Change Notice on Fa0/19

01:07:40.413: %LINEPROTO-5-UPDOWN: Line protocol on Interface FastEthernet0/23,
  changed state to down
```

```
SW2# show spanning-tree vlan 1 | include Fa0

Fa0/2              Desg FWD 3019      128.4    P2p
Fa0/19             Root FWD 3019      128.21   P2p
```

You can see that it *only* took a second for the F0/19 interface to transition into the forwarding state.

To ensure stability and to protect itself from constant link flaps, spanning tree does *not* converge immediately when port F0/23 is enabled. SW2's F0/23 interface does *not* transition into the forwarding state before it transitions through the listening and learning states, which can take up to 30 seconds.

This switchover is delayed by 35 seconds by default (2 * **forward-delay** + 5 seconds). The reason the 5 additional seconds is added is to allow other protocols such as DTP time to negotiate.

It is important to be aware of some of the changes that UplinkFast applies. Once UplinkFast is configured, some of the spanning tree parameters are modified.

The bridge priority of the switch is increased significantly. This ensures the switch will *not* be elected as the root bridge. Now let's verify this information.

The following is before the UplinkFast feature was enabled:

```
SW2# show spanning-tree vlan 1 | include Priority

  Root ID    Priority    24577
  Bridge ID  Priority    32769  (priority 32768 sys-id-ext 1)
```

The following is after the UplinkFast feature was enabled:

```
SW2# show spanning-tree vlan 1 | include Priority

  Root ID    Priority    24577
  Bridge ID  Priority    49153  (priority 49152 sys-id-ext 1)
```

To ensure that ports on the local switch do *not* get elected as the designated ports, all the ports on the local switch will have their cost increased by 3000.

The following is before the UplinkFast feature was enabled:

```
SW2# show spanning-tree vlan 1 | begin Interface
Interface           Role Sts Cost      Prio.Nbr Type
------------------- ---- --- --------- -------- -------

Fa0/2               Desg FWD 19        128.4    P2p
Fa0/19              Altn BLK 19        128.21   P2p
Fa0/23              Root FWD 19        128.25   P2p
```

The following is after the UplinkFast feature was enabled:

```
SW2# show spanning-tree vlan 1 | begin Interface

Interface          Role Sts Cost      Prio.Nbr Type
------------------ ---- --- --------- -------- -------
Fa0/2              Desg FWD 3019      128.4    P2p
Fa0/19             Altn BLK 3019      128.21   P2p
Fa0/23             Root FWD 3019      128.25   P2p
```

Remember, the preceding changes can seriously alter your current spanning tree topology.

Erase the configuration on all routers and switches and reload them before proceeding to the next lab.

Lab 3-7: BPDU Guard

Figure 3-12 illustrates the topology that will be used in the following tasks.

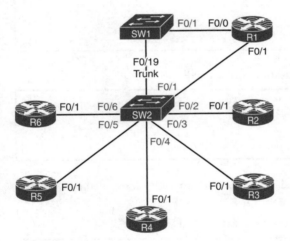

Figure 3-12   *BPDU Guard*

BPDU Guard works with interfaces that have been configured as PortFast or edge ports. BPDU Guard will transition these ports into **err-disable** state if that port receives a single BPDU. The BPDU Guard feature disables these interfaces to avoid a potential bridging loop. The BPDU Guard feature is used to protect the Spanning Tree domain from external influence. BPDU Guard is disabled by default, but it is recommended for all ports on which the PortFast feature has been enabled. This prevents false information from being injected into the Spanning Tree domain on ports that have spanning tree disabled.

When a port is connected to a host device, we can enable PortFast so that we can speed up the port-initialization process and put the port into the forwarding state almost immediately. This process eliminates the 30 seconds of delay that would have been encountered if the STP process went through the listening and learning states. A host is a workstation, and as such it should never send BPDUs or take part in the STP domain; therefore, disabling spanning tree on a port connected to a host should never be an issue.

However, if we removed the host and connected a switch, this new switch would immediately start to generate BPDUs and could possibly take over the role of the root bridge, or it could generate an undesirable loop in the topology. BPDU Guard will prevent this by providing a secure response to invalid configurations or unauthorized switches appearing on the network. This process is considered secure because the administrator must manually reenable the **err-disabled** interface after fixing the invalid configuration or removing the unauthorized switch. It is also possible to set up a timeout interval after which the switch will automatically try to reenable the interface. However, if the invalid configuration or switch is still present, the switch will **err-disable** the interface again.

Task 1

Shut down all ports on SW1 and SW2 and configure an industry-standard trunk between the two switches using port F0/19. *Only* the F0/19 interface should be in **no shutdown** state.

```
On SW1:

SW1(config)# interface range FastEthernet0/1-24
SW1(config-if-range)# shut

SW1(config)# interface FastEthernet0/19
SW1(config-if)# switchport trunk encapsulation dot1q
SW1(config-if)# switchport mode trunk
SW1(config-if)# no shut
```

```
On SW2:

SW2(config)# interface range FastEthernet0/1-24
SW2(config-if-range)# shut

SW2(config)# interface FastEthernet0/19
SW2(config-if)# switchport trunk encapsulation dot1q
SW2(config-if)# switchport mode trunk
SW2(config-if)# no shut
```

Task 2

Configure the F0/1 interface of SW1 such that if it detects any BPDUs, it transitions into **err-disable** mode.

Remember, the F0/1 interface of SW1 is connected to R1's F0/0 interface, and both ports are in administratively down state.

```
On SW1:

SW1# show interface FastEthernet0/1 status

Port        Name            Status          Vlan        Duplex  Speed Type
Fa0/1                       disabled        1              auto    auto 10/100BaseTX
```

BPDU Guard is the feature that can accomplish this task. BPDU Guard can be enabled in two different ways:

- Globally
- On a per-interface basis

When BPDU Guard is enabled globally, it will affect all ports that are PortFast-enabled. If a port that is configured as PortFast receives BPDUs, the BPDU Guard feature will shut down the port in **err-disabled** mode. To enable the BPDU Guard feature globally, you must use the **spanning-tree PortFast bpduguard default** global configuration command.

If BPDU Guard is enabled on a given interface and the port receives BPDUs, it will shut the port down in **err-disabled** mode.

Note   In this mode, PortFast does not need to be enabled.

To enable BPDU Guard on a per-interface basis, you must use the **spanning-tree bpduguard enable** interface configuration command:

```
On SW1:

SW1(config)# interface FastEthernet0/1
SW1(config-if)# spanning-tree bpduguard enable
SW1(config-if)# no shut
```

Let's test and verify the configuration (keep in mind that you must wait for the F0/1 interface of SW1 to transition into the forwarding state):

```
On SW1:

SW1# debug spanning events
Spanning Tree event debugging is on
```

In order to test this feature, R1 is configured as a bridge to send BPDUs:

```
On R1:

R1(config)# bridge 1 protocol ieee

R1(config)# interface FastEthernet0/0
R1(config-if)# bridge-group 1
R1(config-if)# no shut
```

```
On SW1:

set portid: VLAN0001 Fa0/1: new port id 8003

STP: VLAN0001 Fa0/1 -> listening

%SPANTREE-2-BLOCK_BPDUGUARD: Received BPDU on port Fa0/1 with BPDU Guard enabled.

Disabling port.
%PM-4-ERR_DISABLE: bpduguard error detected on Fa0/1, putting Fa0/1 in err-disable
   state
```

Let's verify the result:

```
On SW1:

SW1# show interface FastEthernet0/1 status

Port        Name          Status        Vlan       Duplex  Speed Type
Fa0/1                     err-disabled 1           auto   auto  10/100BaseTX

SW1# sh errdisable detect | inc Err|bpdu

ErrDisable Reason       Detection     Mode
bpduguard               Enabled       port
```

Because the port is *not* in the administratively down state, a **no shutdown** will *not* enable the interface. The **no shutdown** command *only* works if the port's state is administratively down. In order to enable a port that is in **err-disabled** mode, the port must be placed in the administratively down state first, using the **shutdown** interface configuration command. Then it can be enabled by using the **no shutdown** command.

Task 3

Configure SW2 such that the existing and future ports that are PortFast-enabled transition into **err-disabled** mode upon detection of BPDUs.

The following command enables BPDU Guard globally on SW2. When this feature is enabled globally, it must also include the PortFast feature. This affects existing and future ports that are PortFast-enabled.

```
On SW2:

SW2(config)# spanning-tree PortFast bpduguard default
```

Let's verify the configuration:

```
On SW2:

SW2# show spanning-tree summary | include BPDU Guard

PortFast BPDU Guard Default  is enabled
```

Let's test the configuration:

Note   SW2's F0/1 interface is configured with **spanning-tree PortFast**, and the **debug spanning-tree events** is enabled.

```
On SW2:

SW2(config)# interface FastEthernet0/1
SW2(config-if)# spanning-tree PortFast
SW2(config)# no shut

SW2# debug spanning events
Spanning Tree event debugging is on
```

Because R1 is already configured as a bridge, you don't need to configure **bridge 1 protocol ieee** again. All you need to do is to apply the bridge configuration to the F0/1 interface of R1 using the **bridge-group 1** command and then enable the interface:

```
On R1:

R1(config)# interface FastEthernet0/1
R1(config-if)# bridge-group 1
R1(config-if)# no shut
```

You should see the following debug output on SW2:

```
On SW2:


set portid: VLAN0001 Fa0/1: new port id 8003
STP: VLAN0001 Fa0/1 ->jump to forwarding from blocking


%SPANTREE-2-BLOCK_BPDUGUARD: Received BPDU on port Fa0/1 with BPDU Guard enabled.

Disabling port.
%PM-4-ERR_DISABLE: bpduguard error detected on Fa0/1, putting Fa0/1 in err-disable
  state
```

Let's verify the configuration:

```
On SW2:


SW2# show interface FastEthernet0/1 status


Port       Name          Status       Vlan      Duplex  Speed Type
Fa0/1                    err-disabled 1          auto    auto 10/100BaseTX
```

Task 4

Configure SW1's F0/1 interface to automatically recover from **errdisable** mode caused by BPDU Guard. This recovery should occur every 30 seconds. If the interface of the switch detects BPDUs, it should once again transition back into **errdisable** mode. If it does *not* detect BPDUs, it should remain in the up/up state.

```
On SW1:


SW1(config)# errdisable recovery cause bpduguard
SW1(config)# errdisable recovery interval 30
```

Let's verify the configuration:

```
On SW1:

SW1# show errdisable detect | include Err|bpdu

ErrDisable Reason     Detection status
bpduguard             Enabled
```

Every 30 seconds, the port tries to recover from BPDU Guard on the F0/1 interface. You should see the following console messages every 30 seconds as the switch tries to recover from the **errdisable** mode:

```
00:54:19: %PM-4-ERR_RECOVER: Attempting to recover from bpduguard err-disable state
  on Fa0/1
```

The interface comes up:

```
00:54:21: set portid: VLAN0001 Fa0/1: new port id 8003
00:54:21: STP: VLAN0001 Fa0/1 -> listening

00:54:23: %LINK-3-UPDOWN: Interface FastEthernet0/1, changed state to up
```

The interface once again detects BPDUs:

```
00:54:23: %SPANTREE-2-BLOCK_BPDUGUARD: Received BPDU on port
```

The interface (F0/1) has BPDU Guard enabled and transitions into **errdisable** mode:

```
FastEthernet0/1 with BPDU Guard enabled. Disabling port.

00:54:23: %PM-4-ERR_DISABLE: bpduguard error detected on Fa0/1, putting Fa0/1 in
  err-disable state

00:54:25: %LINK-3-UPDOWN: Interface FastEthernet0/1, changed state to down
```

Erase the configuration on all routers and switches and reload them before proceeding to the next lab.

Lab 3-8: BPDU Filter

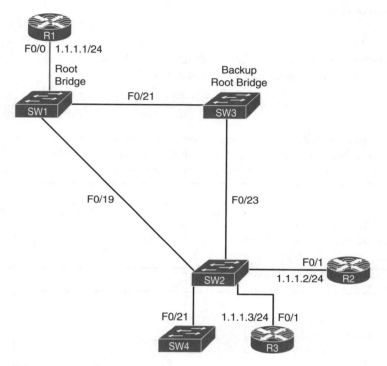

Figure 3-13 *BPDU Filter*

When PortFast is enabled on a port, the port will still send out BPDUs and it will accept and process received BPDUs. The BPDU Guard feature would prevent the port from receiving any BPDUs, but it will not prevent it from sending them. The BPDU Filter feature effectively disables STP on the selected ports by preventing them from sending or receiving any BPDUs.

BPDU filtering supports the ability to prevent switches from sending BPDUs on PortFast-enabled interfaces. Ports configured for the PortFast feature typically connect to host devices. Hosts do not participate in STP and hence drop the received BPDUs. As a result, BPDU filtering prevents unnecessary BPDUs from being transmitted to host devices.

When enabled globally, BPDU filtering has the following effects:

- It affects all operational PortFast ports on switches that do not have BPDU filtering configured.

- If BPDUs are seen, the port loses its PortFast status, BPDU filtering is disabled, and the STP sends and receives BPDUs on the port as it would with any other STP port on the switch.

- Upon startup, the port transmits 10 BPDUs. If this port receives any BPDUs during that time, PortFast and PortFast BPDU filtering will be disabled.

When enabled on an individual port, BPDU filtering has the following effects:

- It ignores all BPDUs received.

- It sends no BPDUs.

If you enable BPDU Guard on the same interface as BPDU filtering, BPDU Guard has no effect because BPDU filtering takes precedence over BPDU Guard.

Task 1

Configure the routers and the switches according to Figure 3-13. The interswitch connections should be configured as a trunk using an industry-standard encapsulation. The unused ports should be configured in administratively down mode.

```
On R1:

R1(config)# interface FastEthernet0/0
R1(config-if)# ip address 1.1.1.1 255.255.255.0
R1(config-if)# no shut
```

```
On R2:

R2(config)# interface FastEthernet0/1
R2(config-if)# ip address 1.1.1.2 255.255.255.0
R2(config-if)# no shut
```

```
On R3:

R3(config)# interface FastEthernet0/1
R3(config-if)# ip address 1.1.1.3 255.255.255.0
R3(config-if)# no shut
```

```
On SW1:

SW1(config)# interface range FastEthernet0/1-24
SW1(config-if-range)# shut

SW1(config)# interface range FastEthernet0/19 , FastEthernet0/21
SW1(config-if-range)# switchport trunk encapsulation dot1q
SW1(config-if-range)# switchport mode trunk
SW1(config-if)# no shut
```

```
On SW2:

SW2(config)# interface range FastEthernet0/1-24
SW2(config-if-range)# shut

SW2(config)# interface range FastEthernet0/19 , FastEthernet0/21 , FastEthernet0/23
SW2(config-if-range)# switchport trunk encapsulation dot1q
SW2(config-if-range)# switchport mode trunk
SW2(config-if)# no shut
```

```
On SW3:

SW3(config)# interface range FastEthernet0/1-24
SW3(config-if-range)# shut


SW3(config)# interface range fastEthernet0/21 , FastEthernet0/23
SW3(config-if-range)# switchport trunk encapsulation dot1q
SW3(config-if-range)# switchport mode trunk
SW3(config-if)# no shut
```

```
On SW4:

SW4(config)# interface FastEthernet0/21
SW4(config-if)# switchport trunk encapsulation dot1q
SW4(config-if)# switchport mode trunk
SW4(config-if)# no shut
```

```
On SW1:

SW1(config)# spanning-tree vlan 1 root primary

SW1(config)# interface FastEthernet0/1
SW1(config-if)# no shut
```

```
On SW3:

SW3(config)# spanning-tree vlan 1 root secondary
```

```
On SW2:

SW2(config)# interface range FastEthernet0/2-3
SW2(config-if)# no shut
```

Let's verify the configuration:

```
On SW1:

SW1# show interface trunk

Port          Mode        Encapsulation   Status          Native vlan
Fa0/19        on          802.1q          trunking        1
Fa0/21        on          802.1q          trunking        1
(The rest of the output is omitted)


SW1# sh spanning vlan 1 | inc ID

  Root ID     Priority     24577
  Bridge ID   Priority     24577   (priority 24576 sys-id-ext 1)
```

Based on the output of the preceding **show** command, you can see that this switch is the root.

```
On SW2:

SW2# show interface trunk

Port          Mode        Encapsulation   Status          Native vlan
Fa0/19        on          802.1q          trunking        1
Fa0/21        on          802.1q          trunking        1
Fa0/23        on          802.1q          trunking        1
(The rest of the output is omitted)


SW2# show spanning-tree vlan 1 | include ID

  Root ID     Priority     24577
  Bridge ID   Priority     32769   (priority 32768 sys-id-ext 1)
```

```
On SW3:


SW3# show interface trunk


Port        Mode        Encapsulation  Status       Native vlan
Fa0/21      on          802.1q         trunking     1
Fa0/23      on          802.1q         trunking     1
(The rest of the output is omitted)


SW3# show spanning-tree vlan 1 | include ID


  Root ID     Priority    24577
  Bridge ID   Priority    28673   (priority 28672 sys-id-ext 1)
```

Based on the output of the preceding **show** command, you can see that this switch is the backup root or root secondary.

```
On SW4:


SW4# show interface trunk


Port        Mode        Encapsulation  Status       Native vlan
Fa0/21      on          802.1q         trunking     1
(The rest of the output is omitted)


SW4# sh spanning vlan 1 | inc ID



  Root ID     Priority    24577
  Bridge ID   Priority    32769   (priority 32768 sys-id-ext 1)
```

Task 2

Configure SW2's F0/21 interface using the following policies:

■ The F0/21 interface of SW2 should be configured to filter sending or receiving BPDUs. If this port receives BPDUs, it should *not* transition into **err-disable** state.

■ If BPDU filtering is enabled on a given interface, the incoming BPDU packets are filtered. Unlike BPDU Guard, it does *not* place the interface of the switch into **err-disabled** state.

Let's check the incoming and outgoing BPDUs before configuring this task:

```
On SW2:

SW2# show spanning-tree interface FastEthernet0/21 detail | include BPDU

   BPDU: sent 339, received 0

SW2# show spanning-tree interface FastEthernet0/21 detail | include BPDU

   BPDU: sent 345, received 0
```

Remember, BPDUs are generated by the root bridge and propagated to downstream switches. Because SW1 is the root, it sends the BPDUs to SW2, and SW2 forwards them downstream to SW4:

```
On SW4:

SW4# show spanning-tree interface FastEthernet0/21 detail | include BPDU

   BPDU: sent 0, received 210

SW4# show spanning-tree interface FastEthernet0/21 detail | include BPDU

   BPDU: sent 0, received 220
```

Let's configure the task:

```
On SW2:

SW2(config)# interface FastEthernet0/21
SW2(config-if)# spanning-tree bpdufilter enable
```

Let's verify the task:

```
On SW2:

SW2# show spanning-tree interface FastEthernet0/21 detail | include BPDU

   BPDU: sent 581, received 0

SW2# show spanning-tree interface FastEthernet0/21 detail | include BPDU

   BPDU: sent 581, received 0
```

Because SW1 is the root bridge, SW2 refloods the BPDU messages that it receives from SW1. Because SW4 is *not* the root bridge, it will *not* generate BPDUs.

Once BPDU filtering is configured on SW2's F0/21 interface, SW4 will no longer see the BPDUs. SW4 will claim to be the root bridge and will start generating BPDUs.

Let's verify the information:

```
On SW4:


SW4# show spanning-tree interface FastEthernet0/21 detail | include BPDU

   BPDU: sent 342, received 291



SW4# show spanning-tree interface FastEthernet0/21 detail | include BPDU

   BPDU: sent 350, received 291

SW4# show spanning-tree vlan 1


VLAN0001
  Spanning tree enabled protocol ieee
  Root ID    Priority    32769


             Address     000c.ced1.fb80
             This bridge is the root
             Hello Time   2 sec  Max Age 20 sec  Forward Delay 15 sec


  Bridge ID  Priority    32769   (priority 32768 sys-id-ext 1)
             Address     000c.ced1.fb80
             Hello Time   2 sec  Max Age 20 sec  Forward Delay 15 sec
             Aging Time 300


Interface          Role Sts Cost      Prio.Nbr Type
------------------ ---- --- --------- -------- -----
Fa0/21             Desg FWD 19        128.21   P2p
```

Note   SW4 is no longer receiving BPDUs from SW2. SW4 claims to be the root bridge and starts generating BPDUs.

However, because SW2 is filtering the incoming BPDUs, the receive BPDU counter on SW2 does not increment. Also, BPDU Filter filters/blocks the incoming and outgoing BPDU messages.

Let's verify the information:

```
On SW2:

SW2# show spanning-tree interface FastEthernet0/21 detail | include BPDU

   BPDU: sent 581, received 0

SW2# show spanning-tree interface FastEthernet0/21 detail | include BPDU

   BPDU: sent 581, received 0
```

Task 3

On the existing topology, demonstrate and prove why and how the BPDU Filter feature can cause a forwarding loop.

Let's verify the communication between R1 and R3:

```
On R1:


R1# ping 1.1.1.2

Type escape sequence to abort.
Sending 5, 100-byte ICMP Echos to 1.1.1.2, timeout is 2 seconds:
.!!!!
Success rate is 80 percent (4/5), round-trip min/avg/max = 1/1/1 ms

R1# ping 1.1.1.3

Type escape sequence to abort.
Sending 5, 100-byte ICMP Echos to 1.1.1.3, timeout is 2 seconds:
.!!!!
Success rate is 80 percent (4/5), round-trip min/avg/max = 1/1/1 ms
```

```
On R2:

R2# ping 1.1.1.3

Type escape sequence to abort.
Sending 5, 100-byte ICMP Echos to 1.1.1.3, timeout is 2 seconds:
.!!!!
Success rate is 80 percent (4/5), round-trip min/avg/max = 1/1/1 ms
```

Let's find out which switch interface is in the blocking state. Because SW1 is the root bridge, all of its interfaces should be in the forwarding state:

```
On SW1:

SW1# show spanning-tree blockedports

Name                    Blocked Interfaces List
------------------      -----------------------------------
Number of blocked ports (segments) in the system : 0
```

```
On SW3:

SW3# show spanning-tree blockedports

Name                    Blocked Interfaces List
------------------      -----------------------------------
Number of blocked ports (segments) in the system : 0
```

```
On SW2:


SW2# show spanning-tree blockedports

Name                    Blocked Interfaces List
------------------      -----------------------------------
VLAN0001                Fa0/23

Number of blocked ports (segments) in the system : 1
```

Because SW1 was configured to be the root bridge and SW3 was configured to be the backup root bridge, the blocked port had to be on SW2. However, because the F0/19 interface of SW2 is the closest interface to the root bridge (root port), the only other interface (F0/23) must be in blocking state.

If BPDU Filter is configured on this interface (F0/23), all interfaces on SW2 will be in the forwarding state. Therefore, we will see a spanning tree forwarding loop. With BPDU Filter configured, the loop-free topology feature of the spanning tree protocol is being prevented from functioning. The following demonstrates this fact:

```
On SW2:

SW2(config)# interface FastEthernet0/23
SW2(config-if)# spanning-tree bpdufilter enable
```

Let's verify the configuration:

```
On SW1:


SW1# show spanning-tree blockedports


Name                     Blocked Interfaces List
-------------------- ------------------------------------
Number of blocked ports (segments) in the system : 0
```

```
On SW3:


SW3# show spanning-tree blockedports


Name                     Blocked Interfaces List
-------------------- ------------------------------------
Number of blocked ports (segments) in the system : 0
```

```
On SW2:


SW2# show spanning-tree blockedports



Name                     Blocked Interfaces List
-------------------- ------------------------------------
Number of blocked ports (segments) in the system : 0
```

If none of the switches are blocking any of their ports, then how is STP performing loop avoidance? It is *not*. This is why the BPDU Filter feature must be configured carefully.

You should see the following console messages:

Note   Depending on the IOS version, you may or may not see these console messages.

```
On SW2:


%SW_MATM-4-MACFLAP_NOTIF: Host 0019.e8d7.6821 in vlan 1 is flapping between port
   Fa0/19 and port Fa0/23


%SW_MATM-4-MACFLAP_NOTIF: Host 0007.b35d.81a1 in vlan 1 is flapping between port
   Fa0/23 and port Fa0/19
```

Let's test the configuration:

```
On R1, R2 and R3:

R1# clear arp

On R1:

R1# ping 1.1.1.3

Type escape sequence to abort.
Sending 5, 100-byte ICMP Echos to 1.1.1.3, timeout is 2 seconds:
.....
Success rate is 0 percent (0/5)

R1# ping 1.1.1.2

Type escape sequence to abort.
Sending 5, 100-byte ICMP Echos to 1.1.1.2, timeout is 2 seconds:
.....
Success rate is 0 percent (0/5)
```

Let's remove the command before proceeding to the next task:

```
On SW2:

SW2(config)# interface FastEthernet0/23
SW2(config-if)# spanning-tree bpdufilter disable
```

Let's verify the configuration:

```
On SW2:

SW2# show spanning-tree blockedports

Name                Blocked Interfaces List
------------------- ------------------------------------
VLAN0001            Fa0/23

Number of blocked ports (segments) in the system : 1

R1# ping 1.1.1.2

Type escape sequence to abort.
Sending 5, 100-byte ICMP Echos to 1.1.1.2, timeout is 2 seconds:
!!!!!
Success rate is 100 percent (5/5), round-trip min/avg/max = 1/1/4 ms
```

Task 4

Configure SW2 based on the following policies:

- Configure the F0/2 interface of this switch to bypass the spanning tree listening and learning states.

- This switch should be configured such that upon detection of BPDU messages on existing and/or future PortFast-enabled ports, it loses its spanning tree PortFast status but does *not* transition into **err-disabled** mode.

```
On SW2:

SW2(config)# spanning-tree PortFast bpdufilter default
```

Let's verify the configuration:

```
On SW2:

SW2# show spanning-tree summary | include BPDU Filter

PortFast BPDU Filter Default is enabled

SW2(config)# int f0/2
SW2(config-if)# spanning portf
```

A **show spanning-tree** command should reveal whether or not PortFast is enabled on a given interface. We will explore this on SW2.

```
On SW2:

SW2# show spanning-tree interface FastEthernet0/2 PortFast

VLAN0001              enabled
```

Let's test and verify the configuration:

```
On SW2:

SW2# debug spanning-tree events
Spanning Tree event debugging is on
```

```
On R2:

R2(config)# bridge 1 protocol ieee

R2(config)# interface FastEthernet0/1
R2(config-if)# shut
R2(config-if)# bridge-group 1
R2(config-if)# no shut
```

You should see the following console messages on SW2:

```
On SW2:

set portid: VLAN0001 Fa0/2: new port id 8004
STP: VLAN0001 Fa0/2 ->jump to forwarding from blocking

%LINK-3-UPDOWN: Interface FastEthernet0/2, changed state to up
%LINEPROTO-5-UPDOWN: Line protocol on Interface FastEthernet0/2, changed state to up

STP: VLAN0001 heard root 32768-0011.9279.1f71 on Fa0/2

STP: VLAN0001 Topology Change rcvd on Fa0/2
STP: VLAN0001 sent Topology Change Notice on Fa0/19
```

You *must* wait for the preceding message on your console before entering the following **show** command:

```
SW2# show spanning-tree interface FastEthernet0/2 PortFast

VLAN0001            disabled

SW2# show interface FastEthernet0/2 status

Port       Name           Status       Vlan      Duplex  Speed Type
Fa0/2                     connected    1         a-full  a-100 10/100BaseTX

SW2# show running-config interface FastEthernet0/2 | begin interface

interface FastEthernet0/2
 spanning-tree PortFast

SW2# show running-config | include spanning-tree PortFast bpdufilter

spanning-tree PortFast bpdufilter default
```

Erase the configuration on all routers and switches and reload them before proceeding to the next lab.

Lab 3-9: Spanning Tree Backbone Fast

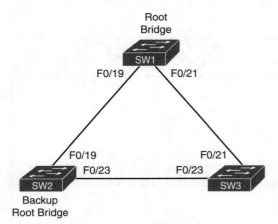

Figure 3-14   *Spanning Tree Backbone Fast*

Task 1

Configure the switches according to Figure 3-14. The unused ports must be in administratively down state.

```
On All Switches:

SWx(config)# interface range FastEthernet0/1-24
SWx(config-if-range)# shut
```

```
On SW1:

SW1(config)# spanning-tree vlan 1 root primary

SW1(config)# interface range FastEthernet0/19 , FastEthernet0/21
SW1(config-if-range)# switchport trunk encapsulation dot1q
SW1(config-if-range)# switchport mode trunk
SW1(config-if-range)# no shut
```

```
On SW2:

SW2(config)# spanning-tree vlan 1 root secondary

SW2(config)# interface range FastEthernet0/19 , FastEthernet0/23
SW2(config-if-range)# switchport trunk encapsulation dot1q
SW2(config-if-range)# switchport mode trunk
SW2(config-if-range)# no shut
```

```
On SW3:

SW3(config)# interface range FastEthernet0/21 , FastEthernet0/23
SW3(config-if-range)# switchport trunk encapsulation dot1q
SW3(config-if-range)# switchport mode trunk
SW3(config-if-range)# no shut
```

Let's verify the configuration:

```
On SW3:

SW3# show spanning-tree root

                                  Root    Hello Max Fwd
Vlan               Root ID        Cost    Time  Age Dly  Root Port
---------------    --------------------  --------- ----- --- ---  -----------
VLAN0001           24577 0014.6a8d.2280       19     2   20  15   Fa0/21
```

The output of the preceding **show** command reveals that SW3 *cannot* be the root bridge. The question is, why?

A root bridge cannot have a root port. You can see the root port is F0/21 with a cost of 19. So what happened to the F0/23 interface?

Well, the output of the following command reveals the F0/23 interface of this switch is in the blocking state:

```
SW3# show spanning-tree blockedports

Name                   Blocked Interfaces List
-------------------    -----------------------------
VLAN0001               Fa0/23

Number of blocked ports (segments) in the system : 1
```

```
On SW2:

SW2# show spanning-tree root

                                    Root    Hello Max Fwd
Vlan                 Root ID        Cost    Time  Age Dly  Root Port
----------------- -------------------- --------- ----- --- ---  ----------
VLAN0001      24577 0014.6a8d.2280         19     2   20  15  Fa0/19
```

Once again, we can see a root port in the output. Therefore, this switch *cannot* be the root. Let's check the state of the F0/23 interface of this switch:

```
SW2# show spanning-tree blockedports

Name                    Blocked Interfaces List
------------------- ------------------------------
Number of blocked ports (segments) in the system : 0
```

Well, it is not in the blocking state. Let's use another command to determine the state of the F0/23 interface of this switch:

```
SW2# show spanning-tree vlan 1 | begin Interface

Interface          Role Sts Cost      Prio.Nbr Type
------------------- ---- --- --------- -------- ----
Fa0/19             Root FWD 19        128.21   P2p
Fa0/23             Desg FWD 19        128.25   P2p
```

You can see the F0/23 interface of this switch is the designated port.

```
On SW1:

SW1# show spanning-tree root

                                    Root    Hello Max Fwd
Vlan                 Root ID        Cost    Time  Age Dly  Root Port
----------------- -------------------- --------- ----- --- ---  ---------
VLAN0001      24577 0014.6a8d.2280          0     2   20  15
```

You can see that this switch (SW1) is the root bridge, because it has no root port. This switch should *not* have any ports in the blocking state. Let's verify this information:

```
SW1# show spanning-tree blockedports

Name                    Blocked Interfaces List
------------------- ------------------------------
Number of blocked ports (segments) in the system : 0
```

Task 2

Configure the appropriate switch(es) such that if an indirectly connected link fails, the STP convergence time is improved. Do *not* manually configure any timers to accomplish this task.

To resolve this task, the **spanning-tree backbonefast** feature must be enabled. Backbone Fast is a spanning tree feature that optimizes the convergence by expiring the **max-age** timer. Backbone Fast *must* be enabled on all switches.

With UplinkFast, the switches detected a failure of a directly connected link; with Backbone Fast, the switches detect a failure of an indirectly connected link.

Backbone Fast works in two stages. In the first stage, when a switch receives inferior BPDUs through a nondesignated port (NDP), it knows the switch that sent the inferior BPDUs has lost its connection to the root bridge. When the local switch receives the inferior BPDUs, it verifies if the source that generated these messages is from a local segment. If the source is from a local segment, it knows that an indirectly connected link failure has occurred. If the source of the inferior BPDUs is from a switch that is *not* on a local segment, the local switch will ignore them.

In the second stage, the local switch goes through a verification process. The switch uses a request and response protocol. This process queries other switches to determine if the connection to the root bridge is lost.

The verification process is done by the local switch that received the inferior BPDUs. The switch generates Root Link Query (RLQ) requests. These messages are sent out of the root port(s).

These messages are sent to query the upstream switch(es) if their connection to the root bridge is up. The receiving switch sends RLQ responses to reply to the RLQ requests *only* if the connection to the root bridge is up. When the switch receives an RLQ response on its root port, it knows the connection to the root bridge is good. Therefore, it expires the **max-age** timer in order to speed up the convergence.

The following steps occur when Backbone Fast is enabled (see Figure 3-15):

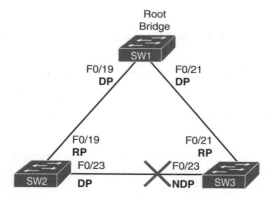

Figure 3-15 *Backbone Fast*

- SW2 loses its connection to SW1. Basically, interface F0/19 goes down.

- SW2 immediately withdraws interface F0/19 as its root port and starts generating configuration BPDUs (C-BPDUs) announcing itself as the root bridge. These messages are sent out of F0/23 interface.

- SW3's F0/23 interface receives these C-BPDUs and realizes they are inferior BPDUs from a switch on a local segment.

- SW3 sends an RLQ request out of its F0/21 interface in order to verify a stable connection to the root bridge.

- SW1 receives the RLQ from SW3. Because it's the root bridge, it replies with an RLQ response.

- SW3 receives the RLQ responses through its root port and immediately expires its **max-age** timer (20 seconds by default).

- SW3 starts sending C-BPDUs out F0/23 and goes through the listening and learning states.

- SW2 receives the C-BPDUs and it knows that it is *not* the root bridge. SW2 changes the state of its F0/23 as the root port.

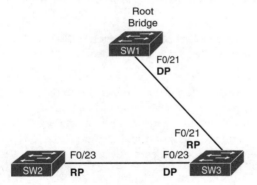

Figure 3-16 *New Topology with Backbone Fast Enabled*

Figure 3-16 illustrates the topology that will be used in the following tasks.

Let's configure Backbone Fast:

```
On All Switches:

SWx(config)# spanning-tree backbonefast
```

Let's test and verify the configuration:

```
On SW3:

SW3# debug spanning events
Spanning Tree event debugging is on
```

```
On SW2:

SW2(config)# interface FastEthernet0/19
SW2(config-if)# shut
```

You should see the following output of the debug on SW3:

```
On SW3:

00:41:21: STP: VLAN0001 heard root 28673-001b.2be5.1200 on Fa0/23
00:41:21: STP: VLAN0001 Fa0/23 -> listening

00:41:22: STP: VLAN0001 Topology Change rcvd on Fa0/23
00:41:22: STP: VLAN0001 sent Topology Change Notice on Fa0/21

00:41:36: STP: VLAN0001 Fa0/23 -> learning

00:41:51: STP: VLAN0001 sent Topology Change Notice on Fa0/21
00:41:51: STP: VLAN0001 Fa0/23 -> forwarding
```

Let's verify the result:

```
On SW1:

SW1# show spanning-tree vlan 1 | begin Interface

Interface        Role Sts Cost      Prio.Nbr Type
---------------- ---- --- --------- -------- -----------------
Fa0/21           Desg FWD 19        128.23   P2p
```

```
On SW3:

SW3# show spanning-tree vlan 1 | begin Interface

Interface          Role Sts Cost      Prio.Nbr Type
------------------ ---- --- --------- -------- ---------------
Fa0/21             Root FWD 19        128.21   P2p
Fa0/23             Desg FWD 19        128.23   P2p

SW3# sh spanning sum | inc Back

BackboneFast              is enabled
BackboneFast statistics
```

```
On SW2:


SW2# show spanning-tree vlan 1 | begin Interface


Interface         Role Sts Cost        Prio.Nbr Type
----------------- ---- --- ---------   -------- -----------------
Fa0/23            Root FWD 19          128.25   P2p
```

Erase the configuration on all routers and switches and reload them before proceeding to the next lab.

Lab 3-10: Spanning Tree Root Guard

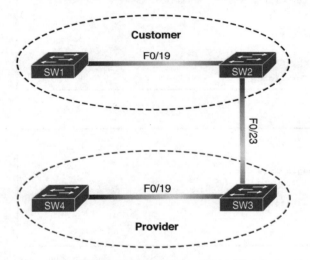

Figure 3-17 *Spanning Tree Root Guard*

Root Guard prevents Layer 2 loops during periods of network anomalies (specifically during reconvergence). The Root Guard feature forces an interface to become a designated port in order to keep any surrounding switches from becoming a root switch. So at the basic level, Root Guard provides us a way to enforce the root bridge placement in the STP topology.

The Root Guard feature prevents a designated port from becoming a root port. In the event that this newly configured port should receive a superior BPDU, the port will transition into a root-inconsistent state, thus protecting the current placement of the root bridge.

In a nutshell, the Root Guard feature prevents a given port from ever becoming a root port by ensuring that the port will always remain in the designated port role. Unlike other STP enhancements we have discussed, Root Guard must always be manually enabled on all ports where the root bridge should not be allowed to appear. This fact makes it important that we have a deterministic topology when we design and implement STP in the LAN.

The current recommended approach is to enable Root Guard on all access ports so that a root bridge cannot be elected out these ports. Once a port in the root-inconsistent state stops receiving superior BPDUs, the port will unblock again and begin to reconverge. This means the port will transition through the normal STP listen and learn states, and eventually move to forwarding. This recovery process is automatic and requires no user intervention.

Task 1

Configure the switches according to Figure 3-17:

```
On All Switches:


SWx(config)# interface range FastEthernet0/1-24
SWx(config-if-range)# shut
```

```
On SW1 and SW4:



SWx(config)# interface FastEthernet0/19
SWx(config-if)# switchport trunk encapsulation dot1q
SWx(config-if)# switchport mode trunk
SWx(config-if)# no shut
```

```
On SW2 and SW3:

SW2(config)# interface range FastEthernet0/19 , FastEthernet0/23
SW2(config-if-range)# switchport trunk encapsulation dot1q
SW2(config-if-range)# switchport mode trunk
SW2(config-if-range)# no shut
```

Task 2

Configure the appropriate switch such that the customer edge switch is never elected as the root bridge of the provider switched network, no matter how it's configured. Do *not* use BPDU Filter to accomplish this task.

This feature is typically seen in the service provider's network. A service provider with a Layer 2 network can have many switch connections to the customer network. Spanning tree can reconfigure itself based on the credentials of the customer's switch, and the customer's switch can become the root bridge for the service provider's switched network.

This situation can be avoided by using the Root Guard feature. Root Guard must be enabled on the interface facing the customer's switch. When this feature is enabled and spanning tree calculations cause the customer's switch to become the root bridge, Root Guard will immediately place the interface facing the customer in the root-inconsistent state (which means the port is in blocking state). This will prevent the customer's switch from becoming the root switch.

To test this configuration, the provider's edge switch (SW3) is set up as the root bridge. In this configuration, the **priority** command is used. The **root primary** macro can also be used to accomplish this.

```
On SW3:

SW3(config)# spanning-tree vlan 1 priority 8192
```

Let's test and verify the configuration:

```
On SW1:

SW1# show spanning-tree vlan 1


VLAN0001
  Spanning tree enabled protocol ieee
  Root ID    Priority    8193
             Address     000a.41f2.1080
             Cost        38
             Port        21 (FastEthernet0/19)
             Hello Time   2 sec  Max Age 20 sec  Forward Delay 15 sec

  Bridge ID  Priority    32769  (priority 32768 sys-id-ext 1)
             Address     0014.a934.b880
             Hello Time   2 sec  Max Age 20 sec  Forward Delay 15 sec
             Aging Time 300


Interface        Role Sts Cost      Prio.Nbr Type
---------------- ---- --- --------- -------- ------
Fa0/19           Root FWD 19        128.21   P2p

SW1# show version | include Base

Base ethernet MAC Address       : 00:14:A9:34:B8:80
```

```
On SW2:

SW2# show spanning-tree vlan 1

VLAN0001
  Spanning tree enabled protocol ieee
  Root ID    Priority    8193
             Address     000a.41f2.1080
             Cost        19
             Port        25 (FastEthernet0/23)
             Hello Time   2 sec  Max Age 20 sec  Forward Delay 15 sec

  Bridge ID  Priority    32769  (priority 32768 sys-id-ext 1)
             Address     001b.2be5.1200
             Hello Time   2 sec  Max Age 20 sec  Forward Delay 15 sec
             Aging Time 300

Interface          Role Sts Cost      Prio.Nbr Type
---------------- ---- --- --------- -------- -----
Fa0/19             Desg FWD 19        128.21   P2p

Fa0/23             Root FWD 19        128.25   P2p

SW2# show version | include Base

Base ethernet MAC Address      : 00:1B:2B:E5:12:00
```

```
On SW3:

SW3# show spanning-tree vlan 1

VLAN0001
  Spanning tree enabled protocol ieee
  Root ID    Priority    8193
             Address     000a.41f2.1080
             This bridge is the root
             Hello Time   2 sec  Max Age 20 sec  Forward Delay 15 sec

  Bridge ID  Priority    8193   (priority 8192 sys-id-ext 1)
             Address     000a.41f2.1080
             Hello Time   2 sec  Max Age 20 sec  Forward Delay 15 sec
             Aging Time 300

Interface          Role Sts Cost      Prio.Nbr Type
---------------- ---- --- --------- -------- -----
Fa0/19             Desg FWD 19        128.19   P2p
Fa0/23             Desg FWD 19        128.23   P2p

SW3# show version | include Base

Base ethernet MAC Address: 00:0A:41:F2:10:80
```

```
On SW4:


SW4# show spanning-tree vlan 1


VLAN0001
  Spanning tree enabled protocol ieee
  Root ID    Priority    8193
             Address     000a.41f2.1080
             Cost        19
             Port        19 (FastEthernet0/19)
             Hello Time   2 sec  Max Age 20 sec  Forward Delay 15 sec


  Bridge ID  Priority    32769   (priority 32768 sys-id-ext 1)



             Address     000a.8a3e.b200
             Hello Time   2 sec  Max Age 20 sec  Forward Delay 15 sec
             Aging Time 300


Interface         Role Sts Cost      Prio.Nbr Type
---------------- ---- --- --------- -------- -----
Fa0/19            Root FWD 19        128.19   P2p


SW4# show version | include Base

Base ethernet MAC Address: 00:0A:8A:3E:B2:00
```

Let's look at the existing situation:

```
On SW2 and SW3:

SWx# debug spanning events
Spanning Tree event debugging is on
```

Let's lower the priority for VLAN 1 on the customer's edge switch, SW2:

```
On SW2:

SW2(config)# spanning-tree vlan 1 priority 4096
```

You should see the following debug output on SW2:

```
setting bridge id (which=1) prio 4097 prio cfg 4096 sysid 1 (on) id
  1001.001b.2be5.1200
STP: VLAN0001 we are the spanning tree root


SW2# show version | include Base

Base ethernet MAC Address        : 00:1B:2B:E5:12:00

On SW3:


STP: VLAN0001 heard root   4097-001b.2be5.1200 on Fa0/23
supersedes  8193-000a.41f2.1080
STP: VLAN0001 new root is 4097, 001b.2be5.1200 on port Fa0/23, cost 19
```

Note   If a switch connecting to your switch has a lower priority, the spanning tree calculations can elect that switch to be the root bridge. We will configure Root Guard and analyze its behavior.

Let's remove the configuration on SW2:

```
On SW2:

SW2(config)# no spanning-tree vlan 1 priority 4096
```

You should wait for spanning tree to converge. Once it converges, SW3 will once again become the root bridge.

Let's verify the configuration:

```
On SW3:

SW3# show spanning-tree vlan 1 | include root

          This bridge is the root
```

Let's configure Root Guard:

```
On SW3:

SW3(config)# interface FastEthernet0/23
SW3(config-if)# spanning-tree guard root
```

You should see the following console message:

```
%SPANTREE-2-ROOTGUARD_CONFIG_CHANGE: Root guard enabled on port FastEthernet0/23.
```

Note   The Root Guard feature is implemented using the **spanning-tree guard root** interface configuration mode command.

Let's test and verify the configuration:

```
On SW2:

SW2(config)# spanning-tree vlan 1 priority 4096
```

You should see the following debug output on SW2.

```
setting bridge id (which=1) prio 4097 prio cfg 4096 sysid 1 (on) id
  1001.001b.2be5.1200
STP: VLAN0001 we are the spanning tree root
```

You should see the following debug output on SW3. This message states that the F0/23 interface of SW3 just heard the switch on the other end of the interface (F0/23) is claiming to be the root bridge.

```
On SW3:

STP: VLAN0001 heard root   4097-001b.2be5.1200 on Fa0/23
```

The following debug output states the switch that claims to be the root has a better BID, and it supersedes our BID:

```
supersedes  8193-000a.41f2.1080
```

The last message states that Root Guard places the F0/23 interface in the blocking state. But you may have missed this message. Stop the debug and scroll up to look for the following message:

```
%SPANTREE-2-ROOTGUARD_BLOCK: Root guard blocking port FastEthernet0/23 on VLAN0001.
```

Every 2 seconds you will see the following debug output:

```
STP: VLAN0001 heard root   4097-001b.2be5.1200 on Fa0/23
     supersedes  8193-000a.41f2.1080
```

Let's disable the debug on SW3:

```
On SW3:


SW3# undebug all
All possible debugging has been turned off
```

Let's test the configuration:

```
On SW2:


SW2# show spanning-tree vlan 1


VLAN0001
  Spanning tree enabled protocol ieee
  Root ID    Priority    4097
             Address       001b.2be5.1200
             This bridge is the root
             Hello Time    2 sec  Max Age 20 sec  Forward Delay 15 sec


  Bridge ID  Priority    4097   (priority 4096 sys-id-ext 1)
             Address       001b.2be5.1200
             Hello Time    2 sec  Max Age 20 sec  Forward Delay 15 sec


             Aging Time 300


Interface         Role Sts Cost      Prio.Nbr Type
---------------- ---- --- --------- -------- -----
Fa0/19                Desg FWD 19        128.21   P2p
Fa0/23                Desg FWD 19        128.25   P2p
```

```
On SW3:


SW3# show spanning-tree vlan 1


VLAN0001
  Spanning tree enabled protocol ieee
  Root ID    Priority    8193
             Address       000a.41f2.1080
             This bridge is the root
             Hello Time    2 sec  Max Age 20 sec  Forward Delay 15 sec


  Bridge ID  Priority    8193   (priority 8192 sys-id-ext 1)
             Address       000a.41f2.1080
```

```
              Hello Time   2 sec  Max Age 20 sec  Forward Delay 15 sec
              Aging Time 300


Interface          Role Sts Cost        Prio.Nbr Type
---------------    ---- --- ---------   -------- ------
Fa0/19             Desg FWD 19          128.19   P2p
Fa0/23             Desg BKN*19          128.23   P2p *ROOT_Inc
```

Erase the configuration on all routers and switches and reload them before proceeding to the next lab.

Lab 3-11: Spanning Tree Loop Guard

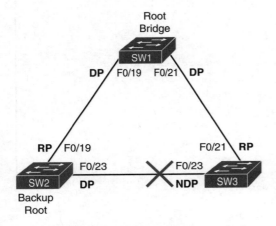

Figure 3-18 *Spanning Tree Loop Guard*

Loop Guard provides additional protection against forwarding loops in our Layer 2 topology. A bridging loop most commonly happens when an STP blocking port in a redundant topology erroneously transitions to the forwarding state. This usually occurs because one of the ports of a physically redundant topology has stopped receiving STP BPDUs. In STP, switches rely on continuous reception or transmission of BPDUs, depending on the port role. Specifically, a designated port will transmit BPDUs, whereas a nondesignated port will expect to receive BPDUs.

If the switch link is up and no BPDUs are received, the switch assumes that it is safe to bring this link up, and then the port transitions to the forwarding state and begins relaying received BPDUs. If a switch is connected to the other end of the link, this effectively creates the loop condition we are discussing.

With the Loop Guard feature enabled, switches do an additional check before transitioning to the STP forwarding state. If switches stop receiving BPDUs on a nondesignated port with the Loop Guard feature enabled, the switch places the port into loop-inconsistent blocking state instead of moving through the listening, learning, and forwarding states. If a switch receives a BPDU on a port in the loop-inconsistent STP state, the port will transition through STP states in accordance with the received BPDU. As a result, recovery is automatic, and no manual intervention is necessary.

When implementing Loop Guard, you should be aware of the following implementation guidelines:

- Loop Guard cannot be enabled simultaneously with Root Guard on the same device.

- Loop Guard does not affect UplinkFast or Backbone Fast operation.

- Loop Guard must be enabled on point-to-point links only.

- Loop Guard operation is not affected by the spanning tree timers.

- Loop Guard cannot actually detect a unidirectional link.

- Loop Guard cannot be enabled on PortFast or dynamic VLAN ports.

You configure the Loop Guard feature on a per-port basis, even though the feature is designed to block inconsistent ports on a per-VLAN basis. In other words, on a given trunk port, if BPDUs are not received for only one particular VLAN, the switch will only block that VLAN (by moving the port for that VLAN to the loop-inconsistent state). However, in a case where we are dealing with an aggregated link between two devices, all of the links in the aggregate will transition into the inconsistent state for the particular VLAN that is no longer receiving BPDUs.

This raises the question, where do we enable the Loop Guard feature? Loop Guard should be enabled on root and alternative ports for all possible combinations of active topologies. This means that before enabling Loop Guard, we need to carefully consider all possible failover scenarios in our topology.

Task 1

Configure the switches according to Figure 3-18. The unused ports should be configured in the administratively down state:

```
On All Switches:

SWx(config)# interface range FastEthernet0/1-24
SWx(config-if-range)# shut
```

```
On SW1:

SW1(config)# spanning-tree vlan 1 root primary

SW1(config)# interface range FastEthernet0/19 , FastEthernet0/21
SW1(config-if-range)# switchport trunk encapsulation dot1q
SW1(config-if-range)# switchport mode trunk
SW1(config-if-range)# no shut
```

```
On SW2:

SW2(config)# spanning-tree vlan 1 root secondary

SW2(config)# interface range FastEthernet0/19 , FastEthernet0/23
SW2(config-if-range)# switchport trunk encapsulation dot1q
SW2(config-if-range)# switchport mode trunk
SW2(config-if-range)# no shut
```

```
On SW3:

SW3(config)# interface range FastEthernet0/21 , FastEthernet0/23
SW3(config-if-range)# switchport trunk encapsulation dot1q
SW3(config-if-range)# switchport mode trunk
SW3(config-if-range)# no shut
```

Task 2

Configure the F0/23 interface of SW3 such that if it does *not* receive BPDUs from SW2's F0/23 interface, Layer 2 loops do *not* occur.

If the Spanning Tree Protocol is running, why would we ever run into loops? Well, let's think about the following scenario:

- SW1 is configured as the root bridge, and SW2 is the backup root bridge.

- SW3 does *not* receive BPDUs from SW2 due to unidirectional link failure.

- The F0/23 interface of SW3 does *not* receive BPDUs from SW2. Therefore, it will transition into the spanning tree listening and learning states. When the **max-age** timer expires, the F0/23 interface of SW3 will transition into the forwarding state.

- This situation creates a spanning tree loop.

The spanning tree Loop Guard feature can prevent spanning tree loops from occurring. The blocked port (F0/23) on SW3 will transition into the loop-inconsistent state after the **max-age** timer expires, thus avoiding a spanning tree loop.

To demonstrate the loop, configure the switches as follows:

Note SW2 is constantly sending BPDUs.

```
On SW2:

SW2# show spanning-tree interface FastEthernet0/23 detail | include BPDU

    BPDU: sent 227, received 0
```

To stop SW2's F0/23 interface from sending BPDUs, configure spanning tree BPDU Filter:

```
SW2(config)# interface FastEthernet0/23
SW2(config-if)# shut
SW2(config-if)# spanning-tree bpdufilter enable
SW2(config-if)# no shut
```

Once the preceding command is entered, SW2 will no longer send any BPDUs out of its F0/23 interface. Let's verify this fact:

```
SW2# show spanning-tree interface FastEthernet0/23 detail | include BPDU

  BPDU: sent 0, received 0

SW2# show spanning-tree interface FastEthernet0/23 detail | include BPDU

  BPDU: sent 0, received 0

SW2# show spanning-tree interface FastEthernet0/23 detail | include BPDU

  BPDU: sent 0, received 0
```

Let's test the configuration:

```
On SW1:

SW1# show spanning-tree vlan 1 | include Fa

Fa0/19              Desg FWD 19        128.21   P2p
Fa0/21              Desg FWD 19        128.23   P2p
```

```
On SW2:

SW2# show spanning-tree vlan 1 | include Fa0

Fa0/19                  Root FWD 19           128.21   P2p
Fa0/23                  Desg FWD 19           128.25   P2p
```

```
On SW3:

SW3# show spanning-tree vlan 1 | include Fa0

Fa0/21                  Root FWD 19           128.21   P2p
Fa0/23                  Desg FWD 19           128.23   P2p
```

Note   We have a spanning tree loop because all ports are in the forwarding state.

Let's remove the BPDU Filter command from the F0/23 interface of SW2:

```
On SW2:

SW2(config)# interface FastEthernet0/23
SW2(config-if)# no spanning bpdufilter enable
```

Let's verify the configuration:

```
On SW3:

SW3# show spanning-tree vlan 1 | include Fa0

Fa0/21                  Root FWD 19           128.21   P2p
Fa0/23                  Altn BLK 19           128.23   P2p
```

Let's configure spanning tree Loop Guard on SW3's F0/23 interface and enable **debug spanning-tree events**:

```
On SW3:

SW3# debug spanning events

SW3(config)# interface FastEthernet0/23
SW3(config-if)# shut
SW3(config-if)# spanning-tree guard loop
SW3(config-if)# no shut
```

Let's verify the configuration:

```
On SW3:


SW3# show spanning-tree vlan 1 | include Fa0



Fa0/21              Root FWD 19        128.21    P2p
Fa0/23              Altn BLK 19        128.23    P2p
```

Let's configure BPDU Filter on the F0/23 interface of SW2:

```
On SW2:

SW2(config)# interface FastEthernet0/23
SW2(config-if)# spanning-tree bpdufilter enable
```

You should see the following console message on SW3 within 30 seconds:

```
On SW3:

%SPANTREE-2-LOOPGUARD_BLOCK: Loop guard blocking port FastEthernet0/23 on VLAN0001
```

Let's verify the configuration:

```
On SW3:


SW3# show spanning-tree vlan 1 | include Fa0

Fa0/21              Root FWD 19        128.21    P2p
Fa0/23              Desg BKN*19        128.23    P2p *LOOP_Inc
```

SW3 places the F0/23 interface in a loop-inconsistent state.

Loop Guard can also be configured in the global configuration mode. Once it's configured, the feature's protection is applied to all interfaces on the local switch. This can be achieved by using the following command:

```
SWx(config)# spanning-tree loopguard default
```

Erase the configuration on all routers and switches and reload them before proceeding to the next lab.

Chapter 4

Point-to-Point Protocol

Point-to-Point Protocol (PPP) is one of the most ubiquitous and arguably well-designed data-link layer protocols still in use. Originally designed for dialed and permanent point-to-point WAN links running over serial interfaces, PPP has been reused in a number of other protocols, such as PPTP, L2TP, and PPPoE. Despite its open nature and wide adoption, though, understanding of PPP operations is often superficial—an administrator usually just activates the PPP encapsulation and optionally configures authentication parameters. This chapter therefore provides a more involved insight into the workings of PPP.

Introduction to PPP

To understand why PPP has become so popular, we need to take a brief look into the history of WAN data-link layer protocols. In the late 1980s, just before PPP was created, there were already a number of data-link layer protocols that could be used over a physical point-to-point link, or at least could provide an emulation of a point-to-point link. The most prominent protocols were HDLC, SLIP, X.25, and Frame Relay. However, all these protocols had certain deficiencies. The first major drawback was the lack of control and management functions, such as negotiation of link operational parameters, a keepalive mechanism, peer authentication, detection of a looped link, negotiation of higher layer protocols to be transported across the link, and provisioning of configuration information to higher layer protocols. While these features might seem to be of marginal usefulness, they are extremely important from a service provider's point of view, and we will have a closer look at them later in the chapter.

The second drawback was much more fundamental: As surprising as it may seem, the frame format of these protocols did not contain a field that would identify the protocol in the payload portion of the frame. In other words, based on the information present in the frame header alone, it was not possible to know what was being carried inside the frame's payload—whether it was, say, an IPv4 packet or an IPv6 packet. This approach made sense in the past when there was usually only a single specific higher protocol carried over a link, so both peers statically configured for this protocol knew what to expect. However, if multiple higher protocols were to be used simultaneously over this link, frame headers did not carry the information necessary to tell these higher protocols apart. There were several methods envisioned to solve this problem, such as inserting IEEE 802.2 LLC, IEEE 802 SNAP, or ISO/IEC NLPID headers identifying the higher protocol into the frame payload along with the higher protocol packet itself, or assuming that the header of the higher protocol already contained a fixed field that uniquely identified it; however, none of these methods became mandatory, so the uncertainty remained. And as if this were not confusing enough, vendors sometimes decided to solve this problem in their own proprietary and incompatible ways by extending the frame formats themselves with an additional "Payload Type"-like field that, initially, was supported only by their own devices. This is the exact case with Cisco's own formats of High-Level Data Link Control (HDLC) and Frame Relay framing.

The design of PPP removes these deficiencies, and adds a set of new useful features not seen with other data-link layer protocols. PPP is an open protocol whose core part is specified in RFCs 1661 and 1662 (the initial RFC was 1134), and additional features are described in various further RFCs. Although we will be talking about PPP running on Cisco routers in particular, at the time of its inception, PPP ran as a software driver on ordinary user computers, workstations, and servers, and only then gradually made its way into ISDN modems, integrated routers, and other network equipment. All discussion about PPP "between routers" should therefore be seen in this broader context as a PPP session between any two directly connected neighbors on a point-to-point link, regardless of what exact devices these neighbors are, as long as they support PPP.

PPP Frame Format

Interestingly enough, PPP does not specify its own entire frame format. Instead, for point-to-point serial links, it reuses the basic HDLC framing and defines additional header and trailer fields that will be added into the basic HDLC frame payload so that, together, they form a valid PPP frame in HDLC framing, as shown in Figure 4-1.

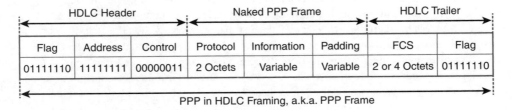

Figure 4-1 *PPP Frame Format*

The Flag, Address, and Control header fields are retained from the basic HDLC frame structure. The Flag field contains a constant value of 01111110 in binary, and serves as a frame delimiter to separate subsequent frames from each other. In a series of frames sent one after another, a single Flag field between individual frames can be used. The

Address field for PPP is set to a constant value of 11111111 (the All-Stations address) in binary, regardless of the sender of the frame, because on a point-to-point link, unique data-link addresses have no meaning. The Control field is also set to a constant value of 00000011, indicating that this is an unnumbered information frame, one of three specific HDLC frame types that carry user information but are not delivered reliably (meaning no sequencing and no acknowledgements).

The Protocol field is a mandatory field present in every PPP frame. Being two octets long, this field identifies the type of higher protocol carried in the Information field. The purpose of the Protocol field is the same as the purpose of the EtherType field in Ethernet frames; however, perhaps somewhat unfortunately, PPP uses different values than Ethernet to enumerate higher protocols. For example, IPv4 uses an EtherType of 0x0800 but a PPP Protocol value of 0x0021; IPv6 uses an EtherType of 0x86DD but a PPP Protocol value of 0x0057. Nonetheless, the Protocol field is a fixed part of every PPP frame and hence it solves one of the major drawbacks of HDLC in terms of identifying the nature of its payload.

The Information field is the actual payload where the higher protocol datagram would be carried—and quite naturally, it is of a variable size. The Padding field allows the sender to artificially fill the frame with dummy bytes so that its size meets a prescribed minimum. Because frame padding is seldom used, the entire Padding field is optional. The "naked PPP frame," therefore, usually consists just of the Protocol header field and the actual higher protocol packet.

The FCS field is the frame checksum computed over the Address, Control, Protocol, Information, and Payload fields (if present). By default, a 16-bit cyclic redundancy check (CRC) is used. It is possible to configure routers to use a 32-bit CRC if necessary.

PPP Control Plane

What truly distinguishes PPP from other similar data-link layer protocols is the fact that along with the framing (the PPP data plane), it comes with its own control plane and a dedicated set of control protocols. These PPP control plane protocols can be divided into two subgroups: the Link Control Protocol (LCP) and the Network Control Protocols (NCPs). LCP is a protocol that takes care of establishing a PPP session between two link partners. NCP is the name for a whole family of protocols that negotiate the transport of specific higher layer protocols over a PPP link and optionally provide configuration parameters to these higher protocols. Both LCP and NCP are carried inside PPP frames as their payload, and each of them uses a unique Protocol value.

Link Control Protocol and Basic PPP Session Establishment

A PPP session between two routers is established in three phases: Link Establishment Phase, Authentication Phase, and Network Layer Protocol Phase. The Link Establishment Phase is the first phase, during which two routers verify whether they speak PPP and negotiate the basic link operation parameters. The key protocol in charge of the Link Establishment Phase is the Link Control Protocol.

LCP is a protocol whose purpose is to set up and maintain a PPP session between routers. In particular, LCP performs the following tasks:

- It verifies that the routers speak PPP.

- It verifies that the link is not looped (if the link is looped, the router will be talking to itself).

- It negotiates the basic parameters of the link operation, such as the maximum packet size a router is willing to receive, partner authentication, link quality monitoring, and Protocol and/or Address/Control header field compression.

- It periodically verifies the liveliness of the session.

- It tears down the session if any of the routers decides to close it.

During the Link Establishment Phase, LCP makes use of four Configure message types: Configure-Request, Configure-Ack, Configure-Nak, and Configure-Reject. Each of these messages contains a one-octet integer called Identification in its header, which is used to properly match a request and a corresponding response (Ack, Nak, or Reject).

The basic start of a PPP session is accomplished by each router sending PPP frames with an LCP Configure-Request (CONFREQ) message, as shown in Figure 4-2. This message may contain a list of options depending on what feature is being requested by a router from its neighbor. Among other options, a CONFREQ message usually contains a so-called *magic number* option, which is simply a random number generated by its sender. If a sender receives a CONFREQ with the same magic number it has sent itself, then either its neighbor has chosen the same magic number, or the link is looped and the sender is seeing its own frame. In such a case, each of the senders will choose another magic number and attempt another exchange of LCP packets. If the received magic numbers are still identical to the sent ones, it is with high probability an indication of a looped link. The number of attempts at arriving at a unique magic number and the reaction to an indication of a looped link is implementation-specific; PPP does not mandate any specific action. The magic number option is not mandatory and may be omitted; however, Cisco routers use it by default.

If a router receives a CONFREQ with a different magic number or no magic number at all, it analyzes the other options in the message. These options may include the maximum receive unit (MRU; the maximum packet size the neighbor is capable of receiving), authentication type, link quality monitoring, selected frame header field compression, and others. If the router recognizes all received options, is in agreement with all of them, and is willing to operate accordingly, it will respond with a Configure-Ack (CONFACK) message. This CONFACK will contain an exact copy of the entire body of the CONFREQ that is being acknowledged. If a router receives a CONFACK from its neighbor to its own CONFREQ, this indicates that the neighbor speaks PPP and fully agrees with all suggested link options. In the simplest case, a PPP session is bidirectionally established after each router both receives a CONFACK for its own CONFREQ and sends a CONFACK for the neighbor's CONFREQ (four messages in total). Note that the precise order of these messages on the link may vary; a router usually sends out CONFREQ

messages without waiting for its neighbor to send anything, and may confirm a received
CONFREQ with a CONFACK right away, without waiting for its own CONFREQ to be
confirmed by the neighbor. Figure 4-2 shows one particular possible ordering.

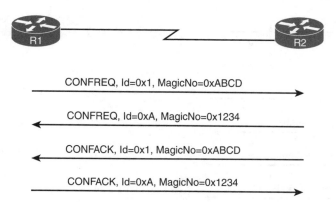

Figure 4-2   *Basic LCP Message Exchange Between PPP Peers*

If a router receives a CONFREQ with a different magic number or no magic number at
all, as well as recognizes all options in the message but considers some of the option
values unacceptable and open for negotiation (for example, the particular authentication
method is not supported by the router but another method is), it will respond by sending
back a Configure-Nak (CONFNAK) message, as shown in Figure 4-3. This CONFNAK
will contain the list of all unacceptable options from the CONFREQ, and their values
will be set to the router's own acceptable values for these options. This way, the router
negotiates alternative values for these options, hoping that its neighbor will still find them
agreeable. If the neighbor receives a CONFNAK and is willing to adapt its own operation
to the option values suggested by the router, it will resend a new CONFREQ with all
options it has included previously, but for the contentious options, it will use the values
as suggested in the received CONFNAK. If the neighbor is unwilling to adapt, then a
deadlock ensues; the neighbor will resend a new CONFREQ with all options unchanged,
prompting the same CONFNAK from the router as before, and the PPP session will not
be established. The "ping-pong" of CONFREQ and CONFNAK messages will be throt-
tled down but will continue until the configuration of either router is changed to match
the neighbor or until the interface is brought down.

Figure 4-3 shows a situation where R1 and R2 are trying to bring up a link, and R2
requires that R1 prove its identity (that is, authenticate itself) to R2 using CHAP.
R1, however, does not support CHAP and suggests using PAP instead, which R2 finds
acceptable. Note that R2 acknowledged R1's CONFREQ right away because R1 did
not have any specific demands; however, R1 objects to R2's request for CHAP and
suggests an alternative, prompting R2 to resend its own CONFREQ with an updated
authentication option.

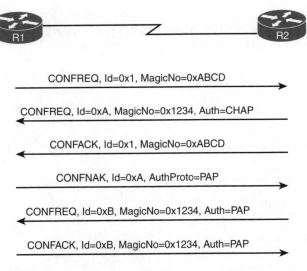

Figure 4-3   *Use of CONFNAK in an LCP Exchange*

If a router receives a CONFREQ with a different magic number, or no magic number at all, and does not recognize some of the options, or their values are unacceptable and nonnegotiable, it will respond by sending back a Configure-Reject (CONFREJ) message, as shown in Figure 4-4. This CONFREJ will contain the list of all unrecognized or unacceptable options, but instead of suggesting acceptable values, the CONFREJ will simply contain the unrecognized/unacceptable options along with their unacceptable values. If the neighbor is willing to operate without the particular features that were rejected, it will send another CONFREQ omitting all rejected options. Otherwise, the routers are in a deadlock, with the one insisting on particular options in its CONFREQ messages and the other rejecting some of these options with CONFREJ messages continuously until the routers are either reconfigured or shut down.

Figure 4-4 shows a situation where R1 suggests using the Protocol Field Compression feature, which would allow shrinking the Protocol field in PPP headers to a single octet. However, R2 refuses to use this feature by sending back a CONFREJ. Therefore, R1 resends its CONFREQ without suggesting the PFC feature anymore, thus allowing the PPP session to come up.

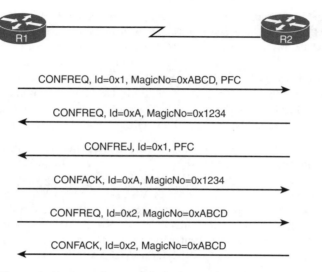

Figure 4-4   *Use of CONFREJ in an LCP Exchange*

The Link Establishment Phase ends when each router has both sent a CONFACK for its neighbor's CONFREQ and received a CONFACK for its own CONFREQ.

Besides the four Configure message types, LCP also uses other message types, the most important being the following:

■ Terminate-Request and Terminate-Ack are used to request and confirm the teardown of a PPP session.

■ Code-Reject is used to reject an entire LCP message whose type is unknown.

■ Protocol-Reject is used to reject a suggestion for a particular higher layer protocol (described in the "Network Control Protocols and Network Layer Protocol Phase" section).

■ Echo-Request and Echo-Reply are used as a keepalive mechanism to verify whether the neighbor is still alive and running the PPP session.

Authentication Phase and Authentication Mechanisms

If, during the Link Establishment Phase, routers agreed on performing authentication, they will enter the Authentication Phase immediately after the Link Establishment Phase ends and then perform the negotiated authentication procedure. In PPP, authentication is fundamentally a one-way procedure in which one router proves its identity to the other router. If mutual authentication is configured, then two entirely independent one-way authentications, one for each router, will take place. This is an important fact that is often overlooked.

Originally, two primary authentication mechanisms were defined for PPP—the Password Authentication Protocol (PAP) and the Challenge-Handshake Authentication Protocol (CHAP). Both PAP and CHAP are discussed in RFC 1334. Later, the set of authentication mechanisms was extended by two CHAP variations authored by Microsoft (MS-CHAP and MS-CHAPv2) and ultimately by the Extensible Authentication Protocol (EAP), which provides a wide variety of authentication methods. PPP MS-CHAP is discussed in RFC 2433, while PPP MS-CHAPv2 is covered in RFC 2759. PPP EAP is discussed in RFC 3748. Still, the PAP- and CHAP-based methods remain prevalent.

PAP is a very simple, two-way authentication method. A router proving its identity sends its preconfigured username and password in plaintext in a PAP Authenticate-Request message to the neighbor, and after the neighbor verifies the information either against its local set of usernames and their passwords, or against an AAA server (either RADIUS or TACACS+), it responds back with an Authenticate-Ack (success) or Authenticate-Nak (failure) message. The disadvantages of this method are obvious—sensitive data is sent in plaintext, and the neighbor who requires the local router to authenticate has no means of requesting a repeated authentication once it has been performed successfully.

In CHAP, the neighbor that requires the local router to authenticate starts by sending a Challenge message. This message contains, among other data, an Identifier value to match requests and responses (just like with LCP), the neighbor's hostname, and a random string of bytes called the challenge string. After the local router receives the challenge, it looks up the appropriate shared password (also called a *secret*) associated with the neighbor based on the hostname indicated in the Challenge message. Then it computes a hash value over the identifier (the secret) and the challenge string. In basic CHAP, MD5 is used as the hashing function; newer CHAP variants may be using different hashes. After the hash value is computed, the local router sends back a Response message that will contain the same identifier as the Challenge message, the computed hash value, and the local router's hostname. The neighbor will compute its own hash value based on the same identifier, the secret associated with the local router's hostname, and the challenge string, and compare this value to the one received in the Response packet. Based on the comparison result, it will respond with either a Success or a Failure message.

CHAP's advantages step in right where PAP fails—sensitive information is carried in a more secure way (even though the simple hashing method used by CHAP has been gradually proven insufficient), and because the CHAP exchange is started by the neighbor that requires the local router to authenticate, repeated authentications are in its direct control and can occur at any time during the PPP session. That being said, Cisco routers do not appear to repeat the CHAP authentication during an existing PPP session once it has been successfully completed.

As mentioned already, the authentication in PPP is essentially a one-way process. With two-way authentication, two independent one-way authentications are performed, meaning that either authentication direction can use a different mechanism (hardly a best practice, but still possible). Also, based on the nature of PAP and CHAP mechanisms, there are certain not-so-obvious facts worth keeping in mind:

- With PAP, the router that performs the validation of user credentials (that is, compares them to the database of usernames and passwords) can store the passwords in an irreversibly hashed format (**username** *login* **secret** *password*) without impacting the PAP functionality. This is because the incoming password in a PAP Authenticate-Request message will be received as plaintext, so the validating router can always apply the hashing function to this plaintext password to yield its hashed form and compare it to the stored value. Conversely, with CHAP, user passwords must be stored in the plaintext form or be encrypted by a reversible mechanism because to compute the MD5 hash, the validating router needs to know the original, plaintext value of the password. If the passwords were stored in an irreversibly hashed format, CHAP would necessarily fail.

- With PAP and mutual authentication, each router can use a different username/ password combination when authenticating to the other router. With CHAP, however, the routers must use the same shared password even though the usernames will be different. This is because in CHAP, the password needed to compute the MD5 hash (both when *sending* a response and *validating* a received response) is either statically tied to the interface (using the **ppp chap password** command) or looked up in the local username/password database based on the hostname of the neighbor. In other words, both when responding to a challenge of a neighbor (the router→neighbor authentication direction) and when validating a neighbor's response (the neighbor→router authentication direction), the router computes the hash using a password based on the neighbor's hostname or the interface configuration; therefore, it is going to be the same for both authentication directions.

Lastly, in PPP, a router sends its credentials to a neighbor only if the neighbor has requested this router to authenticate itself. If the neighbor does not request this router to authenticate, then the router will not send any authentication information, even if it has this information preconfigured.

Network Control Protocols and Network Layer Protocol Phase

After the Link Establishment Phase and the optional Authentication Phase have been successfully completed, the PPP link is considered to be functional and fully operational. This is the moment when Cisco routers will report the interface as "up, line protocol up" (during the Link Establishment and Authentication phases, the interface is "up, line protocol down").

At this point, the PPP session enters the third phase, called the Network Layer Protocol Phase, which allows higher layer protocols and user data to be transmitted across the link. This phase is also called the UP Phase. However, even in this phase, the PPP control plane still keeps a tight grip on the communication by mandating that the routers can speak only those higher layer protocols that have been mutually agreed upon by both routers. Certainly it would be a waste of effort and link bandwidth, as well as a security issue, to send IPv6 packets to a neighbor that does not support IPv6 at all, or to send CDP packets to a neighbor that is not willing to process them in this PPP session. And even if two routers agree on a common protocol (say, IPv4), there are still open questions on how this protocol would be set up. In particular, for IPv4, there are questions that correspond to the elementary configuration variables of an IPv4 stack, such as What is my IP address? What is the neighbor's IP address? What DNS servers should I use?

The task of negotiating a particular higher layer protocol and its settings is handled by the Network Control Protocols (NCPs). Contrary to LCP, which is just a single protocol, NCP is in fact the name for an entire family of negotiation protocols—one NCP for each higher layer protocol carried over a PPP link. The names of individual NCPs are derived from the name/acronym of the particular higher protocol and the addition of the term "Control Protocol (CP)." For example, IPv4 is handled by IPCP, IPv6 is handled by IPv6CP, MPLS is handled by MPLSCP, CDP is handled by CDPCP, and OSI protocols (such as IS-IS) are handled by OSICP. If a particular protocol is not mutually requested and acknowledged between routers by a corresponding NCP, the routers will not attempt to send or receive their packets over the PPP link.

Keep in mind that these NCPs are not additional encapsulations for the corresponding higher level protocols. NCPs only negotiate whether a particular protocol will be running over a PPP link and how the protocol should be set up. After this has been done, however, the higher layer protocol will be encapsulated directly into the Information field of PPP frames. NCPs are used only for control and signaling purposes.

Because NCPs serve different higher layer protocols, which in turn have different features and options, there is no general list of options that each NCP can negotiate—some protocols, such as CDP or MPLS, have no negotiable options whatsoever, whereas, say, IPv4 allows for negotiating IP addresses of peering routers, addresses of DNS servers, and even the addresses of WINS servers. However, in general, NCPs use a set of messages similar to LCP—namely, Configure-Request, Configure-Ack, Configure-Nak, Configure-Reject, Terminate-Request, Terminate-Ack, and Code-Reject—with the same meaning and rules of use.

Figure 4-5 shows two routers negotiating the use of IPv4 and CDP over a PPP link. Both routers agree on using IPv4; however, CDP is suggested by R1 and is refused by R2 via an LCP Protocol-Reject (PROTREJ) message. The fact that a CDPCP CONFREJ message was responded to by an LCP PROTREJ message may be surprising at first. However, it is logical: Assuming that R2 does not support CDP, it also does not support the CDPCP, so it cannot respond using that particular NCP. Therefore, all NCP negotiations for unsupported protocols will be rejected by LCP PROTREJ messages. The Identifier values of these LCP PROTREJ messages do not correspond to the Identifier values of rejected NCP messages (they are numbered independently, so their numbering may overlap); instead, the Identifier value is simply a unique number increased for each PROTREJ message.

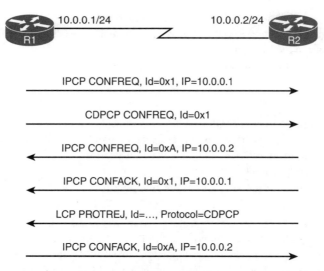

IPCP CONFREQ, Id=0x1, IP=10.0.0.1

CDPCP CONFREQ, Id=0x1

IPCP CONFREQ, Id=0xA, IP=10.0.0.2

IPCP CONFACK, Id=0x1, IP=10.0.0.1

LCP PROTREJ, Id=..., Protocol=CDPCP

IPCP CONFACK, Id=0xA, IP=10.0.0.2

Figure 4-5 *Use of PROTREJ in an NCP/LCP Exchange*

Advanced PPP Features

PPP supports a number of features not commonly seen with other protocols. We will have a brief look at three of them: compression, multilink, and PPPoE.

Compression

PPP supports both header and data payload compression. These features were most usable in the past when the WAN links were slow (tens or hundreds of Kbps) and when the bulk of data traffic contained uncompressed data. Nowadays, the compression mostly has lost its meaning: WAN links are faster by orders of magnitude, the bulk of data traffic is already compressed (think of graphics or video), and performing compression under these circumstances would strain the CPU on routers so much that it would become the new bottleneck. Nonetheless, it is always an advantage to at least have an overview of what is possible.

Header compression in PPP can be divided into several categories based on which header fields are to be compressed:

- Protocol Field Compression (PFC) allows shrinking the two-octet Protocol field to a one-octet value. This functionality is negotiated by LCP.

- Address and Control Field Compression (ACFC) allows omitting the Address and Control fields from the HDLC frame because they carry a constant value all the time. This functionality is negotiated by LCP.

- Compression of IP+TCP and IP+UDP+RTP headers allows for the shrinking of these headers for a particular packet flow by an order of magnitude. This functionality is negotiated by IPCP.

Payload compression applies to the contents of the Information field indiscriminately. Cisco routers may support different compression mechanisms, such as LZS, MPPC, Predictor, and Stac. The use of payload compression is negotiated by a standalone NCP called the Compression Control Protocol (CCP).

Multilink PPP

Multilink PPP (MLPPP) is a unique feature that allows bundling multiple parallel links toward the same neighboring router and utilizing the aggregate bandwidth. This feature was originally designed to make efficient use of multiple B-channels on an ISDN interface, but it can be used to bundle any number of any point-to-point links running PPP between the same neighboring devices, even if the links are not of the same transmission speed.

As opposed to the well-known EtherChannel technology, where frames of a particular data flow are carried only by a single link in the bundle, MLPPP first creates a naked PPP frame by encapsulating each transmitted packet according to the usual PPP rules. It then splits this naked PPP frame into several fragments, adds a new HDLC+PPP+MLPPP header to each of these fragments, and sends them over the multiple links to the neighboring router. The MLPPP header contains a sequence number used to reassemble the fragments into the proper order, and two bits indicating that the particular fragment is either the first or the last fragment of the original naked PPP frame. This way, MLPPP allows even a single data flow to be split among multiple links and thus experience bandwidth improvement.

Multilink PPP is the underlying mechanism for the Link Fragmentation and Interleaving (LFI) QoS tool that allows interspersing short high-priority packets with fragments of longer lower-priority packets to reduce the jitter and queuing delay of high-priority flows.

PPP over Ethernet

PPPoE, which stands for *PPP over Ethernet*, is a technology originally developed to build PPP sessions between possibly multiple clients and an access concentrator, assuming that these clients and the access concentrator are interconnected by a common Ethernet network and are thus located in a single broadcast domain. This application was motivated by the fact that Ethernet has gradually grown into the role of a cost-effective, fast, and reasonably reliable network access technology. With Ethernet as an access technology, clients could connect to a service provider without needing to purchase any special devices or interfaces, using just their Ethernet network interfaces. At the same time, however, providers did not want to change their core networks and internal mechanisms, and if their client connectivity model was built on top of PPP, they wanted to keep PPP in place even if the access technology changed. Quite naturally, this called for some kind of integration of PPP and Ethernet.

PPPoE is the result of this integration. Defined in RFC 2516, PPPoE is basically a control and adaptation mechanism for PPP that allows carrying PPP frames across an Ethernet network between a client and an access concentrator. PPPoE also provides mechanisms for a client to dynamically discover an access concentrator and associate with it. With PPPoE, multiple clients, and even multiple PPP sessions from the same client, can be served by a single access concentrator within the same Ethernet network. Essentially, PPPoE defines the encapsulation procedure to carry PPP frames within Ethernet frames as well as the control procedures required for a client to discover, associate with, and disassociate with an access concentrator.

With regard to encapsulation, PPPoE defines a six-octet-long PPPoE header that is inserted together with each naked PPP frame into the Ethernet frame payload. Among other information, the most important field in the PPPoE header is the Session ID field. This is a unique number assigned to a particular client and that client's PPP session by the access concentrator during the association procedure. This Session ID field allows the access concentrator to distinguish between different clients and their PPP sessions. Client MAC addresses alone are not used to differentiate between clients and individual PPP sessions because a single client can have multiple PPPoE clients and thus multiple PPP sessions running over the same interface. Because the naked PPP frame contains the Protocol field, which is two octets long, the total overhead of PPPoE is $6+2=8$ bytes. This is the reason why on PPPoE virtual interfaces, the MTU is being decreased by a value of 8, to 1492, to provide sufficient space for the additional PPPoE+PPP headers.

PPPoE operates in two distinct stages—the Discovery Stage and the PPP Session Stage. The purpose of the Discovery Stage is to allow the client to discover an access concentrator and associate with it. The Discovery Stage strongly resembles a DHCP operation:

1. The client broadcasts a PPPoE Active Discovery Initiation (PADI) frame, soliciting access concentrators in the same broadcast domain.

2. Each access concentrator that receives the PADI responds by unicasting a PPPoE Active Discovery Offer (PADO) frame to the client.

3. After choosing one particular access concentrator, the client unicasts a PPPoE Active Discovery Request (PADR) frame to the chosen concentrator to associate with it.

4. If the access concentrator is willing to handle this client, it responds with a unicast PPPoE Active Discovery Session-confirmation (PADS) frame, assigning a unique Session ID to this particular client's session.

After receiving the PADS frame, the client moves to the PPP Session Stage. This stage allows the clients to send and receive PPP frames using Ethernet+PPPoE encapsulation. In all outgoing Ethernet+PPPoE frames, the client must use the Session ID assigned by the access concentrator in the PADS message, and, conversely, all incoming Ethernet+PPPoE frames will have the same Session ID filled in by the access concentrator. During the PPP Session Stage, all PPP operations are entirely the same as if PPP were running over a serial link in HDLC framing.

The PPP Session Stage can be terminated by either the client or the access concentrator by sending a PPPoE Active Discovery Termination (PADT) message. Usually, though, this will be a result of PPP itself tearing down the PPP session beforehand using the LCP Terminate-Request and Terminate-Ack messages.

To better distinguish PPPoE control (discovery) frames from data (session) frames, all discovery frames have an EtherType of 0x8863, whereas all session frames have an EtherType of 0x8864.

Although PPPoE was not designed specifically with DSL in mind, DSL has reused PPPoE and is arguably the most extensively deployed access technology that internally relies on PPPoE.

Lab 4-1: PPP

Note   Before proceeding with this lab, you need to copy and paste the running configuration information found in the Lab4-1_PPP.txt file. Once these configurations have been installed, you may proceed with Task 1.

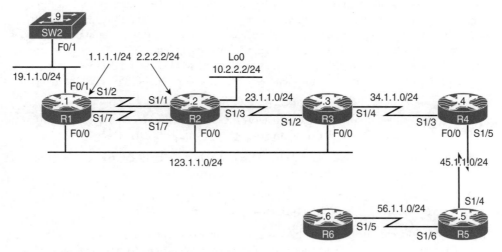

Figure 4-6   *PPP and PPPoE Lab Topology*

Task 1

Configure the S1/2 interface of R1 and the S1/1 interface of R2 so that they can ping each other. Do not configure an IGP, change their IP addresses, or use PBR, NAT, or any global configuration mode command to accomplish this task.

Figure 4-6 shows that the serial interfaces S1/2 on R1 and S1/1 on R2 facing each other are not configured in the same IP network. Without additional configuration, R1 won't be able to reach R2, and vice versa, because neither of these two routers will consider the other to be on a directly connected network. Two manually configured static routes, one on each router, can fix this problem—but the task assignment explicitly prohibits using a global configuration mode command.

However, we are not prohibited from changing the encapsulation on the serial interfaces. If the encapsulation is changed to PPP, each router will automatically add a /32 route toward the other router's IP address. This automatically added route to the neighbor's IP address is also called a *neighbor route*, and adding it is a part of the IPCP operation. As a result, these routers will be able to ping each other as soon as the link comes up.

Let's first change the serial link encapsulation on R1 and R2 to PPP:

```
! On R1:

R1(config)# interface serial1/2
R1(config-if)# encapsulation PPP

! On R2:

R2(config)# interface serial1/1
R2(config-if)# encapsulation PPP
```

To see the IPCP and add the neighbor route in action, let's bring the S1/2 interface on R1 down, activate **debug ppp negotiation,** and then bring the S1/2 interface back up:

```
R1(config)# interface s1/2
R1(config-if)# shutdown

%LINK-5-CHANGED: Interface Serial1/2, changed state to administratively down
%LINEPROTO-5-UPDOWN: Line protocol on Interface Serial1/2, changed state to down

R1(config-if)# do debug ppp negotiation
PPP protocol negotiation debugging is on

R1(config-if)# no shutdown

%LINK-3-UPDOWN: Interface Serial1/2, changed state to up
Se1/2 PPP: Sending cstate UP notification
Se1/2 PPP: Processing CstateUp message
PPP: Alloc Context [49A53484]
ppp4 PPP: Phase is ESTABLISHING
Se1/2 PPP: Using default call direction
Se1/2 PPP: Treating connection as a dedicated line
Se1/2 PPP: Session handle[4B000004] Session id[4]
Se1/2 LCP: Event[OPEN] State[Initial to Starting]
Se1/2 LCP: O CONFREQ [Starting] id 1 len 10
Se1/2 LCP:    MagicNumber 0x0718A653 (0x05060718A653)
Se1/2 LCP: Event[UP] State[Starting to REQsent]
Se1/2 LCP: I CONFREQ [REQsent] id 1 len 10
Se1/2 LCP:    MagicNumber 0x1C631023 (0x05061C631023)
Se1/2 LCP: O CONFACK [REQsent] id 1 len 10
Se1/2 LCP:    MagicNumber 0x1C631023 (0x05061C631023)
Se1/2 LCP: Event[Receive ConfReq+] State[REQsent to ACKsent]
Se1/2 LCP: I CONFACK [ACKsent] id 1 len 10
Se1/2 LCP:    MagicNumber 0x0718A653 (0x05060718A653)
Se1/2 LCP: Event[Receive ConfAck] State[ACKsent to Open]
Se1/2 PPP: Queue IPCP code[1] id[1]
Se1/2 PPP: Phase is FORWARDING, Attempting Forward
```

```
Se1/2 LCP: State is Open
Se1/2 PPP: Phase is ESTABLISHING, Finish LCP
Se1/2 PPP: Phase is UP
Se1/2 IPCP: Protocol configured, start CP. state[Initial]
Se1/2 IPCP: Event[OPEN] State[Initial to Starting]
Se1/2 IPCP: O CONFREQ [Starting] id 1 len 10
Se1/2 IPCP:    Address 1.1.1.1 (0x030601010101)
Se1/2 IPCP: Event[UP] State[Starting to REQsent]
Se1/2 PPP: Process pending ncp packets
Se1/2 IPCP: Redirect packet to Se1/2
Se1/2 IPCP: I CONFREQ [REQsent] id 1 len 10
Se1/2 IPCP:    Address 2.2.2.2 (0x030602020202)
Se1/2 IPCP: O CONFACK [REQsent] id 1 len 10
Se1/2 IPCP:    Address 2.2.2.2 (0x030602020202)
Se1/2 IPCP: Event[Receive ConfReq+] State[REQsent to ACKsent]
%LINEPROTO-5-UPDOWN: Line protocol on Interface Serial1/2, changed state to up
Se1/2 IPCP: I CONFACK [ACKsent] id 1 len 10
Se1/2 IPCP:    Address 1.1.1.1 (0x030601010101)
Se1/2 IPCP: Event[Receive ConfAck] State[ACKsent to Open]
Se1/2 IPCP: State is Open
Se1/2 Added to neighbor route AVL tree: topoid 0, address 2.2.2.2
Se1/2 IPCP: Install route to 2.2.2.2
```

In the preceding transcript, the codes I and O, shown with various LCP and NCP protocol messages, stand for Incoming and Outgoing, respectively.

The neighbor routes can now be seen in the routing tables on both routers, and we can check whether R1 and R2 can reach each other, like so:

```
! On R1:

R1# show ip route | begin Gate
Gateway of last resort is not set

     1.0.0.0/8 is variably subnetted, 2 subnets, 2 masks
C       1.1.1.0/24 is directly connected, Serial1/2
L       1.1.1.1/32 is directly connected, Serial1/2
     2.0.0.0/32 is subnetted, 1 subnets
C       2.2.2.2 is directly connected, Serial1/2
     19.0.0.0/8 is variably subnetted, 2 subnets, 2 masks
C       19.1.1.0/24 is directly connected, FastEthernet0/1
L       19.1.1.1/32 is directly connected, FastEthernet0/1

! On R2:

R2# show ip route | begin Gate

Gateway of last resort is not set
```

```
      1.0.0.0/32 is subnetted, 1 subnets
C        1.1.1.1 is directly connected, Serial1/1
      2.0.0.0/8 is variably subnetted, 2 subnets, 2 masks
C        2.2.2.0/24 is directly connected, Serial1/1
L        2.2.2.2/32 is directly connected, Serial1/1
      10.0.0.0/8 is variably subnetted, 2 subnets, 2 masks
C        10.2.2.0/24 is directly connected, Loopback0
L        10.2.2.2/32 is directly connected, Loopback0

! On R1:

R1# ping 2.2.2.2
Type escape sequence to abort.
Sending 5, 100-byte ICMP Echos to 2.2.2.2, timeout is 2 seconds:
!!!!!
Success rate is 100 percent (5/5), round-trip min/avg/max = 28/29/32 ms
R1# undebug all
All possible debugging has been turned off
```

The adding of a neighbor route to a particular neighbor can also be disabled on a router by configuring the **no peer neighbor-route** command on its serial interface toward this neighbor, although this is seldom necessary.

```
! On R1:

R1# show ppp all
Interface/ID OPEN+ Nego* Fail-      Stage     Peer Address     Peer Name
------------ --------------------- -------- --------------- --------------------
Se1/1        LCP+ IPCP+ CDPCP+      LocalT    2.2.2.2
```

As you can see, the Network Control Protocols LCP, IPCP, and CDPCP have been successfully negotiated and are functioning properly because they are in the OPEN state.

Task 2

Configure R1 so that it can ping R2's loopback0 interface. Do not configure a static route, any routing protocol, NAT, or PBR to accomplish this task.

Let's see if R1 can ping the loopback0 interface of R2 already:

```
R1# ping 10.2.2.2
Type escape sequence to abort.
Sending 5, 100-byte ICMP Echos to 10.2.2.2, timeout is 2 seconds:
.....
Success rate is 0 percent (0/5)
```

Obviously, it cannot, because it does not know the route to this address. This problem can be solved by instructing IPCP to inject a default route on R1 pointing toward R2. Let's configure this feature first:

```
R1(config)# interface serial1/2
R1(config-if)# ppp ipcp route default
R1(config-if)# shutdown

%LINK-5-CHANGED: Interface Serial1/2, changed state to administratively down
%LINEPROTO-5-UPDOWN: Line protocol on Interface Serial1/2, changed state to down

R1(config-if)# no shutdown
```

Now let's verify it:

```
R1# show ip route | begin Gate
Gateway of last resort is 2.2.2.2 to network 0.0.0.0

S*    0.0.0.0/0 [1/0] via 2.2.2.2
      1.0.0.0/8 is variably subnetted, 2 subnets, 2 masks
C        1.1.1.0/24 is directly connected, Serial1/2
L        1.1.1.1/32 is directly connected, Serial1/2
      2.0.0.0/32 is subnetted, 1 subnets
C        2.2.2.2 is directly connected, Serial1/2
      19.0.0.0/8 is variably subnetted, 2 subnets, 2 masks
C        19.1.1.0/24 is directly connected, FastEthernet0/1
L        19.1.1.1/32 is directly connected, FastEthernet0/1

R1# ping 10.2.2.2
Type escape sequence to abort.
Sending 5, 100-byte ICMP Echos to 10.2.2.2, timeout is 2 seconds:
!!!!!
Success rate is 100 percent (5/5), round-trip min/avg/max = 28/29/32 ms
```

Note   If the **no peer neighbor-route** command is configured on the interface toward a neighbor, the default route through this neighbor will not be injected, either.

Task 3

Configure R2 so that it can assign an IP address of 23.1.1.3 to R3's s1/2 interface. Do not configure DHCP to accomplish this task.

One of the benefits of PPP encapsulation is the ability to assign an IP address to a directly connected neighboring host using IPCP.

The following commands must be configured on these two routers:

1. PPP encapsulation must be configured on the serial interfaces of these two routers that face each other.

2. On R2, the **peer default ip address 23.1.1.3** interface command instructs the router to assign the IP address of 23.1.1.3 to R3.

3. On R3, the **ip address negotiated** interface command must be configured.

Let's configure these commands, then:

```
! On R2:

R2(config)# interface serial1/3
R2(config-if)# encapsulation ppp
R2(config-if)# shutdown

%LINK-5-CHANGED: Interface Serial1/3, changed state to administratively down
%LINEPROTO-5-UPDOWN: Line protocol on Interface Serial1/3, changed state to down

R2(config-if)# peer default ip address 23.1.1.3
R2(config-if)# no shutdown

! On R3:

R3(config)# interface serial1/2
R3(config-if)# encapsulation ppp
R3(config-if)# ip address negotiated
R3(config-if)# no shutdown
```

Now let's verify and test the configuration:

```
R3# show ip interface brief serial1/2
Interface       IP-Address      OK? Method Status          Protocol
Serial1/2       23.1.1.3        YES IPCP   up              up

R3# ping 23.1.1.2
Type escape sequence to abort.
Sending 5, 100-byte ICMP Echos to 23.1.1.2, timeout is 2 seconds:
!!!!!
Success rate is 100 percent (5/5), round-trip min/avg/max = 28/29/32 ms
```

Task 4

Configure one-way PAP authentication between the serial interfaces of R3 and R4. R3 should be configured to authenticate R4 (that is, R4 must prove its identity, or authenticate itself, to R3) using PAP. R4 should use "R4" as its username and "Cisco" as its password.

Among the authentication mechanisms supported by PPP are PAP and CHAP. These authentication methods are defined in RFCs 1334 and 1994, respectively. PAP, in particular, provides a simple though unsecure method for authentication. In PAP, the password is sent across the link in cleartext, and there is no protection from playback or trial-and-error attacks. Nor is there a possibility of periodic reauthentication between PPP peers.

To better illustrate how PAP works, consider the following two figures of PAP messages dissected by the Wireshark traffic analyzer. Figure 4-7 shows a PAP AUTH-REQ message from R4 to R3, plainly carrying the sensitive data.

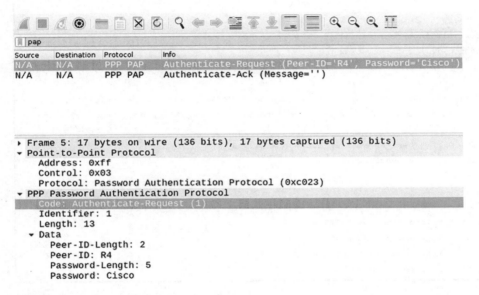

Figure 4-7 *PAP AUTH-REQ Message*

In Figure 4-7, notice that the PAP message is actually a PPP frame's payload with a Protocol identifier of 0xc023. The PAP message contains the following information: Code identifies the actual PAP message, Identifier is a value used to pair together requests and responses, Length describes the length of the entire PAP message, and the Data portion contains the actual credentials.

Figure 4-8 shows a PAP AUTH-ACK message confirming a successful authentication. This message has an empty Data portion because it does not carry any additional information. If this message was a PPP AUTH-NAK message, the Message field in the Data portion would contain an optional error message clarifying why the authentication failed.

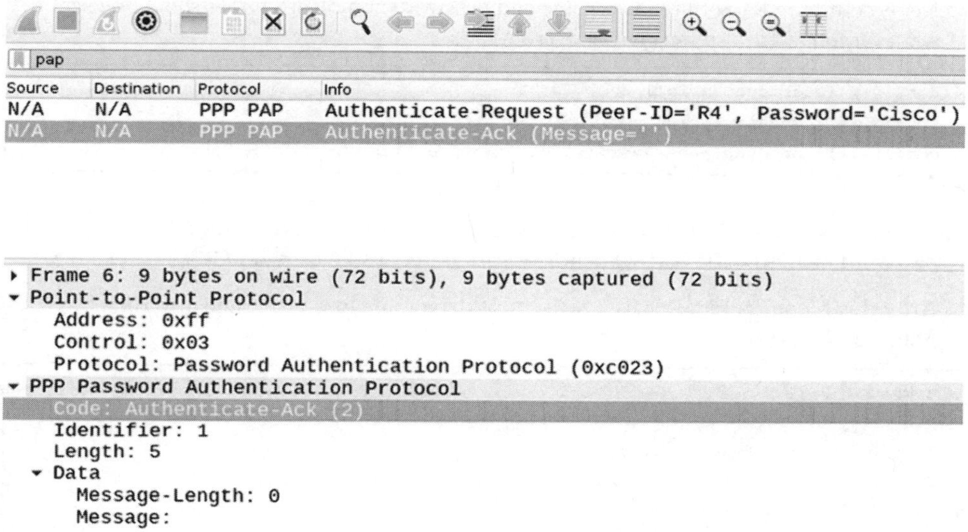

Source	Destination	Protocol	Info
N/A	N/A	PPP PAP	Authenticate-Request (Peer-ID='R4', Password='Cisco')
N/A	N/A	PPP PAP	Authenticate-Ack (Message='')

```
▸ Frame 6: 9 bytes on wire (72 bits), 9 bytes captured (72 bits)
▾ Point-to-Point Protocol
      Address: 0xff
      Control: 0x03
      Protocol: Password Authentication Protocol (0xc023)
▾ PPP Password Authentication Protocol
      Code: Authenticate-Ack (2)
      Identifier: 1
      Length: 5
   ▾ Data
      Message-Length: 0
      Message:
```

Figure 4-8 *PAP AUTH-ACK Message*

According to the task, R3 is the router that will *verify* the identity of R4 using PAP, while R4 needs to *provide* information over PAP that proves that it is what it claims to be. R3 must therefore be configured to ask R4 to provide authentication information, while R4 must be configured with a proper username and password combination to be sent to R3 when it asks for it.

Let's start with the configuration of R3 and enable **debug ppp authentication** along the way, as we configure the task.

```
R3(config)# do debug ppp authentication
PPP authentication debugging is on


R3(config)# interface serial1/4
R3(config-if)# encapsulation ppp
R3(config-if)# ppp authentication pap
```

The **ppp authentication pap** command configures R3 to be the *authenticator*, which requests that the connected peer authenticate itself using PAP. This command instructs R3 to inform R4 during the initial LCP exchange phase that it wants R4 to prove its identity using PAP. Note that the particular authentication method is always negotiated in the LCP phase before the authentication exchange itself.

Next, configure R4 with the username and password combination that should be sent to whoever requests this information over PAP:

```
R4(config)# interface serial1/3
R4(config-if)# encapsulation ppp
R4(config-if)# ppp pap sent-username R4 password Cisco
```

The **ppp pap sent-username** command configures R4 to send the indicated username and password in a PAP AUTH-REQ (Authentication Request) message to R3.

After this is configured, R3 displays a set of debugging messages similar to the following output:

```
! On R3:

Se1/4 PPP: Using default call direction
Se1/4 PPP: Treating connection as a dedicated line
Se1/4 PPP: Session handle[2C000073] Session id[115]
Se1/4 PAP: I AUTH-REQ id 1 len 13 from "R4"
Se1/4 PAP: Authenticating peer R4
Se1/4 PPP: Sent PAP LOGIN Request
Se1/4 PPP: Received LOGIN Response FAIL
Se1/4 PAP: O AUTH-NAK id 1 len 26 msg is "Authentication failed"
```

The output of the preceding debug reveals that R3 received R4's username and password but it sent an AUTH-NAK (Negative Acknowledgment) back to R4, telling it that the authentication failed. This is because R3 checked the received credentials against its user account database and did not find a matching entry.

Here's how to see the number of failed attempts:

```
R3# show ppp statistics | include Counter|PAP
Type PPP MIB Counters                      PEAK        CURRENT
51   PAP authentication attempts           10          10
52   PAP authentication successes          0           0
53   PAP authentication failures           10          10
54   User failed PAP authentication        10          10
```

Let's add the username and password for R4 to R3's user account database:

```
! On R3:

R3(config)# username R4 password Cisco
```

```
Se1/4 PPP: Using default call direction
Se1/4 PPP: Treating connection as a dedicated line
Se1/4 PPP: Session handle[D400000F] Session id[270]
Se1/4 PAP: I AUTH-REQ id 1 len 13 from "R4"
Se1/4 PAP: Authenticating peer R4
Se1/4 PPP: Sent PAP LOGIN Request
Se1/4 PPP: Received LOGIN Response PASS
Se1/4 PAP: O AUTH-ACK id 1 len 5
```

This time, R3 responds with an AUTH-ACK message, indicating to R4 that the authentication is successful.

Now let's test the configuration:

```
R3# ping 34.1.1.4
Type escape sequence to abort.
Sending 5, 100-byte ICMP Echos to 34.1.1.4, timeout is 2 seconds:
!!!!!
Success rate is 100 percent (5/5), round-trip min/avg/max = 28/29/32 ms

R3# undebug all
All possible debugging has been turned off
```

Task 5

Configure two-way PAP authentication between the serial interfaces of R4 and R5 using the following parameters:

- **R4:** Username R4, password R4
- **R5:** Username R5, password R5

Because R4 uses a username of R4 and a password of R4, this username and password must be configured on R5, and the username and the password that is used by R5 should be configured on R4, as shown here:

```
! On R4:
R4(config)# username R5 password R5

! On R5:
R5(config)# username R4 password R4
```

PPP encapsulation must be configured on the serial interfaces of these two routers that face each other:

```
! On R4:

R4(config)# interface serial1/5
R4(config-if)# encapsulation ppp


! On R5:

R5(config)# interface serial1/4
R5(config-if)# encapsulation ppp
```

Configure the username and the password on the serial interfaces of these two routers:

```
! On R4:

R4(config)# interface serial1/5
R4(config-if)# ppp pap sent-username R4 password R4

! On R5:

R5(config)# interface serial1/4
R5(config-if)# ppp pap sent-username R5 password R5
```

The final step is to configure both routers as authenticators to mutually request authentication from each other:

```
! On R4:

R4(config)# interface serial1/5
R4(config-if)# ppp authentication pap


! On R5:

R5(config)# interface serial1/4
R5(config-if)# ppp authentication pap
```

To see and verify the two-way authentication, let's bring down the s1/5 interface of R4, enable **debug ppp authentication**, and then activate the s1/5 interface on R4 again:

```
R4(config)# interface serial1/5
R4(config-if)# shutdown
R4(config-if)# do debug ppp authentication
PPP authentication debugging is on


R4(config-if)# no shutdown


Se1/5 PPP: Using default call direction
Se1/5 PPP: Treating connection as a dedicated line
Se1/5 PPP: Session handle[90000014] Session id[276]
Se1/5 PAP: Using hostname from interface PAP
Se1/5 PAP: Using password from interface PAP
Se1/5 PAP: O AUTH-REQ id 1 len 10 from "R4"
Se1/5 PAP: I AUTH-REQ id 1 len 10 from "R5"
Se1/5 PAP: Authenticating peer R5
Se1/5 PPP: Sent PAP LOGIN Request
Se1/5 PPP: Received LOGIN Response PASS
Se1/5 PAP: O AUTH-ACK id 1 len 5
Se1/5 PAP: I AUTH-ACK id 1 len 5
```

The output shows R4 both sending and receiving an AUTH-REQ message, and subsequently both sending and receiving an AUTH-ACK message, suggesting that both R4 and R5 have mutually authenticated themselves successfully.

Another way to verify whether PAP was successful is with the **show ppp all** command, shown here:

```
R4# show ppp all
Interface/ID OPEN+ Nego* Fail-      Stage    Peer Address    Peer Name
------------ -------------------- -------- --------------- --------------------
Se1/5        LCP+ PAP+ IPCP+ CDPC> LocalT   45.1.1.5        R5
Se1/3        LCP+ IPCP+ CDPCP+     LocalT   34.1.1.3
```

In the output, **CDPC>** simply means that the field has been truncated. Use the **show ppp interface** command to view the full output:

```
R4# show ppp interface serial1/5
PPP Serial Context Info
-------------------
Interface        : Se1/5
PPP Serial Handle: 0x9700002B
PPP Handle       : 0xDD00002B
SSS Handle       : 0xA300002B
```

```
Access IE        : 0xB000029
SHDB Handle      : 0x0
State            : Up
Last State       : Binding
Last Event       : LocalTerm


PPP Session Info
----------------
Interface        : Se1/5
PPP ID           : 0xDD00002B
Phase            : UP
Stage            : Local Termination
Peer Name        : R5
Peer Address     : 45.1.1.5
Control Protocols: LCP[Open] PAP+ IPCP[Open] CDPCP[Open]
Session ID       : 41
AAA Unique ID    : 55
SSS Manager ID   : 0xA300002B
SIP ID           : 0x9700002B
PPP_IN_USE       : 0x11


Se1/5 LCP: [Open]
Our Negotiated Options
Se1/5 LCP:     AuthProto PAP (0x0304C023)
Se1/5 LCP:     MagicNumber 0xBCC153A3 (0x0506BCC153A3)
Peer's Negotiated Options
Se1/5 LCP:     AuthProto PAP (0x0304C023)
Se1/5 LCP:     MagicNumber 0xBCC152D1 (0x0506BCC152D1)


Se1/5 IPCP: [Open]
Our Negotiated Options
Se1/5 IPCP:    Address 45.1.1.4 (0x03062D010104)
Peer's Negotiated Options
Se1/5 IPCP:    Address 45.1.1.5 (0x03062D010105)


Se1/5 CDPCP: [Open]
Our Negotiated Options
  NONE
Peer's Negotiated Options
  NONE
```

PAP authentication is shown as an LCP "negotiated option."

Task 6

Configure one-way CHAP authentication between the serial interfaces of R5 and R6. R5 should be configured to send a challenge to R6. Use the following parameters to accomplish this task:

- **R5**: Username R5, password aaa

- **R6**: Username R6, password aaa

The Challenge Handshake Authentication Protocol, or CHAP, is defined in RFC 1994. CHAP can be used to verify the identity of the peer by exchanging three packets: a Challenge packet, a Response packet, and a Success or Failure indication.

CHAP can be used in one-way or two-way authentication. In this task, we will configure CHAP in a one-way authentication manner. As for the authentication direction, R5 is the authenticator because the task states that R5 should send a challenge to R6, and a challenge is always sent out from the router that asks its peer to prove its identity. This means that R5 will be configured with the **ppp authentication chap** interface command and a username/password combination that matches the credentials configured on R6, whereas R6 will be configured with the credentials necessary to authenticate to R5.

To better understand the processes behind CHAP, we will have a look at the contents of CHAP messages as dissected by Wireshark.

R5 as an authenticator begins the CHAP authentication process by sending a CHAP Challenge packet to R6. Figure 4-9 shows the contents of the CHAP Challenge packet.

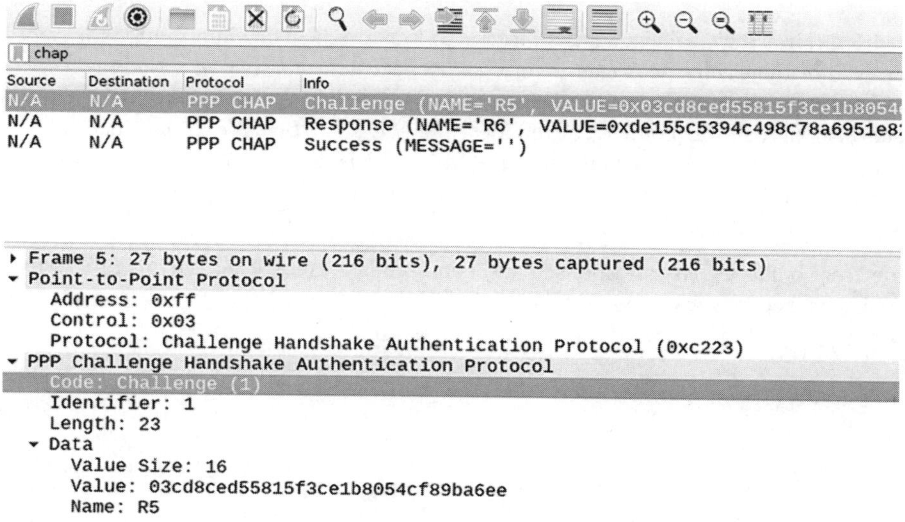

Figure 4-9 *CHAP Challenge Packet Contents*

The Protocol field in the PPP frame header identifies CHAP with its protocol number 0xc223. A CHAP Challenge packet contains the Code field identifying the particular CHAP message type, an Identifier value that is used to pair this message with the Response packet from the peer, a Length field covering the length of the entire CHAP message, and the Data portion. The Data portion itself consists of the challenge size (Value Size), the challenge itself (Value), and the hostname of the sender that originates the challenge (Name).

The Code field can carry one of the four possible values shown in Table 4-1.

Table 4-1   *CHAP Message Types*

Code	Description
1	Challenge
2	Response
3	Success
4	Failure

The Value field is the actual challenge originated by R5 and is sent to R6 for processing. Whenever R5 originates a new challenge, this field carries a new pseudorandom (ideally, a random) value that cannot be predicted.

The Name field, by default, carries the hostname of the router sending the challenge, but it can be changed using the **ppp chap hostname** interface configuration mode command.

After R6 receives the Challenge packet, it tries to look up the name indicated in the Name field of the Challenge packet in its local user account database. If it finds a matching entry, it feeds the password associated with that username into an MD5 hash generator, along with the contents of the Identifier and Value fields from the Challenge packet (the precise order of data fed into the MD5 sum is the Identifier field, then the password, then the Value field). The result of this MD5 hash is the response that needs to be sent back to R5.

R6 therefore builds a CHAP Response packet and sends it to R5. The contents of a CHAP Response packet are shown in Figure 4-10.

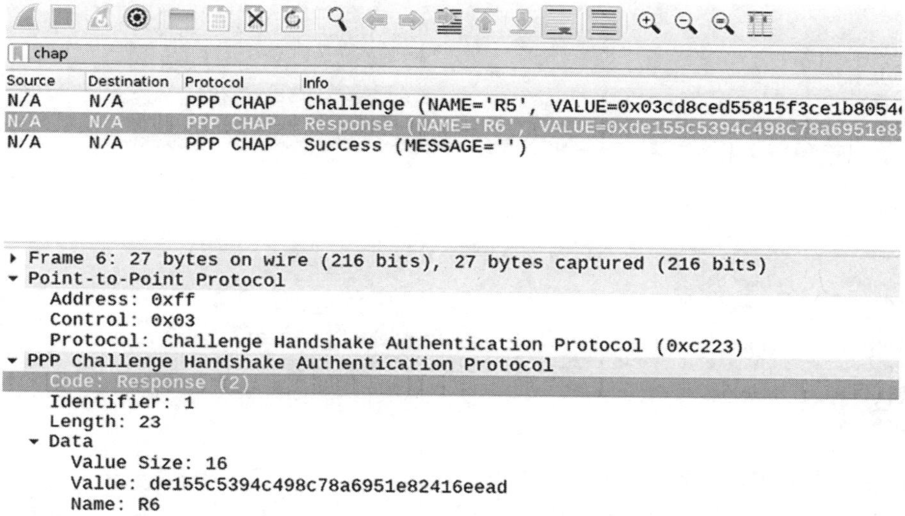

```
▶ Frame 6: 27 bytes on wire (216 bits), 27 bytes captured (216 bits)
▼ Point-to-Point Protocol
      Address: 0xff
      Control: 0x03
      Protocol: Challenge Handshake Authentication Protocol (0xc223)
▼ PPP Challenge Handshake Authentication Protocol
      Code: Response (2)
      Identifier: 1
      Length: 23
    ▼ Data
        Value Size: 16
        Value: de155c5394c498c78a6951e82416eead
        Name: R6
```

Figure 4-10 *CHAP Response Packet Contents*

Note that the format of a CHAP Response packet is very similar to the CHAP Challenge packet. The Code value is set to 2, indicating a Response packet. Identifier is set to 1, identical to the preceding Challenge, allowing R5 to match its former Challenge with this Response. The Length field again indicates the length of the entire CHAP message, and the Data portion contains the length of the response itself (Value Size), the MD5 value comprising the response (Value), and again the hostname of the sending host (Name).

R5 receives this Response message from R6. Using the Name field contents from the Response message, it looks up the matching username in its user account database. R5 then uses the password associated with the matching username together with the Identifier field and the original challenge value to compute its own MD5 hash result and then compares it to the Value field in the received Response packet. If they match, it is clear that R6 knows the same password as R5, that R6 is responding to the same challenge R5 sent it in the first step, and that the Challenge and Response packets' fields processed by the MD5 hash have not been tampered with while in transit. R5 can now claim that R6 is authentic and send a CHAP Success message, as shown in Figure 4-11. If, however, the computed MD5 hash does not match the Value field in the received Response packet, R5 will send back a Failure packet.

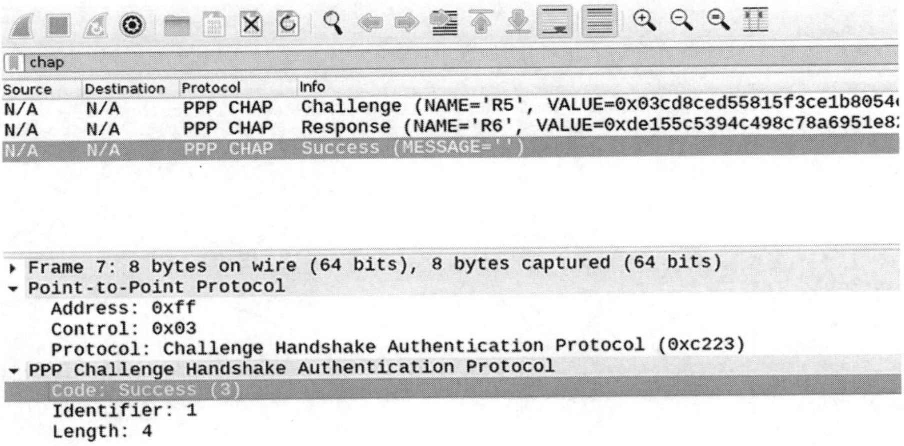
chap
Source Destination Protocol Info
N/A N/A PPP CHAP Challenge (NAME='R5', VALUE=0x03cd8ced55815f3ce1b8054
N/A N/A PPP CHAP Response (NAME='R6', VALUE=0xde155c5394c498c78a6951e8
N/A N/A PPP CHAP Success (MESSAGE='')
Frame 7: 8 bytes on wire (64 bits), 8 bytes captured (64 bits)
Point-to-Point Protocol
Address: 0xff
Control: 0x03
Protocol: Challenge Handshake Authentication Protocol (0xc223)
PPP Challenge Handshake Authentication Protocol
Code: Success (3)
Identifier: 1
Length: 4

Figure 4-11 *CHAP Success Packet Contents*

When you're configuring CHAP authentication, it is useful to follow the path of actual CHAP messages and configure routers in that sequence to minimize configuration errors.

Let's now configure one-way CHAP authentication on R5 and R6. We start by configuring R5 to start the authentication process and send a Challenge packet to R6:

```
R5(config)# interface serial1/6
R5(config-if)# encapsulation ppp
R5(config-if)# ppp authentication chap
```

On R6, PPP needs to be configured:

```
R6(config)# interface serial1/5
R6(config-if)# encapsulation ppp
```

Because R5 includes its own hostname in the Name field of the Challenge packet, and R6 will perform a lookup in its user account database for the associated password to be used with R5, R6 has to be configured with a username and a password for R5:

```
R6(config)# username R5 password aaa
```

With the preceding command configured, R6 can find the password for R5 and use it in computing its Response message contents, but R6 will also include its hostname in the Response packet, so R5 has to find the proper password to validate R6's response. Therefore, R5 must be configured with a username and password for R6, like so:

```
R5(config)# username R6 password aaa
```

To verify the configuration, bring the interface s1/6 on R5 down, enable **debug ppp authentication**, and reactivate the interface:

```
R5(config)# interface serial1/6
R5(config-if)# shutdown
R5(config-if)# do debug ppp authentication
PPP authentication debugging is on

R5(config-if)# no shutdown

Se1/6 PPP: Using default call direction
Se1/6 PPP: Treating connection as a dedicated line
Se1/6 PPP: Session handle[58000028] Session id[38]
Se1/6 CHAP: O CHALLENGE id 1 len 23 from "R5"
Se1/6 PPP: Sent CHAP SENDAUTH Request
Se1/6 PPP: Received SENDAUTH Response PASS
Se1/6 CHAP: Using hostname from configured hostname
Se1/6 CHAP: Using password from AAA
Se1/6 CHAP: I RESPONSE id 1 len 23 from "R6"
Se1/6 PPP: Sent CHAP LOGIN Request
Se1/6 PPP: Received LOGIN Response PASS
Se1/6 CHAP: O SUCCESS id 1 len 4
```

Finally, let's test and verify the configuration:

```
R5# ping 56.1.1.6
Type escape sequence to abort.
Sending 5, 100-byte ICMP Echos to 56.1.1.6, timeout is 2 seconds:
!!!!!
Success rate is 100 percent (5/5), round-trip min/avg/max = 28/29/32 ms
msR5# show ppp all
Interface/ID OPEN+ Nego* Fail-     Stage     Peer Address   Peer Name
------------ -------------------- --------  -------------- --------------------
Se1/6        LCP+ CHAP+ IPCP+ CDP> LocalT   56.1.1.6       R6
Se1/4        LCP+ PAP+ IPCP+ CDPC> LocalT   45.1.1.4       R4
```

Task 7

Reconfigure R5 and R6 to perform two-way CHAP authentication using the credentials from the previous task.

To configure this task, we have to configure R6 to also send a Challenge packet. This takes one additional command to accomplish. R5 will automatically respond with a proper Response packet because it has the necessary credentials for R6 already configured.

```
R6(config)# interface serial1/5
R6(config-if)# ppp authentication chap
```

To verify the configuration, bring the interface s1/5 on R6 down, enable **debug ppp authentication**, and reactivate the interface:

```
R6(config)# interface serial1/5
R6(config-if)# shutdown
R6(config-if)# do debug ppp authentication
PPP authentication debugging is on

R6(config-if)# no shutdown

Se1/5 PPP: Using default call direction
Se1/5 PPP: Treating connection as a dedicated line
Se1/5 PPP: Session handle[15000022] Session id[32]
Se1/5 CHAP: O CHALLENGE id 1 len 23 from "R6"
Se1/5 CHAP: I CHALLENGE id 1 len 23 from "R5"
Se1/5 PPP: Sent CHAP SENDAUTH Request
Se1/5 PPP: Received SENDAUTH Response PASS
Se1/5 CHAP: Using hostname from configured hostname
Se1/5 CHAP: Using password from AAA
Se1/5 CHAP: O RESPONSE id 1 len 23 from "R6"
Se1/5 CHAP: I RESPONSE id 1 len 23 from "R5"
Se1/5 PPP: Sent CHAP LOGIN Request
Se1/5 PPP: Received LOGIN Response PASS
Se1/5 CHAP: O SUCCESS id 1 len 4
Se1/5 CHAP: I SUCCESS id 1 len 4
```

Finally, let's test the connectivity:

```
R6# ping 56.1.1.5
Type escape sequence to abort.
Sending 5, 100-byte ICMP Echos to 56.1.1.5, timeout is 2 seconds:
!!!!!
Success rate is 100 percent (5/5), round-trip min/avg/max = 28/29/32 ms
```

Task 8

In Task 4, R3 is configured to authenticate R4 (that is, verify R4's identity) using PAP. Configure R4 to authenticate R3 (that is, verify R3's identity) using CHAP. If this task is configured properly, R3 will authenticate R4 using PAP, and R4 will authenticate R3 using CHAP. Use the following parameters to accomplish the task:

- **R3 username:** R3
- **R4 username:** router4
- **Shared secret:** aaa

Before we start configuring the routers, we need to analyze the existing configuration on R3 and R4 to properly integrate it with the required changes for this task.

In Task 4, R4 sends a username/password combination of "R4/Cisco" to R3 via PAP to prove its identity. R3 therefore already has a **username R4 password Cisco** command present in its configuration. This task requires that R3 prove its own identity to R4 using a different password. An important observation is that R4 is required to use a different username when sending its Challenge packet to R3—"router4" instead of "R4". Therefore, the existing R4's account on R3 used by PAP is not affected; just a new username/password combination needs to be added to R3 so that when challenged by "router4", it responds using the password "aaa".

According to the task assignment, R4 is the CHAP authenticator and therefore must start the CHAP authentication exchange by sending a CHAP Challenge packet to R3. This is accomplished by configuring **ppp authentication chap** on R4's interface toward R3. However, the assignment also requires that R4 use a username different from its preconfigured hostname. Therefore, R4's interface toward R3 must also be configured with the required username using the **ppp chap hostname** command.

Let's start first with R4, which is supposed to send a CHAP Challenge packet to R3 with a nondefault hostname:

```
R4(config)# interface serial1/3
R4(config-if)# ppp authentication chap
R4(config-if)# ppp chap hostname router4
```

On R3, as the node being authenticated, all that is necessary is to configure a username account for "router4" and a password of "aaa" so that this password is used to construct a Response packet back to "router4" (which is really R4):

```
R3(config)# username router4 password aaa
```

Finally, on R4 as an authenticator, we need to add R3's account:

```
R4(config)# username R3 password aaa
```

To verify the configuration, let's bring down the s1/3 interface of R4, enable **debug ppp authentication**, and then activate the s1/3 interface on R4 again:

```
R4(config)# interface serial1/3
R4(config-if)# shutdown
R4(config-if)# do debug ppp authentication
PPP authentication debugging is on

R4(config-if)# no shutdown
```

```
Se1/3 PPP: Using default call direction
Se1/3 PPP: Treating connection as a dedicated line
Se1/3 PPP: Session handle[E900009E] Session id[668]
Se1/3 PAP: Using hostname from interface PAP
Se1/3 PAP: Using password from interface PAP
Se1/3 PAP: O AUTH-REQ id 1 len 13 from "R4"
Se1/3 CHAP: O CHALLENGE id 1 len 28 from "router4"
Se1/3 CHAP: I RESPONSE id 1 len 23 from "R3"
Se1/3 PPP: Sent CHAP LOGIN Request
Se1/3 PAP: I AUTH-ACK id 1 len 5
Se1/3 PPP: Received LOGIN Response PASS
Se1/3 CHAP: O SUCCESS id 1 len 4
```

Now let's test the configuration:

```
R4# ping 34.1.1.3
Type escape sequence to abort.
Sending 5, 100-byte ICMP Echos to 34.1.1.3, timeout is 2 seconds:
!!!!!
Success rate is 100 percent (5/5), round-trip min/avg/max = 28/33/48 ms
```

Here's how to verify the configuration:

```
R4# show ppp interface serial1/3
PPP Serial Context Info
-------------------
Interface        : Se1/3
PPP Serial Handle: 0xB3000001
PPP Handle       : 0xB9000101
SSS Handle       : 0x16000101
AAA ID           : 269
Access IE        : 0xC50000FD
SHDB Handle      : 0x0
State            : Up
Last State       : Binding
Last Event       : LocalTerm
PPP Session Info
----------------
Interface        : Se1/3
PPP ID           : 0xB9000101
Phase            : UP
Stage            : Local Termination
Peer Name        : R3
Peer Address     : 34.1.1.3
```

```
Control Protocols: LCP[Open] CHAP+ IPCP[Open] CDPCP[Open]
Session ID       : 253
AAA Unique ID    : 269
SSS Manager ID   : 0x16000101
SIP ID           : 0xB3000001
PPP_IN_USE       : 0x11


Se1/3 LCP: [Open]
Our Negotiated Options
Se1/3 LCP:     AuthProto CHAP (0x0305C22305)
Se1/3 LCP:     MagicNumber 0xBD251DF0 (0x0506BD251DF0)
Peer's Negotiated Options
Se1/3 LCP:     AuthProto PAP (0x0304C023)
Se1/3 LCP:     MagicNumber 0xBD251B84 (0x0506BD251B84)


Se1/3 IPCP: [Open]
Our Negotiated Options
Se1/3 IPCP:    Address 34.1.1.4 (0x030622010104)
Peer's Negotiated Options
Se1/3 IPCP:    Address 34.1.1.3 (0x030622010103)


Se1/3 CDPCP: [Open]
Our Negotiated Options
  NONE
Peer's Negotiated Options
  NONE
```

As you can see, our LCP negotiated option is CHAP. Our peer's LCP negotiated option is PAP.

Task 9

Configure PPPoE based on the following parameters:

- R1 should be configured as a PPPoE access concentrator. R2 and R3 should be configured as PPPoE clients.

- R1 should be configured with an IP address of 123.1.1.1/24, and R2 and R3 should be configured to acquire an IP address from R1. R1 should be configured with a range that includes 123.1.1.2 and 123.1.1.3 IP addresses. Do not configure a DHCP to accomplish this task.

- You should use the f0/0 interfaces of these routers to accomplish this task.

- Assign a MAC address of 0000.1111.1111, 0000.2222.2222, and 0000.3333.3333 to R1, R2 and R3, respectively.

With PPPoE, one device is configured as a PPPoE access concentrator that terminates PPPoE sessions from clients. For brevity purposes, we will call this device a "server," although this is not the official terminology. Devices connecting to and establishing a PPPoE session with a PPPoE server are called "PPPoE clients." In this task, R1 should be configured as the server, and R2 and R3 as the clients.

A Cisco IOS-based router can run multiple PPPoE server instances. Each PPPoE server instance is represented in the router configuration by a construct called the bba-group (Broad Band Aggregation). A bba-group holds the configuration details of a particular PPPoE server instance, such as the access concentrator name presented to clients, the maximum number of attached clients, and, most importantly, a reference to a specific Virtual-Template interface. A Virtual-Template interface is a placeholder for the configuration of per-client Virtual-Access interfaces that are created on the fly, one for each connected PPPoE client. Whenever a new PPPoE client connects to a PPPoE server, the server dynamically creates a new Virtual-Access interface for this client that inherits the complete configuration from the Virtual-Template interface. In other words, Virtual-Access interfaces are instances of the Virtual-Template interface, instantiated at the moment of accepting a PPPoE client, and destroyed when the client disconnects. Virtual-Template interfaces are commonly configured with all the configuration that applies to all clients, such as PPP authentication, MTU, TCP MSS manipulation, NAT, ACLs, and so on. The entire bba-group is applied to a physical Ethernet interface or subinterface to make the router listen for PPPoE clients on that particular interface or VLAN.

Let's configure the PPPoE server on R1. In the following configuration snippet, we first configure a loopback interface with an IP address that will subsequently be shared with the Virtual-Template interface, and consequently with all Virtual-Access interfaces cloned off the Virtual-Template. Although the Virtual-Template interface can be configured with an IP address directly, it is customary to use IP Unnumbered with Virtual-Template interfaces. This also saves us from a series of harmless-yet-annoying console messages about overlapping IP networks that would otherwise appear when Virtual-Access interfaces are instantiated. Next, we create a Virtual-Template interface, assign it an IP address, and have all clients handled by Virtual-Access instances of this interface be offered IP addresses from the local address pool named "tst-pool". We do not configure a DHCP pool because this was prohibited in the task assignment. In addition, because PPPoE encapsulation causes 8 bytes from each frame to be consumed by PPPoE and PPP headers while the maximum payload of an Ethernet frame remains fixed at 1500 bytes, we need to decrease the available MTU for the interface by 8 bytes. All IP packets larger than 1492 bytes will therefore need to be fragmented by the router; otherwise, after PPPoE and PPP headers are added, their size would exceed 1500 bytes and they would not fit into Ethernet frames. Specifically for TCP, we configure the router to silently modify the Maximum Segment Size (MSS) value in all TCP SYN and SYN+ACK segments to take into account the 40-byte TCP header so that it does not exceed the value of 1452. Thanks to this, TCP sessions carried by PPPoE will never encounter segments larger than 1452 bytes in payload; therefore, their total size including TCP and IP headers will not exceed 1492 bytes, thus avoiding the need to be fragmented. Finally, we configure the "tst-pool" pool with the desired addresses for PPPoE clients. Note that we do not configure **encapsulation ppp** on the Virtual-Template interface because that is the default encapsulation.

```
R1(config)# interface loopback123
R1(config-if)# ip address 123.1.1.1 255.255.255.0
R1(config-if)# exit
R1(config)# interface virtual-template123
R1(config-if)# ip unnumbered loopback123
R1(config-if)# peer default ip address pool tst-pool
R1(config-if)# mtu 1492
R1(config-if)# ip tcp adjust-mss 1452
R1(config-if)# exit
R1(config)# ip local pool tst-pool 123.1.1.2 123.1.1.3
```

Next, we create a PPPoE server instance and refer it to the Virtual-Template interface created earlier:

```
R1(config)# bba-group pppoe tst
R1(config-bba-group)# virtual-template 123
```

Finally, we attach this PPPoE server instance to the f0/0 interface, along with changing its MAC address:

```
R1(config)# interface fastethernet0/0
R1(config-if)# mac-address 0000.1111.1111
R1(config-if)# pppoe enable group tst
R1(config-if)# no shutdown
```

PPPoE clients are configured using yet another type of virtual interface: a Dialer interface. This interface type is commonly used for dialed connections over analog and ISDN BRI or PRI interfaces. A Dialer interface, sometimes also called a *dialer profile*, holds the configuration necessary to dial a particular destination, but it is not strictly tied to any specific physical interface. Instead, it refers to a pool of interfaces called the *dialer pool*, and whenever the Dialer interface needs to place a call, it picks up the first free interface from the associated dialer pool and then places the call. Now, obviously, PPPoE is not a dialed connection, but most operations of a PPP client carrying its frames over a PPPoE session are the same as with former dialed interfaces. Therefore, Cisco decided to keep the concept of the Dialer interface even for PPPoE client configuration, and instead have the PPPoE client instance act as a dialed interface in a dialer pool. This way, the Dialer interface operates almost the same way as with dialed interfaces, but instead of picking a physical dialed interface from a dialer pool, it picks a PPPoE client instance from a dialer pool to carry the PPP frames.

On R2, we create a Dialer interface. Because the default encapsulation on Dialer interfaces is HDLC, we need to change the encapsulation to PPP. Next, we configure the Dialer interface to acquire its IP address using IPCP, modify the MTU and TCP MSS values as required for PPPoE, and, importantly, reference a dialer pool from which this Dialer interface can pick interfaces to place calls through. Afterward, we move to F0/0. First, we change its MAC address, and then we start a PPPoE client instance on F0/0 that offers its communication services in dialer pool 100, exactly the one used by Dialer123 to choose dialed interfaces to place calls through.

```
R2(config)# interface dialer123
R2(config-if)# encapsulation ppp
R2(config-if)# ip address negotiated
R2(config-if)# mtu 1492
R2(config-if)# ip tcp adjust-mss 1452
R2(config-if)# dialer pool 100
R2(config-if)# interface fastethernet0/0
R2(config-if)# mac-address 0000.2222.2222
R2(config-if)# pppoe-client dial-pool-number 100
R2(config-if)# no shutdown
```

Within the next minute, the following console messages should appear on R2's console:

```
%DIALER-6-BIND: Interface Vi1 bound to profile Di123
%LINK-3-UPDOWN: Interface Virtual-Access1, changed state to up
%LINEPROTO-5-UPDOWN: Line protocol on Interface Virtual-Access1, changed state to up
```

Let's verify the configuration:

```
! On R1:

R1# show pppoe session

    1 session  in LOCALLY_TERMINATED (PTA) State
    1 session  total

Uniq ID  PPPoE  RemMAC          Port            VT  VA        State
         SID    LocMAC                              VA-st     Type

    10     1    0000.2222.2222  Fa0/0            123 Vi2.1     PTA
                0000.1111.1111                       UP
R1# show interface virtual-access 2.1

Virtual-Access2.1 is up, line protocol is up
```

```
Hardware is Virtual Access interface
Interface is unnumbered. Using address of Loopback123 (123.1.1.1)
MTU 1492 bytes, BW 100000 Kbit/sec, DLY 100000 usec,
    reliability 255/255, txload 1/255, rxload 1/255
Encapsulation PPP, LCP Open
Open: IPCP
PPPoE vaccess, cloned from Virtual-Template123
Vaccess status 0x0
Keepalive set (10 sec)
    49 packets input, 662 bytes
    48 packets output, 668 bytes
Last clearing of "show interface" counters never


! On R2:


R2# show ip interface brief dialer 123
Interface            IP-Address       OK? Method Status        Protocol
Dialer123            123.1.1.2        YES IPCP   up            up
```

Now we can test the connectivity from R2 to R1:

```
R2# ping 123.1.1.1
Type escape sequence to abort.
Sending 5, 100-byte ICMP Echos to 12.1.1.1, timeout is 2 seconds:
!!!!!
Success rate is 100 percent (5/5), round-trip min/avg/max = 1/1/4 ms
```

Configuration on R3 will be identical to that on R2, save for the MAC address on f0/0:

```
R3(config)# interface dialer123
R3(config-if)# encapsulation ppp
R3(config-if)# ip address negotiated
R3(config-if)# mtu 1492
R3(config-if)# ip tcp adjust-mss 1452
R3(config-if)# dialer pool 100
R3(config-if)# interface fastethernet0/0
R3(config-if)# mac-address 0000.3333.3333
R3(config-if)# pppoe-client dial-pool-number 100
R3(config-if)# no shutdown
```

Let's verify the configuration again:

```
! On R1:


R1# show pppoe session

    2 sessions in LOCALLY_TERMINATED (PTA) State
    2 sessions total


Uniq ID  PPPoE  RemMAC          Port              VT  VA       State
         SID    LocMAC                                VA-st    Type
    10     1    0000.2222.2222  Fa0/0            123  Vi2.1    PTA
                0000.1111.1111                        UP
    11     2    0000.3333.3333  Fa0/0            123  Vi2.2    PTA
                0000.1111.1111                        UP


R1# show interface virtual-access 2.2

Virtual-Access2.2 is up, line protocol is up
  Hardware is Virtual Access interface
  Interface is unnumbered. Using address of Loopback123 (123.1.1.1)
  MTU 1492 bytes, BW 100000 Kbit/sec, DLY 100000 usec,
     reliability 255/255, txload 1/255, rxload 1/255
  Encapsulation PPP, LCP Open
  Open: IPCP
  PPPoE vaccess, cloned from Virtual-Template123
  Vaccess status 0x0
  Keepalive set (10 sec)
     46 packets input, 618 bytes
     45 packets output, 624 bytes
  Last clearing of "show interface" counters never

R1# show ip local pool

  Pool                 Begin           End          Free  In use  Blocked
  tst-pool             123.1.1.2       123.1.1.3       0     2       0

! We can see that the pool starts with 123.1.1.2 and ends with 123.1.1.3,
! and both IP addresses are in use.


! On R3:

R3# show ip interface brief dialer 123
Interface            IP-Address      OK? Method Status            Protocol
Dialer123            123.1.1.3       YES IPCP   up                up
```

Finally, let's test the configuration:

```
R3# ping 123.1.1.1
Type escape sequence to abort.
Sending 5, 100-byte ICMP Echos to 123.1.1.1, timeout is 2 seconds:
!!!!!
Success rate is 100 percent (5/5), round-trip min/avg/max = 1/2/4 ms
```

Task 10

Configure SW2 as a DHCP server with a pool of IP addresses ranging from 123.1.1.2 to 123.1.1.253. The IP address of the DHCP server should be 19.1.1.9. SW2 connects via its F0/1 interface to R1 and its G0/1 interface. Then, reconfigure the previous task so that R2 and R3 obtain their address via DHCP.

To configure R2 and R3 to use the DHCP server on SW2, R1 must be configured as a DHCP relay agent to forward the requests to SW2. Before this can be accomplished, the **peer default ip address pool** command must be removed from R1 and replaced with an **ip helper-address** command. Although not necessary for this task, let's remove the **ip local pool** command to clean up the configuration. Regarding SW2 configuration, it must have an IP interface in the network 19.1.1.0/24 between R1 and itself; in addition, it must have a route back to the network 123.1.1.0/24 because that is the source network from which the relayed DHCP requests will be sourced.

```
! On SW2:

SW2(config)# ip routing
SW2(config)# interface fastethernet0/1
SW2(config-if)# no switchport
SW2(config-if)# ip address 19.1.1.9 255.255.255.0
SW2(config-if)# exit
SW2(config)# ip route 123.1.1.0 255.255.255.0 19.1.1.1
SW2(config)# ip dhcp excluded-address 123.1.1.1
SW2(config)# ip dhcp excluded-address 123.1.1.254
SW2(config)# ip dhcp pool tst
SW2(dhcp-config)# network 123.1.1.0 /24


! On R1:

R1(config)# interface virtual-template123
R1(config-if)# no peer default ip address pool tst-pool
R1(config-if)# ip helper-address 19.1.1.9
R1(config-if)# exit
R1(config)# no ip local pool tst-pool
```

```
! R2 and R3 should be configured to use the DHCP server (the following
! example only shows R3):

R3(config)# interface dialer123
R3(config-if)# shutdown
R3(config-if)# ip address dhcp
R3(config-if)# no shutdown

%DIALER-6-BIND: Interface Vi1 bound to profile Di123
%LINK-3-UPDOWN: Interface Virtual-Access1, changed state to up
%LINEPROTO-5-UPDOWN: Line protocol on Interface Virtual-Access1, changed state to up
%DHCP-6-ADDRESS_ASSIGN: Interface Dialer123 assigned DHCP address 123.1.1.3, mask
    255.255.255.0, hostname R3
```

According to the logging messages, R3 has obtained an IP address via DHCP, so let's check it and test the connectivity with R1:

```
R3# show ip interface brief dialer 123

Interface            IP-Address      OK? Method Status          Protocol
Dialer123            123.1.1.3       YES DHCP   up              up

R3# ping 123.1.1.1
Type escape sequence to abort.
Sending 5, 100-byte ICMP Echos to 123.1.1.1, timeout is 2 seconds:
!!!!!
Success rate is 100 percent (5/5), round-trip min/avg/max = 1/2/4 ms
```

A similar test should be performed on R2, which is left as an exercise for the reader.

We can also check the DHCP bindings on the DHCP server and the DHCP relay:

```
SW2# show ip dhcp binding
Bindings from all pools not associated with VRF:
IP address     Client-ID/            Lease expiration       Type        State
Interface
               Hardware address/
               User name
123.1.1.2      0063.6973.636f.2d61.   Mar 27 2016 10:18 PM  Automatic   Active
Ethernet0/0
               6162.622e.6363.3030.
               2e30.3230.302d.4469.
               3132.33
```

```
123.1.1.3          0063.6973.636f.2d61.     Mar 27 2016 10:18 PM    Automatic  Active
Ethernet0/0

                   6162.622e.6363.3030.

                   2e30.3330.302d.4469.

                   3132.33


R1# show ip dhcp binding
Bindings from all pools not associated with VRF:
IP address         Client-ID/               Lease expiration        Type
                   Hardware address/
                   User name
123.1.1.2          aabb.cc00.0200           Mar 27 2016 10:18 PM     Relay
123.1.1.3          aabb.cc00.0300           Mar 27 2016 10:18 PM     Relay
```

Task 11

Reconfigure the serial interfaces of R1 and R2 based on the following policy:

- Configure R1 and R2 to exchange Microsoft Point-to-Point Encryption (MPPE) protocol.

- The R1 S1/2 interface should use an IP address of 1.1.1.1/24, and the R2 S1/1 interface should use the IP address of 2.2.2.2/24.

- Configure one-way MS-CHAP authentication between the serial interfaces of R1 and R2. R1 should be configured to authenticate R2 (that is, R1 must prove its identity, or authenticate itself, to R2).

```
! On R1:

R1(config)# default interface serial1/2
Interface Serial1/2 set to default configuration


On R2:

R2(config)# default interface serial1.1

! On R1:

R1(config)# interface serial1/2
R1(config-if)# ip address 1.1.1.1 255.255.255.0
R1(config-if)# clock rate 64000
R1(config-if)# encapsulation ppp
R1(config-if)# ppp encrypt mppe 40 required
R1(config-if)# ppp chap password cisco
R1(config-if)# no shutdown
```

```
! On R2:

R2(config)# interface serial1/1
R2(config-if)# ip address 12.1.1.2 255.255.255.0
R2(config-if)# encapsulation ppp
R2(config-if)# ppp encrypt mppe 40 required
R2(config-if)# ppp authentication ms-chap
R2(config-if)# no shutdown
```

Let's test and verify the configuration:

```
R1(config)# interface serial1/2
R1(config-if)# shutdown
R1(config-if)# do debug ppp mppe events
R1(config-if)# no shutdown


Se1/0 MPPE: Generate keys using local database
Se1/0 MPPE: Initialize keys
Se1/0 MPPE: [40 bit encryption]  [stateless mode]


R1# undebug all


R1# ping 2.2.2.2
Type escape sequence to abort.
Sending 5, 100-byte ICMP Echos to 2.2.2.2, timeout is 2 seconds:
!!!!!
Success rate is 100 percent (5/5), round-trip min/avg/max = 16/19/20 ms



R1# show ppp all
Interface/ID OPEN+ Nego* Fail-      Stage    Peer Address    Peer Name
------------ -------------------- -------- -------------- --------------------
Se1/2        LCP+ IPCP+ CCP+ CDPC> LocalT   2.2.2.2         R2


R1# show ppp interface serial1/2
PPP Serial Context Info
-------------------
Interface       : Se1/2
PPP Serial Handle: 0xB4000006
PPP Handle      : 0xFD00000C
SSS Handle      : 0xD0000013
AAA ID          : 24
Access IE       : 0x3000000B
SHDB Handle     : 0x0
```

```
State              : Up
Last State         : Binding
Last Event         : LocalTerm
PPP Session Info
----------------
Interface          : Se1/2
PPP ID             : 0xFD00000C
Phase              : U
Stage              : Local Termination
Peer Name          : R2
Peer Address       : 2.2.2.2
Control Protocols: LCP[Open] IPCP[Open] CCP[Open] CDPCP[Open]
Session ID         : 11
AAA Unique ID      : 24
SSS Manager ID     : 0xD0000013
SIP ID             : 0xB4000006
PPP_IN_USE         : 0x11


Se1/2 LCP: [Open]
Our Negotiated Options
Se1/2 LCP:    MagicNumber 0xC1AAB3BA (0x0506C1AAB3BA)
Peer's Negotiated Options
Se1/2 LCP:    AuthProto MS-CHAP (0x0305C22380)
Se1/2 LCP:    MagicNumber 0xC1AAB59C (0x0506C1AAB59C)


Se1/2 IPCP: [Open]
Our Negotiated Options
Se1/2 IPCP:    Address 1.1.1.1 (0x030601010101)
Peer's Negotiated Options
Se1/2 IPCP:    Address 2.2.2.2 (0x030602020202)


Se1/2 CCP: [Open]
Our Negotiated Options
Se1/2 CCP:    MS-PPC supported bits 0x01000020 (0x120601000020)
Peer's Negotiated Options
Se1/2 CCP:    MS-PPC supported bits 0x01000020 (0x120601000020)


Se1/2 CDPCP: [Open]
Our Negotiated Options
  NONE
Peer's Negotiated Options
  NONE
```

Task 12

Reconfigure the serial interfaces of R1 and R2 based on the following policy:

■ The R1 S1/2 interface should use an IP address of 1.1.1.1/24, and the R2 S1/1 interface should use the IP address 2.2.2.2/24.

■ Configure one-way EAP authentication between the serial interfaces of R1 and R2. R1 should be configured to authenticate R2 (that is, R1 must prove its identity, or authenticate itself, to R2).

■ R2 should use the identity of "tst" and a password of "tstpassword". Use interface configuration commands on R2.

```
! On R1:

R1(config)# default interface serial1/2
Interface Serial1/2 set to default configuration


On R2:

R2(config)# default interface serial1.1


! On R1:

R1(config)# interface serial1/2
R1(config-if)# ip address 1.1.1.1 255.255.255.0
R1(config-if)# clock rate 64000
R1(config-if)# encapsulation ppp
R1(config-if)# ppp authentication eap
R1(config-if)# ppp eap local
R1(config-if)# no shutdown

! On R2:

R2(config)# interface serial1/1
R2(config-if)# ip address 12.1.1.2 255.255.255.0
R2(config-if)# encapsulation ppp
R2(config-if)# ppp encrypt mppe 40 required
R2(config-if)# ppp authentication ms-chap
R2(config-if)# no shutdown
```

Let's test and verify the configuration:

```
R1(config)# interface serial1/2
R1(config-if)# shutdown
R1(config-if)# do debug ppp mppe events
R1(config-if)# no shutdown


Se1/0 MPPE: Generate keys using local database
Se1/0 MPPE: Initialize keys
Se1/0 MPPE: [40 bit encryption]   [stateless mode]


R1# undebug all


R1# ping 2.2.2.2
Type escape sequence to abort.
Sending 5, 100-byte ICMP Echos to 2.2.2.2, timeout is 2 seconds:
!!!!!
Success rate is 100 percent (5/5), round-trip min/avg/max = 16/19/20 ms



R1# show ppp all
Interface/ID OPEN+ Nego* Fail-      Stage     Peer Address    Peer Name
------------ -------------------- -------- --------------- --------------------
Se1/2         LCP+ IPCP+ CCP+ CDPC> LocalT   2.2.2.2          R2


R1# show ppp interface serial1/0
PPP Serial Context Info
-------------------
Interface         : Se1/0
PPP Serial Handle: 0xB4000006
PPP Handle        : 0xFD00000C
SSS Handle        : 0xD0000013
AAA ID            : 24
Access IE         : 0x3000000B
SHDB Handle       : 0x0
State             : Up
Last State        : Binding
Last Event        : LocalTerm


PPP Session Info
----------------
Interface         : Se1/0
PPP ID            : 0xFD00000C
Phase             : UP
Stage             : Local Termination
```

```
Peer Name         : R2
Peer Address      : 2.2.2.2
Control Protocols: LCP[Open] IPCP[Open] CCP[Open] CDPCP[Open]
Session ID        : 11
AAA Unique ID     : 24
SSS Manager ID    : 0xD0000013
SIP ID            : 0xB4000006
PPP_IN_USE        : 0x11

Se1/0 LCP: [Open]
Our Negotiated Options
Se1/0 LCP:    MagicNumber 0xC1AAB3BA (0x0506C1AAB3BA)
Peer's Negotiated Options
Se1/0 LCP:    AuthProto MS-CHAP (0x0305C22380)
Se1/0 LCP:    MagicNumber 0xC1AAB59C (0x0506C1AAB59C)

Se1/0 IPCP: [Open]
Our Negotiated Options
Se1/0 IPCP:    Address 1.1.1.1 (0x030601010101)
Peer's Negotiated Options
Se1/0 IPCP:    Address 2.2.2.2 (0x030602020202)

Se1/0 CCP: [Open]
Our Negotiated Options
Se1/0 CCP:    MS-PPC supported bits 0x01000020 (0x120601000020)
Peer's Negotiated Options
Se1/0 CCP:    MS-PPC supported bits 0x01000020 (0x120601000020)

Se1/0 CDPCP: [Open]
Our Negotiated Options
  NONE
Peer's Negotiated Options
  NONE
```

Task 13

Reconfigure the serial interfaces of R1 and R2 based on the following policy:

- Configure PPP Multilink using the two serial interfaces that connect these two routers to each other.

- R1 should use an IP address of 12.1.1.1/24, and R2 should use an IP address of 12.1.1.2/24.

Before Multilink PPP is configured, the existing configuration on the serial interfaces of these two routers must be removed.

```
! On R1:


R1(config)# default interface serial1/2
Interface Serial1/2 set to default configuration


! On R2:


R2(config)# default interface serial1/1
Interface Serial1/1 set to default configuration
```

Multilink PPP bundles are represented by Multilink interfaces, similar to how EtherChannel bundles are represented by port-channel interfaces. To configure Multilink PPP, a Multilink interface is first configured with the usual IP addressing and other common configurations, and then physical serial interfaces are assigned to a particular multilink bundle.

```
! On R1:


R1(config)# interface multilink12
R1(config-if)# ip address 12.1.1.1 255.255.255.0
R1(config-if)# exit
R1(config)# interface serial1/2
R1(config-if)# clock rate 64000
R1(config-if)# encapsulation ppp
R1(config-if)# ppp multilink group 12
R1(config-if)# no shutdown
R1(config-if)# exit
R1(config)# interface serial1/7
R1(config-if)# clock rate 64000
R1(config-if)# encapsulation ppp
R1(config-if)# ppp multilink group 12
R1(config-if)# no shutdown


! On R2:


R2(config)# interface multilink21
R2(config-if)# ip address 12.1.1.2 255.255.255.0
R2(config-if)# exit
R2(config)# interface serial1/1
R2(config-if)# encapsulation ppp
R2(config-if)# ppp multilink group 21
R2(config-if)# no shutdown
```

```
R2(config)# interface serial1/7
R2(config-if)# encapsulation ppp
R2(config-if)# ppp multilink group 21
R2(config-if)# no shutdown
```

Let's verify and test the configuration:

```
R1# show ppp multilink

Multilink12

   Bundle name: R2
   Remote Endpoint Discriminator: [1] R2
   Local Endpoint Discriminator: [1] R1
   Bundle up for 00:05:10, total bandwidth 256, load 1/255
   Receive buffer limit 24000 bytes, frag timeout 1000 ms
     0/0 fragments/bytes in reassembly list
     0 lost fragments, 1 reordered
     0/0 discarded fragments/bytes, 0 lost received
     0xE received sequence, 0xE sent sequence
   Member links: 2 active, 0 inactive (max 255, min not set)
     Se1/2, since 00:05:10
     Se1/7, since 00:02:09
No inactive multilink interfaces


R1# ping 12.1.1.2
Type escape sequence to abort.
Sending 5, 100-byte ICMP Echos to 12.1.1.2, timeout is 2 seconds:
!!!!!
Success rate is 100 percent (5/5), round-trip min/avg/max = 16/19/20 ms
```

Erase the startup configuration of these routers and switches and reload them before proceeding to the next lab.

Summary

The use of PPP has improved network operations for years, and it is not going to go away completely any time soon. PPP provides many capabilities that ordinarily would not be available on serial interfaces, and also can be used to bring some of the efficiencies found on serial interfaces to Ethernet. We looked at being able to group these slower serial interfaces in such a fashion as to permit their bandwidth to be aggregated. In short, it should be obvious that so long as serial interfaces exist, PPP will be a technology we continue to rely on.

Chapter 5

DMVPN

Dynamic multipoint virtual private networks (DMVPNs) began simply as what is best described as hub-and-spoke topologies. The main tool employed to create these VPNs is a combination of Multipoint Generic Routing Encapsulation (mGRE) connections employed on the hub and traditional Point-to-Point (P2P) GRE tunnels on the spoke devices.

In this initial deployment methodology, known as a Phase 1 DMVPN, the spokes can only join the hub and they can only communicate with one another through the hub. This phase does not use spoke-to-spoke tunnels. The spokes are configured for Point-to-Point GRE to the hub and register their logical IP with the Non-Broadcast Multi-Access (NBMA) address on the Next Hop Server (NHS) hub.

This registration process can be conducted via static or dynamic means. Static operation implies that each of the spokes will be configured via manual mapping statements. It is important to keep in mind that there is a total of three phases, and each one can influence the following:

- Spoke-to-spoke traffic patterns
- Routing protocol design
- Scalability

Lab 5-1: DMVPN Phase 1 Using Static Mapping

The simplest way to solve the mapping problem between the NBMA address (the "outside" address) and the tunnel IP address is to use static mappings. However, this is normally not done because it kind of removes the dynamic part of DMVPN. Let's explore the concept here because it very clearly illustrates what we are trying to do. Let's say you have the very simple topology outline shown in Figure 5-1. Let's explore almost every aspect of the static method so we can compare it more analytically to the dynamic method in the next lab.

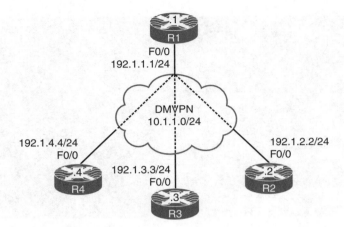

Figure 5-1 *DMVPN Phase 1 Using Static Mapping*

Task 1

SW1 represents the Internet. Configure a static default route on each router pointing to the appropriate interface on SW1. If this configuration is performed correctly, these routers should be able to ping and have reachability to the F0/0 interfaces of all routers in this topology. The switch interface to which the routers are connected should have ".10" in the host portion of the IP address for that subnet.

Let's configure SW1's interfaces for these routers. Because SW1 represents the Internet, the IP addresses in the following configuration should be made the default gateway on the routers.

```
On SW1:

SW1(config)# interface range FastEthernet0/1-4
SW1(config-if-range)# no switchport

SW1(config)# interface FastEthernet0/1
SW1(config-if)# ip address 192.1.1.10 255.255.255.0
SW1(config-if)# no shutdown

SW1(config)# interface FastEthernet0/2
SW1(config-if)# ip address 192.1.2.10 255.255.255.0
SW1(config-if)# no shutdown

SW1(config)# interface FastEthernet0/3
SW1(config-if)# ip address 192.1.3.10 255.255.255.0
SW1(config-if)# no shutdown
```

```
SW1(config)# interface FastEthernet0/4
SW1(config-if)# ip address 192.1.4.10 255.255.255.0
SW1(config-if)# no shutdown
```

Let's *not* forget to enable **ip routing**; otherwise, the switch will not be able to route from one subnet to another:

```
SW1(config)# ip routing
```

Let's configure the routers:

```
On R1:

R1(config)# interface FastEthernet0/0
R1(config-if)# ip address 192.1.1.1 255.255.255.0
R1(config-if)# no shutdown

R1(config)# ip route 0.0.0.0 0.0.0.0 192.1.1.10
```

```
On R2:

R2(config)# interface FastEthernet0/0
R2(config-if)# ip address 192.1.2.2 255.255.255.0
R2(config-if)# no shutdown

R2(config)# ip route 0.0.0.0 0.0.0.0 192.1.2.10
```

```
On R3:

R3(config)# interface FastEthernet0/0
R3(config-if)# ip address 192.1.3.3 255.255.255.0
R3(config-if)# no shutdown

R3(config)# ip route 0.0.0.0 0.0.0.0 192.1.3.10
```

```
On R4:

R4(config)# interface FastEthernet0/0
R4(config-if)# ip address 192.1.4.4 255.255.255.0
R4(config-if)# no shutdown

R4(config)# ip route 0.0.0.0 0.0.0.0 192.1.4.10
```

Now let's verify the configuration:

```
On R1:


R1# ping 192.1.2.2


Type escape sequence to abort.
Sending 5, 100-byte ICMP Echos to 192.1.2.2, timeout is 2 seconds:
!!!!!
Success rate is 100 percent (5/5), round-trip min/avg/max = 1/2/4 ms


R1# ping 192.1.3.3


Type escape sequence to abort.
Sending 5, 100-byte ICMP Echos to 192.1.3.3, timeout is 2 seconds:
!!!!!
Success rate is 100 percent (5/5), round-trip min/avg/max = 1/2/4 ms


R1# ping 192.1.4.4


Type escape sequence to abort.
Sending 5, 100-byte ICMP Echos to 192.1.4.4, timeout is 2 seconds:
!!!!!
Success rate is 100 percent (5/5), round-trip min/avg/max = 1/2/4 ms
```

```
On R2:


R2# ping 192.1.1.1


Type escape sequence to abort.
Sending 5, 100-byte ICMP Echos to 192.1.1.1, timeout is 2 seconds:
!!!!!
Success rate is 100 percent (5/5), round-trip min/avg/max = 1/2/4 ms


R2# ping 192.1.3.3


Type escape sequence to abort.
Sending 5, 100-byte ICMP Echos to 192.1.3.3, timeout is 2 seconds:
!!!!!
Success rate is 100 percent (5/5), round-trip min/avg/max = 1/2/4 ms
```

```
R2# ping 192.1.4.4

Type escape sequence to abort.
Sending 5, 100-byte ICMP Echos to 192.1.4.4, timeout is 2 seconds:
!!!!!
Success rate is 100 percent (5/5), round-trip min/avg/max = 1/1/4 ms
```

Task 2

Configure DMVPN Phase 1 such that R1 is the hub and R2, R3, and R4 are the spokes. You should use 10.1.1.*x*/24, where *x* is the router number. If this configuration is performed correctly, these routers should have reachability to all tunnel endpoints. You should configure static mapping to accomplish this task.

DMVPN is a combination of mGRE, the Next-Hop Resolution Protocol (NHRP), and IPSec (optional). DMVPN can be implemented as Phase 1, Phase 2, or Phase 3.

There are two GRE flavors:

- GRE
- mGRE

GRE, which is a point-to-point logical link, is configured with a tunnel source and tunnel destination. The tunnel source can either be an IP address or an interface. When a tunnel destination is configured, it ties the tunnel to a specific endpoint. This makes a GRE tunnel a point-to-point tunnel. If there are 200 endpoints, each endpoint would need to configure 199 GRE tunnels.

With Multipoint Generic Routing Encapsulation (mGRE), the configuration includes the tunnel source and tunnel mode. The tunnel destination is *not* configured. Therefore, the tunnel can have many endpoints, and only a single tunnel interface is utilized. The end-points can be configured as a GRE tunnel or an mGRE tunnel.

But what if the spokes need to communicate with each other? Especially with the NBMA nature of mGRE? How would we accomplish that?

If a spoke needs to communicate with another spoke in a hub-and-spoke Frame Relay network, a Frame Relay mapping needs to be configured. Is there a mapping that we need to configure in mGRE?

Well, mGRE does not have a mapping capability. This is why another protocol is used. That protocol is called the Next-Hop Resolution Protocol (NHRP) and is defined in RFC 2332. It provides Layer 2 address resolution and a caching service, very much like ARP and inverse ARP.

NHRP is used by the spokes connected to an NBMA network to determine the NBMA IP address of the next-hop router. With NHRP, you can map a tunnel IP address to an NBMA IP address either statically or dynamically. The NBMA IP address is the IP address acquired from the service provider. The tunnel IP address is the IP address that *you* assigned to the tunnel interface, typically using RFC 1918 addressing.

In NHRP, a router is configured either as an NHRP client (NHC) or an NHRP server (NHS). The NHS acts as a mapping agent and stores all registered mappings performed by the NHC. The NHS can reply to the queries made by NHCs. NHCs send a query to the NHS if they need to communicate with another NHC.

NHRP is like the Address Resolution Protocol (ARP). Why is it like ARP? Because it allows NHCs to dynamically register their NBMA-IP-address-to-tunnel-IP-address mapping. This allows the NHCs to join the NBMA network without the NHS needing to be reconfigured. This means that when a new NHC is added to the NBMA network, none of the NHCs or the NHSs need to be reconfigured.

Let's look at a scenario where the NHC has a dynamic physical IP address or the NHC is behind a network address translation (NAT) device. How would you configure the NHS and what IP addresses are you going to use for the NHCs?

This is the reason why dynamic registration and queries are very useful. In these scenarios, it is almost impossible to preconfigure the logical tunnel IP address to the physical NBMA IP address mapping for the NHCs on the NHS. NHRP is a resolution protocol that allows the NHCs to dynamically discover the logical-IP-address-to-physical-IP-address mapping for other NHCs within the same NBMA network.

Without this discovery, packets must traverse through the hub to reach other spokes. This can negatively impact the CPU and the bandwidth of the hub router.

There are three phases in DMVPN: Phase 1, Phase 2, and Phase 3. Here are some important points to remember about DMVPN Phase 1:

■ mGRE is configured on the hub, and GRE is configured on the spokes.

■ Multicast or unicast traffic can *only* flow between the hub and the spokes, *not* from spoke to spoke.

■ This can be configured statically, or the NHCs (spokes) can register themselves dynamically with the NHS (the hub).

Let's configure R1 (the hub router) with static mappings.

The tunnel configuration on the hub, whether static or dynamic, can be broken down into two configuration steps. In the first step, the mGRE tunnel is configured. This step uses three configuration commands: the IP address of the tunnel, the tunnel source, and the tunnel mode, as shown here:

```
On R1:

R1(config)# interface tunnel 1
R1(config-if)# ip address 10.1.1.1 255.255.255.0
R1(config-if)# tunnel source 192.1.1.1
R1(config-if)# tunnel mode gre multipoint
```

In the second step, NHRP is configured. This configuration uses two NHRP configuration commands: the NHRP network ID (which enables NHRP on that tunnel interface) and the NHRP mapping that maps the tunnel IP address to the physical IP address (NBMA IP address) of the spoke(s). This needs to be done for each spoke. An optional third NHRP configuration command allows the mapping of multicast to the physical IP address of the spokes. This enables multicasting and allows the Interior Gateway Protocols (IGPs) to use multicasting over the tunnel interface. (Doesn't this remind you of the Frame Relay days with the **Broadcast** keyword at the end of the **frame-relay map** statement?) In this task, the mapping of multicast to the NBMA IP address is not configured.

```
R1(config-if)# ip nhrp network-id 111
R1(config-if)# ip nhrp map 10.1.1.2 192.1.2.2
R1(config-if)# ip nhrp map 10.1.1.3 192.1.3.3
R1(config-if)# ip nhrp map 10.1.1.4 192.1.4.4
```

Let's verify the configuration:

```
R1# show ip nhrp

10.1.1.2/32 via 10.1.1.2
   Tunnel1 created 00:05:20, never expire

   Type: static, Flags:
   NBMA address: 192.1.2.2
10.1.1.3/32 via 10.1.1.3
   Tunnel1 created 00:05:12, never expire
   Type: static, Flags:
   NBMA address: 192.1.3.3
10.1.1.4/32 via 10.1.1.4
   Tunnel1 created 00:05:05, never expire
   Type: static, Flags:
   NBMA address: 192.1.4.4
```

In the DMVPN Phase 1 configuration on the spokes, the tunnels should be configured as point-to-point GRE tunnels. The configuration includes the tunnel source and the tunnel destination. Because the tunnel destination is configured, it ties that tunnel to that destination *only*. This makes the tunnel a point-to-point tunnel and *not* a multipoint tunnel. Once the tunnel commands are configured, the next step is to configure NHRP. In this configuration on the spokes, NHRP is enabled first and then a single mapping is configured for the hub's tunnel IP address:

```
On R2:


R2(config)# interface tunnel 1
R2(config-if)# ip address 10.1.1.2 255.255.255.0
R2(config-if)# tunnel source 192.1.2.2
R2(config-if)# tunnel destination 192.1.1.1
R2(config-if)# ip nhrp network-id 222
R2(config-if)# ip nhrp map 10.1.1.1 192.1.1.1
```

Let's verify the configuration:

```
R2# show ip nhrp


10.1.1.1/32 via 10.1.1.1
    Tunnel1 created 00:04:03, never expire
    Type: static, Flags:
    NBMA address: 192.1.1.1
```

```
On R3:


R3(config)# interface tunnel 1
R3(config-if)# ip address 10.1.1.3 255.255.255.0
R3(config-if)# tunnel source FastEthernet0/0
R3(config-if)# tunnel destination 192.1.1.1
R3(config-if)# ip nhrp network-id 333
R3(config-if)# ip nhrp map 10.1.1.1 192.1.1.1
```

```
On R4:


R4(config)# interface tunnel 1
R4(config-if)# ip address 10.1.1.4 255.255.255.0
R4(config-if)# tunnel source FastEthernet0/0
R4(config-if)# tunnel destination 192.1.1.1
R4(config-if)# ip nhrp network-id 444
R4(config-if)# ip nhrp map 10.1.1.1 192.1.1.1
```

Now we can test the configuration:

```
On R1:


R1# ping 10.1.1.2


Type escape sequence to abort.
Sending 5, 100-byte ICMP Echos to 10.1.1.2, timeout is 2 seconds:
!!!!!
Success rate is 100 percent (5/5), round-trip min/avg/max = 1/3/4 ms

R1# ping 10.1.1.3
Type escape sequence to abort.
Sending 5, 100-byte ICMP Echos to 10.1.1.3, timeout is 2 seconds:
!!!!!
Success rate is 100 percent (5/5), round-trip min/avg/max = 1/3/4 ms

R1# ping 10.1.1.4

Type escape sequence to abort.
Sending 5, 100-byte ICMP Echos to 10.1.1.4, timeout is 2 seconds:
!!!!!
Success rate is 100 percent (5/5), round-trip min/avg/max = 1/3/4 ms
```

```
On R2:

R2# ping 10.1.1.1

Type escape sequence to abort.
Sending 5, 100-byte ICMP Echos to 10.1.1.1, timeout is 2 seconds:
!!!!!
Success rate is 100 percent (5/5), round-trip min/avg/max = 1/2/4 ms


R2# ping 10.1.1.3

Type escape sequence to abort.
Sending 5, 100-byte ICMP Echos to 10.1.1.3, timeout is 2 seconds:
!!!!!
Success rate is 100 percent (5/5), round-trip min/avg/max = 1/3/4 ms
```

```
R2# ping 10.1.1.4

Type escape sequence to abort.
Sending 5, 100-byte ICMP Echos to 10.1.1.4, timeout is 2 seconds:
!!!!!
Success rate is 100 percent (5/5), round-trip min/avg/max = 1/3/4 ms


To see the traffic path between the spokes:

R2# traceroute 10.1.1.3

Type escape sequence to abort.
Tracing the route to 10.1.1.3
VRF info: (vrf in name/id, vrf out name/id)
  1 10.1.1.1 4 msec 4 msec 4 msec
  2 10.1.1.3 0 msec *  0 msec


R2# traceroute 10.1.1.4

Type escape sequence to abort.
Tracing the route to 10.1.1.4
VRF info: (vrf in name/id, vrf out name/id)
  1 10.1.1.1 4 msec 4 msec 0 msec
  2 10.1.1.4 4 msec *  0 msec
```

```
On R3:

R3# ping 10.1.1.4

Type escape sequence to abort.
Sending 5, 100-byte ICMP Echos to 10.1.1.4, timeout is 2 seconds:
!!!!!
Success rate is 100 percent (5/5), round-trip min/avg/max = 1/2/4 ms


R3# traceroute 10.1.1.4

Type escape sequence to abort.
Tracing the route to 10.1.1.4

VRF info: (vrf in name/id, vrf out name/id)

  1 10.1.1.1 0 msec 4 msec 4 msec
  2 10.1.1.4 0 msec *  0 msec
```

Because the spokes are configured in a point-to-point manner, there is no need to map multicast traffic to the NBMA IP address of a given endpoint.

Erase the startup configuration of the routers and the switch and reload them before proceeding to the next lab.

Lab 5-2: DMVPN Phase 1 Using Dynamic Mapping

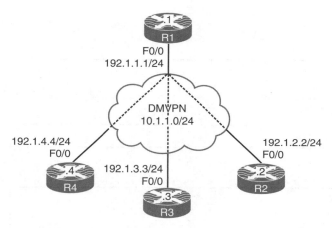

Figure 5-2   *DMVPN Phase 1 Using Dynamic Mapping*

Task 1

In Figure 5.2, we see the topology we will use in this lab. Hidden in the figure we see a cloud, and in this lab that cloud is a switch named SW1. SW1 represents the Internet; configure a static default route on each router pointing to the appropriate interface on SW1. If this
configuration is performed correctly, these routers should be able to ping and have reachability to the F0/0 interfaces of all routers in this topology. The switch interface to which the routers are connected should have ".10" in the host portion of the IP address for that subnet.

Let's configure SW1's interfaces for these routers. Because in this lab SW1 represents the Internet, the IP addresses in the following configuration should be set as the default gateway on the routers.

```
On SW1:

SW1(config)# interface range FastEthernet0/1-4
SW1(config-if-range)# no switchport

SW1(config)# interface FastEthernet0/1
SW1(config-if)# ip address 192.1.1.10 255.255.255.0
SW1(config-if)# no shutdown
```

```
SW1(config)# interface FastEthernet0/2
SW1(config-if)# ip address 192.1.2.10 255.255.255.0
SW1(config-if)# no shutdown

SW1(config)# interface FastEthernet0/3
SW1(config-if)# ip address 192.1.3.10 255.255.255.0
SW1(config-if)# no shutdown

SW1(config)# interface FastEthernet0/4
SW1(config-if)# ip address 192.1.4.10 255.255.255.0
SW1(config-if)# no shutdown
```

Let's *not* forget to enable **ip routing**; otherwise, the switch will not be able to route from one subnet to another:

```
SW1(config)# ip routing
```

Let's configure the routers:

```
On R1:

R1(config)# interface FastEthernet0/0
R1(config-if)# ip address 192.1.1.1 255.255.255.0
R1(config-if)# no shutdown

R1(config)# ip route 0.0.0.0 0.0.0.0 192.1.1.10
```

```
On R2:

R2(config)# interface FastEthernet0/0
R2(config-if)# ip address 192.1.2.2 255.255.255.0
R2(config-if)# no shut

R2(config)# ip route 0.0.0.0 0.0.0.0 192.1.2.10
```

```
On R3:

R3(config)# interface FastEthernet0/0
R3(config-if)# ip address 192.1.3.3 255.255.255.0
R3(config-if)# no shutdown

R3(config)# ip route 0.0.0.0 0.0.0.0 192.1.3.10
```

```
On R4:

R4(config)# interface FastEthernet0/0
R4(config-if)# ip address 192.1.4.4 255.255.255.0
R4(config-if)# no shutdown

R4(config)# ip route 0.0.0.0 0.0.0.0 192.1.4.10
```

Now let's verify the configuration:

```
On R1:


R1# ping 192.1.2.2


Type escape sequence to abort.
Sending 5, 100-byte ICMP Echos to 192.1.2.2, timeout is 2 seconds:
!!!!!
Success rate is 100 percent (5/5), round-trip min/avg/max = 1/2/4 ms


R1# ping 192.1.3.3


Type escape sequence to abort.
Sending 5, 100-byte ICMP Echos to 192.1.3.3, timeout is 2 seconds:
!!!!!
Success rate is 100 percent (5/5), round-trip min/avg/max = 1/2/4 ms


R1# ping 192.1.4.4


Type escape sequence to abort.
Sending 5, 100-byte ICMP Echos to 192.1.4.4, timeout is 2 seconds:
!!!!!
Success rate is 100 percent (5/5), round-trip min/avg/max = 1/2/4 ms
```

```
On R2:


R2# ping 192.1.1.1


Type escape sequence to abort.
Sending 5, 100-byte ICMP Echos to 192.1.1.1, timeout is 2 seconds:
!!!!!
Success rate is 100 percent (5/5), round-trip min/avg/max = 1/2/4 ms
```

```
R2# ping 192.1.3.3

Type escape sequence to abort.
Sending 5, 100-byte ICMP Echos to 192.1.3.3, timeout is 2 seconds:
!!!!!
Success rate is 100 percent (5/5), round-trip min/avg/max = 1/2/4 ms

R2# ping 192.1.4.4

Type escape sequence to abort.
Sending 5, 100-byte ICMP Echos to 192.1.4.4, timeout is 2 seconds:
!!!!!
Success rate is 100 percent (5/5), round-trip min/avg/max = 1/1/4 ms
```

Task 2

Configure DMVPN Phase 1 such that R1 is the hub and R2, R3, and R4 are the spokes. You should use 10.1.1.*x*/24, where *x* is the router number. If this configuration is performed correctly, these routers should have reachability to all tunnel endpoints. You should *not* configure static mappings on the hub router to accomplish this task.

Because the task refers to DMVPN Phase 1, you know that the hub router must be configured in a multipoint manner and the spokes should be configured in a point-to-point manner. The task also specifies that the hub router should *not* be configured with static mappings. This means that the hub should be configured such that the mappings are performed dynamically. This configuration is more scalable than configuring the hub with static mappings. If the hub is configured with static mappings for each spoke, a newly added spoke will require some configuration on the hub. If the mappings are performed dynamically, the spokes can be added dynamically without any configuration performed on the hub. How does that work?

When a spoke router initially connects to the DMVPN network, it registers its tunnel-IP-address-to-NBMA-IP-address mapping with the hub router. The hub router will acknowledge the registration by' sending back the registration message that was initiated by the spoke with a success code. This registration enables the mGRE interface on the hub router to build a dynamic GRE tunnel back to the registering spoke router. This means that the spoke routers *must* be configured with the tunnel IP address of the hub; otherwise, they won't know where to go to register their tunnel-IP-address-to-NBMA-IP-address mapping.

Let's configure the routers, starting with the hub (R1). Remember that this configuration should be done in two steps. In the first step, the tunnel source and tunnel mode are configured:

```
On R1:

R1(config)# interface tunnel 1
R1(config-if)# ip address 10.1.1.1 255.255.255.0
R1(config-if)# tunnel source 192.1.1.1
R1(config-if)# tunnel mode gre multipoint
```

In the second step, NHRP is configured. First, the NHRP network ID is configured, which enables NHRP on that tunnel interface. The NHRP mapping should then be configured. This mapping can be configured dynamically or statically. The previous lab demonstrated the configuration of static mapping. In this lab, the configuration of dynamic mapping is demonstrated. In a dynamic mapping configuration, nothing else is done. As long as NHRP is enabled on that interface, the mappings will occur dynamically. Let's configure the routers and verify.

```
R1(config-if)# ip nhrp network-id 111
```

Since in DMVPN Phase 1 configuration the spoke routers should be configured as "point to point," the configuration includes the tunnel source and the tunnel destination. Because the tunnel destination is configured, it ties that tunnel to that destination only. This makes the tunnel a point-to-point tunnel and *not* a multipoint tunnel. Once the tunnel commands are configured, the next step to configure NHRP. To configure NHRP dynamically on the spokes, first enable NHRP and then configure the NHS.

Note   Because the tunnel on the spoke routers (R2, R3, and R4) is configured in a point-to-point manner, there is no need to configure an NHRP mapping for the NHS's IP address.

```
On R2:

R2(config)# interface tunnel 1
R2(config-if)# ip address 10.1.1.2 255.255.255.0
R2(config-if)# tunnel source FastEthernet0/0
R2(config-if)# tunnel destination 192.1.1.1
R2(config-if)# ip nhrp network-id 222
R2(config-if)# ip nhrp nhs 10.1.1.1
```

Let's verify the configuration:

```
On R1:

R1# show ip nhrp
10.1.1.2/32 via 10.1.1.2
   Tunnel1 created 00:01:05, expire 01:58:54
Type: dynamic, Flags: unique registered
   NBMA address: 192.1.2.2
```

You can see that once R2 was connected to the DMVPN network, the hub router (R1) created a dynamic entry for R2. Let's configure the other spoke routers:

```
On R3:


R3(config)# interface tunnel 1
R3(config-if)# ip address 10.1.1.3 255.255.255.0
R3(config-if)# tunnel source FastEthernet0/0
R3(config-if)# tunnel destination 192.1.1.1
R3(config-if)# ip nhrp network-id 333
R3(config-if)# ip nhrp nhs 10.1.1.1
```

```
On R4:


R4(config)# interface tunnel 1
R4(config-if)# ip address 10.1.1.4 255.255.255.0
R4(config-if)# tunnel source FastEthernet0/0
R4(config-if)# tunnel destination 192.1.1.1
R4(config-if)# ip nhrp network-id 444
R4(config-if)# ip nhrp nhs 10.1.1.1
```

Let's verify the configuration:

```
On R1:


R1# show ip nhrp

10.1.1.2/32 via 10.1.1.2
   Tunnel1 created 00:05:53, expire 01:54:06
   Type: dynamic, Flags: unique registered
   NBMA address: 192.1.2.2
10.1.1.3/32 via 10.1.1.3
   Tunnel1 created 00:02:24, expire 01:57:35
   Type: dynamic, Flags: unique registered
   NBMA address: 192.1.3.3
10.1.1.4/32 via 10.1.1.4

   Tunnel1 created 00:00:21, expire 01:59:38
   Type: dynamic, Flags: unique registered
   NBMA address: 192.1.4.4
```

Now let's test the configuration:

```
On R1:


R1# ping 10.1.1.2
Type escape sequence to abort.
Sending 5, 100-byte ICMP Echos to 10.1.1.2, timeout is 2 seconds:
!!!!!
Success rate is 100 percent (5/5), round-trip min/avg/max = 1/3/4 ms

R1# ping 10.1.1.3
Type escape sequence to abort.
Sending 5, 100-byte ICMP Echos to 10.1.1.3, timeout is 2 seconds:
!!!!!
Success rate is 100 percent (5/5), round-trip min/avg/max = 1/2/4 ms

R1# ping 10.1.1.4
Type escape sequence to abort.
Sending 5, 100-byte ICMP Echos to 10.1.1.4, timeout is 2 seconds:
!!!!!
Success rate is 100 percent (5/5), round-trip min/avg/max = 1/3/4 ms
```

```
On R3:


R3# ping 10.1.1.1
Type escape sequence to abort.
Sending 5, 100-byte ICMP Echos to 10.1.1.1, timeout is 2 seconds:
!!!!!
Success rate is 100 percent (5/5), round-trip min/avg/max = 1/3/4 ms

R3# ping 10.1.1.2
Type escape sequence to abort.
Sending 5, 100-byte ICMP Echos to 10.1.1.2, timeout is 2 seconds:

!!!!!
Success rate is 100 percent (5/5), round-trip min/avg/max = 1/2/4 ms

R3# ping 10.1.1.4
Type escape sequence to abort.
Sending 5, 100-byte ICMP Echos to 10.1.1.4, timeout is 2 seconds:
!!!!!

Success rate is 100 percent (5/5), round-trip min/avg/max = 1/2/4 ms
```

```
R3# traceroute 10.1.1.2 numeric

Type escape sequence to abort.
Tracing the route to 10.1.1.2
VRF info: (vrf in name/id, vrf out name/id)
  1 10.1.1.1 0 msec 4 msec 4 msec
  2 10.1.1.2 4 msec *  0 msec
```

You can see that in DMVPN Phase 1, no matter the configuration (static mapping or dynamic mapping), the spokes will go through the hub to connect to the other spokes.

Erase the startup configuration of the routers and the switch and reload them before proceeding to the next lab.

Lab 5-3: DMVPN Phase 2 Using Static Mapping

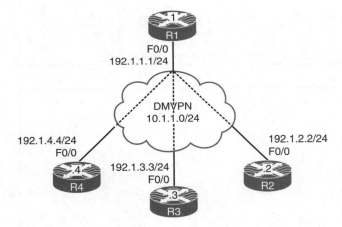

Figure 5-3   *DMVPN Phase 2 Using Static Mapping*

In Figure 5.3, we see the topology we will use in this lab. To allow the dynamic spoke-to-spoke tunnels to form, you need to change the spokes to multipoint tunnels. As you do that, you need to make sure that you also add a static entry for the hub, because without that entry, the NHRP registration cannot be sent. The question then becomes, how does a spoke learn the NHRP mapping of another spoke? A system of requests and replies are used where a spoke sends a request for a particular spoke that it wants to send traffic to. It then gets a reply from the spoke in question. The process looks something like the following:

1. Spoke 1 forwards a packet with a next hop that is another spoke, spoke 2. There is no NHRP map entry for this spoke, so an NHRP resolution request is sent to the hub.

2. The request from spoke 1 contains the tunnel IP address of spoke 2. The hub relays the request to spoke 2.

3. Spoke 2 receives the request, adds its own address mapping to it, and sends it as an NHRP reply directly to spoke 1.

4. Spoke 2 then sends its own request to the hub, which relays it to spoke 1.

5. Spoke 1 receives the request from spoke 2 via the hub and replies by adding its own mapping to the packet and sending it directly to spoke 2.

6. Technically, the requests themselves provide enough information to build a spoke-to-spoke tunnel, but the replies accomplish two things. They acknowledge to the other spoke that the request was received and also verify that spoke-to-spoke NBMA reachability exists.

This phase of DMVPN deployment has some restrictions:

■ Summarization is not allowed on the hub.

■ Default routing is not allowed on the hub.

■ The spokes must always maintain next-hop reachability.

Task 1

SW1 represents the Internet. Configure a static default route on each router pointing to the appropriate interface on SW1. If this configuration is performed correctly, these routers should be able to ping and have reachability to the F0/0 interfaces of all routers in this topology. The switch interface to which the routers are connected should have ".10" in the host portion of the IP address for that subnet.

Let's configure SW1's interfaces for these routers. Since in this lab SW1 represents the Internet, the IP addresses in the following configuration should be set as the default gateway on the routers:

```
On SW1:

SW1(config)# interface range FastEthernet0/1-4
SW1(config-if-range)# no switchport

SW1(config)# interface FastEthernet0/1
SW1(config-if)# ip address 192.1.1.10 255.255.255.0
SW1(config-if)# no shutdown

SW1(config)# interface FastEthernet0/2
SW1(config-if)# ip address 192.1.2.10 255.255.255.0
SW1(config-if)# no shutdown

SW1(config)# interface FastEthernet0/3
SW1(config-if)# ip address 192.1.3.10 255.255.255.0
SW1(config-if)# no shutdown
```

```
SW1(config)# interface FastEthernet0/4
SW1(config-if)# ip address 192.1.4.10 255.255.255.0
SW1(config-if)# no shutdown
```

Let's *not* forget to enable **ip routing**; otherwise, the switch will not be able to route from one subnet to another:

```
SW1(config)# ip routing
```

Let's configure the routers:

```
On R1:

R1(config)# interface FastEthernet0/0
R1(config-if)# ip address 192.1.1.1 255.255.255.0
R1(config-if)# no shutdown

R1(config)# ip route 0.0.0.0 0.0.0.0 192.1.1.10
```

```
On R2:

R2(config)# interface FastEthernet0/0
R2(config-if)# ip address 192.1.2.2 255.255.255.0
R2(config-if)# no shutdown

R2(config)# ip route 0.0.0.0 0.0.0.0 192.1.2.10
```

```
On R3:

R3(config)# interface FastEthernet0/0
R3(config-if)# ip address 192.1.3.3 255.255.255.0
R3(config-if)# no shutdown

R3(config)# ip route 0.0.0.0 0.0.0.0 192.1.3.10
```

```
On R4:

R4(config)# interface FastEthernet0/0
R4(config-if)# ip address 192.1.4.4 255.255.255.0
R4(config-if)# no shutdown

R4(config)# ip route 0.0.0.0 0.0.0.0 192.1.4.10
```

Now let's verify the configuration:

```
On R1:


R1# ping 192.1.2.2


Type escape sequence to abort.
Sending 5, 100-byte ICMP Echos to 192.1.2.2, timeout is 2 seconds:
!!!!!
Success rate is 100 percent (5/5), round-trip min/avg/max = 1/2/4 ms


R1# ping 192.1.3.3


Type escape sequence to abort.
Sending 5, 100-byte ICMP Echos to 192.1.3.3, timeout is 2 seconds:
!!!!!
Success rate is 100 percent (5/5), round-trip min/avg/max = 1/2/4 ms


R1# ping 192.1.4.4


Type escape sequence to abort.
Sending 5, 100-byte ICMP Echos to 192.1.4.4, timeout is 2 seconds:
!!!!!
Success rate is 100 percent (5/5), round-trip min/avg/max = 1/2/4 ms


On R2:


R2# ping 192.1.1.1


Type escape sequence to abort.
Sending 5, 100-byte ICMP Echos to 192.1.1.1, timeout is 2 seconds:
!!!!!
Success rate is 100 percent (5/5), round-trip min/avg/max = 1/2/4 ms


R2# ping 192.1.3.3


Type escape sequence to abort.
Sending 5, 100-byte ICMP Echos to 192.1.3.3, timeout is 2 seconds:
!!!!!
Success rate is 100 percent (5/5), round-trip min/avg/max = 1/2/4 ms


R2# ping 192.1.4.4


Type escape sequence to abort.
Sending 5, 100-byte ICMP Echos to 192.1.4.4, timeout is 2 seconds:
!!!!!
Success rate is 100 percent (5/5), round-trip min/avg/max = 1/1/4 ms
```

Task 2

Configure DMVPN Phase 2 such that R1 is the hub and R2, R3, and R4 are the spokes. You should use 10.1.1.*x*/24, where *x* is the router number. If this configuration is performed correctly, these routers should have reachability to all tunnel endpoints. You should configure static mappings on the hub router to accomplish this task.

Since the task refers to DMVPN Phase 2, the hub and all the spokes are configured with multipoint GRE tunnels. In this phase, the spokes have reachability to the other spokes directly.

Let's configure the routers:

```
On R1:

R1(config)# interface tunnel 1
R1(config-if)# ip address 10.1.1.1 255.255.255.0
R1(config-if)# tunnel source 192.1.1.1
R1(config-if)# tunnel mode gre multipoint
R1(config-if)# ip nhrp network-id 111

R1(config-if)# ip nhrp map 10.1.1.2 192.1.2.2
```

```
On R4:
R4(config-if)# ip nhrp map 10.1.1.3 192.1.3.3
R4(config-if)# ip nhrp map 10.1.1.4 192.1.4.4
```

```
On R2:

R2(config)# interface tunnel 1
R2(config-if)# ip address 10.1.1.2 255.255.255.0
R2(config-if)# tunnel source FastEthernet0/0
R2(config-if)# tunnel mode gre multipoint

R2(config-if)# ip nhrp network-id 222
R2(config-if)# ip nhrp map 10.1.1.1 192.1.1.1
R2(config-if)# ip nhrp map 10.1.1.3 192.1.3.3
R2(config-if)# ip nhrp map 10.1.1.4 192.1.4.4
```

```
On R3:

R3(config)# interface tunnel 1
R3(config-if)# ip address 10.1.1.3 255.255.255.0
R3(config-if)# tunnel source FastEthernet0/0
R3(config-if)# tunnel mode gre multipoint

R3(config-if)# ip nhrp network-id 333
R3(config-if)# ip nhrp map 10.1.1.1 192.1.1.1
R3(config-if)# ip nhrp map 10.1.1.2 192.1.2.2
R3(config-if)# ip nhrp map 10.1.1.4 192.1.4.4
```

```
On R4:

R4(config)# interface tunnel 1
R4(config-if)# ip address 10.1.1.4 255.255.255.0
R4(config-if)# tunnel source FastEthernet0/0
R4(config-if)# tunnel mode gre multipoint

R4(config-if)# ip nhrp network-id 444
R4(config-if)# ip nhrp map 10.1.1.1 192.1.1.1
R4(config-if)# ip nhrp map 10.1.1.2 192.1.2.2
R4(config-if)# ip nhrp map 10.1.1.3 192.1.3.3
```

Let's verify the configuration:

```
On R1:

R1# show ip nhrp

10.1.1.2/32 via 10.1.1.2
   Tunnel1 created 00:19:16, never expire
   Type: static, Flags: used
   NBMA address: 192.1.2.2
10.1.1.3/32 via 10.1.1.3
   Tunnel1 created 00:19:08, never expire
   Type: static, Flags:
   NBMA address: 192.1.3.3
10.1.1.4/32 via 10.1.1.4
   Tunnel1 created 00:01:09, never expire
   Type: static, Flags:
   NBMA address: 192.1.4.4
```

```
On R2:

R2# show ip nhrp

10.1.1.1/32 via 10.1.1.1
   Tunnel1 created 00:15:34, never expire
   Type: static, Flags: used
   NBMA address: 192.1.1.1
10.1.1.3/32 via 10.1.1.3
   Tunnel1 created 00:15:27, never expire
   Type: static, Flags:
   NBMA address: 192.1.3.3
10.1.1.4/32 via 10.1.1.4
   Tunnel1 created 00:15:19, never expire
   Type: static, Flags:
   NBMA address: 192.1.4.4
```

```
On R3:

R3# show ip nhrp

10.1.1.1/32 via 10.1.1.1
   Tunnel1 created 00:15:19, never expire
   Type: static, Flags:
   NBMA address: 192.1.1.1
10.1.1.2/32 via 10.1.1.2
   Tunnel1 created 00:15:11, never expire
   Type: static, Flags:
   NBMA address: 192.1.2.2

10.1.1.4/32 via 10.1.1.4

   Tunnel1 created 00:15:02, never expire
   Type: static, Flags:
   NBMA address: 192.1.4.4
```

```
On R4:

R4# show ip nhrp

10.1.1.1/32 via 10.1.1.1
   Tunnel1 created 00:15:13, never expire
   Type: static, Flags:
   NBMA address: 192.1.1.1
```

```
10.1.1.2/32 via 10.1.1.2
   Tunnel1 created 00:15:04, never expire
   Type: static, Flags:
   NBMA address: 192.1.2.2
10.1.1.3/32 via 10.1.1.3
   Tunnel1 created 00:14:57, never expire
   Type: static, Flags:
   NBMA address: 192.1.3.3
```

Now let's test the configuration:

```
On R1:


R1# ping 10.1.1.2
Type escape sequence to abort.
Sending 5, 100-byte ICMP Echos to 10.1.1.2, timeout is 2 seconds:
!!!!!
Success rate is 100 percent (5/5), round-trip min/avg/max = 1/3/4 ms


R1# ping 10.1.1.3
Type escape sequence to abort.
Sending 5, 100-byte ICMP Echos to 10.1.1.3, timeout is 2 seconds:
!!!!!
Success rate is 100 percent (5/5), round-trip min/avg/max = 1/2/4 ms


R1# ping 10.1.1.4
Type escape sequence to abort.
Sending 5, 100-byte ICMP Echos to 10.1.1.4, timeout is 2 seconds:
!!!!!
Success rate is 100 percent (5/5), round-trip min/avg/max = 1/3/4 ms
```

```
On R3:


R3# ping 10.1.1.1
Type escape sequence to abort.
Sending 5, 100-byte ICMP Echos to 10.1.1.1, timeout is 2 seconds:
!!!!!
Success rate is 100 percent (5/5), round-trip min/avg/max = 1/3/4 ms
```

```
R3# ping 10.1.1.2
Type escape sequence to abort.
Sending 5, 100-byte ICMP Echos to 10.1.1.2, timeout is 2 seconds:
!!!!!
Success rate is 100 percent (5/5), round-trip min/avg/max = 1/2/4 ms

R3# ping 10.1.1.4
Type escape sequence to abort.
Sending 5, 100-byte ICMP Echos to 10.1.1.4, timeout is 2 seconds:
!!!!!
Success rate is 100 percent (5/5), round-trip min/avg/max = 1/2/4 ms

R3# traceroute 10.1.1.2

Type escape sequence to abort.
Tracing the route to 10.1.1.2
VRF info: (vrf in name/id, vrf out name/id)
  1 10.1.1.2 4 msec *  0 msec
```

You can see in DMVPN Phase 2 that the spokes can communicate with and reach other spokes directly.

Erase the startup configuration of the routers and the switch and reload them before proceeding to the next lab.

Lab 5-4: DMVPN Phase 2 Using Dynamic Mapping

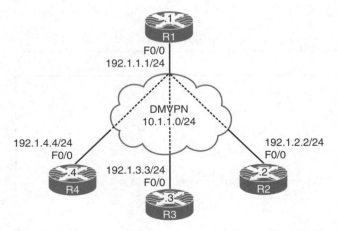

Figure 5-4 *DMVPN Phase 2 Using Dynamic Mapping*

Task 1

In Figure 5.4, we see the topology we will use in this lab. Hidden in the figure we see a cloud, and in this lab that cloud is a switch named SW1. SW1 represents the Internet. Configure a static default route on each router pointing to the appropriate interface on SW1. If this configuration is performed correctly, these routers should be able to ping and have reachability to the F0/0 interfaces of all routers in this topology. The switch interface to which the routers are connected should have ".10" in the host portion of the IP address for the subnet.

Let's configure SW1's interfaces for these routers. Since in this lab SW1 represents the Internet, the IP addresses in the following configuration should be set as the default gateway on the routers:

```
On SW1:

SW1(config)# interface range FastEthernet0/1-4
SW1(config-if-range)# no switchport

SW1(config)# interface FastEthernet0/1
SW1(config-if)# ip address 192.1.1.10 255.255.255.0
SW1(config-if)# no shutdown

SW1(config)# interface FastEthernet0/2
SW1(config-if)# ip address 192.1.2.10 255.255.255.0
SW1(config-if)# no shutdown

SW1(config)# interface FastEthernet0/3
SW1(config-if)# ip address 192.1.3.10 255.255.255.0
SW1(config-if)# no shutdown

SW1(config)# interface FastEthernet0/4
SW1(config-if)# ip address 192.1.4.10 255.255.255.0
SW1(config-if)# no shutdown
```

Let's *not* forget to enable **ip routing**; otherwise, the switch will not be able to route from one subnet to another:

```
SW1(config)# ip routing
```

Let's configure the routers:

```
On R1:

R1(config)# interface FastEthernet0/0
R1(config-if)# ip address 192.1.1.1 255.255.255.0
R1(config-if)# no shutdown

R1(config)# ip route 0.0.0.0 0.0.0.0 192.1.1.10
```

```
On R2:

R2(config)# interface FastEthernet0/0
R2(config-if)# ip address 192.1.2.2 255.255.255.0
R2(config-if)# no shutdown

R2(config)# ip route 0.0.0.0 0.0.0.0 192.1.2.10
```

```
On R3:

R3(config)# interface FastEthernet0/0
R3(config-if)# ip address 192.1.3.3 255.255.255.0
R3(config-if)# no shutdown

R3(config)# ip route 0.0.0.0 0.0.0.0 192.1.3.10
```

```
On R4:

R4(config)# interface FastEthernet0/0
R4(config-if)# ip address 192.1.4.4 255.255.255.0
R4(config-if)# no shutdown

R4(config)# ip route 0.0.0.0 0.0.0.0 192.1.4.10
```

Let's verify the configuration:

```
On R1:

R1# ping 192.1.2.2

Type escape sequence to abort.
Sending 5, 100-byte ICMP Echos to 192.1.2.2, timeout is 2 seconds:
!!!!!
Success rate is 100 percent (5/5), round-trip min/avg/max = 1/2/4 ms

R1# ping 192.1.3.3

Type escape sequence to abort.
Sending 5, 100-byte ICMP Echos to 192.1.3.3, timeout is 2 seconds:
!!!!!
Success rate is 100 percent (5/5), round-trip min/avg/max = 1/2/4 ms
```

```
R1# ping 192.1.4.4

Type escape sequence to abort.
Sending 5, 100-byte ICMP Echos to 192.1.4.4, timeout is 2 seconds:
!!!!!
Success rate is 100 percent (5/5), round-trip min/avg/max = 1/2/4 ms
```

```
On R2:

R2# ping 192.1.1.1

Type escape sequence to abort.
Sending 5, 100-byte ICMP Echos to 192.1.1.1, timeout is 2 seconds:
!!!!!
Success rate is 100 percent (5/5), round-trip min/avg/max = 1/2/4 ms

R2# ping 192.1.3.3

Type escape sequence to abort.
Sending 5, 100-byte ICMP Echos to 192.1.3.3, timeout is 2 seconds:
!!!!!
Success rate is 100 percent (5/5), round-trip min/avg/max = 1/2/4 ms

R2# ping 192.1.4.4

Type escape sequence to abort.
Sending 5, 100-byte ICMP Echos to 192.1.4.4, timeout is 2 seconds:
!!!!!
Success rate is 100 percent (5/5), round-trip min/avg/max = 1/1/4 ms
```

Task 2

Configure DMVPN Phase 2 such that R1 is the hub and R2, R3, and R4 are the spokes. You should use 10.1.1.x/24, where x is the router number. If this configuration is performed correctly, these routers should have reachability to all tunnel endpoints. You should *not* configure static mappings on the hub router to accomplish this task.

Since the task refers to DMVPN Phase 2, the hub and all the spokes are configured with multipoint GRE tunnels. In this phase, the spokes have reachability to the other spokes directly.

> **Note**   The hub router is configured with a tunnel source, a tunnel mode, and an NHRP
> network ID:

```
On R1:

R1(config)# interface tunnel 1
R1(config-if)# ip address 10.1.1.1 255.255.255.0
R1(config-if)# tunnel source 192.1.1.1
R1(config-if)# tunnel mode gre multipoint
R1(config-if)# ip nhrp network-id 111
```

The spokes are configured with a tunnel source, a tunnel mode, and an NHRP network
ID. The configuration **ip nhrp nhs** identifies the NHRP next-hop server. The configuration **ip nhrp map 10.1.1.1 192.1.1.1** maps the hub's tunnel IP address to the hub's NBMA
IP address. If this mapping is *not* configured, the spokes won't be able to communicate
with the hub router. This mapping is needed because the spokes are configured with a
multipoint GRE tunnel.

```
On R2:

R2(config)# interface tunnel 1
R2(config-if)# ip address 10.1.1.2 255.255.255.0
R2(config-if)# tunnel source FastEthernet0/0
R2(config-if)# tunnel mode gre multipoint

R2(config-if)# ip nhrp network-id 222
R2(config-if)# ip nhrp nhs 10.1.1.1
R2(config-if)# ip nhrp map 10.1.1.1 192.1.1.1
```

Before we configure R3, let's enable **debug nhrp packet** and **debug nhrp cache** on both
R1 and R3 and verify the output:

```
On R3:

R3(config)# interface tunnel 1
R3(config-if)# ip address 10.1.1.3 255.255.255.0
R3(config-if)# tunnel source FastEthernet0/0
R3(config-if)# tunnel mode gre multipoint

R3(config-if)# ip nhrp network-id 333
R3(config-if)# ip nhrp nhs 10.1.1.1
R3(config-if)# ip nhrp map 10.1.1.1 192.1.1.1
```

The following debug output was produced once the **ip nhrp map 10.1.1.1 192.1.1.1** command was configured:

```
NHRP: Tunnel1: Cache add for target 10.1.1.1/32 next-hop 10.1.1.1
         192.1.1.1
```

The following debug output sends a registration request to the NHS, which happened because we configured the NHS using the **ip nhrp nhs 10.1.1.1** command:

```
NHRP: Send Registration Request via Tunnel1 vrf 0, packet size: 92
 src: 10.1.1.3, dst: 10.1.1.1
```

```
On R1:

R1 received the registration request and added the entry to its cache.

NHRP: Receive Registration Request via Tunnel1 vrf 0, packet size: 92
 (F) afn: IPv4(1), type: IP(800), hop: 255, ver: 1
     shtl: 4(NSAP), sstl: 0(NSAP)
     pktsz: 92 extoff: 52
 (M) flags: "unique nat ", reqid: 65537
     src NBMA: 192.1.2.2
     src protocol: 10.1.1.2, dst protocol: 10.1.1.1

NHRP: Tunnel1: Cache update for target 10.1.1.2/32 next-hop 10.1.1.2
         192.1.2.2
```

Let's configure R4:

```
On R4:

R4(config)# interface tunnel 1
R4(config-if)# ip address 10.1.1.4 255.255.255.0
R4(config-if)# tunnel source FastEthernet0/0
R4(config-if)# tunnel mode gre multipoint

R4(config-if)# ip nhrp network-id 444
R4(config-if)# ip nhrp nhs 10.1.1.1
R4(config-if)# ip nhrp map 10.1.1.1 192.1.1.1
```

Now we can verify and test the configuration. Let's start by looking at the existing NHRP cache:

```
R4# show ip nhrp

10.1.1.1/32 via 10.1.1.1
   Tunnel1 created 00:00:24, never expire
   Type: static, Flags: used
   NBMA address: 192.1.1.1
```

The following traceroute should go through the hub router to reach 10.1.1.2, because this is the initial communication between the two spokes. R4 needs to send a resolution request to the hub router, R1. R1 receives the message and redirects that request to the destination spoke, R2. Because R4 includes its tunnel-IP-address-to-NBMA-IP-address mapping in the resolution request message, R2 caches the mapping information for R4 when it receives that message. R2 establishes a tunnel to R4 directly. When R4 receives the resolution message from R2, it caches the tunnel-IP-address-to-NBMA-IP-address mapping for R2. From that point on, it goes directly to R4.

```
R4# traceroute 10.1.1.2

Type escape sequence to abort.
Tracing the route to 10.1.1.2

VRF info: (vrf in name/id, vrf out name/id)
  1 10.1.1.1 8 msec 0 msec 4 msec
  2 10.1.1.2 8 msec *  0 msec

R4# show ip nhrp

10.1.1.1/32 via 10.1.1.1
   Tunnel1 created 00:00:44, never expire
   Type: static, Flags: used
   NBMA address: 192.1.1.1
10.1.1.2/32 via 10.1.1.2
   Tunnel1 created 00:00:07, expire 01:59:52
   Type: dynamic, Flags: router used
   NBMA address: 192.1.2.2
10.1.1.4/32 via 10.1.1.4
   Tunnel1 created 00:00:07, expire 01:59:52
   Type: dynamic, Flags: router unique local
   NBMA address: 192.1.4.4
     (no-socket)
```

You can see that in DMVPN Phase 2, the spokes can communicate with and reach other spokes directly.

Erase the startup configuration of the routers and the switch and reload them before proceeding to the next lab.

Lab 5-5: DMVPN Phase 3

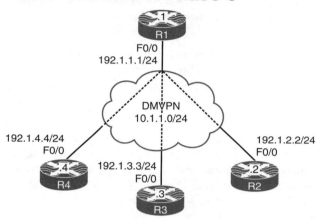

Figure 5-5 *DMVPN Phase 3*

In Figure 5.5, we see the topology we will use in this lab. Phase 3 is just like Phase 2 of mGRE tunnels on the hub and on the spokes of a DMVPN, but adding an NHRP redirect allows the data plane of spoke-to-spoke conversations to join the spokes directly without going through the hub, thus eliminating the requirement to conduct IP CEF (Cisco Express Forwarding) resolution.

NHRP Phase 3 allows the spokes to support *NHRP resolution requests*, meaning that the hub is not the only device that contains the NHRP database.

Operationally, the process follows these guidelines:

Step 1.   The spokes register their mappings with the Hub. This allows the hub and spokes to dynamically discover and establish adjacencies. Then the routing information is exchanged. However, the hub is not obliged to preserve the information. We can summarize routes, given that they are sent to the spokes. One can even send a route-default to the spokes, which improves network scalability.

Step 2.   The spokes receive routing information and fill their CEF tables. In this phase of DMVPN there should be no CEF invalid entries; they are all "complete." They all point to the IP of the hub NBMA, so that all the first packets are CEF switches to the hub, and the invalid CEF no longer triggers the NHRP resolution.

Henceforth, the spoke-to-spoke communications are based on the packet **NHRP Redirect** message.

Step 3.   A tunnel mGRE is configured for **NHRP Redirect** messages (the first major order for Phase 3), which is an operation similar to the **ICMP redirect IP**. When a router receives an incoming IP packet via the mGRE tunnel, which will be returning on the same interface, it sends a source **Redirect NHRP**. This message tells the source that the path is not optimal, and it should find a better way via the **NHRP Resolution**. This first package is still routed through the GDI.

Step 4.   Now the spoke receives the **NHRP Redirect**. The router is thus sending an **NHRP Request** to the same destination IP, which is not the NHS (although the package always goes through there). The **NHRP Request** travels on all spokes until it finds the target. This is the normal operation of **NHRP Request** forwarding, which goes hop by hop.

Step 5.   Now the spoke (not the NHS) has the resolution. Based on the IP source present in the payload package, it finds the corresponding spoke in its routing table. It uses the source NBMA IP router and returns an NHRP reply directly (without re-crossing the hub). The reply arrives on the source router, which then learns the IP NBMA its destination. Now, in addition to rewriting the NHRP table, the router rewrites the CEF entry.

The rewriting of the CEF is called **NHRP Shortcut**. Instead of having a CEF adjacency that triggers the **NHRP Request**, the CEF entry is rewritten when the **NHRP Response** is received. Simple.

Traffic is CEF switched at all times, and NHRP responses update the table of router CEF entries.

In summation:

- NHRP is needed for spoke registration to the hub.

- NHRP is required for spoke-to-spoke resolution.

- When traffic goes from a spoke to the hub, and the hub sees that the destination is reachable via another spoke, it sends an **NHRP Redirect**, which causes the spoke to install routes to each other.

- A spoke-to-spoke tunnel is triggered by the hub via **NHRP Redirect**.

- **NHRP Resolution** is done per true destination and not per next hop, as in Phase 2.

Unlike Phase 2, Phase 3 has far less restrictive behavior:

- Summarization is allowed on the hub.

- Default routing is allowed on the hub.

- Next-hop values on the spokes are always modified.

We will explore these and other aspects of Phase 3 DMVPNs in the following tasks.

Task 1

SW1 represents the Internet. Configure a static default route on each router pointing to the appropriate interface on SW1. If this configuration is performed correctly, these routers should be able to ping and have reachability to the F0/0 interfaces of all routers in this topology. The switch interface to which the routers are connected should have ".10" in the host portion of the IP address for that subnet.

Let's configure SW1's interfaces for these routers. Because in this lab, SW1 represents the Internet, the IP addresses in the following configuration should be set as the default gateway on the routers:

```
On SW1:

SW1(config)# interface range FastEthernet0/1-4
SW1(config-if-range)# no switchport

SW1(config)# interface FastEthernet0/1
SW1(config-if)# ip address 192.1.1.10 255.255.255.0
SW1(config-if)# no shutdown

SW1(config)# interface FastEthernet0/2
SW1(config-if)# ip address 192.1.2.10 255.255.255.0
SW1(config-if)# no shutdown

SW1(config)# interface FastEthernet0/3
SW1(config-if)# ip address 192.1.3.10 255.255.255.0
SW1(config-if)# no shutdown

SW1(config)# interface FastEthernet0/4
SW1(config-if)# ip address 192.1.4.10 255.255.255.0
SW1(config-if)# no shutdown
```

Let's *not* forget to enable **ip routing**; otherwise, the switch will not be able to route from one subnet to another:

```
SW1(config)# ip routing
```

Let's configure the routers:

```
On R1:

R1(config)# interface FastEthernet0/0
R1(config-if)# ip address 192.1.1.1 255.255.255.0
R1(config-if)# no shutdown

R1(config)# ip route 0.0.0.0 0.0.0.0 192.1.1.10
```

```
On R2:

R2(config)# interface FastEthernet0/0
R2(config-if)# ip address 192.1.2.2 255.255.255.0
R2(config-if)# no shutdown

R2(config)# ip route 0.0.0.0 0.0.0.0 192.1.2.10
```

```
On R3:

R3(config)# interface FastEthernet0/0
R3(config-if)# ip address 192.1.3.3 255.255.255.0
R3(config-if)# no shutdown

R3(config)# ip route 0.0.0.0 0.0.0.0 192.1.3.10
```

```
On R4:

R4(config)# interface FastEthernet0/0
R4(config-if)# ip address 192.1.4.4 255.255.255.0
R4(config-if)# no shutdown

R4(config)# ip route 0.0.0.0 0.0.0.0 192.1.4.10
```

Now let's verify the configuration:

```
On R1:

R1# ping 192.1.2.2

Type escape sequence to abort.
Sending 5, 100-byte ICMP Echos to 192.1.2.2, timeout is 2 seconds:
!!!!!
Success rate is 100 percent (5/5), round-trip min/avg/max = 1/2/4 ms

R1# ping 192.1.3.3

Type escape sequence to abort.
Sending 5, 100-byte ICMP Echos to 192.1.3.3, timeout is 2 seconds:
!!!!!
Success rate is 100 percent (5/5), round-trip min/avg/max = 1/2/4 ms
```

```
R1# ping 192.1.4.4

Type escape sequence to abort.
Sending 5, 100-byte ICMP Echos to 192.1.4.4, timeout is 2 seconds:
!!!!!
Success rate is 100 percent (5/5), round-trip min/avg/max = 1/2/4 ms
```

```
On R2:

R2# ping 192.1.1.1

Type escape sequence to abort.
Sending 5, 100-byte ICMP Echos to 192.1.1.1, timeout is 2 seconds:
!!!!!
Success rate is 100 percent (5/5), round-trip min/avg/max = 1/2/4 ms

R2# ping 192.1.3.3

Type escape sequence to abort.
Sending 5, 100-byte ICMP Echos to 192.1.3.3, timeout is 2 seconds:
!!!!!
Success rate is 100 percent (5/5), round-trip min/avg/max = 1/2/4 ms

R2# ping 192.1.4.4

Type escape sequence to abort.
Sending 5, 100-byte ICMP Echos to 192.1.4.4, timeout is 2 seconds:
!!!!!
Success rate is 100 percent (5/5), round-trip min/avg/max = 1/1/4 ms
```

Task 2

Configure DMVPN Phase 3 such that R1 is the hub and R2, R3, and R4 are the spokes. You should use 10.1.1.x/24, where x is the router number. If this configuration is performed correctly, these routers should have reachability to all tunnel endpoints. You should *not* configure static mappings on the hub router to accomplish this task.

Since the task refers to DMVPN Phase 3, the hub and all the spokes are configured with multipoint GRE tunnels, just like in Phase 2. In addition to mGRE being configured on all routers, the hub router is configured with the **ip nhrp redirect** command and the spokes are configured with the **ip nhrp shortcut** command. In this phase, the spokes have reachability to the other spokes directly.

Let's configure the hub:

```
On R1:


R1(config)# interface tunnel 1
R1(config-if)# ip address 10.1.1.1 255.255.255.0
R1(config-if)# tunnel source 192.1.1.1
R1(config-if)# tunnel mode gre multipoint
R1(config-if)# ip nhrp network-id 111
R1(config-if)# ip nhrp redirect
```

Let's configure the spoke routers:

```
On R2:


R2(config)# interface tunnel 1
R2(config-if)# ip address 10.1.1.2 255.255.255.0
R2(config-if)# tunnel source FastEthernet0/0
R2(config-if)# tunnel mode gre multipoint
R2(config-if)# ip nhrp network-id 222
R2(config-if)# ip nhrp nhs 10.1.1.1
R2(config-if)# ip nhrp map 10.1.1.1 192.1.1.1
R2(config-if)# ip nhrp shortcut
```

```
On R3:


R3(config)# interface tunnel 1
R3(config-if)# ip address 10.1.1.3 255.255.255.0
R3(config-if)# tunnel source FastEthernet0/0
R3(config-if)# tunnel mode gre multipoint
R3(config-if)# ip nhrp network-id 333
R3(config-if)# ip nhrp nhs 10.1.1.1
R3(config-if)# ip nhrp map 10.1.1.1 192.1.1.1
R3(config-if)# ip nhrp shortcut
```

```
On R4:


R4(config)# interface tunnel 1
R4(config-if)# ip address 10.1.1.4 255.255.255.0
R4(config-if)# tunnel source FastEthernet0/0
R4(config-if)# tunnel mode gre multipoint
R4(config-if)# ip nhrp network-id 444
R4(config-if)# ip nhrp nhs 10.1.1.1
R4(config-if)# ip nhrp map 10.1.1.1 192.1.1.1
R4(config-if)# ip nhrp shortcut
```

Now we need to verify and test the configuration. First, let's see the existing NHRP cache:

```
R4# show ip nhrp

10.1.1.1/32 via 10.1.1.1
    Tunnel1 created 00:00:24, never expire
    Type: static, Flags: used
    NBMA address: 192.1.1.1
```

One of the major benefits of DMVPN Phase 3 is that the hub router, R1, can inject a default route and suppress the more specific routes that it receives from the spokes.

In this case, the spoke routers will only have a single default route pointing to the hub router, R1. But the spoke routers will be able to access other spoke routers or the network(s) that the other spoke routers are advertising directly without going through the hub router. How is this possible?

Let's configure the following loopback interfaces on the spoke routers and advertise them in EIGRP AS 100 and then configure the hub router to inject a default route using the **ip summary-address** command so that we can test and verify.

Let's configure the loopback interfaces on the routers based on the following chart:

```
On R2:
Lo0 - 2.2.0.2/24
Lo1 - 2.2.1.2/24
Lo2 - 2.2.2.2/24
Lo3 - 2.2.3.2/24
```

```
On R3:
Lo0 - 3.3.0.3/24
Lo1 - 3.3.1.3/24
Lo2 - 3.3.2.3/24
Lo3 - 3.3.3.3/24
```

```
On R4:
Lo0 - 4.4.0.4/24
Lo1 - 4.4.1.4/24
Lo2 - 4.4.2.4/24
Lo3 - 4.4.3.4/24
```

```
On R2:

R2(config)# interface loopback0
R2(config-if)# ip address 2.2.0.2 255.255.255.0

R2(config)# interface loopback1
R2(config-if)# ip address 2.2.1.2 255.255.255.0

R2(config)# interface loopback2
R2(config-if)# ip address 2.2.2.2 255.255.255.0

R2(config)# interface loopback3
R2(config-if)# ip address 2.2.3.2 255.255.255.0
```

```
On R3:

R3(config)# interface loopback0
R3(config-if)# ip address 3.3.0.3 255.255.255.0

R3(config)# interface loopback1
R3(config-if)# ip address 3.3.1.3 255.255.255.0

R3(config)# interface loopback2
R3(config-if)# ip address 3.3.2.3 255.255.255.0

R3(config)# interface loopback3
R3(config-if)# ip address 3.3.3.3 255.255.255.0
```

```
On R4:

R4(config)# interface loopback0
R4(config-if)# ip address 4.4.0.4 255.255.255.0

R4(config)# interface loopback1
R4(config-if)# ip address 4.4.1.4 255.255.255.0

R4(config)# interface loopback2
R4(config-if)# ip address 4.4.2.4 255.255.255.0

R4(config)# interface loopback3
R4(config-if)# ip address 4.4.3.4 255.255.255.0
```

Let's configure EIGRP on all routers. Because IGPs use multicast to form an adjacency, before any IGP is configured, we need to provide multicast capability to all routers:

```
On R1:

R1(config)# interface tunnel 1
R1(config-if)# ip nhrp map multicast dynamic
```

The preceding command provides multicast capability to all the entries in the NHRP table that are learned dynamically. Let's see the entries in the NHRP cache:

```
R1# show ip nhrp

10.1.1.2/32 via 10.1.1.2
    Tunnel1 created 00:34:16, expire 01:32:53
    Type: dynamic, Flags: unique registered
    NBMA address: 192.1.2.2
10.1.1.3/32 via 10.1.1.3
    Tunnel1 created 00:33:38, expire 01:26:21
    Type: dynamic, Flags: unique registered
    NBMA address: 192.1.3.3
10.1.1.4/32 via 10.1.1.4
    Tunnel1 created 00:32:53, expire 01:27:06
    Type: dynamic, Flags: unique registered
    NBMA address: 192.1.4.4
```

The output of the preceding **show** command reveals all the entries/spokes that are learned dynamically (these are R2, R3, and R4).

```
R1(config)# router eigrp 100
R1(config-router)# network 10.1.1.1 0.0.0.0
```

Let's configure the spokes:

```
On R2, R3, and R4:

Rx(config)# interface tunnel 1
Rx(config-if)# ip nhrp map multicast 192.1.1.1
```

The preceding command provides multicast capability for the hub router, R1.

```
On R2:

R2(config)# router eigrp 100
R2(config-router)# network 10.1.1.2 0.0.0.0
R2(config-router)# network 2.2.0.2 0.0.0.0
R2(config-router)# network 2.2.1.2 0.0.0.0
R2(config-router)# network 2.2.2.2 0.0.0.0
R2(config-router)# network 2.2.3.2 0.0.0.0
```

You should see the following console message:

```
%DUAL-5-NBRCHANGE: EIGRP-IPv4 100: Neighbor 10.1.1.1 (Tunnel1) is up: new adjacency
```

Note   If the adjacency is not formed, you may need the spoke routers to re-register their tunnel-IP-to-NBMA-IP mapping with the hub router. One way to achieve this is to configure the **ip nhrp registration timeout 5** command. This command sends a registration request to the hub router every 5 seconds:

```
On R3:

R3(config)# router eigrp 100
R3(config-router)# network 10.1.1.3 0.0.0.0
R3(config-router)# network 3.3.0.3 0.0.0.0
R3(config-router)# network 3.3.1.3 0.0.0.0
R3(config-router)# network 3.3.2.3 0.0.0.0
R3(config-router)# network 3.3.3.3 0.0.0.0
```

You should see the following console message:

```
%DUAL-5-NBRCHANGE: EIGRP-IPv4 100: Neighbor 10.1.1.1 (Tunnel1) is up: new adjacency
```

```
On R4:

R4(config)# router eigrp 100
R4(config-router)# network 10.1.1.4 0.0.0.0
R4(config-router)# network 4.4.0.4 0.0.0.0
R4(config-router)# network 4.4.1.4 0.0.0.0
R4(config-router)# network 4.4.2.4 0.0.0.0
R4(config-router)# network 4.4.3.4 0.0.0.0
```

You should see the following console message:

```
%DUAL-5-NBRCHANGE: EIGRP-IPv4 100: Neighbor 10.1.1.1 (Tunnel1) is up: new adjacency
```

Let's verify the configuration:

```
On R1:


R1# show ip route eigrp | begin Gate
Gateway of last resort is 192.1.1.10 to network 0.0.0.0

      2.0.0.0/24 is subnetted, 4 subnets
D        2.2.0.0 [90/27008000] via 10.1.1.2, 00:06:00, Tunnel1
D        2.2.1.0 [90/27008000] via 10.1.1.2, 00:06:00, Tunnel1
D        2.2.2.0 [90/27008000] via 10.1.1.2, 00:06:00, Tunnel1
D        2.2.3.0 [90/27008000] via 10.1.1.2, 00:06:00, Tunnel1
      3.0.0.0/24 is subnetted, 4 subnets
D        3.3.0.0 [90/27008000] via 10.1.1.3, 00:02:20, Tunnel1
D        3.3.1.0 [90/27008000] via 10.1.1.3, 00:02:16, Tunnel1
D        3.3.2.0 [90/27008000] via 10.1.1.3, 00:02:13, Tunnel1
D        3.3.3.0 [90/27008000] via 10.1.1.3, 00:02:10, Tunnel1
      4.0.0.0/24 is subnetted, 4 subnets
D        4.4.0.0 [90/27008000] via 10.1.1.4, 00:01:03, Tunnel1
D        4.4.1.0 [90/27008000] via 10.1.1.4, 00:01:00, Tunnel1
D        4.4.2.0 [90/27008000] via 10.1.1.4, 00:00:57, Tunnel1
D        4.4.3.0 [90/27008000] via 10.1.1.4, 00:00:54, Tunnel1
```

For the spoke routers to see the routes from the other spokes, EIGRP split-horizon needs to be disabled:

```
On R1:


R1(config)# interface tunnel 1
R1(config-if)# no ip split-horizon eigrp 100
```

Let's verify the configuration:

```
On R2:


R2# show ip route eigrp | begin Gate
Gateway of last resort is 192.1.2.10 to network 0.0.0.0

      3.0.0.0/24 is subnetted, 4 subnets
D        3.3.0.0 [90/28288000] via 10.1.1.1, 00:00:36, Tunnel1
```

```
D          3.3.1.0 [90/28288000] via 10.1.1.1, 00:00:36, Tunnel1
D          3.3.2.0 [90/28288000] via 10.1.1.1, 00:00:36, Tunnel1
D          3.3.3.0 [90/28288000] via 10.1.1.1, 00:00:36, Tunnel1
       4.0.0.0/24 is subnetted, 4 subnets
D          4.4.0.0 [90/28288000] via 10.1.1.1, 00:00:36, Tunnel1
D          4.4.1.0 [90/28288000] via 10.1.1.1, 00:00:36, Tunnel1
D          4.4.2.0 [90/28288000] via 10.1.1.1, 00:00:36, Tunnel1
D          4.4.3.0 [90/28288000] via 10.1.1.1, 00:00:36, Tunnel1
```

Let's configure **ip summary-address** on the hub router to suppress all the specific routes from the other spokes and inject a default route:

```
On R1:

R1(config)# interface tunnel 1
R1(config-if)# ip summary-address eigrp 100 0.0.0.0 0.0.0.0
```

Before the configuration is verified, the static default routes that are configured on the spoke routers must be removed, and specific static routes for the NBMA IP address of the spokes must be configured. Let's see the reason for this:

```
On R2:

R2# show ip route eigrp | begin Gate
Gateway of last resort is 192.1.2.10 to network 0.0.0.0
```

Note   We cannot see the default route configured on the hub router, so let's configure the spoke routers with specific static routes:

```
On R2:

R2(config)# ip route 192.1.1.1 255.255.255.255 192.1.2.10
R2(config)# ip route 192.1.3.3 255.255.255.255 192.1.2.10
R2(config)# ip route 192.1.4.4 255.255.255.255 192.1.2.10
R2(config)# no ip route 0.0.0.0 0.0.0.0
```

```
On R3:

R3(config)# ip route 192.1.1.1 255.255.255.255 192.1.3.10
R3(config)# ip route 192.1.2.2 255.255.255.255 192.1.3.10
R3(config)# ip route 192.1.4.4 255.255.255.255 192.1.3.10
R3(config)# no ip route 0.0.0.0 0.0.0.0
```

```
On R4:

R4(config)# ip route 192.1.1.1 255.255.255.255 192.1.4.10
R4(config)# ip route 192.1.2.2 255.255.255.255 192.1.4.10
R4(config)# ip route 192.1.3.3 255.255.255.255 192.1.4.10
R4(config)# no ip route 0.0.0.0 0.0.0.0
```

Now let's verify the configuration:

```
On R2:

R2# show ip route eigrp | begin Gate
Gateway of last resort is 10.1.1.1 to network 0.0.0.0

D*    0.0.0.0/0 [90/28160000] via 10.1.1.1, 00:02:04, Tunnel1
```

Let's test DMVPN Phase 3 by using **traceroute 3.3.3.3** on R2:

```
On R2:

R2# show adjacency tunnel 1 detail

Protocol Interfac        Address
IP       Tunnel1         10.1.1.1(11)
                         0 packets, 0 bytes
                         epoch 0
                         sourced in sev-epoch 0
                         Encap length 24
                         4500000000000000FF2F38C9C0010202
                         C001010100000800
                         Tun endpt
                         Next chain element:
                         IP adj out of FastEthernet0/0, addr 192.1.2.10
```

You can see a single rewrite for the hub router. The "c0010101" part is the NBMA IP address of the hub router.

Note: c0 in decimal is 192, followed by 010101, or 192.1.1.1.

```
R2# traceroute 3.3.3.3 numeric

Type escape sequence to abort.
Tracing the route to 3.3.3.3
VRF info: (vrf in name/id, vrf out name/id)
  1 10.1.1.1 4 msec 4 msec 4 msec
  2 10.1.1.3 4 msec *  0 msec
```

Let's verify the configuration:

```
R2# show adjacency tunnel 1 detail

Protocol Interface          Address
IP       Tunnel1            10.1.1.1(11)
                            0 packets, 0 bytes
                            epoch 0
                            sourced in sev-epoch 0
                            Encap length 24
                            4500000000000000FF2F38C9C0010202
                            C001010100000800
                            Tun endpt
                            Next chain element:
                            IP adj out of FastEthernet0/0, addr 192.1.2.10
IP       Tunnel1            10.1.1.3(9)
                            0 packets, 0 bytes
                            epoch 0
                            sourced in sev-epoch 0
                            Encap length 24
                            4500000000000000FF2F36C7C0010202
                            C001030300000800
                            Tun endpt
                            Next chain element:
                            IP adj out of FastEthernet0/0, addr 192.1.2.10
```

Now that the second rewrite is in the CEF, the traceroutes should go directly to the destination spoke. Let's verify:

```
R2# traceroute 3.3.3.3 numeric

Type escape sequence to abort.
Tracing the route to 3.3.3.3
VRF info: (vrf in name/id, vrf out name/id)
  1 10.1.1.3 4 msec *  0 msec
```

How did this work?

DMVPN Phase 3 is similar to Phase 2 in that it provides direct spoke-to-spoke tunnels. However, the underlying mechanism is significantly different. The change came with the requirement to allow spoke routers to receive only a summarized set of routes— possibly just a default route—from the hub router, and yet allow direct spoke-to-spoke communication.

The following explains the process in Phase 3:

■ The data packet is forwarded from the originating spoke to the hub based on the routing table of the originating spoke. No NHRP messaging is triggered by the originating spoke at this point, because it is not certain whether the destination is located in a DMVPN or in a normal network.

■ The hub router receives the data packet from the originating spoke and forwards it to the destination spoke according to its routing table. The hub also realizes that the packet is being forwarded within the same DMVPN because the incoming and outgoing interface have the same **ip nhrp network-id** configured. The hub router thus realizes that it is a transit router for the data packets between the spokes.

■ The hub router sends an NHRP Traffic Indication message back to the originating spoke router, telling it that for the original packet whose header is carried in the Traffic Indication body, there might be a more direct way to the destination rather than through the hub.

■ Upon receiving the NHRP Traffic Indication message, the originating spoke triggers an NHRP Resolution Request to map the known destination IP address of the *original packet* to the unknown NBMA address of the destination spoke. As in Phase 2, the spoke router includes its tunnel-IP-to-NBMA-IP mapping in the Resolution Request.

■ The hub router receives the NHRP Resolution Request. Based on the destination address of the original packet indicated in the Resolution Request, it looks up the matching destination network in its routing table, finds the next hop, and forwards the Resolution Request to the next hop.

- The destination spoke receives the NHRP Resolution Request. Using its contents, it learns about the originating spoke's tunnel IP and NBMA IP and adds this mapping into its NHRP table. The destination spoke then creates an NHRP Resolution Reply packet with its own tunnel IP and NBMA IP. In addition, because the Resolution Request asked about the original packet's destination address rather than the tunnel IP address of the destination spoke, the destination spoke will also insert the original packet's destination address and the netmask of the matching destination network from its routing table into its Resolution Reply. This will allow the originating spoke to compute the address of the destination network for which the original packet is intended.

- If IPSec is also configured, before sending the Resolution Reply to the originating spoke, the destination spoke triggers IPSec to create a secured spoke-to-spoke tunnel.

- After the originating spoke receives the Resolution Reply, it will add the mapping for the destination spoke's tunnel IP and NBMA IP into its NHRP table. In addition, using the original packet's destination address and the netmask of the matching network on the destination spoke carried in the Resolution Reply, the originating spoke will compute the address of the destination network and insert this network into its routing table, with the next-hop address pointing to the destination spoke's tunnel IP. Because this added network has a longer prefix than the default route, it will be matched first for every packet going to this destination network. This will cause subsequent packets to be sent to the destination spoke directly, rather than being routed over the hub.

There are two new commands related to DMVPN Phase 3:

- **ip nhrp redirect**: This command allows a hub router to send out NHRP Traffic Indication messages.

- **ip nhrp shortcut**: This command allows a spoke router to accept incoming NHRP Traffic Indication messages, and in turn send an NHRP Resolution Request message for the original packet's destination address and then, after receiving an NHRP Resolution Reply, install the destination network discovered through the Resolution Reply into the routing table with the responding spoke router as a next hop.

Erase the startup configuration of the routers and the switch and reload them before proceeding to the next lab.

Chapter 6

IP Prefix-List

Lab 6-1: Configuring Prefix Lists

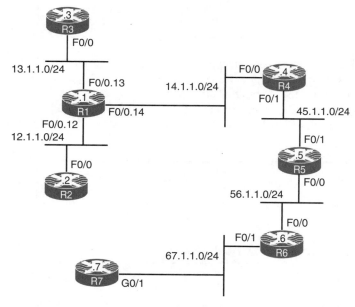

Figure 6-1 *Configuring Prefix Lists*

Figure 6-1 illustrates the topology that will be used in the following task.

Task 1

Configure R1 to filter 192.1.1.32/27 using a prefix list.

Here are some important facts about prefix lists:

- They were introduced in IOS 12.0(3)T.

- They are configured to match on the actual prefix and the prefix length.

- They are parsed and processed from the top to bottom—or to be more accurate, from the lowest sequence number to the highest sequence number.

- Because sequence numbers are used, entries can be added or removed at any time.

- They have an implicit **deny all** statement at the end, just like access lists.

- Like access lists, they can be used to identify, permit, or filter prefixes.

You can see 192.1.1.1/32 and 192.1.1.32/27 in the output of the following **show** command. This task is asking you to filter 192.1.1.32/27.

```
On R1:

R1# show ip route | include 192.1.1.
     192.1.1.0/24 is variably subnetted, 2 subnets, 2 masks
D        192.1.1.1/32 [90/156160] via 12.1.1.2, 00:01:09, FastEthernet0/0.12
D        192.1.1.32/27 [90/156160] via 12.1.1.2, 00:07:31, FastEthernet0/0.12
```

The following **prefix-list**, called NET, has two statements: The first statement denies network 192.1.1.32 with a prefix length of /27, or 255.255.255.224. The second statement permits everything else, as you can see the le option, which means the less-than or equal option, is used. The le option is used to create an entry that matches any prefix (0.0.0.0) with a prefix length between 0 and 32 bits inclusively; this matches all possible IPv4 prefixes.

```
On R1:
R1(config)# ip prefix-list NET deny 192.1.1.32/27
R1(config)# ip prefix-list NET permit 0.0.0.0/0 le 32

R1(config)# router eigrp 1
R1(config-router)# distribute-list prefix NET in fastethernet0/0.12
```

Let's verify the configuration:

```
On R1:

R1# show ip route | include 192.1.1.
     192.1.1.0/32 is subnetted, 1 subnets
D        192.1.1.1 [90/156160] via 12.1.1.2, 00:02:29, FastEthernet0/0.12
As we can see network 192.1.1.32/27 is filtered.
```

As you can see, network 192.1.1.32/27 is filtered.

When you're configuring prefix lists, the prefix and the prefix length must be configured to match the exact prefix and prefix length you are trying to deny, permit, or identify.

Task 2

Configure R1 such that it only allows Class A networks that are *not* subnetted, plus all Class B and C networks.

Before we configure the prefix list, let's verify the routing table of R1:

```
On R1:

R1# show ip route eigrp | begin Gate
Gateway of last resort is not set

D      1.0.0.0/8 [90/156160] via 13.1.1.3, 00:23:35, FastEthernet0/0.13
       6.0.0.0/8 is variably subnetted, 5 subnets, 5 masks
D         6.1.1.0/24 [90/161280] via 14.1.1.4, 00:23:33, FastEthernet0/0.14
D         6.1.2.128/25 [90/161280] via 14.1.1.4, 00:23:33, FastEthernet0/0.14
D         6.1.3.192/26 [90/161280] via 14.1.1.4, 00:23:33, FastEthernet0/0.14
D         6.1.4.224/27 [90/161280] via 14.1.1.4, 00:23:33, FastEthernet0/0.14
D         6.1.5.240/28 [90/161280] via 14.1.1.4, 00:23:33, FastEthernet0/0.14
       10.0.0.0/8 is variably subnetted, 3 subnets, 3 masks
D         10.1.1.0/24 [90/156160] via 13.1.1.3, 00:23:35, FastEthernet0/0.13
11.0.0.0/16 is subnetted, 1 subnets
D         11.1.0.0 [90/156160] via 13.1.1.3, 00:23:35, FastEthernet0/0.13
       22.0.0.0/24 is subnetted, 1 subnets
D         22.1.2.0 [90/156160] via 13.1.1.3, 00:23:35, FastEthernet0/0.13
D      29.0.0.0/8 [90/156160] via 13.1.1.3, 00:23:35, FastEthernet0/0.13
       33.0.0.0/24 is subnetted, 1 subnets
D         33.0.0.0 [90/156160] via 13.1.1.3, 00:23:35, FastEthernet0/0.13
D      44.0.0.0/8 [90/156160] via 13.1.1.3, 00:23:35, FastEthernet0/0.13
       45.0.0.0/24 is subnetted, 1 subnets
D         45.1.1.0 [90/30720] via 14.1.1.4, 00:23:33, FastEthernet0/0.14
       56.0.0.0/24 is subnetted, 1 subnets
D         56.1.1.0 [90/33280] via 14.1.1.4, 00:23:33, FastEthernet0/0.14
       67.0.0.0/24 is subnetted, 1 subnets
D         67.1.1.0 [90/35840] via 14.1.1.4, 00:23:33, FastEthernet0/0.14
D      99.0.0.0/8 [90/158720] via 14.1.1.4, 00:23:33, FastEthernet0/0.14
       146.1.0.0/16 is variably subnetted, 5 subnets, 5 masks
D         146.1.1.0/24 [90/161280] via 14.1.1.4, 00:23:33, FastEthernet0/0.14
D         146.1.2.128/25 [90/161280] via 14.1.1.4, 00:23:33, FastEthernet0/0.14
D         146.1.3.192/26 [90/161280] via 14.1.1.4, 00:23:33, FastEthernet0/0.14
```

```
D         146.1.4.224/27 [90/161280] via 14.1.1.4, 00:23:33, FastEthernet0/0.14
D         146.1.5.240/28 [90/161280] via 14.1.1.4, 00:23:33, FastEthernet0/0.14
     172.16.0.0/24 is subnetted, 4 subnets
D        172.16.0.0 [90/156160] via 12.1.1.2, 00:23:32, FastEthernet0/0.12
D        172.16.1.0 [90/156160] via 12.1.1.2, 00:23:32, FastEthernet0/0.12
D        172.16.2.0 [90/156160] via 12.1.1.2, 00:23:32, FastEthernet0/0.12
D        172.16.3.0 [90/156160] via 12.1.1.2, 00:23:32, FastEthernet0/0.12
D     185.1.0.0/16 [90/158720] via 14.1.1.4, 00:23:33, FastEthernet0/0.14
     186.1.0.0/17 is subnetted, 1 subnets
D        186.1.128.0 [90/158720] via 14.1.1.4, 00:23:33, FastEthernet0/0.14
     189.1.0.0/24 is subnetted, 1 subnets
D        189.1.1.0 [90/158720] via 14.1.1.4, 00:23:33, FastEthernet0/0.14
     192.1.1.0/32 is subnetted, 1 subnets
D        192.1.1.1 [90/156160] via 12.1.1.2, 00:23:32, FastEthernet0/0.12
D     198.1.1.0/24 [90/156160] via 14.1.1.4, 00:23:33, FastEthernet0/0.14
D     199.1.1.0/24 [90/156160] via 14.1.1.4, 00:23:33, FastEthernet0/0.14
D     200.1.1.0/24 [90/156160] via 14.1.1.4, 00:23:33, FastEthernet0/0.14
     200.1.4.0/29 is subnetted, 1 subnets
D        200.1.4.8 [90/156160] via 14.1.1.4, 00:23:33, FastEthernet0/0.14
     200.1.5.0/30 is subnetted, 1 subnets
D        200.1.5.4 [90/156160] via 14.1.1.4, 00:23:33, FastEthernet0/0.14
D     201.1.3.0/24 [90/156160] via 13.1.1.3, 00:23:35, FastEthernet0/0.13
     205.1.1.0/28 is subnetted, 1 subnets
D        205.1.1.240 [90/158720] via 14.1.1.4, 00:23:33, FastEthernet0/0.14
     206.1.1.0/30 is subnetted, 1 subnets
D        206.1.1.248 [90/158720] via 14.1.1.4, 00:23:33, FastEthernet0/0.14
     207.1.1.0/26 is subnetted, 1 subnets
D        207.1.1.192 [90/158720] via 14.1.1.4, 00:23:33, FastEthernet0/0.14
     208.1.1.0/25 is subnetted, 1 subnets
D        208.1.1.128 [90/158720] via 14.1.1.4, 00:23:33, FastEthernet0/0.14
     211.4.4.0/27 is subnetted, 1 subnets
D        211.4.4.32 [90/158720] via 14.1.1.4, 00:23:33, FastEthernet0/0.14
D     223.1.1.0/24 [90/156160] via 14.1.1.4, 00:23:33, FastEthernet0/0.14
```

The preceding highlighted networks are *not* subnetted; therefore, they should be allowed in. These are 1.0.0.0/8, 29.0.0.0/8, 44.0.0.0/8 through F0/0.13, and 99.0.0.0/8 through F0/0.14.

The rest of the Class A networks should be filtered; these are subsets of networks 6.0.0.0, 10.0.0.0, 11.0.0.0, 22.0.0.0, 45.0.0.0, 56.0.0.0, and 67.0.0.0.

Figure 6-2 shows how Class A networks are identified. The letter *N* identifies the network bits, and the letter *H* identifies the host bits.

1st Octet		2nd Octet		3rd Octet		4th Octet
0 N N N N N N N	•	H H H H H H H H	•	H H H H H H H H	•	H H H H H H H H

Figure 6-2   *Class A Native Mask*

Class A networks are identified based on the following:

■ The first bit is set to 0; therefore, there are seven network bits followed by 24 host bits.

■ The initial octet is 0–127.

■ There are 126 Class A networks (0 and 127 are reserved).

■ There are 16,777,214 hosts on each Class A network.

Note   The most significant bit of the first octet is set to a binary 0, and the rest of the bits in the first octet can be zeros or ones. If the most significant bit of the first octet is 0, it must be a Class A network. The **prefix-list** matches on the first bit by using /1 in the prefix length. The ge option used in the following configuration denies any network with a prefix length of /9 or greater.

The following **prefix-list** denies all Class A networks that have a prefix length of /9 or greater; the only way a Class A network will have a prefix length of /9 or greater is when it is subnetted.

```
R1(config)# ip prefix-list Class-A deny 0.0.0.0/1 ge 9
R1(config)# ip prefix-list Class-A permit 0.0.0.0/1 le 32

R1(config)# router eigrp 1
R1(config-router)# distribute-list prefix Class-A in fastethernet0/0.13
R1(config-router)# distribute-list prefix Class-A in fastethernet0/0.14

R1# show ip route eigrp | begin Gate
Gateway of last resort is not set

D     1.0.0.0/8 [90/156160] via 13.1.1.3, 00:06:33, FastEthernet0/0.13
D     29.0.0.0/8 [90/156160] via 13.1.1.3, 00:06:33, FastEthernet0/0.13
D     44.0.0.0/8 [90/156160] via 13.1.1.3, 00:06:33, FastEthernet0/0.13
D     99.0.0.0/8 [90/158720] via 14.1.1.4, 00:06:33, FastEthernet0/0.14
      146.1.0.0/16 is variably subnetted, 5 subnets, 5 masks
D        146.1.1.0/24 [90/161280] via 14.1.1.4, 00:06:33, FastEthernet0/0.14
D        146.1.2.128/25 [90/161280] via 14.1.1.4, 00:06:33, FastEthernet0/0.14
D        146.1.3.192/26 [90/161280] via 14.1.1.4, 00:06:33, FastEthernet0/0.14
D        146.1.4.224/27 [90/161280] via 14.1.1.4, 00:06:33, FastEthernet0/0.14
```

```
D        146.1.5.240/28 [90/161280] via 14.1.1.4, 00:06:33, FastEthernet0/0.14
     172.16.0.0/24 is subnetted, 4 subnets
D        172.16.0.0 [90/156160] via 12.1.1.2, 00:55:01, FastEthernet0/0.12
D        172.16.1.0 [90/156160] via 12.1.1.2, 00:55:01, FastEthernet0/0.12
D        172.16.2.0 [90/156160] via 12.1.1.2, 00:55:01, FastEthernet0/0.12
D        172.16.3.0 [90/156160] via 12.1.1.2, 00:55:01, FastEthernet0/0.12
D     185.1.0.0/16 [90/158720] via 14.1.1.4, 00:06:33, FastEthernet0/0.14
     186.1.0.0/17 is subnetted, 1 subnets
D        186.1.128.0 [90/158720] via 14.1.1.4, 00:06:33, FastEthernet0/0.14
     189.1.0.0/24 is subnetted, 1 subnets
D        189.1.1.0 [90/158720] via 14.1.1.4, 00:06:33, FastEthernet0/0.14
     192.1.1.0/32 is subnetted, 1 subnets

D        192.1.1.1 [90/156160] via 12.1.1.2, 00:55:01, FastEthernet0/0.12
D     198.1.1.0/24 [90/156160] via 14.1.1.4, 00:06:33, FastEthernet0/0.14
D     199.1.1.0/24 [90/156160] via 14.1.1.4, 00:06:33, FastEthernet0/0.14
D     200.1.1.0/24 [90/156160] via 14.1.1.4, 00:06:33, FastEthernet0/0.14
     200.1.4.0/29 is subnetted, 1 subnets
D        200.1.4.8 [90/156160] via 14.1.1.4, 00:06:33, FastEthernet0/0.14
     200.1.5.0/30 is subnetted, 1 subnets
D        200.1.5.4 [90/156160] via 14.1.1.4, 00:06:33, FastEthernet0/0.14
D     201.1.3.0/24 [90/156160] via 13.1.1.3, 00:06:33, FastEthernet0/0.13
     205.1.1.0/28 is subnetted, 1 subnets
D        205.1.1.240 [90/158720] via 14.1.1.4, 00:06:33, FastEthernet0/0.14
     206.1.1.0/30 is subnetted, 1 subnets
D        206.1.1.248 [90/158720] via 14.1.1.4, 00:06:33, FastEthernet0/0.14
     207.1.1.0/26 is subnetted, 1 subnets
D        207.1.1.192 [90/158720] via 14.1.1.4, 00:06:33, FastEthernet0/0.14
     208.1.1.0/25 is subnetted, 1 subnets
D        208.1.1.128 [90/158720] via 14.1.1.4, 00:06:33, FastEthernet0/0.14
     211.4.4.0/27 is subnetted, 1 subnets
D        211.4.4.32 [90/158720] via 14.1.1.4, 00:06:33, FastEthernet0/0.14
D     223.1.1.0/24 [90/156160] via 14.1.1.4, 00:06:33, FastEthernet0/0.14
```

Task 3

Configure R4 such that it only allows Class B networks that are not subnetted from its neighboring routers.

Before the filter is configured and applied, let's check the routing table of R4:

```
On R4:


R4# show ip route eigrp | begin Gate
Gateway of last resort is not set


D     1.0.0.0/8 [90/158720] via 14.1.1.1, 00:22:55, FastEthernet0/0
      6.0.0.0/8 is variably subnetted, 5 subnets, 5 masks
D        6.1.1.0/24 [90/158720] via 45.1.1.5, 01:11:28, FastEthernet0/1
D        6.1.2.128/25 [90/158720] via 45.1.1.5, 01:11:28, FastEthernet0/1
D        6.1.3.192/26 [90/158720] via 45.1.1.5, 01:11:28, FastEthernet0/1
D        6.1.4.224/27 [90/158720] via 45.1.1.5, 01:11:28, FastEthernet0/1
D        6.1.5.240/28 [90/158720] via 45.1.1.5, 01:11:28, FastEthernet0/1
      10.0.0.0/8 is variably subnetted, 2 subnets, 2 masks
12.0.0.0/24 is subnetted, 1 subnets
D        12.1.1.0 [90/30720] via 14.1.1.1, 01:11:24, FastEthernet0/0
      13.0.0.0/24 is subnetted, 1 subnets
D        13.1.1.0 [90/30720] via 14.1.1.1, 01:11:24, FastEthernet0/0
D     29.0.0.0/8 [90/158720] via 14.1.1.1, 00:22:55, FastEthernet0/0
D     44.0.0.0/8 [90/158720] via 14.1.1.1, 00:22:55, FastEthernet0/0
      56.0.0.0/24 is subnetted, 1 subnets
D        56.1.1.0 [90/30720] via 45.1.1.5, 01:11:28, FastEthernet0/1
      67.0.0.0/24 is subnetted, 1 subnets
D        67.1.1.0 [90/33280] via 45.1.1.5, 01:11:28, FastEthernet0/1
D     99.0.0.0/8 [90/156160] via 45.1.1.5, 01:11:28, FastEthernet0/1
D     128.1.0.0/16 [90/156160] via 14.1.1.1, 01:11:24, FastEthernet0/0
D     131.1.0.0/16 [90/156160] via 14.1.1.1, 01:11:24, FastEthernet0/0
      146.1.0.0/16 is variably subnetted, 5 subnets, 5 masks
D        146.1.1.0/24 [90/158720] via 45.1.1.5, 01:11:28, FastEthernet0/1
D        146.1.2.128/25 [90/158720] via 45.1.1.5, 01:11:28, FastEthernet0/1
D        146.1.3.192/26 [90/158720] via 45.1.1.5, 01:11:28, FastEthernet0/1
D        146.1.4.224/27 [90/158720] via 45.1.1.5, 01:11:28, FastEthernet0/1
D        146.1.5.240/28 [90/158720] via 45.1.1.5, 01:11:28, FastEthernet0/1
      172.16.0.0/24 is subnetted, 4 subnets
D        172.16.0.0 [90/158720] via 14.1.1.1, 01:11:19, FastEthernet0/0
D        172.16.1.0 [90/158720] via 14.1.1.1, 01:11:19, FastEthernet0/0
D        172.16.2.0 [90/158720] via 14.1.1.1, 01:11:19, FastEthernet0/0
D        172.16.3.0 [90/158720] via 14.1.1.1, 01:11:19, FastEthernet0/0
      180.1.0.0/24 is subnetted, 3 subnets
D        180.1.4.0 [90/156160] via 14.1.1.1, 01:11:24, FastEthernet0/0
D        180.1.5.0 [90/156160] via 14.1.1.1, 01:11:24, FastEthernet0/0
D        180.1.6.0 [90/156160] via 14.1.1.1, 01:11:24, FastEthernet0/0
D     185.1.0.0/16 [90/156160] via 45.1.1.5, 01:11:28, FastEthernet0/1
      186.1.0.0/17 is subnetted, 1 subnets
```

```
D          186.1.128.0 [90/156160] via 45.1.1.5, 01:11:28, FastEthernet0/1
      189.1.0.0/24 is subnetted, 1 subnets
D          189.1.1.0 [90/156160] via 45.1.1.5, 01:11:28, FastEthernet0/1
      192.1.1.0/32 is subnetted, 1 subnets
D          192.1.1.1 [90/158720] via 14.1.1.1, 01:11:19, FastEthernet0/0
D      201.1.3.0/24 [90/158720] via 14.1.1.1, 00:22:55, FastEthernet0/0
      205.1.1.0/28 is subnetted, 1 subnets
D          205.1.1.240 [90/156160] via 45.1.1.5, 01:11:28, FastEthernet0/1
      206.1.1.0/30 is subnetted, 1 subnets
D          206.1.1.248 [90/156160] via 45.1.1.5, 01:11:28, FastEthernet0/1
      207.1.1.0/26 is subnetted, 1 subnets
D          207.1.1.192 [90/156160] via 45.1.1.5, 01:11:28, FastEthernet0/1
      208.1.1.0/25 is subnetted, 1 subnets
D          208.1.1.128 [90/156160] via 45.1.1.5, 01:11:28, FastEthernet0/1
      211.4.4.0/27 is subnetted, 1 subnets
D          211.4.4.32 [90/156160] via 45.1.1.5, 01:11:28, FastEthernet0/1
```

The highlighted Class B networks should be allowed since they are *not* subnetted; these are networks 128.1.0.0, 131.1.0.0 through R1 (f0/0), and 185.1.0.0/16 through R5 (f0/1).

Figure 6-3 shows how Class B networks are identified. The letter *N* identifies the network bits, and the letter *H* identifies the host bits.

1st Octet		2nd Octet	3rd Octet	4th Octet
1 0 N N N N N N	•	N N N N N N N N	• H H H H H H H H	• H H H H H H H H

Figure 6-3   *Class B Native Network Mask*

Class B networks are identified based on the following:

- First two bits are set to 10; therefore, there are 14 network bits left to identify the networks, and the remaining 16 bits identify the host bits.

- The initial byte is 128–191.

- There are 16,384 Class B networks.

- There are 65,532 hosts on each Class B network.

If the most significant two bits of the first octet are set to 10, the network is a Class B network. The **prefix-list** matches on the most significant two bits of the first octet by using a prefix length of /2.

In the following example the **prefix-list** matches on the first two bits by using a prefix length of /2, with a network address of 128.0.0.0. Because the task states that only Class B networks that are not subnetted should be allowed, the prefix length specifies **ge 16** and **le 16**, as shown here:

```
R4(config)# ip prefix-list NET permit 128.0.0.0/2 ge 16 le 16
R4(config)# Router eigrp 1
R4(config-router)# distribute-list prefix NET in fastethernet0/0
R4(config-router)# distribute-list prefix NET in fastethernet0/1
```

Let's verify the configuration:

```
On R4:


R4# show ip route eigrp | begin Gate
Gateway of last resort is not set


D    128.1.0.0/16 [90/156160] via 14.1.1.1, 01:34:44, FastEthernet0/0
D    131.1.0.0/16 [90/156160] via 14.1.1.1, 01:34:44, FastEthernet0/0
D    185.1.0.0/16 [90/156160] via 45.1.1.5, 01:34:48, FastEthernet0/1
```

Task 4

Configure R5 such that it only allows Class C networks that are not subnetted.

Before configuring this task, you should verify the routing table on R5:

```
On R5:


R5# show ip route eigrp | begin Gate
Gateway of last resort is not set


      6.0.0.0/8 is variably subnetted, 5 subnets, 5 masks
D        6.1.1.0/24 [90/156160] via 56.1.1.6, 01:43:15, FastEthernet0/0
D        6.1.2.128/25 [90/156160] via 56.1.1.6, 01:43:15, FastEthernet0/0
D        6.1.3.192/26 [90/156160] via 56.1.1.6, 01:43:15, FastEthernet0/0
D        6.1.4.224/27 [90/156160] via 56.1.1.6, 01:43:15, FastEthernet0/0
D        6.1.5.240/28 [90/156160] via 56.1.1.6, 01:43:15, FastEthernet0/0
      14.0.0.0/24 is subnetted, 1 subnets
D        14.1.1.0 [90/30720] via 45.1.1.4, 01:42:42, FastEthernet0/1
      67.0.0.0/24 is subnetted, 1 subnets
D        67.1.1.0 [90/30720] via 56.1.1.6, 01:43:15, FastEthernet0/0
D      128.1.0.0/16 [90/158720] via 45.1.1.4, 01:42:38, FastEthernet0/1
D      131.1.0.0/16 [90/158720] via 45.1.1.4, 01:42:38, FastEthernet0/1
      146.1.0.0/16 is variably subnetted, 5 subnets, 5 masks
D        146.1.1.0/24 [90/156160] via 56.1.1.6, 01:43:15, FastEthernet0/0
D        146.1.2.128/25 [90/156160] via 56.1.1.6, 01:43:15, FastEthernet0/0
```

```
D          146.1.3.192/26 [90/156160] via 56.1.1.6, 01:43:15, FastEthernet0/0
D          146.1.4.224/27 [90/156160] via 56.1.1.6, 01:43:15, FastEthernet0/0
D          146.1.5.240/28 [90/156160] via 56.1.1.6, 01:43:15, FastEthernet0/0
D       198.1.1.0/24 [90/156160] via 45.1.1.4, 01:42:42, FastEthernet0/1
D       199.1.1.0/24 [90/156160] via 45.1.1.4, 01:42:42, FastEthernet0/1
D       200.1.1.0/24 [90/156160] via 45.1.1.4, 01:42:42, FastEthernet0/1
        200.1.4.0/29 is subnetted, 1 subnets
D          200.1.4.8 [90/156160] via 45.1.1.4, 01:42:42, FastEthernet0/1
        200.1.5.0/30 is subnetted, 1 subnets
D          200.1.5.4 [90/156160] via 45.1.1.4, 01:42:42, FastEthernet0/1
D       223.1.1.0/24 [90/156160] via 45.1.1.4, 01:42:42, FastEthernet0/1
```

As you can see, only the highlighted networks should be permitted.

In Figure 6-4, the letter *N* identifies the network bits, and the letter *H* identifies the host bits.

1st Octet	2nd Octet	3rd Octet	4th Octet
1 1 0 N N N N N •	N N N N N N N N •	N N N N N N N N •	H H H H H H H H

Figure 6-4   *Class C Native Mask*

Class C networks are identified based on the following:

■ The first three bits of the first octet are reserved as 110. Because the first three octets belong to networks, there are 21 network bits left to identify the networks; therefore, the remaining 8 bits identify the host bits.

■ The first octet is 192–223.

■ There are 2,097,152 Class C networks.

■ Each Class C network can handle 254 hosts.

In the following example we will explore how this would work for Class C addresses specifically.

```
On R5:

R5(config)# ip prefix-list NET permit 192.0.0.0/3 ge 24 le 24
```

In this case, R5 is not receiving any Class B networks that are not subnetted through its f0/0 interface.

The first statement is configured for future Class B networks that are not subnetted that may be advertised to R5 through its f0/0 interface:

```
R5(config)# router eigrp 1
R5(config-router)# distribute-list prefix NET in fastethernet0/0
R5(config-router)# distribute-list prefix NET in fastethernet0/1
```

Let's verify the configuration:

```
On R5:

R5# show ip route eigrp | begin Gate
Gateway of last resort is not set

D    198.1.1.0/24 [90/156160] via 45.1.1.4, 01:48:48, FastEthernet0/1
D    199.1.1.0/24 [90/156160] via 45.1.1.4, 01:48:48, FastEthernet0/1
D    200.1.1.0/24 [90/156160] via 45.1.1.4, 01:48:48, FastEthernet0/1
D    223.1.1.0/24 [90/156160] via 45.1.1.4, 01:48:48, FastEthernet0/1
```

This task can also be configured to deny all subnetted Class C networks and only permit the Class C networks that are not subnetted. Let's configure this:

```
On R5:

R5(config)# no ip prefix-list NET

R5(config)# ip prefix-list NET deny 192.0.0.0/3 ge 25
R5(config)# ip prefix-list NET permit 192.0.0.0/3 ge 24 le 24
```

Now we can verify the configuration:

```
On R5:

R5# show ip route eigrp | begin Gate
Gateway of last resort is not set

D    198.1.1.0/24 [90/156160] via 45.1.1.4, 00:00:18, FastEthernet0/1
D    199.1.1.0/24 [90/156160] via 45.1.1.4, 00:00:18, FastEthernet0/1
D    200.1.1.0/24 [90/156160] via 45.1.1.4, 00:00:18, FastEthernet0/1
D    223.1.1.0/24 [90/156160] via 45.1.1.4, 00:00:18, FastEthernet0/1
```

Task 5

Configure R3 such that it only allows Class C networks that are not subnetted.

Configure the loopback interfaces shown in Table 6-1 on R3 and advertise them in EIGRP AS 1.

Table 6-1 *Loopback Interfaces*

Interface	IP Address
loopback8	203.4.4.34 255.255.255.224
loopback9	203.4.5.66 255.255.255.192

```
On R3:

R3(config)# interface loopback8
R3(config-if)# ip address 203.4.4.34 255.255.255.224

R3(config)# interface loopback9
R3(config-if)# ip address 203.4.5.67 255.255.255.192
```

Because EIGRP on R3 is configured to advertise all existing and future directly connected networks, no additional configuration is required. Let's see how EIGRP is configured:

```
R3# show run | section router eigrp
router eigrp 1
 network 0.0.0.0
```

Now let's verify the configuration:

```
On R1:

R1# show ip route eigrp | include 203.4.
      203.4.4.0/27 is subnetted, 1 subnets
D        203.4.4.32 [90/156160] via 13.1.1.3, 00:04:35, FastEthernet0/0.13
      203.4.5.0/26 is subnetted, 1 subnets
D        203.4.5.64 [90/156160] via 13.1.1.3, 00:04:21, FastEthernet0/0.13
```

Task 6

Configure R1 such that it denies prefixes 203.4.4.33/27 and 203.4.5.65/26 and allows the rest of the prefixes. You should configure the minimum number of lines in the prefix list to accomplish this task. This configuration should not break the previous policies.

Before configuring the prefix list, you should verify the existing routing table on R1:

```
On R1:


R1# show ip route eigrp | begin Gate
Gateway of last resort is not set


D    1.0.0.0/8 [90/156160] via 13.1.1.3, 01:28:26, FastEthernet0/0.13
D    29.0.0.0/8 [90/156160] via 13.1.1.3, 01:28:26, FastEthernet0/0.13
D    44.0.0.0/8 [90/156160] via 13.1.1.3, 01:28:26, FastEthernet0/0.13
     172.16.0.0/24 is subnetted, 4 subnets
D       172.16.0.0 [90/156160] via 12.1.1.2, 02:16:54, FastEthernet0/0.12
D       172.16.1.0 [90/156160] via 12.1.1.2, 02:16:54, FastEthernet0/0.12
D       172.16.2.0 [90/156160] via 12.1.1.2, 02:16:54, FastEthernet0/0.12
D       172.16.3.0 [90/156160] via 12.1.1.2, 02:16:54, FastEthernet0/0.12
D    185.1.0.0/16 [90/158720] via 14.1.1.4, 01:28:26, FastEthernet0/0.14
     192.1.1.0/32 is subnetted, 1 subnets
D       192.1.1.1 [90/156160] via 12.1.1.2, 02:16:54, FastEthernet0/0.12
D    198.1.1.0/24 [90/156160] via 14.1.1.4, 01:28:26, FastEthernet0/0.14
D    199.1.1.0/24 [90/156160] via 14.1.1.4, 01:28:26, FastEthernet0/0.14
D    200.1.1.0/24 [90/156160] via 14.1.1.4, 01:28:26, FastEthernet0/0.14
     200.1.4.0/29 is subnetted, 1 subnets
D       200.1.4.8 [90/156160] via 14.1.1.4, 01:28:26, FastEthernet0/0.14
     200.1.5.0/30 is subnetted, 1 subnets
D       200.1.5.4 [90/156160] via 14.1.1.4, 01:28:26, FastEthernet0/0.14
D    201.1.3.0/24 [90/156160] via 13.1.1.3, 01:28:26, FastEthernet0/0.13
     203.4.4.0/27 is subnetted, 1 subnets
D       203.4.4.32 [90/156160] via 13.1.1.3, 00:06:48, FastEthernet0/0.13
     203.4.5.0/26 is subnetted, 1 subnets
D       203.4.5.64 [90/156160] via 13.1.1.3, 00:06:34, FastEthernet0/0.13
D    223.1.1.0/24 [90/156160] via 14.1.1.4, 01:28:26, FastEthernet0/0.14
```

To figure out how you are going to use the minimum number of lines in the prefix list, you should focus on the third and the fourth octet because the first two octets are identical. Let's convert the third and the fourth octets of these two prefixes to binary, as shown in Figure 6-5.

	3rd Octet									4th Octet							
203.4.4.32	0	0	0	0	0	1	0	0	•	0	0	1	0	0	0	0	0
203.4.5.64	0	0	0	0	0	1	0	1	•	0	1	0	0	0	0	0	0

Figure 6-5 *Binary Conversion*

Once the third and the fourth octets of these two networks are converted to binary, you can identify the contiguous identical binary digits (see Figure 6-6).

	3rd Octet			4th Octet							
10.4.4.32	0 0 0 0 0 1 0 0	•	0 0 1 0 0 0 0 0
10.4.5.64	0 0 0 0 0 1 0 1	•	0 1 0 0 0 0 0 0

Figure 6-6 *Identify Contiguous Identical Bits*

You can see that the first 23 bits are identical; this includes the first two octets (16 bits) plus the most significant 7 bits of the third octet. Because this defines the network (203.4.4.0), we need the first 23 bits to be 203.4.4.0. Therefore, the prefix is written as 203.4.4.0/23. Now, the prefix length needs to be **ge 23** and **le 27**, which will cover the two prefixes.

Remember that we already have a **distribute-list** called **Class-A** applied to f0/0.13; therefore, we need to add the following **prefix-list** to the existing one. You can see how the sequence numbers can be beneficial in cases like this.

Let's view the existing **prefix-list**:

```
R1# show run | include ip prefix-list
ip prefix-list Class-A seq 5 deny 0.0.0.0/1 ge 9
ip prefix-list Class-A seq 10 permit 0.0.0.0/0 le 32
```

Let's configure the **prefix-list**:

```
On R1:

R1(config)# ip prefix-list Class-A seq 7 deny 203.4.4.0/23 ge 24 le 27
```

Now let's verify the configuration:

```
On R1:

R1# show ip route eigrp | begin Gate
Gateway of last resort is not set


D    1.0.0.0/8 [90/156160] via 13.1.1.3, 01:50:41, FastEthernet0/0.13
D    29.0.0.0/8 [90/156160] via 13.1.1.3, 01:50:41, FastEthernet0/0.13
D    44.0.0.0/8 [90/156160] via 13.1.1.3, 01:50:41, FastEthernet0/0.13
     172.16.0.0/24 is subnetted, 4 subnets
D       172.16.0.0 [90/156160] via 12.1.1.2, 02:39:09, FastEthernet0/0.12
D       172.16.1.0 [90/156160] via 12.1.1.2, 02:39:09, FastEthernet0/0.12
D       172.16.2.0 [90/156160] via 12.1.1.2, 02:39:09, FastEthernet0/0.12
D       172.16.3.0 [90/156160] via 12.1.1.2, 02:39:09, FastEthernet0/0.12
```

```
D      185.1.0.0/16 [90/158720] via 14.1.1.4, 01:50:41, FastEthernet0/0.14
       192.1.1.0/32 is subnetted, 1 subnets
D         192.1.1.1 [90/156160] via 12.1.1.2, 02:39:09, FastEthernet0/0.12
D      198.1.1.0/24 [90/156160] via 14.1.1.4, 01:50:41, FastEthernet0/0.14
D      199.1.1.0/24 [90/156160] via 14.1.1.4, 01:50:41, FastEthernet0/0.14
D      200.1.1.0/24 [90/156160] via 14.1.1.4, 01:50:41, FastEthernet0/0.14
       200.1.4.0/29 is subnetted, 1 subnets
D         200.1.4.8 [90/156160] via 14.1.1.4, 01:50:41, FastEthernet0/0.14
       200.1.5.0/30 is subnetted, 1 subnets
D         200.1.5.4 [90/156160] via 14.1.1.4, 01:50:41, FastEthernet0/0.14
D      201.1.3.0/24 [90/156160] via 13.1.1.3, 01:50:41, FastEthernet0/0.13
D      223.1.1.0/24 [90/156160] via 14.1.1.4, 01:50:41, FastEthernet0/0.14
```

Now let's see the **prefix-list** called **Class-A**:

```
R1# show run | include ip prefix-list Class-A

ip prefix-list Class-A seq 5 deny 0.0.0.0/1 ge 9
ip prefix-list Class-A seq 7 deny 203.4.4.0/23 ge 24 le 27
ip prefix-list Class-A seq 10 permit 0.0.0.0/0 le 32
```

Task 7

Configure R5 to inject a default route in the EIGRP routing domain. If this configuration is successful, R6 should see a default route in its routing table.

```
On R5:

R5(config)# ip route 0.0.0.0 0.0.0.0 null0

R5(config)# router eigrp 1
R5(config-router)# redistribute static
```

Let's verify the configuration:

```
On R6:

R6# show ip route eigrp | begin Gate
Gateway of last resort is 56.1.1.5 to network 0.0.0.0

45.0.0.0/24 is subnetted, 1 subnets
D        45.1.1.0 [90/30720] via 56.1.1.5, 02:46:17, FastEthernet0/0
D      99.0.0.0/8 [90/156160] via 56.1.1.5, 02:46:17, FastEthernet0/0
D      185.1.0.0/16 [90/156160] via 56.1.1.5, 02:46:17, FastEthernet0/0
       186.1.0.0/17 is subnetted, 1 subnets
```

```
D          186.1.128.0 [90/156160] via 56.1.1.5, 02:46:17, FastEthernet0/0
        189.1.0.0/24 is subnetted, 1 subnets
D          189.1.1.0 [90/156160] via 56.1.1.5, 02:46:17, FastEthernet0/0
D        198.1.1.0/24 [90/158720] via 56.1.1.5, 00:49:48, FastEthernet0/0
D        199.1.1.0/24 [90/158720] via 56.1.1.5, 00:49:48, FastEthernet0/0
D        200.1.1.0/24 [90/158720] via 56.1.1.5, 00:49:48, FastEthernet0/0
        205.1.1.0/28 is subnetted, 1 subnets
D          205.1.1.240 [90/156160] via 56.1.1.5, 02:46:17, FastEthernet0/0
        206.1.1.0/30 is subnetted, 1 subnets
D          206.1.1.248 [90/156160] via 56.1.1.5, 02:46:17, FastEthernet0/0
        207.1.1.0/26 is subnetted, 1 subnets
D          207.1.1.192 [90/156160] via 56.1.1.5, 02:46:17, FastEthernet0/0
        208.1.1.0/25 is subnetted, 1 subnets
D          208.1.1.128 [90/156160] via 56.1.1.5, 02:46:17, FastEthernet0/0
        211.4.4.0/27 is subnetted, 1 subnets
D          211.4.4.32 [90/156160] via 56.1.1.5, 02:46:17, FastEthernet0/0
D        223.1.1.0/24 [90/158720] via 56.1.1.5, 00:49:48, FastEthernet0/0
```

Note   R4 will not see the default route because it has a filter that *only* allows Class B networks that are not subnetted.

Task 8

R6 should be configured to filter the default route injected in the previous step.

Let's look at the default route in R6's routing table:

```
R6# show ip route eigrp | include 0.0.0.0/0
D*    0.0.0.0/0 [90/28160] via 56.1.1.5, 00:00:08, FastEthernet0/0
```

The output of the preceding **show** command reveals that 0.0.0.0/0 is in the routing table of R6. Let's filter 0.0.0.0/0:

```
On R6:

R6(config)# ip prefix-list DEFAULT deny 0.0.0.0/0
R6(config)# ip prefix-list DEFAULT permit 0.0.0.0/0 le 32


R6(config)# router eigrp 1
R6(config-router)# distribute-list prefix DEFAULT in fastethernet0/0
```

Now let's verify the configuration:

```
On R6:


R6# sh ip route eigrp | b Gate
Gateway of last resort is not set


45.0.0.0/24 is subnetted, 1 subnets
D        45.1.1.0 [90/30720] via 56.1.1.5, 02:52:00, FastEthernet0/0
D      99.0.0.0/8 [90/156160] via 56.1.1.5, 02:52:00, FastEthernet0/0
D      185.1.0.0/16 [90/156160] via 56.1.1.5, 02:52:00, FastEthernet0/0
       186.1.0.0/17 is subnetted, 1 subnets
D        186.1.128.0 [90/156160] via 56.1.1.5, 02:52:00, FastEthernet0/0
       189.1.0.0/24 is subnetted, 1 subnets
D        189.1.1.0 [90/156160] via 56.1.1.5, 02:52:00, FastEthernet0/0
D      198.1.1.0/24 [90/158720] via 56.1.1.5, 00:55:31, FastEthernet0/0
D      199.1.1.0/24 [90/158720] via 56.1.1.5, 00:55:31, FastEthernet0/0
D      200.1.1.0/24 [90/158720] via 56.1.1.5, 00:55:31, FastEthernet0/0
       205.1.1.0/28 is subnetted, 1 subnets
D        205.1.1.240 [90/156160] via 56.1.1.5, 02:52:00, FastEthernet0/0
       206.1.1.0/30 is subnetted, 1 subnets
D        206.1.1.248 [90/156160] via 56.1.1.5, 02:52:00, FastEthernet0/0
       207.1.1.0/26 is subnetted, 1 subnets
D        207.1.1.192 [90/156160] via 56.1.1.5, 02:52:00, FastEthernet0/0
       208.1.1.0/25 is subnetted, 1 subnets
D        208.1.1.128 [90/156160] via 56.1.1.5, 02:52:00, FastEthernet0/0
       211.4.4.0/27 is subnetted, 1 subnets
D        211.4.4.32 [90/156160] via 56.1.1.5, 02:52:00, FastEthernet0/0
D      223.1.1.0/24 [90/158720] via 56.1.1.5, 00:55:31, FastEthernet0/0
```

Task 9

Configure R6 to filter any networks with a prefix length of /26 or less.

Let's verify the routing table of R6 before configuring any prefix list:

```
On R6:


R6# show ip route eigrp | begin Gate
Gateway of last resort is not set


45.0.0.0/24 is subnetted, 1 subnets
D        45.1.1.0 [90/30720] via 56.1.1.5, 02:57:17, FastEthernet0/0
D      99.0.0.0/8 [90/156160] via 56.1.1.5, 02:57:17, FastEthernet0/0
D      185.1.0.0/16 [90/156160] via 56.1.1.5, 02:57:17, FastEthernet0/0
       186.1.0.0/17 is subnetted, 1 subnets
```

```
D        186.1.128.0 [90/156160] via 56.1.1.5, 02:57:17, FastEthernet0/0
      189.1.0.0/24 is subnetted, 1 subnets
D        189.1.1.0 [90/156160] via 56.1.1.5, 02:57:17, FastEthernet0/0
D      198.1.1.0/24 [90/158720] via 56.1.1.5, 01:00:48, FastEthernet0/0
D      199.1.1.0/24 [90/158720] via 56.1.1.5, 01:00:48, FastEthernet0/0
D      200.1.1.0/24 [90/158720] via 56.1.1.5, 01:00:48, FastEthernet0/0
      205.1.1.0/28 is subnetted, 1 subnets
D        205.1.1.240 [90/156160] via 56.1.1.5, 02:57:17, FastEthernet0/0
      206.1.1.0/30 is subnetted, 1 subnets
D        206.1.1.248 [90/156160] via 56.1.1.5, 02:57:17, FastEthernet0/0
      207.1.1.0/26 is subnetted, 1 subnets
D        207.1.1.192 [90/156160] via 56.1.1.5, 02:57:17, FastEthernet0/0
      208.1.1.0/25 is subnetted, 1 subnets
D        208.1.1.128 [90/156160] via 56.1.1.5, 02:57:17, FastEthernet0/0
      211.4.4.0/27 is subnetted, 1 subnets
D        211.4.4.32 [90/156160] via 56.1.1.5, 02:57:17, FastEthernet0/0
D      223.1.1.0/24 [90/158720] via 56.1.1.5, 01:00:48, FastEthernet0/0
```

You can see networks with /8, /16, /17, /24, /25, /26, /27, /28, and /30 as the prefix length. In this task, you need to filter any networks with a prefix length of /26 or less, which leaves you with the following networks:

205.1.1.0/28

206.1.1.0/30

211.4.4.0/27

But the **prefix-list** should be added to the existing one. Let's view the existing **prefix-list**:

```
R6# show run | include ip prefix-list

ip prefix-list DEFAULT seq 5 deny 0.0.0.0/0
ip prefix-list DEFAULT seq 10 permit 0.0.0.0/0 le 32
```

Let's configure this task. The following prefix denies any prefix as long as the prefix length is greater than or equal to 8 and less than or equal to 26:

```
On R6:
R6(config)# ip prefix-list DEFAULT seq 7 deny 0.0.0.0/0 ge 8 le 26
```

Because in the previous task a **distribute-list** named **DEFAULT** was applied inbound to the F0/0 interface, you only need to apply it to the F0/1 interface of R6:

```
R6(config)# router eigrp 1
R6(config-router)# distribute-list prefix DEFAULT in fastethernet0/1
```

Let's verify the configuration:

```
On R6:


R6# show ip route eigrp | begin Gate
Gateway of last resort is not set


205.1.1.0/28 is subnetted, 1 subnets
D        205.1.1.240 [90/156160] via 56.1.1.5, 03:06:51, FastEthernet0/0
     206.1.1.0/30 is subnetted, 1 subnets
D        206.1.1.248 [90/156160] via 56.1.1.5, 03:06:51, FastEthernet0/0
     211.4.4.0/27 is subnetted, 1 subnets
D        211.4.4.32 [90/156160] via 56.1.1.5, 03:06:51, FastEthernet0/0
```

Task 10

Configure loopback10 on R6 and assign it an IP address of 206.6.6.6/32. Make sure that this prefix is advertised to R7.

```
On R6:


R6(config)# interface loopback10
R6(config-if)# ip address 206.6.6.6 255.255.255.255
```

EIGRP is configured such that all existing and future directly connected interfaces are advertised in AS 1.

Let's verify the configuration:

```
On R7:


R7# show ip route 206.6.6.6
Routing entry for 206.6.6.6/32
  Known via "eigrp 1", distance 90, metric 156160, type internal
  Redistributing via eigrp 1
  Last update from 67.1.1.6 on GigabitEthernet0/1, 00:02:07 ago
  Routing Descriptor Blocks:
  * 67.1.1.6, from 67.1.1.6, 00:02:07 ago, via GigabitEthernet0/1
      Route metric is 156160, traffic share count is 1
      Total delay is 5100 microseconds, minimum bandwidth is 100000 Kbit
      Reliability 255/255, minimum MTU 1500 bytes
      Loading 1/255, Hops 1
```

Task 11

Configure R7 to filter existing and future host routes.

Let's check the routing table of R7 for host routes:

```
On R7:

R7# show ip route eigrp | include /32
      206.6.6.0/32 is subnetted, 1 subnets
```

The first line of the prefix list denies any prefix that has a prefix length of 32 or greater. This will deny all host routes.

```
R7(config)# ip prefix-list NET deny 0.0.0.0/0 ge 32
R7(config)# ip prefix-list NET permit 0.0.0.0/0 le 32

R7(config)# router eigrp 1
R7(config-router)# distribute-list prefix NET in gigabitethernet0/1
```

Let's verify the configuration:

```
On R7:

R7# show ip route eigrp | include /32
```

Erase the startup configuration and reload the routers before proceeding to the next lab.

Chapter 7

EIGRP

This chapter focuses on the commands and methodologies necessary to deploy the Enhanced Interior Gateway Routing Protocol (EIGRP) in a Cisco Routing and Switching environment. Each section of this chapter covers a critical aspect of deploying EIGRP.

Lab 7-1: EIGRP

Note   Before proceeding with this lab, you need to copy and paste the running configuration information found in the Lab7-1_EIGRP.txt file. Once these configurations have been installed, you may proceed with Task 1.

Task 1

First, we have to enable **ip routing** on SW1 itself. This enables the device to provide the services necessary to emulate the behavior of the Internet in this lab. Second, we have to configure static routes pointing to the corresponding interfaces on SW1.

```
!On SW1:

SW1(config)# ip routing
```

Now that we have enabled **ip routing** on SW1, we need to configure the prescribed static default routes specified in the task:

```
!On R1:

R1(config)# ip route 0.0.0.0 0.0.0.0 200.1.1.10

!On R2:
```

```
R2(config)# ip route 0.0.0.0 0.0.0.0 200.1.2.10

!On R3:

R3(config)# ip route 0.0.0.0 0.0.0.0 200.1.3.10

!On R4:

R4(config)# ip route 0.0.0.0 0.0.0.0 200.1.4.10
```

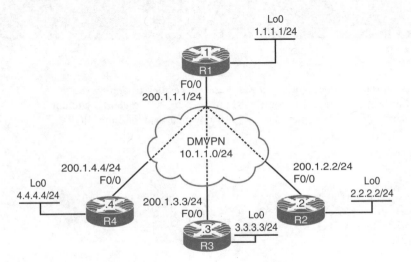

Figure 7-1   *Running EIGRP over DMVPN Lab Topology*

Figure 7-1 shows the topology we will use to explore running EIGRP across a Dynamic Multi-point Virtual Private Network (DMVPN) cloud. In this topology, SW1 represents the Internet. We have configured a static default route on each router pointing to the appropriate interface on SW1. If this configuration has been performed correctly, these routers should be able to ping and have reachability to the F0/0 interfaces of all routers in this topology. The switch interface to which the routers are connected will have ".10" in the host portion of the IP address for that subnet. We can verify this essential reachability as follows:

```
!On R1:

R1# ping 200.1.2.2
Type escape sequence to abort.
Sending 5, 100-byte ICMP Echos to 192.1.2.2, timeout is 2 seconds:
!!!!!
Success rate is 100 percent (5/5), round-trip min/avg/max = 1/2/4 ms
```

```
R1# ping 200.1.3.3
Type escape sequence to abort.
Sending 5, 100-byte ICMP Echos to 192.1.3.3, timeout is 2 seconds:
!!!!!
Success rate is 100 percent (5/5), round-trip min/avg/max = 1/2/4 ms

R1# ping 200.1.4.4
Type escape sequence to abort.
Sending 5, 100-byte ICMP Echos to 192.1.4.4, timeout is 2 seconds:
!!!!!
Success rate is 100 percent (5/5), round-trip min/avg/max = 1/2/4 ms

!On R2:

R2# ping 200.1.3.3
Type escape sequence to abort.
Sending 5, 100-byte ICMP Echos to 192.1.3.3, timeout is 2 seconds:
!!!!!
Success rate is 100 percent (5/5), round-trip min/avg/max = 1/2/4 ms

R2# ping 200.1.4.4
Type escape sequence to abort.
Sending 5, 100-byte ICMP Echos to 192.1.4.4, timeout is 2 seconds:
!!!!!
Success rate is 100 percent (5/5), round-trip min/avg/max = 1/1/4 ms

!On R3:

R3# ping 200.1.4.4
Type escape sequence to abort.
Sending 5, 100-byte ICMP Echos to 200.1.4.4, timeout is 2 seconds:
!!!!!
Success rate is 100 percent (5/5), round-trip min/avg/max = 1/1/4 ms
```

As you can see, the verifications indicate that we have the necessary reachability across the simulated Internet connection to begin building the DMVPN interconnections.

Task 2

Configure DMVPN Phase 1 such that R1 is the hub. R2, R3, and R4 are configured as the spokes. You should use 10.1.1.x/24, where "x" is the router number for the tunnel IP address. If this configuration is performed correctly, these routers should have reachability to all tunnel endpoints. Do *not* provide multicast capability.

```
!On R1:

R1(config)# interface tunnel1
R1(config-if)# ip address 10.1.1.1 255.255.255.0
R1(config-if)# tunnel source 200.1.1.1
R1(config-if)# tunnel mode gre multipoint
R1(config-if)# ip nhrp network-id 111


!On R2:

R2(config)# interface tunnel1
R2(config-if)# ip address 10.1.1.2 255.255.255.0
R2(config-if)# tunnel source 200.1.2.2
R2(config-if)# tunnel destination 200.1.1.1
R2(config-if)# ip nhrp network-id 222
R2(config-if)# ip nhrp nhs 10.1.1.1
R2(config-if)# ip nhrp map 10.1.1.1 200.1.1.1


!On R3:

R3(config)# interface tunnel1
R3(config-if)# ip address 10.1.1.3 255.255.255.0
R3(config-if)# tunnel source 200.1.3.3
R3(config-if)# tunnel destination 200.1.1.1
R3(config-if)# ip nhrp network-id 333
R3(config-if)# ip nhrp nhs 10.1.1.1
R3(config-if)# ip nhrp map 10.1.1.1 200.1.1.1


!On R4:

R4(config)# interface tunnel1
R4(config-if)# ip address 10.1.1.4 255.255.255.0
R4(config-if)# tunnel source 200.1.4.4
R4(config-if)# tunnel destination 200.1.1.1
R4(config-if)# ip nhrp network-id 444
R4(config-if)# ip nhrp nhs 10.1.1.1
R4(config-if)# ip nhrp map 10.1.1.1 200.1.1.1
```

With this accomplished, we need to verify that the DMVPN cloud is working as expected:

```
!On R1:

R1# show ip nhrp
10.1.1.2/32 via 10.1.1.2
   Tunnel1 created 00:00:31, expire 01:59:58
   Type: dynamic, Flags: unique registered used
   NBMA address: 200.1.2.2
10.1.1.3/32 via 10.1.1.3
   Tunnel1 created 00:00:20, expire 01:59:59
   Type: dynamic, Flags: unique registered used
   NBMA address: 200.1.3.3
10.1.1.4/32 via 10.1.1.4
   Tunnel1 created 00:00:12, expire 01:59:57
   Type: dynamic, Flags: unique registered used
   NBMA address: 200.1.4.4


R1# ping 10.1.1.2
Type escape sequence to abort.
Sending 5, 100-byte ICMP Echos to 10.1.1.2, timeout is 2 seconds:
!!!!!
Success rate is 100 percent (5/5), round-trip min/avg/max = 1/3/4 ms


R1# ping 10.1.1.3
Type escape sequence to abort.
Sending 5, 100-byte ICMP Echos to 10.1.1.3, timeout is 2 seconds:
!!!!!
Success rate is 100 percent (5/5), round-trip min/avg/max = 1/3/4 ms


R1# ping 10.1.1.4
Type escape sequence to abort.
Sending 5, 100-byte ICMP Echos to 10.1.1.4, timeout is 2 seconds:
!!!!!
Success rate is 100 percent (5/5), round-trip min/avg/max = 1/3/4 ms


!On R2:

R2# ping 10.1.1.3
Type escape sequence to abort.
Sending 5, 100-byte ICMP Echos to 10.1.1.3, timeout is 2 seconds:
!!!!!
Success rate is 100 percent (5/5), round-trip min/avg/max = 1/3/4 ms


R2# ping 10.1.1.4
Type escape sequence to abort.
Sending 5, 100-byte ICMP Echos to 10.1.1.4, timeout is 2 seconds:
```

```
!!!!!
Success rate is 100 percent (5/5), round-trip min/avg/max = 1/3/4 ms

!On R3:

R3# ping 10.1.1.4
Type escape sequence to abort.
Sending 5, 100-byte ICMP Echos to 10.1.1.4, timeout is 2 seconds:
!!!!!
Success rate is 100 percent (5/5), round-trip min/avg/max = 1/2/4 ms
```

Use the **traceroute** command to see the traffic path between the spokes. Run the command twice to see if there are any changes:

```
R2# traceroute 10.1.1.3 numeric
Type escape sequence to abort.
Tracing the route to 10.1.1.3
VRF info: (vrf in name/id, vrf out name/id)
  1 10.1.1.1 4 msec 4 msec 4 msec
  2 10.1.1.3 0 msec *  0 msec

R2# traceroute 10.1.1.3 numeric
Type escape sequence to abort.
Tracing the route to 10.1.1.3
VRF info: (vrf in name/id, vrf out name/id)
  1 10.1.1.1 0 msec 4 msec 4 msec
  2 10.1.1.3 4 msec *  0 msec

R2# traceroute 10.1.1.4 numeric
Type escape sequence to abort.
Tracing the route to 10.1.1.4
VRF info: (vrf in name/id, vrf out name/id)
  1 10.1.1.1 4 msec 4 msec 0 msec
  2 10.1.1.4 4 msec *  0 msec

R2# traceroute 10.1.1.4 numeric
Type escape sequence to abort.
Tracing the route to 10.1.1.4
VRF info: (vrf in name/id, vrf out name/id)
  1 10.1.1.1 4 msec 4 msec 0 msec
  2 10.1.1.4 4 msec *  0 msec
```

Task 3

Configure EIGRP AS 100 on the tunnel and the loopback interfaces of these routers. You may break one of the rules in the previous task. These routers must use multicast for EIGRP adjacency.

```
!On R1:


R1(config)# router eigrp 100
R1(config-router)# network 1.1.1.1 0.0.0.0
R1(config-router)# network 10.1.1.1 0.0.0.0


!On R2:


R2(config)# router eigrp 100
R2(config-router)# network 2.2.2.2 0.0.0.0
R2(config-router)# network 10.1.1.2 0.0.0.0


!On R3:


R3(config)# router eigrp 100
R3(config-router)# network 3.3.3.3 0.0.0.0
R3(config-router)# network 10.1.1.3 0.0.0.0


!On R4:


R4(config)# router eigrp 100
R4(config-router)# network 4.4.4.4 0.0.0.0
R4(config-router)# network 10.1.1.4 0.0.0.0
```

You can see that the adjacency is not stable. On R1, the adjacency keeps on going up and then down:

```
%DUAL-5-NBRCHANGE: EIGRP-IPv4 100: Neighbor 10.1.1.2 (Tunnel1) is up: new adjacency
%DUAL-5-NBRCHANGE: EIGRP-IPv4 100: Neighbor 10.1.1.3 (Tunnel1) is up: new adjacency
%DUAL-5-NBRCHANGE: EIGRP-IPv4 100: Neighbor 10.1.1.4 (Tunnel1) is up: new adjacency
%DUAL-5-NBRCHANGE: EIGRP-IPv4 100: Neighbor 10.1.1.2 (Tunnel1) is down: retry limit
  exceeded
%DUAL-5-NBRCHANGE: EIGRP-IPv4 100: Neighbor 10.1.1.2 (Tunnel1) is up: new adjacency
%DUAL-5-NBRCHANGE: EIGRP-IPv4 100: Neighbor 10.1.1.3 (Tunnel1) is down: retry limit
  exceeded
%DUAL-5-NBRCHANGE: EIGRP-IPv4 100: Neighbor 10.1.1.3 (Tunnel1) is up: new adjacency
%DUAL-5-NBRCHANGE: EIGRP-IPv4 100: Neighbor 10.1.1.4 (Tunnel1) is down: retry limit
  exceeded
%DUAL-5-NBRCHANGE: EIGRP-IPv4 100: Neighbor 10.1.1.4 (Tunnel1) is up: new adjacency
```

This happens because, by default, EIGRP uses a multicast address of 224.0.0.10 and we have *not* provided multicast capability. Let's provide multicast capability to these routers using the following commands:

```
!On R1:


R1(config)# interface tunnel1
R1(config-if)# ip nhrp map multicast 200.1.2.2
R1(config-if)# ip nhrp map multicast 200.1.3.3
R1(config-if)# ip nhrp map multicast 200.1.4.4
```

Because the spokes are configured in a point-to-point manner and the point-to-point networks have the capability to support both unicast and multicast traffic, there is no need to map multicast traffic to the Non-Broadcast Multi-Access (NBMA) IP address of a given endpoint. We will conduct verification by looking at the EIGRP neighbor table output on the hub and by looking at the routing tables of the spoke routers to verify a successful configuration.

```
!On R1:


R1# show ip eigrp neighbor
EIGRP-IPv4 Neighbors for AS(100)
H   Address              Interface        Hold Uptime    SRTT   RTO  Q  Seq
                                          (sec)          (ms)        Cnt Num
2   10.1.1.4             Tu1                13 00:03:06    13   1434  0  3
1   10.1.1.3             Tu1                14 00:03:29     2   1434  0  3
0   10.1.1.2             Tu1                12 00:03:57     1   1434  0  3


R1# show ip route eigrp | begin Gate
Gateway of last resort is 200.1.1.10 to network 0.0.0.0


      2.0.0.0/24 is subnetted, 1 subnets
D        2.2.2.0 [90/27008000] via 10.1.1.2, 00:03:21, Tunnel1
      3.0.0.0/24 is subnetted, 1 subnets
D        3.3.3.0 [90/27008000] via 10.1.1.3, 00:03:18, Tunnel1
      4.0.0.0/24 is subnetted, 1 subnets
D        4.4.4.0 [90/27008000] via 10.1.1.4, 00:03:26, Tunnel1


!On R2:


R2# show ip route eigrp | begin Gate
Gateway of last resort is 200.1.2.10 to network 0.0.0.0


      1.0.0.0/24 is subnetted, 1 subnets
D        1.1.1.0 [90/27008000] via 10.1.1.1, 00:04:03, Tunnel1
```

```
!On R3:


R3# show ip route eigrp | begin Gate
Gateway of last resort is 200.1.3.10 to network 0.0.0.0


     1.0.0.0/24 is subnetted, 1 subnets
D        1.1.1.0 [90/27008000] via 10.1.1.1, 00:04:31, Tunnel1

!On R4:


R4# show ip route eigrp | begin Gate
Gateway of last resort is 200.1.4.10 to network 0.0.0.0


     1.0.0.0/24 is subnetted, 1 subnets
D        1.1.1.0 [90/27008000] via 10.1.1.1, 00:05:03, Tunnel1
```

This output seems suspect. As you can see, the hub router (R1) can see the loopback interfaces of the spokes, but the spokes can only see the loopback interface of the hub. This raises the question, "Why can't the spoke routers see each other's loopback interfaces?"

The answer is split horizon. The rule for split horizon states that if you receive a route through a given interface, you cannot advertise that same route out of that same interface. The command **no ip split-horizon** is used to disable split horizon for the Routing Information Protocol (RIP). This will allow routes to be advertised out the same interface on which they were received. With EIGRP, we must use **no ip split-horizon eigrp** and specify the autonomous-system number.

Let's disable the split horizon on R1 for EIGRP:

```
!On R1:


R1(config)# interface tunnel1
R1(config-if)# no ip split-horizon eigrp 100


%DUAL-5-NBRCHANGE: EIGRP-IPv4 100: Neighbor 10.1.1.4 (Tunnel1) is resync: split
  horizon changed
%DUAL-5-NBRCHANGE: EIGRP-IPv4 100: Neighbor 10.1.1.3 (Tunnel1) is resync: split
  horizon changed
%DUAL-5-NBRCHANGE: EIGRP-IPv4 100: Neighbor 10.1.1.2 (Tunnel1) is resync: split
  horizon changed
```

Now we need to re-verify the status of the spokes to see if this modification to the hub has any impact on their routing tables. We should now expect to see the previously "missing" prefixes.

```
!On R2:

R2# show ip route eigrp | begin Gate
Gateway of last resort is 200.1.2.10 to network 0.0.0.0

      1.0.0.0/24 is subnetted, 1 subnets
D        1.1.1.0 [90/27008000] via 10.1.1.1, 00:11:46, Tunnel1
      3.0.0.0/24 is subnetted, 1 subnets
D        3.3.3.0 [90/28288000] via 10.1.1.1, 00:03:01, Tunnel1
      4.0.0.0/24 is subnetted, 1 subnets
D        4.4.4.0 [90/28288000] via 10.1.1.1, 00:03:01, Tunnel1


!On R3:

R3# show ip route eigrp | begin Gate
Gateway of last resort is 200.1.3.10 to network 0.0.0.0

      1.0.0.0/24 is subnetted, 1 subnets
D        1.1.1.0 [90/27008000] via 10.1.1.1, 00:12:04, Tunnel1
      2.0.0.0/24 is subnetted, 1 subnets
D        2.2.2.0 [90/28288000] via 10.1.1.1, 00:03:22, Tunnel1
      4.0.0.0/24 is subnetted, 1 subnets
D        4.4.4.0 [90/28288000] via 10.1.1.1, 00:03:22, Tunnel1


!On R4:

R4# show ip route eigrp | begin Gate
Gateway of last resort is 200.1.4.10 to network 0.0.0.0

      1.0.0.0/24 is subnetted, 1 subnets
D        1.1.1.0 [90/27008000] via 10.1.1.1, 00:12:27, Tunnel1
      2.0.0.0/24 is subnetted, 1 subnets
D        2.2.2.0 [90/28288000] via 10.1.1.1, 00:03:37, Tunnel1
      3.0.0.0/24 is subnetted, 1 subnets
D        3.3.3.0 [90/28288000] via 10.1.1.1, 00:03:37, Tunnel1
```

You can see that full reachability has been achieved. Now, the next thing we need to verify is the specific traffic pattern between the loopback interfaces of the spoke routers:

```
!On R2:

R2# traceroute 3.3.3.3 source loopback0 numeric
Type escape sequence to abort.
Tracing the route to 3.3.3.3
```

```
VRF info: (vrf in name/id, vrf out name/id)
  1 10.1.1.1 4 msec 4 msec 0 msec
  2 10.1.1.3 4 msec *   0 msec


R2# traceroute 3.3.3.3 source loopback0 numeric
Type escape sequence to abort.
Tracing the route to 3.3.3.3
VRF info: (vrf in name/id, vrf out name/id)
  1 10.1.1.1 4 msec 4 msec 0 msec
  2 10.1.1.3 0 msec *   0 msec


R2# traceroute 4.4.4.4 source loopback0 numeric
Type escape sequence to abort.
Tracing the route to 4.4.4.4
VRF info: (vrf in name/id, vrf out name/id)
  1 10.1.1.1 4 msec 4 msec 0 msec
  2 10.1.1.4 4 msec *   0 msec


R2# traceroute 4.4.4.4 source loopback0 numeric
Type escape sequence to abort.
Tracing the route to 4.4.4.4
VRF info: (vrf in name/id, vrf out name/id)
  1 10.1.1.1 4 msec 0 msec 4 msec
  2 10.1.1.4 4 msec *   0 msec


!On R3:


R3# traceroute 4.4.4.4 source loopback0 numeric
Type escape sequence to abort.
Tracing the route to 4.4.4.4
VRF info: (vrf in name/id, vrf out name/id)
  1 10.1.1.1 0 msec 4 msec 4 msec
  2 10.1.1.4 0 msec *   0 msec


R3# traceroute 4.4.4.4 source loopback0 numeric
Type escape sequence to abort.
Tracing the route to 4.4.4.4
VRF info: (vrf in name/id, vrf out name/id)
  1 10.1.1.1 4 msec 4 msec 0 msec
  2 10.1.1.4 4 msec *   0 msec
```

You can see that the traffic from one spoke to another is traversing the hub router. This happens because the spokes are configured in a point-to-point manner and the tunnel endpoint for the spoke routers is the hub router.

Task 4

Convert the DMVPN tunnel to Phase 2. To do this, the spokes must be configured as multipoint, as follows:

```
!On R2, R3 and R4:


Rx(config)# interface tunnel1
Rx(config-if)# tunnel mode gre multipoint
```

The tunnel destination must be unconfigured before we can modify the configuration:

```
Rx(config-if)# no tunnel destination 200.1.1.1
Rx(config-if)# tunnel mode gre multipoint
```

Now that the spokes are changed from point-to-point to multipoint, we must provide multicast capability to the spokes as well. Multicast is mapped to the NBMA IP address and not the tunnel IP address.

```
Rx(config-if)# ip nhrp map multicast 200.1.1.1
```

Let's verify the configuration:

```
!On R2:


R2# show ip route eigrp | begin Gate
Gateway of last resort is 200.1.2.10 to network 0.0.0.0


      1.0.0.0/24 is subnetted, 1 subnets
D        1.1.1.0 [90/27008000] via 10.1.1.1, 00:02:36, Tunnel1
      3.0.0.0/24 is subnetted, 1 subnets
D        3.3.3.0 [90/28288000] via 10.1.1.1, 00:01:23, Tunnel1
      4.0.0.0/24 is subnetted, 1 subnets
D        4.4.4.0 [90/28288000] via 10.1.1.1, 00:01:03, Tunnel1


!On R3:


R3# show ip route eigrp | begin Gate
Gateway of last resort is 200.1.3.10 to network 0.0.0.0


      1.0.0.0/24 is subnetted, 1 subnets
D        1.1.1.0 [90/27008000] via 10.1.1.1, 00:01:55, Tunnel1
      2.0.0.0/24 is subnetted, 1 subnets
```

```
D        2.2.2.0 [90/28288000] via 10.1.1.1, 00:01:55, Tunnel1
      4.0.0.0/24 is subnetted, 1 subnets
D        4.4.4.0 [90/28288000] via 10.1.1.1, 00:01:36, Tunnel1

!On R4:

R4# show ip route eigrp | begin Gate
Gateway of last resort is 200.1.4.10 to network 0.0.0.0


      1.0.0.0/24 is subnetted, 1 subnets
D        1.1.1.0 [90/27008000] via 10.1.1.1, 00:02:04, Tunnel1
      2.0.0.0/24 is subnetted, 1 subnets
D        2.2.2.0 [90/28288000] via 10.1.1.1, 00:02:04, Tunnel1
      3.0.0.0/24 is subnetted, 1 subnets
D        3.3.3.0 [90/28288000] via 10.1.1.1, 00:02:04, Tunnel1
```

Let's see the traffic pattern between the spoke routers:

```
!On R2:

R2# traceroute 3.3.3.3 numeric
Type escape sequence to abort.
Tracing the route to 3.3.3.3
VRF info: (vrf in name/id, vrf out name/id)
  1 10.1.1.1 0 msec 0 msec 4 msec
  2 10.1.1.3 4 msec *  0 msec


R2# traceroute 3.3.3.3 numeric
Type escape sequence to abort.
Tracing the route to 3.3.3.3
VRF info: (vrf in name/id, vrf out name/id)
  1 10.1.1.1 0 msec 4 msec 4 msec
  2 10.1.1.3 4 msec *  0 msec
```

Why is R2 going through the hub router to reach R3? This is Phase 2.

Let's check the routing table of R2 again:

```
R2# show ip route 3.3.3.3

Routing entry for 3.3.3.0/24
  Known via "eigrp 100", distance 90, metric 28288000, type internal
  Redistributing via eigrp 100
  Last update from 10.1.1.1 on Tunnel1, 00:07:11 ago
  Routing Descriptor Blocks:
```

```
* 10.1.1.1, from 10.1.1.1, 00:07:11 ago, via Tunnel1
    Route metric is 28288000, traffic share count is 1
    Total delay is 105000 microseconds, minimum bandwidth is 100 Kbit
    Reliability 255/255, minimum MTU 1476 bytes
    Loading 1/255, Hops 2
```

In order for R2 to reach 3.3.3.0/24, the next-hop IP address is 10.1.1.1. In Phase 2, the direct communication between the spokes can *only* occur through the routing protocols.

Normally when a spoke router (say, R2) sends an EIGRP update to the hub router, R2 sets the next-hop IP address to be its tunnel IP address (in this case, 10.1.1.2). When the hub router receives the EIGRP update from R2, it changes the next-hop IP address to be its own tunnel IP address (in this case, 10.1.1.1). With the following command, we are instructing the hub router not to change the next-hop IP address when it receives EIGRP updates from the spokes. Let's configure this feature and then verify it:

```
!On R1:

R1(config)# interface tunnel1
R1(config-if)# no ip next-hop-self eigrp 100
```

Let's verify the configuration:

```
!On R2:

R2# show ip route eigrp | begin Gate
Gateway of last resort is 200.1.2.10 to network 0.0.0.0

      1.0.0.0/24 is subnetted, 1 subnets
D        1.1.1.0 [90/27008000] via 10.1.1.1, 00:00:34, Tunnel1
      3.0.0.0/24 is subnetted, 1 subnets
D        3.3.3.0 [90/28288000] via 10.1.1.3, 00:00:34, Tunnel1
      4.0.0.0/24 is subnetted, 1 subnets
D        4.4.4.0 [90/28288000] via 10.1.1.4, 00:00:34, Tunnel1
```

As you can see, the next-hop IP address has changed from 10.1.1.1 to 10.1.1.3. Here's how to test the configuration:

```
!On R2:

R2# traceroute 3.3.3.3 numeric
Type escape sequence to abort.
Tracing the route to 3.3.3.3
VRF info: (vrf in name/id, vrf out name/id)
  1 10.1.1.3 0 msec *  0 msec
```

Let's verify the NHRP table of R2:

```
R2# show ip nhrp 10.1.1.3
10.1.1.3/32 via 10.1.1.3
   Tunnel1 created 00:13:32, expire 01:46:27
   Type: dynamic, Flags: router implicit used
   NBMA address: 200.1.3.3
```

Because R2 has reachability to the NBMA IP address of R3, it knows how to reach R3 directly. The routing table of R2 has 10.1.1.3 as the next-hop IP address to reach 3.3.3.0/24. Therefore, R2 goes to R3 directly.

When you disabled **ip next-hop-self** in EIGRP, the route on the spoke router was pointing to the far-end spoke (instead of the hub). But let's see what happens in the background:

- The data packet is forwarded to the hub router because there is no NHRP information (Tunnel-IP-to-NBMA-IP mapping) for the remote spoke.

- The spoke router at the same time triggers an NHRP Resolution request for the remote spoke's NBMA IP address. This resolution request includes the Tunnel-IP-to-NBMA-IP mapping.

- The hub router receives the NHRP Resolution request and forwards it to the destination spoke.

- The destination spoke gets that NHRP Resolution request and creates an NHRP Reply packet (thanks to the information in the NHRP Resolution request that contains the Tunnel-IP-to-NBMA-IP mapping of the originating spoke).

- The destination spoke sends out an NHRP Resolution reply to the originating spoke *directly*.

- If IPSec is also configured, before the NHRP Resolution reply is sent to the originating spoke, IPSec is triggered to create a direct spoke-to-spoke tunnel.

- When the originating spoke receives the NHRP Resolution reply, it adds the remote spoke's Tunnel-IP-to-NBMA-IP mapping to its NHRP table, and it switches the traffic path to the direct spoke-to-spoke tunnel.

Task 5

Configure the loopback interfaces shown in Table 7-1 on the spoke routers and advertise them in EIGRP AS 100. This may override the Lo0 interfaces of the spokes.

Table 7-1 *Loopback Interfaces*

Router	Interface–IP Address
R2	
R2	Lo0–2.2.0.2/24
R2	Lo1–2.2.1.2/24
R2	Lo2–2.2.2.2/24
R2	Lo3–2.2.3.2/24
R3	
R3	Lo0–3.3.0.3/24
R3	Lo1–3.3.1.3/24
R3	Lo2–3.3.2.3/24
R3	Lo3–3.3.3.3/24
R4	
R4	Lo0–4.4.0.4/24
R4	Lo1–4.4.1.4/24
R4	Lo2–4.4.2.4/24
R4	Lo3–4.4.3.4/24

```
!On R2:

R2(config)# interface loopback0
R2(config-if)# ip address 2.2.0.2 255.255.255.0

R2(config)# interface loopback1
R2(config-if)# ip address 2.2.1.2 255.255.255.0

R2(config)# interface loopback2
R2(config-if)# ip address 2.2.2.2 255.255.255.0

R2(config)# interface loopback3
R2(config-if)# ip address 2.2.3.2 255.255.255.0

R2(config)# router eigrp 100
R2(config-router)# network 2.2.0.2 0.0.0.0
```

```
R2(config-router)# network 2.2.1.2 0.0.0.0
R2(config-router)# network 2.2.2.2 0.0.0.0
R2(config-router)# network 2.2.3.2 0.0.0.0

!On R3:

R3(config)# interface loopback0
R3(config-if)# ip address 3.3.0.3 255.255.255.0

R3(config)# interface loopback1
R3(config-if)# ip address 3.3.1.3 255.255.255.0

R3(config)# interface loopback2
R3(config-if)# ip address 3.3.2.3 255.255.255.0

R3(config)# interface loopback3
R3(config-if)# ip address 3.3.3.3 255.255.255.0

R3(config)# router eigrp 100
R3(config-router)# network 3.3.0.3 0.0.0.0
R3(config-router)# network 3.3.1.3 0.0.0.0
R3(config-router)# network 3.3.2.3 0.0.0.0

!On R4:

R4(config)# interface loopback0
R4(config-if)# ip address 4.4.0.4 255.255.255.0

R4(config)# interface loopback1
R4(config-if)# ip address 4.4.1.4 255.255.255.0

R4(config)# interface loopback2
R4(config-if)# ip address 4.4.4.4 255.255.255.0

R4(config)# interface loopback3
R4(config-if)# ip address 4.4.3.4 255.255.255.0

R4(config)# router eigrp 100
R4(config-router)# network 4.4.0.4 0.0.0.0
R4(config-router)# network 4.4.1.4 0.0.0.0
R4(config-router)# network 4.4.2.4 0.0.0.0
R4(config-router)# network 4.4.3.4 0.0.0.0
```

Let's verify the configuration:

```
!On R2:

R2# show ip route eigrp | begin Gate
Gateway of last resort is 200.1.2.10 to network 0.0.0.0


     1.0.0.0/24 is subnetted, 1 subnets
D        1.1.1.0 [90/27008000] via 10.1.1.1, 00:20:03, Tunnel1
     3.0.0.0/24 is subnetted, 4 subnets
D        3.3.0.0 [90/28288000] via 10.1.1.3, 00:01:33, Tunnel1
D        3.3.1.0 [90/28288000] via 10.1.1.3, 00:01:29, Tunnel1
D        3.3.2.0 [90/28288000] via 10.1.1.3, 00:01:25, Tunnel1
D        3.3.3.0 [90/28288000] via 10.1.1.3, 00:01:40, Tunnel1
     4.0.0.0/24 is subnetted, 4 subnets
D        4.4.0.0 [90/28288000] via 10.1.1.4, 00:00:29, Tunnel1
D        4.4.1.0 [90/28288000] via 10.1.1.4, 00:00:26, Tunnel1
D        4.4.2.0 [90/28288000] via 10.1.1.4, 00:00:22, Tunnel1
D        4.4.3.0 [90/28288000] via 10.1.1.4, 00:00:18, Tunnel1
```

Task 6

In the future, another 1000 spokes will be added to this DMVPN network. The future spokes will have some networks that they will advertise in this routing domain. In order to cut down on the number of entries in the routing table of the spokes, we decide to summarize existing and future routes on the hub router using the **ip summary-address eigrp 100 0.0.0.0 0.0.0.0** command. After summarizing on the hub router, we realize that the communication between the spokes is no longer direct and it traverses the hub router to reach the other spokes. We need to provide a solution through DMVPN so that the communication between the spokes is direct.

Let's summarize on the hub router based on this task:

```
!On R1:

R1(config)# interface tunnel1
R1(config-if)# ip summary-address eigrp 100 0.0.0.0 0.0.0.0
```

Let's verify the configuration:

```
!On R2:

R2# show ip route eigrp | begin Gate
Gateway of last resort is 200.1.2.10 to network 0.0.0.0
```

Why can't we see the default route injected into the EIGRP routing domain by R1?

The reason we don't see the default route injected within the EIGRP routing domain is because we have a static default route pointing to the NBMA IP address of the switch to which we are connected. This was done in Task 1. Because static routes have a lower administrative distance, EIGRP's default route is not injected into the routing table.

Let's remove the static default route from all routers:

```
!On All Routers:

Rx(config)# no ip route 0.0.0.0 0.0.0.0
```

With that accomplished, we can configure specific static routes for the NBMA IP addresses of the other spokes:

```
!On R1:

R1(config)# ip route 200.1.2.2 255.255.255.255 200.1.1.10
R1(config)# ip route 200.1.3.3 255.255.255.255 200.1.1.10
R1(config)# ip route 200.1.4.4 255.255.255.255 200.1.1.10

!On R2:

R2(config)# ip route 200.1.1.1 255.255.255.255 200.1.2.10
R2(config)# ip route 200.1.3.3 255.255.255.255 200.1.2.10
R2(config)# ip route 200.1.4.4 255.255.255.255 200.1.2.10

!On R3:

R3(config)# ip route 200.1.1.1 255.255.255.255 200.1.3.10
R3(config)# ip route 200.1.2.2 255.255.255.255 200.1.3.10
R3(config)# ip route 200.1.4.4 255.255.255.255 200.1.3.10

!On R4:

R4(config)# ip route 200.1.1.1 255.255.255.255 200.1.4.10
R4(config)# ip route 200.1.2.2 255.255.255.255 200.1.4.10
R4(config)# ip route 200.1.3.3 255.255.255.255 200.1.4.10
```

We will verify the configuration on R2 to simplify the number of **show** commands needed to see the impact of this change. Feel free to repeat the verification on the other spoke devices if you like.

Note   Once the summarization is configured on the hub router, all spokes point to the hub again, so the main requirement of DMVPN Phase 2 is broken.

```
R2# show ip route eigrp | begin Gate
Gateway of last resort is 10.1.1.1 to network 0.0.0.0

D*    0.0.0.0/0 [90/27008000] via 10.1.1.1, 00:01:29, Tunnel1
```

The output of the preceding **show** command reveals that the next-hop IP address to reach any destination is the hub router (R1) with an IP address of 10.1.1.1.

Let's test the configuration:

```
!On R2:


R2# traceroute 3.3.3.3 numeric
Type escape sequence to abort.
Tracing the route to 3.3.3.3
VRF info: (vrf in name/id, vrf out name/id)
  1 10.1.1.1 0 msec 4 msec 4 msec
  2 10.1.1.3 4 msec *  0 msec


R2# traceroute 3.3.3.3 numeric
Type escape sequence to abort.
Tracing the route to 3.3.3.3
VRF info: (vrf in name/id, vrf out name/id)
  1 10.1.1.1 4 msec 4 msec 0 msec
  2 10.1.1.3 4 msec *  0 msec
```

Note   The direct spoke-to-spoke communication is no longer available.

What if the DMVPN is converted into Phase 3? The process in Phase 3 is similar to Phase 2 with one major difference. In Phase 3, we have CEF adjacency always resolved because we're pointing to the hub. So there must be another mechanism used to switch the traffic path to direct spoke-to-spoke tunnels.

The following explains the process:

■ The data packet is forwarded to the hub router. This is based on Routing Information-Base (RIB) and Forwarding Information-Base.

■ The hub router gets the data packet from the originating spoke and forwards it to the destination spoke via its tunnel interface. It also realizes that the packet is being forwarded out the same tunnel interface (the hub router knows this because the "incoming" and "outgoing" interfaces have the same **ip nhrp network-id** configured). The hub router now realizes that it is a transit router for the data packets between the spokes.

■ The hub router sends an NHRP Redirect message to the originating spoke router requesting an NHRP Resolution.

■ The originating spoke router gets the NHRP Redirect and triggers an NHRP Resolution request for the destination spoke's NBMA IP address. The spoke router includes its Tunnel-IP-to-NBMA-IP mapping.

■ The hub router receives the NHRP Resolution request and forwards it to the destination spoke router.

■ The destination spoke router receives the NHRP Resolution request and creates an NHRP Resolution reply packet (thanks to the information in the NHRP Resolution request that contains the originating spoke's Tunnel-IP-to-NBMA-IP mapping).

■ The destination spoke sends out an NHRP Resolution reply to the originating spoke directly. If IPSec is configured, the destination spoke triggers IPSec to create a direct spoke-to-spoke tunnel before the NHRP Resolution reply is sent.

■ When the originating spoke receives the NHRP Resolution reply, it adds the destination spoke's Tunnel-IP-to-NBMA-IP mapping to its NHRP table. It then overrides the previous CEF information for the destination spoke, and then it switches the traffic path to the direct spoke-to-spoke tunnel.

We will configure **ip nhrp redirect**, thus converting our DMVPN to a Phase 3 DMVPN. Here's how to examine the impact while running EIGRP:

```
!On R1:

R1(config)# interface tunnel1
R1(config-if)# ip nhrp redirect
```

Note In Phase 3, we no longer need to instruct the hop router not to change the next-hop IP address.

```
R1(config-if)# ip next-hop-self eigrp 100

!On R2, R3, and R4:

Rx(config)# interface tunnel1
Rx(config-if)# ip nhrp shortcut
```

Let's verify the NHRP table of R1:

```
!On R1:


R1# show ip nhrp
10.1.1.2/32 via 10.1.1.2
   Tunnel1 created 00:00:16, expire 01:59:58
   Type: dynamic, Flags: unique registered used
   NBMA address: 200.1.2.2
10.1.1.3/32 via 10.1.1.3
   Tunnel1 created 00:00:19, expire 01:59:55
   Type: dynamic, Flags: unique registered used
   NBMA address: 200.1.3.3
10.1.1.4/32 via 10.1.1.4
   Tunnel1 created 00:00:16, expire 01:59:58
   Type: dynamic, Flags: unique registered used
   NBMA address: 200.1.4.4
```

Let's test the configuration:

```
!On R2:


R2# show adjacency tunnel1 detail
Protocol Interface        Address
IP       Tunnel1          10.1.1.1(11)
                          0 packets, 0 bytes
                          epoch 1
                          sourced in sev-epoch 3
                          Encap length 24
                          4500000000000000FF2F28C9C8010202
                          C801010100000800
                          Tun endpt
                          Next chain element:
                            IP adj out of FastEthernet0/0, addr 200.1.2.10


R2# traceroute 3.3.3.3 numeric
Type escape sequence to abort.
Tracing the route to 3.3.3.3
VRF info: (vrf in name/id, vrf out name/id)
  1 10.1.1.1 4 msec 0 msec 4 msec
  2 10.1.1.3 4 msec *  0 msec
```

We can see a single rewrite for the hub router. The "c8010101" is the NBMA IP address of the hub router.

Note   "C8" in decimal is 200, followed by 010101 (or 200.1.1.1).

We can also see a rewrite for the spoke router.

```
R2# show adjacency tunnel1 detail
Protocol Interface       Address
IP       Tunnel1         10.1.1.1(11)
                         0 packets, 0 bytes
                         epoch 1
                         sourced in sev-epoch 3
                         Encap length 24
                         4500000000000000FF2F28C9C8010202
                         C801010100000800
                         Tun endpt
                         Next chain element:
                          IP adj out of FastEthernet0/0, addr 200.1.2.10
IP       Tunnel1         10.1.1.3(8)
                         0 packets, 0 bytes
                         epoch 1
                         sourced in sev-epoch 3
                         Encap length 24
                         4500000000000000FF2F26C7C8010202
                         C801030300000800
                         Tun endpt
                         Next chain element:
                          IP adj out of FastEthernet0/0, addr 200.1.2.10
```

Now that the second rewrite is in the CEF, the traceroutes should go directly to the destination spoke:

```
R2# traceroute 3.3.3.3 numeric
Type escape sequence to abort.
Tracing the route to 3.3.3.3
VRF info: (vrf in name/id, vrf out name/id)
  1 10.1.1.3 0 msec *  0 msec
```

This is one major benefit of converting to Phase 3, but how did it happen?

Let's check the routing and the NHRP table of R2:

```
R2# show ip route eigrp | begin Gate
Gateway of last resort is 10.1.1.1 to network 0.0.0.0


D*    0.0.0.0/0 [90/27008000] via 10.1.1.1, 00:08:34, Tunnel1


R2# show ip nhrp
3.3.3.0/24 via 10.1.1.3
   Tunnel1 created 00:13:04, expire 01:46:55
   Type: dynamic, Flags: router
   NBMA address: 200.1.3.3
10.1.1.1/32 via 10.1.1.1
   Tunnel1 created 01:41:35, never expire
   Type: static, Flags: used
   NBMA address: 200.1.1.1
10.1.1.2/32 via 10.1.1.2
   Tunnel1 created 00:13:04, expire 01:46:55
   Type: dynamic, Flags: router unique local
   NBMA address: 200.1.2.2
     (no-socket)
10.1.1.3/32 via 10.1.1.3
   Tunnel1 created 00:13:04, expire 01:46:55
   Type: dynamic, Flags: router implicit
   NBMA address: 200.1.3.3
```

The **ip nhrp shortcut** command instructs the spoke routers to look at their NHRP table and override CEF. This is why the NHRP table can grow. To verify this, let's ping 4.4.3.4 and look at the NHRP table:

```
R2# ping 4.4.3.4

Type escape sequence to abort.
Sending 5, 100-byte ICMP Echos to 4.4.4.4, timeout is 2 seconds:
!!!!!
Success rate is 100 percent (5/5), round-trip min/avg/max = 1/3/8 ms
```

Let's now verify the NHRP table of R2:

```
R2# show ip nhrp 4.4.3.0
4.4.3.0/24 via 10.1.1.4
   Tunnel1 created 00:01:00, expire 01:58:59
   Type: dynamic, Flags: router
   NBMA address: 200.1.4.4
```

Erase the startup configuration of the routers and the switch and reload them before proceeding to the next lab.

Lab 7-2: EIGRP Named Mode

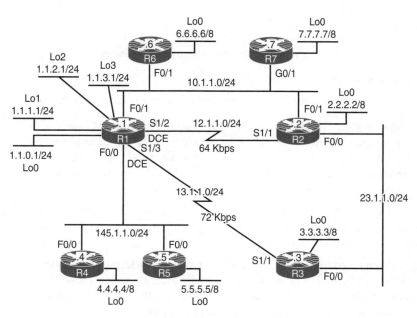

Figure 7-2 *EIGRP Named Mode Lab Topology*

Task 1

Figure 7-2 illustrates the topology used in the following tasks. Configure EIGRP on R1, R2, and R3 based on the policy shown in Table 7-2.

Table 7-2 *Policy for Configuring EIGRP*

Router	Interface	AS Number
R1	F0/1	200
	F0/0	100
	S1/2	100
		100
	S1/3	100
	loopback0 - 3	
R2	F0/1	200
	F0/0	100
	S1/1	100
	loopback0	100

Router	Interface	AS Number
R3	F0/0	100
	S1/1	100
	loopback0	100

Here are some key points to keep in mind:

- R1 should be configured to use unicast to establish a neighbor adjacency with R2.
- R1 should use multicast to establish a neighbor adjacency with R3.
- R1, R2, and R3 should use an EIGRP named configuration to accomplish this task.

Configuring EIGRP with a virtual instance name creates an EIGRP named configuration. If you need to configure another EIGRP instance in another ASN, on the local router you must use another EIGRP virtual instance with a different name and specify the ASN in the **address-family** command. Between the two routers, the virtual instance name does not need to match; the virtual instance name is locally significant.

The **auto-summary** is disabled by default. If you enter the **no auto-summary** command, it will not be displayed in the output of the **show run | section router eigrp** command, unless it is specifically enabled.

Using the EIGRP named configuration, you configure the **network** statement under the **address-family** configuration mode and *not* directly under the router EIGRP configuration mode. The named configuration supports IPv4, IPv6, and VRF instances using different **address-family** types in a single EIGRP instance.

The named configuration provides a single place for all EIGRP commands, and it can be displayed using a single **show** command.

```
!On R1:

R1(config)# router eigrp AS100
R1(config-router)# address-family ipv4 unicast autonomous-system 100
R1(config-router-af)# network 12.1.1.1 0.0.0.0
R1(config-router-af)# network 13.1.1.1 0.0.0.0
R1(config-router-af)# network 145.1.1.1 0.0.0.0
R1(config-router-af)# network 1.1.0.1 0.0.0.0
R1(config-router-af)# network 1.1.1.1 0.0.0.0
R1(config-router-af)# network 1.1.2.1 0.0.0.0
R1(config-router-af)# network 1.1.3.1 0.0.0.0
```

You can see that the **neighbor** command is configured under the **address-family** and *not* directly under the **router eigrp** configuration mode:

```
R1(config-router-af)# neighbor 12.1.1.2 serial1/2
```

Note   R1 could have been configured using the **network 0.0.0.0** statement instead of seven **network** statements. With the **network 0.0.0.0** statement, you are running EIGRP on all existing and future interface(s) in the specified AS. Some engineers configure EIGRP using the following method:

```
network 12.1.1.0 0.0.0.255
network 13.1.1.0 0.0.0.255
```

In the preceding example, you are running EIGRP AS 100 on all interfaces in networks 12.1.1.0/24 and 13.1.1.0/24. This means that if these networks use variable-length subnet masking (VLSM), then EIGRP AS 100 is running on all subsets of these two networks. The best way to configure EIGRP is to be very specific, like the configuration performed on R1. Let's continue with our configuration:

Note   You can use **as** instead of **autonomous-system**.

```
R1(config)# router eigrp AS200
R1(config-router)# address-family ipv4 unicast as 200
R1(config-router-af)# network 10.1.1.1 0.0.0.0
```

Tip   In order to minimize the amount of typing you have to do when configuring EIGRP named mode, once one end is configured, you should issue a **show run | section router eigrp** command.

```
R1# show run | section router eigrp AS100
router eigrp AS100
 !
 address-family ipv4 unicast autonomous-system 100
  !
  topology base
  exit-af-topology
  neighbor 12.1.1.2 Serial1/2
  network 1.1.0.1 0.0.0.0
```

```
   network 1.1.1.1 0.0.0.0
   network 1.1.2.1 0.0.0.0
   network 1.1.3.1 0.0.0.0
   network 12.1.1.1 0.0.0.0
   network 13.1.1.1 0.0.0.0
   network 145.1.1.1 0.0.0.0
 exit-address-family
```

Copy the first three lines after the **show** command and paste them on the other router(s) running in the same AS; then all you have to do is enter the **network** command:

```
!On R2:

R2(config)# router eigrp AS100

R2(config-router)# address-family ipv4 unicast autonomous-system 100
R2(config-router-af)# network 12.1.1.2 0.0.0.0
R2(config-router-af)# network 23.1.1.2 0.0.0.0
R2(config-router-af)# network 2.2.2.2 0.0.0.0
```

In EIGRP, if one neighbor is configured for unicast, the other end has to be configured for unicast as well; you cannot have one end configured for unicast and the other for multicast.

```
R2(config-router-af)# neighbor 12.1.1.1 serial1/1
```

You should see the following console message stating that a neighbor adjacency has been established between the local router and R1 (12.1.1.1):

```
%DUAL-5-NBRCHANGE: EIGRP-IPv4 100: Neighbor 12.1.1.1 (Serial1/1) is up: new
  adjacency

R2(config)# router eigrp AS200
R2(config-router)# address-family ipv4 unicast as 200
R2(config-router-af)# network 10.1.1.2 0.0.0.0
```

You should see the following console message stating that the local router has established an adjacency with R1 (10.1.1.1):

```
%DUAL-5-NBRCHANGE: EIGRP-IPv4 200: Neighbor 10.1.1.1 (FastEthernet0/1) is
up: new adjacency

!On R3:
```

```
R3(config)# router eigrp AS100
R3(config-router)# address-family ipv4 unicast as 100
R3(config-router-af)# network 23.1.1.3 0.0.0.0
R3(config-router-af)# network 13.1.1.3 0.0.0.0
R3(config-router-af)# network 3.3.3.3 0.0.0.0
```

You should see the following console message stating that the local router has established an adjacency with R1 (13.1.1.1) and R2 (23.1.1.2):

```
%DUAL-5-NBRCHANGE: EIGRP-IPv4 100: Neighbor 23.1.1.2 (FastEthernet0/0) is up: new
  adjacency
%DUAL-5-NBRCHANGE: EIGRP-IPv4 100: Neighbor 13.1.1.1 (Serial1/1) is up: new
  adjacency
```

Let's verify the configuration:

```
!On R3:

R3# show ip route eigrp 100 | begin Gate
Gateway of last resort is not set


      1.0.0.0/24 is subnetted, 4 subnets
D        1.1.0.0 [90/36195328] via 13.1.1.1, 00:01:29, Serial1/1
D        1.1.1.0 [90/36195328] via 13.1.1.1, 00:01:29, Serial1/1
D        1.1.2.0 [90/36195328] via 13.1.1.1, 00:01:29, Serial1/1
D        1.1.3.0 [90/36195328] via 13.1.1.1, 00:01:29, Serial1/1
D     2.0.0.0/8 [90/156160] via 23.1.1.2, 00:01:31, FastEthernet0/0
      12.0.0.0/24 is subnetted, 1 subnets
D        12.1.1.0 [90/40514560] via 23.1.1.2, 00:01:31, FastEthernet0/0
      145.1.0.0/24 is subnetted, 1 subnets
D        145.1.1.0 [90/36069888] via 13.1.1.1, 00:01:29, Serial1/1

!On R1:


R1# show ip route eigrp | begin Gate
Gateway of last resort is not set

D     2.0.0.0/8 [90/36197888] via 13.1.1.3, 00:09:23, Serial1/3
D     3.0.0.0/8 [90/36195328] via 13.1.1.3, 00:09:18, Serial1/3
      23.0.0.0/24 is subnetted, 1 subnets
D        23.1.1.0 [90/36069888] via 13.1.1.3, 00:09:23, Serial1/3
```

You can see that EIGRP has the capability to establish unicast or multicast—or in this case, both simultaneously.

Task 2

Configure EIGRP on R4 and R5 in AS 100. You must use named mode to accomplish this task.

```
!On R4:

R4(config)# router eigrp AS100
R4(config-router)# address-family ipv4 unicast as 100
R4(config-router-af)# network 145.1.1.4 0.0.0.0
R4(config-router-af)# network 4.4.4.4 0.0.0.0
```

You should see the following console message:

```
%DUAL-5-NBRCHANGE: EIGRP-IPv4 100: Neighbor 145.1.1.1 (FastEthernet0/0) is up: new
  adjacency

!On R5:

R5(config)# router eigrp AS100
R5(config-router)# address-family ipv4 unicast as 100
R5(config-router-af)# network 5.5.5.5 0.0.0.0
R5(config-router-af)# network 145.1.1.5 0.0.0.0
```

You should see the following console messages as well:

```
%DUAL-5-NBRCHANGE: EIGRP-IPv4 100: Neighbor 145.1.1.4 (FastEthernet0/0) is up: new
  adjacency
%DUAL-5-NBRCHANGE: EIGRP-IPv4 100: Neighbor 145.1.1.1 (FastEthernet0/0) is up: new
  adjacency
```

Let's verify the configuration:

```
!On R5:

R5# show ip route eigrp | begin Gate
Gateway of last resort is not set

     1.0.0.0/24 is subnetted, 4 subnets
D       1.1.0.0 [90/156160] via 145.1.1.1, 00:01:04, FastEthernet0/0
D       1.1.1.0 [90/156160] via 145.1.1.1, 00:01:04, FastEthernet0/0
D       1.1.2.0 [90/156160] via 145.1.1.1, 00:01:04, FastEthernet0/0
D       1.1.3.0 [90/156160] via 145.1.1.1, 00:01:04, FastEthernet0/0
D     2.0.0.0/8 [90/36200448] via 145.1.1.1, 00:01:04, FastEthernet0/0
D     3.0.0.0/8 [90/36197888] via 145.1.1.1, 00:01:04, FastEthernet0/0
D     4.0.0.0/8 [90/156160] via 145.1.1.4, 00:01:04, FastEthernet0/0
     12.0.0.0/24 is subnetted, 1 subnets
```

```
D        12.1.1.0 [90/40514560] via 145.1.1.1, 00:01:04, FastEthernet0/0
    13.0.0.0/24 is subnetted, 1 subnets
D        13.1.1.0 [90/36069888] via 145.1.1.1, 00:01:04, FastEthernet0/0
    23.0.0.0/24 is subnetted, 1 subnets
D        23.1.1.0 [90/36072448] via 145.1.1.1, 00:01:04, FastEthernet0/0
```

Task 3

Configure R1, R4, and R5 to use unicast to establish their neighbor adjacency:

```
!On R1:

R1(config)# router eigrp AS100
R1(config-router)# address-family ipv4 unicast as 100
R1(config-router-af)# neighbor 145.1.1.4 fastEthernet0/0
R1(config-router-af)# neighbor 145.1.1.5 fastEthernet0/0
```

Once the preceding **neighbor** commands are configured, you should see the following console messages, which state that both neighbors (R4 and R5) lost their adjacency to the local router:

```
%DUAL-5-NBRCHANGE: EIGRP-IPv4 100: Neighbor 145.1.1.5 (FastEthernet0/0) is down:
Static peer configured
%DUAL-5-NBRCHANGE: EIGRP-IPv4 100: Neighbor 145.1.1.4 (FastEthernet0/0) is down:
Static peer configured
```

But why didn't R5 reestablish its adjacency?

In Task 1, you saw that EIGRP established a unicast adjacency with R2 and a multicast adjacency with R3. But in this case, once the **neighbor** command was configured, all adjacencies on that segment were torn down. So what is different about R1, R4, and R5 versus R1, R2, and R3?

R1, R2, and R3 were configured in a point-to-point manner, whereas R1, R4 and R5 are on the same Ethernet segment. On a broadcast network, EIGRP *cannot* unicast to one or more neighbors and multicast to others. It's either one or the other.

Let's configure R4 and R5:

```
!On R4:

R4(config)# router eigrp AS100
R4(config-router)# address-family ipv4 unicast as 100
R4(config-router-af)# neighbor 145.1.1.1 fastEthernet0/0
R4(config-router-af)# neighbor 145.1.1.5 fastEthernet0/0
```

You should see the following console message:

```
%DUAL-5-NBRCHANGE: EIGRP-IPv4 100: Neighbor 145.1.1.1 (FastEthernet0/0) is up: new
  adjacency


!On R5:


R5(config)# router eigrp AS100
R5(config-router)# address-family ipv4 unicast as 100
R5(config-router-af)# neighbor 145.1.1.1 fastethernet0/0
R5(config-router-af)# neighbor 145.1.1.4 fastethernet0/0
```

You should also see the following console messages:

```
%DUAL-5-NBRCHANGE: EIGRP-IPv4 100: Neighbor 145.1.1.1 (FastEthernet0/0) is up: new
  adjacency
%DUAL-5-NBRCHANGE: EIGRP-IPv4 100: Neighbor 145.1.1.4 (FastEthernet0/0) is up: new
  adjacency
```

Let's verify the configuration:

```
!On R4:


R4# show ip route eigrp | begin Gate
Gateway of last resort is not set


     1.0.0.0/24 is subnetted, 4 subnets
D       1.1.0.0 [90/156160] via 145.1.1.1, 00:07:46, FastEthernet0/0
D       1.1.1.0 [90/156160] via 145.1.1.1, 00:07:46, FastEthernet0/0
D       1.1.2.0 [90/156160] via 145.1.1.1, 00:07:46, FastEthernet0/0
D       1.1.3.0 [90/156160] via 145.1.1.1, 00:07:46, FastEthernet0/0
D    2.0.0.0/8 [90/36200448] via 145.1.1.1, 00:07:46, FastEthernet0/0
D    3.0.0.0/8 [90/36197888] via 145.1.1.1, 00:07:46, FastEthernet0/0
D    5.0.0.0/8 [90/156160] via 145.1.1.5, 00:00:17, FastEthernet0/0
     12.0.0.0/24 is subnetted, 1 subnets
D       12.1.1.0 [90/40514560] via 145.1.1.1, 00:07:46, FastEthernet0/0
     13.0.0.0/24 is subnetted, 1 subnets
D       13.1.1.0 [90/36069888] via 145.1.1.1, 00:07:46, FastEthernet0/0
     23.0.0.0/24 is subnetted, 1 subnets
D       23.1.1.0 [90/36072448] via 145.1.1.1, 00:07:46, FastEthernet0/0
```

Task 4

Configure R6 in EIGRP AS 200. This router should run EIGRP AS 200 on its F0/1 and loopback0 interfaces. You should use an EIGRP named mode to accomplish this task.

```
!On R6:

R6(config)# router eigrp AS200
R6(config-router)# address-family ipv4 unicast as 200
R6(config-router-af)# network 6.6.6.6 0.0.0.0
R6(config-router-af)# network 10.1.1.6 0.0.0.0
```

You should see the following console messages:

```
%DUAL-5-NBRCHANGE: EIGRP-IPv4 200: Neighbor 10.1.1.2 (FastEthernet0/1) is up: new
  adjacency
%DUAL-5-NBRCHANGE: EIGRP-IPv4 200: Neighbor 10.1.1.1 (FastEthernet0/1) is up: new
  adjacency
```

Let's verify the configuration:

```
!On R1:

R1# show ip route eigrp 200 | begin Gate
Gateway of last resort is not set

D    6.0.0.0/8 [90/156160] via 10.1.1.6, 00:03:03, FastEthernet0/1
```

Task 5

Configure OSPF area 0 on the F0/1 interfaces of R6 and R7 and on the loopback0 interface of R7. You should use a router ID of your choice. Change the OSPF network type of R7's loopback0 interface to point-to-point.

Note   The Open Shortest Path First (OSPF) protocol will be covered in later labs.

```
!On R6:

R6(config)# router ospf 1
R6(config-router)# router-id 0.0.0.6
R6(config-router)# network 10.1.1.6 0.0.0.0 area 0

!On R7:

R7(config)# interface loopback0
R7(config-if)# ip ospf network point-to-point
```

```
R7(config)# router ospf 1
R7(config-router)# router-id 0.0.0.7
R7(config-router)# network 10.1.1.7 0.0.0.0 area 0
R7(config-router)# network 7.7.7.7 0.0.0.0 area 0
```

You should see the following console message:

```
%OSPF-5-ADJCHG: Process 1, Nbr 0.0.0.6 on GigabitEthernet0/1 from LOADING to FULL,
    Loading Done
```

Let's verify the configuration:

```
!On R6:

R6# show ip route ospf | begin Gate
Gateway of last resort is not set

O      7.0.0.0/8 [110/2] via 10.1.1.7, 00:00:25, FastEthernet0/1
```

Task 6

Configure R6 to redistribute OSPF into EIGRP such that R1 and R2 go directly to R7 to reach network 7.0.0.0/8 (R7's Lo0).

In the **address-family** configuration mode, you will see the "topology base." The route redistribution is configured in this subconfiguration mode. The following commands are configured in this mode:

```
R6(config)# router eigrp AS200
R6(config-router)# address-family ipv4 unicast as 200
R6(config-router-af)# topology base
R6(config-router-af-topology)#?
Address Family Topology configuration commands:
  auto-summary        Enable automatic network number summarization
  default             Set a command to its defaults
  default-information Control distribution of default information
  default-metric      Set metric of redistributed routes
  distance            Define an administrative distance
  distribute-list     Filter entries in eigrp updates
  eigrp               EIGRP specific commands
  exit-af-topology    Exit from Address Family Topology configuration mode
  maximum-paths       Forward packets over multiple paths
  metric              Modify metrics and parameters for advertisement
```

```
no                   Negate a command or set its defaults
offset-list          Add or subtract offset from EIGRP metrics
redistribute         Redistribute IPv4 routes from another routing protocol
snmp                 Modify snmp parameters
summary-metric       Specify summary to apply metric/filtering
timers               Adjust topology specific timers
traffic-share        How to compute traffic share over alternate paths
variance             Control load balancing variance
```

Note   Redistribution is covered in detail in Chapter 9, "Redistribution."

```
!On R6

R6(config)# router eigrp AS200
R6(config-router)# address-family ipv4 unicast as 200
R6(config-router-af)# topology base
R6(config-router-af-topology)# redistribute ospf 1 metric 1 1 1 1 1
```

Let's verify the configuration:

```
!On R1:

R1# show ip route 7.7.7.7
Routing entry for 7.0.0.0/8
  Known via "eigrp 200", distance 170, metric 2560002816, type external
  Redistributing via eigrp 200
  Last update from 10.1.1.6 on FastEthernet0/1, 00:11:13 ago
  Routing Descriptor Blocks:
  * 10.1.1.6, from 10.1.1.6, 00:11:13 ago, via FastEthernet0/1
      Route metric is 2560002816, traffic share count is 1
      Total delay is 110 microseconds, minimum bandwidth is 1 Kbit
      Reliability 1/255, minimum MTU 1 bytes
      Loading 1/255, Hops 1

R1# traceroute 7.7.7.7 numeric
Type escape sequence to abort.
Tracing the route to 7.7.7.7
VRF info: (vrf in name/id, vrf out name/id)
  1 10.1.1.6 4 msec 0 msec 4 msec
  2 10.1.1.7 0 msec *  0 msec
```

You can see that the next hop is pointing to R6 and *not* R7. To resolve this task, we can use the third-party next hop; in classic EIGRP configuration, this feature was configured directly under the interface, but in the EIGRP named mode, it's configured in the **af-interface** mode directly under the **address-family** configuration mode. Let's look at our options in the **af-interface** mode:

```
!On R6:


R6(config)# router eigrp AS200
R6(config-router)# address-family ipv4 unicast as 200
R6(config-router-af)# af-interface fastEthernet0/1
R6(config-router-af-interface)#?
Address Family Interfaces configuration commands:
  authentication        authentication subcommands
  bandwidth-percent     Set percentage of bandwidth percentage limit
  bfd                   Enable Bidirectional Forwarding Detection
  dampening-change      Percent interface metric must change to cause update
  dampening-interval    Time in seconds to check interface metrics
  default               Set a command to its defaults
  exit-af-interface     Exit from Address Family Interface configuration mode
  hello-interval        Configures hello interval
  hold-time             Configures hold time
  next-hop-self         Configures EIGRP next-hop-self
  no                    Negate a command or set its defaults
  passive-interface     Suppress address updates on an interface
  shutdown              Disable Address-Family on interface
  split-horizon         Perform split horizon
  summary-address       Perform address summarization
```

You can see that most if not all the interface-configuration commands for EIGRP are listed in this mode. Let's configure the third-party next hop:

```
R6(config-router-af-interface)# no next-hop-self
```

Now let's verify the configuration:

```
!On R1:


R1# show ip route 7.7.7.7
Routing entry for 7.0.0.0/8
  Known via "eigrp 200", distance 170, metric 2560002816, type external
  Redistributing via eigrp 200
  Last update from 10.1.1.7 on FastEthernet0/1, 00:01:09 ago
  Routing Descriptor Blocks:
```

```
   * 10.1.1.7, from 10.1.1.6, 00:01:09 ago, via FastEthernet0/1
        Route metric is 2560002816, traffic share count is 1
        Total delay is 110 microseconds, minimum bandwidth is 1 Kbit
        Reliability 1/255, minimum MTU 1 bytes
        Loading 1/255, Hops 1


R1# traceroute 7.7.7.7 numeric
Type escape sequence to abort.
Tracing the route to 7.7.7.7
VRF info: (vrf in name/id, vrf out name/id)
  1 10.1.1.7 0 msec *   0 msec
```

Task 7

Configure the hello interval of all routers in AS 200 to be twice as much as the default.

To start, let's look at the default value for the hello interval on R1:

```
R1# show ip eigrp 200 interface detail
EIGRP-IPv4 VR(tst200) Address-Family Interfaces for AS(200)
                        Xmit Queue    Mean   Pacing Time   Multicast    Pending
Interface       Peers   Un/Reliable   SRTT   Un/Reliable   Flow Timer   Routes
Fa0/1             2       0/0           6       0/1           50           0
  Hello-interval is 5, Hold-time is 15
  Split-horizon is enabled
  Next xmit serial <none>
  Un/reliable mcasts: 0/4  Un/reliable ucasts: 6/8
  Mcast exceptions: 0  CR packets: 0  ACKs suppressed: 0
  Retransmissions sent: 3  Out-of-sequence rcvd: 0
  Topology-ids on interface - 0
  Authentication mode is not set
```

Now that we know the default values, let's change the hello interval to 10 seconds:

```
!On R1, R2, and R6:


Rx(config)# router eigrp AS200
Rx(config-router)# address-family ipv4 unicast as 200
Rx(config-router-af)# af-interface fastEthernet0/1
Rx(config-router-af-interface)# hello-interval 10
```

Now let's verify the configuration:

```
!On R1:

R1# show ip eigrp 200 interface detail
EIGRP-IPv4 VR(tst200) Address-Family Interfaces for AS(200)
                         Xmit Queue  Mean   Pacing Time  Multicast   Pending
Interface        Peers  Un/Reliable SRTT   Un/Reliable  Flow Timer  Routes
Fa0/1              2       0/0        6       0/1          50          0
  Hello-interval is 10, Hold-time is 15
  Split-horizon is enabled
  Next xmit serial <none>
  Un/reliable mcasts: 0/4  Un/reliable ucasts: 6/8
  Mcast exceptions: 0  CR packets: 0  ACKs suppressed: 0
  Retransmissions sent: 3  Out-of-sequence rcvd: 0
  Topology-ids on interface - 0
  Authentication mode is not set
```

Note   When the hello interval is changed, the hold time is *not* changed automatically.

Task 8

R4 should be configured such that in the worst-case scenario, it uses 10% of the bandwidth for its EIGRP updates. This policy should apply to the existing and future interfaces.

By default, EIGRP will *only* consume 50% of its interface's bandwidth; this can be changed using the **bandwidth-percent** command in interface-configuration mode or in the **af-interface** configuration mode under the **address-family**. Let's configure this feature in the **af-interface** configuration mode:

```
!On R4:

R4(config)# router eigrp AS100
R4(config-router)# address-family ipv4 unicast as 100
```

When **af-interface default** is used, instead of referencing a given interface, the configuration is applied to all existing and future interfaces on this router:

```
R4(config-router-af)# af-interface default
R4(config-router-af-interface)# bandwidth-percent 10
```

Let's verify the configuration:

```
!On R4:


R4# show ip eigrp 100 interface detail
EIGRP-IPv4 VR(AS100) Address-Family Interfaces for AS(100)
                                  Xmit Queue    PeerQ       Mean   Pacing Time   Multi-
   cast     Pending
Interface             Peers  Un/Reliable  Un/Reliable  SRTT   Un/Reliable   Flow
   Timer    Routes
Fa0/0                   2        0/0          0/0         5        0/1          50
   0
   Hello-interval is 5, Hold-time is 15
   Split-horizon is enabled
   Next xmit serial <none>
   Packetized sent/expedited: 28/1
   Hello's sent/expedited: 16855/5
   Un/reliable mcasts: 0/9  Un/reliable ucasts: 41/19
   Mcast exceptions: 0  CR packets: 0  ACKs suppressed: 1
   Retransmissions sent: 2  Out-of-sequence rcvd: 1
   Topology-ids on interface - 0
   Interface BW percentage is 10
   Authentication mode is not set
Lo0                     0        0/0          0/0         0        0/0           0
   0
   Hello-interval is 5, Hold-time is 15
   Split-horizon is enabled
   Next xmit serial <none>
   Packetized sent/expedited: 0/0
   Hello's sent/expedited: 0/1
   Un/reliable mcasts: 0/0  Un/reliable ucasts: 0/0
   Mcast exceptions: 0  CR packets: 0  ACKs suppressed: 0
   Retransmissions sent: 0  Out-of-sequence rcvd: 0
   Topology-ids on interface - 0
   Interface BW percentage is 10
   Authentication mode is not set
```

Task 9

Configure R1 to summarize its loopback interfaces and advertise a single summary.

Note The **af-interface default** command *cannot* be used for summarization. The interface(s) must be specified, like so:

```
!On R1:

R1(config)# router eigrp AS100
R1(config-router)# address-family ipv4 unicast as 100
R1(config-router-af)# af-interface serial1/2
R1(config-router-af-interface)# summary-address 1.1.0.0 255.255.252.0
R1(config-router-af)# af-interface serial1/3
R1(config-router-af-interface)# summary-address 1.1.0.0 255.255.252.0
```

Let's verify the configuration:

```
!On R2:

R2# show ip route eigrp | begin Gate
Gateway of last resort is not set

      1.0.0.0/22 is subnetted, 1 subnets
D        1.1.0.0 [90/36197888] via 23.1.1.3, 00:02:24, FastEthernet0/0
D     3.0.0.0/8 [90/156160] via 23.1.1.3, 02:19:11, FastEthernet0/0
D     4.0.0.0/8 [90/36200448] via 23.1.1.3, 01:47:13, FastEthernet0/0
D     5.0.0.0/8 [90/36200448] via 23.1.1.3, 01:46:18, FastEthernet0/0
D     6.0.0.0/8 [90/156160] via 10.1.1.6, 00:46:08, FastEthernet0/1
      7.0.0.0/32 is subnetted, 1 subnets
D EX    7.7.7.7 [170/2560002816] via 10.1.1.7, 00:46:08, FastEthernet0/1
      13.0.0.0/24 is subnetted, 1 subnets
D        13.1.1.0 [90/36069888] via 23.1.1.3, 02:19:17, FastEthernet0/0
      145.1.0.0/24 is subnetted, 1 subnets
D        145.1.1.0 [90/36072448] via 23.1.1.3, 02:04:01, FastEthernet0/0

!On R3:

R3# show ip route eigrp | begin Gate
Gateway of last resort is not set

      1.0.0.0/22 is subnetted, 1 subnets
D        1.1.0.0 [90/36195328] via 13.1.1.1, 00:03:23, Serial1/1
D     2.0.0.0/8 [90/156160] via 23.1.1.2, 02:20:14, FastEthernet0/0
D     4.0.0.0/8 [90/36197888] via 13.1.1.1, 01:48:13, Serial1/1
D     5.0.0.0/8 [90/36197888] via 13.1.1.1, 01:47:18, Serial1/1
      12.0.0.0/24 is subnetted, 1 subnets
D        12.1.1.0 [90/40514560] via 23.1.1.2, 02:20:14, FastEthernet0/0
      145.1.0.0/24 is subnetted, 1 subnets
D        145.1.1.0 [90/36069888] via 13.1.1.1, 02:05:01, Serial1/1
```

You can see that R2 traverses through R3 to get to the loopback interfaces or to the summary for the loopback interfaces, whereas R3 goes directly to R1 to reach the summary route. This is because the bandwidth of R2's link to R1 is set to 64 Kbps, whereas the bandwidth of R3's link to R1 is set to 72 Kbps. Here's how to test this:

```
!On R2:


R2# traceroute 1.1.1.1 numeric
Type escape sequence to abort.
Tracing the route to 1.1.1.1
VRF info: (vrf in name/id, vrf out name/id)
  1 23.1.1.3 0 msec 0 msec 0 msec
  2 13.1.1.1 16 msec *  12 msec


!On R3:


R3# traceroute 1.1.1.1 numeric
Type escape sequence to abort.
Tracing the route to 1.1.1.1
VRF info: (vrf in name/id, vrf out name/id)
  1 13.1.1.1 12 msec *  12 msec
```

Task 10

Configure R1 to assign a fixed metric to its summary route such that R2 and R3 both use R1 as the next hop to reach the more specific routes of the summary, regardless of the bandwidth command on the serial links to R2 and R3.

Before we configure this task, let's look at the cost of the summary route on R2 and R3:

```
!On R2:


R2# show ip route 1.1.0.0 | include metric

  Known via "eigrp 100", distance 90, metric 36197888, type internal
     Route metric is 36197888, traffic share count is 1


!On R3:


R3# show ip route 1.1.0.0 | include metric

  Known via "eigrp 100", distance 90, metric 36195328, type internal
     Route metric is 36195328, traffic share count is 1
```

The traceroutes performed at the end of the previous task revealed that R2 goes through R3 to reach the more specific routes of the summary. Let's assign a *fixed* cost to the summary so that both R2 and R3 use R1 as the next hop to reach the components of the summary route:

```
!On R1:

R1(config)# router eigrp AS100
R1(config-router)# address-family ipv4 unicast as 100
R1(config-router-af)# topology base
R1(config-router-af-topology)# summary-metric 1.1.0.0/22 1 1 1 1 1
```

The preceding command assigns a *fixed* metric for the EIGRP summary route. You can use the metric of the actual interface instead of **1 1 1 1 1**.

Let's verify the configuration:

```
!On R2:

R2# show ip route 1.1.0.0 | include metric
  Known via "eigrp 100", distance 90, metric 2560512256, type internal
     Route metric is 2560512256, traffic share count is 1


!On R3:

R3# show ip route 1.1.0.0 | include metric
  Known via "eigrp 100", distance 90, metric 2560512256, type internal
     Route metric is 2560512256, traffic share count is 1
```

Now let's test the configuration:

```
!On R2:

R2# traceroute 1.1.1.1 numeric
Type escape sequence to abort.
Tracing the route to 1.1.1.1
VRF info: (vrf in name/id, vrf out name/id)
  1 12.1.1.1 12 msec *  12 msec


!On R3:

R3# traceroute 1.1.1.1 numeric
Type escape sequence to abort.
Tracing the route to 1.1.1.1
VRF info: (vrf in name/id, vrf out name/id)
  1 13.1.1.1 16 msec *  12 msec
```

Task 11

Configure R1 to limit the number of received prefixes from R5 to 10. R1 should be configured to receive a warning message once 50% of this threshold is reached and a warning message for every additional route that exceeds the threshold.

To test this feature, let's configure 10 additional loopback interfaces on R5 and then advertise one at a time and verify the result:

```
!On R5:

R5(config)# interface loopback1
R5(config-if)# ip address 51.1.1.5 255.0.0.0

R5(config-if)# interface loopback2
R5(config-if)# ip address 52.1.1.5 255.0.0.0

R5(config-if)# interface loopback3
R5(config-if)# ip address 53.1.1.5 255.0.0.0

R5(config-if)# interface loopback4
R5(config-if)# ip address 54.1.1.5 255.0.0.0

R5(config-if)# interface loopback5
R5(config-if)# ip address 55.1.1.5 255.0.0.0

R5(config-if)# interface loopback6
R5(config-if)# ip address 56.1.1.5 255.0.0.0

R5(config-if)# interface loopback7
R5(config-if)# ip address 57.1.1.5 255.0.0.0

R5(config-if)# interface loopback8
R5(config-if)# ip address 58.1.1.5 255.0.0.0

R5(config-if)# interface loopback9
R5(config-if)# ip address 59.1.1.5 255.0.0.0

R5(config-if)# interface loopback10
R5(config-if)# ip address 60.1.1.5 255.0.0.0
```

Let's configure R1 for this feature:

```
!On R1:

R1(config)# router eigrp AS100
R1(config-router)# address-family ipv4 unicast as 100
R1(config-router-af)# neighbor 145.1.1.5 maximum-prefix 10 50 warning-only
```

Now let's test and verify the configuration:

```
!On R5:

R5(config)# router eigrp AS100
R5(config-router)# address-family ipv4 unicast as 100
R5(config-router-af)# network 51.1.1.5 0.0.0.0
R5(config-router-af)# network 52.1.1.5 0.0.0.0
R5(config-router-af)# network 53.1.1.5 0.0.0.0


R1# show ip route eigrp | include 145.1.1.5

D     5.0.0.0/8 [90/156160] via 145.1.1.5, 00:19:51, FastEthernet0/0
D     51.0.0.0/8 [90/156160] via 145.1.1.5, 00:01:03, FastEthernet0/0
D        52.1.1.0 [90/156160] via 145.1.1.5, 00:00:57, FastEthernet0/0
D        53.1.1.0 [90/156160] via 145.1.1.5, 00:00:51, FastEthernet0/0
```

So far, R1 has not received any warning messages because it is only receiving four networks from R5 (R5's Lo0, Lo1, Lo2, and Lo3). Let's advertise one more and verify the result:

```
R5(config-router-af)# network 54.1.1.5 0.0.0.0
```

Now let's check the console messages on R1. Here's the first message received:

```
!On R1:

%DUAL-4-PFXLIMITTHR: EIGRP-IPv4 100: Neighbor threshold prefix level(5) reached.
```

Let's advertise another network on R5 and verify the result:

```
!On R5:

R5(config-router-af)# network 55.1.1.5 0.0.0.0
```

No console messages on R1 yet, so let's advertise another network on R5:

```
R5(config-router-af)# network 56.1.1.5 0.0.0.0
```

Still no console messages on R1, so let's advertise another three networks on R5 to reach the threshold of 10 networks:

```
R5(config-router-af)# network 57.1.1.5 0.0.0.0
R5(config-router-af)# network 58.1.1.5 0.0.0.0
R5(config-router-af)# network 59.1.1.5 0.0.0.0
```

Now if we look at R1, we should see the following output:

```
!On R1:

%DUAL-4-PFXLIMITTHR: EIGRP-IPv4 100: Neighbor threshold prefix level(5) reached.

%DUAL-3-PFXLIMIT: EIGRP-IPv4 100: Neighbor prefix limit reached(10).
```

Let's advertise another network on R5 and verify the result:

```
!On R5:

R5(config-router-af)# network 60.1.1.5 0.0.0.0
```

You can see that for every additional network above the set threshold, a console message is generated on R1's console:

```
!On R1

%DUAL-3-PFXLIMIT: EIGRP-IPv4 100: Neighbor prefix limit reached(10).
```

Task 12

Configure R1 to limit the number of prefixes received from R4 to five; R1 should be configured to tear down the adjacency if R4 exceeds the specified threshold.

Let's configure five more loopback interfaces on R4 so we can test this feature:

```
!On R4:

R4(config)# interface loopback1
R4(config-if)# ip address 41.1.1.4 255.0.0.0

R4(config)# interface loopback2
R4(config-if)# ip address 42.1.1.4 255.0.0.0

R4(config)# interface loopback3
R4(config-if)# ip address 43.1.1.4 255.0.0.0

R4(config)# interface loopback4
R4(config-if)# ip address 44.1.1.4 255.0.0.0

R4(config)# interface loopback5
R4(config-if)# ip address 45.1.1.4 255.0.0.0
```

Let's configure R1 for this feature:

```
!On R1:

R1(config)# router eigrp AS100
R1(config-router)# address-family ipv4 unicast as 100
R1(config-router-af)# neighbor 145.1.1.4 maximum-prefix 5
```

Let's go back to R1 and advertise an extra network and verify the results:

```
!On R4:

R4(config)# router eigrp AS100
R4(config-router)# address-family ipv4 unicast as 100
R4(config-router-af)# network 41.1.1.4 0.0.0.0
```

So far R1 has not received any console messages because it is only receiving two networks from R4, so let's advertise three more and verify the result:

```
R4(config-router-af)# network 42.1.1.4 0.0.0.0
R4(config-router-af)# network 43.1.1.4 0.0.0.0
```

Sure enough, the following console message is shown on R1 because 80% of the configured threshold was reached:

```
%DUAL-4-PFXLIMITTHR: EIGRP-IPv4 100: Neighbor threshold prefix level(3) reached.
```

Let's advertise one more and verify the console messages on R1:

```
R4(config-router-af)# network 44.1.1.4 0.0.0.0
```

You should see the following two console messages on R1 stating that the maximum threshold has been reached:

```
!On R1:

%DUAL-3-PFXLIMIT: EIGRP-IPv4 100: Neighbor prefix limit reached(5).

%DUAL-5-NBRCHANGE: EIGRP-IPv4 100: Neighbor 145.1.1.4 (FastEthernet0/0) is down:
prefix-limit exceeded
```

You can see that the neighbor adjacency is torn down, so let's verify the neighbor table of R4:

```
R4# show ip eigrp neighbor
EIGRP-IPv4 VR(tst) Address-Family Neighbors for AS(100)
H   Address                 Interface       Hold Uptime   SRTT   RTO  Q   Seq
                                            (sec)         (ms)       Cnt Num
1   145.1.1.5               Fa0/0            12 00:14:24    1    200  0   23


R4# show ip route eigrp | begin Gate
Gateway of last resort is not set

D     5.0.0.0/8 [90/156160] via 145.1.1.5, 00:13:57, FastEthernet0/0
D     51.0.0.0/8 [90/156160] via 145.1.1.5, 00:13:57, FastEthernet0/0
D     52.0.0.0/8 [90/156160] via 145.1.1.5, 00:13:57, FastEthernet0/0
D     53.0.0.0/8 [90/156160] via 145.1.1.5, 00:13:57, FastEthernet0/0
D     54.0.0.0/8 [90/156160] via 145.1.1.5, 00:13:57, FastEthernet0/0
D     55.0.0.0/8 [90/156160] via 145.1.1.5, 00:13:57, FastEthernet0/0
D     56.0.0.0/8 [90/156160] via 145.1.1.5, 00:13:57, FastEthernet0/0
D     57.0.0.0/8 [90/156160] via 145.1.1.5, 00:13:57, FastEthernet0/0
D     58.0.0.0/8 [90/156160] via 145.1.1.5, 00:13:57, FastEthernet0/0
D     59.0.0.0/8 [90/156160] via 145.1.1.5, 00:13:57, FastEthernet0/0
D     60.0.0.0/8 [90/156160] via 145.1.1.5, 00:13:57, FastEthernet0/0
```

You can now see that R4 only exchanges routes with R5 and *not* R1.

Erase the startup config and reload the routers before proceeding to the next lab.

Lab 7-3: EIGRP Metrics (Classic and Wide)

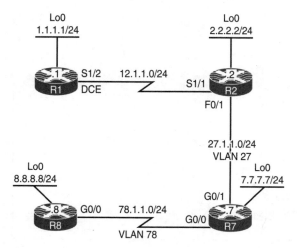

Figure 7-3 *EIGRP Metrics Topology*

Task 1

Figure 7-3 illustrates the topology used in the following tasks. Configure RIPv2 on R1 and R2. R1 should advertise all of its directly connected interfaces in the RIPv2 routing domain. R2 should be configured to advertise its S1/1 interface in RIPv2. Disable auto summary in RIPv2.

Configure EIGRP AS 100 on the F0/1 and Lo0 interfaces of R2 as well as all interfaces of R7 and R8:

```
!On R1:

R1(config)# router rip
R1(config-router)# no auto-summary
R1(config-router)# version 2
R1(config-router)# network 1.0.0.0
R1(config-router)# network 12.0.0.0

!On R2

R2(config-subif)# router rip
R2(config-router)# no auto-summary
R2(config-router)# version 2
R2(config-router)# network 12.0.0.0
```

Let's verify the configuration:

```
!On R2:

R2# show ip route rip | begin Gate
Gateway of last resort is not set

     1.0.0.0/24 is subnetted, 1 subnets
R        1.1.1.0 [120/1] via 12.1.1.1, 00:00:11, Serial1/1

R2(config-router)# router eigrp 100
R2(config-router)# network 2.2.2.2 0.0.0.0
R2(config-router)# network 27.1.1.2 0.0.0.0

!On R7:

R7(config)# router eigrp 100
R7(config-router)# network 27.1.1.7 0.0.0.0
R7(config-router)# network 7.7.7.7 0.0.0.0
R7(config-router)# network 78.1.1.7 0.0.0.0
```

You should see the following console message:

```
%DUAL-5-NBRCHANGE: EIGRP-IPv4 100: Neighbor 27.1.1.2 (GigabitEthernet0/1) is up: new
  adjacency


!On R8:


R8(config)# router eigrp 100
R8(config-router)# network 78.1.1.8 0.0.0.0
R8(config-router)# network 8.8.8.8 0.0.0.0
```

You should also see the following console message:

```
%DUAL-5-NBRCHANGE: EIGRP-IPv4 100: Neighbor 78.1.1.7 (GigabitEthernet0/0) is up: new
  adjacency
```

Let's verify the configuration:

```
!On R7:


R7# show ip route eigrp | begin Gate
Gateway of last resort is not set


     2.0.0.0/24 is subnetted, 1 subnets
D       2.2.2.0 [90/156160] via 27.1.1.2, 00:03:40, GigabitEthernet0/1
     8.0.0.0/24 is subnetted, 1 subnets
D       8.8.8.0 [90/156160] via 78.1.1.8, 00:01:47, GigabitEthernet0/0
```

Task 2

Perform a mutual redistribution between RIPv2 and EIGRP such that R1 sees the EIGRP
routes with the correct hop count. For example, R1 should see network 2.2.2.0/24 with
a hop count of 1, and network 7.7.7.0/24 with a hop count of 2. Future networks should
be redistributed with a hop count of 1.

To resolve this task, an access list is configured to identify every network in the EIGRP
routing domain; a route map will be configured to reference a given access list and assign
a hop count using the **set metric** command.

> **Tip**   Always issue a **show access-lists** command before configuring an access list;
> otherwise, you may add the new access list to an existing one.

```
!On R2

R2# show access-lists

R2(config)# access-list 2 permit 2.2.2.0 0.0.0.255
R2(config)# access-list 7 permit 7.7.7.0 0.0.0.255
R2(config)# access-list 8 permit 8.8.8.0 0.0.0.255
R2(config)# access-list 27 permit 27.1.1.0 0.0.0.255
R2(config)# access-list 78 permit 78.1.1.0 0.0.0.255

R2(config)# route-map TST permit 10
R2(config-route-map)# match ip address 2
R2(config-route-map)# set metric 1

R2(config)# route-map TST permit 20
R2(config-route-map)# match ip address 7
R2(config-route-map)# set metric 2

R2(config)# route-map TST permit 30
R2(config-route-map)# match ip address 8
R2(config-route-map)# set metric 3

R2(config)# route-map TST permit 40
R2(config-route-map)# match ip address 27
R2(config-route-map)# set metric 1

R2(config)# route-map TST permit 50
R2(config-route-map)# match ip address 78
R2(config-route-map)# set metric 2

R2(config)# route-map TST permit 60
R2(config-route-map)# set metric 1
```

Note The route-map TST permit 60 command must be configured for the future networks that may be redistributed into RIPv2. These networks will be assigned a hop count
of 1, per requirement of this task.

```
R2(config-router)# router rip
R2(config-router)# redistribute eigrp 100 route-map TST

R2(config)# router eigrp 100
R2(config-router)# redistribute rip metric 1500 20000 255 1 1500
```

Let's verify the configuration:

```
!On R1:


R1# show ip route rip | begin Gate
Gateway of last resort is not set


      2.0.0.0/24 is subnetted, 1 subnets
R        2.2.2.0 [120/1] via 12.1.1.2, 00:00:26, Serial1/2
      7.0.0.0/24 is subnetted, 1 subnets
R        7.7.7.0 [120/2] via 12.1.1.2, 00:00:26, Serial1/2
      8.0.0.0/24 is subnetted, 1 subnets
R        8.8.8.0 [120/3] via 12.1.1.2, 00:00:26, Serial1/2
      27.0.0.0/24 is subnetted, 1 subnets
R        27.1.1.0 [120/1] via 12.1.1.2, 00:00:26, Serial1/2
      78.0.0.0/24 is subnetted, 1 subnets
R        78.1.1.0 [120/2] via 12.1.1.2, 00:00:26, Serial1/2
```

Task 3

Explain EIGRP's composite metric in classic mode configuration. You should explain the formula that EIGRP uses to calculate the composite metric for R2's loopback0 interface from R7's perspective.

EIGRP in classic mode uses the following formula:

```
((K1*BW)+(K2*BW)/(256-load)+(K3*DLY)*(K5/(K4 + Reliability)))*256
```

The **K** parameters are multipliers and by default are set to the following:

```
K1=1, K2=0, K3=1, K4=0, K5=0
```

The last part of the formula, **K5/(K4 + Reliability)**, *only* comes into play if the value of **K5** is any value except zero. **K4** and **K5** can be used to allow packet loss and reliability to influence routing decisions. If **K5** is equal to zero, the resulting quotient is set to 1. Therefore, by default, the formula that EIGRP uses is

```
(BW+DLY)*256
```

Let's verify the routing table of R7 for the Lo0 interface of R2:

```
!On R7:


R7# show ip route 2.2.2.2


Routing entry for 2.2.2.0/24
  Known via "eigrp 100", distance 90, metric 156160, type internal
  Redistributing via eigrp 100
  Last update from 27.1.1.2 on GigabitEthernet0/1, 01:05:18 ago
  Routing Descriptor Blocks:
```

```
* 27.1.1.2, from 27.1.1.2, 01:05:18 ago, via GigabitEthernet0/1
    Route metric is 156160, traffic share count is 1
    Total delay is 5100 microseconds, minimum bandwidth is 100000 Kbit
    Reliability 255/255, minimum MTU 1500 bytes
    Loading 1/255, Hops 1
```

You can see that the cost is 156160.

EIGRP takes the lowest bandwidth (BW) along the path to a given destination. Let's check the BW of R7's G0/1 and R2's Lo0 interfaces:

```
R7# show interface gigabitEthernet0/1 | include BW

 MTU 1500 bytes, BW 100000 Kbit/sec, DLY 100 usec,

R2# show interface loopback0 | include BW

 MTU 1514 bytes, BW 8000000 Kbit/sec, DLY 5000 usec,
```

Therefore, the lowest BW along the path to network 2.2.2.0/24 is 100,000 Kb.

We then divide 10,000,000 Kb (a set value that cannot be changed) by 100,000 Kb, which yields 100.

Now, let's look at the delay (DLY). EIGRP takes the sum of all DLYs along the path to a given destination. Based on the preceding **show** commands, you can see that the DLY value of the G0/1 interface of R7 is 100, and the DLY value of the Lo0 interface is 5000. Thus, 5000+100=5100. EIGRP calculates the DLY in tens of microseconds. Therefore, the total DLY value should be divided by 10. Thus, 5100/10=510.

The final step is to add 510 to 100, which is 610, and then multiply that by 256. This gives us a value of 156,160.

Task 4

Reconfigure the EIGRP named mode on the G0/0 interfaces of R7 and R8 as well as the Lo0 interface of R8:

```
!On R7:

R7(config)# no router eigrp 100

R7(config)# router eigrp tst
R7(config-router)# address-family ipv4 unicast as 100
R7(config-router-af)# network 78.1.1.7 0.0.0.0
```

```
!On R8:

R8(config)# no router eigrp 100

R8(config)# router eigrp tst
R8(config-router)# address-family ipv4 unicast as 100
R8(config-router-af)# network 8.8.8.8 0.0.0.0
R8(config-router-af)# network 78.1.1.8 0.0.0.0
```

You should see the following console message stating that the two routers have established an EIGRP adjacency:

```
%DUAL-5-NBRCHANGE: EIGRP-IPv4 100: Neighbor 78.1.1.7 (GigabitEthernet0/0) is up: new
  adjacency
```

Let's verify the routing table of R7:

```
!On R7:

R7# show ip route eigrp | begin Gate
Gateway of last resort is not set

      8.0.0.0/24 is subnetted, 1 subnets
D        8.8.8.0 [90/103040] via 78.1.1.8, 00:00:25, GigabitEthernet0/0
```

Task 5

Explain EIGRP's composite metric in the named mode configuration. You should explain the formula and the constant values that EIGRP named mode uses to calculate the composite metric for R8's Lo0 interface.

Let's display the routing table of R7:

```
!On R7:

R7# show ip route eigrp | begin Gate
Gateway of last resort is not set

      8.0.0.0/24 is subnetted, 1 subnets
D        8.8.8.0 [90/103040] via 78.1.1.8, 00:00:25, GigabitEthernet0/0
```

You can see that the local router's cost to get to prefix 8.8.8.0/24 is 103,040. Let's check the topology table for this prefix:

```
!On R7:


R7# show ip eigrp topology 8.8.8.0/24
EIGRP-IPv4 VR(tst) Topology Entry for AS(100)/ID(8.8.8.8) for 8.8.8.0/24
  State is Passive, Query origin flag is 1, 1 Successor(s), FD is 13189120, RIB is
  103040
  Descriptor Blocks:
  78.1.1.8 (GigabitEthernet0/0), from 78.1.1.8, Send flag is 0x0
      Composite metric is (13189120/163840), route is Internal
      Vector metric:
        Minimum bandwidth is 100000 Kbit
        Total delay is 101250000 picoseconds
        Reliability is 255/255
        Load is 1/255
        Minimum MTU is 1500
        Hop count is 1
        Originating router is 78.1.1.8
```

The feasible distance is 13,189,120, but the RIB is 103,040. What is going on?

In the EIGRP named mode configuration, we see a **metric rib-scale** command set to 128 by default. Therefore, if the feasible distance is divided by the **rib-scale** value, we should see what is entered in the routing table. Let's verify:

```
!On R8:


R8# show eigrp protocol
EIGRP-IPv4 VR(tst) Address-Family Protocol for AS(100)
  Metric weight K1=1, K2=0, K3=1, K4=0, K5=0 K6=0
  Metric rib-scale 128
  Metric version 64bit
  NSF-aware route hold timer is 240
  Router-ID: 8.8.8.8
  Topology : 0 (base)
    Active Timer: 3 min
    Distance: internal 90 external 170
    Maximum path: 4
    Maximum hopcount 100
    Maximum metric variance 1
    Total Prefix Count: 2
    Total Redist Count: 0
```

Thus, 13,189,120 / 128 = 103,040. But why did Cisco do that?

The composite metric with EIGRP Wide Metrics is 64 bits. The metric variable in the routing table is a 32-bit value. Larger numbers can't be installed. Therefore, the **rib-scale** command can reduce the composite metric so it can fit.

So how does the local router calculate the feasible distance? EIGRP uses a number of defined constants for the calculation of the metric value, and they are based on the following:

```
EIGRP_BANDWIDTH                    10,000,000
EIGRP_DELAY_PICO                    1,000,000
    Multiplier                                    65536
```

Now, that we know the constants, the formula for calculating the composite metric is

```
Throughput + Latency
```

But let's see how these are calculated:

```
Throughput = EIGRP_BANDWIDTH * 65536 / Min Bandwidth
```

Here, **EIGRP_BANDWIDTH** is a constant value and cannot be changed. Also, **65536** is the multiplier and cannot be changed. The **Min Bandwidth** is taken from the output of the **show ip eigrp topology 8.8.8.0/24** command. This means the following:

```
10,000,000 * 65536 / 100,000 = 6,553,600
```

Let's see how the latency is calculated:

```
Latency = Total delay (In picoseconds) * 65536 / EIGRP_DELAY_PICO
```

The "total delay in picoseconds" is taken from the output of the **show ip eigrp topology 8.8.8.0/24** command. The **65536** is the multiplier and cannot be changed, and **EIGRP_DELAY_PICO** is a constant value and cannot be changed. This means the following:

```
101,250,000 * 65536 / 1,000,000 = 6,635,520
```

The "total delay" is also taken from the output of the **show ip EIGRP topology 8.8.8.0/24** command, and **EIGRP_DELAY_PICO** is the constant value described previously. Now that we have calculated the latency, let's add the latency to the throughput:

```
6,553,600 + 6,635,520 = 13,189,120 → The Feasible Distance
```

Task 6

In the preceding topology, R1 and R2 are Cisco 2811 series routers running c2800nm-adventerprisek9-mz.151-4.M7.bin. R7 and R8 are Cisco 1900 series running c1900-universalk9-mz.SPA.154-1.T.bin. How do we know if these routers support EIGRP Wide Metric?

Here is a way to figure out if the local router has EIGRP Wide Metric support:

```
!On R8:

R8# show eigrp tech-support | include release

    eigrp-release      :  14.00.00 : Portable EIGRP Release

On R2:

R2# show eigrp tech-support | include release

    eigrp-release      :  6.00.00 : Portable EIGRP Release
```

If the EIGRP release is 8.00.00 or higher, the local router has support for EIGRP Wide Metric. As you can see, R2 does not support it. Another way to see the EIGRP release is to use the following **show** commands:

```
!On R8:

R8# show eigrp plugins | include release

    eigrp-release      :  14.00.00 : Portable EIGRP Release

!On R2:

R2# show eigrp plugins | include release

    eigrp-release      :  6.00.00 : Portable EIGRP Release
```

Task 7

Configure the F0/1 interface of R2 and the G0/1 interface to simulate an Ethernet connection. Use **bandwidth 10000** and **delay 100** to accomplish this. On R2, reconfigure the metric set for RIP routes redistributed into EIGRP to use the lowest possible values. Ensure R8 can ping the Lo0 interface on R1.

EIGRP Wide Metrics can potentially cause problems with slow network connections. In particular, if the metric values are set to **1 1 1 1 1** for prefixes that traverse a slow link, the resulting composite metric will be too large and the FD will be set to **Infinity**. A prefix with an FD of **Infinity** will not have a successor and will not be installed into the RIB. This problem can be encountered with older network devices or virtual router environments that have Ethernet interfaces.

Because the computed composite metric is a 64-bit unsigned value, the largest possible value is 18,446,744,073,709,551,615. This value is divided by the **rib-scale** value. The result is displayed in the EIGRP table as the RIB value. The RIB value is a 32-bit unsigned value. The largest possible RIB value is 4,294,967,295. If the composite metric divided by the **rib-scale** value is larger than the largest possible RIB value, the RIB value is set to the maximum and the feasible distance (FD) is set to **Infinity**. An FD of **Infinity** means the prefix is unreachable, similar to how a RIP prefix that has a hop count of 16 is unreachable. A router will not advertise an unreachable prefix.

Per RFC 7868, with Wide Metrics, a delay value of 0xFFFFFFFFFF (or decimal 281,474,976,719,655) also indicates an unreachable route.

There are two ways to resolve FD being set to **Infinity**. The first is to use sane values when setting EIGRP metrics. In short, do not use **1 1 1 1 1** when setting metric values. One method is to use bandwidth and delay settings that are normally seen on FastEthernet or GigabitEthernet interfaces. You can use the **show interface** command to view these values. The second method of avoiding FD being set to **Infinity** is to increase the **rib-scale** value.

Before we make any configuration changes, let's look at the current bandwidth, delay, reliability, and load settings on F0/1 of R2 and G0/1 of R7:

```
!On R2:

R2# show interface fastethernet0/1 | include BW|load
  MTU 1500 bytes, BW 100000 Kbit/sec, DLY 100 usec,
     reliability 255/255, txload 1/255, rxload 1/255

!On R7;
R7# show interface gigabitethernet0/1 | include BW|load
  MTU 1500 bytes, BW 100000 Kbit/sec, DLY 100 usec,
     reliability 255/255, txload 1/255, rxload 1/255
```

For the first part of the task, set the bandwidth and delay on the interfaces:

```
!On R2:

R2(config)# interface fastethernet0/1
R2(config-if)# bandwidth 10000
R2(config-if)# delay 100

!On R7:

R7(config)# interface gigabitethernet0/1
R7(config-if)# bandwidth 10000
R7(config-if)# delay 100
```

Let's verify this:

```
!On R2:

R2# show interface fastethernet0/1 | include BW|load
  MTU 1500 bytes, BW 10000 Kbit/sec, DLY 1000 usec,
     reliability 255/255, txload 1/255, rxload 1/255


!On R7:

R7# show interface gigabitethernet0/1 | include BW|load
  MTU 1500 bytes, BW 10000 Kbit/sec, DLY 1000 usec,
     reliability 255/255, txload 1/255, rxload 1/255
```

For the next part of the task, change the metric that is set on the routes redistributed from RIP:

```
!On R2:

R2(config)# router eigrp 100
R2(config-router)# redistribute rip metric 1 1 1 1 1
```

Now let's see what happened on R8:

```
!On R8:

R8# show ip route eigrp | begin Gate
Gateway of last resort is not set


      2.0.0.0/24 is subnetted, 1 subnets
D        2.2.2.0 [90/3635200] via 78.1.1.7, 00:05:41, GigabitEthernet0/0
      27.0.0.0/24 is subnetted, 1 subnets
D        27.1.1.0 [90/1075200] via 78.1.1.7, 00:05:41, GigabitEthernet0/0
```

As you can see, the prefixes from R1 are no longer present. What happened to them?

```
R8# show ip eigrp topology
EIGRP-IPv4 VR(tst) Topology Table for AS(100)/ID(8.8.8.8)
Codes: P - Passive, A - Active, U - Update, Q - Query, R - Reply,
       r - reply Status, s - sia Status


P 2.2.2.0/24, 1 successors, FD is 465305600
        via 78.1.1.7 (465305600/458752000), GigabitEthernet0/0
```

```
P 27.1.1.0/24, 1 successors, FD is 137625600
        via 78.1.1.7 (137625600/131072000), GigabitEthernet0/0
P 78.1.1.0/24, 1 successors, FD is 13107200
        via Connected, GigabitEthernet0/0
P 8.8.8.0/24, 1 successors, FD is 163840
        via Connected, Loopback0
```

The prefixes are not present in the EIGRP topology table. Let's check R7:

```
!On R7:

R7# show ip route eigrp | begin Gate
Gateway of last resort is not set

      2.0.0.0/24 is subnetted, 1 subnets
D        2.2.2.0 [90/3584000] via 27.1.1.2, 00:08:14, GigabitEthernet0/1
      8.0.0.0/24 is subnetted, 1 subnets
D        8.8.8.0 [90/103040] via 78.1.1.8, 02:53:09, GigabitEthernet0/0

R7# show ip eigrp topology
EIGRP-IPv4 VR(tst) Topology Table for AS(100)/ID(7.7.7.7)
Codes: P - Passive, A - Active, U - Update, Q - Query, R - Reply,
       r - reply Status, s - sia Status

P 2.2.2.0/24, 1 successors, FD is 340787200
        via 27.1.1.2 (458752000/327745536), GigabitEthernet0/1
P 27.1.1.0/24, 1 successors, FD is 131072000
        via Connected, GigabitEthernet0/1
P 78.1.1.0/24, 1 successors, FD is 13107200
        via Connected, GigabitEthernet0/0
P 12.1.1.0/24, 0 successors, FD is Infinity
        via 27.1.1.2 (655426191360/655360655360), GigabitEthernet0/1
P 8.8.8.0/24, 1 successors, FD is 13189120
        via 78.1.1.8 (13189120/163840), GigabitEthernet0/0
P 1.1.1.0/24, 0 successors, FD is Infinity
        via 27.1.1.2 (655426191360/655360655360), GigabitEthernet0/1
```

The prefixes from R1 have an FD of **Infinity** and are therefore unreachable. Because the prefixes are unreachable, R7 is not advertising them to R8. You can see that the composite metric value for the prefixes is **655426191360**. Take this value and divide by the default **rib-scale** value of 128, and you get 5,120,517,120. This value is larger than the largest RIB value. This means that the prefix is unreachable. The FD is set to **Infinity**. If you look at the details of the prefix entry in the EIGRP topology table, you'll see that the RIB is set to the maximum value, or 4,294,967,295.

Let's check the details of the EIGRP topology table:

```
R7# show ip eigrp topology 1.1.1.0/24
EIGRP-IPv4 VR(tst) Topology Entry for AS(100)/ID(7.7.7.7) for 1.1.1.0/24
  State is Passive, Query origin flag is 1, 0 Successor(s), FD is Infinity, RIB is
    4294967295
  Descriptor Blocks:
  27.1.1.2 (GigabitEthernet0/1), from 27.1.1.2, Send flag is 0x0
      Composite metric is (655426191360/655360655360), route is External
      Vector metric:
        Minimum bandwidth is 1 Kbit
        Total delay is 1010000000 picoseconds
        Reliability is 1/255
        Load is 1/255
        Minimum MTU is 1
        Hop count is 1
      External data:
        Originating router is 2.2.2.2
        AS number of route is 0
        External protocol is RIP, external metric is 1
        Administrator tag is 0 (0x00000000)

R7# show ip eigrp topology zero-successors
EIGRP-IPv4 VR(tst) Topology Table for AS(100)/ID(7.7.7.7)
Codes: P - Passive, A - Active, U - Update, Q - Query, R - Reply,
       r - reply Status, s - sia Status

P 12.1.1.0/24, 0 successors, FD is Infinity
        via 27.1.1.2 (655426191360/655360655360), GigabitEthernet0/1
P 1.1.1.0/24, 0 successors, FD is Infinity
        via 27.1.1.2 (655426191360/655360655360), GigabitEthernet0/1
```

Because the task asked you to set the metric to the lowest possible value, we'll have to change the **rib-scale** value to resolve this problem:

```
R7(config)# router eigrp tst
R7(config-router)# address-family ipv4 unicast as 100
R7(config-router-af)# metric rib-scale 255
```

Let's verify the change:

```
R7# show eigrp protocols
EIGRP-IPv4 VR(tst) Address-Family Protocol for AS(100)
  Metric weight K1=1, K2=0, K3=1, K4=0, K5=0 K6=0
  Metric rib-scale 255
  Metric version 64bit
```

```
    NSF-aware route hold timer is 240
    Router-ID: 7.7.7.7
    Topology : 0 (base)
      Active Timer: 3 min
      Distance: internal 90 external 170
      Maximum path: 4
      Maximum hopcount 100
      Maximum metric variance 1
      Total Prefix Count: 6
      Total Redist Count: 0


R7# show ip route eigrp | begin Gate
Gateway of last resort is not set


      1.0.0.0/24 is subnetted, 1 subnets
D EX      1.1.1.0 [170/2570298789] via 27.1.1.2, 00:02:43, GigabitEthernet0/1
      2.0.0.0/24 is subnetted, 1 subnets
D         2.2.2.0 [90/1799027] via 27.1.1.2, 00:02:43, GigabitEthernet0/1
      8.0.0.0/24 is subnetted, 1 subnets
D         8.8.8.0 [90/51722] via 78.1.1.8, 00:02:43, GigabitEthernet0/0
      12.0.0.0/24 is subnetted, 1 subnets
D EX     12.1.1.0 [170/2570298789] via 27.1.1.2, 00:02:43, GigabitEthernet0/1
```

The prefixes are now present in the RIB. Here's what you see in the EIGRP topology table:

```
R7# show ip eigrp topology 1.1.1.0/24
EIGRP-IPv4 VR(tst) Topology Entry for AS(100)/ID(7.7.7.7) for 1.1.1.0/24
  State is Passive, Query origin flag is 1, 1 Successor(s), FD is 655426191360, RIB
    is 2570298789
  Descriptor Blocks:
  27.1.1.2 (GigabitEthernet0/1), from 27.1.1.2, Send flag is 0x0
      Composite metric is (655426191360/655360655360), route is External
      Vector metric:
        Minimum bandwidth is 1 Kbit
        Total delay is 1010000000 picoseconds
        Reliability is 1/255
        Load is 1/255
        Minimum MTU is 1
        Hop count is 1
      External data:
        Originating router is 2.2.2.2
        AS number of route is 0
        External protocol is RIP, external metric is 1
        Administrator tag is 0 (0x00000000)
```

You can see that the composite metric value for the prefixes is still **655426191360**. Take this value and divide by the **rib-scale** value of 255 and you get 2,570,298,789. The FD is set to the value of the composite metric. Let's check R8:

```
!On R8:


R8# show ip route eigrp | begin Gate
Gateway of last resort is not set


      2.0.0.0/24 is subnetted, 1 subnets
D        2.2.2.0 [90/3635200] via 78.1.1.7, 00:17:25, GigabitEthernet0/0
      27.0.0.0/24 is subnetted, 1 subnets
D        27.1.1.0 [90/1075200] via 78.1.1.7, 00:17:25, GigabitEthernet0/0
```

The **rib-scale** value only affects the locally calculated composite metric. We will have to change the **rib-scale** value on R8:

```
R8(config)# router eigrp tst
R8(config-router)# address-family ipv4 unicast as 100
R8(config-router-af)# metric rib-scale 255
```

Let's verify:

```
R8# show ip route eigrp | begin Gate
Gateway of last resort is not set


      1.0.0.0/24 is subnetted, 1 subnets
D EX    1.1.1.0 [170/2570324490] via 78.1.1.7, 00:00:13, GigabitEthernet0/0
      2.0.0.0/24 is subnetted, 1 subnets
D        2.2.2.0 [90/1824727] via 78.1.1.7, 00:00:13, GigabitEthernet0/0
      12.0.0.0/24 is subnetted, 1 subnets
D EX    12.1.1.0 [170/2570324490] via 78.1.1.7, 00:00:13, GigabitEthernet0/0
      27.0.0.0/24 is subnetted, 1 subnets
D        27.1.1.0 [90/539708] via 78.1.1.7, 00:00:13, GigabitEthernet0/0


R8# ping 1.1.1.1
Type escape sequence to abort.
Sending 5, 100-byte ICMP Echos to 1.1.1.1, timeout is 2 seconds:
!!!!!
Success rate is 100 percent (5/5), round-trip min/avg/max = 28/29/32 ms
```

Note Erase the startup config and reload the routers and the switches before proceeding to the next lab.

Lab 7-4: EIGRP Summarization

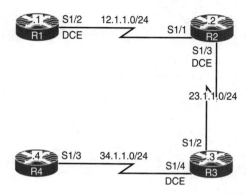

Figure 7-4 *EIGRP Summarization Topology*

Task 1

Figure 7-4 illustrates the topology used in the following tasks. Configure the loopback interfaces in Table 7-3 on R1 and advertise them in the EIGRP routing domain.

Table 7-3 *Loopback Interfaces for R1*

Interface	IP Address
Lo0	1.1.0.1/24
Lo1	1.1.1.1/24
Lo2	1.1.2.1/24
Lo3	1.1.3.1/24

```
!On R1:


R1(config)# interface loopback0
R1(config-if)# ip address 1.1.0.1 255.255.255.0


R1(config-if)# interface loopback1
R1(config-if)# ip address 1.1.1.1 255.255.255.0


R1(config-if)# interface loopback2
R1(config-if)# ip address 1.1.2.1 255.255.255.0
```

```
R1(config-if)# interface loopback3
R1(config-if)# ip address 1.1.3.1 255.255.255.0

R1(config)# router eigrp 100
R1(config-router)# network 12.1.1.1 0.0.0.0
R1(config-router)# network 1.0.0.0
```

Task 2

Configure the loopback interfaces in Table 7-4 on R2 and advertise them in the EIGRP routing domain.

Table 7-4   *Loopback Interfaces for R2*

Interface	IP Address
Lo0	2.2.4.2/24
Lo1	2.2.5.2/24
Lo2	2.2.6.2/24
Lo3	2.2.7.2/24

```
!On R2:

R2(config)# interface loopback0
R2(config-if)# ip address 2.2.4.2 255.255.255.0

R2(config-if)# interface loopback1
R2(config-if)# ip address 2.2.5.2 255.255.255.0

R2(config-if)# interface loopback2
R2(config-if)# ip address 2.2.6.2 255.255.255.0

R2(config-if)# interface loopback3
R2(config-if)# ip address 2.2.7.2 255.255.255.0

R2(config)# router eigrp 100
R2(config-router)# network 12.1.1.2 0.0.0.0
R2(config-router)# network 23.1.1.2 0.0.0.0
R2(config-router)# network 2.2.4.2 0.0.0.0
R2(config-router)# network 2.2.5.2 0.0.0.0
R2(config-router)# network 2.2.6.2 0.0.0.0
R2(config-router)# network 2.2.7.2 0.0.0.0
```

Task 3

Configure the loopback interfaces shown in Table 7-5 on R3 and advertise them in EIGRP 100.

Table 7-5   *Loopback Interfaces for R3*

Interface	IP Address
Lo0	3.3.8.3/24
Lo1	3.3.9.3/24
Lo2	3.3.10.3/24
Lo3	3.3.11.3/24

```
!On R3:

R3(config)# interface loopback0
R3(config-if)# ip address 3.3.8.3 255.255.255.0

R3(config)# interface loopback1
R3(config-if)# ip address 3.3.9.3 255.255.255.0

R3(config)# interface loopback2
R3(config-if)# ip address 3.3.10.3 255.255.255.0

R3(config)# interface loopback3
R3(config-if)# ip address 3.3.11.3 255.255.255.0

R3(config)# router eigrp 100
R3(config-router)# network 23.1.1.3 0.0.0.0
R3(config-router)# network 34.1.1.3 0.0.0.0
R3(config-router)# network 3.3.8.3 0.0.0.0
R3(config-router)# network 3.3.9.3 0.0.0.0
R3(config-router)# network 3.3.10.3 0.0.0.0
R3(config-router)# network 3.3.11.3 0.0.0.0
```

Task 4

Configure the loopback interfaces in Table 7-6 on R4 and advertise them in EIGRP 100.

Table 7-6   *Loopback Interfaces for R4*

Interface	IP Address
Lo0	4.4.12.4/24
Lo1	4.4.13.4/24
Lo2	4.4.14.4/24
Lo3	4.4.15.4/24

```
!On R4:

R4(config)# interface loopback0
R4(config-if)# ip address 4.4.12.4 255.255.255.0

R4(config)# interface loopback1
R4(config-if)# ip address 4.4.13.4 255.255.255.0

R4(config)# interface loopback2
R4(config-if)# ip address 4.4.14.4 255.255.255.0

R4(config)# interface loopback3
R4(config-if)# ip address 4.4.15.4 255.255.255.0

R4(config)# router eigrp 100
R4(config-router)# network 34.1.1.4 0.0.0.0
R4(config-router)# network 4.4.12.4 0.0.0.0
R4(config-router)# network 4.4.13.4 0.0.0.0
R4(config-router)# network 4.4.14.4 0.0.0.0
R4(config-router)# network 4.4.15.4 0.0.0.0
```

Let's verify the configuration:

```
!On R4:

R4# show ip route eigrp | begin Gate
Gateway of last resort is not set

      1.0.0.0/24 is subnetted, 4 subnets
D        1.1.0.0 [90/21664000] via 34.1.1.3, 00:08:22, Serial1/3
D        1.1.1.0 [90/21664000] via 34.1.1.3, 00:08:22, Serial1/3
D        1.1.2.0 [90/21664000] via 34.1.1.3, 00:08:22, Serial1/3
D        1.1.3.0 [90/21664000] via 34.1.1.3, 00:08:22, Serial1/3
      2.0.0.0/24 is subnetted, 4 subnets
```

```
D          2.2.4.0 [90/21152000] via 34.1.1.3, 00:05:17, Serial1/3
D          2.2.5.0 [90/21152000] via 34.1.1.3, 00:05:17, Serial1/3
D          2.2.6.0 [90/21152000] via 34.1.1.3, 00:05:17, Serial1/3
D          2.2.7.0 [90/21152000] via 34.1.1.3, 00:05:17, Serial1/3
       3.0.0.0/24 is subnetted, 4 subnets
D          3.3.8.0 [90/20640000] via 34.1.1.3, 00:03:44, Serial1/3
D          3.3.9.0 [90/20640000] via 34.1.1.3, 00:03:44, Serial1/3
D          3.3.10.0 [90/20640000] via 34.1.1.3, 00:03:44, Serial1/3
D          3.3.11.0 [90/20640000] via 34.1.1.3, 00:03:44, Serial1/3
       12.0.0.0/24 is subnetted, 1 subnets
D          12.1.1.0 [90/21536000] via 34.1.1.3, 00:08:22, Serial1/3
       23.0.0.0/24 is subnetted, 1 subnets
D          23.1.1.0 [90/21024000] via 34.1.1.3, 00:08:22, Serial1/3

!On R1:


R1# show ip route eigrp | begin Gate
Gateway of last resort is not set


       2.0.0.0/24 is subnetted, 4 subnets
D          2.2.4.0 [90/20640000] via 12.1.1.2, 00:06:20, Serial1/2
D          2.2.5.0 [90/20640000] via 12.1.1.2, 00:06:20, Serial1/2
D          2.2.6.0 [90/20640000] via 12.1.1.2, 00:06:20, Serial1/2
D          2.2.7.0 [90/20640000] via 12.1.1.2, 00:06:20, Serial1/2
       3.0.0.0/24 is subnetted, 4 subnets
D          3.3.8.0 [90/21152000] via 12.1.1.2, 00:04:47, Serial1/2
D          3.3.9.0 [90/21152000] via 12.1.1.2, 00:04:47, Serial1/2
D          3.3.10.0 [90/21152000] via 12.1.1.2, 00:04:47, Serial1/2
D          3.3.11.0 [90/21152000] via 12.1.1.2, 00:04:47, Serial1/2
       4.0.0.0/24 is subnetted, 4 subnets
D          4.4.12.0 [90/21664000] via 12.1.1.2, 00:03:37, Serial1/2
D          4.4.13.0 [90/21664000] via 12.1.1.2, 00:03:37, Serial1/2
D          4.4.14.0 [90/21664000] via 12.1.1.2, 00:03:37, Serial1/2
D          4.4.15.0 [90/21664000] via 12.1.1.2, 00:03:37, Serial1/2
       23.0.0.0/24 is subnetted, 1 subnets
D          23.1.1.0 [90/21024000] via 12.1.1.2, 00:09:47, Serial1/2
       34.0.0.0/24 is subnetted, 1 subnets
D          34.1.1.0 [90/21536000] via 12.1.1.2, 00:09:25, Serial1/2
```

Task 5

Configure R2 such that it advertises a summary route for its loopback interfaces to R3.

Unlike OSPF, summarization can be performed on any router anywhere within the topology in EIGRP. Summarization is configured in the interface configuration mode, making it very specific. This means that only the neighbor(s) through that interface will receive the summary route.

```
!On R2:


R2(config)# interface serial1/3
R2(config-if)# ip summary-address eigrp 100 2.2.4.0 255.255.252.0
```

Let's verify the configuration:

Note   When summarization is configured, EIGRP will inject a discard route for loop avoidance, highlighted here.

```
!On R2:


R2# show ip route eigrp | include 2.2.4.0

D       2.2.4.0/22 is a summary, 00:01:17, Null0

R2# show ip route 2.2.4.0 255.255.252.0
Routing entry for 2.2.4.0/22
  Known via "eigrp 100", distance 5, metric 128256, type internal
  Redistributing via eigrp 100
  Routing Descriptor Blocks:
  * directly connected, via Null0
      Route metric is 128256, traffic share count is 1
      Total delay is 5000 microseconds, minimum bandwidth is 10000000 Kbit
      Reliability 255/255, minimum MTU 9676 bytes
      Loading 1/255, Hops 0


!On R3:


R3# show ip route eigrp | begin Gate
Gateway of last resort is not set


     1.0.0.0/24 is subnetted, 4 subnets
D        1.1.0.0 [90/21152000] via 23.1.1.2, 00:11:43, Serial1/2
D        1.1.1.0 [90/21152000] via 23.1.1.2, 00:11:43, Serial1/2
D        1.1.2.0 [90/21152000] via 23.1.1.2, 00:11:43, Serial1/2
D        1.1.3.0 [90/21152000] via 23.1.1.2, 00:11:43, Serial1/2
     2.0.0.0/22 is subnetted, 1 subnets
D        2.2.4.0 [90/20640000] via 23.1.1.2, 00:00:53, Serial1/2
```

```
        4.0.0.0/24 is subnetted, 4 subnets
D          4.4.12.0 [90/20640000] via 34.1.1.4, 00:05:56, Serial1/4
D          4.4.13.0 [90/20640000] via 34.1.1.4, 00:05:56, Serial1/4
D          4.4.14.0 [90/20640000] via 34.1.1.4, 00:05:56, Serial1/4
D          4.4.15.0 [90/20640000] via 34.1.1.4, 00:05:56, Serial1/4
        12.0.0.0/24 is subnetted, 1 subnets
D          12.1.1.0 [90/21024000] via 23.1.1.2, 00:11:43, Serial1/2
```

Task 6

R2 should summarize its loopback interfaces and advertise a single summary route plus all the specific routes of the summary to R1.

The **leak-map** option was introduced in IOS 12.3(14)T, and it must be configured under the physical interface and *not* a subinterface. Configuring the **leak-map** option allows us to advertise a component route (one or more specific networks of the summary route) that would otherwise be suppressed by manual summarization.

There are three rules to remember:

- If **leak-map** is configured to reference a route map that does not exist, only the summary route is advertised and the more specific routes are suppressed.

- If **leak-map** is configured to reference a route map, and the route map is referencing an access list that does *not* exist, then the summary route plus all the specific routes are advertised.

- If **leak-map** is configured to reference a route map, and the route map matches on an access list, all the permitted networks by the access list will be advertised along with the summary route.

```
!On R2:

R2(config)# interface serial1/1
R2(config-if)# ip summary-address eigrp 100 2.2.4.0 255.255.252.0 leak-map TEST21

R2(config)# route-map TEST21 permit 10
```

Note   The **leak-map** option is referencing a route map, and the route map is *not* referencing an access list. Therefore, the summary route plus all the specific routes are advertised. If the route map references an access list that does *not* exist, you will see the same result.

Let's verify the configuration:

```
!On R1:


R1# show ip route eigrp | begin Gate
Gateway of last resort is not set


     2.0.0.0/8 is variably subnetted, 5 subnets, 2 masks
D       2.2.4.0/22 [90/20640000] via 12.1.1.2, 00:00:48, Serial1/2
D       2.2.4.0/24 [90/20640000] via 12.1.1.2, 00:00:28, Serial1/2
D       2.2.5.0/24 [90/20640000] via 12.1.1.2, 00:00:28, Serial1/2
D       2.2.6.0/24 [90/20640000] via 12.1.1.2, 00:00:28, Serial1/2
D       2.2.7.0/24 [90/20640000] via 12.1.1.2, 00:00:28, Serial1/2
     3.0.0.0/24 is subnetted, 4 subnets
D       3.3.8.0 [90/21152000] via 12.1.1.2, 00:11:39, Serial1/2
D       3.3.9.0 [90/21152000] via 12.1.1.2, 00:11:39, Serial1/2
D       3.3.10.0 [90/21152000] via 12.1.1.2, 00:11:39, Serial1/2
D       3.3.11.0 [90/21152000] via 12.1.1.2, 00:11:39, Serial1/2
     4.0.0.0/24 is subnetted, 4 subnets
D       4.4.12.0 [90/21664000] via 12.1.1.2, 00:10:29, Serial1/2
D       4.4.13.0 [90/21664000] via 12.1.1.2, 00:10:29, Serial1/2
D       4.4.14.0 [90/21664000] via 12.1.1.2, 00:10:29, Serial1/2
D       4.4.15.0 [90/21664000] via 12.1.1.2, 00:10:29, Serial1/2
     23.0.0.0/24 is subnetted, 1 subnets
D       23.1.1.0 [90/21024000] via 12.1.1.2, 00:16:39, Serial1/2
     34.0.0.0/24 is subnetted, 1 subnets
D       34.1.1.0 [90/21536000] via 12.1.1.2, 00:16:17, Serial1/2
```

Task 7

Configure R4 to summarize its loopback interfaces and advertise a summary route plus
network 4.4.13.0/24 to R3.

```
!On R4:


R4# show access-lists

R4(config)# interface serial1/3
R4(config-if)# ip summary-address eigrp 100 4.4.12.0 255.255.252.0 leak-map TEST43

R4(config)# access-list 13 permit 4.4.13.0 0.0.0.255

R4(config)# route-map TEST43 permit 10
R4(config-route-map)# match ip address 13
```

Let's verify the configuration:

```
!On R4:

R4# show ip route eigrp | include Null0

D       4.4.12.0/22 is a summary, 00:01:49, Null0
```

The output of the preceding **show** command reveals the Null0 discard route that is created whenever summarization is configured:

```
!On R3:

R3# show ip route eigrp | begin Gate
Gateway of last resort is not set

     1.0.0.0/24 is subnetted, 4 subnets
D        1.1.0.0 [90/21152000] via 23.1.1.2, 00:19:34, Serial1/2
D        1.1.1.0 [90/21152000] via 23.1.1.2, 00:19:34, Serial1/2
D        1.1.2.0 [90/21152000] via 23.1.1.2, 00:19:34, Serial1/2
D        1.1.3.0 [90/21152000] via 23.1.1.2, 00:19:34, Serial1/2
     2.0.0.0/22 is subnetted, 1 subnets
D        2.2.4.0 [90/20640000] via 23.1.1.2, 00:08:44, Serial1/2
     4.0.0.0/8 is variably subnetted, 2 subnets, 2 masks
D        4.4.12.0/22 [90/20640000] via 34.1.1.4, 00:01:21, Serial1/4
D        4.4.13.0/24 [90/20640000] via 34.1.1.4, 00:00:57, Serial1/4
     12.0.0.0/24 is subnetted, 1 subnets
D        12.1.1.0 [90/21024000] via 23.1.1.2, 00:19:34, Serial1/2
```

Task 8

Configure R3 to summarize its loopback interfaces and advertise a single summary plus 3.3.10.0/24 and 3.3.11.0/24 to R4:

```
!On R3:

R3# show access-lists

R3(config)# interface serial1/4
R3(config-if)# ip summary-address eigrp 100 3.3.8.0 255.255.252.0 leak-map TEST34
```

```
R3(config-if)# access-list 34 permit 3.3.10.0 0.0.0.255
R3(config)# access-list 34 permit 3.3.11.0 0.0.0.255

R3(config)# route-map TEST34 permit 10
R3(config-route-map)# match ip address 34
```

Let's verify the configuration:

```
!On R4:

R4# show ip route eigrp | begin Gate
Gateway of last resort is not set


      1.0.0.0/24 is subnetted, 4 subnets
D        1.1.0.0 [90/21664000] via 34.1.1.3, 00:22:02, Serial1/3
D        1.1.1.0 [90/21664000] via 34.1.1.3, 00:22:02, Serial1/3
D        1.1.2.0 [90/21664000] via 34.1.1.3, 00:22:02, Serial1/3
D        1.1.3.0 [90/21664000] via 34.1.1.3, 00:22:02, Serial1/3
      2.0.0.0/22 is subnetted, 1 subnets
D        2.2.4.0 [90/21152000] via 34.1.1.3, 00:11:11, Serial1/3
      3.0.0.0/8 is variably subnetted, 3 subnets, 2 masks
D        3.3.8.0/22 [90/20640000] via 34.1.1.3, 00:00:47, Serial1/3
D        3.3.10.0/24 [90/20640000] via 34.1.1.3, 00:00:24, Serial1/3
D        3.3.11.0/24 [90/20640000] via 34.1.1.3, 00:00:24, Serial1/3
      4.0.0.0/8 is variably subnetted, 9 subnets, 3 masks
D        4.4.12.0/22 is a summary, 00:03:48, Null0
      12.0.0.0/24 is subnetted, 1 subnets
D        12.1.1.0 [90/21536000] via 34.1.1.3, 00:22:02, Serial1/3
      23.0.0.0/24 is subnetted, 1 subnets
D        23.1.1.0 [90/21024000] via 34.1.1.3, 00:22:02, Serial1/3
```

Task 9

Configure R1 to inject a default route into the EIGRP 100 routing domain. Do *not* use any global or router-configuration command as part of the solution to accomplish this task.

The following command summarizes all Class A, Class B, and Class C networks; it's the mother of all summaries:

```
!On R1:

R1(config)# interface serial1/2
R1(config-if)# ip summary-address eigrp 100 0.0.0.0 0.0.0.0
```

Let's look at the discard route:

```
!On R1:


R1# show ip route eigrp | include Null0
D*   0.0.0.0/0 is a summary, 00:03:19, Null0


!On R2:


R2# show ip route eigrp | include Serial1/1
D*   0.0.0.0/0 [90/20640000] via 12.1.1.1, 00:00:37, Serial1/1
```

Note   All the specific routes are suppressed and *only* the summary route is advertised.

Erase the startup config and reload the routers before proceeding to the next lab.

Lab 7-5: EIGRP Authentication

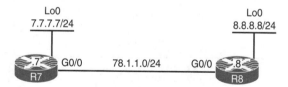

Figure 7-5   *EIGRP Authentication Topology*

Task 1

Configure the routers based on the diagram shown in Figure 7-5.

```
!On SW1:


SW1(config)# interface range fastethernet0/7 - 8
SW1(config-if)# switchport mode access
SW1(config-if)# switchport access vlan 78
SW1(config-if)# no shutdown


!On R7:


R7(config)# interface gigabitethernet0/0
R7(config-if)# ip address 78.1.1.7 255.255.255.0
R7(config-if)# no shutdown
```

```
R7(config)# interface loopback0
R7(config-if)# ip address 7.7.7.7 255.255.255.0

!On R8:

R8(config)# interface gigabitethernet0/0
R8(config-if)# ip address 78.1.1.8 255.255.255.0
R8(config-if)# no shutdown

R8(config)# interface loopback0
R8(config-if)# ip address 8.8.8.8 255.255.255.0
```

Let's verify the configuration:

```
!On R7:

R7# ping 78.1.1.8

Type escape sequence to abort.
Sending 5, 100-byte ICMP Echos to 78.1.1.8, timeout is 2 seconds:
.!!!!
Success rate is 80 percent (4/5), round-trip min/avg/max = 1/1/1 ms
```

Task 2

Configure EIGRP in AS 100 on both routers and advertise their directly connected networks. You should use classic mode EIGRP to accomplish this task:

```
!On R7:

R7(config)# router eigrp 100
R7(config-router)# network 78.1.1.7 0.0.0.0
R7(config-router)# network 7.7.7.7 0.0.0.0

!On R8:

R8(config)# router eigrp 100
R8(config-router)# network 78.1.1.8 0.0.0.0
R8(config-router)# network 8.8.8.8 0.0.0.0
```

You should see the following console message:

```
%DUAL-5-NBRCHANGE: EIGRP-IPv4 100: Neighbor 78.1.1.7 (GigabitEthernet0/0) is up: new
  adjacency                                                              .
```

Let's verify the configuration:

```
!On R7:

R7# show ip route eigrp | begin Gate
Gateway of last resort is not set

      8.0.0.0/24 is subnetted, 1 subnets
D        8.8.8.0 [90/156160] via 78.1.1.8, 00:01:18, GigabitEthernet0/0
```

Task 3

Enable MD5 EIGRP authentication between R7 and R8. Use "cisco" as the password.

EIGRP uses keychain-based authentication, just like RIPv2:

```
!On Both Routers:

Rx(config)# key chain TST
Rx(config-keychain)# key 1
Rx(config-keychain-key)# key-string cisco

Rx(config)# interface gigabitethernet0/0
Rx(config-if)# ip authentication key-chain eigrp 100 TST
Rx(config-if)# ip authentication mode eigrp 100 md5
```

Let's verify the configuration:

```
!On R7:

R7# show ip route eigrp | begin Gate
Gateway of last resort is not set

      8.0.0.0/24 is subnetted, 1 subnets
D        8.8.8.0 [90/156160] via 78.1.1.8, 00:00:33, GigabitEthernet0/0

R7# show ip eigrp interface detail | include Authen

  Authentication mode is md5,  key-chain is "TST"
  Authentication mode is not set
```

Task 4

Configure the strongest authentication method on R7 and R8. You must use "C?IE" as the password.

In EIGRP, when authentication is enabled, every packet that is exchanged between the neighbors must be authenticated to ensure the identity of the neighbor. This is done by using identical pre-shared authentication keys, meaning the two neighbors must use the same pre-shared authentication key. EIGRP authentication is configured in the interface-configuration mode. This means that packets exchanged between neighbors connected through an interface are authenticated.

EIGRP supports MD5 authentication in the classic mode, and the Hashed Message Authentication Code-Secure Hash Algorithm-256 (HMAC-SHA-256) authentication method in the named mode. Because the task states that the strongest authentication method must be used, it is referring to HMAC-SHA-256.

Before authentication is configured, you must remove EIGRP and reconfigure EIGRP in the named mode. Let's configure this task:

```
!On R8:


R8(config)# no router eigrp 100


R8(config)# router eigrp tst
R8(config-router)# address-family ipv4 unicast as 100
R8(config-router-af)# network 78.1.1.8 0.0.0.0
R8(config-router-af)# network 8.8.8.8 0.0.0.0
```

When configuring the address family, you have two choices to identify the AS number: One way is to use the **autonomous-system** keyword at the end, and the second choice is to use the **as** keyword.

```
!On R7:


R7(config)# no router eigrp 100


R7(config)# router eigrp tst
R7(config-router)# address-family ipv4 unicast as 100
R7(config-router-af)# network 78.1.1.7 0.0.0.0
```

Because authentication is configured in the interface-configuration mode, you must enter the **address-family** mode for a given interface:

```
!On R7 and R8:


Rx(config)# router eigrp tst
Rx(config-router)# address-family ipv4 unicast as 100
Rx(config-router-af)# af-interface GigabitEthernet0/0
Rx(config-router-af-interface)# authentication mode hmac-sha-256 C?IE
```

So how do you enter "C?IE"? Before pressing the **?** key, you must press **Esc** and then let go, then press **q** and let go before a "?" can be entered.

Let's verify the configuration:

```
!On R7:


R7# show ip route eigrp | begin Gate
Gateway of last resort is not set

      8.0.0.0/24 is subnetted, 1 subnets
D        8.8.8.0 [90/103040] via 78.1.1.8, 00:01:21, GigabitEthernet0/0
```

Erase the startup config and reload the routers before proceeding to the next lab.

Lab 7-6: Default Route Injection

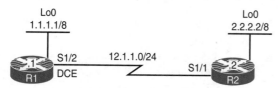

Figure 7-6 *Default Route Injection*

Task 1

Figure 7-6 illustrates the topology used in the following tasks. Configure EIGRP in AS 100 on both routers and advertise their directly connected networks.

```
!On R1:

R1(config)# router eigrp 100
R1(config-router)# network 12.1.1.1 0.0.0.0
R1(config-router)# network 1.1.1.1 0.0.0.0

!On R2:

R2(config)# router eigrp 100
R2(config-router)# network 2.2.2.2 0.0.0.0
R2(config-router)# network 12.1.1.2 0.0.0.0
```

Let's verify the configuration:

```
!On R1:

R1# show ip route eigrp | begin Gate

D    2.0.0.0/8 [90/20640000] via 12.1.1.2, 00:00:20, Serial1/2
```

Task 2

Configure R1 to inject a default route into the EIGRP routing domain.

There are many ways to inject a default route in EIGRP; in this task, we'll test four ways of injecting a default route.

Option #1

One way to inject a default route into EIGRP is to configure a static default route pointing to Null0 and then redistribute the default route into EIGRP. When redistributing a static, connected, or EIGRP route for another AS, the metric does not need to be assigned. The default route will be an external EIGRP route.

```
!On R1:

R1(config)# ip route 0.0.0.0 0.0.0.0 null0

R1(config)# router eigrp 100
R1(config-router)# redistribute static
```

Let's verify the configuration:

```
!On R2:


R2# show ip route eigrp | begin Gate
Gateway of last resort is 12.1.1.1 to network 0.0.0.0


D*EX  0.0.0.0/0 [170/20512000] via 12.1.1.1, 00:03:01, Serial1/1
D     1.0.0.0/8 [90/20640000] via 12.1.1.1, 00:04:52, Serial1/1


R2# show ip eigrp topology 0.0.0.0/0
EIGRP-IPv4 Topology Entry for AS(100)/ID(2.2.2.2) for 0.0.0.0/0
  State is Passive, Query origin flag is 1, 1 Successor(s), FD is 20512000
  Descriptor Blocks:
  12.1.1.1 (Serial1/1), from 12.1.1.1, Send flag is 0x0
      Composite metric is (20512000/256), route is External
      Vector metric:
        Minimum bandwidth is 128 Kbit
        Total delay is 20000 microseconds
        Reliability is 0/255
        Load is 1/255
        Minimum MTU is 1500
        Hop count is 1
        Originating router is 1.1.1.1
      External data:
        AS number of route is 0
        External protocol is Static, external metric is 0
        Administrator tag is 0 (0x00000000)
        Exterior flag is set
```

Option #2

The second method for injecting a default route into EIGRP is to configure a **network** command with **0.0.0.0**. You must have the static default route configured; otherwise, with **network 0.0.0.0**, all existing and future directly connected interfaces will be advertised in the configured AS. The default route will be an internal EIGRP route.

```
R1(config)# ip route 0.0.0.0 0.0.0.0 null0


R1(config)# router eigrp 100
R1(config-router)# no redistribute static
R1(config-router)# network 0.0.0.0
```

Let's verify the configuration:

```
!On R2:


R2# show ip route eigrp | begin Gate
Gateway of last resort is 12.1.1.1 to network 0.0.0.0


D*     0.0.0.0/0 [90/20512000] via 12.1.1.1, 00:00:09, Serial1/1
D      1.0.0.0/8 [90/20640000] via 12.1.1.1, 00:11:11, Serial1/1


R2# sh ip eigrp topology 0.0.0.0/0
EIGRP-IPv4 Topology Entry for AS(100)/ID(2.2.2.2) for 0.0.0.0/0
  State is Passive, Query origin flag is 1, 1 Successor(s), FD is 20512000
  Descriptor Blocks:
  12.1.1.1 (Serial1/1), from 12.1.1.1, Send flag is 0x0
      Composite metric is (20512000/256), route is Internal
      Vector metric:
        Minimum bandwidth is 128 Kbit
        Total delay is 20000 microseconds
        Reliability is 0/255
        Load is 1/255
        Minimum MTU is 1500
        Hop count is 1
        Originating router is 1.1.1.1
      Exterior flag is set
```

Option #3

The third method for injecting a default route into EIGRP is to configure the **ip summary-address eigrp** interface-configuration command. With this command, you are summarizing all Class A, B, and C networks. This means that you are suppressing every route in your routing table, but if you must advertise a specific network, you must leak it. The default route will be an internal EIGRP route.

```
!On R1:


R1(config)# no ip route 0.0.0.0 0.0.0.0 null0


R1(config)# interface serial1/2
R1(config-if)# ip summary-address eigrp 100 0.0.0.0 0.0.0.0
```

Let's verify the configuration:

```
!On R2:


R2# show ip route eigrp | begin Gate
Gateway of last resort is 12.1.1.1 to network 0.0.0.0


D*    0.0.0.0/0 [90/20640000] via 12.1.1.1, 00:00:36, Serial1/1


R2# show ip eigrp topology 0.0.0.0/0
EIGRP-IPv4 Topology Entry for AS(100)/ID(2.2.2.2) for 0.0.0.0/0
  State is Passive, Query origin flag is 1, 1 Successor(s), FD is 20640000
  Descriptor Blocks:
  12.1.1.1 (Serial1/1), from 12.1.1.1, Send flag is 0x0
      Composite metric is (20640000/128256), route is Internal
      Vector metric:
        Minimum bandwidth is 128 Kbit
        Total delay is 25000 microseconds
        Reliability is 255/255
        Load is 1/255
        Minimum MTU is 1500
        Hop count is 1
        Originating router is 1.1.1.1
```

As you can see, all the specific routes are suppressed.

Option #4

The fourth method of injecting a default route is to use **ip default-network**. In this method, R1 is injecting a candidate default, and the candidate route must be advertised to R2. Let's configure this and verify:

```
R1(config)# interface serial1/2
R1(config-if)# no ip summary-address eigrp 100 0.0.0.0 0.0.0.0
```

Because network 1.0.0.0/8 is already advertised to R2, this network can be set to be the candidate network.

```
R1(config)# ip default-network 1.0.0.0
R1(config)# router eigrp 100
R1(config-router)# network 1.0.0.0
```

> **Note**   The network specified must be a classful network, meaning that it cannot be a subnetted network; it must be a major network (either Class A, B, or C).

Let's verify the configuration:

```
!On R2:

R2# show ip route eigrp | begin Gate
Gateway of last resort is not set

D*    1.0.0.0/8 [90/20640000] via 12.1.1.1, 00:05:24, Serial1/1
```

The asterisk next to the letter *D* means "candidate default." This means that if R2 doesn't have the route it needs to reach in its routing table, it will use the candidate default (in this case, network 1.0.0.0). Because R1 was the router that advertised network 1.0.0.0/8 to R2, R2 will use R1 to reach that network.

Erase the startup config and reload the routers before proceeding to the next lab.

Lab 7-7: EIGRP Stub

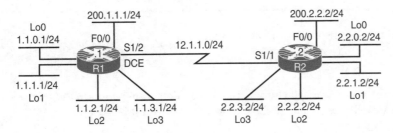

Figure 7-7   *EIGRP Stub Topology*

Task 1

Figure 7-7 illustrates the topology used in the following tasks. Configure EIGRP AS 100 on the serial interface and all loopback interfaces of these two routers. R1 should configure EIGRP using the classic method, and R2 should use EIGRP named mode configuration to accomplish this task. Do *not* run EIGRP on the F0/0 interfaces of these two routers.

```
!On R1:

R1(config)# router eigrp 100
R1(config-router)# network 1.1.0.1 0.0.0.0
R1(config-router)# network 1.1.1.1 0.0.0.0
R1(config-router)# network 1.1.2.1 0.0.0.0
```

```
R1(config-router)# network 1.1.3.1 0.0.0.0
R1(config-router)# network 12.1.1.1 0.0.0.0

!On R2:


R2(config)# router eigrp AS100
R2(config-router)# address-family ipv4 unicast autonomous-system 100
R2(config-router-af)# network 2.2.0.2 0.0.0.0
R2(config-router-af)# network 2.2.1.2 0.0.0.0
R2(config-router-af)# network 2.2.2.2 0.0.0.0
R2(config-router-af)# network 2.2.3.2 0.0.0.0
R2(config-router-af)# network 12.1.1.2 0.0.0.0
```

You should see the following console message:

```
%DUAL-5-NBRCHANGE: EIGRP-IPv4 100: Neighbor 12.1.1.1 (Serial1/1) is up: new adja-
  cency
```

Let's verify the configuration:

```
!On R1:


R1# show ip route eigrp | begin Gate
Gateway of last resort is not set


     2.0.0.0/24 is subnetted, 4 subnets
D       2.2.0.0 [90/20640000] via 12.1.1.2, 00:03:18, Serial1/2
D       2.2.1.0 [90/20640000] via 12.1.1.2, 00:03:18, Serial1/2
D       2.2.2.0 [90/20640000] via 12.1.1.2, 00:03:18, Serial1/2
D       2.2.3.0 [90/20640000] via 12.1.1.2, 00:03:18, Serial1/2

!On R2:


R2# show ip route eigrp | begin Gate
Gateway of last resort is not set


     1.0.0.0/24 is subnetted, 4 subnets
D       1.1.0.0 [90/20640000] via 12.1.1.1, 00:03:42, Serial1/1
D       1.1.1.0 [90/20640000] via 12.1.1.1, 00:03:42, Serial1/1
D       1.1.2.0 [90/20640000] via 12.1.1.1, 00:03:42, Serial1/1
D       1.1.3.0 [90/20640000] via 12.1.1.1, 00:03:42, Serial1/1
```

Task 2

Configure R1 and R2 to summarize their loopback interfaces in EIGRP:

```
!On R1:

R1(config)# interface serial1/2
R1(config-if)# ip summary-address eigrp 100 1.1.0.0 255.255.252.0

!On R2:

R2(config)# router eigrp AS100
R2(config-router)# address-family ipv4 unicast autonomous-system 100
R2(config-router-af)# af-interface serial1/1
R2(config-router-af-interface)# summary-address 2.2.0.0 255.255.252.0
```

Let's verify the configuration:

```
!On R1:

R1# show ip route eigrp | begin Gate
Gateway of last resort is not set

     1.0.0.0/8 is variably subnetted, 9 subnets, 3 masks
D       1.1.0.0/22 is a summary, 00:00:09, Null0
     2.0.0.0/22 is subnetted, 1 subnets
D       2.2.0.0 [90/20640000] via 12.1.1.2, 00:01:54, Serial1/2

!On R2:

R2# show ip route eigrp | begin Gate
Gateway of last resort is not set

     1.0.0.0/22 is subnetted, 1 subnets
D       1.1.0.0 [90/20640000] via 12.1.1.1, 00:00:27, Serial1/1
     2.0.0.0/8 is variably subnetted, 9 subnets, 3 masks
D       2.2.0.0/22 is a summary, 00:02:13, Null0
```

Task 3

Configure the static routes shown in Table 7-7 on R1 and R2 and redistribute them into EIGRP.

Table 7-7   *Static Routes*

Router	Static route
R1	Create a static route to network 11.0.0.0/8 via F0/0.
R2	Create a static route to network 22.0.0.0/8 via F0/0.

```
!On R1:

R1(config)# ip route 11.0.0.0 255.0.0.0 fastEthernet0/0

R1(config)# router eigrp 100
R1(config-router)# redistribute static

!On R2:

R2(config)# ip route 22.0.0.0 255.0.0.0 fastEthernet0/0

R2(config)# router eigrp AS100
R2(config-router)# address-family ipv4 unicast autonomous-system 100
R2(config-router-af)# topology base

R2(config-router-af-topology)# redistribute static
```

Let's verify the configuration:

```
!On R1:

R1# show ip route eigrp | begin Gate
Gateway of last resort is not set

      1.0.0.0/8 is variably subnetted, 9 subnets, 3 masks
D        1.1.0.0/22 is a summary, 00:03:09, Null0
      2.0.0.0/22 is subnetted, 1 subnets
D        2.2.0.0 [90/20640000] via 12.1.1.2, 00:04:54, Serial1/2
D EX  22.0.0.0/8 [170/20514560] via 12.1.1.2, 00:00:34, Serial1/2

!On R2:

R2# show ip route eigrp | begin Gate
Gateway of last resort is not set
```

```
       1.0.0.0/22 is subnetted, 1 subnets
D        1.1.0.0 [90/20640000] via 12.1.1.1, 00:02:44, Serial1/1
       2.0.0.0/8 is variably subnetted, 9 subnets, 3 masks
D        2.2.0.0/22 is a summary, 00:04:30, Null0
D EX  11.0.0.0/8 [170/20514560] via 12.1.1.1, 00:01:00, Serial1/1
```

Task 4

Advertise the FastEthernet interfaces of these two routers in RIPv2 and disable auto-summarization. You should redistribute RIP into EIGRP. Use any metric for redistributed routes.

```
!On R1:

R1(config)# router rip
R1(config-router)# no auto-summary
R1(config-router)# version 2
R1(config-router)# network 200.1.1.0

R1(config)# router eigrp 100
R1(config-router)# redistribute rip metric 1 1 1 1 1

!On R2:

R2(config)# router rip
R2(config-router)# no auto-summary
R2(config-router)# version 2
R2(config-router)# network 200.2.2.0

R2(config)# router eigrp AS100
R2(config-router)# address-family ipv4 unicast autonomous-system 100
R2(config-router-af)# topology base
R2(config-router-af-topology)# redistribute rip metric 1 1 1 1 1
```

Let's verify the configuration:

```
!On R1:

R1# show ip route eigrp | begin Gate
Gateway of last resort is not set

       1.0.0.0/8 is variably subnetted, 9 subnets, 3 masks
D        1.1.0.0/22 is a summary, 00:06:20, Null0
       2.0.0.0/22 is subnetted, 1 subnets
```

```
D        2.2.0.0 [90/20640000] via 12.1.1.2, 00:08:05, Serial1/2
D EX  22.0.0.0/8 [170/20514560] via 12.1.1.2, 00:03:45, Serial1/2
D EX  200.2.2.0/24 [170/2560512256] via 12.1.1.2, 00:00:29, Serial1/2


!On R2:


R2# show ip route eigrp | begin Gate
Gateway of last resort is not set


      1.0.0.0/22 is subnetted, 1 subnets
D         1.1.0.0 [90/20640000] via 12.1.1.1, 00:06:48, Serial1/1
      2.0.0.0/8 is variably subnetted, 9 subnets, 3 masks
D         2.2.0.0/22 is a summary, 00:08:34, Null0
D EX  11.0.0.0/8 [170/20514560] via 12.1.1.1, 00:05:04, Serial1/1
D EX  200.1.1.0/24 [170/2560512256] via 12.1.1.1, 00:01:43, Serial1/1
```

Task 5

Configure EIGRP stub routing on R1 using the **eigrp stub connected** option. Test this option and verify the routes in the routing tables of both routers.

```
!On R1:


R1(config)# router eigrp 100
R1(config-router)# eigrp stub connected
```

You should see the following console message stating that the neighbor adjacency was reset:

```
%DUAL-5-NBRCHANGE: EIGRP-IPv4 100: Neighbor 12.1.1.2 (Serial1/2) is down: peer info
  changed
%DUAL-5-NBRCHANGE: EIGRP-IPv4 100: Neighbor 12.1.1.2 (Serial1/2) is up: new
  adjacency
```

The **eigrp stub** routing can also be configured in EIGRP named mode, but in this case it is *only* configured on R1. The following shows how EIGRP stub routing can be configured in an EIGRP named configuration:

```
R2(config)# router eigrp AS100
R2(config-router)# address-family ipv4 unicast autonomous-system 100
R2(config-router-af)# eigrp stub ?
  connected     Do advertise connected routes
  leak-map      Allow dynamic prefixes based on the leak-map
```

```
receive-only    Set receive only neighbor
redistributed   Do advertise redistributed routes
static          Do advertise static routes
summary         Do advertise summary routes
```

Let's verify the configuration:

```
!On R2:

R2# show ip route eigrp | begin Gate
Gateway of last resort is not set

      1.0.0.0/24 is subnetted, 4 subnets
D        1.1.0.0 [90/20640000] via 12.1.1.1, 00:02:06, Serial1/1
D        1.1.1.0 [90/20640000] via 12.1.1.1, 00:02:06, Serial1/1
D        1.1.2.0 [90/20640000] via 12.1.1.1, 00:02:06, Serial1/1
D        1.1.3.0 [90/20640000] via 12.1.1.1, 00:02:06, Serial1/1
      2.0.0.0/8 is variably subnetted, 9 subnets, 3 masks
D        2.2.0.0/22 is a summary, 00:11:21, Null0
```

Note   Only the directly connected networks that R1 used a network command to advertise were advertised to R2.

```
!On R1:

R1# show ip route eigrp | begin Gate
Gateway of last resort is not set

      1.0.0.0/8 is variably subnetted, 9 subnets, 3 masks
D        1.1.0.0/22 is a summary, 00:10:09, Null0
      2.0.0.0/22 is subnetted, 1 subnets
D        2.2.0.0 [90/20640000] via 12.1.1.2, 00:02:39, Serial1/2
D EX  22.0.0.0/8 [170/20514560] via 12.1.1.2, 00:02:39, Serial1/2
D EX  200.2.2.0/24 [170/2560512256] via 12.1.1.2, 00:02:39, Serial1/2
```

Note   The routing table of R1 was *not* affected at all.

Task 6

Remove the **eigrp stub connected** option configured in the previous task and then reconfigure EIGRP stub routing on R1 using the **eigrp stub summary** option. Test this option
and verify the routes in the routing tables of both routers:

```
!On R1:

R1(config)# router eigrp 100
R1(config-router)# no eigrp stub connected
R1(config-router)# eigrp stub summary
```

Let's verify the configuration:

```
!On R2:

R2# show ip route eigrp | include 12.1.1.1
Gateway of last resort is not set

      1.0.0.0/22 is subnetted, 1 subnets
D        1.1.0.0 [90/20640000] via 12.1.1.1, 00:00:17, Serial1/1
      2.0.0.0/8 is variably subnetted, 9 subnets, 3 masks
D        2.2.0.0/22 is a summary, 00:15:23, Null0

!On R1:

R1# show ip route eigrp | begin Gate
Gateway of last resort is not set

      1.0.0.0/8 is variably subnetted, 9 subnets, 3 masks
D        1.1.0.0/22 is a summary, 01:12:59, Null0
      2.0.0.0/22 is subnetted, 1 subnets
D        2.2.0.0 [90/20640000] via 12.1.1.2, 00:00:57, Serial1/2
D EX  22.0.0.0/8 [170/20514560] via 12.1.1.2, 00:00:57, Serial1/2
D EX  200.2.2.0/24 [170/2560512256] via 12.1.1.2, 00:00:57, Serial1/2
```

By looking at the routing table of these two routers, you can clearly see that *only* the
summarized route(s) were advertised to R2, but once again the routing table of R1 was
not affected at all.

Task 7

Remove the **eigrp stub summary** option configured in the previous task and reconfigure
EIGRP stub routing on R1 using **eigrp stub static**. Test this option and verify the routes
in the routing tables of both routers.

```
!On R1:

R1(config)# router eigrp 100
R1(config-router)# no eigrp stub summary
R1(config-router)# eigrp stub static
```

Let's verify the configuration:

```
!On R2:

R2# show ip route eigrp | begin Gate
Gateway of last resort is not set

     2.0.0.0/8 is variably subnetted, 9 subnets, 3 masks
D       2.2.0.0/22 is a summary, 00:17:25, Null0
D EX  11.0.0.0/8 [170/20514560] via 12.1.1.1, 00:00:09, Serial1/1

!On R1:

R1# show ip route eigrp | begin Gate
Gateway of last resort is not set

     1.0.0.0/8 is variably subnetted, 9 subnets, 3 masks
D       1.1.0.0/22 is a summary, 01:16:33, Null0
     2.0.0.0/22 is subnetted, 1 subnets
D       2.2.0.0 [90/20640000] via 12.1.1.2, 00:01:41, Serial1/2
D EX  22.0.0.0/8 [170/20514560] via 12.1.1.2, 00:01:41, Serial1/2
D EX  200.2.2.0/24 [170/2560512256] via 12.1.1.2, 00:01:41, Serial1/2
```

The output of the preceding **show** command reveals that R1's routing table was *not* affected at all, but R2 received the static routes that R1 redistributed into its routing table.

Note   The routing protocol that is redistributed into EIGRP is *not* advertised and *only* the static routes are advertised.

Task 8

Remove the **eigrp stub static** option configured in the previous task and reconfigure EIGRP stub routing on R1 using **eigrp stub redistributed**. Test this option and verify the routes in the routing tables of both routers:

```
!On R1:

R1(config)# router eigrp 100
R1(config-router)# no eigrp stub static
R1(config-router)# eigrp stub redistributed
```

Let's verify the configuration:

```
!On R2:

R2# show ip route eigrp | begin Gate
Gateway of last resort is not set

      2.0.0.0/8 is variably subnetted, 9 subnets, 3 masks
D         2.2.0.0/22 is a summary, 00:20:05, Null0
D EX   11.0.0.0/8 [170/20514560] via 12.1.1.1, 00:00:10, Serial1/1
D EX   200.1.1.0/24 [170/2560512256] via 12.1.1.1, 00:00:10, Serial1/1
```

Note   All the redistributed routes are advertised to R2, which means that the static routes and the routing protocols that were redistributed into EIGRP were advertised with this option.

Task 9

Remove the **eigrp stub redistributed** option configured in the previous task and reconfigure EIGRP stub routing on R1 using **eigrp stub receive-only**. Test this option and verify the routes in the routing tables of both routers:

```
!On R1:

R1(config)# router eigrp 100
R1(config-router)# no eigrp stub redistributed
R1(config-router)# eigrp stub receive-only
```

Let's verify the configuration:

```
!On R2:

R2# show ip route eigrp | begin Gate
Gateway of last resort is not set

      2.0.0.0/8 is variably subnetted, 9 subnets, 3 masks
D         2.2.0.0/22 is a summary, 00:21:28, Null0
```

You can clearly see that nothing was advertised to R2. With this option configured on R1, R1 receives all the routes from R2 but does *not* advertise any routes to R2.

```
!On R1:

R1# show ip route eigrp | begin Gate
Gateway of last resort is not set

      1.0.0.0/8 is variably subnetted, 9 subnets, 3 masks
D        1.1.0.0/22 is a summary, 01:31:37, Null0
      2.0.0.0/22 is subnetted, 1 subnets
D        2.2.0.0 [90/20640000] via 12.1.1.2, 00:01:27, Serial1/2
D EX  22.0.0.0/8 [170/20514560] via 12.1.1.2, 00:01:27, Serial1/2
D EX  200.2.2.0/24 [170/2560512256] via 12.1.1.2, 00:01:27, Serial1/2
```

Task 10

Remove the **eigrp stub receive-only** option configured in the previous task and reconfigure EIGRP stub routing on R1 using **eigrp stub**. Test this option and verify the routes in the routing tables of both routers:

```
!On R1:

R1(config)# router eigrp 100
R1(config-router)# no eigrp stub receive-only
R1(config-router)# eigrp stub
```

Let's verify the configuration:

```
!On R2:

R2# show ip route eigrp | begin Gate
Gateway of last resort is not set

      1.0.0.0/22 is subnetted, 1 subnets
D        1.1.0.0 [90/20640000] via 12.1.1.1, 00:00:05, Serial1/1
      2.0.0.0/8 is variably subnetted, 9 subnets, 3 masks
D        2.2.0.0/22 is a summary, 00:22:37, Null0
```

Note   All the directly connected routes and the summary route are advertised to R2. The reason you only see a single summary route is because when summarization is performed, the specific routes that are included in the summary are suppressed. To prove this fact, let's configure the loopback100 interface on R1 and assign an IP address of 100.1.1.1/24 and advertise this route in EIGRP AS 100. If this is performed successfully, R2 should see the summary plus the 100.1.1.0/24 routes:

```
!On R1:

R1(config)# interface loopback100
R1(config-if)# ip address 100.1.1.1 255.255.255.0

R1(config)# router eigrp 100
R1(config-router)# network 100.1.1.1 0.0.0.0
```

Let's verify the configuration:

```
!On R2:

R2# show ip route eigrp | begin Gate
Gateway of last resort is not set

     1.0.0.0/22 is subnetted, 1 subnets
D       1.1.0.0 [90/20640000] via 12.1.1.1, 00:01:36, Serial1/1
     2.0.0.0/8 is variably subnetted, 9 subnets, 3 masks
D       2.2.0.0/22 is a summary, 00:24:08, Null0
     100.0.0.0/24 is subnetted, 1 subnets
D       100.1.1.0 [90/20640000] via 12.1.1.1, 00:00:10, Serial1/1
```

Erase the startup config and reload the routers before proceeding to the next lab.

Chapter 8

OSPF

Lab 8-1: Advertising Networks

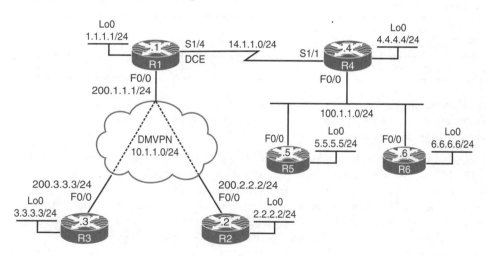

Figure 8-1 *Advertising Networks*

Figure 8-1 illustrates the topology that will used in the following tasks.

Task 1

Configure the connections between R4, R5, and R6 and run OSPF Area 0 on the f0/0 and the lo0 interfaces of these three routers. Configure the router IDs to be 0.0.0.x, where x is the router number. The loopback interfaces should be advertised with their correct mask.

```
On SW1:

SW1(config)# interface range FastEthernet0/4-6
SW1(config-if-range)# switchport
SW1(config-if-range)# switchport mode access
SW1(config-if-range)# switchport access vlan 456
SW1(config-if-range)# no shutdown
```

```
On R4:

R4(config)# interface loopback0
R4(config-if)# ip address 4.4.4.4 255.255.255.0
R4(config-if)# ip ospf network point-to-point

R4(config)# interface FastEthernet0/0
R4(config-if)# ip address 100.1.1.4 255.255.255.0
R4(config-if)# no shutdown
```

Let's configure OSPF:

```
R4(config)# router ospf 1
```

In the following configuration, OSPF's **router-id** is set to 0.0.0.4. In OSPF, the router ID uniquely identifies the router within the entire routing domain and *must* be unique within the entire OSPF routing domain.

The OSPF router ID is a 32-bit dotted decimal value, *it is not an IP address*. However, since IP addresses are also 32-bit dotted decimal values, a value that looks like an IP address can also be used as the OSPF router ID. If the **router-id** is not configured, the numerically highest IP address of any loopback interface will be chosen as the router ID; if one does not exist, then the highest IP address configured on the local router will be chosen as the OSPF router ID. It's a good practice to always configure OSPF's **router-id**, unless you are in the CCIE lab and the task states not to.

```
R4(config-router)# router-id 0.0.0.4
```

In OSPF, the **network** statement can be configured in different ways; the following **network** statement could have been configured in the following ways:

- **network 0.0.0.0 0.0.0.0 area 0**: This **network** statement means that the existing and future interface(s) that have an IP address will run in Area 0. Remember that if an interface is redistributed into the OSPF routing protocol, the redistributed interface will show up in the routing table as an intra-area route and *not* an external route, because intra-area is preferred over inter-area, which in turn is preferred over external routes.

- **network 100.0.0.0 0.255.255.255 area 0:** This **network** statement means that any subnet within the major network (100.0.0.0/8) should run in Area 0.

- **network 100.1.1.0 0.0.0.255 area 0:** This **network** statement means that any host within network 100.1.1.0/24 will run in area 0.

- **network 100.1.1.4 0.0.0.0 area 0:** This **network** statement is by far the best way to go. You are being very specific and are running OSPF on that given interface only.

```
R4(config-router)# network 100.1.1.4 0.0.0.0 area 0
R4(config-router)# network 4.4.4.4 0.0.0.0 area 0
```

```
On R5:

R5(config)# interface FastEthernet0/0
R5(config-if)# ip address 100.1.1.5 255.255.255.0
R5(config-if)# no shutdown

R5(config)# interface loopback0
R5(config-if)# ip address 5.5.5.5 255.255.255.0
R5(config-if)# ip ospf network point-to-point

R5(config)# router ospf 1
R5(config-router)# router-id 0.0.0.5
R5(config-router)# network 5.5.5.5 0.0.0.0 area 0
R5(config-router)# network 100.1.1.5 0.0.0.0 area 0
```

You should see the following console message:

```
%OSPF-5-ADJCHG: Process 1, Nbr 0.0.0.4 on FastEthernet0/0 from LOADING to FULL,
Loading Done
```

When running OSPF on any Layer 2 protocol, you must know the capabilities of that protocol from OSPF's perspective. The following list details the important aspects of an Ethernet segment:

- By default, OSPF's network type is broadcast.

- By default, the timers are set to 10/40, meaning that the OSPF hellos are exchanged every 10 seconds, and the dead interval is set to 40 seconds.

- There must be a DR election. The router with the highest OSPF interface priority is elected as the DR, the default priority is set to 1, and the range is 0–255. A priority of 0 means that the local router will *not* participate in the DR/BDR election.

- Next hop is the IP address of the router that originated the route.

- The routers use multicast addresses of 224.0.0.5 and 224.0.0.6.

Let's verify these items:

```
R5# show ip ospf interface FastEthernet0/0 | include Network

  Internet Address 100.1.1.5/24, Area 0, Attached via Network Statement
  Process ID 1, Router ID 0.0.0.5, Network Type BROADCAST, Cost: 1

R5# show ip ospf interface f0/0 | i Timer

  Timer intervals configured, Hello 10, Dead 40, Wait 40, Retransmit 5

R5# Show ip ospf neighbor

Neighbor ID     Pri    State      Dead Time    Address         Interface
0.0.0.4           1    FULL/DR    00:00:37     100.1.1.4       FastEthernet0/0

R5# Show ip route 4.4.4.0

Routing entry for 4.4.4.0/24
  Known via "ospf 1", distance 110, metric 2, type intra area
  Last update from 100.1.1.4 on FastEthernet0/0, 00:00:09 ago
  Routing Descriptor Blocks:
  * 100.1.1.4, from 0.0.0.4, 00:00:09 ago, via FastEthernet0/0
      Route metric is 2, traffic share count is 1

R5# show ip interface FastEthernet0/0 | include 224

  Multicast reserved groups joined: 224.0.0.5 224.0.0.6
```

Let's configure R6:

```
On R6:

R6(config)# interface FastEthernet0/0
R6(config-if)# ip address 100.1.1.6 255.255.255.0
R6(config-if)# no shutdown

R6(config)# interface loopback0
R6(config-if)# ip address 6.6.6.6 255.255.255.0
R6(config-if)# ip ospf network point-to-point

R6(config)# router ospf 1
R6(config-router)# router-id 0.0.0.6
R6(config-router)# network 6.6.6.6 0.0.0.0 area 0
R6(config-router)# network 100.1.1.6 0.0.0.0 area 0
```

You should see the following console messages:

```
%OSPF-5-ADJCHG: Process 1, Nbr 0.0.0.4 on FastEthernet0/0 from LOADING to FULL,
Loading Done

%OSPF-5-ADJCHG: Process 1, Nbr 0.0.0.5 on FastEthernet0/0 from LOADING to FULL,
Loading Done
```

Let's verify the configuration:

```
On R6:

R6# show ip route ospf | begin Gate
Gateway of last resort is not set

      4.0.0.0/24 is subnetted, 1 subnets
O        4.4.4.0 [110/2] via 100.1.1.4, 00:04:54, FastEthernet0/0
      5.0.0.0/24 is subnetted, 1 subnets
O        5.5.5.0 [110/2] via 100.1.1.5, 00:04:44, FastEthernet0/0
```

Task 2

Configure the serial connection that links R1 to R4 as well as their loopback interfaces. Configure OSPF Area 0 on the serial interfaces of R1 and R4 and their loopback0 interfaces. R1's **router-id** should be configured to be 0.0.0.1. R1's loopback interface must be advertised with its correct mask.

```
On R1:

R1(config)# interface serial 1/4
R1(config-if)# clock rate 64000
R1(config-if)# ip address 14.1.1.1 255.255.255.0
R1(config-if)# no shutdown

R1(config)# interface loopback0
R1(config-if)# ip address 1.1.1.1 255.255.255.0
R1(config-if)# ip ospf network point-to-point

R1(config)# router ospf 1
R1(config-router)# router-id 0.0.0.1
R1(config-router)# network 1.1.1.1 0.0.0.0 area 0
R1(config-router)# network 14.1.1.1 0.0.0.0 area 0
```

```
On R4:

R4(config)# interface serial1/1
R4(config-if)# ip address 14.1.1.4 255.255.255.0
R4(config-if)# no shutdown

R4(config)# router ospf 1
R4(config-router)# network 14.1.1.4 0.0.0.0 area 0
```

You should see the following console message:

```
%OSPF-5-ADJCHG: Process 1, Nbr 0.0.0.1 on Serial1/1 from LOADING to FULL,
Loading Done
```

Let's verify the configuration:

```
On R1:

R1# show ip route ospf | begin Gate
Gateway of last resort is not set

      4.0.0.0/24 is subnetted, 1 subnets
O        4.4.4.0 [110/782] via 14.1.1.4, 00:02:17, Serial1/4
      5.0.0.0/24 is subnetted, 1 subnets
O        5.5.5.0 [110/783] via 14.1.1.4, 00:02:17, Serial1/4
      6.0.0.0/24 is subnetted, 1 subnets
O        6.6.6.0 [110/783] via 14.1.1.4, 00:02:17, Serial1/4
    100.0.0.0/24 is subnetted, 1 subnets
O      100.1.1.0 [110/782] via 14.1.1.4, 00:02:17, Serial1/4


R1# show ip ospf neighbor

Neighbor ID   Pri   State      Dead Time   Address     Interface
0.0.0.4         0   FULL/  -   00:00:32    14.1.1.4    Serial1/4
```

You can see that the local router has established an adjacency with R4 (0.0.0.4).

```
R1# show ip ospf interface brief

Interface   PID   Area   IP Address/Mask   Cost   State  Nbrs F/C
Lo0         1     0      1.1.1.1/24        1      P2P    0/0
Se1/4       1     0      14.1.1.1/24       781    P2P    1/1
```

The output of the preceding **show** command reveals the following:

- The OSPF process ID (PID) is 1.
- The local router's Se1/4 and Lo0 interfaces are configured in Area 0.
- The IP addresses in this area are 1.1.1.1/24 and 14.1.1.1/24.
- The OSPF cost of the Se1/4 interface is 781, and the cost of the Lo0 interface is 1.
- The local router has two neighbors.

Task 3

Configure the addresses shown in Table 8-1.

Table 8-1 *IP Addressing*

Router	Interface	IP Address
R1	F0/0	200.1.1.1/24
R2	F0/0	200.2.2.2/24
	Lo0	2.2.2.2/24
R3	F0/0	200.3.3.3/24
	Lo0	3.3.3.3/24

```
On R1:

R1(config)# interface FastEthernet0/0
R1(config-if)# ip address 200.1.1.1 255.255.255.0
R1(config-if)# no shutdown
```

```
On R2:

R2(config)# interface FastEthernet0/0
R2(config-if)# ip address 200.2.2.2 255.255.255.0
R2(config-if)# no shutdown

R2(config)# interface loopback0
R2(config-if)# ip address 2.2.2.2 255.255.255.0
```

```
On R3:

R3(config)# interface FastEthernet0/0
R3(config-if)# ip address 200.3.3.3 255.255.255.0
R3(config-if)# no shutdown

R3(config)# interface loopback0
R3(config-if)# ip address 3.3.3.3 255.255.255.0
```

OSPF can be configured in one of two different modes: router configuration mode or interface configuration mode. This task states that a **network** command cannot be used; therefore, the interface configuration mode is used to run OSPF Area 0 on the S1/2 interface of R1. When OSPF is configured directly on the interface, the IOS will automatically start the OSPF process for you.

Task 4

SW1 represents the Internet. Configure a static default route on each router pointing to the appropriate interface on SW1. If this configuration is performed correctly, these routers should be able to ping and have reachability to the F0/0 interfaces of all routers in this topology. The switch interface to which the routers are connected should have ".10" in the host portion of the IP address for that subnet.

Let's configure SW1's interfaces for these routers. Since in this lab SW1 represents the Internet, the IP addresses in the following configuration should be set as the default gateway on the routers.

```
On SW1:

SW1(config)# interface range FastEthernet0/1-3
SW1(config-if-range)# no switchport

SW1(config)# interface FastEthernet0/1
SW1(config-if)# ip address 200.1.1.10 255.255.255.0
SW1(config-if)# no shut

SW1(config)# interface FastEthernet0/2
SW1(config-if)# ip addr 200.2.2.10 255.255.255.0
SW1(config-if)# no shut

SW1(config)# interface f0/3
SW1(config-if)# ip addr 200.3.3.10 255.255.255.0
SW1(config-if)# no shut
```

Let's *not* forget to enable **ip routing**; otherwise, the switch will not be able to route from one subnet to another:

```
SW1(config)# ip routing
```

Let's configure the routers:

```
On R1:

R1(config)# ip route 0.0.0.0 0.0.0.0 200.1.1.10
```

```
On R2:

R2(config)# ip route 0.0.0.0 0.0.0.0 200.1.2.10
```

```
On R3:

R3(config)# ip route 0.0.0.0 0.0.0.0 200.1.3.10
```

Now let's verify the configuration:

```
On R1:

R1# ping 200.2.2.2

Type escape sequence to abort.
Sending 5, 100-byte ICMP Echos to 200.2.2.2, timeout is 2 seconds:
!!!!!
Success rate is 100 percent (5/5), round-trip min/avg/max = 1/2/4 ms

R1# ping 200.3.3.3

Type escape sequence to abort.
Sending 5, 100-byte ICMP Echos to 200.3.3.3, timeout is 2 seconds:
!!!!!
Success rate is 100 percent (5/5), round-trip min/avg/max = 1/2/4 ms
```

```
On R2:

R2# ping 200.3.3.3

Type escape sequence to abort.
Sending 5, 100-byte ICMP Echos to 200.3.3.3, timeout is 2 seconds:
!!!!!
Success rate is 100 percent (5/5), round-trip min/avg/max = 1/2/4 ms
```

Task 5

SW1 represents the Internet. Configure a static default route on each router pointing
to the appropriate interface on SW1. If this configuration is performed correctly, these
routers should be able to ping and have reachability to the F0/0 interfaces of all routers in
this topology. The switch interface to which the routers are connected should have ".10"
in the host portion of the IP address for that subnet.

Configure the dynamic multipoint virtual private network (DMVPN) based on the following policies:

- R1 should be the Next-Hop Resolution Protocol server (NHS), and R2 and R3 should be the spokes.

- R1 should not be configured with any static mappings.

- R2 and R3 should be configured in a point-to-point manner.

- The tunnel source of these routers should be based on their f0/0 interfaces.

- Provide multicast capability on the appropriate router(s).

```
On R1:

R1(config)# interface tunnel 1
R1(config-if)# ip address 10.1.1.1 255.255.255.0
R1(config-if)# tunnel source FastEthernet0/0
R1(config-if)# tunnel mode gre multipoint
R1(config-if)# ip nhrp network-id 111
R1(config-if)# ip nhrp map multicast dynamic
```

```
On R2:

R2(config)# interface tunnel 1
R2(config-if)# ip address 10.1.1.2 255.255.255.0
R2(config-if)# tunnel source FastEthernet0/0
R2(config-if)# tunnel destination 200.1.1.1
R2(config-if)# ip nhrp network-id 222
R2(config-if)# ip nhrp nhs 10.1.1.1
R2(config-if)# ip nhrp map 10.1.1.1 200.1.1.1
```

Let's verify the configuration:

```
On R2:

R2# ping 10.1.1.1

Type escape sequence to abort.
Sending 5, 100-byte ICMP Echos to 10.1.1.1, timeout is 2 seconds:
!!!!!
Success rate is 100 percent (5/5), round-trip min/avg/max = 1/2/4 ms
```

```
On R3:

R3(config)# interface tunnel 1
R3(config-if)# ip address 10.1.1.3 255.255.255.0
R3(config-if)# tunnel source FastEthernet0/0
R3(config-if)# tunnel destination 200.1.1.1
R3(config-if)# ip nhrp network-id 333
R3(config-if)# ip nhrp nhs 10.1.1.1
R3(config-if)# ip nhrp map 10.1.1.1 200.1.1.1
```

Pings will let us know if we have reachability

```
On R3:

R3# ping 10.1.1.1

Type escape sequence to abort.
Sending 5, 100-byte ICMP Echos to 10.1.1.1, timeout is 2 seconds:
!!!!!
Success rate is 100 percent (5/5), round-trip min/avg/max = 1/3/4 ms

R3# ping 10.1.1.2

Type escape sequence to abort.
Sending 5, 100-byte ICMP Echos to 10.1.1.2, timeout is 2 seconds:
!!!!!
Success rate is 100 percent (5/5), round-trip min/avg/max = 1/3/4 ms
```

Task 6

Configure OSPF Area 0 on the tunnel interfaces of R1, R2, and R3 as well as the
loopback0 interfaces of R2 and R3. The loopback interfaces must be advertised with
their correct mask. The OSPF router IDs of R2 and R3 should be configured to be 0.0.0.2
and 0.0.0.3, respectively. There should not be any designated router (DR) or backup
designated router (BDR) on this segment.

```
On R1:

R1(config)# router ospf 1
R1(config-router)# network 10.1.1.1 0.0.0.0 area 0
```

```
On R2:

R2(config)# router ospf 1
R2(config-router)# router-id 0.0.0.2
R2(config-router)# network 2.2.2.2 0.0.0.0 area 0
R2(config-router)# network 10.1.1.2 0.0.0.0 area 0
```

```
On R5:
R5(config)# interface lo0
R5(config-if)# ip ospf network point-to-point
```

You should see the following console message:

```
%OSPF-5-ADJCHG: Process 1, Nbr 0.0.0.1 on Tunnel1 from LOADING to FULL,
Loading Done
```

```
On R3:

R3(config)# router ospf 1
R3(config-router)# router-id 0.0.0.3
R3(config-router)# network 3.3.3.3 0.0.0.0 area 0
R3(config-router)# network 10.1.1.3 0.0.0.0 area 0

R3(config)# interface loopback0
R3(config-if)# ip ospf network point-to-point
```

You should also see the following console messages:

```
%OSPF-5-ADJCHG: Process 1, Nbr 0.0.0.1 on Tunnel1 from LOADING to FULL,
Loading Done

%OSPF-5-ADJCHG: Process 1, Nbr 0.0.0.1 on Tunnel1 from LOADING to FULL,
Loading Done

%OSPF-5-ADJCHG: Process 1, Nbr 0.0.0.1 on Tunnel1 from LOADING to FULL,
Loading Done
```

It seems like the local router (R3) keeps reestablishing an OSPF adjacency with R1. Let's see why.

Let's look at the rules and conditions that must be met before two OSPF routers form an adjacency:

- Timers must match.

- Area IDs must match.

- The two routers must be on the same subnet.

- The authentication type and passwords must match.

- The MTUs must match.

Let's verify these items.

On R1, you can see that the Tunnel 1 interface keeps on flapping: It establishes an OSPF adjacency with 0.0.0.2 and then drops the adjacency and forms an adjacency with 0.0.0.3, and then the cycle repeats. You cannot even access the console of R1 because of the messages. In order to have access to R1's console, let's shut down the f0/1 interface on SW1:

```
On SW1:

SW1(config)# interface FastEthernet0/1
SW1(config-if)# shutdown
```

Once the f0/1 interface is shut down, you can access the console. Let's verify the information on the tunnel interface of R1:

```
On R1:

R1# show ip ospf interface tunnel 1 | inc Timer

  Timer intervals configured, Hello 10, Dead 40, Wait 40, Retransmit 5
```

The tunnel interface is configured in a multipoint manner, but why are the hello and dead intervals set to 10 and 40 seconds, respectively?

Let's check the network type:

```
R1# show ip ospf interface tunnel 1 | include Network

  Internet Address 10.1.1.1/24, Area 0, Attached via Network Statement
  Process ID 1, Router ID 0.0.0.1, Network Type POINT_TO_POINT, Cost: 1000
```

You can see the problem: OSPF does not read or process the "tunnel mode GRE multipoint." OSPF sees a tunnel interface and assumes that it is a point-to-point tunnel; therefore, it sets the OSPF network type to point-to-point. Because you cannot have a DR/BDR (based on the task's requirements), let's change the network type to "point-to-multipoint" and then **no shutdown** the f0/1 interface on SW1 and test the adjacency again:

```
R1(config)# interface tunnel 1
R1(config-if)# ip ospf network point-to-multipoint
```

```
On SW1:

SW1(config)# interface FastEthernet0/1
SW1(config-if)# no shutdown
```

Let's verify the neighbor adjacency on R1:

```
On R1:

R1# show ip ospf neighbor

Neighbor ID    Pri   State        Dead Time   Address      Interface
0.0.0.4          0   FULL/ -      00:00:33    14.1.1.4     Serial1/4
```

Let's see if the spoke routers have registered themselves with the hub router:

```
R1# show ip nhrp
```

Nothing in the NHRP table. There are many ways to fix this problem. One way is to configure the spoke routers to send a registration request every 5 seconds. Let's test this:

```
On R2 and R3:

Rx(config)# interface tunnel 1
Rx(config-if)# ip nhrp registration timeout 5
```

Now let's verify the configuration:

```
On R1:

R1# show ip nhrp

10.1.1.2/32 via 10.1.1.2
   Tunnel1 created 00:01:01, expire 01:59:58
   Type: dynamic, Flags: unique registered used
   NBMA address: 200.2.2.2
10.1.1.3/32 via 10.1.1.3
   Tunnel1 created 00:00:06, expire 01:59:58
   Type: dynamic, Flags: unique registered used
   NBMA address: 200.3.3.3
```

The spoke routers, R2 and R3, have successfully registered themselves with the hub router, R1. However, the routers have not formed an adjacency. Let's verify the timers:

```
R1# show ip ospf interface tunnel 1 | include Timer

  Timer intervals configured, Hello 30, Dead 120, Wait 120, Retransmit 5
```

```
On R2:

R2# show ip ospf interface tunnel 1 | include Timer

  Timer intervals configured, Hello 10, Dead 40, Wait 40, Retransmit 5
```

```
On R3:

R3# show ip ospf interface tunnel 1 | include Timer

  Timer intervals configured, Hello 10, Dead 40, Wait 40, Retransmit 5
```

You can see the problem: The timers do not match. Let's configure the hello and dead intervals on R1's tunnel interface to match R2 and R3:

```
On R1:

R1(config)# interface tunnel 1
R1(config-if)# ip ospf hello-interval 10
```

Note   Once the preceding command is entered, you should see the following console messages:

```
%OSPF-5-ADJCHG: Process 1, Nbr 0.0.0.3 on Tunnel1 from LOADING to FULL,
Loading Done

%OSPF-5-ADJCHG: Process 1, Nbr 0.0.0.2 on Tunnel1 from LOADING to FULL,
Loading Done
```

However, we didn't change the dead interval. Did the dead interval automatically adjust? Let's verify:

```
R1# show ip ospf interface tunnel 1 | include Timer

  Timer intervals configured, Hello 10, Dead 40, Wait 40, Retransmit 5
```

Yes, if the hello interval is changed, the dead interval will automatically be set to four times the hello interval.

Let's verify the configuration:

```
On R3:

R3# show ip route ospf | begin Gate
Gateway of last resort is 200.3.3.10 to network 0.0.0.0

        1.0.0.0/24 is subnetted, 1 subnets
O          1.1.1.0 [110/1001] via 10.1.1.1, 00:03:16, Tunnel1
        2.0.0.0/24 is subnetted, 1 subnets
O          2.2.2.0 [110/2001] via 10.1.1.1, 00:03:06, Tunnel1
        4.0.0.0/24 is subnetted, 1 subnets
O          4.4.4.0 [110/1782] via 10.1.1.1, 00:03:16, Tunnel1
        5.0.0.0/24 is subnetted, 1 subnets
O          5.5.5.0 [110/1783] via 10.1.1.1, 00:03:16, Tunnel1
        6.0.0.0/24 is subnetted, 1 subnets
O          6.6.6.0 [110/1783] via 10.1.1.1, 00:03:16, Tunnel1
        10.0.0.0/8 is variably subnetted, 3 subnets, 2 masks
O          10.1.1.1/32 [110/1000] via 10.1.1.1, 00:03:16, Tunnel1
        14.0.0.0/24 is subnetted, 1 subnets
O          14.1.1.0 [110/1781] via 10.1.1.1, 00:03:16, Tunnel1
        100.0.0.0/24 is subnetted, 1 subnets
O          100.1.1.0 [110/1782] via 10.1.1.1, 00:03:16, Tunnel1
```

```
On R2:

R2# show ip route ospf | begin Gate
Gateway of last resort is 200.2.2.10 to network 0.0.0.0

        1.0.0.0/24 is subnetted, 1 subnets
O          1.1.1.0 [110/1001] via 10.1.1.1, 00:03:41, Tunnel1
        3.0.0.0/24 is subnetted, 1 subnets
O          3.3.3.0 [110/2001] via 10.1.1.1, 00:03:41, Tunnel1
        4.0.0.0/24 is subnetted, 1 subnets
O          4.4.4.0 [110/1782] via 10.1.1.1, 00:03:41, Tunnel1
        5.0.0.0/24 is subnetted, 1 subnets
O          5.5.5.0 [110/1783] via 10.1.1.1, 00:03:41, Tunnel1
        6.0.0.0/24 is subnetted, 1 subnets
O          6.6.6.0 [110/1783] via 10.1.1.1, 00:03:41, Tunnel1
        10.0.0.0/8 is variably subnetted, 3 subnets, 2 masks
```

```
O         10.1.1.1/32 [110/1000] via 10.1.1.1, 00:03:41, Tunnel1
        14.0.0.0/24 is subnetted, 1 subnets
O         14.1.1.0 [110/1781] via 10.1.1.1, 00:03:41, Tunnel1
        100.0.0.0/24 is subnetted, 1 subnets
O         100.1.1.0 [110/1782] via 10.1.1.1, 00:03:41, Tunnel1
```

Erase the startup configuration and reload the routers before proceeding to the next lab.

Lab 8-2: OSPF Broadcast Networks

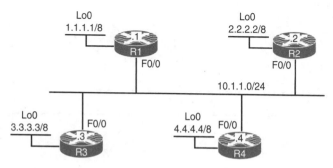

Figure 8-2 *OSPF Broadcast Networks*

Task 1

Configure OSPF Area 0 on the f0/0 and lo0 interfaces in Figure 8-2. Configure the loopback interfaces such that they are advertised with their correct mask. You should configure 0.0.0.1, 0.0.0.2, 0.0.0.3, and 0.0.0.4 with the router IDs of R1, R2, R3, and R4, respectively.

```
On R1:


R1(config)# router ospf 1
R1(config-router)# router-id 0.0.0.1
R1(config-router)# network 10.1.1.1 0.0.0.0 area 0
R1(config-router)# network 1.1.1.1 0.0.0.0 area 0

R1(config-router)# interface loopback0
R1(config-if)# ip ospf network point-to-point
```

```
On R2:


R2(config)# router ospf 1
R2(config-router)# router-id 0.0.0.2
```

```
R2(config-router)# network 10.1.1.2 0.0.0.0 area 0
R2(config-router)# network 2.2.2.2 0.0.0.0 area 0

R2(config-router)# interface loopback0
R2(config-if)# ip ospf network point-to-point
```

```
On R3:

R3(config)# router ospf 1
R3(config-router)# router-id 0.0.0.3
R3(config-router)# network 10.1.1.3 0.0.0.0 area 0
R3(config-router)# network 3.3.3.3 0.0.0.0 area 0

R3(config-router)# interface loopback0
R3(config-if)# ip ospf network point-to-point
```

```
On R4:

R4(config)# router ospf 1
R4(config-router)# router-id 0.0.0.4
R4(config-router)# network 10.1.1.4 0.0.0.0 area 0
R4(config-router)# network 4.4.4.4 0.0.0.0 area 0

R4(config-router)# interface loopback0
R4(config-if)# ip ospf network point-to-point
```

Let's verify the configuration:

```
On R1:

R1# show ip route ospf | begin Gate
Gateway of last resort is not set

O    2.0.0.0/8 [110/2] via 10.1.1.2, 00:00:20, FastEthernet0/0
O    3.0.0.0/8 [110/2] via 10.1.1.3, 00:00:20, FastEthernet0/0
O    4.0.0.0/8 [110/2] via 10.1.1.4, 00:00:30, FastEthernet0/0

R1# show ip ospf database

          OSPF router with ID (0.0.0.1) (Process ID 1)

             router Link States (Area 0)
```

```
Link ID          ADV router        Age        Seq#         Checksum Link count
0.0.0.1          0.0.0.1           90         0x80000004   0x00D02E 2
0.0.0.2          0.0.0.2           91         0x80000004   0x00E119 2
0.0.0.3          0.0.0.3           91         0x80000004   0x00F204 2
0.0.0.4          0.0.0.4           91         0x80000004   0x0004EE 2


                 Net Link States (Area 0)


Link ID          ADV router        Age        Seq#         Checksum
10.1.1.4         0.0.0.4           90         0x80000001   0x0072A1

R1# show ip ospf database network

              OSPF router with ID (0.0.0.1) (Process ID 1)

                 Net Link States (Area 0)

 Routing Bit Set on this LSA in topology Base with MTID 0
 LS age: 189
 Options: (No TOS-capability, DC)
 LS Type: network Links
 Link State ID: 10.1.1.4 (address of Designated Router)
 Advertising Router: 0.0.0.4
 LS Seq Number: 80000001
 Checksum: 0x72A1
 Length: 40
 network Mask: /24
       Attached Router: 0.0.0.4
       Attached Router: 0.0.0.1
       Attached Router: 0.0.0.2
       Attached Router: 0.0.0.3
```

You can see that it's the DR that floods Type-2 LSAs, and on this segment R4 is the DR with an IP address of 10.1.1.4/24, which means 10.1.1.0/24 is the network address of this segment. This segment will not be advertised by the other routers; *only* the DR is responsible for this. Network LSAs or Type-2 LSAs also reveal the router IDs of the other routers that are attached to this broadcast multi-access network.

```
R1# show ip ospf neighbor


Neighbor ID      Pri   State          Dead Time    Address      Interface
0.0.0.2          1     2WAY/DROTHER   00:00:32     10.1.1.2     FastEthernet0/0
0.0.0.3          1     FULL/BDR       00:00:37     10.1.1.3     FastEthernet0/0
0.0.0.4          1     FULL/DR        00:00:37     10.1.1.4     FastEthernet0/0
```

Based on the preceding output, you can see that the local router is in the 2WAY state with R2 and in the FULL state with the DR and BDR. Let's check the routing table of R1:

```
R1# show ip route ospf | begin Gate
Gateway of last resort is not set


O    2.0.0.0/8 [110/2] via 10.1.1.2, 00:13:30, FastEthernet0/0
O    3.0.0.0/8 [110/2] via 10.1.1.3, 00:13:30, FastEthernet0/0
O    4.0.0.0/8 [110/2] via 10.1.1.4, 00:13:40, FastEthernet0/0
```

You can see the next hop to reach any network is the router that originated that particular network. Let's see how often these routers exchange hellos:

```
R1# show ip ospf interface FastEthernet0/0 | include Timer

  Timer intervals configured, Hello 10, Dead 40, Wait 40, Retransmit 5
```

Let's see the destination address of OSPF hello messages on OSPF broadcast network types:

```
R1# debug ip ospf hello
OSPF hello debugging is on


OSPF-1 HELLO Fa0/0: Send hello to 224.0.0.5 area 0 from 10.1.1.1


R1# undebug all
All possible debugging has been turned off
```

Let's identify the major points of an OSPF broadcast network type:

- Ethernet networks default to OSPF broadcast network types.

- The timers are 10/40, meaning that the hello interval is 10 seconds and the dead interval is set to 40 seconds.

- The next hop does *not* change. In the output of the preceding **show ip route ospf** command, you can see that the next-hop IP address is the IP address of the f0/0 interface of the router that originated the route.

- DR and BDR election will take place in broadcast multi-access networks.

- With broadcast network types, the hellos are sent to the multicast destination of 224.0.0.5.

Task 2

Reload the routers and configure them by copying and pasting the initial config file called Lab8-2_OSPF Broadcast Network_Task2.txt.

Figure 8-3 introduces the topology we will use to explore OSPF functionality via a non-broadcast multi-access network using DMVPN.

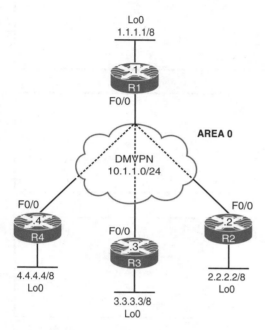

Figure 8-3 *OSPF DMVPN Topology*

Configure OSPF on the tunnel and loopback0 interfaces of all routers based on the following policies:

- R1 is the hub, and R2, R3, and R4 are configured as the spokes. Do *not* change the topology. All routers are configured in a multipoint manner.

- Configure the tunnel interfaces of all routers to be the OSPF broadcast network type.

- The loopback interfaces should be advertised with their correct mask.

- Configure the router IDs of 0.0.0.1, 0.0.0.2, 0.0.0.3, and 0.0.0.4 for R1, R2, R3, and R4, respectively.

```
On All Routers:


Rx(config-router)# interface loopback0
Rx(config-if)# ip ospf network point-to-point


Rx(config)# interface tunnel 1234
Rx(config-if)# ip ospf network broadcast
```

```
On R1:

R1(config)# router ospf 1
R1(config-router)# router-id 0.0.0.1
R1(config-router)# network 10.1.1.1 0.0.0.0 area 0
R1(config-router)# network 1.1.1.1 0.0.0.0 area 0
```

```
On R2:

R2(config)# router ospf 1
R2(config-router)# router-id 0.0.0.2
R2(config-router)# network 2.2.2.2 0.0.0.0 area 0
R2(config-router)# network 10.1.1.2 0.0.0.0 area 0
```

```
On R3:

R3(config)# router ospf 1
R3(config-router)# router-id 0.0.0.3
R3(config-router)# network 3.3.3.3 0.0.0.0 area 0
R3(config-router)# network 10.1.1.3 0.0.0.0 area 0
```

```
On R4:

R4(config)# router ospf 1
R4(config-router)# router-id 0.0.0.4
R4(config-router)# network 4.4.4.4 0.0.0.0 area 0
R4(config-router)# network 10.1.1.4 0.0.0.0 area 0
```

Let's verify the configuration:

```
On R1:

R1# show ip ospf neighbor
```

You can see that the routers did not establish an OSPF adjacency. We know that in OSPF broadcast network types, the hellos are sent to a destination multicast address of 224.0.0.5, so let's check and see if our network allows multicast traffic through:

```
On R1:

R1# show run interface tunnel 1234 | begin interface

interface Tunnel1234
 ip address 10.1.1.1 255.255.255.0
 no ip redirects
 ip nhrp map 10.1.1.4 192.1.4.4
 ip nhrp map 10.1.1.3 192.1.3.3
 ip nhrp map 10.1.1.2 192.1.2.2
 ip nhrp network-id 111
 ip ospf network broadcast
 tunnel source FastEthernet0/0
 tunnel mode gre multipoint
end
```

Based on the preceding output, you can see that multicast is *not* mapped. Let's check R2:

```
On R2:

R2# show run interface tunnel 1234 | begin interface

interface Tunnel1234
 ip address 10.1.1.2 255.255.255.0
 no ip redirects
 ip nhrp map 10.1.1.1 192.1.1.1
 ip nhrp network-id 222
 ip ospf network broadcast
 tunnel source FastEthernet0/0
 tunnel mode gre multipoint
end
```

R2 is configured the same. Let's map multicast on R1 and R2 and see the result before we move on to the other routers:

```
On R2:

R2(config)# interface tunnel 1234
R2(config-if)# ip nhrp map multicast 192.1.1.1
```

```
On R1:

R1(config)# interface tunnel 1234
R1(config-if)# ip nhrp map multicast 192.1.2.2
```

If both ends are not configured to map multicast for each other's tunnel IP addresses, the OSPF adjacency will be established and torn down, and you will get the following console message:

```
%OSPF-5-ADJCHG: Process 1, Nbr 0.0.0.2 on Tunnel1234 from LOADING to FULL,
Loading Done

%OSPF-5-ADJCHG: Process 1, Nbr 0.0.0.2 on Tunnel1234 from FULL to DOWN,
neighbor Down: Dead timer expired
```

Let's verify the adjacency and see if these two routers are exchanging routes:

```
On R1:

R1# show ip ospf neighbor

Neighbor ID     Pri   State        Dead Time   Address      Interface
0.0.0.2          1    FULL/DR      00:00:37    10.1.1.2     Tunnel1234

R1# show ip route ospf | be Gate
Gateway of last resort is not set

O    2.0.0.0/8 [110/1001] via 10.1.1.2, 00:01:08, Tunnel1234
```

Let's configure the other spokes to map multicast traffic:

```
On R1:

R1(config)# interface tunnel 1234
R1(config-if)# ip nhrp map multicast 192.1.3.3
R1(config-if)# ip nhrp map multicast 192.1.4.4
```

```
On R3:

R3(config)# interface tunnel 1234
R3(config-if)# ip nhrp map multicast 192.1.1.1
```

```
On R4:

R4(config)# interface tunnel 1234
R4(config-if)# ip nhrp map multicast 192.1.1.1
```

Let's verify the configuration:

```
On R1:


R1# show ip ospf neighbor


Neighbor ID    Pri    State         Dead Time    Address      Interface
0.0.0.2         1     FULL/DROTHER   00:00:35     10.1.1.2     Tunnel1234
0.0.0.3         1     FULL/DROTHER   00:00:30     10.1.1.3     Tunnel1234
0.0.0.4         1     FULL/DR        00:00:31     10.1.1.4     Tunnel1234
```

You can see that R4, which happens to be one of the spokes, is the DR. You should always configure the hub router as the DR, so let's configure this and verify:

```
On R2, R3, and R4:


Rx(config)# interface tunnel 1234
Rx(config-if)# ip ospf priority 0
```

```
On All Routers:


Rx# Clear ip ospf process
Reset ALL OSPF processes? [no]: Yes
```

```
On R1:


R1# show ip ospf neighbor


neighbor ID    Pri    State         Dead Time    Address      Interface
0.0.0.2          0    FULL/DROTHER   00:00:31     10.1.1.2     Tunnel1234
0.0.0.3          0    FULL/DROTHER   00:00:32     10.1.1.3     Tunnel1234
0.0.0.4          0    FULL/DROTHER   00:00:32     10.1.1.4     Tunnel1234


R1# show ip route ospf | begin Gate
Gateway of last resort is not set


O    2.0.0.0/8 [110/1001] via 10.1.1.2, 00:01:58, Tunnel1234
O    3.0.0.0/8 [110/1001] via 10.1.1.3, 00:01:58, Tunnel1234
O    4.0.0.0/8 [110/1001] via 10.1.1.4, 00:01:58, Tunnel1234
```

Note We know that on broadcast network types, the next-hop IP address is set based on the originating router. From R1's perspective, this is not a problem, but let's check R2 and the other spokes:

```
On R2:

R2# show ip route ospf | begin Gate
Gateway of last resort is not set

O      1.0.0.0/8 [110/1001] via 10.1.1.1, 00:03:18, Tunnel1234
O      3.0.0.0/8 [110/1001] via 10.1.1.3, 00:03:08, Tunnel1234
O      4.0.0.0/8 [110/1001] via 10.1.1.4, 00:03:18, Tunnel1234
```

Does R2 have reachability to the advertised networks? Let's verify:

```
R2# ping 1.1.1.1

Type escape sequence to abort.
Sending 5, 100-byte ICMP Echos to 1.1.1.1, timeout is 2 seconds:
!!!!!
Success rate is 100 percent (5/5), round-trip min/avg/max = 1/2/4 ms

R2# ping 3.3.3.3

Type escape sequence to abort.
Sending 5, 100-byte ICMP Echos to 3.3.3.3, timeout is 2 seconds:
.....
Success rate is 0 percent (0/5)

R2# ping 4.4.4.4

Type escape sequence to abort.
Sending 5, 100-byte ICMP Echos to 4.4.4.4, timeout is 2 seconds:
.....
Success rate is 0 percent (0/5)
```

R2 has reachability to the 1.1.1.1 prefix only. Does R2 have reachability to the next-hop IP address of the other spoke routers? Let's verify:

```
R2# ping 10.1.1.3

Type escape sequence to abort.
Sending 5, 100-byte ICMP Echos to 10.1.1.3, timeout is 2 seconds:
.....
Success rate is 0 percent (0/5)
```

```
R2# ping 10.1.1.4

Type escape sequence to abort.
Sending 5, 100-byte ICMP Echos to 10.1.1.4, timeout is 2 seconds:
.....
Success rate is 0 percent (0/5)
```

No, it doesn't. If the network is configured in a point-to-point manner, the routers have unicast, multicast, and/or broadcast capability. In a point-to-point network, because there can only be another node/router on the other end of the link/tunnel, as long as the destination network is in the routing table, you should be able to reach the destination.

On the other hand, if the network is configured as multipoint, you have unicast reachability, but broadcast/multicast capability is only available if it's provided.

Because in a multipoint network there can potentially be more than one router on the other end of the tunnel, the local router *must* have a mapping to the next-hop IP address(es). Otherwise, Network Layer Reachability Information (NLRI) cannot be achieved.

Because the spoke routers don't have mapping for each other's tunnel IP address, they cannot reach the advertised networks. Let's provide this reachability and verify:

```
On R2:

R2(config)# interface tunnel 1234
R2(config-if)# ip nhrp map 10.1.1.3 192.1.3.3
```

```
On R3:

R3(config)# interface tunnel 1234
R3(config-if)# ip nhrp map 10.1.1.2 192.1.2.2
```

Let's verify the configuration:

```
On R3:

R3# ping 10.1.1.2

Type escape sequence to abort.
Sending 5, 100-byte ICMP Echos to 10.1.1.2, timeout is 2 seconds:
!!!!!
Success rate is 100 percent (5/5), round-trip min/avg/max = 1/2/4 ms
```

This is great. Let's configure full mesh logical mapping between the spoke routers:

```
On R2:


R2(config)# interface tunnel 1234
R2(config-if)# ip nhrp map 10.1.1.4 192.1.4.4
```

```
On R3:


R3(config)# interface tunnel 1234
R3(config-if)# ip nhrp map 10.1.1.4 192.1.4.4
```

```
On R4:


R4(config)# interface tunnel 1234
R4(config-if)# ip nhrp map 10.1.1.2 192.1.2.2
R4(config-if)# ip nhrp map 10.1.1.3 192.1.3.3
```

Let's verify the mappings:

```
On R2:


R2# show ip nhrp


10.1.1.1/32 via 10.1.1.1
   Tunnel1234 created 00:50:36, never expire
   Type: static, Flags: used
   NBMA address: 192.1.1.1
10.1.1.3/32 via 10.1.1.3
   Tunnel1234 created 00:04:57, never expire
   Type: static, Flags:
   NBMA address: 192.1.1.1
10.1.1.4/32 via 10.1.1.4
   Tunnel1234 created 00:01:41, never expire
   Type: static, Flags:
   NBMA address: 192.1.1.1
```

```
On R3:


R3# show ip nhrp


10.1.1.1/32 via 10.1.1.1
   Tunnel1234 created 00:50:50, never expire
```

```
    Type: static, Flags: used
    NBMA address: 192.1.1.1
10.1.1.2/32 via 10.1.1.2
    Tunnel1234 created 00:05:11, never expire
    Type: static, Flags:
    NBMA address: 192.1.1.1
10.1.1.4/32 via 10.1.1.4
    Tunnel1234 created 00:02:28, never expire
    Type: static, Flags:
    NBMA address: 192.1.1.1
```

```
On R4:

R4# show ip nhrp

10.1.1.1/32 via 10.1.1.1
    Tunnel1234 created 00:50:54, never expire
    Type: static, Flags: used
    NBMA address: 192.1.1.1
10.1.1.2/32 via 10.1.1.2
    Tunnel1234 created 00:01:33, never expire
    Type: static, Flags:
    NBMA address: 192.1.1.1
10.1.1.3/32 via 10.1.1.3
    Tunnel1234 created 00:01:25, never expire
    Type: static, Flags:
    NBMA address: 192.1.1.1
```

Let's test the configuration:

```
On R2:

R2# ping 3.3.3.3

Type escape sequence to abort.
Sending 5, 100-byte ICMP Echos to 3.3.3.3, timeout is 2 seconds:
!!!!!
Success rate is 100 percent (5/5), round-trip min/avg/max = 1/3/4 ms
```

```
R2# ping 4.4.4.4

Type escape sequence to abort.
Sending 5, 100-byte ICMP Echos to 4.4.4.4, timeout is 2 seconds:
!!!!!
Success rate is 100 percent (5/5), round-trip min/avg/max = 1/2/4 ms

R2# traceroute 3.3.3.3 numeric

Type escape sequence to abort.
Tracing the route to 3.3.3.3
VRF info: (vrf in name/id, vrf out name/id)
 1 10.1.1.3 4 msec *  0 msec
```

```
On R3:

R3# ping 4.4.4.4

Type escape sequence to abort.
Sending 5, 100-byte ICMP Echos to 4.4.4.4, timeout is 2 seconds:
!!!!!
Success rate is 100 percent (5/5), round-trip min/avg/max = 1/2/4 ms
```

In broadcast network types, the next-hop IP address is not changed. If the network is Non-Broadcast Multi-Access (NBMA) in nature and it's configured in a multipoint manner, you have to remember the following:

- Multicast capability must be provided.

- Spokes must have mapping to the next-hop IP address to have reachability to the networks that other spokes are advertising.

Erase the startup configuration of the routers as well as the config.text and vlan.dat files of the switches and reload them before proceeding to the next lab.

Lab 8-3: Non-Broadcast Networks

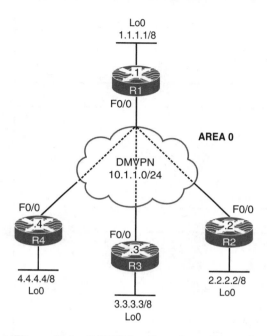

Figure 8-4 *OSPF Non-Broadcast Networks*

The DMVPN is configured in Phase 2 using static maps. R1 (the hub router) is configured with two static maps—one for each spoke. Routers R2 and R3 are configured with a single map for the hub.

Task 1

Configure OSPF Area 0 on the tunnel and the loopback interfaces of all routers in the topology shown in Figure 8-4. You should configure the tunnel interfaces as the OSPF non-broadcast network type. Use the following list for the router IDs:

> **R1:** 0.0.0.1
>
> **R2:** 0.0.0.2
>
> **R3:** 0.0.0.3
>
> **R4:** 0.0.0.4

```
On All Routers:

Rx(config)# interface tunnel 1234
Rx(config-if)# ip ospf network non-broadcast
```

```
On R1:

R1(config)# router ospf 1
R1(config-router)# router-id 0.0.0.1
R1(config-router)# network 10.1.1.1 0.0.0.0 area 0
R1(config-router)# network 1.1.1.1 0.0.0.0 area 0
```

```
On R2:

R2(config)# router ospf 1
R2(config-router)# router-id 0.0.0.2
R2(config-router)# network 10.1.1.2 0.0.0.0 area 0
R2(config-router)# network 2.2.2.2 0.0.0.0 area 0
```

```
On R3:

R3(config)# router ospf 1
R3(config-router)# router-id 0.0.0.3
R3(config-router)# network 3.3.3.3 0.0.0.0 area 0
R3(config-router)# network 10.1.1.3 0.0.0.0 area 0
```

```
On R4:

R4(config)# router ospf 1
R4(config-router)# router-id 0.0.0.4
R4(config-router)# network 4.4.4.4 0.0.0.0 area 0
R4(config-router)# network 10.1.1.4 0.0.0.0 area 0
```

Let's verify the configuration:

```
On R1:

R1# show ip ospf neighbor

R1# show ip ospf interface brief

Interface   PID   Area        IP Address/Mask    Cost  State Nbrs F/C
Lo0         1     0           1.1.1.1/8          1     LOOP  0/0
Tu1234      1     0           10.1.1.1/24        1000  DR    0/0
```

Let's check OSPF's configuration on the Tunnel 1234 interface:

```
R1# show ip ospf interface tunnel 1234

Tunnel1234 is up, line protocol is up
  Internet Address 10.1.1.1/24, Area 0, Attached via network Statement
  Process ID 1, router ID 0.0.0.1, network Type NON_BROADCAST, Cost: 1000
  Topology-MTID    Cost    Disabled    Shutdown      Topology Name
       0           1000       no          no             Base
  Transmit Delay is 1 sec, State DR, Priority 1
  Designated router (ID) 0.0.0.1, Interface address 10.1.1.1
  No backup designated router on this network
  Timer intervals configured, Hello 30, Dead 120, Wait 120, Retransmit 5
    oob-resync timeout 120
(The rest of the output is omitted for brevity)
```

You can see that the network type is set to **NON_BROADCAST**, which means that one way to get the local router to establish an adjacency with another OSPF-speaking router is to use the **neighbor** command and change the multicast destination of 224.0.0.5 to unicast destinations of 10.1.1.2, 10.1.1.3, and 10.1.1.4. Thus, as you can see, the rules did not change at all; the same rules apply to all NBMA networks.

Let's configure the **neighbor** commands on the routers:

```
On R1:

R1(config)# router ospf 1
R1(config-router)# neighbor 10.1.1.2
R1(config-router)# neighbor 10.1.1.3
R1(config-router)# neighbor 10.1.1.4
```

You should see the following console messages stating that the adjacencies are established with the OSPF 0.0.0.2, 0.0.0.3, and 0.0.0.4 neighbors:

```
%OSPF-5-ADJCHG: Process 1, Nbr 0.0.0.2 on Tunnel1234 from LOADING to FULL,
Loading Done

%OSPF-5-ADJCHG: Process 1, Nbr 0.0.0.3 on Tunnel1234 from LOADING to FULL,
Loading Done

%OSPF-5-ADJCHG: Process 1, Nbr 0.0.0.4 on Tunnel1234 from LOADING to FULL,
Loading Done
```

This worked, but let's review some important points about OSPF non-broadcast networks:

- The **neighbor** command must be used because non-broadcast network types don't have multicast capability.

- The hello intervals are 30 seconds, and the dead interval is set to 120 seconds.

- DR election is required.

- In this network type, the next-hop IP address is based on the router that originated the route.

Let's go through every item and verify it.

If the routers don't have multicast capability, then the **neighbor** command must be configured. In hub-and-spoke networks, the hub *must* be the DR, and the spokes are configured with a priority of 0 so that they don't participate in the DR/BDR election.

```
On R2:

R2# show ip ospf interface tunnel 1234 | include Priority

  Transmit Delay is 1 sec, State WAITING, Priority 1
```

```
On R3:

R3# show ip ospf interface tunnel 1234 | include Priority

  Transmit Delay is 1 sec, State BDR, Priority 1
```

```
On R4:

R4# show ip ospf interface tunnel 1234 | include Priority

  Transmit Delay is 1 sec, State BDR, Priority 1
```

Let's configure the priority of the spoke routers as 0 and clear the OSPF process to implement the changes:

```
On R2, R3, and R4:

Rx(config)# interface tunnel 1234
Rx(config-if)# ip ospf priority 0

Rx# Clear ip ospf process
Reset ALL OSPF processes? [no]: Yes
```

Let's verify the configuration:

```
On R1:


R1# show ip ospf neighbor


neighbor ID      Pri    State           Dead Time    Address        Interface
0.0.0.2            0    FULL/DROTHER    00:01:46     10.1.1.2       Tunnel123
0.0.0.3            0    FULL/DROTHER    00:01:46     10.1.1.3       Tunnel1234
0.0.0.4            0    FULL/DROTHER    00:01:46     10.1.1.4       Tunnel1234
```

```
On All Routers:


On R1:


R1# show ip route ospf | begin Gate
Gateway of last resort is not set


      2.0.0.0/32 is subnetted, 1 subnets
O        2.2.2.2 [110/1001] via 10.1.1.2, 00:03:13, Tunnel1234
      3.0.0.0/32 is subnetted, 1 subnets
O        3.3.3.3 [110/1001] via 10.1.1.3, 00:03:13, Tunnel1234
      4.0.0.0/32 is subnetted, 1 subnets
O        4.4.4.4 [110/1001] via 10.1.1.4, 00:03:13, Tunnel1234
```

Let's check the routing table of the spokes:

```
On R2:


R2# show ip route ospf | begin Gate
Gateway of last resort is not set


      1.0.0.0/32 is subnetted, 1 subnets
O        1.1.1.1 [110/1001] via 10.1.1.1, 00:04:16, Tunnel1234
      3.0.0.0/32 is subnetted, 1 subnets
O        3.3.3.3 [110/1001] via 10.1.1.3, 00:04:06, Tunnel1234
      4.0.0.0/32 is subnetted, 1 subnets
O        4.4.4.4 [110/1001] via 10.1.1.4, 00:04:06, Tunnel1234
```

```
On R3:


R3# show ip route ospf | begin Gate
Gateway of last resort is not set
```

```
      1.0.0.0/32 is subnetted, 1 subnets
O        1.1.1.1 [110/1001] via 10.1.1.1, 00:05:03, Tunnel1234
      2.0.0.0/32 is subnetted, 1 subnets
O        2.2.2.2 [110/1001] via 10.1.1.2, 00:05:03, Tunnel1234
      4.0.0.0/32 is subnetted, 1 subnets
O        4.4.4.4 [110/1001] via 10.1.1.4, 00:04:53, Tunnel1234
```

```
On R4:

R4# show ip route ospf | begin Gate
Gateway of last resort is not set

      1.0.0.0/32 is subnetted, 1 subnets
O        1.1.1.1 [110/1001] via 10.1.1.1, 00:05:12, Tunnel1234
      2.0.0.0/32 is subnetted, 1 subnets
O        2.2.2.2 [110/1001] via 10.1.1.2, 00:05:12, Tunnel1234
      3.0.0.0/32 is subnetted, 1 subnets
O        3.3.3.3 [110/1001] via 10.1.1.3, 00:05:02, Tunnel1234
```

As you can see, in OSPF non-broadcast networks, the next hop is based on the IP address of the router that originated the route. Do we have reachability to these addresses? Let's verify:

```
R4# ping 10.1.1.1

Type escape sequence to abort.
Sending 5, 100-byte ICMP Echos to 10.1.1.1, timeout is 2 seconds:
!!!!!
Success rate is 100 percent (5/5), round-trip min/avg/max = 1/3/4 ms

R4# ping 10.1.1.2

Type escape sequence to abort.
Sending 5, 100-byte ICMP Echos to 10.1.1.2, timeout is 2 seconds:
.....
Success rate is 0 percent (0/5)

R4# ping 10.1.1.3

Type escape sequence to abort.
Sending 5, 100-byte ICMP Echos to 10.1.1.3, timeout is 2 seconds:
.....
Success rate is 0 percent (0/5)
```

As you can see, the spokes do not have reachability to the routes that are advertised by the other spokes. Let's check their NHRP mapping (does that remind you of Frame Relay?):

```
R4# show ip nhrp

10.1.1.1/32 via 10.1.1.1
   Tunnel1234 created 01:13:32, never expire
   Type: static, Flags: used
   NBMA address: 192.1.1.1
```

The only mapping is for the hub router, and that's why the ping to the 1.1.1.1 prefix was successful. On R4, we should configure a mapping for R2 and another one for R3, and for the return traffic, a mapping from R2 and R3 to R4 is required. Let's configure and verify:

```
On R4:

R4(config)# interface tunnel 1234
R4(config-if)# ip nhrp map 10.1.1.2 192.1.1.1
R4(config-if)# ip nhrp map 10.1.1.3 192.1.1.1
```

Note   R4 is mapping the next-hop IP address (the tunnel IP address) to the NBMA IP address of the hub, so the topology does not change.

```
R4# show ip nhrp

10.1.1.1/32 via 10.1.1.1
   Tunnel1234 created 00:48:05, never expire
   Type: static, Flags: used
   NBMA address: 192.1.1.1
10.1.1.2/32 via 10.1.1.2
   Tunnel1234 created 00:01:34, never expire
   Type: static, Flags:
   NBMA address: 192.1.1.1
10.1.1.3/32 via 10.1.1.3
   Tunnel1234 created 00:01:27, never expire
   Type: static, Flags:
   NBMA address: 192.1.1.1
```

```
On R2:

R2(config)# interface tunnel 1234
R2(config-if)# ip nhrp map 10.1.1.3 192.1.1.1
R2(config-if)# ip nhrp map 10.1.1.4 192.1.1.1
```

Let's verify the configuration:

```
R2# show ip nhrp

10.1.1.1/32 via 10.1.1.1
   Tunnel1234 created 00:50:07, never expire
   Type: static, Flags: used
   NBMA address: 192.1.1.1
10.1.1.3/32 via 10.1.1.3
   Tunnel1234 created 00:00:31, never expire
   Type: static, Flags:
   NBMA address: 192.1.1.1
10.1.1.4/32 via 10.1.1.4
   Tunnel1234 created 00:00:24, never expire
   Type: static, Flags:
   NBMA address: 192.1.1.1
```

```
On R3:

R3(config)# interface tunnel 1234
R3(config-if)# ip nhrp map 10.1.1.2 192.1.1.1
R3(config-if)# ip nhrp map 10.1.1.4 192.1.1.1
```

Another excellent verification step is to look at the **show ip nhrp** output below.

```
R3# show ip nhrp

10.1.1.1/32 via 10.1.1.1
   Tunnel1234 created 00:51:19, never expire
   Type: static, Flags: used
   NBMA address: 192.1.1.1
10.1.1.2/32 via 10.1.1.2
   Tunnel1234 created 00:00:28, never expire
   Type: static, Flags:
   NBMA address: 192.1.1.1
10.1.1.4/32 via 10.1.1.4
   Tunnel1234 created 00:00:21, never expire

   Type: static, Flags:
   NBMA address: 192.1.1.1
```

Let's verify the routing table and reachability on the spoke routers:

```
On R2:


R2# show ip route ospf | begin Gate
Gateway of last resort is not set


      1.0.0.0/32 is subnetted, 1 subnets
O        1.1.1.1 [110/1001] via 10.1.1.1, 00:22:19, Tunnel1234
      3.0.0.0/32 is subnetted, 1 subnets
O        3.3.3.3 [110/1001] via 10.1.1.3, 00:22:09, Tunnel1234
      4.0.0.0/32 is subnetted, 1 subnets
O        4.4.4.4 [110/1001] via 10.1.1.4, 00:22:09, Tunnel1234


R2# ping 1.1.1.1


Type escape sequence to abort.
Sending 5, 100-byte ICMP Echos to 1.1.1.1, timeout is 2 seconds:
!!!!!
Success rate is 100 percent (5/5), round-trip min/avg/max = 1/2/4 ms


R2# ping 3.3.3.3


Type escape sequence to abort.
Sending 5, 100-byte ICMP Echos to 3.3.3.3, timeout is 2 seconds:
!!!!!
Success rate is 100 percent (5/5), round-trip min/avg/max = 1/2/4 ms


R2# ping 4.4.4.4


Type escape sequence to abort.
Sending 5, 100-byte ICMP Echos to 4.4.4.4, timeout is 2 seconds:
!!!!!
Success rate is 100 percent (5/5), round-trip min/avg/max = 1/2/4 ms
```

```
On R3:


R3# show ip route ospf | began Gate
Gateway of last resort is not set


      1.0.0.0/32 is subnetted, 1 subnets
O        1.1.1.1 [110/1001] via 10.1.1.1, 00:32:39, Tunnel1234
      2.0.0.0/32 is subnetted, 1 subnets
O        2.2.2.2 [110/1001] via 10.1.1.2, 00:32:39, Tunnel1234
      4.0.0.0/32 is subnetted, 1 subnets
O        4.4.4.4 [110/1001] via 10.1.1.4, 00:32:29, Tunnel1234
```

```
R3# ping 10.1.1.1

Type escape sequence to abort.
Sending 5, 100-byte ICMP Echos to 10.1.1.1, timeout is 2 seconds:
!!!!!
Success rate is 100 percent (5/5), round-trip min/avg/max = 1/2/4 ms


R3# ping 2.2.2.2

Type escape sequence to abort.
Sending 5, 100-byte ICMP Echos to 2.2.2.2, timeout is 2 seconds:
!!!!!
Success rate is 100 percent (5/5), round-trip min/avg/max = 1/3/4 ms


R3# ping 4.4.4.4

Type escape sequence to abort.
Sending 5, 100-byte ICMP Echos to 4.4.4.4, timeout is 2 seconds:
!!!!!
Success rate is 100 percent (5/5), round-trip min/avg/max = 1/3/4 ms
```

```
On R4:

R4# show ip route ospf | begin Gate
Gateway of last resort is not set

      1.0.0.0/32 is subnetted, 1 subnets
O        1.1.1.1 [110/1001] via 10.1.1.1, 00:33:16, Tunnel1234
      2.0.0.0/32 is subnetted, 1 subnets
O        2.2.2.2 [110/1001] via 10.1.1.2, 00:33:16, Tunnel1234
      3.0.0.0/32 is subnetted, 1 subnets
O        3.3.3.3 [110/1001] via 10.1.1.3, 00:33:06, Tunnel1234


R4# ping 1.1.1.1

Type escape sequence to abort.
Sending 5, 100-byte ICMP Echos to 1.1.1.1, timeout is 2 seconds:
!!!!!
Success rate is 100 percent (5/5), round-trip min/avg/max = 1/3/4 ms


R4# ping 2.2.2.2

Type escape sequence to abort.
```

```
Sending 5, 100-byte ICMP Echos to 2.2.2.2, timeout is 2 seconds:
!!!!!
Success rate is 100 percent (5/5), round-trip min/avg/max = 1/3/4 ms


R4# ping 3.3.3.3

Type escape sequence to abort.
Sending 5, 100-byte ICMP Echos to 3.3.3.3, timeout is 2 seconds:
!!!!!
Success rate is 100 percent (5/5), round-trip min/avg/max = 1/3/4 ms
```

Let's review the important points about non-broadcast networks:

- They require a DR.

- There are no broadcast/multicast capabilities; only unicast is available.

- The next-hop IP address does *not* change.

- Hello intervals are 30 seconds, and the dead interval is set to 120 seconds.

Erase the startup configuration of the routers as well as the config.text and vlan.dat files of the switches and then reload them before proceeding to the next lab.

Lab 8-4: OSPF Point-to-Point Networks

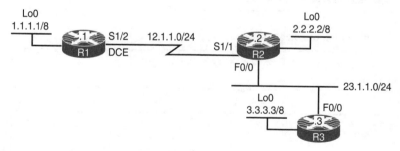

Figure 8-5 *OSPF Point-to-Point Network Types*

Task 1

Configure OSPF Area 0 on the routers in Figure 8-5 based on the following policies:

- The loopback0 interface of these routers should be advertised with their correct mask.

- Use 0.0.0.1, 0.0.0.2, and 0.0.0.3 as the router IDs of R1, R2, and R3, respectively.

- There should not be any DR/BDR election on any of the links.

- Do *not* configure "point-to-multipoint" or "point-to-multipoint non-broadcast" on any of the links.

```
On R1:

R1(config-if)# router ospf 1
R1(config-router)# router-id 0.0.0.1
R1(config-router)# network 1.1.1.1 0.0.0.0 area 0
R1(config-router)# network 12.1.1.1 0.0.0.0 area 0

R1(config-router)# interface loopback0
R1(config-if)# ip ospf network point-to-point
```

```
On R2:

R2(config)# router ospf 1
R2(config-router)# router-id 0.0.0.2
R2(config-router)# network 2.2.2.2 0.0.0.0 area 0
R2(config-router)# network 12.1.1.2 0.0.0.0 area 0
R2(config-router)# network 23.1.1.2 0.0.0.0 area 0

R2(config-router)# interface loopback0
R2(config-if)# ip ospf network point-to-point
```

You should see the following console message:

```
%OSPF-5-ADJCHG: Process 1, Nbr 0.0.0.1 on Serial1/1 from LOADING to FULL,
Loading Done
```

```
On R3:

R3(config)# router ospf 1
R3(config-router)# router-id 0.0.0.3
R3(config-router)# network 3.3.3.3 0.0.0.0 area 0
R3(config-router)# network 23.1.1.3 0.0.0.0 area 0

R3(config-router)# interface loopback0
R3(config-if)# ip ospf network point-to-point
```

You should also see the following console message:

```
%OSPF-5-ADJCHG: Process 1, Nbr 0.0.0.2 on FastEthernet0/0 from LOADING to FULL,
Loading Done
```

Let's verify the configuration:

```
On R1:


R1# show ip route ospf | begin Gate
Gateway of last resort is not set

O     2.0.0.0/8 [110/782] via 12.1.1.2, 00:00:17, Serial1/2
O     3.0.0.0/8 [110/783] via 12.1.1.2, 00:00:17, Serial1/2
      23.0.0.0/24 is subnetted, 1 subnets
O        23.1.1.0 [110/782] via 12.1.1.2, 00:00:17, Serial1/2
```

```
On R2:


R2# show ip route ospf | begin Gate
Gateway of last resort is not set

O     1.0.0.0/8 [110/782] via 12.1.1.1, 00:01:10, Serial1/1
O     3.0.0.0/8 [110/2] via 23.1.1.3, 00:02:02, FastEthernet0/0
```

```
On R3:


R3# show ip route ospf | begin Gate
Gateway of last resort is not set

O     1.0.0.0/8 [110/783] via 23.1.1.2, 00:01:39, FastEthernet0/0
O     2.0.0.0/8 [110/2] via 23.1.1.2, 00:02:41, FastEthernet0/0
      12.0.0.0/24 is subnetted, 1 subnets
O        12.1.1.0 [110/782] via 23.1.1.2, 00:01:49, FastEthernet0/0

R3# show ip ospf neighbor

neighbor ID     Pri   State       Dead Time   Address      Interface
0.0.0.2          1    FULL/BDR    00:00:33    23.1.1.2     FastEthernet0/0
```

The task states that there should no DR/BDR election, and because the use of both point-to-multipoint and point-to-multipoint non-broadcast is prohibited, the network type of the f0/0 interfaces of R2 and R3 should be changed to **point-to-point**:

```
On R2 and R3:


Rx(config)# interface FastEthernet0/0
Rx(config-if)# ip ospf network point-to-point
```

Let's verify the configuration:

```
On R3:


R3# show ip route ospf | begin Gate
Gateway of last resort is not set

O     1.0.0.0/8 [110/783] via 23.1.1.2, 00:00:09, FastEthernet0/0
O     2.0.0.0/8 [110/2] via 23.1.1.2, 00:00:09, FastEthernet0/0
      12.0.0.0/24 is subnetted, 1 subnets
O        12.1.1.0 [110/782] via 23.1.1.2, 00:00:09, FastEthernet0/0
```

Let's verify some of the parameters on the interfaces that have a point-to-point network type:

```
On R1:


R1# show ip ospf interface serial1/2 | include Network|Hello

  Internet Address 12.1.1.1/24, Area 0, Attached via network Statement
  Process ID 1, router ID 0.0.0.1, network Type POINT_TO_POINT, Cost: 781
  Timer intervals configured, Hello 10, Dead 40, Wait 40, Retransmit 5
    Hello due in 00:00:01
```

You can see that with the OSPF point-to-point network type, there are no DR/BDR elections, and the hello and dead intervals are set to 10 and 40, respectively. You can also see that we did not experience any problems forming adjacency using multicast.

Here are the important points concerning OSPF point-to-point network types:

- Hellos are exchanged every 10 seconds, and the dead interval is set to 40 seconds.

- There is no DR/BDR election.

- The routers use 224.0.0.5 to form an adjacency and send hello messages.

- The next hop is the router that advertised the route; this is the neighboring router.

Erase the startup configuration of the routers as well as the config.text and vlan.dat files of the switches and then reload them before proceeding to the next lab.

Lab 8-5: OSPF Point-to-Multipoint and Point-to-Multipoint Non-Broadcast Networks

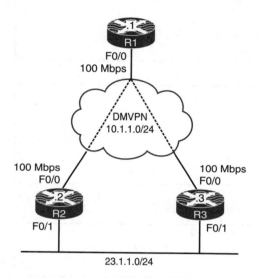

Figure 8-6 *OSPF Point-to-Multipoint and Point-to-Multipoint Non-Broadcast Network*

Figure 8-6 illustrates the topology that will used in the following tasks.

The DMVPN is configured in Phase 2 using static maps. R1 (the hub router) is configured with two static maps—one for each spoke. Routers R2 and R3 are configured with a single map for the hub.

Task 1

Configure OSPF Area 0 on the tunnel interfaces of these three routers. R2 and R3 should also run OSPF Area 0 on their f0/1 interface. If this configuration is performed successfully, the routers in this topology should have full reachability to every network in the topology. The tunnel interface of these routers should be configured as point-to-multipoint OSPF networks.

Use 0.0.0.1, 0.0.0.2, and 0.0.0.3 as the router IDs of R1, R2, and R3, respectively:

```
On All routers:

Rx(config)# interface tunnel 123
Rx(config-if)# ip ospf network point-to-multipoint
```

```
On R1:

R1(config)# router ospf 1
R1(config-router)# router-id 0.0.0.1
R1(config-router)# network 10.1.1.1 0.0.0.0 area 0
```

```
On R2:

R2(config)# router ospf 1
R2(config-router)# router-id 0.0.0.2
R2(config-router)# network 10.1.1.2 0.0.0.0 area 0
R2(config-router)# network 23.1.1.2 0.0.0.0 area 0
```

```
On R3:

R3(config)# router ospf 1
R3(config-router)# router-id 0.0.0.3
R3(config-router)# network 10.1.1.3 0.0.0.0 area 0
R3(config-router)# network 23.1.1.3 0.0.0.0 area 0
```

Let's verify the configuration:

```
On R1:

R1# show ip ospf neighbor
```

The routers did *not* form an OSPF adjacency, so let's look at the important points in OSPF point-to-multipoint network types:

- The routers use 224.0.0.5.

- There is no requirement for a DR or BDR.

- The next hop is the advertising router.

- Host routes are advertised automatically for NLRI in partial mesh topologies.

Because the routers use a multicast address of 224.0.0.5, let's see if the tunnel interfaces have multicast capability:

```
On R1:

R1# show run interface tunnel 123 | begin interface

interface Tunnel123
 ip address 10.1.1.1 255.255.255.0
 no ip redirects
 ip nhrp map 10.1.1.3 192.1.3.3
 ip nhrp map 10.1.1.2 192.1.2.2
```

```
 ip nhrp network-id 111
 ip ospf network point-to-multipoint
 tunnel source FastEthernet0/0
 tunnel mode gre multipoint
end
```

```
On R2:

R2# show run interface tunnel 123 | begin interface

interface Tunnel123
 ip address 10.1.1.2 255.255.255.0
 no ip redirects
 ip nhrp map 10.1.1.1 192.1.1.1
 ip nhrp network-id 222
 ip ospf network point-to-multipoint
 tunnel source FastEthernet0/0
 tunnel mode gre multipoint
end
```

```
On R3:

R3# show run interface tunnel 123 | begin inter

interface Tunnel123
 ip address 10.1.1.3 255.255.255.0
 no ip redirects
 ip nhrp map 10.1.1.1 192.1.1.1
 ip nhrp network-id 333
 ip ospf network point-to-multipoint
 tunnel source FastEthernet0/0
 tunnel mode gre multipoint
end
```

You can see the problem—the routers don't have mapping for multicast. Let's configure them:

```
On R1:

R1(config)# interface tunnel 123
R1(config-if)# ip nhrp map multicast 192.1.2.2
R1(config-if)# ip nhrp map multicast 192.1.3.3
```

```
On R2:

R2(config)# interface tunnel 123
R2(config-if)# ip nhrp map multicast 192.1.1.1
```

```
On R3:

R3(config)# interface tunnel 123
R3(config-if)# ip nhrp map multicast 192.1.1.1
```

Now let's verify the configuration:

```
On R1:

R1# show ip ospf neighbor

neighbor ID     Pri    State        Dead Time    Address      Interface
0.0.0.2          0     FULL/  -     00:01:57     10.1.1.2     Tunnel123
0.0.0.3          0     FULL/  -     00:01:57     10.1.1.3     Tunnel123


R1# show ip route ospf | begin Gate
Gateway of last resort is not set

      10.0.0.0/8 is variably subnetted, 4 subnets, 2 masks
O        10.1.1.2/32 [110/1000] via 10.1.1.2, 00:02:06, Tunnel123
O        10.1.1.3/32 [110/1000] via 10.1.1.3, 00:02:06, Tunnel123
      23.0.0.0/24 is subnetted, 1 subnets
O        23.1.1.0 [110/1001] via 10.1.1.3, 00:02:06, Tunnel123
                  [110/1001] via 10.1.1.2, 00:02:06, Tunnel123
```

Here's a summary of some of the important points in OSPF point-to-multipoint networks:

- The routers use 224.0.0.5.
- There is no requirement for a DR or BDR.
- The next hop is the advertising router.
- Host routes are advertised automatically for NLRI in partial Mesh topologies.

We have fixed the first point by mapping multicast. Let's verify the second point:

```
R1# show ip ospf neighbor

neighbor ID     Pri    State        Dead Time    Address      Interface
0.0.0.2          0     FULL/  -     00:01:54     10.1.1.2     Tunnel123
0.0.0.3          0     FULL/  -     00:01:58     10.1.1.3     Tunnel123
```

Note The routers are in full state, and there are no DRs or BDRs.

Now let's verify the third and fourth points:

```
On R2:


R2# show ip route ospf | begin Gate
Gateway of last resort is not set


       10.0.0.0/8 is variably subnetted, 4 subnets, 2 masks
O          10.1.1.1/32 [110/1000] via 10.1.1.1, 00:06:48, Tunnel123
O          10.1.1.3/32 [110/1] via 23.1.1.3, 00:20:03, FastEthernet0/1
```

You can see that the next-hop IP address is the IP address of the router that originated the route. You can also see the host routes that are advertised for reachability.

Task 2

Because R2's connection to the cloud is 10 Mbps and R3's connection is 100 Mbps, R1 should not perform equal-cost load sharing, and R1 should go through R3 to reach network 23.1.1.0/24. Do *not* configure Policy Based Routing (PBR) or use the **ip ospf cost** command to accomplish this task.

As you can see, R2's f0/0 is configured as 10 Mbps, whereas the f0/0 interfaces of R1 and R3 are configured as 100 Mbps. Since OSPF is running on the tunnel interfaces of these routers, OSPF will not see the actual cost of the f0/0 interfaces; therefore, a suboptimal routing can result.

In order to accomplish this task, you can change the OSPF network type. If the network type is changed to point-to-multipoint non-broadcast, then **neighbor** commands *must* be configured on the hub router. In this network type, the **neighbor** command can be configured with a cost that can make the connection through a given neighbor more attractive. Let's configure this.

First, let's verify the routing table of R1:

```
R1# show ip route ospf | begin Gate
Gateway of last resort is not set


       10.0.0.0/8 is variably subnetted, 4 subnets, 2 masks
O          10.1.1.2/32 [110/1000] via 10.1.1.2, 00:02:06, Tunnel123
O          10.1.1.3/32 [110/1000] via 10.1.1.3, 00:02:06, Tunnel123
       23.0.0.0/24 is subnetted, 1 subnets
O          23.1.1.0 [110/1001] via 10.1.1.3, 00:02:06, Tunnel123
                    [110/1001] via 10.1.1.2, 00:02:06, Tunnel123
```

```
On All Routers:

Rx(config)# interface tunnel 123
Rx(config-if)# ip ospf network point-to-multipointerface non-broadcast

R1(config)# router ospf 1
R1(config-router)# neighbor 10.1.1.2 cost 20
R1(config-router)# neighbor 10.1.1.3 cost 1
```

You should see the following console messages stating that the neighbor adjacency has
been established:

```
%OSPF-5-ADJCHG: Process 1, Nbr 0.0.0.3 on Tunnel123 from LOADING to FULL,
Loading Done

%OSPF-5-ADJCHG: Process 1, Nbr 0.0.0.2 on Tunnel123 from LOADING to FULL,
Loading Done
```

Let's verify the configuration:

```
On R1:

R1# show ip route ospf | begin Gate
Gateway of last resort is not set

      10.0.0.0/8 is variably subnetted, 4 subnets, 2 masks
O        10.1.1.2/32 [110/2] via 10.1.1.3, 00:02:55, Tunnel123
O        10.1.1.3/32 [110/1] via 10.1.1.3, 00:02:55, Tunnel123
      23.0.0.0/24 is subnetted, 1 subnets
O        23.1.1.0 [110/2] via 10.1.1.3, 00:02:55, Tunnel123
```

Let's summarize the important points in OSPF point-to-multipoint network types:

- There is no DR/BDR requirement.

- Hello and dead intervals are 30 and 120 seconds, respectively.

- The next hop is the neighboring router.

- There is no multicast capability, so **neighbor** commands must be configured to
  establish OSPF adjacencies.

Erase the startup configuration of the routers as well as the config.text and vlan.dat files
of the switches and then reload them before proceeding to the next lab.

Lab 8-6: OSPF Authentication

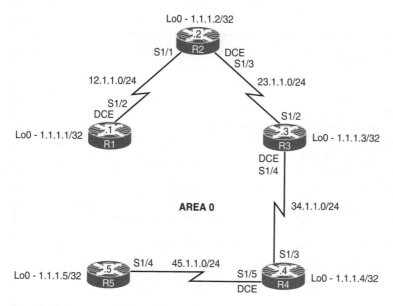

Figure 8-7   *OSPF Authentication*

Figure 8-7 illustrates the topology that will used in the following tasks.

Task 1

Configure the directly connected interfaces of all routers in Area 0. Configure the router IDs to be 0.0.0.x, where x is the router number:

```
On R1:


R1(config)# router ospf 1
R1(config-router)# router-id 0.0.0.1
R1(config-router)# network 1.1.1.1 0.0.0.0 area 0
R1(config-router)# network 12.1.1.1 0.0.0.0 area 0
```

```
On R2:

R2(config-if)# router ospf 1
R2(config-router)# router-id 0.0.0.2
R2(config-router)# network 1.1.1.2 0.0.0.0 area 0
R2(config-router)# network 12.1.1.2 0.0.0.0 area 0
R2(config-router)# network 23.1.1.2 0.0.0.0 area 0
```

You should see the following console message:

```
%OSPF-5-ADJCHG: Process 1, Nbr 0.0.0.1 on Serial1/1 from LOADING to FULL,
Loading Done
```

```
On R3:

R3(config-if)# router ospf 1
R3(config-router)# router-id 0.0.0.3
R3(config-router)# network 1.1.1.3 0.0.0.0 area 0
R3(config-router)# network 23.1.1.3 0.0.0.0 area 0
R3(config-router)# network 34.1.1.3 0.0.0.0 area 0
```

The peering with 0.0.0.2 will come up quickly.

```
%OSPF-5-ADJCHG: Process 1, Nbr 0.0.0.2 on Serial1/2 from LOADING to FULL,
Loading Done
```

```
On R4:

R4(config-if)# router ospf 1
R4(config-router)# router-id 0.0.0.4
R4(config-router)# network 1.1.1.4 0.0.0.0 area 0
R4(config-router)# network 34.1.1.4 0.0.0.0 area 0
R4(config-router)# network 45.1.1.4 0.0.0.0 area 0
```

Now 0.0.0.3 becomes a peer as evidenced by the console output.

```
%OSPF-5-ADJCHG: Process 1, Nbr 0.0.0.3 on Serial1/3 from LOADING to FULL,
Loading Done
```

```
On R5:

R5(config-if)# router ospf 1
R5(config-router)# router-id 0.0.0.5
R5(config-router)# network 45.1.1.5 0.0.0.0 area 0
R5(config-router)# network 1.1.1.5 0.0.0.0 area 0
```

Lastly, 0.0.0.4 joins the OSPF domain.

```
%OSPF-5-ADJCHG: Process 1, Nbr 0.0.0.4 on Serial1/4 from LOADING to FULL,
Loading Done
```

Let's verify the configuration:

```
On R1:


R1# show ip route ospf | begin Gate
Gateway of last resort is not set


     1.0.0.0/32 is subnetted, 5 subnets
O        1.1.1.2 [110/782] via 12.1.1.2, 00:01:52, Serial1/2
O        1.1.1.3 [110/1563] via 12.1.1.2, 00:01:19, Serial1/2
O        1.1.1.4 [110/2344] via 12.1.1.2, 00:01:03, Serial1/2
O        1.1.1.5 [110/3125] via 12.1.1.2, 00:00:39, Serial1/2
     23.0.0.0/24 is subnetted, 1 subnets
O        23.1.1.0 [110/1562] via 12.1.1.2, 00:01:42, Serial1/2
     34.0.0.0/24 is subnetted, 1 subnets
O        34.1.1.0 [110/2343] via 12.1.1.2, 00:01:19, Serial1/2
     45.0.0.0/24 is subnetted, 1 subnets
O        45.1.1.0 [110/3124] via 12.1.1.2, 00:00:53, Serial1/2
```

```
On R5:


R5# show ip route ospf | begin Gate
Gateway of last resort is not set


     1.0.0.0/32 is subnetted, 5 subnets
O        1.1.1.1 [110/3125] via 45.1.1.4, 00:01:56, Serial1/4
O        1.1.1.2 [110/2344] via 45.1.1.4, 00:01:56, Serial1/4
O        1.1.1.3 [110/1563] via 45.1.1.4, 00:01:56, Serial1/4
O        1.1.1.4 [110/782] via 45.1.1.4, 00:01:56, Serial1/4
     12.0.0.0/24 is subnetted, 1 subnets
O        12.1.1.0 [110/3124] via 45.1.1.4, 00:01:56, Serial1/4
     23.0.0.0/24 is subnetted, 1 subnets
O        23.1.1.0 [110/2343] via 45.1.1.4, 00:01:56, Serial1/4
     34.0.0.0/24 is subnetted, 1 subnets
O        34.1.1.0 [110/1562] via 45.1.1.4, 00:01:56, Serial1/4
```

Task 2

Configure plaintext authentication on all routers in Area 0. You must use a router configuration command as part of the solution to this task. Use "Cisco" as the password for this authentication.

OSPF supports two types of authentication: plaintext (64-bit password) and MD5 (which consists of a key ID and 128-bit password). In OSPF, authentication must be enabled and then applied.

In OSPF, authentication can be enabled in two different ways. One way to enable OSPF authentication is to configure it in the router configuration mode, in which case authentication is enabled globally on all OSPF-enabled interfaces in the specified area. The second way is to enable authentication directly on the interface for which authentication is required.

Because this task states that a router configuration mode must be used, OSPF authentication is enabled in the router configuration mode.

So that you understand OSPF's authentication, let's enable **debug ip ospf packet** on R1:

```
On R1:


R1# debug ip ospf packet
OSPF packet debugging is on
```

You should see the following debug messages:

```
OSPF-1 PAK  : rcv. v:2 t:1 l:48 rid:0.0.0.2 aid:0.0.0.0 chk:EC97 aut:0 auk:
from Serial1/2
```

The output of the preceding debug message shows the following:

- **V:2**—This indicates OSPF version 2

- **T:1**—This identifies the packet type (in this case, packet type 1, a hello message).

- **l:48**—The length of these messages is 48 bytes.

- **rid:0.0.0.2**—This is the router ID of R2, the sending router.

- **aid:0.0.0.0**—This is the area ID.

- **aut:0**—This means that there is no authentication.

- **auk:**—No authentication key is defined.

- **from Serial1/2**—The packet is received through the local router's S1/2 interface.

```
On R1:

R1(config)# router ospf 1
R1(config-router)# area 0 authentication

R1(config-router)# interface serial1/2
R1(config-subif)# ip ospf authentication-key Cisco
```

```
On R2:

R2(config)# router ospf 1
R2(config-router)# area 0 authentication

R2(config-router)# interface s1/1
R2(config-subif)# ip ospf authentication-key Cisco
```

On R1, you should now see in the output of the OSPF debug packets that the authentication type is set to 1, which means cleartext authentication (you will see the MD5 authentication type later in this lab):

```
OSPF-1 PAK  : rcv. v:2 t:1 l:48 rid:0.0.0.2 aid:0.0.0.0 chk:EC96 aut:1 auk:
from Serial1/2
```

Let's turn off the debug packets:

```
R1# undebug all
All possible debugging has been turned off
```

Now we can continue with R2's configuration:

```
On R2:

R2(config-if)# interface serial1/3
R2(config-if)# ip ospf authentication-key Cisco
```

Let's verify the configuration:

```
On R2:

R2# show ip ospf interface serial1/1 | include auth

 Simple password authentication enabled
```

Note the output of the preceding **show** command, which verifies that simple password authentication is enabled and applied to the s1/1 interface.

```
R2# show ip ospf neighbor

neighbor ID    Pri   State        Dead Time    Address      Interface
0.0.0.1          0   FULL/  -     00:00:34     12.1.1.1     Serial1/1
```

```
R2# show ip route ospf | be Gate
Gateway of last resort is not set

     1.0.0.0/32 is subnetted, 2 subnets
O       1.1.1.1 [110/782] via 12.1.1.1, 00:06:32, Serial1/1
```

Let's configure R3 and R4:

```
On R3:

R3(config)# router ospf 1
R3(config-router)# area 0 authentication

R3(config)# interface serial1/2
R3(config-if)# ip ospf authentication-key Cisco

R3(config)# interface serial1/4
R3(config-if)# ip ospf authentication-key Cisco
```

You should see the following console message stating that the adjacency transitioned from FULL to DOWN (this is because authentication is not configured on R4):

```
%OSPF-5-ADJCHG: Process 1, Nbr 0.0.0.4 on Serial1/4 from FULL to DOWN,
Neighbor Down: Dead timer expired
```

Let's verify the configuration:

```
On R3:

R3# show ip route ospf | begin Gate
Gateway of last resort is not set

     1.0.0.0/32 is subnetted, 3 subnets
O       1.1.1.1 [110/1563] via 23.1.1.2, 00:00:29, Serial1/2
O       1.1.1.2 [110/782] via 23.1.1.2, 00:00:29, Serial1/2
     12.0.0.0/24 is subnetted, 1 subnets
O       12.1.1.0 [110/1562] via 23.1.1.2, 00:00:29, Serial1/2
```

```
On R4:

R4(config)# router ospf 1
R4(config-router)# area 0 authentication

R4(config)# interface serial1/3
R4(config-if)# ip ospf authentication-key Cisco
```

You should see the following console message:

```
%OSPF-5-ADJCHG: Process 1, Nbr 0.0.0.3 on Serial1/3 from LOADING to FULL,
Loading Done
```

```
R4(config-if)# interface serial1/5
R4(config-if)# ip ospf authentication-key Cisco
```

Let's verify the configuration. On R4, you should *not* see the 1.1.1.5/32 prefix in the routing table. If you still see this prefix in R4's routing table, you may have to wait for the adjacency to R5 to go down before entering the following **show** command:

```
R4# show ip route ospf | begin Gate
Gateway of last resort is not set

      1.0.0.0/32 is subnetted, 4 subnets
O        1.1.1.1 [110/2344] via 34.1.1.3, 00:00:41, Serial1/3
O        1.1.1.2 [110/1563] via 34.1.1.3, 00:00:41, Serial1/3
O        1.1.1.3 [110/782] via 34.1.1.3, 00:00:41, Serial1/3
      12.0.0.0/24 is subnetted, 1 subnets
O        12.1.1.0 [110/2343] via 34.1.1.3, 00:00:41, Serial1/3
      23.0.0.0/24 is subnetted, 1 subnets
O        23.1.1.0 [110/1562] via 34.1.1.3, 00:00:41, Serial1/3
```

Let's configure R5:

```
On R5:

R5(config)# router ospf 1
R5(config-router)# area 0 authentication

R5(config-router)# interface serial1/4
R5(config-if)# ip ospf authentication-key Cisco
```

You should see the following console message:

```
%OSPF-5-ADJCHG: Process 1, Nbr 0.0.0.4 on Serial1/4 from LOADING to FULL,
Loading Done
```

Let's verify the configuration:

```
On R5:

R5# show ip route ospf | begin Gate
Gateway of last resort is not set

     1.0.0.0/32 is subnetted, 5 subnets
O       1.1.1.1 [110/3125] via 45.1.1.4, 00:00:10, Serial1/4
O       1.1.1.2 [110/2344] via 45.1.1.4, 00:00:10, Serial1/4
O       1.1.1.3 [110/1563] via 45.1.1.4, 00:00:10, Serial1/4
O       1.1.1.4 [110/782] via 45.1.1.4, 00:00:10, Serial1/4
     12.0.0.0/24 is subnetted, 1 subnets
O       12.1.1.0 [110/3124] via 45.1.1.4, 00:00:10, Serial1/4
     23.0.0.0/24 is subnetted, 1 subnets
O       23.1.1.0 [110/2343] via 45.1.1.4, 00:00:10, Serial1/4
     34.0.0.0/24 is subnetted, 1 subnets
O       34.1.1.0 [110/1562] via 45.1.1.4, 00:00:10, Serial1/4
```

Task 3

Remove the authentication configuration from the previous task and ensure that every router sees every route advertised in Area 0:

```
On All Routers:

Rx(config)# router ospf 1
Rx(config-router)# no area 0 authentication
```

```
On R1:

R1(config)# interface serial1/2
R1(config-if)# no ip ospf authentication-key Cisco
```

```
On R2:

R2(config)# interface serial1/1
R2(config-if)# no ip ospf authentication-key Cisco

R2(config-if)# interface serial1/3
R2(config-if)# no ip ospf authentication-key Cisco
```

```
On R3:

R3(config-if)# interface s1/2
R3(config-if)# no ip ospf authentication-key Cisco

R3(config-if)# interface s1/4
R3(config-if)# no ip ospf authentication-key Cisco
```

```
On R4:

R4(config)# interface serial1/3
R4(config-if)# no ip ospf authentication-key Cisco

R4(config)# interface s1/5
R4(config-if)# no ip ospf authentication-key Cisco
```

```
On R5:

R5(config)# interface serial1/4
R5(config-if)# no ip ospf authentication-key Cisco
```

Let's verify the configuration:

```
On R1:

R1# show ip route ospf | include O
Gateway of last resort is not set

      1.0.0.0/32 is subnetted, 5 subnets
O       1.1.1.2 [110/782] via 12.1.1.2, 00:09:49, Serial1/2
O       1.1.1.3 [110/1563] via 12.1.1.2, 00:06:40, Serial1/2
O       1.1.1.4 [110/2344] via 12.1.1.2, 00:05:25, Serial1/2
O       1.1.1.5 [110/3125] via 12.1.1.2, 00:03:57, Serial1/2
      23.0.0.0/24 is subnetted, 1 subnets
O       23.1.1.0 [110/1562] via 12.1.1.2, 00:09:49, Serial1/2
      34.0.0.0/24 is subnetted, 1 subnets
O       34.1.1.0 [110/2343] via 12.1.1.2, 00:06:40, Serial1/2
      45.0.0.0/24 is subnetted, 1 subnets
O       45.1.1.0 [110/3124] via 12.1.1.2, 00:05:25, Serial1/2
```

Task 4

Configure MD5 authentication on all the serial links in this area. You should use a router configuration command as part of the solution to this task. Use "Cisco" as the password for this authentication.

The following command enables MD5 authentication on the routers using the router configuration mode:

```
On All Routers:

Rx(config)# router ospf 1
Rx(config-router)# area 0 authentication message-digest
```

```
On R1:

R1(config)# interface serial1/2
R1(config-if)# ip ospf message-digest-key 1 md5 Cisco
```

```
On R2:

R2(config)# interface serial1/1
R2(config-if)# ip ospf message-digest-key 1 md5 Cisco
```

Let's see the debug output and verify the authentication type and key:

```
On R1:

R1# debug ip ospf packet
OSPF packet debugging is on
```

You should see the following debug output on your console:

```
OSPF-1 PAK  : rcv. v:2 t:1 l:48 rid:0.0.0.2 aid:0.0.0.0 chk:0 aut:2 keyid:1
seq:0x536538E9 from Serial1/2
```

You can clearly see **aut:2**. This identifies the authentication type, which is set to 2, meaning that it's MD5 authentication. You can also see **keyid:1**, which means that the key value used in the configuration is 1.

```
On R2:

R2(config-if)# interface serial1/3
R2(config-if)# ip ospf message-digest-key 1 MD5 Cisco
```

Let's verify the configuration. Before doing so, however, we need to disable the debug on R1:

```
On R1:

R1# undebug all
All possible debugging has been turned off
```

```
On R2:

R2# show ip ospf interface serial1/1 | begin Message

  Message digest authentication enabled
    Youngest key id is 1
```

Note   The output of the preceding **show** command reveals that MD5 authentication is enabled and applied and that the key ID is set to 1.

```
R2# show ip route ospf | begin Gate
Gateway of last resort is not set

     1.0.0.0/32 is subnetted, 2 subnets
O        1.1.1.1 [110/782] via 12.1.1.1, 00:18:36, Serial1/1
```

```
On R3:

R3(config)# interface serial1/2
R3(config-if)# ip ospf message-digest-key 1 md5 Cisco

R3(config)# interface serial1/4
R3(config-if)# ip ospf message-digest-key 1 md5 Cisco
```

Let's verify the configuration. Once the OSPF adjacency to R2 comes up and the adjacency to R4 goes down, you should see the following output:

```
On R3:

R3# show ip route ospf | begin Gate
Gateway of last resort is not set

     1.0.0.0/32 is subnetted, 3 subnets
O        1.1.1.1 [110/1563] via 23.1.1.2, 00:00:54, Serial1/2
O        1.1.1.2 [110/782] via 23.1.1.2, 00:00:54, Serial1/2
     12.0.0.0/24 is subnetted, 1 subnets
O        12.1.1.0 [110/1562] via 23.1.1.2, 00:00:54, Serial1/2
```

```
On R4:


R4(config)# interface serial1/3
R4(config-if)# ip ospf message-digest-key 1 md5 Cisco


R4(config)# interface serial1/5
R4(config-if)# ip ospf message-digest-key 1 MD5 Cisco
```

Let's verify the configuration. Once the OSPF adjacency to R3 comes up and the adjacency to R5 goes down, you should see the following output:

```
On R4:


R4# show ip route ospf | begin Gate
Gateway of last resort is not set


      1.0.0.0/32 is subnetted, 4 subnets
O        1.1.1.1 [110/2344] via 34.1.1.3, 00:00:58, Serial1/3
O        1.1.1.2 [110/1563] via 34.1.1.3, 00:00:58, Serial1/3
O        1.1.1.3 [110/782] via 34.1.1.3, 00:00:58, Serial1/3
      12.0.0.0/24 is subnetted, 1 subnets
O        12.1.1.0 [110/2343] via 34.1.1.3, 00:00:58, Serial1/3
      23.0.0.0/24 is subnetted, 1 subnets
O        23.1.1.0 [110/1562] via 34.1.1.3, 00:00:58, Serial1/3
```

```
On R5:


R5(config)# interface serial1/4
R5(config-subif)# ip ospf message-digest-key 1 md5 Cisco
```

Let's verify the configuration:

```
On R5:


R5# show ip route ospf | begin Gate
Gateway of last resort is not set


      1.0.0.0/32 is subnetted, 5 subnets
O        1.1.1.1 [110/3125] via 45.1.1.4, 00:00:07, Serial1/4
O        1.1.1.2 [110/2344] via 45.1.1.4, 00:00:07, Serial1/4
O        1.1.1.3 [110/1563] via 45.1.1.4, 00:00:07, Serial1/4
O        1.1.1.4 [110/782] via 45.1.1.4, 00:00:07, Serial1/4
      12.0.0.0/24 is subnetted, 1 subnets
O        12.1.1.0 [110/3124] via 45.1.1.4, 00:00:07, Serial1/4
```

```
      23.0.0.0/24 is subnetted, 1 subnets
O        23.1.1.0 [110/2343] via 45.1.1.4, 00:00:07, Serial1/4
      34.0.0.0/24 is subnetted, 1 subnets
O        34.1.1.0 [110/1562] via 45.1.1.4, 00:00:07, Serial1/4
```

Task 5

Remove the authentication configuration from the previous task and ensure that every router sees every route advertised in Area 0:

```
On All Routers:

Rx(config)# router ospf 1
Rx(config-router)# no area 0 authentication message-digest
```

```
On R1:

R1(config)# interface serial1/2
R1(config-if)# no ip ospf message-digest-key 1 MD5 Cisco
```

```
On R2:

R2(config)# interface serial1/1
R2(config-if)# no ip ospf message-digest-key 1 MD5 Cisco

R2(config)# interface serial1/3
R2(config-if)# no ip ospf message-digest-key 1 MD5 Cisco
```

```
On R3:

R3(config)# interface serial1/2
R3(config-if)# no ip ospf message-digest-key 1 MD5 Cisco

R3(config)# interface serial1/4
R3(config-if)# no ip ospf message-digest-key 1 MD5 Cisco
```

```
On R4:

R4(config)# interface serial1/3
R4(config-if)# no ip ospf message-digest-key 1 MD5 Cisco

R4(config)# interface serial1/5
R4(config-if)# no ip ospf message-digest-key 1 MD5 Cisco
```

```
On R5:

R5(config)# interface serial1/4
R5(config-if)# no ip ospf message-digest-key 1 MD5 Cisco
```

Let's verify the configuration:

```
On R5:

R5# show ip route ospf | begin Gate
Gateway of last resort is not set


      1.0.0.0/32 is subnetted, 5 subnets
O        1.1.1.1 [110/3125] via 45.1.1.4, 00:04:50, Serial1/4
O        1.1.1.2 [110/2344] via 45.1.1.4, 00:04:50, Serial1/4
O        1.1.1.3 [110/1563] via 45.1.1.4, 00:04:50, Serial1/4
O        1.1.1.4 [110/782] via 45.1.1.4, 00:04:50, Serial1/4
      12.0.0.0/24 is subnetted, 1 subnets
O        12.1.1.0 [110/3124] via 45.1.1.4, 00:04:50, Serial1/4
      23.0.0.0/24 is subnetted, 1 subnets
O        23.1.1.0 [110/2343] via 45.1.1.4, 00:04:50, Serial1/4
      34.0.0.0/24 is subnetted, 1 subnets
O        34.1.1.0 [110/1562] via 45.1.1.4, 00:04:50, Serial1/4
```

Task 6

Configure MD5 authentication between R1 and R2. You should use a router configuration command as part of the solution to this task. Also, use "ccie" as the password.

```
On Both Routers:

Rx(config)# router ospf 1
Rx(config-router)# area 0 authentication message-digest
```

```
On R1:

R1(config)# interface serial1/2
R1(config-if)# ip ospf message-digest-key 1 MD5 ccie
```

```
On R2:

R2(config)# interface serial1/1
R2(config-if)# ip ospf message-digest-key 1 MD5 ccie
```

You should see the following console messages:

```
%OSPF-5-ADJCHG: Process 1, Nbr 0.0.0.1 on Serial1/1 from LOADING to FULL,
Loading Done
```

Then, you should see the following console message stating that the local router no longer has an adjacency with R3 with a router ID of 0.0.0.3:

```
%OSPF-5-ADJCHG: Process 1, Nbr 0.0.0.3 on Serial1/3 from FULL to DOWN,
neighbor Down: Dead timer expired
```

Let's verify the configuration:

```
On R2:

R2# show ip route ospf | begin Gate
Gateway of last resort is not set

      1.0.0.0/32 is subnetted, 2 subnets
O        1.1.1.1 [110/782] via 12.1.1.1, 00:36:55, Serial1/1
```

Note that because authentication is enabled in the router configuration mode, it is applied to every interface that is running in Area 0; therefore, every router in Area 0 *must* have the **area 0 authentication message-digest** command configured. Because R3 does not have MD5 authentication enabled, these routers will drop their adjacency.

Let's verify the configuration:

```
On R2:

R2# show ip ospf neighbors

neighbor ID    Pri   State       Dead Time   Address       Interface
0.0.0.1          0   FULL/  -    00:00:39    12.1.1.1      Serial1/1
```

Here are two solutions to fix this problem:

■ Enable authentication on R3. However, if authentication is enabled on R3 under router OSPF, then R4 will drop the adjacency. Therefore, if router configuration mode must be used as part of the solution (based on the task), authentication needs to be enabled on R3, R4, and R5.

■ Disable authentication under the S1/3 interface. If authentication is disabled on the interface facing R3, then R3, R4, and R5 won't need to have authentication enabled.

Let's configure the preceding solutions and verify them. We'll start with Solution 1:

```
On R3, R4 and R5:


Rx(config)# router ospf 1
Rx(config-router)# area 0 authentication message-digest
```

You should see the following console message on R3:

```
%OSPF-5-ADJCHG: Process 1, Nbr 0.0.0.2 on Serial1/2 from LOADING to FULL,
Loading Done
```

Let's verify the configuration:

```
On R2:


R2# show ip route ospf | begin Gate
Gateway of last resort is not set


     1.0.0.0/32 is subnetted, 5 subnets
O       1.1.1.1 [110/782] via 12.1.1.1, 00:43:45, Serial1/1
O       1.1.1.3 [110/782] via 23.1.1.3, 00:00:57, Serial1/3
O       1.1.1.4 [110/1563] via 23.1.1.3, 00:00:57, Serial1/3
O       1.1.1.5 [110/2344] via 23.1.1.3, 00:00:57, Serial1/3
     34.0.0.0/24 is subnetted, 1 subnets
O       34.1.1.0 [110/1562] via 23.1.1.3, 00:00:57, Serial1/3
     45.0.0.0/24 is subnetted, 1 subnets
O       45.1.1.0 [110/2343] via 23.1.1.3, 00:00:57, Serial1/3
```

Now let's try Solution 2:

```
On R3, R4 and R5:


Rx(config)# router ospf 1
Rx(config-router)# no area 0 authentication message-digest
```

You should see the following console message after the dead interval expires:

```
%OSPF-5-ADJCHG: Process 1, Nbr 0.0.0.3 on Serial1/3 from FULL to DOWN,
neighbor Down: Dead timer expired
```

Let's verify the configuration:

```
On R2:


R2# show ip route ospf | begin Gate
Gateway of last resort is not set


     1.0.0.0/32 is subnetted, 2 subnets
O        1.1.1.1 [110/782] via 12.1.1.1, 00:45:32, Serial1/1
```

In this solution, authentication is disabled on R2's interface facing R3 using the **ip ospf authentication null** interface configuration command, meaning that there is no need to have authentication downstream to the S1/3 interface of R2. Therefore, R3, R4, and R5 do *not* need to have authentication enabled.

```
On R2:


R2(config)# interface serial1/3
R2(config-if)# ip ospf authentication null
```

You should see the following console message on R2:

```
%OSPF-5-ADJCHG: Process 1, Nbr 0.0.0.3 on Serial1/3 from LOADING to FULL,
Loading Done
```

Let's verify the configuration:

```
On R2:


R2# show ip route ospf | include O
Gateway of last resort is not set


     1.0.0.0/32 is subnetted, 5 subnets
O        1.1.1.1 [110/782] via 12.1.1.1, 00:47:16, Serial1/1
O        1.1.1.3 [110/782] via 23.1.1.3, 00:00:20, Serial1/3
O        1.1.1.4 [110/1563] via 23.1.1.3, 00:00:20, Serial1/3


O        1.1.1.5 [110/2344] via 23.1.1.3, 00:00:20, Serial1/3
     34.0.0.0/24 is subnetted, 1 subnets
O        34.1.1.0 [110/1562] via 23.1.1.3, 00:00:20, Serial1/3
     45.0.0.0/24 is subnetted, 1 subnets
O        45.1.1.0 [110/2343] via 23.1.1.3, 00:00:20, Serial1/3
```

Task 7

Reconfigure the authentication password on R1 and R2 to be "CCIE12" without interrupting the link's operation.

Let's view the current configuration:

```
On R1:

R1# show ip ospf interface serial1/2 | begin Mess

  Message digest authentication enabled
    Youngest key id is 1

R1# show run interface serial1/2 | include ip ospf

ip ospf message-digest-key 1 md5 ccie
```

```
On R2:

R2# show ip ospf interface serial1/1 | begin Mess

  Message digest authentication enabled
    Youngest key id is 1

R2# show run interface serial1/1 | include ip ospf

ip ospf message-digest-key 1 md5 ccie

R2# show ip route ospf | begin Gate
Gateway of last resort is not set

      1.0.0.0/32 is subnetted, 5 subnets
O        1.1.1.1 [110/782] via 12.1.1.1, 00:50:19, Serial1/1
O        1.1.1.3 [110/782] via 23.1.1.3, 00:03:23, Serial1/3

O        1.1.1.4 [110/1563] via 23.1.1.3, 00:03:23, Serial1/3
O        1.1.1.5 [110/2344] via 23.1.1.3, 00:03:23, Serial1/3
      34.0.0.0/24 is subnetted, 1 subnets
O        34.1.1.0 [110/1562] via 23.1.1.3, 00:03:23, Serial1/3
      45.0.0.0/24 is subnetted, 1 subnets
O        45.1.1.0 [110/2343] via 23.1.1.3, 00:03:23, Serial1/3
```

In order to change the password without any interruption to the link, you need to enter the second key with the required password:

```
On R1:

R1(config)# interface serial1/2
R1(config-if)# ip ospf message-digest-key 2 md5 CCIE12
```

Let's verify the configuration:

```
On R1:

R1# show run interface serial1/2 | include ip ospf

ip ospf message-digest-key 1 md5 ccie
ip ospf message-digest-key 2 md5 CCIE12

R1# show ip ospf inter Serial1/2 | begin Message

  Message digest authentication enabled
    Youngest key id is 2
    Rollover in progress, 1 neighbor(s) using the old key(s):
      key id 1
```

Even though the second key (key 2) is only configured on R1, R1 and R2 are still authenticating based on the first key (key 1). This is revealed in the second line of the preceding **show** command.

R1 knows that the second key is configured (the second line in the preceding display) and that the rollover is in progress (the third line), but the other end (R2) has not been configured yet.

```
On R2:

R2(config)# interface serial1/1
R2(config-if)# ip ospf message-digest-key 2 md5 CCIE12
```

Let's verify the configuration:

```
On R2:

R2# show ip ospf inter serial1/1 | begin Message

Message digest authentication enabled
    Youngest key id is 2
```

Note   Once R2 is configured, both routers (R1 and R2) will switch over and use the second key for their authentication.

```
On R1:


R1# show ip ospf interface serial1/2 | begin Message

 Message digest authentication enabled
   Youngest key id is 2
```

Once R1 and R2's key rollover is completed and both routers display the same youngest key without the "rollover in progress" message, you can safely remove the prior key (in this case, key ID 1). Remember that the newest key is not determined based on the numerically higher value.

```
On R1:


R1# show run interface serial1/2 | include ip ospf

 ip ospf message-digest-key 1 md5 ccie
 ip ospf message-digest-key 2 md5 CCIE12


R1(config)# interface serial1/2
R1(config-subif)# no ip ospf message-digest-key 1 md5 ccie
```

```
On R2:


R2# show run interface serial1/1 | include ip ospf

 ip ospf message-digest-key 1 md5 ccie
 ip ospf message-digest-key 2 md5 CCIE12


R2(config)# interface serial1/1
R2(config-subif)# no ip ospf message-digest-key 1 md5 ccie
```

Task 8

Reconfigure the authentication password on R4 and R5 to be "Cisco45" without interrupting the link's operation.

```
On R5:


R5(config)# interface serial1/4
R5(config-if)# ip ospf authentication message-digest
R5(config-if)# ip ospf message-digest-key 1 md5 Cisco45
```

```
On R4:


R4(config)# interface serial1/5
R4(config-if)# ip ospf authentication message-digest
R4(config-if)# ip ospf message-digest-key 1 md5 Cisco45
```

Note The authentication is enabled and applied directly under the interface for which authentication was required. When authentication is enabled directly under a given interface, authentication is enabled on that given interface *only*. Therefore, *only* the neighbor through that interface should have authentication enabled. This is called *per-interface authentication*.

Let's verify the configuration:

```
On R5:


R5# show ip route ospf | begin Gate
Gateway of last resort is not set


     1.0.0.0/32 is subnetted, 5 subnets
O        1.1.1.1 [110/3125] via 45.1.1.4, 00:00:09, Serial1/4
O        1.1.1.2 [110/2344] via 45.1.1.4, 00:00:09, Serial1/4
O        1.1.1.3 [110/1563] via 45.1.1.4, 00:00:09, Serial1/4
O        1.1.1.4 [110/782] via 45.1.1.4, 00:00:09, Serial1/4
     12.0.0.0/24 is subnetted, 1 subnets
O        12.1.1.0 [110/3124] via 45.1.1.4, 00:00:09, Serial1/4
     23.0.0.0/24 is subnetted, 1 subnets
O        23.1.1.0 [110/2343] via 45.1.1.4, 00:00:09, Serial1/4
     34.0.0.0/24 is subnetted, 1 subnets
O        34.1.1.0 [110/1562] via 45.1.1.4, 00:00:09, Serial1/4
```

Task 9

Reconfigure the OSPF areas based on Table 8-2 and remove all the authentications configured on the routers. These routers should see all the routes advertised in this routing domain.

Table 8-2　*Reconfigure the OSPF Areas*

Router	Interface	Area
R1	s1/2	0
	loopback0	0
R2	s1/1	0
	s1/3	1
	loopback0	1
R3	s1/2	1
	s1/4	2
	loopback0	2
R4	s1/3	2
	s1/5	3
	loopback0	3
R5	s1/4	3
	loopback0	3

```
On All Routers:

Rx(config)# no router ospf 1
```

```
On R1:

R1(config)# router ospf 1
R1(config-router)# router-id 0.0.0.1
R1(config-router)# network 1.1.1.1 0.0.0.0 area 0
R1(config-router)# network 12.1.1.1 0.0.0.0 area 0

R1(config)# interface serial1/2
R1(config-subif)# no ip ospf message-digest-key 2 md5 CCIE12
```

```
On R2:

R2(config)# router ospf 1
R2(config-router)# router-id 0.0.0.2
R2(config-router)# network 12.1.1.2 0.0.0.0 area 0
R2(config-router)# network 23.1.1.2 0.0.0.0 area 1
R2(config-router)# network 1.1.1.2 0.0.0.0 area 1
```

```
R2(config)# interface serial1/1
R2(config-subif)# no ip ospf message-digest-key 2 md5 CCIE12

R2(config)# interface serial1/3
R2(config-subif)# no ip ospf authentication null
```

```
On R3:

R3(config)# router ospf 1
R3(config-router)# router-id 0.0.0.3
R3(config-router)# network 1.1.1.3 0.0.0.0 area 2
R3(config-router)# network 34.1.1.3 0.0.0.0 area 2
R3(config-router)# network 23.1.1.3 0.0.0.0 area 1
```

```
On R4:

R4(config)# router ospf 1
R4(config-router)# router-id 0.0.0.4
R4(config-router)# network 1.1.1.4 0.0.0.0 area 3
R4(config-router)# network 45.1.1.4 0.0.0.0 area 3
R4(config-router)# network 34.1.1.4 0.0.0.0 area 2

R4(config)# interface serial1/5
R4(config-if)# no ip ospf message-digest-key 1 md5 Cisco45
R4(config-if)# no ip ospf authentication message-digest
```

```
On R5:

R5(config)# router ospf 1
R5(config-router)# router-id 0.0.0.5
R5(config-router)# network 1.1.1.5 0.0.0.0 area 3
R5(config-router)# network 45.1.1.5 0.0.0.0 area 3

R5(config)# interface Serial1/4
R5(config-if)# no ip ospf message-digest-key 1 md5 Cisco45
R5(config-if)# no ip ospf authentication message-digest
```

In order for these routers to see all the routes advertised in this routing domain, you *must* configure virtual links because not all areas have connectivity to Area 0.

Area 1 has a connection to Area 0, but Areas 2 and 3 do not. Let's begin with Area 2:

```
On R2:

R2(config)# router ospf 1

R2(config-router)# area 1 virtual-link 0.0.0.3
```

```
On R3:

R3(config)# router ospf 1
R3(config-router)# area 1 virtual-link 0.0.0.2
```

You should see the following console message:

```
%OSPF-5-ADJCHG: Process 1, Nbr 0.0.0.2 on OSPF_VL0 from LOADING to FULL,
Loading Done
```

Let's connect Area 3 to Area 0:

```
On R3:

R3(config)# router ospf 1
R3(config-router)# area 2 virtual-link 0.0.0.4
```

```
On R4:

R4(config)# router ospf 1
R4(config-router)# area 2 virtual-link 0.0.0.3
```

You should see the following console message:

```
%OSPF-5-ADJCHG: Process 1, Nbr 0.0.0.3 on OSPF_VL2 from LOADING to FULL,
Loading Done
```

Let's verify the configuration:

```
On R5:


R5# show ip route ospf | begin Gate
Gateway of last resort is not set


      1.0.0.0/32 is subnetted, 5 subnets
O IA     1.1.1.1 [110/3125] via 45.1.1.4, 00:00:40, Serial1/4
O IA     1.1.1.2 [110/2344] via 45.1.1.4, 00:00:40, Serial1/4
O IA     1.1.1.3 [110/1563] via 45.1.1.4, 00:00:45, Serial1/4
O        1.1.1.4 [110/782] via 45.1.1.4, 00:03:17, Serial1/4
      12.0.0.0/24 is subnetted, 1 subnets
O IA     12.1.1.0 [110/3124] via 45.1.1.4, 00:00:40, Serial1/4
      23.0.0.0/24 is subnetted, 1 subnets

O IA     23.1.1.0 [110/2343] via 45.1.1.4, 00:00:40, Serial1/4
      34.0.0.0/24 is subnetted, 1 subnets
O IA     34.1.1.0 [110/1562] via 45.1.1.4, 00:00:45, Serial1/4
```

Task 10

Configure MD5 authentication on the link between R1 and R2 in area 0. The password for this authentication should be set to "Micronics". You should use router configuration mode to accomplish this task.

```
On R1 and R2:


Rx(config)# router ospf 1
Rx(config-router)# area 0 authentication message-digest
```

```
On R1:


R1(config)# interface serial1/2
R1(config-subif)# ip ospf message-digest-key 1 md5 Micronics
```

```
On R2:


R2(config)# interface serial1/1
R2(config-subif)# ip ospf message-digest-key 1 md5 Micronics
```

Let's verify the configuration:

```
On R2:

R2# show ip route ospf | begin Gate
Gateway of last resort is not set


      1.0.0.0/32 is subnetted, 5 subnets
O         1.1.1.1 [110/782] via 12.1.1.1, 00:07:10, Serial1/1
O IA      1.1.1.3 [110/782] via 23.1.1.3, 00:02:49, Serial1/3
O IA      1.1.1.4 [110/1563] via 23.1.1.3, 00:02:02, Serial1/3
O IA      1.1.1.5 [110/2344] via 23.1.1.3, 00:02:02, Serial1/3
      34.0.0.0/24 is subnetted, 1 subnets
O IA      34.1.1.0 [110/1562] via 23.1.1.3, 00:02:49, Serial1/3
      45.0.0.0/24 is subnetted, 1 subnets
O IA      45.1.1.0 [110/2343] via 23.1.1.3, 00:02:02, Serial1/3
```

Why do we see all the routes?

Let's shut down the lo0 interface of R2, and then **no shutdown** the interface, and you should see the following console message within 40 seconds:

```
R2(config)# interface loopback 0
R2(config-if)# shutdown
```

Wait for the link to go down before entering the following command:

```
R2(config-if)# no shutdown
```

```
%OSPF-5-ADJCHG: Process 1, Nbr 0.0.0.3 on OSPF_VL0 from FULL to DOWN,
neighbor Down: Dead timer expired
```

```
R2# show ip route ospf | begin Gate
Gateway of last resort is not set

      1.0.0.0/32 is subnetted, 2 subnets
O         1.1.1.1 [110/782] via 12.1.1.1, 00:24:18, Serial1/1
```

The reason we had to **shutdown** and then **no shutdown** an advertised route is because virtual links are demand circuits, and when a link is a demand circuit, OSPF suppresses the OSPF hello and refresh messages. Demand circuits are typically configured on switched virtual circuits (SVCs) such as ISDN, so when OSPF is enabled on a demand circuit, OSPF hello messages will keep that link up indefinitely. To handle this issue, you can configure the **ip ospf demand-circuit** command. With this command configured, OSPF will form an adjacency, and when the link goes down, the OSPF adjacency stays up. Because hello and refresh messages are suppressed, the link can stay down.

So when does this link ever come up? When there is a topology change. Enabling authentication is not a topology change, so this is the reason we had to **shutdown** and then **no shutdown** the interface; this triggers a topology change.

When a topology change is detected, the link comes up. When the link comes up and you have enabled authentication on one end of the link and not the other, the virtual link goes down and stays down until authentication is enabled on the other end of the link.

Note R2 does not have any other prefix in its routing table. This is because authentication is enabled directly under the router configuration mode of R1 and R2. When authentication is enabled in the router configuration mode, it is enabled on all links in the configured area—in this case, Area 0—and because virtual links are always in Area 0 (which cannot be changed), authentication must also be enabled on those links. There are three ways to fix this problem:

■ Enable authentication on R3 and R4 in their router configuration mode. Remember R5 does not have a virtual link configured.

■ Enable authentication directly on the virtual links configured on R2, R3, and R4.

■ Disable authentication on R2's virtual link.

Let's implement the first solution:

```
On R3 and R4:


Rx(config)# router ospf 1
Rx(config-router)# area 0 authentication message-digest
```

Let's verify the configuration:

```
On R5:


R5# show ip route ospf | begin Gate
Gateway of last resort is not set


     1.0.0.0/32 is subnetted, 5 subnets
O IA    1.1.1.1 [110/3125] via 45.1.1.4, 00:00:17, Serial1/4
O IA    1.1.1.2 [110/2344] via 45.1.1.4, 00:08:25, Serial1/4
O IA    1.1.1.3 [110/1563] via 45.1.1.4, 00:08:30, Serial1/4
```

```
O          1.1.1.4 [110/782] via 45.1.1.4, 00:11:02, Serial1/4
        12.0.0.0/24 is subnetted, 1 subnets
O IA    12.1.1.0 [110/3124] via 45.1.1.4, 00:00:17, Serial1/4
        23.0.0.0/24 is subnetted, 1 subnets
O IA    23.1.1.0 [110/2343] via 45.1.1.4, 00:08:25, Serial1/4
        34.0.0.0/24 is subnetted, 1 subnets
O IA    34.1.1.0 [110/1562] via 45.1.1.4, 00:08:30, Serial1/4
```

```
On R2:

R2# show ip route ospf | begin Gate
Gateway of last resort is not set

     1.0.0.0/32 is subnetted, 5 subnets
O          1.1.1.1 [110/782] via 12.1.1.1, 00:14:03, Serial1/1
O IA    1.1.1.3 [110/782] via 23.1.1.3, 00:01:07, Serial1/3
O IA    1.1.1.4 [110/1563] via 23.1.1.3, 00:01:07, Serial1/3
O IA    1.1.1.5 [110/2344] via 23.1.1.3, 00:01:07, Serial1/3
     34.0.0.0/24 is subnetted, 1 subnets
O IA    34.1.1.0 [110/1562] via 23.1.1.3, 00:01:07, Serial1/3
     45.0.0.0/24 is subnetted, 1 subnets
O IA    45.1.1.0 [110/2343] via 23.1.1.3, 00:01:07, Serial1/3
```

Remember that when authentication is enabled in router configuration mode, authentication is enabled on all links/interfaces in the specified area. Because virtual links are always in Area 0, authentication will be enabled on all virtual links.

Let's now implement the second solution. First, however, you need to remove the configuration from the previous solution:

```
On R3 and R4:

Rx(config)# router ospf 1
Rx(config-router)# no area 0 authentication message-digest

Rx# clear ip ospf process
Reset ALL OSPF processes? [no]: y
```

Let's verify the configuration:

```
On R2:


R2# show ip route ospf | begin Gate
Gateway of last resort is not set


     1.0.0.0/32 is subnetted, 2 subnets
O        1.1.1.1 [110/782] via 12.1.1.1, 00:16:26, Serial1/1
```

Let's enable authentication on the virtual links:

```
R2(config)# router ospf 1
R2(config-router)# area 1 virtual-link 0.0.0.3 authentication message-digest
```

```
On R3:


R3(config)# router ospf 1
R3(config-router)# area 1 virtual-link 0.0.0.2 authentication message-digest
R3(config-router)# area 2 virtual-link 0.0.0.4 authentication message-digest
```

You should see the following console message:

```
%OSPF-5-ADJCHG: Process 1, Nbr 0.0.0.2 on OSPF_VL0 from LOADING to FULL,
Loading Done
```

```
On R4:


R4(config)# router ospf 1
R4(config-router)# area 2 virtual-link 0.0.0.3 authentication message-digest
```

Let's verify the configuration:

```
On R5:


R5# show ip route ospf | begin Gate


Gateway of last resort is not set


     1.0.0.0/32 is subnetted, 5 subnets
O IA    1.1.1.1 [110/3125] via 45.1.1.4, 00:01:22, Serial1/4
O IA    1.1.1.2 [110/2344] via 45.1.1.4, 00:04:19, Serial1/4
```

```
O IA    1.1.1.3 [110/1563] via 45.1.1.4, 00:04:24, Serial1/4
O       1.1.1.4 [110/782] via 45.1.1.4, 00:04:24, Serial1/4
     12.0.0.0/24 is subnetted, 1 subnets
O IA    12.1.1.0 [110/3124] via 45.1.1.4, 00:01:22, Serial1/4
     23.0.0.0/24 is subnetted, 1 subnets
O IA    23.1.1.0 [110/2343] via 45.1.1.4, 00:04:09, Serial1/4
     34.0.0.0/24 is subnetted, 1 subnets
O IA    34.1.1.0 [110/1562] via 45.1.1.4, 00:04:24, Serial1/4
```

Now let's implement the third solution. First, however, you need to remove the configuration from the previous solution:

```
On R2:

R2(config)# router ospf 1
R2(config-router)# no Area 1 virtual-link 0.0.0.3
R2(config-router)# area 1 virtual-link 0.0.0.3
```

```
On R3:

R3(config)# router ospf 1
R3(config-router)# no area 1 virtual-link 0.0.0.2
R3(config-router)# no area 2 virtual-link 0.0.0.4

R3(config-router)# area 1 virtual-link 0.0.0.2
R3(config-router)# area 2 virtual-link 0.0.0.4
```

```
On R4:

R4(config)# router ospf 1
R4(config-router)# no area 2 virtual-link 0.0.0.3
R4(config-router)# area 2 virtual-link 0.0.0.3
```

Let's verify the configuration:

```
On R1:


R1# show ip route ospf | begin Gate
Gateway of last resort is not set


      1.0.0.0/32 is subnetted, 2 subnets
O IA    1.1.1.2 [110/782] via 12.1.1.2, 00:15:54, Serial1/2
      23.0.0.0/24 is subnetted, 1 subnets
O IA    23.1.1.0 [110/1562] via 12.1.1.2, 00:23:52, Serial1/2
```

Let's implement the third solution:

```
On R2:


R2(config)# router ospf 1
R2(config-router)# area 1 virtual-link 0.0.0.3 authentication null
```

You should see the following console message:

```
%OSPF-5-ADJCHG: Process 1, Nbr 0.0.0.3 on OSPF_VL2 from LOADING to FULL,
Loading Done
```

```
On R2:


R2# show ip route ospf | begin Gate
Gateway of last resort is not set


      1.0.0.0/32 is subnetted, 5 subnets
O        1.1.1.1 [110/782] via 12.1.1.1, 00:25:40, Serial1/1
O IA    1.1.1.3 [110/782] via 23.1.1.3, 00:00:48, Serial1/3
O IA    1.1.1.4 [110/1563] via 23.1.1.3, 00:00:48, Serial1/3
O IA    1.1.1.5 [110/2344] via 23.1.1.3, 00:00:48, Serial1/3
      34.0.0.0/24 is subnetted, 1 subnets
O IA    34.1.1.0 [110/1562] via 23.1.1.3, 00:00:48, Serial1/3
      45.0.0.0/24 is subnetted, 1 subnets
O IA    45.1.1.0 [110/2343] via 23.1.1.3, 00:00:48, Serial1/3
```

```
On R5:


R5# show ip route ospf | begin Gate
Gateway of last resort is not set
```

```
        1.0.0.0/32 is subnetted, 5 subnets
O IA      1.1.1.1 [110/3125] via 45.1.1.4, 00:01:10, Serial1/4
O IA      1.1.1.2 [110/2344] via 45.1.1.4, 00:04:02, Serial1/4
O IA      1.1.1.3 [110/1563] via 45.1.1.4, 00:04:07, Serial1/4
O         1.1.1.4 [110/782] via 45.1.1.4, 00:10:34, Serial1/4
        12.0.0.0/24 is subnetted, 1 subnets
O IA      12.1.1.0 [110/3124] via 45.1.1.4, 00:01:10, Serial1/4
        23.0.0.0/24 is subnetted, 1 subnets
O IA      23.1.1.0 [110/2343] via 45.1.1.4, 00:04:02, Serial1/4
        34.0.0.0/24 is subnetted, 1 subnets
O IA      34.1.1.0 [110/1562] via 45.1.1.4, 00:04:07, Serial1/4
```

Erase the startup configuration and reload the routers before proceeding to the next lab.

Lab 8-7: OSPF Summarization

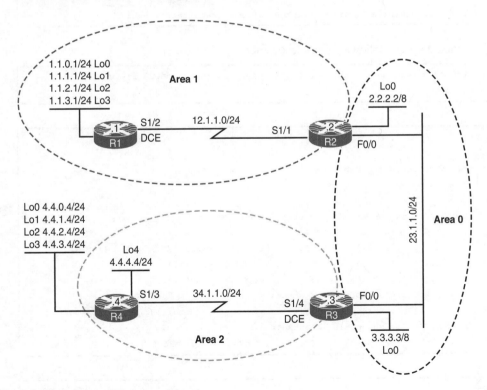

Figure 8-8   *OSPF Summarization*

Figure 8-8 illustrates the topology that will used in the following tasks.

Task 1

Configure R4 based on the following policy:

- R4 should run OSPF Area 2 on its loopback4 and s1/3 interfaces. This loopback interface should be advertised with its correct mask.

- R4 should redistribute Lo0, Lo1, Lo2, and Lo3 in this routing domain.

- R4's router ID should be configured as 0.0.0.4.

```
On R4:

R4(config)# interface loopback 4
R4(config-if)# ip ospf network point-to-point

R4(config)# route-map tst
R4(config-route-map)# match interface lo0 lo1 lo2 lo3

R4(config)# router ospf 1
R4(config-router)# router-id 0.0.0.4
R4(config-router)# network 34.1.1.4 0.0.0.0 area 2
R4(config-router)# network 4.4.4.4 0.0.0.0 area 2
R4(config-router)# redistribute connected route-map tst subnets
```

Task 2

Configure R3 based on the following policy:

- R3 should run OSPF Area 0 on its loopback0 and f0/0 interfaces, and run OSPF Area 2 on its s1/4 interface. This loopback interface should be advertised with its correct mask.

- R3's router ID should be configured as 0.0.0.3.

```
On R3:

R3(config)# interface loopback 0
R3(config-if)# ip ospf network point-to-point

R3(config)# router ospf 1
R3(config-router)# router-id 0.0.0.3
R3(config-router)# network 3.3.3.3 0.0.0.0 area 0
R3(config-router)# network 23.1.1.3 0.0.0.0 area 0
R3(config-router)# network 34.1.1.3 0.0.0.0 area 2
```

You should see the following console message:

```
%OSPF-5-ADJCHG: Process 1, Nbr 0.0.0.4 on Serial1/4 from LOADING to FULL,
Loading Done
```

Let's verify the configuration:

```
On R3:

R3# show ip route ospf | begin Gate
Gateway of last resort is not set

     4.0.0.0/24 is subnetted, 5 subnets
O E2    4.4.0.0 [110/20] via 34.1.1.4, 00:00:13, Serial1/4
O E2    4.4.1.0 [110/20] via 34.1.1.4, 00:00:13, Serial1/4
O E2    4.4.2.0 [110/20] via 34.1.1.4, 00:00:13, Serial1/4
O E2    4.4.3.0 [110/20] via 34.1.1.4, 00:00:13, Serial1/4
O       4.4.4.0 [110/782] via 34.1.1.4, 00:00:13, Serial1/4
```

Task 3

Configure R2 based on the following policy:

- R2 should advertise its loopback0 and f0/0 interfaces in Area 0 and its s1/1 interface in Area 1. This loopback interface should be advertised with its correct mask.

- R2's router ID should be configured as 0.0.0.2.

```
On R2:

R2(config)# interface loopback 0
R2(config-if)# ip ospf network point-to-point

R2(config)# router ospf 1
R2(config-router)# router-id 0.0.0.2
R2(config-router)# network 2.2.2.2 0.0.0.0 area 0
R2(config-router)# network 23.1.1.2 0.0.0.0 area 0
R2(config-router)# network 12.1.1.2 0.0.0.0 area 1
```

You should see the following console message:

```
%OSPF-5-ADJCHG: Process 1, Nbr 0.0.0.3 on FastEthernet0/0 from LOADING to FULL,
Loading Done
```

Let's verify the configuration:

```
On R2:


R2# show ip route ospf | begin Gate
Gateway of last resort is not set

O     3.0.0.0/8 [110/2] via 23.1.1.3, 00:00:10, FastEthernet0/0
      4.0.0.0/24 is subnetted, 5 subnets
O E2     4.4.0.0 [110/20] via 23.1.1.3, 00:00:10, FastEthernet0/0
O E2     4.4.1.0 [110/20] via 23.1.1.3, 00:00:10, FastEthernet0/0
O E2     4.4.2.0 [110/20] via 23.1.1.3, 00:00:10, FastEthernet0/0
O E2     4.4.3.0 [110/20] via 23.1.1.3, 00:00:10, FastEthernet0/0
O IA     4.4.4.0 [110/783] via 23.1.1.3, 00:00:10, FastEthernet0/0
      34.0.0.0/24 is subnetted, 1 subnets
O IA     34.1.1.0 [110/782] via 23.1.1.3, 00:00:10, FastEthernet0/0
```

Task 4

Configure R1 based on the following policy:

- R1 should run OSPF Area 1 on all of its directly connected interfaces. You should use the minimum number of **network** statements to accomplish this task. The loopback interfaces must be advertised with their correct mask.

- R1's router ID should be configured as 0.0.0.1.

```
On R1:

R1(config)# interface loopback 0
R1(config-if)# ip ospf network point-to-point

R1(config)# interface loopback 1
R1(config-if)# ip ospf network point-to-point

R1(config)# interface loopback 2
R1(config-if)# ip ospf network point-to-point

R1(config)# interface loopback 3
R1(config-if)# ip ospf network point-to-point

R1(config)# router ospf 1
R1(config-router)# router-id 0.0.0.1
R1(config-router)# network 0.0.0.0 0.0.0.0 area 1
```

You should see the following console message:

```
%OSPF-5-ADJCHG: Process 1, Nbr 0.0.0.2 on Serial1/2 from LOADING to FULL,
Loading Done
```

Let's verify the configuration:

```
On R1:


R1# show ip route ospf | include O
Gateway of last resort is not set


O IA  2.0.0.0/8 [110/782] via 12.1.1.2, 00:00:08, Serial1/2
O IA  3.0.0.0/8 [110/783] via 12.1.1.2, 00:00:08, Serial1/2
      4.0.0.0/24 is subnetted, 5 subnets
O E2    4.4.0.0 [110/20] via 12.1.1.2, 00:00:08, Serial1/2
O E2    4.4.1.0 [110/20] via 12.1.1.2, 00:00:08, Serial1/2
O E2    4.4.2.0 [110/20] via 12.1.1.2, 00:00:08, Serial1/2
O E2    4.4.3.0 [110/20] via 12.1.1.2, 00:00:08, Serial1/2
O IA    4.4.4.0 [110/1564] via 12.1.1.2, 00:00:08, Serial1/2
      23.0.0.0/24 is subnetted, 1 subnets
O IA    23.1.1.0 [110/782] via 12.1.1.2, 00:00:08, Serial1/2
      34.0.0.0/24 is subnetted, 1 subnets
O IA    34.1.1.0 [110/1563] via 12.1.1.2, 00:00:08, Serial1/2
```

```
On R2:


R2# show ip route ospf | begin Gate
Gateway of last resort is not set


      1.0.0.0/24 is subnetted, 4 subnets
O        1.1.0.0 [110/782] via 12.1.1.1, 00:00:39, Serial1/1
O        1.1.1.0 [110/782] via 12.1.1.1, 00:00:39, Serial1/1
O        1.1.2.0 [110/782] via 12.1.1.1, 00:00:39, Serial1/1
O        1.1.3.0 [110/782] via 12.1.1.1, 00:00:39, Serial1/1
O     3.0.0.0/8 [110/2] via 23.1.1.3, 00:03:43, FastEthernet0/0
      4.0.0.0/24 is subnetted, 5 subnets
O E2    4.4.0.0 [110/20] via 23.1.1.3, 00:03:43, FastEthernet0/0
O E2    4.4.1.0 [110/20] via 23.1.1.3, 00:03:43, FastEthernet0/0
O E2    4.4.2.0 [110/20] via 23.1.1.3, 00:03:43, FastEthernet0/0
O E2    4.4.3.0 [110/20] via 23.1.1.3, 00:03:43, FastEthernet0/0
O IA    4.4.4.0 [110/783] via 23.1.1.3, 00:03:43, FastEthernet0/0
      34.0.0.0/24 is subnetted, 1 subnets
O IA    34.1.1.0 [110/782] via 23.1.1.3, 00:03:43, FastEthernet0/0
```

Task 5

Configure the appropriate router in Area 2 to summarize all the external (E2) routes.

In OSPF, summarization can be configured on two types of routers: an Area Border Router (ABR) and/or an Autonomous System Boundary Router (ASBR). OSPF intra-area routes can only be summarized on the ABRs, whereas the external (redistributed) routes can be summarized on the router that originates the external routes. This can be the ASBR or an ABR in a not-so-stubby-area (NSSA).

In an NSSA area, the ABR of that area receives the "N" routes, converts them to "E" routes, and then injects them into Area 0. In this case, because the ABR is the router that originates the E routes, the ABR can summarize the external routes (the E routes) and inject a single summary into Area 0.

When summarizing internal routes on an ABR, you must use the **Area *xx* range** command, where *xx* is the area ID where the specific routes were originated.

Summarization of external routes can be accomplished by using the **summary-address** router configuration mode command. In this case, because R4 is the router that originates Type-5 LSAs, summarization can *only* be performed on R4.

```
On R4:


R4(config)# router ospf 1
R4(config-router)# summary-address 4.4.0.0 255.255.252.0
```

Note   Whenever summarization is performed on a given router, a discard route is auto-injected into the routing table for loop avoidance. This is a summary route pointing to the Null0 interface.

Let's view the Null0 route for the summary:

```
On R4:


R4# show ip route | include Null0


O        4.4.0.0/22 is a summary, 00:09:31, Null0
```

Now let's verify the configuration:

```
On R1:


R1# show ip route ospf | begin Gate
Gateway of last resort is not set

O IA  2.0.0.0/8 [110/782] via 12.1.1.2, 00:02:07, Serial1/2
O IA  3.0.0.0/8 [110/783] via 12.1.1.2, 00:02:07, Serial1/2
      4.0.0.0/8 is variably subnetted, 2 subnets, 2 masks
O E2    4.4.0.0/22 [110/20] via 12.1.1.2, 00:00:30, Serial1/2
O IA    4.4.4.0/24 [110/1564] via 12.1.1.2, 00:02:07, Serial1/2
      23.0.0.0/24 is subnetted, 1 subnets
O IA    23.1.1.0 [110/782] via 12.1.1.2, 00:02:07, Serial1/2
      34.0.0.0/24 is subnetted, 1 subnets
O IA    34.1.1.0 [110/1563] via 12.1.1.2, 00:02:07, Serial1/2
```

Note   The external routes are summarized.

Task 6

R4 should be configured to advertise the summary plus network 4.4.0.0/24.

This task can be accomplished in two different ways. First, you can add another **summary-address** command for network 4.4.0.0/24. Let's test this method:

```
R4(config)# router ospf 1
R4(config-router)# summary-address 4.4.0.0 255.255.255.0
```

Now let's verify the configuration:

```
On R1:


R1# show ip route ospf | begin Gate
Gateway of last resort is not set

O IA  2.0.0.0/8 [110/782] via 12.1.1.2, 00:06:39, Serial1/2
O IA  3.0.0.0/8 [110/783] via 12.1.1.2, 00:06:39, Serial1/2
      4.0.0.0/8 is variably subnetted, 3 subnets, 2 masks
O E2    4.4.0.0/22 [110/20] via 12.1.1.2, 00:05:02, Serial1/2
O E2    4.4.0.0/24 [110/20] via 12.1.1.2, 00:00:46, Serial1/2
O IA    4.4.4.0/24 [110/1564] via 12.1.1.2, 00:06:39, Serial1/2
```

```
      23.0.0.0/24 is subnetted, 1 subnets
O IA     23.1.1.0 [110/782] via 12.1.1.2, 00:06:39, Serial1/2
      34.0.0.0/24 is subnetted, 1 subnets
O IA     34.1.1.0 [110/1563] via 12.1.1.2, 00:06:39, Serial1/2
```

Run the loopback0 interface in OSPF Area 2. Because the **summary-address** command *only* summarizes the external routes, if one of the specific routes is advertised as an intra-area route in Area 2, it won't be summarized. Let's verify this method.

First, we need to remove the second **summary-address** command:

```
On R4:

R4(config)# router ospf 1
R4(config-router)# no summary-address 4.4.0.0 255.255.255.0
```

Let's run OSPF Area 2 on the loopback0 interface of R4, but we must advertise the loopback with its correct mask:

```
R4(config-router)# network 4.4.0.4 0.0.0.0 area 2

R4(config)# interface loopback 0
R4(config-if)# ip ospf network point-to-point
```

Let's verify the configuration:

```
On R1:

R1# show ip route ospf | begin Gate
Gateway of last resort is not set

O IA  2.0.0.0/8 [110/782] via 12.1.1.2, 00:26:23, Serial1/2
O IA  3.0.0.0/8 [110/783] via 12.1.1.2, 00:26:23, Serial1/2
      4.0.0.0/8 is variably subnetted, 3 subnets, 2 masks
O E2     4.4.0.0/22 [110/20] via 12.1.1.2, 00:24:46, Serial1/2
O IA     4.4.0.0/24 [110/1564] via 12.1.1.2, 00:02:40, Serial1/2
O IA     4.4.4.0/24 [110/1564] via 12.1.1.2, 00:26:23, Serial1/2
      23.0.0.0/24 is subnetted, 1 subnets
O IA     23.1.1.0 [110/782] via 12.1.1.2, 00:26:23, Serial1/2
      34.0.0.0/24 is subnetted, 1 subnets
O IA     34.1.1.0 [110/1563] via 12.1.1.2, 00:26:23, Serial1/2
```

> **Note**   Network 4.4.0.0/24 shows up as an inter-area route and not external route; hence, it's not summarized.

Task 7

Configure the appropriate router in Area 1 to summarize networks 1.1.0.0/24, 1.1.1.0/24, 1.1.2.0/24, and 1.1.3.0/24 into the OSPF routing domain.

The routes that are identified in this task are originated by R1, and they can only be summarized by the ABR of Area 1 (in this topology, the ABR for Area 1 is R2).

```
On R2:

R2(config)# router ospf 1
R2(config-router)# area 1 range 1.1.0.0 255.255.252.0
```

> **Note**   Whenever summarization is performed on a given router, a discard route is auto-injected into the routing table for loop avoidance. This is a summary route pointing to the Null0 interface.

Let's view the Null0 route for the summary:

```
On R2:

R2# show ip route ospf | include Null0

O       1.1.0.0/22 is a summary, 00:00:15, Null0
```

Now let's verify the configuration:

```
On R3:

R3# show ip route ospf | begin Gate
Gateway of last resort is not set

      1.0.0.0/22 is subnetted, 1 subnets
O IA     1.1.0.0 [110/783] via 23.1.1.2, 00:01:29, FastEthernet0/0
O       2.0.0.0/8 [110/2] via 23.1.1.2, 00:35:27, FastEthernet0/0
        4.0.0.0/8 is variably subnetted, 3 subnets, 2 masks
O E2     4.4.0.0/22 [110/20] via 34.1.1.4, 00:29:45, Serial1/4
O        4.4.0.0/24 [110/782] via 34.1.1.4, 00:07:39, Serial1/4
O        4.4.4.0/24 [110/782] via 34.1.1.4, 00:37:30, Serial1/4
      12.0.0.0/24 is subnetted, 1 subnets
O IA     12.1.1.0 [110/782] via 23.1.1.2, 00:34:16, FastEthernet0/0
```

Task 8

The routers should not install a Null 0 route in the routing table when summarization is performed. You should test two different methods to accomplish this task.

In OSPF, the discard route is installed in the routing table automatically whenever summarization is configured. There are two types of summary routes: internal and external.

When summarization is configured for intra-area routes, OSPF will auto-inject an internal discard route, and when summarization is configured for an external OSPF route, the OSPF process will create an external discard route. The discard routes are created to stop forwarding loops.

Here's one way to remove the internal discard route:

```
On R2:

R2# show ip route ospf | include Null0

O        1.1.0.0/22 is a summary, 00:05:14, Null0

R2(config)# router ospf 1
R2(config-router)# no discard-route internal
```

Let's verify the configuration:

```
On R2:

R2# show ip route ospf | include Null0
```

Let's use another method, where we raise the administrative distance of this route to 255:

```
R2(config)# router ospf 1
R2(config-router)# discard-route internal

R2# show ip route ospf | include Null0

O        1.1.0.0/22 is a summary, 00:00:14, Null0

R2(config)# router ospf 1
R2(config-router)# discard-route internal 255
```

Let's verify the configuration:

```
On R2:

R2# show ip route ospf | include Null0
```

Here's one way to remove the external discard route:

```
On R4:

R4# show ip route ospf | include Null0

O        4.4.0.0/22 is a summary, 00:06:13, Null0

R4(config)# router ospf 1
R4(config-router)# no discard-route external
```

Let's verify the configuration:

```
On R4:

R4# show ip route ospf | include Null0
```

To use the second method, just like we did for internal routes, we will raise the administrative distance to 255:

```
R4(config)# router ospf 1
R4(config-router)# discard-route external 255
```

Let's verify the configuration:

```
On R4:

R4# show ip route ospf | include Null0
```

Task 9

Configure R2 to advertise 1.1.0.0/24 plus the summary route. You should demonstrate two different methods to accomplishing this task.

This task can be accomplished in two different ways. First, you can add another **area range** command for network 1.1.0.0/24. Let's test this method:

On R2:

```
R2(config)# router ospf 1
R2(config-router)# area 1 range 1.1.0.0 255.255.255.0
```

Let's verify the configuration:

```
On R4:

R4# show ip route ospf | begin Gate
Gateway of last resort is not set


      1.0.0.0/8 is variably subnetted, 2 subnets, 2 masks
O IA    1.1.0.0/22 [110/1564] via 34.1.1.3, 00:07:37, Serial1/3
O IA    1.1.0.0/24 [110/1564] via 34.1.1.3, 00:00:34, Serial1/3
O IA    2.0.0.0/8 [110/783] via 34.1.1.3, 00:07:37, Serial1/3
O IA    3.0.0.0/8 [110/782] via 34.1.1.3, 00:07:37, Serial1/3
      12.0.0.0/24 is subnetted, 1 subnets
O IA    12.1.1.0 [110/1563] via 34.1.1.3, 00:07:37, Serial1/3
      23.0.0.0/24 is subnetted, 1 subnets
O IA    23.1.1.0 [110/782] via 34.1.1.3, 00:07:37, Serial1/3
```

Another way to accomplish the same task is to redistribute the loopback1 interface of R1.

Let's remove the second **area-range** command:

```
R2(config)# router ospf 1
R2(config-router)# no area 1 range 1.1.0.0 255.255.255.0
```

Let's verify the configuration:

```
On R4:

R4# show ip route ospf | begin Gate
Gateway of last resort is not set


      1.0.0.0/22 is subnetted, 1 subnets
O IA    1.1.0.0 [110/1564] via 34.1.1.3, 00:12:45, Serial1/3
O IA    2.0.0.0/8 [110/783] via 34.1.1.3, 00:12:45, Serial1/3
O IA    3.0.0.0/8 [110/782] via 34.1.1.3, 00:12:45, Serial1/3
      12.0.0.0/24 is subnetted, 1 subnets
O IA    12.1.1.0 [110/1563] via 34.1.1.3, 00:12:45, Serial1/3
      23.0.0.0/24 is subnetted, 1 subnets
O IA    23.1.1.0 [110/782] via 34.1.1.3, 00:12:45, Serial1/3
```

You can see that the specific route (1.1.0.0/24) is no longer in the routing table of R4. Let's redistribute that loopback interface into the OSPF routing domain on R1. Because the **area-range** command *only* summarizes the internal routes, if the loopback0 interface of R1 is redistributed into the OSPF routing domain, it won't be summarized. Before this task can be accomplished, the **network** statement configured on R1 should be changed. The **network** statement of R1 states that the existing and future directly connected interfaces should be advertised in Area 1. Let's have a look at the way OSPF is configured:

```
R1# Show run | section router ospf

router ospf 1
 router-id 0.0.0.1
 network 0.0.0.0 255.255.255.255 area 1
```

With the preceding configuration, even if the loopback0 interface is redistributed into the OSPF routing domain, it will still be advertised as an internal route. Let's redistribute:

```
R1(config)# route-map tst
R1(config-route-map)# match interface loopback 0

R1(config)# router ospf 1
R1(config-router)# redistribute connected route-map tst subnets
```

Let's verify the configuration:

```
On R4:

R4# show ip route ospf | begin Gate
Gateway of last resort is not set

      1.0.0.0/22 is subnetted, 1 subnets
O IA    1.1.0.0 [110/1564] via 34.1.1.3, 00:22:06, Serial1/3
O IA  2.0.0.0/8 [110/783] via 34.1.1.3, 00:22:06, Serial1/3
O IA  3.0.0.0/8 [110/782] via 34.1.1.3, 00:22:06, Serial1/3
      12.0.0.0/24 is subnetted, 1 subnets
O IA    12.1.1.0 [110/1563] via 34.1.1.3, 00:22:06, Serial1/3
      23.0.0.0/24 is subnetted, 1 subnets
O IA    23.1.1.0 [110/782] via 34.1.1.3, 00:22:06, Serial1/3
```

The output of the preceding **show** command reveals that the loopback0 interface of R1 is summarized. Let's reconfigure the network statement on R1 and verify again:

```
R1(config)# router ospf 1
R1(config-router)# network 1.1.1.1 0.0.0.0 area 1
R1(config-router)# network 1.1.2.1 0.0.0.0 area 1
R1(config-router)# network 1.1.3.1 0.0.0.0 area 1
R1(config-router)# network 12.1.1.1 0.0.0.0 area 1
```

Now let's remove the original **network** statement:

```
R1(config-router)# no network 0.0.0.0 0.0.0.0 area 1
```

Let's view the OSPF configuration after this change:

```
R1# show run | section router ospf
router ospf 1
 router-id 0.0.0.1
 redistribute connected subnets route-map tst
 network 1.1.1.1 0.0.0.0 area 1
 network 1.1.2.1 0.0.0.0 area 1
 network 1.1.3.1 0.0.0.0 area 1
 network 12.1.1.1 0.0.0.0 area 1
```

Now let's verify the configuration:

```
On R4:

R4# show ip route ospf | be Gate
Gateway of last resort is not set

      1.0.0.0/8 is variably subnetted, 2 subnets, 2 masks
O IA     1.1.0.0/22 [110/1564] via 34.1.1.3, 00:25:38, Serial1/3
O E2     1.1.0.0/24 [110/20] via 34.1.1.3, 00:01:12, Serial1/3
O IA  2.0.0.0/8 [110/783] via 34.1.1.3, 00:25:38, Serial1/3
O IA  3.0.0.0/8 [110/782] via 34.1.1.3, 00:25:38, Serial1/3
      12.0.0.0/24 is subnetted, 1 subnets
O IA     12.1.1.0 [110/1563] via 34.1.1.3, 00:25:38, Serial1/3
      23.0.0.0/24 is subnetted, 1 subnets
O IA     23.1.1.0 [110/782] via 34.1.1.3, 00:25:38, Serial1/3
```

Erase the startup config and reload the routers before proceeding to the next lab.

Lab 8-8: OSPF Filtering

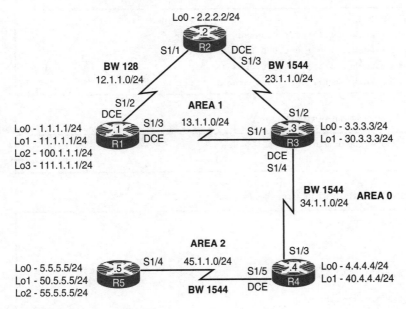

Figure 8-9   *OSPF Filtering*

Figure 8-9 illustrates the topology that will used in the following tasks.

Task 1

Configure R1 and R2's directly connected interfaces, and configure R3's serial
connections to R2 and R1 in Area 1. Configure 0.0.0.1, 0.0.0.2, and 0.0.0.3 to be the
OSPF RIDs of R1, R2, and R3, respectively.

```
On R1:

R1(config)# router ospf 1
R1(config-router)# router-id 0.0.0.1
R1(config-router)# network 12.1.1.1 0.0.0.0 area 1
R1(config-router)# network 13.1.1.1 0.0.0.0 area 1
R1(config-router)# network 1.1.1.1 0.0.0.0 area 1
R1(config-router)# network 11.1.1.1 0.0.0.0 area 1
R1(config-router)# network 100.1.1.1 0.0.0.0 area 1
R1(config-router)# network 111.1.1.1 0.0.0.0 area 1
```

```
On R2:

R2(config)# router ospf 1
R2(config-router)# router-id 0.0.0.2
R2(config-router)# network 12.1.1.2 0.0.0.0 area 1
R2(config-router)# network 23.1.1.2 0.0.0.0 area 1
R2(config-router)# network 2.2.2.2 0.0.0.0 area 1
```

You should see the following console message:

```
%OSPF-5-ADJCHG: Process 1, Nbr 0.0.0.1 on Serial1/1 from LOADING to FULL,
Loading Done
```

```
On R3:

R3(config)# router ospf 1
R3(config-router)# router-id 0.0.0.3
R3(config-router)# network 23.1.1.3 0.0.0.0 area 1
R3(config-router)# network 13.1.1.3 0.0.0.0 area 1
```

You should also see these console messages:

```
%OSPF-5-ADJCHG: Process 1, Nbr 0.0.0.2 on Serial1/2 from LOADING to FULL,
Loading Done

%OSPF-5-ADJCHG: Process 1, Nbr 0.0.0.1 on Serial1/1 from LOADING to FULL,
Loading Done
```

Let's verify the configuration:

```
On R1:

R1# show ip route ospf | begin Gate
Gateway of last resort is not set

      2.0.0.0/32 is subnetted, 1 subnets
O        2.2.2.2 [110/129] via 13.1.1.3, 00:00:29, Serial1/3
      23.0.0.0/24 is subnetted, 1 subnets
O        23.1.1.0 [110/128] via 13.1.1.3, 00:00:29, Serial1/3
```

```
On R3:

R3# show ip route ospf | begin Gate
Gateway of last resort is not set

      1.0.0.0/32 is subnetted, 1 subnets
O        1.1.1.1 [110/65] via 13.1.1.1, 00:01:23, Serial1/1
      2.0.0.0/32 is subnetted, 1 subnets
O        2.2.2.2 [110/65] via 23.1.1.2, 00:01:33, Serial1/2
      11.0.0.0/32 is subnetted, 1 subnets
O        11.1.1.1 [110/65] via 13.1.1.1, 00:01:23, Serial1/1
      12.0.0.0/24 is subnetted, 1 subnets
O        12.1.1.0 [110/845] via 23.1.1.2, 00:01:33, Serial1/2
                  [110/845] via 13.1.1.1, 00:01:23, Serial1/1
      100.0.0.0/32 is subnetted, 1 subnets
O        100.1.1.1 [110/65] via 13.1.1.1, 00:01:23, Serial1/1
      111.0.0.0/32 is subnetted, 1 subnets
O        111.1.1.1 [110/65] via 13.1.1.1, 00:01:23, Serial1/1
```

```
On R2:

R2# show ip route ospf | begin Gate
Gateway of last resort is not set

      1.0.0.0/32 is subnetted, 1 subnets
O        1.1.1.1 [110/129] via 23.1.1.3, 00:02:04, Serial1/3
      11.0.0.0/32 is subnetted, 1 subnets
O        11.1.1.1 [110/129] via 23.1.1.3, 00:02:04, Serial1/3
      13.0.0.0/24 is subnetted, 1 subnets
O        13.1.1.0 [110/128] via 23.1.1.3, 00:02:04, Serial1/3
      100.0.0.0/32 is subnetted, 1 subnets
O        100.1.1.1 [110/129] via 23.1.1.3, 00:02:04, Serial1/3
      111.0.0.0/32 is subnetted, 1 subnets
O        111.1.1.1 [110/129] via 23.1.1.3, 00:02:04, Serial1/3
```

Task 2

Configure the serial connection between R3 and R4 in Area 0. R4's OSPF RID should be
set to 0.0.0.4.

```
On R3:

R3(config)# router ospf 1
R3(config-router)# network 34.1.1.3 0.0.0.0 area 0
```

```
On R4:

R4(config)# router ospf 1
R4(config-router)# router-id 0.0.0.4
R4(config-router)# network 34.1.1.4 0.0.0.0 area 0
```

You should see the following console message:

```
%OSPF-5-ADJCHG: Process 1, Nbr 0.0.0.3 on Serial1/3 from LOADING to FULL,
Loading Done
```

Let's verify the configuration:

```
On R4:

R4# show ip route ospf | begin Gate
Gateway of last resort is not set

      1.0.0.0/32 is subnetted, 1 subnets
O IA     1.1.1.1 [110/129] via 34.1.1.3, 00:00:38, Serial1/3
      2.0.0.0/32 is subnetted, 1 subnets
O IA     2.2.2.2 [110/129] via 34.1.1.3, 00:00:38, Serial1/3
      11.0.0.0/32 is subnetted, 1 subnets
O IA     11.1.1.1 [110/129] via 34.1.1.3, 00:00:38, Serial1/3
      12.0.0.0/24 is subnetted, 1 subnets
O IA     12.1.1.0 [110/909] via 34.1.1.3, 00:00:38, Serial1/3
     13.0.0.0/24 is subnetted, 1 subnets
O IA     13.1.1.0 [110/128] via 34.1.1.3, 00:00:38, Serial1/3
     23.0.0.0/24 is subnetted, 1 subnets
O IA     23.1.1.0 [110/128] via 34.1.1.3, 00:00:38, Serial1/3
      100.0.0.0/32 is subnetted, 1 subnets
O IA     100.1.1.1 [110/129] via 34.1.1.3, 00:00:38, Serial1/3
      111.0.0.0/32 is subnetted, 1 subnets
O IA     111.1.1.1 [110/129] via 34.1.1.3, 00:00:38, Serial1/3
```

Task 3

Configure the serial connection between R4 and R5 in Area 2. R5's OSPF RID should be set to 0.0.0.5.

```
On R4:

R4(config)# router ospf 1
R4(config-router)# network 45.1.1.4 0.0.0.0 area 2
```

```
On R5:

R5(config)# router ospf 1
R5(config-router)# router-id 0.0.0.5
R5(config-router)# network 45.1.1.5 0.0.0.0 area 2
```

You should see the following console message:

```
%OSPF-5-ADJCHG: Process 1, Nbr 0.0.0.4 on Serial1/4 from LOADING to FULL,
Loading Done
```

Let's verify the configuration:

```
On R5:

R5# show ip route ospf | begin Gate
Gateway of last resort is not set

      1.0.0.0/32 is subnetted, 1 subnets
O IA     1.1.1.1 [110/193] via 45.1.1.4, 00:00:43, Serial1/4
      2.0.0.0/32 is subnetted, 1 subnets
O IA     2.2.2.2 [110/193] via 45.1.1.4, 00:00:43, Serial1/4
      11.0.0.0/32 is subnetted, 1 subnets
O IA     11.1.1.1 [110/193] via 45.1.1.4, 00:00:43, Serial1/4
      12.0.0.0/24 is subnetted, 1 subnets
O IA     12.1.1.0 [110/973] via 45.1.1.4, 00:00:43, Serial1/4
      13.0.0.0/24 is subnetted, 1 subnets
O IA     13.1.1.0 [110/192] via 45.1.1.4, 00:00:43, Serial1/4
      23.0.0.0/24 is subnetted, 1 subnets
O IA     23.1.1.0 [110/192] via 45.1.1.4, 00:00:43, Serial1/4
```

```
      34.0.0.0/24 is subnetted, 1 subnets
O IA     34.1.1.0 [110/128] via 45.1.1.4, 00:00:43, Serial1/4
      100.0.0.0/32 is subnetted, 1 subnets
O IA     100.1.1.1 [110/193] via 45.1.1.4, 00:00:43, Serial1/4
      111.0.0.0/32 is subnetted, 1 subnets
O IA     111.1.1.1 [110/193] via 45.1.1.4, 00:00:43, Serial1/4
```

Task 4

Configure the loopback interfaces of R1 and R2 with their correct mask.

```
On R1:

R1(config)# interface range loopback 0 - 3
R1(config-if)# ip ospf network point-to-point
```

```
On R2:

R2(config)# interface lo0
R2(config-if)# ip ospf network point-to-point
```

Let's verify the configuration:

```
On R5:

R5# show ip route ospf | begin Gate
Gateway of last resort is not set


      1.0.0.0/24 is subnetted, 1 subnets
O IA     1.1.1.0 [110/193] via 45.1.1.4, 00:00:37, Serial1/4
      2.0.0.0/24 is subnetted, 1 subnets
O IA     2.2.2.0 [110/193] via 45.1.1.4, 00:00:20, Serial1/4
      11.0.0.0/24 is subnetted, 1 subnets
O IA     11.1.1.0 [110/193] via 45.1.1.4, 00:00:37, Serial1/4
      12.0.0.0/24 is subnetted, 1 subnets
O IA     12.1.1.0 [110/973] via 45.1.1.4, 00:02:26, Serial1/4
      13.0.0.0/24 is subnetted, 1 subnets
O IA     13.1.1.0 [110/192] via 45.1.1.4, 00:02:26, Serial1/4
```

```
        23.0.0.0/24 is subnetted, 1 subnets
O IA     23.1.1.0 [110/192] via 45.1.1.4, 00:02:26, Serial1/4
        34.0.0.0/24 is subnetted, 1 subnets
O IA     34.1.1.0 [110/128] via 45.1.1.4, 00:02:26, Serial1/4
        100.0.0.0/24 is subnetted, 1 subnets
O IA     100.1.1.0 [110/193] via 45.1.1.4, 00:00:37, Serial1/4
        111.0.0.0/24 is subnetted, 1 subnets
O IA     111.1.1.0 [110/193] via 45.1.1.4, 00:00:37, Serial1/4
```

Task 5

Configure R2 to filter network 1.1.1.0/24 from its routing table. Ensure that R3, R4, and R5 have full reachability to this network. You should use an **ip prefix-list** to accomplish this task.

In this case, the following solution only affects the router it's configured on:

```
On R2:

R2(config)# ip prefix-list TST seq 5 deny 1.1.1.0/24
R2(config)# ip prefix-list TST seq 10 permit 0.0.0.0/0 le 32

R2(config)# router ospf 1
R2(config-router)# distribute-list Prefix TST in
```

Let's verify the configuration:

```
On R2:

R2# show ip route 1.1.1.0
% network not in table
```

Note that the **distribute-list in** router configuration mode command can be used when filtering any route on any given router. This command *only* filters the prefix(es) from the local router's routing table and *not* the database. The output of the following **show** command reveals that R2 still has the prefix in its database:

```
R2# show ip ospf database router adv-router 0.0.0.1

        OSPF router with ID (0.0.0.2) (Process ID 1)

            router Link States (Area 1)

  LS age: 383
  Options: (No TOS-capability, DC)
```

```
   LS Type: router Links
   Link State ID: 0.0.0.1
   Advertising Router: 0.0.0.1
   LS Seq Number: 80000009
   Checksum: 0xD11D
   Length: 120
   Number of Links: 8


     Link connected to: a Stub Network
      (Link ID) Network/subnet number: 1.1.1.0
      (Link Data) network Mask: 255.255.255.0
       Number of MTID metrics: 0
        TOS 0 Metrics: 1
(The rest of the output is omitted for brevity)
```

Let's verify and test the configuration:

```
On R3:

R3# ping 1.1.1.1

Type escape sequence to abort.
Sending 5, 100-byte ICMP Echos to 1.1.1.1, timeout is 2 seconds:
!!!!!
Success rate is 100 percent (5/5), round-trip min/avg/max = 28/28/32 ms
```

```
On R4:

R4# ping 1.1.1.1

Type escape sequence to abort.

Sending 5, 100-byte ICMP Echos to 1.1.1.1, timeout is 2 seconds:
!!!!!
Success rate is 100 percent (5/5), round-trip min/avg/max = 80/81/84 ms
```

```
On R5:

R5# ping 1.1.1.1

Type escape sequence to abort.
Sending 5, 100-byte ICMP Echos to 1.1.1.1, timeout is 2 seconds:
!!!!!
Success rate is 100 percent (5/5), round-trip min/avg/max = 128/130/132 ms
```

Task 6

Configure filtering on the appropriate router(s) such that the existing and future routers in Area 2 do not see network 11.1.1.0/24 in their routing table and/or database.

The following method *only* works for filtering Type-3 LSAs. You must remember the following two points:

- LSA Type-3 filtering can only be configured on the ABR(s).

- You must use a prefix list.

The first step is to configure a prefix list to deny network 11.1.1.0/24 and permit everything else:

```
On R4:

R4(config)# ip prefix-list TST seq 5 deny 11.1.1.0/24
R4(config)# ip prefix-list TST seq 10 permit 0.0.0.0/0 le 32
```

The prefix list can reference Area 0 or Area 2. If it references Area 0, the direction must be "out," meaning that you are filtering the prefix out of Area 0. In this case, it will affect the existing and future downstream areas that connect to Area 0.

The prefix can also reference Area 2. If it references Area 2, the direction must be "in," meaning that you are filtering the prefix from getting into Area 2.

In this case, Area 2 is referenced in the command:

```
R4(config)# router ospf 1
R4(config-router)# area 2 filter-list prefix TST in
```

Let's verify the configuration:

```
On R5:

R5# show ip route 11.1.1.0
% network not in table
```

The preceding **show** command reveals that R5 does *not* have the route in its routing table, and the following command verifies that R5 does not have the prefix in its database:

```
R5# show ip ospf database summary 11.1.1.0

              OSPF router with ID (0.0.0.5) (Process ID 1)
```

```
On R4:


R4# show ip route 11.1.1.0


Routing entry for 11.1.1.0/24
  Known via "ospf 1", distance 110, metric 129, type inter area
  Last update from 34.1.1.3 on Serial1/3, 00:21:56 ago
  Routing Descriptor Blocks:
  * 34.1.1.3, from 0.0.0.3, 00:21:56 ago, via Serial1/3
      Route metric is 129, traffic share count is 1
```

Note Even though the output of the preceding **show** command reveals that network 11.1.1.0/24 is in R4's routing table, the output of the following **show** command clearly shows that it's in the database of Area 0 and *not* in the database that belongs to Area 2:

```
R4# show ip ospf database summary 11.1.1.0


              OSPF router with ID (0.0.0.4) (Process ID 1)


                  Summary Net Link States (Area 0)


  Routing Bit Set on this LSA in topology Base with MTID 0
  LS age: 1369
  Options: (No TOS-capability, DC, Upward)
  LS Type: Summary Links(Network)
  Link State ID: 11.1.1.0 (summary network Number)
  Advertising Router: 0.0.0.3
  LS Seq Number: 80000001
  Checksum: 0x5D8E
  Length: 28
  network Mask: /24
        MTID: 0          Metric: 65
```

Let's check another prefix, such as 1.1.1.0/24, and see the difference. This prefix should be in the database of Area 0 and Area 2:

```
R4# show ip ospf database summary 1.1.1.0


              OSPF router with ID (0.0.0.4) (Process ID 1)


                  Summary Net Link States (Area 0)
```

```
Routing Bit Set on this LSA in topology Base with MTID 0
LS age: 1406
Options: (No TOS-capability, DC, Upward)
LS Type: Summary Links(Network)
Link State ID: 1.1.1.0 (summary network Number)
Advertising Router: 0.0.0.3
LS Seq Number: 80000001
Checksum: 0xDF16
Length: 28
network Mask: /24
      MTID: 0          Metric: 65


              Summary Net Link States (Area 2)


LS age: 1405
Options: (No TOS-capability, DC, Upward)
LS Type: Summary Links(Network)
Link State ID: 1.1.1.0 (summary network Number)
Advertising Router: 0.0.0.4
LS Seq Number: 80000001
Checksum: 0x5C58
Length: 28
network Mask: /24
       MTID: 0          Metric: 129
```

You can see that from R4's perspective, network 1.1.1.0/24 shows up in the database of Areas 0 and 2. From Area 0's perspective, the cost is 65; from Area 2's perspective, the cost is 129.

Task 7

Configure the appropriate router such that the routers in Area 0 do not see network 11.1.1.0/24 in their routing table or link state database. You should use the same solution as the one in the previous task, but it should be implemented in the outbound direction.

In the previous task, this network (11.1.1.0/24) was filtered from getting into Area 2. Now, you need to filter it from getting into Area 0. Once this filtering is accomplished, any existing and future area(s) downstream to Area 0 will be affected.

```
On R4:


R4# show ip route 11.1.1.0


Routing entry for 11.1.1.0/24
  Known via "ospf 1", distance 110, metric 129, type inter area
  Last update from 34.1.1.3 on Serial1/3, 00:33:58 ago
  Routing Descriptor Blocks:
  * 34.1.1.3, from 0.0.0.3, 00:33:58 ago, via Serial1/3
      Route metric is 129, traffic share count is 1
```

```
On R3:


R3(config)# ip prefix-list TST seq 5 deny 11.1.1.0/24
R3(config)# ip prefix-list TST seq 10 permit 0.0.0.0/0 le 32


R3(config)# router ospf 1
R3(config-router)# area 1 filter-list prefix TST out
```

Let's verify the configuration. The output of the following command reveals that prefix 11.1.1.0/24 is no longer in the routing table of R4:

```
On R4:


R4# show ip route 11.1.1.0
% network not in table
```

Note   The prefix is still in the routing table of R3, where the filtering was performed, but the prefix is in the routing table of R3 as a route from Area 1 (an intra-area route) and *not* a prefix from Area 0 (from Area 0's perspective this prefix is an inter-area route).

```
On R3:


R3# show ip route 11.1.1.0


Routing entry for 11.1.1.0/24
  Known via "ospf 1", distance 110, metric 65, type intra area
  Last update from 13.1.1.1 on Serial1/1, 00:37:55 ago
  Routing Descriptor Blocks:
  * 13.1.1.1, from 0.0.0.1, 00:37:55 ago, via Serial1/1
      Route metric is 65, traffic share count is 1
```

Let's prove this further:

```
On R3:


R3# show ip ospf database summary 11.1.1.0


            OSPF router with ID (0.0.0.3) (Process ID 1)
```

Note that the output of the preceding **show** command reveals that network 11.1.1.0 /24 is *not* in Area 0. If it was in Area 0, it would have been in the link state database of this router as a summary LSA or Type-3 LSA. However, the following **show** command reveals that the prefix is in Area 1 as a router LSA or Type-1 LSA.

```
R3# show ip ospf database router | include Area 1|_11.1.1.0


            Router Link States (Area 1)
    (Link ID) Network/subnet number: 11.1.1.0
```

Task 8

Configure the appropriate router(s) to filter network 111.1.1.0/24 such that the routers in Area 0 or Area 2 do *not* have this network in their routing table or database. Use the minimum number of commands to accomplish this task.

The output of the following **show** command verifies that network 111.1.1.0/24 is in the database of R3 belonging to Area 1 as a router LSA or Type-1 LSA:

```
On R3:


R3# show ip ospf database router | Include Area 1|_111.1.1.0


            router Link States (Area 1)
    (Link ID) Network/subnet number: 111.1.1.0
```

The output of the following **show** command reveals that prefix 111.1.1.0/24 is also in the database of R3 as a summary LSA or Type-3 LSA, but from Area 0's perspective:

```
R3# show ip ospf database summary 111.1.1.0


            OSPF router with ID (0.0.0.3) (Process ID 1)


            Summary Net Link States (Area 0)
```

```
LS age: 120

Options: (No TOS-capability, DC, Upward)

LS Type: Summary Links(Network)

Link State ID: 111.1.1.0 (summary network Number)

Advertising Router: 0.0.0.3

LS Seq Number: 80000003

Checksum: 0x4045

Length: 28

network Mask: /24

     MTID: 0           Metric: 65
```

The following command reveals that prefix 111.1.1.0/24 is in the routing table of R3 as an intra-area route:

```
R3# show ip route ospf | include 111.1.1.0


O         111.1.1.0 [110/65] via 13.1.1.1, 01:07:30, Serial1/1


R3# show ip ospf route | Inc 111.1.1.0/24


*>  111.1.1.0/24, Intra, cost 65, area 1
```

The following OSPF filtering mechanism works only on intra-area routes. It instructs the router not to generate a Type-3 LSA for this prefix.

```
On R3:


R3(config)# router ospf 1
R3(config-router)# area 1 range 111.1.1.0 255.255.255.0 not-advertise
```

Note that, as stated earlier, the **area range not-advertise** command stops the generation of Type-3 LSAs, and this is why you see the prefix in the routing table of R3 as an intra-area route:

```
R3# show ip route 111.1.1.0


Routing entry for 111.1.1.0/24
  Known via "ospf 1", distance 110, metric 65, type intra area
  Last update from 13.1.1.1 on Serial1/1, 00:00:27 ago


  Routing Descriptor Blocks:
  * 13.1.1.1, from 0.0.0.1, 00:00:27 ago, via Serial1/1
      Route metric is 65, traffic share count is 1
```

The prefix is no longer in the database of R3 as Type-3 LSAs, which means that the routers in Area 0 or any other area downstream of Area 0 will not have this prefix in their routing table or their link state database.

```
R3# show ip ospf database summary 111.1.1.0

              OSPF router with ID (0.0.0.3) (Process ID 1)


R3# show ip ospf database router | Inc Area 1|_111.1.1.0

              router Link States (Area 1)
     (Link ID) Network/subnet number: 111.1.1.0
```

```
On R4 or R5:


Rx# show ip route 111.1.1.0

% network not in table
```

Task 9

Configure the appropriate routers such that none of the routers except R1 can see network 100.1.1.0/24 in their routing table; do *not* stop advertising this network. You should use a distribute list to accomplish this task.

You should always display the existing access lists and distribute lists before configuring one:

```
On R2:


R2# Show ip prefix-list

ip prefix-list TST: 2 entries
    seq 5 deny 1.1.1.0/24
    seq 10 permit 0.0.0.0/0 le 32


R2# show run | section router ospf 1

router ospf 1

 router-id 0.0.0.2
 log-adjacency-changes
 network 2.2.2.2 0.0.0.0 area 1
 network 12.1.1.2 0.0.0.0 area 1
 network 23.1.1.2 0.0.0.0 area 1
 distribute-list prefix TST in
```

Note The preceding **show** command verifies that there is already a **distribute-list** configured in the router configuration mode; therefore, you should try to modify the existing **prefix-list** that is applied by the existing **distribute-list**.

```
R2(config)# ip prefix-list TST seq 7 deny 100.1.1.0/24
```

Let's view the prefix list after this addition:

```
On R2:

R2# show run | Include ip pref

ip prefix-list TST seq 5 deny 1.1.1.0/24
ip prefix-list TST seq 7 deny 100.1.1.0/24
ip prefix-list TST seq 10 permit 0.0.0.0/0 le 32
```

Now let's verify the configuration:

```
On R2:

R2# show ip route 100.1.1.0

% network not in table
```

Let's check R3:

```
On R3:

R3# show ip prefix-list

ip prefix-list TST: 2 entries
   seq 5 deny 11.1.1.0/24
   seq 10 permit 0.0.0.0/0 le 32

R3# show run | section ospf

router ospf 1

 router-id 0.0.0.3
```

```
area 1 range 111.1.1.0 255.255.255.0 not-advertise
area 1 filter-list prefix TST out
network 13.1.1.3 0.0.0.0 area 1
network 23.1.1.3 0.0.0.0 area 1
network 34.1.1.3 0.0.0.0 area 0

R3# show ip route | Include 100.1.1.0

O        100.1.1.0 [110/65] via 13.1.1.1, 00:08:38, Serial1/1
```

Let's configure R3:

```
R3(config)# ip prefix-list NET seq 5 deny 100.1.1.0/24
R3(config)# ip prefix-list NET seq 10 permit 0.0.0.0/0 LE 32

R3(config)# router ospf 1
R3(config-router)# distribute-list prefix NET in
```

Now let's verify the configuration:

```
On R3:

R3# show ip route ospf | Include 100.1.1.0
```

On R4, the **distance** command can be used to reference network 100.1.1.0/24 in **access-list 1**, and the **distance** command sets the AD of the network referenced in **access-list 1** to 255 sourcing from R3 (0.0.0.3 0.0.0.0); AD of 255 is unreachable and won't be injected into the routing table:

```
 On R4:

R4(config)# access-list 1 permit 100.1.1.0 0.0.0.255

R4(config)# router ospf 1
R4(config-router)# distance 255 0.0.0.3 0.0.0.0 1
```

```
On R5:

R5# show ip route 100.1.1.0 255.255.255.0

% network not in table

R5# show ip ospf database summary 100.1.1.0

            OSPF router with ID (0.0.0.5) (Process ID 1)
```

Note that the preceding solution utilizes the behavior of OSPF when prefixes are advertised from Area 0 into a non-zero area; when inter-area prefixes are advertised from Area 0 into other areas, the behavior is like an internal redistribution. Basically, if R4 does not have the route in its routing table, it will not redistribute the route into Area 2; therefore, R5 or any other router in Area 2 will not see the prefix(es) in its routing table or database.

Task 10

Configure R5 to redistribute the loopback0, 1, and 2 interfaces into the OSPF routing domain using the default cost.

```
On R5:

R5(config)# route-map TST permit 10
R5(config-route-map)# match interface lo0 lo1 lo2

R5(config)# router ospf 1
R5(config-router)# redistribute connected subnets route-map TST
```

Let's verify the configuration:

```
On R4:

R4# show ip route ospf | Include E2
       E1 - OSPF external type 1, E2 - OSPF external type 2

O E2     5.5.5.0 [110/20] via 45.1.1.5, 00:00:08, Serial1/5
O E2     50.5.5.0 [110/20] via 45.1.1.5, 00:00:08, Serial1/5
O E2     55.5.5.0 [110/20] via 45.1.1.5, 00:00:08, Serial1/5
```

Task 11

Configure the appropriate router such that none of the routers except R5 can see network 5.5.5.0/24 in their routing table.

```
On R5:


R5(config)# ip prefix-list NET seq 5 deny 5.5.5.0/24
R5(config)# ip prefix-list NET seq 10 permit 0.0.0.0/0 LE 32


R5(config)# router ospf 1
R5(config-router)# distribute-list prefix NET OUT
```

Let's verify the configuration:

```
On R4:


R4# show ip route ospf | Include E2
       E1 - OSPF external type 1, E2 - OSPF external type 2


O E2    50.5.5.0 [110/20] via 45.1.1.5, 00:02:07, Serial1/5
O E2    55.5.5.0 [110/20] via 45.1.1.5, 00:02:07, Serial1/5
```

```
On R1:


R1# show ip route ospf | Include E2
       E1 - OSPF external type 1, E2 - OSPF external type 2


O E2    50.5.5.0 [110/20] via 13.1.1.3, 00:02:55, Serial1/3
O E2    55.5.5.0 [110/20] via 13.1.1.3, 00:02:55, Serial1/3
```

Note that this is the only scenario where the **distribute-list OUT** command works in OSPF. This command must be configured on the ASBR; otherwise, it will not have any effect whatsoever. This command filters external routes.

```
R5# show ip ospf database external | Include 5


           OSPF router with ID (0.0.0.5) (Process ID 1)
             Type-5 AS External Link States
Link State ID: 50.5.5.0 (External network Number )
Advertising Router: 0.0.0.5
Checksum: 0xC995
Link State ID: 55.5.5.0 (External network Number )
Advertising Router: 0.0.0.5
```

Task 12

Configure the appropriate router such that none of the routers except R5 can see network 50.5.5.0/24 in their routing table or database. You should not use the solution that was implemented in the previous task.

The following command is used to filter the external routes ("E" and/or "N"). This command must be configured on an ASBR or the router that originated the external route(s), and when configured, it filters the specified prefix from the OSPF link state database.

```
On R5:

R5(config)# router ospf 1
R5(config-router)# summary-address 50.5.5.0 255.255.255.0 not-advertise
```

The following **show** command reveals that network 50.5.5.0/24 is not in the link state database of R5:

```
R5# show ip ospf database external | Include 5

            OSPF router with ID (0.0.0.5) (Process ID 1)
              Type-5 AS External Link States
   Link State ID: 55.5.5.0 (External network Number )
   Advertising Router: 0.0.0.5
```

Let's verify the configuration:

```
On R4:

R4# show ip route 50.5.5.0

% network not in table
```

```
On R1:

R1# show ip route 50.5.5.0

% network not in table
```

Task 13

Configure the appropriate router such that R1 does not have network 55.5.5.0/24 in its routing table.

Let's view R1's existing routing table:

```
On R1:

R1# show ip route 55.5.5.0

Routing entry for 55.5.5.0/24
  Known via "ospf 1", distance 110, metric 20, type extern 2, forward metric 192
  Last update from 13.1.1.3 on Serial1/3, 00:10:17 ago
  Routing Descriptor Blocks:
  * 13.1.1.3, from 0.0.0.5, 00:10:17 ago, via Serial1/3
      Route metric is 20, traffic share count is 1
```

Note   There is no **access-list** or **ip prefix-list** configured on this router:

```
R1# show access-list

R1# show ip prefix-list

R1(config)# ip prefix-list NET seq 5 deny 55.5.5.0/24
R1(config)# ip prefix-list NET seq 10 permit 0.0.0.0/0 LE 32
R1(config)# router ospf 1
R1(config-router)# distribute-list prefix NET in
```

Let's verify the configuration:

```
On R1:

R1# show ip route 55.5.5.0

% network not in table
```

Task 14

Remove any filtering used in the previous tasks. If this configuration is performed successfully, all the routers in this routing domain should have every route advertised and redistributed in this lab.

```
On R1:


R1(config)# No ip prefix NET


R1(config)# router ospf 1
R1(config-router)# No distribute-list prefix NET in


R1# Show run | section router ospf

router ospf 1
 router-id 0.0.0.1
 network 1.1.1.1 0.0.0.0 area 1
 network 11.1.1.1 0.0.0.0 area 1
 network 12.1.1.1 0.0.0.0 area 1
 network 13.1.1.1 0.0.0.0 area 1
 network 100.1.1.1 0.0.0.0 area 1
 network 111.1.1.1 0.0.0.0 area 1
```

```
On R2:


R2(config)# No ip prefix-list TST


R2(config)# router ospf 1
R2(config-router)# No distribute-list prefix TST in


R2# show run | section ospf
ip ospf network point-to-point
router ospf 1
 router-id 0.0.0.2
 network 2.2.2.2 0.0.0.0 area 1
 network 12.1.1.2 0.0.0.0 area 1
 network 23.1.1.2 0.0.0.0 area 1
```

```
On R3:

R3(config)# No ip prefix-list NET
R3(config)# No ip prefix-list TST

R3(config)# router ospf 1
R3(config-router)# No area 1 range 111.1.1.0 255.255.255.0 not-advertise
R3(config-router)# No distribute-list prefix NET in
R3(config-router)# No area 1 filter-list prefix TST out

R3# Show run | section ospf

router ospf 1
 router-id 0.0.0.3
 network 13.1.1.3 0.0.0.0 area 1
 network 23.1.1.3 0.0.0.0 area 1
 network 34.1.1.3 0.0.0.0 area 0
```

```
On R4:

R4(config)# No ip prefix-list TST
R4(config)# No access-list 1

R4(config)# router ospf 1
R4(config-router)# No distance 255 0.0.0.3 0.0.0.0 1
R4(config-router)# No area 2 filter-list prefix TST in

R4# show run | section ospf

router ospf 1
 router-id 0.0.0.4
 network 34.1.1.4 0.0.0.0 area 0
 network 45.1.1.4 0.0.0.0 area 2
```

```
On R5:

R5(config)# No ip prefix-list NET

R5(config)# router ospf 1
R5(config-router)# No distribute-list prefix NET out
R5(config-router)# No summary-address 50.5.5.0 255.255.255.0 not-advertise
```

```
R5# show run | section ospf

router ospf 1
 router-id 0.0.0.5
 summary-address 50.5.5.0 255.255.255.0
 redistribute connected subnets route-map TST
 network 45.1.1.5 0.0.0.0 area 2
```

Let's verify the configuration:

```
On R4:

R4# show ip route ospf | begin Gate
Gateway of last resort is not set


      1.0.0.0/24 is subnetted, 1 subnets
O IA    1.1.1.0 [110/129] via 34.1.1.3, 00:04:14, Serial1/3
      2.0.0.0/24 is subnetted, 1 subnets
O IA    2.2.2.0 [110/129] via 34.1.1.3, 00:04:14, Serial1/3
      5.0.0.0/24 is subnetted, 1 subnets
O E2    5.5.5.0 [110/20] via 45.1.1.5, 00:02:45, Serial1/5
      11.0.0.0/24 is subnetted, 1 subnets
O IA    11.1.1.0 [110/129] via 34.1.1.3, 00:04:14, Serial1/3
      12.0.0.0/24 is subnetted, 1 subnets
O IA    12.1.1.0 [110/909] via 34.1.1.3, 00:04:14, Serial1/3
      13.0.0.0/24 is subnetted, 1 subnets
O IA    13.1.1.0 [110/128] via 34.1.1.3, 00:04:14, Serial1/3
      23.0.0.0/24 is subnetted, 1 subnets
O IA    23.1.1.0 [110/128] via 34.1.1.3, 00:04:14, Serial1/3
      50.0.0.0/24 is subnetted, 1 subnets
O E2    50.5.5.0 [110/20] via 45.1.1.5, 00:02:12, Serial1/5
      55.0.0.0/24 is subnetted, 1 subnets
O E2    55.5.5.0 [110/20] via 45.1.1.5, 00:04:14, Serial1/5
      100.0.0.0/24 is subnetted, 1 subnets
O IA    100.1.1.0 [110/129] via 34.1.1.3, 00:04:14, Serial1/3
      111.0.0.0/24 is subnetted, 1 subnets
O IA    111.1.1.0 [110/129] via 34.1.1.3, 00:04:14, Serial1/3
```

```
On R3:


R5# show ip route ospf | begin Gate
Gateway of last resort is not set


      1.0.0.0/24 is subnetted, 1 subnets
O        1.1.1.0 [110/65] via 13.1.1.1, 00:07:02, Serial1/1
      2.0.0.0/24 is subnetted, 1 subnets
O        2.2.2.0 [110/65] via 23.1.1.2, 00:07:02, Serial1/2
      5.0.0.0/24 is subnetted, 1 subnets
O E2  5.5.5.0 [110/20] via 34.1.1.4, 00:03:48, Serial1/4
      11.0.0.0/24 is subnetted, 1 subnets
O        11.1.1.0 [110/65] via 13.1.1.1, 00:07:02, Serial1/1
      12.0.0.0/24 is subnetted, 1 subnets
O        12.1.1.0 [110/845] via 23.1.1.2, 00:07:02, Serial1/2


                  [110/845] via 13.1.1.1, 00:07:02, Serial1/1
      45.0.0.0/24 is subnetted, 1 subnets
O IA     45.1.1.0 [110/128] via 34.1.1.4, 00:07:02, Serial1/4
      50.0.0.0/24 is subnetted, 1 subnets
O E2  50.5.5.0 [110/20] via 34.1.1.4, 00:03:15, Serial1/4
      55.0.0.0/24 is subnetted, 1 subnets
O E2  55.5.5.0 [110/20] via 34.1.1.4, 00:07:02, Serial1/4
      100.0.0.0/24 is subnetted, 1 subnets
O        100.1.1.0 [110/65] via 13.1.1.1, 00:07:02, Serial1/1
      111.0.0.0/24 is subnetted, 1 subnets
O        111.1.1.0 [110/65] via 13.1.1.1, 00:07:02, Serial1/1
```

```
On R2:


R3# show ip route ospf | begin Gate
Gateway of last resort is not set


      1.0.0.0/24 is subnetted, 1 subnets
O        1.1.1.0 [110/129] via 23.1.1.3, 00:10:15, Serial1/3
      5.0.0.0/24 is subnetted, 1 subnets
O E2  5.5.5.0 [110/20] via 23.1.1.3, 00:04:28, Serial1/3
      11.0.0.0/24 is subnetted, 1 subnets
O        11.1.1.0 [110/129] via 23.1.1.3, 00:10:15, Serial1/3
      13.0.0.0/24 is subnetted, 1 subnets
O        13.1.1.0 [110/128] via 23.1.1.3, 00:10:15, Serial1/3
      34.0.0.0/24 is subnetted, 1 subnets
O IA     34.1.1.0 [110/128] via 23.1.1.3, 00:10:15, Serial1/3
```

```
      45.0.0.0/24 is subnetted, 1 subnets
O IA     45.1.1.0 [110/192] via 23.1.1.3, 00:10:15, Serial1/3
      50.0.0.0/24 is subnetted, 1 subnets
O E2     50.5.5.0 [110/20] via 23.1.1.3, 00:03:56, Serial1/3
      55.0.0.0/24 is subnetted, 1 subnets
O E2     55.5.5.0 [110/20] via 23.1.1.3, 00:10:15, Serial1/3
      100.0.0.0/24 is subnetted, 1 subnets
O        100.1.1.0 [110/129] via 23.1.1.3, 00:10:15, Serial1/3
      111.0.0.0/24 is subnetted, 1 subnets
O        111.1.1.0 [110/129] via 23.1.1.3, 00:10:15, Serial1/3
```

Task 15

Advertise the Lo0 interface of R3 in Area 1, the Lo1 interfaces of R3 and R4 in Area 0, and the Lo0 interface of R4 in Area 2. These loopback interfaces must be advertised with their correct mask.

```
On R3:

R3(config)# interface range loopback 0 - 1
R3(config-if-range)# ip ospf net point-to-point

R3(config-if)# router ospf 1
R3(config-router)# network 3.3.3.3 0.0.0.0 area 1
R3(config-router)# network 30.3.3.3 0.0.0.0 area 0
```

```
On R4:

R4(config)# interface range loopback 0 - 1
R4(config-if-range)# ip ospf network point-to-point

R4(config-if)# router ospf 1
R4(config-router)# network 4.4.4.4 0.0.0.0 area 2
R4(config-router)# network 40.4.4.4 0.0.0.0 area 0
```

Let's verify the configuration:

```
On R1:

R1# show ip route ospf | begin Gate
Gateway of last resort is not set

      2.0.0.0/24 is subnetted, 1 subnets
O        2.2.2.0 [110/129] via 13.1.1.3, 00:15:41, Serial1/3
```

```
         3.0.0.0/24 is subnetted, 1 subnets
O          3.3.3.0 [110/65] via 13.1.1.3, 00:01:35, Serial1/3
         4.0.0.0/24 is subnetted, 1 subnets
O IA     4.4.4.0 [110/129] via 13.1.1.3, 00:00:19, Serial1/3
         5.0.0.0/24 is subnetted, 1 subnets
O E2     5.5.5.0 [110/20] via 13.1.1.3, 00:08:47, Serial1/3
         23.0.0.0/24 is subnetted, 1 subnets
O          23.1.1.0 [110/128] via 13.1.1.3, 00:15:41, Serial1/3
         30.0.0.0/24 is subnetted, 1 subnets
O IA     30.3.3.0 [110/65] via 13.1.1.3, 00:01:18, Serial1/3
         34.0.0.0/24 is subnetted, 1 subnets

O IA     34.1.1.0 [110/128] via 13.1.1.3, 00:15:41, Serial1/3
         40.0.0.0/24 is subnetted, 1 subnets
O IA     40.4.4.0 [110/129] via 13.1.1.3, 00:00:14, Serial1/3
         45.0.0.0/24 is subnetted, 1 subnets
O IA     45.1.1.0 [110/192] via 13.1.1.3, 00:15:41, Serial1/3
         50.0.0.0/24 is subnetted, 1 subnets
O E2     50.5.5.0 [110/20] via 13.1.1.3, 00:08:14, Serial1/3
         55.0.0.0/24 is subnetted, 1 subnets
O E2     55.5.5.0 [110/20] via 13.1.1.3, 00:15:41, Serial1/3
```

Task 16

Configure the appropriate router(s) such that the routers in Area 2 do not see any of the networks advertised by any of the routers in this topology, but routers R1, R2, R3, and R4 should see all the networks advertised by the existing and future router(s) advertised in Area 2.

By default, all outgoing LSAs are flooded to the interface. The following configuration prevents flooding of *all* OSPF LSAs out of a given interface (in this case, R4's S1/5 interface):

```
On R4:

R4(config)# interface Serial 1/5
R4(config-subif)# ip ospf database-filter all out
```

For this filtering mechanism to work, the OSPF process must be cleared:

```
On R5:

R5# Clear ip ospf proc
Reset ALL OSPF processes? [no]: y
```

Note R4 and R5 are still maintaining their neighbor adjacency:

```
R5# Sh ip ospf neighbor


neighbor ID    Pri   State        Dead Time    Address      Interface
0.0.0.4          0   FULL/  -     00:00:39     45.1.1.4     Serial1/4
```

You can see that R5 does not have any of the routes from the other routers; this includes R4's routes that are advertised within the same area. Remember that the filtering is done on the S1/5 interface of R4, meaning that all LSAs (regardless of their area) are filtered.

```
On R5:


R5# show ip route ospf | begin Gate
Gateway of last resort is not set
```

Note that R1 has all the routes, including the ones advertised by R5:

```
On R1:


R1# show ip route ospf | begin Gate
Gateway of last resort is not set


     2.0.0.0/24 is subnetted, 1 subnets
O       2.2.2.0 [110/129] via 13.1.1.3, 00:20:22, Serial1/3
     3.0.0.0/24 is subnetted, 1 subnets
O       3.3.3.0 [110/65] via 13.1.1.3, 00:06:16, Serial1/3
     4.0.0.0/24 is subnetted, 1 subnets
O IA    4.4.4.0 [110/129] via 13.1.1.3, 00:05:00, Serial1/3
     5.0.0.0/24 is subnetted, 1 subnets
O E2    5.5.5.0 [110/20] via 13.1.1.3, 00:01:59, Serial1/3
     23.0.0.0/24 is subnetted, 1 subnets
O       23.1.1.0 [110/128] via 13.1.1.3, 00:20:22, Serial1/3
     30.0.0.0/24 is subnetted, 1 subnets
O IA    30.3.3.0 [110/65] via 13.1.1.3, 00:05:59, Serial1/3
     34.0.0.0/24 is subnetted, 1 subnets
O IA    34.1.1.0 [110/128] via 13.1.1.3, 00:20:22, Serial1/3
     40.0.0.0/24 is subnetted, 1 subnets
O IA    40.4.4.0 [110/129] via 13.1.1.3, 00:04:55, Serial1/3
     45.0.0.0/24 is subnetted, 1 subnets
O IA    45.1.1.0 [110/192] via 13.1.1.3, 00:20:22, Serial1/3
     50.0.0.0/24 is subnetted, 1 subnets
O E2    50.5.5.0 [110/20] via 13.1.1.3, 00:01:59, Serial1/3
     55.0.0.0/24 is subnetted, 1 subnets
O E2    55.5.5.0 [110/20] via 13.1.1.3, 00:01:59, Serial1/3
```

Erase the startup configuration of the routers and reload them before proceeding to the next lab.

Lab 8-9: Virtual Links and GRE Tunnels

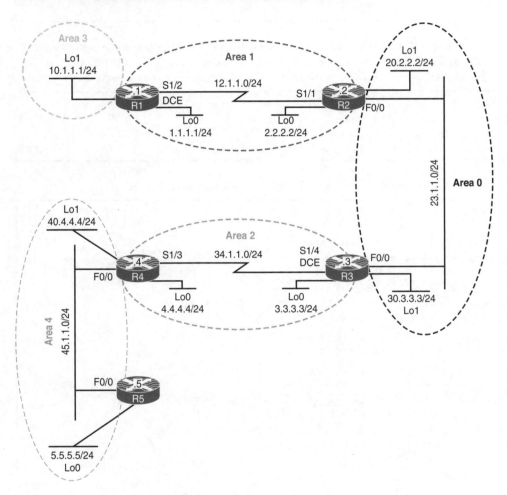

Figure 8-10   *Virtual Links and GRE Tunnels*

Figure 8-10 illustrates the topology that will used in the following tasks.

The same rules governing how all OSPF areas must be adjacent to Area 0 are maintained in OSPFv3. To maintain a logical capacity to support this, we have the same tools we used in OSPFv2. Virtual links are among the most efficient ways to maintain this adjacency to Area 0, even in OSPFv3. Remember that we are using the 32-bit address from a loopback interface or from a manually configured router ID, so this process will look exactly like it does on OSPFv2.

Let's create a loopback100 interface on R4 and assign it an IPv6 address. This loopback will be advertised in OSPF Area 2.

```
R4(config)# interface loopback 100
R4(config-if)# ipv6 address 44:44:44:44::44/64
R4(config-if)# ipv6 ospf 1 area 2
R4(config-if)# ipv6 ospf network point-to-point
R4(config-if)# !
R4(config-if)# ipv6 router ospf 1
R4(config-rtr)# area 1 virtual-link 1.1.1.1
```

Now we will go to R1 to complete the link:

```
R1# conf t
Enter configuration commands, one per line.  End with CNTL/Z.
R1(config)# !
R1(config)# ipv6 router ospf 1
R1(config-rtr)# area 1 virtual-link 4.4.4.4
R1(config-rtr)# end
```

You can see the status of the virtual link via the console messages on R1 and R4:

```
R1(config-rtr)#
%OSPFv3-5-ADJCHG: Process 1, Nbr 4.4.4.4 on OSPFv3_VL0 from LOADING to FULL,
Loading Done
```

```
R4(config-rtr)#
%OSPFv3-5-ADJCHG: Process 1, Nbr 1.1.1.1 on OSPFv3_VL0 from LOADING to FULL,
Loading Done
```

Once the virtual link is operational, you should now see the 44:44:44:44::44/64 prefix on R2:

```
R2# show ipv6 route ospf
IPv6 Routing Table - Default - 13 entries
Codes: C - Connected, L - Local, S - Static, U - Per-user Static route
       B - BGP, M - MIPv6, R - RIP, I1 - ISIS L1
       I2 - ISIS L2, IA - ISIS interarea, IS - ISIS summary, D - EIGRP
       EX - EIGRP external
       O - OSPF Intra, OI - OSPF Inter, OE1 - OSPF ext 1, OE2 - OSPF ext 2
       ON1 - OSPF NSSA ext 1, ON2 - OSPF NSSA ext 2
O   1:1:1:1::/64 [110/2]
     via FE80::1, FastEthernet0/0
```

```
Q   3:3:3:3::/64 [110/2]
     via FE80::3, FastEthernet0/0
OI  4:4:4:4::/64 [110/783]
     via FE80::3, FastEthernet0/0
     via FE80::1, FastEthernet0/0
OI  4:4:4:4::4/128 [110/782]
     via FE80::3, FastEthernet0/0
     via FE80::1, FastEthernet0/0
OI  10:1:41::/64 [110/782]
     via FE80::1, FastEthernet0/0
OI  10:1:41::1/128 [110/1]
     via FE80::1, FastEthernet0/0
OI  10:1:43::/64 [110/782]
     via FE80::3, FastEthernet0/0
OI  44:44:44:44::/64 [110/783]
     via FE80::1, FastEthernet0/0
```

Let's remove the virtual link configuration and stop advertising loopback100 into OSPF before we move any further in our command exploration:

```
R4(config)# interface loopback 100
R4(config-if)# ipv6 address 44:44:44:44::44/64
R4(config-if)# no ipv6 ospf 1 area 2
R4(config-if)# no ipv6 ospf network point-to-point
R4(config-if)# !
```

We need to remove the virtual link from R2 as well:

```
R4(config)# interface loopback 100
R4(config-if)# ipv6 address 44:44:44:44::44/64
R4(config-if)# no ipv6 ospf 1 area 2
R4(config-if)# no ipv6 ospf network point-to-point
```

Task 1

Configure OSPF based on Table 8-3.

Table 8-3 *Configure OSPF*

Router	Interface	OSPF Area	Router ID
R1	Lo0	1	0.0.0.1
	S1/2	1	
	Lo1	3	
R2	Lo0	1	0.0.0.2
	S1/1	1	
	f0/0	0	
	Lo1	0	
R3	Lo1	0	0.0.0.3
	f0/0	0	
	S1/4	2	
	Lo0	2	
R4	S1/3	2	0.0.0.4
	Lo0	2	
	Lo1	4	
	f0/0	4	
R5	f0/0	4	0.0.0.5
	Lo0	4	

```
On R1:

R1(config)# router ospf 1
R1(config-router)# router-id 0.0.0.1
R1(config-router)# network 10.1.1.1 0.0.0.0 are 3
R1(config-router)# network 12.1.1.1 0.0.0.0 are 1
R1(config-router)# network 1.1.1.1 0.0.0.0 are 1
```

```
On R2:

R2(config)# router ospf 1
R2(config-router)# router-id 0.0.0.2
R2(config-router)# network 12.1.1.2 0.0.0.0 are 1
R2(config-router)# network 2.2.2.2 0.0.0.0 are 1
R2(config-router)# network 23.1.1.2 0.0.0.0 are 0
R2(config-router)# network 20.2.2.2 0.0.0.0 are 0
```

You should see the following console message:

```
%OSPF-5-ADJCHG: Process 1, Nbr 0.0.0.1 on Serial1/1 from LOADING to FULL,
Loading Done
```

```
On R3:

R3(config-if)# router ospf 1
R3(config-router)# router-id 0.0.0.3
R3(config-router)# network 23.1.1.3 0.0.0.0 are 0
R3(config-router)# network 3.3.3.3 0.0.0.0 are 2
R3(config-router)# network 34.1.1.3 0.0.0.0 are 2
R3(config-router)# network 30.3.3.3 0.0.0.0 are 0
```

You should see the following console message:

```
%OSPF-5-ADJCHG: Process 1, Nbr 0.0.0.2 on FastEthernet0/0 from LOADING to FULL,
Loading Done
```

```
On R4:

R4(config)# router ospf 1
R4(config-router)# router-id 0.0.0.4
R4(config-router)# network 34.1.1.4 0.0.0.0 area 2
R4(config-router)# network 4.4.4.4 0.0.0.0 are 2
R4(config-router)# network 45.1.1.4 0.0.0.0 are 4
R4(config-router)# network 40.4.4.4 0.0.0.0 are 4
```

You should also see this console message:

```
%OSPF-5-ADJCHG: Process 1, Nbr 0.0.0.3 on Serial1/3 from LOADING to FULL,
Loading Done
```

The following console message states that a virtual link is needed but it is not configured:

```
%OSPF-4-ERRRCV: Received invalid packet: mismatched area ID, from backbone area
must be virtual-link but not found from 23.1.1.3, FastEthernet0/0
```

```
On R5:

R5(config)# router ospf 1
R5(config-router)# router-id 0.0.0.5
R5(config-router)# network 45.1.1.5 0.0.0.0 are 4
R5(config-router)# network 5.5.5.5 0.0.0.0 are 4
```

Finally, you should see the following console message:

```
%OSPF-5-ADJCHG: Process 1, Nbr 0.0.0.4 on FastEthernet0/0 from LOADING to FULL,
Loading Done
```

Task 2

Ensure that the networks from Area 3 are reachable by R2, R3, and R4. Do not use a GRE tunnel to accomplish this task.

In OSPF, every non-zero area *must* be connected to Area 0 (the backbone area). This connection can be a physical or a logical connection. The area through which the virtual link is configured is called the *transit area*, and this area must have full routing information and can't be a stub area of any kind.

When the virtual link is first configured, it is in the down state because R1 (0.0.0.1) and R2 (0.0.0.2) don't have network layer reachability information (NLRI) to each other; therefore, all the LSAs need to be flooded and the SPF algorithm needs to be calculated so that these routers know how to reach each other through Area 1. Once the routers have NLRI for each other, they form an adjacency across the virtual link.

It is important to note that the OSPF packets between the endpoints of the virtual link are *not* multicast packets; they are tunneled packets from 12.1.1.1 (R1) to 12.1.1.2 (R2), or vice versa.

The virtual link configuration must be performed on the ABRs, and if one of the endpoints is not an ABR, the virtual link will not transition into the up state; to be a backbone (BB) router, there must be a minimum of one link in the BB area. Once the routers form an adjacency on the virtual link, R1 becomes a backbone router; once R1 becomes a BB router, because it has another connection to Area 3, it becomes an ABR.

Because Area 3 is *not* connected to Area 0, the routers in the other areas won't be able to see the route(s) advertised by this area; therefore, a virtual link or a GRE tunnel must be configured to connect R1 (the router that connects Area 3 to Area 1) to R2 in Area 0.

Use the following steps to configure a virtual link:

Step 1.   Because the virtual link is terminated on the ABRs using their router IDs, the router ID of these routers must be determined:

```
On R1:


R1# show ip ospf | include ID
 Routing Process "ospf 1" with ID 0.0.0.1
```

```
On R2:


R2# show ip ospf | include ID

 Routing Process "ospf 1" with ID 0.0.0.2
```

Step 2.   Ensure that the router IDs are stable, meaning that they are statically configured on the routers—unless you are in the CCIE lab and are asked not to configure the router IDs. Even though in this case this can be bypassed (because the router IDs are 0.0.0.x, where x is the router number), it is still a good practice to go through so that you have a process.

```
On R1:


R1# show run | section router ospf


router ospf 1
 router-id 0.0.0.1
 network 1.1.1.1 0.0.0.0 area 1
 network 10.1.1.1 0.0.0.0 area 3
 network 12.1.1.1 0.0.0.0 area 1
```

```
On R2:


R2# show run | section router ospf


router ospf 1
 router-id 0.0.0.2
 network 2.2.2.2 0.0.0.0 area 1
 network 12.1.1.2 0.0.0.0 area 1
 network 20.2.2.2 0.0.0.0 area 0
 network 23.1.1.2 0.0.0.0 area 0
```

Step 3. Ensure that the transit area is not a stub. Based on the preceding **show** command, you can see that the transit area, Area 1, is not a stub area.

Step 4. Configure the virtual links:

```
On R1:


R1(config)# router ospf 1
R1(config-router)# area 1 virtual-link 0.0.0.2
```

You should see the following console message every hello interval. These messages should stop once the virtual link is configured successfully:

```
On R2:


%OSPF-4-ERRRCV: Received invalid packet: mismatched area ID, from backbone area
must be virtual-link but not found from 12.1.1.1, Serial1/1


R2(config)# router ospf 1
R2(config-router)# area 1 virtual-link 0.0.0.1
```

You should see the following console message stating that an OSPF adjacency is established using the virtual link:

```
%OSPF-5-ADJCHG: Process 1, Nbr 0.0.0.1 on OSPF_VL0 from LOADING to FULL,
Loading Done
```

Step 5. The cost of the virtual link should not exceed 65534:

```
R2# show ip ospf virtual-links


Virtual Link OSPF_VL0 to router 0.0.0.1 is up
  Run as demand circuit
  DoNotAge LSA allowed.
  Transit area 1, via interface Serial1/1
 Topology-MTID    Cost     Disabled      Shutdown      Topology Name
      0            781        no            no          Base
  Transmit Delay is 1 sec, State POINT_TO_POINT,
  Timer intervals configured, Hello 10, Dead 40, Wait 40, Retransmit 5
    Hello due in 00:00:05
    Adjacency State FULL (Hello suppressed)
    Index 2/3, retransmission queue length 0, number of retransmission 0
    First 0x0(0)/0x0(0) Next 0x0(0)/0x0(0)
    Last retransmission scan length is 0, maximum is 0
    Last retransmission scan time is 0 msec, maximum is 0 msec
```

You can see that the virtual link is up and its cost is 781. Because OSPF packets are tunneled packets from 12.1.1.1 (R1) to 12.1.1.2 (R2), the cost of the virtual link is based on the OSPF cost of all links from R1's s1/2 interface to R2's s1/1 interface. Let's see the OSPF cost of the serial link between R1 and R2:

```
On R2:

R2# show ip ospf interface serial1/1 | include Cost

  Process ID 1, router ID 0.0.0.2, network Type POINT_TO_POINT, Cost: 781
  Topology-MTID    Cost    Disabled    Shutdown    Topology Name
```

Now let's verify and test the configuration:

```
On R2:

R2# show ip route ospf | begin Gate
Gateway of last resort is not set

      1.0.0.0/32 is subnetted, 1 subnets
O        1.1.1.1 [110/782] via 12.1.1.1, 00:46:58, Serial1/1
      3.0.0.0/32 is subnetted, 1 subnets
O IA     3.3.3.3 [110/2] via 23.1.1.3, 00:45:18, FastEthernet0/0
      4.0.0.0/32 is subnetted, 1 subnets
O IA     4.4.4.4 [110/783] via 23.1.1.3, 00:44:25, FastEthernet0/0
      10.0.0.0/32 is subnetted, 1 subnets
O IA     10.1.1.1 [110/782] via 12.1.1.1, 00:00:18, Serial1/1
      30.0.0.0/32 is subnetted, 1 subnets
O        30.3.3.3 [110/2] via 23.1.1.3, 00:45:18, FastEthernet0/0
      34.0.0.0/24 is subnetted, 1 subnets
O IA     34.1.1.0 [110/782] via 23.1.1.3, 00:45:18, FastEthernet0/0


R2# ping 10.1.1.1

Type escape sequence to abort.
Sending 5, 100-byte ICMP Echos to 10.1.1.1, timeout is 2 seconds:
!!!!!
Success rate is 100 percent (5/5), round-trip min/avg/max = 48/50/52 ms
```

```
On R3:


R3# show ip route ospf | begin Gate
Gateway of last resort is not set


      1.0.0.0/32 is subnetted, 1 subnets
O IA    1.1.1.1 [110/783] via 23.1.1.2, 00:54:56, FastEthernet0/0
      2.0.0.0/32 is subnetted, 1 subnets
O IA    2.2.2.2 [110/2] via 23.1.1.2, 00:54:56, FastEthernet0/0
      4.0.0.0/32 is subnetted, 1 subnets
O       4.4.4.4 [110/782] via 34.1.1.4, 00:54:01, Serial1/4
      10.0.0.0/32 is subnetted, 1 subnets
O IA    10.1.1.1 [110/783] via 23.1.1.2, 00:09:53, FastEthernet0/0
      12.0.0.0/24 is subnetted, 1 subnets
O IA    12.1.1.0 [110/782] via 23.1.1.2, 00:54:56, FastEthernet0/0
      20.0.0.0/32 is subnetted, 1 subnets
O       20.2.2.2 [110/2] via 23.1.1.2, 00:54:56, FastEthernet0/0


R3# ping 10.1.1.1


Type escape sequence to abort.
Sending 5, 100-byte ICMP Echos to 10.1.1.1, timeout is 2 seconds:
!!!!!
Success rate is 100 percent (5/5), round-trip min/avg/max = 48/50/52 ms
```

Task 3

Ensure that the routers in Area 4 can see and have NLRI for all routes advertised in this routing domain. You should use loopback0 IP addresses. Do *not* change the area in which they are already configured. Also, do *not* use a virtual link to accomplish this task.

Let's check the routing table of R5:

```
On R5:


R5# show ip route ospf | begin Gate
Gateway of last resort is not set


      40.0.0.0/32 is subnetted, 1 subnets
O        40.4.4.4 [110/2] via 45.1.1.4, 01:00:16, FastEthernet0/0
```

The reason R5 only sees network 40.4.4.0/24 is because Area 4 does not have a connection (logical or physical) to Area 0. In order to rectify this problem, you must configure a virtual link. Because configuring virtual links is prohibited by the condition of this task, a GRE tunnel is configured instead. The task also states that you must use loopback0 IP addresses.

```
On R4:

R4(config)# interface tunnel 43
R4(config-if)# ip unnumbered loopback 0
R4(config-if)# tunnel source 34.1.1.4
R4(config-if)# tunnel destination 34.1.1.3
```

```
On R3:

R3(config)# interface tunnel 34
R3(config-if)# ip unnumbered loopback 0
R3(config-if)# tunnel source 34.1.1.3
R3(config-if)# tunnel destination 34.1.1.4
```

You should see the following console message:

```
%LINEPROTO-5-UPDOWN: Line protocol on Interface Tunnel34, changed state to up
```

When configuring a GRE tunnel, you *must* configure the IP address of the tunnel in Area 0. This can become a major problem when "IP unnumbered loopback" interface configuration commands are used, especially when the loopback interfaces are configured in different areas.

Let's verify the configuration:

```
On R5:

R5# show ip route ospf | begin Gate
Gateway of last resort is not set

     40.0.0.0/32 is subnetted, 1 subnets
O       40.4.4.4 [110/2] via 45.1.1.4, 01:07:31, FastEthernet0/0
```

R5 cannot see any routes from the other areas. Why?

The tunnel interface must be configured in Area 0. Let's verify this:

```
R4# show ip ospf interface brief

Interface    PID    Area        IP Address/Mask    Cost    State  Nbrs F/C
Lo0          1      2           4.4.4.4/24         1       LOOP   0/0
Tu43         1      2           Unnumbered Lo0     1000    P2P    1/1
Se1/3        1      2           34.1.1.4/24        781     P2P    1/1
Lo1          1      4           40.4.4.4/24        1       LOOP   0/0
Fa0/0        1      4           45.1.1.4/24        1       DR     1/1
```

You can see the problem: The tunnel interface is configured based on the loopback0 interface, which is running in Area 2. Because the task states that you cannot change the area assignment of any interface, you'll need to go to the tunnel interface and configure OSPF directly under the tunnel interface:

```
On R4:

R4(config)# interface tunnel 43
R4(config-if)# ip ospf 1 area 0
```

```
On R3:

R3(config)# interface tunnel 34
R3(config-if)# ip ospf 1 area 0
```

You should see the following console message:

```
%OSPF-5-ADJCHG: Process 1, Nbr 0.0.0.4 on Tunnel34 from LOADING to FULL,
Loading Done
```

Let's verify and test the configuration:

```
On R5:

R5# show ip route ospf | begin Gate
Gateway of last resort is not set

     1.0.0.0/32 is subnetted, 1 subnets
O IA    1.1.1.1 [110/1784] via 45.1.1.4, 00:00:50, FastEthernet0/0


     2.0.0.0/32 is subnetted, 1 subnets
O IA    2.2.2.2 [110/1003] via 45.1.1.4, 00:00:50, FastEthernet0/0
     3.0.0.0/32 is subnetted, 1 subnets
O IA    3.3.3.3 [110/783] via 45.1.1.4, 00:01:15, FastEthernet0/0
```

```
        4.0.0.0/32 is subnetted, 1 subnets
O IA    4.4.4.4 [110/2] via 45.1.1.4, 00:01:15, FastEthernet0/0
        10.0.0.0/32 is subnetted, 1 subnets
O IA    10.1.1.1 [110/1784] via 45.1.1.4, 00:00:50, FastEthernet0/0
        12.0.0.0/24 is subnetted, 1 subnets
O IA    12.1.1.0 [110/1783] via 45.1.1.4, 00:00:50, FastEthernet0/0
        20.0.0.0/32 is subnetted, 1 subnets
O IA    20.2.2.2 [110/1003] via 45.1.1.4, 00:00:50, FastEthernet0/0
        23.0.0.0/24 is subnetted, 1 subnets
O IA    23.1.1.0 [110/1002] via 45.1.1.4, 00:00:50, FastEthernet0/0
        30.0.0.0/32 is subnetted, 1 subnets
O IA    30.3.3.3 [110/1002] via 45.1.1.4, 00:00:50, FastEthernet0/0
        34.0.0.0/24 is subnetted, 1 subnets
O IA    34.1.1.0 [110/782] via 45.1.1.4, 00:01:15, FastEthernet0/0
        40.0.0.0/32 is subnetted, 1 subnets
O       40.4.4.4 [110/2] via 45.1.1.4, 01:13:26, FastEthernet0/0


R5# ping 10.1.1.1

Type escape sequence to abort.
Sending 5, 100-byte ICMP Echos to 10.1.1.1, timeout is 2 seconds:
!!!!!
Success rate is 100 percent (5/5), round-trip min/avg/max = 64/64/64 ms


R4# show ip ospf interface brief


Interface   PID   Area     IP Address/Mask    Cost   State Nbrs F/C
Tu43        1     0        Unnumbered Lo0     1000   P2P   1/1
Lo0         1     2        4.4.4.4/24           1    LOOP  0/0
Se1/3       1     2        34.1.1.4/24        781    P2P   1/1
Lo1         1     4        40.4.4.4/24          1    LOOP  0/0
Fa0/0       1     4        45.1.1.4/24          1    DR    1/1
```

Unlike virtual links, whose cost is based on the OSPF cost of all links between the ABRs, the cost of the GRE tunnel is *not* based on the cost of all links between the endpoints of the tunnel. Let's verify:

```
On R4:


R4# show ip ospf interface tunnel 43 | Include Cost

  Process ID 1, router ID 0.0.0.4, network Type POINT_TO_POINT, Cost: 1000
  Topology-MTID    Cost    Disabled    Shutdown     Topology Name
```

Erase the startup config and reload the routers before proceeding to the next lab.

Lab 8-10: OSPF Stub, Totally Stubby, and NSSA Areas

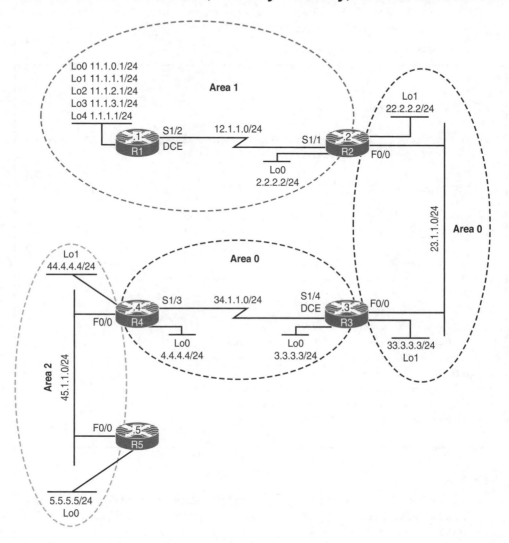

Figure 8-11 *OSPF Stub, Totally Stubby, and NSSA Areas*

Figure 8-11 illustrates the topology that will used in the following tasks.

The router IDSs in this lab should be configured as follows:

> **R1:** 0.0.0.1
>
> **R2:** 0.0.0.2
>
> **R3:** 0.0.0.3
>
> **R4:** 0.0.0.4
>
> **R5:** 0.0.0.5

Task 1

Configure OSPF Area 1 on all directly connected interfaces of R1. The loopback interfaces should be advertised with their correct mask.

Let's see R1's directly connected interfaces:

```
On R1:


R1# show ip interface brief | exclude unassigned

Interface                IP-Address       OK? Method Status        Protocol
Serial1/2                12.1.1.1         YES manual up            up
Loopback0                11.1.0.1         YES manual up            up
Loopback1                11.1.1.1         YES manual up            up
Loopback2                11.1.2.1         YES manual up            up
Loopback3                11.1.3.1         YES manual up            up
Loopback4                1.1.1.1          YES manual up            up


R1(config)# interface range lo0 - 4
R1(config-if-range)# ip ospf network point-to-point


R1(config)# router ospf 1
R1(config-router)# router-id 0.0.0.1
R1(config-router)# network 11.1.0.1 0.0.0.0 area 1
R1(config-router)# network 11.1.1.1 0.0.0.0 area 1
R1(config-router)# network 11.1.2.1 0.0.0.0 area 1
R1(config-router)# network 11.1.3.1 0.0.0.0 area 1
R1(config-router)# network 1.1.1.1 0.0.0.0 area 1
R1(config-router)# network 12.1.1.1 0.0.0.0 area 1
```

Task 2

Configure R2's s1/1 and loopback0 interfaces in OSPF Area 1 and then configure R2's f0/0 and loopback1 interfaces in Area 0. The loopback interfaces should be advertised with their correct mask.

Let's see R2's directly connected interfaces:

```
On R2:


R2# show ip interface brief | exclude unassigned

Interface                IP-Address       OK? Method Status        Protocol
FastEthernet0/0          23.1.1.2         YES manual up            up
```

```
Serial1/1                    12.1.1.2         YES manual up              up
Loopback0                    2.2.2.2          YES manual up              up
Loopback1                    22.2.2.2         YES manual up              up


R2(config)# interface range lo 0 - 1
R2(config-if-range)# ip ospf network point-to-point


R2(config)# router ospf 1
R2(config-router)# router-id 0.0.0.2
R2(config-router)# network 12.1.1.2 0.0.0.0 area 1
R2(config-router)# network 2.2.2.2 0.0.0.0 area 1
R2(config-router)# network 22.2.2.2 0.0.0.0 area 0
R2(config-router)# network 23.1.1.2 0.0.0.0 area 0
```

You should see the following console message:

```
%OSPF-5-ADJCHG: Process 1, Nbr 0.0.0.1 on Serial1/1 from LOADING to FULL,
Loading Done
```

Let's verify the configuration:

```
R2# show ip route ospf | begin Gate
Gateway of last resort is not set


     1.0.0.0/24 is subnetted, 1 subnets
O        1.1.1.0 [110/782] via 12.1.1.1, 00:06:32, Serial1/1
     11.0.0.0/24 is subnetted, 4 subnets
O        11.1.0.0 [110/782] via 12.1.1.1, 00:06:32, Serial1/1
O        11.1.1.0 [110/782] via 12.1.1.1, 00:06:32, Serial1/1
O        11.1.2.0 [110/782] via 12.1.1.1, 00:06:32, Serial1/1
O        11.1.3.0 [110/782] via 12.1.1.1, 00:06:32, Serial1/1
```

Task 3

Configure all of R3's directly connected interfaces in Area 0.

Let's see R3's directly connected interfaces:

```
On R3:


R3# show ip interface brief | exclude unassigned


Interface                IP-Address       OK? Method Status           Protocol
FastEthernet0/0          23.1.1.3         YES manual up               up
Serial1/4                34.1.1.3         YES manual up               up
```

```
Loopback0                    3.3.3.3         YES manual up            up
Loopback1                    33.3.3.3        YES manual up            up


R3(config)# interface range loopback 0 - 1
R3(config-if-range)# ip ospf network point-to-point


R3(config)# router ospf 1
R3(config-router)# router-id 0.0.0.3
R3(config-router)# network 3.3.3.3 0.0.0.0 area 0
R3(config-router)# network 33.3.3.3 0.0.0.0 area 0
R3(config-router)# network 23.1.1.3 0.0.0.0 area 0
R3(config-router)# network 34.1.1.3 0.0.0.0 area 0
```

You should see the following console message:

```
%OSPF-5-ADJCHG: Process 1, Nbr 0.0.0.2 on FastEthernet0/0 from LOADING to FULL,
  Loading Done
```

Let's verify the configuration:

```
R3# show ip route ospf | begin Gate
Gateway of last resort is not set


      1.0.0.0/24 is subnetted, 1 subnets
O IA    1.1.1.0 [110/783] via 23.1.1.2, 00:04:23, FastEthernet0/0
      2.0.0.0/24 is subnetted, 1 subnets
O IA    2.2.2.0 [110/2] via 23.1.1.2, 00:04:23, FastEthernet0/0
      11.0.0.0/24 is subnetted, 4 subnets
O IA    11.1.0.0 [110/783] via 23.1.1.2, 00:04:23, FastEthernet0/0
O IA    11.1.1.0 [110/783] via 23.1.1.2, 00:04:23, FastEthernet0/0
O IA    11.1.2.0 [110/783] via 23.1.1.2, 00:04:23, FastEthernet0/0
O IA    11.1.3.0 [110/783] via 23.1.1.2, 00:04:23, FastEthernet0/0
      12.0.0.0/24 is subnetted, 1 subnets
O IA    12.1.1.0 [110/782] via 23.1.1.2, 00:02:11, FastEthernet0/0
      22.0.0.0/24 is subnetted, 1 subnets
O       22.2.2.0 [110/2] via 23.1.1.2, 00:04:23, FastEthernet0/0
```

Task 4

Configure OSPF Area 2 based on Table 8-4.

Table 8-4 *Configuration of OSPF Area 2*

Router	Interface	Area	Router ID
R4	Lo1	2	0.0.0.4
	f0/0	2	
	s1/3	0	
	Lo0	0	
R5	Lo0	2	0.0.0.5
	f0/0	2	

Let's see R4's directly connected interfaces:

```
On R4:


R4# show ip interface brief | exclude unassigned


Interface               IP-Address     OK? Method Status          Protocol
FastEthernet0/0         45.1.1.4       YES manual up              up
Serial1/3               34.1.1.4       YES manual up              up
Loopback0               4.4.4.4        YES manual up              up
Loopback1               44.4.4.4       YES manual up              up


R4(config)# interface range loopback 0 - 1
R4(config-if-range)# ip ospf network point-to-point


R4(config)# router ospf 1
R4(config-router)# router-id 0.0.0.4
R4(config-router)# network 44.4.4.4 0.0.0.0 area 2
R4(config-router)# network 45.1.1.4 0.0.0.0 area 2
R4(config-router)# network 34.1.1.4 0.0.0.0 area 0
R4(config-router)# network 4.4.4.4 0.0.0.0 area 0
```

You should see the following console message:

```
%OSPF-5-ADJCHG: Process 1, Nbr 0.0.0.3 on Serial1/3 from LOADING to FULL,
Loading Done
```

```
On R5:

R5# show ip interface brief | exclude unassigned

Interface                IP-Address      OK? Method Status        Protocol
FastEthernet0/0          45.1.1.5        YES manual up            up
Loopback0                5.5.5.5         YES manual up            up


R5(config)# interface loopback 0
R5(config-if)# ip ospf network point-to-point


R5(config)# router ospf 1
R5(config-router)# router-id 0.0.0.5
R5(config-router)# network 5.5.5.5 0.0.0.0 area 2
R5(config-router)# network 45.1.1.5 0.0.0.0 area 2
```

You should see the following console message:

```
%OSPF-5-ADJCHG: Process 1, Nbr 0.0.0.4 on FastEthernet0/0 from LOADING to FULL,
Loading Done
```

Let's verify the configuration:

```
On R5:

R5# show ip route ospf | begin Gate
Gateway of last resort is not set

      1.0.0.0/24 is subnetted, 1 subnets
O IA    1.1.1.0 [110/1565] via 45.1.1.4, 00:00:46, FastEthernet0/0
      2.0.0.0/24 is subnetted, 1 subnets
O IA    2.2.2.0 [110/784] via 45.1.1.4, 00:00:46, FastEthernet0/0
      3.0.0.0/24 is subnetted, 1 subnets
O IA    3.3.3.0 [110/783] via 45.1.1.4, 00:00:46, FastEthernet0/0
      4.0.0.0/24 is subnetted, 1 subnets
O IA    4.4.4.0 [110/2] via 45.1.1.4, 00:00:46, FastEthernet0/0
      11.0.0.0/24 is subnetted, 4 subnets
O IA    11.1.0.0 [110/1565] via 45.1.1.4, 00:00:46, FastEthernet0/0
O IA    11.1.1.0 [110/1565] via 45.1.1.4, 00:00:46, FastEthernet0/0
O IA    11.1.2.0 [110/1565] via 45.1.1.4, 00:00:46, FastEthernet0/0
O IA    11.1.3.0 [110/1565] via 45.1.1.4, 00:00:46, FastEthernet0/0
      12.0.0.0/24 is subnetted, 1 subnets
O IA    12.1.1.0 [110/1564] via 45.1.1.4, 00:00:46, FastEthernet0/0
      22.0.0.0/24 is subnetted, 1 subnets
O IA    22.2.2.0 [110/784] via 45.1.1.4, 00:00:46, FastEthernet0/0
```

```
      23.0.0.0/24 is subnetted, 1 subnets
O IA     23.1.1.0 [110/783] via 45.1.1.4, 00:00:46, FastEthernet0/0
      33.0.0.0/24 is subnetted, 1 subnets
O IA     33.3.3.0 [110/783] via 45.1.1.4, 00:00:46, FastEthernet0/0
      34.0.0.0/24 is subnetted, 1 subnets
O IA     34.1.1.0 [110/782] via 45.1.1.4, 00:00:46, FastEthernet0/0
      44.0.0.0/24 is subnetted, 1 subnets
O        44.4.4.0 [110/2] via 45.1.1.4, 00:00:46, FastEthernet0/0
```

Task 5

Configure and redistribute the loopback30 interface as 130.1.1.3/32 on R3:

```
On R3:

R3(config)# interface loopback 30
R3(config-if)# ip address 130.1.1.3 255.255.255.255

R3(config)# route-map tst permit 10
R3(config-route-map)# match interface loopback 30

R3(config)# router ospf 1
R3(config-router)# redistribute connected route-map tst subnets
```

Let's verify the configuration:

```
On R1:

R1# show ip route ospf | include 130

      130.1.0.0/32 is subnetted, 1 subnets
O E2     130.1.1.3 [110/20] via 12.1.1.2, 00:00:55, Serial1/2
```

Task 6

Configure Area 1 such that it does not receive Type-4 or Type-5 LSAs, but the routers in this area should still maintain the inter-area routes in their routing table. These routers should have reachability to the existing and future external routes redistributed into this routing domain.

We can configure the OSPF stub area to accomplish this task. Here are *some* important points to understand about a stub area:

■ A stub area cannot be a transit area for virtual links. GRE tunnels should be used instead.

- A stub area cannot have an ASBR.

- The backbone area cannot be configured as a stub area.

- Every router and the ABR(s) of that area should be configured with the **area *xx* stub** command to match the area stub flag; otherwise, the adjacency will be torn down.

- External routes are *not* allowed in a stub area, but the routers in the stub area can connect to the external routes via the default route that is injected by their ABR.

- A stub area *cannot* have Type-4 or Type-5 LSAs.

- By default, the cost of the default route injected into this area by the ABR is 1; this can be verified using the **show ip ospf** and/or **show ip route** commands. The cost of the default route can be changed using **area *xx* default-cost *cc***, where *xx* is the area number and *cc* is the desired cost.

```
On R1:

R1(config)# router ospf 1
R1(config-router)# area 1 stub
```

You should see the following console message:

```
%OSPF-5-ADJCHG: Process 1, Nbr 0.0.0.2 on Serial1/2 from FULL to DOWN,
neighbor Down: Adjacency forced to reset
```

Note   The adjacency with R2 (0.0.0.2) transitioned from FULL to DOWN because the area stub flag no longer matches:

```
On R2:

R2(config)# router ospf 1
R2(config-router)# area 1 stub
```

You should see the following console message stating that the adjacency is in the FULL state:

```
%OSPF-5-ADJCHG: Process 1, Nbr 0.0.0.1 on Serial1/1 from LOADING to FULL,
Loading Done
```

Let's verify the configuration:

```
On R1:


R1# show ip ospf | include area


 Supports area transit capability
 Number of areas in this router is 1. 0 normal 1 stub 0 nssa
 Number of areas transit capable is 0
        Number of interfaces in this area is 6
        It is a stub area


R1# show ip route ospf | include 0.0.0.0/0


O*IA   0.0.0.0/0 [110/782] via 12.1.1.2, 00:01:40, Serial1/2
```

The output of the preceding **show** command reveals that the cost of the default route from R1's perspective is 782. Why 782? The default cost of the default route is 1 *plus* the cost of the serial link, which is 781.

Let's verify this:

```
On R2:


R2# show ip ospf | include cost


        generates stub default route with cost 1


R2# show ip ospf interface serial 1/1 | include Cost


 Process ID 1, router ID 0.0.0.1, network Type POINT_TO_POINT, Cost: 781
 Topology-MTID    Cost    Disabled    Shutdown    Topology Name
```

Therefore, if 1 is added to 781, you should see a resulting cost of 782.

The following command is a hidden command. Therefore, pressing the Tab key will not complete it.

```
 On R1:


R1# show ip ospf route | include 0.0.0.0


*>  0.0.0.0/0, Inter, cost 782, area 1
```

Based on the following successful ping, you can see that the routers in Area 1 have reachability to the external routes that are redistributed in other areas of this routing domain:

```
R1# ping 130.1.1.3

Type escape sequence to abort.
Sending 5, 100-byte ICMP Echos to 130.1.1.3, timeout is 2 seconds:
!!!!!
Success rate is 100 percent (5/5), round-trip min/avg/max = 28/29/32 ms
```

Task 7

Area 2 should not receive Type-3, -4, or -5 LSAs. These routers should have reachability to the existing and future inter-area and external routes redistributed into this routing domain.

You can reduce the size of the routing table further by configuring an area as "totally stubby." Because all the "IA" and "E" (inter-area and external) routes can be reached via a default route, which is injected by the ABR of this area, there is no reason to maintain these routes.

```
On R5:

R5(config)# router ospf 1
R5(config-router)# area 2 stub
```

You should see the following console message stating that the adjacency transitioned from the FULL state to the DOWN state. This happened because the area stub flag no longer matches (remember that if the area stub flag does *not* match, the adjacency *cannot* be established). Therefore, the preceding command must be configured on all the routers within Area 2.

```
%OSPF-5-ADJCHG: Process 1, Nbr 0.0.0.4 on FastEthernet0/0 from FULL to DOWN,
neighbor Down: Adjacency forced to reset
```

```
On R4:

R4(config)# router ospf 1
R4(config-router)# area 2 stub no-summary
```

The preceding command must only be configured on the ABR of this area.

Let's verify the configuration:

```
On R5:


R5# show ip route ospf | begin Gate
Gateway of last resort is 45.1.1.4 to network 0.0.0.0


O*IA  0.0.0.0/0 [110/2] via 45.1.1.4, 00:00:14, FastEthernet0/0
      44.0.0.0/24 is subnetted, 1 subnets
O        44.4.4.0 [110/2] via 45.1.1.4, 00:00:14, FastEthernet0/0
```

Here are some important points to understand about a "*totally stubby*" area:

- A totally stub area cannot be a transit area for virtual links. GRE tunnels should be used instead.

- A totally stub area cannot have an ASBR.

- The backbone area cannot be configured as a totally stub area.

- The routers within the area should be configured with the **area *xx* stub** command, whereas the ABR of the totally stub area *must* be configured with **area *xx* stub no-summary**.

- External routes are *not* allowed in a totally stub area, but the routers in the totally stub area can connect to the external routes via the default route that is injected into the area by their ABR.

- By default, the cost of the default route injected into this area by the ABR is 1. This can be verified using the **show ip ospf** command on the ABR and/or the **show ip route** command on the other routers in the area. The cost of the default route can be changed using **area *xx* default-cost *cc***, where *xx* is the area number and *cc* is the desired cost.

- The routers in a totally stub area don't get inter-area routes, but they have NLRI for the inter-area routes via the default route that is injected by the ABR.

Let's see why the default route is the *only* inter-area route injected into this area:

```
R4# show ip ospf database summary 0.0.0.0


            OSPF router with ID (0.0.0.4) (Process ID 1)


                Summary Net Link States (Area 2)


  LS age: 331
  Options: (No TOS-capability, DC, Upward)
  LS Type: Summary Links(Network)
```

```
Link State ID: 0.0.0.0 (summary network Number)
Advertising Router: 0.0.0.4
LS Seq Number: 80000001
Checksum: 0x99A0
Length: 28
network Mask: /0
     MTID: 0          Metric: 1
```

You can see that the default route is injected by the ABR—in this case, R4 (0.0.0.4)—and it was generated within Area 2. Therefore, it is wrong to say that the default route is the *only* inter-area route injected into the totally stubby area.

The inter-area routes that have originated in the other areas are the only routes that are blocked. Because the default route is originated in Area 2, it is not blocked.

Task 8

Redistribute Lo0–4 interfaces of R1 into this routing domain. Reconfigure Area 1 such that it only receives and propagates LSA Types 1, 2, 3, and 7. This area should not have the ability to connect to any external routes redistributed elsewhere within this routing domain.

Because a stub area *cannot* have external routes, Area 1 must be converted into an NSSA, meaning that Area 1 wants to be a stub area but at the same time allow the existence of external routes.

Let's remove the following commands from R1:

```
On R1:

R1(config)# router ospf 1
R1(config-router)# no network 1.1.1.1 0.0.0.0 area 1
R1(config-router)# no network 11.1.0.1 0.0.0.0 area 1
R1(config-router)# no network 11.1.1.1 0.0.0.0 area 1
R1(config-router)# no network 11.1.2.1 0.0.0.0 area 1
R1(config-router)# no network 11.1.3.1 0.0.0.0 area 1

R1(config-router)# no area 1 stub
R1(config-router)# area 1 nssa
```

You should see the following console message:

```
%OSPF-5-ADJCHG: Process 1, Nbr 0.0.0.2 on Serial1/2 from DOWN to DOWN,
neighbor Down: Adjacency forced to reset
```

```
R1(config)# route-map TST permit 10
R1(config-route-map)# match interface lo0 lo1 lo2 lo3 lo4

R1(config)# router ospf 1
R1(config-router)# redistribute connected route-map TST subnets
```

```
On R2:

R2(config)# router ospf 1
R2(config-router)# no area 1 stub
R2(config-router)# area 1 nssa
```

You should see this console message as well:

```
%OSPF-5-ADJCHG: Process 1, Nbr 0.0.0.1 on Serial1/1 from LOADING to FULL,
Loading Done
```

Let's verify the configuration:

Note R1 does *not* have a default route because the ABR (R2) did *not* inject one.

```
On R2:

R1# show ip route ospf | include 0.0.0.0/0
```

```
On R2:

R2# show ip route ospf | begin Gate
Gateway of last resort is not set

      1.0.0.0/24 is subnetted, 1 subnets
O N2    1.1.1.0 [110/20] via 12.1.1.1, 00:02:43, Serial1/1
      3.0.0.0/24 is subnetted, 1 subnets
O       3.3.3.0 [110/2] via 23.1.1.3, 00:02:53, FastEthernet0/0
      4.0.0.0/24 is subnetted, 1 subnets
O       4.4.4.0 [110/783] via 23.1.1.3, 00:02:53, FastEthernet0/0
      5.0.0.0/24 is subnetted, 1 subnets
O IA    5.5.5.0 [110/784] via 23.1.1.3, 00:02:53, FastEthernet0/0
      11.0.0.0/24 is subnetted, 4 subnets
```

```
O N2     11.1.0.0 [110/20] via 12.1.1.1, 00:02:43, Serial1/1
O N2     11.1.1.0 [110/20] via 12.1.1.1, 00:02:43, Serial1/1
O N2     11.1.2.0 [110/20] via 12.1.1.1, 00:02:43, Serial1/1
O N2     11.1.3.0 [110/20] via 12.1.1.1, 00:02:43, Serial1/1
         33.0.0.0/24 is subnetted, 1 subnets
O           33.3.3.0 [110/2] via 23.1.1.3, 00:02:53, FastEthernet0/0
         34.0.0.0/24 is subnetted, 1 subnets
O           34.1.1.0 [110/782] via 23.1.1.3, 00:02:53, FastEthernet0/0
         44.0.0.0/24 is subnetted, 1 subnets
O IA        44.4.4.0 [110/783] via 23.1.1.3, 00:02:53, FastEthernet0/0
         45.0.0.0/24 is subnetted, 1 subnets
O IA        45.1.1.0 [110/783] via 23.1.1.3, 00:02:53, FastEthernet0/0
         130.1.0.0/32 is subnetted, 1 subnets
O E2        130.1.1.3 [110/20] via 23.1.1.3, 00:02:53, FastEthernet0/0
```

Note   R2 received the external routes from Area 1 as "N2" and converts them all to "E2."

```
On R4:

R4# show ip route ospf | begin Gate
Gateway of last resort is not set

      1.0.0.0/24 is subnetted, 1 subnets
O E2     1.1.1.0 [110/20] via 34.1.1.3, 00:03:29, Serial1/3
      2.0.0.0/24 is subnetted, 1 subnets
O IA     2.2.2.0 [110/783] via 34.1.1.3, 00:22:15, Serial1/3
      3.0.0.0/24 is subnetted, 1 subnets
O         3.3.3.0 [110/782] via 34.1.1.3, 00:22:15, Serial1/3
      5.0.0.0/24 is subnetted, 1 subnets
O         5.5.5.0 [110/2] via 45.1.1.5, 00:22:03, FastEthernet0/0
      11.0.0.0/24 is subnetted, 4 subnets
O E2     11.1.0.0 [110/20] via 34.1.1.3, 00:03:29, Serial1/3
O E2     11.1.1.0 [110/20] via 34.1.1.3, 00:03:29, Serial1/3
O E2     11.1.2.0 [110/20] via 34.1.1.3, 00:03:29, Serial1/3
O E2     11.1.3.0 [110/20] via 34.1.1.3, 00:03:29, Serial1/3
      12.0.0.0/24 is subnetted, 1 subnets
O IA     12.1.1.0 [110/1563] via 34.1.1.3, 00:22:15, Serial1/3
      22.0.0.0/24 is subnetted, 1 subnets
O         22.2.2.0 [110/783] via 34.1.1.3, 00:22:15, Serial1/3
      23.0.0.0/24 is subnetted, 1 subnets
O         23.1.1.0 [110/782] via 34.1.1.3, 00:22:15, Serial1/3
```

```
        33.0.0.0/24 is subnetted, 1 subnets
O          33.3.3.0 [110/782] via 34.1.1.3, 00:22:15, Serial1/3
        130.1.0.0/32 is subnetted, 1 subnets
O E2     130.1.1.3 [110/20] via 34.1.1.3, 00:15:19, Serial1/3
```

In an NSSA area, the ABR receives the Type-7 LSAs and converts them into Type-5 LSAs. The following can confirm this fact:

```
R2# show ip ospf database nssa-external | include Link State


                Type-7 AS External Link States (Area 1)
  Link State ID: 1.1.1.0 (External network Number )
  Link State ID: 11.1.0.0 (External network Number )
  Link State ID: 11.1.1.0 (External network Number )
  Link State ID: 11.1.2.0 (External network Number )
  Link State ID: 11.1.3.0 (External network Number )


R2# show ip ospf database external | include Link State


                Type-5 AS External Link States
  Link State ID: 1.1.1.0 (External network Number )
  Link State ID: 11.1.0.0 (External network Number )
  Link State ID: 11.1.1.0 (External network Number )
  Link State ID: 11.1.2.0 (External network Number )
  Link State ID: 11.1.3.0 (External network Number )
  Link State ID: 130.1.1.3 (External Network Number )
```

This happens because the ASBR in an NSSA area sets the "P" bit when it redistributes external routes. This bit instructs the ABR(s) to translate the Type-7 LSAs to Type-5 LSAs. You can see the P bit in the output of the following **show** command on R1:

```
On R1:

R1# show ip ospf database nssa-external


           OSPF Router with ID (0.0.0.1) (Process ID 1)


               Type-7 AS External Link States (Area 1)


  LS age: 566
  Options: (No TOS-capability, Type 7/5 translation, DC)
  LS Type: AS External Link
  Link State ID: 1.1.1.0 (External Network Number )
  Advertising Router: 0.0.0.1
```

```
    LS Seq Number: 80000001
    Checksum: 0xD4AE
    Length: 36
    Network Mask: /24
          Metric Type: 2 (Larger than any link state path)
          MTID: 0
          Metric: 20
          Forward Address: 12.1.1.1
          External Route Tag: 0
(The rest of the output is omitted for brevity)
```

Task 9

Configure the following loopback interfaces on R5:

Lo1: 55.5.1.5/24

Lo2: 55.5.2.5/24

Lo3: 55.5.3.5/24

Lo4: 55.5.4.5/24

```
On R5:

R5(config-if)# interface loopback 1
R5(config-if)# ip address 55.5.1.5 255.255.255.0

R5(config-if)# interface loopback 2
R5(config-if)# ip address 55.5.2.5 255.255.255.0

R5(config-if)# interface loopback 3
R5(config-if)# ip address 55.5.3.5 255.255.255.0

R5(config-if)# interface loopback 4
R5(config-if)# ip address 55.5.4.5 255.255.255.0
```

Let's verify the configuration:

```
On R5:


R5# show ip interface brief | exclude unassociated


Interface              IP-Address       OK? Method Status        Protocol
FastEthernet0/0        45.1.1.5         YES manual up            up
Loopback0              5.5.5.5          YES manual up            up
Loopback1              55.5.1.5         YES manual up            up
Loopback2              55.5.2.5         YES manual up            up
Loopback3              55.5.3.5         YES manual up            up
Loopback4              55.5.4.5         YES manual up            up
```

Task 10

Redistribute the Lo1–4 interfaces on R5. Configure the appropriate router(s) such that the routers in this area only maintain and propagate LSA Types 1, 2, 3, and 7 and a default route.

Because Area 2 is a totally stubby area, it can't have external routes unless it's converted into an NSSA because the task states that the routers of this area should also get a default route. The ABR of this area (R4) is configured to inject a default route using the **default-information-originate** keyword.

```
On R5:


R5(config-if)# route-map TST permit 10
R5(config-route-map)# match interface lo1 lo2 lo3 lo4


R5(config)# router ospf 1
R5(config-router)# no area 2 stub
R5(config-router)# area 2 nssa
R5(config-router)# redistribute connected subnets route-map TST
```

```
On R4:


R4(config)# router ospf 1
R4(config-router)# no area 2 stub
R4(config-router)# area 2 nssa default-information-originate
```

You should see the following console message:

```
%OSPF-5-ADJCHG: Process 1, Nbr 0.0.0.5 on FastEthernet0/0 from LOADING to FULL,
Loading Done
```

The **default-information-originate** keyword at the end of the **area 2 nssa** command will inject a default route into the area. This default route will be injected as "N2" and *not* "IA." Also, note that you didn't have to have a default route in your routing table to originate one.

Let's verify the configuration:

```
On R5:

R5# show ip route ospf | include 0.0.0.0/0

O*N2  0.0.0.0/0 [110/1] via 45.1.1.4, 00:02:19, FastEthernet0/0
```

Task 11

Area 1 should be changed such that it receives and propagates LSA Types 1, 2, and 7 plus a default route. This area should not maintain inter-area routes but must have the ability to connect to these routes.

```
On R2:

R2(config)# router ospf 1
R2(config-router)# area 1 nssa no-summary
```

The **no-summary** keyword blocks the summary LSAs that are the inter-area routes. Whenever the inter-area routes are blocked using the **no-summary** keyword, the ABR will always inject a default route.

Let's verify the configuration:

```
On R1:

R1# show ip route ospf | begin Gate
Gateway of last resort is 12.1.1.2 to network 0.0.0.0

O*IA  0.0.0.0/0 [110/782] via 12.1.1.2, 00:03:14, Serial1/2
      2.0.0.0/24 is subnetted, 1 subnets
O        2.2.2.0 [110/782] via 12.1.1.2, 00:26:23, Serial1/2
```

Task 12

The default route that was injected into Area 1 should have a cost of 50.

Let's look at the cost of the default route that was injected:

```
On R1:

R1# show ip route ospf | include 0.0.0.0/0

O*IA  0.0.0.0/0 [110/782] via 12.1.1.2, 00:04:17, Serial1/2

R1# show ip ospf interface serial1/2 | include Cost

  Process ID 1, router ID 0.0.0.1, network Type POINT_TO_POINT, Cost: 781
  Topology-MTID    Cost    Disabled    Shutdown      Topology Name
```

You can see that the cost of the s1/2 interface is 781 and that the total cost of the default route injected is 782. Therefore, by default, the cost of the default route is 1. Let's change it to 50 and verify.

The default cost of the injected default route can be changed using the **area** *xx* **default-cost** *cc* command, where *cc* is the new cost replacing the default value:

```
On R2:

R2(config)# router ospf 1
R2(config-router)# area 1 default-cost 50
```

Let's verify the configuration:

```
On R1:

R1# Show ip ospf route | begin Inter-area

    Inter-area Route List
*>  0.0.0.0/0, Inter, cost 831, area 1
      via 12.1.1.2, Serial1/2
```

If you subtract the OSPF cost of the S1/2 interface from 831, you should see the cost of the default route injected into this area:

$$831 - 781 = 50$$

```
R1# show ip route ospf | include 0.0.0.0/0

O*IA  0.0.0.0/0 [110/831] via 12.1.1.2, 00:03:18, Serial1/2

Let's verify the cost in the database:

R1# show ip ospf database summary

          OSPF router with ID (0.0.0.1) (Process ID 1)

             Summary Net Link States (Area 1)

  Routing Bit Set on this LSA in topology Base with MTID 0

  LS age: 242
  Options: (No TOS-capability, DC, Upward)

  LS Type: Summary Links (Network)
  Link State ID: 0.0.0.0 (summary network Number)
  Advertising Router: 0.0.0.2
  LS Seq Number: 80000002
  Checksum: 0x17EA
  Length: 28
  network Mask: /0
       MTID: 0          Metric: 50
```

Erase the startup config and reload the routers before proceeding to the next lab.

Lab 8-11: How Is This Possible?

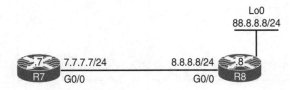

Lo0
88.8.8.8/24

.7   7.7.7.7/24   8.8.8.8/24 .8
R7   G0/0   G0/0   R8

Figure 8-12 *How Is This Possible?*

Task 1

Configure OSPF Area 0 on all links in the topology shown in Figure 8-12. If this configuration is done properly, R7 should have reachability to R8's loopback0 interface. Do not configure a GRE tunnel, IPnIP tunnel, or PPP or change an IP address to accomplish this task.

To resolve this scenario, you can configure OSPFv3. This solution works because the packets are encapsulated in IPv6 and not IPv4. Therefore, it does not matter what their IP addresses are. Let's configure and verify this solution.

If IPv6 unicast routing is not configured on these two routers, a routing protocol cannot be configured.

```
On Both Routers:

Rx(config)# ipv6 unicast-routing
```

```
On R7:

R7(config)# router ospfv3 1
R7(config-router)# address-family ipv4 unicast
R7(config-router-af)# router-id 0.0.0.7

R7(config)# interface GigabitEthernet0/0
R7(config-if)# ipv6 enable
R7(config-if)# ospfv3 1 ipv4 area 0
```

```
On R8:

R8(config)# router ospfv3 1
R8(config-router)# address-family ipv4 unicast
R8(config-router-af)# router-id 0.0.0.8

R8(config)# interface lo0
R8(config-if)# ipv6 enable
R8(config-if)# ospfv3 1 ipv4 area 0

R8(config)# interface GigabitEthernet0/0
R8(config-if)# ipv6 enable
R8(config-if)# ospfv3 1 ipv4 area 0
```

You should see the following console message:

```
%OSPFv3-5-ADJCHG: Process 1, IPv4, Nbr 0.0.0.7 on GigabitEthernet0/0 from LOADING
to FULL, Loading Done
```

Let's verify and test the configuration:

```
On R7:

R7# show ip route ospfv3 | begin Gate
Gateway of last resort is not set

      8.0.0.0/24 is subnetted, 1 subnets
O        8.8.8.0 is directly connected, 00:00:59, GigabitEthernet0/0
      88.0.0.0/32 is subnetted, 1 subnets
O        88.8.8.8 [110/1] via 8.8.8.8, 00:00:59, GigabitEthernet0/0

R7# ping 88.8.8.8

Type escape sequence to abort.
Sending 5, 100-byte ICMP Echos to 88.8.8.8, timeout is 2 seconds:
.!!!!
Success rate is 80 percent (4/5), round-trip min/avg/max = 1/1/1 ms

R7# ping 8.8.8.8

Type escape sequence to abort.
Sending 5, 100-byte ICMP Echos to 8.8.8.8, timeout is 2 seconds:
!!!!!
Success rate is 100 percent (5/5), round-trip min/avg/max = 1/1/4 ms
```

Erase the startup configuration and reload the routers before proceeding to the next lab.

Lab 8-12: LSA Type 4 and Suppress FA

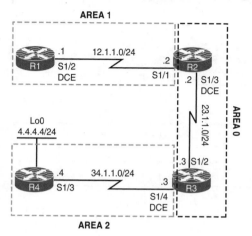

Figure 8-13 *LSA Type 4 and Suppress FA*

Task 1

Configure OSPF based on the topology shown in Figure 8-13. R4 should redistribute its loopback0 interface into the OSPF routing domain. Configure router IDs of 0.0.0.1, 0.0.0.2, 0.0.0.3, and 0.0.0.4 for R1, R2, R3, and R4, respectively.

```
On R1:


R1(config)# router ospf 1
R1(config-router)# router-id 0.0.0.1
R1(config-router)# network 12.1.1.1 0.0.0.0 area 1
```

```
On R2:


R2(config)# router ospf 1
R2(config-router)# router-id 0.0.0.2
R2(config-router)# network 12.1.1.2 0.0.0.0 area 1
R2(config-router)# network 23.1.1.2 0.0.0.0 area 0
```

You should see the following console message:

```
%OSPF-5-ADJCHG: Process 1, Nbr 0.0.0.1 on Serial1/1 from LOADING to FULL,
Loading Done
```

```
On R3:

R3(config)# router ospf 1
R3(config-router)# router-id 0.0.0.3
R3(config-router)# network 23.1.1.3 0.0.0.0 area 0
R3(config-router)# network 34.1.1.3 0.0.0.0 area 2
```

You should see the following console message:

```
%OSPF-5-ADJCHG: Process 1, Nbr 0.0.0.2 on Serial1/2 from LOADING to FULL,
Loading Done
```

```
On R4:

R4(config)# route-map tst
R4(config-route-map)# match interface loopback 0

R4(config)# router ospf 1
R4(config-router)# router-id 0.0.0.4
R4(config-router)# network 34.1.1.4 0.0.0.0 area 2
R4(config-router)# redistribute connected route-map tst subnets
```

You should see the following console message:

```
%OSPF-5-ADJCHG: Process 1, Nbr 0.0.0.3 on Serial1/3 from LOADING to FULL,
Loading Done
```

Let's verify the configuration:

```
On R1:

R1# show ip route ospf | begin Gate
Gateway of last resort is not set

      4.0.0.0/24 is subnetted, 1 subnets
O E2    4.4.4.0 [110/20] via 12.1.1.2, 00:03:37, Serial1/2
      23.0.0.0/24 is subnetted, 1 subnets
O IA    23.1.1.0 [110/1562] via 12.1.1.2, 00:08:13, Serial1/2
      34.0.0.0/24 is subnetted, 1 subnets
O IA    34.1.1.0 [110/2343] via 12.1.1.2, 00:06:25, Serial1/2
```

R1 can see network 4.4.4.0/24. Let's check the database and see the details of this Type-5 LSA:

```
R1# show ip ospf database external 4.4.4.0

            OSPF Router with ID (0.0.0.1) (Process ID 1)

                Type-5 AS External Link States

 Routing Bit Set on this LSA in topology Base with MTID 0
 LS age: 306
 Options: (No TOS-capability, DC)
 LS Type: AS External Link
 Link State ID: 4.4.4.0 (External Network Number )
 Advertising Router: 0.0.0.4
 LS Seq Number: 80000001
 Checksum: 0x3F51
 Length: 36
 Network Mask: /24
       Metric Type: 2 (Larger than any link state path)
       MTID: 0
       Metric: 20
       Forward Address: 0.0.0.0
       External Route Tag: 0
```

The Link State ID in LSAs Type 3, 5, and 7 describes the actual network. The Advertising Router in this case is R4 (0.0.0.4). The Network Mask for network 4.4.4.0 is /24. Even though the output states Network Mask, in reality it is the prefix length. The Metric Type is 2. This is the default OSPF behavior for redistributed routes, unless this is statically changed to 1 using the **metric-type 1** keyword in the **redistribute** command. The Metric setting (or the cost) is 20. This is the default cost of any redistributed route in OSPF unless it is changed. The Forward Address setting is 0.0.0.0. The forward address is the next hop; when the next hop is set to 0.0.0.0, it means that to reach the next hop, you should go to the advertising router (in this case, 0.0.0.4).

But how do you reach 0.0.0.4? This is not an IP address. This is where LSA Type 4 comes to rescue. Let's verify this information:

```
R1# show ip ospf database asbr-summary 0.0.0.4

            OSPF Router with ID (0.0.0.1) (Process ID 1)

                Summary ASB Link States (Area 1)

 Routing Bit Set on this LSA in topology Base with MTID 0
```

```
LS age: 925
Options: (No TOS-capability, DC, Upward)
LS Type: Summary Links(AS Boundary Router)
Link State ID: 0.0.0.4 (AS Boundary Router address)
Advertising Router: 0.0.0.2
LS Seq Number: 80000001
Checksum: 0x8293
Length: 28
Network Mask: /0
       MTID: 0           Metric: 1562
```

The Link State ID setting in LSA Type 4 describes the router ID—in this case, the RID of R4, which happens to be an ASBR. The Advertising Router setting is 0.0.0.2, or R2. The Metric setting specifies the cost; the cost to reach 0.0.0.4 is set to 1562. Why 1562? Let's calculate it.

To calculate the cost, you must add the cost of the serial link that connects R3 to R4 to the cost of the link that connects R2 to R3. Let's find out the cost of these interfaces:

```
On R3:

R3# show ip ospf interface serial 1/4 | include Cost

 Process ID 1, Router ID 0.0.0.3, Network Type POINT_TO_POINT, Cost: 781
 Topology-MTID    Cost    Disabled    Shutdown      Topology Name
```

```
On R2:

R2# show ip ospf interface serial 1/3 | include Cost

 Process ID 1, Router ID 0.0.0.2, Network Type POINT_TO_POINT, Cost: 781
 Topology-MTID    Cost    Disabled    Shutdown      Topology Name
```

In other words, 781 + 781 = 1562.

Let's go to R2 and verify the same information:

Based on the output of the following **show** command, you can see that the information in LSA Type 5 did not change at all:

```
On R2:

R2# show ip ospf database external 4.4.4.0

            OSPF Router with ID (0.0.0.2) (Process ID 1)
```

```
                Type-5 AS External Link States


  Routing Bit Set on this LSA in topology Base with MTID 0
  LS age: 1857
  Options: (No TOS-capability, DC)
  LS Type: AS External Link
  Link State ID: 4.4.4.0 (External Network Number )
  Advertising Router: 0.0.0.4
  LS Seq Number: 80000001
  Checksum: 0x3F51
  Length: 36
  Network Mask: /24
        Metric Type: 2 (Larger than any link state path)
        MTID: 0
        Metric: 20
        Forward Address: 0.0.0.0
        External Route Tag: 0
```

Let's check LSA Type-4:

R2# **show ip ospf database asbr-summary 0.0.0.4**

```
             OSPF Router with ID (0.0.0.2) (Process ID 1)


                 Summary ASB Link States (Area 0)


  Routing Bit Set on this LSA in topology Base with MTID 0
  LS age: 195
  Options: (No TOS-capability, DC, Upward)
  LS Type: Summary Links(AS Boundary Router)
  Link State ID: 0.0.0.4 (AS Boundary Router address)
  Advertising Router: 0.0.0.3
  LS Seq Number: 80000002
  Checksum: 0xDC47
  Length: 28
  Network Mask: /0
        MTID: 0          Metric: 781


                 Summary ASB Link States (Area 1)


  LS age: 17
  Options: (No TOS-capability, DC, Upward)
  LS Type: Summary Links(AS Boundary Router)
  Link State ID: 0.0.0.4 (AS Boundary Router address)
  Advertising Router: 0.0.0.2
```

```
LS Seq Number: 80000002
Checksum: 0x8094
Length: 28
Network Mask: /0
      MTID: 0            Metric: 1562
```

As you can see, there are two Type-4 LSAs: One is propagated into Area 0 with a cost of 781, and the second one is propagated into Area 1 with a cost of 1562.

The reason we see two Type-4 LSAs is because R3 injects a Type-4 LSA into Area 0 with the cost of the R3–R4 link, which is 781. R3 does that so the routers in Area 0 will have reachability to the ASBR. R2 is another ABR, so R2 does the same for the routers in Area 1; otherwise, they won't have reachability to the ASBR.

Now that you know how Type-4 LSAs provide reachability to the ASBR, let's convert Area 2 to an NSSA area:

```
On R3 and R4:

Rx(config)# router ospf 1
Rx(config-router)# area 2 nssa
```

Let's verify the routing table and the database on R1 and see the difference:

```
On R1

R1# show ip route ospf | begin Gate
Gateway of last resort is not set

     4.0.0.0/24 is subnetted, 1 subnets
O E2    4.4.4.0 [110/20] via 12.1.1.2, 00:00:47, Serial1/2
     23.0.0.0/24 is subnetted, 1 subnets
O IA    23.1.1.0 [110/1562] via 12.1.1.2, 00:49:29, Serial1/2
     34.0.0.0/24 is subnetted, 1 subnets
O IA    34.1.1.0 [110/2343] via 12.1.1.2, 00:47:41, Serial1/2
```

Based on the output of the preceding **show** command, there's no change from the routing table's perspective. Let's view the external database of R1:

```
R1# show ip ospf database external 4.4.4.0

            OSPF Router with ID (0.0.0.1) (Process ID 1)

            Type-5 AS External Link States
```

```
Routing Bit Set on this LSA in topology Base with MTID 0
LS age: 143
Options: (No TOS-capability, DC)
LS Type: AS External Link
Link State ID: 4.4.4.0 (External Network Number )
Advertising Router: 0.0.0.3
LS Seq Number: 80000001
Checksum: 0xE5B
Length: 36
Network Mask: /24
      Metric Type: 2 (Larger than any link state path)
      MTID: 0
      Metric: 20
      Forward Address: 34.1.1.4
      External Route Tag: 0
```

The output of the preceding **show** command reveals that the advertising router is 0.0.0.3,
which is R3. Once Area 1 was converted to an NSSA area, the ASBR (R4) originated
the external routes in Type-7 LSAs and then the ABR (R3) received a Type-7 LSA and
converted it to LSA Type 5. Therefore, it became a pseudo-ASBR, and this is why the
advertising router is set based on R3. The final change is the forward address (FA), or
the next hop. It is now set to the IP address of R4 (34.1.1.4). Because the FA is set to the
actual IP address of R4, there is no requirement to propagate a Type-4 LSA into Area 0.
Let's verify the Type-4 LSA on R1:

```
R1# show ip ospf database asbr-summary 0.0.0.3

            OSPF Router with ID (0.0.0.1) (Process ID 1)


            Summary ASB Link States (Area 1)


Routing Bit Set on this LSA in topology Base with MTID 0
LS age: 520
Options: (No TOS-capability, DC, Upward)
LS Type: Summary Links(AS Boundary Router)
Link State ID: 0.0.0.3 (AS Boundary Router address)
Advertising Router: 0.0.0.2
LS Seq Number: 80000001
Checksum: 0xEE38
Length: 28
Network Mask: /0
      MTID: 0          Metric: 781
```

Note In the preceding output, you can see that R3 is stated as an ASBR. The reason is because R3 is originating an LSA Type 5, and to reach this ASBR you need to go to R2 (0.0.0.2).

Let's go to R2 and verify the same information:

```
On R2:

R2# show ip ospf database external 4.4.4.0

            OSPF Router with ID (0.0.0.2) (Process ID 1)

              Type-5 AS External Link States

  Routing Bit Set on this LSA in topology Base with MTID 0
  LS age: 726
  Options: (No TOS-capability, DC)
  LS Type: AS External Link
  Link State ID: 4.4.4.0 (External Network Number )
  Advertising Router: 0.0.0.3
  LS Seq Number: 80000001
  Checksum: 0xE5B
  Length: 36
  Network Mask: /24
        Metric Type: 2 (Larger than any link state path)
        MTID: 0
        Metric: 20
        Forward Address: 34.1.1.4
        External Route Tag: 0
```

Let's verify the Type-4 LSA:

```
R2# show ip ospf database asbr-summary

            OSPF Router with ID (0.0.0.2) (Process ID 1)

              Summary ASB Link States (Area 1)

  LS age: 843
  Options: (No TOS-capability, DC, Upward)
  LS Type: Summary Links(AS Boundary Router)
  Link State ID: 0.0.0.3 (AS Boundary Router address)
  Advertising Router: 0.0.0.2
```

```
LS Seq Number: 80000001
Checksum: 0xEE38
Length: 28
Network Mask: /0
      MTID: 0          Metric: 781
```

Note The only Type-4 LSA is propagated in Area 1. Because R3 is claiming to be an ASBR, there is no need to propagate a Type-4 LSA to provide reachability to R3, because R3 has an interface in Area 0.

What will happen if the link that connects R3 to R4 is filtered? Will R1 have network 4.4.4.0/24 in its routing table? Let's verify:

```
On R3:

R3(config)# router ospf 1
R3(config-router)# area 2 range 34.1.1.0 255.255.255.0 not-advertise
```

So if R1 does not have reachability to network 34.1.1.0/24, then it shouldn't have reachability to a host (34.1.1.4, the FA) on that network. If this is the case, then R1 should not have network 4.4.4.0/24 in its routing table. Let's verify:

```
On R1

R1# show ip route ospf | begin Gate
Gateway of last resort is not set

      23.0.0.0/24 is subnetted, 1 subnets
O IA    23.1.1.0 [110/1562] via 12.1.1.2, 01:09:46, Serial1/2
```

Sure enough, R1 does not have network 4.4.4.0/24 in its routing table.

What if the FA is changed to R3? Will R1 have the external route in its routing table? It should because R1 has reachability to R3. Let's verify.

You need to change the FA to R3. The following command instructs R3 to translate Type-7 LSAs to Type-5 LSAs but to suppress the FA:

```
On R3

R3(config)# router ospf 1
R3(config-router)# area 2 nssa translate type7 suppress-fa
```

Let's verify the configuration:

```
On R1


R1# show ip route ospf | begin Gate
Gateway of last resort is not set


      4.0.0.0/24 is subnetted, 1 subnets
O E2     4.4.4.0 [110/20] via 12.1.1.2, 00:00:14, Serial1/2
      23.0.0.0/24 is subnetted, 1 subnets
O IA     23.1.1.0 [110/1562] via 12.1.1.2, 01:15:10, Serial1/2
```

Does R1 have reachability to 34.1.1.4?

```
R1# ping 4.4.4.4

Type escape sequence to abort.
Sending 5, 100-byte ICMP Echos to 4.4.4.4, timeout is 2 seconds:
!!!!!
Success rate is 100 percent (5/5), round-trip min/avg/max = 160/160/160 ms
```

This can be used in certain designs to save resources on the routers. Imagine that there is a hub-and-spoke topology with 1000 spokes, and each spoke is redistributing a single external route. The routers upstream to the hub router will have 2000 routes in their routing table: 1000 routes for the links that connect the hub to the spokes, and another 1000 external routes.

If the spokes are all converted into an NSSA area, and the links that connect the hub to the spokes are all filtered, then the hub router is configured to suppress the FA, and the routers upstream to the hub router will only have 1000 external routes in their routing table, thus saving resources.

Erase the startup configuration and reload the routers before proceeding to the next lab.

Lab 8-13: Can OSPF Take a Suboptimal Path?

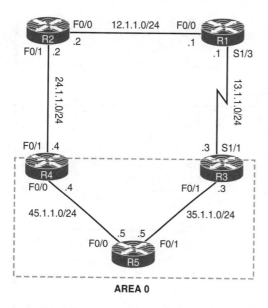

Figure 8-14 *Can OSPF Take a Suboptimal Path?*

Task 1

Configure OSPF Area 0 on R3, R4, and R5 based on the following policies:

- These routers should run OSPF Area 0 on all existing and future directly connected interfaces.

- Configure the RIDs to be 0.0.0.3, 0.0.0.4, and 0.0.0.5 for R3, R4, and R5, respectively.

```
On R3:

R3(config)# router ospf 1
R3(config-router)# router-id 0.0.0.3
R3(config-router)# network 0.0.0.0 0.0.0.0 area 0
```

```
On R4:

R4(config)# router ospf 1
R4(config-router)# router-id 0.0.0.4
R4(config-router)# network 0.0.0.0 0.0.0.0 area 0
```

```
On R5:

R5(config)# router ospf 1
R5(config-router)# router-id 0.0.0.5
R5(config-router)# network 0.0.0.0 0.0.0.0 area 0
```

You should see the following console messages:

```
%OSPF-5-ADJCHG: Process 1, Nbr 0.0.0.4 on FastEthernet0/0 from LOADING to FULL,
Loading Done

%OSPF-5-ADJCHG: Process 1, Nbr 0.0.0.3 on FastEthernet0/1 from LOADING to FULL,
Loading Done
```

Let's verify the configuration:

```
On R5:

R5# show ip ospf neighbor

Neighbor ID    Pri   State      Dead Time    Address       Interface
0.0.0.3         1    FULL/DR    00:00:33     35.1.1.3      FastEthernet0/1
0.0.0.4         1    FULL/BDR   00:00:32     45.1.1.4      FastEthernet0/0
```

Task 2

Configure the following policies on the routers in the topology shown in Figure 8-14:

- Configure a static default route on R1 pointing to R3 (13.1.1.3).

- Configure a static default route on R2 pointing to R4 (24.1.1.4).

- Configure a static route for network 12.1.1.0/24 on R3 pointing to R1 (13.1.1.1) and redistribute this static route into the OSPF routing domain using metric type 1.

- Configure a static route for network 12.1.1.0/24 on R4 pointing to R2 (24.1.1.2) and redistribute this static route into the OSPF routing domain using metric type 1.

```
On R1

R1(config)# ip route 0.0.0.0 0.0.0.0 13.1.1.3
```

```
On R2

R2(config)# ip route 0.0.0.0 0.0.0.0 24.1.1.4
```

```
On R3

R3(config)# ip route 12.1.1.0 255.255.255.0 13.1.1.1

R3(config)# router ospf 1
R3(config-router)# redistribute static subnets metric-type 1
```

```
On R4

R4(config)# ip route 12.1.1.0 255.255.255.0 24.1.1.2

R4(config)# Router ospf 1
R4(config-router)# redistribute static subnets metric-type 1
```

Let's verify the configuration:

```
On R5:

R5# show ip route ospf | begin Gate
Gateway of last resort is not set


     12.0.0.0/24 is subnetted, 1 subnets
O E1    12.1.1.0 [110/21] via 35.1.1.3, 00:01:13, FastEthernet0/1
     13.0.0.0/24 is subnetted, 1 subnets
O        13.1.1.0 [110/782] via 35.1.1.3, 00:05:39, FastEthernet0/1
     24.0.0.0/24 is subnetted, 1 subnets
O        24.1.1.0 [110/2] via 45.1.1.4, 00:05:10, FastEthernet0/0
```

R5 has two ways to reach network 12.1.1.0/24: one through R4, in which case it has to traverse through two FastEthernet links, and the other through R3, in which case it has to traverse the FastEthernet and a serial link. Why is R5 taking a suboptimal path through R3?

Let's verify R5's cost to the two ASBRs (R3 and R4):

```
R5# Show ip ospf border-routers
OSPF Process 1 internal Routing Table


Codes: i - Intra-area route, I - Inter-area route

i 0.0.0.3 [1] via 35.1.1.3, FastEthernet0/1, ASBR, Area 0, SPF 5
i 0.0.0.4 [1] via 45.1.1.4, FastEthernet0/0, ASBR, Area 0, SPF 5
```

You can see that R5 has a cost of 1 to reach both ASBRs, R3 (0.0.0.3) and R4 (0.0.0.4), and by default when the ASBRs redistribute external routes, they assign a cost of 20. Therefore, the cost should be 21 through both ASBRs, so why is R5 taking R3?

Let's verify the cost for the s1/1 interface of R3:

```
On R3:


R3# show ip ospf interface serial 1/1 | include Cost

 Process ID 1, Router ID 0.0.0.3, Network Type POINT_TO_POINT, Cost: 781
 Topology-MTID    Cost    Disabled    Shutdown       Topology Name
```

Let's verify the cost for the f0/1 interface of R4:

```
On R4:


R4# show ip ospf interface FastEthernet0/1 | include Cost

 Process ID 1, Router ID 0.0.0.4, Network Type BROADCAST, Cost: 1
 Topology-MTID    Cost    Disabled    Shutdown       Topology Name
```

The cost is lower through R4, but R5 is taking R3 to reach network 12.1.1.0/24.

Let's shut down the F0/1 interface of R5 and see if R5 will go through R4 to reach 12.1.1.0/24:

```
R5(config)# int FastEthernet0/1
R5(config-if)# shutdown
```

```
R5# Show ip route ospf | begin Gate
Gateway of last resort is not set


     12.0.0.0/24 is subnetted, 1 subnets
O E1    12.1.1.0 [110/22] via 45.1.1.4, 00:00:15, FastEthernet0/0
     24.0.0.0/24 is subnetted, 1 subnets
O        24.1.1.0 [110/2] via 45.1.1.4, 00:18:16, FastEthernet0/0
```

R5's cost to R4 is 1, and R4 is redistributing the external routes with a default cost of 20. This should be 21 and not 22. Let's use **no shutdown** on the F0/1 interface of R5 and check the Link State Database (LSDB) of this router:

```
On R5


R5(config)# interface FastEthernet0/1
R5(config-if)# no shutdown

R5# show ip ospf database external 12.1.1.0

            OSPF Router with ID (0.0.0.5) (Process ID 1)


            Type-5 AS External Link States


  Routing Bit Set on this LSA in topology Base with MTID 0
  LS age: 1895
  Options: (No TOS-capability, DC)
  LS Type: AS External Link
  Link State ID: 12.1.1.0 (External Network Number )
  Advertising Router: 0.0.0.3
  LS Seq Number: 80000001
  Checksum: 0x9E71
  Length: 36
  Network Mask: /24
       Metric Type: 1 (Comparable directly to link state metric)
       MTID: 0
       Metric: 20
       Forward Address: 0.0.0.0
       External Route Tag: 0

  LS age: 1857
  Options: (No TOS-capability, DC)
  LS Type: AS External Link
  Link State ID: 12.1.1.0 (External Network Number )
  Advertising Router: 0.0.0.4
```

```
LS Seq Number: 80000001
Checksum: 0xD61C
Length: 36
Network Mask: /24
        Metric Type: 1 (Comparable directly to link state metric)
        MTID: 0
        Metric: 20
        Forward Address: 24.1.1.2
        External Route Tag: 0
```

Okay, you can see the problem: R4 has set the FA to 24.1.1.2; therefore, the cost is calculated from R5 all the way to R2's F0/1 interface, whereas the FA from R3 is set to R3 (0.0.0.0). Let's calculate the cost:

- **The cost through R3:** R3 is advertising an FA of 0.0.0.0; therefore, R5 calculates the cost right up to R3. R3 redistributes the static route with a default cost of 20. R5's cost to R3 is 1. Therefore, the cost through R3 is 21.

- **The cost through R4:** R4 is advertising an FA of 24.1.1.2; therefore, R5 calculates the cost right up to R2's f0/1 interface. R5 redistributes the static route with a default cost of 20. R5's cost to R4 is 1, and R4's cost to R2 is also 1. Therefore, R5's cost through R4 is 22.

The question is, Why?

The answer is the network type. R4's external interface to R2 has a network type of broadcast. Let's verify:

```
R4# show ip ospf interface FastEthernet0/1 | include Network
 Process ID 1, Router ID 0.0.0.4, Network Type BROADCAST, Cost: 1
```

Because on a broadcast network we can have many neighbors, the next-hop/FA is set based on the advertising router's IP address (in this case, 24.1.1.2).

Let's verify the network type of the s1/1 interface of R3:

```
R3# show ip ospf interface serial 1/1 | include Network
 Process ID 1, Router ID 0.0.0.3, Network Type POINT_TO_POINT, Cost: 64
```

Because the network type is set to be point-to-point, R3 simply says there is *only* one potential neighbor, so it sets the NH/FA to its interface's IP address.

Let's change the network types on the external interfaces of R3 and R4 such that R5 takes an optimal path to reach 12.1.1.0/24. To accomplish this, the network types are swapped:

```
On R3:

R3(config)# interface serial 1/1
R3(config-if)# ip ospf network broadcast
```

```
On R4:

R4(config)# interface FastEthernet0/1
R4(config-if)# ip ospf network point-to-point
```

Let's verify the configuration:

```
On R5:

R5# show ip route ospf | begin Gate
Gateway of last resort is not set


     12.0.0.0/24 is subnetted, 1 subnets
O E1    12.1.1.0 [110/21] via 45.1.1.4, 00:00:28, FastEthernet0/0
     13.0.0.0/24 is subnetted, 1 subnets
O       13.1.1.0 [110/782] via 35.1.1.3, 00:16:28, FastEthernet0/1
     24.0.0.0/24 is subnetted, 1 subnets
O       24.1.1.0 [110/2] via 45.1.1.4, 00:51:40, FastEthernet0/0

R5# show ip ospf database external 12.1.1.0 | include Advertising|Forward

  Advertising Router: 0.0.0.3
       Forward Address: 13.1.1.1
  Advertising Router: 0.0.0.4
       Forward Address: 0.0.0.0
```

Erase the startup configuration of the routers and reload them before proceeding to the next lab.

Lab 8-14: RFC 3101 and RFC 1587

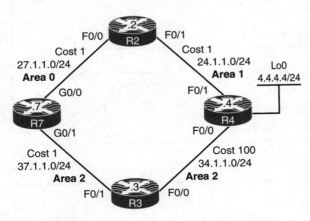

Figure 8-15   *RFC 3101 and RFC 1587*

Task 1

Configure OSPF based on the topology shown in Figure 8-15. R4 should be configured to redistribute its loopback0 interface in this routing domain using the default parameters. The router IDs should be configured as 0.0.0.*x*, where *x* is the router number. Explain which path R7 takes to reach network 4.4.4.0/24.

```
On R7:

R7(config)# router ospf 1
R7(config-router)# router-id 0.0.0.7
R7(config-router)# network 27.1.1.7 0.0.0.0 area 0
R7(config-router)# network 37.1.1.7 0.0.0.0 area 2
```

```
On R2:

R2(config)# router ospf 1
R2(config-router)# router-id 0.0.0.2
R2(config-router)# network 27.1.1.2 0.0.0.0 area 0
R2(config-router)# network 24.1.1.2 0.0.0.0 area 1
```

You should see the following console message:

```
%OSPF-5-ADJCHG: Process 1, Nbr 0.0.0.7 on FastEthernet0/0 from LOADING to FULL,
Loading Done
```

```
On R3:

R3(config)# router ospf 1
R3(config-router)# router-id 0.0.0.3
R3(config-router)# network 37.1.1.3 0.0.0.0 area 2
R3(config-router)# network 34.1.1.3 0.0.0.0 area 2
```

You should see the following console message as well:

```
%OSPF-5-ADJCHG: Process 1, Nbr 0.0.0.7 on FastEthernet0/1 from LOADING to FULL,
Loading Done
```

```
On R4:

R4(config)# route-map tst
R4(config-route-map)# match interface loopback 0

R4(config)# router ospf 1
R4(config-router)# router-id 0.0.0.4
R4(config-router)# network 34.1.1.4 0.0.0.0 area 2
R4(config-router)# network 24.1.1.4 0.0.0.0 area 1
R4(config-router)# redistribute connected route-map tst subnets
```

You should also see the following console messages:

```
%OSPF-5-ADJCHG: Process 1, Nbr 0.0.0.3 on FastEthernet0/0 from LOADING to FULL,
Loading Done

%OSPF-5-ADJCHG: Process 1, Nbr 0.0.0.2 on FastEthernet0/1 from LOADING to FULL,
Loading Done
```

Let's verify the configuration:

```
On R7:

R7# show ip route ospf | begin Gate
Gateway of last resort is not set

      4.0.0.0/24 is subnetted, 1 subnets
O E2     4.4.4.0 [110/20] via 37.1.1.3, 00:00:11, GigabitEthernet0/1
      24.0.0.0/24 is subnetted, 1 subnets
O IA     24.1.1.0 [110/2] via 27.1.1.2, 00:02:07, GigabitEthernet0/0
      34.0.0.0/24 is subnetted, 1 subnets
O        34.1.1.0 [110/101] via 37.1.1.3, 00:01:15, GigabitEthernet0/1
```

We can see that R7 takes the path through R3 to reach network 4.4.4.0/24. But why? Let's check R7's route to network 4.4.4.0/24:

```
R7# show ip route 4.4.4.0

Routing entry for 4.4.4.0/24
  Known via "ospf 1", distance 110, metric 20, type extern 2, forward metric 101
  Last update from 37.1.1.3 on GigabitEthernet0/1, 00:01:19 ago
  Routing Descriptor Blocks:
  * 37.1.1.3, from 0.0.0.4, 00:01:19 ago, via GigabitEthernet0/1
      Route metric is 20, traffic share count is 1
```

Let's check the LSDB of R7 for network 4.4.4.0/24:

```
R7# show ip ospf database external 4.4.4.0

            OSPF Router with ID (0.0.0.1) (Process ID 1)

              Type-5 AS External Link States

Routing Bit Set on this LSA in topology Base with MTID 0
LS age: 170
Options: (No TOS-capability, DC, Upward)
LS Type: AS External Link
Link State ID: 4.4.4.0 (External Network Number )
Advertising Router: 0.0.0.4
LS Seq Number: 80000001
Checksum: 0x3F51
Length: 36
Network Mask: /24
        Metric Type: 2 (Larger than any link state path)
        MTID: 0
        Metric: 20
        Forward Address: 0.0.0.0
        External Route Tag: 0
```

The output of the preceding **show** command reveals the following:

■ The link state ID, which describes the network as 4.4.4.0.

■ The advertising router is 0.0.0.4, or R4.

■ The metric type is 2. This is the default behavior in OSPF.

■ The forward address is set to 0.0.0.0, meaning that R4 is the next hop.

R7 has two paths to reach network 4.4.4.0/24:

- **An intra-area route via R3 with a cost of 101**: This cost is displayed in the output of the **show ip route 4.4.4.0** command as the forward metric.

- **An inter-area route via R2 with a cost of 2**: From R7's perspective, this is the cumulative cost of reaching R2 (the ABR), which is 1, plus the ABR's cost to reach R4, which is also 1. Therefore, the total cost is 2. We can see the cost by looking at the Type-4 LSA that is injected by the ABR (R2) and/or by using the **show ip ospf border-routers** command:

```
R7# show ip ospf border-routers

            OSPF Router with ID (0.0.0.1) (Process ID 1)

               Base Topology (MTID 0)

Internal Router Routing Table
Codes: i - Intra-area route, I - Inter-area route


i 0.0.0.2 [1] via 27.1.1.2, GigabitEthernet0/0, ABR, Area 0, SPF 4
i 0.0.0.4 [101] via 37.1.1.3, GigabitEthernet0/1, ASBR, Area 2, SPF 8


R7# show ip ospf database asbr-summary adv-router 0.0.0.2

            OSPF Router with ID (0.0.0.1) (Process ID 1)

               Summary ASB Link States (Area 0)


  LS age: 1616
  Options: (No TOS-capability, DC, Upward)
  LS Type: Summary Links(AS Boundary Router)
  Link State ID: 0.0.0.4 (AS Boundary Router address)
  Advertising Router: 0.0.0.2
  LS Seq Number: 80000001
  Checksum: 0x51E3
  Length: 28
  Network Mask: /0
        MTID: 0          Metric: 1
```

Let's traceroute to 4.4.4.4 and verify the path:

```
R7# traceroute 4.4.4.4 numeric

Type escape sequence to abort.
Tracing the route to 4.4.4.4
VRF info: (vrf in name/id, vrf out name/id)
  1 37.1.1.3 4 msec 0 msec 4 msec
  2 34.1.1.4 0 msec *  0 msec
```

In OSPF, intra-area routes are preferred over inter-area routes. R7 takes the intra-area route versus inter-area route to reach 4.4.4.0/24.

Task 2

Convert Areas 1 and 2 to NSSA. Once the areas are converted to NSSA, describe the path that R7 takes to reach network 4.4.4.0/24.

```
On R7, R3, and R4:

Rx(config)# router ospf 1
Rx(config-router)# area 2 nssa
```

```
On R2, and R4:

Rx(config)# router ospf 1
Rx(config-router)# area 1 nssa
```

Let's verify the configuration:

```
On R7:

R7# show ip route ospf | begin Gate
Gateway of last resort is not set

      4.0.0.0/24 is subnetted, 1 subnets
O E2    4.4.4.0 [110/20] via 27.1.1.2, 00:00:41, GigabitEthernet0/0
      24.0.0.0/24 is subnetted, 1 subnets
O IA    24.1.1.0 [110/2] via 27.1.1.2, 00:01:43, GigabitEthernet0/0
      34.0.0.0/24 is subnetted, 1 subnets
O       34.1.1.0 [110/101] via 37.1.1.3, 00:01:00, GigabitEthernet0/1


R7# show ip route 4.4.4.0
```

```
Routing entry for 4.4.4.0/24
  Known via "ospf 1", distance 110, metric 20, type extern 2, forward metric 2
  Last update from 27.1.1.2 on GigabitEthernet0/0, 00:01:18 ago
  Routing Descriptor Blocks:
  * 27.1.1.2, from 0.0.0.2, 00:01:18 ago, via GigabitEthernet0/0
      Route metric is 20, traffic share count is 1
```

Why is R7 installing an "E2" route through R2 and not an "N2" route through R3?

R4 advertises two Type-7 LSAs:

- A Type-7 LSA with a forward address of 24.1.1.4. This is the IP address of R4's F0/1 interface, and this LSA is flooded into Area 1. The ABR (R2) translates this Type-7 LSA into a Type-5 LSA, copies the forward address from LSA Type 7 into LSA Type 5, and floods it into Area 0.

- A Type-7 LSA with a forward address of 34.1.1.4. This is R4's F0/0 interface; it is flooded into Area 2.

```
R7# show ip ospf database external 4.4.4.0

            OSPF Router with ID (0.0.0.1) (Process ID 1)


            Type-5 AS External Link States


  Routing Bit Set on this LSA in topology Base with MTID 0
  LS age: 552
  Options: (No TOS-capability, DC)
  LS Type: AS External Link
  Link State ID: 4.4.4.0 (External Network Number )
  Advertising Router: 0.0.0.2
  LS Seq Number: 80000001
  Checksum: 0xA5CE
  Length: 36
  Network Mask: /24
        Metric Type: 2 (Larger than any link state path)
        MTID: 0
        Metric: 20
        Forward Address: 24.1.1.4
        External Route Tag: 0

R7# show ip ospf database nssa-external 4.4.4.0

            OSPF Router with ID (0.0.0.1) (Process ID 1)


            Type-7 AS External Link States (Area 2)
```

```
LS age: 659
Options: (No TOS-capability, Type 7/5 translation, DC)
LS Type: AS External Link
Link State ID: 4.4.4.0 (External Network Number )
Advertising Router: 0.0.0.4
LS Seq Number: 80000002
Checksum: 0x71EB
Length: 36
Network Mask: /24
        Metric Type: 2 (Larger than any link state path)
        MTID: 0
        Metric: 20
        Forward Address: 34.1.1.4
        External Route Tag: 0
```

R7 chooses the best path to reach the two forward addresses using an intra-area route (through R3) and an inter-area route (through R2):

```
R7# show ip route 24.1.1.4

Routing entry for 24.1.1.0/24
  Known via "ospf 1", distance 110, metric 2, type inter area
  Last update from 27.1.1.2 on GigabitEthernet0/0, 00:06:32 ago
  Routing Descriptor Blocks:
  * 27.1.1.2, from 0.0.0.2, 00:06:32 ago, via GigabitEthernet0/0
      Route metric is 2, traffic share count is 1

R7# show ip route 34.1.1.4

Routing entry for 34.1.1.0/24
  Known via "ospf 1", distance 110, metric 101, type intra area
  Last update from 37.1.1.3 on GigabitEthernet0/1, 00:06:24 ago
  Routing Descriptor Blocks:
  * 37.1.1.3, from 0.0.0.4, 00:06:24 ago, via GigabitEthernet0/1
      Route metric is 101, traffic share count is 1
```

Because the two OSPF routes (intra-area and inter-area) are pointing to different destinations, R7 can no longer prefer the intra-area route over the inter-area route. Therefore, R7 chooses the lowest cost through R2. Let's verify:

```
R1# traceroute 4.4.4.4 numeric

Type escape sequence to abort.
Tracing the route to 4.4.4.4
VRF info: (vrf in name/id, vrf out name/id)
  1 27.1.1.2 4 msec 0 msec 0 msec
  2 24.1.1.4 0 msec *  0 msec
```

To prove this, let's change the cost of R7's link to R2 to 200:

```
R7(config)# int GigabitEthernet0/0
R7(config-if)# ip ospf cost 200
```

Let's verify the configuration:

```
R71# traceroute 4.4.4.4 numeric

Type escape sequence to abort.
Tracing the route to 4.4.4.4
VRF info: (vrf in name/id, vrf out name/id)
  1 37.1.1.3 0 msec 0 msec 0 msec
  2 34.1.1.4 4 msec *  0 msec
```

The following **show** command displays that the "N" route is preferred over the "E" route:

```
R7# show ip route ospf | begin Gate
Gateway of last resort is not set

      4.0.0.0/24 is subnetted, 1 subnets
O N2    4.4.4.0 [110/20] via 37.1.1.3, 00:01:08, GigabitEthernet0/1
      24.0.0.0/24 is subnetted, 1 subnets
O IA    24.1.1.0 [110/201] via 27.1.1.2, 00:01:08, GigabitEthernet0/0
      34.0.0.0/24 is subnetted, 1 subnets
O       34.1.1.0 [110/101] via 37.1.1.3, 00:13:08, GigabitEthernet0/1
```

Let's reconfigure the cost on R7's g0/0 as well as R3 and R4's f0/0 to 1. This way, from R7's perspective, the cost will be identical no matter which path R7 takes:

```
On R3 and R4:

Rx(config)# interface FastEthernet0/0
Rx(config-if)# ip ospf cost 1
```

```
On R7:


R7(config)# interface GigabitEthernet0/0
R7(config-if)# ip ospf cost 1
```

Let's verify the configuration:

```
On R7:


R7# show ip route ospf | begin Gate
Gateway of last resort is not set

      4.0.0.0/24 is subnetted, 1 subnets
O N2    4.4.4.0 [110/20] via 37.1.1.3, 00:01:10, GigabitEthernet0/1
      24.0.0.0/24 is subnetted, 1 subnets
O IA    24.1.1.0 [110/2] via 27.1.1.2, 00:03:05, GigabitEthernet0/0
      34.0.0.0/24 is subnetted, 1 subnets
O       34.1.1.0 [110/2] via 37.1.1.3, 00:01:10, GigabitEthernet0/1
```

In this case, the cost from R7's perspective is identical no matter which path it takes, but R7 is taking the "N" route over the "E" route. Why?

Let's verify:

```
On R7:


R7# show ip ospf | include RFC
 Supports NSSA (compatible with RFC 3101)
```

You can see that R7 is implementing RFC 3101. RFC 3101 states the following: If the current LSA is functionally the same as an installed LSA (that is, same destination, cost, and non-zero forwarding address), then apply the following priorities in deciding which LSA is preferred:

1. A Type-7 LSA with the P-bit set.

2. A Type-5 LSA.

3. The LSA with the higher router ID.

Let's see if the P-bit is set:

```
R7# Show ip ospf database nssa-external 4.4.4.0

              OSPF Router with ID (0.0.0.7) (Process ID 1)

                 Type-7 AS External Link States (Area 2)

  Routing Bit Set on this LSA in topology Base with MTID 0
  LS age: 1670
  Options: (No TOS-capability, Type 7/5 translation, DC, Upward)
  LS Type: AS External Link
  Link State ID: 4.4.4.0 (External Network Number )
  Advertising Router: 0.0.0.4
  LS Seq Number: 80000001
  Checksum: 0x73EA
  Length: 36
  Network Mask: /24
        Metric Type: 2 (Larger than any link state path)
        MTID: 0
        Metric: 20
        Forward Address: 34.1.1.4
        External Route Tag: 0
```

What if RFC 1587 is implemented? RFC 1587 states the following: When a Type-5 LSA and a Type-7 LSA are found to have the same type and an equal distance, the following priorities apply (listed from highest to lowest) for breaking the tie:

1. Any Type-5 LSA.

2. A Type-7 LSA with the P-bit set and a non-zero forwarding address.

3. Any other Type-7 LSA.

Let's change the RFC to implement RFC 1587:

```
R7(config)# router ospf 1
R7(config-router)# compatible rfc1587
```

Note To implement RFC 3101, the preceding command must be negated.

Let's verify the configuration:

```
On R7:


R7# show ip route ospf | begin Gate
Gateway of last resort is not set


     4.0.0.0/24 is subnetted, 1 subnets
O E2    4.4.4.0 [110/20] via 27.1.1.2, 00:01:35, GigabitEthernet0/0
     24.0.0.0/24 is subnetted, 1 subnets
O IA    24.1.1.0 [110/2] via 27.1.1.2, 00:19:18, GigabitEthernet0/0
     34.0.0.0/24 is subnetted, 1 subnets
O       34.1.1.0 [110/2] via 37.1.1.3, 00:17:23, GigabitEthernet0/1
```

Erase the startup configuration of the routers and reload them before proceeding to the next lab.

Chapter 9

Redistribution

Lab 9-1: Basic Redistribution 1

Task 1

Figure 9-1 illustrates the topology that will be used in the following tasks. Configure the link between R1 and R3 to be in OSPF area 0. Configure the Lo0 interface of R3 in area 2. Do not use the **network** command to accomplish this task. The OSPF router IDs should be configured as 0.0.0.1 and 0.0.0.3 for R1 and R3, respectively.

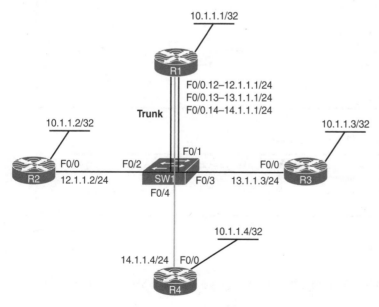

Figure 9-1 *Configuring Basic Redistribution*

```
On R1:


R1(config)# interface FastEthernet0/0.13
R1(config-subif)# ip ospf 1 area 0


R1(config)# router ospf 1
R1(config-router)# router-id 0.0.0.1


On R3:


R3(config)# interface FastEthernet0/0
R3(config-if)# ip ospf 1 area 0


R3(config)# interface loopback 0
R3(config-if)# ip ospf 1 area 2
```

When you run the Open Shortest Path First (OSPF) protocol on a given interface by using the interface-configuration command, IOS starts the OSPF process automatically:

```
R3# show run | section router ospf 1

router ospf 1
 log-adjacency-changes

R3(config)# router ospf 1
R3(config-router)# router-id 0.0.0.3
% OSPF: Reload or use "clear ip ospf process" command, for this to take effect

R3# clear ip ospf process
Reset ALL OSPF processes? [no]: yes
```

You should see the following console message:

```
%OSPF-5-ADJCHG: Process 1, Nbr 0.0.0.1 on Ethernet0/0 from FULL to DOWN, Neighbor
  Down: Interface down or detached
%OSPF-5-ADJCHG: Process 1, Nbr 0.0.0.1 on FastEthernet0/0 from LOADING to FULL,
  Loading Done
```

Let's verify the configuration:

Note   R1 should see R3's Lo0 as an "O IA" route in its routing table.

```
On R1:

R1# show ip route ospf | begin gate
gateway of last resort is not set

     10.0.0.0/8 is variably subnetted, 9 subnets, 2 masks

O IA    10.1.1.3/32 [110/2] via 10.1.13.3, 00:01:33, Fastethernet0/0.13
```

Task 2

Add the following loopback interfaces to R3:

- **Lo31**: 192.168.31.3/24
- **Lo32**: 192.168.32.3/24
- **Lo33**: 192.168.33.3/24

Redistribute Lo31 and Lo33 into OSPF. Do not redistribute Lo32 into OSPF. Do not use **access-list** or **prefix-list** to accomplish the task.

The first step in configuring this task is to configure the loopback interfaces on R3:

```
On R3:

R3(config)# interface loopback31
R3(config-if)# ip address 192.168.31.3 255.255.255.0

R3(config-if)# interface loopback32
R3(config-if)# ip address 192.168.32.3 255.255.255.0

R3(config-if)# interface loopback33
R3(config-if)# ip address 192.168.33.3 255.255.255.0
```

Because using an access list or a prefix list is not allowed, a route map is configured and the required interfaces are matched using the **match interface** option in the route map configuration mode.

Note   The task states that Lo32 should *not* be redistributed; therefore, the route map could be configured to deny Lo32 and permit the rest of the networks, or the route map could simply permit the Lo31 and Lo33 interfaces and deny Lo32 from being redistributed.

Once the route map is configured, it's referenced in the **redistribute connected** command in the router configuration mode.

We have two options as far as configuring a route map goes.

Option #1

In this option, only Lo32 is denied. If **route-map tst permit 90** is not configured, the rest of the interfaces will also be denied from being redistributed, because if the logic of the route map is not completed, IOS will try to protect you and in the process will drop the rest of the interfaces. Therefore, **route-map tst permit 90** is configured to permit the rest of the interfaces.

```
!On R3:

R3(config)# route-map tst deny 10
R3(config-route-map)# match interface loopback32
R3(config)# route-map tst permit 90
```

Option #2

This option is more specific and should be used in this configuration. This option is more specific because it will *not* redistribute future directly connected routes in this process.

```
R3(config)# route-map tst permit 10
R3(config-route-map)# match interface loopback31 loopback33
```

In the final step, the connected interfaces that are referenced in the **route-map** are redistributed into the OSPF routing protocol.

```
R3(config-route-map)# router ospf 1
R3(config-router)# redistribute connected subnets route-map tst
```

The **subnets** keyword is required; otherwise, only the classful networks (networks that are not subnetted) will be redistributed.

Let's verify the configuration:

```
!On R3:

R3# show ip ospf database external | include Type-5|192

              Type-5 AS External Link States
  link state id: 192.168.31.0 (External Network Number )
  link state id: 192.168.33.0 (External Network Number )
```

```
!On R1:

R1# show ip route ospf | begin Gate
gateway of last resort is not set

        10.0.0.0/8 is variably subnetted, 9 subnets, 2 masks
O IA     10.1.1.3/32 [110/2] via 10.1.13.3, 00:10:39, Fastethernet0/0.13
O E2 192.168.31.0/24 [110/20] via 10.1.13.3, 00:01:45, Fastethernet0/0.13
O E2 192.168.33.0/24 [110/20] via 10.1.13.3, 00:01:45, Fastethernet0/0.13
```

Task 3

Configure R1 and R2 based on the following policy:

- Configure RIPv2 between R1 and R2. Disable auto-summary.

- R1 should be configured to redistribute OSPF routes into the RIP routing domain.

- R1 should filter R3's Lo33. Do not use **distribute-list** or **offset-list** to accomplish this task.

The first step is to configure RIPv2 on both R1 and R2:

```
!On R1:
R1(config)# router rip
R1(config-router)# version 2
R1(config-router)# no auto-summary
R1(config-router)# network 12.0.0.0
R1(config-router)# network 10.0.0.0
R1(config-router)# passive-interface FastEthernet0/0.13
R1(config-router)# passive-interface FastEthernet0/0.14
```

Note   In the preceding configuration, the **passive-interface** commands are required because the task requires RIPv2 to run between R1 and R2. The **passive-interface** commands turn the specified subinterfaces into receive-only mode.

```
!On R2:

R2(config)# router rip
R2(config-router)# version 2
R2(config-router)# no auto-summary
R2(config-router)# network 12.0.0.0
R2(config-router)# network 10.0.0.0
```

Let's verify the configuration:

```
!On R2:


R2# show ip route rip | begin Gate
Gateway of last resort is not set

      10.0.0.0/32 is subnetted, 2 subnets
R        10.1.1.1 [120/1] via 12.1.1.1, 00:00:17, FastEthernet0/0
```

In the second step, OSPF is redistributed into RIP on R1:

```
!On R1:


R1(config)# router rip
R1(config-router)# redistribute ospf 1
```

Let's verify the configuration:

```
!On R2:


R2# show ip route rip | begin Gate
Gateway of last resort is not set

      10.0.0.0/32 is subnetted, 2 subnets
R        10.1.1.1 [120/1] via 12.1.1.1, 00:00:05, FastEthernet0/0
```

Note R3's Lo0, Lo31, and Lo33 that were redistributed from the OSPF routing domain are not in the routing table of R2.

One of the biggest problems of redistribution is that each routing protocol has its own metric:

- **RIP**: Hop count
- **EIGRP**: Composite of bandwidth, delay, reliability, load, and K values
- **OSPF**: Cost, which is based on bandwidth

When redistributing from OSPF into the RIP routing protocol, what should be the metric?

Well, there are many choices:

■ The metric can be configured such that it applies to all existing and future redistributed routes.

■ The metric can be set separately on each configured **redistribute** command.

■ The metric can be set based on usage of a **route-map**.

One notable exception is directly connected routes to which RIP applies a default metric of 0. To correct the problem, a metric of 3 is assigned to the OSPF routes that are redistributed into RIPv2:

```
!On R1:

R1(config)# router rip
R1(config-router)# redistribute ospf 1 metric 3
```

Let's verify the configuration:

```
!On R2:

R2# show ip route rip | begin Gate
Gateway of last resort is not set

      10.0.0.0/32 is subnetted, 3 subnets
R        10.1.1.1 [120/1] via 12.1.1.1, 00:00:13, FastEthernet0/0
R        10.1.1.3 [120/3] via 12.1.1.1, 00:00:13, FastEthernet0/0
      13.0.0.0/24 is subnetted, 1 subnets
R        13.1.1.0 [120/3] via 12.1.1.1, 00:00:13, FastEthernet0/0
R     192.168.31.0/24 [120/3] via 12.1.1.1, 00:00:13, FastEthernet0/0
R     192.168.33.0/24 [120/3] via 12.1.1.1, 00:00:13, FastEthernet0/0
```

The output of the preceding **show** command verifies that all OSPF routes have been redistributed into RIPv2. The last step of this task requires filtering of R3's Lo33 (192.168.33.0/24). Remember that the use of **distribute-list** or **offset-list** is not allowed. Therefore, a **route-map** is used to set the metric of Lo33's interface to **Infinity**. This will cause R1 to poison that route.

The steps required to configure this task are as follows:

1. A **prefix-list** is configured to identify the IP address of R3's Lo33.

2. A **route-map** is configured to reference the **prefix-list** from the previous step and to set the metric to 16 (infinity).

3. The **redistribute** command is reconfigured to reference the route map.

Here's the first step:

```
!On R1

 R1(config)# ip prefix-list lo33 permit 192.168.33.0/24
```

Here's the second step:

```
R1(config)# route-map tst permit 10
R1(config-route-map)# match ip address prefix-list lo33

R1(config-route-map)# set metric 16
R1(config-route-map)# route-map tst permit 90
```

And here's the third and the final step:

```
R1(config-route-map)# router rip
R1(config-router)# redistribute ospf 1 metric 3 route-map tst
```

Let's verify the configuration:

```
!On R2:

R2# show ip route rip | begin Gate
Gateway of last resort is not set

      10.0.0.0/32 is subnetted, 3 subnets
R        10.1.1.1 [120/1] via 12.1.1.1, 00:00:11, FastEthernet0/0
R        10.1.1.3 [120/3] via 12.1.1.1, 00:00:11, FastEthernet0/0
      13.0.0.0/24 is subnetted, 1 subnets
R        13.1.1.0 [120/3] via 12.1.1.1, 00:00:11, FastEthernet0/0
R     192.168.31.0/24 [120/3] via 12.1.1.1, 00:00:11, FastEthernet0/0
```

To see the routes advertised to R2, let's enable RIP debugging on R1 and R2:

```
!On R1:

R1# debug ip rip

RIP: sending v2 update to 224.0.0.9 via FastEthernet0/0.12 (12.1.1.1)
RIP: build update entries
        10.1.1.1/32 via 0.0.0.0, metric 1, tag 0
```

```
     10.1.1.3/32 via 0.0.0.0, metric 3, tag 0
     13.1.1.0/24 via 0.0.0.0, metric 3, tag 0
     192.168.31.0/24 via 0.0.0.0, metric 3, tag 0
     192.168.33.0/24 via 0.0.0.0, metric 16, tag 0
```

In the output of the preceding **debug,** you can clearly see that network 192.168.33.0/24 is advertised with a hop count of 16, and the output of the following **debug** reveals that R2 discards the route because a hop count of 16 is inaccessible in the RIP routing protocol:

```
!On R2

R2# debug ip rip

RIP: received v2 update from 12.1.1.1 on FastEthernet0/0
     10.1.1.1/32 via 0.0.0.0 in 1 hops
     10.1.1.3/32 via 0.0.0.0 in 3 hops
     13.1.1.0/24 via 0.0.0.0 in 3 hops
     192.168.31.0/24 via 0.0.0.0 in 3 hops
     192.168.33.0/24 via 0.0.0.0 in 16 hops  (inaccessible)
```

Here's how to disable debug on R1 and R2:

```
!On R1 and R2:

Rx# undebug all
```

Task 4

Add the following loopback interfaces to R2 and R3:

- **R2:** Lo23: 192.168.23.2 /24

- **R3:** Lo23: 192.168.23.3 /24

Advertise R2's Lo23 into the RIPv2 routing protocol. R3's Lo23 should be configured in OSPF area 2 and advertised with its correct mask.

```
!On R2:

R2(config)# interface loopback 23
R2(config-if)# ip address 192.168.23.2 255.255.255.0

R2(config-if)# router rip
R2(config-router)# network 192.168.23.0
```

```
On R3:

R3(config)# interface loopback 23
R3(config-if)# ip address 192.168.23.3 255.255.255.0
R3(config-if)# ip ospf network point-to-point

R3(config-if)# router ospf 1
R3(config-router)# network 192.168.23.3 0.0.0.0 area 2
```

Let's verify the configuration:

```
!On R1:

R1# show ip route | include 192.168.23

    192.168.23.0/24 is subnetted, 1 subnets
O IA  192.168.23.0/24 [110/2] via 13.1.1.3, 00:00:24, FastEthernet0/0.13
```

The route does not appear as a RIP route. Did RIP advertise the route? If so, what happened?

Let's check R1's RIP database:

```
R1# show ip rip database 192.168.23.0 255.255.255.0

192.168.23.0/24    redistributed
    [3] via 13.1.1.3, from 0.0.0.3,

R1# show ip route 192.168.23.0
Routing entry for 192.168.23.0/24
  Known via "ospf 1", distance 110, metric 2, type inter area
  Redistributing via rip
  Advertised by rip metric 3 route-map tst
  Last update from 13.1.1.3 on FastEthernet0/0.13, 00:04:05 ago
  Routing Descriptor Blocks:
  * 13.1.1.3, from 0.0.0.3, 00:04:05 ago, via FastEthernet0/0.13
      Route metric is 2, traffic share count is 1
```

Note   The route is in RIP's database, but it is in the database as a "redistributed" route. It is in the database as "redistributed" because of the redistribution of OSPF into RIP on R1 in Task 3. The routing table shows that route as **Known via "ospf 1"**.

So where is the update from R2?

Maybe R2 is not sending that update at all? Let's debug RIP's updates and verify:

```
R1# debug ip rip
RIP protocol debugging is on

RIP: sending v2 update to 224.0.0.9 via FastEthernet0/0.12 (12.1.1.1)
RIP: build update entries
        10.1.1.1/32 via 0.0.0.0, metric 1, tag 0
        10.1.1.3/32 via 0.0.0.0, metric 3, tag 0
        13.1.1.0/24 via 0.0.0.0, metric 3, tag 0
        192.168.23.0/24 via 0.0.0.0, metric 3, tag 0
        192.168.31.0/24 via 0.0.0.0, metric 3, tag 0
        192.168.33.0/24 via 0.0.0.0, metric 16, tag 0

RIP: received v2 update from 12.1.1.2 on FastEthernet0/0.12
        10.1.1.2/32 via 0.0.0.0 in 1 hops
        192.168.23.0/24 via 0.0.0.0 in 1 hops
```

R1 received an update for network 192.168.23.0/24 from R2, but it does not install it into its RIP database because the RIP database contains only redistributed routes and learned RIP routes that are actually installed in the router's routing table.

Because the "administrative distance" of RIP is higher than OSPF's administrative distance, IOS prefers the OSPF route and rejects the RIP route.

Let's verify this fact:

```
!On R3

R3(config)# interface loopback 23
R3(config-if)# shutdown

!On R1

R1# show ip route rip | begin Gate
Gateway of last resort is not set

      10.0.0.0/32 is subnetted, 3 subnets
R        10.1.1.2 [120/1] via 12.1.1.2, 00:00:15, FastEthernet0/0.12
R        192.168.23.0/24 [120/1] via 12.1.1.2, 00:00:15, FastEthernet0/0.12

R1# show ip rip database 192.168.23.0 255.255.255.0

192.168.23.0/24
    [1] via 12.1.1.2, 00:00:21, FastEthernet0/0.12
```

The output of the preceding **show** commands reveals that network 192.168.23.0/24 is a RIP route.

To verify and reveal the comparison of administrative distance of RIP versus OSPF, **debug ip routing** is enabled on R1 and then the Lo23 interface of R3 is enabled (**no shut**).

Here's how to disable the existing debug:

```
R1# undebug all
```

Here's how to enable debugging for IP routing:

```
R1# debug ip routing
IP routing debugging is on


!On R3


R3(config)# interface loopback 23
R3(config-if)# no shutdown
```

Let's check the debug output on R1:

```
!On R1:


RT: closer admin distance for 192.168.23.0, flushing 1 routes
RT: add 192.168.23.0/24 via 13.1.1.3, ospf metric [110/2]
```

The first line of the preceding output reveals the comparison of the administrative distance of RIP and OSPF, and **add 192.168.23.0/24 via 13.1.1.3, ospf metric [110/2]** is what is injected into the routing table of this router to verify that information:

```
R1# show ip route ospf | include 192.168.23.0

O IA  192.168.23.0/24 [110/2] via 13.1.1.3, 00:01:25, FastEthernet0/0.13
```

Let's disable the debugging:

```
R1# undebug all
```

Task 5

Configure EIGRP AS 100 on R1's F0/0.14 interface and R4's F0/0 interface. R4 should redistribute its loopback0 interface into this routing domain.

```
!On R1:

R1(config)# router eigrp 100
R1(config-router)# network 14.1.1.1 0.0.0.0

!On R4:

R4(config)# router eigrp 100
R4(config-router)# network 14.1.1.4 0.0.0.0
```

You should see the following console message:

```
%DUAL-5-NBRCHANGE: EIGRP-IPv4 100: Neighbor 14.1.1.1 (FastEthernet0/0) is up: new
  adjacency
```

Let's verify the configuration:

```
!On R4:

R4# show ip eigrp neighbors

EIGRP-IPv4 Neighbors for AS(100)
H   Address                 Interface       Hold Uptime   SRTT   RTO  Q  Seq
                                            (sec)         (ms)       Cnt Num
0   14.1.1.1                Fa0/0             13 00:00:45    8   300  0  1
```

First, a **route-map** is configured and the Lo0 interface is referenced:

```
R4(config)# route-map tst permit 10
R4(config-route-map)# match interface loopback0
```

Second, the **redistribute connected** command is configured to reference the **route-map**. When redistributing routes into EIGRP, the metric should also be configured. The metric is in the following order:

Bandwidth, Delay, Reliability, Load, and MTU.

Note   EIGRP does not use MTU as a parameter for metric calculation, but it's still a required value that must be configured.

The only exception to configuring a metric with EIGRP is when redistributing connected routes, static routes, or routes from another EIGRP routing domain.

```
R4(config)# router eigrp 100
R4(config-router)# redistribute connected route-map tst
```

Let's verify the configuration:

```
!On R1:

R1# show ip route eigrp | begin Gate
Gateway of last resort is not set

     10.0.0.0/32 is subnetted, 4 subnets
D EX    10.1.1.4 [170/156160] via 14.1.1.4, 00:00:10, FastEthernet0/0.14
```

Task 6

Redistribute RIP into EIGRP. Ensure that R4 installs a route for network 192.168.23.0/24 into its routing table:

```
!On R1:

R1# show interface fastethernet0/0.12 | include BW|load
  MTU 1500 bytes, BW 100000 Kbit/sec, DLY 100 usec,
     reliability 255/255, txload 1/255, rxload 1/255

R1(config)# router eigrp 100
R1(config-router)# redistribute rip metric 100000 10 255 1 1500
```

Let's verify the configuration:

```
!On R4:

R4# show ip route eigrp | begin Gate
Gateway of last resort is not set

     10.0.0.0/32 is subnetted, 3 subnets
D EX    10.1.1.1 [170/30720] via 14.1.1.1, 00:00:27, FastEthernet0/0
D EX    10.1.1.2 [170/30720] via 14.1.1.1, 00:00:27, FastEthernet0/0
     12.0.0.0/24 is subnetted, 1 subnets
D EX    12.1.1.0 [170/30720] via 14.1.1.1, 00:00:27, FastEthernet0/0
```

Network 192.168.23.0/24 is not being redistributed, as shown here:

```
R4# show ip route 192.168.23.0
% Network not in table


R4# show ip eigrp topology 192.168.23.0/24
EIGRP-IPv4 Topology Entry for AS(100)/ID(10.1.1.4)
%Entry 192.168.23.0/24 not in topology table
```

Warning   IOS will redistribute the 192.168.23.0/24 network only if this network is in the routing table of R2 as a RIP route. Let's say the routes from routing protocol A are to be redistributed into routing protocol B; the IOS will only redistribute the routes that are in its routing table as A into routing protocol B's routing table.

Let's verify the routing table of R1 for network 192.168.23.0/24:

```
!On R1


R1# show ip rip database 192.168.23.0 255.255.255.0


192.168.23.0/24    redistributed
    [3] via 13.1.1.3, from 0.0.0.3,


R1# show ip route 192.168.23.0


Routing entry for 192.168.23.0/24
  Known via "ospf 1", distance 110, metric 2, type inter area
  Redistributing via rip
  Advertised by rip metric 3 route-map tst
  Last update from 13.1.1.3 on FastEthernet0/0.13, 00:18:17 ago
  Routing Descriptor Blocks:
  * 13.1.1.3, from 0.0.0.3, 00:18:17 ago, via FastEthernet0/0.13
              Route metric is 2, traffic share count is 1
```

The output of the preceding **show** commands reveals that the route is present in RIP's database, but the route in R1 is known via OSPF. The problem is, we are redistributing RIP into EIGRP.

To accomplish this task, the administrative distance of 192.168.23.0/24 is raised in OSPF by a value that is higher than RIP's default administrative distance. The first step is to create an access list that matches 192.168.23.0/24. The next step is to change the administrative distance. The **distance** command will specify an administrative distance that is greater than the default RIP administrative distance. We will then specify the route source or the router ID of the router that advertises the route to R1. Finally, we will reference the access list.

```
!On R1:          The desired ad value


R1# show access-lists
R1#


R1(config)# access-list 1 permit 192.168.23.0 0.0.0.255
R1(config)# router ospf 1
R1(config-router)# distance 121 0.0.0.3 0.0.0.0 1
```

Let's verify the configuration:

```
!On R1:


R1# show ip route ospf | begin Gate
Gateway of last resort is not set


      10.0.0.0/32 is subnetted, 4 subnets
O IA    10.1.1.3 [121/2] via 13.1.1.3, 00:01:11, FastEthernet0/0.13
O E2  192.168.31.0/24 [121/20] via 13.1.1.3, 00:01:11, FastEthernet0/0.13
O E2  192.168.33.0/24 [121/20] via 13.1.1.3, 00:01:11, FastEthernet0/0.13
```

Note   The route is no longer in the routing table as an OSPF route.

Because of the adjusted AD, the route is now a RIP route. Specifically, the administrative distance of the 192.168.23.0/24 route advertised by R3 via OSPF was increased to be higher than the default RIP administrative distance. This allows the RIP route for 192.168.23.0/24 to be selected and inserted into the routing table. Let's verify:

```
R1# show ip route rip | begin Gate
Gateway of last resort is not set


      10.0.0.0/32 is subnetted, 4 subnets
R        10.1.1.2 [120/1] via 12.1.1.2, 00:00:21, FastEthernet0/0.12
R      192.168.23.0/24 [120/1] via 12.1.1.2, 00:00:21, FastEthernet0/0.12
```

Now let's go to R4 and verify the configuration:

```
!On R4:


R4# show ip route 192.168.23.0


Routing entry for 192.168.23.0/24
  Known via "eigrp 100", distance 170, metric 2560002816, type external
```

```
Redistributing via eigrp 100
Last update from 14.1.1.1 on FastEthernet0/0, 00:02:40 ago
Routing Descriptor Blocks:
* 14.1.1.1, from 14.1.1.1, 00:02:40 ago, via FastEthernet0/0
    Route metric is 30720, traffic share count is 1
    Total delay is 110 microseconds, minimum bandwidth is 1 Kbit
    Reliability 1/255, minimum MTU 1 bytes
    Loading 1/255, Hops 1
```

Task 7

Configure the following loopback interface on R2:

- Lo40: 172.16.0.2/24.

- R2 should be configured to advertise this loopback interface in RIPv2.

- Ensure that the only 172.16.x.x route present in R1's routing table is 172.16.0.0/24.

- R3 should see this route as 172.16.0.0/16.

First, configure loopback40 on R2 and advertise this network in RIPv2:

```
!On R2:

R2(config)# interface loopback40
R2(config-if)# ip address 172.16.0.2 255.255.255.0

R2(config-if)# router rip
R2(config-router)# network 172.16.0.0
```

Let's verify the configuration:

```
!On R1:

R1# show ip route rip | begin Gate
Gateway of last resort is not set

      10.0.0.0/32 is subnetted, 4 subnets
R        10.1.1.2 [120/1] via 12.1.1.2, 00:00:20, FastEthernet0/0.12
      172.16.0.0/24 is subnetted, 1 subnets
R         172.16.0.0 [120/1] via 12.1.1.2, 00:00:20, FastEthernet0/0.12
R      192.168.23.0/24 [120/1] via 12.1.1.2, 00:00:20, FastEthernet0/0.12
```

R1 has the route based on the requirement of the task. To perform the last step of this task, R1 should be configured to redistribute RIPv2 into OSPF.

By default, OSPF assigns a metric of 20 and a metric type of 2 to all redistributed routes. Therefore, there is no need to assign the cost when redistributing routes into OSPF.

```
!On R1:

R1(config)# router ospf 1
R1(config-router)# redistribute rip subnets
```

Let's verify the configuration:

```
!On R3:

R3# show ip route ospf | begin Gate
Gateway of last resort is not set

      10.0.0.0/32 is subnetted, 3 subnets
O E2     10.1.1.1 [110/20] via 13.1.1.1, 00:00:32, FastEthernet0/0
O E2     10.1.1.2 [110/20] via 13.1.1.1, 00:00:32, FastEthernet0/0
      12.0.0.0/24 is subnetted, 1 subnets
O E2     12.1.1.0 [110/20] via 13.1.1.1, 00:00:32, FastEthernet0/0
      172.16.0.0/24 is subnetted, 1 subnets
O E2     172.16.0.0 [110/20] via 13.1.1.1, 00:00:32, FastEthernet0/0
```

Note   This task specified that network 172.16.0.0 should appear in the routing table of R3 as "/16." To accomplish this task, we need to summarize this network as follows:

```
!On R1:

R1(config)# router ospf 1
R1(config-router)# summary-address 172.16.0.0 255.255.0.0
```

Let's verify the configuration:

```
!On R3:

R3# show ip route ospf | begin Gate
Gateway of last resort is not set

      10.0.0.0/32 is subnetted, 3 subnets
```

```
O E2     10.1.1.1 [110/20] via 13.1.1.1, 00:02:37, FastEthernet0/0
O E2     10.1.1.2 [110/20] via 13.1.1.1, 00:02:37, FastEthernet0/0
      12.0.0.0/24 is subnetted, 1 subnets
O E2     12.1.1.0 [110/20] via 13.1.1.1, 00:02:37, FastEthernet0/0
O E2 172.16.0.0/16 [110/20] via 13.1.1.1, 00:00:16, FastEthernet0/0
```

Note This fulfills the requirement of the last task, but remember that this task specified that R1 should only have 172.16.0.0/24 in its routing table.

Again, let's verify the configuration:

```
!On R1:

R1# show ip route | include 172.16

      172.16.0.0/16 is variably subnetted, 2 subnets, 2 masks
O         172.16.0.0/16 is a summary, 00:01:20, Null0
R         172.16.0.0/24 [120/1] via 12.1.1.2, 00:00:23, FastEthernet0/0.12
```

R1 has two 172.16.*x*.*x* routes in its routing table: 172.16.0.0/24, which was learned from RIP, and 172.16.0.0/16, which is the direct result of summarization. When summarization is configured in OSPF, a discard route is injected to avoid forwarding loops. The injected discard route can be for internal OSPF routes that were summarized or external OSPF routes that were summarized.

If the discard route is internal and needs to be removed, then the **no discard-route internal** command can be used. However, in this case it's for external routes, so it should be removed using the following configuration:

```
!On R1:

R1(config)# router ospf 1
R1(config-router)# no discard-route external
```

We could have used the **discard-route external 255** command to accomplish this task. Remember, any route that has an administrative distance of 255 will not be injected into the routing table.

Let's verify the configuration:

```
!On R1:


R1# show ip route | include 172.16


    172.16.0.0/24 is subnetted, 1 subnets
R      172.16.0.0 [120/1] via 12.1.1.2, 00:00:10, FastEthernet0/0.12

!On R3:


R3# show ip route ospf | begin Gate
Gateway of last resort is not set


    10.0.0.0/32 is subnetted, 3 subnets
O E2    10.1.1.1 [110/20] via 13.1.1.1, 00:08:37, FastEthernet0/0
O E2    10.1.1.2 [110/20] via 13.1.1.1, 00:08:37, FastEthernet0/0
    12.0.0.0/24 is subnetted, 1 subnets
O E2    12.1.1.0 [110/20] via 13.1.1.1, 00:08:37, FastEthernet0/0
O E2  172.16.0.0/16 [110/20] via 13.1.1.1, 00:06:16, FastEthernet0/0
```

Erase the startup configuration and reload the routers before proceeding to the next task.

Lab 9-2: Basic Redistribution 2

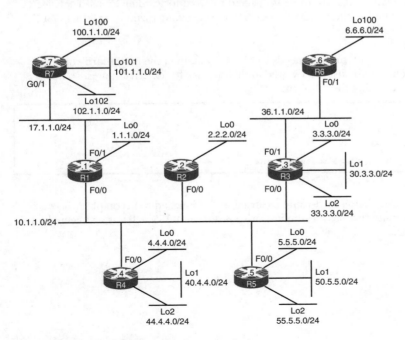

Figure 9-2 *Basic Redistribution part 2*

Task 1

Figure 9-2 illustrates the topology that will be used in the following tasks. Configure OSPF area 0 on the following routers and their interfaces:

- R3: F0/0 and Lo1.

- R4 and R5: F0/0, Lo0, Lo1, and Lo2.

- Loopback interfaces should be advertised with their correct mask.

- Assign the following OSPF costs to the loopback interfaces of R4 and R5:

    - R4 and R5's Lo0 should have a cost of 10, Lo1 should have a cost of 20, and Lo2 should have a cost of 30.

You should use an OSPF process ID of 1 to accomplish this task. Also, you should configure the OSPF RIDs to be 0.0.0.x, where x is the router number.

```
!On R3:

R3(config)# router ospf 1
R3(config-router)# router-id 0.0.0.3
R3(config-router)# network 10.1.1.3 0.0.0.0 area 0
R3(config-router)# network 30.3.3.3 0.0.0.0 area 0

R3(config)# interface loopback 1
R3(config-if)# ip ospf network point-to-point

!On R4:

R4(config-router)# interface loopback 0
R4(config-if)# ip ospf network point-to-point
R4(config-if)# ip ospf cost 10

R4(config-router)# interface loopback 1
R4(config-if)# ip ospf network point-to-point
R4(config-if)# ip ospf cost 20

R4(config-router)# interface loopback 2
R4(config-if)# ip ospf network point-to-point
R4(config-if)# ip ospf cost 30

R4(config)# router ospf 1
R4(config-router)# router-id 0.0.0.4
R4(config-router)# network 10.1.1.4 0.0.0.0 area 0
R4(config-router)# network 4.4.4.4 0.0.0.0 area 0
R4(config-router)# network 40.4.4.4 0.0.0.0 area 0
R4(config-router)# network 44.4.4.4 0.0.0.0 area 0
```

You should see the following console message:

```
%OSPF-5-ADJCHG: Process 1, Nbr 0.0.0.3 on FastEthernet0/0 from LOADING to FULL,
  Loading Done
!On R5:


R5(config-router)# interface loopback 0
R5(config-if)# ip ospf network point-to-point
R5(config-if)# ip ospf cost 10

R5(config-router)# interface loopback 1
R5(config-if)# ip ospf network point-to-point
R5(config-if)# ip ospf cost 20

R5(config-router)# interface loopback 2
R5(config-if)# ip ospf network point-to-point
R5(config-if)# ip ospf cost 30

R5(config)# router ospf 1
R5(config-router)# router-id 0.0.0.5
R5(config-router)# network 10.1.1.5 0.0.0.0 area 0
R5(config-router)# network 5.5.5.5 0.0.0.0 area 0
R5(config-router)# network 50.5.5.5 0.0.0.0 area 0
R5(config-router)# network 55.5.5.5 0.0.0.0 area 0
```

You should also see this console message:

```
%OSPF-5-ADJCHG: Process 1, Nbr 0.0.0.3 on FastEthernet0/0 from LOADING to FULL,
  Loading Done

%OSPF-5-ADJCHG: Process 1, Nbr 0.0.0.4 on FastEthernet0/0 from LOADING to FULL,
  Loading Done
```

Let's verify the configuration:

```
!On R3:


R3# show ip route ospf | begin Gate
Gateway of last resort is not set

     4.0.0.0/24 is subnetted, 1 subnets
O       4.4.4.0 [110/11] via 10.1.1.4, 00:03:29, FastEthernet0/0
     5.0.0.0/24 is subnetted, 1 subnets
O       5.5.5.0 [110/11] via 10.1.1.5, 00:01:21, FastEthernet0/0
     40.0.0.0/24 is subnetted, 1 subnets
```

```
O          40.4.4.0 [110/21] via 10.1.1.4, 00:03:29, FastEthernet0/0
       44.0.0.0/24 is subnetted, 1 subnets
O          44.4.4.0 [110/31] via 10.1.1.4, 00:03:29, FastEthernet0/0
       50.0.0.0/24 is subnetted, 1 subnets
O          50.5.5.0 [110/21] via 10.1.1.5, 00:01:21, FastEthernet0/0
       55.0.0.0/24 is subnetted, 1 subnets
O          55.5.5.0 [110/31] via 10.1.1.5, 00:01:11, FastEthernet0/0
```

Task 2

Configure EIGRP AS 100 on the following routers and their interfaces:

- R1, R2, and R3's F0/0 and loopback0 interfaces
- The F0/1 interfaces of R1 and R7
- The Lo100, Lo101, and Lo102 interfaces of R7

```
!On R3:

R3(config)# router eigrp 100
R3(config-router)# network 10.1.1.3 0.0.0.0
R3(config-router)# network 3.3.3.3 0.0.0.0

!On R2:

R2(config)# router eigrp 100
R2(config-router)# network 10.1.1.2 0.0.0.0
R2(config-router)# network 2.2.2.2 0.0.0.0
```

You should see the following console message:

```
%DUAL-5-NBRCHANGE: EIGRP-IPv4 100: Neighbor 10.1.1.3 (FastEthernet0/0) is up: new
  adjacency

!On R1:

R1(config)# router eigrp 100
R1(config-router)# network 10.1.1.1 0.0.0.0
R1(config-router)# network 17.1.1.1 0.0.0.0
R1(config-router)# network  1.1.1.1 0.0.0.0
```

You should also see this console message:

```
%DUAL-5-NBRCHANGE: EIGRP-IPv4 100: Neighbor 10.1.1.3 (FastEthernet0/0) is up:
  new adjacency

%DUAL-5-NBRCHANGE: EIGRP-IPv4 100: Neighbor 10.1.1.2 (FastEthernet0/0) is up:
  new adjacency

!On R7:

R7(config)# router eigrp 100
R7(config-router)# network 17.1.1.7 0.0.0.0
R7(config-router)# network 7.7.7.7 0.0.0.0
R7(config-router)# network 70.7.7.7 0.0.0.0
R7(config-router)# network 77.7.7.7 0.0.0.0
```

You should see the following console message as well:

```
%DUAL-5-NBRCHANGE: EIGRP-IPv4 100: Neighbor 17.1.1.1 (GigabitEthernet0/1) is up:
  new adjacency
```

Let's verify the configuration:

```
!On R3:

R3# show ip route eigrp | begin Gate
Gateway of last resort is not set


      1.0.0.0/24 is subnetted, 1 subnets
D        1.1.1.0 [90/156160] via 10.1.1.1, 00:03:16, FastEthernet0/0
      2.0.0.0/24 is subnetted, 1 subnets
D        2.2.2.0 [90/156160] via 10.1.1.2, 00:03:46, FastEthernet0/0
      7.0.0.0/24 is subnetted, 1 subnets
D        7.7.7.0 [90/158720] via 10.1.1.1, 00:02:31, FastEthernet0/0
      17.0.0.0/24 is subnetted, 1 subnets
D        17.1.1.0 [90/30720] via 10.1.1.1, 00:03:11, FastEthernet0/0
      70.0.0.0/24 is subnetted, 1 subnets
D        70.7.7.0 [90/158720] via 10.1.1.1, 00:02:27, FastEthernet0/0
      77.0.0.0/24 is subnetted, 1 subnets
D        77.7.7.0 [90/158720] via 10.1.1.1, 00:02:24, FastEthernet0/0
```

Task 3

Configure OSPF area 0 with the process ID of 36 on the following routers and their interfaces:

- The F0/1 interfaces of R3 and R6

- The Lo0 interface of R6

- The Lo2 interface of R3

These loopback interfaces should be advertised with their correct masks:

```
!On R3:

R3(config-if)# interface loopback 2
R3(config-if)# ip ospf network point-to-point

R3(config)# router ospf 36
R3(config-router)# network 36.1.1.3 0.0.0.0 area 0
R3(config-router)# network 33.3.3.3 0.0.0.0 area 0

On R6:

R6(config)# interface loopback 0
R6(config-if)# ip ospf network point-to-point

R6(config)# router ospf 36
R6(config-router)# network 36.1.1.6 0.0.0.0 area 0
R6(config-router)# network 6.6.6.6 0.0.0.0 area 0
```

You should see the following console message:

```
%OSPF-5-ADJCHG: Process 36, Nbr 33.3.3.3 on FastEthernet0/1 from LOADING to FULL,
  Loading Done
```

Let's verify the configuration:

```
!On R3:

R3# show ip route ospf 36 | begin Gate
Gateway of last resort is not set

      6.0.0.0/24 is subnetted, 1 subnets
O        6.6.6.0 [110/2] via 36.1.1.6, 00:00:54, FastEthernet0/1
```

Task 4

Configure R3 to redistribute **eigrp 100** into **ospf 1** such that networks 1.1.1.0/24 and 2.2.2.0/24 carry a route tag of 111 and 222, respectively. The rest of the routes should have a route tag of 333.

```
!On R3:


R3# show access-lists

R3(config)# access-list 1 permit 1.1.1.0 0.0.0.255
R3(config)# access-list 2 permit 2.2.2.0 0.0.0.255


R3(config)# route-map tst permit 10
R3(config-route-map)# match ip address 1
R3(config-route-map)# set tag 111


R3(config)# route-map tst permit 20
R3(config-route-map)# match ip address 2
R3(config-route-map)# set tag 222


R3(config)# route-map tst permit 30
R3(config-route-map)# set tag 333
R3(config)# router ospf 1
R3(config-router)# redistribute eigrp 100 subnets route-map tst
```

Let's verify the configuration:

```
On R3:


R3# show ip ospf 1 database | begin Type-5
             Type-5 AS External Link States


Link ID        ADV Router     Age     Seq#        Checksum Tag
1.1.1.0        0.0.0.3        52      0x80000001 0x001D01 111
2.2.2.0        0.0.0.3        52      0x80000001 0x00DCCD 222
3.3.3.0        0.0.0.3        52      0x80000001 0x00E95C 333
7.7.7.0        0.0.0.3        52      0x80000001 0x00EE3E 333
17.1.1.0       0.0.0.3        52      0x80000001 0x00F638 333
70.7.7.0       0.0.0.3        52      0x80000001 0x00B835 333
77.7.7.0       0.0.0.3        52      0x80000001 0x005D89 333
```

```
On R4:

R4# show ip route ospf | include E2
        E1 - OSPF external type 1, E2 - OSPF external type 2
O E2     1.1.1.0 [110/20] via 10.1.1.1, 00:11:07, FastEthernet0/0
O E2     2.2.2.0 [110/20] via 10.1.1.2, 00:11:07, FastEthernet0/0
O E2     3.3.3.0 [110/20] via 10.1.1.3, 00:11:07, FastEthernet0/0
O E2     7.7.7.0 [110/20] via 10.1.1.1, 00:11:07, FastEthernet0/0
O E2    17.1.1.0 [110/20] via 10.1.1.1, 00:11:07, FastEthernet0/0
O E2    70.7.7.0 [110/20] via 10.1.1.1, 00:11:07, FastEthernet0/0
O E2    77.7.7.0 [110/20] via 10.1.1.1, 00:11:07, FastEthernet0/0


R4# show ip ospf database | begin Type-5
                Type-5 AS external link states

Link ID          ADV Router        Age       Seq#          Checksum Tag
1.1.1.0          0.0.0.3           171       0x80000001 0x001D01 111
2.2.2.0          0.0.0.3           171       0x80000001 0x00DCCD 222
3.3.3.0          0.0.0.3           171       0x80000001 0x00E95C 333
7.7.7.0          0.0.0.3           711       0x80000001 0x00EE3E 333
17.1.1.0         0.0.0.3           711       0x80000001 0x00F638 333
70.7.7.0         0.0.0.3           711       0x80000001 0x00B835 333
77.7.7.0         0.0.0.3           711       0x80000001 0x005D89 333
```

Task 5

Configure R4 to filter all routes that are tagged with 111. You should not use an **access-list** or a **prefix-list** to accomplish this task.

```
!On R4:

R4# show ip ospf rib | include 111
*>  1.1.1.0/24, Ext2, cost 20, tag 111

R4(config)# route-map tst deny 10
R4(config-route-map)# match tag 111
R4(config)# route-map tst permit 90

R4(config)# router ospf 1
R4(config-router)# distribute-list route-map tst in
```

Let's verify the configuration:

```
!On R4:

R4# show ip route ospf | include E2
       E1 - OSPF external type 1, E2 - OSPF external type 2
O E2    2.2.2.0 [110/20] via 10.1.1.2, 00:00:20, FastEthernet0/0
O E2    3.3.3.0 [110/20] via 10.1.1.3, 00:00:20, FastEthernet0/0
O E2    7.7.7.0 [110/20] via 10.1.1.1, 00:00:20, FastEthernet0/0
O E2    17.1.1.0 [110/20] via 10.1.1.1, 00:00:20, FastEthernet0/0
O E2    70.7.7.0 [110/20] via 10.1.1.1, 00:00:20, FastEthernet0/0
O E2    77.7.7.0 [110/20] via 10.1.1.1, 00:00:20, FastEthernet0/0
```

Route tags are very handy tools; once a given route is tagged with a value, that route can be manipulated using the tag that it carries.

Note   Network 1.1.1.0/24 is no longer in the routing table of R1. Keep in mind that it is still in the database of this router. The output of the following **show** command reveals that information:

```
R4# show ip ospf database external 1.1.1.0


            OSPF Router with ID (0.0.0.4) (Process ID 1)


                Type-5 AS External Link States

Routing Bit Set on this LSA in topology Base with MTID 0
LS age: 493
Options: (No TOS-capability, DC)
LS Type: AS External Link
Link State ID: 1.1.1.0 (External Network Number )
Advertising Router: 0.0.0.3
LS Seq Number: 80000001
Checksum: 0x1D01
Length: 36
Network Mask: /24
      Metric Type: 2 (Larger than any link state path)
      MTID: 0
      Metric: 20
      Forward Address: 10.1.1.1
      External Route Tag: 111
```

Task 6

Configure R5 to filter all routes that carry a route tag of 222. You should not use an **access-list** or a **prefix-list** to accomplish this task.

```
!On R5:

R5# show ip ospf rib | include 222
*   2.2.2.0/24, Ext2, cost 20, tag 222

R5(config)# route-map tst deny 10
R5(config-route-map)# match tag 222
R5(config)# route-map tst permit 90

R5(config)# router ospf 1
R5(config-router)# distribute-list route-map tst in
```

Let's verify the configuration:

```
!On R5:

R5# show ip route ospf | include E2
        E1 - OSPF external type 1, E2 - OSPF external type 2
O E2    1.1.1.0 [110/20] via 10.1.1.1, 00:00:31, FastEthernet0/0
O E2    3.3.3.0 [110/20] via 10.1.1.3, 00:00:31, FastEthernet0/0
O E2    7.7.7.0 [110/20] via 10.1.1.1, 00:00:31, FastEthernet0/0
O E2    17.1.1.0 [110/20] via 10.1.1.1, 00:00:31, FastEthernet0/0
O E2    70.7.7.0 [110/20] via 10.1.1.1, 00:00:31, FastEthernet0/0
O E2    77.7.7.0 [110/20] via 10.1.1.1, 00:00:31, FastEthernet0/0
```

Task 7

Configure R3 to redistribute **ospf 1** into **eigrp 100** such that network 4.4.4.0/24 and 5.5.5.0/24 are tagged with 444 and 555, respectively.

```
!On R3:

R3# show access-list

Standard IP access list 1
    10 permit 1.1.1.0, wildcard bits 0.0.0.255 (1 match)
Standard IP access list 2
    10 permit 2.2.2.0, wildcard bits 0.0.0.255 (1 match)
```

```
R3(config)# access-list 4 permit 4.4.4.0 0.0.0.255


R3(config)# access-list 5 permit 5.5.5.0 0.0.0.255


R3(config)# route-map tst1 permit 10
R3(config-route-map)# match ip address 4
R3(config-route-map)# set tag 444


R3(config)# route-map tst1 permit 20
R3(config-route-map)# match ip address 5
R3(config-route-map)# set tag 555


R3(config)# route-map tst1 permit 90


R3# show interface fastethernet0/0 | include BW|load
  MTU 1500 bytes, BW 100000 Kbit/sec, DLY 100 usec,
      reliability 255/255, txload 1/255, rxload 1/255


R3(config)# router eigrp 100
R3(config-router)# redistribute ospf 1 route-map tst1 metric 100000 10 255 1 1500
```

Let's verify the configuration:

```
!On R3:


R3# show ip eigrp topology | include 444|555
P 5.5.5.0/24, 1 successors, FD is 28160, tag is 555
P 4.4.4.0/24, 1 successors, FD is 28160, tag is 444
```

Task 8

Configure R2 to filter network 4.4.4.0/24. Do not use an **access-list** or a **prefix-list** to accomplish this task.

```
!On R2:


R2# show ip eigrp topology | include 444
P 4.4.4.0/24, 1 successors, FD is 30720, tag is 444
```

Note   R2 sees the tag that was assigned in the previous task.

```
R2(config)# route-map tst deny 10
R2(config-route-map)# match tag 444
R2(config)# route-map tst permit 90

R2(config)# router eigrp 100
R2(config-router)# distribute-list route-map tst in
```

You should see the following console messages verifying that some route configuration has changed:

```
%DUAL-5-NBRCHANGE: EIGRP-IPv4 100: Neighbor 10.1.1.1 (FastEthernet0/0) is resync:
  route configuration changed

%DUAL-5-NBRCHANGE: EIGRP-IPv4 100: Neighbor 10.1.1.3 (FastEthernet0/0) is resync:
  route configuration changed
```

Let's verify the configuration:

```
!On R2:

R2# show ip route eigrp | include EX
       D - EIGRP, EX - EIGRP external, O - OSPF, IA - OSPF inter area
D EX     5.5.5.0 [170/30720] via 10.1.1.3, 00:42:00, FastEthernet0/0
D EX     30.3.3.0 [170/30720] via 10.1.1.3, 00:42:00, FastEthernet0/0
D EX     40.4.4.0 [170/30720] via 10.1.1.3, 00:42:00, FastEthernet0/0
D EX     44.4.4.0 [170/30720] via 10.1.1.3, 00:42:00, FastEthernet0/0
D EX     50.5.5.0 [170/30720] via 10.1.1.3, 00:42:00, FastEthernet0/0
D EX     55.5.5.0 [170/30720] via 10.1.1.3, 00:42:00, FastEthernet0/0
```

Task 9

Configure R5 to filter all routes that are originated by R4. Do not use a prefix list or route tags to accomplish this task.

Note R5 receives the following three routes from R4:

```
!On R5:

R5# show ip route | include 10.1.1.4

O        4.4.4.0 [110/11] via 10.1.1.4, 00:15:53, FastEthernet0/0
O        40.4.4.0 [110/21] via 10.1.1.4, 00:15:53, FastEthernet0/0
O        44.4.4.0 [110/31] via 10.1.1.4, 00:15:53, FastEthernet0/0
```

The **match ip route-source** command can be used to accomplish this task. In OSPF, the **route-source** is not the next-hop IP address; it is the router ID of the router that originated the routes. Here's how to see the router ID of R4:

```
!On R4:

R4# show ip ospf | include ID
 Routing Process "ospf 1" with ID 0.0.0.4

!On R5:

R5# show access-list

R5(config)# access-list 4 permit host 0.0.0.4
```

In Task 6, we configured a **route-map**. Let's look at that **route-map**:

```
R5# show run | section route-map

 distribute-list route-map tst in
route-map tst deny 10
 match tag 222
route-map tst permit 90
```

In the preceding output, you can see that **route-map tst** denies any routes that carry a route tag of 222, and this **route-map** is applied inbound on R5. To resolve this task, we can add the following line to the existing **route-map**:

```
R5(config)# route-map tst deny 20
R5(config-route-map)# match ip route-source 4
```

The preceding configuration denies any prefix originated from a route source with a router ID that is referenced in access list **4**. Because the preceding configuration is added to the existing **route-map**, the new **route-map** should look like the following:

```
!On R5:

R5# show run | section route-map

 distribute-list route-map tst in
route-map tst deny 10
 match tag 222
route-map tst deny 20
 match ip route-source 4
route-map tst permit 90
```

> **Note**   We have the sequence numbers in the **route-map** so we can add configuration lines in the beginning, middle, or end of the **route-map** (in this case, **route-map** sequence number 20 is added between **route-map** 10 and 90).

Because the **route-map** is already applied, no further configuration is necessary. Let's verify the configuration:

```
!On R5:

R5# show ip route | include 10.1.1.4
```

> **Note**   The networks that were advertised by R4 are filtered.

Task 10

Configure R3 to redistribute **ospf 1** and **eigrp 100** into the **ospf 36** routing domain using the following policy:

- The routes from the **ospf 1** routing domain with an OSPF cost of 11 should be redistributed as **E2**. These routes should have a tag of 11.

- The routes from the **ospf 1** routing domain with an OSPF cost of 21 should be redistributed as **E2**. These routes should have a tag of 21.

- The routes from the **ospf 1** routing domain with an OSPF cost of 31 should be redistributed as **E2**. These routes should have a tag of 31.

- EIGRP AS 100 routes should be redistributed as **E1** with a route tag of 99.

- Do not use an **access-list** or **prefix-list** to accomplish this task.

Let's see the OSPF routes and their cost:

```
R3# show ip route ospf | begin Gate
Gateway of last resort is not set


     4.0.0.0/24 is subnetted, 1 subnets
O       4.4.4.0 [110/11] via 10.1.1.4, 01:11:06, FastEthernet0/0
     5.0.0.0/24 is subnetted, 1 subnets
O       5.5.5.0 [110/11] via 10.1.1.5, 01:08:58, FastEthernet0/0
     6.0.0.0/24 is subnetted, 1 subnets
O       6.6.6.0 [110/2] via 36.1.1.6, 00:45:39, FastEthernet0/1
     40.0.0.0/24 is subnetted, 1 subnets
```

```
O          40.4.4.0 [110/21] via 10.1.1.4, 01:11:06, FastEthernet0/0
      44.0.0.0/24 is subnetted, 1 subnets
O          44.4.4.0 [110/31] via 10.1.1.4, 01:11:06, FastEthernet0/0
      50.0.0.0/24 is subnetted, 1 subnets
O          50.5.5.0 [110/21] via 10.1.1.5, 01:08:58, FastEthernet0/0
      55.0.0.0/24 is subnetted, 1 subnets
O          55.5.5.0 [110/31] via 10.1.1.5, 01:08:48, FastEthernet0/0
```

The **source-protocol** option is another useful and effective tool you can use to achieve certain results. The **source-protocol** option specifies a **match** clause that matches external routes from sources that match the source protocol.

The following **route-map** says that if the source protocol is OSPF 1 and the metric is 11, then the tag should be set to 11:

```
!On R3:

R3(config)# route-map task10 permit 10
R3(config-route-map)# match source-protocol ospf 1
R3(config-route-map)# match metric 11
R3(config-route-map)# set tag 11
```

The following **route-map** says that if the source protocol is OSPF 1 and the metric is 21, then the tag should be set to 21:

```
R3(config)# route-map task10 permit 20
R3(config-route-map)# match source-protocol ospf 1
R3(config-route-map)# match metric 21
R3(config-route-map)# set tag 21
```

The following **route-map** says that if the source protocol is OSPF 1 and the metric is 31, then the tag should be set to 31:

```
R3(config)# route-map task10 permit 30
R3(config-route-map)# match source-protocol ospf 1
R3(config-route-map)# match metric 31
R3(config-route-map)# set tag 31
R3(config)# route-map task10 permit 90
```

The following **route-map** says that if the source protocol is EIGRP 100, then the tag should be set to 99 and the **route-type** should be set to **type-1**:

```
R3(config)# route-map eigrp permit 10
R3(config-route-map)# match source-protocol eigrp 100
R3(config-route-map)# set tag 99
R3(config-route-map)# set metric-type type-1


R3(config)# router ospf 36
R3(config-router)# redistribute ospf 1 subnets route-map task10
R3(config-router)# redistribute eigrp 100 subnets route-map eigrp
```

Let's verify the configuration:

```
!On R6:

R6# show ip route ospf | include E1
        E1 - OSPF external type 1, E2 - OSPF external type 2
O E1    1.1.1.0 [110/21] via 36.1.1.3, 00:00:24, FastEthernet0/1
O E1    2.2.2.0 [110/21] via 36.1.1.3, 00:00:24, FastEthernet0/1
O E1    3.3.3.0 [110/21] via 36.1.1.3, 00:00:24, FastEthernet0/1
O E1    7.7.7.0 [110/21] via 36.1.1.3, 00:00:24, FastEthernet0/1
O E1    10.1.1.0 [110/21] via 36.1.1.3, 00:00:24, FastEthernet0/1
O E1    17.1.1.0 [110/21] via 36.1.1.3, 00:00:24, FastEthernet0/1
O E1    70.7.7.0 [110/21] via 36.1.1.3, 00:00:24, FastEthernet0/1
O E1    77.7.7.0 [110/21] via 36.1.1.3, 00:00:24, FastEthernet0/1


R6# show ip route ospf | include E2


        E1 - OSPF external type 1, E2 - OSPF external type 2
O E2    4.4.4.0 [110/11] via 36.1.1.3, 00:04:44, FastEthernet0/1
O E2    5.5.5.0 [110/11] via 36.1.1.3, 00:04:44, FastEthernet0/1
O E2    30.3.3.0 [110/1] via 36.1.1.3, 00:04:44, FastEthernet0/1
O E2    40.4.4.0 [110/21] via 36.1.1.3, 00:04:44, FastEthernet0/1
O E2    44.4.4.0 [110/31] via 36.1.1.3, 00:04:44, FastEthernet0/1
O E2    50.5.5.0 [110/21] via 36.1.1.3, 00:04:44, FastEthernet0/1
O E2    55.5.5.0 [110/31] via 36.1.1.3, 00:04:44, FastEthernet0/1


R6# show ip ospf database | include 11_


4.4.4.0         33.3.3.3        341        0x80000001 0x005A0E 11
5.5.5.0         33.3.3.3        341        0x80000001 0x00362F 11
```

```
R6# show ip ospf database | include 21_

40.4.4.0        33.3.3.3        381        0x80000001 0x009D92 21
50.5.5.0        33.3.3.3        381        0x80000001 0x000420 21

R6# show ip ospf database | include 31_

44.4.4.0        33.3.3.3        429        0x80000001 0x008295 31
55.5.5.0        33.3.3.3        429        0x80000001 0x00DB2F 31

R6# show ip ospf database | include 99_
1.1.1.0         33.3.3.3        1780       0x80000001 0x00D3BC 99
2.2.2.0         33.3.3.3        1780       0x80000001 0x00AFDD 99
3.3.3.0         33.3.3.3        1780       0x80000001 0x008BFE 99
7.7.7.0         33.3.3.3        1780       0x80000001 0x00FA83 99
10.1.1.0        33.3.3.3        1780       0x80000002 0x005C2A 99
17.1.1.0        33.3.3.3        1780       0x80000001 0x00037D 99
70.7.7.0        33.3.3.3        1780       0x80000001 0x00C47A 99
77.7.7.0        33.3.3.3        1780       0x80000001 0x0069CE 99
```

Task 11

Configure R3 such that EIGRP routes that have a composite metric of 156160 to 158720 are not redistributed into the **ospf 36** routing domain. None of the previous configurations should be removed or overridden to accomplish this task.

This task is asking you to filter the routes that have a composite metric of 156160 to 158720; the formula to calculate the metric and the deviation value is shown here (add the two numbers together and then divide by two):

```
156160 + 158720 = 314880
314880 / 2 = 157440 → this gives us the metric value
```

To calculate the deviation value, subtract the start of the number range (the lower value, or the *from* value; in this case, 156160) from the *to* value (in this case, 158720) and then divide the result by two:

```
158720 - 156160 = 2560
2560 / 2 = 1280
```

Thus, the **match metric** statement in the **route-map** should have the following values. This statement says that if 1280 is subtracted from 157440, we will get the lowest value within the range, and if it is added, we will get the highest value within the range:

```
match metric 157440 +-1280
```

Let's test the values:

```
157440 - 1280 = 156160 → this is the lowest value within the range.
157440 + 1280 = 158720 → this is the highest value within the range.
```

Now let's look at the existing EIGRP routes:

```
!On R3:


R3# show ip route eigrp | begin Gate
Gateway of last resort is not set


      1.0.0.0/24 is subnetted, 1 subnets
D        1.1.1.0 [90/156160] via 10.1.1.1, 01:57:21, FastEthernet0/0
      2.0.0.0/24 is subnetted, 1 subnets
D        2.2.2.0 [90/156160] via 10.1.1.2, 01:57:45, FastEthernet0/0
      7.0.0.0/24 is subnetted, 1 subnets
D        7.7.7.0 [90/158720] via 10.1.1.1, 01:56:37, FastEthernet0/0
      17.0.0.0/24 is subnetted, 1 subnets
D        17.1.1.0 [90/30720] via 10.1.1.1, 01:57:22, FastEthernet0/0
      70.0.0.0/24 is subnetted, 1 subnets
D        70.7.7.0 [90/158720] via 10.1.1.1, 01:56:32, FastEthernet0/0
      77.0.0.0/24 is subnetted, 1 subnets
D        77.7.7.0 [90/158720] via 10.1.1.1, 01:56:26, FastEthernet0/0
```

A **route-map** is configured to deny any route that has a composite metric of 156160 to 158720, inclusive:

```
R3(config)# route-map task11 deny 10
R3(config-route-map)# match metric 157440 +- 1280


R3(config)# route-map task11 permit 90


R3(config-route-map)# router eigrp 100
R3(config-router)# distribute-list route-map task11 in
```

Let's verify the configuration:

```
!On R3:


%DUAL-5-NBRCHANGE: EIGRP-IPv4 100: Neighbor 10.1.1.1 (FastEthernet0/0) is resync:
  route configuration changed
%DUAL-5-NBRCHANGE: EIGRP-IPv4 100: Neighbor 10.1.1.2 (FastEthernet0/0) is resync:
  route configuration changed
R3# show ip route eigrp | begin Gate
Gateway of last resort is not set


      17.0.0.0/24 is subnetted, 1 subnets
D        17.1.1.0 [90/30720] via 10.1.1.1, 01:15:07, FastEthernet0/0
```

> **Note**   If a given prefix is not in the routing table of R3 as an EIGRP route, it will not be redistributed.

Erase the startup configuration and reload the routers before proceeding to the next task.

Lab 9-3: Redistribute RIPv2 and EIGRP

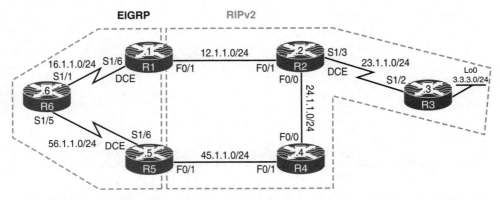

Figure 9-3   *Configuring Redistribution of RIPv2 and EIGRP*

Figure 9-3 illustrates the topology that will be used in the following tasks. EIGRP needs five metrics when redistributing other protocols: bandwidth, delay, reliability, load, and MTU, as detailed in Table 9-1.

Table 9-1   *EIGRP Metrics*

Metric	Value
Bandwidth	In units of kilobits per second. 10000 for Ethernet; 100000 for FastEthernet.
Delay	In units of tens of microseconds. For Ethernet it is 100×10 microseconds = 1 ms.
Reliability	255 for 100% reliability.
Load	Effective load on the link expressed as a number from 1 to 255 (255 is 100% loading).
MTU	Minimum MTU of the path. Usually equals the MTU for the Ethernet interface, which is 1500 bytes.

Multiple EIGRP processes can run on the same router, with redistribution between them. For example, EIGRP1 and EIGRP2 can run on the same router. However, running two processes of the same protocol on the same router is rarely necessary, and can consume the router's memory and CPU.

The redistribution of EIGRP into another EIGRP process does not require any metric conversion, so there is no need to define metrics or use the **default-metric** command during redistribution.

A redistributed static route takes precedence over the summary route because the static route has an administrative distance of 1, whereas EIGRP summary routes have an administrative distance of 5. This happens when a static route is redistributed with the use of **redistribute static** under the EIGRP process and the EIGRP process has a default route.

The RIP metric is composed of hop count, and the maximum valid metric is 15. Anything above 15 is considered infinite. You can use 16 to describe an infinite metric in RIP. When redistributing a protocol into RIP, Cisco recommends that you use a low metric, such as 1. A high metric, such as 10, limits RIP even further. If you define a metric of 10 for redistributed routes, these routes can only be advertised to routers up to five hops away, at which point the metric (hop count) exceeds 15. By defining a metric of 1, you enable a route to travel the maximum number of hops in a RIP domain. However, doing this increases the possibility of routing loops if there are multiple redistribution points and a router learns about the network with a better metric from the redistribution point than from the original source. Therefore, you have to make sure that the metric is neither too high, preventing it from being advertised to all the routers, nor too low, leading to routing loops when there are multiple redistribution points.

You can see that there is a vast difference in how RIP perceives metric values. As an example, RIPv2 may see a prefix with a metric of 16 as unreachable or infinite. However, a metric of 16 in EIGRP would be considered a very attractive metric that most likely would be used for forwarding data.

Task 1

Configure RIPv2 on R2, R3, and R4. These routers should advertise their directly connected interfaces in this routing domain. You should disable auto-summary.

```
!On R2:

R2(config)# router rip
R2(config-router)# no auto-summary
R2(config-router)# version 2
R2(config-router)# network 12.0.0.0
R2(config-router)# network 23.0.0.0
R2(config-router)# network 24.0.0.0

!On R3:

R3(config)# router rip
R3(config-router)# no auto-summary
R3(config-router)# version 2
R3(config-router)# network 3.0.0.0
R3(config-router)# network 23.0.0.0
```

```
!On R4:

R4(config)# router rip
R4(config-router)# no auto-summary
R4(config-router)# version 2
R4(config-router)# network 24.0.0.0
R4(config-router)# network 45.0.0.0
```

Let's verify the configuration:

```
!On R4:

R5# show ip route rip | begin Gate
Gateway of last resort is not set

      3.0.0.0/24 is subnetted, 1 subnets
R        3.3.3.0 [120/2] via 24.1.1.2, 00:00:02, FastEthernet0/0
      12.0.0.0/24 is subnetted, 1 subnets
R        12.1.1.0 [120/1] via 24.1.1.2, 00:00:02, FastEthernet0/0
      23.0.0.0/24 is subnetted, 1 subnets
R        23.1.1.0 [120/1] via 24.1.1.2, 00:00:02, FastEthernet0/0
```

Task 2

Configure RIPv2 on the F0/1 interfaces of R1 and R5. Disable auto-summary.

```
!On R1:

R1(config)# router rip
R1(config-router)# no auto-summary
R1(config-router)# version 2
R1(config-router)# network 12.0.0.0

!On R5:
R4(config)# router rip
R4(config-router)# no auto-summary
R4(config-router)# version 2
R4(config-router)# network 45.0.0.0
```

Let's verify the configuration:

```
!On R1:

R1# show ip route rip | begin Gate
Gateway of last resort is not set
```

```
        3.0.0.0/24 is subnetted, 1 subnets
R           3.3.3.0 [120/2] via 12.1.1.2, 00:00:23, FastEthernet0/1
        23.0.0.0/24 is subnetted, 1 subnets
R           23.1.1.0 [120/1] via 12.1.1.2, 00:00:23, FastEthernet0/1
        24.0.0.0/24 is subnetted, 1 subnets
R           24.1.1.0 [120/1] via 12.1.1.2, 00:00:23, FastEthernet0/1
        45.0.0.0/24 is subnetted, 1 subnets
R           45.1.1.0 [120/2] via 12.1.1.2, 00:00:23, FastEthernet0/1
```

Task 3

R3's loopback0 interface should be advertised with a hop count of 5.

```
!On R3:

R3# show access-lists

R3(config)# access-list 3 permit 3.3.3.0 0.0.0.255

R3(config)# router rip
R3(config-router)# offset-list 3 out 4
```

Let's verify the configuration:

```
!On R2:

R2# show ip route | include 3.3.3.0

R           3.3.3.0 [120/5] via 23.1.1.3, 00:00:11, Serial1/3
```

Task 4

Configure EIGRP AS 100 based on the following policy:

- Configure EIGRP AS 100 on the S1/6 interfaces of R1 and R5.
- Configure EIGRP AS 100 on the S1/1 and S1/5 interfaces of R6.
- Set the administrative distance of all external routes to 110.

```
!On R1:

R1(config)# router eigrp 100
R1(config-router)# network 16.1.1.1 0.0.0.0
R1(config-router)# distance eigrp 90 110


!On R5:

R5(config)# router eigrp 100
R5(config-router)# network 56.1.1.5 0.0.0.0
R5(config-router)# distance eigrp 90 110


!On R6:

R6(config)# router eigrp 100
R6(config-router)# network 16.1.1.6 0.0.0.0
R6(config-router)# network 56.1.1.6 0.0.0.0
```

You should see the following console message:

```
%DUAL-5-NBRCHANGE: EIGRP-IPv4 100: Neighbor 16.1.1.1 (Serial1/1) is up:
  new adjacency

%DUAL-5-NBRCHANGE: EIGRP-IPv4 100: Neighbor 56.1.1.5 (Serial1/5) is up:
  new adjacency
```

Let's verify the configuration:

```
On R1:

R1# show ip route eigrp | begin Gate
Gateway of last resort is not set

     56.0.0.0/24 is subnetted, 1 subnets
D        56.1.1.0 [90/21024000] via 16.1.1.6, 00:02:36, Serial1/6
```

Task 5

Perform a mutual redistribution between RIPv2 and EIGRP on routers R1 and R5. EIGRP routes should be redistributed into the RIPv2 routing domain with a hop count of 1. RIPv2 routes should be redistributed into EIGRP using the interface metrics. You should use **clear ip route** * once this redistribution is completed.

Ensure that every router has reachability to the 3.3.3.3 IP address, and use **ping** to verify it.

```
!On R1:

R1(config)# router rip
R1(config-router)# redistribute eigrp 100 metric 1

R1# show interface serial1/6 | include BW|load
  MTU 1500 bytes, BW 128 Kbit/sec, DLY 20000 usec,
     reliability 255/255, txload 1/255, rxload 1/255

R1(config)# router eigrp 100
R1(config-router)# redistribute rip metric 128 2000 255 1 1500

!On R5:

R5(config)# router rip
R5(config-router)# redistribute eigrp 100 metric 1

R5# show interface serial1/6 | include BW|load
  MTU 1500 bytes, BW 128 Kbit/sec, DLY 20000 usec,
     reliability 255/255, txload 1/255, rxload 1/255

R5(config)# router eigrp 100
R5(config-router)# redistribute rip metric 128 2000 255 1 1500

On All Routers:

rx# clear ip route *
```

Let's verify the configuration:

```
On R1:

R1# show ip route | begin Gate
Gateway of last resort is not set


     3.0.0.0/24 is subnetted, 1 subnets
R       3.3.3.0 [120/3] via 12.1.1.2, 00:00:15, FastEthernet0/1
     12.0.0.0/8 is variably subnetted, 2 subnets, 2 masks
C       12.1.1.0/24 is directly connected, FastEthernet0/1
L       12.1.1.1/32 is directly connected, FastEthernet0/1
     16.0.0.0/8 is variably subnetted, 2 subnets, 2 masks
C       16.1.1.0/24 is directly connected, Serial1/6
```

```
L            16.1.1.1/32 is directly connected, Serial1/6
        23.0.0.0/24 is subnetted, 1 subnets
R            23.1.1.0 [120/1] via 12.1.1.2, 00:00:15, FastEthernet0/1
        24.0.0.0/24 is subnetted, 1 subnets
R            24.1.1.0 [120/1] via 12.1.1.2, 00:00:15, FastEthernet0/1
        45.0.0.0/24 is subnetted, 1 subnets
D EX         45.1.1.0 [110/21536000] via 16.1.1.6, 00:00:15, Serial1/6
        56.0.0.0/24 is subnetted, 1 subnets
D            56.1.1.0 [90/21024000] via 16.1.1.6, 00:00:15, Serial1/6


!On R2:


R2# show ip route rip | begin Gate
Gateway of last resort is not set


        3.0.0.0/24 is subnetted, 1 subnets
R            3.3.3.0 [120/2] via 24.1.1.4, 00:00:24, FastEthernet0/0
        16.0.0.0/24 is subnetted, 1 subnets
R            16.1.1.0 [120/1] via 12.1.1.1, 00:00:25, FastEthernet0/1
        45.0.0.0/24 is subnetted, 1 subnets
R            45.1.1.0 [120/1] via 24.1.1.4, 00:00:24, FastEthernet0/0
                     [120/1] via 12.1.1.1, 00:00:25, FastEthernet0/1
        56.0.0.0/24 is subnetted, 1 subnets
R            56.1.1.0 [120/1] via 12.1.1.1, 00:00:25, FastEthernet0/1


!On R3:


R3# show ip route rip | begin Gate
Gateway of last resort is not set


        12.0.0.0/24 is subnetted, 1 subnets
R            12.1.1.0 [120/1] via 23.1.1.2, 00:00:09, Serial1/2
        16.0.0.0/24 is subnetted, 1 subnets
R            16.1.1.0 [120/2] via 23.1.1.2, 00:00:09, Serial1/2
        24.0.0.0/24 is subnetted, 1 subnets
R            24.1.1.0 [120/1] via 23.1.1.2, 00:00:09, Serial1/2
        45.0.0.0/24 is subnetted, 1 subnets
R            45.1.1.0 [120/2] via 23.1.1.2, 00:00:09, Serial1/2
        56.0.0.0/24 is subnetted, 1 subnets
R            56.1.1.0 [120/2] via 23.1.1.2, 00:00:09, Serial1/2


!On R4:


R4# show ip route rip | begin Gate
Gateway of last resort is not set
```

```
      3.0.0.0/24 is subnetted, 1 subnets
R        3.3.3.0 [120/1] via 45.1.1.5, 00:00:20, FastEthernet0/1
      12.0.0.0/24 is subnetted, 1 subnets
R       12.1.1.0 [120/1] via 45.1.1.5, 00:00:20, FastEthernet0/1
                 [120/1] via 24.1.1.2, 00:00:20, FastEthernet0/0
      16.0.0.0/24 is subnetted, 1 subnets
R       16.1.1.0 [120/1] via 45.1.1.5, 00:00:20, FastEthernet0/1
      23.0.0.0/24 is subnetted, 1 subnets
R       23.1.1.0 [120/1] via 45.1.1.5, 00:00:20, FastEthernet0/1
                 [120/1] via 24.1.1.2, 00:00:20, FastEthernet0/0
      56.0.0.0/24 is subnetted, 1 subnets
R       56.1.1.0 [120/1] via 45.1.1.5, 00:00:20, FastEthernet0/1

!On R5:

R5# show ip route | begin Gate
Gateway of last resort is not set


      3.0.0.0/24 is subnetted, 1 subnets
D EX    3.3.3.0 [110/21536000] via 56.1.1.6, 00:04:48, Serial1/6
      12.0.0.0/24 is subnetted, 1 subnets
D EX   12.1.1.0 [110/21536000] via 56.1.1.6, 00:04:53, Serial1/6
      16.0.0.0/24 is subnetted, 1 subnets
D      16.1.1.0 [90/21024000] via 56.1.1.6, 00:04:53, Serial1/6
      23.0.0.0/24 is subnetted, 1 subnets
D EX   23.1.1.0 [110/21536000] via 56.1.1.6, 00:04:48, Serial1/6
      24.0.0.0/24 is subnetted, 1 subnets
D EX   24.1.1.0 [110/21536000] via 56.1.1.6, 00:04:48, Serial1/6
      45.0.0.0/8 is variably subnetted, 2 subnets, 2 masks
C       45.1.1.0/24 is directly connected, FastEthernet0/1
L       45.1.1.5/32 is directly connected, FastEthernet0/1
      56.0.0.0/8 is variably subnetted, 2 subnets, 2 masks
C       56.1.1.0/24 is directly connected, Serial1/6
L       56.1.1.5/32 is directly connected, Serial1/6
!On R6:

R6# show ip route eigrp | begin Gate
Gateway of last resort is not set


      3.0.0.0/24 is subnetted, 1 subnets
D EX    3.3.3.0 [170/21024000] via 16.1.1.1, 00:05:40, Serial1/1
      12.0.0.0/24 is subnetted, 1 subnets
D EX   12.1.1.0 [170/21024000] via 16.1.1.1, 00:06:28, Serial1/1
      23.0.0.0/24 is subnetted, 1 subnets
```

```
D EX     23.1.1.0 [170/21024000] via 16.1.1.1, 00:05:40, Serial1/1
      24.0.0.0/24 is subnetted, 1 subnets
D EX     24.1.1.0 [170/21024000] via 16.1.1.1, 00:05:40, Serial1/1
      45.0.0.0/24 is subnetted, 1 subnets
D EX     45.1.1.0 [170/21024000] via 56.1.1.5, 00:05:40, Serial1/5
```

The output of the preceding **show** commands reveals that every router has every route in its routing table, but this only means that the control plane has worked properly. Let's verify and test the data plane by pinging 3.3.3.3 from R6:

```
!On R6:

R6# ping 3.3.3.3

Type escape sequence to abort.
Sending 5, 100-byte ICMP Echos to 3.3.3.3, timeout is 2 seconds:
.....
Success rate is 0 percent (0/5)
```

Let's see the next-hop router toward network 3.3.3.0/24:

```
R6# show ip route | include 3.3.3.0
D EX     3.3.3.0 [170/21024000] via 16.1.1.1, 00:06:58, Serial1/1
```

Now let's go to R1 and see the next-hop router toward network 3.3.3.0/24:

```
!On R1:

R1# show ip route | include 3.3.3.0

R       3.3.3.0 [120/3] via 12.1.1.2, 00:00:14, FastEthernet0/1
```

It looks like R1 is going through R2 to reach network 3.3.3.0/24. Let's see the next-hop router that R2 takes to reach network 3.3.3.0/24:

```
!On R2:

R2# show ip route | include 3.3.3.0

R       3.3.3.0 [120/2] via 24.1.1.4, 00:00:18, FastEthernet0/0
```

It looks like R2 is going through R4 to reach network 3.3.3.0/24. Let's see the next-hop router that R4 takes to reach network 3.3.3.0/24:

```
!On R4:

R4# show ip route | include 3.3.3.0

R         3.3.3.0 [120/1] via 45.1.1.5, 00:00:14, FastEthernet0/1
```

It looks like R4 is going through R5 to reach network 3.3.3.0/24. Let's see the next-hop router that R5 takes to reach network 3.3.3.0/24:

```
!On R5:

R5# show ip route | include 3.3.3.0

D EX      3.3.3.0 [110/21536000] via 56.1.1.6, 00:09:27, Serial1/6
```

This looks like a perfect loop, because R6 is using R1 as its next-hop router to reach network 3.3.3.0/24. Let's use **traceroute** to verify this:

```
!On R6:

R6# traceroute 3.3.3.3 numeric

Type escape sequence to abort.
Tracing the route to 3.3.3.3
VRF info: (vrf in name/id, vrf out name/id)
  1 16.1.1.1 28 msec 12 msec 12 msec
  2 12.1.1.2 16 msec 36 msec 16 msec
  3 24.1.1.4 16 msec 12 msec 20 msec
  4 45.1.1.5 16 msec 16 msec 16 msec
  5 56.1.1.6 28 msec 28 msec 32 msec
  6 16.1.1.1 24 msec 28 msec 24 msec
  7 12.1.1.2 24 msec 28 msec 24 msec
  8 24.1.1.4 28 msec 28 msec 24 msec
  9 45.1.1.5 24 msec 24 msec 24 msec
 10 56.1.1.6 44 msec 40 msec 40 msec
 11 16.1.1.1 36 msec 36 msec 36 msec
 12 12.1.1.2 36 msec 36 msec 36 msec
 13 24.1.1.4 36 msec 36 msec 36 msec
 14 45.1.1.5 36 msec 36 msec 36 msec
 15 56.1.1.6 52 msec 48 msec 48 msec
```

```
16 16.1.1.1 44 msec 44 msec 44 msec

17 12.1.1.2 48 msec 44 msec 48 msec

18 24.1.1.4 48 msec 44 msec 48 msec

19 45.1.1.5 44 msec 44 msec 48 msec

20 56.1.1.6 60 msec 60 msec 60 msec

21 16.1.1.1 56 msec 56 msec 56 msec

22 12.1.1.2 56 msec 56 msec 56 msec

23 24.1.1.4 56 msec 56 msec 56 msec

24 45.1.1.5 56 msec 56 msec 56 msec

25 56.1.1.6 72 msec 68 msec 72 msec

26 16.1.1.1 64 msec 68 msec 100 msec

27 12.1.1.2 64 msec 68 msec 68 msec

28 24.1.1.4 68 msec 68 msec 64 msec

29 45.1.1.5 64 msec 68 msec 68 msec

30 56.1.1.6 80 msec 80 msec 84 msec
```

You can see very clearly that the data in this lab is looping. We have analyzed the control plan mechanism used to generate this situation, but for clarity's sake, we need to take a look at it from a higher-order view. Figure 9-4 illustrates the process from the perspective of the control plane mechanism we configured in the first portion of this lab and explores the actual mechanism that leads to the loop in our topology.

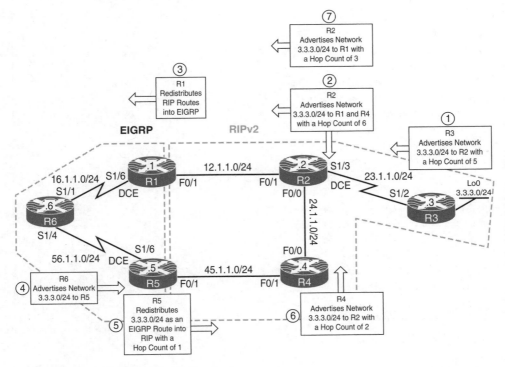

Figure 9-4 *Control Plane Mechanism*

After looking closely at Figure 9-4, you can see that the control plan has led to the generation of the routing loop. In Figure 9-5, you see the "data plane" which is the path the data actually follows. By looking at this, you can see where the problem originates and then adopt a methodology to correct it.

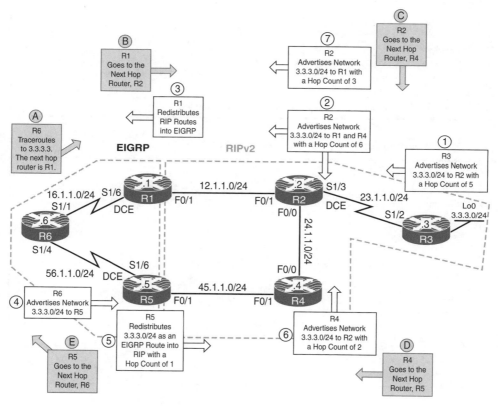

Figure 9-5 *Control Plane Mechanism*

Now that we know the reason, we need to ask ourselves, how do we fix this problem?

Solution #1

There is no reason for R1 and R5 to advertise the RIP routes back into the RIP routing domain. Therefore, we will configure R1 and R5 to filter RIP routes from being advertised out of their F0/1 interface into the RIP routing domain.

Let's try this solution and verify it:

```
!On R1 and R5:


Rx# show access-lists
Rx#


Rx(config)# access-list 1 deny 3.3.3.0 0.0.0.255
Rx(config)# access-list 1 permit any


Rx(config)# router rip
Rx(config-router)# distribute-list 1 out FastEthernet0/1
```

Let's run **clear ip route** * on all routers and verify the result:

```
!On All Routers:


Rx# clear ip route *


!On R6:


R6# traceroute 3.3.3.3 numeric


Type escape sequence to abort.
Tracing the route to 3.3.3.3
VRF info: (vrf in name/id, vrf out name/id)
  1 16.1.1.1 16 msec 12 msec 16 msec
  2 12.1.1.2 16 msec 16 msec 16 msec
  3 23.1.1.3 28 msec *  28 msec
```

You can see that R6 goes to R1, R1 goes to R2, and R2 goes to R3. But why are we getting the asterisk (*) in the third line of the **traceroute?**

The reason we get this kind of timeout is because of the IOS default value for **icmp rate-limit.** Let's verify this parameter:

```
R6# show ip icmp rate-limit


                          DF bit unreachables    All other unreachables
Interval (millisecond)    500                    500


Interface                 #  DF bit unreachables   #  All other unreachables
---------                 --------------------    ------------------------
Serial1/1                 0                      0
Serial1/5                 0                      0
```

The output of the preceding command reveals that the ICMP timeout is 500 ms. This value can be increased, decreased, or negated altogether. Let's negate the timeout:

```
!On All Routers:

Rx(config)# no ip icmp rate-limit unreachable

!On R6:

R6# traceroute 3.3.3.3 numeric

Type escape sequence to abort.
Tracing the route to 3.3.3.3
VRF info: (vrf in name/id, vrf out name/id)
  1 16.1.1.1 12 msec 16 msec 16 msec
  2 12.1.1.2 16 msec 16 msec 16 msec
  3 23.1.1.3 28 msec 28 msec 32 msec
```

Solution #2

Another way to perform this redistribution is to only allow the required routes to be redistributed; in this case, on R1 and R5, we only need to redistribute the EIGRP routes into RIP and nothing else.

Before we configure the second solution, let's remove the first solution:

```
!On R1 and R5:

Rx(config)# no access-list 1
Rx(config)# router rip
Rx(config-router)# no distribute-list 1 out FastEthernet0/1

Rx# clear ip route *
```

Note   You may have to run **clear ip route** * a few times for RIP to converge.

Let's verify the configuration:

```
!On R6:

R6# traceroute 3.3.3.3 numeric

Type escape sequence to abort.
Tracing the route to 3.3.3.3
```

```
VRF info: (vrf in name/id, vrf out name/id)
  1 16.1.1.1 12 msec 12 msec 16 msec
  2 12.1.1.2 16 msec 16 msec 16 msec
  3 24.1.1.4 16 msec 12 msec 12 msec
  4 45.1.1.5 16 msec 16 msec 16 msec
  5 56.1.1.6 28 msec 28 msec 36 msec
  6 16.1.1.1 24 msec 24 msec 28 msec
  7 12.1.1.2 24 msec 28 msec 24 msec
  8 24.1.1.4 24 msec 24 msec 24 msec
  9 45.1.1.5 24 msec 28 msec 24 msec
 10 56.1.1.6 40 msec 40 msec 40 msec
 11 16.1.1.1 36 msec 36 msec 36 msec
 12 12.1.1.2 36 msec 36 msec 36 msec
 13 24.1.1.4 36 msec 36 msec 36 msec
 14 45.1.1.5 36 msec 36 msec 36 msec
 15 56.1.1.6 48 msec 52 msec 48 msec
 16 16.1.1.1 48 msec 44 msec 48 msec
 17 12.1.1.2 48 msec 44 msec 48 msec
 18 24.1.1.4 44 msec 48 msec 48 msec
 19 45.1.1.5 44 msec 48 msec 48 msec
 20 56.1.1.6 60 msec 60 msec 60 msec
 21 16.1.1.1 56 msec 56 msec 56 msec
 22 12.1.1.2 56 msec 56 msec 60 msec
 23 24.1.1.4 56 msec 56 msec 56 msec
 24 45.1.1.5 56 msec 56 msec 56 msec
 25 56.1.1.6 68 msec 72 msec 72 msec
 26 16.1.1.1 64 msec 68 msec 68 msec
 27 12.1.1.2 68 msec 64 msec 64 msec
 28 24.1.1.4 68 msec 76 msec 68 msec
 29 45.1.1.5 68 msec 68 msec 68 msec
 30 56.1.1.6 80 msec 80 msec 84 msec
```

Now we can configure the second solution:

```
!On R1 and R5:

Rx(config)# ip prefix-list net deny 12.1.1.0/24
Rx(config)# ip prefix-list net deny 25.1.1.0/24
Rx(config)# ip prefix-list net deny 45.1.1.0/24
Rx(config)# ip prefix-list net deny 3.3.3.0/24
Rx(config)# ip prefix-list net permit 0.0.0.0/0 le 32

Rx(config)# route-map tst permit 10
Rx(config-route-map)# match ip address prefix net
```

```
Rx(config)# router rip
Rx(config-router)# redistribute eigrp 100 route-map tst metric 1

!On R1 - R5:

Rx# clear ip route *

!On R1, R5 and R6:

Rx# clear ip eigrp neighbor
```

Let's verify and test the configuration:

```
!On R6:

R6# traceroute 3.3.3.3 numeric

Type escape sequence to abort.
Tracing the route to 3.3.3.3
VRF info: (vrf in name/id, vrf out name/id)
  1 16.1.1.1 12 msec 16 msec 16 msec
  2 12.1.1.2 16 msec 16 msec 16 msec
  3 23.1.1.3 28 msec 28 msec 28 msec
```

Solution #3

To avoid routing loops when mutual redistribution is configured at multiple points, the routes originating in a routing domain must be denied from being redistributed back into the same routing domain. Let's say a mutual redistribution is being performed between protocols A and B. The routes from protocol A are tagged with a value (say, 111). And the routes from protocol B are tagged with a value (say, 222). When the redistribution is performed in a mutual manner, the routing table of protocols A and B will consist of routes that are tagged with values of 111 and 222, respectively. Therefore, when you're redistributing protocol B into protocol A, any route that carries a tag of 111 is filtered inbound. When you're redistributing protocol A into protocol B, any route that carries a tag of 222 is filtered inbound.

A common method of tagging routes is using the administrative distance of the originating routing protocol. EIGRP routes are tagged with 90, OSPF routes are tagged with 110, and RIP routes are tagged with 120. This makes it easy to look at the route tag associated with a route and know where the route originated.

Let's configure this task and verify the result. However, before configuring solution #3, let's remove the configuration from the previous solution:

```
!On R1 and R5:

Rx(config)# no ip prefix-list net

Rx(config)# no route-map tst

Rx(config)# router rip
Rx(config-router)# no redistribute eigrp 100
Rx(config-router)# redistribute eigrp 100 metric 1
```

Let's test the configuration:

```
!On R6:

R6# traceroute 3.3.3.3 numeric

Type escape sequence to abort.
Tracing the route to 3.3.3.3
VRF info: (vrf in name/id, vrf out name/id)
  1 16.1.1.1 16 msec 16 msec 16 msec
  2 12.1.1.2 16 msec 16 msec 16 msec
  3 24.1.1.4 16 msec 16 msec 12 msec
  4 45.1.1.5 12 msec 16 msec 16 msec
  5 56.1.1.6 28 msec 32 msec 32 msec
  6 16.1.1.1 28 msec 24 msec 24 msec
  7 12.1.1.2 28 msec 24 msec 28 msec
  8 24.1.1.4 24 msec 28 msec 24 msec
  9 45.1.1.5 28 msec 24 msec 24 msec
 10 56.1.1.6 36 msec 40 msec 40 msec
 11 16.1.1.1 36 msec 36 msec 36 msec
 12 12.1.1.2 36 msec 36 msec 36 msec
 13 24.1.1.4 36 msec 36 msec 36 msec
 14 45.1.1.5 36 msec 36 msec 36 msec
 15 56.1.1.6 48 msec 48 msec 48 msec
 16 16.1.1.1 44 msec 44 msec 48 msec
 17 12.1.1.2 44 msec 48 msec 44 msec
 18 24.1.1.4 48 msec 48 msec 44 msec
 19 45.1.1.5 48 msec 48 msec 44 msec
 20 56.1.1.6 60 msec 64 msec 56 msec
```

```
21 16.1.1.1 56 msec 56 msec 56 msec
22 12.1.1.2 56 msec 56 msec 56 msec
23 24.1.1.4 56 msec 56 msec 56 msec
24 45.1.1.5 56 msec 60 msec 56 msec
25 56.1.1.6 68 msec 72 msec 72 msec
26 16.1.1.1 64 msec 68 msec 68 msec
27 12.1.1.2 68 msec 68 msec 64 msec
28 24.1.1.4 64 msec 68 msec 68 msec
29 45.1.1.5 64 msec 64 msec 68 msec
30 56.1.1.6 80 msec 80 msec 80 msec
```

Now we can configure solution #3 and verify it:

```
!On R1 and R5:

Rx(config)# route-map RIPtoEIGRP deny 10
Rx(config-route-map)# match tag 90
Rx(config)# route-map RIPtoEIGRP permit 90
Rx(config-route-map)# set tag 120

Rx(config)# route-map EIGRPtoRIP deny 10
Rx(config-route-map)# match tag 120
Rx(config)# route-map EIGRPtoRIP permit 90
Rx(config-route-map)# set tag 90
```

The best way to understand the following route maps is to read them from bottom to top:

route-map eigrp→rip permit 90: This route map tags all EIGRP routes with a value of 90.

route-map rip→eigrp deny 10: This route map denies any route that carries a tag value of 90.

route-map rip→eigrp permit 90: This route map tags all RIP routes with a value of 120.

route-map eigrp→rip deny 10: This route map denies any route that carries a tag value of 120.

```
Rx(config)# router rip
Rx(config-router)# redistribute eigrp 100 route-map EIGRPtoRIP metric 1

Rx(config)# router eigrp 100
Rx(config-router)# redistribute rip route-map RIPtoEIGRP metric 128 2000 255 1 1500
```

Let's test the configuration:

```
!On R6:


R6# traceroute 3.3.3.3 numeric


Type escape sequence to abort.
Tracing the route to 3.3.3.3
VRF info: (vrf in name/id, vrf out name/id)
  1 16.1.1.1 16 msec 16 msec 16 msec
  2 12.1.1.2 16 msec 12 msec 16 msec
  3 23.1.1.3 32 msec 28 msec 28 msec
```

Solution #4

We can use summarization to fix this problem. Let's configure this solution and verify it. However, before we try solution #4, we should remove the previous solution:

```
!On R1 and R5:


Rx(config)# no route-map RIPtoEIGRP
Rx(config)# no route-map EIGRPtoRIP


Rx(config)# router rip
Rx(config-router)# no redistribute eigrp 100 route-map EIGRPtoRIP
Rx(config-router)# redistribute eigrp 100 metric 1


Rx(config-router)# router eigrp 100
Rx(config-router)# no redistribute rip route-map RIPtoEIGRP
Rx(config-router)# redistribute rip metric 128 2000 255 1 1500
```

Let's verify the configuration:

```
!On R6:
R6# traceroute 3.3.3.3 numeric


Type escape sequence to abort.
Tracing the route to 3.3.3.3
VRF info: (vrf in name/id, vrf out name/id)
  1 56.1.1.5 16 msec 16 msec 12 msec
  2 45.1.1.4 16 msec 16 msec 16 msec
  3 24.1.1.2 16 msec 16 msec 16 msec
  4 12.1.1.1 16 msec 12 msec 16 msec
  5 16.1.1.6 32 msec 28 msec 28 msec
```

```
 6 56.1.1.5 28 msec 24 msec 24 msec
 7 45.1.1.4 24 msec 28 msec 24 msec
 8 24.1.1.2 24 msec 24 msec 24 msec
 9 12.1.1.1 28 msec 24 msec 28 msec
10 16.1.1.6 40 msec 40 msec 40 msec
11 56.1.1.5 36 msec 36 msec 36 msec
12 45.1.1.4 36 msec 36 msec 36 msec
13 24.1.1.2 36 msec 36 msec 36 msec
14 12.1.1.1 36 msec 36 msec 36 msec
15 16.1.1.6 52 msec 48 msec 52 msec
16 56.1.1.5 44 msec 48 msec 44 msec
17 45.1.1.4 48 msec 48 msec 44 msec
18 24.1.1.2 44 msec 48 msec 48 msec
19 12.1.1.1 44 msec 48 msec 44 msec
20 16.1.1.6 60 msec 60 msec 60 msec
21 56.1.1.5 56 msec 56 msec 56 msec
22 45.1.1.4 56 msec 76 msec 56 msec
23 24.1.1.2 56 msec 68 msec 56 msec
24 12.1.1.1 56 msec 56 msec 56 msec
25 16.1.1.6 72 msec 68 msec 72 msec
26 56.1.1.5 68 msec 68 msec 64 msec
27 45.1.1.4 68 msec 68 msec 68 msec
28 24.1.1.2 68 msec 64 msec 68 msec
29 12.1.1.1 68 msec 68 msec 68 msec
30 16.1.1.6 80 msec 80 msec 84 msec
```

Now we can configure solution #4:

```
!On R1 and R6:

Rx(config)# interface serial1/6
Rx(config-if)# ip summary-address eigrp 100 3.0.0.0 255.0.0.0
```

When summarization is configured, the more specific routes are suppressed; therefore, a single summary route is injected into the EIGRP routing domain, and because the more specific routes are suppressed, the RIP routes are reachable through RIP routing domain.

Let's test the configuration:

```
On R6:

R6# show ip route eigrp | begin Gate
Gateway of last resort is not set
```

```
          3.0.0.0/24 is subnetted, 1 subnets
D EX      3.3.3.0 [170/21024000] via 16.1.1.1, 00:05:40, Serial1/1
          12.0.0.0/24 is subnetted, 1 subnets
D EX      12.1.1.0 [170/21024000] via 16.1.1.1, 00:06:28, Serial1/1
          23.0.0.0/24 is subnetted, 1 subnets
D EX      23.1.1.0 [170/21024000] via 16.1.1.1, 00:05:40, Serial1/1
          24.0.0.0/24 is subnetted, 1 subnets
D EX      24.1.1.0 [170/21024000] via 16.1.1.1, 00:05:40, Serial1/1
          45.0.0.0/24 is subnetted, 1 subnets
D EX      45.1.1.0 [170/21024000] via 56.1.1.5, 00:05:40, Serial1/5


On R1:


R1# show ip route 3.3.3.0


Routing entry for 3.3.3.0/24
  Known via "rip", distance 120, metric 6
  Redistributing via rip, eigrp 100
  Advertised by eigrp 100 metric 128 2000 255 1 1500
  Last update from 12.1.1.2 on FastEthernet0/1, 00:00:14 ago
  Routing Descriptor Blocks:
  * 12.1.1.2, from 12.1.1.2, 00:00:14 ago, via FastEthernet0/1
      Route metric is 6, traffic share count is 1


!On R2:
R2# show ip route 3.3.3.0


Routing entry for 3.3.3.0/24
  Known via "rip", distance 120, metric 5
  Redistributing via rip
  Last update from 23.1.1.3 on Serial1/3, 00:00:28 ago
  Routing Descriptor Blocks:
  * 23.1.1.3, from 23.1.1.3, 00:00:28 ago, via Serial1/3
      Route metric is 5, traffic share count is 1


!On R6:


R6# traceroute 3.3.3.3 numeric


Type escape sequence to abort.
Tracing the route to 3.3.3.3
VRF info: (vrf in name/id, vrf out name/id)
  1 16.1.1.1 12 msec
    56.1.1.5 16 msec
    16.1.1.1 16 msec
```

```
  2 45.1.1.4 16 msec
    12.1.1.2 16 msec
    45.1.1.4 16 msec
  3 23.1.1.3 28 msec
    24.1.1.2 16 msec
    23.1.1.3 28 msec
```

Erase the startup configuration of the routers and switches and reload them before proceeding to the next lab.

Lab 9-4: Redistribute RIPv2 and OSPF

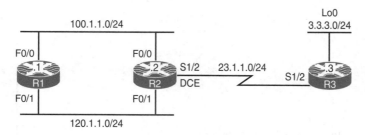

Figure 9-6   *Configuring Redistribution RIPv2 and OSPF*

Figure 9-6 illustrates the topology that will be used in the following tasks. As mentioned in the previous lab involving RIP, you should remember that the metric is composed of a hop count and that the maximum valid metric is 15. Anything above 15 is considered infinite; you can use 16 to describe an infinite metric in RIP. When you're redistributing a protocol into RIP, Cisco recommends that you use a low metric, such as 1. A high metric, such as 10, limits RIP even further. If you define a metric of 10 for redistributed routes, these routes can only be advertised to routers up to five hops away, at which point the metric (hop count) exceeds 15. By defining a metric of 1, you enable a route to travel the maximum number of hops in a RIP domain. However, doing this increases the possibility of routing loops if there are multiple redistribution points and a router learns about the network with a better metric from the redistribution point than from the original source. Therefore, you have to make sure that the metric is neither too high, preventing it from being advertised to all the routers, nor too low, leading to routing loops when there are multiple redistribution points.

With OSPF, the metric is a cost value based on 10^8 divided by the bandwidth of the link in bits/sec. For example, the OSPF cost of Ethernet is 10: $10^8/10^7 = 10$

Note   If a metric is not specified, OSPF uses a default value of 20 with the default metric type, or type-2, when redistributing routes from all protocols except Border Gateway Protocol (BGP) routes, which get a metric of 1.

When there is a major network that is subnetted, you need to use the keyword **subnets** to redistribute protocols into OSPF. Without this keyword, OSPF only redistributes major networks that are not subnetted.

It is possible to run more than one OSPF process on the same router. However, running more than one process of the same protocol is rarely needed and consumes the router's memory and CPU. Also, you do not need to define the metric or use the **default-metric** command when redistributing one OSPF process into another.

Now we will experiment with redistribution between these two protocols.

Task 1

Configure OSPF area 0 on the F0/0 interfaces of R1 and R2:

```
!On R1:

R1(config)# router ospf 1
R1(config-router)# router-id 0.0.0.1
R1(config-router)# network 110.1.1.1 0.0.0.0 area 0

!On R2:

R2(config)# router ospf 1
R2(config-router)# router-id 0.0.0.2
R2(config-router)# network 110.1.1.2 0.0.0.0 area 0
```

You should see the following console message:

```
OSPF-5-ADJCHG: Process 1, Nbr 0.0.0.1.1.1.1 on FastEthernet0/0 from LOADING to FULL,
  Loading Done
```

Let's verify the configuration:

```
!On R2:

R2# show ip ospf neighbor

Neighbor ID     Pri    State      Dead Time    Address        Interface
0.0.0.1           1    FULL/DR    00:00:36     110.1.1.1      FastEthernet0/0
```

Task 2

Configure RIPv2 on R1, R2, and R3 based on the following requirement:

- On R1, configure RIPv2 on the F0/1 interface.

- On R2, configure RIPv2 on the F0/1 and S1/3 interfaces.

- On R3, configure RIPv2 on the S1/2 and loopback0 interfaces.

- Disable auto-summarization on all three routers.

```
!On R1:

R1(config)# router rip
R1(config-router)# version 2
R1(config-router)# no auto-summary
R1(config-router)# network 120.0.0.0

On R2:

R2(config)# router rip
R2(config-router)# version 2
R2(config-router)# no auto-summary
R2(config-router)# network 120.0.0.0
R2(config-router)# network 23.0.0.0

On R3:

R3(config)# router rip
R3(config-router)# version 2
R3(config-router)# no auto-summary
R3(config-router)# network 3.0.0.0
R3(config-router)# network 23.0.0.0
```

Let's verify the configuration:

```
!On R1:

R1# show ip route rip | begin Gate
Gateway of last resort is not set


      3.0.0.0/24 is subnetted, 1 subnets
R        3.3.3.0 [120/2] via 120.1.1.2, 00:00:01, FastEthernet0/1
      23.0.0.0/24 is subnetted, 1 subnets
R        23.1.1.0 [120/1] via 120.1.1.2, 00:00:01, FastEthernet0/1

On R2:

R2# show ip route rip | begin Gate
Gateway of last resort is not set


      3.0.0.0/24 is subnetted, 1 subnets
R        3.3.3.0 [120/1] via 23.1.1.3, 00:00:03, Serial1/3
```

Task 3

Configure the update, invalidation, and flush timers to be one-third of their default values:

```
!On R1:

Rx# show ip protocols | section rip
Routing Protocol is "rip"
  Outgoing update filter list for all interfaces is not set
  Incoming update filter list for all interfaces is not set
  Sending updates every 30 seconds, next due in 13 seconds
  Invalid after 180 seconds, hold down 180, flushed after 240
  Redistributing: rip
  Default version control: send version 2, receive version 2
    Interface            Send  Recv  Triggered RIP  Key-chain
    FastEthernet0/1       2     2
  Automatic network summarization is not in effect
  Maximum path: 4
  Routing for Networks:  `
    120.0.0.0
  Routing Information Sources:
    Gateway         Distance      Last Update
    120.1.1.2            120      00:00:05
  Distance: (default is 120)


!On All Routers:

Rx(config)# router rip
Rx(config-router)# timers basic 10 60 60 80
```

Let's verify the configuration:

```
!On R1:

R1# show ip protocols | section rip
Routing Protocol is "rip"
  Outgoing update filter list for all interfaces is not set
  Incoming update filter list for all interfaces is not set
  Sending updates every 10 seconds, next due in 0 seconds
  Invalid after 60 seconds, hold down 60, flushed after 80
  Redistributing: rip
  Default version control: send version 2, receive version 2
    Interface            Send  Recv  Triggered RIP  Key-chain
    Ethernet0/1           2     2
```

```
Automatic network summarization is not in effect
Maximum path: 4
Routing for Networks:
  120.0.0.0
Routing Information Sources:
  Gateway          Distance      Last Update
  120.1.1.2              120      00:00:04
Distance: (default is 120)
```

Task 4

Perform a mutual redistribution between OSPF and RIPv2 on R1. R1 should redistribute the OSPF routes into RIPv2 with a metric of 1. RIP routes should be redistributed into OSPF using the default cost and metric type. Ensure full reachability using **ping**.

```
!On R1:

R1(config)# router rip
R1(config-router)# redistribute ospf 1 metric 1

R1(config)# router ospf 1
R1(config-router)# redistribute rip subnets
```

Let's verify the configuration:

Note   You only have to type the command **show ip route | include 3.3.3.0** once. After pressing the Enter key, press the up-arrow key once and then the Enter key again.

```
!On R2:

R2# show ip route | include 3.3.3.0

R        3.3.3.0 [120/1] via 23.1.1.3, 00:00:00, Serial1/3

R2# show ip route | include 3.3.3.0

R        3.3.3.0 [120/1] via 23.1.1.3, 00:00:01, Serial1/3

R2# show ip route | include 3.3.3.0

R        3.3.3.0 [120/1] via 23.1.1.3, 00:00:02, Serial1/3
```

```
R2# show ip route | include 3.3.3.0

R       3.3.3.0 [120/1] via 23.1.1.3, 00:00:03, Serial1/3

R2# show ip route | include 3.3.3.0

R       3.3.3.0 [120/1] via 23.1.1.3, 00:00:04, Serial1/3

R2# show ip route | include 3.3.3.0

R       3.3.3.0 [120/1] via 23.1.1.3, 00:00:04, Serial1/3

R2# show ip route | include 3.3.3.0

O E2    3.3.3.0 [110/20] via 110.1.1.1, 00:00:00, FastEthernet0/0

R2# show ip route | include 3.3.3.0

O E2    3.3.3.0 [110/20] via 110.1.1.1, 00:00:01, FastEthernet0/0

R2# show ip route | include 3.3.3.0

O E2    3.3.3.0 [110/20] via 110.1.1.1, 00:00:02, FastEthernet0/0

R2# show ip route | include 3.3.3.0

O E2    3.3.3.0 [110/20] via 110.1.1.1, 00:00:02, FastEthernet0/0

R2# show ip route | include 3.3.3.0

O E2    3.3.3.0 [110/20] via 110.1.1.1, 00:00:03, FastEthernet0/0

R2# show ip route | include 3.3.3.0

O E2    3.3.3.0 [110/20] via 110.1.1.1, 00:00:04, FastEthernet0/0

R2# show ip route | include 3.3.3.0

O E2    3.3.3.0 [110/20] via 110.1.1.1, 00:00:04, FastEthernet0/0

R2# show ip route | include 3.3.3.0

O E2    3.3.3.0 [110/20] via 110.1.1.1, 00:00:05, FastEthernet0/0
```

```
R2# show ip route | include 3.3.3.0

O E2    3.3.3.0 [110/20] via 110.1.1.1, 00:00:06, FastEthernet0/0

R2# show ip route | include 3.3.3.0

O E2    3.3.3.0 [110/20] via 110.1.1.1, 00:00:07, FastEthernet0/0

R2# show ip route | include 3.3.3.0

O E2    3.3.3.0 [110/20] via 110.1.1.1, 00:00:07, FastEthernet0/0

R2# show ip route | include 3.3.3.0

O E2    3.3.3.0 [110/20] via 110.1.1.1, 00:00:08, FastEthernet0/0

R2# show ip route | include 3.3.3.0
R2# show ip route | include 3.3.3.0
```

The route was not in the routing table, then it showed up as RIP, then it showed up as OSPF **O E2**, and then the route disappeared.

Let's enable some debugging to find the problem so we can fix it. Let's enable **debug ip routing** and **debug ip rip** on R2 and **debug ip ospf lsa-generation** on R1:

```
!On R1:

R1# debug ip ospf lsa-generation
ospf summary lsa generation debugging is on

!On R2:

R2# debug ip routing
IP routing debugging is on

R2# debug ip rip
RIP protocol debugging is on
```

When you see **RT: add 3.3.3.0/24 via 23.1.1.3, rip metric [120/1]** on R2 twice, disable all debugging on R1 and R2.

Let's now analyze the output of the debug commands.

Step #1:

R3 advertises network 3.3.3.0/24 to R2, and R2 adds that entry to its RIB:

```
!On R2:

RT: add 3.3.3.0/24 via 23.1.1.3, rip metric [120/1]

RT: updating rip 3.3.3.0/24 (0x0):
   via 23.1.1.3 Se1/3
```

Let's check the routing table of R2:

```
R2# show ip route | include 3.3.3.0
R      3.3.3.0 [120/1] via 23.1.1.3, 00:00:08, Serial1/3
```

Once R2 receives network 3.3.3.0/24, it advertises the network to R1.

Step #2:

R1 receives network 3.3.3.0/24 from R2 and redistributes it into OSPF, and it sends an LSA type 5 to R2:

```
!On R1:

OSPF-1 LSGEN: Generate external LSA 3.3.3.0, mask 255.255.255.0, type 5, age 0, seq
  0x80000059

OSPF-1 LSGEN: Generate external LSA 3.3.3.0, mask 255.255.255.0, type 5, age 0, seq
  0x8000009B
OSPF-1 LSGEN: MTID   Metric   Metric-type   FA         Tag       Topology Name
OSPF-1 LSGEN: 0      20       2             0.0.0.0    0         Base
```

Let's look at this on R1:

```
R1# show ip ospf database external | include 3.3.3.0
  link state id: 3.3.3.0 (external network number )
```

Step #3:

R2 receives the OSPF external update from R1. Because OSPF has a lower administrative distance, it flushes the RIP-learned route and replaces it with OSPF with a next-hop IP address of 110.1.1.1. R2 also sends a RIP update to R1 notifying it that network 3.3.3.0/24 is no longer available. Let's go to R2 and see this in the debug output:

```
RT: closer admin distance for 3.3.3.0, flushing 1 routes
RT: add 3.3.3.0/24 via 110.1.1.1, ospf metric [110/20]

RT: updating rip 110.1.1.0/24 (0x0):
    via 120.1.1.1 Fa0/1
```

Let's look at this on R2:

```
R2# show ip route | include 3.3.3.0

O E2     3.3.3.0 [110/20] via 110.1.1.1, 00:00:07, FastEthernet0/0
```

Step #4:

Since R2 flushed the RIP-learned (3.3.3.0/24) network and replaced it with OSPF, it sent an update to R1 for network 3.3.3.0/24, telling R1 that this is no longer available (meaning this prefix is inaccessible). This means that it's 16 hops away from the local router. Because R1 no longer has network 3.3.3.0/24 in its routing table, it can no longer redistribute the route into OSPF, so it advertises network 3.3.3.0/24 with a metric of 16,777,215.

Because R1 does not have network 3.3.3.0/24 in its routing table, it can no longer redistribute it into OSPF, so it advertises network 3.3.3.0/24 with its maximum metric, poisoning the route.

```
OSPF-1 LSGEN: generate external lsa 3.3.3.0, mask 255.255.255.0, type 5, age 3600,
  seq 0x80000016
OSPF-1 LSGEN: MITD    Metric    Metric-type    FA         Tag      Topology Name
OSPF-1 LSGEN: 0       16777215  2              0.0.0.0    0        Base
```

This is when the route totally disappeared:

```
R2# show ip route | include 3.3.3.0
R2#
```

But a few seconds later, R2 receives a RIP update from R3 for network 3.3.3.0/24 and adds it to its RIB, and the cycle repeats:

```
R2# show ip route | include 3.3.3.0
R       3.3.3.0 [120/1] via 23.1.1.3, 00:00:04, Serial1/3
```

To fix this problem, R2 should always trust RIP's information for network 3.3.3.0/24 over OSPF. Therefore, let's change the administrative distance of RIP to be lower than OSPF's administrative distance. Once this configuration is performed, R3 will ignore OSPF's update regarding network 3.3.3.0/24.

```
!On R2:

R2(config)# router rip
R2(config-router)# distance 109
```

Let's test and verify the configuration:

```
!On R1:

R1# ping 3.3.3.3

Type escape sequence to abort.
sending 5, 100-byte icmp echos to 3.3.3.3, timeout is 2 seconds:
!!!!!
Success rate is 100 percent (5/5), round-trip min/avg/max = 28/30/32 ms

!On R2:

R2# ping 3.3.3.3

Type escape sequence to abort.
sending 5, 100-byte icmp echos to 3.3.3.3, timeout is 2 seconds:
!!!!!
Success rate is 100 percent (5/5), round-trip min/avg/max = 28/28/32 ms
```

Erase the startup configuration of the routers and switches and reload them before proceeding to the next lab.

Chapter 10

Border Gateway Protocol

Lab 10-1: Establishing Neighbor Adjacencies

In the following labs, we will explore the deployment of the Border Gateway Protocol (BGP) in the network topology illustrated in Figure 10-1.

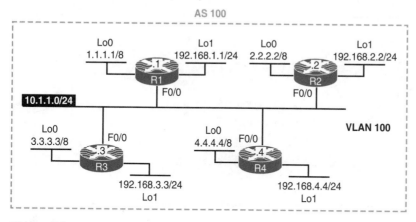

Figure 10-1 *iBGP Lab Topology*

We will begin by turning our focus toward iBGP peering relationships.

The initial configuration files used in this lab can be found by downloading the BGP-Lab-1.txt file and subsequently applying those configurations on a device-by-device basis.

Task 1

Configure routers R1–R4 in AS 100. These routers should create interior-BGP peer sessions between them in a full-mesh manner. Ensure that these routers advertise

their loopback0 interface in this autonomous system (AS). Use their F0/0 interface
for establishing an adjacency.

```
!On R1:


R1(config)# router bgp 100
R1(config-router)# neighbor 10.1.1.2 remote-as 100
R1(config-router)# neighbor 10.1.1.3 remote-as 100
R1(config-router)# neighbor 10.1.1.4 remote-as 100
R1(config-router)# network 1.0.0.0


!On R2:


R2(config)# router bgp 100
R2(config-router)# neighbor 10.1.1.1 remote-as 100
R2(config-router)# neighbor 10.1.1.3 remote-as 100
R2(config-router)# neighbor 10.1.1.4 remote-as 100
R2(config-router)# network 2.0.0.0
```

You should see the following console message stating that an adjacency is established
with neighbor 10.1.1.1:

```
%BGP-5-ADJCHANGE: neighbor 10.1.1.1 Up


!On R3:


R3(config)# router bgp 100
R3(config-router)# neighbor 10.1.1.1 remote-as 100
R3(config-router)# neighbor 10.1.1.2 remote-as 100
R3(config-router)# neighbor 10.1.1.4 remote-as 100
R3(config-router)# network 3.0.0.0
```

You should see the following console messages:

```
%BGP-5-ADJCHANGE: neighbor 10.1.1.1 Up
%BGP-5-ADJCHANGE: neighbor 10.1.1.2 Up


!On R4:


R1(config)# router bgp 100
R4(config-router)# neighbor 10.1.1.1 remote-as 100
R4(config-router)# neighbor 10.1.1.2 remote-as 100
R4(config-router)# neighbor 10.1.1.3 remote-as 100
R4(config-router)# network 4.0.0.0
```

You should also see these console messages:

```
%BGP-5-ADJCHANGE: neighbor 10.1.1.1 Up
%BGP-5-ADJCHANGE: neighbor 10.1.1.3 Up
%BGP-5-ADJCHANGE: neighbor 10.1.1.2 Up
```

Let's verify the configuration:

```
!On R1:

R1# show ip bgp | begin Network

    Network          Next Hop          Metric LocPrf Weight Path
*>  1.0.0.0          0.0.0.0                0          32768 i
*>i2.0.0.0           10.1.1.2               0    100       0 i
*>i3.0.0.0           10.1.1.3               0    100       0 i
*>i4.0.0.0           10.1.1.4               0    100       0 i
```

The following explains the output of the preceding **show** command:

- The * means that the entry in the table is valid.

- The **>** means that this is the best entry for a given prefix.

- The i means that the entry was learned via an iBGP; this is the i to the right of the greater-than sign (>) in the network column. The letter i under the path column specifies the origin of the route.

- The **Network** column identifies the prefix entry for the network(s). If the mask is omitted, the default mask is assumed.

- The **Next Hop** column identifies the next hop's IP address to reach the specified network address. If it's set to 0.0.0.0, it identifies a prefix that the local router has advertised.

- The **Metric** column identifies the **inter-as** metric, or the **MED** attribute, which is set to zero by default.

- The **LocPrf** column identifies the "local preference" attribute. This is used in the route selection process carried out within the local AS *only*. With the **local-pref** attribute, the higher value has more preference. By default, the prefixes that are received from a peer AS are tagged with a **local-pref** value of 100; this behavior can be changed to influence the best-path-selection process. The changed value is only advertised to iBGP peers. When the local router advertises a prefix, no **local-pref** value is seen in the output of the **show ip bgp** command. The default value of 100 can be changed by the **bgp default local-preference** command.

- The **Weight** column identifies the **weight** attribute. The prefixes that are received via a neighbor (iBGP or exterior Border Gateway Protocol [eBGP]) will have a **weight** attribute of 0, but the prefixes that are originated by the local router will have a **weight** value of 32768. This attribute overrides any other attribute for performing best-path determination.

■ The **Path** column identifies the **path** attribute. If the prefixes were originated or learned via an iBGP neighbor, the path column will have the letter **i** without any AS number (ASN). If the prefix was learned through another AS, then this column will have the AS number(s) followed by the letter **i**. The ASNs indicate which AS advertised the prefix. The maximum number of AS instances a prefix can traverse through is 255.

```
R4# show ip bgp summary | begin Neighbor

Neighbor        V         AS MsgRcvd MsgSent   TblVer  InQ OutQ Up/Down  State/PfxRcd
10.1.1.1        4        100      13      13        6    0    0 00:07:34           1
10.1.1.2        4        100      13      13        6    0    0 00:07:32           1
10.1.1.3        4        100      12      13        6    0    0 00:07:23           1
```

Task 2

Reconfigure the routers in AS 100 based on the following policy:

■ Authentication must be enabled between the peers using "cisco" as the password.

■ The peer session must be established based on the loopback0's IP address.

■ These routers should only advertise their loopback1 interface in BGP.

■ Provide Network Layer Reachability Information (NLRI) to the loopback0 interface using RIPv2.

■ Use peer groups to accomplish this task.

Cisco's implementation of BGP in IOS 12.0(5)T and earlier releases supports BGP versions 2, 3, and 4, with dynamic negotiation down to Version 2. However, in IOS version 12.0(6)T and later, Cisco routers only support version 4, and they do *not* support dynamic negotiation down to version 2.

```
!On R1:

R1(config)# no router bgp 100

R1(config)# router bgp 100
R1(config-router)# network 192.168.1.0
R1(config-router)# neighbor TST peer-group
R1(config-router)# neighbor TST remote-as 100
```

```
R1(config-router)# neighbor TST update-source loopback0
R1(config-router)# neighbor TST password cisco

R1(config-router)# neighbor 2.2.2.2 peer-group TST
R1(config-router)# neighbor 3.3.3.3 peer-group TST
R1(config-router)# neighbor 4.4.4.4 peer-group TST

R1(config-router)# router rip
R1(config-router)# no auto-summary
R1(config-router)# version 2
R1(config-router)# network 10.0.0.0
R1(config-router)# network 1.0.0.0

!On R2:

R2(config)# no router bgp 100

R2(config)# router bgp 100
R2(config-router)# network 192.168.2.0
R2(config-router)# neighbor TST peer-group
R2(config-router)# neighbor TST remote-as 100
R2(config-router)# neighbor TST update-source loopback0
R2(config-router)# neighbor TST password cisco

R2(config-router)# neighbor 1.1.1.1 peer-group TST
R2(config-router)# neighbor 3.3.3.3 peer-group TST
R2(config-router)# neighbor 4.4.4.4 peer-group TST

R2(config-router)# router rip
R2(config-router)# no auto-summary
R2(config-router)# version 2
R2(config-router)# network 10.0.0.0
R2(config-router)# network 2.0.0.0
```

You should see the following console message stating that an adjacency was established with 1.1.1.1 (R1):

```
%BGP-5-ADJCHANGE: neighbor 1.1.1.1 Up

!On R3:

R3(config)# no router bgp 100

R3(config)# router bgp 100
```

```
R3(config-router)# network 192.168.3.0
R3(config-router)# neighbor TST peer-group

R3(config-router)# neighbor TST remote-as 100
R3(config-router)# neighbor TST update-source loopback0
R3(config-router)# neighbor TST password cisco

R3(config-router)# neighbor 1.1.1.1 peer-group TST
R3(config-router)# neighbor 2.2.2.2 peer-group TST
R3(config-router)# neighbor 4.4.4.4 peer-group TST

R3(config-router)# router rip
R3(config-router)# no auto-summary
R3(config-router)# version 2
R3(config-router)# network 10.0.0.0
R3(config-router)# network 3.0.0.0
```

You should see the following console messages stating that an adjacency was established with 1.1.1.1 (R1) and 2.2.2.2 (R2):

```
%BGP-5-ADJCHANGE: neighbor 1.1.1.1 Up
%BGP-5-ADJCHANGE: neighbor 2.2.2.2 Up

!On R4:

R4(config)# no router bgp 100

R4(config)# router bgp 100
R4(config-router)# network 192.168.4.0
R4(config-router)# neighbor TST peer-group
R4(config-router)# neighbor TST remote-as 100
R4(config-router)# neighbor TST update-source loopback0
R4(config-router)# neighbor TST password cisco

R4(config-router)# neighbor 1.1.1.1 peer-group TST
R4(config-router)# neighbor 2.2.2.2 peer-group TST
R4(config-router)# neighbor 3.3.3.3 peer-group TST

R4(config-router)# router rip
R4(config-router)# no auto-summary
R4(config-router)# version 2
R4(config-router)# network 10.0.0.0
R4(config-router)# network 4.0.0.0
```

You should see the following console messages stating that an adjacency was established with 1.1.1.1 (R1), 2.2.2.2 (R2), and 3.3.3.3 (R3):

```
%BGP-5-ADJCHANGE: neighbor 1.1.1.1 Up
%BGP-5-ADJCHANGE: neighbor 3.3.3.3 Up
%BGP-5-ADJCHANGE: neighbor 2.2.2.2 Up
```

To verify the configuration:

```
!On R1:

R1# show ip bgp | begin Network

   Network          Next Hop          Metric LocPrf Weight Path
*> 192.168.1.0      0.0.0.0                0          32768 i
*>i192.168.2.0      2.2.2.2                0    100       0 i
*>i192.168.3.0      3.3.3.3                0    100       0 i
*>i192.168.4.0      4.4.4.4                0    100       0 i
```

Now let's move to R1 and continue the verification process there.

```
!On R1:

R1# show ip bgp peer-group TST

BGP peer-group is TST,  remote AS 100
  BGP version 4
  Default minimum time between advertisement runs is 0 seconds
 For address family: IPv4 Unicast
  BGP neighbor is TST, peer-group internal, members:
  2.2.2.2 3.3.3.3 4.4.4.4
  Index 0, Offset 0, Mask 0x0
  Update messages formatted 0, replicated 0
  Number of NLRIs in the update sent: max 0, min 0
```

Note   The output of the **show ip bgp peer-group TST** command reveals the IP address of the members of the peer group. One of the major benefits of a peer group is that it can reduce the administrative overhead by cutting down redundant configuration on the routers.

Erase the startup configuration and reload the routers before proceeding to the next lab.

Lab 10-2: Router Reflectors

A *route reflector* is a BGP router that is allowed to ignore the iBGP loop avoidance rule and, as such, is allowed to advertise updates received from an iBGP peer to another iBGP peer under specific conditions. This means that the deployment of route reflectors can eliminate the BGP full-mesh requirement. Just this one simple change in behavior allows us to simplify the building of our iBGP networks. Plus, it makes them more readily scalable. RFC 4456 describes BGP route reflection. Route reflectors make all this possible, as follows:

- By dividing iBGP routers into route reflectors, route reflector clients, and non-client peers.

- Routes received from a route reflector client are reflected to both client and non-client neighbors.

- Routes received from a non-client neighbor are reflected to route reflector clients only.

- By setting the nontransitive **Originator-ID** attribute in the reflected update if it is not already set. The **Originator-ID** is set to the peer **Router-ID** that advertised the prefix to the router reflector.

- By adding the **Cluster-ID** to the nontransitive **Cluster-list** attribute in the reflected update. By default, the **Cluster-ID** is set to the BGP **Router-ID**.

- A route reflector will only reflect BGP best routes. If more than one update is received for the same destination, only the BGP best route will be reflected.

- A route reflector is not allowed to change any of the following attributes of the reflected routes: **NEXT_HOP, AS_PATH, LOCAL_PREF**, and **MED**.

The issue with the deployment of route reflectors is the fact that route reflectors ignore the primary iBGP loop-prevention mechanism. This would be an untenable situation if route reflectors did not introduce their own loop-detection and -prevention mechanism:

- If a router receives an iBGP route with the **Originator-ID** attribute set to its own **Router-ID**, the route is discarded.

- If a route reflector receives a route with a **Cluster-list** attribute containing its **Cluster-ID**, the route is discarded.

Figure 10-2 illustrates the simple topology we will use to explore the configuration and benefits of employing route reflectors as a solution to prevent the administrative overhead associated with the full-mesh requirement for iBGP peers we explored in the previous lab.

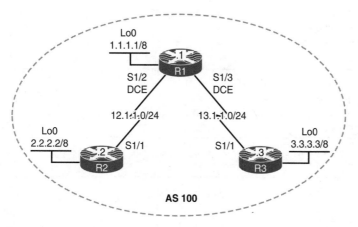

Figure 10-2   *Route Reflector Lab Topology*

The initial configuration files used in this lab can be found by downloading the BGP-Lab-2.txt file and subsequently applying those configurations on a device-by-device basis.

Task 1

Configure BGP AS 100 on all routers and ensure that the routers can successfully establish an iBGP peer session with each other. These routers should only advertise their loopback0 interface in BGP.

```
!On R1:

R1(config)# router bgp 100
R1(config-router)# network 1.0.0.0
R1(config-router)# neighbor 12.1.1.2 remote-as 100
R1(config-router)# neighbor 13.1.1.3 remote-as 100

!On R2:

R2(config)# router bgp 100
R2(config-router)# network 2.0.0.0
R2(config-router)# neighbor 12.1.1.1 remote-as 100
R2(config-router)# neighbor 13.1.1.3 remote-as 100
```

You should see the following console message:

```
%BGP-5-ADJCHANGE: neighbor 12.1.1.1 Up

!On R3:

R3(config)# router bgp 100
```

```
R3(config-router)# network 3.0.0.0
R3(config-router)# neighbor 13.1.1.1 remote-as 100
R3(config-router)# neighbor 12.1.1.2 remote-as 100
```

You should also see this console message:

```
%BGP-5-ADJCHANGE: neighbor 13.1.1.1 Up
```

Let's verify the configuration:

```
!On R1:


R1# show ip bgp | begin Network

   Network          Next Hop          Metric LocPrf Weight Path
*> 1.0.0.0          0.0.0.0                0          32768 i
*>i2.0.0.0          12.1.1.2               0    100      0 i
*>i3.0.0.0          13.1.1.3               0    100      0 i


R1# show ip route bgp | include B

Codes: L - local, C - connected, S - static, R - RIP, M - mobile, B - BGP
B     2.0.0.0/8 [200/0] via 12.1.1.2, 00:07:34
B     3.0.0.0/8 [200/0] via 13.1.1.3, 00:05:27

!On R2:

R2# show ip bgp | begin Network

   Network          Next Hop         Metric LocPrf Weight Path
*>i1.0.0.0          12.1.1.1              0    100      0 i
*> 2.0.0.0          0.0.0.0               0          32768 i

R2# show ip route bgp | include B

Codes: L - local, C - connected, S - static, R - RIP, M - mobile, B - BGP
B     1.0.0.0/8 [200/0] via 12.1.1.1, 00:08:56
```

Network 3.0.0.0 is *not* in the BGP table of R2. Let's check the neighbor adjacency:

```
R2# show ip bgp summary | begin Neighbor

Neighbor       V    AS MsgRcvd MsgSent   TblVer  InQ OutQ Up/Down   State/PfxRcd
12.1.1.1       4   100      16      16        4    0    0 00:10:33             1
13.1.1.3       4   100       0       0        1    0    0 never     Idle
```

The neighbor is in an idle state. Do we have reachability to this neighbor? Let's verify using **ping**:

```
R2# ping 13.1.1.3

Type escape sequence to abort.
Sending 5, 100-byte ICMP Echos to 13.1.1.3, timeout is 2 seconds:
.....
Success rate is 0 percent (0/5)

Let's check the routing table:

R2# show ip route 13.1.1.3
% Network not in table
```

We *cannot* see 13.1.1.3 in the routing table. This is one reason why an IGP should be configured within an AS. This IGP should provide reachability to the links within the AS. Let's run Open Shortest Path First (OSPF) on the links that interconnect the routers:

```
!On R1:

R1(config)# router ospf 1
R1(config-router)# router-id 0.0.0.1
R1(config-router)# network 12.1.1.1 0.0.0.0 area 0
R1(config-router)# network 13.1.1.1 0.0.0.0 area 0

!On R2:

R2(config)# router ospf 1
R2(config-router)# router-id 0.0.0.2
R2(config-router)# network 12.1.1.2 0.0.0.0 area 0

!On R3:

R3(config)# router ospf 1
R3(config-router)# router-id 0.0.0.3
R3(config-router)# network 13.1.1.3 0.0.0.0 area 0
```

You should see the following console message:

```
%BGP-5-ADJCHANGE: neighbor 12.1.1.2 Up

R3# show ip bgp | begin Network

   Network          Next Hop            Metric LocPrf Weight Path
*>i1.0.0.0          13.1.1.1                 0    100      0 i
```

```
*>i2.0.0.0          12.1.1.2                0    100      0 i
*> 3.0.0.0          0.0.0.0                 0           32768 i

R3# ping 2.2.2.2

Type escape sequence to abort.
Sending 5, 100-byte ICMP Echos to 2.2.2.2, timeout is 2 seconds:
!!!!!
Success rate is 100 percent (5/5), round-trip min/avg/max = 56/57/60 ms

R3# ping 2.2.2.2 source loopback0loopback 0

Type escape sequence to abort.
Sending 5, 100-byte ICMP Echos to 2.2.2.2, timeout is 2 seconds:
Packet sent with a source address of 3.3.3.3
!!!!!
Success rate is 100 percent (5/5), round-trip min/avg/max = 56/57/60 ms
```

Task 2

You receive an email from management stating that within the next 12 months, 20 additional routers will be added to this AS. In order to minimize the number of peer sessions within this AS, you decide to implement route reflectors.

Configure R1 as a route reflector for this AS:

```
!On R1:

R1(config)# router bgp 100
R1(config-router)# neighbor 12.1.1.2 route-reflector-client
R1(config-router)# neighbor 13.1.1.3 route-reflector-client
```

You should see that the adjacency resets itself and then it comes up:

```
%BGP-5-ADJCHANGE: neighbor 12.1.1.2 Down RR client config change
%BGP_SESSION-5-ADJCHANGE: neighbor 12.1.1.2 IPv4 Unicast topology base removed
  from session  RR client config change
%BGP-5-ADJCHANGE: neighbor 12.1.1.2 Up

%BGP-5-ADJCHANGE: neighbor 13.1.1.3 Down RR client config change
%BGP_SESSION-5-ADJCHANGE: neighbor 13.1.1.3 IPv4 Unicast topology base removed
  from session  RR client config change
%BGP-5-ADJCHANGE: neighbor 13.1.1.3 Up
```

> **Note**   Once the route reflector is configured, there is no need for R2 and R3 to establish an iBGP peer session. The route reflector (R1) will reflect the prefixes from one iBGP neighbor to another:

```
!On R2:

R2(config)# router bgp 100
R2(config-router)# no neighbor 13.1.1.3 remote-as 100

!On R3:

R3(config)# router bgp 100
R3(config-router)# no neighbor 12.1.1.2 remote-as 100
```

Let's verify the configuration:

```
!On R3:

R3# show ip bgp summary | begin Neighbor

Neighbor        V         AS MsgRcvd MsgSent   TblVer  InQ OutQ Up/Down  State/PfxRcd
13.1.1.1        4        100      11       8        7    0    0 00:04:50           2

R3# show ip bgp | begin Net

   Network          Next Hop         Metric LocPrf Weight Path
*>i1.0.0.0          13.1.1.1              0    100      0 i
*>i2.0.0.0          12.1.1.2              0    100      0 i
*> 3.0.0.0          0.0.0.0               0           32768 i

R3# ping 2.2.2.2

Type escape sequence to abort.
Sending 5, 100-byte ICMP Echos to 2.2.2.2, timeout is 2 seconds:
!!!!!
Success rate is 100 percent (5/5), round-trip min/avg/max = 56/58/60 ms
```

```
R3# ping 2.2.2.2 source loopback0loopback 0

Type escape sequence to abort.
Sending 5, 100-byte ICMP Echos to 2.2.2.2, timeout is 2 seconds:
Packet sent with a source address of 3.3.3.3
!!!!!
Success rate is 100 percent (5/5), round-trip min/avg/max = 56/58/60 ms
```

In order for all iBGP speakers in an AS to exchange routes with one another, they must be fully meshed (every router must establish a peer session with every other router). This is because of a rule called *iBGP split-horizon*, which states that when a BGP speaker receives an update from an iBGP peer, it will *not* advertise that update to another iBGP peer.

Route reflectors can be configured to reduce the number of peer sessions that must be established between the routers within a given AS. If a route reflector is used, all iBGP speakers need not be fully meshed. In this model, the router that is configured to be the route reflector must have a peer session established to every client, and the clients must establish a peer session with the route reflector *only*. The route reflector will reflect prefixes learned from one client to another client (or clients).

Let's verify the configuration:

```
!On R1:

R1# show ip bgp | begin Network

   Network          Next Hop          Metric LocPrf Weight Path
*>  1.0.0.0          0.0.0.0                0        32768 i
*>i2.0.0.0          12.1.1.2               0    100      0 i
*>i3.0.0.0          13.1.1.3               0    100      0 i
```

The output of the following **show** commands reveal the fact that prefixes 2.0.0.0/8 and 3.0.0.0/8 were received from a route reflector client:

```
R1# show ip bgp 2.0.0.0

BGP routing table entry for 2.0.0.0/8, version 6
Paths: (1 available, best # 1, table Default-IP-Routing-Table)
  Advertised to update-groups:
      2
  Local, (Received from a RR-client)
    10.1.12.2 from 10.1.12.2 (2.2.2.2)
      Origin IGP, metric 0, localpref 100, valid, internal, best
```

```
R1# show ip bgp 3.0.0.0

BGP routing table entry for 3.0.0.0/8, version 9
Paths: (1 available, best # 1, table default)
  Advertised to update-groups:
     2
  Local, (Received from a RR-client)
    13.1.1.3 from 13.1.1.3 (3.3.3.3)
      Origin IGP, metric 0, localpref 100, valid, internal, best
```

The output of the following **show** commands reveals the **Originator-ID** and the **Cluster-list** of prefix 3.0.0.0/8:

```
!On R2:

R2# show ip bgp | begin Network

   Network          Next Hop          Metric LocPrf Weight Path
*>i1.0.0.0          12.1.1.1               0    100      0 i
*> 2.0.0.0          0.0.0.0                0         32768 i
*>i3.0.0.0          13.1.1.3               0    100      0 i

R2# show ip bgp 3.0.0.0
BGP routing table entry for 3.0.0.0/8, version 7
Paths: (1 available, best # 1, table default)
  Not advertised to any peer
  Refresh Epoch 1
  Local
    13.1.1.3 (metric 128) from 12.1.1.1 (1.1.1.1)
      Origin IGP, metric 0, localpref 100, valid, internal, best
      Originator: 3.3.3.3, Cluster list: 1.1.1.1
      rx pathid: 0, tx pathid: 0x0

R2# ping 3.3.3.3

Type escape sequence to abort.
Sending 5, 100-byte ICMP Echos to 3.3.3.3, timeout is 2 seconds:
!!!!!
Success rate is 100 percent (5/5), round-trip min/avg/max = 56/58/60 ms
```

Erase the startup config and reload the routers before proceeding to the next lab.

Lab 10-3: Conditional Advertisement and BGP Backdoor (Figure 10-3)

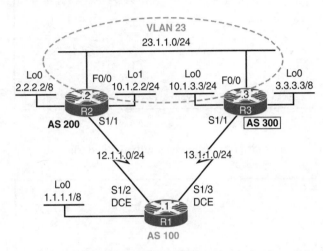

Figure 10-3 *Conditional Advertisement and Backdoor Lab Topology*

The initial configuration files used in this lab can be found by downloading the BGP-Lab-3.txt file and subsequently applying those configurations on a device-by-device basis.

Task 1

Configure R1 in AS 100 to establish an eBGP peer session with R2 and R3 in AS 200 and 300, respectively. R2 should *not* have a BGP peer session with R3. You should use their serial interface's IP address to accomplish this task.

```
!On R1:

R1(config)# router bgp 100
R1(config-router)# neighbor 12.1.1.2 remote-as 200
R1(config-router)# neighbor 13.1.1.3 remote-as 300


!On R2:

R2(config)# router bgp 200
R2(config-router)# neighbor 12.1.1.1 remote-as 100


!On R3:

R3(config)# router bgp 300
R3(config-router)# neighbor 13.1.1.1 remote-as 100
```

Let's verify the configuration:

```
!On R1:

R1# show ip bgp summary | begin Neighbor

Neighbor        V    AS MsgRcvd MsgSent    TblVer  InQ OutQ Up/Down   State/PfxRcd
10.1.12.2       4   200       3       3         1    0    0 00:00:39            0
10.1.13.3       4   300       3       3         1    0    0 00:00:32            0
```

Task 2

Configure R1, R2, and R3 to advertise their loopback0 interface in BGP:

```
!On R1:

R1(config)# router bgp 100
R1(config-router)# network 1.0.0.0

!On R2:

R2(config)# router bgp 200
R2(config-router)# network 2.0.0.0

!On R3:

R3(config)# router bgp 300
R3(config-router)# network 3.0.0.0
```

Let's verify the configuration:

```
!On R3:

R3# show ip bgp | begin Network

   Network          Next Hop         Metric LocPrf Weight Path
*> 1.0.0.0          13.1.1.1              0             0 100 i
*> 2.0.0.0          13.1.1.1                            0 100 200 i
*> 3.0.0.0          0.0.0.0               0         32768 i
```

Task 3

Configure RIPv2 and EIGRP 100 on the routers as follows:

■ Configure RIPv2 on networks 12.1.1.0/24 and 13.1.1.0/24; disable auto-summarization.

■ R2 and R3 should advertise their F0/0 and loopback1 interfaces in EIGRP AS 100.

```
!On R1:

R1(config)# router rip
R1(config-router)# no auto-summary
R1(config-router)# version 2
R1(config-router)# network 12.0.0.0
R1(config-router)# network 13.0.0.0

!On R2:

R2(config)# router rip
R2(config-router)# no auto-summary
R2(config-router)# version 2
R2(config-router)# network 12.0.0.0

R2(config)# router eigrp 100
R2(config-router)# network 23.1.1.2 0.0.0.0
R2(config-router)# network 10.1.2.2 0.0.0.0

!On R3:

R3(config)# router rip
R3(config-router)# no auto-summary
R3(config-router)# version 2
R3(config-router)# network 13.0.0.0

R3(config)# router eigrp 100
R3(config-router)# network 23.1.1.3 0.0.0.0
R3(config-router)# network 10.1.3.3 0.0.0.0
```

Let's verify the configuration:

```
!On R2:

R2# show ip route eigrp | begin Gate
Gateway of last resort is not set

     10.0.0.0/8 is variably subnetted, 5 subnets, 2 masks
D       10.1.3.0/24 [90/156160] via 10.1.23.3, 00:00:52, FastEthernet0/0

R2# show ip route rip | begin Gate
Gateway of last resort is not set

     13.0.0.0/24 is subnetted, 1 subnets
R       13.1.1.0 [120/1] via 12.1.1.1, 00:00:15, Serial1/1
```

Task 4

Because network 23.1.1.0/24 is *not* advertised in BGP, if the Ethernet link between R2 and R3 goes down, the loopback1 networks of these two routers won't have reachability to each other, even though there is a redundant link between the two routers through BGP. Therefore, the administrator of R2 and R3 has decided that the loopback1 interfaces of R2 and R3 should be advertised in BGP to provide redundancy.

Configure these routers to accommodate this decision:

```
!On R2:

R2(config)# router bgp 200
R2(config-router)# network 10.1.2.0 mask 255.255.255.0

!On R3:

R3(config)# router bgp 300
R3(config-router)# network 10.1.3.0 mask 255.255.255.0
```

Let's verify the configuration:

```
!On R2:

R2# show ip route bgp | begin Gate
Gateway of last resort is not set

B     1.0.0.0/8 [20/0] via 12.1.1.1, 00:16:27
B     3.0.0.0/8 [20/0] via 12.1.1.1, 00:15:57
      10.0.0.0/8 is variably subnetted, 5 subnets, 2 masks
B        10.1.3.0/24 [20/0] via 12.1.1.1, 00:00:13

!On R3:

R3# show ip route bgp | begin Gate
Gateway of last resort is not set

B     1.0.0.0/8 [20/0] via 13.1.1.1, 00:17:06
B     2.0.0.0/8 [20/0] via 13.1.1.1, 00:16:05
      10.0.0.0/8 is variably subnetted, 5 subnets, 2 masks
B        10.1.2.0/24 [20/0] via 13.1.1.1, 00:01:22
```

Task 5

After you implement the previous task, the administrator realizes that the traffic between networks 10.1.2.0/24 and 10.1.3.0/24 is taking a suboptimal path and is not using the direct path between R2 and R3.

Implement a BGP solution to fix this problem. You should *not* use the distance, PBR, or any global config mode command to accomplish this task.

Let's look at the suboptimal path:

```
!On R3:

R3# traceroute 10.1.2.2 numeric

Type escape sequence to abort.
Tracing the route to 10.1.2.2
VRF info: (vrf in name/id, vrf out name/id)
  1 13.1.1.1 16 msec 16 msec 12 msec
  2 12.1.1.2 32 msec *  28 msec

R3# show ip route 10.1.2.2

Routing entry for 10.1.2.0/24
  Known via "bgp 300", distance 20, metric 0
  Tag 100, type external
  Last update from 13.1.1.1 00:07:02 ago
  Routing Descriptor Blocks:
  * 13.1.1.1, from 13.1.1.1, 00:07:02 ago
      Route metric is 0, traffic share count is 1
      AS Hops 2
      Route tag 100
      MPLS label: none
```

We can see that R2 and R3 are taking a suboptimal path to reach each other's loopback1 interface.

The BGP **backdoor** option can help you accomplish this task. The **backdoor** keyword is added to the **network** statement. You should reference the network that is advertised to you and *not* the network that your local router is advertising:

```
!On R2:

R2(config)# router bgp 200
R2(config-router)# network 10.1.3.0 mask 255.255.255.0 backdoor
```

Let's verify the configuration:

```
!On R2:


R2# show ip route 10.1.3.3


Routing entry for 10.1.3.0/24
  Known via "eigrp 100", distance 90, metric 156160, type internal
  Redistributing via eigrp 100
  Last update from 10.1.23.3 on FastEthernet0/0, 00:00:56 ago
  Routing Descriptor Blocks:
  * 10.1.23.3, from 10.1.23.3, 00:00:56 ago, via FastEthernet0/0
      Route metric is 156160, traffic share count is 1
      Total delay is 5100 microseconds, minimum bandwidth is 100000 Kbit
      Reliability 255/255, minimum MTU 1500 bytes
      Loading 1/255, Hops 1


R2# traceroute 10.1.3.3 numeric


Type escape sequence to abort.
Tracing the route to 10.1.3.3
VRF info: (vrf in name/id, vrf out name/id)
  1 23.1.1.3 0 msec *  0 msec
```

We can see that R2 uses its direct connection (F0/0 interface) to reach the loopback1 interface of R3. The **backdoor** keyword causes BGP to use the administrative distance for BGP local routes, which by default is 200, instead of the administrative distance for BGP external routes. This allows the Routing Information Base (RIB) to select the IGP advertised route instead of eBGP's advertisement.

Let's look at the changes in the BGP table and table entry:

```
R2# show ip bgp
BGP table version is 6, local router ID is 10.1.2.2
Status codes: s suppressed, d damped, h history, * valid, > best, i - internal,
              r RIB-failure, S Stale, m multipath, b backup-path, f RT-Filter,
              x best-external, a additional-path, c RIB-compressed,
Origin codes: i - IGP, e - EGP, ? - incomplete
RPKI validation codes: V valid, I invalid, N Not found

     Network          Next Hop            Metric LocPrf Weight Path
 *>  1.0.0.0          12.1.1.1                 0             0 100 i
 *>  2.0.0.0          0.0.0.0                  0         32768 i
 *>  3.0.0.0          12.1.1.1                               0 100 300 i
 *>  10.1.2.0/24      0.0.0.0                  0         32768 i
 r>  10.1.3.0/24      12.1.1.1                               0 100 300 i
```

```
R2# show ip bgp 10.1.3.0
BGP routing table entry for 10.1.3.0/24, version 3
Paths: (1 available, best # 1, table default, RIB-failure(17) - next-hop mismatch)
  Not advertised to any peer
  Refresh Epoch 1
  100 300
    12.1.1.1 from 12.1.1.1 (1.1.1.1)
      Origin IGP, localpref 100, valid, external, best
      rx pathid: 0, tx pathid: 0x0


R2# show ip bgp rib-failure
  Network              Next Hop                          RIB-failure     RIB-NH Matches
  10.1.3.0/24          12.1.1.1                  Higher admin distance         n/a
```

As you can see, the Routing Information Base rejected the router because it now has a higher administrative distance.

Let's see the configured administrative distance for BGP local routes:

```
R2# show ip protocols | section bgp
Routing Protocol is "bgp 200"
  Outgoing update filter list for all interfaces is not set
  Incoming update filter list for all interfaces is not set
  IGP synchronization is disabled
  Automatic route summarization is disabled
  Neighbor(s):
    Address           FiltIn FiltOut DistIn DistOut Weight RouteMap
    12.1.1.1
  Maximum path: 1
  Routing Information Sources:
    Gateway           Distance        Last Update
    12.1.1.1                20         00:16:39
  Distance: external 20 internal 200 local 200
```

Now we need to test the redundancy. First, on R2, let's shut down the F0/0 interface and verify reachability:

```
!On R2:

R2(config)# interface FastEthernet0/0
R2(config-if)# shutdown


R2# show ip route 10.1.3.3
```

```
Routing entry for 10.1.3.0/24
  Known via "bgp 200", distance 200, metric 0
  Tag 100, type locally generated
  Last update from 12.1.1.1 00:00:42 ago
  Routing Descriptor Blocks:
  * 12.1.1.1, from 12.1.1.1, 00:00:42 ago
      Route metric is 0, traffic share count is 1
      AS Hops 2
      Route tag 100
      MPLS label: none

R2# traceroute 10.1.3.3 numeric

Type escape sequence to abort.
Tracing the route to 10.1.3.3
VRF info: (vrf in name/id, vrf out name/id)
  1 12.1.1.1 16 msec 16 msec 12 msec
  2 13.1.1.3 32 msec *  28 msec
```

Next, let's enable the F0/0 interface of R2 and configure the same on R3:

```
!On R2:

R2(config)# interface FastEthernet0/0
R2(config-if)# no shutdown

R2# show ip route 10.1.3.3

Routing entry for 10.1.3.0/24
  Known via "eigrp 100", distance 90, metric 156160, type internal
  Redistributing via eigrp 100
  Last update from 10.1.23.3 on FastEthernet0/0, 00:00:33 ago
  Routing Descriptor Blocks:
  * 10.1.23.3, from 10.1.23.3, 00:00:33 ago, via FastEthernet0/0
      Route metric is 156160, traffic share count is 1
      Total delay is 5100 microseconds, minimum bandwidth is 100000 Kbit
      Reliability 255/255, minimum MTU 1500 bytes
      Loading 1/255, Hops 1

!On R3:

R3(config)# router bgp 300
R3(config-router)# network 10.1.2.0 mask 255.255.255.0 backdoor
```

Let's verify the configuration:

```
!On R3:

R3# show ip route eigrp | begin Gate
Gateway of last resort is not set

     10.0.0.0/8 is variably subnetted, 5 subnets, 2 masks
D        10.1.2.0/24 [90/156160] via 10.1.23.2, 00:00:20, FastEthernet0/0

!On R2:

R2# show ip route eigrp | begin Gate
Gateway of last resort is not set

     10.0.0.0/8 is variably subnetted, 5 subnets, 2 masks
D        10.1.3.0/24 [90/156160] via 10.1.23.3, 00:07:07, FastEthernet0/0
```

Here's a summary of what you learned:

- R2 and R3 were receiving routing information for networks 10.1.2.0/24 and 10.1.3.0/24 from two different sources: BGP and EIGRP.

- R2 and R3 were using the routing information from BGP because it had a lower administrative distance (20 for eBGP versus 90 for EIGRP).

- The **network** statement with the **backdoor** option is a BGP solution to this problem. The BGP **backdoor** option assigns the BGP local route administrative distance of 200 to the advertised network, making the EIGRP-learned routes more attractive.

Task 6

Remove the IP address from the F0/0 interfaces of R2 and R3 and ensure that the F0/0 interfaces of both routers are in the administratively down state. You should also remove the loopback1 interface from these two routers.

```
!On R2 and R3:

Rx(config)# default interface FastEthernet0/0

Rx(config)# interface FastEthernet0/0
Rx(config-if)# shutdown

Rx(config)# no interface loopback 1
```

Task 7

Configure R1 based on the following policy:

- If network 2.0.0.0/8 is up and it's advertised to R1, R1 should *not* advertise its network 1.0.0.0/8 to R3.

- R1 should advertise network 1.0.0.0/8 to R3 *only* if network 2.0.0.0/8 is down.

Before configuring this task, let's verify the current BGP table of these routers:

```
!On R1:


R1# show ip bgp | begin Network

   Network          Next Hop            Metric LocPrf Weight Path
*> 1.0.0.0          0.0.0.0                  0         32768 i
*> 2.0.0.0          12.1.1.2                 0             0 200 i
*> 3.0.0.0          13.1.1.3                 0             0 300 i

R2# show ip bgp | begin Network

   Network          Next Hop            Metric LocPrf Weight Path
*> 1.0.0.0          12.1.1.1                 0             0 100 i
*> 2.0.0.0          0.0.0.0                  0         32768 i
*> 3.0.0.0          12.1.1.1                               0 100 300 i

R3# show ip bgp | begin Network

   Network          Next Hop            Metric LocPrf Weight Path
*> 1.0.0.0          13.1.1.1                 0             0 100 i
*> 2.0.0.0          13.1.1.1                               0 100 200 i
*> 3.0.0.0          0.0.0.0                  0         32768 i
```

To implement conditional advertisement in BGP, the following reserved maps can be used:

- **advertise-map**
- **non-exist-map**
- **exist-map**
- **inject-map**

This situation calls for the use of the **advertise-map** and **non-exist-map**. Basically, using these two commands, we are saying, "Advertise network 1.0.0.0 *only* if network 2.0.0.0 is down; if network 2.0.0.0 is *not* down, then don't advertise network 1.0.0.0."

Let's configure this task:

Step 1.   Identify the prefixes using two access lists/prefix lists:

```
!On R1:

R1# sh access-lists

R1(config)# access-list 1 permit 1.0.0.0 0.255.255.255
R1(config)# access-list 2 permit 2.0.0.0 0.255.255.255
```

Step 2.   Configure two route maps: one to reference **access-list 1** and the second to reference **access-list 2**. To prevent confusion, you should choose meaningful names when configuring the route maps:

```
R1(config)# route-map Advertise permit 10
R1(config-route-map)# match ip address 1
R1(config-route-map)# exit

R1(config)# route-map NotThere permit 10
R1(config-route-map)# match ip address 2
R1(config-route-map)# exit
```

Step 3.   The route maps are referenced by the **advertise-map** and **non-exist-map** options:

```
R1(config)# router bgp 100
R1(config-router)# neighbor 13.1.1.3 advertise-map Advertise non-exist-map NotThere
```

The **neighbor** command has the following route maps:

- **advertise-map:** Specifies the name of the route map that will be advertised if the condition of the **non-exist-map** is met.

- **non-exist-map:** Specifies the name of the route map that will be compared to the **advertise-map**. If the condition is met and no match occurs, the route will be advertised. If a match occurs, then the condition is *not* met and the route is withdrawn.

If network 2.0.0.0 is up, then network 1.0.0.0 should *not* be advertised to R3. Because all the networks are up and advertised, R1 should withdraw its network (1.0.0.0/8):

Note   Network 2.0.0.0 is up, so network 1.0.0.0/8 should *not* be advertised to R3.

```
!On R1:

R1# show ip bgp | begin Network

   Network          Next Hop          Metric LocPrf Weight Path
*> 1.0.0.0          0.0.0.0                0          32768 i
*> 2.0.0.0          12.1.1.2               0              0 200 i
*> 3.0.0.0          13.1.1.3               0              0 300 i
```

The following **show** command reveals that R1 does *not* advertise its network (1.0.0.0/8) to R3:

```
R1# show ip bgp neighbors 13.1.1.3 advertised-routes | begin Network

   Network          Next Hop          Metric LocPrf Weight Path
*> 2.0.0.0          12.1.1.2               0              0 200 i
```

Let's look at the status of the **advertise-map**:

```
R1# show ip bgp neighbor 13.1.1.3 | include map
  Condition-map NotThere, Advertise-map Advertise, status: Withdraw
```

Now let's verify this configuration:

```
!On R3:

R3# show ip bgp | begin Network

   Network          Next Hop          Metric LocPrf Weight Path
*> 2.0.0.0          13.1.1.1                              0 100 200 i
*> 3.0.0.0          0.0.0.0                0          32768 i
```

Now we need to test the condition:

```
!On R2:

R2(config)# interface loopback 0
R2(config-if)# shutdown
```

The output of the following **show** command reveals that network 2.0.0.0 is down and that R1 is advertising its network (1.0.0.0/8) to R3. It may take few seconds for this policy to be implemented.

```
!On R1:

R1# show ip bgp neighbors 13.1.1.3 advertised-routes | begin Network

   Network          Next Hop              Metric LocPrf Weight Path
*> 1.0.0.0          0.0.0.0                    0           32768 i
```

Let's see the status of the **advertise-map**:

```
R1# show ip bgp neighbor 13.1.1.3 | include map
   Condition-map NotThere, Advertise-map Advertise, status: Advertise
```

Now let's look at the test on R3:

```
!On R3:

R3# show ip bgp | begin Network

   Network          Next Hop              Metric LocPrf Weight Path
*> 1.0.0.0          13.1.1.1                   0          0 100 i
*> 3.0.0.0          0.0.0.0                    0           32768 i
```

Task 8

Remove the configuration commands entered in the previous task before you proceed to
the next task. Ensure that the routers have the advertised networks in their BGP table:

```
!On R1:

R1(config)# no access-list 1
R1(config)# no access-list 2

R1(config)# no route-map Advertise
R1(config)# no route-map NotThere

R1(config)# router bgp 100
R1(config-router)# no neighbor 13.1.1.3 advertise-map Advertise non-exist-map NotThere

R1# clear ip bgp *

!On R2:

R2(config)# interface loopback 0
R2(config-if)# no shutdown
```

```
!On R1:


R1# show ip bgp | begin Network

   Network          Next Hop         Metric LocPrf Weight Path
*> 1.0.0.0          0.0.0.0              0        32768 i         .
*> 2.0.0.0          12.1.1.2             0            0 200 i
*> 3.0.0.0          13.1.1.3             0            0 300 i

!On R2:


R2# show ip bgp | begin Network

   Network          Next Hop         Metric LocPrf Weight Path
*> 1.0.0.0          12.1.1.1             0            0 100 i
*> 2.0.0.0          0.0.0.0              0        32768 i
*> 3.0.0.0          12.1.1.1                          0 100 300 i

!On R3:


R3# show ip bgp | begin Network

   Network          Next Hop         Metric LocPrf Weight Path
*> 1.0.0.0          13.1.1.1             0            0 100 i
*> 2.0.0.0          13.1.1.1                          0 100 200 i
*> 3.0.0.0          0.0.0.0              0        32768 i
```

Task 9

R1 should be configured based on the following policy:

1. If both networks (1.0.0.0/8 and 2.0.0.0/8) are up, then both networks should be advertised to R3.

2. If network 1.0.0.0/8 is down, R1 should *not* advertise network 2.0.0.0/8 to R3.

3. If network 2.0.0.0/8 is down, R1 should *only* advertise network 1.0.0.0/8 to R3.

The logic in the following configuration says, "*Only* advertise network 2.0.0.0/8 if network 1.0.0.0/8 is up, so if network 1.0.0.0/8 is *not* up, do *not* advertise network 2.0.0.0/8."

Step 1.   The following two access lists identify the two networks (1.0.0.0/8 and 2.0.0.0/8):

```
!On R1:

R1(config)# access-list 1 permit 1.0.0.0 0.255.255.255
R1(config)# access-list 2 permit 2.0.0.0 0.255.255.255
```

Step 2.   The following route maps are configured to reference the two access lists from the previous step:

```
R1(config)# route-map Advertise permit 10
R1(config-route-map)# match ip address 2

R1(config)# route-map Exist permit 10
R1(config-route-map)# match ip address 1
```

Step 3.   With the following configuration, we are instructing BGP for the conditions of the task's requirements:

```
R1(config)# router bgp 100
R1(config-router)# neighbor 13.1.1.3 advertise-map Advertise exist-map Exist
```

To test the first condition, if both networks (1.0.0.0/8 and 2.0.0.0/8) are up, then both networks should be advertised to R3.

Note   Both prefixes are up:

```
!On R1:

R1# show ip bgp | begin Network

   Network          Next Hop          Metric LocPrf Weight Path
*> 1.0.0.0          0.0.0.0                0         32768 i
*> 2.0.0.0          12.1.1.2               0             0 200 i
*> 3.0.0.0          13.1.1.3               0             0 300 i
```

Let's see the prefixes that R1 is advertising to R3:

```
!On R1:

R1# show ip bgp neighbor 13.1.1.3 advertised-routes | begin Network

   Network          Next Hop          Metric LocPrf Weight Path
*> 1.0.0.0          0.0.0.0                0         32768 i
*> 2.0.0.0          12.1.1.2               0             0 200 i
```

As you can see, both prefixes are being advertised to R3. Let's look at the status of the **advertise-map:**

```
R1# show ip bgp neighbor 13.1.1.3 | include map
  Condition-map Exist, Advertise-map Advertise, status: Advertise
```

Let's check R3's BGP table:

```
!On R3:

R3# show ip bgp | begin Network

   Network          Next Hop          Metric LocPrf Weight Path
*> 1.0.0.0          13.1.1.1               0          0 100 i
*> 2.0.0.0          13.1.1.1                          0 100 200 i
*> 3.0.0.0          0.0.0.0                0      32768 i
```

To test the second condition, if network 1.0.0.0/8 is down, R1 should *not* advertise network 2.0.0.0/8 to R3.

Let's shut down R1's Lo0 interface:

```
!On R1:

R1(config)# interface loopback 0
R1(config-if)# shutdown
```

Now let's force the change much faster:

```
!On R1:

R1# clear ip bgp *
```

Now we need to look at the prefixes that R1 is advertising to R3. You may have to wait for the changes to be implemented.

```
R1# show ip bgp neighbor 13.1.1.3 advertised-routes | begin Network


R1# show ip bgp 2.0.0.0

BGP routing table entry for 2.0.0.0/8, version 4
Paths: (1 available, best # 1, table default)
  Not advertised to any peer
  200
    12.1.1.2 from 12.1.1.2 (10.1.2.2)
      Origin IGP, metric 0, localpref 100, valid, external, best
```

> **Note**   The output of the preceding **show** command reveals that R1 is *not* advertising any prefixes to R3.

Let's look at the status of the **advertise-map**:

```
R1# show ip bgp neighbor 13.1.1.3 | include map
  Condition-map Exist, Advertise-map Advertise, status: Withdraw
```

Now let's check R3's BGP table to verify:

```
!On R3:

R3# show ip bgp | begin Network

  Network          Next Hop          Metric LocPrf Weight Path
*> 3.0.0.0          0.0.0.0                0        32768 i
```

Now we need to test the third condition. If network 2.0.0.0/8 is down, R1 should only advertise network 1.0.0.0/8 to R3.

Let's apply **no shutdown** to R1's Lo0 and **shutdown** R2's Lo0:

```
!On R1:

R1(config)# interface loopback 0
R1(config-if)# no shutdown

!On R2:

R2(config)# interface loopback 0
R2(config-if)# shutdown
```

Now let's force the change much faster:

```
!On R1:

R1# clear ip bgp *
```

Let's see which prefixes are advertised to R3 by R1. You may have to wait a little for the changes to be implemented:

```
R1# show ip bgp neighbor 13.1.1.3 advertised-routes | begin Network


   Network          Next Hop            Metric LocPrf Weight Path
*> 1.0.0.0          0.0.0.0                  0         32768 i


R1# show ip bgp neighbor 13.1.1.3 | include map
  Condition-map Exist, Advertise-map Advertise, status: Advertise
```

Let's verify the configuration:

```
!On R3:

R3# show ip bgp | begin Network

   Network          Next Hop            Metric LocPrf Weight Path

*> 1.0.0.0          13.1.1.1                 0             0 100 i
*> 3.0.0.0          0.0.0.0                  0         32768 i
```

Erase the startup config and reload the routers before proceeding to the next lab.

Lab 10-4: Community Attribute

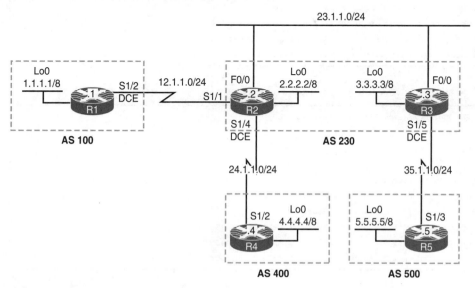

Figure 10-4 *Community Attribute Lab Topology*

The initial configuration files used in this lab can be found by downloading the BGP-Lab-4.txt file and subsequently applying those configurations on a device-by-device basis.

Task 1

Configure BGP peering based on the topology shown in Figure 10-4. These routers should advertise their loopback0 interfaces in BGP. Ensure reachability between the loopback interfaces. Do *not* configure an IGP or default routes to accomplish this task.

The task states, "Ensure reachability between the loopback interfaces without configuring an IGP or default routes." This is another way of asking you to establish BGP peering using the links that interconnect the routers. If the peering is configured based on the loopback0 interfaces, the peering will not come up because you need to have NLRI to those loopback0 IP addresses.

```
!On R1:

R1(config)# router bgp 100
R1(config-router)# network 1.0.0.0
R1(config-router)# no auto-summary
R1(config-router)# neighbor 12.1.1.2 remote-as 230

!On R2:

R2(config)# router bgp 230
R2(config-router)# network 2.0.0.0
R2(config-router)# no auto-summary
R2(config-router)# neighbor 12.1.1.1 remote-as 100
R2(config-router)# neighbor 23.1.1.3 remote-as 230
R2(config-router)# neighbor 23.1.1.3 next-hop-self
R2(config-router)# neighbor 24.1.1.4 remote-as 400
```

You should see the following console message:

```
%BGP-5-ADJCHANGE: neighbor 12.1.1.1 Up

!On R3:

R3(config)# router bgp 230
R3(config-router)# network 3.0.0.0
R3(config-router)# no auto-summary
R3(config-router)# neighbor 23.1.1.2 remote-as 230
R3(config-router)# neighbor 23.1.1.2 next-hop-self
R3(config-router)# neighbor 35.1.1.5 remote-as 500
```

You should also see this console message:

```
%BGP-5-ADJCHANGE: neighbor 23.1.1.2 Up


!On R4:


R4(config)# router bgp 400
R4(config-router)# network 4.0.0.0
R4(config-router)# no auto-summary
R4(config-router)# neighbor 24.1.1.2 remote-as 230
```

And you should see this console message:

```
%BGP-5-ADJCHANGE: neighbor 24.1.1.2 Up


!On R5:


R5(config)# router bgp 500
R5(config-router)# network 5.0.0.0
R5(config-router)# no auto-summary
R5(config-router)# neighbor 35.1.1.3 remote-as 230
```

And this console message:

```
%BGP-5-ADJCHANGE: neighbor 35.1.1.3 Up
```

Let's verify the configuration:

```
!On R1:


R1# show ip bgp | begin Network

   Network          Next Hop         Metric LocPrf Weight Path
*> 1.0.0.0          0.0.0.0               0         32768 i
*> 2.0.0.0          12.1.1.2              0             0 230 i
*> 3.0.0.0          12.1.1.2                            0 230 i
*> 4.0.0.0          12.1.1.2                            0 230 400 i
*> 5.0.0.0          12.1.1.2                            0 230 500 i

!On R2:


R2# show ip bgp | begin Network

   Network          Next Hop         Metric LocPrf Weight Path
*> 1.0.0.0          12.1.1.1              0             0 100 i
```

```
*>  2.0.0.0          0.0.0.0              0            32768 i
*>i3.0.0.0           23.1.1.3             0     100       0 i
*>  4.0.0.0          24.1.1.4             0               0 400 i
*>i5.0.0.0           23.1.1.3             0     100       0 500 i
```

!On R3:

R3# **show ip bgp | begin Network**

```
    Network          Next Hop        Metric LocPrf Weight Path
*>i1.0.0.0           23.1.1.2             0     100       0 100 i
*>i2.0.0.0           23.1.1.2             0     100       0 i
*>  3.0.0.0          0.0.0.0              0            32768 i
*>i4.0.0.0           23.1.1.2             0     100       0 400 i
*>  5.0.0.0          35.1.1.5             0               0 500 i
```

!On R4:

R4# **show ip bgp | begin Network**

```
    Network          Next Hop        Metric LocPrf Weight Path
*>  1.0.0.0          24.1.1.2                           0 230 100 i
*>  2.0.0.0          24.1.1.2             0             0 230 i
*>  3.0.0.0          24.1.1.2                           0 230 i
*>  4.0.0.0          0.0.0.0              0            32768 i
*>  5.0.0.0          24.1.1.2                           0 230 500 i
```

!On R5:

R5# **show ip bgp | begin Network**

```
    Network          Next Hop        Metric LocPrf Weight Path
*>  1.0.0.0          35.1.1.3                           0 230 100 i
*>  2.0.0.0          35.1.1.3                           0 230 i
*>  3.0.0.0          35.1.1.3             0             0 230 i
*>  4.0.0.0          35.1.1.3                           0 230 400 i
*>  5.0.0.0          0.0.0.0              0            32768 i
```

Now let's test the configuration:

```
!On R1:

R1# ping 2.2.2.2 source 1.1.1.1

Type escape sequence to abort.
Sending 5, 100-byte ICMP Echos to 2.2.2.2, timeout is 2 seconds:
```

```
Packet sent with a source address of 1.1.1.1
!!!!!
Success rate is 100 percent (5/5), round-trip min/avg/max = 28/29/32 ms

R1# ping 3.3.3.3 source 1.1.1.1

Type escape sequence to abort.
Sending 5, 100-byte ICMP Echos to 3.3.3.3, timeout is 2 seconds:
Packet sent with a source address of 1.1.1.1
!!!!!
Success rate is 100 percent (5/5), round-trip min/avg/max = 28/30/32 ms

R1# ping 4.4.4.4 source 1.1.1.1

Type escape sequence to abort.
Sending 5, 100-byte ICMP Echos to 4.4.4.4, timeout is 2 seconds:
Packet sent with a source address of 1.1.1.1
!!!!!
Success rate is 100 percent (5/5), round-trip min/avg/max = 56/58/60 ms

R1# ping 5.5.5.5 source 1.1.1.1

Type escape sequence to abort.
Sending 5, 100-byte ICMP Echos to 5.5.5.5, timeout is 2 seconds:
Packet sent with a source address of 1.1.1.1
!!!!!
Success rate is 100 percent (5/5), round-trip min/avg/max = 56/57/60 ms

!On R3:

R3# ping 4.4.4.4 source 3.3.3.3

Type escape sequence to abort.
Sending 5, 100-byte ICMP Echos to 4.4.4.4, timeout is 2 seconds:
Packet sent with a source address of 3.3.3.3
!!!!!
Success rate is 100 percent (5/5), round-trip min/avg/max = 28/30/32 ms

!On R2:

R2# ping 5.5.5.5 source 2.2.2.2

Type escape sequence to abort.
Sending 5, 100-byte ICMP Echos to 5.5.5.5, timeout is 2 seconds:
Packet sent with a source address of 2.2.2.2
!!!!!
Success rate is 100 percent (5/5), round-trip min/avg/max = 28/29/32 ms
```

Task 2

Using the **community** attribute, configure R1 such that when it advertises network 1.0.0.0/8 to R2 in AS 230, the network is not advertised to any of R2's iBGP or eBGP neighbors.

The **community** attribute is a numerical value that can be attached to a given prefix and advertised to a specific neighbor. Once the neighbor receives the prefix, it will examine the community value and will perform either filtering or use that value for the route-selection process.

By default, the **community** attribute is *not* sent to any neighbor. To specify that a community attribute should be sent to a BGP neighbor, the **neighbor send-community** command must be configured in the router config mode.

Here are the well-known communities:

- **local-as:** If **local-as** is assigned to a network, that network should only be advertised within that AS.

- **no-advertise:** If **no-advertise** is assigned to a network, that network should *not* be advertised to any BGP neighbor.

- **no-export:** If **no-export** is assigned to a network, that network should *not* be advertised to any eBGP neighbor.

Step 1. An access list or a prefix list is configured to identify the network.

Note Before configuring an access list, always perform a **show access-lists** command to ensure that one does not exist.

```
!On R1:

R1# show access-lists
R1(config)# access-list 1 permit 1.0.0.0 0.255.255.255
```

Step 2. A route map is configured to reference the access list and sets the community to **no-advertise**. This well-known **community** attribute tells the receiving router not to advertise that prefix to any of its neighbors (iBGP or eBGP).

The **route-map TEST permit 90** clause is the catchall **route-map** clause. It matches any network *not* referenced with the **match** keyword in **route-map TST permit 10**.

```
R1(config)# route-map TEST permit 10
R1(config-route-map)# match ip address 1
R1(config-route-map)# set community no-advertise

R1(config-route-map)# route-map TEST permit 90
```

Step 3. Send the community; this is done with the **neighbor send-community** command.

Once the community is sent, then the policy through the route map is configured. The direction of the route map specifies which neighbor/router's decision should be influenced by this policy. If it should affect the neighbor's decision, the direction of the route map should be "out," but if the policy should affect the local router, the direction of the route map should be "in."

```
R1(config)# router bgp 100
R1(config-router)# neighbor 12.1.1.2 send-community
R1(config-router)# neighbor 12.1.1.2 route-map TEST out
```

Let's verify the configuration:

```
!On R2:

R2# show ip bgp 1.0.0.0

BGP routing table entry for 1.0.0.0/8, version 18
Paths: (1 available, best # 1, table default, not advertised to any peer)
  Not advertised to any peer
  100
    12.1.1.1 from 12.1.1.1 (1.1.1.1)
      Origin IGP, metric 0, localpref 100, valid, external, best
      Community: no-advertise
```

Because R2 does not advertise the network, R3 and the other eBGP and/or iBGP neighbors will not have any knowledge of this prefix.

```
!On R3:

R3# show ip bgp 1.0.0.0

% Network not in table

!On R4:

R4# show ip bgp 1.0.0.0
% Network not in table

!On R5:

R5# show ip bgp 1.0.0.0
% Network not in table
```

Task 3

Configure R5 such that when it advertises its network 5.0.0.0 to R3 in AS 230, the routers in AS 230 do *not* advertise that network to any of their eBGP peers. Do not configure filtering on R3 to accomplish this task.

Because in the previous task an access list was used, in this task a prefix list is configured to reference the prefix:

```
!On R5:

R5(config)# ip prefix-list NET5 permit 5.0.0.0/8
```

A route map is configured to reference the prefix list, and a policy of **no-export** is applied:

```
R5(config)# route-map TST permit 10
R5(config-route-map)# match ip address prefix-list NET5
R5(config-route-map)# set community no-export

R5(config-route-map)# route-map TST permit 90
```

The community and the policy are sent using the route map in the outbound direction:

```
R5(config)# router bgp 500
R5(config-router)# neighbor 35.1.1.3 send-community
R5(config-router)# neighbor 35.1.1.3 route-map TST out
```

This is another well-known community attribute. In this case, network 5.0.0.0 will only be advertised to the routers in AS 230. The routers in AS 230 will not advertise this network to any of their eBGP neighbors.

Note   By default, routers will strip the **community** attribute when they send the community in the route map to a given neighbor (iBGP or eBGP). Therefore, in this case, R3 should be configured to send the community to R2; otherwise, R2 will advertise that network to its eBGP peers.

```
!On R3:

R3(config)# router bgp 230
R3(config-router)# neighbor 23.1.1.2 send-community
```

Let's verify the configuration:

```
!On R3:


R3# show ip bgp 5.0.0.0


BGP routing table entry for 5.0.0.0/8, version 8
Paths: (1 available, best # 1, table default, not advertised to EBGP peer)
  Advertised to update-groups:
     10
  500
    35.1.1.5 from 35.1.1.5 (5.5.5.5)
      Origin IGP, metric 0, localpref 100, valid, external, best
      Community: no-export

!On R2:


R2# show ip bgp 5.0.0.0


BGP routing table entry for 5.0.0.0/8, version 19
Paths: (1 available, best # 1, table default, not advertised to EBGP peer)
  Not advertised to any peer
  500
    23.1.1.3 from 23.1.1.3 (3.3.3.3)
      Origin IGP, metric 0, localpref 100, valid, internal, best
      Community: no-export

!On R4:


R4# show ip bgp 5.0.0.0


% Network not in table

!On R1:


R1# show ip bgp 5.0.0.0


% Network not in table
```

Task 4

Configure R3 in AS 230 to advertise network 3.0.0.0/8 to the routers in its own AS *only*.
You *must* use a **network** command to accomplish this task.

To configure this task, a route map is configured to assign a **local-as** community and then
the **network** command references the route map:

```
!On R3:

R3(config)# route-map TST permit 10
R3(config-route-map)# set community local-as

R3(config)# router bgp 230
R3(config-router)# network 3.0.0.0 route-map TST
R3(config-router)# neighbor 23.1.1.2 send-community
```

Let's verify the configuration:

```
!On R3:

R3# show ip bgp 3.0.0.0

BGP routing table entry for 3.0.0.0/8, version 9
Paths: (1 available, best # 1, table default, not advertised outside local AS)
  Advertised to update-groups:
      10
  Local
      0.0.0.0 from 0.0.0.0 (3.3.3.3)
        Origin IGP, metric 0, localpref 100, weight 32768, valid, sourced, local, best
        Community: local-AS

!On R5:

R5# show ip bgp 3.0.0.0

% Network not in table

!On R2:

R2# show ip bgp 3.0.0.0

BGP routing table entry for 3.0.0.0/8, version 20
Paths: (1 available, best # 1, table default, not advertised outside local AS)

 Not advertised to any peer
  Local
      23.1.1.3 from 23.1.1.3 (3.3.3.3)
        Origin IGP, metric 0, localpref 100, valid, internal, best
        Community: local-AS
```

```
!On R1:

R1# show ip bgp 3.0.0.0

% Network not in table
```

In this topology, **no-export** and **local-as** have the same behavior. The **no-export** community does not look at the **BGP Confederation identifier** command; therefore, it will keep the prefix(es) local in the AS number that the BGP router is configured in. On the other hand, the **local-as** community looks at the **BGP Confederation identifier** command first; if it's configured, it will keep the prefix(es) within that AS, but if the **BGP Confederation identifier** is *not* configured, it will keep the prefix(es) local to the AS that the BGP is configured in.

Task 5

R1 is advertising network 1.0.0.0, which has an attached community attribute of **no-advertise** to R2 (see Task 2). R2 should be configured to advertise network 1.0.0.0 to all of its iBGP and eBGP peers. You should utilize a **community** attribute to accomplish this task.

Before configuring R2, we should display the prefix in the BGP table:

```
!On R2:

R2# show ip bgp 1.0.0.0

BGP routing table entry for 1.0.0.0/8, version 18
Paths: (1 available, best # 1, table default, not advertised to any peer)
  Not advertised to any peer
  100
    12.1.1.1 from 12.1.1.1 (1.1.1.1)
      Origin IGP, metric 0, localpref 100, valid, external, best
      Community: no-advertise
```

The output of the preceding **show** command reveals that network 1.0.0.0/8 is not going to be advertised to any of its peers, but you can configure R2 to override the set community by assigning the **internet** community to this network. With the **internet** community assigned, network 1.0.0.0/8 will be advertised to all peers.

Let's configure the task:

```
!On R2:

R2# show access-lists

R2(config)# access-list 1 permit 1.0.0.0

R2(config)# route-map TST permit 10
R2(config-route-map)# match ip address 1
R2(config-route-map)# set community internet

R2(config)# router bgp 230
R2(config-router)# neighbor 12.1.1.1 route-map TST in
```

Let's verify the configuration:

```
!On R2:

R2# clear ip bgp * in

R2# show ip bgp 1.0.0.0

BGP routing table entry for 1.0.0.0/8, version 21
Paths: (1 available, best # 1, table default)
  Advertised to update-groups:
     6           7
  100
    12.1.1.1 from 12.1.1.1 (1.1.1.1)
      Origin IGP, metric 0, localpref 100, valid, external, best
      Community: internet

!On R4:

R4# show ip bgp | begin Network

  Network          Next Hop         Metric LocPrf Weight Path
*> 1.0.0.0          24.1.1.2                         0 230 100 i
*> 2.0.0.0          24.1.1.2              0           0 230 i
*> 4.0.0.0          0.0.0.0              0       32768 i
```

```
!On R5:


R5# show ip bgp | begin Network

    Network         Next Hop         Metric LocPrf Weight Path
*> 1.0.0.0         35.1.1.3                           0 230 100 i
*> 2.0.0.0         35.1.1.3                           0 230 i
*> 4.0.0.0         35.1.1.3                           0 230 400 i
*> 5.0.0.0         0.0.0.0              0         32768 i
```

Erase the startup config and reload the routers before proceeding to the next lab.

Lab 10-5: The AS-path Attribute

This lab demonstrates how to use **AS-path** manipulation to affect how an external AS will route traffic to networks into an internal AS. By prepending the autonomous system value of a prefix as it is advertised to an external AS, we can affect how traffic will enter the local AS. The shortest **AS-path** will be selected, and that path will be the path used by an external AS to reach a given prefix. This will be demonstrated in our lab topology when we apply an outbound policy, making the current path be selected by BGP via the topology illustrated in Figure 10-5.

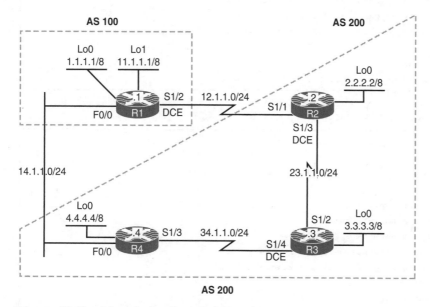

Figure 10-5 AS-path *Attribute Lab Topology*

The initial configuration files used in this lab can be found by downloading the BGP-Lab-5.txt file and subsequently applying those configurations on a device-by-device basis.

Task 1

Configure R2, R3, and R4 in AS 200; these routers should have a full-mesh peer session between them. R2 and R4 should have an eBGP peer session with R1 in AS 100. These routers should *only* advertise their loopback interfaces in BGP. Provide NLRI for the links using OSPF.

```
!On R1:

R1(config)# router bgp 100
R1(config-router)# no auto-summary
R1(config-router)# network 1.0.0.0
R1(config-router)# network 11.0.0.0
R1(config-router)# neighbor 12.1.1.2 remote-as 200
R1(config-router)# neighbor 14.1.1.4 remote-as 200


!On R2:

R2(config)# router bgp 200
R2(config-router)# no auto-summary
R2(config-router)# network 2.0.0.0
R2(config-router)# neighbor 12.1.1.1 remote-as 100
R2(config-router)# neighbor 23.1.1.3 remote-as 200
R2(config-router)# neighbor 23.1.1.3 next-hop-self
R2(config-router)# neighbor 34.1.1.4 next-hop-self
R2(config-router)# neighbor 34.1.1.4 remote-as 200


R2(config)# router ospf 1
R2(config-router)# network 23.1.1.2 0.0.0.0 area 0
```

You should see the following console message:

```
%BGP-5-ADJCHANGE: neighbor 12.1.1.1 Up

!On R3:

R3(config)# router bgp 200
R3(config-router)# no auto-summary
R3(config-router)# network 3.0.0.0
R3(config-router)# neighbor 34.1.1.4 remote-as 200
R3(config-router)# neighbor 23.1.1.2 remote-as 200

R3(config)# router ospf 1
R3(config-router)# network 23.1.1.3 0.0.0.0 area 0
R3(config-router)# network 34.1.1.3 0.0.0.0 area 0
```

You should also see this console message:

```
%BGP-5-ADJCHANGE: neighbor 23.1.1.2 Up

%OSPF-5-ADJCHG: Process 1, Nbr 2.2.2.2 on Serial1/2 from LOADING to FULL, Loading
  Done

!On R4:

R4(config)# router bgp 200
R4(config-router)# no auto-summary
R4(config-router)# network 4.0.0.0
R4(config-router)# neighbor 34.1.1.3 remote-as 200
R4(config-router)# neighbor 34.1.1.3 next-hop-self
R4(config-router)# neighbor 23.1.1.2 remote-as 200
R4(config-router)# neighbor 23.1.1.2 next-hop-self
R4(config-router)# neighbor 14.1.1.1 remote-as 100

R4(config)# router ospf 1
R4(config-router)# network 34.1.1.4 0.0.0.0 area 0
```

You should see this console message as well:

```
%BGP-5-ADJCHANGE: neighbor 34.1.1.3 Up
%BGP-5-ADJCHANGE: neighbor 14.1.1.1 Up
%BGP-5-ADJCHANGE: neighbor 23.1.1.2 Up

%OSPF-5-ADJCHG: Process 1, Nbr 3.3.3.3 on Serial1/3 from LOADING to FULL, Loading
  Done
```

Let's verify the configuration:

```
!On R1:

R1# show ip bgp | begin Network

   Network          Next Hop         Metric LocPrf Weight Path
*> 1.0.0.0          0.0.0.0               0        32768 i
*  2.0.0.0          14.1.1.4                          0 200 i
*>                  12.1.1.2              0            0 200 i
*> 3.0.0.0          12.1.1.2                          0 200 i
*                   14.1.1.4                          0 200 i
*> 4.0.0.0          12.1.1.2                          0 200 i
*                   14.1.1.4              0            0 200 i
*> 11.0.0.0         0.0.0.0               0        32768 i
```

```
!On R2:


R2# show ip bgp | begin Network

   Network           Next Hop        Metric LocPrf Weight Path
 * i1.0.0.0          34.1.1.4             0    100      0 100 i
 *>                  12.1.1.1             0             0 100 i
 *> 2.0.0.0          0.0.0.0              0         32768 i
 *>i3.0.0.0          23.1.1.3             0    100      0 i
 *>i4.0.0.0          34.1.1.4             0    100      0 i
 * i11.0.0.0         34.1.1.4             0    100      0 100 i
 *>                  12.1.1.1             0             0 100 i


!On R3:


R3# show ip bgp | begin Network

   Network           Next Hop        Metric LocPrf Weight Path
 *>i1.0.0.0          23.1.1.2             0    100      0 100 i
 * i                 34.1.1.4             0    100      0 100 i
 *>i2.0.0.0          23.1.1.2             0    100      0 i
 *> 3.0.0.0          0.0.0.0              0         32768 i
 *>i4.0.0.0          34.1.1.4             0    100      0 i
 *>i11.0.0.0         23.1.1.2             0    100      0 100 i
 * i                 34.1.1.4             0    100      0 100 i


!On R4:


R4# show ip bgp | begin Network

   Network           Next Hop        Metric LocPrf Weight Path
 * i1.0.0.0          23.1.1.2             0    100      0 100 i
 *>                  14.1.1.1             0             0 100 i
 *>i2.0.0.0          23.1.1.2             0    100      0 i
 *>i3.0.0.0          34.1.1.3             0    100      0 i
 *> 4.0.0.0          0.0.0.0              0         32768 i
 * i11.0.0.0         23.1.1.2             0    100      0 100 i
 *>                  14.1.1.1             0             0 100 i
```

Task 2

Configure R1 in AS 100 such that routers in AS 200 use the link through R4–R1 to reach its network 1.0.0.0/8. Use the **AS-path** attribute to accomplish this task.

The **AS-path** attribute can be manipulated to accomplish this task. This attribute can be manipulated by prepending the AS number to existing AS paths one or more times.

Typically, you perform an **AS-path** prepending on the outgoing eBGP updates over the undesired return path, making the **AS-path** over the undesired link become longer than the desired path, and as a result making the desired path the primary one.

```
!On R1:


R1# show access-lists


R1(config)# access-list 1 permit 1.0.0.0 0.255.255.255


R1(config)# route-map TST1 permit 10
R1(config-route-map)# match ip address 1
R1(config-route-map)# set as-path prepend 100
R1(config)# route-map TST1 permit 90


R1(config)# router bgp 100
R1(config-router)# neighbor 12.1.1.2 route-map TST1 out
```

Let's enforce the policy:

```
R1# clear ip bgp * out
```

Let's verify the configuration:

```
!On R2:


R2# show ip bgp | begin Network

   Network          Next Hop         Metric LocPrf Weight Path
*>i1.0.0.0          34.1.1.4              0    100      0 100 i
*                   12.1.1.1              0             0 100 100 i
*> 2.0.0.0          0.0.0.0               0         32768 i
*>i3.0.0.0          23.1.1.3              0    100      0 i
*>i4.0.0.0          34.1.1.4              0    100      0 i
*  i11.0.0.0        34.1.1.4              0    100      0 100 i
*>                  12.1.1.1              0             0 100 i
```

The following configuration injects a default route into AS 100; this is done for return traffic:

```
!On R2:


R2(config)# router bgp 200
R2(config-router)# neighbor 12.1.1.1 default-originate


R2# clear ip bgp * out
```

```
!On R4:

R4(config)# router bgp 200
R4(config-router)# neighbor 14.1.1.1 default-originate

R4# clear ip bgp * out

!On R2:

R2# traceroute 1.1.1.1 numeric

Type escape sequence to abort.
Tracing the route to 1.1.1.1
VRF info: (vrf in name/id, vrf out name/id)
  1 23.1.1.3 12 msec 12 msec 16 msec
  2 34.1.1.4 28 msec 32 msec 28 msec
  3 14.1.1.1 20 msec *  20 msec

!On R3:

R3# traceroute 1.1.1.1 numeric

Type escape sequence to abort.
Tracing the route to 1.1.1.1
VRF info: (vrf in name/id, vrf out name/id)
  1 34.1.1.4 16 msec 16 msec 12 msec
  2 14.1.1.1 20 msec *  24 msec

!On R4:

R4# traceroute 1.1.1.1 numeric

Type escape sequence to abort.
Tracing the route to 1.1.1.1
  1 14.1.1.1 0 msec *  0 msec
```

Note   The AS-path attribute is used to influence the degree of preference in another AS. R2, R3, and R4 will go through R4 to reach network 1.0.0.0/8 because by going through R4, they traverse through fewer AS hops.

Task 3

Configure R1 in AS 100 such that the routers in AS 200 use the link through R2–R1 to reach network 11.0.0.0/8. Use the **AS-path** attribute and an **IP Prefix-list** to accomplish this task.

Even though a prefix list is used instead of an access list, the process and the steps are identical.

```
!On R1:

R1(config)# ip prefix-list NET11 permit 11.0.0.0/8

R1(config)# route-map TST11 permit 10
R1(config-route-map)# match ip address prefix-list NET11
R1(config-route-map)# set as-path prepend 100 100
R1(config)# route-map TST11 permit 90

R1(config-route-map)# router bgp 100
R1(config-router)# neighbor 14.1.1.4 route-map TST11 out

R1# clear ip bgp * out
```

Let's verify the configuration:

```
!On R2:

R2# traceroute 11.1.1.1 numeric

Type escape sequence to abort.
Tracing the route to 11.1.1.1
VRF info: (vrf in name/id, vrf out name/id)
  1 12.1.1.1 16 msec *  12 msec

!On R3:

R3# traceroute 11.1.1.1 numeric

Type escape sequence to abort.
Tracing the route to 11.1.1.1

  1 23.1.1.2 12 msec 12 msec 16 msec
  2 12.1.1.1 28 msec *  28 msec
```

```
!On R4:

R4# traceroute 11.1.1.1 numeric

Type escape sequence to abort.
Tracing the route to 11.1.1.1

  1 34.1.1.3 12 msec 12 msec 16 msec
  2 23.1.1.2 28 msec 28 msec 32 msec
  3 12.1.1.1 40 msec *  40 msec
```

Erase the startup configuration and reload the routers before proceeding to the next lab.

Lab 10-6: The Weight Attribute

There are two options to manipulate the Cisco proprietary **weight** attribute. It can be done on either a per-neighbor basis or on specific-prefix basis. Manipulating the **weight** attribute is only going to affect the best-path-selection process on an individual router; this alteration will not affect the other BGP speakers in the same AS. We will explore these mechanisms via the topology illustrated in Figure 10-6.

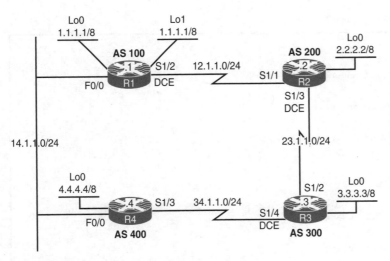

Figure 10-6   *The* **weight** *Attribute Lab Topology*

The initial configuration files used in this lab can be found by downloading the BGP-Lab-6.txt file and subsequently applying those configurations on a device-by-device basis.

Task 1

Configure R1 in AS 100 to establish an eBGP peer session with R2 in AS 200 and R4 in AS 400.

- Router R2 should establish eBGP peer sessions with R1 in AS 100 and R3 in AS 300.

- Router R3 should establish eBGP peer sessions with R2 in AS 200 and R4 in AS 400.

- Router R4 should establish eBGP peer sessions with R1 in AS 100 and R3 in AS 300.

- The BGP routers should *only* advertise their loopback(s) in BGP.

- Do *not* use the loopback interfaces to establish BGP peer sessions.

```
!On R1:

R1(config-if)# router bgp 100
R1(config-router)# no auto-summary
R1(config-router)# network 1.0.0.0
R1(config-router)# network 11.0.0.0
R1(config-router)# neighbor 14.1.1.4 remote-as 400
R1(config-router)# neighbor 12.1.1.2 remote-as 200

!On R2:

R2(config)# router bgp 200
R2(config-router)# no auto-summary
R2(config-router)# network 2.0.0.0
R2(config-router)# neighbor 12.1.1.1 remote-as 100
R2(config-router)# neighbor 23.1.1.3 remote-as 300
```

You should see the following console message:

```
%BGP-5-ADJCHANGE: neighbor 12.1.1.1 Up

!On R3:

R3(config)# router bgp 300
R3(config-router)# no auto-summary
R3(config-router)# network 3.0.0.0
R3(config-router)# neighbor 34.1.1.4 remote-as 400
R3(config-router)# neighbor 23.1.1.2 remote-as 200
```

You should also see this console message:

```
%BGP-5-ADJCHANGE: neighbor 23.1.1.2 Up


!On R4:


R4(config)# router bgp 400
R4(config-router)# no auto-summary
R4(config-router)# network 4.0.0.0
R4(config-router)# neighbor 34.1.1.3 remote-as 300
R4(config-router)# neighbor 14.1.1.1 remote-as 100
```

You should see this console message as well:

```
%BGP-5-ADJCHANGE: neighbor 14.1.1.1 Up
%BGP-5-ADJCHANGE: neighbor 34.1.1.3 Up
```

Let's verify the configuration:

```
!On R4:


R4# show ip bgp | begin Network

   Network          Next Hop          Metric LocPrf Weight Path
*  1.0.0.0          34.1.1.3                            0 300 200 100 i
*>                  14.1.1.1              0              0 100 i
*  2.0.0.0          34.1.1.3                            0 300 200 i
*>                  14.1.1.1                             0 100 200 i
*  3.0.0.0          14.1.1.1                             0 100 200 300 i
*>                  34.1.1.3              0              0 300 i
*> 4.0.0.0          0.0.0.0              0          32768 i
*  11.0.0.0         34.1.1.3                            0 300 200 100 i
*>                  14.1.1.1              0              0 100 i


!On R1:


R1# show ip bgp | begin Network

   Network          Next Hop          Metric LocPrf Weight Path
*> 1.0.0.0          0.0.0.0              0          32768 i
*> 2.0.0.0          12.1.1.2             0              0 200 i
*  3.0.0.0          14.1.1.4                             0 400 300 i
*>                  12.1.1.2                             0 200 300 i
*> 4.0.0.0          14.1.1.4             0              0 400 i
*> 11.0.0.0         0.0.0.0              0          32768 i
```

Task 2

Configure R1 in AS 100 to use AS 200 to reach all the prefixes within this topology. You must use the **weight** attribute to accomplish this task.

The **weight** attribute is a Cisco-defined attribute that is local to the router. This attribute is *not* advertised to any BGP neighbors. If there is more than one route for a given destination, the **weight** attribute can decide which path is the best path. The higher the value, the better the preference.

The following assigns a **weight** attribute of 40000 to all existing and future prefixes:

```
!On R1:


R1(config)# router bgp 100
R1(config-router)# neighbor 12.1.1.2 weight 40000


R1# clear ip bgp *
```

Let's verify and test the configuration:

```
!On R1:


R1# show ip bgp | begin Network

   Network          Next Hop        Metric LocPrf Weight Path
*> 1.0.0.0          0.0.0.0              0         32768 i
*  2.0.0.0          14.1.1.4                           0 400 300 200 i
*>                  12.1.1.2             0         40000 200 i
*  3.0.0.0          14.1.1.4                           0 400 300 i
*>                  12.1.1.2                       40000 200 300 i
*  4.0.0.0          14.1.1.4             0             0 400 i
*>                  12.1.1.2                       40000 200 300 400 i
*> 11.0.0.0         0.0.0.0              0         32768 i
```

You can see that R1 has to traverse through R2 to reach all the prefixes within this topology. To test this configuration, RIPv2 is configured on all routers to advertise the links that interconnect the routers. This is done for return traffic for pings and traceroutes.

```
R1(config)# router rip
R1(config-router)# no auto-summary
R1(config-router)# version 2
R1(config-router)# network 12.0.0.0
R1(config-router)# network 14.0.0.0
```

```
!On R2:

R2(config)# router rip
R2(config-router)# no auto-summary
R2(config-router)# version 2
R2(config-router)# network 12.0.0.0
R2(config-router)# network 23.0.0.0

!On R3:

R3(config)# router rip
R3(config-router)# no auto-summary
R3(config-router)# version 2
R3(config-router)# network 23.0.0.0
R3(config-router)# network 34.0.0.0

!On R4:

R4(config)# router rip
R4(config-router)# no auto-summary
R4(config-router)# version 2
R4(config-router)# network 34.0.0.0
R4(config-router)# network 14.0.0.0
```

Let's verify the configuration:

```
!On R1:

R1# show ip route rip | begin Gate
Gateway of last resort is not set

     23.0.0.0/24 is subnetted, 1 subnets
R       23.1.1.0 [120/1] via 12.1.1.2, 00:00:23, Serial1/2
     34.0.0.0/24 is subnetted, 1 subnets
R       34.1.1.0 [120/1] via 14.1.1.4, 00:00:08, FastEthernet0/0

R1# traceroute 4.4.4.4 numeric

Type escape sequence to abort.
Tracing the route to 4.4.4.4
VRF info: (vrf in name/id, vrf out name/id)
  1 12.1.1.2 52 msec 16 msec 16 msec
  2 23.1.1.3 28 msec 28 msec 32 msec
  3 34.1.1.4 16 msec *  16 msec
```

```
R1# traceroute 3.3.3.3 numeric

Type escape sequence to abort.
Tracing the route to 3.3.3.3
VRF info: (vrf in name/id, vrf out name/id)
  1 12.1.1.2 16 msec 12 msec 16 msec
  2 23.1.1.3 32 msec *  28 msec


R1# traceroute 2.2.2.2 numeric

Type escape sequence to abort.
Tracing the route to 2.2.2.2
VRF info: (vrf in name/id, vrf out name/id)
  1 12.1.1.2 16 msec *  12 msec
```

Task 3

Configure the following loopback interface on R3 and advertise it in BGP:

> **loopback1**: 33.3.3.3/24

```
!On R3:

R3(config)# interface loopback 1
R3(config-if)# ip address 33.3.3.3 255.255.255.0

R3(config)# router bgp 300
R3(config-router)# network 33.3.3.0 mask 255.255.255.0
```

Note The preceding **network** statement has to include the **mask** option because **auto-summary** is disabled. When **auto-summary** is disabled, the network must be advertised using the exact mask, but if **auto-summary** is enabled, all subsets of a given major network can be advertised by simply advertising the major network.

Let's verify the configuration:

```
!On R3:

R3# show ip bgp 33.3.3.0/24
BGP routing table entry for 33.3.3.0/24, version 11
Paths: (1 available, best # 1, table default)
  Advertised to update-groups:
     2
  Local
```

```
      0.0.0.0 from 0.0.0.0 (3.3.3.3)
        Origin IGP, metric 0, localpref 100, weight 32768, valid, sourced, local, best

!On R1:


R1# show ip bgp | begin Network

   Network          Next Hop           Metric LocPrf Weight Path
*> 1.0.0.0          0.0.0.0                 0        32768 i
*  2.0.0.0          14.1.1.4                             0 400 300 200 i
*>                  12.1.1.2                0        40000 200 i
*  3.0.0.0          14.1.1.4                             0 400 300 i
*>                  12.1.1.2                         40000 200 300 i
*  4.0.0.0          14.1.1.4                0            0 400 i
*>                  12.1.1.2                         40000 200 300 400 i
*> 11.0.0.0         0.0.0.0                 0        32768 i
*> 33.3.3.0/24      12.1.1.2                         40000 200 300 i
*                   14.1.1.4                             0 400 300 i
```

Note   The **weight** attribute configured in Task 3 affected the existing and the future prefixes within the topology.

Let's verify this information:

```
R1# traceroute 33.3.3.3 numeric

Type escape sequence to abort.
Tracing the route to 33.3.3.3

VRF info: (vrf in name/id, vrf out name/id)
  1 12.1.1.2 12 msec 16 msec 16 msec
  2 23.1.1.3 28 msec *  28 msec
```

Task 4

Reconfigure R1 based on the following policy; this policy may override the previously implemented policy:

- R1 in AS 100 should use R4 in AS 400 to reach network 33.0.0.0/8 and network 4.0.0.0/8.

- R1 in AS 100 should use R2 in AS 200 to reach network 3.0.0.0/8, as well as existing and future prefixes advertised in AS 200.

Let's remove the **weight** configuration that was implemented in Task 3:

```
!On R1:


R1(config)# router bgp 100
R1(config-router)# no neighbor 12.1.1.2 weight 40000


R1# clear ip bgp *
```

To configure this task, we configure two access lists: the first access list identifies networks 4.0.0.0/8 and 33.3.3.0/24, and the second one identifies network 3.0.0.0/8.

But how do we identify the existing and future prefixes advertised in AS 200? The easiest way to accomplish this is to configure an **AS-path** access list identifying the AS number, because the AS number remains the same for existing and future routes in AS 200.

The following access list identifies networks 33.3.3.0/24 and 4.0.0.0/8:

```
R1# show access-list

R1(config)# access-list 1 permit 33.3.3.0 0.0.0.255
R1(config)# access-list 1 permit 4.0.0.0 0.255.255.255
```

The following access list identifies networks 3.0.0.0/8:

```
R1(config)# access-list 2 permit 3.0.0.0 0.255.255.255
```

With access lists or prefix lists, IP addresses are identified. Using **ip as-path access-list**, we can identify the AS (in this case, AS 200):

```
R1(config)# ip as-path access-list 1 permit ^200$
```

Once the prefixes are all identified, they are referenced in a route map and the **weight** attribute is assigned to them based on the requirements of this task.

The following route map (TST) assigns a **weight** attribute of 45000 to the networks identified in **access-list 1**:

```
R1(config)# route-map TST permit 10
R1(config-route-map)# match ip address 1
R1(config-route-map)# set weight 45000
R1(config)# route-map TST permit 90
```

The following route map (TEST) assigns a **weight** attribute of 50000 to the networks identified in **access-list 2** and AS 200:

```
R1(config)# route-map TEST permit 10
R1(config-route-map)# match as-path 1
R1(config-route-map)# set weight 50000

R1(config)# route-map TEST permit 20
R1(config-route-map)# match ip address 2
R1(config-route-map)# set weight 50000
R1(config)# route-map TEST permit 90

R1(config)# router bgp 100
R1(config-router)# neighbor 14.1.1.4 route-map TST in
R1(config-router)# neighbor 12.1.1.2 route-map TEST in
```

The preceding commands assign the attributes to neighbors R2 and R4:

```
R1# clear ip bgp *
```

Let's verify the configuration:

```
!On R1:

R1# show ip bgp | begin Network

   Network          Next Hop         Metric LocPrf Weight Path
*> 1.0.0.0          0.0.0.0               0        32768 i
*  2.0.0.0          14.1.1.4                           0 400 300 200 i
*>                  12.1.1.2              0        50000 200 i
*  3.0.0.0          14.1.1.4                           0 400 300 i
*>                  12.1.1.2                       50000 200 300 i
*> 4.0.0.0          14.1.1.4              0        45000 400 i
*                   12.1.1.2                           0 200 300 400 i
*> 11.0.0.0         0.0.0.0               0        32768 i
*> 33.3.3.0/24      14.1.1.4                       45000 400 300 i
*                   12.1.1.2                           0 200 300 i
```

> **Note**   Network 3.0.0.0/8 and networks that originated with and are advertised by AS 200 are assigned a **weight** value of 50000, and networks 4.0.0.0/8 and 33.3.3.0/24 are assigned a **weight** value of 45000. Therefore, R1 goes through R4 to reach networks 33.3.3.0/24 and 4.0.0.0/8. R1 also goes through R2 for all existing and future prefixes that originated in AS 200 and network 3.0.0.0/8. Let's verify:

```
R1# traceroute 4.4.4.4 numeric

Type escape sequence to abort.
Tracing the route to 4.4.4.4
VRF info: (vrf in name/id, vrf out name/id)
  1 14.1.1.4 0 msec *  0 msec


R1# traceroute 33.3.3.3 numeric

Type escape sequence to abort.
Tracing the route to 33.3.3.3
VRF info: (vrf in name/id, vrf out name/id)
  1 14.1.1.4 4 msec 0 msec 0 msec
  2 34.1.1.3 12 msec *  12 msec


R1# traceroute 2.2.2.2 numeric

Type escape sequence to abort.
Tracing the route to 2.2.2.2
VRF info: (vrf in name/id, vrf out name/id)
  1 12.1.1.2 32 msec *  12 msec


R1# traceroute 3.3.3.3 numeric

Type escape sequence to abort.
Tracing the route to 3.3.3.3
VRF info: (vrf in name/id, vrf out name/id)
  1 12.1.1.2 16 msec 16 msec 16 msec
  2 23.1.1.3 28 msec *  28 msec
```

Do *not* erase the configuration; instead, proceed to the next lab.

Lab 10-7: Multi-Exit Discriminator Attribute

One other BGP attribute we can use to manipulate how an external AS will enter our local AS is the multiple exit discriminator, which is very useful in this scenario. However, for this to work, the external AS must be configured to accept the **MED** attribute. Additionally, by default, **MED** will only work in scenarios where the local AS is multi-homed to the same external AS, as illustrated in Figure 10-7.

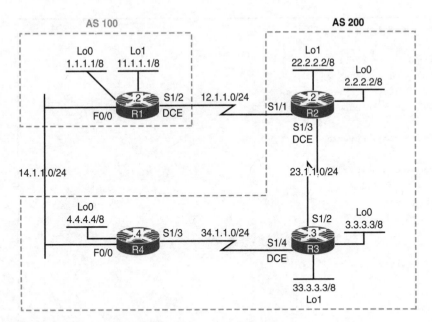

Figure 10-7 *Multi-Exit Discriminator Lab Topology*

The initial configuration files used in this lab can be found by downloading the BGP-Lab-7.txt file and subsequently applying those configurations on a device-by-device basis.

Task 1

Configure routers R2, R3, and R4 in AS 200; these routers should have a full-mesh peer session between them. R2 and R4 should have an eBGP peer session with R1 in AS 100. BGP routers should only advertise their loopback interface(s) in BGP.

```
!On R1:

R1(config-if)# router bgp 100
R1(config-router)# no auto-summary
R1(config-router)# network 11.0.0.0
R1(config-router)# network 1.0.0.0
R1(config-router)# neighbor 14.1.1.4 remote-as 200
R1(config-router)# neighbor 12.1.1.2 remote-as 200


!On R2:

R2(config)# router bgp 200
R2(config-router)# no auto-summary
```

```
R2(config-router)# network 2.0.0.0
R2(config-router)# network 22.0.0.0
R2(config-router)# neighbor 12.1.1.1 remote-as 100
R2(config-router)# neighbor 23.1.1.3 remote-as 200
R2(config-router)# neighbor 23.1.1.3 next-hop-self
R2(config-router)# neighbor 34.1.1.4 remote-as 200
R2(config-router)# neighbor 34.1.1.4 next-hop-self
```

You should see the following console messages:

```
%BGP-5-ADJCHANGE: neighbor 12.1.1.1 Up


!On R3:


R3(config)# router bgp 200
R3(config-router)# no auto-summary
R3(config-router)# network 3.0.0.0
R3(config-router)# network 33.0.0.0
R3(config-router)# neighbor 34.1.1.4 remote-as 200
R3(config-router)# neighbor 23.1.1.2 remote-as 200
```

You should also see these console messages:

```
%BGP-5-ADJCHANGE: neighbor 23.1.1.2 Up


!On R4:


R4(config)# router bgp 200
R4(config-router)# no auto-summary
R4(config-router)# network 4.0.0.0
R4(config-router)# neighbor 34.1.1.3 remote-as 200
R4(config-router)# neighbor 34.1.1.3 next-hop-self
R4(config-router)# neighbor 23.1.1.2 remote-as 200
R4(config-router)# neighbor 23.1.1.2 next-hop-self
R4(config-router)# neighbor 14.1.1.1 remote-as 100
```

You should see these console messages as well:

```
%BGP-5-ADJCHANGE: neighbor 14.1.1.1 Up
%BGP-5-ADJCHANGE: neighbor 34.1.1.3 Up
%BGP-5-ADJCHANGE: neighbor 23.1.1.2 Up
```

Let's verify the configuration:

```
!On R1:

R1# show ip bgp | begin Network

   Network          Next Hop          Metric LocPrf Weight Path
*> 1.0.0.0          0.0.0.0                0         32768 i
*  2.0.0.0          14.1.1.4                             0 200 i
*>                  12.1.1.2               0             0 200 i
*  3.0.0.0          14.1.1.4                             0 200 i
*>                  12.1.1.2                             0 200 i
*  4.0.0.0          12.1.1.2                             0 200 i
*>                  14.1.1.4               0             0 200 i
*> 11.0.0.0         0.0.0.0                0         32768 i
*  22.0.0.0         14.1.1.4                             0 200 i
*>                  12.1.1.2               0             0 200 i
*  33.0.0.0         14.1.1.4                             0 200 i
*>                  12.1.1.2                             0 200 i


!On R2:

R2# show ip bgp | begin Network

   Network          Next Hop          Metric LocPrf Weight Path
*  i1.0.0.0         34.1.1.4               0    100      0 100 i
*>                  12.1.1.1               0             0 100 i
*> 2.0.0.0          0.0.0.0                0         32768 i
*>i3.0.0.0          23.1.1.3               0    100      0 i
*>i4.0.0.0          34.1.1.4               0    100      0 i
*  i11.0.0.0        34.1.1.4               0    100      0 100 i
*>                  12.1.1.1               0             0 100 i
*> 22.0.0.0         0.0.0.0                0         32768 i
*>i33.0.0.0         23.1.1.3               0    100      0 i


!On R3:

R3# show ip bgp | begin Network

   Network          Next Hop          Metric LocPrf Weight Path
*>i1.0.0.0          34.1.1.4               0    100      0 100 i
*  i                23.1.1.2               0    100      0 100 i
*>i2.0.0.0          23.1.1.2               0    100      0 i
```

```
*>  3.0.0.0          0.0.0.0              0          32768 i
*>i4.0.0.0           34.1.1.4             0    100     0 i
*>i11.0.0.0          34.1.1.4             0    100     0 100 i
*  i                 23.1.1.2             0    100     0 100 i
*>i22.0.0.0          23.1.1.2             0    100     0 i
*> 33.0.0.0          0.0.0.0              0          32768 i


!On R4:


R4# show ip bgp | begin Network


    Network          Next Hop           Metric LocPrf Weight Path
*  i1.0.0.0          23.1.1.2             0    100     0 100 i
*>                   14.1.1.1             0            0 100 i
*>i2.0.0.0           23.1.1.2             0    100     0 i
*>i3.0.0.0           34.1.1.3             0    100     0 i
*> 4.0.0.0           0.0.0.0              0          32768 i
*  i11.0.0.0         23.1.1.2             0    100     0 100 i
*>                   14.1.1.1             0            0 100 i
*>i22.0.0.0          23.1.1.2             0    100     0 i
*>i33.0.0.0          34.1.1.3             0    100     0 i
```

Task 2

Configure AS 200 such that R1 in AS 100 takes R4 to reach any prefix advertised in AS 200. You should manipulate **MED** to accomplish this task.

MED is used as a suggestion to an external AS regarding the preferred path into the AS that is advertising the metric. This suggestion is used here because the AS receiving the **MED** attribute could use another attribute such as **weight** that overrides the **MED** attribute. As far as **MED** is concerned, the lower value has better preference.

```
!On R2:

R2(config)# route-map TST permit 10
R2(config-route-map)# set metric 100

R2(config)# router bgp 200
R2(config-router)# neighbor 12.1.1.1 route-map TST out

R2# clear ip bgp * out
```

Let's verify the configuration:

```
!On R1:

R1# show ip bgp | begin Network

   Network           Next Hop              Metric LocPrf Weight Path
*> 1.0.0.0           0.0.0.0                    0          32768 i
*> 2.0.0.0           14.1.1.4                              0 200 i
*                    12.1.1.2                 100          0 200 i
*> 3.0.0.0           14.1.1.4                              0 200 i
*                    12.1.1.2                 100          0 200 i
*  4.0.0.0           12.1.1.2                 100          0 200 i
*>                   14.1.1.4                   0          0 200 i
*> 11.0.0.0          0.0.0.0                    0          32768 i
*> 22.0.0.0          14.1.1.4                              0 200 i
*                    12.1.1.2                 100          0 200 i
*> 33.0.0.0          14.1.1.4                              0 200 i
*                    12.1.1.2                 100          0 200 i

R1# traceroute 2.2.2.2 source 1.1.1.1 numeric

Type escape sequence to abort.
Tracing the route to 2.2.2.2
VRF info: (vrf in name/id, vrf out name/id)
  1 14.1.1.4 0 msec 4 msec 0 msec
  2 34.1.1.3 16 msec 16 msec 16 msec
  3 23.1.1.2 20 msec *  20 msec
```

Note   R1 receives a **MED** value of 100 for all prefixes from R2 because R1 does not receive a **MED** value from R4. R1 considers the **MED** value coming from R4 to be zero. When R1 compares the two **MED** values coming from the same AS, it takes the path with a lower **MED** value, which is R4.

Task 3

Remove the configuration command from the previous task before proceeding to the next task:

```
!On R2:

R2(config)# no route-map TST

R2(config)# router bgp 200
R2(config-router)# no neighbor 12.1.1.1 route-map TST out

R2# clear ip bgp *
```

Task 4

Configure the appropriate router(s) in AS 200 such that AS 100 goes through R4 to reach network 33.0.0.0/8 and R2 to reach network 3.0.0.0/8. You should utilize **MED** to accomplish this task.

The following output shows the existing BGP table of R1 before the **MED** attribute is manipulated:

```
!On R1:

R1# show ip bgp | begin Network

    Network          Next Hop         Metric LocPrf Weight Path
*> 1.0.0.0           0.0.0.0               0         32768 i
*  2.0.0.0           14.1.1.4                            0 200 i
*>                   12.1.1.2              0             0 200 i
*  3.0.0.0           12.1.1.2                            0 200 i
*>                   14.1.1.4                            0 200 i
*  4.0.0.0           12.1.1.2                            0 200 i
*>                   14.1.1.4              0             0 200 i
*> 11.0.0.0          0.0.0.0               0         32768 i
*  22.0.0.0          14.1.1.4                            0 200 i
*>                   12.1.1.2              0             0 200 i
*  33.0.0.0          12.1.1.2                            0 200 i
*>                   14.1.1.4                            0 200 i
```

Note   R1 goes through R4 to reach both networks.

On R2, configure the following two prefix lists (NET3 and NET33), which reference prefixes 3.0.0.0/8 and 33.0.0.0/8, respectively:

Note   It is very easy to remember that prefix list NET3 is referencing network 3.0.0.0/8 and prefix list NET33 is referencing network 33.0.0.0/8. If possible, though, you should choose a meaningful name.

```
R2# show ip prefix-list

R2(config)# ip prefix-list NET3 permit 3.0.0.0/8
R2(config)# ip prefix-list NET33 permit 33.0.0.0/8
```

The following configuration sets the **metric**, which is the **MED** value, to 50 for network 3.0.0.0/8 and to 100 for network 33.0.0.0/8. On R4, the **MED** values are reversed, meaning that the **MED** value for network 3.0.0.0/8 is set to 100 and for network 33.0.0.0/8 it is set to 50.

```
R2(config)# route-map TST permit 10
R2(config-route-map)# match ip address prefix-list NET3
R2(config-route-map)# set metric 50

R2(config)# route-map TST permit 20
R2(config-route-map)# match ip address prefix-list NET33
R2(config-route-map)# set metric 100

R2(config)# route-map TST permit 90

R2(config)# router bgp 200
R2(config-router)# neighbor 12.1.1.1 route-map TST out

R2# clear ip bgp *

 !On R4:

R4# sh ip prefix-list

R4(config)# ip prefix-list NET3 permit 3.0.0.0/8
R4(config)# ip prefix-list NET33 permit 33.0.0.0/8

R4(config)# route-map TST permit 10
R4(config-route-map)# match ip address prefix-list NET3
R4(config-route-map)# set metric 100

R4(config)# route-map TST permit 20
R4(config-route-map)# match ip address prefix-list NET33
R4(config-route-map)# set metric 50

R4(config)# route-map TST permit 90

R4(config)# router bgp 200
R4(config-router)# neighbor 14.1.1.1 route-map TST out

R4# clear ip bgp *
```

Let's verify the configuration:

```
!On R1:


R1# show ip bgp | begin Network

    Network          Next Hop            Metric LocPrf Weight Path
*>  1.0.0.0          0.0.0.0                  0         32768 i
*   2.0.0.0          14.1.1.4                           0 200 i
*>                   12.1.1.2                 0         0 200 i
*   3.0.0.0          14.1.1.4               100         0 200 i
*>                   12.1.1.2                50         0 200 i
*   4.0.0.0          12.1.1.2                           0 200 i
*>                   14.1.1.4                 0         0 200 i
*>  11.0.0.0         0.0.0.0                  0         32768 i
*   22.0.0.0         14.1.1.4                           0 200 i
*>                   12.1.1.2                 0         0 200 i
*>  33.0.0.0         14.1.1.4                50         0 200 i
*                    12.1.1.2               100         0 200 i
```

Note   Network 3.0.0.0/8 is reachable via R2, and network 33.0.0.0/8 is reachable via R4.

Let's test the configuration:

```
!On R1:


R1# traceroute 3.3.3.3 source 1.1.1.1 numeric

Type escape sequence to abort.

Tracing the route to 3.3.3.3
VRF info: (vrf in name/id, vrf out name/id)
  1 12.1.1.2 16 msec 16 msec 12 msec
  2 23.1.1.3 24 msec *  20 msec


R1# traceroute 33.3.3.3 source 1.1.1.1 numeric

Type escape sequence to abort.

Tracing the route to 33.3.3.3
VRF info: (vrf in name/id, vrf out name/id)
  1 14.1.1.4 4 msec 0 msec 0 msec
  2 34.1.1.3 12 msec *  12 msec
```

Erase the startup config and reload the routers before proceeding to the next lab.

Lab 10-8: Filtering Using Access Lists and Prefix Lists

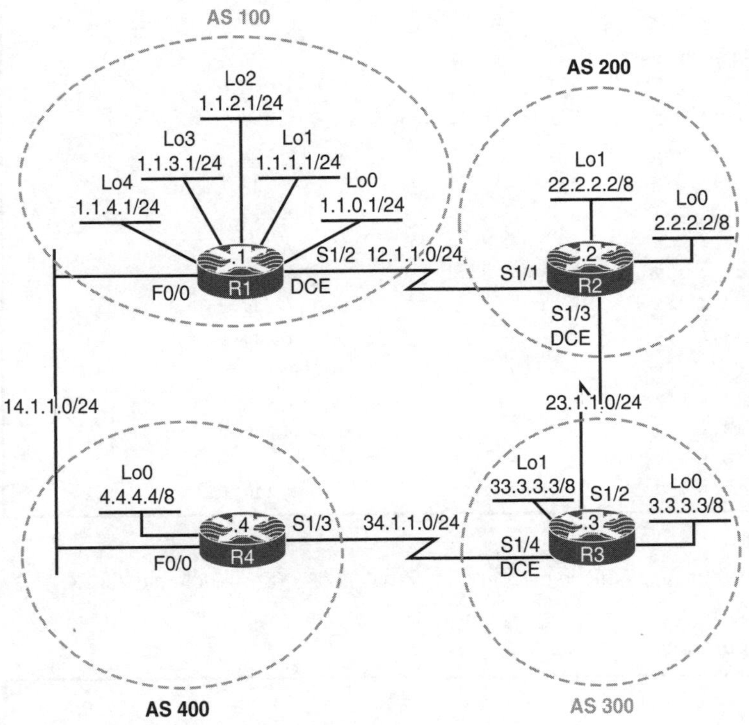

Figure 10-8   *BGP Filtering Lab Topology*

The initial configuration files used in this lab can be found by downloading the BGP-Lab-8.txt file and subsequently applying those configurations on a device-by-device basis.

Task 1

Configure the BGP peering based on Figure 10-8:

```
!On R1:

R1(config)# router bgp 100
R1(config-router)# no auto-summary
R1(config-router)# network 1.1.0.0 mask 255.255.255.0
R1(config-router)# network 1.1.1.0 mask 255.255.255.0
R1(config-router)# network 1.1.2.0 mask 255.255.255.0
R1(config-router)# network 1.1.3.0 mask 255.255.255.0
R1(config-router)# network 1.1.4.0 mask 255.255.255.0
R1(config-router)# neighbor 12.1.1.2 remote-as 200
R1(config-router)# neighbor 14.1.1.4 remote-as 400
```

```
!On R2:

R2(config)# router bgp 200
R2(config-router)# no auto-summary
R2(config-router)# network 2.0.0.0
R2(config-router)# network 22.0.0.0
R2(config-router)# neighbor 12.1.1.1 remote-as 100
R2(config-router)# neighbor 23.1.1.3 remote-as 300
```

You should see the following console message:

```
%BGP-5-ADJCHANGE: neighbor 12.1.1.1 Up

!On R3:

R3(config)# router bgp 300
R3(config-router)# no auto-summary
R3(config-router)# network 3.0.0.0
R3(config-router)# network 33.0.0.0
R3(config-router)# neighbor 23.1.1.2 remote-as 200
R3(config-router)# neighbor 34.1.1.4 remote-as 400
```

You should also see this console message:

```
%BGP-5-ADJCHANGE: neighbor 23.1.1.2 Up

!On R4:

R4(config)# router bgp 400
R4(config-router)# no auto-summary
R4(config-router)# network 4.0.0.0
R4(config-router)# neighbor 14.1.1.1 remote-as 100
R4(config-router)# neighbor 34.1.1.3 remote-as 300
```

You should see the following console message as well:

```
%BGP-5-ADJCHANGE: neighbor 14.1.1.1 Up
%BGP-5-ADJCHANGE: neighbor 34.1.1.3 Up
```

Let's verify the configuration:

Note   If you don't see all the entries in the BGP table, run **clear ip bgp** *.

```
!On R1:

R1# show ip bgp | begin Network
     Network          Next Hop         Metric LocPrf Weight Path
 *>  1.1.0.0/24       0.0.0.0              0            32768 i
 *>  1.1.1.0/24       0.0.0.0              0            32768 i
 *>  1.1.2.0/24       0.0.0.0              0            32768 i
 *>  1.1.3.0/24       0.0.0.0              0            32768 i
 *>  1.1.4.0/24       0.0.0.0              0            32768 i
 *>  2.0.0.0          12.1.1.2             0                0 200 i
 *                    14.1.1.4                             0 400 300 200 i
 *   3.0.0.0          12.1.1.2                             0 200 300 i
 *>                   14.1.1.4                             0 400 300 i
 *   4.0.0.0          12.1.1.2                             0 200 300 400 i
 *>                   14.1.1.4              0                0 400 i
 *>  22.0.0.0         12.1.1.2             0                0 200 i
 *                    14.1.1.4                             0 400 300 200 i
 *   33.0.0.0         12.1.1.2                             0 200 300 i
 *>                   14.1.1.4                             0 400 300 i

!On R2:

R2# show ip bgp | begin Network
     Network          Next Hop         Metric LocPrf Weight Path
 *   1.1.0.0/24       23.1.1.3                             0 300 400 100 i
 *>                   12.1.1.1             0                0 100 i
 *   1.1.1.0/24       23.1.1.3                             0 300 400 100 i
 *>                   12.1.1.1             0                0 100 i
 *   1.1.2.0/24       23.1.1.3                             0 300 400 100 i
 *>                   12.1.1.1             0                0 100 i
 *   1.1.3.0/24       23.1.1.3                             0 300 400 100 i
 *>                   12.1.1.1             0                0 100 i
 *   1.1.4.0/24       23.1.1.3                             0 300 400 100 i
 *>                   12.1.1.1             0                0 100 i
 *>  2.0.0.0          0.0.0.0              0            32768 i
 *>  3.0.0.0          23.1.1.3             0                0 300 i
 *                    12.1.1.1                             0 100 400 300 i
 *   4.0.0.0          23.1.1.3                             0 300 400 i
 *>                   12.1.1.1                             0 100 400 i
 *>  22.0.0.0         0.0.0.0              0            32768 i
 *>  33.0.0.0         23.1.1.3             0                0 300 i
 *                    12.1.1.1                             0 100 400 300 i
```

```
!On R3:


R3# show ip bgp | begin Network

     Network            Next Hop         Metric LocPrf Weight Path
 *   1.1.0.0/24         34.1.1.4                          0 400 100 i
 *>                     23.1.1.2                          0 200 100 i
 *   1.1.1.0/24         34.1.1.4                          0 400 100 i
 *>                     23.1.1.2                          0 200 100 i
 *   1.1.2.0/24         34.1.1.4                          0 400 100 i
 *>                     23.1.1.2                          0 200 100 i
 *   1.1.3.0/24         34.1.1.4                          0 400 100 i
 *>                     23.1.1.2                          0 200 100 i
 *   1.1.4.0/24         23.1.1.2                          0 200 100 i
 *>                     34.1.1.4                          0 400 100 i
 *   2.0.0.0            34.1.1.4                          0 400 100 200 i
 *>                     23.1.1.2              0            0 200 i
 *>  3.0.0.0            0.0.0.0              0        32768 i
 *>  4.0.0.0            34.1.1.4             0            0 400 i
 *                      23.1.1.2                          0 200 100 400 i
 *   22.0.0.0           34.1.1.4                          0 400 100 200 i
 *>                     23.1.1.2             0            0 200 i
 *>  33.0.0.0           0.0.0.0              0        32768 i


!On R4:


R4# show ip bgp | begin Network

     Network            Next Hop         Metric LocPrf Weight Path
 *   1.1.0.0/24         34.1.1.3                          0 300 200 100 i
 *>                     14.1.1.1             0            0 100 i
 *   1.1.1.0/24         34.1.1.3                          0 300 200 100 i
 *>                     14.1.1.1             0            0 100 i
 *   1.1.2.0/24         34.1.1.3                          0 300 200 100 i
 *>                     14.1.1.1             0            0 100 i
 *   1.1.3.0/24         34.1.1.3                          0 300 200 100 i
 *>                     14.1.1.1             0            0 100 i
 *   1.1.4.0/24         34.1.1.3                          0 300 200 100 i
 *>                     14.1.1.1             0            0 100 i
 *   2.0.0.0            34.1.1.3                          0 300 200 i
 *>                     14.1.1.1                          0 100 200 i
 *>  3.0.0.0            34.1.1.3             0            0 300 i
 *                      14.1.1.1                          0 100 200 300 i
 *>  4.0.0.0            0.0.0.0              0        32768 i
```

```
*   22.0.0.0          34.1.1.3                              0 300 200 i
*>                    14.1.1.1                              0 100 200 i
*>  33.0.0.0          34.1.1.3              0               0 300 i
*                     14.1.1.1                              0 100 200 300 i
```

Task 2

Configure R2 to filter network 1.1.4.0/24. Use **distribute-list** and **access-list** to accomplish this task.

Let's see the existing entry for this network:

```
!On R2:

R2# show ip bgp 1.1.4.0/24
BGP routing table entry for 1.1.4.0/24, version 57
Paths: (2 available, best # 2, table default)
  Advertised to update-groups:
     2
  Refresh Epoch 1
  300 400 100
    23.1.1.3 from 23.1.1.3 (33.3.3.3)
      Origin IGP, localpref 100, valid, external
      rx pathid: 0, tx pathid: 0
  Refresh Epoch 1
  100
    12.1.1.1 from 12.1.1.1 (1.1.4.1)
      Origin IGP, metric 0, localpref 100, valid, external, best
      rx pathid: 0, tx pathid: 0x0
```

To filter the prefix, an access list is configured to deny the prefix that needs to be filtered and to permit everything else:

```
R2# show access-lists

R2(config)# access-list 4 deny 1.1.4.0 0.0.0.255
R2(config)# access-list 4 permit any
```

Two distribute lists are configured to filter the prefix inbound from both neighbors, R1 and R3:

```
R2(config)# router bgp 200
R2(config-router)# neighbor 12.1.1.1 distribute-list 4 in
R2(config-router)# neighbor 23.1.1.3 distribute-list 4 in
```

The tricky part here is to understand the topology. If you do not understand the topology, silly mistakes can occur, which can cost you points in the CCIE lab. Particularly tricky is blocking the prefix from both neighbors.

Let's verify the configuration:

```
!On R2:

R2# clear ip bgp * in

R2# show ip route 1.1.4.0

% Subnet not in table

R2# show ip bgp 1.1.4.0

% Network not in table
```

Task 3

Remove the configuration command from the previous task and then accomplish the same objective using **prefix-list** and **distribute-list**:

```
!On R2:

R2(config)# no access-list 4

R2(config)# router bgp 200
R2(config-router)# no neighbor 12.1.1.1 distribute-list 4 in
R2(config-router)# no neighbor 23.1.1.3 distribute-list 4 in

R2# clear ip bgp * in
```

Let's verify the configuration:

```
!On R2:

R2# show ip bgp 1.1.4.0

BGP routing table entry for 1.1.4.0/24, version 11
Paths: (2 available, best # 2, table default)
  Advertised to update-groups:
     2
  300 400 100
    23.1.1.3 from 23.1.1.3 (33.3.3.3)
```

```
      Origin IGP, localpref 100, valid, external
  100
    12.1.1.1 from 12.1.1.1 (1.1.4.1)
      Origin IGP, metric 0, localpref 100, valid, external, best

R2# show ip route 1.1.4.0

Routing entry for 1.1.4.0/24
  Known via "bgp 200", distance 20, metric 0
  Tag 100, type external
  Last update from 12.1.1.1 00:00:57 ago
  Routing Descriptor Blocks:
  * 12.1.1.1, from 12.1.1.1, 00:00:57 ago
      Route metric is 0, traffic share count is 1
      AS Hops 1
      Route tag 100
      MPLS label: none

R2# show ip prefix-list
R2(config)# ip prefix-list TST seq 5 deny 1.1.4.0/24
R2(config)# ip prefix-list TST seq 10 permit 0.0.0.0/0 le 32

R2(config)# router bgp 200
R2(config-router)# neighbor 12.1.1.1 prefix-list TST in
R2(config-router)# neighbor 23.1.1.3 prefix-list TST in

R2# clear ip bgp * in
```

Note   There are multiple ways to accomplish a given task—understanding and remembering the different ways can be the key to success.

Let's verify the configuration:

```
!On R2:

R2# show ip bgp 1.1.4.0
% Network not in table

R2# show ip route 1.1.4.0
% Subnet not in table
```

Task 4

Configure R3 in AS 300 to filter network 22.0.0.0/8. Do *not* use **distribute-list** or **prefix-list**. Instead, **route-map** and **access-list** should be used to accomplish this task.

Let's verify the existing entry in the BGP table:

```
!On R3:

R3# show ip bgp 22.0.0.0

BGP routing table entry for 22.0.0.0/8, version 8
Paths: (2 available, best # 2, table default)
  Advertised to update-groups:
     1
 400 100 200
   34.1.1.4 from 34.1.1.4 (4.4.4.4)

     Origin IGP, localpref 100, valid, external
 200
   23.1.1.2 from 23.1.1.2 (22.2.2.2)
     Origin IGP, metric 0, localpref 100, valid, external, best
```

You can see that the local router is learning the prefix (22.0.0.0/8) from two neighbors: R2 and R4.

To filter the prefix, an access list is configured to deny the prefix that needs to be filtered and to allow the rest:

```
R3# show access-lists

R3(config)# access-list 22 deny 22.0.0.0 0.255.255.255
R3(config)# access-list 22 permit any
```

A route map is configured to reference the access list:

```
R3(config)# route-map TST permit 10
R3(config-route-map)# match ip address 22
```

A **neighbor route-map** command is used for each neighbor:

```
R3(config)# router bgp 300
R3(config-router)# neighbor 23.1.1.2 route-map TST in
R3(config-router)# neighbor 34.1.1.4 route-map TST in

R3# clear ip bgp * in
```

Let's verify the configuration:

```
!On R3:

R3# show ip route 22.0.0.0
% Network not in table

R3# show ip bgp 22.0.0.0
% Network not in table
```

Task 5

Remove the **access-list** and **route-map** configuration from the previous task. Use a minimum number of lines in the access list to filter network 22.0.0.0/8. You should use **access-list** and **route-map** to accomplish this task.

```
!On R3:

R3(config)# no access-list 22
R3(config)# no route-map TST

R3(config)# access-list 22 permit 22.0.0.0 0.255.255.255

R3(config)# route-map TST deny 10
R3(config-route-map)# match ip address 22

R3(config)# route-map TST permit 90
```

Note   Remember that the **neighbor** command is already configured.

Let's verify the configuration:

```
!On R3:

R3# clear ip bgp * in

R3# show ip route 22.0.0.0
% Network not in table

R3# show ip bgp 22.0.0.0
% Network not in table
```

When you are asked to configure an access list with a minimum number of lines, you should always see whether the task can be accomplished using a single statement in the access list. Sometimes a single line can accomplish the task, and sometimes more lines are required in the access list to accomplish the given task.

Task 6

R4 should *not* see networks 1.1.0.0/24–1.1.4.0/24 in its BGP or routing table; you should configure a prefix list to accomplish this task. Do *not* use a route map or configure the solution on R4.

Let's verify the existing BGP table of R4 for all the prefixes that originated in AS 100 (the regular expression will be covered in the next lab):

```
R4# show ip bgp regexp ^100$

BGP table version is 11, local router ID is 4.4.4.4
Status codes: s suppressed, d damped, h history, * valid, > best, i - internal,
              r RIB-failure, S Stale, m multipath, b backup-path, x best-external,
  f RT-Filter

Origin codes: i - IGP, e - EGP, ? - incomplete

   Network          Next Hop         Metric LocPrf Weight Path
*> 1.1.0.0/24       14.1.1.1              0          0 100 i
*> 1.1.1.0/24       14.1.1.1              0          0 100 i
*> 1.1.2.0/24       14.1.1.1              0          0 100 i
*> 1.1.3.0/24       14.1.1.1              0          0 100 i
*> 1.1.4.0/24       14.1.1.1              0          0 100 i
```

Because R4 cannot be configured to accomplish this task, R4's neighbors are configured to filter the prefixes outbound toward R4:

```
!On R1 and R3:

Rx# show ip prefix-list

Rx(config)# ip prefix-list TST seq 5 deny 1.1.0.0/24
Rx(config)# ip prefix-list TST seq 10 deny 1.1.1.0/24
Rx(config)# ip prefix-list TST seq 15 deny 1.1.2.0/24
Rx(config)# ip prefix-list TST seq 20 deny 1.1.3.0/24
Rx(config)# ip prefix-list TST seq 25 deny 1.1.4.0/24
Rx(config)# ip prefix-list TST seq 30 permit 0.0.0.0/0 le 32

!On R1:

R1(config)# router bgp 100
R1(config-router)# neighbor 14.1.1.4 prefix-list TST out

R1# clear ip bgp * out
```

```
!On R3:

R3(config)# router bgp 300
R3(config-router)# neighbor 34.1.1.4 prefix-list TST out

R3# clear ip bgp * out

To verify the configuration:

!On R4:

R4# show ip bgp | begin Network

     Network          Next Hop         Metric LocPrf Weight Path
*    2.0.0.0          34.1.1.3                        0 300 200 i
*>                    14.1.1.1                        0 100 200 i
*>   3.0.0.0          34.1.1.3              0         0 300 i
*                     14.1.1.1                        0 100 200 300 i
*>   4.0.0.0          0.0.0.0               0     32768 i
*>   22.0.0.0         14.1.1.1                        0 100 200 i
*>   33.0.0.0         34.1.1.3              0         0 300 i
*                     14.1.1.1                        0 100 200 300 i
```

Erase the startup config and reload the routers before proceeding to the next lab.

Lab 10-9: Regular Expressions (Figure 10-9)

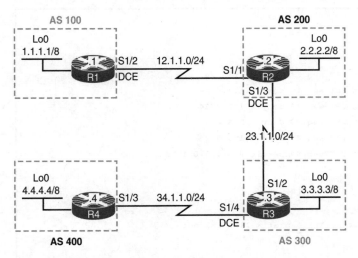

Figure 10-9 *BGP Regular Expression Lab Topology*

The initial configuration files used in this lab can be found by downloading the BGP-Lab-9.txt file and subsequently applying those configurations on a device-by-device basis.

Task 1

Configure BGP peering based on the following policy:

- R1 in AS 100 should establish eBGP peer sessions with R2 in AS 200.

- R2 should establish eBGP peer sessions with R1 and R3 in AS 100 and 300, respectively.

- R3 should establish eBGP peer sessions with R2 and R4 in AS 200 and 400, respectively.

- R4 should establish eBGP peer sessions with R3 in AS 300.

- Advertise the loopback interfaces in BGP.

- Do not use loopback interfaces for peering.

```
!On R1:

R1(config)# router bgp 100
R1(config-router)# no auto-summary
R1(config-router)# network 1.0.0.0
R1(config-router)# neighbor 12.1.1.2 remote-as 200


!On R2:

R2(config)# router bgp 200
R2(config-router)# no auto-summary
R2(config-router)# network 2.0.0.0
R2(config-router)# neighbor 12.1.1.1 remote-as 100
R2(config-router)# neighbor 23.1.1.3 remote-as 300
```

You should see the following console message:

```
%BGP-5-ADJCHANGE: neighbor 12.1.1.1 Up

!On R3:

R3(config)# router bgp 300
R3(config-router)# no auto-summary
R3(config-router)# network 3.0.0.0
R3(config-router)# neighbor 23.1.1.2 remote-as 200
R3(config-router)# neighbor 34.1.1.4 remote-as 400
```

You should also see this console message:

```
%BGP-5-ADJCHANGE: neighbor 23.1.1.2 Up


!On R4:


R4(config)# router bgp 400
R4(config-router)# no auto-summary
R4(config-router)# network 4.0.0.0
R4(config-router)# neighbor 34.1.1.3 remote-as 300
```

You should see the following console message as well:

```
%BGP-5-ADJCHANGE: neighbor 34.1.1.3 Up
```

Let's verify the configuration:

```
!On R1:


R1# show ip bgp | begin Network

   Network          Next Hop          Metric LocPrf Weight Path
*> 1.0.0.0          0.0.0.0                0          32768 i
*> 2.0.0.0          12.1.1.2               0              0 200 i
*> 3.0.0.0          12.1.1.2                              0 200 300 i
*> 4.0.0.0          12.1.1.2                              0 200 300 400 i


!On R2:


R2# show ip bgp | begin Network

   Network          Next Hop          Metric LocPrf Weight Path
*> 1.0.0.0          12.1.1.1               0              0 100 i
*> 2.0.0.0          0.0.0.0                0          32768 i
*> 3.0.0.0          23.1.1.3               0              0 300 i
*> 4.0.0.0          23.1.1.3                              0 300 400 i


!On R3:


R3# show ip bgp | begin Network

   Network          Next Hop          Metric LocPrf Weight Path
*> 1.0.0.0          23.1.1.2                              0 200 100 i
*> 2.0.0.0          23.1.1.2               0              0 200 i
```

```
*> 3.0.0.0            0.0.0.0                      0       32768 i
*> 4.0.0.0            34.1.1.4                     0           0 400 i


!On R4:


R4# show ip bgp | begin Network

   Network           Next Hop         Metric LocPrf Weight Path
*> 1.0.0.0            34.1.1.3                             0 300 200 100 i
*> 2.0.0.0            34.1.1.3                             0 300 200 i
*> 3.0.0.0            34.1.1.3             0               0 300 i
*> 4.0.0.0            0.0.0.0              0           32768 i


R1# ping 4.4.4.4 source loopback0Loopback 0

Type escape sequence to abort.
Sending 5, 100-byte ICMP Echos to 4.4.4.4, timeout is 2 seconds:
Packet sent with a source address of 1.1.1.1
!!!!!
Success rate is 100 percent (5/5), round-trip min/avg/max = 84/86/88 ms
```

Task 2

Configure R1 such that it filters all the prefixes that have originated in AS 300.

Table 10-1 translates the meaning of the parts of the regular expression used in this task.

Table 10-1   *Regular Expression Used in Task 2*

Regular Expression	Meaning
_	The underscore matches a space or comma.
{ }	The left and right braces denote the beginning and the end of an input string.
$	The dollar sign means the end of a string.

Basically, you are referencing the first AS number in the path. Another way of looking at this is to say that you don't care about the prefixes that have been advertised by any other AS instances in the path, but you want to match the prefix that has been advertised or originated by the last ASN in the path. In this task, you are asked to filter prefixes that have originated from and *not* traversed through AS 300. Let's look at the difference.

First, we'll look at the prefixes that have traversed through AS 300:

```
R1# show ip bgp regexp _300_

BGP table version is 7, local router ID is 1.1.1.1
Status codes: s suppressed, d damped, h history, * valid, > best, i - internal,
              r RIB-failure, S Stale, m multipath, b backup-path, x best-external,
  f RT-Filter
Origin codes: i - IGP, e - EGP, ? - incomplete

   Network          Next Hop            Metric LocPrf Weight Path
*> 3.0.0.0          12.1.1.2                             0 200 300 i
*> 4.0.0.0          12.1.1.2                             0 200 300 400 i
```

Now let's see the prefixes that have originated in AS 300:

```
R1# show ip bgp regexp _300$

BGP table version is 7, local router ID is 1.1.1.1
Status codes: s suppressed, d damped, h history, * valid, > best, i - internal,
              r RIB-failure, S Stale, m multipath, b backup-path, x best-external,
  f RT-Filter
Origin codes: i - IGP, e - EGP, ? - incomplete

   Network          Next Hop            Metric LocPrf Weight Path
*> 3.0.0.0          12.1.1.2                             0 200 300 i
```

An **ip as-path access-list** is configured to deny any prefixes that have originated in AS 300 and to permit everything else:

```
!On R1:

R1(config)# ip as-path access-list 1 deny _300$
R1(config)# ip as-path access-list 1 permit .*
```

The **ip as-path access-list** is referenced in the **neighbor filter-list** command inbound through the neighbor 12.1.1.2 (R2):

```
R1(config)# router bgp 100
R1(config-router)# neighbor 12.1.1.2 filter-list 1 in

R1# clear ip bgp * in
```

Let's verify the configuration:

```
!On R1:

R1# show ip bgp regexp _300$

R1# show ip bgp | begin Network

   Network          Next Hop          Metric LocPrf Weight Path
*> 1.0.0.0          0.0.0.0                0         32768 i
*> 2.0.0.0          12.1.1.2               0             0 200 i
*> 4.0.0.0          12.1.1.2                             0 200 300 400 i
```

Task 3

Remove the configuration from the previous task before proceeding to the next task:

```
!On R1:

R1(config)# no ip as-path access-list 1

R1(config)# router bgp 100
R1(config-router)# no neighbor 12.1.1.2 filter-list 1 in

R1# clear ip bgp * in
```

Let's verify the configuration:

```
!On R1:

R1# show ip bgp | begin Network

   Network          Next Hop          Metric LocPrf Weight Path
*> 1.0.0.0          0.0.0.0                0         32768 i
*> 2.0.0.0          12.1.1.2               0             0 200 i
*> 3.0.0.0          12.1.1.2                             0 200 300 i
*> 4.0.0.0          12.1.1.2                             0 200 300 400 i
```

Task 4

Configure R1 such that it blocks all the prefixes that have AS 300 in their **AS-path** list.

Let's see all the prefixes that have traversed or have AS 300 in their **AS-path** list:

```
R1# show ip bgp regexp _300_


BGP table version is 5, local router ID is 1.1.1.1
Status codes: s suppressed, d damped, h history, * valid, > best, i - internal,
              r RIB-failure, S Stale, m multipath, b backup-path, x best-external,
  f RT-Filter
Origin codes: i - IGP, e - EGP, ? - incomplete


   Network          Next Hop            Metric LocPrf Weight Path
*> 3.0.0.0          12.1.1.2                             0 200 300 i
*> 4.0.0.0          12.1.1.2                             0 200 300 400 i


!On R1:


R1(config)# ip as-path access-list 1 deny _300_
R1(config)# ip as-path access-list 1 permit .*


R1(config)# router bgp 100
R1(config-router)# neighbor 12.1.1.2 filter-list 1 in


R1# clear ip bgp * in
```

Let's verify the configuration:

```
!On R1:


R1# show ip bgp | begin Network


   Network          Next Hop          Metric LocPrf Weight Path
*> 1.0.0.0          0.0.0.0                0          32768 i
*> 2.0.0.0          12.1.1.2               0              0 200 i
```

Task 5

Remove the configuration from the previous task before proceeding to the next task.

```
!On R1:


R1(config)# no ip as-path access-list 1


R1(config)# router bgp 100
R1(config-router)# no neighbor 12.1.1.2 filter-list 1 in


R1# clear ip bgp * in
```

Let's verify the configuration:

```
!On R1:


R1# show ip bgp | begin Network

   Network          Next Hop         Metric LocPrf Weight Path
*> 1.0.0.0          0.0.0.0              0         32768 i
*> 2.0.0.0          12.1.1.2             0             0 200 i
*> 3.0.0.0          12.1.1.2                           0 200 300 i
*> 4.0.0.0          12.1.1.2                           0 200 300 400 i
```

Task 6

Configure R3 such that it doesn't advertise the prefixes that have originated in its own AS to any of its neighbors.

Let's translate and test the regular expression shown in Table 10-2 before we start the configuration. Remember that the prefixes that originated in the local AS will *not* have their own ASN in the **AS-path**. The prefixes are only prepended when they are advertised to an eBGP neighbor. This method is used so the upstream AS instances will *not* use the local AS as a transit AS.

Table 10-2   *Regular Expression Used in Task 6*

Regular Expression	Meaning
^	Start of string. In BGP, it means a directly connected AS.
$	End of string.

Let's test the regular expression:

```
!On R3:


R3# show ip bgp regexp ^$

BGP table version is 7, local router ID is 3.3.3.3
Status codes: s suppressed, d damped, h history, * valid, > best, i - internal,
              r RIB-failure, S Stale, m multipath, b backup-path, x best-external,
   f RT-Filter
Origin codes: i - IGP, e - EGP, ? - incomplete

   Network          Next Hop         Metric LocPrf Weight Path
*> 3.0.0.0          0.0.0.0              0         32768 i
```

Now that we know the regular expression works, we can perform the configuration:

```
!On R3:

R3(config)# ip as-path access-list 1 deny ^$
R3(config)# ip as-path access-list 1 permit .*

R3(config)# router bgp 300
R3(config-router)# neighbor 23.1.1.2 filter-list 1 out
R3(config-router)# neighbor 34.1.1.4 filter-list 1 out

R3# clear ip bgp * out
```

Let's verify the configuration:

```
!On R4:

R4# show ip bgp | begin Network

   Network          Next Hop         Metric LocPrf Weight Path
*> 1.0.0.0          34.1.1.3                          0 300 200 100 i
*> 2.0.0.0          34.1.1.3                          0 300 200 i
*> 4.0.0.0          0.0.0.0               0       32768 i

!On R2:

R2# show ip bgp | begin Network

   Network          Next Hop         Metric LocPrf Weight Path
*> 1.0.0.0          12.1.1.1              0           0 100 i
*> 2.0.0.0          0.0.0.0               0       32768 i
*> 4.0.0.0          23.1.1.3                          0 300 400 i
```

Task 7

Remove the configuration from the previous task before proceeding to the next task:

```
!On R3:

R3(config)# no ip as-path access-list 1

R3(config)# router bgp 300
R3(config-router)# no neighbor 23.1.1.2 filter-list 1 out
R3(config-router)# no neighbor 34.1.1.4 filter-list 1 out

R3# clear ip bgp * out
```

Let's verify the configuration:

```
!On R1:


R1# show ip bgp | begin Network

   Network          Next Hop         Metric LocPrf Weight Path
*> 1.0.0.0          0.0.0.0               0         32768 i
*> 2.0.0.0          12.1.1.2              0             0 200 i
*> 3.0.0.0          12.1.1.2                            0 200 300 i
*> 4.0.0.0          12.1.1.2                            0 200 300 400 i

!On R2:


R2# show ip bgp | begin Network

   Network          Next Hop         Metric LocPrf Weight Path
*> 1.0.0.0          12.1.1.1              0             0 100 i
*> 2.0.0.0          0.0.0.0               0         32768 i
*> 3.0.0.0          23.1.1.3              0             0 300 i
*> 4.0.0.0          23.1.1.3                            0 300 400 i

!On R4:


R4# show ip bgp | begin Network

   Network          Next Hop         Metric LocPrf Weight Path
*> 1.0.0.0          34.1.1.3                            0 300 200 100 i
*> 2.0.0.0          34.1.1.3                            0 300 200 i
*> 3.0.0.0          34.1.1.3              0             0 300 i
*> 4.0.0.0          0.0.0.0               0         32768 i
```

Task 8

Configure R3 such that it blocks all the prefixes that have originated in the neighboring AS 200.

You know that ^ means the start of the string or a directly connected AS; therefore, the regular expression can start with ^, followed by the ASN, and then end with $, which indicates the end of the string. Let's test this:

```
R3# show ip bgp regexp ^200$

BGP table version is 7, local router ID is 3.3.3.3
Status codes: s suppressed, d damped, h history, * valid, > best, i - internal,
              r RIB-failure, S Stale, m multipath, b backup-path, x best-external,
   f RT-Filter
```

```
Origin codes: i - IGP, e - EGP, ? - incomplete


   Network           Next Hop           Metric LocPrf Weight Path
*> 2.0.0.0           23.1.1.2                0            0 200 i


!On R3:


R3(config)# ip as-path access-list 1 deny ^200$
R3(config)# ip as-path access-list 1 permit .*


R3(config)# router bgp 300
R3(config-router)# neighbor 23.1.1.2 filter-list 1 in


R3# clear ip bgp * in
```

Let's verify the configuration:

```
!On R3:


R3# show ip bgp | begin Network


   Network           Next Hop           Metric LocPrf Weight Path
*> 1.0.0.0           23.1.1.2                            0 200 100 i
*> 3.0.0.0           0.0.0.0                 0      32768 i
*> 4.0.0.0           34.1.1.4                0            0 400 i
```

Task 9

Remove the configuration from the previous task before proceeding to the next task:

```
!On R3:


R3(config)# no ip as-path access-list 1


R3(config)# router bgp 300
R3(config-router)# no neighbor 23.1.1.2 filter-list 1 in


R3# clear ip bgp * in
```

Let's verify the configuration:

```
!On R3:

R3# show ip bgp | begin Network

   Network          Next Hop         Metric LocPrf Weight Path
*> 1.0.0.0          23.1.1.2                          0 200 100 i
*> 2.0.0.0          23.1.1.2              0            0 200 i
*> 3.0.0.0          0.0.0.0              0        32768 i
*> 4.0.0.0          34.1.1.4              0            0 400 i
```

Task 10

Configure R3 such that it blocks all the prefixes from its existing directly connected neighbors.

Use Table 10-3 to translate the parts of the regular expression used in this task.

Table 10-3   *Regular Expression for Task 10*

Regular Expression	Meaning
^	Start of string. In BGP, it means a directly connected AS.
[0-9]	Range of characters. In BGP, it means any value from 0 to 9, inclusive.
+	Means one or more of the instances; in this configuration, it means one or more instance of [0-9].
$	End of string.

Therefore, the regular expression (**regexp**) used in this solution means any AS number as long as it's directly connected.

Let's test the solution before implementing it:

```
R3# show ip bgp regexp ^[0-9]+$

BGP table version is 9, local router ID is 3.3.3.3
Status codes: s suppressed, d damped, h history, * valid, > best, i - internal,
              r RIB-failure, S Stale, m multipath, b backup-path, x best-external,
  f RT-Filter
Origin codes: i - IGP, e - EGP, ? - incomplete

   Network          Next Hop         Metric LocPrf Weight Path
*> 2.0.0.0          23.1.1.2              0            0 200 i
*> 4.0.0.0          34.1.1.4              0            0 400 i
```

```
!On R3:

R3(config)# ip as-path access-list 1 deny ^[0-9]+$
R3(config)# ip as-path access-list 1 permit .*

R3(config)# router bgp 300
R3(config-router)# neighbor 23.1.1.2 filter-list 1 in
R3(config-router)# neighbor 34.1.1.4 filter-list 1 in

R3# clear ip bgp * in
```

Let's verify the configuration:

```
!On R3:

R3# show ip bgp | beginBegin Network

   Network          Next Hop         Metric LocPrf Weight Path
*> 1.0.0.0          23.1.1.2                          0 200 100 i
*> 3.0.0.0          0.0.0.0               0       32768 i
```

Task 11

Remove the configuration from the previous task before proceeding to the next task:

```
!On R3:

R3(config)# no ip as-path access-list 1

R3(config)# router bgp 300
R3(config-router)# no neighbor 23.1.1.2 filter-list 1 in
R3(config-router)# no neighbor 34.1.1.4 filter-list 1 in

R3# clear ip bgp * in
```

Let's verify the configuration:

```
!On R3:

R3# show ip bgp | begin Network

   Network          Next Hop         Metric LocPrf Weight Path
*> 1.0.0.0          23.1.1.2                          0 200 100 i
*> 2.0.0.0          23.1.1.2              0           0 200 i
*> 3.0.0.0          0.0.0.0               0       32768 i
*> 4.0.0.0          34.1.1.4              0           0 400 i
```

Task 12

Configure R1 such that it blocks all the prefixes that have originated in AS 300 and traversed through AS 200.

Let's test the regular expression:

```
R1# show ip bgp regexp _200_300$

BGP table version is 13, local router ID is 1.1.1.1
Status codes: s suppressed, d damped, h history, * valid, > best, i - internal,
              r RIB-failure, S Stale, m multipath, b backup-path, x best-external,
  f RT-Filter
Origin codes: i - IGP, e - EGP, ? - incomplete

  Network          Next Hop            Metric LocPrf Weight Path
*> 3.0.0.0          12.1.1.2                             0 200 300 i

!On R1:

R1(config)# ip as-path access-list 1 deny _200_300$
R1(config)# ip as-path access-list 1 permit .*

R1(config)# router bgp 100
R1(config-router)# neighbor 12.1.1.2 filter-list 1 in

R1# clear ip bgp * in
```

Let's verify the configuration:

```
!On R1:

R1# show ip bgp | begin  Network

  Network          Next Hop            Metric LocPrf Weight Path
*> 1.0.0.0          0.0.0.0                  0         32768 i
*> 2.0.0.0          12.1.1.2                 0             0 200 i
*> 4.0.0.0          12.1.1.2                               0 200 300 400 i
```

Task 13

Remove the configuration command from the previous task before proceeding to the next task:

```
!On R1:

R1(config)# no ip as-path access-list 1

R1(config)# router bgp 100
R1(config-router)# no neighbor 12.1.1.2 filter-list 1 in

R1# clear ip bgp * in
```

Let's verify the configuration:

```
!On R1:

R1# show ip bgp | begin Network

   Network          Next Hop          Metric LocPrf Weight Path
*> 1.0.0.0          0.0.0.0                0         32768 i
*> 2.0.0.0          12.1.1.2               0             0 200 i
*> 3.0.0.0          12.1.1.2                             0 200 300 i
*> 4.0.0.0          12.1.1.2                             0 200 300 400 i
```

Task 14

Configure R1 in AS 100 to filter prefixes from the directly connected AS 200 if their AS number has been prepended multiple times.

Before writing and applying the **as-path access-list**, you should issue a **show ip bgp regexp** command. If the desired output is displayed, the **as-path access-list** should be written and applied.

Note   In the following regular expression, the (_\1) section can be thought of as the memory button in a calculator; basically, the expression before it, ^([0-9]+), is what you are putting in memory location 1, and the asterisk (*) specifies zero or more occurrences of the expression in memory location 1.

```
!On R1:

R1# show ip bgp regexp ^([0-9]+)(_\1)*$

BGP table version is 19, local router ID is 1.1.1.1
```

```
Status codes: s suppressed, d damped, h history, * valid, > best, i - internal,
              r RIB-failure, S Stale
Origin codes: i - IGP, e - EGP, ? - incomplete


   Network          Next Hop          Metric LocPrf Weight Path
*> 2.0.0.0          12.1.1.2               0             0 200 i
```

Because the * before the $ means zero or more occurrences, the preceding regular expression will reference the prefixes regardless of whether or not the neighboring AS 200 has prepended its ASN. Therefore, let's replace * with +, which will only match if AS 200 has prepended its ASN.

```
R1# show ip bgp regexp ^([0-9]+)(_\1)+$
```

Obviously AS 200 is *not* prepending its AS number, and that's why we don't see any prefixes in the **AS-path.** Let's configure and test this:

```
R1(config)# ip as-path access-list 1 deny ^([0-9]+)(_\1)+$
R1(config)# ip as-path access-list 1 permit .*
```

There are two ways to test the regular expression before applying it to a given neighbor:

```
1. show ip bgp regexp
2. show ip bgp filter-list
```

The next step is to apply the regular expression to the neighbor(s):

```
R1(config)# router bgp 100
R1(config-router)# neighbor 12.1.1.2 filter-list 1 in
```

The following uses the refresh messages so the changes can apply to the existing and new prefixes:

```
R1# clear ip bgp * in
```

Let's verify the configuration:

```
!On R1:


R1# show ip bgp | begin Network

   Network          Next Hop          Metric LocPrf Weight Path
*> 1.0.0.0          0.0.0.0                0         32768 i
*> 2.0.0.0          12.1.1.2               0             0 200 i
*> 3.0.0.0          12.1.1.2                             0 200 300 i
*> 4.0.0.0          12.1.1.2                             0 200 300 400 i
```

To properly test this, let's configure R2 to prepend its AS number multiple times:

```
R2(config)# ip prefix-list NET permit 2.0.0.0/8

R2(config)# route-map TST permit 10
R2(config-route-map)# match ip address prefix-list NET
R2(config-route-map)# set as-path prepend 200
R2(config-route-map)# route-map TST permit 90

R2(config)# router bgp 200
R2(config-router)# neighbor 12.1.1.1 route-map TST out

R2# clear ip bgp * out
```

Let's verify and test the configuration:

```
!On R1:

R1# show ip bgp | begin Network

   Network          Next Hop         Metric LocPrf Weight Path
*> 1.0.0.0          0.0.0.0              0         32768 i
*> 3.0.0.0          12.1.1.2                           0 200 300 i
*> 4.0.0.0          12.1.1.2                           0 200 300 400 i

R1# show ip bgp filter-list 1
BGP table version is 18, local router ID is 1.1.1.1
Status codes: s suppressed, d damped, h history, * valid, > best, i - internal,
              r RIB-failure, S Stale, m multipath, b backup-path, f RT-Filter,
              x best-external, a additional-path, c RIB-compressed,
Origin codes: i - IGP, e - EGP, ? - incomplete
RPKI validation codes: V valid, I invalid, N Not found

     Network          Next Hop         Metric LocPrf Weight Path
 *>  1.0.0.0          0.0.0.0              0         32768 i
 *>  3.0.0.0          12.1.1.2                           0 200 300 i
 *>  4.0.0.0          12.1.1.2                           0 200 300 400 i
```

Because R2 is prepending its AS number multiple times, R1 filters the prefix. Let's remove the filtering configuration from R1 and verify:

```
!On R1:

R1(config)# no ip as-path access-list 1

R1(config)# router bgp 100
```

```
R1(config-router)# no neighbor 12.1.1.2 filter-list 1 in

R1# clear ip bgp * in

R1# show ip bgp | begin Network

   Network          Next Hop          Metric LocPrf Weight Path
*> 1.0.0.0          0.0.0.0                0      32768 i
*> 2.0.0.0          12.1.1.2               0          0 200 200 i
*> 3.0.0.0          12.1.1.2                          0 200 300 i
*> 4.0.0.0          12.1.1.2                          0 200 300 400 i
```

Let's remove the configuration from R2:

```
!On R2:

R2(config)# no ip prefix-list NET
R2(config)# no route-map TST

R2(config)# router bgp 200
R2(config-router)# no neighbor 12.1.1.1 route-map TST out

R2# clear ip bgp * out
```

Let's test and verify the configuration:

```
!On R1:

R1# show ip bgp | begin Network

   Network          Next Hop          Metric LocPrf Weight Path
*> 1.0.0.0          0.0.0.0                0      32768 i
*> 2.0.0.0          12.1.1.2               0          0 200 i
*> 3.0.0.0          12.1.1.2                          0 200 300 i
*> 4.0.0.0          12.1.1.2                          0 200 300 400 i
```

Erase the startup config and reload the routers before proceeding to the next lab.

Lab 10-10: BGP Confederation

BGP confederations are designed to help manage iBGP meshing. They can be used instead of or in combination with route reflectors, which we discussed in detail in Lab 10-2. The most basic functionality of BGP confederations is to split up the autonomous system into smaller, more manageable autonomous systems, which are represented as one single autonomous system to eBGP peers outside the confederation. BGP confederations were originally defined in RFC 3065 (currently RFC 5065).

By creating smaller autonomous system domains—or sub-AS domains, as they are often called—it is possible to restrict the number of iBGP sessions required to create a full mesh. This is made possible by only requiring the full mesh configuration within each independent sub-AS. We illustrate this in our working environment by creating three distinct sub-autonomous systems. We will use the private AS range to accomplish this. The autonomous system numbers within the range 64,512 through 65,535 are reserved for private use. Confederations often employ these private AS numbers. At this juncture of our conversation, we will utilized the autonomous system numbers 65511, C65522, and 65534 to apply confederations under AS 100. The first stage will be to create the topology outlined in Figure 10-10.

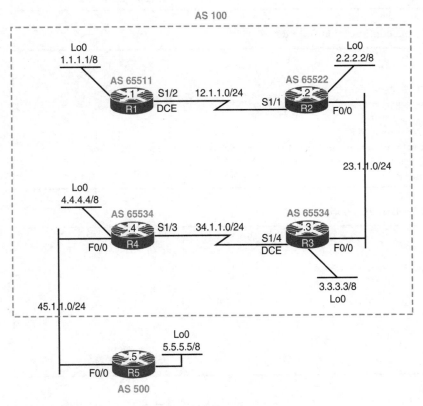

Figure 10-10 *BGP Confederation Topology*

The initial configuration files used in this lab can be found by downloading the BGP-Lab-10.txt file and subsequently applying those configurations on a device-by-device basis.

Task 1

Configure BGP peering on the routers as follows:

- Configure routers R1–R4 in a confederation with a public AS number of 100.

- R1 in sub-AS 65511 should establish an eBGP peer session with R2 in sub-AS 65522.

- R2 in sub-AS 65522 should establish eBGP peer sessions with R1 and R3 in sub-AS 65511 and sub-AS 65534, respectively.

- R3 in sub-AS 65534 should establish an eBGP peer session with R2 in sub-AS 65522 and an iBGP peer session with R4 in AS 65534.

- R4 in sub-AS 65534 should establish an iBGP peer session with R3 and an eBGP peer session with R5 in AS 500.

- R5 in AS 500 should establish an eBGP peer session with R4 in AS 100.

- These routers should advertise their loopback interface in BGP.

- AS 100 should use OSPF for the links within the AS.

```
!On R1:

R1(config)# router ospf 1
R1(config-router)# network 12.1.1.1 0.0.0.0 area 0

R1(config)# router bgp 65511
R1(config-router)# no auto-summary
R1(config-router)# network 1.0.0.0
R1(config-router)# neighbor 12.1.1.2 remote-as 65522
R1(config-router)# bgp confederation identifier 100
```

The **BGP confederation identifier** command is used to configure a single AS number to identify a group of smaller autonomous systems as a single confederation. This command *must* be configured on all the routers within the confederation.

A confederation can be used to reduce the iBGP mesh by dividing a large single AS into multiple sub-AS instances and then grouping them into a single confederation.

```
R1(config-router)# bgp confederation peers 65522
```

The preceding command is used to identify the directly connected eBGP sub-confederation peers.

```
!On R2:

R2(config)# router ospf 1
R2(config-router)# network 12.1.1.2 0.0.0.0 area 0
R2(config-router)# network 23.1.1.2 0.0.0.0 area 0


R2(config)# router bgp 65522
R2(config-router)# no auto-summary
R2(config-router)# network 2.0.0.0
R2(config-router)# neighbor 12.1.1.1 remote-as 65511
R2(config-router)# neighbor 23.1.1.3 remote-as 65534
R2(config-router)# bgp confederation identifier 100
R2(config-router)# bgp confederation peers 65511 65534

!On R3:

R3(config)# router ospf 1
R3(config-router)# network 34.1.1.3 0.0.0.0 area 0
R3(config-router)# network 23.1.1.3 0.0.0.0 area 0


R3(config)# router bgp 65534
R3(config-router)# no auto-summary
R3(config-router)# neighbor 34.1.1.4 remote-as 65534
R3(config-router)# neighbor 23.1.1.2 remote-as 65522
R3(config-router)# network 3.0.0.0
R3(config-router)# bgp confederation identifier 100
```

Note   R3 did not configure R4 (AS 65534) as a confederation peer because the local router (R3) is in the same sub-confederation as R4.

```
R3(config-router)# bgp confederation peers 65522
```

Note   R4 runs OSPF on the external link (45.1.1.0/24). This is configured so the routers within AS 100 can have reachability to the next-hop IP address for all the prefixes advertised by R5 in AS 500. Also, **passive-interface fastethernet0/0** is configured so that if R5 runs OSPF on the same link, it will not be able to establish an OSPF adjacency with R4 and have information on all the private IP addresses advertised in AS 100.

```
R4(config)# router ospf 1
R4(config-router)# network 34.1.1.4 0.0.0.0 area 0

R4(config-router)# network 45.1.1.4 0.0.0.0 area 0
R4(config-router)# passive-interface fastethernet0FastEtherenet0/0

R4(config)# router bgp 65534
R4(config-router)# no auto-summary
R4(config-router)# network 4.0.0.0
R4(config-router)# bgp confederation identifier 100
R4(config-router)# neighbor 45.1.1.5 remote-as 500
R4(config-router)# neighbor 34.1.1.3 remote-as 65534
```

Note R4 does *not* have any directly connected eBGP sub-confederation peers. Therefore, the **bgp confederation peers** command is *not* configured.

```
!On R5:

R5(config)# router bgp 500
R5(config-router)# no auto-summary
R5(config-router)# network 5.0.0.0
R5(config-router)# neighbor 45.1.1.4 remote-as 100
```

Let's verify the configuration:

```
!On R5:

R5# show ip bgp | begin Network

   Network          Next Hop          Metric LocPrf Weight Path
*> 1.0.0.0          45.1.1.4                          0 100 i
*> 2.0.0.0          45.1.1.4                          0 100 i
*> 3.0.0.0          45.1.1.4                          0 100 i
*> 4.0.0.0          45.1.1.4               0          0 100 i
*> 5.0.0.0          0.0.0.0                0      32768 i
```

From R5's perspective, all the prefixes are from AS 100:

```
!On R1:

R1# show ip bgp | begin Network

   Network          Next Hop         Metric LocPrf Weight Path
*> 1.0.0.0          0.0.0.0               0         32768 i
*> 2.0.0.0          10.1.12.2             0    100      0 (65522) i
*> 3.0.0.0          10.1.23.3             0    100      0 (65522 65534) i
*> 4.0.0.0          10.1.34.4             0    100      0 (65522 65534) i
*> 5.0.0.0          10.1.45.5             0    100      0 (65522 65534) 500 i
```

Note   The AS paths in parentheses are the private AS numbers within the confederation; AS 500 is outside of the parentheses because it's *not* part of the confederation.

Erase the startup config and reload the routers before proceeding to the next lab.

Chapter 11

IPv6

Lab 11-1: Acquiring an IPv6 Address

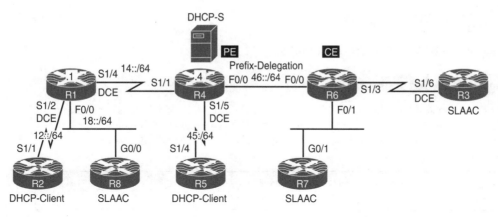

Figure 11-1 *Acquiring an IPv6 Address*

Figure 11-1 illustrates the topology that will be used in the following lab.

Modified EUI-64 Addressing

Modified Extended Unique Identifier 64 (EUI-64) is the process that allows a host to assign itself a unique IPv6 address. The host's MAC address is converted into a 64-bit identifier, called a Modified EUI-64, and this value is appended to a 64-bit network prefix learned by other means. This feature is an enhancement over IPv4 because it eliminates the need for manual configuration or DHCP. The IPv6 Modified EUI-64 format address is created based on the 48-bit MAC address of the interface. The MAC address is first separated into two 24-bit groups, the first being the OUI (organizationally unique identifier) and the other being NIC-specific. The 16-bit value of FFFE is then inserted between these two 24-bit groups to form the 64-bit EUI address. IEEE has chosen FFFE as a reserved value that can only appear in EUI-64 generated from the EUI-48 MAC address.

Finally, the seventh bit from the left, or the universal/local (U/L) bit, needs to be inverted. This process can be seen in Figure 11-2. This bit identifies whether this Modified EUI-64 interface identifier is officially assigned or locally generated; in other words, whether it is universally or locally administered. If it is 0, the address is locally administered; if it is 1, the address is globally unique. It is worth noticing that in the original OUI portion, the globally unique addresses assigned by the IEEE have their U/L bit always set to 0, whereas locally created addresses have it set to 1. In other words, the meaning of the U/L bit in the Modified EUI-64 is inverted when compared to the meaning assigned by IEEE. This is the reason for calling this address the *Modified* EUI-64. Therefore, when the bit is inverted, it maintains its original value.

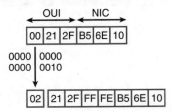

Figure 11-2   *Modified EUI-64 Addressing*

Using EUI-64 Addressing

At the command line, the configuration of Modified EUI-64 addressing is very simple, but we are interested in the outcome rather than just the process of implementation here. Therefore, we will first look to see what the 48-bit MAC address of the FastEthernet0/1 interface is:

```
R1# show interface FastEthernet0/1 | include bia
  Hardware is Gt96k FE, address is 0017.942f.10f1 (bia 0017.942f.10f1)
```

You can see that the address is 0017.942f.10f1, so let's first break this address up into two 24-bit groups.:

```
0017.94    2f.10f1
```

Now we will insert the prescribed FFFE value to get a 64-bit product:

```
0017.94FF.FE2f.10f1
```

Finally, we will invert the seventh least significant bit in the second byte of this value. The second byte in this address is the second zero, which would be 00000000 if we converted it to decimal. We see that the seventh zero in binary stream is 0, and we will invert it to a 1. This means that the value would now be a binary 00000010, which would be a value of 2 if we converted it back to hexadecimal. This means that the modified value would now be the following:

```
0217:94FF:FE2F:10F1
```

After removing leading zeros, we have a final value of 217:94FF:FE2F:10F1. This is the Modified EUI-64 value that will be assigned when we configure the command under R1's FastEthernet0/1 interface. You can see that here:

```
R1# conf t
Enter configuration commands, one per line.  End with CNTL/Z.
R1(config)# interface FastEthernet0/1
R1(config-if)# ipv6 address 2001::/64 eui-64
```

Now you can see what IPv6 address was assigned by using the **show ipv6 interface** command:

```
R1# show ipv6 interface FastEthernet0/1 | include EUI
    2001::217:94FF:FE2F:10F1, subnet is 2001::/64 [EUI/TEN]
```

This matches our calculations exactly.

Implement IPv6 Neighbor Discovery

Neighbor Discovery protocol is in fact an umbrella term for many interrelated subprotocols and mechanisms whose main responsibilities include the following:

- Resolution of IPv6 addresses into MAC addresses of neighboring hosts

- Duplicate address detection

- Router discovery

- Stateless address auto-configuration

- Host redirection

The common denominator for all these operations is the ICMPv6 protocol, which has been extended with the necessary message types to accomplish all these tasks. Similar to ICMP in IPv4, ICMPv6 is still used for various purposes, such as performing connectivity tests (pings) and indicating errors during packet delivery (TTL expiration, packet too big, unknown destination, communication prohibited, and so on). In addition, however, ICMPv6 has also taken on the role of Address Resolution Protocol (ARP) as well as some other protocols.

As the name suggests, the Neighbor Discovery functions added to ICMPv6 are related to facilitating communication between directly connected neighbors:

- **Router Advertisement:** Routers send Route Advertisement messages out of each IPv6-enabled interface, informing attached hosts of their presence. Router Advertisement messages may also contain vital information allowing the hosts to automatically configure their IPv6 stack: the IPv6 prefix of the particular network, the first-hop MTU, the router's MAC address (allowing hosts to learn about the router's MAC address right away), and even the list of DNS domains and DNS servers. Using the information in a received Router Advertisement, a host can automatically configure its IPv6 stack and obtain IPv6 connectivity without the need for any dedicated DHCP service on a network. Router Advertisements are sent periodically, though infrequently, and they are also sent immediately as a response to a Router Solicitation message originated by an end host.

■ **Router Solicitation:** Upon an interface of a node being enabled, Router Solicitation messages can be used to request all routers on the same local link to send Router Advertisements immediately, rather than waiting until the next periodically scheduled advertisement.

■ **Redirect:** Redirect messages are used by routers to tell hosts that a better on-link router exists for a given destination address.

■ **Neighbor Solicitation:** Neighbor Solicitation messages have three main purposes. The first one is to discover the link layer address of a neighbor as part of the MAC address resolution process. This process replaces the use of ARP requests and replies in IPv4. The second purpose is to determine the reachability of a neighbor. The last purpose is to detect the presence of duplicate IPv6 addresses.

■ **Neighbor Advertisement:** Neighbor Advertisement messages are either sent in response to Neighbor Solicitations or are sent by a neighbor to announce a change in its link layer address. Upon receipt of a Neighbor Advertisement, a node will update its neighbor cache, which contains mappings between IPv6 and link layer addresses of neighbors.

■ **Host auto-configuration:** Throughout this section, the term *global address* is used to describe a unicast IPv6 address that is not a link-local address. A global address does not necessarily need to be from the Global Aggregatable scope; however, it might very well be a unique local address, for example.

When the interface of a host is first connected to the network, it must acquire information necessary for the host to communicate on the local link and the entire network. It must obtain link-local and global unicast IPv6 addresses, a list of on-link routers, a list of on-link prefixes, and other related information.

The process begins with the automatic generation of a link-local IPv6 address. Because it is also possible to manually configure link layer addresses, there is a chance that a duplicate link-local address exists on the same link of the network. To determine if this is the case, the Duplicate Address Detection procedure is invoked.

■ **Duplicate Address Detection:** The host interface to be auto-configured sends a Neighbor Solicitation to all node interfaces on the same link belonging to the same solicited node multicast address. This type of multicast address ensures that the Neighbor Solicitation will only be received by member nodes of the same multicast group (that is, those that match the last 24 bits of their IPv6 address). The source address included in the IPv6 header is the unspecified address (::). The body of the Neighbor Solicitation contains the complete link-local address, which is to be checked for duplication.

If no host responds within a given time period, the host undergoing auto-configuration may keep its link-local address. Otherwise, the host containing the duplicate address responds with a Neighbor Advertisement. This advertisement is sent to all nodes on the same link by using the all-nodes multicast address FF02::1 as its IPv6 destination address. The message contains its link layer address and a flag to indicate whether the responding node is a router.

All nodes on the same link will therefore be forced to update their neighbor caches if their entries are not up to date. Receipt of a Neighbor Advertisement also updates the reachability status entry in the neighbor cache. A duplicate address on the local link may require the manual configuration of the new host interface link-local address.

■ **Router Discovery**: Once a unique link-local address has been obtained, the newly connected host needs to discover routers on its local link and also prefix lists that are used on the local link. This is performed in the next stage of auto-configuration: Router Discovery.

The newly connected host sends out a Router Solicitation to all routers on the local link using the all-router multicast address FF02::2 as the destination address. In doing so, the host provides all such routers with its newly created local link address and its corresponding link layer address, so that all routers may update their records. All routers then respond in turn with a Router Advertisement. This message contains the following important data to be used by a host in the auto-configuration process:

■ A router's link layer address

■ A router's lifetime (that is, how long a host is able to keep using this router until subsequent advertisements update this value)

■ Flags used to determine the process by which the host's global unicast address is created

■ Periodic timer values used in the Address Resolution and Neighbor Unreachability Detection procedures

■ Global prefixes that should be cached in the host's prefix list

Upon receipt of the Router Advertisements, a host updates the relevant fields of its default router list, neighbor cache, and prefix list. Now the host has the link-local IPv6 and link layer addresses of all on-link routers, a list of on-link prefixes, and other relevant data. At this point, the host can use its own MAC address to create a Modified EUI-64 interface identifier and append it to the prefixes acquired from the Router Advertisement message, generating a set of unique global IPv6 addresses, one for each global prefix. In the end, the host has all information to achieve full IPv6 connectivity: its own global address and the address of its gateway. This process is called stateless address auto-configuration, or SLAAC.

■ **Implementing auto-configuration:** Let's look at how to configure IPv6 auto-configuration between R1 and R2. We will configure R2 such that it obtains its IPv6 address from R1. First, we need to make our configuration on R1:

```
R1# conf t
Enter configuration commands, one per line.  End with CNTL/Z.
R1(config)# ipv6 unicast-routing
R1(config)# int FastEthernet0/0
R1(config-if)# ipv6 address FE80::1 link-local
R1(config-if)# ipv6 address 2001:12::1/64
R1(config-if)# no shut
```

Now we need to tell R2 to obtain its interface IPv6 address via auto-configuration:

```
R2# conf t
Enter configuration commands, one per line.  End with CNTL/Z.
R2(config)# ipv6 unicast-routing
R2(config)# interface FastEthernet0/0
R2(config-if)# ipv6 enable
R2(config-if)# ipv6 address autoconfig
R2(config-if)# no shut
R2(config-if)# end
```

Before we do anything else, we need to check whether R2 sees any routers on the Ethernet segment connected to R1:

```
R2# show ipv6 routers
Router FE80::1 on FastEthernet0/0, last update 1 min
  Hops 64, Lifetime 1800 sec, AddrFlag=0, OtherFlag=0, MTU=1500
  HomeAgentFlag=0, Preference=Medium
  Reachable time 0 msec, Retransmit time 0 msec
  Prefix 2001:12::/64 onlink autoconfig
    Valid lifetime 2592000, preferred lifetime 604800
```

Note that R2 sees R1 as the router on this segment (ID FE80::1), and that the prefix 2001:12::/64 will be issued as the auto-configurable network address. Lastly, observe that the lifetime of this auto-configuration will be 30 days. Now let's look at the address that was auto-configured on R2:

```
R2# show ipv6 interface FastEthernet0/0
FastEthernet0/0 is up, line protocol is up
  IPv6 is enabled, link-local address is FE80::20F:8FFF:FE4A:1060
  No Virtual link-local address(es):
  Global unicast address(es):
    2001:12::20F:8FFF:FE4A:1060, subnet is 2001:12::/64 [EUI/CAL/PRE]
      valid lifetime 2591899 preferred lifetime 604699
  Joined group address(es):
    FF02::1
    FF02::2
    FF02::1:FF4A:1060
  MTU is 1500 bytes
  ICMP error messages limited to one every 100 milliseconds
  ICMP redirects are enabled
  ICMP unreachables are sent
  ND DAD is enabled, number of DAD attempts: 1
  ND reachable time is 30000 milliseconds
  ND advertised reachable time is 0 milliseconds
  ND advertised retransmit interval is 0 milliseconds
  ND router advertisements are sent every 200 seconds
  ND router advertisements live for 1800 seconds
  ND advertised default router preference is Medium
  Hosts use stateless autoconfig for addresses.
```

Observe that R2 has created a host portion for the IPv6 address based on the Modified EUI-64 scheme for both the global and link local addresses. Also notice that R2 joined three multicast groups: FF02::1 as an IPv6-enabled node, FF02::2 as an IPv6-enabled router, and FF02::1:FF4A:1060 as a solicited-node multicast address that corresponds to both the link-local address and the global unicast address.

Task 1

R8 should be configured to acquire an IPv6 address through the SLAAC process from R1. Use the following MAC addresses for these two routers:

- **R1**: 0000.1111.1111

- **R8**: 0000.8888.8888

Stateless address auto-configuration (SLAAC) is a method used for IPv6 hosts to acquire the prefix portion of their IPv6 address. SLAAC provides a very simple process where the clients self-assign an IPv6 address based on the IPv6 prefix.

This process is achieved based on the following:

- A host sends a Router Solicitation (RS) message.

- A router with IPv6 unicast routing enabled will reply with a Router Advertisement (RA) message.

- The host takes the IPv6 prefix from the Router Advertisement message and combines it with the 64-bit Modified EUI-64 address to create a global unicast address.

- The host also uses the source IPv6 address of the Router Advertisement message as its default gateway. This address would be a link-local address.

- Duplicate Address Detection is performed by IPv6 clients to ensure the uniqueness of the new IPv6 address.

In IPv6, unicast routing is disabled by default, and in order for R1 to respond to the Router Solicitation (RS) messages, the IPv6 unicast routing must be enabled:

```
! On R1:
R1(config)# ipv6 unicast-routing

R1(config)# interface FastEthernet0/0
R1(config)# ipv6 enable
R1(config-if)# mac-address 0000.1111.1111
R1(config-if)# shutdown   → wait for the interface to go down
R1(config-if)# no shutdown
```

Now you need to verify the configuration. You need to understand that when IPv6 is enabled on a router, it will automatically join certain multicast groups. The following **show** command reveals the multicast addresses:

```
! On R1 ("SNM" stands for Solicited Node Multicast):

R1# show ipv6 interface FastEthernet0/0 | include FF

  IPv6 is enabled, link-local address is FE80::200:11FF:FE11:1111
    FF02::1 → All hosts within the local segment
    FF02::2 → All routers within the local segment
    FF02::1:FF00:1 → SNM based on the Global unicast IPv6 address
    FF02::1:FF11:1111 → SNM based on the Link Local IPv6 address
```

In the output of this **show** command, you can see that the local router has auto-generated a link-local address based on the Modified EUI-64 format.

Recall that whenever a Layer 3 multicast packet is encapsulated into a Layer 2 Ethernet frame, the destination MAC address must be a group address. For IPv6 in particular, the group MAC address is computed using the prefix of 33-33 in hexadecimal, concatenated with the lowermost four bytes of the multicast IPv6 address, as shown in Table 11-1.

Table 11-1   *MAC Addresses for IPv6*

Multicast Address	MAC Address
FF02::1	33-33-00-00-00-01
FF02::2	33-33-00-00-00-02
FF02::1:FF00:1	33-33-FF-00-00-01
FF02::1:FF11:1111	33-33-FF-11-11-11

Now configure R8 to obtain its IPv6 address using SLAAC:

```
! On R8:


R8(config)# interface GigabitEthernet0/0
R8(config-if)# mac-address 0000.8888.8888
R8(config-if)# ipv6 enable
R8(config-if)# ipv6 address autoconfig default
R8(config-if)# no shutdown
```

Once the **ipv6 enable** and **no shutdown** commands are entered, R8 will automatically generate its link-local address (FE80::200:88FF:FE88:8888) and use Duplicate Address Detection (DAD) to ensure the uniqueness of this link-local IPv6 address. The additional **ipv6 address autoconfig default** command tells R8 to also acquire a network prefix using SLAAC, and to install a default route automatically through neighboring routers discovered during SLAAC.

Let's verify the configuration:

```
R8# show ipv6 interface brief GigabitEthernet0/0

GigabitEthernet0/0      [up/up]
    FE80::200:88FF:FE88:8888
    18::200:88FF:FE88:8888


R8# show ipv6 interface GigabitEthernet0/0

GigabitEthernet0/0 is up, line protocol is up
  IPv6 is enabled, link-local address is FE80::200:88FF:FE88:8888
  No Virtual link-local address(es):
  Stateless address autoconfig enabled
  Global unicast address(es):
    18::200:88FF:FE88:8888, subnet is 18::/64 [EUI/CAL/PRE]
      valid lifetime 2591856 preferred lifetime 604656
```

```
Joined group address(es):
   FF02::1
   FF02::FB → This Multicast address is used for mDNS
   FF02::1:FF88:8888
MTU is 1500 bytes
ICMP error messages limited to one every 100 milliseconds
ICMP redirects are enabled
ICMP unreachables are sent
ND DAD is enabled, number of DAD attempts: 1
ND reachable time is 30000 milliseconds (using 30000)
ND NS retransmit interval is 1000 milliseconds
Default router is FE80::200:11FF:FE11:1111 on GigabitEthernet0/0
```

The next hop for the automatically added default route is the link-local IPv6 address of R1. The verification of this fact is left as an exercise for the reader.

Task 2

R4 should be configured as a DHCP server, and R5 should be configured as a DHCP client acquiring an IPv6 address from R4. R5 should also get its domain name (example.com) and the DNS server's IPv6 address (2001:1111::1) from R4.

Let's configure R4 as a DHCP server using the options stated in the task. To work as a DHCP server, unicast routing must be enabled:

```
! On R4:

R4(config)# ipv6 unicast-routing
R4(config)# ipv6 dhcp pool TST
```

The following specifies the address range to provide in the pool:

```
R4(config-dhcpv6)# address prefix 45::/64
```

The following configuration provides the DNS server and the domain name option to DHCP clients:

```
R4(config-dhcpv6)# dns-server 2001:1:1111::1
R4(config-dhcpv6)# domain-name example.com
```

Let's view the configuration of R4's s1/5 interface:

```
R4# show run interface Serial 1/5 | begin interface

interface Serial1/5
 no ip address
 ipv6 address 45::4/64
 ipv6 enable
 clock rate 64000
end
```

The following command associates the DHCP pool with the interface facing the client (R5), effectively starting the particular DHCP server instance on s1/5:

```
R4(config)# interface Serial 1/5
R4(config-if)# no ipv6 nd ra suppress
R4(config-if)# ipv6 dhcp server TST
```

Serial interfaces do not send the Router Advertisement messages by default—this is different from Ethernet interfaces, where RA messages are sent automatically. Because they will be required later, we are configuring the s1/5 interface to send them.

As opposed to IPv4, where starting a DHCP server was essentially enough for the hosts to obtain their configuration via DHCP, in IPv6, the hosts must actually be instructed to use DHCP. Without this indication, they will continue using SLAAC. This is accomplished using the Router Advertisement (RA) messages.

RA messages contain two specific bits, or flags, that are used to inform hosts about the mechanism hosts should use to obtain their IPv6 settings. These flags are commonly called the M-flag and the O-flag.

The M-flag, or the *managed address configuration* flag, tells hosts to obtain their entire IPv6 configuration using DHCP, including their address, prefix length, DNS server address, domain name, and so on. The only parameter that will still remain discovered using RA messages is the default gateway address. DHCP for IPv6 does not support conveying the default gateway address information to clients because this information can always be learned from RA messages, which must have been received by hosts in the first place; otherwise, they would not be contacting DHCP at all. The M-flag can be set in outgoing RA messages using the **ipv6 nd managed-config-flag** interface configuration command.

The O-flag, or the *other configuration* flag, tells hosts to obtain their IPv6 address and gateway using SLAAC, and to acquire all other configuration (DNS address, domain name, and so on) using DHCP. The O-flag can be set in outgoing RA messages using the **ipv6 nd other-config-flag** interface configuration command.

It is important to note that these flags are indications only. It is entirely up to the software running on the host to honor them. Some operating systems may choose to ignore these flags and behave according to their preset configuration. This is also valid for IOS—obviously, when an interface is statically configured to obtain its configuration via DHCP, it will attempt to talk to DHCP even if the RA messages do not have the M-flag set. Nonetheless, we will set up the flags diligently—it is considered a best practice, as well as a very safe approach, to accommodate most operating systems.

The following command sets the M-flag in the RA messages. This tells the hosts not to rely on SLAAC and instead to use DHCP to obtain their IPv6 configuration. (Without this command, some hosts would continue using SLAAC even if the DHCP server was running.)

```
R4(config-if)# ipv6 nd managed-config-flag
```

Let's enable **debug ipv6 dhcp** on R5:

```
! On R5:

R5# debug ipv6 dhcp
   IPv6 DHCP debugging is on
```

Before configuring R5, let's view the existing configuration of R5's s1/4 interface:

```
interface Serial1/4
 no ip address
 shutdown
end

R5(config)# interface Serial 1/4
R5(config-if)# ipv6 enable
R5(config-if)# ipv6 address dhcp
R5(config-if)# no shutdown
```

Here, the **ipv6 enable** command is required to allow the interface to have a link-local address. Without it, the interface would be unable to send DHCP requests because it would have no source IPv6 address. Based on the following output, we can see that the local router (R5) sends a Solicit message to FF02::1:2. Because there is no broadcast in IPv6, this is a special multicast address that the clients use to communicate with a DHCP server.

The local router receives an Advertise message from the link-local IPv6 address of R4, the DHCP server.

The local router then sends a request to use the IPv6 address given to it by the DHCP server, and it receives a reply from the server. In IPv4 DHCP, we also had four messages: Discover, Offer, Request, and Acknowledge, all with a similar meaning.

```
IPv6 DHCP: Sending SOLICIT to FF02::1:2 on Serial1/4
IPv6 DHCP: Received ADVERTISE from FE80::217:59FF:FECE:2B8 on Serial1/4
IPv6 DHCP: Adding server FE80::217:59FF:FECE:2B8
IPv6 DHCP: Sending REQUEST to FF02::1:2 on Serial1/4
IPv6 DHCP: DHCPv6 address changes state from SOLICIT to REQUEST (ADDR_ADVERTISE_
  RECEIVED) on Serial1/4
IPv6 DHCP: Received REPLY from FE80::217:59FF:FECE:2B8 on Serial1/4
IPv6 DHCP: Processing options

IPv6 DHCP: Adding address 45::A58D:F28F:9901:DA14/128 to Serial1/4
IPv6 DHCP: T1 set to expire in 43200 seconds
IPv6 DHCP: T2 set to expire in 69120 seconds
IPv6 DHCP: Configuring DNS server 2001:1:1111::1
IPv6 DHCP: Configuring domain name example.com
IPv6 DHCP: DHCPv6 address changes state from REQUEST to OPEN (ADDR_REPLY_RECEIVED)
  on Serial1/4
```

Let's verify the configuration:

```
! On R5:

R5# show ipv6 interface brief Serial 1/4

Serial1/4                      [up/up]
    FE80::21B:D4FF:FEBE:69D0
    45::A58D:F28F:9901:DA14
```

You can see that the local router acquired an IPv6 address from the DHCP server. How do we display the DHCP optional parameters that the local router acquired from the DHCP server?

```
R5# show ipv6 dhcp interface

Serial1/4 is in client mode
  Prefix State is IDLE
  Address State is OPEN
  Renew for address will be sent in 10:35:25
  List of known servers:
    Reachable via address: FE80::217:59FF:FECE:2B8
    DUID: 00030001001759CE02B8
    Preference: 0
    Configuration parameters:
      IA NA: IA ID 0x00090001, T1 43200, T2 69120
        Address: 45::A58D:F28F:9901:DA14/128
```

```
                     preferred lifetime 86400, valid lifetime 172800
                     expires at Jul 07 2016 07:58 PM (167726 seconds)
      DNS server: 2001:1:1111::1
      Domain name: example.com
      Information refresh time: 0
  Prefix Rapid-Commit: disabled
  Address Rapid-Commit: disabled
```

Rapid commit will be discussed and experimented with later in this chapter. We can continue our verification by looking at the IPv6 binding database on R4, the DHCP server, and comparing it to the IPv6 address assigned to R5's Serial1/4 interface.

```
! On R4:

R4# show ipv6 dhcp binding

Client: FE80::21B:D4FF:FEBE:69D0
  DUID: 00030001001BD4BE69D0
  Username : unassigned
  IA NA: IA ID 0x00090001, T1 43200, T2 69120
    Address: 45::A58D:F28F:9901:DA14
            preferred lifetime 86400, valid lifetime 172800
            expires at Jul 07 2016 08:24 PM (167588 seconds)

R5# show ipv6 interface brief Serial1/4

Serial1/4                      [up/up]
    FE80::21B:D4FF:FEBE:69D0
    45::A58D:F28F:9901:DA14
```

Even though not shown here, the **show ipv6 route** command would be somewhat disappointing because no default route would be installed.

The default route in DHCPv6 environments is somewhat confusing. Because IPv6 routers are required to send RA messages, the creators of DHCPv6 decided not to have a default gateway option for DHCPv6, and instead simply rely on the hosts discovering their gateways using RA messages. As a result, even in a DHCPv6 environment, RA messages are required for hosts to discover their gateway, while DHCPv6 provides the rest of the IPv6 configuration.

On Cisco IOS-based routers, having a router obtain its interface configuration through **ipv6 address dhcp** will cause it to obtain its address and other optional information via DHCP, but this will not make it install a default route through a neighbor sourcing RA messages. If you want to do that as well, you must add the **ipv6 address autoconfig default** command to the same interface to have the router install a default route discovered via SLAAC.

Finally, having an interface configured both with **ipv6 address dhcp** and **ipv6 address autoconfig default** will cause the interface to have two addresses: one obtained via DHCP, the other via SLAAC. Although this may appear to defeat the purpose of DHCP, that is not entirely true: You can configure R4's s1/5 interface with the **ipv6 nd prefix default no-advertise** command, which will prevent R4 from advertising any prefix in its RA messages. Although R4 will continue to send RAs, there will be no global prefix advertised, so R5 would only install a default route through R4 without generating a SLAAC-derived address itself.

Task 3

R2 should be configured to acquire an IPv6 address from the DHCP server. R2 should acquire the following from the DHCP server (R4):

- An address from the range 12::/64

- DNS server: 2000:2222::2

- Domain name: example.com

R1 should be configured as a DHCP relay agent.

Let's verify the configuration of R4's s1/1 interface before adding additional configuration:

```
! On R4:

R4# show run interface Serial 1/1 | begin interface

interface Serial1/1
 no ip address
 ipv6 address 14::4/64
 ipv6 enable
end

R4# ping 14::1

Type escape sequence to abort.
Sending 5, 100-byte ICMP Echos to 14::1, timeout is 2 seconds:
!!!!!
Success rate is 100 percent (5/5), round-trip min/avg/max = 28/28/28 ms
```

Let's configure the DHCP server on R4 for the network where R2 resides:

```
R4(config)# ipv6 dhcp pool R2
R4(config-dhcpv6)# address prefix 12::/64
R4(config-dhcpv6)# dns-server 2000:2222::2
R4(config-dhcpv6)# domain-name example.com
```

Let's apply the pool called "R2" to the closest interface toward R2:

```
R4(config)# interface Serial 1/1
R4(config-if)# ipv6 dhcp server R2
```

Let's move to R1:

```
! On R1:

R1# show run interface Serial 1/2 | begin interface
interface Serial1/2
 no ip address
 ipv6 address 12::1/64
 ipv6 enable
 clock rate 64000
end
```

R1's s1/2 interface should be configured to set the M-flag and then relay the Solicit messages to the DHCP server:

```
R1(config)# interface Serial 1/2
```

The following command configures the IPv6 address of the DHCP server by using the **destination** keyword; the reference to s1/4 as an outgoing interface is optional in this scenario. Referencing the outgoing interface would be required if the **destination** keyword pointed to the link-local IPv6 address of R4.

```
R1(config-if)# ipv6 dhcp relay destination 14::4 serial1/4
R1(config-if)# ipv6 nd managed-config-flag
R1(config-if)# no ipv6 nd ra suppress
```

As an aside, the configuration of IPv6 DHCP relay is much more intuitive than its IPv4 counterpart whose command, **ip helper-address**, does not even readily resemble anything related to DHCP.

In this case, R2 is going to be the DHCP client. R2 will multicast a DHCP Solicit message. R1 will receive this message and relay it to R4, the DHCP server. The Solicit message will have the Link Address field populated with the IPv6 address of R1's link facing R2. R4 will go through its DHCP scopes and will find one that matches the same network. Subsequently, it will lease out an IPv6 address from that scope and offer it to R2 using the Advertise message. Note, however, that the Advertise response will be unicast to R1's address learned from the Solicit message.

R1 will receive the Advertise message and will relay it down to R2. After R2 receives the Advertise message, it will continue with multicasting a DHCP Request message, which will again be relayed by R2 to R4. Then, R4 will respond with a DHCP Reply message to R2, which in turn forwards it to R1. At this point, R1 has a usable address. The entire process is very similar to IPv4 DHCP.

> **Note**   If the address prefix 12::/64 is configured in the previous pool (**TST**), R2 will get two IPv6 addresses: one from the 12::/64 network, and the second from the 45::/64 network. A DHCP pool in IPv6 can contain multiple IPv6 prefixes at the same time.

Let's now configure the DHCP client on R2:

```
! On R2:

R2# show run interface Serial1/1 | begin interface

interface Serial1/1
 no ip address
 shutdown
end

R2(config)# interface Serial 1/1
R2(config-if)# ipv6 enable
R2(config-if)# ipv6 address dhcp
R2(config-if)# no shutdown
```

Now let's verify the configuration:

```
! On R2:

R2# show ipv6 interface brief Serial 1/1

Serial1/1                     [up/up]
    FE80::21C:58FF:FEB9:F778
    12::8C35:DAD7:B0C2:10BD

R2# show ipv6 dhcp interface

Serial1/1 is in client mode
  Prefix State is IDLE
  Address State is OPEN
  Renew for address will be sent in 11:58:21
  List of known servers:
    Reachable via address: FE80::FEFB:FBFF:FEA1:1520
    DUID: 00030001001759CE02B8
```

```
Preference: 0
Configuration parameters:
    IA NA: IA ID 0x00060001, T1 43200, T2 69120
      Address: 12::8C35:DAD7:B0C2:10BD/128
              preferred lifetime 86400, valid lifetime 172800
              expires at Jul 08 2016 04:15 AM (172701 seconds)
    DNS server: 2000:2222::2
    Domain name: example.com
    Information refresh time: 0
Prefix Rapid-Commit: disabled
Address Rapid-Commit: disabled
```

Task 4

Reconfigure R5 to acquire its IPv6 address from R4 (the DHCP server) using two messages instead of four.

The DHCPv6 client can acquire its IPv6 address and optional parameters from a DHCP server in two ways:

- **Rapid-commit:** In this process, only two messages are exchanged: a Solicit from the client to the server, and a Reply from the server to the client.

- **Default:** The DHCP client and server exchange four DHCP messages: Solicit, Advertise, Request, and Reply.

Before the task is configured, let's enable **debug ipv6 dhcp**, reset the s1/4 interface on R5 to the default configuration, and then set up the **rapid-commit** feature:

```
! On R5:

R5(config)# default interface Serial 1/4
Interface Serial1/4 set to default configuration


R5# debug ipv6 dhcp
   IPv6 DHCP debugging is on


R5(config)# interface Serial 1/4
R5(config-if)# shutdown
R5(config-if)# ipv6 enable
R5(config-if)# ipv6 address dhcp rapid-commit
```

The **rapid-commit** option must be configured both on the DHCP client and the DHCP server to be effective. Here's how to configure the DHCP server for **rapid-commit**:

```
! On R4:

R4(config)# interface Serial 1/5
R4(config-if)# shutdown
R4(config-if)# ipv6 dhcp server TST rapid-commit
R4(config-if)# no shutdown

! On R5:

R5(config-if)# interface Serial 1/4
R5(config-if)# no shutdown
```

Let's verify the output of the **debug** command:

```
IPv6 DHCP: Sending SOLICIT to FF02::1:2 on Serial1/4
IPv6 DHCP: Received REPLY from FE80::217:59FF:FECE:2B8 on Serial1/4
IPv6 DHCP: Adding server FE80::217:59FF:FECE:2B8
IPv6 DHCP: Processing options
IPv6 DHCP: Adding address 45::A58D:F28F:9901:DA14/128 to Serial1/4
IPv6 DHCP: T1 set to expire in 43200 seconds
IPv6 DHCP: T2 set to expire in 69120 seconds
IPv6 DHCP: Configuring DNS server 2001:1:1111::1
IPv6 DHCP: Configuring domain name example.com
```

As you can see, only two messages were exchanged.

Task 5

ISP-A (represented by R4) has an IPv6 prefix of 46:1:1::/48, and it needs to automatically subnet this prefix into /56 subnets for its existing and future clients as well as assign the entire resulting /56 prefixes to the customers dynamically.

Company A (represented by R6) should acquire a /56 prefix from the ISP-A (R4) and automatically subnet this prefix into /64 subnetworks. The third subnet should be automatically assigned to its s1/3 interface, with the host portion of its IPv6 address as ::33. The seventh subnet should be automatically assigned to its F0/1 interface, with the host portion of its IPv6 address as ::77.

R3 and R7 should automatically acquire the network portion of their IPv6 addresses from R6 as well as auto-generate the host portion of their IPv6 addresses using the Modified EUI-64 format. Also, R3 and R7 should use R6 as their default gateway. Both R3 and R7 should have reachability to R4's F0/0 IPv6 address.

Do not configure any static routes, dynamic routing, or complete static IPv6 addresses to accomplish this task.

Figure 11-3 shows the bits used by the provider to generate /56 subnets. When a customer requests a prefix, it is given one of these /56 subnets on a first-come-first-serve basis.

	Subnet Bits Used by ISP							Bits NOT Subnetted				Bits Subnetted by the customer				Subnets Used by the Provider
49	50	51	52	53	54	55	56	57	58	59	60	61	62	63	64	
0	0	0	0	0	0	0	0	0	0	0	0	0	0	0	0	46:1:1::/56
0	0	0	0	0	0	0	1	0	0	0	0	0	0	0	0	46:1:1:100::/56
0	0	0	0	0	0	1	0	0	0	0	0	0	0	0	0	46:1:1:200::/56
0	0	0	0	0	0	1	1	0	0	0	0	0	0	0	0	46:1:1:300::/56
⋮	⋮	⋮	⋮	⋮	⋮	⋮	⋮	⋮	⋮	⋮	⋮	⋮	⋮	⋮	⋮	
1	1	1	1	1	1	1	1	0	0	0	0	0	0	0	0	46:1:1:FF00::/56

Figure 11-3   *Provider Bits Used to Generate /56 Subnets*

Figure 11-4 shows the bits that are given to the customer. The customer can use the remaining bits to generate up to 256 networks.

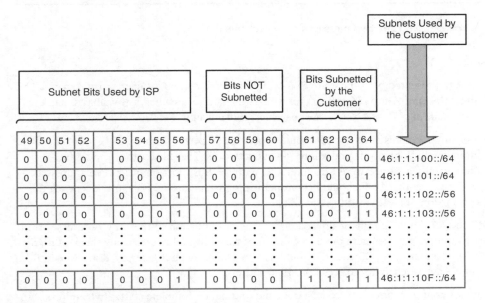

	Subnet Bits Used by ISP							Bits NOT Subnetted				Bits Subnetted by the Customer				Subnets Used by the Customer
49	50	51	52	53	54	55	56	57	58	59	60	61	62	63	64	
0	0	0	0	0	0	0	1	0	0	0	0	0	0	0	0	46:1:1:100::/64
0	0	0	0	0	0	0	1	0	0	0	0	0	0	0	1	46:1:1:101::/64
0	0	0	0	0	0	0	1	0	0	0	0	0	0	1	0	46:1:1:102::/56
0	0	0	0	0	0	0	1	0	0	0	0	0	0	1	1	46:1:1:103::/56
⋮	⋮	⋮	⋮	⋮	⋮	⋮	⋮	⋮	⋮	⋮	⋮	⋮	⋮	⋮	⋮	
0	0	0	0	0	0	0	1	0	0	0	0	1	1	1	1	46:1:1:10F::/64

Figure 11-4   *Bits Provided to the Customer*

To resolve this task, you need to configure a DHCP feature called *prefix delegation*. The purpose of the prefix delegation mechanism is to delegate entire prefixes (not just individual address from within a prefix) to customer routers automatically. A prefix delegated to a customer can then be freely subnetted by the customer according to their needs.

In this topology, R4 is the delegating router. Let's see the existing configuration of R4's f0/0 interface:

```
! On R4:


R4# show run interface FastEthernet 0/0 | begin interface


interface FastEthernet0/0
 no ip address
 duplex auto
 speed auto
 ipv6 address FE80::4 link-local
 ipv6 address 46::4/64
 ipv6 enable
end
```

In order to accomplish this task, you need to configure a local pool that instructs the router to hand out /56 prefixes from the 46:1:1::/48 range:

```
! On R4:


R4(config)# ipv6 local pool 123 46:1:1::/48 56
```

Let's verify the configuration:

```
R4# show ipv6 local pool

Pool                  Prefix                             Free  In use
123                   46:1:1::/48                        256       0
```

Next, you need to configure a regular DHCPv6 pool called "ISP." The DHCP pool will reference the local pool called "123" and assign a lifetime of infinity to every prefix leased from the pool.

The name of the DHCP pool can be anything (in this case, "ISP" is used).

```
R4(config)# ipv6 dhcp pool ISP
R4(config-dhcpv6)# prefix-delegation pool 123 lifetime infinite infinite
```

Assign the pool to the f0/0 interface of R4 facing R6:

```
R4(config)# interface FastEthernet 0/0
R4(config-if)# ipv6 dhcp server ISP
```

Next, R6 will act as the typical CPE (customer premises equipment) router. Its f0/0 interface will be considered a wide area network (WAN) interface for this exercise. R6 will acquire its IPv6 interface on f0/0 using SLAAC:

```
! On R6:

R6(config)# ipv6 unicast-routing
R6(config)# interface FastEthernet 0/0
R6(config-if)# ipv6 enable
R6(config-if)# ipv6 address autoconfig default
R6(config-if)# no shutdown
```

Let's verify the configuration:

```
R6# show ipv6 interface brief FastEthernet 0/0

FastEthernet0/0            [up/up]
    FE80::217:5AFF:FEAD:52AA
    46::217:5AFF:FEAD:52AA
```

Next, the **ipv6 dhcp client pd** command enables R6 to ask for a delegated prefix using DHCP and to store the assigned prefix under a tag (or a variable) named **TST**. Later on, we will refer to **TST** to use the assigned prefix and subnet it further.

```
R6(config)# interface Fast Ethernet 0/0
R6(config-if)# ipv6 dhcp client pd TST
```

Let's verify the configuration:

```
R6# show ipv6 dhcp interface

FastEthernet0/0 is in client mode
  Prefix State is OPEN
  Renew will be sent in 3d11h
  Address State is IDLE
  List of known servers:
    Reachable via address: FE80::4
    DUID: 00030001001759CE02B8
    Preference: 0
    Configuration parameters:
      IA PD: IA ID 0x00030001, T1 302400, T2 483840
```

```
      Prefix: 46:1:1::/56
                  preferred lifetime INFINITY, valid lifetime INFINITY
      Information refresh time: 0
  Prefix name: TST
  Prefix Rapid-Commit: disabled
  Address Rapid-Commit: disabled
```

You can see that prefix 46:1:1::/56 is given to R6, the Customer Edge (CE) device. Let's configure the f0/1 and s1/3 interfaces of R6:

```
R6(config)# interface FastEthernet 0/1
R6(config-if)# ipv6 enable
```

The following example shows how to enable IPv6 processing on the interface and configure an address based on the prefix tag. In the **ipv6 address** command, you refer to **TST** as the name of the variable that stores the actual assigned prefix, and then specify the remainder of the address that should be appended to the prefix stored under **TST**. Note that the value of **TST** undergoes an OR operation and demonstrates the specified remainder, and that the remainder has to be 128 bits long, obviously having leading zeros in the part that will be copied from **TST**. That is the reason for the double-colon at the beginning of the address remainder. Note that ::7:... is the seventh subnet, meaning that you are assigning the seventh subnet to this interface; if you wanted to assign the second subnet, for example, you would use ::2:... instead.

```
R6(config-if)# ipv6 address TST ::7:0:0:0:77/64
R6(config-if)# no shutdown
```

Let's verify the configuration:

```
R6# show ipv6 inter brief FastEthernet 0/1

FastEthernet0/1                [up/up]
    FE80::217:5AFF:FEAD:52AB
    46:1:1:7::77


R6# show ipv6 interface FastEthernet 0/1 | include subnet

    46:1:1:7::77, subnet is 46:1:1:7::/64


R6# ping 46::4

Type escape sequence to abort.
Sending 5, 100-byte ICMP Echos to 46::4, timeout is 2 seconds:
!!!!!
Success rate is 100 percent (5/5), round-trip min/avg/max = 28/28/28 ms
```

Because R6 is a SLAAC client, it should get a default route from R4. Let's verify this information:

```
R6# show ipv6 route static

IPv6 Routing Table - default - 7 entries
Codes: C - Connected, L - Local, S - Static, U - Per-user Static route
       B - BGP, HA - Home Agent, MR - Mobile Router, R - RIP
       I1 - ISIS L1, I2 - ISIS L2, IA - ISIS interarea, IS - ISIS summary
       D - EIGRP, EX - EIGRP external, NM - NEMO, ND - Neighbor Discovery
       l - LISP
       O - OSPF Intra, OI - OSPF Inter, OE1 - OSPF ext 1, OE2 - OSPF ext 2
       ON1 - OSPF NSSA ext 1, ON2 - OSPF NSSA ext 2
S   ::/0 [2/0]
    via FE80::4, FastEthernet0/0
S   46:1:1::/56 [1/0]
    via Null0, directly connected
```

Let's configure the s1/3 interface of R6:

```
R6(config)# interface Serial 1/3
R6(config-if)# ipv6 enable
R6(config-if)# ipv6 address TST ::3:0:0:0:33/64
R6(config-if)# no shutdown
To verify the configuration:
R6# show ipv6 interface Serial 1/3 | include subnet
    46:1:1:3::33, subnet is 46:1:1:3::/64
```

Let's configure R7 and R3 as a SLAAC client to R6:

```
! On R7:

R7(config)# interface GigabitEthernet 0/1
R7(config-if)# ipv6 enable
R7(config-if)# ipv6 address autoconfig default
R7(config-if)# no shutdown
```

Let's verify the configuration:

```
R7# show ipv6 interface brief GigabitEthernet 0/1

GigabitEthernet0/1    [up/up]
    FE80::26E9:B3FF:FEAB:4B21
    46:1:1:7:26E9:B3FF:FEAB:4B21

! On R3:
```

```
R3(config)# interface Serial 1/6
R3(config-if)# clock rate 64000
R3(config-if)# ipv6 enable
R3(config-if)# ipv6 address autoconfig default
R3(config-if)# no shutdown
```

Let's take a closer look at the ipv6 address that is assigned to R7's Serial1/6 interface.

```
! On R3:


R7# show ipv6 interface brief Serial 1/6


Serial1/6                    [up/up]
    FE80::21C:58FF:FEF6:F660
    46:1:1:3:21C:58FF:FEF6:F660
```

You can see that R7 has two injected routes, both injected via SLAAC: the first one is the default route, and the second is the global address prefix.

```
! On R7:


R7# show ipv6 route


IPv6 Routing Table - default - 4 entries
Codes: C - Connected, L - Local, S - Static, U - Per-user Static route
       B - BGP, HA - Home Agent, MR - Mobile Router, R - RIP
       H - NHRP, I1 - ISIS L1, I2 - ISIS L2, IA - ISIS interarea
       IS - ISIS summary, D - EIGRP, EX - EIGRP external, NM - NEMO
       ND - ND Default, NDp - ND Prefix, DCE - Destination, NDr - Redirect
       O - OSPF Intra, OI - OSPF Inter, OE1 - OSPF ext 1, OE2 - OSPF ext 2
       ON1 - OSPF NSSA ext 1, ON2 - OSPF NSSA ext 2, ls - LISP site
       ld - LISP dyn-EID, a - Application
ND   ::/0 [2/0]
     via FE80::217:5AFF:FEAD:52AB, GigabitEthernet0/1
NDp 46:1:1:7::/64 [2/0]
     via GigabitEthernet0/1, directly connected
L    46:1:1:7:26E9:B3FF:FEAB:4B21/128 [0/0]
     via GigabitEthernet0/1, receive
L    FF00::/8 [0/0]
     via Null0, receive


R7# ping 46::4


Type escape sequence to abort.
Sending 5, 100-byte ICMP Echos to 46::4, timeout is 2 seconds:
```

```
! ! ! ! !
Success rate is 100 percent (5/5), round-trip min/avg/max = 1/3/12 ms


R7# ping 46:1:1:3:21C:58FF:FEF6:F660


Type escape sequence to abort.
Sending 5, 100-byte ICMP Echos to ping 46:1:1:3:21C:58FF:FEF6:F660, timeout is 2
  seconds:
! ! ! ! !
Success rate is 100 percent (5/5), round-trip min/avg/max = 28/28/32 ms


! On R3:


R3# show ipv6 inter brief serial1/6


Serial1/6                      [up/up]
    FE80::21C:58FF:FEF6:F660
    46:1:1:3:21C:58FF:FEF6:F660
```

You can see that R3 has a default route that was given to it because of the SLAAC
process. Note how different IOS versions display routes differently. Because R7 is
running 15.4T, it shows the default route as ND and the connected route as NDp. R3 is
running 15.1(4), and the ND and NDp designations are not there.

```
R3# show ipv6 route


IPv6 Routing Table - default - 4 entries
Codes: C - Connected, L - Local, S - Static, U - Per-user Static route
       B - BGP, HA - Home Agent, MR - Mobile Router, R - RIP
       I1 - ISIS L1, I2 - ISIS L2, IA - ISIS interarea, IS - ISIS summary
       D - EIGRP, EX - EIGRP external, NM - NEMO, ND - Neighbor Discovery
       l - LISP
       O - OSPF Intra, OI - OSPF Inter, OE1 - OSPF ext 1, OE2 - OSPF ext 2
       ON1 - OSPF NSSA ext 1, ON2 - OSPF NSSA ext 2
S   ::/0 [2/0]
     via FE80::217:5AFF:FEAD:52AA, Serial1/6
C   46:1:1:3::/64 [0/0]
     via Serial1/6, directly connected
L   46:1:1:3:21C:58FF:FEF6:F660/128 [0/0]
     via Serial1/6, receive
L   FF00::/8 [0/0]
     via Null0, receive
```

```
R3# ping 46::4

Type escape sequence to abort.
Sending 5, 100-byte ICMP Echos to 46::4, timeout is 2 seconds:
!!!!!
Success rate is 100 percent (5/5), round-trip min/avg/max = 28/29/32 ms


R3# ping 46:1:1:7:26E9:B3FF:FEAB:4B21

Type escape sequence to abort.
Sending 5, 100-byte ICMP Echos to 46:1:1:7:26E9:B3FF:FEAB:4B21, timeout is 2
  seconds:
!!!!!
Success rate is 100 percent (5/5), round-trip min/avg/max = 28/28/32 ms
```

Erase the startup configuration of the routers and reload them before proceeding to the next lab.

Lab 11-2: Configuring OSPFv3

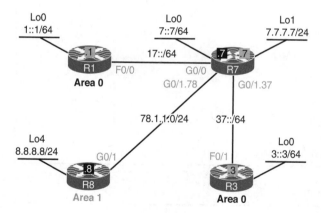

Figure 11-5   *Configuring OSPFv3*

Figure 11-5 illustrates the topology that will be used in the following lab.

Task 1

Configure OSPF and OSPFv3 on the routers in this topology based on the following policy:

- Configure the F0/0 interface of R1, the G0/0 interface of R7, and their loopback0 interfaces in Area 0.

- Configure R8 and its loopback interface in Area 1.

- R7's G0/1.78 should be configured in Area 1, and its G0/1.37 should be configured in Area 0.

- R7 and R8 should accomplish this task using an **address-family** configuration section.

- The loopback interface prefixes should be advertised with their correct mask.

IPv6 unicast routing must be explicitly enabled before any routing protocol can be configured:

```
! On R1:

R1(config)# ipv6 unicast-routing

R1(config)# ipv6 router ospf 1
```

You should see the following console message stating that since OSPFv3 could not find an IPv4-configured interface, it could not assign a router ID. Let's statically assign a router ID to this process:

```
%OSPFv3-4-NORTRID: OSPFv3 process 1 could not pick a router-id, please configure
  manually

R1(config-rtr)# router-id 0.0.0.1

R1(config)# interface loopback 0
R1(config-if)# ipv6 address 1::1/64
R1(config-if)# ipv6 ospf 1 area 0

R1(config)# interface FastEthernet0/0
R1(config-if)# ipv6 address 17::1/64
R1(config-if)# ipv6 ospf 1 area 0
```

Now let's verify the configuration:

```
! On R1:

R1# show ipv6 ospf interface brief

Interface    PID   Area          Intf ID   Cost  State Nbrs F/C
Lo0          1     0             22        1     LOOP  0/0
Fa0/0        1     0             3         1     DR    0/0


R1# show ipv6 ospf inter loopback 0

Loopback0 is up, line protocol is up
```

```
Link Local Address FE80::20A:B8FF:FE6B:DFD0, Interface ID 22
Area 0, Process ID 1, Instance ID 0, Router ID 0.0.0.1
Network Type LOOPBACK, Cost: 1
Loopback interface is treated as a stub Host
```

You can see that the loopback0 interface for R1 is treated as a host. This is the same behavior you know from OSPFv2. This will also cause any global address configured on the loopback0 interface to be advertised with a prefix length of 128 regardless of the true configured prefix length. Let's therefore change the network type to **point-to-point**:

```
R1(config)# interface loopback 0
R1(config-if)# ipv6 ospf network point-to-point
```

Let's verify the configuration:

```
! On R1:

R1# show ipv6 ospf interface loopback 0

Loopback0 is up, line protocol is up
  Link Local Address FE80::20A:B8FF:FE6B:DFD0, Interface ID 22
  Area 0, Process ID 1, Instance ID 0, Router ID 0.0.0.1
  Network Type POINT_TO_POINT, Cost: 1

(The rest of the output is omitted for brevity)
```

OSPF on Cisco IOS-based routers can be configured in three ways: OSPFv2 configuration for IPv4 (**router ospf**), OSPFv3 configuration (**ipv6 router ospf**), and OSPFv3 using an address family (**router ospfv3**). The benefit of configuring OSPFv3 using the address family concept is that this configuration leverages the recently added OSPFv3 support to advertise both IPv4 and IPv6 prefixes, even though the transport always will be IPv6-based, and for each address family, OSPFv3 will start a separate instance.

```
! On R7:

R7(config)# ipv6 unicast-routing
```

The configuration starts with **router ospfv3** followed by the process ID:

```
R7(config)# router ospfv3 1
```

The router ID is configured directly under **address-family**:

```
R7(config-router)# address-family ipv6 unicast
R7(config-router)# router-id 0.0.0.7
```

Running OSPFv3 on the interfaces is done by configuring **ospfv3** followed by the process ID 1, followed by the **ipv6** keyword to indicate that this instance is being started for IPv6. If this instance were intended for IPv4, the **ipv4** keyword would be used instead. Finally, the **area** keyword is used to indicate the area.

```
R7(config)# interface loopback 0
R7(config-if)# ipv6 address 7::7/64
R7(config-if)# ospfv3 1 ipv6 area 0


R7(config-if)# ospfv3 network point-to-point


R7(config)# interface GigabitEthernet 0/0
R7(config-if)# ipv6 address 17::7/64
R7(config-if)# ospfv3 1 ipv6 area 0
```

You should see the following console message:

```
%OSPFv3-5-ADJCHG: Process 1, IPv6, Nbr 0.0.0.1 on GigabitEthernet0/0 from LOADING
to FULL, Loading Done
```

Let's verify the configuration:

```
! On R7:

R7# show ipv6 route ospf

IPv6 Routing Table - default - 8 entries
Codes: C - Connected, L - Local, S - Static, U - Per-user Static route
       B - BGP, HA - Home Agent, MR - Mobile Router, R - RIP
       H - NHRP, I1 - ISIS L1, I2 - ISIS L2, IA - ISIS interarea
       IS - ISIS summary, D - EIGRP, EX - EIGRP external, NM - NEMO
       ND - ND Default, NDp - ND Prefix, DCE - Destination, NDr - Redirect
       O - OSPF Intra, OI - OSPF Inter, OE1 - OSPF ext 1, OE2 - OSPF ext 2
       ON1 - OSPF NSSA ext 1, ON2 - OSPF NSSA ext 2, ls - LISP site
       ld - LISP dyn-EID, a - Application
O   1::/64 [110/2]
      via FE80::1, GigabitEthernet0/0
```

```
R7# show ipv6 ospf neighbor

            OSPFv3 Router with ID (0.0.0.7) (Process ID 1)


Neighbor ID     Pri   State       Dead Time   Interface ID   Interface
0.0.0.1           1   FULL/DR     00:00:39    3              GigabitEthernet0/0
```

You can do the preceding **show** command using the following command:

```
R7# show ospfv3 neighbor

            OSPFv3 1 address-family ipv6 (router-id 0.0.0.7)


Neighbor ID     Pri   State       Dead Time   Interface ID   Interface
0.0.0.1           1   FULL/DR     00:00:32    3              GigabitEthernet0/0
```

Let's configure OSPFv3 on the g0/1.37 interface:

```
R7(config)# interface GigabitEthernet0/1.37
R7(config-subif)# ipv6 address 37::7/64
R7(config-subif)# ospfv3 1 ipv6 area 0
```

Now you should configure R3 and verify its adjacency with R7:

```
! On R3:

R3(config)# ipv6 unicast-routing

R3(config)# ipv6 router ospf 1
R3(config-rtr)# router-id 0.0.0.3

R3(config)# interface FastEthernet 0/1
R3(config-if)# ipv6 address 37::3/64
R3(config-if)# ipv6 ospf 1 area 0
```

You should see the following console message:

```
%OSPFv3-5-ADJCHG: Process 1, Nbr 0.0.0.7 on FastEthernet0/1 from LOADING to FULL,
  Loading Done

R3(config-if)# interface loopback 0
R3(config-if)# ipv6 address 3::3/64
R3(config-if)# ipv6 ospf network point-to-point
R3(config-if)# ipv6 ospf 1 area 0
```

Let's verify the configuration:

```
! On R3:

R3# show ipv6 route ospf

IPv6 Routing Table - default - 8 entries
Codes: C - Connected, L - Local, S - Static, U - Per-user Static route
       B - BGP, HA - Home Agent, MR - Mobile Router, R - RIP
       I1 - ISIS L1, I2 - ISIS L2, IA - ISIS interarea, IS - ISIS summary
       D - EIGRP, EX - EIGRP external, NM - NEMO, ND - Neighbor Discovery
       l - LISP
       O - OSPF Intra, OI - OSPF Inter, OE1 - OSPF ext 1, OE2 - OSPF ext 2
       ON1 - OSPF NSSA ext 1, ON2 - OSPF NSSA ext 2
O    1::/64 [110/3]
     via FE80::7, FastEthernet0/1
O    7::/64 [110/2]
     via FE80::7, FastEthernet0/1
O    17::/64 [110/2]
     via FE80::7, FastEthernet0/1


R3# ping 7::7

Type escape sequence to abort.
Sending 5, 100-byte ICMP Echos to 7::7, timeout is 2 seconds:
!!!!!
Success rate is 100 percent (5/5), round-trip min/avg/max = 0/0/4 ms


R3# ping 7::7 source lo0

Type escape sequence to abort.
Sending 5, 100-byte ICMP Echos to 7::7, timeout is 2 seconds:
Packet sent with a source address of 3::3
!!!!!
Success rate is 100 percent (5/5), round-trip min/avg/max = 0/0/0 ms
```

Let's configure OSPFv3 on R7 and R8 for IPv4:

```
! On R7:
R7(config)# router ospfv3 1
R7(config-router)# address-family ipv4 unicast
R7(config-router-af)# router-id 0.0.0.7

R7(config)# interface GigabitEthernet 0/1.78
R7(config-subif)# ip address 78.1.1.7 255.255.255.0
R7(config-subif)# ospfv3 1 ipv4 area 1
```

You should see the following console message:

```
% OSPFv3: IPV6 is not enabled on this interface
```

The reason you get this notification is that even though you are forming an OSPFv3 adjacency through the g0/1.78 subinterface, which should advertise IPv4 networks, OSPFv3 always uses IPv6 to exchange messages. To fix this problem, you need to enable IPv6 on this interface. This will allow the interface to have its own link-local address that is entirely sufficient to run OSPFv3.

```
R7(config-subif)# ipv6 enable
R7(config-subif)# ospfv3 1 ipv4 area 1

R7(config)# interface loopback 1
R7(config-if)# ip address 7.7.7.7 255.255.255.0
R7(config-if)# ipv6 enable
R7(config-if)# ospfv3 1 ipv4 area 1
R7(config-if)# ospfv3 network point-to-point
```

Now let's configure R8:

```
! On R8:

R8(config)# router ospfv3 1
```

You should see the following console message:

```
%OSPFv3: IPv6 routing not enabled
```

Note The preceding console message states that **ipv6 unicast-routing** must be enabled in order for you to configure OSPFv3.

Let's enable IPv6 unicast routing:

```
R8(config)# ipv6 unicast-routing

R8(config)# router ospfv3 1
R8(config-router)# address-family ipv4 unicast
R8(config-router-af)# router-id 0.0.0.8

R8(config)# interface GigabitEthernet 0/1
R8(config-if)# ip address 78.1.1.8 255.255.255.0
R8(config-if)# ipv6 enable
R8(config-if)# ospfv3 1 ipv4 area 1
```

```
R8(config)# interface loopback 0
R8(config-if)# ip address 8.8.8.8 255.255.255.0
R8(config-if)# ipv6 enable
R8(config-if)# ospfv3 1 ipv4 area 1
```

You should see the following console message:

```
%OSPFv3-5-ADJCHG: Process 1, IPv4, Nbr 0.0.0.7 on GigabitEthernet0/1 from LOADING
to FULL, Loading Done
```

Let's verify the configuration:

```
! On R7:

R7# show ipv6 route ospf

IPv6 Routing Table - default - 9 entries
Codes: C - Connected, L - Local, S - Static, U - Per-user Static route
       B - BGP, HA - Home Agent, MR - Mobile Router, R - RIP
       H - NHRP, I1 - ISIS L1, I2 - ISIS L2, IA - ISIS interarea
       IS - ISIS summary, D - EIGRP, EX - EIGRP external, NM - NEMO
       ND - ND Default, NDp - ND Prefix, DCE - Destination, NDr - Redirect
       O - OSPF Intra, OI - OSPF Inter, OE1 - OSPF ext 1, OE2 - OSPF ext 2
       ON1 - OSPF NSSA ext 1, ON2 - OSPF NSSA ext 2, ls - LISP site
       ld - LISP dyn-EID, a - Application
O   1::/64 [110/2]
     via FE80::1, GigabitEthernet0/0
O   3::/64 [110/2]
     via FE80::3, GigabitEthernet0/1.37


R7# show ip route ospfv3 | begin Gate
Gateway of last resort is not set

     8.0.0.0/32 is subnetted, 1 subnets
O       8.8.8.8 [110/1] via 78.1.1.8, 00:03:48, GigabitEthernet0/1.78
```

You can see that loopback0 on R8 is not advertised with its correct mask. Let's change the network type and verify:

Note The **ip ospf network point-to-point** command will not work because that is an OSPFv2 command. Because we have configured OSPFv3, the OSPFv3 command should be used to accomplish this task.

```
! On R8:


R8(config)# interface loopback 0
R8(config-if)# ospfv3 network point-to-point


! On R7:


R7# show ip route ospfv3 | begin Gate
Gateway of last resort is not set

     8.0.0.0/24 is subnetted, 1 subnets
O        8.8.8.0 [110/2] via 78.1.1.8, 00:00:23, GigabitEthernet0/1.78
```

Erase the startup configuration of the routers and reload before proceeding to the next lab.

Lab 11-3: Summarization of Internal and External Networks

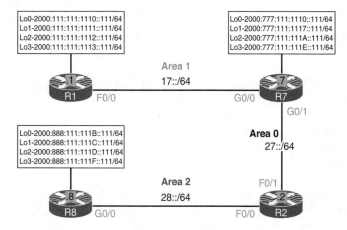

Figure 11-6 *Summarization of Internal and External Networks*

Figure 11-6 illustrates the topology that will be used in the following lab.

Task 1

Configure OSPFv3 based on the following requirements:

■ Configure OSPFv3 on R1 and run all its directly connected interfaces in Area 1. Do not use **address-family** to configure this router. Configure and advertise the loopback interfaces with their correct mask. The RID of this router should be set to 0.0.0.1.

■ Configure OSPFv3 on R7 using **address-family**. This router should run OSPFv3 Area 1 on its G0/0 interface and OSPFv3 Area 0 on its G0/1 interface. The loopback interfaces of this router should be configured in Area 0. Configure and advertise the loopback interfaces with their correct mask. The RID of this router should be set to 0.0.0.7.

■ Configure OSPFv3 on R2 and run its F0/1 interface in Area 0 and its F0/0 interface in Area 2. Do not use **address-family** to configure this router. The RID of this router should be set to 0.0.0.2.

■ Configure OSPFv3 on R8 using **address-family**. This router should run OSPFv3 Area 2 on its G0/0 interface. The loopback interfaces of this router should be injected into the OSPFv3 routing domain. The RID of this router should be set to 0.0.0.8.

```
! On R1:

R1(config)# ipv6 unicast-routing

R1(config)# ipv6 router ospf 1
R1(config-rtr)# router-id 0.0.0.1

R1(config)# interface FastEthernet 0/0
R1(config-if)# ipv6 address 17::1/64
R1(config-if)# ipv6 ospf 1 area 1

R1(config)# interface Loopback 0
R1(config-if)# ipv6 address 2000:111:111:1110::111/64
R1(config-if)# interface Loopback 1
R1(config-if)# ipv6 address 2000:111:111:1111::111/64
R1(config-if)# interface Loopback 2
R1(config-if)# ipv6 address 2000:111:111:1112::111/64
R1(config-if)# interface Loopback 3
R1(config-if)# ipv6 address 2000:111:111:1113::111/64
R1(config-if)# interface range Loopback 0 - 3
R1(config-if-range)# ipv6 ospf 1 area 1
R1(config-if-range)# ipv6 ospf network point-to-point
```

Let's verify the configuration:

```
R1# show ipv6 ospf interface brief

Interface    PID    Area        Intf ID    Cost    State  Nbrs F/C
Lo1          1      1           23         1       P2P    0/0
Lo2          1      1           24         1       P2P    0/0
Lo3          1      1           25         1       P2P    0/0
Lo0          1      1           22         1       P2P    0/0
Fa0/0        1      1           3          1       DR     0/0
```

```
! On R7:

R7(config)# ipv6 unicast-routing

R7(config)# router ospfv3 1
R7(config-router)# address-family ipv6 unicast
R7(config-router-af)# router-id 0.0.0.7

R7(config)# interface GigabitEthernet 0/1
R7(config-if)# ipv6 address 27::7/64
R7(config-if)# ospfv3 1 ipv6 area 0

R7(config)# interface GigabitEthernet 0/0
R7(config-if)# ipv6 address 17::7/64
R7(config-if)# ospfv3 1 ipv6 area 1
```

You should see the following console message:

```
%OSPFv3-5-ADJCHG: Process 1, IPv6, Nbr 0.0.0.1 on GigabitEthernet0/0 from LOADING
to FULL, Loading Done
```

```
R7(config)# interface Loopback 0
R7(config-if)# ipv6 address 2000:777:111:1110::111/64
R7(config-if)# interface Loopback 1
R7(config-if)# ipv6 address 2000:777:111:1117::111/64
R7(config-if)# interface Loopback 2
R7(config-if)# ipv6 address 2000:777:111:111A::111/64
R7(config-if)# interface Loopback 3
R7(config-if)# ipv6 address 2000:777:111:111E::111/64
R7(config-if)# interface range Loopback 0 - 3
R7(config-if-range)# ospfv3 1 ipv6 area 0
R7(config-if-range)# ospfv3 network point-to-point
```

Let's verify the configuration:

```
R7# show ospfv3 interface brief

Interface    PID   Area          AF        Cost  State Nbrs F/C
Lo0          1     0             ipv6      1     P2P   0/0
Lo1          1     0             ipv6      1     P2P   0/0
Lo2          1     0             ipv6      1     P2P   0/0
Lo3          1     0             ipv6      1     P2P   0/0
```

```
Gi0/1        1     0              ipv6     1    DR     0/0
Gi0/0        1     1              ipv6     1    BDR    1/1


R7# show ipv6 route ospf


IPv6 Routing Table - default - 17 entries
Codes: C - Connected, L - Local, S - Static, U - Per-user Static route
       B - BGP, HA - Home Agent, MR - Mobile Router, R - RIP
       H - NHRP, I1 - ISIS L1, I2 - ISIS L2, IA - ISIS interarea
       IS - ISIS summary, D - EIGRP, EX - EIGRP external, NM - NEMO
       ND - ND Default, NDp - ND Prefix, DCE - Destination, NDr - Redirect
       O - OSPF Intra, OI - OSPF Inter, OE1 - OSPF ext 1, OE2 - OSPF ext 2
       ON1 - OSPF NSSA ext 1, ON2 - OSPF NSSA ext 2, ls - LISP site
       ld - LISP dyn-EID, a - Application
O    2000:111:111:1110::/64 [110/2]
     via FE80::1, GigabitEthernet0/0
O    2000:111:111:1111::/64 [110/2]
     via FE80::1, GigabitEthernet0/0
O    2000:111:111:1112::/64 [110/2]
     via FE80::1, GigabitEthernet0/0
O    2000:111:111:1113::/64 [110/2]
     via FE80::1, GigabitEthernet0/0


R7# show ospfv3 neighbor


         OSPFv3 1 address-family ipv6 (router-id 0.0.0.7)


Neighbor ID      Pri   State      Dead Time   Interface ID   Interface
0.0.0.1            1   FULL/DR    00:00:37    3              GigabitEthernet0/0


! On R2:


R2(config)# ipv6 unicast-routing

R2(config)# ipv6 router ospf 1
R2(config-rtr)# router-id 0.0.0.2

R2(config)# interface FastEthernet 0/1
R2(config-if)# ipv6 address 27::2/64
R2(config-if)# ipv6 ospf 1 area 0

R2(config)# interface FastEthernet 0/0
R2(config-if)# ipv6 address 28::2/64
R2(config-if)# ipv6 ospf 1 area 2
```

You should see the following console message:

```
%OSPFv3-5-ADJCHG: Process 1, Nbr 0.0.0.7 on FastEthernet0/1 from LOADING to FULL,
Loading Done
```

Let's verify the configuration:

```
! On R2:

R2# show ipv6 route ospf

IPv6 Routing Table - default - 14 entries
Codes: C - Connected, L - Local, S - Static, U - Per-user Static route
       B - BGP, HA - Home Agent, MR - Mobile Router, R - RIP
       I1 - ISIS L1, I2 - ISIS L2, IA - ISIS interarea, IS - ISIS summary
       D - EIGRP, EX - EIGRP external, NM - NEMO, ND - Neighbor Discovery
       l - LISP
       O - OSPF Intra, OI - OSPF Inter, OE1 - OSPF ext 1, OE2 - OSPF ext 2
       ON1 - OSPF NSSA ext 1, ON2 - OSPF NSSA ext 2
OI  17::/64 [110/2]
     via FE80::7, FastEthernet0/1
OI  2000:111:111:1110::/64 [110/3]
     via FE80::7, FastEthernet0/1
OI  2000:111:111:1111::/64 [110/3]
     via FE80::7, FastEthernet0/1
OI  2000:111:111:1112::/64 [110/3]
     via FE80::7, FastEthernet0/1
OI  2000:111:111:1113::/64 [110/3]
     via FE80::7, FastEthernet0/1
O   2000:111:111:1117::/64 [110/2]
     via FE80::7, FastEthernet0/1
O   2000:111:111:111A::/64 [110/2]
     via FE80::7, FastEthernet0/1
O   2000:111:111:111E::/64 [110/2]
     via FE80::7, FastEthernet0/1
O   2000:777:111:1110::/64 [110/2]
     via FE80::7, FastEthernet0/1
```

Because the task does not specify the area in which the loopback interfaces on R8 should be configured, the only other way to run them in OSPF is to redistribute them into the OSPF routing domain. Let's configure R8 based on the requirements of this task:

```
! On R8:

R8(config)# ipv6 unicast-routing

R8(config)# interface Loopback 0
R8(config-if)# ipv6 address 2000:888:111:111B::111/64
R8(config-if)# interface Loopback 1
R8(config-if)# ipv6 address 2000:888:111:111C::111/64
R8(config-if)# interface Loopback 2
R8(config-if)# ipv6 address 2000:888:111:111D::111/64
R8(config-if)# interface Loopback 3
R8(config-if)# ipv6 address 2000:888:111:111F::111/64

R8(config)# interface GigabitEthernet 0/0
R8(config-if)# ipv6 address 28::8/64
R8(config-if)# ospfv3 1 ipv6 area 2

R8(config)# route-map tst
R8(config-route-map)# match interface lo0 lo1 lo2 lo3

R8(config)# router ospfv3 1
R8(config-router)# address-family ipv6 unicast
R8(config-router-af)# router-id 0.0.0.8
R8(config-router-af)# redistribute connected route-map tst
```

You should see the following console message:

```
%OSPFv3-5-ADJCHG: Process 1, IPv6, Nbr 0.0.0.2 on GigabitEthernet0/0 from LOADING
to FULL, Loading Done
```

Let's verify the configuration:

```
! On R8:

R8# show ipv6 route ospf

IPv6 Routing Table - default - 21 entries
Codes: C - Connected, L - Local, S - Static, U - Per-user Static route
       B - BGP, HA - Home Agent, MR - Mobile Router, R - RIP
       H - NHRP, I1 - ISIS L1, I2 - ISIS L2, IA - ISIS interarea
       IS - ISIS summary, D - EIGRP, EX - EIGRP external, NM - NEMO
       ND - ND Default, NDp - ND Prefix, DCE - Destination, NDr - Redirect
       O - OSPF Intra, OI - OSPF Inter, OE1 - OSPF ext 1, OE2 - OSPF ext 2
       ON1 - OSPF NSSA ext 1, ON2 - OSPF NSSA ext 2, ls - LISP site
       ld - LISP dyn-EID, a - Application
```

```
OI  17::/64 [110/3]
     via FE80::2, GigabitEthernet0/0
OI  27::/64 [110/2]
     via FE80::2, GigabitEthernet0/0
OI  2000:111:111:1110::/64 [110/4]
     via FE80::2, GigabitEthernet0/0
OI  2000:111:111:1111::/64 [110/4]
     via FE80::2, GigabitEthernet0/0
OI  2000:111:111:1112::/64 [110/4]
     via FE80::2, GigabitEthernet0/0
OI  2000:111:111:1113::/64 [110/4]
     via FE80::2, GigabitEthernet0/0
OI  2000:111:111:1117::/64 [110/3]
     via FE80::2, GigabitEthernet0/0
OI  2000:111:111:111A::/64 [110/3]
     via FE80::2, GigabitEthernet0/0
OI  2000:111:111:111E::/64 [110/3]
     via FE80::2, GigabitEthernet0/0
OI  2000:777:111:1110::/64 [110/3]
     via FE80::2, GigabitEthernet0/0


! On R1:


R1# show ipv6 route ospf

IPv6 Routing Table - default - 18 entries
Codes: C - Connected, L - Local, S - Static, U - Per-user Static route
       B - BGP, HA - Home Agent, MR - Mobile Router, R - RIP
       I1 - ISIS L1, I2 - ISIS L2, IA - ISIS interarea, IS - ISIS summary
       D - EIGRP, EX - EIGRP external, NM - NEMO, ND - Neighbor Discovery
       l - LISP
       O - OSPF Intra, OI - OSPF Inter, OE1 - OSPF ext 1, OE2 - OSPF ext 2
       ON1 - OSPF NSSA ext 1, ON2 - OSPF NSSA ext 2
OI  27::/64 [110/2]
     via FE80::7, FastEthernet0/0
OI  28::/64 [110/3]
     via FE80::7, FastEthernet0/0
OI  2000:111:111:1117::/64 [110/2]
     via FE80::7, FastEthernet0/0
OI  2000:111:111:111A::/64 [110/2]
     via FE80::7, FastEthernet0/0
OI  2000:111:111:111E::/64 [110/2]
     via FE80::7, FastEthernet0/0
```

```
OI   2000:777:111:1110::/64 [110/2]
     via FE80::7, FastEthernet0/0
OE2 2000:888:111:111B::/64 [110/20]
     via FE80::7, FastEthernet0/0
OE2 2000:888:111:111C::/64 [110/20]
     via FE80::7, FastEthernet0/0
OE2 2000:888:111:111D::/64 [110/20]
     via FE80::7, FastEthernet0/0
OE2 2000:888:111:111F::/64 [110/20]
```

Task 2

Summarize the loopback interfaces configured on R1 and R7 in all OSPF areas. There should be a single summary route for the loopback interfaces of R1 and R7. Do not configure more than two different summary routes to accomplish this task.

In OSPF, summarization can be configured on an Area Border Router (ABR) and an Autonomous System Boundary Router (ASBR), and it's applied either to all routes coming from a given area or to redistributed networks. Because R7 is the ABR between Areas 0 and 1, you should configure R7 to summarize the networks coming from R1 when advertising them to R2.

The process of summarization in IPv6 is identical to IPv4. Let's look at the IPv6 addresses on R1:

> **Lo0:** 2000:111:111:1110::111/64
>
> **Lo1:** 2000:111:111:1111::111/64
>
> **Lo2:** 2000:111:111:1112::111/64
>
> **Lo3:** 2000:111:111:1113::111/64

You can see that they all start with 2000:111:111:111, but the last hex digit in the fourth hextet is where they differ. Let's convert the last hex digit of the fourth hextet to binary (remember that every hex digit represents four bits):

> 0 = 0 0 0 0
>
> 1 = 0 0 0 1
>
> 2 = 0 0 1 0
>
> 3 = 0 0 1 1

Counting the common identical prefixing contiguous bits, you should see the following:

> 0 = 0 0 0 0
>
> 1 = 0 0 0 1
>
> 2 = 0 0 1 0
>
> 3 = 0 0 1 1

You can see that the last two binary digits is where these hex digits differ; therefore, all the bits up to the third binary digit of the fourth hextet are identical. In other words, these four addresses are common in their first 62 bits (16 : 16 : 16 : 14) and differ afterward. Therefore, the following statement summarizes these four networks:

2000:111:111:1110::/62

Let's configure OSPFv3 to summarize these networks, but before we summarize, let's verify the routing table of R7 and look for these networks:

```
! On R7:


R7# show ipv6 route ospf | include 2000:111:111


O    2000:111:111:1110::/64 [110/2]
O    2000:111:111:1111::/64 [110/2]
O    2000:111:111:1112::/64 [110/2]
O    2000:111:111:1113::/64 [110/2]
```

Let's summarize:

```
R7(config)# router ospfv3 1
R7(config-router)# address-family ipv6 unicast
R7(config-router-af)# area 1 range 2000:111:111:1110::/62
```

Now let's verify the configuration:

```
! On R2:


R2# show ipv6 route ospf | include 2000:111:111:1110


OI   2000:111:111:1110::/62 [110/3]
```

When routes are summarized in OSPFv2, a discard route is injected. Let's verify whether the behavior is the same in OSPFv3:

```
! On R7:


R7# show ipv6 route ospf | include /62|Null


O    2000:111:111:1110::/62 [110/2]
        via Null0, directly connected
```

You can see that the discard route is injected to avoid forwarding loops just like OSPFv2.

Let's summarize the loopback interfaces configured on R7 as advertised from Area 0 into Area 1:

Lo0: 2000:777:111:1110::111/64

Lo1: 2000:777:111:1117::111/64

Lo2: 2000:777:111:111A::111/64

Lo3: 2000:777:111:111E::111/64

Once again, the last hex digit of the fourth hextet is where they differ, so let's go through the same process:

0 = 0 0 0 0

7 = 0 1 1 1

A = 1 0 1 0

E = 1 1 1 0

In this case, these four values do not share any common bit prefix. If you wanted to be very precise, the four loopbacks on R7 cannot be correctly summarized because the networks do not constitute a contiguous address space at all. However, you can always configure a larger summary network that covers all loopback networks on R7, even if it also includes networks that do not exist on R7. This is necessary to meet the requirements of this task.

The four loopback addresses on R7 match in their first 16 : 16 : 16 : 12 bits, and looking at the matching bits, you see that the summary network is

2000:777:111:1110::/60

```
R7(config)# router ospfv3 1
R7(config-router)# address-family ipv6 unicast
R7(config-router-af)# area 0 range 2000:777:111:1110::/60
```

Let's verify the configuration:

```
! On R1:

R1# show ipv6 route ospf | inc/60

OI  2000:777:111:1110::/60 [110/2]

R1# ping 2000:777:111:1117::111

Type escape sequence to abort.
Sending 5, 100-byte ICMP Echos to 2000:777:111:1117::111, timeout is 2 seconds:
!!!!!
Success rate is 100 percent (5/5), round-trip min/avg/max = 0/1/4 ms
```

You need to repeat the same configuration on R2 when advertising networks into Area 2, but before we configure the summary route for R7's loopback interfaces, let's verify the routing table of R8:

```
! On R8:


R8# show ipv6 route ospf

IPv6 Routing Table - default - 18 entries
Codes: C - Connected, L - Local, S - Static, U - Per-user Static route
       B - BGP, HA - Home Agent, MR - Mobile Router, R - RIP
       H - NHRP, I1 - ISIS L1, I2 - ISIS L2, IA - ISIS interarea
       IS - ISIS summary, D - EIGRP, EX - EIGRP external, NM - NEMO
       ND - ND Default, NDp - ND Prefix, DCE - Destination, NDr - Redirect
       O - OSPF Intra, OI - OSPF Inter, OE1 - OSPF ext 1, OE2 - OSPF ext 2
       ON1 - OSPF NSSA ext 1, ON2 - OSPF NSSA ext 2, ls - LISP site
       ld - LISP dyn-EID, a - Application


OI  17::/64 [110/3]
     via FE80::2, GigabitEthernet0/0
OI  27::/64 [110/2]
     via FE80::2, GigabitEthernet0/0
OI  2000:111:111:1110::/62 [110/4]
     via FE80::2, GigabitEthernet0/0
OI  2000:777:111:1110::/64 [110/3]
     via FE80::2, GigabitEthernet0/0
OI  2000:777:111:1117::/64 [110/3]
     via FE80::2, GigabitEthernet0/0
OI  2000:777:111:111A::/64 [110/3]
     via FE80::2, GigabitEthernet0/0
OI  2000:777:111:111E::/64 [110/3]
     via FE80::2, GigabitEthernet0/0

! On R2:

R2(config)# ipv6 router ospf 1
R2(config-rtr)# area 0 range 2000:777:111:1110::/60
```

Now let's verify the configuration:

```
! On R8:


R8# show ipv6 route ospf


IPv6 Routing Table - default - 15 entries
Codes: C - Connected, L - Local, S - Static, U - Per-user Static route
       B - BGP, HA - Home Agent, MR - Mobile Router, R - RIP
       H - NHRP, I1 - ISIS L1, I2 - ISIS L2, IA - ISIS interarea
       IS - ISIS summary, D - EIGRP, EX - EIGRP external, NM - NEMO
       ND - ND Default, NDp - ND Prefix, DCE - Destination, NDr - Redirect
       O - OSPF Intra, OI - OSPF Inter, OE1 - OSPF ext 1, OE2 - OSPF ext 2
       ON1 - OSPF NSSA ext 1, ON2 - OSPF NSSA ext 2, ls - LISP site
       ld - LISP dyn-EID, a - Application
OI  17::/64 [110/3]
     via FE80::2, GigabitEthernet0/0
OI  27::/64 [110/2]
     via FE80::2, GigabitEthernet0/0
OI  2000:111:111:1110::/62 [110/4]
     via FE80::2, GigabitEthernet0/0
OI  2000:777:111:1110::/60 [110/3]
     via FE80::2, GigabitEthernet0/0


R8# ping 2000:777:111:1117::111


Type escape sequence to abort.
Sending 5, 100-byte ICMP Echos to 2000:777:111:1117::111, timeout is 2 seconds:
!!!!!
Success rate is 100 percent (5/5), round-trip min/avg/max = 1/1/4 ms
```

Task 3

Summarize the external routes redistributed on R8. If this summarization is performed correctly, the rest of the routers should see a single summary route for the four networks redistributed into the OSPF routing domain.

Let's look at the IPv6 addresses that you are going to summarize:

Lo0: 2000:888:111:111B::111/64

Lo1: 2000:888:111:111C::111/64

Lo2: 2000:888:111:111D::111/64

Lo3: 2000:888:111:111F::111/64

Let's configure the last digit of the fourth hextet to binary:

B = 1 0 1 1

C = 1 1 0 0

D = 1 1 0 1

F = 1 1 1 1

You need to take a relaxed approach to summarizing these networks again. Note that the only leading bit common to these networks is the first one. Therefore, the summary route should be 2000:888:111:1118::/61. Let's configure it and verify.

In OSPFv2, you use the **area range** command for internal routes and **summary-address** for summarizing external routes. In OSPFv3, you still use the **area range** command for internal routes, but for external routes, instead of the **summary-address** command, you use the **summary-prefix** command, like so:

```
! On R8:

R8(config)# router ospfv3 1
R8(config-router)# address-family ipv6 unicast
R8(config-router-af)# summary-prefix 2000:888:111:1118::/61
```

Let's verify the configuration:

```
! On R1:

R1# show ipv6 route ospf | inc /61

OE2 2000:888:111:1118::/61 [110/20]

R1# ping 2000:888:111:111f::111

Type escape sequence to abort.
Sending 5, 100-byte ICMP Echos to 2000:888:111:111F::111, timeout is 2 seconds:
!!!!!
Success rate is 100 percent (5/5), round-trip min/avg/max = 0/0/4 ms
```

Task 4

The policy for summarizing external routes has changed. The routers in Area 2 should see all specific external routes, whereas the routers in the other areas should see a single summary route for the four external routes.

Let's remove the **summary-prefix** command configured in the previous step:

```
! On R8:

R8(config)# router ospfv3 1
R8(config-router)# address-family ipv6 unicast
R8(config-router-af)# no summary-prefix 2000:888:111:1118::/61
```

Let's verify the configuration:

```
! On R1:

R1# show ipv6 route ospf | inc /61

R1# show ipv6 route ospf | inc OE2

      O - OSPF Intra, OI - OSPF Inter, OE1 - OSPF ext 1, OE2 - OSPF ext 2
OE2 2000:888:111:111B::/64 [110/20]
OE2 2000:888:111:111C::/64 [110/20]
OE2 2000:888:111:111D::/64 [110/20]
OE2 2000:888:111:111F::/64 [110/20]
```

Note Summarization in OSPFv3 is identical to that in OSPFv2. Summarization can be configured for two router types, depending on what routes are to be summarized:

- **The routes are internal.** If the routes are internal, the summarization can only be configured on the ABRs using the **area range** command.

- **The routes are external.** There are two types of external routes: the "E" routes and the "N" routes. Both of them can only be summarized at ASBRs that originate them. The small trick here comes from the fact that when N routes are translated into E routes (also called 7-to-5 translation, because Type-7 LSAs are translated into Type-5 LSAs), the ABR performing the 7-to-5 translation effectively becomes an ASBR as well and is thus allowed to perform the summarization of translated external routes.

Because the routers in Area 2 should see all the specific routes, and the routers in the other areas should only see a single summary route, Area 2 is converted into a Not-So-Stubby Area (NSSA). Once that happens, R2 will receive the N routes, and it will translate them into E routes. Because R2 is the one that originates the external E routes, it can summarize the routes redistributed by R8.

```
! On R8:

R8(config)# router ospfv3 1
R8(config-router)# address-family ipv6 unicast
R8(config-router-af)# area 2 nssa
```

You should see the following console message stating that the adjacency to R2 is down. This is because the area NSSA flag no longer matches. Once R2 is configured with **area 2 nssa**, the area NSSA flag will match and the adjacency will be reestablished.

```
%OSPFv3-5-ADJCHG: Process 1, IPv6, Nbr 0.0.0.2 on GigabitEthernet0/0 from FULL to
DOWN, Neighbor Down: Adjacency forced to reset
```

```
! On R2:

R2(config)# ipv6 router ospf 1
R2(config-rtr)# area 2 nssa
R2(config-rtr)# summary-prefix 2000:888:111:1118::/61
```

You should see the following console message stating that the adjacency with 0.0.0.8 or R8 is in the FULL state:

```
%OSPFv3-5-ADJCHG: Process 1, Nbr 0.0.0.8 on FastEthernet0/0 from LOADING to FULL,
Loading Done
```

Let's verify the configuration:

```
! On R1:

R1# show ipv6 route ospf | inc/61

        O - OSPF Intra, OI - OSPF Inter, OE1 - OSPF ext 1, OE2 - OSPF ext 2
OE2 2000:888:111:1118::/61 [110/20]


R1# ping 2000:888:111:111f::111

Type escape sequence to abort.
Sending 5, 100-byte ICMP Echos to 2000:888:111:111F::111, timeout is 2 seconds:
!!!!!
Success rate is 100 percent (5/5), round-trip min/avg/max = 0/1/4 ms
```

```
! On R2:

R2# show ipv6 route ospf

IPv6 Routing Table - default - 17 entries
Codes: C - Connected, L - Local, S - Static, U - Per-user Static route
       B - BGP, HA - Home Agent, MR - Mobile Router, R - RIP
       I1 - ISIS L1, I2 - ISIS L2, IA - ISIS interarea, IS - ISIS summary
       D - EIGRP, EX - EIGRP external, NM - NEMO, ND - Neighbor Discovery
       l - LISP
       O - OSPF Intra, OI - OSPF Inter, OE1 - OSPF ext 1, OE2 - OSPF ext 2
       ON1 - OSPF NSSA ext 1, ON2 - OSPF NSSA ext 2
OI   17::/64 [110/2]
     via FE80::7, FastEthernet0/1
OI   2000:111:111:1110::/62 [110/3]
     via FE80::7, FastEthernet0/1
O    2000:777:111:1110::/60 [110/0]
     via Null0, directly connected
O    2000:777:111:1110::/64 [110/2]
     via FE80::7, FastEthernet0/1
O    2000:777:111:1117::/64 [110/2]
     via FE80::7, FastEthernet0/1
O    2000:777:111:111A::/64 [110/2]
     via FE80::7, FastEthernet0/1
O    2000:777:111:111E::/64 [110/2]
     via FE80::7, FastEthernet0/1
O    2000:888:111:1118::/61 [110/0]
     via Null0, directly connected
ON2 2000:888:111:111B::/64 [110/20]
     via 28::8, FastEthernet0/0
ON2 2000:888:111:111C::/64 [110/20]
     via 28::8, FastEthernet0/0
ON2 2000:888:111:111D::/64 [110/20]
     via 28::8, FastEthernet0/0
ON2 2000:888:111:111F::/64 [110/20]
     via 28::8, FastEthernet0/0
```

Task 5

None of the routers should have a discard route in their routing table.

In OSPF, the discard routes are auto-injected on the router that performs summarization. Let's verify the existence of the discard routes on R7 and R2:

```
! On R2:


R2# show ipv6 route ospf


IPv6 Routing Table - default - 17 entries
Codes: C - Connected, L - Local, S - Static, U - Per-user Static route
       B - BGP, HA - Home Agent, MR - Mobile Router, R - RIP
       I1 - ISIS L1, I2 - ISIS L2, IA - ISIS interarea, IS - ISIS summary
       D - EIGRP, EX - EIGRP external, NM - NEMO, ND - Neighbor Discovery
       l - LISP
       O - OSPF Intra, OI - OSPF Inter, OE1 - OSPF ext 1, OE2 - OSPF ext 2
       ON1 - OSPF NSSA ext 1, ON2 - OSPF NSSA ext 2
OI  17::/64 [110/2]
     via FE80::7, FastEthernet0/1
OI  2000:111:111:1110::/62 [110/3]
     via FE80::7, FastEthernet0/1
O   2000:777:111:1110::/60 [110/0]
     via Null0, directly connected
O   2000:777:111:1110::/64 [110/2]
     via FE80::7, FastEthernet0/1
O   2000:777:111:1117::/64 [110/2]
     via FE80::7, FastEthernet0/1
O   2000:777:111:111A::/64 [110/2]
     via FE80::7, FastEthernet0/1
O   2000:777:111:111E::/64 [110/2]
     via FE80::7, FastEthernet0/1
O   2000:888:111:1118::/61 [110/0]
     via Null0, directly connected
ON2 2000:888:111:111B::/64 [110/20]
     via 28::8, FastEthernet0/0
ON2 2000:888:111:111C::/64 [110/20]
     via 28::8, FastEthernet0/0
ON2 2000:888:111:111D::/64 [110/20]
     via 28::8, FastEthernet0/0
ON2 2000:888:111:111F::/64 [110/20]
     via 28::8, FastEthernet0/0
```

The output of the preceding **show** command reveals that R2 has two discard routes: 2000:777:111:1110::/60, which is the discard route for internal networks within Area 0, and 2000:888:111:1118::/61, which is the discard route for external networks. Let's remove the discard route for the internal routes:

```
R2(config)# ipv6 router ospf 1
R2(config-rtr)# no discard-route internal
```

Now let's verify this configuration:

```
! On R2:


R2# show ipv6 route ospf | inc /60
```

You can see that the discard route for internal networks is removed. Let's remove the discard route for the external routes:

```
R2(config)# ipv6 router ospf 1
R2(config-rtr)# no discard-route external
```

Let's verify this configuration:

```
! On R2:


R2# show ipv6 route ospf | inc /61
```

Now let's remove the discard route on R7:

```
! On R7:


R7# show ipv6 route ospf


IPv6 Routing Table - default - 21 entries
Codes: C - Connected, L - Local, S - Static, U - Per-user Static route
       B - BGP, HA - Home Agent, MR - Mobile Router, R - RIP
       H - NHRP, I1 - ISIS L1, I2 - ISIS L2, IA - ISIS interarea
       IS - ISIS summary, D - EIGRP, EX - EIGRP external, NM - NEMO
       ND - ND Default, NDp - ND Prefix, DCE - Destination, NDr - Redirect
       O - OSPF Intra, OI - OSPF Inter, OE1 - OSPF ext 1, OE2 - OSPF ext 2
       ON1 - OSPF NSSA ext 1, ON2 - OSPF NSSA ext 2, ls - LISP site
       ld - LISP dyn-EID, a - Application
OI  28::/64 [110/2]
    via FE80::2, GigabitEthernet0/1
O   2000:111:111:1110::/62 [110/2]
    via Null0, directly connected
O   2000:111:111:1110::/64 [110/2]
    via FE80::1, GigabitEthernet0/0
O   2000:111:111:1111::/64 [110/2]
    via FE80::1, GigabitEthernet0/0
O   2000:111:111:1112::/64 [110/2]
    via FE80::1, GigabitEthernet0/0
```

```
O   2000:111:111:1113::/64 [110/2]
     via FE80::1, GigabitEthernet0/0
O   2000:777:111:1110::/60 [110/1]
     via Null0, directly connected
OE2 2000:888:111:1118::/61 [110/20]
     via FE80::2, GigabitEthernet0/1
```

Because both discard routes are for internal networks, they can be removed using a single command:

```
R7(config)# router ospfv3 1
R7(config-router)# address-family ipv6 unicast
R7(config-router-af)# no discard-route internal
```

Let's verify the configuration:

```
! On R7:

R7# show ipv6 route ospf

IPv6 Routing Table - default - 19 entries
Codes: C - Connected, L - Local, S - Static, U - Per-user Static route
       B - BGP, HA - Home Agent, MR - Mobile Router, R - RIP
       H - NHRP, I1 - ISIS L1, I2 - ISIS L2, IA - ISIS interarea
       IS - ISIS summary, D - EIGRP, EX - EIGRP external, NM - NEMO
       ND - ND Default, NDp - ND Prefix, DCE - Destination, NDr - Redirect
       O - OSPF Intra, OI - OSPF Inter, OE1 - OSPF ext 1, OE2 - OSPF ext 2
       ON1 - OSPF NSSA ext 1, ON2 - OSPF NSSA ext 2, ls - LISP site
       ld - LISP dyn-EID, a - Application
OI  28::/64 [110/2]
     via FE80::2, GigabitEthernet0/1
O   2000:111:111:1110::/64 [110/2]
     via FE80::1, GigabitEthernet0/0
O   2000:111:111:1111::/64 [110/2]
     via FE80::1, GigabitEthernet0/0
O   2000:111:111:1112::/64 [110/2]
     via FE80::1, GigabitEthernet0/0
O   2000:111:111:1113::/64 [110/2]
     via FE80::1, GigabitEthernet0/0
OE2 2000:888:111:1118::/61 [110/20]
     via FE80::2, GigabitEthernet0/1
```

Erase the startup configuration of the routers, config.text, and the VLAN.dat file of the switches and reload them before proceeding to the next lab.

Lab 11-4: LSAs in OSPFv3

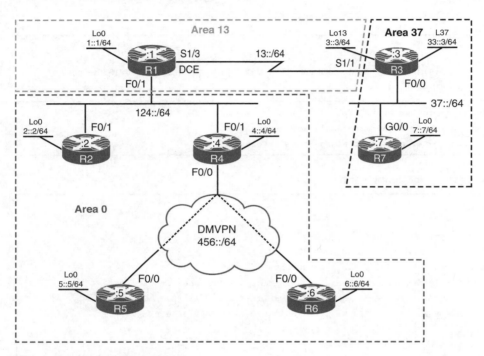

Figure 11-7   *LSAs in OSPFv3*

Figure 11-7 illustrates the topology that will be used in the following lab.

Task 1

Configure OSPF Area 0 on the F0/1 and loopback0 interfaces of R1, R2, and R4:

```
! On R1, R2, and R4:

Rx(config)# ipv6 unicast-routing

Rx(config)# interface loopback 0
Rx(config-if)# ipv6 ospf 1 area 0
Rx(config-if)# ipv6 ospf network point-to-point

Rx(config)# interface FastEthernet 0/1
Rx(config-if)# ipv6 ospf 1 area 0
```

```
! On R1:

R1(config)# ipv6 router ospf 1
R1(config-rtr)# router-id 0.0.0.1

R1# clear ipv6 ospf process
Reset ALL OSPF processes? [no]: Y

! On R2:

R2(config)# ipv6 router ospf 1
R2(config-rtr)# router-id 0.0.0.2

R2# clear ipv6 ospf process
Reset ALL OSPF processes? [no]: Y

! On R4:

R4(config)# ipv6 router ospf 1
R4(config-rtr)# router-id 0.0.0.4

R4# clear ipv6 ospf process
Reset ALL OSPF processes? [no]: Y
```

You should see the following console messages:

```
%OSPFv3-5-ADJCHG: Process 1, Nbr 0.0.0.1 on FastEthernet0/1 from LOADING to FULL,
Loading Done

%OSPFv3-5-ADJCHG: Process 1, Nbr 0.0.0.2 on FastEthernet0/1 from LOADING to FULL,
Loading Done
```

Let's verify the configuration:

```
! On R1

R1# show ipv6 ospf neighbor

Neighbor ID     Pri   State          Dead Time   Interface ID   Interface
0.0.0.2          1    FULL/DR        00:00:31    4              FastEthernet0/1
0.0.0.4          1    FULL/DROTHER   00:00:35    4              FastEthernet0/1
```

```
R1# show ipv6 route ospf

IPv6 Routing Table - default - 9 entries
Codes: C - Connected, L - Local, S - Static, U - Per-user Static route
       B - BGP, HA - Home Agent, MR - Mobile Router, R - RIP
       I1 - ISIS L1, I2 - ISIS L2, IA - ISIS interarea, IS - ISIS summary
       D - EIGRP, EX - EIGRP external, NM - NEMO, ND - Neighbor Discovery
       l - LISP
       O - OSPF Intra, OI - OSPF Inter, OE1 - OSPF ext 1, OE2 - OSPF ext 2
       ON1 - OSPF NSSA ext 1, ON2 - OSPF NSSA ext 2
O   2::/64 [110/2]
     via FE80::2, FastEthernet0/1
O   4::/64 [110/2]
     via FE80::4, FastEthernet0/1
```

Now let's see which LSAs are propagated in this area so far:

```
R1# show ipv6 ospf database

            OSPFv3 Router with ID (0.0.0.1) (Process ID 1)

                Router Link States (Area 0)

ADV Router      Age         Seq#        Fragment ID  Link count   Bits
0.0.0.1         511         0x80000002  0            1            None
0.0.0.2         512         0x80000002  0            1            None
0.0.0.4         368         0x80000001  0            1            None

                Net Link States (Area 0)

ADV Router      Age         Seq#        Link ID   Rtr count
0.0.0.2         328         0x80000004  4         3

                Link (Type-8) Link States (Area 0)

ADV Router      Age         Seq#        Link ID   Interface
0.0.0.1         716         0x80000001  22        Lo0
0.0.0.1         511         0x80000001  4         Fa0/1
0.0.0.2         561         0x80000001  4         Fa0/1
0.0.0.4         368         0x80000001  4         Fa0/1
```

```
                Intra Area Prefix Link States (Area 0)

ADV Router        Age         Seq#          Link ID    Ref-lstype   Ref-LSID
  0.0.0.1         506         0x80000004    0          0x2001       0
  0.0.0.2         512         0x80000003    0          0x2001       0
  0.0.0.2         512         0x80000001    4096       0x2002       4
  0.0.0.4         368         0x80000001    0          0x2001       0
```

You can see that four different types of LSAs are propagated: Router LSA, Network LSA, Link (Type-8) LSA, and Intra-Area Prefix (Type-9) LSA. Let's examine each LSA type, starting with Router LSA.

Based on the preceding output, you can see that there are three Router LSAs, one per router:

```
R1# show ipv6 ospf database router adv-router 0.0.0.1

           OSPFv3 Router with ID (0.0.0.1) (Process ID 1)

             Router Link States (Area 0)

  LS age: 827
  Options: (V6-Bit, E-Bit, R-bit, DC-Bit)
  LS Type: Router Links
  Link State ID: 0
  Advertising Router: 0.0.0.1
  LS Seq Number: 80000002
  Checksum: 0xCB27
  Length: 40
  Number of Links: 1

    Link connected to: a Transit Network
      Link Metric: 1
      Local Interface ID: 4
      Neighbor (DR) Interface ID: 4
      Neighbor (DR) Router ID: 0.0.0.2
```

Router LSAs (Type-1) describe the link states and the cost of the local router's links to the neighboring network objects (routers, multi-access networks, stub networks, or virtual links) within the same area. Just like in the previous OSPF version, Router LSAs are flooded within an area only. This LSA type also describes the router's role, indicating whether the router is an ABR or ASBR, and if it's one end of a given virtual link. As opposed to OSPFv2, however, Router LSAs in OSPFv3 only describe the topology relations but carry no addressing information. The question is, why?

The major drawback of OSPFv2, as opposed to Intermediate System to Intermediate System (IS-IS), was its inability to distinguish between a topology change and an addressing change. The addressing information in OSPFv2's Router and Network LSA was so closely intertwined with the topological information that a change to an interface addressing was indistinguishable from a topology change where one interface or an entire router went away and a new one was brought up. These two categories of events require different handling, however: If a topology changes, OSPF must run the SPF algorithm to compute a new shortest path tree. On the other hand, if addressing changes, there is no need to run SPF and compute a new shortest path tree because that tree already exists and has not changed—just the addressing information present in the tree needs to be updated. OSPF could save a lot of work if it were able to tell a change to the topology from a change to the addressing.

This is where OSPFv3 is arguably an improvement. Router and Network LSAs no longer carry addressing information and instead are used exclusively to describe the topology. All addressing information from these LSA types has been moved out to the Intra-Area Prefix LSA (Type-9 LSA). Thanks to this, if only addressing changes, the affected router originates an updated Intra-Area Prefix LSA while keeping the existing Router and Network LSAs unchanged. As a result, other routers in the area won't run SPF and instead will only update the addressing information already present in the shortest path tree, thus saving precious CPU cycles.

The output of the preceding **show** command reveals that Router LSAs do not carry the IPv6 addressing; instead, they only identify the following:

- Options field:
  - V6-Bit identifies that the router has the capability of forwarding transit IPv6 packets.
  - E-Bit identifies the capability of the local router to accept external LSAs.
  - R-Bit indicates that the router can be used to route transit traffic.
  - DC-Bit identifies that the router is capable of running demand circuits.
- Advertising the router's RID (in this case, 0.0.0.1).
- The number of its own links this router advertises information about (in this case, just one).
- The individual interfaces of this router that connect to other network objects. In this case, this router's interface connects to a transit network that is represented by its Designated Router (here, it is R2) and the corresponding Network LSA the Designated Router (DR) has originated.
- The cost of the interface. In this case, the cost is 1 because the link operates at 100 Mbps.
- The interface IDs of this router and its neighbor connected by this link. In OSPFv3, interface IDs are used instead of IPv6 addresses to precisely indicate the interfaces

that are connected together. Every interface on a router is assigned an interface ID, and the local router can learn about its neighbor's interface ID from the received Hello packets.

■ The RID of the DR (in this case, 0.0.0.2). This means that R2 is the DR for this segment.

Let's examine LSA Type-2 or the Network LSAs. We will only see Network LSAs if there are multi-access segments in the topology with at least two routers. If we do not have multi-access segments (Broadcast or Non-Broadcast) in the topology, there will not be any Network LSAs. In the output of the **show ipv6 ospf database** command, we only saw a single Network LSA, and it was originated by R2 (0.0.0.2) because R2 is currently acting as the DR on the Ethernet network between R1, R2 and R4.

```
R1# show ipv6 ospf database network

            OSPFv3 Router with ID (0.0.0.1) (Process ID 1)

              Net Link States (Area 0)


  LS age: 223
  Options: (V6-Bit, E-Bit, R-bit, DC-Bit)
  LS Type: Network Links
  Link State ID: 4 (Interface ID of Designated Router)
  Advertising Router: 0.0.0.2


  LS Seq Number: 80000005
  Checksum: 0x27CC
  Length: 36
        Attached Router: 0.0.0.2
        Attached Router: 0.0.0.1
        Attached Router: 0.0.0.4
```

Note   Network LSAs no longer contain the address of the link. This information has also been moved out to Intra-Area Prefix LSAs. Network LSAs only state the RID of the routers that are attached to the multi-access segment. Remember, Router and Network LSAs in OSPFv3 no longer carry addressing information; they only describe how routers and networks are connected together.

Let's now examine the Link LSAs or Type-8 LSAs. Keep in mind that these LSAs have only a link-wide flooding scope, meaning that a Link LSA advertised from an interface will be received and processed by the neighboring routers, but they will not flood it further. This can be slightly confusing because it causes different routers to have different link state database contents. Each router will only know its own Link LSAs and the Link

LSAs originated by its neighbors for the common links. Nonetheless, this is expected behavior. When observing the following output, keep in mind that we are looking at the database of R1:

```
R1# show ipv6 ospf database

            OSPFv3 Router with ID (0.0.0.1) (Process ID 1)

            Router Link States (Area 0)

ADV Router        Age        Seq#          Fragment ID  Link count  Bits
0.0.0.1           911        0x80000003    0            1           None
0.0.0.2           965        0x80000003    0            1           None
0.0.0.4           839        0x80000002    0            1           None

            Net Link States (Area 0)

ADV Router        Age        Seq#          Link ID    Rtr count
0.0.0.2           720        0x80000005    4          3

            Link (Type-8) Link States (Area 0)

ADV Router        Age        Seq#          Link ID    Interface
0.0.0.1           1157       0x80000002    22         Lo0
0.0.0.1           911        0x80000002    4          Fa0/1
0.0.0.2           965        0x80000002    4          Fa0/1
0.0.0.4           839        0x80000002    4          Fa0/1

            Intra Area Prefix Link States (Area 0)

ADV Router        Age        Seq#          Link ID    Ref-lstype   Ref-LSID
0.0.0.1           911        0x80000005    0          0x2001       0
0.0.0.2           965        0x80000004    0          0x2001       0
0.0.0.2           965        0x80000002    4096       0x2002       4

0.0.0.4           839        0x80000002    0          0x2001       0
```

There are four Link LSAs in R1's link state database: two from 0.0.0.1, one from 0.0.0.2, and another one from 0.0.0.4. The reason R1 has originated two entries is because it is running OSPFv3 on two interfaces: loopback0 and F0/1. Other Link LSAs are received from the neighbors R2 and R4. Note that both R2 and R4 might have originated multiple Link LSAs, but each Link LSA is related only to a particular interface and is only sent out from that interface.

Let's now check the link state database on R2:

```
! On R2:

R2# show ipv6 ospf database link

              Link (Type-8) Link States (Area 0)

ADV Router        Age         Seq#           Link ID     Interface
  0.0.0.2         1159        0x80000002     22          Lo0
  0.0.0.1         1107        0x80000002     4           Fa0/1
  0.0.0.2         1159        0x80000002     4           Fa0/1
  0.0.0.4         1035        0x80000002     4           Fa0/1

(The output is modified to show the section for LSA Type-8s only)
```

```
! On R4:

R4# show ipv6 ospf database link

              Link (Type-8) Link States (Area 0)

ADV Router        Age         Seq#           Link ID     Interface
  0.0.0.4         1209        0x80000002     22          Lo0
  0.0.0.1         1282        0x80000002     4           Fa0/1
  0.0.0.2         1336        0x80000002     4           Fa0/1
  0.0.0.4         1209        0x80000002     4           Fa0/1

(The output is modified to show the section for LSA Type-8s only)
```

Let's examine these LSAs in detail. Link LSAs provide the link-local IPv6 address of the local router to all other routers attached to the link. Link LSAs also convey all IPv6 prefixes associated with the interface for which the Link LSA was originated.

```
! On R1:

R1# show ipv6 ospf database Link adv-router 0.0.0.1

              OSPFv3 Router with ID (0.0.0.1) (Process ID 1)

              Link (Type-8) Link States (Area 0)
```

```
LS age: 1637
Options: (V6-Bit, E-Bit, R-bit, DC-Bit)
LS Type: Link-LSA (Interface: Loopback0)

Link State ID: 22 (Interface ID)
Advertising Router: 0.0.0.1
LS Seq Number: 80000002
Checksum: 0xCEB7
Length: 56
Router Priority: 1
Link Local Address: FE80::213:7FFF:FE10:7590
Number of Prefixes: 1
Prefix Address: 1::
Prefix Length: 64, Options: None

LS age: 1390
Options: (V6-Bit, E-Bit, R-bit, DC-Bit)
LS Type: Link-LSA (Interface: FastEthernet0/1)
Link State ID: 4 (Interface ID)
Advertising Router: 0.0.0.1
LS Seq Number: 80000002
Checksum: 0x1904
Length: 56
Router Priority: 1
Link Local Address: FE80::1
Number of Prefixes: 1
Prefix Address: 124::
Prefix Length: 64, Options: None
```

You can see two Link LSAs—one per interface. You can also see the link local IPv6 address associated with each interface. Because the link-local IPv6 address of the Lo0 interface was not statically configured, a Modified EUI-64 format was used to generate one.

Let's look at the last two lines of the preceding output. Currently, these lines say that F0/1 uses a prefix of 124:: with a length of /64. If we configure another IPv6 address on the F0/1 interface, we should see two prefixes.

```
! On R1:

R1(config)# interface FastEthernet 0/1
R1(config-if)# ipv6 address 111::111/64
```

Let's verify:

```
R1# show ipv6 ospf database Link interface FastEthernet 0/1 adv-router 0.0.0.1

            OSPFv3 Router with ID (0.0.0.1) (Process ID 1)

                Link (Type-8) Link States (Area 0)

  LS age: 17
  Options: (V6-Bit, E-Bit, R-bit, DC-Bit)
  LS Type: Link-LSA (Interface: FastEthernet0/1)
  Link State ID: 4 (Interface ID)
  Advertising Router: 0.0.0.1
  LS Seq Number: 80000004
  Checksum: 0x10AB
  Length: 68
  Router Priority: 1
  Link Local Address: FE80::1
  Number of Prefixes: 2
  Prefix Address: 111::
  Prefix Length: 64, Options: None
  Prefix Address: 124::
  Prefix Length: 64, Options: None
```

Now, there are two prefixes advertised for the interface, confirming the assumption. Let's remove the added prefix:

```
R1(config)# interface FastEthernet 0/1
R1(config-if)# no ipv6 address 111::111/64
```

The last LSA type is the Intra-Area Prefix LSA, or Type-9 LSA (Type-9 LSA will be used here for brevity). Let's examine this LSA:

```
R1# show ipv6 ospf database prefix adv-router 0.0.0.1

            OSPFv3 Router with ID (0.0.0.1) (Process ID 1)

                Intra Area Prefix Link States (Area 0)

  Routing Bit Set on this LSA
  LS age: 221
  LS Type: Intra-Area-Prefix-LSA
  Link State ID: 0
```

```
Advertising Router: 0.0.0.1
LS Seq Number: 80000006
Checksum: 0x6B7
Length: 44

Referenced LSA Type: 2001
Referenced Link State ID: 0
Referenced Advertising Router: 0.0.0.1
Number of Prefixes: 1
Prefix Address: 1::
Prefix Length: 64, Options: None, Metric: 1
```

The output of the preceding **show** command reveals the intra-area prefixes carried by Type-9 LSAs. Every router advertises its directly connected networks in Type-9 LSAs, which are then flooded across the area. In fact, a single router can originate multiple Type-9 LSAs—recall that OSPFv2 used to advertise directly connected networks in Router LSAs (stub networks) and in Network LSAs (transit networks). OSPFv3 moved this addressing information out from Router and Network LSAs into Intra-Area Prefix LSAs (Type-9 LSAs), but the information in these Type-9 LSAs refers back to either Router or Network LSAs where the information was previously stored. Therefore, a router will originate one Type-9 LSA for all stub networks that were formerly present in its Router LSA, plus one Type-9 LSA for each transit network where the router is a DR and has originated a corresponding Network LSA. The specific LSA (Router or Network) a Type-9 LSA refers back to is identified by the entries "Referenced LSA Type" (Router or Network LSA), "Referenced Link State ID" (0 for Router LSA, Interface ID for Network LSA), or "Referenced Advertising Router."

Task 2

Configure OSPF Area 13 on the S1/3 interface of R1 and the S1/1 and loopback13 interfaces of R3:

```
! On R1:

R1(config)# interface Serial 1/3
R1(config-if)# ipv6 ospf 1 area 13
```

```
! On R3:

R3(config)# ipv6 unicast-routing
```

```
R3(config)# int loopback 13
R3(config-if)# ipv6 ospf 1 area 13
R3(config-if)# ipv6 ospf network point-to-point

R3(config)# interface Serial 1/1
R3(config-if)# ipv6 ospf 1 area 13
```

You should see the following console messages:

```
%OSPFv3-5-ADJCHG: Process 1, Nbr 0.0.0.1 on Serial1/1 from LOADING to FULL,
Loading Done
```

Let's verify the configuration:

```
! On R3:

R3# show ipv6 route ospf

IPv6 Routing Table - default - 11 entries
Codes: C - Connected, L - Local, S - Static, U - Per-user Static route
       B - BGP, HA - Home Agent, MR - Mobile Router, R - RIP
       I1 - ISIS L1, I2 - ISIS L2, IA - ISIS interarea, IS - ISIS summary
       D - EIGRP, EX - EIGRP external, NM - NEMO, ND - Neighbor Discovery
       l - LISP
       O - OSPF Intra, OI - OSPF Inter, OE1 - OSPF ext 1, OE2 - OSPF ext 2
       ON1 - OSPF NSSA ext 1, ON2 - OSPF NSSA ext 2
OI  1::/64 [110/65]
     via FE80::1, Serial1/1
OI  2::/64 [110/66]
     via FE80::1, Serial1/1
OI  4::/64 [110/66]
     via FE80::1, Serial1/1
OI  124::/64 [110/65]
     via FE80::1, Serial1/1
```

```
! On R1:

R1# show ipv6 route ospf

IPv6 Routing Table - default - 10 entries
Codes: C - Connected, L - Local, S - Static, U - Per-user Static route
       B - BGP, HA - Home Agent, MR - Mobile Router, R - RIP
       I1 - ISIS L1, I2 - ISIS L2, IA - ISIS interarea, IS - ISIS summary
       D - EIGRP, EX - EIGRP external, NM - NEMO, ND - Neighbor Discovery
```

```
        1 - LISP
        O - OSPF Intra, OI - OSPF Inter, OE1 - OSPF ext 1, OE2 - OSPF ext 2
        ON1 - OSPF NSSA ext 1, ON2 - OSPF NSSA ext 2
O    2::/64 [110/2]
      via FE80::2, FastEthernet0/1
O    3::/64 [110/65]
      via FE80::3, Serial1/3
O    4::/64 [110/2]
      via FE80::4, FastEthernet0/1
```

Let's see the OSPFv3 database on R3:

```
! On R3:

R3# show ipv6 ospf database

            OSPFv3 Router with ID (0.0.0.3) (Process ID 1)

            Router Link States (Area 13)

ADV Router      Age         Seq#         Fragment ID  Link count  Bits
0.0.0.1         156         0x80000002   0            1           B
0.0.0.3         156         0x80000002   0            1           None


            Inter Area Prefix Link States (Area 13)

ADV Router      Age         Seq#         Prefix
0.0.0.1         433         0x80000001   1::/64
0.0.0.1         433         0x80000001   2::/64
0.0.0.1         433         0x80000001   4::/64
0.0.0.1         433         0x80000001   124::/64


            Link (Type-8) Link States (Area 13)

ADV Router      Age         Seq#         Link ID    Interface
0.0.0.3         311         0x80000001   23         Lo13
0.0.0.1         433         0x80000001   8          Se1/1
0.0.0.3         156         0x80000001   6          Se1/1


            Intra Area Prefix Link States (Area 13)

ADV Router      Age         Seq#         Link ID    Ref-lstype   Ref-LSID
0.0.0.1         433         0x80000001   0          0x2001       0
0.0.0.3         156         0x80000003   0          0x2001       0
```

Here, you can see LSA Types 1 (Router), 3 (Inter-Area Prefix), 8 (Link), and 9 (Intra-Area Prefix).

NOTE   Because there is no multi-access network with at least two OSPF routers in Area 13, there is no DR/BDR election, and consequently no Network LSA is originated.

Let's examine these LSAs starting with the Router LSA:

```
R3# show ipv6 ospf database router adv-router 0.0.0.3

              OSPFv3 Router with ID (0.0.0.3) (Process ID 1)

                Router Link States (Area 13)

  LS age: 1040
  Options: (V6-Bit, E-Bit, R-bit, DC-Bit)
  LS Type: Router Links

  Link State ID: 0
  Advertising Router: 0.0.0.3
  LS Seq Number: 80000029
  Checksum: 0x3155
  Length: 40
  Number of Links: 1

    Link connected to: another Router (point-to-point)
      Link Metric: 64
      Local Interface ID: 6
      Neighbor Interface ID: 8
      Neighbor Router ID: 0.0.0.1
```

You can see that the link is a point-to-point interface for which there is no requirement for DR/BDR. Router LSAs describe routers present in the topology and their interfaces to directly attached network objects. In this case, you can see that the local router is connected to R1 (0.0.0.1) and the cost of the local router's interface toward R1 is 64. Again, addressing information is no longer present.

Router LSAs also describe the role of the router, whether the router is an ABR or ASBR, and whether it is a virtual-link endpoint. Because R1 is an ABR, you should see this role identified in its Router LSAs. Let's verify:

```
! On R1:

R1# show ipv6 ospf database router adv-router 0.0.0.1 | begin Area 13
               Router Link States (Area 13)


  LS age: 1605
  Options: (V6-Bit, E-Bit, R-bit, DC-Bit)
  LS Type: Router Links
  Link State ID: 0
  Advertising Router: 0.0.0.1
  LS Seq Number: 80000029
  Checksum: 0x6421
  Length: 40
  Area Border Router
  Number of Links: 1


    Link connected to: another Router (point-to-point)
      Link Metric: 64
      Local Interface ID: 8
      Neighbor Interface ID: 6
      Neighbor Router ID: 0.0.0.3
```

Let's now examine the Inter-Area Prefix LSAs on R3:

```
! On R3:

R3# show ipv6 ospf database inter-area prefix

          OSPFv3 Router with ID (0.0.0.3) (Process ID 1)


             Inter Area Prefix Link States (Area 13)


  Routing Bit Set on this LSA
  LS age: 698
  LS Type: Inter Area Prefix Links
  Link State ID: 0
  Advertising Router: 0.0.0.1
  LS Seq Number: 80000029
  Checksum: 0x3596
```

```
Length: 36
Metric: 1
Prefix Address: 1::
Prefix Length: 64, Options: None


Routing Bit Set on this LSA
LS age: 698
LS Type: Inter Area Prefix Links
Link State ID: 1
Advertising Router: 0.0.0.1
LS Seq Number: 80000029
Checksum: 0x3D8B
Length: 36
Metric: 2
Prefix Address: 2::
Prefix Length: 64, Options: None


Routing Bit Set on this LSA
LS age: 698
LS Type: Inter Area Prefix Links
Link State ID: 2
Advertising Router: 0.0.0.1
LS Seq Number: 80000029
Checksum: 0x4B7A
Length: 36
Metric: 2
Prefix Address: 4::
Prefix Length: 64, Options: None


Routing Bit Set on this LSA

LS age: 698
LS Type: Inter Area Prefix Links
Link State ID: 3
Advertising Router: 0.0.0.1
LS Seq Number: 80000029
Checksum: 0xC7DC
Length: 36
Metric: 1
Prefix Address: 124::
Prefix Length: 64, Options: None
```

Let's verify these prefixes on R1. Remember that from R1's perspective, these routes are intra-area prefixes. Let's verify the cost from R1's perspective:

```
! On R1:

R1# show ipv6 ospf inter FastEthernet 0/1 | include Cost

  Network Type BROADCAST, Cost: 1

R1# show ipv6 route 4::/64 | include metric

  Known via "ospf 1", distance 110, metric 2, type intra area

R1# show ipv6 route 2::/64 | include metric

  Known via "ospf 1", distance 110, metric 2, type intra area

R1# show ipv6 ospf inter lo0 | include Cost

  Network Type POINT_TO_POINT, Cost: 1
```

Now, these routes are inter-area routes from R3's perspective, and because the cost in OSPF is cumulative, it will be the sum of what R1 advertised plus the cost of the link to R1. Let's verify this information:

```
! On R3:

R3# show ipv6 route ospf

IPv6 Routing Table - default - 11 entries
Codes: C - Connected, L - Local, S - Static, U - Per-user Static route
       B - BGP, HA - Home Agent, MR - Mobile Router, R - RIP
       I1 - ISIS L1, I2 - ISIS L2, IA - ISIS interarea, IS - ISIS summary
       D - EIGRP, EX - EIGRP external, NM - NEMO, ND - Neighbor Discovery
       l - LISP

       O - OSPF Intra, OI - OSPF Inter, OE1 - OSPF ext 1, OE2 - OSPF ext 2
       ON1 - OSPF NSSA ext 1, ON2 - OSPF NSSA ext 2
OI  1::/64 [110/65]
     via FE80::1, Serial1/1
OI  2::/64 [110/66]
     via FE80::1, Serial1/1
OI  4::/64 [110/66]
     via FE80::1, Serial1/1
OI  124::/64 [110/65]
     via FE80::1, Serial1/1
```

You can see that the prefixes are inter-area, so let's examine the database of R3 for one of these prefixes:

```
R3# show ipv6 ospf database inter-area prefix 1::/64

            OSPFv3 Router with ID (0.0.0.3) (Process ID 1)


            Inter Area Prefix Link States (Area 13)


  Routing Bit Set on this LSA
  LS age: 1508
  LS Type: Inter Area Prefix Links
  Link State ID: 0
  Advertising Router: 0.0.0.1
  LS Seq Number: 80000029
  Checksum: 0x3596
  Length: 36
  Metric: 1
  Prefix Address: 1::
  Prefix Length: 64, Options: None
```

You can see that the advertising router is R1 (0.0.0.1). Let's see what R3's cost is to reach R1 by looking at the cost of the interface between R3 and R1:

```
R3# show ipv6 ospf interface Serial 1/1 | include Cost

  Network Type POINT_TO_POINT, Cost: 64
```

So R3's cost to R1 is 64, and R1's cost to the 1::/64 prefix is 1; therefore, R3's overall cost to network 1::/64 is 65.

Let's examine Link LSAs:

```
R3# show ipv6 ospf database

            OSPFv3 Router with ID (0.0.0.3) (Process ID 1)


            Link (Type-8) Link States (Area 13)

ADV Router      Age        Seq#        Link ID    Interface
0.0.0.3         1569       0x80000029  23         Lo13
0.0.0.1         1992       0x80000029  8          Se1/1
0.0.0.3         1569       0x80000029  6          Se1/1
```

You can see that R3 (0.0.0.3) has two entries: one for its Lo0 interface and one for its S1/1 interface. Let's examine these closer:

```
R3# show ipv6 ospf database link adv-router 0.0.0.3

            OSPFv3 Router with ID (0.0.0.3) (Process ID 1)

              Link (Type-8) Link States (Area 13)


  LS age: 1491
  Options: (V6-Bit, E-Bit, R-bit, DC-Bit)
  LS Type: Link-LSA (Interface: Loopback13)
  Link State ID: 23 (Interface ID)
  Advertising Router: 0.0.0.3
  LS Seq Number: 80000029
  Checksum: 0xCD26
  Length: 56
  Router Priority: 1
  Link Local Address: FE80::21B:54FF:FEB7:7770
  Number of Prefixes: 1
  Prefix Address: 3::
  Prefix Length: 64, Options: None


  LS age: 1491
  Options: (V6-Bit, E-Bit, R-bit, DC-Bit)
  LS Type: Link-LSA (Interface: Serial1/1)
  Link State ID: 6 (Interface ID)
  Advertising Router: 0.0.0.3
  LS Seq Number: 80000029
  Checksum: 0x956C
  Length: 56
  Router Priority: 1
  Link Local Address: FE80::3
  Number of Prefixes: 1
  Prefix Address: 13::
  Prefix Length: 64, Options: None
```

These were explained in the previous task, so let's move on to intra-area prefixes:

```
R3# show ipv6 ospf database prefix adv-router 0.0.0.3

            OSPFv3 Router with ID (0.0.0.3) (Process ID 1)

              Intra Area Prefix Link States (Area 13)


  Routing Bit Set on this LSA
  LS age: 1844
```

```
LS Type: Intra-Area-Prefix-LSA
Link State ID: 0
Advertising Router: 0.0.0.3
LS Seq Number: 8000002B
Checksum: 0xC031
Length: 56
Referenced LSA Type: 2001
Referenced Link State ID: 0
Referenced Advertising Router: 0.0.0.3
Number of Prefixes: 2
Prefix Address: 3::
Prefix Length: 64, Options: None, Metric: 1
Prefix Address: 13::
Prefix Length: 64, Options: None, Metric: 64
```

Task 3

Configure OSPF Area 37 on the F0/0 and Lo37 interfaces of R3 and the G0/0 and Lo0 interfaces of R7. These routers should see all the routes from the other areas in this routing domain.

Once the routers in Area 37 are configured, a virtual link must be configured to extend Area 0 to the routers in Area 37:

```
! On R3:

R3(config)# interface FastEthernet 0/0
R3(config-if)# ipv6 ospf 1 area 37

R3(config)# interface loopback 37
R3(config-if)# ipv6 ospf 1 area 37
R3(config-if)# ipv6 ospf network point-to-point
```

```
! On R7:

R7(config)# ipv6 unicast-routing

R7(config)# router ospfv3 1
R7(config-router)# address-family ipv6 unicast
R7(config-router-af)# router-id 0.0.0.7

R7(config)# interface GigabitEthernet 0/0
R7(config-if)# ospfv3 1 ipv6 area 37
```

You should see the following console message:

```
%OSPFv3-5-ADJCHG: Process 1, IPv6, Nbr 0.0.0.3 on GigabitEthernet0/0 from LOADING
to FULL, Loading Done
```

```
R7(config)# interface loopback 0
R7(config-if)# ospfv3 1 ipv6 area 37
R7(config-if)# ospfv3 network point-to-point
```

Let's verify the configuration:

```
! On R7:

R7# show ipv6 route ospf

IPv6 Routing Table - default - 6 entries
Codes: C - Connected, L - Local, S - Static, U - Per-user Static route
       B - BGP, HA - Home Agent, MR - Mobile Router, R - RIP
       H - NHRP, I1 - ISIS L1, I2 - ISIS L2, IA - ISIS interarea
       IS - ISIS summary, D - EIGRP, EX - EIGRP external, NM - NEMO
       ND - ND Default, NDp - ND Prefix, DCE - Destination, NDr - Redirect
       O - OSPF Intra, OI - OSPF Inter, OE1 - OSPF ext 1, OE2 - OSPF ext 2
       ON1 - OSPF NSSA ext 1, ON2 - OSPF NSSA ext 2, ls - LISP site
       ld - LISP dyn-EID, a - Application
O   33::/64 [110/2]
     via FE80::3, GigabitEthernet0/0
```

You can only see the prefix that is advertised by R3. The reason is that Area 37 is not
touching Area 0. Let's configure the virtual link on R3 and R1. Because a virtual link uses
Router IDs to identify its endpoints, let's find out the RID of R1 and R3:

```
! On R1:

R1# show ipv6 ospf | inc ID

 Routing Process "ospfv3 1" with ID 0.0.0.1

! On R3:

R3# show ipv6 ospf | inc ID

 Routing Process "ospfv3 1" with ID 0.0.0.3
```

Next, you should check and see if filtering was configured in the transit area, or if the transit area is a stub of any kind. Because you have configured these routers and know that you have not filtered any prefixes or configured any of the areas as stubs, you can bypass this verification.

Next to be verified is the cumulative cost between the virtual-link endpoints R1 and R3. The reason is that the cost of a virtual link is inherited from the cost of the shortest path between the virtual-link endpoints and cannot be configured manually. Because a virtual link is treated as a point-to-point unnumbered interface, its cost must be less than 65535, which is the maximum OSPF metric for an interface and is used to indicate a nontransit link. Therefore, it is advisable that you verify whether the path between R1 and R3 reaches or even exceeds this metric; in such case, the virtual link would not come up.

The last step is to configure the virtual link:

```
! On R1:

R1(config)# ipv6 router ospf 1
R1(config-rtr)# area 13 virtual-link 0.0.0.3
```

```
! On R3:

R3(config)# ipv6 router ospf 1
R3(config-rtr)# area 13 virtual-link 0.0.0.1
```

You should see the following console message:

```
%OSPFv3-5-ADJCHG: Process 1, Nbr 0.0.0.1 on OSPFv3_VL0 from LOADING to FULL,
Loading Done
```

Let's verify the configuration:

```
! On R3:

R3# show ipv6 ospf neighbor

Neighbor ID     Pri    State       Dead Time    Interface ID    Interface
0.0.0.1          0    FULL/   -    00:00:03     23              OSPFv3_VL0
0.0.0.1          0    FULL/   -    00:00:36     8               Serial1/1
0.0.0.7          1    FULL/BDR    00:00:32     3               FastEthernet0/0

R3# show ipv6 ospf virtual-links

Virtual Link OSPFv3_VL0 to router 0.0.0.1 is up
  Interface ID 25, IPv6 address 13::1
  Run as demand circuit
```

```
DoNotAge LSA allowed.
Transit area 13, via interface Serial1/1, Cost of using 64
Transmit Delay is 1 sec, State POINT_TO_POINT,
Timer intervals configured, Hello 10, Dead 40, Wait 40, Retransmit 5
  Adjacency State FULL (Hello suppressed)
  (The rest of the output is omitted for brevity)
```

Let's verify the database of R3:

```
! On R3:


R3# show ipv6 ospf database router adv-router 0.0.0.1


            OSPFv3 Router with ID (0.0.0.3) (Process ID 1)


                Router Link States (Area 0)


  Routing Bit Set on this LSA
  LS age: 1 (DoNotAge)
  Options: (V6-Bit, E-Bit, R-bit, DC-Bit)
  LS Type: Router Links
  Link State ID: 0
  Advertising Router: 0.0.0.1
  LS Seq Number: 8000002F
  Checksum: 0x4DEF
  Length: 56
  Area Border Router
  Number of Links: 2

    Link connected to: a Virtual Link
      Link Metric: 64


      Local Interface ID: 23
      Neighbor Interface ID: 25
      Neighbor Router ID: 0.0.0.3
    (The rest of the output is omitted for brevity)
```

```
! On R7:


R7# show ipv6 route ospf


IPv6 Routing Table - default - 14 entries
Codes: C - Connected, L - Local, S - Static, U - Per-user Static route
       B - BGP, HA - Home Agent, MR - Mobile Router, R - RIP
       H - NHRP, I1 - ISIS L1, I2 - ISIS L2, IA - ISIS interarea
```

```
        IS - ISIS summary, D - EIGRP, EX - EIGRP external, NM - NEMO
        ND - ND Default, NDp - ND Prefix, DCE - Destination, NDr - Redirect
        O - OSPF Intra, OI - OSPF Inter, OE1 - OSPF ext 1, OE2 - OSPF ext 2
        ON1 - OSPF NSSA ext 1, ON2 - OSPF NSSA ext 2, ls - LISP site
        ld - LISP dyn-EID, a - Application
OI  1::/64 [110/66]
    via FE80::3, GigabitEthernet0/0
OI  2::/64 [110/67]
    via FE80::3, GigabitEthernet0/0
OI  3::/64 [110/2]
    via FE80::3, GigabitEthernet0/0
OI  3::3/128 [110/1]
    via FE80::3, GigabitEthernet0/0
OI  4::/64 [110/67]
    via FE80::3, GigabitEthernet0/0
OI  13::/64 [110/65]
    via FE80::3, GigabitEthernet0/0
OI  13::1/128 [110/65]
    via FE80::3, GigabitEthernet0/0
O   33::/64 [110/2]
    via FE80::3, GigabitEthernet0/0
OI  124::/64 [110/66]
    via FE80::3, GigabitEthernet0/0
```

Task 4

Configure OSPF Area 0 on the DMVPN network. The OSPFv3 network type for the DMVPN network should be configured as broadcast, like so:

```
! On R4:

R4(config)# interface tunnel 1
R4(config-if)# ipv6 ospf network broadcast
R4(config-if)# ipv6 ospf 1 area 0
```

```
! On R5:

R5(config)# ipv6 unicast-routing

R5(config)# ipv6 router ospf 1
R5(config-rtr)# router-id 0.0.0.5
```

```
R5(config)# interface tunnel 1
R5(config-if)# ipv6 ospf priority 0
R5(config-if)# ipv6 ospf network broadcast
R5(config-if)# ipv6 ospf 1 area 0
```

You should see the following console message:

```
%OSPFv3-5-ADJCHG: Process 1, Nbr 0.0.0.4 on Tunnel1 from LOADING to FULL,
Loading Done
```

```
! On R6:

R6(config)# ipv6 unicast-routing

R6(config)# ipv6 router ospf 1
R6(config-rtr)# router-id 0.0.0.6

R6(config)# interface tunnel 1
R6(config-if)# ipv6 ospf priority 0
R6(config-if)# ipv6 ospf network broadcast
R6(config-if)# ipv6 ospf 1 area 0
```

You should also see this console message:

```
%OSPFv3-5-ADJCHG: Process 1, Nbr 0.0.0.4 on Tunnel1 from LOADING to FULL, Loading
  Done
```

Let's verify the configuration:

```
! On R6:

R6# show ipv6 route ospf

IPv6 Routing Table - default - 16 entries
Codes: C - Connected, L - Local, S - Static, U - Per-user Static route
       B - BGP, HA - Home Agent, MR - Mobile Router, R - RIP
       I1 - ISIS L1, I2 - ISIS L2, IA - ISIS interarea, IS - ISIS summary
       D - EIGRP, EX - EIGRP external, NM - NEMO, ND - Neighbor Discovery
       l - LISP
       O - OSPF Intra, OI - OSPF Inter, OE1 - OSPF ext 1, OE2 - OSPF ext 2
       ON1 - OSPF NSSA ext 1, ON2 - OSPF NSSA ext 2
```

```
O    1::/64 [110/1002]
        via FE80::4, Tunnel1
O    2::/64 [110/1002]
        via FE80::4, Tunnel1
OI   3::/64 [110/1066]
        via FE80::4, Tunnel1
OI   3::3/128 [110/1065]
        via FE80::4, Tunnel1
O    4::/64 [110/1001]
        via FE80::4, Tunnel1
OI   7::/64 [110/1067]
        via FE80::4, Tunnel1
OI   13::/64 [110/1065]
        via FE80::4, Tunnel1
OI   13::1/128 [110/1001]
        via FE80::4, Tunnel1
OI   33::/64 [110/1066]
        via FE80::4, Tunnel1
OI   37::/64 [110/1066]
        via FE80::4, Tunnel1
O    124::/64 [110/1001]
        via FE80::4, Tunnel1
```

```
R6# show ipv6 ospf database

            OSPFv3 Router with ID (0.0.0.6) (Process ID 1)

            Router Link States (Area 0)

ADV Router      Age         Seq#        Fragment ID  Link count  Bits
 0.0.0.1        1172        0x80000030  0            2           B
 0.0.0.2        2048        0x8000002E  0            1           None
 0.0.0.3        3    (DNA)  0x80000002  0            1           B
 0.0.0.4        253         0x8000002E  0            2           None
 0.0.0.5        164         0x80000001  0            1           None
 0.0.0.6        83          0x80000001  0            1           None

            Net Link States (Area 0)

ADV Router      Age         Seq#        Link ID   Rtr count
 0.0.0.2        1785        0x80000030  4         3
 0.0.0.4        84          0x80000004  23        3
```

```
                Inter Area Prefix Link States (Area 0)

ADV Router        Age           Seq#          Prefix
 0.0.0.1          1172          0x8000002B    13::/64
 0.0.0.1          669           0x8000002B    3::/64
 0.0.0.1          1437          0x80000001    13::1/128
 0.0.0.1          1401          0x80000001    3::3/128
 0.0.0.3          8      (DNA)  0x80000001    13::/64
 0.0.0.3          8      (DNA)  0x80000001    13::1/128
 0.0.0.3          8      (DNA)  0x80000001    3::/64
 0.0.0.3          8      (DNA)  0x80000001    33::/64
 0.0.0.3          8      (DNA)  0x80000001    7::/64
 0.0.0.3          8      (DNA)  0x80000001    37::/64
 0.0.0.3          3      (DNA)  0x80000001    3::3/128


                Link (Type-8) Link States (Area 0)

ADV Router        Age           Seq#          Link ID    Interface
 0.0.0.4          305           0x80000001    23         Tu1
 0.0.0.5          164           0x80000001    23         Tu1
 0.0.0.6          84            0x80000001    23         Tu1


                Intra Area Prefix Link States (Area 0)

ADV Router        Age           Seq#          Link ID    Ref-lstype    Ref-LSID
 0.0.0.1          180           0x80000031    0          0x2001        0
 0.0.0.2          2048          0x8000002F    0          0x2001        0
 0.0.0.2          2048          0x8000002F    4096       0x2002        4
 0.0.0.4          253           0x8000002F    0          0x2001        0
 0.0.0.4          253           0x80000001    23552      0x2002        23
```

In the output of the preceding command, the entries with **(DNA)** are the prefixes learned over the virtual link. Remember that a virtual link runs as a demand circuit, which is similar to running the **ip ospf demand-circuit** command on a dial-up link such as ISDN. Let's verify:

```
! On R3:

R3# show ipv6 ospf virtual-links | include demand

  Run as demand circuit
```

Erase the startup configuration and reload the routers before proceeding to the next lab.

Lab 11-5: EIGRPv6

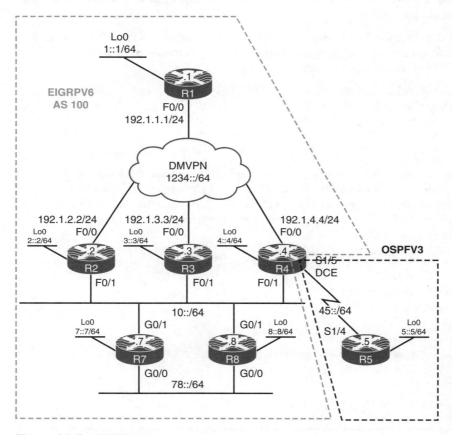

Figure 11-8 *EIGRPv6*

Figure 11-8 illustrates the topology that will be used in the following lab.

EIGRPv6—which is only a fancy name for IPv6-enabled EIGRP and does not really refer to a specific EIGRP version—operates in a very similar manner to its predecessor, EIGRP for IPv4. Both versions of EIGRP perform the following tasks:

■ EIGRP routers build a topology table using each of their neighbors' advertisements, and then only the best routes from the topology table are placed into the routers' routing tables. For each route, the next hop that provides the shortest loop-free path is called a *successor*, while a next hop that provides a higher-cost loop-free path is called a *feasible successor*.

■ Both versions of EIGRP use the same Diffusing Update Algorithm (DUAL) for fast convergence and to guarantee loop-free operation.

■ Both versions of EIGRP only send routing updates about paths that have changed once an EIGRP network has converged.

- Both versions of EIGRP send out Hello packets every 5 seconds on high-bandwidth links and every 60 seconds on low-bandwidth multipoint links to verify neighboring router connectivity.

- Both versions of EIGRP rely on the metrics of Bandwidth, Delay, Reliability, and Load to compute the composite metric of individual routes. By default, only Bandwidth and Delay are taken into account.

- Both versions of EIGRP use the Reliable Transport Protocol (RTP) to guarantee the delivery of EIGRP packets.

Task 1

Configure OSPFv3 Area 0 on the loopback0 and s1/4 interfaces of R5 and the s1/5 interface of R4. The loopback0 interface of R5 should be advertised with its correct mask. R4 and R5's RIDs should be configured to be 0.0.0.4 and 0.0.0.5, respectively.

```
! On R5:

R5(config)# ipv6 unicast-routing

R5(config)# ipv6 router ospf 1
R5(config-rtr)# router-id 0.0.0.5

R5(config)# interface loopback 0
R5(config-if)# ipv6 ospf network point-to-point
R5(config-if)# ipv6 ospf 1 area 0

R5(config)# interface Serial 1/4
R5(config-if)# ipv6 ospf 1 area 0
```

```
! On R4:

R4(config)# ipv6 unicast-routing

R4(config)# ipv6 router ospf 1
R4(config-rtr)# router-id 0.0.0.4

R4(config)# interface Serial 1/5
R4(config-if)# ipv6 ospf 1 area 0
```

You should see the following console message:

```
%OSPFv3-5-ADJCHG: Process 1, Nbr 0.0.0.5 on Serial1/5 from LOADING to FULL, Loading
  Done
```

```
R4# show ipv6 route ospf

IPv6 Routing Table - default - 10 entries
Codes: C - Connected, L - Local, S - Static, U - Per-user Static route
       B - BGP, HA - Home Agent, MR - Mobile Router, R - RIP
       I1 - ISIS L1, I2 - ISIS L2, IA - ISIS interarea, IS - ISIS summary
       D - EIGRP, EX - EIGRP external, NM - NEMO, ND - Neighbor Discovery
       l - LISP
       O - OSPF Intra, OI - OSPF Inter, OE1 - OSPF ext 1, OE2 - OSPF ext 2
       ON1 - OSPF NSSA ext 1, ON2 - OSPF NSSA ext 2
O   5::/64 [110/782]
     via FE80::5, Serial1/5

R4# ping 5::5

Type escape sequence to abort.
Sending 5, 100-byte ICMP Echos to 5::5, timeout is 2 seconds:

!!!!!
Success rate is 100 percent (5/5), round-trip min/avg/max = 28/29/32 ms
```

Task 2

Configure EIGRPv6 AS 100 on the loopback0, G0/1, and G0/0 interfaces of R7 and R8. These routers should be configured with EIGRPv6 named mode. The RIDs of the R7 and R8 routers should be configured as 0.0.0.7 and 0.0.0.8, respectively.

When configuring EIGRPv6, you must configure the EIGRP RID; otherwise, the EIGRP process will not start.

```
! On R7:

R7(config)# ipv6 unicast-routing

R7(config)# router eigrp A
R7(config-router)# address-family ipv6 unicast as 100
R7(config-router-af)# eigrp router-id 0.0.0.7
```

```
! On R8:

R8(config)# ipv6 unicast-routing

R8(config)# router eigrp B
R8(config-router)# address-family ipv6 unicast as 100
R8(config-router-af)# eigrp router-id 0.0.0.8
```

You should see the following console message:

```
%DUAL-5-NBRCHANGE: EIGRP-IPv6 100: Neighbor FE80::7 (GigabitEthernet0/0) is up:
new adjacency

%DUAL-5-NBRCHANGE: EIGRP-IPv6 100: Neighbor FE80::7 (GigabitEthernet0/1) is up:
new adjacency
```

Note   You did not have to run EIGRPv6 on any interface. When you're configuring EIGRPv6 in the named mode, by default, EIGRPv6 will run on all IPv6-enabled interfaces.

You can see that the two routers have established two EIGRPv6 neighbor adjacencies: one through their G0/0 interface and another through their G0/1 interface.

Let's verify the configuration:

```
! On R8:

R8# show ipv6 eigrp neighbors
EIGRP-IPv6 VR(B) Address-Family Neighbors for AS(100)

H   Address              Interface     Hold Uptime    SRTT   RTO   Q  Seq
                                       (sec)          (ms)         Cnt Num
1   Link-local address:  Gi0/1          11 00:01:41   1596   5000  0  6
    FE80::7
0   Link-local address:  Gi0/0          13 00:01:41   1596   5000  0  5
    FE80::7
```

```
! On R7:

R7# show ipv6 route eigrp

IPv6 Routing Table - default - 8 entries
Codes: C - Connected, L - Local, S - Static, U - Per-user Static route
       B - BGP, HA - Home Agent, MR - Mobile Router, R - RIP
       H - NHRP, I1 - ISIS L1, I2 - ISIS L2, IA - ISIS interarea
       IS - ISIS summary, D - EIGRP, EX - EIGRP external, NM - NEMO
       ND - ND Default, NDp - ND Prefix, DCE - Destination, NDr - Redirect
       O - OSPF Intra, OI - OSPF Inter, OE1 - OSPF ext 1, OE2 - OSPF ext 2
       ON1 - OSPF NSSA ext 1, ON2 - OSPF NSSA ext 2, ls - LISP site
       ld - LISP dyn-EID, a - Application
D   8::/64 [90/103040]
    via FE80::8, GigabitEthernet0/0
    via FE80::8, GigabitEthernet0/1
```

Note In IPv6, routers use their link-local IPv6 addresses to establish a neighbor adjacency and as the next-hop IPv6 addresses.

Task 3

Configure EIGRPv6 on all directly connected interfaces of R1, R2, and R3, as well as the loopback0, F0/1, and tunnel interfaces of R4. The EIGRP Router IDs should be configured to be 0.0.0.1, 0.0.0.2, 0.0.0.3, and 0.0.0.4 for R1, R2, R3, and R4, respectively.

```
! On R1:

R1(config)# ipv6 unicast-routing

R1(config)# ipv6 router eigrp 100
R1(config-rtr)# eigrp router-id 0.0.0.1
```

If EIGRPv6 is configured in the classic mode, it must be enabled on the interfaces for which EIGRP should run.

```
R1(config)# interface tunnel 1
R1(config-if)# ipv6 eigrp 100

R1(config)# interface loopback 0
R1(config-if)# ipv6 eigrp 100
```

```
! On R2:

R2(config)# ipv6 unicast-routing

R2(config)# ipv6 router eigrp 100
R2(config-rtr)# eigrp router-id 0.0.0.2

R2(config)# interface loopback 0
R2(config-if)# ipv6 eigrp 100

R2(config)# interface tunnel 1
R2(config-if)# ipv6 eigrp 100
```

You should see the following console message:

```
%DUAL-5-NBRCHANGE: EIGRP-IPv6 100: Neighbor FE80::1 (Tunnel1) is up:
new adjacency
```

```
R2(config)# interface FastEthernet 0/1
R2(config-if)# ipv6 eigrp 100
```

After this command is entered we should see adjacencies form with R8 and R7.

```
%DUAL-5-NBRCHANGE: EIGRP-IPv6 100: Neighbor FE80::8 (FastEthernet0/1) is up:
new adjacency
%DUAL-5-NBRCHANGE: EIGRP-IPv6 100: Neighbor FE80::7 (FastEthernet0/1) is up:
new adjacency
```

```
! On R3:

R3(config)# ipv6 unicast-routing

R3(config)# ipv6 router eigrp 100
R3(config-rtr)# eigrp router-id 0.0.0.3

R3(config)# interface loopback 0
R3(config-if)# ipv6 eigrp 100

R3(config)# interface tunnel 1
R3(config-if)# ipv6 eigrp 100
```

Now a neighbor relationship will form with R1.

```
%DUAL-5-NBRCHANGE: EIGRP-IPv6 100: Neighbor FE80::1 (Tunnel1) is up:
new adjacency
```

```
R3(config)# interface FastEthernet 0/1
R3(config-if)# ipv6 eigrp 100
```

Three adjacencies will result.

```
%DUAL-5-NBRCHANGE: EIGRP-IPv6 100: Neighbor FE80::7 (FastEthernet0/1) is up:
new adjacency

%DUAL-5-NBRCHANGE: EIGRP-IPv6 100: Neighbor FE80::8 (FastEthernet0/1) is up:
new adjacency

%DUAL-5-NBRCHANGE: EIGRP-IPv6 100: Neighbor FE80::2 (FastEthernet0/1) is up:
new adjacency
```

```
! On R4:

R4(config)# ipv6 router eigrp 100
R4(config-rtr)# eigrp router-id 0.0.0.4

R4(config)# interface loopback 0
R4(config-if)# ipv6 eigrp 100

R4(config)# interface tunnel 1
R4(config-if)# ipv6 eigrp 100
```

Notice that the tunnel interface to R1 now comes up.

```
%DUAL-5-NBRCHANGE: EIGRP-IPv6 100: Neighbor FE80::1 (Tunnel1) is up:
new adjacency
```

```
R4(config)# interface FastEthernet 0/1
R4(config-if)# ipv6 eigrp 100
```

Lastly, you should see the following console messages:

```
%DUAL-5-NBRCHANGE: EIGRP-IPv6 100: Neighbor FE80::7 (FastEthernet0/1) is up:
new adjacency

%DUAL-5-NBRCHANGE: EIGRP-IPv6 100: Neighbor FE80::2 (FastEthernet0/1) is up:
new adjacency

%DUAL-5-NBRCHANGE: EIGRP-IPv6 100: Neighbor FE80::8 (FastEthernet0/1) is up:
new adjacency

%DUAL-5-NBRCHANGE: EIGRP-IPv6 100: Neighbor FE80::3 (FastEthernet0/1) is up:
new adjacency
```

Let's verify the configuration:

```
! On R1:

R1# show ipv6 route eigrp

IPv6 Routing Table - default - 12 entries
Codes: C - Connected, L - Local, S - Static, U - Per-user Static route
       B - BGP, HA - Home Agent, MR - Mobile Router, R - RIP
       I1 - ISIS L1, I2 - ISIS L2, IA - ISIS interarea, IS - ISIS summary
       D - EIGRP, EX - EIGRP external, NM - NEMO, ND - Neighbor Discovery
```

```
      1 - LISP
      O - OSPF Intra, OI - OSPF Inter, OE1 - OSPF ext 1, OE2 - OSPF ext 2
      ON1 - OSPF NSSA ext 1, ON2 - OSPF NSSA ext 2
D   2::/64 [90/27008000]
    via FE80::2, Tunnel1
D   3::/64 [90/27008000]
    via FE80::3, Tunnel1
D   4::/64 [90/27008000]
    via FE80::4, Tunnel1
D   7::/64 [90/26882592]
    via FE80::3, Tunnel1
    via FE80::2, Tunnel1
    via FE80::4, Tunnel1
D   8::/64 [90/26882592]
    via FE80::3, Tunnel1
    via FE80::2, Tunnel1
    via FE80::4, Tunnel1
D   10::/64 [90/26882560]
    via FE80::3, Tunnel1
    via FE80::2, Tunnel1
    via FE80::4, Tunnel1
D   78::/64 [90/26885120]
    via FE80::3, Tunnel1
    via FE80::2, Tunnel1
    via FE80::4, Tunnel1
```

Task 4

Configure R4 to redistribute OSPFv3 into EIGRPv6 and inject a default route into the OSPFv3 routing domain.

The following command injects a default route into OSPF's routing domain. The use of the **always** keyword eliminates the need for maintaining a default route locally:

```
! On R4:

R4(config)# ipv6 router ospf 1
R4(config-rtr)# default-information originate always

R4(config-rtr)# ipv6 router eigrp 100
R4(config-rtr)# redistribute ospf 1 include-connected metric 1 1 1 1 1
```

Note in the preceding configuration that the **include-connected** keyword also redistributes the connected interfaces that are in OSPF's routing domain on R4.

Let's verify the configuration:

```
! On R1:


R1# show ipv6 route eigrp | include EX


      D - EIGRP, EX - EIGRP external, NM - NEMO, ND - Neighbor Discovery
EX  5::/64 [170/2561280256]
EX  45::/64 [170/2561280256]
```

Note   Network 45::/64 is redistributed into EIGRP's routing domain because on R4 you used the **include-connected** keyword when the redistribution was performed.

```
R1# ping 5::5
Type escape sequence to abort.
Sending 5, 100-byte ICMP Echos to 5::5, timeout is 2 seconds:
!!!!!
Success rate is 100 percent (5/5), round-trip min/avg/max = 28/29/32 ms
```

Task 5

Configure the Hello interval and Hold timer of R7 and R8 to 10 and 40 seconds, respectively. This policy should only be enforced for the G0/0 segment.

Let's see the default Hello interval:

```
! On R7:


R7# show ipv6 eigrp interface detail GigabitEthernet 0/0 | include Hold


  Hello-interval is 5, Hold-time is 15


R7(config)# router eigrp A
R7(config-router)# address-family ipv6 unicast autonomous-system 100


R7(config-router-af)# af-interface GigabitEthernet 0/0
R7(config-router-af-interface)# hello-interval 10
R7(config-router-af-interface)# hold-time 40
```

```
! On R8:


R8(config)# router eigrp B
R8(config-router)# address-family ipv6 unicast autonomous-system 100


R8(config-router-af)# af-interface GigabitEthernet 0/0
R8(config-router-af-interface)# hello-interval 10
R8(config-router-af-interface)# hold-time 40
```

Let's verify the configuration:

```
! On R7:


R7# show ipv6 eigrp interface detail Gigabit 0/0 | include Hold


  Hello-interval is 10, Hold-time is 40
```

Task 6

Configure a loopback1 interface on R2 using 2:2::2/64 as its IPv6 address. This loopback interface should be advertised in EIGRPv6 AS 100. Ensure that all routers in AS 100 know the path to this network and make use of redundant paths if and when they are available:

```
! On R2:


R2(config)# interface loopback 1
R2(config-if)# ipv6 address 2:2::2/64
R2(config-if)# ipv6 address fe80::2 link-local
R2(config-if)# ipv6 eigrp 100
```

Let's verify the configuration:

```
! On R1:


R1# show ipv6 route 2:2::/64


Routing entry for 2:2::/64
  Known via "eigrp 100", distance 90, metric 27008000, type internal
  Route count is 1/1, share count 0
  Routing paths:
    FE80::2, Tunnel1
      Last updated 13:18:12 ago
```

You can also verify this by looking for the same prefix on one of the other spokes:

```
! On R3:


R3# show ipv6 route 2:2::/64


Routing entry for 2:2::/64

  Known via "eigrp 100", distance 90, metric 156160, type internal
  Route count is 1/1, share count 0
  Routing paths:
    FE80::2, FastEthernet0/1
      Last updated 13:19:43 ago
```

Note R3 learns the route through its F0/1 segment and not through the DMVPN cloud. If the F0/1 interface of this router is shut down, the router will not see the route through the DMVPN cloud.

This is because EIGRP for IPv6 has IPv6 split-horizon for EIGRPv6 enabled on multipoint interfaces; therefore, a given spoke will not see the routes advertised by the other spokes unless IPv6 split-horizon is disabled for EIGRP in AS 100. Let's do a traceroute and see the paths that R3 takes to reach the 2:2::/64 network:

```
! On R3:


R3# traceroute
Protocol [ip]: ipv6
Target IPv6 address: 2:2::2
Source address: 3::3
Insert source routing header? [no]: → Hit Enter to accept the default
Numeric display? [no]: → Hit Enter to accept the default
Timeout in seconds [3]: → Hit Enter to accept the default
Probe count [3]: → Hit Enter to accept the default
Minimum Time to Live [1]: → Hit Enter to accept the default
Maximum Time to Live [30]: → Hit Enter to accept the default
Priority [0]: → Hit Enter to accept the default
Port Number [0]: → Hit Enter to accept the default
Type escape sequence to abort.
Tracing the route to 2:2::2

  1 10::2 8 msec 0 msec 4 msec
```

Let's shut down the F0/1 interface of R3 and see if the path changes from going through the F0/1 interface to DMVPN:

```
R3(config)# interface FastEthernet 0/1
R3(config-if)# shut
```

Let's verify:

```
R3# show ipv6 route 2:2::/64

% Route not found
```

You can see that R3 does not take the redundant path to reach 2:2::/64. Let's disable the IPv6 split-horizon on R1:

```
! On R1:

R1(config)# interface tunnel 1
R1(config-if)# no ipv6 split-horizon eigrp 100
```

Let's verify the configuration:

```
! On R3:

R3# show ipv6 route 2:2::/64

Routing entry for 2:2::/64
  Known via "eigrp 100", distance 90, metric 28288000, type internal
  Route count is 1/1, share count 0
  Routing paths:
    FE80::1, Tunnel1
      Last updated 00:00:45 ago
```

You can see that you have redundancy. Let's enable the F0/1 interface of R3:

```
R3(config)# interface FastEthernet 0/1
R3(config-if)# no shutdown
```

Let's verify the configuration:

```
! On R3:


R3# show ipv6 route 2:2::/64


Routing entry for 2:2::/64
  Known via "eigrp 100", distance 90, metric 156160, type internal
  Route count is 1/1, share count 0
  Routing paths:
    FE80::2, FastEthernet0/1
      Last updated 00:00:23 ago


R3# show ipv6 eigrp topology 2:2::/64


EIGRP-IPv6 Topology Entry for AS(100)/ID(0.0.0.3) for 2:2::/64
  State is Passive, Query origin flag is 1, 1 Successor(s), FD is 156160
  Descriptor Blocks:
  FE80::2 (FastEthernet0/1), from FE80::2, Send flag is 0x0


      Composite metric is (156160/128256), route is Internal
      Vector metric:
        Minimum bandwidth is 100000 Kbit
        Total delay is 5100 microseconds
        Reliability is 255/255
        Load is 1/255
        Minimum MTU is 1500
        Hop count is 1
        Originating router is 0.0.0.2
  FE80::1 (Tunnel1), from FE80::1, Send flag is 0x0
      Composite metric is (28288000/27008000), route is Internal
      Vector metric:
        Minimum bandwidth is 100 Kbit
        Total delay is 105000 microseconds
        Reliability is 255/255
        Load is 2/255
        Minimum MTU is 1476
        Hop count is 2
        Originating router is 0.0.0.2
```

Task 7

R4 should never use more than 25% of its bandwidth for EIGRPv6 traffic on its tunnel and F0/1 interfaces. You should use an EIGRP-specific command to accomplish this task.

By default, EIGRP packets use up to 50% of the link's bandwidth, but this percentage can be changed using the **ipv6 bandwidth-percent eigrp** interface configuration command:

```
On R4:

R4(config)# interface range tunnel 1 , FastEthernet 0/1
R4(config-if-range)# ipv6 bandwidth-percent eigrp 100 25
```

Task 8

Configure a loopback1 interface on R1 using 1:1::1/64 as its IPv6 address. Ensure that all routers in AS 100 can reach this network. Do not advertise or redistribute this particular network in EIGRP to solve this task.

One way to accomplish this task is to configure R1 to send a summary that includes the network 1:1::/64. One such summary network is a default route:

```
! On R1:

R1(config)# interface loopback 1
R1(config-if)# ipv6 address 1:1::1/64
R1(config-if)# ipv6 address fe80::1 1
```

Note Just like EIGRP for IPv4, the summary address can be configured to inject a default route.

```
R1(config)# interface tunnel 1
R1(config-if)# ipv6 summary-address eigrp 100 ::/0
```

Let's test and verify the configuration:

```
! On R7:

R7# show ipv6 route eigrp

IPv6 Routing Table - default - 16 entries
Codes: C - Connected, L - Local, S - Static, U - Per-user Static route
       B - BGP, HA - Home Agent, MR - Mobile Router, R - RIP
```

```
        H - NHRP, I1 - ISIS L1, I2 - ISIS L2, IA - ISIS interarea
        IS - ISIS summary, D - EIGRP, EX - EIGRP external, NM - NEMO
        ND - ND Default, NDp - ND Prefix, DCE - Destination, NDr - Redirect
        O - OSPF Intra, OI - OSPF Inter, OE1 - OSPF ext 1, OE2 - OSPF ext 2
        ON1 - OSPF NSSA ext 1, ON2 - OSPF NSSA ext 2, ls - LISP site
        ld - LISP dyn-EID, a - Application
D    ::/0 [90/79411200]
     via FE80::4, GigabitEthernet0/1
     via FE80::2, GigabitEthernet0/1
     via FE80::3, GigabitEthernet0/1
D    2::/64 [90/2662400]
     via FE80::2, GigabitEthernet0/1
D    2:2::/64 [90/2662400]
     via FE80::2, GigabitEthernet0/1
D    3::/64 [90/2662400]
     via FE80::3, GigabitEthernet0/1
D    4::/64 [90/2662400]
     via FE80::4, GigabitEthernet0/1
EX   5::/64 [170/4294967295]
     via FE80::4, GigabitEthernet0/1
     via FE80::8, GigabitEthernet0/0
D    8::/64 [90/103040]
     via FE80::8, GigabitEthernet0/0
     via FE80::8, GigabitEthernet0/1
EX   45::/64 [170/4294967295]
     via FE80::4, GigabitEthernet0/1
     via FE80::8, GigabitEthernet0/0
D    1234::/64 [90/76851200]
     via FE80::2, GigabitEthernet0/1
     via FE80::4, GigabitEthernet0/1
     via FE80::3, GigabitEthernet0/1

R7# ping 1:1::1

Type escape sequence to abort.
Sending 5, 100-byte ICMP Echos to 1:1::1, timeout is 2 seconds:
!!!!!
Success rate is 100 percent (5/5), round-trip min/avg/max = 1/2/4 ms
```

Task 9

Configure MD5 authentication on all routers connected to the 10::/64 segment. You should use "eigrpv6" as the password to accomplish this task:

```
! On R2, R3, R4, R7 and R8:

Rx(config)# key chain TST
Rx(config-keychain)# key 1
Rx(config-keychain-key)# key-string eigrpv6
```

```
! On R2:

R2(config)# interface FastEthernet 0/1
R2(config-if)# ipv6 authentication key-chain eigrp 100 TST
R2(config-if)# ipv6 authentication mode eigrp 100 md5
```

```
! On R3:

R3(config)# interface FastEthernet 0/1
R3(config-if)# ipv6 authentication key-chain eigrp 100 TST
R3(config-if)# ipv6 authentication mode eigrp 100 md5
```

```
! On R4:

R4(config)# interface FastEthernet 0/1
R4(config-if)# ipv6 authentication key-chain eigrp 100 TST
R4(config-if)# ipv6 authentication mode eigrp 100 md5
```

```
! On R7:

R7(config)# router eigrp A
R7(config-router)# address-family ipv6 unicast autonomous-system 100

R7(config-router-af)# af-interface GigabitEthernet 0/1
R7(config-router-af-interface)# authentication key-chain TST
R7(config-router-af-interface)# authentication mode md5
```

```
! On R8:

R8(config)# router eigrp B
R8(config-router)# address-family ipv6 unicast autonomous-system 100

R8(config-router-af)# af-interface GigabitEthernet0/1
R8(config-router-af-interface)# authentication key-chain TST
R8(config-router-af-interface)# authentication mode md5
```

You should see the following console messages:

```
%DUAL-5-NBRCHANGE: EIGRP-IPv6 100: Neighbor FE80::4 (GigabitEthernet0/1) is up:
new adjacency


%DUAL-5-NBRCHANGE: EIGRP-IPv6 100: Neighbor FE80::7 (GigabitEthernet0/1) is up:
new adjacency


%DUAL-5-NBRCHANGE: EIGRP-IPv6 100: Neighbor FE80::2 (GigabitEthernet0/1) is up:
new adjacency


%DUAL-5-NBRCHANGE: EIGRP-IPv6 100: Neighbor FE80::3 (GigabitEthernet0/1) is up:
new adjacency
```

Let's verify the configuration:

```
! On R8:

R8# show ipv6 eigrp interface detail GigabitEthernet 0/1 | include Auth

  Authentication mode is md5,  key-chain is "TST"
```

Task 10

Configure authentication on the 78::/64 segment. You must use the strongest
authentication mechanism to accomplish this task. Use "Cisco" as the password. Do
not configure a key chain to accomplish this task.

In EIGRP, authentication is configured on a per-interface basis, which means that the
packet exchange between the two neighbors through that given interface is authenticated.

When HMAC-SHA-256 authentication is configured, each EIGRP packet is authenticated using the preshared key. The preshared key is used to generate and verify a message digest that is added to the packet. The message digest is a one-way function of the
packet and the secret key.

```
! On R7:

R7(config)# router eigrp A
R7(config-router)# address-family ipv6 unicast autonomous-system 100

R7(config-router-af)# af-interface GigabitEthernet 0/0
R7(config-router-af-interface)# authentication mode hmac-sha-256 Cisco
```

```
! On R8:

R8(config)# router eigrp B
R8(config-router)# address-family ipv6 unicast autonomous-system 100

R8(config-router-af)# af-interface GigabitEthernet 0/0
R8(config-router-af-interface)# authentication mode hmac-sha-256 Cisco
```

Let's verify the configuration:

```
! On R7:

R7# show ipv6 eigrp interface detail GigabitEthernet 0/0 | include Auth

  Authentication mode is HMAC-SHA-256, key-chain is not set
```

Task 11

Configure R2 such that it filters existing and future external routes. Do not use a prefix list or a route map to accomplish this task.

Let's see if we can verify the existing external routes on R2:

```
! On R2:

R2# show ipv6 route eigrp | include EX

      D - EIGRP, EX - EIGRP external, NM - NEMO, ND - Neighbor Discovery
EX  5::/64 [170/2560002816]
EX  45::/64 [170/2560002816]
```

Note In the following command, the first value (90) is the administrative distance that is applied to all internal EIGRP routes, whereas the second value is the administrative distance applied to all external EIGRP routes:

```
R2(config)# ipv6 router eigrp 100
R2(config-rtr)# distance eigrp 90 255
```

Let's verify the configuration:

```
! On R2:


R2# show ipv6 route eigrp


IPv6 Routing Table - default - 15 entries
Codes: C - Connected, L - Local, S - Static, U - Per-user Static route
       B - BGP, HA - Home Agent, MR - Mobile Router, R - RIP
       I1 - ISIS L1, I2 - ISIS L2, IA - ISIS interarea, IS - ISIS summary
       D - EIGRP, EX - EIGRP external, NM - NEMO, ND - Neighbor Discovery
       l - LISP
       O - OSPF Intra, OI - OSPF Inter, OE1 - OSPF ext 1, OE2 - OSPF ext 2
       ON1 - OSPF NSSA ext 1, ON2 - OSPF NSSA ext 2
D    ::/0 [90/27008000]
     via FE80::1, Tunnel1
D    3::/64 [90/156160]
     via FE80::3, FastEthernet0/1
D    4::/64 [90/156160]
     via FE80::4, FastEthernet0/1
D    7::/64 [90/28192]
     via FE80::7, FastEthernet0/1
D    8::/64 [90/28192]
     via FE80::8, FastEthernet0/1
D    78::/64 [90/30720]
     via FE80::8, FastEthernet0/1
     via FE80::7, FastEthernet0/1
```

Task 12

R3 should be configured to filter prefix 2:2::/64:

```
! On R3:


R3# show ipv6 route 2:2::/64


Routing entry for 2:2::/64
  Known via "eigrp 100", distance 90, metric 156160, type internal
  Route count is 1/1, share count 0
  Routing paths:
    FE80::2, FastEthernet0/1
      Last updated 00:13:41 ago
```

Note In EIGRPv6, **distribute-list prefix-list** is supported, but the use of **route-map** is
not supported. Therefore, a prefix list is configured, and the distribute list is configured to
reference the prefix list as follows:

```
! On R3:

R3(config)# ipv6 prefix-list TST seq 5 deny 2:2::/64
R3(config)# ipv6 prefix-list TST seq 10 permit ::0/0 le 128

R3(config)# ipv6 router eigrp 100
R3(config-rtr)# distribute-list prefix TST in FastEthernet 0/1
R3(config-rtr)# distribute-list prefix TST in tunnel 1
```

Let's verify the configuration:

```
! On R3:

R3# show ipv6 route eigrp

IPv6 Routing Table - default - 15 entries
Codes: C - Connected, L - Local, S - Static, U - Per-user Static route
       B - BGP, HA - Home Agent, MR - Mobile Router, R - RIP
       I1 - ISIS L1, I2 - ISIS L2, IA - ISIS interarea, IS - ISIS summary
       D - EIGRP, EX - EIGRP external, NM - NEMO, ND - Neighbor Discovery
       l - LISP
       O - OSPF Intra, OI - OSPF Inter, OE1 - OSPF ext 1, OE2 - OSPF ext 2
       ON1 - OSPF NSSA ext 1, ON2 - OSPF NSSA ext 2
D    ::/0 [90/27008000]
     via FE80::1, Tunnel1
D    2::/64 [90/156160]
     via FE80::2, FastEthernet0/1
D    4::/64 [90/156160]
     via FE80::4, FastEthernet0/1
EX   5::/64 [170/2560002816]
     via FE80::4, FastEthernet0/1
D    7::/64 [90/28192]
     via FE80::7, FastEthernet0/1
```

```
D    8::/64 [90/28192]
      via FE80::8, FastEthernet0/1
EX   45::/64 [170/2560002816]
      via FE80::4, FastEthernet0/1
D    78::/64 [90/30720]
      via FE80::7, FastEthernet0/1
      via FE80::8, FastEthernet0/1
```

Erase the startup configuration and reload the routers before proceeding to the next lab.

Chapter 12

Quality of Service

Quality of service (QOS) involves how we as network administrators ensure that different types of traffic can be managed differently. In this chapter, we are going to delve into the underlying mechanisms that allow us to be able to select which particular type of traffic we want to provide preferential treatment to.

Preferential treatment means that out of all the available bandwidth we have, we want to cut out a portion and assign it to one particular type of traffic such that it is going to be receiving better treatment than the traffic it's sharing the overall bandwidth with. On the other hand, non-preferential treatment means that we're taking away privilege. The important rule to understand here is that there is only so much bandwidth available. There is absolutely no quality of service mechanism we can employ that's going to allow us to get more bandwidth out of our links than they can natively support. The only thing we can do is designate who gets the lion's share of that bandwidth and also put into place certain mechanisms that allow us to ensure that certain types of traffic are not starved.

We have two types of QOS mechanisms, each operating at separate levels of the OSI model. Layer 2 quality of service is made possible by the Class of Service (COS Byte) field found in 802.1 Q trunk headers. Layer 3 QOS is supported by the Type of Services (TOS Byte) field found in the Layer 3 IP headers. Due to the absence of advanced Layer 2 application-specific integrated circuits (ASICs) in the virtualized equipment employed in the CCIE exam, Cisco has removed almost all of the complex Layer 2 mechanisms for quality of service.

If we want to support the idea of distributed switching, we're going to be moving functionality and capabilities to the hardware in our switch in order to relieve the strain from the main processor. Ports have specialized hardware with their own coprocessors that allow them to perform a lot of functions directly applicable to quality of service (QOS) at Layer 2. Because we use all virtualized gear in the Routing and Switching Version 5 exam, we're missing these ASICs. They're gone. They're not part of the equation, so we can't use many of the advanced quality of service mechanisms that operate at Layer 2. In other words, many of the more complicated L2 QOS features have been removed from the blueprint.

In the following series of labs, we explore the Layer 2 QOS topics remaining in the blueprint.

Lab 12-1: MLS QOS

12.1.1.0/24

VTP Domain
tst

Figure 12-1   *Configuring MLS QOS*

Figure 12-1 illustrates the topology that will be used in the following tasks.

Task 1

Configure R1 to send all traffic with a COS marking of 1. R2 should be used for verification purposes and should be configured to match on COS values of 0–7 ingress on its f0/1.21 subinterface.

In this task, R2 is configured to match on incoming traffic with COS values of 0–7; this is done so the policy can be tested and verified.

```
On R2:

R2(config)# class-map cos0
R2(config-cmap)# match cos 0

R2(config)# class-map cos1
R2(config-cmap)# match cos 1

R2(config)# class-map cos2
R2(config-cmap)# match cos 2

R2(config)# class-map cos3
R2(config-cmap)# match cos 3

R2(config)# class-map cos4
R2(config-cmap)# match cos 4

R2(config)# class-map cos5
R2(config-cmap)# match cos 5
```

```
R2(config)# class-map cos6
R2(config-cmap)# match cos 6

R2(config)# class-map cos7
R2(config-cmap)# match cos 7

R2(config)# policy-map TST
R2(config-pmap)# class cos0
R2(config-pmap)# class cos1
R2(config-pmap)# class cos2
R2(config-pmap)# class cos3
R2(config-pmap)# class cos4
R2(config-pmap)# class cos5
R2(config-pmap)# class cos6
R2(config-pmap)# class cos7

R2(config)# interface FastEthernet0/1.21
R2(config-subif)# service-policy in TST
```

The following configures R1 to generate all traffic with a COS value of 1:

```
On R1:

R1(config)# policy-map TST
R1(config-pmap)# class class-default
R1(config-pmap-c)# set cos 1

R1(config-pmap-c)# interface FastEthernet0/0.12
R1(config-subif)# service-policy out TST
```

Let's test the configuration:

```
On R1:

R1# ping 12.1.1.2
Type escape sequence to abort.
Sending 5, 100-byte ICMP Echos to 12.1.1.2, timeout is 2 seconds:
!!!!!
Success rate is 100 percent (5/5), round-trip min/avg/max = 1/3/4 ms

On R2:

R3# show policy-map interface | section cos1
    Class-map: cos1 (match-all)
      5 packets, 590 bytes
      5 minute offered rate 0 bps
      Match: cos  1
```

You can see that the test was successful. Let's verify the configuration of **mls qos** on SW1 and SW2:

```
On SW1:

SW1# show mls qos
QOS is disabled
QOS ip packet dscp rewrite is enabled


On SW2:

SW2# show mls qos
QOS is disabled
QOS ip packet dscp rewrite is enabled
```

The test was successful because **mls qos** was disabled. When **mls qos** is disabled, the switch does *not* drop or change the marking of incoming traffic.

Task 2

Enable **mls qos** on SW1 and ensure that the test in the previous task is still successful:

```
On SW1:

SW1(config)# mls qos
```

Let's verify the configuration:

```
SW1# show mls qos
QOS is enabled
QOS ip packet dscp rewrite is enabled
```

When **mls qos** is enabled, the switch drops the marking of all incoming traffic, unless that marking is trusted on the interface through which the traffic is received. Once **mls qos** is configured on SW1, SW1 will drop the marking of all incoming traffic; therefore, R2 will see all traffic generated by R1 with a COS value of 0.

If the f0/1 interface of SW1 is configured to trust COS, when SW1 receives the traffic, it will *not* rewrite or drop the Layer 2 marking.

```
On R2:

R2# clear counters
Clear "show interface" counters on all interfaces [confirm]
Press Enter to confirm
```

Let's test the configuration:

```
On R1:

R1# ping 12.1.1.2
Type escape sequence to abort.
Sending 5, 100-byte ICMP Echos to 12.1.1.2, timeout is 2 seconds:
!!!!!
Success rate is 100 percent (5/5), round-trip min/avg/max = 4/4/4 ms

On R2:

R2# show policy-map interface | section cos1
    Class-map: cos1 (match-all)
      0 packets, 0 bytes
      5 minute offered rate 0 bps
      Match: cos  1
```

Note Because the marking was dropped by SW1, R2 no longer sees incoming traffic marked with a COS value of 1. However, if the marking is dropped, it should match COS 0, correct? Let's verify:

```
On R2:

R2# show policy-map interface | section cos0
    Class-map: cos0 (match-all)
      5 packets, 590 bytes
      5 minute offered rate 0 bps
      Match: cos  0
```

In order for SW1 to trust the COS marking of incoming traffic, the switchport that R1 is connected to must trust the COS marking in incoming traffic. Let's configure SW1's f0/1 interface to trust the COS marking of all incoming traffic:

```
On SW1:

SW1(config)# interface FastEthernet0/1
SW1(config-if)# mls qos trust cos
```

Let's test the configuration:

```
On R2:


R2# clear counters
Clear "show interface" counters on all interfaces [confirm]
Press Enter to confirm


On R1:


R1# ping 12.1.1.2 repeat 10
Type escape sequence to abort.
Sending 10, 100-byte ICMP Echos to 12.1.1.2, timeout is 2 seconds:
!!!!!!!!!!
Success rate is 100 percent (10/10), round-trip min/avg/max = 1/3/4 ms


On R2:


R2# show policy-map interface | section cos0
    Class-map: cos0 (match-all)
      0 packets, 0 bytes
      5 minute offered rate 0 bps
      Match: cos  0

R2# show policy-map interface | section cos1
    Class-map: cos1 (match-all)
      10 packets, 1180 bytes
      5 minute offered rate 0 bps
      Match: cos  1
```

Task 3

Configure SW1's f0/1 interface such that it marks all ingress traffic with a COS marking
of 2. Do *not* configure Modular Quality of Service Command Line Interface (MQC) for
this purpose.

The following command assigns a COS value of 2:

```
On SW1:
SW1(config)# interface FastEthernet0/1
SW1(config-if)# mls qos cos 2
```

Let's remove the **mls qos trust cos** command and verify the configuration of the f0/1 interface of SW1:

```
SW1(config)# interface FastEthernet0/1
SW1(config-if)# no mls qos trust cos

SW1# sh run int f0/1
Building configuration...

Current configuration : 128 bytes
!
interface FastEthernet0/1
 switchport trunk encapsulation dot1q
 switchport mode trunk
 mls qos cos 2
end
```

Let's verify the configuration:

```
On SW1:

SW1# show mls qos interface FastEthernet0/1
FastEthernet0/1
trust state: not trusted
trust mode: not trusted
trust enabled flag: ena
COS override: dis
default COS: 2
DSCP Mutation Map: Default DSCP Mutation Map
Trust device: none
qos mode: port-based
```

Now we can test the configuration:

```
On R2:

R2# clear counters
Clear "show interface" counters on all interfaces [confirm]
Press Enter to confirm

On R1:

R1# ping 12.1.1.2 rep 20
Type escape sequence to abort.
Sending 20, 100-byte ICMP Echos to 12.1.1.2, timeout is 2 seconds:
!!!!!!!!!!!!!!!!!!!!
Success rate is 100 percent (20/20), round-trip min/avg/max = 1/3/4 ms
```

Let's verify the test:

```
On R2:

R2# show policy-map interface | section cos0
    Class-map: cos0 (match-all)
      20 packets, 2360 bytes
      5 minute offered rate 1000 bps
      Match: cos  0

R2# show policy-map interface | section cos1
    Class-map: cos1 (match-all)
      0 packets, 0 bytes
      5 minute offered rate 0 bps
      Match: cos  1

R2# show policy-map interface | section cos2
    Class-map: cos2 (match-all)
      0 packets, 0 bytes
      5 minute offered rate 0 bps
      Match: cos  2
```

The **mls qos cos 2** command on its own does *nothing*. It should be combined with either **mls qos cos override** or **mls qos trust cos**. When it's combined with **MLS qos trust cos**, *only* the untagged traffic is affected, but if it is combined with **mls qos cos override**, then all traffic (tagged or untagged) is affected. Tagged traffic is traffic that contains the VLAN ID.

Let's test this by adding **mls qos trust cos** to the f0/1 interface of SW1 and view the result:

```
On SW1:

SW1(config)# interface FastEthernet0/1
SW1(config-if)# mls qos trust cos


On R2:


R2# clear counters
Clear "show interface" counters on all interfaces [confirm]
Press Enter to confirm


On R1:


R1# ping 12.1.1.2 rep 20
Type escape sequence to abort.
Sending 20, 100-byte ICMP Echos to 12.1.1.2, timeout is 2 seconds:
```

```
!!!!!!!!!!!!!!!!!!!!!
Success rate is 100 percent (20/20), round-trip min/avg/max = 1/3/4 ms

On R2:

R2# show policy-map interface | section cos0
    Class-map: cos0 (match-all)
      0 packets, 0 bytes
      5 minute offered rate 0 bps
      Match: cos   0

R2# show policy-map interface | section cos1
    Class-map: cos1 (match-all)
      20 packets, 2360 bytes
      5 minute offered rate 0 bps
      Match: cos   1

R2# show policy-map interface | section cos2
    Class-map: cos2 (match-all)
      0 packets, 0 bytes
      5 minute offered rate 0 bps
      Match: cos   2
```

Note Even though the interface is configured with **mls qos cos 2** and **mls qos trust cos**, the traffic coming in on that interface is *not* affected. To mark *all* traffic with a COS marking of 2, which means tagged or untagged, the port must be configured to override the existing COS.

The following command configures the switch port with the **mls qos cos override** command:

```
On SW1:

SW1(config)# interface FastEthernet0/1
SW1(config-if)# mls qos cos override
```

Let's look at the configuration on the f0/1 interface of SW1:

```
On SW1:

SW1# show run interface FastEthernet0/1
Building configuration...
```

```
Current configuration : 131 bytes
!
interface FastEthernet0/1
 switchport trunk encapsulation dot1q
 switchport mode trunk
 mls qos cos 2
 mls qos cos override
end
```

You can see that the **mls qos trust cos** command was auto-replaced with the **mls qos cos override** command. Let's test and verify:

```
On R2:


R2# clear counters
Clear "show interface" counters on all interfaces [confirm]
Press Enter to confirm

On R1:


R1# ping 12.1.1.2 rep 20
Type escape sequence to abort.
Sending 20, 100-byte ICMP Echos to 12.1.1.2, timeout is 2 seconds:
!!!!!!!!!!!!!!!!!!!!
Success rate is 100 percent (20/20), round-trip min/avg/max = 1/3/4 ms


On R2:


R2# show policy-map interface | section cos0
    Class-map: cos0 (match-all)
      0 packets, 0 bytes
      5 minute offered rate 0 bps
      Match: cos  0


R2# show policy-map interface | section cos1
    Class-map: cos1 (match-all)
      0 packets, 0 bytes
      5 minute offered rate 0 bps
      Match: cos  1


R2# show policy-map interface | section cos2
    Class-map: cos2 (match-all)
      20 packets, 2360 bytes
      5 minute offered rate 1000 bps
      Match: cos  2
```

You can see that the traffic generated by R1 that had a COS value of 1 was overridden with a COS value of 2.

What if the f0/1 interface of SW1 is configured with **mls qos trust cos** and **mls qos cos 2** and we want the traffic generated by R1 to be rewritten to a COS value of 2? Can we accomplish this task by configuring R1?

Let's test and verify:

```
On SW1:

SW1(config)# interface FastEthernet0/1
SW1(config-if)# mls qos trust cos
```

Now let's verify the configuration:

```
SW1# show run interface FastEthernet0/1
Building configuration...

Current configuration : 128 bytes
!
interface FastEthernet0/1
 switchport trunk encapsulation dot1q
 switchport mode trunk
 mls qos cos 2
 mls qos trust cos
end
```

Note The **mls qos trust cos** command automatically removed the **mls qos cos override** command.

We know that with the preceding configuration, only untagged traffic will be affected, but how do we untag the traffic generated by R1 without having to reconfigure R1?

```
On R1:

R1(config)# interface FastEthernet0/0.12
R1(config-subif)# encapsulation dot1Q 100 native
```

Note With the **native** keyword, we are instructing R1 to remove the tag; therefore, the value before **native** is irrelevant.

Let's test the configuration:

```
On R2:


R2# clear counters
Clear "show interface" counters on all interfaces [confirm]
Press Enter to confirm


On R1:


R1# ping 12.1.1.2 rep 20
Type escape sequence to abort.
Sending 20, 100-byte ICMP Echos to 12.1.1.2, timeout is 2 seconds:
!!!!!!!!!!!!!!!!!!!!
Success rate is 100 percent (20/20), round-trip min/avg/max = 1/3/4 ms


On R2:


R2# show policy-map interface | section cos0
    Class-map: cos0 (match-all)
      0 packets, 0 bytes
      5 minute offered rate 0 bps
      Match: cos  0


R2# show policy-map interface | section cos1
    Class-map: cos1 (match-all)
      0 packets, 0 bytes
      5 minute offered rate 0 bps
      Match: cos  1


R2# show policy-map interface | section cos2
    Class-map: cos2 (match-all)
      20 packets, 2360 bytes
      5 minute offered rate 0 bps
      Match: cos  2
```

Because the traffic is no longer tagged, the traffic generated by R1 with a COS value of 1 is rewritten to a COS value of 2.

Erase the startup configuration on R1–R3 and on SW1 and SW2 and reload these routers and switches before proceeding to the next lab.

Lab 12-2: Differential Service Code Point-Mutation

12.1.1.0/24
VTP Domain
tst

Figure 12-2 *Configuring DSCP-Mutation*

Figure 12-2 illustrates the topology that will be used in the following tasks.

Task 1

Configure an MQC on R1 such that all packets going out of its F0/0 interface are marked with a DSCP value of 1. For verification purposes, R2's F0/1 interface should be configured to match on DSCP values of 0–7 for all ingress traffic. Ensure that **mls qos** is disabled on both switches.

```
On both switches:

SWx# show mls qos
QOS is disabled
QOS ip packet dscp rewrite is enabled
```

The following configuration marks all egress traffic with a DSCP value of 1:

```
On R1:

R1(config)# policy-map TST
R1(config-pmap)# class class-default
R1(config-pmap-c)# set ip dscp 1

R1(config)# interface FastEthernet0/0
R1(config-if)# service-policy out TST
```

The following configuration is done for verification and testing purposes:

```
On R2:
R2(config)# class-map dscp0
R2(config-cmap)# match ip dscp 0

R2(config)# class-map dscp1
R2(config-cmap)# match ip dscp 1

R2(config)# class-map dscp2
R2(config-cmap)# match ip dscp 2
```

```
R2(config)# class-map dscp3
R2(config-cmap)# match ip dscp 3

R2(config)# class-map dscp4
R2(config-cmap)# match ip dscp 4

R2(config)# class-map dscp5
R2(config-cmap)# match ip dscp 5

R2(config)# class-map dscp6
R2(config-cmap)# match ip dscp 6

R2(config)# class-map dscp7
R2(config-cmap)# match ip dscp 7

R2(config)# policy-map TST
R2(config-pmap)# class dscp0
R2(config-pmap)# class dscp1
R2(config-pmap)# class dscp2
R2(config-pmap)# class dscp3
R2(config-pmap)# class dscp4
R2(config-pmap)# class dscp5
R2(config-pmap)# class dscp6
R2(config-pmap)# class dscp7

R2(config)# interface FastEthernet0/1
R2(config-if)# service-policy in TST
```

Let's test the configuration:

```
On R1:


R1# ping 12.1.1.2 rep 10
Type escape sequence to abort.
Sending 10, 100-byte ICMP Echos to 12.1.1.2, timeout is 2 seconds:
!!!!!!!!!!
Success rate is 100 percent (10/10), round-trip min/avg/max = 1/3/4 ms


On R2:


R2# show policy-map inter | section dscp1
    Class-map: dscp1 (match-all)
      10 packets, 1140 bytes
      5 minute offered rate 0 bps
      Match: ip dscp 1
```

Task 2

Configure SW2 such that if the incoming traffic is marked with a DSCP value of 1, it is overwritten with a DSCP value of 60. Do *not* configure a class map or a policy map to accomplish this task. Use R2 to verify the configuration.

DSCP-mutation can be configured on SW2 to accomplish this task. Configuring DSCP-mutation requires four steps.

Step 1

First, **mls qos** *must* be enabled:

```
On SW2:

SW2(config)# mls qos
```

Once **mls qos** is enabled, the marking of all traffic is zeroed out, meaning that incoming traffic that is marked with any DSCP value will match to a DSCP value of 0. This can be seen on R2. The following proves this point:

```
On SW2:

SW2# show mls qos
QOS is enabled
QOS ip packet dscp rewrite is enabled
```

Let's test the configuration:

```
On R2:

R2# clear counters
Clear "show interface" counters on all interfaces [confirm]

Press Enter to confirm

On R1:

R1# ping 12.1.1.2 rep 100

Type escape sequence to abort.
Sending 100, 100-byte ICMP Echos to 12.1.1.2, timeout is 2 seconds:
!!!!!!!!!!!!!!!!!!!!!!!!!!!!!!!!!!!!!!!!!!!!!!!!!!!!!!!!!!!!!!!!!!!!!!!!!!!!
!!!!!!!!!!!!!!!!!!!!!!!!!!!!!!!!
Success rate is 100 percent (100/100), round-trip min/avg/max = 1/1/4 ms
```

Now we can verify the configuration:

```
On R2:

R2# show policy-map interface | section dscp1

    Class-map: DSCP1 (match-all)
      0 packets, 0 bytes
      5 minute offered rate 0 bps
      Match:  dscp 1

R3# show policy-map interface | section dscp0

    Class-map: DSCP0 (match-all)
      100 packets, 11400 bytes
      5 minute offered rate 2000 bps
      Match:  dscp default (0)
```

Step 2

If **mls qos trust dscp** is *not* configured, the configuration will not have any effect on the packets because SW2 will drop the marking of all incoming traffic:

```
On SW2:

SW2(config)# interface FastEthernet0/19
SW2(config-if)# mls qos trust dscp
```

Let's verify this information:

```
On SW2:

SW2# show mls qos interface FastEthernet0/19 | include trust state
trust state: trust dscp
```

Note   If COS was trusted, the output of the preceding command would have stated **trust state: trust cos** since *only* DSCP is trusted. In other words, the trust state is DSCP.

Let's test this information:

```
On R2:


R2# clear counters
Clear "show interface" counters on all interfaces [confirm]
Press Enter to confirm


On R1:


R1# ping 12.1.1.2 rep 100


Type escape sequence to abort.
Sending 100, 100-byte ICMP Echos to 12.1.1.2, timeout is 2 seconds:
!!!!!!!!!!!!!!!!!!!!!!!!!!!!!!!!!!!!!!!!!!!!!!!!!!!!!!!!!!!!!!!!!!!!!!!!
!!!!!!!!!!!!!!!!!!!!!!!!!!!!!!!!
Success rate is 100 percent (100/100), round-trip min/avg/max = 1/1/4 ms


On R2:


R2# show policy-map interface | section dscp0


    Class-map: DSCP0 (match-all)
      0 packets, 0 bytes
      5 minute offered rate 0 bps
      Match:  dscp default (0)


R2# show policy-map interface | section dscp1


    Class-map: DSCP1 (match-all)
      100 packets, 11400 bytes
      5 minute offered rate 0 bps
      Match:  dscp 1
```

Step 3

In this step, a custom DSCP-mutation map is configured. Remember that if this custom mapping is *not* configured, the default DSCP-mutation map will be used.

The default DSCP-mutation map cannot be changed, and it is configured as "one to one," meaning that the DSCP marking in the incoming traffic will always match the DSCP marking in the outgoing traffic.

In this step, a custom DSCP-mutation map named TST is configured. This custom DSCP-mutation map maps the incoming DSCP value (in this case 1) to an outgoing DSCP value of 60.

Let's look at the default DSCP-mutation map:

```
SW2# show mls qos map dscp-mutation

  Dscp-dscp mutation map:
  Default DSCP Mutation Map:

   d1 :  d2 0   1   2   3   4   5   6   7   8   9
  ----------------------------------------
    0 :     00  01  02  03  04  05  06  07  08  09
    1 :     10  11  12  13  14  15  16  17  18  19
    2 :     20  21  22  23  24  25  26  27  28  29
    3 :     30  31  32  33  34  35  36  37  38  39
    4 :     40  41  42  43  44  45  46  47  48  49
    5 :     50  51  52  53  54  55  56  57  58  59
    6 :     60  61  62  63
```

Note that the "d1" column specifies the most significant digit of the DSCP value of incoming packets, whereas the "d2" row specifies the least significant digit of the DSCP value in incoming packets.

The intersection of the "d1" and "d2" values in the body of the output provides the DSCP value of the outgoing traffic.

Note   The output of the preceding **show** command reveals that the incoming DSCP value of 1 is rewritten to the outgoing DSCP value of 1.

Let's configure a custom DSCP-mutation map called "TST" that maps the incoming DSCP value of 1 to an outgoing DSCP value of 60:

```
SW2(config)# mls qos map dscp-mutation TST 1 to 60
```

Let's verify the configuration:

```
On SW2:

SW2# show mls qos map dscp-mutation TST

  Dscp-dscp mutation map:
  TST:
   d1 :  d2 0   1   2   3   4   5   6   7   8   9
  ----------------------------------------
    0 :     00  60  02  03  04  05  06  07  08  09
    1 :     10  11  12  13  14  15  16  17  18  19
```

```
2 :      20 21 22 23 24 25 26 27 28 29
3 :      30 31 32 33 34 35 36 37 38 39
4 :      40 41 42 43 44 45 46 47 48 49
5 :      50 51 52 53 54 55 56 57 58 59
6 :      60 61 62 63
```

Once the custom DSCP-mutation map is configured, it must be applied to the F0/19 interface (trunk interface) of SW2:

```
SW2(config)# interface FastEthernet0/19
SW2(config-if)# mls qos dscp-mutation TST
```

Let's verify the configuration:

```
On SW2:

SW2# show mls qos interface FastEthernet0/19

FastEthernet0/19
trust state: trust dscp
trust mode: trust dscp
trust enabled flag: ena
COS override: dis
default COS: 0
DSCP Mutation Map: TST
Trust device: none
qos mode: port-based
```

Step 4

In the final step of this configuration, you *must* ensure that DSCP rewrites are enabled. If this feature is disabled, the DSCP marking will *not* be rewritten.

Let's verify whether DSCP rewrites are enabled:

```
On SW2:

SW2# Show mls qos

QOS is enabled
QOS ip packet dscp rewrite is enabled
```

By default, DSCP rewrites are enabled *only* if **mls qos** is enabled. I recommend that you enter the following command and *not* rely on memory to check to see if it is enabled:

```
SW2(config)# mls qos rewrite ip dscp
```

Let's test and see if the incoming DSCP value of 1 is rewritten to a DSCP value of 60 (remember that on R3 we need to match on DSCP 60 so we can test and verify the configuration):

```
On R2:

R2(config)# class-map dscp60
R2(config-cmap)# match ip dscp 60

R2(config)# policy-map TST
R2(config-pmap)# class dscp60
```

When we add a class (or classes) to an existing policy map, the new classes are added to the end of all the classes within that policy map. Let's look at this:

```
On R2:

R2# show policy-map TST

 Policy Map TST
   Class dscp0
   Class dscp1
   Class dscp2
   Class dscp3
   Class dscp4
   Class dscp5
   Class dscp6
   Class dscp7
   Class dscp60
```

Now let's test the configuration:

```
On R2:

R2# clear counters
Clear "show interface" counters on all interfaces [confirm]
Press Enter to confirm
```

```
On R1:


R1# ping 12.1.1.2 rep 60


Type escape sequence to abort.
Sending 60, 100-byte ICMP Echos to 12.1.1.2, timeout is 2 seconds:
!!!!!!!!!!!!!!!!!!!!!!!!!!!!!!!!!!!!!!!!!!!!!!!!!!!!!!!!!!!!!!!
Success rate is 100 percent (60/60), round-trip min/avg/max = 1/1/4 ms


On R2:


R2# show policy-map interface | section dscp60


    Class-map: DSCP60 (match-all)
      60 packets, 6840 bytes
      5 minute offered rate 2000 bps
      Match: ip dscp 60
```

Let's disable the rewrites:

```
On SW2:

SW2(config)# no mls qos rewrite ip dscp
```

Now let's verify the configuration:

```
On SW2:

SW2# Show mls qos

QOS is enabled
QOS ip packet dscp rewrite is disabled
```

We also need to test the configuration:

```
On R2:

R2# clear counters
Clear "show interface" counters on all interfaces [confirm]
Press Enter to confirm


On R1:


R1# ping 12.1.1.2 rep 10
```

```
Type escape sequence to abort.
Sending 100, 100-byte ICMP Echos to 12.1.1.2, timeout is 2 seconds:
!!!!!!!!!!
Success rate is 100 percent (10/10), round-trip min/avg/max = 1/1/4 ms


On R2:


R2# show policy-map interface | section dscp60
    Class-map: dscp60 (match-all)
      0 packets, 0 bytes
      5 minute offered rate 0 bps
      Match: ip dscp 60


R2# show policy-map interface | section dscp1
    Class-map: dscp1 (match-all)
      10 packets, 1140 bytes
      5 minute offered rate 0 bps
      Match: ip dscp 1
```

> **Note** Because the rewriting of DSCP markings is disabled, the incoming DSCP value was *not* modified. Let's enable IP DSCP rewrites:

```
On SW2:


SW2(config)# mls qos rewrite ip dscp
```

Erase the startup configuration on R1–R3 and SW1 and SW2 and reload these routers and switches before proceeding to the next lab.

Lab 12-3: DSCP-COS Mapping

12.1.1.0/24
VTP Domain
tst

R1 .1 F0/0   F0/1 SW1 F0/19   F0/19 SW2 F0/2   F0/1.12 .2 R2
                         Trunk   Trunk

VLAN 12

Figure 12-3 *Configuring DSCP-COS Mapping*

Figure 12-3 illustrates the topology that will be used in the following tasks.

Task 1

For testing and verification of this lab, configure R2 to match on incoming COS markings of 0–7 using an MQC; this policy should be applied inbound to R2's F0/1.12 subinterface.

```
On R2:

R2(config)# class-map cos0
R2(config-cmap)# match cos 0

R2(config)# class-map cos1
R2(config-cmap)# match cos 1

R2(config)# class-map cos2
R2(config-cmap)# match cos 2

R2(config)# class-map cos3
R2(config-cmap)# match cos 3

R2(config)# class-map cos4
R2(config-cmap)# match cos 4

R2(config)# class-map cos5
R2(config-cmap)# match cos 5

R2(config)# class-map cos6
R2(config-cmap)# match cos 6

R2(config)# class-map cos7
R2(config-cmap)# match cos 7

R2(config)# policy-map TST
R2(config-pmap)# class cos0
R2(config-pmap)# class cos1
R2(config-pmap)# class cos2
R2(config-pmap)# class cos3
R2(config-pmap)# class cos4
R2(config-pmap)# class cos5
R2(config-pmap)# class cos6
R2(config-pmap)# class cos7

R2(config)# interface FastEthernet0/1.21
R2(config-subif)# service-policy in TST
```

Task 2

Configure R1 such that it marks all outgoing traffic with a DSCP value of 5:

```
On R1:

R1(config)# policy-map TST
R1(config-pmap)# class class-default
R1(config-pmap-c)# set ip dscp 5


R1(config)# interface FastEthernet0/0
R1(config-if)# service-policy out TST
```

Task 3

Configure SW2 such that it rewrites the incoming traffic marked with a DSCP value of 5 to an outgoing COS value of 1.

Before configuring this task, you need to display the default **dscp-cos** mapping using the following command:

```
On SW2:

SW2# show mls qos map dscp-cos

  Dscp-cos map:
    d1 :  d2 0  1  2  3  4  5  6  7  8  9
    ---------------------------------------
    0 :     00 00 00 00 00 00 00 00 01 01
    1 :     01 01 01 01 01 01 02 02 02 02
    2 :     02 02 02 02 03 03 03 03 03 03
    3 :     03 03 04 04 04 04 04 04 04 04
    4 :     05 05 05 05 05 05 05 05 06 06
    5 :     06 06 06 06 06 06 07 07 07 07
    6 :     07 07 07 07
```

Note The output of the preceding **show** command displays the default DSCP-to-COS mapping, which means that *if* the **mls qos trust dscp** command is configured, then the DSCP markings of incoming packets are mapped to the outgoing COS value according to the DSCP-COS map.

The incoming DSCP values are shown in the "d1" column and the "d2" row, whereas the outgoing COS values are identified in the body of this display; this is the intersection of the "d1" column and the "d2" row.

Note   Every eight DSCP values are mapped to a single COS value. Because there is no default mapping for **dscp-cos**, this mapping can affect the entire switch.

By default, an incoming DSCP value of 5 is mapped to an outgoing COS value of 0. To accomplish this task, you have to modify this mapping so the incoming DSCP value of 5 is mapped to an outgoing COS value of 1. Figure 12-4 illustrates this process.

Note   The DSCP marking is not changed at all; therefore, you are rewriting the outgoing COS value based on the incoming DSCP value.

Figure 12-4   *Modifying the Mapping of DSCP Values to COS Values*

To test and verify the default configuration, the following command *must* be configured so that the incoming DSCP values are trusted. If this is not configured, the incoming DSCP values will *not* be mapped to an outgoing COS value.

```
On SW2:

SW2(config)# mls qos

SW2(config)# interface FastEthernet0/19
SW2(config-if)# mls qos trust dscp
```

Let's verify the configuration:

```
On SW2:

SW2# show mls qos interface FastEthernet0/19 | include trust state

trust state: trust dscp
```

To test the configuration, a **ping** is generated from R1 with a repeat count of 50 that's verified on R2:

```
On R1:

R1# ping 12.1.1.2 repeat 50

Type escape sequence to abort.
Sending 50, 100-byte ICMP Echos to 12.1.1.2, timeout is 2 seconds:
!!!!!!!!!!!!!!!!!!!!!!!!!!!!!!!!!!!!!!!!!!!!!!!!!!!!
Success rate is 100 percent (50/50), round-trip min/avg/max = 1/3/4 ms
```

Let's verify the configuration:

```
On R2:

R2# show policy-map interface | section cos0

    Class-map: cos0 (match-all)
      50 packets, 5900 bytes
      5 minute offered rate 0 bps
      Match: cos  0
```

Note   DSCP 5 is mapped to a COS value of 0 because of the default mapping that is in use.

In the next step, the default **dscp-cos** mapping is changed to map an incoming DSCP value of 5 to an outgoing COS value of 1:

```
On SW2:

SW2(config)# mls qos map dscp-cos 5 to 1
```

Note   The first value (5) is the DSCP value in the incoming packets, and the second value (1) is the COS value in the outgoing packets.

Let's now test and verify the configuration:

```
On R2:

R3# clear counters
Clear "show interface" counters on all interfaces [confirm]

Press Enter to confirm
```

```
On R1:


R1# ping 12.1.1.2 repeat 50


Type escape sequence to abort.
Sending 50, 100-byte ICMP Echos to 12.1.1.2, timeout is 2 seconds:
!!!!!!!!!!!!!!!!!!!!!!!!!!!!!!!!!!!!!!!!!!!!!!!!!!!!
Success rate is 100 percent (50/50), round-trip min/avg/max = 1/3/4 ms
```

Note Incoming packets that are marked with a DSCP value of 5 are mapped to an outgoing COS value of 1 and *nor* 0:

```
On R2:
R2# show policy-map interface | section cos0
    Class-map: cos0 (match-all)
      0 packets, 0 bytes
      5 minute offered rate 0 bps
      Match: cos  0


R2# show policy-map interface | section cos1
    Class-map: cos1 (match-all)
      50 packets, 5900 bytes
      5 minute offered rate 0 bps
      Match: cos  1
```

Erase the startup configuration on R1–R3 and SW1 and SW2 and reload these routers and switches before proceeding to the next lab.

Lab 12-4: COS-DSCP Mapping

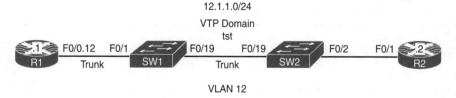

Figure 12-5 *Configuring COS-DSCP Mapping*

Figure 12-5 illustrates the topology that will be used in the following tasks.

Task 1

Configure the F0/1 interface of R2 to match all its incoming traffic marked as DSCP 0, 30, or 56 using an MQC:

```
On R2:

R2(config)# class-map d0
R2(config-cmap)# match ip dscp 0

R2(config-cmap)# class-map d30
R2(config-cmap)# match ip dscp 30

R2(config-cmap)# class-map d56
R2(config-cmap)# match ip dscp 56

R2(config)# policy-map TST
R2(config-pmap)# class d0
R2(config-pmap-c)# class d30
R2(config-pmap-c)# class d56

R2(config-pmap-c)# interface FastEthernet0/1
R2(config-if)# service-policy in TST
```

Task 2

Configure the F0/1 interface of SW1 so that it marks all incoming traffic with a COS value of 7. This should apply to both tagged and untagged traffic.

```
On SW1:

SW2(config)# mls qos

SW2(config)# interface FastEthernet0/1
SW2(config-if)# mls qos cos 7
SW2(config-if)# mls qos cos override
```

Task 3

Configure the F0/19 interface of SW2 so that it maps incoming traffic with a COS value of 7 to outgoing traffic with a DSCP value of 30.

Before configuring this task, you should display the default mapping. The following command reveals the default mapping of COS to DSCP:

```
On SW2:

SW2# show mls qos map cos-dscp

  Cos-dscp map:
      cos:   0  1  2  3  4  5  6  7 ←← The Cos value of incoming packets
      --------------------------------
      dscp:  0  8 16 24 32 40 48 56  ← The DSCP value of outgoing packets
```

The preceding displays the existing COS-to-DSCP map. You can see that COS value of 0 is mapped to an outgoing DSCP value of 0, and an incoming COS value of 1 is mapped to a DSCP value of 8, and so forth.

To test this, R1 will ping R2 because the switchport that R1 is connected to is configured to assign a COS value of 7 to all incoming traffic; it should be matched to a DSCP value of 56 on R2. Before this can be accomplished, **mls qos** must be enabled on SW2:

```
On SW2:

SW1(config)# mls qos

SW1(config)# interface FastEthernet0/19
SW1(config-if)# mls qos trust cos
```

Let's verify the configuration:

```
On SW2:

SW2# Show mls qos

QOS is enabled
QOS ip packet dscp rewrite is enabled

SW2# show mls qos interface FastEthernet0/19 | include trust state

trust state: trust cos
```

Now we can test the configuration:

```
On R1:


R1# ping 12.1.1.2 rep 30


Type escape sequence to abort.
Sending 30, 100-byte ICMP Echos to 12.1.1.2, timeout is 2 seconds:
!!!!!!!!!!!!!!!!!!!!!!!!!!!!!!
Success rate is 100 percent (30/30), round-trip min/avg/max = 1/2/4 ms


On R2:


R2# show policy-map interface | section d56


    Class-map: d56 (match-all)
      30 packets, 3420 bytes
      5 minute offered rate 0 bps
      Match: ip dscp cs7 (56)
```

To configure this task, you need to change the default mapping. SW2 should be config-ured as follows:

```
                                                COS 0       COS 1      COS 2
COS 3         COS 4     COS 5     COS 6     COS 7
On SW2:


SW2(config)# mls qos map cos-dscp 0    8    16   24   32   40   48   30
```

For this command, you *must* configure all eight DSCP values. The values entered are the DSCP values, and the position of the DSCP values identifies the COS values. The first DSCP value (0) maps to a COS value of 0, and the second DSCP value (8) maps to a COS value of 1. The third DSCP value (16) maps to a COS value of 2, the fourth DSCP value (24) maps to a COS value of 3, the fifth DSCP value (32) maps to a COS value of 4, the sixth DSCP value (40) maps to a COS value of 5, the seventh DSCP value (48) maps to a COS value of 6, and the last DSCP value (30) maps to a COS value of 7.

Let's verify and test the configuration:

```
On SW2:


SW1# show mls qos map cos-dscp

   Cos-dscp map:
        cos:   0  1  2  3  4  5  6  7
        -------------------------------
        dscp:  0  8 16 24 32 40 48 30

On R2:


R2# clear counters
Clear "show interface" counters on all interfaces [confirm]

Press Enter to confirm

On R1:


R1# ping 12.1.1.2 rep 30

Type escape sequence to abort.
Sending 30, 100-byte ICMP Echos to 12.1.1.2, timeout is 2 seconds:
!!!!!!!!!!!!!!!!!!!!!!!!!!!!!!
Success rate is 100 percent (30/30), round-trip min/avg/max = 1/2/4 ms

On R2:


R2# show policy-map interface | section d56
    Class-map: d56 (match-all)
      0 packets, 0 bytes
      5 minute offered rate 0 bps
      Match: ip dscp cs7 (56)

R2# show policy-map interface | section d30
    Class-map: d30 (match-all)
      30 packets, 3420 bytes
      5 minute offered rate 2000 bps
      Match: ip dscp af33 (30)
```

Erase the startup configuration on R1–R3 and SW1 and SW2 and reload these routers and switches before proceeding to the next lab.

Lab 12-5: IP-Precedence-DSCP Mapping

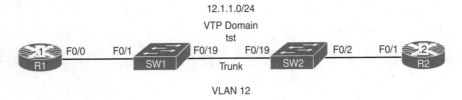

12.1.1.0/24
VTP Domain
tst

R1 · F0/0 — F0/1 [SW1] F0/19 — F0/19 [SW2] F0/2 — F0/1 R2

Trunk

VLAN 12

Figure 12-6 *Configuring IP-Precedence-DSCP Mapping*

Figure 12-6 illustrates the topology that will be used in the following tasks.

Task 1

Configure SW2 so that it overwrites the IP-Precedence value of 5 in incoming traffic with a DSCP value of 50 in the outgoing traffic. Configure R2 to match on DSCP markings of 0, 5, and 40 in incoming packets; this should be done for testing purpose.

```
On R2:

R2(config)# class-map d0
R2(config-cmap)# match ip dscp 0

R2(config)# class-map d5
R2(config-cmap)# match ip dscp 5

R2(config)# class-map d50
R2(config-cmap)# match ip dscp 50

R2(config)# policy-map TST
R2(config-pmap)# class d0
R2(config-pmap)# class d5
R2(config-pmap)# class d50

R2(config)# interface FastEthernet0/1
R2(config-if)# service-policy in TST
```

Before this task is configured, the existing IP-Precedence-to-DSCP mapping should be examined:

```
On SW2:

SW2# Show mls qos map ip-prec-dscp

IpPrecedence-dscp map:
      ipprec:   0  1  2  3  4  5  6  7 ← The IPP value of incoming packets
      --------------------------------
        dscp:   0  8 16 24 32 40 48 56 ← The DSCP value of Outgoing packets
```

> **Note**   The IP-Precedence value of 0 is mapped to an outgoing DSCP value of 0, and the incoming IP-Precedence value of 1 is mapped to a DSCP value of 8, and so forth.

Configure the following to test this default mapping:

- Configure R1 to mark all egress traffic with an IP-Precedence value of 5.

- Enable **mls qos** on both switches.

- The F0/1 interface of SW1 and the F0/19 interface of SW2 should be configured to trust IP-Precedence.

Ping R2 from R1. If the devices are configured correctly, R2 should see the ping traffic from R1 match to a DSCP value of 40.

```
On R1:

R1(config)# policy-map TST
R1(config-pmap)# class class-default
R1(config-pmap-c)# Set ip precedence 5

R1(config)# interface FastEthernet0/0
R1(config-if)# service-policy output TST

On SW1:

SW1(config)# mls qos

SW1(config)# interface FastEthernet0/1
SW1(config-if)# mls qos trust ip-precedence

On SW2:

SW2(config)# mls qos

SW2(config)# interface FastEthernet0/19
SW2(config-if)# mls qos trust ip-precedence
```

Let's test and verify the configuration:

```
On R2:

R2# clear counters
Clear "show interface" counters on all interfaces [confirm]
Press Enter to confirm

On R1:

R1# ping 12.1.1.2 rep 50

Type escape sequence to abort.
```

```
Sending 50, 100-byte ICMP Echos to 12.1.1.2, timeout is 2 seconds:
!!!!!!!!!!!!!!!!!!!!!!!!!!!!!!!!!!!!!!!!!!!!!!!!!!!!
Success rate is 100 percent (50/50), round-trip min/avg/max = 1/3/8 ms


On R2:


R1# show policy-map interface | section d40

    Class-map: D40 (match-all)
      50 packets, 5700 bytes
      5 minute offered rate 0 bps
      Match: ip dscp cs5 (40)
```

Note   *All* traffic is matched to a DSCP value of 40 on R1.

Let's configure this task:

```
On SW2:

SW2(config)# mls qos map ip-prec-dscp 0 8 16 24 32 50 48 56
```

Now we can verify the configuration:

```
SW2# show mls qos map ip-prec-dscp

   IpPrecedence-dscp map:
     ipprec:   0   1   2   3   4   5   6   7
     --------------------------------------
      dscp:    0   8  16  24  32  50  48  56
```

Let's test the configuration:

```
On R2:


R2# clear counters
Clear "show interface" counters on all interfaces [confirm]
Press Enter to confirm


On R1:


R1# ping 12.1.1.2 rep 50
```

```
Type escape sequence to abort.
Sending 50, 100-byte ICMP Echos to 12.1.1.2, timeout is 2 seconds:
!!!!!!!!!!!!!!!!!!!!!!!!!!!!!!!!!!!!!!!!!!!!!!!!!!!!!
Success rate is 100 percent (50/50), round-trip min/avg/max = 1/3/4 ms


On R2:


R2# show policy-map interface | section d50

   Class-map: d50 (match-all)
     50 packets, 5700 bytes
     5 minute offered rate 2000 bps
     Match: ip dscp 50
```

Erase the startup config and reload these devices with a clean configuration before proceeding to the next lab.

Lab 12-6: Match Input-Interface and Match NOT

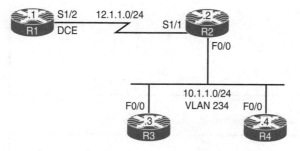

Figure 12-7 *Configuring Input-Interface and Match NOT*

Figure 12-7 illustrates the topology that will be used in the following tasks.

Task 1

Configure R4's f0/0 to mark all egress traffic with a DSCP value of 40:

```
On R4:


R4(config)# policy-map tst
R4(config-pmap)# class class-default
R4(config-pmap-c)# Set ip dscp 40


R4(config)# interface FastEthernet0/0
R4(config-if)# service-policy out tst
```

Let's verify and test the configuration:

```
On R4:

R4# show policy-map interface
 FastEthernet0/0

  Service-policy output: tst

    Class-map: class-default (match-any)
      12 packets, 1304 bytes
      5 minute offered rate 0 bps, drop rate 0 bps
      Match: any
      QOS Set
        dscp cs5
          Packets marked 0
```

To test the configuration, a class map is configured to match on the DSCP value of 40, and a policy-map is configured that references the class map. The policy map is applied to the F0/0 interface of R2 inbound.

```
R2(config)# class-map DSCP40
R2(config-cmap)# match ip dscp 40

R2(config)# policy-map tst
R2(config-pmap)# class DSCP40

R2(config)# interface FastEthernet0/0
R2(config-if)# service-policy in tst
```

To test this configuration, R4 will ping R2. The result is verified on R2:

```
On R2:

R2# show policy-map interface
 FastEthernet0/0

  Service-policy input: tst

    Class-map: DSCP40 (match-all)
      0 packets, 0 bytes
      5 minute offered rate 0 bps
      Match: ip dscp cs5 (40)

    Class-map: class-default (match-any)
      0 packets, 0 bytes
      5 minute offered rate 0 bps, drop rate 0 bps
      Match: any
```

Note   The packet count is set to 0.

```
On R4:

R4# ping 10.1.1.2 rep 40

Type escape sequence to abort.
Sending 40, 100-byte ICMP Echos to 10.1.1.2, timeout is 2 seconds:
!!!!!!!!!!!!!!!!!!!!!!!!!!!!!!!!!!!!!!!!!!
Success rate is 100 percent (40/40), round-trip min/avg/max = 1/3/4 ms

On R2:

R2# show policy-map interface
FastEthernet0/0

  Service-policy input: tst

    Class-map: DSCP40 (match-all)
      0 packets, 0 bytes
      5 minute offered rate 0 bps
      Match: ip dscp cs5 (40)

    Class-map: class-default (match-any)
      40 packets, 4560 bytes
      5 minute offered rate 2000 bps, drop rate 0 bps
      Match: any
```

The output of the preceding **show** command reveals that 40 packets were matched to class **class-default** and *not* DSCP 40. What went wrong?

Well, R2, R3, and R4 are connected to each other via SW1, and if SW1 has **mls qos** enabled, it will drop all the markings. Let's check **mls qos** on SW1:

```
On SW1:

SW1# show mls qos
QOS is enabled
QOS ip packet dscp rewrite is enabled
```

Now let's disable **mls qos**:

```
SW1(config)# no mls qos
```

Let's test and verify the configuration:

```
On R2:

R2# clear counters
Clear "show interface" counters on all interfaces [confirm]
Press Enter to confirm

On R4:

R4# ping 10.1.1.2 rep 40

Type escape sequence to abort.
Sending 40, 100-byte ICMP Echos to 10.1.1.2, timeout is 2 seconds:
!!!!!!!!!!!!!!!!!!!!!!!!!!!!!!!!!!!!!!!!!!
Success rate is 100 percent (40/40), round-trip min/avg/max = 1/3/4 ms

On R2:

R2# show policy-map interface
 FastEthernet0/0

  Service-policy input: tst

    Class-map: DSCP40 (match-all)
      40 packets, 4560 bytes
      5 minute offered rate 0 bps
      Match: ip dscp cs5 (40)


    Class-map: class-default (match-any)
      0 packets, 0 bytes
      5 minute offered rate 0 bps, drop rate 0 bps
      Match: any
```

You can see that 40 packets matched on the class that matches the DSCP value 40. Let's remove the MQC configured on R2 and proceed to the next task:

```
On R2:

R2(config)# interface FastEthernet0/0
R2(config-if)# no service-policy in tst

R2(config)# no policy-map tst
R2(config)# no class-map DSCP40
```

Task 2

Configure R2 based on the following policy:

- The ingress traffic through the s1/1 interface should be classified and marked with a DSCP value of 10.

- The ingress traffic through the f0/0 interface should be classified and marked with a DSCP value of 20. This policy should *not* affect any ingress traffic that is marked with a DSCP value of 40. Do *not* configure an access list to accomplish this task.

Let's configure the policy for the s1/1 interface:

```
On R2:
R2(config)# class-map S1/1
R2(config-cmap)# match input-interface serial1/1

R2(config)# policy-map TST-S1/1
R2(config-pmap)# class S1/1
R2(config-pmap-c)# set ip dscp 10

R2(config-pmap)# int serial1/1
R2(config-if)# service-policy in TST-S1/1
```

Finally, let's configure the policy for the f0/0 interface:

```
R2(config)# class-map F0/0
R2(config-cmap)# match not dscp 40
R2(config-cmap)# match input-interface FastEthernet0/0

R2(config)# policy-map TST-F0/0
R2(config-pmap)# class F0/0
R2(config-pmap-c)# Set ip dscp 20

R2(config-pmap-c)# interface FastEthernet0/1
R2(config-if)# service-policy in TST-F0/0
```

Now we need to verify the configuration:

```
On R2:

R2# show policy-map interface serial1/1
Serial1/1

  Service-policy input: TST-S1/1

    Class-map: S1/1 (match-all)
      0 packets, 0 bytes
      5 minute offered rate 0 bps, drop rate 0 bps
```

```
        Match: input-interface Serial1/1
        QOS Set
          dscp af11
            Packets marked 0


      Class-map: class-default (match-any)
        0 packets, 0 bytes
        5 minute offered rate 0 bps, drop rate 0 bps
        Match: any

R2# show policy-map interface FastEthernet0/0
FastEthernet0/0

  Service-policy input: TST-F0/0

    Class-map: F0/0 (match-all)
      0 packets, 0 bytes
      5 minute offered rate 0 bps, drop rate 0 bps
      Match: not  dscp cs5 (40)
      Match: input-interface FastEthernet0/0
      QOS Set
        dscp af22
          Packets marked 0

    Class-map: class-default (match-any)
      0 packets, 0 bytes
      5 minute offered rate 0 bps, drop rate 0 bps
      Match: any
```

Let's test this configuration:

```
On R1:


R1# ping 12.1.1.2 rep 10

Type escape sequence to abort.
Sending 10, 100-byte ICMP Echos to 12.1.1.2, timeout is 2 seconds:
!!!!!!!!!!
Success rate is 100 percent (10/10), round-trip min/avg/max = 1/2/4 ms


On R2:


R2# show policy-map interface serial1/1
Serial1/1
```

```
    Service-policy input: TST-S1/1

      Class-map: S1/1 (match-all)
        10 packets, 1040 bytes
        5 minute offered rate 0 bps, drop rate 0 bps
        Match: input-interface Serial1/1
        QOS Set
          dscp af11
            Packets marked 10

      Class-map: class-default (match-any)
        0 packets, 0 bytes
        5 minute offered rate 0 bps, drop rate 0 bps
        Match: any
```

Based on the output of the preceding **show** command, you can see that 10 packets matched the DSCP value of 10.

Now let's test the second policy:

```
On R3:


R3# ping 10.1.1.2 rep 30


Type escape sequence to abort.
Sending 30, 100-byte ICMP Echos to 10.1.1.2, timeout is 2 seconds:
!!!!!!!!!!!!!!!!!!!!!!!!!!!!!!
Success rate is 100 percent (30/30), round-trip min/avg/max = 1/2/4 ms
```

We also need to verify the test:

```
On R2:


R2# show policy-map interface FastEthernet0/0
FastEthernet0/0

  Service-policy input: TST-F0/0

    Class-map: F0/0 (match-all)
      30 packets, 3420 bytes
      5 minute offered rate 0 bps, drop rate 0 bps
      Match: not  dscp cs5 (40)
      Match: input-interface FastEthernet0/0
      QOS Set
```

```
        dscp af22
          Packets marked 30

  Class-map: class-default (match-any)
     0 packets, 0 bytes
     5 minute offered rate 0 bps, drop rate 0 bps
     Match: any
```

Because R3's traffic had no markings, the pings generated by R3 were marked with a DSCP value of 20. Let's conduct the same test, but this time the ping will be generated by R4. Remember that R4 was marking all egress traffic with a DSCP value of 40.

```
On R4:

R4# ping 10.1.1.2 rep 40

Type escape sequence to abort.
Sending 40, 100-byte ICMP Echos to 10.1.1.2, timeout is 2 seconds:
!!!!!!!!!!!!!!!!!!!!!!!!!!!!!!!!!!!!!!!!!!
Success rate is 100 percent (40/40), round-trip min/avg/max = 1/3/4 ms
```

Let's verify the test:

```
On R2:

R2# show policy-map interface FastEthernet0/0
 FastEthernet0/0

  Service-policy input: TST-F0/0

    Class-map: F0/0 (match-all)
       30 packets, 3420 bytes
       5 minute offered rate 0 bps, drop rate 0 bps
       Match: not  dscp cs5 (40)
       Match: input-interface FastEthernet0/0
       QOS Set
         dscp af22
           Packets marked 30

    Class-map: class-default (match-any)
       40 packets, 4560 bytes
       5 minute offered rate 0 bps, drop rate 0 bps
       Match: any
```

> **Note**   Because R4 was generating traffic with a DSCP value of 40, R2 did not mark that traffic. Therefore, it matched on class **class-default**.

Erase the startup configuration on the routers and reload them before proceeding to the next task

Lab 12-7: Match Destination and Source Address MAC

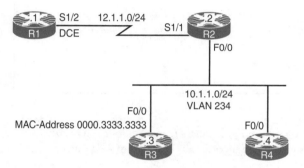

Figure 12-8   *Configuring Match Destination and Source Address MAC*

Figure 12-8 illustrates the topology that will be used in the following tasks.

Task 1

Configure RIPv2 on all routers and advertise their directly connected interface(s):

```
On All Routers:


Rx(config)# router rip
Rx(config-router)# no auto-summary
Rx(config-router)# version 2
Rx(config-router)# network 0.0.0.0
```

Let's verify the configuration:

```
On R4:


R4# Show ip route rip | begin Gate
Gateway of last resort is not set

     12.0.0.0/24 is subnetted, 1 subnets
R       12.1.1.0 [120/1] via 10.1.1.2, 00:00:07, FastEthernet0/1
```

Task 2

Configure R2 to classify and mark all IP routed traffic from any source destined to the MAC address of R3's F0/0 interface with an IP-Precedence level of 1.

R2 is configured to match any packet destined to the MAC address of 0000.3333.3333, which is R3's configured MAC address:

```
On R2:
R2(config)# class-map QOS
R2(config-cmap)# match destination-address mac 0000.3333.3333

R2(config)# policy-map TST
R2(config-pmap)# class QOS
R2(config-pmap-c)# set ip precedence 1

R2(config-pmap-c)# interface FastEthernet0/0
R2(config-if)# service-policy out TST
```

Note If **destination-address Mac** is configured in the class map, the policy map *cannot* be applied inbound because the logic will be incorrect; it must be applied outbound, meaning out toward the MAC address of R3.

Let's verify the configuration:

```
On R2:

R2# show policy-map TST

  Policy Map TST
    Class QOS
      set ip precedence 1

R2# show policy-map interface | section QOS

Class-map: QOS (match-all)
      0 packets, 0 bytes
      5 minute offered rate 0 bps, drop rate 0 bps
      Match: destination-address mac 0000.3333.3333
      QOS Set
        precedence 1
          Packets marked 0
```

Let's test the configuration:

```
On R3:
R3(config)# access-list 100 permit ip any any precedence 1 log
R3(config)# access-list 100 permit udp any any eq 520

R3(config)# interface FastEthernet0/0
R3(config-if)# ip access-group 100 in

On R1:

R1# ping 10.1.1.3 rep 10

Type escape sequence to abort.
Sending 10, 100-byte ICMP Echos to 10.1.1.3, timeout is 2 seconds:
!!!!!!!!!!
Success rate is 100 percent (10/10), round-trip min/avg/max = 1/2/4 ms
```

The preceding configures an access list with the **log** option to match on packets that are marked with an IP-Precedence level of 1. RIP also has been allowed.

Note   The output of the following **show** command indicates that 10 packets were marked with an IP-Precedence value of 1:

```
R2# show policy-map interface
FastEthernet0/0

  Service-policy output: TST

    Class-map: QOS (match-all)
      10 packets, 1140 bytes
      5 minute offered rate 0 bps, drop rate 0 bps
      Match: destination-address mac 0000.3333.3333
      QOS Set
        precedence 1
          Packets marked 10

    Class-map: class-default (match-any)
      40 packets, 3931 bytes
      5 minute offered rate 0 bps, drop rate 0 bps
      Match: any
```

You can see that 10 packets matched the access list:

```
On R3:
R3# show access-list 100

Extended IP access list 100
    10 permit ip any any precedence priority log (10 matches)
    20 permit udp any any eq rip (2 matches)
```

Task 3

Configure R2 to classify and mark all IP-routed traffic from the MAC address of R3 to any destination with IP-Precedence level of 2.

```
On R2:

R2(config)# class-map Task4
R2(config-cmap)# match source-address mac 0000.3333.3333

R2(config)# policy-map QOS
R2(config-pmap)# class Task4
R2(config-pmap-c)# set ip precedence 2

R2(config-pmap-c)# interface FastEthernet0/0
R2(config-if)# service-policy in QOS

On R2:

R2# clear counters
Clear "show interface" counters on all interfaces [confirm]
Press Enter to confirm

On R3:

R3# ping 12.1.1.1 rep 100

Type escape sequence to abort.
Sending 100, 100-byte ICMP Echos to 12.1.1.1, timeout is 2 seconds:
!!!!!!!!!!!!!!!!!!!!!!!!!!!!!!!!!!!!!!!!!!!!!!!!!!!!!!!!!!!!!!!!!!!!!!!!!!!
!!!!!!!!!!!!!!!!!!!!!!!!!!!!!!!!!
Success rate is 100 percent (100/100), round-trip min/avg/max = 1/2/4 ms
```

Let's verify the configuration:

```
On R2:
R2# show policy-map interface | section Task4

   Class-map: Task4 (match-all)
     100 packets, 11400 bytes
     5 minute offered rate 0 bps, drop rate 0 bps
     Match: source-address mac 0000.3333.3333
     QOS Set
       precedence 2
         Packets marked 100
```

You can see that 100 packets were marked with an IP-Precedence value of 2.

Erase the startup configuration on the routers and reload them before proceeding to the next task.

Lab 12-8: Match IP DSCP/Precedence vs. Match DSCP

Figure 12-9 *Configuring Match IP DSCP/Precedence vs. Match DSCP*

Figure 12-9 illustrates the topology that will be used in the following tasks.

Task 1

R1's F0/0 interface should be configured such that it can verify the IP-Precedence marking of incoming traffic. Use R2 to generate traffic with an IP-Precedence value of 1. Do *not* use an MQC or an access list to accomplish this task.

For verification, eight class maps are configured on R1, each matching different IP-Precedence levels. Also, a policy map called "TST" is configured to reference the eight class maps, and the policy map "TST" is applied to the F0/0 interface of R1 in the inbound direction.

```
On R1:

R1(config)# class-map P0
R1(config-cmap)# match ip precedence 0

R1(config)# class-map P1
R1(config-cmap)# match ip precedence 1

R1(config)# class-map P2
R1(config-cmap)# match ip precedence 2

R1(config)# class-map P3
R1(config-cmap)# match ip precedence 3

R1(config)# class-map P4
R1(config-cmap)# match ip precedence 4

R1(config)# class-map P5
R1(config-cmap)# match ip precedence 5

R1(config)# class-map P6
R1(config-cmap)# match ip precedence 6

R1(config)# class-map P7
R1(config-cmap)# match ip precedence 7

R1(config)# policy-map TST
R1(config-pmap)# class P0
R1(config-pmap)# class P1
R1(config-pmap)# class P2
R1(config-pmap)# class P3
R1(config-pmap)# class P4
R1(config-pmap)# class P5
R1(config-pmap)# class P6
R1(config-pmap)# class P7

R1(config)# interface FastEthernet0/0
R1(config-if)# service-policy input TST
```

An extended ping can be used to generate traffic with different IP-Precedence levels. Remember that IP-Precedence uses the three most significant bits of the TOS byte. The decimal values of these bits are 128 (the most significant), 64 (the second most significant), and 32 (the third most significant). Table 12-1 identifies the TOS byte values and their corresponding IP-Precedence values.

Table 12-1   *TOS Byte Values and Corresponding IP-Precedence Values*

→								TOS Byte ←		
IPP	IPP	IPP	D	T	R	ECN	ECN	Decimal	IPP Level	TOS Levels
0	0	0	0	0	0	0	0	0	0	0–31
0	0	1	0	0	0	0	0	32	1	32–63
0	1	0	0	0	0	0	0	64	2	64–95
0	1	1	0	0	0	0	0	96	3	96–127
1	0	0	0	0	0	0	0	128	4	128–159
1	0	1	0	0	0	0	0	160	5	160–191
1	1	0	0	0	0	0	0	192	6	192–223
1	1	1	0	0	0	0	0	224	7	224–255
128	64	32	16	8	4	2	1	Decimal Conversion		

```
On R2:

R2# ping
Protocol [ip]: →

Target IP address: 12.1.1.1
Repeat count [5]: →
Datagram size [100]: →
Timeout in seconds [2]: →
Extended commands [n]: y
Source address or interface: 12.1.1.2
Type of service [0]: 32
Set DF bit in IP header? [no]: →
Validate reply data? [no]: →
Data pattern [0xABCD]: →
Loose, Strict, Record, Timestamp, Verbose[none]: →
Sweep range of sizes [n]: →
Type escape sequence to abort.
Sending 5, 100-byte ICMP Echos to 10.1.12.1, timeout is 2 seconds:
Packet sent with a source address of 10.1.12.2
!!!!!
Success rate is 100 percent (5/5), round-trip min/avg/max = 1/2/4 ms
```

```
On R1:

R1# show policy-map interface | section P1

    Class-map: P1 (match-all)
      5 packets, 570 bytes
      5 minute offered rate 0 bps
      Match: ip precedence 1
```

Note The output of the preceding **show** command reveals that five packets were matched to IP-Precedence level 1.

Based on Table 12-1, if R2 pings R1 using a TOS value of 32 to 63, the result will be the same, meaning that the traffic will be generated with an IP-Precedence value of 1. Let's test this:

```
On R2:

R2# ping
Protocol [ip]: →
Target IP address: 12.1.1.1
Repeat count [5]: →
Datagram size [100]: →
Timeout in seconds [2]: →
Extended commands [n]: y
Source address or interface: 12.1.1.2
Type of service [0]: 63
Set DF bit in IP header? [no]: →
Validate reply data? [no]: →
Data pattern [0xABCD]: →
Loose, Strict, Record, Timestamp, Verbose[none]: →
Sweep range of sizes [n]: →
Type escape sequence to abort.
Sending 5, 100-byte ICMP Echos to 10.1.12.1, timeout is 2 seconds:
Packet sent with a source address of 10.1.12.2
!!!!!
Success rate is 100 percent (5/5), round-trip min/avg/max = 1/2/4 ms
```

Now we can verify the configuration:

```
On R1:


R1# show policy-map interface | section P1

   Class-map: P1 (match-all)
     10 packets, 1140 bytes
     5 minute offered rate 0 bps
     Match: ip precedence 1
```

Let's test the same scenario using IPv6:

```
On R1:


R1# clear counters
Clear "show interface" counters on all interfaces [confirm]
Press Enter to confirm


On R2:


R2# ping ipv6
Target IPv6 address: 12::1
Repeat count [5]: →
Datagram size [100]: →
Timeout in seconds [2]: →
Extended commands? [no]: Y
Source address or interface: 12::2
UDP protocol? [no]: →
Verbose? [no]: →
Precedence [0]: 1
Include hop by hop option? [no]: →
Include destination option? [no]: →
Sweep range of sizes? [no]: →
Type escape sequence to abort.
Sending 5, 100-byte ICMP Echos to 12::1, timeout is 2 seconds:
Packet sent with a source address of 12::2
!!!!!
Success rate is 100 percent (5/5), round-trip min/avg/max = 0/1/4 ms
```

Now let's verify the configuration:

```
On R1:


R1# show policy-map interface | section P1


   Class-map: P1 (match-all)
     0 packets, 0 bytes
     5 minute offered rate 0 bps
     Match: ip precedence 1
```

Note: IPv6 traffic was *not* matched to class P1.

Task 2

Remove the service policy, policy map, and class map from R1 configured in the previous task:

```
On R1:


R1(config)# interface FastEthernet0/0
R1(config-if)# no service-policy input TST
R1(config)# no policy-map TST


R1(config)# no class-map P0
R1(config)# no class-map P1
R1(config)# no class-map P2
R1(config)# no class-map P3
R1(config)# no class-map P4
R1(config)# no class-map P5
R1(config)# no class-map P6
R1(config)# no class-map P7
```

Task 3

R2 should ping R1's F0/0 IPv6 address (12::1); this traffic should be generated with a DSCP value of 20. You should use an MQC to verify the traffic's DSCP marking *only* for IPv6 packets on R1.

Because the DSCP value of IPv6 traffic must be matched, the **match** statement in the class map includes two statements: **match dscp** and **match protocol ipv6**.

```
On R1:

R1(config)# class-map D20
R1(config-cmap)# match protocol ipv6
R1(config-cmap)# match dscp 20

R1(config)# policy-map TST
R1(config-pmap)# class D20

R1(config-pmap)# interface FastEthernet0/0
R1(config-if)# service-policy in TST
```

Let's test the configuration:

```
On R2:

R2(config)# policy-map tst
R2(config-pmap)# class class-default
R2(config-pmap-c)# set dscp 20

R2(config-pmap-c)# interface FastEthernet0/0
R2(config-if)# service-policy output tst

R2# ping ipv6 12::1 repeat 100

Type escape sequence to abort.

Sending 100, 100-byte ICMP Echos to 12::1, timeout is 2 seconds:
!!!!!!!!!!!!!!!!!!!!!!!!!!!!!!!!!!!!!!!!!!!!!!!!!!!!!!!!!!!!!!!!!!!!!!!!!!
!!!!!!!!!!!!!!!!!!!!!!!!!!!!!!!!!
Success rate is 100 percent (100/100), round-trip min/avg/max = 0/0/0 ms
```

Now let's verify the configuration:

```
On R1:

R1# show policy-map interface | section D20

    Class-map: D20 (match-all)
      103 packets, 11642 bytes
      5 minute offered rate 0 bps
      Match: protocol ipv6
      Match:  dscp af22 (20)
```

You can see that the DSCP value was matched in the IPv6 packets. Let's ping R1's IP address to see if it matches the D20 class map:

```
On R1:

R1# clear counters
Clear "show interface" counters on all interfaces [confirm]
Press Enter to confirm


On R2:

R2# ping 12.1.1.1 repeat 100

Type escape sequence to abort.
Sending 100, 100-byte ICMP Echos to 10.1.12.1, timeout is 2 seconds:
!!!!!!!!!!!!!!!!!!!!!!!!!!!!!!!!!!!!!!!!!!!!!!!!!!!!!!!!!!!!!!!!!!!!!!!!!!
!!!!!!!!!!!!!!!!!!!!!!!!!!!!!!!!!!
Success rate is 100 percent (100/100), round-trip min/avg/max = 1/1/4 ms
```

Let's verify the test:

```
On R1:

R1# show policy-map interface
FastEthernet0/0

  Service-policy input: TST

    Class-map: D20 (match-all)
      0 packets, 0 bytes
      5 minute offered rate 0 bps
      Match: protocol ipv6
      Match:  dscp af22 (20)


    Class-map: class-default (match-any)
      100 packets, 11400 bytes
      5 minute offered rate 0 bps, drop rate 0 bps
      Match: any
```

You can see that if **match ip dscp** or **match ip precedence** is used, the match is based on IPv4 traffic, whereas **match dscp** or **match precedence** can match on IPv4 or IPv6. If the **match** statement must match the marking on the IPv6 traffic *only*, then a route map should be configured with two **match** statements: one to match the IPv6 protocol using **match protocol ipv6**, and the second to match on the actual DSCP value using **match dscp**.

Erase the startup configuration on the routers and reload them before proceeding to the next task.

Lab 12-9: Match Protocol HTTP URL, MIME, and Host

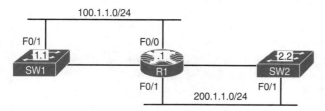

Figure 12-10 *Configuring Match Protocol HTTP URL, MIME, and Host*

Figure 12-10 illustrates the topology that will be used in the following tasks.

Task 1

Save the configuration of SW1 and copy the startup configuration of this switch (config.text) to compact flash as config.mpeg, config.jpeg, and config.txt.

```
On SW1:


SW1# write


SW1# dir
Directory of flash:/


 2  -rwx    7899301   Mar 1 1993 00:19:35 +00:00   c3560-advipservicesk9-mz.122-25.
   SEE.bin
    3  -rwx       1320   Mar 1 1993 00:11:17 +00:00  config.text
    4  -rwx         24   Mar 1 1993 00:11:17 +00:00  private-config.text


SW1# copy config.text config.mpeg
Destination filename [config.mpeg]? → Press Enter


SW1# copy config.text config.txt
Destination filename [config.txt]? → Press Enter


SW1# copy config.text config.jpeg


Destination filename [config.jpeg]? → Press Enter
```

Let's verify the configuration:

```
On SW1:


Switch# dir


Directory of flash:/


    2  -rwx      7899301   Mar 1 1993 00:19:35 +00:00  c3560-advipservicesk9-
       mz.122-25.SEE.bin
    3  -rwx         1320   Mar 1 1993 00:11:17 +00:00  config.text
    4  -rwx           24   Mar 1 1993 00:11:17 +00:00  private-config.text
    5  -rwx         1320   Mar 1 1993 00:13:35 +00:00  config.mpeg
    6  -rwx         1320   Mar 1 1993 00:13:44 +00:00  config.txt
    7  -rwx         1320   Mar 1 1993 00:13:55 +00:00  config.jpeg


15998976 bytes total (8091648 bytes free)
```

Task 2

Enable the Cisco web browser interface on SW1 and set the HTTP path used to locate the files created in the previous step:

```
On SW1:


SW1(config)# ip http server
SW1(config)# ip http path flash:
```

Let's verify the configuration:

```
On SW1:


SW1# show ip http server status


HTTP server status: Enabled
HTTP server port: 80
HTTP server authentication method: enable
HTTP server access class: 0
HTTP server base path: flash:
Maximum number of concurrent server connections allowed: 16
 (The rest of the output is omitted)
```

Task 3

Configure R1's F0/1 interface such that it blocks any URL that contains any file type with an extension of ".mpeg":

```
On R1:

R1(config)# class-map QOS
R1(config-cmap)# match protocol http url *.mpeg

R1(config)# policy-map TST
R1(config-pmap)# class QOS
R1(config-pmap-c)# drop

R1(config-pmap-c)# interface FastEthernet0/1
R1(config-if)# service-policy input TST
```

Let's verify the configuration:

```
On R1:

R1# show class-map QOS

 Class Map match-all QOS (id 1)
   Match protocol http url "*.mpeg"

R1# show policy-map TST

  Policy Map TST
    Class QOS
      drop

R1# show policy-map interface FastEthernet0/1

FastEthernet0/1

  Service-policy input: TST

    Class-map: QOS (match-all)
      0 packets, 0 bytes
      5 minute offered rate 0 bps, drop rate 0 bps
      Match: protocol http url "*.mpeg"
      drop

    Class-map: class-default (match-any)
      0 packets, 0 bytes
      5 minute offered rate 0 bps, drop rate 0 bps
      Match: any
```

For testing purposes, config.txt is copied first; you should be able to copy this file successfully:

```
On SW2:
SW2# copy http://100.1.1.11/config.txt Null:
Loading http://100.1.1.11/config.txt !
1711 bytes copied in 0.026 secs (65808 bytes/sec)
```

> **Note**   The file size on your switch may be different.

The following operation fails because of the ".mpeg" extension, which is blocked on R1:

```
SW2# copy http://100.1.1.11/config.mpeg NULL:
%Error opening http://100.1.1.11/config.mpeg (I/O error)
```

Task 4

Reconfigure R1 such that it blocks any URL that contains any file type with an extension of ".mpeg" or ".jpeg":

```
On R1:

R1(config)# class-map QOS
R1(config-cmap)# no match protocol http url *.mpeg

R1(config-cmap)# match protocol http url *.mpeg|*.jpeg
```

Let's verify the configuration:

```
On R1:

R1# show class-map QOS

 Class Map match-all QOS (id 1)
   Match protocol http url "*.mpeg|*.jpeg"

R1# show policy-map interface FastEthernet0/1
FastEthernet0/1

  Service-policy input: TST

    Class-map: QOS (match-all)
      8 packets, 1320 bytes
```

```
     5 minute offered rate 0 bps, drop rate 0 bps
     Match: protocol http url "*.mpeg|*.jpeg"
     drop

   Class-map: class-default (match-any)
     18 packets, 1481 bytes
     5 minute offered rate 0 bps, drop rate 0 bps
     Match: any
```

Let's test the configuration:

```
On SW2:
SW2# copy http://100.1.1.11/config.mpeg NULL:
```

> **Note** These two **copy** operations fail because the file extensions are blocked on R1.

You should receive the following console message:

```
%Error opening http://100.1.1.11/config.mpeg (I/O error)

SW2# copy http://100.1.1.11/config.jpeg NULL:

You should receive the following console message:

%Error opening http://100.1.1.11/config.jpeg (I/O error)
```

> **Note** The following **copy** operation is successful because the ".txt" extension is *not* blocked by R1:

```
SW2# copy http://100.1.1.11/config.txt NULL:
Loading http://100.1.1.11/config.txt !
1711 bytes copied in 0.017 secs (100647 bytes/sec)
```

Task 5

Reconfigure R1 such that any HTTP call to the server located at 100.1.1.11 is dropped:

```
On R1:

R1(config-if)# class-map QOS
R1(config-cmap)# no match protocol http url *.mpeg|*.jpeg
R1(config-cmap)# match protocol http host 100.1.1.11
```

Let's test the configuration:

```
On SW2:

SW2# copy http://100.1.1.11/config.txt NULL:
```

You should see the following console message:

```
%Error opening http://12.1.1.10/config.txt (I/O error)

SW2# copy http://12.1.1.10/config.mpeg NULL:
```

You should also see this console message:

```
%Error opening http://12.1.1.10/config.mpeg (I/O error)

SW2# copy http://12.1.1.10/config.jpeg NULL:
```

You should see the following console message as well:

```
%Error opening http://12.1.1.10/config.jpeg (I/O error)
```

Erase the startup configuration on the routers and reload them before proceeding to the next task.

Lab 12-10: Class-Based Policing

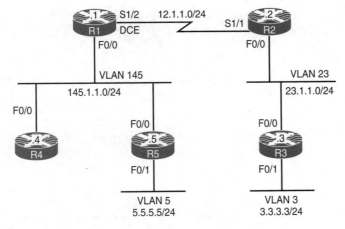

Figure 12-11 *Configuring a Match Based on DSCP Values*

Figure 12-11 illustrates the topology that will be used in the following tasks.

Task 1

Configure R1's S1/2 interface using the following policy:

- ICMP traffic should be rate-limited to 10 Kbps outbound.

- Traffic conforming to this threshold should be marked with a DSCP value of 30 and transmitted, and traffic exceeding this threshold should be marked with a DSCP value of 10 and transmitted.

Because access lists cannot be used, using Network Based Application Recognition is probably the *only* way to identify these traffic types. With NBAR, you must have "IP CEF" enabled. All the new IOS releases have CEF enabled on most of the platforms.

When you're configuring class-based policing, if the **Bc** value is *not* specified, it will default to CIR / 32 or 1500 bytes, whichever is the higher value. Remember that in a single-rate single bucket, **Be** is disabled, and if it is configured, the system will ignore it. The **Be** rate can *only* be utilized when a violate action is configured.

> **Note** To configure a match for the specified protocols, NBAR is used. NBAR uses the **match protocol** command to match on different protocols. When the first **match** command is entered, there will be a slight delay before the cursor is available again, but the subsequent **match** statements will not have this behavior. This happens because when NBAR is used for the first time, it needs to download and decompress the Packet Description Language Modules (PDLM) from the Flash memory into the main memory. Once they are loaded and decompressed, they can be used and accessed very quickly.

```
On R1:

R1(config)# class-map ICMP
```

> **Note** Because neither **match-any** or **match-all** is configured, the **match-all** option is the default:

```
R1(config-cmap)# match protocol icmp

R1(config)# policy-map tst
R1(config-pmap)# class ICMP
R1(config-pmap-c)# police 10000 conform-act set-dscp-tra 30 exceed-act
  set-dscp-tran 10
```

> **Note**   When configuring the **rate-limit** interface command, you *must* configure the normal burst and maximum burst. When configuring the **police** command through the MQC, you do not have to configure these values. If they are *not* configured, the system will use the CIR / 32 or 1500 bytes, whichever one is higher, as the normal burst. Also, the **conform-action** will be to transmit, and the **exceed-action** will be automatically set to drop.

```
R1(config-pmap-c)# interface serial1/2
R1(config-if)# service-policy output tst
```

Let's verify the configuration:

```
On R1:

R1# show policy-map interface serial1/2
  Serial1/2

  Service-policy output: tst

    Class-map: ICMP (match-all)
      0 packets, 0 bytes
      5 minute offered rate 0 bps, drop rate 0 bps
      Match: protocol icmp
      police:
          cir 10000 bps, bc 1500 bytes
        conformed 0 packets, 0 bytes; actions:
          set-dscp-transmit af33
        exceeded 0 packets, 0 bytes; actions:
          set-dscp-transmit af11
        conformed 0 bps, exceed 0 bps

    Class-map: class-default (match-any)
      5 packets, 428 bytes
      5 minute offered rate 0 bps, drop rate 0 bps
      Match: any
```

To test this configuration, R2 is configured to match on DSCP values of 30 and 10:

```
On R2:

R2(config)# class-map d30
R2(config-cmap)# match ip dscp 30

R2(config)# class-map d10
R2(config-cmap)# match ip dscp 10
```

```
R2(config)# policy-map tst
R2(config-pmap)# class d30
R2(config-pmap)# class d10


R2(config)# interface serial1/1
R2(config-if)# service-policy input tst
```

Let's set the **load-interval** to 30 seconds, which is the minimum value. If this is not set to 30 seconds, the load calculation will be performed every 5 minutes:

```
R2(config)# interface serial1/1
R2(config-if)# load-interval 30
```

Let's ping R2 from R1 with a high repeat count and verify the output on R2:

```
R1# ping 12.1.1.2 rep 9999999

Type escape sequence to abort.
Sending 9999999, 100-byte ICMP Echos to 12.1.1.2, timeout is 2 seconds:
!!!!!!!!!!!!!!!!!!!!!!!!!!!!!!!!!!!!!!!!!!!!!!!!!!!!!!!!!!!!!!!!!!!!!!!!
```

Now, while the ICMP packets are running, let's verify the output on R2:

```
R2# show policy-map interface
 Serial1/1

  Service-policy input: tst

    Class-map: d30 (match-all)
      471 packets, 48984 bytes
      30 second offered rate 8000 bps
      Match: ip dscp af33 (30)

    Class-map: d10 (match-all)
      1726 packets, 179504 bytes
      30 second offered rate 26000 bps
      Match: ip dscp af11 (10)

    Class-map: class-default (match-any)
      0 packets, 0 bytes
      30 second offered rate 0 bps, drop rate 0 bps
      Match: any
```

```
R2# show policy-map interface
 Serial1/1

  Service-policy input: tst

    Class-map: d30 (match-all)
      1095 packets, 113880 bytes
      30 second offered rate 9000 bps
      Match: ip dscp af33 (30)

    Class-map: d10 (match-all)
      4104 packets, 426816 bytes
      30 second offered rate 38000 bps
      Match: ip dscp af11 (10)

    Class-map: class-default (match-any)
      0 packets, 0 bytes
      30 second offered rate 0 bps, drop rate 0 bps
      Match: any

R2# show policy-map interface
 Serial1/1

  Service-policy input: tst

    Class-map: d30 (match-all)
      1711 packets, 177944 bytes
      30 second offered rate 10000 bps
      Match: ip dscp af33 (30)

    Class-map: d10 (match-all)
      6451 packets, 670904 bytes
      30 second offered rate 38000 bps
      Match: ip dscp af11 (10)

    Class-map: class-default (match-any)
      0 packets, 0 bytes
      30 second offered rate 0 bps, drop rate 0 bps
      Match: any
```

You can see that the rate remains around 10,000 Kbps.

Task 2

Configure R2's F0/0 interface using the following policy:

- The outgoing Telnet traffic should be rate-limited to 10 Mbps. This traffic should be configured with a minimum amount of normal burst.

- The outgoing TFTP traffic should be limited to 8 Mbps, with 40,000 bps of normal bursts.

- Both Telnet and TFTP traffic exceeding this policy should be dropped; if they conform to this policy, they should be transmitted.

- Do *not* create an access list to accomplish this task.

```
On R2:

R2(config)# class-map TELNET
R2(config-cmap)# match protocol telnet

R2(config)# class-map TFTP
R2(config-cmap)# match protocol tftp

R2(config)# policy-map TST
R2(config-pmap)# class TELNET
R2(config-pmap-c)# police 10000000 1000 conform-ac trans exceed-ac drop
```

You should receive the following console message telling you that the minimum normal burst size for a CIR of 10 Mbps should be 5000 bytes, so the system sets the normal burst to 5000:Conform burst size increased to 5000.

IOS looks at the configured CIR and uses the following formula: CIR/32 or 1500, or whichever one is higher. IOS will *not* allow a **Bc** size lower than 5000 for a CIR of 10 Mbps.

```
R2(config-pmap)# class TFTP
R2(config-pmap-c)# police 8000000 5000 conform-ac trans exceed-ac drop

R2(config-pmap-c-police)# interface FastEthernet0/0
R2(config-if)# service-policy out TST
```

Let's verify the configuration:

```
On R2:

R2# show policy-map interface FastEthernet0/0
FastEthernet0/0

  Service-policy output: TST

    Class-map: TELNET (match-all)
      0 packets, 0 bytes
      5 minute offered rate 0 bps, drop rate 0 bps
```

```
   Match: protocol telnet
   police:
        cir 10000000 bps, bc 5000 bytes
      conformed 0 packets, 0 bytes; actions:
        transmit
      exceeded 0 packets, 0 bytes; actions:
        drop
      conformed 0 bps, exceed 0 bps

 Class-map: TFTP (match-all)
   0 packets, 0 bytes
   5 minute offered rate 0 bps, drop rate 0 bps
   Match: protocol tftp
   police:
        cir 8000000 bps, bc 5000 bytes
      conformed 0 packets, 0 bytes; actions:
        transmit
      exceeded 0 packets, 0 bytes; actions:
        drop
      conformed 0 bps, exceed 0 bps

 Class-map: class-default (match-any)
   7 packets, 721 bytes
   5 minute offered rate 0 bps, drop rate 0 bps
   Match: any
```

The last entry (**Class-map class-default**) is always created automatically by the system. It is the catchall condition. Basically, any traffic that was not specified will use the class **class-default**.

Task 3

R1 has two hosts (R4 and R5) connected to its F0/0 interface with the following MAC addresses:

- **R4**: 0000.4444.4444

- **R5**: 0000.5555.5555

The traffic with a source MAC address of 0000.4444.4444 should be policed to 10 Kbps inbound, whereas the traffic with a source MAC address of 0000.5555.5555 should be policed to 20 Kbps inbound. Traffic from these hosts should *only* be processed if they conform to this policy. Do not use **match source-address** to accomplish this task.

The task states that the **match source-address mac** command cannot be used; because of this restriction, two MAC address access lists should be configured: one identifying R4's MAC address and the other identifying R5's MAC address as follows:

Note   You may have to use **Ctrl+Shift+6** to stop the pings on R1 before continuing with the configuration of this task.

```
On R1:

R1(config)# access-list 700 permit 0000.4444.4444

R1(config)# class-map R4
R1(config-cmap)# match access-group 700

R1(config)# access-list 701 permit 0000.5555.5555

R1(config)# class-map R5
R1(config-cmap)# match access-group 701

R1(config)# policy-map TEST
R1(config-pmap)# class R4
R1(config-pmap-c)# police 10000 conform-ac trans exceed-ac drop
R1(config-pmap)# class R5
R1(config-pmap-c)# police 20000 conform-ac trans exceed-ac drop

R1(config)# interface FastEthernet0/0
R1(config-if)# service-policy in TEST
```

Let's verify the configuration:

```
On R1:

R1# Show policy-map interface FastEthernet0/0
FastEthernet0/0

  Service-policy input: TEST

    Class-map: R4 (match-all)
      0 packets, 0 bytes
      5 minute offered rate 0 bps, drop rate 0 bps
      Match: access-group 700
      police:
          cir 10000 bps, bc 1500 bytes
        conformed 0 packets, 0 bytes; actions:
          transmit
        exceeded 0 packets, 0 bytes; actions:
          drop
        conformed 0 bps, exceed 0 bps
```

```
Class-map: R5 (match-all)
   0 packets, 0 bytes
   5 minute offered rate 0 bps, drop rate 0 bps
   Match: access-group 701
   police:
        cir 20000 bps, bc 1500 bytes
      conformed 0 packets, 0 bytes; actions:
        transmit
      exceeded 0 packets, 0 bytes; actions:
        drop
      conformed 0 bps, exceed 0 bps

Class-map: class-default (match-any)
   0 packets, 0 bytes
   5 minute offered rate 0 bps, drop rate 0 bps
   Match: any
```

Task 4

Ensure that HTTP, FTP, and ICMP traffic on R3's F0/1 interface is policed to 10 Mbps on weekdays from 11:00 a.m. to 3:00 p.m. Traffic exceeding this policy should be dropped, and traffic conforming to this policy should be transmitted.

```
On R3:

R3(config)# time-range weekdays
R3(config-time-range)# periodic weekdays 11:00 to 15:00

R3(config)# access-list 100 permit tcp any any eq www time-range weekdays
R3(config)# access-list 100 permit icmp any any time-range weekdays

R3(config)# access-list 100 permit tcp any any eq 20 time-range weekdays
R3(config)# access-list 100 permit tcp any any eq 21 time-range weekdays

R3(config)# class-map QOS
R3(config-cmap)# match access-group 100

R3(config)# policy-map Task5
R3(config-pmap)# class QOS
R3(config-pmap-c)# police 10000000 conform-act trans exceed-act drop

R3(config-pmap-c)# interface FastEthernet0/0
R3(config-if)# service-policy out Task5
```

Let's verify the configuration:

```
On R3:


R3# Show policy-map interface FastEthernet0/1
 FastEthernet0/1

  Service-policy output: Task5

    Class-map: QOS (match-all)
      0 packets, 0 bytes
      5 minute offered rate 0 bps, drop rate 0 bps
      Match: access-group 100
      police:
          cir 10000000 bps, bc 312500 bytes
        conformed 0 packets, 0 bytes; actions:
          transmit
        exceeded 0 packets, 0 bytes; actions:
          drop
        conformed 0 bps, exceed 0 bps

    Class-map: class-default (match-any)
      8 packets, 781 bytes
      5 minute offered rate 0 bps, drop rate 0 bps
      Match: any
```

Erase the startup configuration and reload the routers before proceeding to the next lab.

Lab 12-11: Class-Based Shaping

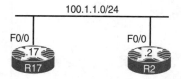

Figure 12-12 *Configuring Class-Based Shaping*

Figure 12-12 illustrates the topology that will be used in the following tasks.

Task 1

Traffic from R17 to R2 should be shaped to 16,000 bps. R17 should be configured to send a **Bc** worth of data every **Tc**. Configure **Tc** to be 4 seconds; R17 should send 8000 bytes per **Tc**.

Traffic can be rate-limited in two ways: You can rate-limit traffic with buffering capabilities, in which case it's called *shaping*, or you can rate-limit traffic without any buffering capabilities, which is called *policing*.

In traffic shaping, you have two choices: shape average and shape peak. When you send a **Bc** worth of data every **Tc**, you are performing a shape average, but if you send **Bc + Be** every **Tc**, you are performing a shape peak.

The task states that R17 should send a **Bc** worth of data every **Tc**, which means that a shape average should be configured. Because R17 should be configured to send 8000 bytes per **Tc**, this means that the **Bc** value should be set to $8 \times 8000 = 64,000$.

Although task doesn't specify the **Be** value, it *must* be configured as zero. If the **Be** value is *not* configured at all (not even as zero), **Be** will equal to **Bc**.

```
On R17:

R17(config)# policy-map tst
R17(config-pmap)# class class-default
R17(config-pmap-c)# shape average 16000 64000 0

R17(config)# interface FastEthernet0/0
R17(config-if)# service-policy out tst
```

Let's verify the configuration:

```
On R17:

R17# show policy-map interface
  FastEthernet0/0

  Service-policy output: tst

    Class-map: class-default (match-any)
      8 packets, 773 bytes
      5 minute offered rate 0 bps, drop rate 0 bps
      Match: any
      Traffic Shaping
            Target/Average   Byte    Sustain    Excess     Interval   Increment
              Rate           Limit   bits/int   bits/int   (ms)       (bytes)
            16000/16000      8000    64000      0          4000       8000


        Adapt   Queue    Packets   Bytes    Packets   Bytes     Shaping
        Active  Depth                       Delayed   Delayed   Active
          -       0         8       773       0         0         no
```

Based on the shaping parameters configured, if **Bc** is divided by the CIR, it should give us the **Tc** value, which in this case is 64,000 / 16,000 = 4 seconds.

Therefore, every 4 seconds, R17 will be sending a **Bc** worth of data because a shape average is configured.

So, every 4 seconds R17 will send 64,000 bps. Because we are going to test this using a **ping** command, and the size of the packets in **ping** is defined in bytes, let's divide 64,000 by 8, which will give us 8000 bytes (the amount of data that R17 will send every 4 seconds). Let's configure and test:

```
On R17:

R17# Debug ip icmp
ICMP packet debugging is on

R17(config)# line con 0
R17(config-line)# logging synchronous

R17# ping 100.1.1.2 size 1000 timeout 0 repeat 32

Type escape sequence to abort.
Sending 32, 1000-byte ICMP Echos to 100.1.1.2, timeout is 0 seconds:
................................
Success rate is 0 percent (0/32)

*Sep 27 21:29:34.743: ICMP: echo reply rcvd, src 100.1.1.2, dst 100.1.1.17
*Sep 27 21:29:34.743: ICMP: echo reply rcvd, src 100.1.1.2, dst 100.1.1.17
*Sep 27 21:29:34.743: ICMP: echo reply rcvd, src 100.1.1.2, dst 100.1.1.17
*Sep 27 21:29:34.743: ICMP: echo reply rcvd, src 100.1.1.2, dst 100.1.1.17
*Sep 27 21:29:34.743: ICMP: echo reply rcvd, src 100.1.1.2, dst 100.1.1.17
*Sep 27 21:29:34.743: ICMP: echo reply rcvd, src 100.1.1.2, dst 100.1.1.17
*Sep 27 21:29:34.743: ICMP: echo reply rcvd, src 100.1.1.2, dst 100.1.1.17
*Sep 27 21:29:34.743: ICMP: echo reply rcvd, src 100.1.1.2, dst 100.1.1.17

*Sep 27 21:29:38.739: ICMP: echo reply rcvd, src 100.1.1.2, dst 100.1.1.17
*Sep 27 21:29:38.739: ICMP: echo reply rcvd, src 100.1.1.2, dst 100.1.1.17
*Sep 27 21:29:38.739: ICMP: echo reply rcvd, src 100.1.1.2, dst 100.1.1.17
*Sep 27 21:29:38.739: ICMP: echo reply rcvd, src 100.1.1.2, dst 100.1.1.17
*Sep 27 21:29:38.739: ICMP: echo reply rcvd, src 100.1.1.2, dst 100.1.1.17
*Sep 27 21:29:38.743: ICMP: echo reply rcvd, src 100.1.1.2, dst 100.1.1.17
*Sep 27 21:29:38.743: ICMP: echo reply rcvd, src 100.1.1.2, dst 100.1.1.17
*Sep 27 21:29:38.743: ICMP: echo reply rcvd, src 100.1.1.2, dst 100.1.1.17

*Sep 27 21:29:42.739: ICMP: echo reply rcvd, src 100.1.1.2, dst 100.1.1.17
*Sep 27 21:29:42.739: ICMP: echo reply rcvd, src 100.1.1.2, dst 100.1.1.17
*Sep 27 21:29:42.739: ICMP: echo reply rcvd, src 100.1.1.2, dst 100.1.1.17
```

```
*Sep 27 21:29:42.739: ICMP: echo reply rcvd, src 100.1.1.2, dst 100.1.1.17
*Sep 27 21:29:42.739: ICMP: echo reply rcvd, src 100.1.1.2, dst 100.1.1.17
*Sep 27 21:29:42.743: ICMP: echo reply rcvd, src 100.1.1.2, dst 100.1.1.17
*Sep 27 21:29:42.743: ICMP: echo reply rcvd, src 100.1.1.2, dst 100.1.1.17
*Sep 27 21:29:42.743: ICMP: echo reply rcvd, src 100.1.1.2, dst 100.1.1.17

*Sep 27 21:29:46.739: ICMP: echo reply rcvd, src 100.1.1.2, dst 100.1.1.17
*Sep 27 21:29:46.739: ICMP: echo reply rcvd, src 100.1.1.2, dst 100.1.1.17
*Sep 27 21:29:46.739: ICMP: echo reply rcvd, src 100.1.1.2, dst 100.1.1.17
*Sep 27 21:29:46.739: ICMP: echo reply rcvd, src 100.1.1.2, dst 100.1.1.17
*Sep 27 21:29:46.739: ICMP: echo reply rcvd, src 100.1.1.2, dst 100.1.1.17
*Sep 27 21:29:46.743: ICMP: echo reply rcvd, src 100.1.1.2, dst 100.1.1.17
*Sep 27 21:29:46.743: ICMP: echo reply rcvd, src 100.1.1.2, dst 100.1.1.17
*Sep 27 21:29:46.743: ICMP: echo reply rcvd, src 100.1.1.2, dst 100.1.1.17
```

The **ping** command is sending 1000-byte packets. Because the shape average is configured to send 8000 bytes every Tc, which is 4 seconds, we can see that every 4 seconds the local router is sending eight 1000-byte packets.

Erase the startup configuration of the routers and reload them before proceeding to the next lab.

Chapter 13

IPSec VPN

VPN tunnels are used to connect physically isolated networks that are more often than not separated by nonsecure internetworks. To protect these connections, we employ the IP Security (IPSec) protocol to make secure the transmission of data, voice, and video between sites. These secure tunnels over the Internet public network are encrypted using a number of advanced algorithms to provide confidentiality of data that is transmitted between multiple sites. This chapter explores how to configure routers to create a permanent secure site-to-site VPN tunnel.

Encryption will be provided by IPSec in concert with VPN tunnels. The Internet Security Association and Key Management Protocol (ISAKMP) and IPSec are essential to building and encrypting VPN tunnels. ISAKMP, also called IKE (Internet Key Exchange), is the negotiation protocol that allows hosts to agree on how to build an IPSec security association.

ISAKMP negotiation consists of two phases:

- Phase 1 creates the first tunnel, which protects later ISAKMP negotiation messages.
- Phase 2 creates the tunnel that protects data.

IPSec then encrypts exchanged data by employing encryption algorithms that result in authentication, encryption, and critical anti-replay services.

Lab 13-1: Basic Site-to-Site IPSec VPN

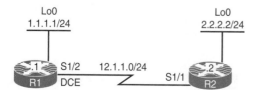

Figure 13-1 *Configuring Basic Site-to-Site IPSec VPN (Main Mode)*

Figure 13-1 illustrates the topology that will be used in the following lab.

Task 1

Configure a basic site-to-site IPSec VPN to protect traffic between IP addresses 1.1.1.1 and 2.2.2.2 using the policy shown in Table 13-1.

Table 13-1 *Policy Guidelines for Configuring Task 1*

ISAKMP Policy	IPSec Policy
Authentication: Pre-shared	Encryption: ESP-3DES
Hash: MD5	Hash: ESP-MD5-HMAC
DH Group: 2	Proxy-ID/Crypto ACL: 1.1.1.1 ←→ 2.2.2.2
Encryption: 3DES	
PSK: cisco	

Reachability to the loopback0 interfaces is provided in the initial configuration.

ISAKMP, originally defined in RFC 7296, covers the following:

- Procedures to authenticate a communicating peer

- How to create and manage security associations (SAs)

- Key-generation techniques

- Threat mitigation, such as denial-of-service (DoS) and replay attacks

IKE does not specify any details of key management or key exchange, and it's not bound to any key-generation techniques. Inside IKE, Cisco uses OAKLEY for the key exchange protocol.

OAKLEY enables you to choose between different well-known Diffie-Hellman (DH) groups. RFC 2412 describes the OAKLEY protocol and covers DH groups 1 through 5. Of these groups, Cisco supports DH groups 1, 2, and 5. RFC 3526 describes DH group 5 and groups 14 through 18. Cisco supports DH groups 5, 14, 15, and 16. RFC 5114 covers DH groups 19 through 26. Of these DH groups, Cisco supports 19, 20, 21, and 24. The following is a list of the DH groups supported by Cisco:

- **1**: Diffie-Hellman group 1 (768 bit)

- **2**: Diffie-Hellman group 2 (1024 bit)

- **5**: Diffie-Hellman group 5 (1536 bit)

- **14**: Diffie-Hellman group 14 (2048 bit)

- **15**: Diffie-Hellman group 15 (3072 bit)

- **16**: Diffie-Hellman group 16 (4096 bit)

- **19**: Diffie-Hellman group 19 (256-bit ECP)

- **20**: Diffie-Hellman group 20 (384-bit ECP)

- **21**: Diffie-Hellman group 21 (521-bit ECP)

- **24**: Diffie-Hellman group 24 (2048 bit, 256-bit subgroup)

ISAKMP and OAKLEY create an authenticated, secure tunnel between two entities, and then negotiate the SA for IPSec. Both peers must authenticate each other and establish a shared key.

Three authentication methods are available: RSA signatures (PKI), RSA encrypted pseudorandom numbers (nonces), and preshared keys (PSK). The DH protocol is used to agree on a common session key.

IPSec uses a different shared key from ISAKMP and OAKLEY. The IPSec shared key can be derived by using DH again to ensure Perfect Forward Secrecy (PFS) or by refreshing the shared secret derived from the original DH exchange.

IKE is a hybrid protocol that establishes a shared security policy and authenticated keys for services that require keys, such as IPSec. Before an IPSec tunnel is established, each device must be able to identify its peer. ISAKMP and IKE are both used interchangeably; however, these two items are somewhat different. IKE was originally defined by RFC 2409. IKE version 2 is currently described by RFC 7296.

> **IKE Phase 1:** The two ISAKMP peers establish a secure and an authenticated channel. This channel is known as the ISAKMP SA. There are two modes defined by ISAKMP: Main Mode and Aggressive Mode.

> **IKE Phase 2:** SAs are negotiated on behalf of services such as IPSec that need keying material. This phase is called Quick Mode.

To configure IKE Phase 1, you need to configure ISAKMP policies. It is possible to configure multiple policies with different configuration statements and then let the two hosts negotiate the policies. The first matched policy on the responder will be used.

Let's start configuring Phase 1 on both routers:

```
On R1:

R1(config)# crypto isakmp policy 10
R1(config-isakmp)# hash md5
R1(config-isakmp)# authentication pre-share
R1(config-isakmp)# group 2
R1(config-isakmp)# encryption 3des
R1(config-isakmp)# exit
```

The IP address of a loopback interface can be used when there are multiple paths to reach the peer's IP address:

```
R1(config)# crypto isakmp key cisco address 12.1.1.2

On R2:

R2(config)# crypto isakmp policy 10
R2(config-isakmp)# hash md5
R2(config-isakmp)# authentication pre-share
R2(config-isakmp)# group 2
R2(config-isakmp)# encryption 3des
R2(config-isakmp)# exit

R2(config)# crypto isakmp key cisco address 12.1.1.1
```

To configure the Phase 2, we need to define the **transform-set**, which specifies the hashing, the security protocol, and the encryption used for Phase 2:

```
On Both Routers:
Rx(config)# crypto ipsec transform-set TSET esp-3des esp-md5-hmac
Rx(cfg-config-trans)# exit
```

Next, we need to define the crypto ACL/proxy ID, which defines the interesting traffic:

```
On R1:

R1(config)# access-list 100 permit ip host 1.1.1.1 host 2.2.2.2

On R2:

R2(config)# access-list 100 permit ip host 2.2.2.2 host 1.1.1.1
```

In the last step, a crypto map is configured to specify the peer, crypto ACL, and the transform set. There are three choices when configuring the following crypto map:

- **IPSec-ISAKMP:** This is the best option. It states that we are using ISAKMP to encrypt and decrypt the key.

- **IPSec-manual:** This is the worst choice. It means that the key needs to be entered manually. (Can you imagine entering a 512-bit key manually?)

- **GDOI:** This choice is used for GETVPN configuration. It stands for *group domain of interpretation.*

```
On R1:
R1(config)# crypto map TST 10 ipsec-isakmp
```

You should see the following console message:

```
% NOTE: This new crypto map will remain disabled until a peer
        and a valid access list have been configured.

R1(config-crypto-map)# set peer 12.1.1.2
R1(config-crypto-map)# match address 100
R1(config-crypto-map)# set transform-set TSET
R1(config-crypto-map)# exit


On R2:


R2(config)# crypto map TST 10 ipsec-isakmp
R2(config-crypto-map)# set peer 12.1.1.1
R2(config-crypto-map)# match address 100
R2(config-crypto-map)# set transform-set TSET
R2(config-crypto-map)# exit
```

The final step applies the crypto map to the interface facing the other peer:

```
On R1:

R1(config)# interface Serial 1/2
R1(config-if)# crypto map TST
```

You should see the following console message:

```
%CRYPTO-6-ISAKMP_ON_OFF: ISAKMP is ON

On R2:

R2(config)# interface Serial 1/1
R2(config-if)# crypto map TST
```

Let's verify the configuration before testing:

```
On R1:


R1# show crypto isakmp policy

Global IKE policy


Protection suite of priority 10
        encryption algorithm:   Three key triple DES
        hash algorithm:         Message Digest 5
        authentication method:  Pre-Shared Key
```

```
        Diffie-Hellman group:   # 2 (1024 bit)
        lifetime:               86400 seconds, no volume limit

R1# show crypto isakmp key

Keyring       Hostname/Address                        Preshared Key
default       12.1.1.2                                cisco
```

Now we can test the configuration:

```
On R1:

R1# debug crypto isakmp
Crypto ISAKMP debugging is on

R1# debug crypto ipsec
Crypto IPSEC debugging is on

R1# ping 2.2.2.2 source loopback0
Type escape sequence to abort.
Sending 5, 100-byte ICMP Echos to 2.2.2.2, timeout is 2 seconds:
Packet sent with a source address of 1.1.1.1
```

The first ICMP packet triggers the ISAKMP process, as this is our interesting traffic matching the configured crypto ACL.

Before we actually start sending IKE packets to the peer, the router first checks whether there is a local SA (security association) matching that traffic. This check is against the IPSec SA and not an IKE SA.

We can see the outbound and remote IP addresses, port number, local proxy, and remote proxy. The protocol used is ESP, and the **transform-set** is the default mode of tunnel.

```
IPSEC(sa_request): ,
  (key eng. msg.) OUTBOUND local= 12.1.1.1:500, remote= 12.1.1.2:500,
    local_proxy= 1.1.1.1/255.255.255.255/0/0 (type=1),
    remote_proxy= 2.2.2.2/255.255.255.255/0/0 (type=1),
    protocol= ESP, transform= esp-3des esp-md5-hmac  (Tunnel),
    lifedur= 3600s and 4608000kb,
    spi= 0x0(0), conn_id= 0, keysize= 0, flags= 0x0
```

The following highlighted line specifies that no SA was found. The router first tried to find an IPSec SA matching the outgoing connection, but it failed to find one.

```
ISAKMP:(0): SA request profile is (NULL)
ISAKMP: Created a peer struct for 12.1.1.2, peer port 500
ISAKMP: New peer created peer = 0x4B24E100 peer_handle = 0x80000003
ISAKMP: Locking peer struct 0x4B24E100, refcount 1 for isakmp_initiator
ISAKMP: local port 500, remote port 500
ISAKMP: set new node 0 to QM_IDLE
ISAKMP: Find a dup sa in the avl tree during calling isadb_insert sa = 4B331BEC
```

IKE Phase 1 (Main Mode) Message 1

By default, IKE Main Mode is used, so we should expect six packets for Phase 1. The following highlighted message states that the Aggressive Mode cannot start. However, this does not mean that we are experiencing errors; it just means that Aggressive Mode is not configured on the local router.

```
ISAKMP:(0):Can not start Aggressive mode, trying Main mode.
```

The router checks for the configured ISAKMP policy and sees that pre-shared key (PSK) authentication is configured. It has to check whether there is a key for the configured peer as well. After that, the first IKE packet is sent out to the peer's IP address on port UDP 500.

The packet contains locally configured ISAKMP policies to be negotiated by the peer. The pre-shared key for the remote peer is found, which means that ISAKMP is going to use it to authenticate the peer. This will happen in the last stage of IKE Phase 1.

```
ISAKMP:(0):found peer pre-shared key matching 12.1.1.2
ISAKMP:(0): constructed NAT-T vendor-rfc3947 ID
ISAKMP:(0): constructed NAT-T vendor-07 ID
ISAKMP:(0): constructed NAT-T vendor-03 ID
ISAKMP:(0): constructed NAT-T vendor-02 ID
ISAKMP:(0):Input = IKE_MESG_FROM_IPSEC, IKE_SA_REQ_MM
ISAKMP:(0):Old State = IKE_READY  New State = IKE_I_MM1

ISAKMP:(0): beginning Main Mode exchange
ISAKMP:(0): sending packet to 12.1.1.2 my_port 500 peer_port 500 (I) MM_NO_STATE
```

The router initiating the IKE exchange is called *the initiator*, and the router responding to IKE request is called *the responder*. The initiator (R1) has sent the ISAKMP policy along with vendor-specific IDs that are part of the IKE packet payload. **MM_NO_STATE** indicates that ISAKMP SA has been created, but nothing else has happened yet.

IKE Phase 1 (Main Mode) Message 2

It looks like everything is going smoothly. We received a response packet from the peer. However, this is one area where things can typically go wrong.

The received packet contains the SA chosen by the peer and some other useful information, such as vendor IDs. Those vendor-specific payloads are used to discover network address translation (NAT) along the path and to maintain keepalives. The router matches the ISAKMP policy from the packet to one that's locally configured. If there is a match, the tunnel-establishment process continues. If the policy configured on both routers is not the same, the crosscheck process fails and the tunnel is down.

```
ISAKMP:(0):Sending an IKE IPv4 Packet.
ISAKMP (0): received packet from 12.1.1.2 dport 500 sport 500 Global (I) MM_NO_STATE
ISAKMP:(0):Input = IKE_MESG_FROM_PEER, IKE_MM_EXCH
ISAKMP:(0):Old State = IKE_I_MM1  New State = IKE_I_MM2

ISAKMP:(0): processing SA payload. message ID = 0
ISAKMP:(0): processing vendor id payload
ISAKMP:(0): vendor ID seems Unity/DPD but major 69 mismatch
ISAKMP (0): vendor ID is NAT-T RFC 3947
ISAKMP:(0):found peer pre-shared key matching 12.1.1.2
ISAKMP:(0): local preshared key found
ISAKMP : Scanning profiles for xauth ...
IS.!!!!
Success rate is 80 percent (4/5), round-trip min/avg/max = 44/45/48 ms
```

The router is processing ISAKMP parameters that have been sent as the reply. The vendor IDs are processed to determine whether the peer supports the NAT-Traversal, Dead Peer Detection feature. ISAKMP policy is checked against policies defined locally. The **atts are acceptable** message indicates that the ISAKMP policy matches with remote peer:

```
R1# AKMP:(0):Checking ISAKMP transform 1 against priority 10 policy
ISAKMP:        encryption 3DES-CBC
ISAKMP:        hash MD5
ISAKMP:        default group 2
ISAKMP:        auth pre-share
ISAKMP:        life type in seconds
ISAKMP:        life duration (VPI) of  0x0 0x1 0x51 0x80
ISAKMP:(0):atts are acceptable. Next payload is 0
```

The lifetime timer has been started. Note that default value is used (86,400 seconds). This is the lifetime for ISAKMP SA. Note that IPSec SAs have their own **lifetime** parameters, which may be defined as number of seconds or kilobytes of transmitted traffic.

```
ISAKMP:(0):Acceptable atts:actual life: 0
ISAKMP:(0):Acceptable atts:life: 0
ISAKMP:(0):Fill atts in sa vpi_length:4
ISAKMP:(0):Fill atts in sa life_in_seconds:86400
ISAKMP:(0):Returning Actual lifetime: 86400
ISAKMP:(0)::Started lifetime timer: 86400.


ISAKMP:(0): processing vendor id payload
ISAKMP:(0): vendor ID seems Unity/DPD but major 69 mismatch
ISAKMP (0): vendor ID is NAT-T RFC 3947
ISAKMP:(0):Input = IKE_MESG_INTERNAL, IKE_PROCESS_MAIN_MODE
ISAKMP:(0):Old State = IKE_I_MM2  New State = IKE_I_MM2
```

IKE Phase 1 (Main Mode) Message 3

The third message is sent out containing key-exchange (KE) information for the Diffie-Hellman (DH) secure key-exchange process:

```
ISAKMP:(0): sending packet to 12.1.1.2 my_port 500 peer_port 500 (I) MM_SA_SETUP
ISAKMP:(0):Sending an IKE IPv4 Packet.
ISAKMP:(0):Input = IKE_MESG_INTERNAL, IKE_PROCESS_COMPLETE
ISAKMP:(0):Old State = IKE_I_MM2  New State = IKE_I_MM3
```

IKE Phase 1 (Main Mode) Message 4

The fourth message has been received from the peer. This message contains the KE payload, and based on that information, both peers can generate a common session key to be used in securing further communication. The pre-shared key configured locally for the peer is used in this calculation.

After receiving this message, peers can determine whether there is NAT along the path.

```
ISAKMP (0): received packet from 12.1.1.2 dport 500 sport 500 Global (I) MM_SA_SETUP
ISAKMP:(0):Input = IKE_MESG_FROM_PEER, IKE_MM_EXCH
ISAKMP:(0):Old State = IKE_I_MM3  New State = IKE_I_MM4


ISAKMP:(0): processing KE payload. message ID = 0
ISAKMP:(0): processing NONCE payload. message ID = 0
ISAKMP:(0):found peer pre-shared key matching 12.1.1.2
ISAKMP:(1002): processing vendor id payload
ISAKMP:(1002): vendor ID is Unity
ISAKMP:(1002): processing vendor id payload
ISAKMP:(1002): vendor ID is DPD
ISAKMP:(1002): processing vendor id payload
```

```
ISAKMP:(1002): speaking to another IOS box!
ISAKMP:received payload type 20
ISAKMP (1002): His hash no match - this node outside NAT
ISAKMP:received payload type 20
ISAKMP (1002): No NAT Found for self or peer
ISAKMP:(1002):Input = IKE_MESG_INTERNAL, IKE_PROCESS_MAIN_MODE
ISAKMP:(1002):Old State = IKE_I_MM4  New State = IKE_I_MM4
```

IKE Phase 1 (Main Mode) Message 5

The fifth message is used for sending out authentication information to the peer. This information is transmitted under the protection of the common shared secret.

```
ISAKMP:(1002):Send initial contact
ISAKMP:(1002):SA is doing pre-shared key authentication using id type ID_IPV4_ADDR
ISAKMP (1002): ID payload
        next-payload : 8
        type         : 1
        address      : 12.1.1.1
        protocol     : 17
        port         : 500
        length       : 12
ISAKMP:(1002):Total payload length: 12
ISAKMP:(1002): sending packet to 12.1.1.2 my_port 500 peer_port 500 (I) MM_KEY_EXCH
```

MM_KEY_EXCH indicates that the peers have exchanged Diffie-Hellman public keys and have generated a shared secret. The ISAKMP SA remains unauthenticated. Note that the process of authentication has just been started.

```
ISAKMP:(1002):Sending an IKE IPv4 Packet.
ISAKMP:(1002):Input = IKE_MESG_INTERNAL, IKE_PROCESS_COMPLETE
ISAKMP:(1002):Old State = IKE_I_MM4  New State = IKE_I_MM5
```

IKE Phase 1 (Main Mode) Message 6

The peer identity is verified by the local router and the SA is established.
This message finishes ISAKMP Main Mode (Phase I), and the status is changed to **IKE_P1_COMPLETE**.

```
ISAKMP (1002): received packet from 12.1.1.2 dport 500 sport 500 Global (I)
   MM_KEY_EXCH
ISAKMP (1002): processing ID payload. message ID = 0
ISAKMP (1002): ID payload
        next-payload : 8
        type         : 1
```

```
        address     : 12.1.1.2
        protocol    : 17
        port        : 500
        length      : 12
ISAKMP:(0):: peer matches *none* of the profiles
ISAKMP:(1002): processing HASH payload. message ID = 0
ISAKMP:(1002):SA authentication status:
    authenticated
ISAKMP:(1002):SA has been authenticated with 12.1.1.2
ISAKMP: Trying to insert a peer 12.1.1.1/12.1.1.2/500/,  and inserted successfully
  4B24E100.
ISAKMP:(1002):Input = IKE_MESG_FROM_PEER, IKE_MM_EXCH
ISAKMP:(1002):Old State = IKE_I_MM5  New State = IKE_I_MM6


ISAKMP:(1002):Input = IKE_MESG_INTERNAL, IKE_PROCESS_MAIN_MODE
ISAKMP:(1002):Old State = IKE_I_MM6  New State = IKE_I_MM6


ISAKMP:(1002):Input = IKE_MESG_INTERNAL, IKE_PROCESS_COMPLETE
ISAKMP:(1002):Old State = IKE_I_MM6  New State = IKE_P1_COMPLETE
```

IKE Phase 2 (Quick Mode) Message 1

Now it's time for Phase 2, which is Quick Mode (QM). The router sends out the packet containing local proxy IDs (network/host addresses to be protected by the IPSec tunnel) and the security policy defined by the transform set.

The state of IKE is **QM_IDLE**. This indicates that the ISAKMP SA is idle. It remains authenticated with its peer and may be used for subsequent Quick Mode exchanges. It is in a quiescent state.

```
ISAKMP:(1002):beginning Quick Mode exchange, M-ID of 623921701
ISAKMP:(1002):QM Initiator gets spi
ISAKMP:(1002): sending packet to 12.1.1.2 my_port 500 peer_port 500 (I) QM_IDLE
ISAKMP:(1002):Sending an IKE IPv4 Packet.
ISAKMP:(1002):Node 623921701, Input = IKE_MESG_INTERNAL, IKE_INIT_QM
ISAKMP:(1002):Old State = IKE_QM_READY  New State = IKE_QM_I_QM1
ISAKMP:(1002):Input = IKE_MESG_INTERNAL, IKE_PHASE1_COMPLETE
ISAKMP:(1002):Old State = IKE_P1_COMPLETE  New State = IKE_P1_COMPLETE


ISAKMP (1002): received packet from 12.1.1.2 dport 500 sport 500 Global (I) QM_IDLE
```

The routers are negotiating the parameters for the IPSec tunnel that will be used for traffic transmission. These parameters are defined by the **crypto ipsec transform-set** command.

Note that lifetime values of the IPSec SA are visible at this moment. You are able to set this both globally and in the crypto map entry. The **attr are acceptable** message indicates that the IPSec parameters defined as the IPSec transform-set match on both sides.

```
ISAKMP:(1002): processing HASH payload. message ID = 623921701
ISAKMP:(1002): processing SA payload. message ID = 623921701
ISAKMP:(1002):Checking IPSec proposal 1
ISAKMP: transform 1, ESP_3DES
ISAKMP:    attributes in transform:
ISAKMP:        encaps is 1 (Tunnel)
ISAKMP:        SA life type in seconds
ISAKMP:        SA life duration (basic) of 3600
ISAKMP:        SA life type in kilobytes
ISAKMP:        SA life duration (VPI) of  0x0 0x46 0x50 0x0
ISAKMP:        authenticator is HMAC-MD5
ISAKMP:(1002):atts are acceptable.
IPSEC(validate_proposal_request): proposal part # 1
IPSEC(validate_proposal_request): proposal part # 1,

  (key eng. msg.) INBOUND local= 12.1.1.1:0, remote= 12.1.1.2:0,
    local_proxy= 1.1.1.1/255.255.255.255/0/0 (type=1),

    remote_proxy= 2.2.2.2/255.255.255.255/0/0 (type=1),
    protocol= ESP, transform= NONE  (Tunnel),
    lifedur= 0s and 0kb,
    spi= 0x0(0), conn_id= 0, keysize= 0, flags= 0x0
Crypto mapdb : proxy_match
        src addr    : 1.1.1.1
        dst addr    : 2.2.2.2
        protocol    : 0
        src port    : 0
        dst port    : 0
ISAKMP:(1002): processing NONCE payload. message ID = 623921701
ISAKMP:(1002): processing ID payload. message ID = 623921701
ISAKMP:(1002): processing ID payload. message ID = 623921701
```

The local and remote proxies are defined. This indicates the sources and destinations set in crypto ACL, which defines the interesting traffic for the IPSec tunnel. Remember that it is enough when only one entry is mirrored. If not, you may get the following entry in the debug output: **PSEC(initialize_sas): invalid proxy IDs.**

```
ISAKMP:(1002): Creating IPSec SAs
        inbound SA from 12.1.1.2 to 12.1.1.1 (f/i)  0/ 0
        (proxy 2.2.2.2 to 1.1.1.1)
        has spi 0x2E5593AE and conn_id 0
        lifetime of 3600 seconds
        lifetime of 4608000 kilobytes
```

```
outbound SA from 12.1.1.1 to 12.1.1.2 (f/i) 0/0
(proxy 1.1.1.1 to 2.2.2.2)
has spi  0x5AEFD96D and conn_id 0
lifetime of 3600 seconds
lifetime of 4608000 kilobytes
```

The IPSec SAs have been created and inserted into the router's security associations database (SADB). SAs are distinguished by Security Parameter Index (SPI) values, which are also used to differentiate many tunnels terminated on the same router. Note that two SPI values are generated for one tunnel: one SPI for the inbound SA and one SPI for the outbound SA.

The SPI value is inserted in the ESP header of the packet leaving the router. At the other side of the tunnel, the SPI value inserted into the ESP header enables the router to reach parameters and keys that have been dynamically agreed upon during IKE negotiations, or session key refreshment in case of lifetime timeout.

```
ISAKMP:(1002): sending packet to 12.1.1.2 my_port 500 peer_port 500 (I) QM_IDLE
ISAKMP:(1002):Sending an IKE IPv4 Packet.
ISAKMP:(1002):deleting node 623921701 error FALSE reason "No Error"
ISAKMP:(1002):Node 623921701, Input = IKE_MESG_FROM_PEER, IKE_QM_EXCH
ISAKMP:(1002):Old State = IKE_QM_I_QM1  New State = IKE_QM_PHASE2_COMPLETE
IPSEC(key_engine): got a queue event with 1 KMI message(s)
Crypto mapdb : proxy_match


        src addr    : 1.1.1.1
        dst addr    : 2.2.2.2
        protocol    : 0
        src port    : 0
        dst port    : 0
IPSEC(crypto_ipsec_sa_find_ident_head): reconnecting with the same proxies and peer
  12.1.1.2
IPSEC(policy_db_add_ident): src 1.1.1.1, dest 2.2.2.2, dest_port 0

IPSEC(create_sa): sa created,
  (sa) sa_dest= 12.1.1.1, sa_proto= 50,
    sa_spi= 0x2E5593AE(777360302),
    sa_trans= esp-3des esp-md5-hmac , sa_conn_id= 2003
    sa_lifetime(k/sec)= (4571378/3600)
IPSEC(create_sa): sa created,
  (sa) sa_dest= 12.1.1.2, sa_proto= 50,
    sa_spi= 0x5AEFD96D(1525668205),
    sa_trans= esp-3des esp-md5-hmac , sa_conn_id= 2004
    sa_lifetime(k/sec)= (4571378/3600)
```

```
IPSEC(update_current_outbound_sa): get enable SA peer 12.1.1.2 current outbound sa
  to SPI 5AEFD96D
IPSEC(update_current_outbound_sa): updated peer 12.1.1.2 current outbound sa to SPI
  5AEFD96D


ISAKMP:(1001):purging SA., sa=4B23D6D0, delme=4B23D6D0


R1# show crypto isakmp sa

IPv4 Crypto ISAKMP SA
dst              src              state          conn-id status
12.1.1.2         12.1.1.1         QM_IDLE           1002 ACTIVE


IPv6 Crypto ISAKMP SA

R1# show crypto ipsec sa

interface: Serial1/2
    Crypto map tag: TST, local addr 12.1.1.1


   protected vrf: (none)
   local  ident (addr/mask/prot/port): (1.1.1.1/255.255.255.255/0/0)
   remote ident (addr/mask/prot/port): (2.2.2.2/255.255.255.255/0/0)
   current_peer 12.1.1.2 port 500
     PERMIT, flags={origin_is_acl,}
    # pkts encaps: 4, # pkts encrypt: 4, # pkts digest: 4
    # pkts decaps: 4, # pkts decrypt: 4, # pkts verify: 4
    # pkts compressed: 0, # pkts decompressed: 0
    # pkts not compressed: 0, # pkts compr. failed: 0
    # pkts not decompressed: 0, # pkts decompress failed: 0
    # send errors 1, # recv errors 0


     local crypto endpt.: 12.1.1.1, remote crypto endpt.: 12.1.1.2
     path mtu 1500, ip mtu 1500, ip mtu idb Serial1/2
     current outbound spi: 0xE53B1D2(240366034)
     PFS (Y/N): N, DH group: none


     inbound esp sas:
      spi: 0xBDAF9A28(3182402088)
        transform: esp-3des esp-md5-hmac ,
        in use settings ={Tunnel, }
        conn id: 2005, flow_id: NETGX:5, sibling_flags 80000046, crypto map: TST
        sa timing: remaining key lifetime (k/sec): (4405715/2686)
        IV size: 8 bytes
```

```
      replay detection support: Y
      Status: ACTIVE

  inbound ah sas:
  inbound pcp sas:

  outbound esp sas:
   spi: 0xE53B1D2(240366034)
     transform: esp-3des esp-md5-hmac ,
     in use settings ={Tunnel, }
     conn id: 2006, flow_id: NETGX:6, sibling_flags 80000046, crypto map: TST
     sa timing: remaining key lifetime (k/sec): (4405715/2686)
     IV size: 8 bytes
     replay detection support: Y
     Status: ACTIVE

  outbound ah sas:
  outbound pcp sas:
```

Task 2

Erase the startup configuration of the routers and reload them before proceeding
to the next lab.

Lab 13-2: Basic Site-to-Site IPSec VPN and NAT

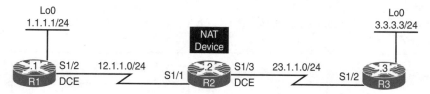

Figure 13-2 *Configuring Basic Site-to-Site IPSec VPN and NAT*

Figure 13-2 illustrates the topology that will be used in the following lab.

Task 1

Reachability to the loopback interfaces of R1 and R3 should be provided using static
routes based on the following policy:

■ R1 and R3 should be configured with a static default route pointing to R2.

■ R2 should be configured with two static routes: one for network 1.1.1.0/24 through
R1, and the second for 3.3.3.0/24 through R3.

```
On R1:

R1(config)# ip route 0.0.0.0 0.0.0.0 12.1.1.2

On R3:

R3(config)# ip route 0.0.0.0 0.0.0.0 23.1.1.2

On R2:

R2(config)# ip route 1.1.1.0 255.255.255.0 12.1.1.1
R2(config)# ip route 3.3.3.0 255.255.255.0 23.1.1.3
```

Let's test the configuration:

```
On R1:

R1# ping 3.3.3.3 source loopback0

Type escape sequence to abort.
Sending 5, 100-byte ICMP Echos to 3.3.3.3, timeout is 2 seconds:
Packet sent with a source address of 1.1.1.1
!!!!!
Success rate is 100 percent (5/5), round-trip min/avg/max = 56/56/60 ms
```

Task 2

Configure static network address translation (NAT) on R2 so that R1's S1/2 IP address is seen on R3 as 23.1.1.1:

```
On R2:

R2(config)# interface Serial1/1
R2(config-if)# ip nat inside

R2(config)# interface Serial1/3
R2(config-if)# ip nat outside
R2(config-if)# exit

R2(config)# ip nat inside source static 12.1.1.1 23.1.1.1
```

Let's verify the configuration:

```
On R2:


R2# show ip nat translations


Pro Inside global     Inside local      Outside local      Outside global
--- 23.1.1.1          12.1.1.1          ---                ---
```

Task 3

Configure a basic site-to-site IPSec VPN to protect traffic between 1.1.1.1 and 3.3.3.3 networks using the policy shown in Table 13-2.

Table 13-2 *Policy Guidelines for Configuring Task 3*

ISAKMP Policy	IPSec Policy
Authentication: Pre-shared	Encryption: ESP-3DES
Hash: MD5	Hash: ESP-MD5-HMAC
DH Group: 2	Proxy-ID/Crypto ACL: 1.1.1.1 $\longleftrightarrow$ 3.3.3.3
Encryption: 3DES	
PSK: cisco	

By now we have a step-by-step process for IPSec configuration that we can use:

Step 1.   Configure ISAKMP using pre-shared authentication, MD5 hashing, DH group 2, and a PSK of "cisco" on both R1 and R3:

```
On R1:


R1(config)# crypto isakmp policy 10
R1(config-isakmp)# hash md5
R1(config-isakmp)# authentication pre-share
R1(config-isakmp)# group 2
R1(config-isakmp)# encryption 3des
R1(config-isakmp)# exit


On R3:


R3(config)# crypto isakmp policy 10
R3(config-isakmp)# hash md5
R3(config-isakmp)# authentication pre-share
R3(config-isakmp)# group 2
R3(config-isakmp)# encryption 3des
R3(config-isakmp)# exit
```

Step 2. Configure the ISAKMP key and identify the peer:

```
On R1:

R1(config)# crypto isakmp key cisco address 23.1.1.3
```

Note R3 has to use the translated IP address because, from its perspective, it's establishing an IPSec tunnel with 23.1.1.1:

```
On R3:

R3(config)# crypto isakmp key cisco address 23.1.1.1
```

Step 3. Configure the IPSec transform set to use DES for encryption and MD5 for hashing:

```
On R1 and R3:

Rx(config)# crypto ipsec transform-set TSET esp-des esp-md5-hmac
Rx(cfg-config-trans)# exit
```

Step 4. Define interesting traffic:

```
On R1:

R1(config)# access-list 100 permit ip host 1.1.1.1 host 3.3.3.3

On R3:

R1(config)# access-list 100 permit ip host 3.3.3.3 host 1.1.1.1
```

Step 5. Configure a crypto map and reference the peer, the crypto ACL, and the transform set configured in the previous steps:

```
On R1:

R1(config)# crypto map TST 10 ipsec-isakmp
R1(config-crypto-map)# set peer 23.1.1.3
R1(config-crypto-map)# match address 100
R1(config-crypto-map)# set transform-set TSET
R1(config-crypto-map)# exit

On R3:

R3(config)# crypto map TST 10 ipsec-isakmp
```

The peer IP address should be the translated IP address:

```
R3(config-crypto-map)# set peer 23.1.1.1
R3(config-crypto-map)# match address 100
R3(config-crypto-map)# set transform-set TSET
R3(config-crypto-map)# exit
```

Step 6.   Apply the crypto map to the outside interface:

```
On R1:

R1(config)# interface Serial1/2
R1(config-if)# crypto map TST

On R3:

R3(config)# interface Serial1/2
R3(config-if)# crypto map TST
```

Now let's test the configuration:

```
On R1:

R1# ping 3.3.3.3 source 1.1.1.1

Type escape sequence to abort.
Sending 5, 100-byte ICMP Echos to 3.3.3.3, timeout is 2 seconds:
Packet sent with a source address of 1.1.1.1
.!!!!
Success rate is 80 percent (4/5), round-trip min/avg/max = 88/91/92 ms

R1# show crypto isakmp sa

IPv4 Crypto ISAKMP SA
dst              src             state          conn-id status
23.1.1.3         12.1.1.1        QM_IDLE            1001 ACTIVE

IPv6 Crypto ISAKMP SA

R1# show crypto ipsec sa | include #pkts

    # pkts encaps: 4, # pkts encrypt: 4, # pkts digest: 4
    # pkts decaps: 4, # pkts decrypt: 4, # pkts verify: 4
    # pkts compressed: 0, # pkts decompressed: 0
```

```
   # pkts not compressed: 0, # pkts compr. failed: 0
   # pkts not decompressed: 0, # pkts decompress failed: 0

R1# show crypto engine connections active
Crypto Engine Connections

   ID  Type   Algorithm          Encrypt  Decrypt LastSeqN IP-Address
  1001  IKE   MD5+3DES                 0        0        0 12.1.1.1
  2001  IPsec  DES+MD5                 0        4        4 12.1.1.1
  2002  IPsec  DES+MD5                 4        0        0 12.1.1.1
```

Erase the startup configuration of the routers and reload them before proceeding to the next lab.

Lab 13-3: Configuring GRE/IPSec Tunnel Mode, Transport Mode, and S-VTI

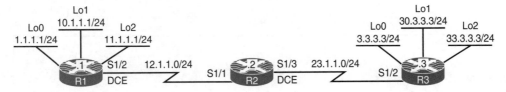

Figure 13-3 *Configuring GRE/IPSec Tunnel Mode, Transport Mode, and S-VTI*

Figure 13-3 illustrates the topology that will be used in the following lab.

Task 1

Configure a basic site-to-site IPSec VPN to protect traffic between the 1.1.1.0/24, 11.1.1.0/24, 2.2.2.0/24, and 22.2.2.0/24 networks using the policies shown in Table 13-3.

Table 13-3 *Policy Guidelines for Configuring Task 1*

ISAKMP Policy	IPSec Policy
Authentication: Pre-shared	Encryption: ESP-3DES
Hash: MD5	Hash: ESP-MD5-HMAC
DH Group: 2	Proxy-ID/Crypto ACL: 1.1.1.1←→ 2.2.2.2
Encryption: 3DES	
PSK: cisco	

Reachability is provided in the initial configuration.

Step 1.   Configure ISAKMP using pre-shared authentication, MD5 hashing, DH group 2, and a PSK of "cisco" on both R1 and R3:

```
On R1:

R1(config)# crypto isakmp policy 10
R1(config-isakmp)# hash md5
R1(config-isakmp)# authentication pre-share
R1(config-isakmp)# group 2
R1(config-isakmp)# encryption 3des
R1(config-isakmp)# exit


On R3:

R3(config)# crypto isakmp policy 10
R3(config-isakmp)# hash md5
R3(config-isakmp)# authentication pre-share
R3(config-isakmp)# group 2
R3(config-isakmp)# encryption 3des
R3(config-isakmp)# exit
```

Step 2.   Configure the ISAKMP key and identify the peer:

```
On R1:

R1(config)# crypto isakmp key cisco address 23.1.1.3

On R3:

R3(config)# crypto isakmp key cisco address 12.1.1.1
```

Step 3.   Configure the IPSec transform set to use DES for encryption and MD5 for hashing:

```
On R1 and R3:

Rx(config)# crypto ipsec transform-set TSET esp-des esp-md5-hmac
Rx(cfg-config-trans)# exit
```

Step 4.   Define interesting traffic. You can see how the crypto ACL can grow and grow. Can you imagine having 500 subnets trying to communicate with another 500 or more networks in a secure manner? The crypto ACL must be configured in a full mesh manner.

```
On R1:

R1(config)# access-list 100 permit ip host 1.1.1.1 host 3.3.3.3
R1(config)# access-list 100 permit ip host 1.1.1.1 host 30.3.3.3
R1(config)# access-list 100 permit ip host 1.1.1.1 host 33.3.3.3
```

```
R1(config)# access-list 100 permit ip host 10.1.1.1 host 3.3.3.3
R1(config)# access-list 100 permit ip host 10.1.1.1 host 30.3.3.3
R1(config)# access-list 100 permit ip host 10.1.1.1 host 33.3.3.3

R1(config)# access-list 100 permit ip host 11.1.1.1 host 3.3.3.3
R1(config)# access-list 100 permit ip host 11.1.1.1 host 30.3.3.3
R1(config)# access-list 100 permit ip host 11.1.1.1 host 33.3.3.3

On R3:

R3(config)# access-list 100 permit ip host 3.3.3.3 host 1.1.1.1
R3(config)# access-list 100 permit ip host 30.3.3.3 host 1.1.1.1
R3(config)# access-list 100 permit ip host 33.3.3.3 host 1.1.1.1

R3(config)# access-list 100 permit ip host 3.3.3.3 host 10.1.1.1
R3(config)# access-list 100 permit ip host 30.3.3.3 host 10.1.1.1
R3(config)# access-list 100 permit ip host 33.3.3.3 host 10.1.1.1

R3(config)# access-list 100 permit ip host 3.3.3.3 host 11.1.1.1
R3(config)# access-list 100 permit ip host 30.3.3.3 host 11.1.1.1
R3(config)# access-list 100 permit ip host 33.3.3.3 host 11.1.1.1
```

Step 5.   Configure the crypto map and reference the peer, the crypto ACL, and the transform set configured in the previous steps:

```
On R1:

R1(config)# crypto map TST 10 ipsec-isakmp
R1(config-crypto-map)# set peer 23.1.1.3
R1(config-crypto-map)# match address 100
R1(config-crypto-map)# set transform-set TSET

On R3:

R3(config)# crypto map TST 10 ipsec-isakmp
R3(config-crypto-map)# set peer 12.1.1.1
R3(config-crypto-map)# match address 100
R3(config-crypto-map)# set transform-set TSET
```

Step 6.   Apply the crypto map to the outside interface:

```
On R1:

R1(config)# interface Serial1/2
R1(config-if)# crypto map TST
```

```
On R3:


R3(config)# interface Serial1/2
R3(config-if)# crypto map TST
```

Let's test the configuration:

```
On R1:


R1# ping 3.3.3.3 source loopback0

Type escape sequence to abort.
Sending 5, 100-byte ICMP Echos to 3.3.3.3, timeout is 2 seconds:
Packet sent with a source address of 1.1.1.1
.!!!!
Success rate is 80 percent (4/5), round-trip min/avg/max = 84/87/88 ms

R1# ping 3.3.3.3 source loopback1

Type escape sequence to abort.
Sending 5, 100-byte ICMP Echos to 3.3.3.3, timeout is 2 seconds:
Packet sent with a source address of 10.1.1.1
.!!!!
Success rate is 80 percent (4/5), round-trip min/avg/max = 84/87/88 ms

R1# ping 3.3.3.3 source loopback2

Type escape sequence to abort.
Sending 5, 100-byte ICMP Echos to 3.3.3.3, timeout is 2 seconds:
Packet sent with a source address of 11.1.1.1
.!!!!
Success rate is 80 percent (4/5), round-trip min/avg/max = 84/87/88 ms

R1# ping 30.3.3.3 source loopback0

Type escape sequence to abort.
Sending 5, 100-byte ICMP Echos to 30.3.3.3, timeout is 2 seconds:
Packet sent with a source address of 1.1.1.1
.!!!!
Success rate is 80 percent (4/5), round-trip min/avg/max = 84/87/88 ms

R1# ping 30.3.3.3 source loopback1

Type escape sequence to abort.
Sending 5, 100-byte ICMP Echos to 30.3.3.3, timeout is 2 seconds:
```

```
Packet sent with a source address of 10.1.1.1
.!!!!
Success rate is 80 percent (4/5), round-trip min/avg/max = 84/87/88 ms

R1# ping 30.3.3.3 source loopback2

Type escape sequence to abort.
Sending 5, 100-byte ICMP Echos to 30.3.3.3, timeout is 2 seconds:
Packet sent with a source address of 11.1.1.1
.!!!!
Success rate is 80 percent (4/5), round-trip min/avg/max = 84/87/88 ms

R1# ping 33.3.3.3 source loopback0

Type escape sequence to abort.
Sending 5, 100-byte ICMP Echos to 33.3.3.3, timeout is 2 seconds:
Packet sent with a source address of 1.1.1.1
.!!!!
Success rate is 80 percent (4/5), round-trip min/avg/max = 84/87/88 ms

R1# ping 33.3.3.3 source loopback1

Type escape sequence to abort.
Sending 5, 100-byte ICMP Echos to 33.3.3.3, timeout is 2 seconds:
Packet sent with a source address of 10.1.1.1
.!!!!
Success rate is 80 percent (4/5), round-trip min/avg/max = 84/87/88 ms

R1# ping 33.3.3.3 source loopback2

Type escape sequence to abort.
Sending 5, 100-byte ICMP Echos to 33.3.3.3, timeout is 2 seconds:
Packet sent with a source address of 11.1.1.1
.!!!!
Success rate is 80 percent (4/5), round-trip min/avg/max = 84/87/88 ms

R1# show crypto isakmp sa

IPv4 Crypto ISAKMP SA
dst             src             state           conn-id status
23.1.1.3        12.1.1.1        QM_IDLE              1001 ACTIVE

IPv6 Crypto ISAKMP SA
```

```
R1# show crypto ipsec sa | include local|remote|#pkts

      Crypto map tag: TST, local addr 12.1.1.1
 local  ident (addr/mask/prot/port): (1.1.1.1/255.255.255.255/0/0)
 remote ident (addr/mask/prot/port): (3.3.3.3/255.255.255.255/0/0)
  # pkts encaps: 4, # pkts encrypt: 4, # pkts digest: 4
  # pkts decaps: 4, # pkts decrypt: 4, # pkts verify: 4
  # pkts compressed: 0, # pkts decompressed: 0
  # pkts not compressed: 0, # pkts compr. failed: 0
  # pkts not decompressed: 0, # pkts decompress failed: 0
   local crypto endpt.: 12.1.1.1, remote crypto endpt.: 23.1.1.3
 local  ident (addr/mask/prot/port): (10.1.1.1/255.255.255.255/0/0)
 remote ident (addr/mask/prot/port): (3.3.3.3/255.255.255.255/0/0)
  # pkts encaps: 4, # pkts encrypt: 4, # pkts digest: 4
  # pkts decaps: 4, # pkts decrypt: 4, # pkts verify: 4
  # pkts compressed: 0, # pkts decompressed: 0
  # pkts not compressed: 0, # pkts compr. failed: 0
  # pkts not decompressed: 0, # pkts decompress failed: 0
   local crypto endpt.: 12.1.1.1, remote crypto endpt.: 23.1.1.3
 local  ident (addr/mask/prot/port): (11.1.1.1/255.255.255.255/0/0)
 remote ident (addr/mask/prot/port): (3.3.3.3/255.255.255.255/0/0)
  # pkts encaps: 4, # pkts encrypt: 4, # pkts digest: 4
  # pkts decaps: 4, # pkts decrypt: 4, # pkts verify: 4
  # pkts compressed: 0, # pkts decompressed: 0
  # pkts not compressed: 0, # pkts compr. failed: 0
  # pkts not decompressed: 0, # pkts decompress failed: 0
   local crypto endpt.: 12.1.1.1, remote crypto endpt.: 23.1.1.3
 local  ident (addr/mask/prot/port): (1.1.1.1/255.255.255.255/0/0)
 remote ident (addr/mask/prot/port): (30.3.3.3/255.255.255.255/0/0)
  # pkts encaps: 4, # pkts encrypt: 4, # pkts digest: 4
  # pkts decaps: 4, # pkts decrypt: 4, # pkts verify: 4
  # pkts compressed: 0, # pkts decompressed: 0
  # pkts not compressed: 0, # pkts compr. failed: 0
  # pkts not decompressed: 0, # pkts decompress failed: 0
   local crypto endpt.: 12.1.1.1, remote crypto endpt.: 23.1.1.3
 local  ident (addr/mask/prot/port): (1.1.1.1/255.255.255.255/0/0)
 remote ident (addr/mask/prot/port): (33.3.3.3/255.255.255.255/0/0)
  # pkts encaps: 4, # pkts encrypt: 4, # pkts digest: 4
  # pkts decaps: 4, # pkts decrypt: 4, # pkts verify: 4
  # pkts compressed: 0, # pkts decompressed: 0
  # pkts not compressed: 0, # pkts compr. failed: 0
  # pkts not decompressed: 0, # pkts decompress failed: 0
   local crypto endpt.: 12.1.1.1, remote crypto endpt.: 23.1.1.3
```

```
   local  ident (addr/mask/prot/port): (10.1.1.1/255.255.255.255/0/0)
   remote ident (addr/mask/prot/port): (30.3.3.3/255.255.255.255/0/0)
    # pkts encaps: 4, # pkts encrypt: 4, # pkts digest: 4
    # pkts decaps: 4, # pkts decrypt: 4, # pkts verify: 4
    # pkts compressed: 0, # pkts decompressed: 0
    # pkts not compressed: 0, # pkts compr. failed: 0
    # pkts not decompressed: 0, # pkts decompress failed: 0
     local crypto endpt.: 12.1.1.1, remote crypto endpt.: 23.1.1.3
   local  ident (addr/mask/prot/port): (11.1.1.1/255.255.255.255/0/0)
   remote ident (addr/mask/prot/port): (30.3.3.3/255.255.255.255/0/0)
    # pkts encaps: 4, # pkts encrypt: 4, # pkts digest: 4
    # pkts decaps: 4, # pkts decrypt: 4, # pkts verify: 4
    # pkts compressed: 0, # pkts decompressed: 0
    # pkts not compressed: 0, # pkts compr. failed: 0
    # pkts not decompressed: 0, # pkts decompress failed: 0
     local crypto endpt.: 12.1.1.1, remote crypto endpt.: 23.1.1.3
   local  ident (addr/mask/prot/port): (10.1.1.1/255.255.255.255/0/0)
   remote ident (addr/mask/prot/port): (33.3.3.3/255.255.255.255/0/0)
    # pkts encaps: 4, # pkts encrypt: 4, # pkts digest: 4
    # pkts decaps: 4, # pkts decrypt: 4, # pkts verify: 4
    # pkts compressed: 0, # pkts decompressed: 0
    # pkts not compressed: 0, # pkts compr. failed: 0
    # pkts not decompressed: 0, # pkts decompress failed: 0
     local crypto endpt.: 12.1.1.1, remote crypto endpt.: 23.1.1.3
   local  ident (addr/mask/prot/port): (11.1.1.1/255.255.255.255/0/0)
   remote ident (addr/mask/prot/port): (33.3.3.3/255.255.255.255/0/0)
    # pkts encaps: 4, # pkts encrypt: 4, # pkts digest: 4
    # pkts decaps: 4, # pkts decrypt: 4, # pkts verify: 4
    # pkts compressed: 0, # pkts decompressed: 0
    # pkts not compressed: 0, # pkts compr. failed: 0
    # pkts not decompressed: 0, # pkts decompress failed: 0
     local crypto endpt.: 12.1.1.1, remote crypto endpt.: 23.1.1.3
```

This is definitely *not* scalable.

```
R1# show crypto engine connections active
Crypto Engine Connections

   ID  Type   Algorithm      Encrypt  Decrypt LastSeqN IP-Address
  1001  IKE    MD5+3DES            0        0        0 12.1.1.1
  2001  IPsec  DES+MD5             0        4        4 12.1.1.1
  2002  IPsec  DES+MD5             4        0        0 12.1.1.1
  2003  IPsec  DES+MD5             0        4        4 12.1.1.1
  2004  IPsec  DES+MD5             4        0        0 12.1.1.1
  2005  IPsec  DES+MD5             0        4        4 12.1.1.1
```

2006	IPsec	DES+MD5	4	0	0 12.1.1.1
2007	IPsec	DES+MD5	0	4	4 12.1.1.1
2008	IPsec	DES+MD5	4	0	0 12.1.1.1
2009	IPsec	DES+MD5	0	4	4 12.1.1.1
2010	IPsec	DES+MD5	4	0	0 12.1.1.1
2011	IPsec	DES+MD5	0	4	4 12.1.1.1
2012	IPsec	DES+MD5	4	0	0 12.1.1.1
2013	IPsec	DES+MD5	0	4	4 12.1.1.1
2014	IPsec	DES+MD5	4	0	0 12.1.1.1
2015	IPsec	DES+MD5	0	4	4 12.1.1.1
2016	IPsec	DES+MD5	4	0	0 12.1.1.1
2017	IPsec	DES+MD5	0	4	4 12.1.1.1
2018	IPsec	DES+MD5	4	0	0 12.1.1.1

You can see the number of SPIs in the output of the preceding **show** command. You can also see that the legacy site-to-site IPSec VPNs are not scalable when the number networks that need to communicate increases.

Task 2

You are getting ready to add 500 more subnets to R1 and 500 more subnets to R3. Therefore, you need to configure a scalable solution that does not require the need for crypto ACLs. You will use GRE/IPSEC with Tunnel Mode to accomplish this task.

Because you need to totally cross-eliminate crypto ACLs, you can configure a GRE tunnel and encrypt all traffic that traverses the tunnel. Let's configure it:

Step 1.   Configure the GRE tunnels.

When you're configuring the GRE tunnels, the **tunnel source** must reference the outside interface of the local router, and the **tunnel destination** must be the outside interface of the peer router. Also, the tunnel IP address should be a private IP address.

```
On R1:


R1(config)# interface tunnel13
R1(config-if)# ip address 10.1.13.1 255.255.255.0
R1(config-if)# tunnel source 12.1.1.1
R1(config-if)# tunnel destination 23.1.1.3


On R3:


R3(config)# interface tunnel31
R3(config-if)# ip address 10.1.13.3 255.255.255.0
R3(config-if)# tunnel source 23.1.1.3
R3(config-if)# tunnel destination 12.1.1.1
```

Step 2. Use an Interior Gateway Protocol (IGP) to advertise the networks in through the tunnel.

In this case, EIGRP AS 100 is used, but you can use any IGP to accomplish this step.

```
On R1:

R1(config)# router eigrp 100
R1(config-router)# netw 10.1.13.1 0.0.0.0

On R3:

R3(config)# router eigrp 100
R3(config-router)# netw 10.1.13.3 0.0.0.0
```

You should see the following console message:

```
%DUAL-5-NBRCHANGE: EIGRP-IPv4 100: Neighbor 10.1.13.1 (Tunnel31) is up:
new adjacency
```

Let's verify the configuration:

```
On R3:

R3# show ip route eigrp | begin Gate
Gateway of last resort is 23.1.1.2 to network 0.0.0.0

      1.0.0.0/24 is subnetted, 1 subnets
D        1.1.1.0 [90/27008000] via 10.1.13.1, 00:02:15, Tunnel31
      10.0.0.0/8 is variably subnetted, 3 subnets, 2 masks
D        10.1.1.0/24 [90/27008000] via 10.1.13.1, 00:02:15, Tunnel31
      11.0.0.0/24 is subnetted, 1 subnets
D        11.1.1.0 [90/27008000] via 10.1.13.1, 00:02:15, Tunnel31
```

Step 3. We need to delete the crypto ACLs and crypto maps. To remove the crypto map we previously applied to the interfaces:

```
On R1 and R3:

Rx(config)# no access-list 100

Rx(config)# interface Serial1/2
Rx(config-if)# no crypto map TST
Rx(config-if)# exit

Rx(config)# no crypto map TST
```

Step 4.   Configure a crypto IPSec profile and reference the transform set:

```
On R1 and R3:

Rx(config)# crypto ipsec profile ABC
Rx(ipsec-profile)# set transform-set TSET
```

Step 5.   Apply the crypto IPSec profile to the tunnel interface:

```
On R1:

R1(config)# interface tunnel13
R1(config-if)# tunnel protection ipsec profile ABC
```

Note   EIGRP adjacency will go down because you are encrypting on one end and not the other. You should also see ISAKMP being enabled in the following console message:

```
%CRYPTO-6-ISAKMP_ON_OFF: ISAKMP is ON

%DUAL-5-NBRCHANGE: EIGRP-IPv4 100: Neighbor 10.1.13.3 (Tunnel13) is down:
holding time expired
```

```
On R3:

R3(config)# interface tunnel31
R3(config-if)# tunnel protection ipsec profile ABC
```

You should see the following console messages:

```
%CRYPTO-6-ISAKMP_ON_OFF: ISAKMP is ON

%DUAL-5-NBRCHANGE: EIGRP-IPv4 100: Neighbor 10.1.13.1 (Tunnel31) is up:
new adjacency
```

The **tunnel protection ipsec profile** command states that any traffic that traverses the tunnel should be encrypted with the IPSec profile called **ABC**.

Note   In the legacy configuration, the crypto map had the following commands:

■ **Set Transform-set:** In the legacy configuration, this is done in the **crypto ipsec profile**.

■ **Set address:** This references the interesting traffic, and we saw in the previous task that this configuration is not scalable at all. In this configuration, the crypto ACLs are no longer required because any traffic that traverses the tunnel will be encrypted, and as long as the configured routing protocol is pointing to the tunnel interface, all traffic from all subnets will be affected.

- **Set peer:** In the legacy configuration, this is achieved through the tunnel destination command when the actual GRE tunnel is configured.

Step 6.   Now we need to verify that GRE/IPSec are running on the tunnels and that we are using Tunnel Mode:

```
R3# show crypto ipsec sa | section spi

    current outbound spi: 0xFA948BE8(4204039144)
    spi: 0xD090B49D(3499144349)
      transform: esp-des esp-md5-hmac ,
      in use settings ={Tunnel, }
      conn id: 2019, flow_id: NETGX:19, sibling_flags 80000046, crypto map:
        Tunnel31-head-0
      sa timing: remaining key lifetime (k/sec): (4598347/3082)
      IV size: 8 bytes
      replay detection support: Y
      Status: ACTIVE

    spi: 0xFA948BE8(4204039144)
      transform: esp-des esp-md5-hmac ,
      in use settings ={Tunnel, }
      conn id: 2020, flow_id: NETGX:20, sibling_flags 80000046, crypto map:
        Tunnel31-head-0
      sa timing: remaining key lifetime (k/sec): (4598347/3082)
      IV size: 8 bytes
      replay detection support: Y
      Status: ACTIVE

R3# show interface tunnel31 | include Tunnel protocol
  Tunnel protocol/transport GRE/IP
```

Task 3

After implementing the previous solution, you realize that every packet has duplicate IP addresses in the header. You need to keep the GRE tunnel but eliminate the duplicate IP addresses in the header of every packet.

To resolve this task, you must change the mode to Transport. Let's do that now:

```
On R1 and R3:


Rx(config)# crypto ipsec transform-set TSET esp-des esp-md5-hmac
Rx(cfg-crypto-trans)# mode transport
```

To verify this, you must clear **crypto ipsec sas**:

```
On Both Routers:


Rx# clear crypto sa


R1# show crypto ipsec sa

interface: Tunnel13
    Crypto map tag: Tunnel13-head-0, local addr 12.1.1.1

   protected vrf: (none)
   local  ident (addr/mask/prot/port): (12.1.1.1/255.255.255.255/47/0)
   remote ident (addr/mask/prot/port): (23.1.1.3/255.255.255.255/47/0)
   current_peer 23.1.1.3 port 500
     PERMIT, flags={origin_is_acl,}
    # pkts encaps: 9, # pkts encrypt: 9, # pkts digest: 9
    # pkts decaps: 7, # pkts decrypt: 7, # pkts verify: 7

    # pkts compressed: 0, # pkts decompressed: 0
    # pkts not compressed: 0, # pkts compr. failed: 0
    # pkts not decompressed: 0, # pkts decompress failed: 0
    # send errors 0, # recv errors 0

     local crypto endpt.: 12.1.1.1, remote crypto endpt.: 23.1.1.3
     path mtu 1500, ip mtu 1500, ip mtu idb Serial1/2
     current outbound spi: 0x58BF5B22(1488935714)
     PFS (Y/N): N, DH group: none

     inbound esp sas:
      spi: 0x31C3E03A(834920506)
        transform: esp-des esp-md5-hmac ,
        in use settings ={Transport, }
        conn id: 2025, flow_id: NETGX:25, sibling_flags 80000006, crypto map:
          Tunnel13-head-0
        sa timing: remaining key lifetime (k/sec): (4430829/3568)
```

```
        IV size: 8 bytes
        replay detection support: Y
        Status: ACTIVE

    inbound ah sas:

    inbound pcp sas:

    outbound esp sas:
     spi: 0x58BF5B22(1488935714)
       transform: esp-des esp-md5-hmac ,
       in use settings ={Transport, }
       conn id: 2026, flow_id: NETGX:26, sibling_flags 80000006, crypto map:
         Tunnel13-head-0
       sa timing: remaining key lifetime (k/sec): (4430829/3568)
       IV size: 8 bytes
       replay detection support: Y
       Status: ACTIVE

    outbound ah sas:

    outbound pcp sas:
```

The transport protocol is still GRE. Let's verify this:

```
On R1:

R1# show interface tunnel13 | include Tunnel protocol

  Tunnel protocol/transport GRE/IP
```

Task 4

Reconfigure R1 and R3 so that the tunnel protocol is IPSec; this way, the extra GRE overhead is no longer there.

In order to eliminate GRE altogether, you can change the tunnel mode to IPSec. Let's configure this and verify:

```
On R1:

R1(config)# interface tunnel13
R1(config-if)# tunnel mode ipsec ipv4
```

You should see the following console message:

```
%DUAL-5-NBRCHANGE: EIGRP-IPv4 100: Neighbor 10.1.13.3 (Tunnel13) is down: holding
  time expired

On R3:

R3(config)# interface tunnel31
R3(config-if)# tunnel mode ipsec ipv4
```

You should see EIGRP coming up again. This means that packets are being encrypted.

```
%DUAL-5-NBRCHANGE: EIGRP-IPv4 100: Neighbor 10.1.13.1 (Tunnel31) is up: new
  adjacency
```

Let's verify the configuration:

```
On R1:


R1# show crypto ipsec sa

interface: Tunnel13
    Crypto map tag: Tunnel13-head-0, local addr 12.1.1.1

   protected vrf: (none)
   local  ident (addr/mask/prot/port): (0.0.0.0/0.0.0.0/0/0)
   remote ident (addr/mask/prot/port): (0.0.0.0/0.0.0.0/0/0)
   current_peer 23.1.1.3 port 500
     PERMIT, flags={origin_is_acl,}
    # pkts encaps: 26, # pkts encrypt: 26, # pkts digest: 26
    # pkts decaps: 27, # pkts decrypt: 27, # pkts verify: 27
    # pkts compressed: 0, # pkts decompressed: 0
    # pkts not compressed: 0, # pkts compr. failed: 0
    # pkts not decompressed: 0, # pkts decompress failed: 0
    # send errors 8, # recv errors 0

     local crypto endpt.: 12.1.1.1, remote crypto endpt.: 23.1.1.3
     path mtu 1500, ip mtu 1500, ip mtu idb Serial1/2
     current outbound spi: 0x653D25F9(1698506233)
     PFS (Y/N): N, DH group: none

     inbound esp sas:
      spi: 0xF08E7802(4035868674)
        transform: esp-des esp-md5-hmac ,
        in use settings ={Tunnel, }
```

```
        conn id: 2029, flow_id: NETGX:29, sibling_flags 80000046, crypto map:
         Tunnel13-head-0
        sa timing: remaining key lifetime (k/sec): (4571849/3511)
        IV size: 8 bytes
        replay detection support: Y
        Status: ACTIVE

     inbound ah sas:

     inbound pcp sas:

     outbound esp sas:
      spi: 0x653D25F9(1698506233)
        transform: esp-des esp-md5-hmac ,
        in use settings ={Tunnel, }
        conn id: 2030, flow_id: NETGX:30, sibling_flags 80000046, crypto map:
         Tunnel13-head-0
        sa timing: remaining key lifetime (k/sec): (4571849/3511)
        IV size: 8 bytes
        replay detection support: Y
        Status: ACTIVE

     outbound ah sas:

     outbound pcp sas:

R1# show interface tunnel13 | include Tunnel protocol

  Tunnel protocol/transport IPSEC/IP
```

Do not forget to make the following configuration on both routers in the topology.

```
Rx(config)# crypto ipsec transform-set TSET esp-des esp-md5-hmac
Rx(cfg-crypto-trans)# mode tunnel

Rx# clear crypto sa
```

You should wait for the tunnel to come up:

```
R1# show crypto ipsec sa

interface: Tunnel13
    Crypto map tag: Tunnel13-head-0, local addr 12.1.1.1

  protected vrf: (none)
    local  ident (addr/mask/prot/port): (0.0.0.0/0.0.0.0/0/0)
```

```
remote ident (addr/mask/prot/port): (0.0.0.0/0.0.0.0/0/0)
current_peer 23.1.1.3 port 500
  PERMIT, flags={origin_is_acl,}
 # pkts encaps: 14, # pkts encrypt: 14, # pkts digest: 14
 # pkts decaps: 13, # pkts decrypt: 13, # pkts verify: 13
 # pkts compressed: 0, # pkts decompressed: 0
 # pkts not compressed: 0, # pkts compr. failed: 0
 # pkts not decompressed: 0, # pkts decompress failed: 0
 # send errors 0, # recv errors 0

  local crypto endpt.: 12.1.1.1, remote crypto endpt.: 23.1.1.3
  path mtu 1500, ip mtu 1500, ip mtu idb Serial1/2
  current outbound spi: 0x8CD7122B(2362905131)
  PFS (Y/N): N, DH group: none

  inbound esp sas:
   spi: 0xD5DFBB05(3588209413)
     transform: esp-des esp-md5-hmac ,
     in use settings ={Tunnel, }
     conn id: 2031, flow_id: NETGX:31, sibling_flags 80000046, crypto map:
       Tunnel13-head-0
     sa timing: remaining key lifetime (k/sec): (4580543/3568)
     IV size: 8 bytes
     replay detection support: Y
     Status: ACTIVE

  inbound ah sas:

  inbound pcp sas:

  outbound esp sas:
   spi: 0x8CD7122B(2362905131)
     transform: esp-des esp-md5-hmac ,
     in use settings ={Tunnel, }
     conn id: 2032, flow_id: NETGX:32, sibling_flags 80000046, crypto map:
       Tunnel13-head-0
     sa timing: remaining key lifetime (k/sec): (4580543/3568)
     IV size: 8 bytes
     replay detection support: Y
     Status: ACTIVE

  outbound ah sas:

  outbound pcp sas:
```

Erase the startup configuration of the routers and reload them before proceeding to the next lab.

Lab 13-4: Protecting DMVPN Tunnels

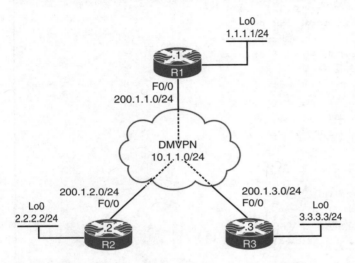

Figure 13-4 *Configuring Protecting DMVPN Tunnels*

Figure 13-4 illustrates the topology that will be used in the following lab.

Task 1

SW1 represents the Internet; configure the ports on the switch based on the following and then enable IP routing:

- **F0/1:** 200.1.1.10/24
- **F0/2:** 200.1.2.10/24
- **F0/3:** 200.1.3.10/24

```
On SW1:

SW1(config)# interface FastEthernet 0/1
SW1(config-if)# no switchport
SW1(config-if)# ip address 200.1.1.10 255.255.255.0
SW1(config-if)# no shutdown

SW1(config)# interface FastEthernet 0/2
SW1(config-if)# no switchport
SW1(config-if)# ip address 200.1.2.10 255.255.255.0
SW1(config-if)# no shutdown
```

```
SW1(config)# interface FastEthernet 0/3
SW1(config-if)# no switchport
SW1(config-if)# ip address 200.1.3.10 255.255.255.0
SW1(config-if)# no shutdown


SW1(config)# ip routing
```

Task 2

Configure the F0/0 and loopback0 interfaces of R1, R2, and R3 based on the configurations shown in Table 13-4.

Table 13-4   *Configurations for Task 2*

Router	Interfaces
R1	loopback0: 1.1.1.1/24 F0/0: 200.1.1.1/24
R2	loopback0: 2.2.2.2/24 F0/0: 200.1.2.2/24
R3	loopback0: 3.3.3.3/24 F0/0: 200.1.3.3/24

Ensure that these routers have full reachability to each other using static routes:

```
On R1:

R1(config)# interface loopback0
R1(config-if)# ip address 1.1.1.1 255.255.255.0


R1(config)# interface FastEthernet 0/0
R1(config-if)# ip address 200.1.1.1 255.255.255.0
R1(config-if)# no shutdown


R1(config)# ip route 200.1.2.0 255.255.255.0 200.1.1.10
R1(config)# ip route 200.1.3.0 255.255.255.0 200.1.1.10


On R2:

R2(config)# interface loopback0
R2(config-if)# ip address 2.2.2.2 255.255.255.0


R2(config)# interface FastEthernet 0/0
R2(config-if)# ip address 200.1.2.2 255.255.255.0
R2(config-if)# no shutdown
```

```
R2(config)# ip route 200.1.1.0 255.255.255.0 200.1.2.10
R2(config)# ip route 200.1.3.0 255.255.255.0 200.1.2.10

On R3:

R3(config)# interface loopback 0
R3(config-if)# ip address 3.3.3.3 255.255.255.0

R3(config)# interface FastEthernet 0/0
R3(config-if)# ip address 200.1.3.3 255.255.255.0
R3(config-if)# no shutdown

R3(config)# ip route 200.1.1.0 255.255.255.0 200.1.3.10
R3(config)# ip route 200.1.2.0 255.255.255.0 200.1.3.10
```

Let's verify the configuration:

```
On R1:

R1# ping 200.1.2.2

Type escape sequence to abort.
Sending 5, 100-byte ICMP Echos to 200.1.2.2, timeout is 2 seconds:
!!!!!
Success rate is 100 percent (5/5), round-trip min/avg/max = 1/2/4 ms

R1# ping 200.1.3.3

Type escape sequence to abort.
Sending 5, 100-byte ICMP Echos to 200.1.3.3, timeout is 2 seconds:
!!!!!
Success rate is 100 percent (5/5), round-trip min/avg/max = 1/2/4 ms

On R2:

R2# ping 200.1.3.3

Type escape sequence to abort.
Sending 5, 100-byte ICMP Echos to 200.1.3.3, timeout is 2 seconds:
!!!!!
Success rate is 100 percent (5/5), round-trip min/avg/max = 1/2/4 ms
```

Task 3

Configure DMVPN Phase 2 such that R1 is the hub. R2 and R3 should be configured as the spokes. You should use 10.1.1.*x*/24, where *x* is the router number. If this configuration is performed correctly, these routers should have full reachability to all loopback interfaces and tunnel endpoints. You should *not* configure static mappings on the hub router to accomplish this task. Use EIGRP to provide reachability.

```
On R1:


R1(config)# interface tunnel123
R1(config-if)# ip address 10.1.1.1 255.255.255.0
R1(config-if)# tunnel source FastEthernet 0/0
R1(config-if)# tunnel mode gre multipoint
R1(config-if)# ip nhrp network-id 111
R1(config-if)# ip nhrp map multicast dynamic


On R2:


R2(config)# interface tunnel123
R2(config-if)# ip address 10.1.1.2 255.255.255.0
R2(config-if)# tunnel source FastEthernet 0/0
R2(config-if)# tunnel mode gre multipoint
R2(config-if)# ip nhrp network-id 222
R2(config-if)# ip nhrp nhs 10.1.1.1
R2(config-if)# ip nhrp map 10.1.1.1 200.1.1.1


On R3:


R3(config)# interface tunnel123
R3(config-if)# ip address 10.1.1.3 255.255.255.0
R3(config-if)# tunnel source FastEthernet 0/0
R3(config-if)# tunnel mode gre multipoint
R3(config-if)# ip nhrp network-id 333
R3(config-if)# ip nhrp nhs 10.1.1.1
R3(config-if)# ip nhrp map 10.1.1.1 200.1.1.1
```

Let's verify the configuration:

```
On R1:


R1# show ip nhrp


10.1.1.2/32 via 10.1.1.2
   Tunnel123 created 00:03:43, expire 01:56:16
   Type: dynamic, Flags: unique registered
   NBMA address: 200.1.2.2
```

```
10.1.1.3/32 via 10.1.1.3
   Tunnel123 created 00:02:18, expire 01:57:41
   Type: dynamic, Flags: unique registered
   NBMA address: 200.1.3.3

R1# show dmvpn detail

Legend: Attrb --> S - Static, D - Dynamic, I - Incomplete
        N - NATed, L - Local, X - No Socket
        #  Ent --> Number of NHRP entries with same NBMA peer
        NHS Status: E --> Expecting Replies, R --> Responding, W --> Waiting
        UpDn Time --> Up or Down Time for a Tunnel
==============================================================================

Interface Tunnel123 is up/up, Addr. is 10.1.1.1, VRF ""
   Tunnel Src./Dest. addr: 200.1.1.1/MGRE, Tunnel VRF ""
   Protocol/Transport: "multi-GRE/IP", Protect ""
   Interface State Control: Disabled
Type:Hub, Total NBMA Peers (v4/v6): 2

# Ent   Peer NBMA Addr Peer Tunnel Add State  UpDn Tm Attrb  Target Network
-----  --------------- --------------- ----- -------- ----- ---------------
    1      200.1.2.2       10.1.1.2     UP 00:04:47    D      10.1.1.2/32
    1      200.1.3.3       10.1.1.3     UP 00:03:22    D      10.1.1.3/32

Crypto Session Details:
------------------------------------------------------------------

Pending DMVPN Sessions:

R1# ping 10.1.1.2

Type escape sequence to abort.
Sending 5, 100-byte ICMP Echos to 10.1.1.2, timeout is 2 seconds:
!!!!!
Success rate is 100 percent (5/5), round-trip min/avg/max = 1/3/4 ms

R1# ping 10.1.1.3

Type escape sequence to abort.
Sending 5, 100-byte ICMP Echos to 10.1.1.3, timeout is 2 seconds:
!!!!!
Success rate is 100 percent (5/5), round-trip min/avg/max = 1/2/4 ms
```

Now we can run EIGRP:

```
R1(config)# router eigrp 100
R1(config-router)# network 1.1.1.1 0.0.0.0
R1(config-router)# network 10.1.1.1 0.0.0.0

R1(config)# interface tunnel123
R1(config-if)# no ip split-horizon eigrp 100
R1(config-if)# no ip next-hop-self eigrp 100

On R2:

R2(config)# router eigrp 100
R2(config-router)# network 2.2.2.2 0.0.0.0
R2(config-router)# network 10.1.1.2 0.0.0.0
```

You should see the following console message:

```
%DUAL-5-NBRCHANGE: EIGRP-IPv4 100: Neighbor 10.1.1.1 (Tunnel123) is up:
new adjacency

R2(config)# interface tunnel123
R2(config-if)# ip nhrp map multicast 200.1.1.1

On R3:

R3(config)# router eigrp 100
R3(config-router)# network 3.3.3.3 0.0.0.0
R3(config-router)# network 10.1.1.3 0.0.0.0
```

You should also see this console message:

```
%DUAL-5-NBRCHANGE: EIGRP-IPv4 100: Neighbor 10.1.1.1 (Tunnel123) is up:
  new adjacency

R3(config)# interface tunnel123
R3(config-if)# ip nhrp map multicast 200.1.1.1
```

Let's verify the configuration:

```
On R2:

R2# show ip route eigrp | begin Gate
Gateway of last resort is not set

      1.0.0.0/24 is subnetted, 1 subnets
D        1.1.1.0 [90/27008000] via 10.1.1.1, 00:02:19, Tunnel123
```

```
      3.0.0.0/24 is subnetted, 1 subnets
D        3.3.3.0 [90/28288000] via 10.1.1.3, 00:01:31, Tunnel123


R2# ping 1.1.1.1

Type escape sequence to abort.
Sending 5, 100-byte ICMP Echos to 1.1.1.1, timeout is 2 seconds:
!!!!!
Success rate is 100 percent (5/5), round-trip min/avg/max = 1/2/4 ms


R2# ping 3.3.3.3

Type escape sequence to abort.
Sending 5, 100-byte ICMP Echos to 3.3.3.3, timeout is 2 seconds:
!!!!!
Success rate is 100 percent (5/5), round-trip min/avg/max = 4/4/8 ms
```

Task 4

Protect the traffic between 1.1.1.0/24, 2.2.2.0/24, and 3.3.3.0/24 using an IPSec VPN based on the policy shown in Table 13-5.

Table 13-5 *Policy Guidelines for Configuring Task 4*

ISAKMP Policy	IPSec Policy
Authentication: Pre-shared	Encryption: ESP-3DES
Hash: MD5	Hash: ESP-MD5-HMAC
DH Group: 2	Proxy-ID/Crypto ACL: 1.1.1.1 $\longleftrightarrow$ 2.2.2.2
Encryption: 3DES	
PSK: cisco	

Let's go through the steps.

First, we begin by configuring IKE Phase 1:

```
On R1:

R1(config)# crypto isakmp policy 10
R1(config-isakmp)# hash md5
R1(config-isakmp)# authentication pre-share
R1(config-isakmp)# group 2
R1(config-isakmp)# encryption 3des
```

Note The address is set to 0.0.0.0 because the edge devices may acquire different IP addresses, and/or spoke-to-spoke communication may occur between any spokes. Therefore, the IP address *must* be set to 0.0.0.0:

```
R1(config)# crypto isakmp key cisco address 0.0.0.0
```

Now with that done, we can create a transform set based on the requirement in the task:

```
R1(config)# crypto ipsec transform-set TSET esp-des esp-md5-hmac
R1(cfg-crypto-trans)# mode transport
```

Next, we configure **crypto ipsec profile** to reference the transform set:

```
R1(config)# crypto ipsec profile TST
R1(ipsec-profile)# set transform-set TSET
```

The **crypto ipsec profile** is configured in the tunnel to protect all traffic traversing the tunnel interface:

```
R1(config)# interface tunnel123
R1(config-if)# tunnel protection ipsec profile TST
```

Once this is configured on R1, you will see that ISAKMP is enabled. Because this is the only site configured, EIGRP neighbor adjacency will be lost to R2 and R3:

```
%CRYPTO-6-ISAKMP_ON_OFF: ISAKMP is ON

%DUAL-5-NBRCHANGE: EIGRP-IPv4 100: Neighbor 10.1.1.2 (Tunnel123) is down:
holding time expired

%DUAL-5-NBRCHANGE: EIGRP-IPv4 100: Neighbor 10.1.1.3 (Tunnel123) is down:
holding time expired
```

You will also see the following console messages stating that you are receiving packets that are not encrypted:

```
%CRYPTO-4-RECVD_PKT_NOT_IPSEC: Rec'd packet not an IPSEC packet. (ip)
vrf/dest_addr= /200.1.1.1, src_addr= 200.1.2.2, prot= 47

On R2:

R2(config)# crypto isakmp policy 10
R2(config-isakmp)# hash md5
```

```
R2(config-isakmp)# authentication pre-share
R2(config-isakmp)# group 2
R2(config-isakmp)# encryption 3des


R2(config)# crypto isakmp key cisco address 0.0.0.0


R2(config)# crypto ipsec transform-set TSET esp-des esp-md5-hmac
R2(cfg-crypto-trans)# mode transport


R2(config)# crypto ipsec profile TST
R2(ipsec-profile)# set transform-set TSET


R2(config)# interface tunnel 123
R2(config-if)# tunnel protection ipsec profile TST
```

You should see the following console message:

```
%CRYPTO-6-ISAKMP_ON_OFF: ISAKMP is ON


%DUAL-5-NBRCHANGE: EIGRP-IPv4 100: Neighbor 10.1.1.1 (Tunnel123) is up:
new adjacency


On R3:

R3(config)# crypto isakmp policy 10
R3(config-isakmp)# hash md5
R3(config-isakmp)# authentication pre-share
R3(config-isakmp)# group 2
R3(config-isakmp)# encryption 3des


R3(config)# crypto isakmp key cisco address 0.0.0.0


R3(config)# crypto ipsec transform-set TSET esp-des esp-md5-hmac
R3(cfg-crypto-trans)# mode transport


R3(config)# crypto ipsec profile TST
R3(ipsec-profile)# set transform-set TSET


R3(config)# interface tunnel 123
R3(config-if)# tunnel protection ipsec profile TST


%CRYPTO-6-ISAKMP_ON_OFF: ISAKMP is ON


%DUAL-5-NBRCHANGE: EIGRP-IPv4 100: Neighbor 10.1.1.1 (Tunnel123) is up:
new adjacency
```

Let's verify the configuration:

```
On R2:

R2# show crypto ipsec sa

interface: Tunnel123
    Crypto map tag: Tunnel123-head-0, local addr 200.1.2.2

  protected vrf: (none)
  local  ident (addr/mask/prot/port): (200.1.2.2/255.255.255.255/47/0)
  remote ident (addr/mask/prot/port): (200.1.1.1/255.255.255.255/47/0)
  current_peer 200.1.1.1 port 500
    PERMIT, flags={origin_is_acl,}
   # pkts encaps: 176, # pkts encrypt: 176, # pkts digest: 176
   # pkts decaps: 178, # pkts decrypt: 178, # pkts verify: 178
   # pkts compressed: 0, # pkts decompressed: 0
   # pkts not compressed: 0, # pkts compr. failed: 0

   # pkts not decompressed: 0, # pkts decompress failed: 0
   # send errors 0, # recv errors 0

    local crypto endpt.: 200.1.2.2, remote crypto endpt.: 200.1.1.1
    path mtu 1500, ip mtu 1500, ip mtu idb (none)
    current outbound spi: 0x97BEF376(2545873782)
    PFS (Y/N): N, DH group: none

    inbound esp sas:
     spi: 0x7AC150C4(2059489476)
       transform: esp-des esp-md5-hmac ,
       in use settings ={Transport, }
       conn id: 2003, flow_id: NETGX:3, sibling_flags 80000006, crypto map:
         Tunnel123-head-0
       sa timing: remaining key lifetime (k/sec): (4428305/2843)
       IV size: 8 bytes
       replay detection support: Y
       Status: ACTIVE

    inbound ah sas:

    inbound pcp sas:

    outbound esp sas:
     spi: 0x97BEF376(2545873782)
       transform: esp-des esp-md5-hmac ,
```

```
        in use settings ={Transport, }
         conn id: 2004, flow_id: NETGX:4, sibling_flags 80000006, crypto map:
           Tunnel123-head-0
         sa timing: remaining key lifetime (k/sec): (4428305/2843)
         IV size: 8 bytes
         replay detection support: Y
         Status: ACTIVE

     outbound ah sas:

     outbound pcp sas:

protected vrf: (none)
local  ident (addr/mask/prot/port): (200.1.2.2/255.255.255.255/47/0)
remote ident (addr/mask/prot/port): (200.1.3.3/255.255.255.255/47/0)
current_peer 200.1.3.3 port 500
  PERMIT, flags={origin_is_acl,}
 # pkts encaps: 0, # pkts encrypt: 0, # pkts digest: 0
 # pkts decaps: 0, # pkts decrypt: 0, # pkts verify: 0

 # pkts compressed: 0, # pkts decompressed: 0
 # pkts not compressed: 0, # pkts compr. failed: 0
 # pkts not decompressed: 0, # pkts decompress failed: 0
 # send errors 0, # recv errors 0

  local crypto endpt.: 200.1.2.2, remote crypto endpt.: 200.1.3.3
  path mtu 1500, ip mtu 1500, ip mtu idb (none)
  current outbound spi: 0x539AB1EC(1402647020)
  PFS (Y/N): N, DH group: none

  inbound esp sas:
   spi: 0xCC3D2892(3426560146)
     transform: esp-des esp-md5-hmac ,
     in use settings ={Transport, }
     conn id: 2007, flow_id: NETGX:7, sibling_flags 80000006, crypto map:
       Tunnel123-head-0
     sa timing: remaining key lifetime (k/sec): (4529448/2854)
     IV size: 8 bytes
     replay detection support: Y
     Status: ACTIVE

   inbound ah sas:

   inbound pcp sas:
```

```
      outbound esp sas:
       spi: 0x539AB1EC(1402647020)
         transform: esp-des esp-md5-hmac ,
         in use settings ={Transport, }
         conn id: 2008, flow_id: NETGX:8, sibling_flags 80000006, crypto map: Tun-
           nel123-head-0
         sa timing: remaining key lifetime (k/sec): (4529448/2854)
         IV size: 8 bytes
         replay detection support: Y
         Status: ACTIVE

      outbound ah sas:

      outbound pcp sas:

R2# show crypto isakmp sa

IPv4 Crypto ISAKMP SA
dst               src               state          conn-id status
200.1.2.2         200.1.3.3         QM_IDLE           1003 ACTIVE
200.1.2.2         200.1.1.1         QM_IDLE           1002 ACTIVE
200.1.1.1         200.1.2.2         QM_IDLE           1001 ACTIVE
200.1.3.3         200.1.2.2         QM_IDLE           1004 ACTIVE

IPv6 Crypto ISAKMP SA

R2# ping 3.3.3.3 source loopback0

Type escape sequence to abort.
Sending 5, 100-byte ICMP Echos to 3.3.3.3, timeout is 2 seconds:
Packet sent with a source address of 2.2.2.2
!!!!!
Success rate is 100 percent (5/5), round-trip min/avg/max = 4/4/4 ms

R2# show crypto ipsec sa | include local|remote|#pkts

   Crypto map tag: Tunnel123-head-0, local addr 200.1.2.2
   local  ident (addr/mask/prot/port): (200.1.2.2/255.255.255.255/47/0)
   remote ident (addr/mask/prot/port): (200.1.1.1/255.255.255.255/47/0)
    # pkts encaps: 304, # pkts encrypt: 304, # pkts digest: 304
    # pkts decaps: 306, # pkts decrypt: 306, # pkts verify: 306
    # pkts compressed: 0, # pkts decompressed: 0
    # pkts not compressed: 0, # pkts compr. failed: 0
    # pkts not decompressed: 0, # pkts decompress failed: 0
     local crypto endpt.: 200.1.2.2, remote crypto endpt.: 200.1.1.1
```

```
local  ident (addr/mask/prot/port): (200.1.2.2/255.255.255.255/47/0)
remote ident (addr/mask/prot/port): (200.1.3.3/255.255.255.255/47/0)
 # pkts encaps: 5, # pkts encrypt: 5, # pkts digest: 5
 # pkts decaps: 5, # pkts decrypt: 5, # pkts verify: 5
 # pkts compressed: 0, # pkts decompressed: 0
 # pkts not compressed: 0, # pkts compr. failed: 0
 # pkts not decompressed: 0, # pkts decompress failed: 0
  local crypto endpt.: 200.1.2.2, remote crypto endpt.: 200.1.3.3
```

Erase the startup configuration of the routers and reload them before proceeding to the next lab.

Chapter 14

Multicast

Lab 14-1: IGMP

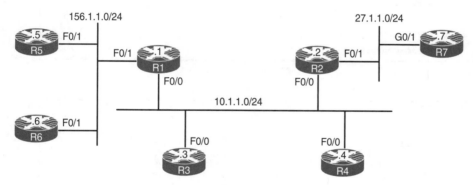

Figure 14-1 *Configuring Internet Group Management Protocol (IGMP)*

Figure 14-1 illustrates the topology that will be used in the following lab.

Task 1

Enable multicast routing on R1 and R2 and configure their F0/0 and F0/1 interfaces in PIM dense mode.

There are two types of multicast routing protocols: dense mode and sparse mode. Dense mode uses a push model, meaning that the multicast traffic is flooded throughout the network. This is called a flood and prune model because initially the traffic is flooded to the network, but after the initial flood the routers with no receivers are pruned.

On both R1 and R2, IP multicast routing is disabled by default and needs to be enabled using the **ip multicast-routing** command on all devices.

The following commands enable PIM dense mode for the requested interfaces; in order to enable any multicasting on a given interface, you must have **IP multicast-routing**. If it is not configured, you will receive a console warning message:

```
WARNING: "ip multicast-routing" is not configured,
         IP Multicast packets will not be forwarded
```

Let's enable Protocol Independent Multicast (PIM) dense mode:

```
On R1:
R1(config)# interface FastEthernet0/0
R1(config-if)# ip pim dense-mode

R1(config)# interface FastEthernet0/1
R1(config-if)# ip pim dense-mode

On R2:
R2(config)# interface FastEthernet0/0
R2(config-if)# ip pim dense-mode

R2(config)# interface FastEthernet0/1
R2(config-if)# ip pim dense-mode
```

Now let's verify the configuration:

```
On R1:

R1# show ip pim interface

Address          Interface        Ver/   Nbr    Query  DR      DR
                                  Mode   Count  Intvl  Prior
10.1.1.1         FastEthernet0/0  v2/D   1      30     1       10.1.1.2
156.1.1.1        FastEthernet0/1  v2/D   0      30     1       156.1.1.1

On R2:

R2# show ip pim interface

Address          Interface        Ver/   Nbr    Query  DR      DR
                                  Mode   Count  Intvl  Prior
10.1.1.2         FastEthernet0/0  v2/D   1      30     1       10.1.1.2
27.1.1.2         FastEthernet0/1  v2/D   0      30     1       27.1.1.2
```

By looking at the DR column in the preceding output, you can see that 10.1.1.2 (R2) is the Designated Router (DR) for 10.1.1.0/24 segment, and 27.1.1.2 (R2) is also the DR for its F0/1 segment.

```
On R1:


R1# show ip mroute


IP Multicast Routing Table
Flags: D - Dense, S - Sparse, B - Bidir Group, s - SSM Group, C - Connected,
       L - Local, P - Pruned, R - RP-bit set, F - Register flag,
       T - SPT-bit set, J - Join SPT, M - MSDP created entry, E - Extranet,
       X - Proxy Join Timer Running, A - Candidate for MSDP Advertisement,
       U - URD, I - Received Source Specific Host Report,
       Z - Multicast Tunnel, z - MDT-data group sender,
       Y - Joined MDT-data group, y - Sending to MDT-data group,
       V - RD & Vector, v - Vector
Outgoing interface flags: H - Hardware switched, A - Assert winner
 Timers: Uptime/Expires
 Interface state: Interface, Next-Hop or VCD, State/Mode


(*, 224.0.1.40), 06:35:29/00:02:35, RP 0.0.0.0, flags: DCL
  Incoming interface: Null, RPF nbr 0.0.0.0
  Outgoing interface list:
    FastEthernet0/0, Forward/Dense, 06:35:28/stopped
```

When PIM is enabled on a given interface, IGMP is also enabled.

Note   The **(*, 224.0.1.40)** entry is always created when PIM is enabled on a Cisco router. Each router will start generating V2 general queries on their multicast-enabled interfaces for group 224.0.1.40. This multicast group is used by Auto-RP, which is discussed later in this chapter.

Let's verify the configuration:

```
On R1:


R1# show ip igmp interface FastEthernet0/0


FastEthernet0/0 is up, line protocol is up
  Internet address is 10.1.1.1/24
  IGMP is enabled on interface <--------------------------------- Line 1
  Current IGMP host version is 2 <------------------------------- Line 2
  Current IGMP router version is 2
  IGMP query interval is 60 seconds <--------------------------- Line 3
  IGMP configured query interval is 60 seconds
  IGMP querier timeout is 120 seconds <------------------------- Line 4
  IGMP configured querier timeout is 120 seconds
```

```
IGMP max query response time is 10 seconds <------------------- Line 5
Last member query count is 2
Last member query response interval is 1000 ms
Inbound IGMP access group is not set
IGMP activity: 1 joins, 0 leaves
Multicast routing is enabled on interface
Multicast TTL threshold is 0
Multicast designated router (DR) is 10.1.1.2 <----------------- Line 6
IGMP querying router is 10.1.1.1 (this system)<---------------- Line 7
Multicast groups joined by this system (number of users):
    224.0.1.40(1)
```

Here are some points to keep in mind:

- **Lines 1 and 2:** By default, when PIM is configured on an interface, IGMPv2 is also enabled; the version of IGMP can be changed using the **ip igmp version** command.

- **Lines 3 and 4:** The IGMP query interval states the frequency at which the IGMP querier sends IGMP-Host-Query messages through this interface. These messages are sent by the querier in order to discover which multicast groups have members on the interface. The default value is 60 seconds; this value can be changed using the **ip igmp query-interval** interface configuration command.

    By default, if the querier misses two queries in a row, the other router(s) on the segment will trigger an election to elect a new querier. Therefore, when the IP IGMP query interval is changed, IOS will automatically change the IGMP querier timeout value to twice the query interval. However, the querier timeout can be changed using the **ip igmp querier-timeout** interface command.

- **Line 5:** By default, the IGMP max query response time is set to 10 seconds; in IGMP version 2 (IGMPv2), this counter is advertised in IGMP queries to the hosts, informing them of the maximum time within which they must respond to a general query. This improves the "burstiness" of the responses. This default value can be changed using the interface configuration **ip igmp query-max-response-time** command.

- **Lines 6 and 7:** Note that the querier is responsible for forwarding the multicast flows. IGMPv1 did not have a querier election; therefore, it was the decision of the multicast routing protocol to elect a DR for this purpose.

    A formal querying router election process was specified within the IGMPv2 protocol. In IGMPv2, each router on a multi-access network will initially assume that it is the querier and begins by sending queries; each router connected to that multi-access network will see the queries from the other IGMPv2 routers and will examine the source IP address of the query messages. All IGMPv2 routers will then elect the router with the lowest source IP address as the IGMP querier. If the elected router fails to send query messages within a specified time limit, the routers on that multi-access network will initiate the query election once again. IGMPv2 is described in RFC 2236.

The concept of a Designated Router (DR) will be covered in later labs.

Task 2

Disable IP routing on R3 and R4 and configure their F0/0 interface to join 224.1.1.1 multicast group:

```
On R3 and R4:
Rx(config)# no ip routing
```

Two commands that are somewhat identical are **ip igmp static-group** and **ip igmp join-group**.

The **ip igmp static-group** command configures a static group membership entry on an interface, which allows the router to join the multicast group. This configuration of the **ip igmp static-group** command will cause the upstream router(s) to maintain the multicast routing table information for that group, which ensures that all the paths to that multicast group are active. Remember that this command does not process the ping packets; it just joins the group and floods the multicast flow.

The **ip igmp join-group** command allows the router to process and respond to **ping** commands. This can be a useful administrative and debugging tool. This command can configure the router to emulate a client connected to a last-hop router, whereas the **ping** command performed on a router can configure the router to act as a server.

We will have both R3 and R4 join the same multicast group. This is accomplished as follows:

```
On R3 and R4:
Rx(config)# interface FastEthernet0/0
Rx(config-if)# ip igmp join-group 224.1.1.1
```

Let's verify the configuration:

```
On R1:

R1# show ip igmp groups

IGMP Connected Group Membership
Group Address  Interface       Uptime    Expires  Last Reporter Group Accounted
224.1.1.1      FastEthernet0/0 00:00:36  00:02:46 10.1.1.4
224.0.1.40     FastEthernet0/0 00:30:04  00:01:57 10.1.1.2
```

Note   R4 (10.1.1.4) is the last host to report being a member of the 224.1.1.1 multicast group (in your configuration this could be 10.1.1.3). The **Uptime** column specifies how long the multicast group has been known. The **Expires** column specifies how long until the entry expires. The entry starts with 2 minutes and 59 seconds, and it counts down all the way to 2 minutes and then back up to 2:59, because every 60 seconds the querier sends IGMP-Host-Query messages. If there is an active group member, it will reply within 10 seconds; therefore, this counter should not go below 2 minutes unless there are no active group members.

Task 3

Disable IP routing on R5 and R6 and configure their F0/1 interfaces to join the 224.56.56.56 multicast group:

```
On R5 and R6:

Rx(config)# no ip routing

Rx(config)# interface FastEthernet0/1
Rx(config-if)# ip igmp Join-group 224.56.56.56
```

Let's verify the configuration:

```
On R1:

R1# show ip igmp groups

IGMP Connected Group Membership
Group Address  Interface        Uptime    Expires    Last Reporter  Group Accounted

224.56.56.56   FastEthernet0/1  00:02:38  00:02:05   156.1.1.5
224.1.1.1      FastEthernet0/0  00:21:41  00:02:06   10.1.1.4
224.0.1.40     FastEthernet0/0  01:25:26  00:02:11   10.1.1.1

On R5:

R5# show ip igmp interface FastEthernet0/1 | begin Multicast groups

  Multicast groups joined by this system (number of users):
      224.56.56.56(1)

R5# show ip igmp groups

IGMP Connected Group Membership
Group Address  Interface        Uptime    Expires Last Reporter  Group Accounted
224.56.56.56   FastEthernet0/1  00:06:10  never   156.1.1.5
```

Note   Because the router's interface is configured with an **igmp join-group** command, the **Expires** column shows **never.**

Task 4

Disable IP routing on R7 and configure its G0/1 interface to join the 224.7.7.7 multicast group:

```
On R7:


R7(config)# no ip routing


R7(config)# interface GigabitEthernet0/1
R7(config-if)# ip igmp join-group 224.7.7.7
```

Let's verify the configuration:

```
On R7:


R7# show ip igmp interface GigabitEthernet0/1 | begin Multicast groups

  Multicast groups joined by this system (number of users):
      224.7.7.7(1)

On R2:


R2# show ip igmp groups | exclude 224.0.1.40


IGMP Connected Group Membership
Group Address  Interface        Uptime     Expires    Last Reporter Group Accounted
224.7.7.7      FastEthernet0/1  00:00:09   00:02:50   27.1.1.7
224.1.1.1      FastEthernet0/0  00:18:22   00:02:34   10.1.1.3
```

Task 5

Configure R1 to restrict hosts connected to its F0/1 interface from joining the 224.5.5.5 and 224.6.6.6 multicast groups.

> **Note** The following standard access list denies the two groups and allows the others:

```
On R1:


R1# show access-lists


R1(config)# ip access-list standard TST
R1(config-std-nacl)# deny 224.5.5.5
```

```
R1(config-std-nacl)# deny 224.6.6.6
R1(config-std-nacl)# permit any

The Access-list is applied to the F0/1 interface of R1

R1(config)# interface FastEthernet0/1
R1(config-if)# ip igmp access-group TST

The following debug is enabled for verification purpose:

R1# debug ip igmp
IGMP debugging is on
```

Let's verify and test the configuration:

```
On R5:

R5(config)# interface FastEthernet0/1
R5(config-if)# ip igmp join-group 224.5.5.5

On R6:

R6(config)# interface FastEthernet0/1
R6(config-if)# ip igmp join-group 224.6.6.6

On R1:

Note: You should see the following messages in the output of the debug:

Received v2 Report on FastEthernet0/1 from 10.1.156.5 for 224.5.5.5
Group 224.5.5.5 access denied on FastEthernet0/1

Received v2 Report on FastEthernet0/1 from 10.1.156.6 for 224.6.6.6
Group 224.6.6.6 access denied on FastEthernet0/1
```

Let's disable the debug:

```
R1# undebug all
All possible debugging has been turned off

R1# show ip igmp groups | exclude 224.0.1.40

IGMP Connected Group Membership
Group Address    Interface       Uptime    Expires   Last Reporter  Group Accounted
224.56.56.56     FastEthernet0/1 00:27:54  00:02:57  156.1.1.6
224.1.1.1        FastEthernet0/0 00:46:56  00:02:51  10.1.1.4
```

```
R1# show ip igmp interface FastEthernet0/1

FastEthernet0/1 is up, line protocol is up
  Internet address is 156.1.1.1/24
  IGMP is enabled on interface
  Current IGMP host version is 2
  Current IGMP router version is 2
  IGMP query interval is 60 seconds
  IGMP configured query interval is 60 seconds
  IGMP querier timeout is 120 seconds
  IGMP configured querier timeout is 120 seconds
  IGMP max query response time is 10 seconds
  Last member query count is 2
  Last member query response interval is 1000 ms
  Inbound IGMP access group is TST
  IGMP activity: 2 joins, 1 leaves
  Multicast routing is enabled on interface
  Multicast TTL threshold is 0
  Multicast designated router (DR) is 156.1.1.1 (this system)
  IGMP querying router is 156.1.1.1 (this system)
  No multicast groups joined by this system
```

Task 6

Because there is only a single host connected to the F0/1 interface of R2, R2 should be configured such that it stops forwarding multicast traffic for all groups immediately upon receipt of an IGMPv2 group leave message:

```
On R2:

R2(config)# interface FastEthernet0/1
R2(config-if)# ip igmp immediate-leave group-list 1

R2# show access-list

R2(config)# access-list 1 permit 224.0.0.0 15.255.255.255
```

Note If **ip igmp immediate-leave group-list 1** is configured in the global configuration mode, it is applied to all interfaces. In this case, it is applied to the F0/1 interface; therefore, it affects hosts that are connected to the F0/1 interface of R2. Note that the access list matches all Class D addresses, thus affecting all multicast groups.

To see how this command works, let's enable **debug ip igmp** on R2 and remove the
ip igmp join-group 224.2.2.2 command and view the results:

```
R2# debug ip igmp
IGMP debugging is on

On R7:


R7(config)# interface GigabitEthernet0/1
R7(config-if)# no ip igmp join-group 224.7.7.7


On R2:


IGMP(0): Received Leave from 27.1.1.7 (FastEthernet0/1) for 224.7.7.7
IGMP(0): Leave group 224.2.2.2 immediately on FastEthernet0/1
IGMP(0): Deleting 224.7.7.7 on FastEthernet0/1
IGMP(0): MRT delete FastEthernet0/1 for (*,224.7.7.7) by 3
```

Based on this output, you can see that once R7 was configured to remove the **ip igmp
join-group** command, it sent a leave message for group 224.7.7.7, and R7 immediately
removed the group.

In the next test, we will add the **ip igmp join-group 224.7.7.7** command on R7 and
remove the **ip igmp immediate-leave group-list 1** command from R2. Then we will
remove the **ip igmp join-group 224.7.7.7** command from R7 and view the result:

```
On R7:


R7(config)# interface GigabitEthernet0/1
R7(config-if)# ip igmp join-group 224.7.7.7


On R2:


R2(config)# interface FastEthernet0/1
R2(config-if)# no ip igmp immediate-leave group-list 1


On R7:


R7(config)# interface GigabitEthernet0/1
R7(config-if)# no ip igmp join-group 224.7.7.7
```

Now, let's examine the output of the debug on R2:

```
On R2:

IGMP(0): Received Leave from 27.1.1.7 (FastEthernet0/1) for 224.7.7.7
IGMP(0): Received Group record for group 224.7.7.7, mode 3 from 27.1.1.7 for 0
   sources
IGMP(0): Lower expiration timer to 2000 msec for 224.7.7.7 on FastEthernet0/1
IGMP(0): Send v2 Query on FastEthernet0/1 for group 224.7.7.7
IGMP(0): Send v2 Query on FastEthernet0/1 for group 224.7.7.7
IGMP(0): Switching to INCLUDE mode for 224.7.7.7 on FastEthernet0/1
IGMP(0): MRT delete FastEthernet0/1 for (*,224.7.7.7) by 0
```

You can see that the local router (R2) sent a query once it received the leave message from R7. Let's disable **debug ip igmp**, add **ip igmp immediate-leave group-list 1** on R2, and add **igmp join-group** on R7:

```
On R2:

R2# undebug all
All possible debugging has been turned off

R2(config)# interface FastEthernet0/1
R2(config-if)# ip igmp immediate-leave group-list 1

On R7:

R7(config)# interface GigabitEthernet0/1
R7(config-if)# ip igmp join-group 224.7.7.7
```

Task 7

Configure R1 such that before it stops forwarding the multicast traffic out of its F0/0 interface, it sends three IGMP query messages at 500-ms intervals after receiving an IGMP group-specific leave message.

Let's begin by viewing the default value:

```
On R1:

R1# show ip igmp interface FastEthernet0/0

FastEthernet0/0 is up, line protocol is up
   Internet address is 10.1.1.1/24
   IGMP is enabled on interface
```

```
Current IGMP host version is 2
Current IGMP router version is 2
IGMP query interval is 60 seconds
IGMP configured query interval is 60 seconds
IGMP querier timeout is 120 seconds
IGMP configured querier timeout is 120 seconds
IGMP max query response time is 10 seconds
Last member query count is 2
Last member query response interval is 1000 ms
Inbound IGMP access group is not set
IGMP activity: 3 joins, 1 leaves
Multicast routing is enabled on interface
Multicast TTL threshold is 0
Multicast designated router (DR) is 10.1.1.2
IGMP querying router is 10.1.1.1 (this system)
Multicast groups joined by this system (number of users):
    224.0.1.40(1)
```

Note   The default last member query count (LMQC) is set to 2, and the interval is set to 1 second (1000 ms). The following command sets the LMQC to 3:

```
On R1:

R1(config)# interface FastEthernet0/0
R1(config-if)# ip igmp last-member-query-count 3
```

Let's verify the configuration:

```
On R1:

R1# show ip igmp interface FastEthernet0/0 | include Last

  Last member query count is 3
  Last member query response interval is 1000 ms
```

Now let's set the interval for these messages:

```
On R1:

R1(config)# interface FastEthernet0/0
R1(config-if)# ip igmp last-member-query-interval 500
```

Now we'll verify the configuration:

```
On R1:

R1# show ip igmp interface FastEthernet0/0 | include Last

  Last member query count is 3
  Last member query response interval is 500 ms
```

Task 8

Configure R2 such that the number of **mroute** states created as a result of host membership reports is 3. This policy should only affect R2's F0/1 interface.

The following solution can be applied in global configuration mode or interface configuration mode. When it's configured in global config mode, it's applied to the entire router and it's referred to as "Global IGMP State Limiter," which means that it affects the router globally. However, if it is configured in the interface config mode, the effect is for the hosts connected to that given interface only.

```
On R2:

R2(config)# interface FastEthernet0/1
R2(config-if)# ip igmp limit 3
```

Let's verify the configuration:

```
On R2:

R2# show ip igmp interface FastEthernet0/1 | include Limit

Interface IGMP State Limit : 1 active out of 3 max
```

Note The output of the preceding **show** command states that there is one active group out of a maximum of three groups, whereas the output of the following **show** command reveals that there is a single group on R2's F0/1 interface:

```
R2# show ip igmp groups FastEthernet0/1

IGMP Connected Group Membership
Group Address Interface         Uptime   Expires  Last Reporter  Group Accounted
224.7.7.7     FastEthernet0/1 00:11:59  00:02:26 27.1.1.7          Ac
```

Now let's test the configuration. In testing the solution, R7 is configured to join additional groups and the **mroute** state is verified on R2; once the limit is reached, R2 denies creating additional **mroute** states:

```
On R7:


R7(config)# interface GigabitEthernet0/1
R7(config-if)# ip igmp join-group 224.22.22.22


On R2:


R2# show ip igmp group FastEthernet0/1


IGMP Connected Group Membership
Group Address   Interface       Uptime    Expires   Last Reporter   Group Accounted
224.22.22.22    FastEthernet0/1 00:00:24  00:02:35  27.1.1.7                    Ac
224.7.7.7       FastEthernet0/1 00:17:14  00:02:35  27.1.1.7                    Ac
```

Note   An **mroute** state is created for group 224.22.22.22, as shown here:

```
R2# show ip igmp interface FastEthernet0/1 | include Limit

   Interface IGMP State Limit : 2 active out of 3 max

R2# show ip mroute | include 224.22.22.22

 (*, 224.22.22.22), 00:02:15/00:02:02, RP 0.0.0.0, flags: DC


On R7:


!Note: The following is the third group:


R7(config)# interface GigabitEthernet0/1
R7(config-if)# ip igmp join-group 224.222.222.222


On R2:


R2# show ip igmp group FastEthernet0/1


IGMP Connected Group Membership
Group Address Interface       Uptime    Expires   Last Reporter Group Accounted
224.22.22.22  FastEthernet0/1 00:02:08  00:02:52  27.1.1.7                  Ac
224.7.7.7     FastEthernet0/1 00:18:57  00:02:52  27.1.1.7                  Ac
224.222.222.222 FastEthernet0/1 00:00:07  00:02:52  27.1.1.7                Ac
```

```
R2# show ip mroute | include 224.222.222.222

(*, 224.222.222.222), 00:00:58/00:02:01, RP 0.0.0.0, flags: DC

R2# show ip igmp interface FastEthernet0/1 | include Limit


Interface IGMP State Limit : 3 active out of 3 max
```

Note R2 has created an **mroute** state and has reached its maximum allowable **mroute** states. To see the effect of the **ip igmp limit** command, configure the **debug ip igmp** command on R2, as follows:

```
On R2:

R2# debug ip igmp
IGMP debugging is on
```

Let's configure R7 with the fourth group:

```
On R7:
R7(config)# interface GigabitEthernet0/1
R7(config-if)# ip igmp join-group 224.220.220.220
```

On R2, you should see the following debug output:

```
On R2:
IGMP(0): Received v2 Report on FastEthernet0/1 from 27.1.1.7 for 224.220.220.220
IGMP(0): Received Group record for group 224.220.220.220, mode 2 from 27.1.1.7 for 0
   sources
IGMP_ACL(0): Group 224.220.220.220 access denied on FastEthernet0/1


R2# show ip igmp groups FastEthernet0/1

IGMP Connected Group Membership
Group Address     Interface       Uptime    Expires   Last Reporter Group Accounted
224.22.22.22      FastEthernet0/1 00:02:08 00:02:52   27.1.1.7                  Ac
224.7.7.7         FastEthernet0/1 00:18:57 00:02:52   27.1.1.7                  Ac
224.222.222.222   FastEthernet0/1 00:00:07 00:02:52   27.1.1.7                  Ac
```

Note As shown here, there are three groups, which is the maximum allowed number:

```
R2# show ip igmp interface FastEthernet0/1 | include Limit

  Interface IGMP State Limit : 3 active out of 3 max
```

Let's disable the **debug ip igmp** command on R2:

```
On R2

R2# undebug all
```

Task 9

Configure R1 and R2 such that if the existing querier is down for longer than 90 seconds, a new querier is elected for the 10.1.1.0/24 network.

The output of the following **show** command displays the existing querying router and the query interval:

```
On R1:

R1# show ip igmp interface FastEthernet0/0 | include IGMP quer

  IGMP query interval is 60 seconds
  IGMP querier timeout is 120 seconds
  IGMP querying router is 10.1.1.1 (this system)

On R2:

R2# show ip igmp interface FastEthernet0/0 | include IGMP quer

  IGMP query interval is 60 seconds
  IGMP querier timeout is 120 seconds
  IGMP querying router is 10.1.1.1
```

You can see that both R1 and R2 agree that R1 (10.1.1.1) is the querying router and that the timers match.

Let's configure the task.

Note   By default, if the querier is down, the other routers on the same subnet will wait twice the query interval specified by **ip igmp query-interval** before the election is reinitiated.

The following command changes the wait time to 90 seconds:

```
On R1 and R2:
Rx(config)# interface FastEthernet0/0
Rx(config-if)# ip igmp querier-timeout 90
```

Let's verify the configuration:

```
On R1:

R1# show ip igmp interface FastEthernet0/0 | include IGMP quer

  IGMP query interval is 60 seconds
  IGMP querier timeout is 90 seconds
  IGMP querying router is 10.1.1.1 (this system)

On R2:

R2# show ip igmp interface FastEthernet0/0 | include IGMP quer

  IGMP query interval is 60 seconds
  IGMP querier timeout is 90 seconds
  IGMP querying router is 10.1.1.1
```

Now we need to verify and test the configuration.

The existing querier is R1 (10.1.1.1). Let's shut down the F0/0 interface of R1 and see the change take effect in 90 seconds:

```
On R1:

R1(config)# interface FastEthernet0/0
R1(config-if)# shutdown
```

You should see the following console message:

```
%PIM-5-NBRCHG: neighbor 10.1.1.2 DOWN on interface FastEthernet0/0 DR
```

The following **show** command is entered within 90 seconds, and as you can see, R2 is the new querying router:

```
R2# show ip igmp interface DastWthernet0/0 | include IGMP quer

  IGMP query interval is 60 seconds
  IGMP querier timeout is 90 seconds
  IGMP querying router is 10.1.1.2 (this system)
```

Let's reconfigure R1 as the querier:

```
On R1:


R1(config)# interface FastEthernet0/0
R1(config-if)# no shutdown
```

Now let's verify the configuration:

```
On R2:
R2# show ip igmp interface FastEthernet0/0 | include IGMP quer

  IGMP query interval is 60 seconds
  IGMP querier timeout is 90 seconds
  IGMP querying router is 10.1.1.1
```

The second the F0/0 interface of R1 is up, it becomes the querier immediately.

Task 10

The F0/0 interfaces of R1 and R2 should be configured to advertise the period during which the responder can respond to an IGMP query message before these routers delete the group to its maximum allowable value.

This is controlled through the **ip igmp query-max-response-time** interface configuration command:

```
On R1 and R2:


RX# show ip igmp interface FastEthernet0/0 | include IGMP max

 IGMP max query response time is 10 seconds
```

The default is 10 seconds. The following command changes this value, whose range is 1–25 seconds:

```
On R1 and R2:


Rx(config)# interface FastEthernet0/0
Rx(config-if)# ip igmp query-max-response-time ?
  <1-25>  query response value in seconds

Rx(config-if)# ip igmp query-max-response-time 25
```

Let's verify the configuration:

```
RX# show ip igmp interface FastEthernet0/0 | include IGMP max

 IGMP max query response time is 25 seconds
```

Erase the startup configuration and reload the routers before proceeding to the next lab.

Lab 14-2: Static RP

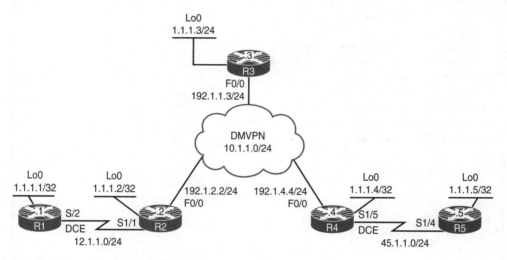

Figure 14-2   *Configuring Static RP*

Task 1

Configure the topology shown in Figure 14-2 based on the policy detailed in Table 14-1.

Table 14-1   *Policy Configuration for Task 1*

Router	NBMA IP	Tunnel IP	Role
R2	192.1.2.2/24	10.1.1.2/24	Spoke
R3	192.1.3.3/24	10.1.1.3/24	Hub
R4	192.1.4.4/24	10.1.1.4/24	Spoke

You should use specific static routes to provide reachability for the dynamic multipoint virtual private network (DMVPN) NBMA IP addresses. The DMVPN should be configured in Phase 1:

```
On SW1:

SW1(config)# interface range FastEthernet0/2 - 4
SW1(config-if-range)# no switchport

SW1(config)# interface FastEthernet0/2
SW1(config-if)# ip address 192.1.2.10 255.255.255.0
SW1(config-if)# no shutdown

SW1(config)# interface FastEthernet0/3
SW1(config-if)# ip address 192.1.3.10 255.255.255.0
SW1(config-if)# no shutdown

SW1(config)# interface FfastEthernet0/4
SW1(config-if)# ip address 192.1.4.10 255.255.255.0
SW1(config-if)# no shutdown

SW1(config)# ip routing

On R1:

R1(config)# interface loopback0
R1(config-if)# ip address 1.1.1.1 255.255.255.255

R1(config)# interface serial1/2
R1(config-if)# clock rate 64000
R1(config-if)# ip address 12.1.1.1 255.255.255.0
R1(config-if)# no shutdown

On R2:

R2(config)# interface loopback0
R2(config-if)# ip address 1.1.1.2 255.255.255.255

R2(config)# interface serial1/1
R2(config-if)# ip address 12.1.1.2 255.255.255.0
R2(config-if)# no shutdown

R2(config)# interface FastEthernet0/0
R2(config-if)# ip address 192.1.2.2 255.255.255.0
R2(config-if)# no shutdown
```

```
R2(config)# ip route 192.1.4.4 255.255.255.255 192.1.2.10
R2(config)# ip route 192.1.3.3 255.255.255.255 192.1.2.10

R2(config)# interface tunnel1
R2(config-if)# ip address 10.1.1.2 255.255.255.0
R2(config-if)# tunnel source FastEthernet0/0
R2(config-if)# tunnel destination 192.1.3.3
R2(config-if)# ip nhrp network 222
R2(config-if)# ip nhrp nhs 10.1.1.3
R2(config-if)# ip nhrp map 10.1.1.3 192.1.3.3
R2(config-if)# ip nhrp map multicast 192.1.3.3

On R3:

R3(config)# interface loopback0
R3(config-if)# ip address 1.1.1.3 255.255.255.255

R3(config)# interface FastEthernet0/0
R3(config-if)# ip address 192.1.3.3 255.255.255.0
R3(config-if)# no shutdown

R3(config)# ip route 192.1.2.2 255.255.255.255 192.1.3.10
R3(config)# ip route 192.1.4.4 255.255.255.255 192.1.3.10

R3(config)# interface tunnel1
R3(config-if)# ip address 10.1.1.3 255.255.255.0
R3(config-if)# tunnel source FastEthernet/0
R3(config-if)# tunnel mode gre multipoint
R3(config-if)# ip nhrp network 333
R3(config-if)# ip nhrp map multicast dynamic

On R4:

R4(config)# interface loopback0
R4(config-if)# ip address 1.1.1.4 255.255.255.255

R4(config)# interface FastEthernet0/0
R4(config-if)# ip address 192.1.4.4 255.255.255.0
R4(config-if)# no shutdown

R4(config)# interface serial1/5
R4(config-if)# clock rate 64000
R4(config-if)# ip address 45.1.1.4 255.255.255.0
R4(config-if)# no shutdown
```

```
R4(config)# ip route 192.1.3.3 255.255.255.255 192.1.4.10
R4(config)# ip route 192.1.2.2 255.255.255.255 192.1.4.10

R4(config)# interface tunnel1
R4(config-if)# ip address 10.1.1.4 255.255.255.0
R4(config-if)# tunnel source FastEthernet0/0
R4(config-if)# tunnel destination 192.1.3.3
R4(config-if)# ip nhrp network 444
R4(config-if)# ip nhrp nhs 10.1.1.3
R4(config-if)# ip nhrp map 10.1.1.3 192.1.3.3
R4(config-if)# ip nhrp map multi 192.1.3.3


On R5:

R5(config)# interface loopback0
R5(config-if)# ip address 1.1.1.5 255.255.255.255

R5(config)# interface serial1/4
R5(config-if)# ip address 45.1.1.5 255.255.255.0
R5(config-if)# no shutdown
```

Let's verify the configuration:

```
On R2:

R2# ping 12.1.1.1

Type escape sequence to abort.
Sending 5, 100-byte ICMP Echos to 12.1.1.1, timeout is 2 seconds:
!!!!!
Success rate is 100 percent (5/5), round-trip min/avg/max = 28/29/32 ms


R2# ping 10.1.1.3

Type escape sequence to abort.
Sending 5, 100-byte ICMP Echos to 10.1.1.3, timeout is 2 seconds:
!!!!!
Success rate is 100 percent (5/5), round-trip min/avg/max = 1/2/4 ms


R2# ping 10.1.1.4

Type escape sequence to abort.
Sending 5, 100-byte ICMP Echos to 10.1.1.4, timeout is 2 seconds:
!!!!!
Success rate is 100 percent (5/5), round-trip min/avg/max = 4/5/8 ms
```

```
On R5:

R5# ping 45.1.1.4

Type escape sequence to abort.
Sending 5, 100-byte ICMP Echos to 45.1.1.4, timeout is 2 seconds:
!!!!!
Success rate is 100 percent (5/5), round-trip min/avg/max = 28/28/32 ms
```

Task 2

Configure OSPF Area 0 on all routers in the topology shown in Figure 14-2 and ensure reachability to all links and loopback interfaces in this diagram. The DMVPN tunnel is configured in Phase 2 and should not be changed to another phase.

```
On R1:

R1(config)# router ospf 1
R1(config-router)# network 12.1.1.1 0.0.0.0 area 0
R1(config-router)# network 1.1.1.1 0.0.0.0 area 0

On R2:

R2(config)# router ospf 1
R2(config-router)# network 1.1.1.2 0.0.0.0 area 0
R2(config-router)# network 12.1.1.2 0.0.0.0 area 0
R2(config-router)# network 10.1.1.2 0.0.0.0 area 0

R2(config-router)# interface tunnel1
R2(config-if)# ip ospf hello-interval 10
```

You should see the following console message:

```
%OSPF-5-ADJCHG: Process 1, Nbr 1.1.1.1 on Serial1/1 from LOADING to FULL, Loading
  Done
```

```
On R3:

R3(config)# interface tunnel1
R3(config-if)# ip ospf network point-to-multipoint
R3(config-if)# ip ospf hello-interval 10

R3(config)# router ospf 1
R3(config-router)# network 1.1.1.3 0.0.0.0 area 0
R3(config-router)# network 10.1.1.3 0.0.0.0 area 0
```

You should also see this console message:

```
%OSPF-5-ADJCHG: Process 1, Nbr 1.1.1.2 on Tunnel1 from LOADING to FULL, Loading Done
```

```
On R4:

R4(config)# router ospf 1
R4(config-router)# network 1.1.1.4 0.0.0.0 area 0
R4(config-router)# network 10.1.1.4 0.0.0.0 area 0
R4(config-router)# network 45.1.1.4 0.0.0.0 area 0

R4(config-router)# interface tunnel1
R4(config-if)# ip ospf hello-interval 10
```

You should see this console message as well:

```
%OSPF-5-ADJCHG: Process 1, Nbr 1.1.1.3 on Tunnel1 from LOADING to FULL, Loading Done
```

```
On R5:

R5(config)# router ospf 1
R5(config-router)# network 1.1.1.5 0.0.0.0 area 0
R5(config-router)# network 45.1.1.5 0.0.0.0 area 0
```

Finally, you should see this console message:

```
%OSPF-5-ADJCHG: Process 1, Nbr 1.1.1.4 on Serial1/4 from LOADING to FULL,
Loading Done
```

Let's verify the configuration:

```
On R1:

R1# show ip route ospf | begin Gate
Gateway of last resort is not set

      1.0.0.0/32 is subnetted, 5 subnets
O        1.1.1.2 [110/782] via 12.1.1.2, 00:04:33, Serial1/2
O        1.1.1.3 [110/1782] via 12.1.1.2, 00:02:33, Serial1/2
O        1.1.1.4 [110/2782] via 12.1.1.2, 00:01:33, Serial1/2
O        1.1.1.5 [110/3563] via 12.1.1.2, 00:00:33, Serial1/2
      10.0.0.0/8 is variably subnetted, 2 subnets, 2 masks
```

```
O          10.1.1.0/24 [110/1781] via 12.1.1.2, 00:04:33, Serial1/2
O          10.1.1.3/32 [110/1781] via 12.1.1.2, 00:02:43, Serial1/2
      45.0.0.0/24 is subnetted, 1 subnets
O          45.1.1.0 [110/3562] via 12.1.1.2, 00:01:23, Serial1/2

R1# ping 1.1.1.5

Type escape sequence to abort.
Sending 5, 100-byte ICMP Echos to 1.1.1.5, timeout is 2 seconds:
!!!!!
Success rate is 100 percent (5/5), round-trip min/avg/max = 56/57/60 ms
```

Task 3

Configure PIM sparse mode on all the interfaces in the topology. Do *not* configure PIM on the F0/0 interfaces of R2, R3, and R4.

The first step is to enable multicast routing. Once multicast routing is enabled, you can enable PIM sparse mode on the interfaces:

```
On R1:

R1(config)# ip multicast-routing

R1(config)# interface loopback0
R1(config-if)# ip pim sparse-mode

R1(config)# interface serial1/2
R1(config-if)# ip pim sparse-mode

On R2:

R2(config)# ip multicast-routing

R2(config)# interface loopback0
R2(config-if)# ip pim sparse-mode

R2(config)# interface serial1/1
R2(config-if)# ip pim sparse-mode

R2(config)# interface tunnel1
R2(config-if)# ip pim sparse-mode
```

You should see the following console message:

```
%PIM-5-NBRCHG: neighbor 12.1.1.1 UP on interface Serial1/1

On R3:

R3(config)# ip multicast-routing

R3(config)# interface loopback0
R3(config-if)# ip pim sparse-mode

R3(config)# interface tunnel1
R3(config-if)# ip pim sparse-mode
```

You should also see this console message:

```
%PIM-5-NBRCHG: neighbor 10.1.1.2 UP on interface Tunnel1

On R4:

R4(config)# ip multicast-routing

R4(config)# interface loopback0
R4(config-if)# ip pim sparse-mode

R4(config)# interface tunnel1
R4(config-if)# ip pim sparse-mode

R4(config)# interface serial1/5
R4(config-if)# ip pim sparse-mode
```

You should see the following console message as well:

```
%PIM-5-NBRCHG: neighbor 10.1.1.3 UP on interface Tunnel1

On R5:

R5(config)# ip multicast-routing

R5(config)# interface loopback0
R5(config-if)# ip pim sparse-mode

R5(config)# interface serial1/4
R5(config-if)# ip pim sparse-mode
```

Finally, you should see this console message:

```
%PIM-5-NBRCHG: neighbor 45.1.1.4 UP on interface Serial1/4
```

To verify the configuration, let's use the following **show ip pim neighbor** commands, which enable us to verify that the directly connected routers are PIM neighbors:

```
On R1:


R1# show ip pim neighbor | begin Interface


Neighbor              Interface              Uptime/Expires    Ver   DR
Address                                                             Prio/Mode
12.1.1.2              Serial1/2              00:07:45/00:01:22 v2    1 / S P G


On R2:


R2# show ip pim neighbor | begin Interface


Neighbor              Interface              Uptime/Expires    Ver   DR
Address                                                             Prio/Mode
12.1.1.1              Serial1/1              00:05:45/00:01:23 v2    1 / S P G
10.1.1.3              Tunnel1                00:05:17/00:01:40 v2    1 / S P G


On R3:


R3# show ip pim neighbor | begin Interface


Neighbor              Interface              Uptime/Expires    Ver   DR
Address                                                             Prio/Mode
10.1.1.4              Tunnel1                00:03:45/00:01:27 v2    1 / DR S P G
10.1.1.2              Tunnel1                00:04:45/00:01:24 v2    1 / S P G


On R4:


R4# show ip pim neighbor | begin Interface


Neighbor              Interface              Uptime/Expires    Ver   DR
Address                                                             Prio/Mode
10.1.1.3              Tunnel1                00:03:34/00:01:38 v2    1 / S P G
45.1.1.5              Serial1/5              00:03:33/00:01:38 v2    1 / S P G


On R5:


R5# show ip pim neighbor | begin Interface


Neighbor              Interface              Uptime/Expires    Ver   DR
Address                                                             Prio/Mode
45.1.1.4              Serial1/4              00:01:36/00:01:35 v2    1 / S P G
```

Task 4

R2 should be configured as the Rendezvous Point (RP) for the private group addresses, whereas R3 should be configured as the RP for the remaining groups. You should use static configuration and loopback0 interfaces to accomplish this task.

Even though static RP configuration is the most popular and simplest solution, it is extremely easy to make configuration typos because the same exact configuration needs to be replicated accurately on all routers including the RP.

Here are the configuration tasks:

- R2's Lo0 interface is to be configured as the RP for the private group addresses.

- R3's Lo0 interface is to be configured as the RP for all other groups.

For RP's requirement, you need to configure an access list to identify the private multicast group address range as well as configure the static RP command to reference the access list. This configuration must be done on all routers, including the RP.

Note   When an access list is not referenced, the IP address specified in the configuration is configured to be the RP for all groups (224.0.0.0 15.255.255.255):

```
On All Routers:

Rx# show access-lists

Rx(config)# access-list 2 permit 239.0.0.0 0.255.255.255

Rx(config)# ip pim rp-address 1.1.1.2 2
Rx(config)# ip pim rp-address 1.1.1.3
```

You should see new tunnel interfaces coming up. On R1 and R5, you should see Tunnel 0 and 1. On R2 and R3, you should see Tunnels 0, 2, and 3. On R4, you should see Tunnels 0 and 2.

Let's see the reason for these tunnel interfaces:

```
On R1:

%LINEPROTO-5-UPDOWN: Line protocol on Interface Tunnel0, changed state to up

%LINEPROTO-5-UPDOWN: Line protocol on Interface Tunnel1, changed state to up
```

```
R1# show interface tunnel0

Tunnel0 is up, line protocol is up
  Hardware is Tunnel
  Interface is unnumbered. Using address of Serial1/2 (12.1.1.1)
  MTU 17912 bytes, BW 100 Kbit/sec, DLY 50000 usec,
      reliability 255/255, txload 1/255, rxload 1/255
  Encapsulation TUNNEL, loopback not set
  Keepalive not set
  Tunnel source 12.1.1.1 (Serial1/2), destination 1.1.1.2
   Tunnel Subblocks:
      src-track:
          Tunnel0 source tracking subblock associated with Serial1/2
           Set of tunnels with source Serial1/2, 2 members (includes iterators), on
  interface <OK>
  Tunnel protocol/transport PIM/IPv4
  Tunnel TOS/Traffic Class 0xC0,  Tunnel TTL 255
  Tunnel transport MTU 1472 bytes
  Tunnel is transmit only
(The rest of the output is omitted for brevity)

R1# show interface tunnel1

Tunnel1 is up, line protocol is up
  Hardware is Tunnel
  Interface is unnumbered. Using address of Serial1/2 (12.1.1.1)
  MTU 17912 bytes, BW 100 Kbit/sec, DLY 50000 usec,
      reliability 255/255, txload 1/255, rxload 1/255
  Encapsulation TUNNEL, loopback not set
  Keepalive not set
  Tunnel source 12.1.1.1 (Serial1/2), destination 1.1.1.3
   Tunnel Subblocks:
      src-track:
          Tunnel1 source tracking subblock associated with Serial1/2
           Set of tunnels with source Serial1/2, 2 members (includes iterators), on
  interface <OK>
  Tunnel protocol/transport PIM/IPv4
  Tunnel TOS/Traffic Class 0xC0,  Tunnel TTL 255
  Tunnel transport MTU 1472 bytes
  Tunnel is transmit only
(The rest of the output is omitted for brevity)
```

When multicasting is enabled and the RPs are defined, the non-RP routers assume that they are going to be directly connected to the source. In 12.4 and earlier IOS versions, when the source is initiated, the first-hop router receives the multicast data and encapsulates the multicast data in register messages that are unicasted to the RP.

In IOS releases 15 and later, the register messages are sent through the tunnel that is auto-configured. You can see that these two tunnels are in transmit mode *only*. The reason you see two tunnels is because you have defined two RPs (1.1.1.2 and 1.1.1.3); therefore, the first tunnel has a destination of 1.1.1.2 and the second tunnel interface has a destination of 1.1.1.3. You can see a similar behavior when multicasting is configured in IPv6. Let's verify that the tunnel interfaces are used for register messages:

```
R1(config)# interface tunnel0
%Tunnel0 used by PIM for Registering, configuration not allowed

R1(config)# interface tunnel1
%Tunnel1 used by PIM for Registering, configuration not allowed
```

The PIM tunnels can also be displayed with the following command:

```
R1# show ip pim tunnel
Tunnel0
  Type  : PIM Encap
  RP    : 1.1.1.2
  Source: 12.1.1.1
Tunnel1
  Type  : PIM Encap
  RP    : 1.1.1.3
  Source: 12.1.1.1
```

You should see the following console messages on R2 and R3:

```
%LINEPROTO-5-UPDOWN: Line protocol on Interface Tunnel0, changed state to up
%LINEPROTO-5-UPDOWN: Line protocol on Interface Tunnel2, changed state to up
%LINEPROTO-5-UPDOWN: Line protocol on Interface Tunnel3, changed state to up
```

Let's check the tunnels on R2 and R3, which are identical. Tunnel 0 is auto-configured in case the local router is a first-hop router and it needs to send register messages to the RP. As you can see, the destination of the tunnel is 1.1.1.2:

```
On R2 or R3:

Rx# show interface tunnel0 | include destination|only

  Tunnel source 1.1.1.2 (Loopback0), destination 1.1.1.2
  Tunnel is transmit only
```

Tunnel 1 cannot be used because you have configured DMVPN using Tunnel 1; therefore, Tunnel 2 is auto-configured in receive-only mode, as shown next. This tunnel is used for receiving the register messages.

```
Rx# show interface tunnel2 | include destination|only

  Tunnel source 1.1.1.2 (Loopback0), destination 1.1.1.2
  Tunnel is receive only
```

Tunnel 3 is auto-configured for sending stop register messages, and that's why it's in transmit-only mode, as shown here:

```
Rx# show interface tunnel3 | include destination|only

  Tunnel source 10.1.1.2 (Tunnel1), destination 1.1.1.3
  Tunnel is transmit only
```

The PIM tunnels can also be displayed with the following command:

```
R2# show ip pim tunnel
Tunnel0
  Type  : PIM Encap
  RP    : 1.1.1.2*
  Source: 1.1.1.2
Tunnel3
  Type  : PIM Encap
  RP    : 1.1.1.3
  Source: 10.1.1.2
Tunnel2
  Type  : PIM Decap
  RP    : 1.1.1.2*
  Source: -
```

The asterisk (*) indicates that this router is the RP.

You should see the following console messages on R4:

```
%LINEPROTO-5-UPDOWN: Line protocol on Interface Tunnel0, changed state to up
%LINEPROTO-5-UPDOWN: Line protocol on Interface Tunnel2, changed state to up
```

Let's check Tunnels 0 and 2 on R4:

```
On R4:

R4# show interface tunnel0 | include destination|only

  Tunnel source 10.1.1.4 (Tunnel1), destination 1.1.1.2
  Tunnel is transmit only
```

```
R4# show interface tunnel2 | include destination|only

 Tunnel source 10.1.1.4 (Tunnel1), destination 1.1.1.3
 Tunnel is transmit only
```

The PIM tunnels can also be displayed with the following command:

```
R4# show ip pim tunnel
Tunnel0
  Type  : PIM Encap
  RP    : 1.1.1.2
  Source: 10.1.1.4
Tunnel2
  Type  : PIM Encap
  RP    : 1.1.1.3
  Source: 10.1.1.4
```

Let's verify the configuration:

```
On R1:


R1# show ip pim rp mapping


PIM Group-to-RP Mappings
              Note since an access-list was NOT referenced, the router
Acl: 2, Static               becomes the RP for ALL Mcast groups
    RP: 1.1.1.2 (?)
Group(s): 224.0.0.0/4, Static
    RP: 1.1.1.3 (?)
```

Note   The output of the preceding **show** command reveals that the lo0 interface of R2 is the RP for the groups that are referenced in ACL 2, whereas the lo0 interface of R3 is the RP for the group range of 224.0.0.0/4, meaning all groups.

Because in the preceding configuration the private group addresses are overlapping, the RP with the highest IP address will become the RP for all groups. In this case, R3 is the RP for all groups.

Based on the existing configuration, R3 is chosen as the RP for all groups, and R2 will not be used at all. The correct solution is to configure another access list, deny group 239.0.0.0/8 and allow all other groups, and then reference the access list for R3. This has to be configured on all routers.

```
On All Routers:


R1# show access-lists
Standard IP access list 2
    10 permit 239.0.0.0, wildcard bits 0.255.255.255


Rx(config)# access-list 3 deny 239.0.0.0 0.255.255.255
Rx(config)# access-list 3 permit any


Rx(config)# ip pim rp-address 1.1.1.3 3
```

Let's verify the configuration:

```
On R1:


R1# show ip pim rp mapping
PIM Group-to-RP Mappings


Acl: 2, Static
    RP: 1.1.1.2 (?)
Acl: 3, Static
    RP: 1.1.1.3 (?)
```

Note   R2 is the RP for the groups defined in ACL #2, and R3 is the RP for groups defined in ACL #3. Remember that the configuration should be performed on all routers, including the RPs.

Task 5

Configure R5's S1/4 interface to join group 224.5.5.5.

All routers must be able to ping this group:

```
On R5:


R5(config)# interface s1/4
R5(config-if)# ip igmp join-group 224.5.5.5
```

Let's verify the configuration:

```
On R5:


R5# show ip mroute | section 224.5.5.5

(*, 225.5.5.5), 00:00:08/00:02:51, RP 1.1.1.3, flags: SJPL
  Incoming interface: Serial1/4, RPF nbr 45.1.1.4
  Outgoing interface list: Null
```

```
On R4:

R4# show ip mroute | section 224.5.5.5

(*, 224.5.5.5), 00:01:10/00:03:18, RP 1.1.1.3, flags: S
  Incoming interface: Tunnel1, RPF nbr 10.1.1.3
  Outgoing interface list:
    Serial1/5, Forward/Sparse, 00:01:10/00:03:18

On R3:

R3# show ip mroute | section 224.5.5.5

(*, 224.5.5.5), 00:04:17/00:03:08, RP 1.1.1.3, flags: S
  Incoming interface: Null, RPF nbr 0.0.0.0
  Outgoing interface list:
    Tunnel1, Forward/Sparse, 00:04:17/00:03:08

On R1 and R2:

Rx# show ip mroute | section 224.5.5.5
```

Note Every PIM-enabled router will create the parent entry **(*, 224.5.5.5)** in their **mroute** table. This is created as the join messages are sent from R5 to the RP; R2 and R1 will not have any entry for this group. The RP for this group is 1.1.1.3 (R3). Remember that R3 is the RP for all scopes (local and global scopes) except for the private/admin scope.

Let's verify the configuration:

```
On R1:

R1# ping 224.5.5.5

Type escape sequence to abort.
Sending 1, 100-byte ICMP Echos to 224.5.5.5, timeout is 2 seconds:
Reply to request 0 from 45.1.1.5, 76 ms
Reply to request 0 from 45.1.1.5, 88 ms
```

The reason you see two replies back is because the ping is originated from every multicast-enabled interface.

Let's verify the configuration:

```
On R1:
R1# show ip mroute | section 225.5.5.5

(*, 224.5.5.5), 00:00:24/stopped, RP 1.1.1.3, flags: SPF
  Incoming interface: Serial1/2, RPF nbr 12.1.1.2
  Outgoing interface list: Null
(12.1.1.1, 224.5.5.5), 00:00:24/00:03:05, flags: PFT
  Incoming interface: Serial1/2, RPF nbr 0.0.0.0, Registering
  Outgoing interface list: Null
(1.1.1.1, 224.5.5.5), 00:00:24/00:02:35, flags: FT
  Incoming interface: Loopback0, RPF nbr 0.0.0.0, Registering
  Outgoing interface list:
    Serial1/2, Forward/Sparse, 00:00:24/00:03:05
```

Note You can see two entries: one sourcing from loopback0 and the second one sourcing from the S1/2 interfaces of R1. With multicasting, when a **ping** command is performed, it is sourced from every multicast-enabled interface on that router.

Erase the startup configuration and reload the routers before proceeding to the next lab.

Lab 14-3: Dynamic Rendezvous Point Learning and Auto-RP

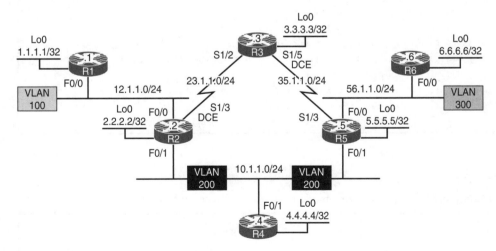

Figure 14-3 *Configuring Auto-RP*

Figure 14-3 illustrates the topology that will be used in the following lab.

Cisco developed a mechanism to dynamically elect and advertise the identity of a Rendezvous Point. This mechanism has several components and will be explored in the following lab.

Task 1

Configure OSPF Area 0 on all interfaces.

```
On All Routers:

Rx(config)# router ospf 1
Rx(config-router)# network 0.0.0.0 0.0.0.0 area 0
```

Let's verify the configuration:

```
On R1:

R1# show ip route ospf | begin Gate
Gateway of last resort is not set

      2.0.0.0/32 is subnetted, 1 subnets
O        2.2.2.2 [110/2] via 12.1.1.2, 00:00:18, FastEthernet0/0
      3.0.0.0/32 is subnetted, 1 subnets
O        3.3.3.3 [110/783] via 12.1.1.2, 00:00:18, FastEthernet0/0
      4.0.0.0/32 is subnetted, 1 subnets
O        4.4.4.4 [110/3] via 12.1.1.2, 00:00:08, FastEthernet0/0
      5.0.0.0/32 is subnetted, 1 subnets
O        5.5.5.5 [110/3] via 12.1.1.2, 00:00:08, FastEthernet0/0
      6.0.0.0/32 is subnetted, 1 subnets
O        6.6.6.6 [110/4] via 12.1.1.2, 00:00:08, FastEthernet0/0
      10.0.0.0/24 is subnetted, 1 subnets
O        10.1.1.0 [110/2] via 12.1.1.2, 00:00:08, FastEthernet0/0
      23.0.0.0/24 is subnetted, 1 subnets
O        23.1.1.0 [110/782] via 12.1.1.2, 00:00:18, FastEthernet0/0
      35.0.0.0/24 is subnetted, 1 subnets
O        35.1.1.0 [110/783] via 12.1.1.2, 00:00:08, FastEthernet0/0
      56.0.0.0/24 is subnetted, 1 subnets
O        56.1.1.0 [110/3] via 12.1.1.2, 00:00:08, FastEthernet0/0
```

Task 2

Configure PIM **sparse-dense-mode** on all the interfaces in this topology:

```
On R1:

R1(config)# ip multicast-routing

R1(config)# interface loopback0
R1(config-if)# ip pim sparse-dense-mode
```

```
R1(config-if)# interface FastEthernet0/0
R1(config-if)# ip pim sparse-dense-mode


On R2:


R2(config)# ip multicast-routing


R2(config)# interface loopback0
R2(config-if)# ip pim sparse-dense-mode


R2(config)# interface FastEthernet0/0
R2(config-if)# ip pim sparse-dense-mode


R2(config)# interface FastEthernet0/1
R2(config-if)# ip pim sparse-dense-mode


R2(config)# interface serial1/3
R2(config-if)# ip pim sparse-dense-mode


On R3:


R3(config)# ip multicast-routing


R3(config)# interface loopback0
R3(config-if)# ip pim sparse-dense-mode


R3(config)# interface serial1/2
R3(config-if)# ip pim sparse-dense-mode


R3(config)# interface serial1/5
R3(config-if)# ip pim sparse-dense-mode


On R4:


R4(config)# ip multicast-routing


R4(config)# interface loopback0
R4(config-if)# ip pim sparse-dense-mode


R4(config)# interface FastEthernet0/1
R4(config-if)# ip pim sparse-dense-mode


On R5:


R5(config)# ip multicast-routing
```

```
R5(config)# interface loopback0
R5(config-if)# ip pim sparse-dense-mode

R5(config)# interface FastEthernet0/0
R5(config-if)# ip pim sparse-dense-mode

R5(config)# interface FastEthernet0/1
R5(config-if)# ip pim sparse-dense-mode

R5(config-)# interface serial1/3
R5(config-if)# ip pim sparse-dense-mode

On R6:

R6(config)# ip multicast-routing

R6(config)# interface loopback0
R6(config-if)# ip pim sparse-dense-mode

R6(config-if)# interface FastEthernet0/0
R6(config-if)# ip pim sparse-dense-mode
```

Let's verify the configuration:

```
On R1:

R1# show ip pim neighbor | begin Interface

Neighbor        Interface            Uptime/Expires      Ver    DR
Address                                                         Prio/Mode
12.1.1.2        FastEthernet0/0      00:03:20/00:01:20 v2    1 / DR S P G

On R2:

R2# show ip pim neighbor | begin Interface

Neighbor        Interface            Uptime/Expires      Ver    DR
Address                                                         Prio/Mode
12.1.1.1        FastEthernet0/0      00:04:30/00:01:40 v2    1 / S P G
10.1.1.5        FastEthernet0/1      00:02:15/00:01:26 v2    1 / DR S P G
10.1.1.4        FastEthernet0/1      00:03:02/00:01:26 v2    1 / S P G
23.1.1.3        Serial1/3            00:03:41/00:01:29 v2    1 / S P G
```

```
On R3:

R3# show ip pim neighbor | begin Interface

Neighbor              Interface              Uptime/Expires      Ver    DR
Address                                                                Prio/Mode
23.1.1.2              Serial1/2              00:03:41/00:01:29 v2    1 / S P G
35.1.1.5              Serial1/5              00:02:26/00:01:16 v2    1 / S P G

On R4:

R4# show ip pim neighbor | begin Interface

Neighbor              Interface              Uptime/Expires      Ver    DR
Address                                                                Prio/Mode
10.1.1.5              FastEthernet0/1        00:02:15/00:01:26 v2    1 / DR S P G
10.1.1.2              FastEthernet0/1        00:03:02/00:01:27 v2    1 / S P G

On R5:

R5# show ip pim neighbor | begin Interface

Neighbor              Interface              Uptime/Expires      Ver    DR
Address                                                                Prio/Mode
35.1.1.3              Serial1/3              00:02:26/00:01:16 v2    1 / S P G
56.1.1.6              FastEthernet0/0        00:02:20/00:01:21 v2    1 / DR S P G
10.1.1.2              FastEthernet0/1        00:02:15/00:01:27 v2    1 / S P G
10.1.1.4              FastEthernet0/1        00:02:15/00:01:26 v2    1 / S P G

On R6:

R6# show ip pim neighbor | begin Interface

Neighbor              Interface              Uptime/Expires      Ver    DR
Address                                                                Prio/Mode
56.1.1.5              FastEthernet0/0        00:02:20/00:01:22 v2    1 / S P
```

Task 3

Configure R4 as the primary RP for 238.0.0.0/8 and R3 as the backup RP. You should use Auto-RP to distribute the RP mapping information through R5.

In Auto-RP, two roles must be defined:

- **Candidate RPs:** The routers configured to be the RP will announce themselves as the RP for all or specific groups. They accomplish this by sending **RP-announce** messages. The destination address of these announcements is 224.0.1.39. All routers will hear these announcements, but only the router configured as the mapping agent will process them.

- **Mapping agent:** The router that is configured to be the mapping agent will process the **RP-announce** messages and decide the RP-to-group mapping. If there is more than one RP announcement for a given group, the mapping agent will elect the RP with the highest source IP address as the RP for that group; this behavior *cannot* be changed. The MA will send **RP-discover** messages to announce the RP-to-group mapping.

We need to explore the caveats and rational behind how Auto-RP works. This extends into its functionality and its operational requirements.

- **Why sparse-dense-mode?** Because 224.0.1.39 and 224.0.1.40 can only work in **dense-mode**, configuring **sparse-mode** will not work. Therefore, **sparse-dense-mode** is required for Auto-RP configuration.

  Auto-RP can work with interfaces configured as **sparse-mode** only if the routers are configured with **ip pim autorp listener.**

- **Why do these groups have to operate in dense-mode?** In Auto-RP, the multicast packets are forwarded on the shared tree, which means that the routers need to be aware of the RP. The router that's listening for 224.0.1.40 should notify its RP that it needs to join 224.0.1.40 so it can receive and process the **RP-discover** messages, but the big question is how would that router know where the RP is if it has not received the **RP-discover** messages for that specific group? In other words, to join the group, the router needs to know the RP, but to know the RP, it needs to join the group.

  The **ip pim sparse-dense-mode** command was created to fix this problem for groups 224.0.1.39 and 224.0.1.40. Remember that in **sparse-dense-mode** configuration, if the RP is known for the group, the interfaces use **sparse-mode**; however, if the RP is not known, they will use **dense-mode**.

In this task, both R3 and R4 should advertise themselves as the RP for the specific group, and R5 will be configured to collect the RP announcements and decide which router will be the primary RP and which will be the backup RP.

```
On R3:


R3# show access-lists


R3(config)# access-list 1 permit 238.0.0.0 0.255.255.255
R3(config)# ip pim send-rp-announce loopback0 scope 2 group-list 1
```

Note The **group-list** keyword limits the RP announcements only for the 238.0.0.0/8 group. The **scope** keyword defines the TTL of these packets, since it was not mentioned in the requirements; a **scope** of 2 was configured so only the mapping agent within *this* topology can receive the announcements.

In order for a router to use its loopback interface as the source IP address of **RP-announce** messages, multicast must be enabled on that loopback interface. If it's not enabled, you will receive the following message:

```
Must first configure PIM mode on the interface: Loopback0
```

Note If you enter **debug ip pim auto-rp** before configuring the mapping agent, the following output will result every 60 seconds. This interval can be changed using the **interval** keyword on the **ip pim send-rp-announce** command.

```
Auto-RP(0): Build RP-Announce for 3.3.3.3, PIMv2/v1, ttl 2, ht 181
Auto-RP(0): Build announce entry for (238.0.0.0/8)
Auto-RP(0): Send RP-Announce packet of length 48 on Serial1/2
Auto-RP(0): Send RP-Announce packet of length 48 on Serial1/5
Auto-RP(0): Send RP-Announce packet of length 48 on Loopback0(*)


On R4:


R4# show access-lists
R4(config)# access-list 1 permit 238.0.0.0 0.255.255.255
R4(config)# ip pim send-rp-announce loopback0 scope 2 group-list 1


On R5:


R5(config)# ip pim send-rp-discovery loopback0 scope 5
```

Let's verify the configuration:

```
On R1:


R1# show ip pim rp mapping
PIM Group-to-RP Mappings


Group(s) 238.0.0.0/8
  RP 4.4.4.4 (?), v2v1
    Info source: 5.5.5.5 (?), elected via Auto-RP
        Uptime: 00:22:04, expires: 00:02:45
```

The output of the preceding **show** command reveals the following:

- R4 (4.4.4.4) is the RP for group 238.0.0.0/8.

- The **?** indicates a failure in the name resolution.

- The **Info source** section identifies the mapping agent (in this case, 5.5.5.5, or R5).

- This election was managed by the Auto-RP process.

- The **Uptime** section shows the uptime of the existing RP for this multicast group.

- The **expires** section indicates the expiration time for the RP; this timer is refreshed when the local router receives the **RP-Discovery** messages, which occur every 60 seconds by default.

Let's verify the name resolution (the second bullet point from the preceding explanation):

```
On R1:

R1(config)# ip host R4 4.4.4.4

R1(config)# ip host R5 5.5.5.5

R1# show ip pim rp mapping
PIM Group-to-RP Mappings

Group(s) 238.0.0.0/8
  RP 4.4.4.4 (R4), v2v1
    Info source: 5.5.5.5 (R5), elected via Auto-RP
        Uptime: 00:03:34, expires: 00:02:24

On R2:

R2# show ip pim rp mapping
PIM Group-to-RP Mappings

Group(s) 238.0.0.0/8
  RP 4.4.4.4 (?), v2v1
    Info source: 5.5.5.5 (?), elected via Auto-RP
        Uptime: 00:21:52, expires: 00:02:19

On R3:

R3# show ip pim rp mapping
PIM Group-to-RP Mappings
This system is an RP (Auto-RP)
```

```
Group(s) 238.0.0.0/8
  RP 4.4.4.4 (?), v2v1
    Info source: 5.5.5.5 (?), elected via Auto-RP
         Uptime: 00:22:17, expires: 00:02:52


On R4:


R4# show ip pim rp mapping
PIM Group-to-RP Mappings
This system is an RP (Auto-RP)


Group(s) 238.0.0.0/8
  RP 4.4.4.4 (?), v2v1
    Info source: 5.5.5.5 (?), elected via Auto-RP
         Uptime: 00:22:51, expires: 00:02:18


On R5:


R5# show ip pim rp mapping
PIM Group-to-RP Mappings
This system is an RP-mapping agent (Loopback0)


Group(s) 238.0.0.0/8
  RP 4.4.4.4 (?), v2v1
    Info source: 4.4.4.4 (?), elected via Auto-RP
         Uptime: 01:12:09, expires: 00:02:55
  RP 3.3.3.3 (?), v2v1
    Info source: 3.3.3.3 (?), via Auto-RP           Source IP address.
         Uptime: 01:10:50, expires: 00:02:12
```

Note   R5 (the MA) is aware of both RPs, but it elected R4 (4.4.4.4) because it has a higher IP address. After making this decision, it advertises R4 to the rest of the routers in **RP-Discovery** messages.

Let's test the backup RP:

```
On R4:


R4(config)# interface loopback0
R4(config-if)# shutdown
```

Note   The **expires** counter is counting down. Because R4 is down, R5 (the MA) will not receive the **RP-announce** messages; therefore, the counter expires and the entry is removed, as follows:

```
R5# show ip pim rp mapping | section 4.4.4.4

  RP 4.4.4.4 (?), v2v1
    Info source: 4.4.4.4 (?), elected via Auto-RP
         Uptime: 00:25:32, expires: 00:02:27

R5# show ip pim rp mapping | section 4.4.4.4

  RP 4.4.4.4 (?), v2v1
    Info source: 4.4.4.4 (?), elected via Auto-RP
         Uptime: 00:26:11, expires: 00:01:49

R5# show ip pim rp mapping | section 4.4.4.4

  RP 4.4.4.4 (?), v2v1
    Info source: 4.4.4.4 (?), elected via Auto-RP
         Uptime: 00:26:40, expires: 00:01:19

R5# show ip pim rp mapping | section 4.4.4.4

  RP 4.4.4.4 (?), v2v1
    Info source: 4.4.4.4 (?), elected via Auto-RP
         Uptime: 00:27:02, expires: 00:00:58

R5# show ip pim rp mapping | section 4.4.4.4

  RP 4.4.4.4 (?), v2v1
    Info source: 4.4.4.4 (?), elected via Auto-RP
         Uptime: 00:27:48, expires: 00:00:11

R5# show ip pim rp mapping | section 4.4.4.4

  RP 4.4.4.4 (?), v2v1
    Info source: 4.4.4.4 (?), elected via Auto-RP
         Uptime: 00:27:55, expires: 00:00:04
```

```
R5# show ip pim rp mapping | section 4.4.4.4

  RP 4.4.4.4 (?), v2v1
    Info source: 4.4.4.4 (?), elected via Auto-RP
        Uptime: 00:27:59, expires: 00:00:01

R5# show ip pim rp mapping | section 4.4.4.4

R5# show ip pim rp mapping
PIM Group-to-RP Mappings

This system is an RP-mapping agent (Loopback0)

Group(s) 238.0.0.0/8
  RP 3.3.3.3 (?), v2v1
    Info source: 3.3.3.3 (?), elected via Auto-RP Uptime: 00:31:26, expires:
    00:02:34
```

Finally, the entry has expired and has been removed; therefore, R3 (3.3.3.3) is the RP for groups in the 238.0.0.0/8 range. If the Lo0 interface of R4 is brought back up, it should once again resume its role as the primary RP. Let's test this:

```
On R4:

R4(config)# interface loopback0
R4(config-if)# no shutdown
```

It may take up to 3 minutes for 3.3.3.3 information to show up in the output of the following **show** command:

```
On R5:
R5# show ip pim rp mapping
PIM Group-to-RP Mappings
This system is an RP-mapping agent (Loopback0)

Group(s) 238.0.0.0/8
  RP 4.4.4.4 (?), v2v1
    Info source: 4.4.4.4 (?), elected via Auto-RP
        Uptime: 00:00:05, expires: 00:02:50
  RP 3.3.3.3 (?), v2v1
    Info source: 3.3.3.3 (?), via Auto-RP
        Uptime: 00:18:20, expires: 00:00:15
```

Task 4

Configure R5 such that R6 does not receive the RP announcements.

Let's view the RP mapping on R6 before the configuration:

```
On R6:

R6# show ip pim rp mapping
PIM Group-to-RP Mappings

Group(s) 238.0.0.0/8
  RP 4.4.4.4 (?), v2v1
    Info source: 5.5.5.5 (?), elected via Auto-RP
          Uptime: 00:01:25, expires: 00:02:31
```

The output of the preceding **show** command reveals that R6 receives the RP mapping information from R5 (the MA). The following steps configure filtering of these announcements.

First, configure an access list to deny 224.0.1.40 and permit **any**:

```
R5# show access-lists

R5(config)# access-list 1 deny host 224.0.1.40
R5(config)# access-list 1 permit any
```

Once the access list is configured, you should apply it to the interface facing R6 (in this case, the F0/0 interface). In this configuration, the **ip multicast boundary** command is used. This command sets a boundary for administratively scoped multicast addresses. The purpose of this boundary is to restrict the flooding of multicast packets, especially in asymmetrical networks.

```
R5(config)# interface FastEthernet0/0
R5(config-if)# ip multicast boundary 1
```

Let's verify the configuration.

Note R5 will no longer send the **RP-Discovery** messages to R6, and as a result of that, the RP mapping will expire, as shown here:

```
On R6:
R6# show ip pim rp mapping
PIM Group-to-RP Mappings
```

```
Group(s) 238.0.0.0/8
  RP 4.4.4.4 (?), v2v1
    Info source: 5.5.5.5 (?), elected via Auto-RP
        Uptime: 00:02:19, expires: 00:02:37

R6# show ip pim rp mapping
PIM Group-to-RP Mappings

Group(s) 238.0.0.0/8
  RP 4.4.4.4 (?), v2v1
    Info source: 5.5.5.5 (?), elected via Auto-RP
        Uptime: 00:02:59, expires: 00:01:57

R6# show ip pim rp mapping

PIM Group-to-RP Mappings

Group(s) 238.0.0.0/8
  RP 4.4.4.4 (?), v2v1
    Info source: 5.5.5.5 (?), elected via Auto-RP
        Uptime: 00:04:28, expires: 00:00:28

R6# show ip pim rp mapping
PIM Group-to-RP Mappings

Group(s) 238.0.0.0/8
  RP 4.4.4.4 (?), v2v1
    Info source: 5.5.5.5 (?), elected via Auto-RP
        Uptime: 00:04:54, expires: 00:00:03

R6# show ip pim rp mapping
PIM Group-to-RP Mappings
```

Once the timer expires, R6 will no longer have the RP mappings.

Task 5

Configure R3 to be the RP for 224.1.1.1 only.

Since the task states "only," you *must* remove the previously configured access list and configure a new one to permit 224.1.1.1:

```
On R3:

R3(config)# no access-list 1
R3(config)# access-list 1 permit host 224.1.1.1
```

```
R3# show ip pim rp mapping
PIM Group-to-RP Mappings
This system is an RP (Auto-RP)


Group(s) 224.0.0.0/4
  RP 3.3.3.3 (?), v2v1
    Info source: 5.5.5.5 (?), elected via Auto-RP
        Uptime: 00:00:18, expires: 00:02:52
Group(s) 224.1.1.1/32
  RP 3.3.3.3 (?), v2v1
    Info source: 5.5.5.5 (?), elected via Auto-RP
        Uptime: 00:00:08, expires: 00:02:50
Group(s) 238.0.0.0/8
  RP 4.4.4.4 (?), v2v1
    Info source: 5.5.5.5 (?), elected via Auto-RP
        Uptime: 00:12:51, expires: 00:02:49


On R1:


R1# show ip pim rp mapping
PIM Group-to-RP Mappings


Group(s) 224.0.0.0/4
  RP 3.3.3.3 (?), v2v1
    Info source: 5.5.5.5 (R5), elected via Auto-RP
        Uptime: 00:01:22, expires: 00:01:48
Group(s) 224.1.1.1/32
  RP 3.3.3.3 (?), v2v1
    Info source: 5.5.5.5 (R5), elected via Auto-RP
        Uptime: 00:01:12, expires: 00:02:58
Group(s) 238.0.0.0/8
  RP 4.4.4.4 (R4), v2v1
    Info source: 5.5.5.5 (R5), elected via Auto-RP
        Uptime: 00:13:55, expires: 00:02:58
```

Task 6

Configure the Lo0 interface of R1 to join the group 224.1.1.1. This router should be
configured such that it responds to pings generated by all routers in this topology:

```
On R1:


R1(config)# interface loopback0
R1(config-if)# ip igmp join-group 224.1.1.1
```

Let's test the configuration:

```
On R2:


R2# ping 224.1.1.1


Type escape sequence to abort.
Sending 1, 100-byte ICMP Echos to 224.1.1.1, timeout is 2 seconds:

Reply to request 0 from 1.1.1.1, 4 ms
Reply to request 0 from 1.1.1.1, 8 ms


On R3:


R3# ping 224.1.1.1


Type escape sequence to abort.
Sending 1, 100-byte ICMP Echos to 224.1.1.1, timeout is 2 seconds:

Reply to request 0 from 1.1.1.1, 32 ms
Reply to request 0 from 1.1.1.1, 44 ms
Reply to request 0 from 1.1.1.1, 32 ms


On R4:


R4# ping 224.1.1.1


Type escape sequence to abort.
Sending 1, 100-byte ICMP Echos to 224.1.1.1, timeout is 2 seconds:

Reply to request 0 from 1.1.1.1, 4 ms
Reply to request 0 from 1.1.1.1, 4 ms


On R5:


R5# ping 224.1.1.1


Type escape sequence to abort.
Sending 1, 100-byte ICMP Echos to 224.1.1.1, timeout is 2 seconds:

Reply to request 0 from 1.1.1.1, 4 ms
Reply to request 0 from 1.1.1.1, 32 ms
Reply to request 0 from 1.1.1.1, 4 ms


On R6:


R6# ping 224.1.1.1
```

```
Type escape sequence to abort.
Sending 1, 100-byte ICMP Echos to 224.1.1.1, timeout is 2 seconds:
.


!Since Auto-RP will not work on R6, as RP-Discovery messages are blocked by R5,
!static RP mapping is implemented as the solution to this task.


On R6:

R6# show access-lists

R6(config)# access-list 1 permit host 224.1.1.1
R6(config)# ip pim rp-address 3.3.3.3 1


R6# ping 224.1.1.1

Type escape sequence to abort.
Sending 1, 100-byte ICMP Echos to 224.1.1.1, timeout is 2 seconds:

Reply to request 0 from 1.1.1.1, 52 ms
Reply to request 0 from 1.1.1.1, 72 ms
```

Task 7

Configure the Lo0 interface of R1 to join group 224.10.10.10. This router should be
configured such that it responds to pings generated by all routers in this topology:

```
On R1:

R1(config-if)# interface loopback0
R1(config-if)# ip igmp join-group 224.10.10.10
```

Let's verify the configuration:

```
On R1:

R1# show ip igmp groups

IGMP Connected Group Membership
Group Address    Interface    Uptime     Expires   Last Reporter  Group Accounted
224.10.10.10     Loopback0    00:00:10   00:02:49  1.1.1.1
224.1.1.1        Loopback0    00:05:19   00:02:41  1.1.1.1
224.0.1.40       Loopback0    01:11:23   00:02:37  1.1.1.1
```

Now we can test the configuration:

```
On R2:


R2# ping 224.10.10.10


Type escape sequence to abort.
Sending 1, 100-byte ICMP Echos to 224.10.10.10, timeout is 2 seconds:

Reply to request 0 from 1.1.1.1, 4 ms
Reply to request 0 from 1.1.1.1, 12 ms


On R3:

R3# ping 224.10.10.10


Type escape sequence to abort.
Sending 1, 100-byte ICMP Echos to 224.10.10.10, timeout is 2 seconds:

Reply to request 0 from 1.1.1.1, 32 ms
Reply to request 0 from 1.1.1.1, 44 ms
Reply to request 0 from 1.1.1.1, 32 ms


On R4:

R4# ping 224.10.10.10


Type escape sequence to abort.
Sending 1, 100-byte ICMP Echos to 224.10.10.10, timeout is 2 seconds:

Reply to request 0 from 1.1.1.1, 4 ms
Reply to request 0 from 1.1.1.1, 8 ms


On R5:

R5# ping 224.10.10.10


Type escape sequence to abort.
Sending 1, 100-byte ICMP Echos to 224.10.10.10, timeout is 2 seconds:

Reply to request 0 from 1.1.1.1, 4 ms
Reply to request 0 from 1.1.1.1, 8 ms
```

```
On R6:

R6# ping 224.10.10.10

Type escape sequence to abort.
Sending 1, 100-byte ICMP Echos to 224.10.10.10, timeout is 2 seconds:

Reply to request 0 from 1.1.1.1, 4 ms
Reply to request 0 from 1.1.1.1, 8 ms

R6# show ip mroute | s 224.10.10.10

(*, 224.10.10.10), 00:08:37/00:00:45, RP 0.0.0.0, flags: D
  Incoming interface: Null, RPF nbr 0.0.0.0
  Outgoing interface list:
    FastEthernet0/0, Forward/Sparse-Dense, 00:02:00/stopped
(The rest of the output is omitted for brevity)
```

Note   R6 was able to reach 224.10.10.10 because the interface of this router is configured as **sparse-dense-mode**. By default, when an interface is configured with **ip pim sparse-dense-mode**, the router will use PIM sparse mode (SM) for groups it has an RP mappings for and use PIM dense mode (DM) for groups it does not. In the event of an RP failure, all traffic will be *dense mode forwarded*. This situation may be undesirable and can be prevented with the use of the **no ip pim dm-fallback** command. We explore this feature in the following task.

Task 8

Configure the routers to disable the use of PIM DM for groups with no RP:

```
On All Routers:

Rx(config)# no ip pim dm-fallback
```

Let's test the configuration:

```
On R2:

R2# ping 224.10.10.10

Type escape sequence to abort.
Sending 1, 100-byte ICMP Echos to 224.10.10.10, timeout is 2 seconds:
.
```

```
On R3:


R3# ping 224.10.10.10


Type escape sequence to abort.
Sending 1, 100-byte ICMP Echos to 224.10.10.10, timeout is 2 seconds:
.


On R4:


R4# ping 224.10.10.10


Type escape sequence to abort.
Sending 1, 100-byte ICMP Echos to 224.10.10.10, timeout is 2 seconds:
.


On R5:


R5# ping 224.10.10.10


Type escape sequence to abort.
Sending 1, 100-byte ICMP Echos to 224.10.10.10, timeout is 2 seconds:

.


On R6:


R6# ping 224.10.10.10


Type escape sequence to abort.
Sending 1, 100-byte ICMP Echos to 224.10.10.10, timeout is 2 seconds:
.
```

The pings failed because there are no RPs for 224.10.10.10 group.

Let's test the configuration further:

```
On All Routers


Rx(config)# ip pim dm-fallback


On R2:


R2# ping 224.10.10.10


Type escape sequence to abort.
Sending 1, 100-byte ICMP Echos to 224.10.10.10, timeout is 2 seconds:
```

```
Reply to request 0 from 1.1.1.1, 8 ms
Reply to request 0 from 1.1.1.1, 48 ms


On R3:


R3# ping 224.10.10.10

Type escape sequence to abort.
Sending 1, 100-byte ICMP Echos to 224.10.10.10, timeout is 2 seconds:

Reply to request 0 from 1.1.1.1, 144 ms
Reply to request 0 from 1.1.1.1, 200 ms
Reply to request 0 from 1.1.1.1, 160 ms


On R4:


R4# ping 224.10.10.10

Type escape sequence to abort.
Sending 1, 100-byte ICMP Echos to 224.10.10.10, timeout is 2 seconds:

Reply to request 0 from 1.1.1.1, 44 ms
Reply to request 0 from 1.1.1.1, 72 ms


On R5:


R5# ping 224.10.10.10

Type escape sequence to abort.
Sending 1, 100-byte ICMP Echos to 224.10.10.10, timeout is 2 seconds:

Reply to request 0 from 1.1.1.1, 44 ms
Reply to request 0 from 1.1.1.1, 72 ms


On R6:


R6# ping 224.10.10.10

Type escape sequence to abort.
Sending 1, 100-byte ICMP Echos to 224.10.10.10, timeout is 2 seconds:

Reply to request 0 from 1.1.1.1, 72 ms
Reply to request 0 from 1.1.1.1, 72 ms
```

> **Note**   The routers can reach 224.10.10.10 once again using PIM dense mode.

Erase the startup configuration of the routers and SW1 and reload them before proceeding to the next lab.

Lab 14-4: Bootstrap Router (BSR)

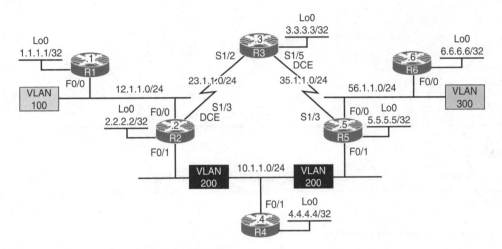

Figure 14-4   *Configuring Boot Strap Router*

Figure 14-4 illustrates the topology that will be used in the following lab.

Task 1

Configure OSPF Area 0 on all interfaces:

```
On All Routers:

Rx(config)# router ospf 1
Rx(config-router)# network 0.0.0.0 0.0.0.0 area 0
```

Let's verify the configuration:

```
On R1:

R1# show ip route ospf | begin Gate
Gateway of last resort is not set

      2.0.0.0/32 is subnetted, 1 subnets
O        2.2.2.2 [110/2] via 12.1.1.2, 00:00:18, FastEthernet0/0
```

```
       3.0.0.0/32 is subnetted, 1 subnets
O         3.3.3.3 [110/783] via 12.1.1.2, 00:00:18, FastEthernet0/0
       4.0.0.0/32 is subnetted, 1 subnets
O         4.4.4.4 [110/3] via 12.1.1.2, 00:00:08, FastEthernet0/0
       5.0.0.0/32 is subnetted, 1 subnets
O         5.5.5.5 [110/3] via 12.1.1.2, 00:00:08, FastEthernet0/0
       6.0.0.0/32 is subnetted, 1 subnets
O         6.6.6.6 [110/4] via 12.1.1.2, 00:00:08, FastEthernet0/0
       10.0.0.0/24 is subnetted, 1 subnets
O         10.1.1.0 [110/2] via 12.1.1.2, 00:00:08, FastEthernet0/0
       23.0.0.0/24 is subnetted, 1 subnets
O         23.1.1.0 [110/782] via 12.1.1.2, 00:00:18, FastEthernet0/0
       35.0.0.0/24 is subnetted, 1 subnets
O         35.1.1.0 [110/783] via 12.1.1.2, 00:00:08, FastEthernet0/0
       56.0.0.0/24 is subnetted, 1 subnets
O         56.1.1.0 [110/3] via 12.1.1.2, 00:00:08, FastEthernet0/0
```

Task 2

Configure **pim sparse-mode** on all the interfaces in this topology:

```
On R1:

R1(config)# ip multicast-routing

R1(config)# interface loopback0
R1(config-if)# ip pim sparse-mode

R1(config-if)# interface FastEthernet0/0
R1(config-if)# ip pim sparse-mode

On R2:

R2(config)# ip multicast-routing

R2(config)# interface loopback0
R2(config-if)# ip pim sparse-mode

R2(config)# interface FastEthernet0/0
R2(config-if)# ip pim sparse-mode

R2(config)# interface FastEthernet0/1
R2(config-if)# ip pim sparse-mode
```

```
R2(config)# interface serial1/3
R2(config-if)# ip pim sparse-mode

On R3:

R3(config)# ip multicast-routing

R3(config)# interface loopback0
R3(config-if)# ip pim sparse-mode

R3(config)# interface serial1/2
R3(config-if)# ip pim sparse-mode

R3(config)# interface serial1/5
R3(config-if)# ip pim sparse-mode

On R4:

R4(config)# ip multicast-routing

R4(config)# interface loopback0
R4(config-if)# ip pim sparse-mode

R4(config)# interface FastEthernet0/1
R4(config-if)# ip pim sparse-mode

On R5:

R5(config)# ip multicast-routing

R5(config)# interface loopback0
R5(config-if)# ip pim sparse-mode

R5(config)# interface FastEthernet0/0
R5(config-if)# ip pim sparse-mode

R5(config)# interface FastEthernet0/1
R5(config-if)# ip pim sparse-mode

R5(config)# interface serial1/3
R5(config-if)# ip pim sparse-mode

On R6:

R6(config)# ip multicast-routing
```

```
R6(config)# interface loopback0
R6(config-if)# ip pim sparse-mode

R6(config)# interface FastEthernet0/0
R6(config-if)# ip pim sparse-mode
```

Let's verify the configuration:

```
On R1:

R1# show ip pim neighbor | begin Interface

Neighbor         Interface          Uptime/Expires    Ver   DR
Address                                                     Prio/Mode
12.1.1.2         FastEthernet0/0    00:03:42/00:01:29 v2    1 / DR S P G


On R2:

R2# show ip pim neighbor | begin Interface

Neighbor         Interface          Uptime/Expires    Ver   DR
Address                                                     Prio/Mode
12.1.1.1         FastEthernet0/0    00:03:42/00:01:28 v2    1 / S P G
10.1.1.5         FastEthernet0/1    00:01:28/00:01:15 v2    1 / DR S P G
10.1.1.4         FastEthernet0/1    00:02:03/00:01:15 v2    1 / S P G
23.1.1.3         Serial1/3          00:03:06/00:01:36 v2    1 / S P G


On R3:

R3# show ip pim neighbor | begin Interface

Neighbor         Interface          Uptime/Expires    Ver   DR
Address                                                     Prio/Mode
23.1.1.2         Serial1/2          00:03:06/00:01:36 v2    1 / S P G
35.1.1.5         Serial1/5          00:01:33/00:01:40 v2    1 / S P G


On R4:

R4# show ip pim neighbor | begin Interface

Neighbor         Interface          Uptime/Expires    Ver   DR
Address                                                     Prio/Mode
10.1.1.5         FastEthernet0/1    00:01:28/00:01:15 v2    1 / DR S P G
10.1.1.2         FastEthernet0/1    00:02:03/00:01:15 v2    1 / S P G
```

```
On R5:

R5# show ip pim neighbor

Neighbor           Interface                Uptime/Expires      Ver    DR
Address                                                                Prio/Mode
35.1.1.3           Serial1/3                00:01:33/00:01:40 v2     1 / S P G
10.1.1.2           FastEthernet0/1          00:01:28/00:01:15 v2     1 / S P G
10.1.1.4           FastEthernet0/1          00:01:28/00:01:15 v2     1 / S P G
56.1.1.6           FastEthernet0/0          00:00:23/00:01:20 v2     1 / DR S P G

On R6:

R6# show ip pim neighbor

Neighbor           Interface                Uptime/Expires      Ver    DR
Address                                                                Prio/Mode
56.1.1.5           FastEthernet0/0          00:00:23/00:01:20 v2     1 / S P G
```

Task 3

Configure R3 and R4 as the RP for all groups; R3 should be the primary and R4 should be the backup. These routers should use their Lo0's IP address as the source of their announcements every 30 seconds. You should not change the PIM mode or change the IP addressing of the interface(s) to accomplish this task.

The following are the possible choices:

- Auto-RP
- Static RP
- BSR
- Anycast RP

To resolve this task, Auto-RP or static RP cannot be used because R4 has a higher IP address and it will always be chosen as the primary RP. Therefore, BSR is the only choice.

The question should be where to place the bootstrap routers. The answer is, any two routers. Why two? Well, the task asks for a redundant mapping.

In the following solution, RP candidates are also configured as the BSRs. A **debug ip pim bsr** command is configured to see the messages generated by the RP and the BSR.

```
On R3:

R3# debug ip pim bsr
PIM-BSR debugging is on

R3(config)# ip pim rp-candidate loopback0 interval 30
```

You should see the following debug output on your console:

```
PIM-BSR(0): Build v2 Candidate-RP advertisement for 3.3.3.3 priority 0, holdtime 150
PIM-BSR(0):   Candidate RP's group prefix 224.0.0.0/4
PIM-BSR(0): no bootstrap router address
```

Note   The advertisements are generated from the IP address of the loopback0 interface. The priority is set to zero and the holdtime is set to 150. The holdtime is 2.5 times the interval in which these messages are generated; by default these messages are generated every 60 seconds. Because a BSR is not configured, the last line of the debug states that the local router does not see a BSR.

Let's configure the BSR:

```
R3(config)# ip pim bsr-candidate loopback0

PIM-BSR(0): Build v2 Candidate-RP advertisement for 3.3.3.3 priority 0,
holdtime 150
PIM-BSR(0):   Candidate RP's group prefix 224.0.0.0/4
PIM-BSR(0): Send Candidate RP Advertisement to 3.3.3.3
PIM-BSR(0):   RP 3.3.3.3, 1 Group Prefixes, Priority 0, Holdtime 150
PIM-BSR(0): RP-set for 224.0.0.0/4
PIM-BSR(0):   RP(1) 3.3.3.3, holdtime 150 sec priority 0
PIM-BSR(0): Bootstrap message for 3.3.3.3 originated
```

Note   Now that candidate RP knows the IP address of the BSR, it sends a unicast message to the bootstrap router to identify itself as a candidate RP.

In the following configuration, R4 is configured as candidate RP with a priority of 200, because a lower priority value has more preference; R3 is elected as the RP:

```
On R4:

R4(config)# ip pim rp-candidate loopback0 interval 30 priority 200
R4(config)# ip pim bsr-candidate loopback0
```

Contrary to RP election, where lower priority has more preference, in BSR election, the higher priority has more preference and the higher IP address is used as the tiebreaker.

Let's verify the configuration:

```
On R3:


R3# undebug all


R3# show ip pim rp mapping
PIM Group-to-RP Mappings
This system is a candidate RP (v2)


Group(s) 224.0.0.0/4
  RP 3.3.3.3 (?), v2
    Info source: 4.4.4.4 (?), via bootstrap, priority 0, holdtime 150
        Uptime: 00:06:14, expires: 00:02:06
  RP 4.4.4.4 (?), v2
    Info source: 4.4.4.4 (?), via bootstrap, priority 200, holdtime 150
        Uptime: 00:04:26, expires: 00:02:05
```

R4 and R3 are both configured as Candidate-BSRs. By default, the priority of these routers is set to zero; therefore, the router with a higher source IP address (4.4.4.4 versus 3.3.3.3) is elected as the BSR.

Contrary to Auto-RP, in BSR, the C-BSR collects all RP announcements and creates a Rendezvous Point Set (RP-SET); the RP-SET is then advertised to all DRs.

Once the DRs receive the RP-SET, they will elect an RP from the list for a given group. Luckily, all DR routers use the same calculations to elect an RP; therefore, the result of the election will be consistent across all routers.

Let's verify the configuration:

```
On R1:


R1# show ip pim rp mapping
PIM Group-to-RP Mappings


Group(s) 224.0.0.0/4
  RP 3.3.3.3 (?), v2
    Info source: 4.4.4.4 (?), via bootstrap, priority 0, holdtime 150
        Uptime: 00:05:19, expires: 00:02:04
  RP 4.4.4.4 (?), v2
    Info source: 4.4.4.4 (?), via bootstrap, priority 200, holdtime 150
        Uptime: 00:03:29, expires: 00:02:04
```

```
On R2:


R2# show ip pim rp mapping
PIM Group-to-RP Mappings


Group(s) 224.0.0.0/4
  RP 3.3.3.3 (?), v2
    Info source: 4.4.4.4 (?), via bootstrap, priority 0, holdtime 150
        Uptime: 00:11:58, expires: 00:02:24
  RP 4.4.4.4 (?), v2
    Info source: 4.4.4.4 (?), via bootstrap, priority 200, holdtime 150
        Uptime: 00:10:10, expires: 00:02:22


On R5:


R5# show ip pim rp mapping
PIM Group-to-RP Mappings


Group(s) 224.0.0.0/4
  RP 3.3.3.3 (?), v2
    Info source: 4.4.4.4 (?), via bootstrap, priority 0, holdtime 150
        Uptime: 00:12:27, expires: 00:01:57
  RP 4.4.4.4 (?), v2
    Info source: 4.4.4.4 (?), via bootstrap, priority 200, holdtime 150
        Uptime: 00:10:38, expires: 00:01:56


On R6:


R6# show ip pim rp mapping

PIM Group-to-RP Mappings

Group(s) 224.0.0.0/4
  RP 3.3.3.3 (?), v2
    Info source: 4.4.4.4 (?), via bootstrap, priority 0, holdtime 150
        Uptime: 00:12:58, expires: 00:02:21
  RP 4.4.4.4 (?), v2
    Info source: 4.4.4.4 (?), via bootstrap, priority 200, holdtime 150
        Uptime: 00:11:10, expires: 00:02:22
```

Let's further verify the configuration:

```
On R1:


R1# show ip pim bsr-router


PIMv2 Bootstrap information
  BSR address: 4.4.4.4 (?)
  Uptime:       00:11:33, BSR Priority: 0, Hash mask length: 0
  Expires:      00:01:36


On R2:


R2# show ip pim bsr-router


PIMv2 Bootstrap information
  BSR address: 4.4.4.4 (?)
  Uptime:       00:12:12, BSR Priority: 0, Hash mask length: 0
  Expires:      00:01:57


On R3:


R3# show ip pim bsr-router


PIMv2 Bootstrap information
  BSR address: 4.4.4.4 (?)
  Uptime:       00:12:55, BSR Priority: 0, Hash mask length: 0
  Expires:      00:01:14
This system is a candidate BSR
  Candidate BSR address: 3.3.3.3, priority: 0, hash mask length: 0
  Candidate RP: 3.3.3.3(Loopback0)
    Holdtime 75 seconds
    Advertisement interval 30 seconds
    Next advertisement in 00:00:04


On R4:


R4# show ip pim bsr-router


PIMv2 Bootstrap information
This system is the Bootstrap Router (BSR)
  BSR address: 4.4.4.4 (?)
  Uptime:       00:12:13, BSR Priority: 0, Hash mask length: 0
  Next bootstrap message in 00:00:47
```

```
Candidate RP: 4.4.4.4(Loopback0)
    Holdtime 75 seconds
    Advertisement interval 30 seconds
    Next advertisement in 00:00:18
    Candidate RP priority : 200


On R5:


R5# show ip pim bsr-router


PIMv2 Bootstrap information
  BSR address: 4.4.4.4 (?)
  Uptime:       00:12:12, BSR Priority: 0, Hash mask length: 0
  Expires:      00:01:57


On R6:


R6# show ip pim bsr-router


PIMv2 Bootstrap information
  BSR address: 4.4.4.4 (?)
  Uptime:       00:12:12, BSR Priority: 0, Hash mask length: 0
  Expires:      00:01:57
```

Task 4

Configure the Lo0 interface of R1 to join 239.1.1.1 and then ensure that R3, R4, and R5 can successfully ping this group:

```
On R1:


R1(config)# interface loopback0
R1(config-if)# ip igmp join-group 239.1.1.1


On R3:


R3# ping 239.1.1.1


Type escape sequence to abort.
Sending 1, 100-byte ICMP Echos to 239.1.1.1, timeout is 2 seconds:


Reply to request 0 from 1.1.1.1, 72 ms
Reply to request 0 from 1.1.1.1, 104 ms
Reply to request 0 from 1.1.1.1, 92 ms
```

```
On R4:

R4# ping 239.1.1.1

Type escape sequence to abort.
Sending 1, 100-byte ICMP Echos to 239.1.1.1, timeout is 2 seconds:

Reply to request 0 from 1.1.1.1, 4 ms
Reply to request 0 from 1.1.1.1, 20 ms

On R5:

R5# ping 239.1.1.1

Type escape sequence to abort.
Sending 1, 100-byte ICMP Echos to 239.1.1.1, timeout is 2 seconds:

Reply to request 0 from 1.1.1.1, 4 ms
Reply to request 0 from 1.1.1.1, 60 ms
Reply to request 0 from 1.1.1.1, 36 ms
Reply to request 0 from 1.1.1.1, 12 ms

On R5:

R5# show ip mroute | section 239.1.1.1

(*, 239.1.1.1), 00:01:52/stopped, RP 3.3.3.3, flags: SPF
  Incoming interface: Serial1/3, RPF nbr 35.1.1.3
  Outgoing interface list: Null
     (The rest of the output is omitted for brevity)
```

As expected, the RP for the group is R3 because it has a lower RP priority.

Erase the startup configuration and reload the routers before proceeding to the next lab.

Chapter 15

MPLS and L3VPNs

Multiprotocol Label Switching (MPLS) is a label switching technology. With MPLS, instead of relying on IP addresses in the IP header to route packets, the router actually builds a label switching path, or LSP, for packets that require sustained forwarding treatment. This is also known as a *forwarding equivalence class* (FEC) and includes source destination IPs, IP precedents, and so on.

In the packet, we can switch based on the MPLS label that the packet carries, while the MPLS label itself is swapped along the way until the packet reaches the last MPLS router closest to the destination. Before the packet label switching can happen, the router needs to know what label to use, and that is through a label distribution protocol, or LDP.

A router allocates local labels to the route it has in its routing table; then it exchanges labels with its LDP neighbors to complete the label switching path. There's actually a lot more detail that goes on underneath the protocols in how the labels are actually distributed. Because LDP is a fundamental component of MPLS, the first lab in our MPLS exploration starts with looking at LDP and its configuration.

In this chapter, we're going to be looking at LDP, including the LDP label exchange and how it actually happens. Then we're going to look deep into the packet of LDP and see what that looks like.

Lab 15-1: Label Distribution Protocol

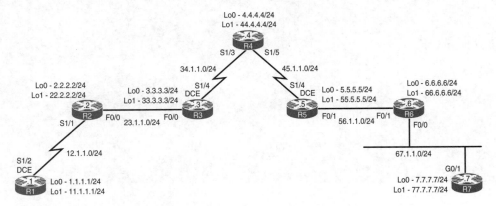

Figure 15-1 *Configuring the Label Distribution Protocol*

Task 1

Configure the topology shown in Figure 15-1. Do not configure any routing protocol.
Use a VLAN ID of your choice.

```
On SW1:

SW1(config)# interface range FastEthernet0/2-3
SW1(config-if-range)# switchport mode access
SW1(config-if-range)# switchport access vlan 23
% Access VLAN does not exist. Creating vlan 23
SW1(config-if-range)# no shutdown

SW1(config)# interface range FastEthernet0/6-7
SW1(config-if-range)# switchport mode access
SW1(config-if-range)# switchport access vlan 67
% Access VLAN does not exist. Creating vlan 67
SW1(config-if-range)# no shutdown


On SW2:

SW2(config)# interface range FastEthernet0/5-6
SW2(config-if-range)# switchport mode access
SW2(config-if-range)# switchport access vlan 56
% Access VLAN does not exist. Creating vlan 56
SW2(config-if-range)# no shutdown
```

```
On R1:

R1(config)# interface loopback0
R1(config-if)# ip address 1.1.1.1 255.255.255.0

R1(config)# interface loopback1
R1(config-if)# ip address 11.1.1.1 255.255.255.0

R1(config)# interface serial1/2
R1(config-if)# clock rate 64000
R1(config-if)# ip address 12.1.1.1 255.255.255.0
R1(config-if)# no shutdown

On R2:

R2(config)# interface loopback0
R2(config-if)# ip address 2.2.2.2 255.255.255.0

R2(config)# interface loopback1
R2(config-if)# ip address 22.2.2.2 255.255.255.0

R2(config)# interface serial1/1
R2(config-if)# ip address 12.1.1.2 255.255.255.0
R2(config-if)# no shutdown

R2(config-if)# interface FastEthernet0/0
R2(config-if)# ip address 23.1.1.2 255.255.255.0
R2(config-if)# no shutdown

On R3:

R3(config)# interface loopback0
R3(config-if)# ip address 3.3.3.3 255.255.255.0

R3(config)# interface loopback1
R3(config-if)# ip address 33.3.3.3 255.255.255.0

R3(config)# interface FastEthernet0/0
R3(config-if)# ip address 23.1.1.3 255.255.255.0
R3(config-if)# no shutdown

R3(config)# interface serial1/4
R3(config-if)# clock rate 64000
R3(config-if)# ip address 34.1.1.3 255.255.255.0
R3(config-if)# no shutdown
```

On R4:

```
R4(config)# interface loopback0
R4(config-if)# ip address 4.4.4.4 255.255.255.0

R4(config)# interface loopback1
R4(config-if)# ip address 44.4.4.4 255.255.255.0

R4(config)# interface serial1/3
R4(config-if)# ip address 34.1.1.4 255.255.255.0
R4(config-if)# no shutdown

R4(config)# interface serial1/5
R4(config-if)# clock rate 64000
R4(config-if)# ip address 45.1.1.4 255.255.255.0
R4(config-if)# no shutdown
```

On R5:

```
R5(config)# interface loopback0
R5(config-if)# ip address 5.5.5.5 255.255.255.0

R5(config)# interface loopback1
R5(config-if)# ip address 55.5.5.5 255.255.255.0

R5(config)# interface serial1/4
R5(config-if)# ip address 45.1.1.5 255.255.255.0
R5(config-if)# no shutdown

R5(config)# interface FastEthernet0/1
R5(config-if)# ip address 56.1.1.5 255.255.255.0
R5(config-if)# no shutdown
```

On R6:

```
R6(config)# interface loopback0
R6(config-if)# ip address 6.6.6.6 255.255.255.0

R6(config)# interface loopback1
R6(config-if)# ip address 66.6.6.6 255.255.255.0

R6(config)# interface FastEthernet0/1
R6(config-if)# ip address 56.1.1.6 255.255.255.0
R6(config-if)# no shutdown
```

```
R6(config)# interface FastEthernet0/0
R6(config-if)# ip address 67.1.1.6 255.255.255.0
R6(config-if)# no shutdown


On R7:


R7(config)# interface loopback0
R7(config-if)# ip address 7.7.7.7 255.255.255.0


R7(config)# interface loopback1
R7(config-if)# ip address 77.7.7.7 255.255.255.0


R7(config)# interface GigabitEthernet0/0
R7(config-if)# ip address 67.1.1.7 255.255.255.0
R7(config-if)# no shutdown
```

Task 2

Configure OSPF Area 0 on all links in the topology shown in Figure 15-1, except loopback1 interfaces. Configure the OSPF router ID (RID) of these routers to be 0.0.0.x, where x is the router number. The loopback0 interface of R7 should be advertised with its correct mask.

```
On R1:


R1(config)# router ospf 1
R1(config-router)# router-id 0.0.0.1
R1(config-router)# network 12.1.1.1 0.0.0.0 area 0
R1(config-router)# network 1.1.1.1 0.0.0.0 area 0


On R2:


R2(config)# router ospf 1
R2(config-router)# router-id 0.0.0.2
R2(config-router)# network 12.1.1.2 0.0.0.0 area 0
R2(config-router)# network 2.2.2.2 0.0.0.0 area 0
R2(config-router)# network 23.1.1.2 0.0.0.0 area 0
```

You should see the following console message:

```
%OSPF-5-ADJCHG: Process 1, Nbr 0.0.0.1 on Serial1/1 from LOADING to FULL,
Loading Done
```

```
On R3:

R3(config)# router ospf 1
R3(config-router)# router-id 0.0.0.3
R3(config-router)# network 3.3.3.3 0.0.0.0 area 0
R3(config-router)# network 34.1.1.3 0.0.0.0 area 0
R3(config-router)# network 23.1.1.3 0.0.0.0 area 0
```

As adjacencies form we will see the system post notifications on the console.

```
%OSPF-5-ADJCHG: Process 1, Nbr 0.0.0.2 on FastEthernet0/0 from LOADING to FULL,
Loading Done
```

```
On R4:

R4(config)# router ospf 1
R4(config-router)# router-id 0.0.0.4
R4(config-router)# network 45.1.1.4 0.0.0.0 area 0
R4(config-router)# network 4.4.4.4 0.0.0.0 area 0
R4(config-router)# network 34.1.1.4 0.0.0.0 area 0
```

Again, console notifications will inform us as neighbor adjacencies come up.

```
%OSPF-5-ADJCHG: Process 1, Nbr 0.0.0.3 on Serial1/3 from LOADING to FULL,
Loading Done
```

```
On R5:

R5(config)# router ospf 1
R5(config-router)# router-id 0.0.0.5
R5(config-router)# network 5.5.5.5 0.0.0.0 area 0
R5(config-router)# network 56.1.1.5 0.0.0.0 area 0
R5(config-router)# network 45.1.1.5 0.0.0.0 area 0
```

You should see the following console message:

```
%OSPF-5-ADJCHG: Process 1, Nbr 0.0.0.4 on Serial1/4 from LOADING to FULL,
Loading Done
```

```
On R6:

R6(config)# router ospf 1
R6(config-router)# router-id 0.0.0.6
R6(config-router)# network 6.6.6.6 0.0.0.0 area 0
R6(config-router)# network 67.1.1.6 0.0.0.0 area 0
R6(config-router)# network 56.1.1.6 0.0.0.0 area 0
```

At this point an adjacency should form with the neighbor identified as 0.0.0.5.

```
%OSPF-5-ADJCHG: Process 1, Nbr 0.0.0.5 on FastEthernet0/1 from LOADING to FULL,
Loading Done
```

```
On R7:

R7(config)# interface loopback0
R7(config-if)# ip ospf net point-to-point

R7(config)# router ospf 1
R7(config-router)# router-id 0.0.0.7
R7(config-router)# network 67.1.1.7 0.0.0.0 area 0
R7(config-router)# network 7.7.7.7 0.0.0.0 area 0
```

We should see the last adjacency form.

```
%OSPF-5-ADJCHG: Process 1, Nbr 0.0.0.6 on GigabitEthernet0/0 from LOADING to
FULL, Loading Done
```

Let's verify the configuration:

```
On R1:

R1# show ip route ospf | begin Gate
 Gateway of last resort is not set

      2.0.0.0/32 is subnetted, 1 subnets
O        2.2.2.2 [110/65] via 12.1.1.2, 00:00:59, Serial1/2
      3.0.0.0/32 is subnetted, 1 subnets
O        3.3.3.3 [110/66] via 12.1.1.2, 00:00:10, Serial1/2
      4.0.0.0/32 is subnetted, 1 subnets
O        4.4.4.4 [110/130] via 12.1.1.2, 00:00:10, Serial1/2
      5.0.0.0/32 is subnetted, 1 subnets
O        5.5.5.5 [110/194] via 12.1.1.2, 00:00:10, Serial1/2
```

```
        6.0.0.0/32 is subnetted, 1 subnets
O          6.6.6.6 [110/195] via 12.1.1.2, 00:00:10, Serial1/2
        7.0.0.0/24 is subnetted, 1 subnets
O          7.7.7.0 [110/196] via 12.1.1.2, 00:00:10, Serial1/2
        23.0.0.0/24 is subnetted, 1 subnets
O          23.1.1.0 [110/65] via 12.1.1.2, 00:00:20, Serial1/2
        34.0.0.0/24 is subnetted, 1 subnets
O          34.1.1.0 [110/129] via 12.1.1.2, 00:00:10, Serial1/2
        45.0.0.0/24 is subnetted, 1 subnets
O          45.1.1.0 [110/193] via 12.1.1.2, 00:00:10, Serial1/2
        56.0.0.0/24 is subnetted, 1 subnets
O          56.1.1.0 [110/194] via 12.1.1.2, 00:00:10, Serial1/2
        67.0.0.0/24 is subnetted, 1 subnets
O          67.1.1.0 [110/195] via 12.1.1.2, 00:00:10, Serial1/2


On R7:


R7# show ip route ospf | begin Gate
Gateway of last resort is not set


        1.0.0.0/32 is subnetted, 1 subnets
O          1.1.1.1 [110/196] via 67.1.1.6, 00:00:05, GigabitEthernet0/0
        2.0.0.0/32 is subnetted, 1 subnets
O          2.2.2.2 [110/132] via 67.1.1.6, 00:00:05, GigabitEthernet0/0
        3.0.0.0/32 is subnetted, 1 subnets
O          3.3.3.3 [110/131] via 67.1.1.6, 00:00:05, GigabitEthernet0/0
        4.0.0.0/32 is subnetted, 1 subnets
O          4.4.4.4 [110/67] via 67.1.1.6, 00:00:05, GigabitEthernet0/0
        5.0.0.0/32 is subnetted, 1 subnets
O          5.5.5.5 [110/3] via 67.1.1.6, 00:00:05, GigabitEthernet0/0
        6.0.0.0/32 is subnetted, 1 subnets
O          6.6.6.6 [110/2] via 67.1.1.6, 00:00:59, GigabitEthernet0/0
        12.0.0.0/24 is subnetted, 1 subnets
O          12.1.1.0 [110/195] via 67.1.1.6, 00:00:05, GigabitEthernet0/0
        23.0.0.0/24 is subnetted, 1 subnets
O          23.1.1.0 [110/131] via 67.1.1.6, 00:00:05, GigabitEthernet0/0
        34.0.0.0/24 is subnetted, 1 subnets
O          34.1.1.0 [110/130] via 67.1.1.6, 00:00:05, GigabitEthernet0/0
        45.0.0.0/24 is subnetted, 1 subnets
O          45.1.1.0 [110/66] via 67.1.1.6, 00:00:05, GigabitEthernet0/0
        56.0.0.0/24 is subnetted, 1 subnets
O          56.1.1.0 [110/2] via 67.1.1.6, 00:00:59, GigabitEthernet0/0
```

Task 3

Configure the label distribution protocol on the links interconnecting the routers in this topology. Ensure that the LDP router ID (RID) is based on the IP address assigned to the loopback0 interfaces of these routers. You may override a command from the previous task to accomplish this task.

When configuring the label distribution protocol, you must specify the actual protocol that creates and distributes labels. This protocol can be either LDP or TDP; TDP is a Cisco proprietary tag distribution protocol that is obsolete. Therefore, this lab strictly focuses on LDP and *not* TDP.

The **mpls label protocol** command can be configured to specify the label distribution protocol. In IOS releases prior to 12.4, TDP was the default protocol used. The **mpls label protocol ldp** command should be configured in the global configuration mode to enable LDP.

Each label switch router (LSR) that is running LDP will be assigned a router ID. The **mpls ldp router-id** command can be used to set the router ID for a given LSR. The LDP RID defaults to similar rules as OSPF, EIGRP, and BGP, which means that if it is not configured statically, then the numerically highest IP address of any loopback interface is selected as the LDP RID. If a loopback interface does not exist, then the highest IP address configured on the router is chosen as the LDP RID.

It is a good practice to configure the LDP RID manually to ensure that the transport address of the MPLS peer is stable. Remember that LDP advertises its LDP RID as the transport address in the LDP discovery hello messages sent from the interface. Therefore, you must provide reachability for that router ID, where it must be an exact match with the LDP RID in the routing table.

The **mpls ip** command enables MPLS forwarding of IPv4 packets along the normally routed paths; in some documents, this is called *dynamic label switching*.

The following command configures LDP as the label distribution protocol:

```
On All routers:

Rx(config)# mpls label protocol ldp
```

The following command configures the LDP ID of the LSRs based on the IP address of the Lo0 interface:

```
Rx(config)# mpls ldp router-id loopback 0
```

Finally, enable the MPLS forwarding of IPv4 packets along the normal routed paths:

```
On R1:

R1(config)# interface Serial1/2
R1(config-if)# mpls ip

On R2:

R2(config)# interface Serial1/1
R2(config-if)# mpls ip
```

You should receive the following console message stating that the local router has discovered a neighbor—in this case, R1 (1.1.1.1):

```
%LDP-5-NBRCHG: LDP Neighbor 1.1.1.1:0 is UP
```

Note   LDP uses a 6-byte quantity, and the first 4 bytes are the LDP router ID. The LDP router ID was specified earlier using the **MPLS ldp router-id** command, and the last 2 bytes (:0) identify the label space; for a platform-wide label space, the last 2 bytes are always set to 0.

We will continue the configuration by enabling MPLS on the physical interface of R2.

```
R2(config)# interface FastEthernet0/0
R2(config-if)# mpls ip
```

Let's verify the configuration:

```
On R2:

R2# show mpls interfaces

Interface           IP          Tunnel    BGP Static Operational
FastEthernet0/0     Yes (ldp)   No        No  No     Yes
Serial1/1           Yes (ldp)   No        No  No     Yes
```

Note   The output of the preceding command reveals that LDP is running on the F0/0 and S1/1 interfaces of R2.

Let's configure R3:

```
On R3:


R3(config)# interface Serial1/4
R3(config-if)# mpls ip


R3(config)# interface FastEthernet0/0
R3(config-if)# mpls ip
```

You should see the following console message:

```
%LDP-5-NBRCHG: LDP Neighbor 2.2.2.2:0 (1) is UP
```

Let's verify the configuration:

```
On R3:

R3# show mpls interfaces

Interface              IP           Tunnel   BGP Static Operational
FastEthernet0/0        Yes (ldp)    No       No  No     Yes
Serial1/4              Yes (ldp)    No       No  No     Yes
```

Let's configure R4:

```
On R4:


R4(config)# interface Serial1/3
R4(config-if)# mpls ip


R4(config)# interface Serial1/5
R4(config-if)# mpls ip
```

You should see the following console message:

```
%LDP-5-NBRCHG: LDP Neighbor 3.3.3.3:0 (1) is UP
```

Let's verify the configuration:

```
On R4:


R4# show mpls interfaces

Interface            IP            Tunnel    BGP Static Operational
Serial1/3            Yes (ldp)     No        No  No     Yes
Serial1/5            Yes (ldp)     No        No  No     Yes
```

Let's configure R5:

```
On R5:


R5(config)# interface FastEthernet0/1
R5(config-if)# mpls ip

R5(config)# interface Serial1/4
R5(config-if)# mpls ip
```

You should see the following console message:

```
%LDP-5-NBRCHG: LDP Neighbor 4.4.4.4:0 (1) is UP
```

Let's verify the configuration:

```
On R5:


R5# show mpls interfaces

Interface            IP            Tunnel    BGP Static Operational
FastEthernet0/1      Yes (ldp)     No        No  No     Yes
Serial1/4            Yes (ldp)     No        No  No     Yes
```

Let's configure R6:

```
On R6:


R6(config)# interface FastEthernet0/1
R6(config-if)# mpls ip

R6(config)# interface FastEthernet0/0
R6(config-if)# mpls ip
```

You should see the following console message:

```
%LDP-5-NBRCHG: LDP Neighbor 5.5.5.5:0 (1) is UP
```

Let's verify the configuration:

```
On R6:

R6# show mpls interface

Interface              IP            Tunnel    BGP Static Operational
FastEthernet0/0        Yes (ldp)     No        No  No     Yes
FastEthernet0/1        Yes (ldp)     No        No  No     Yes
```

Let's configure R7:

```
On R7:

R7(config)# interface GigabitEthernet0/0
R7(config-if)# mpls ip
```

You should see the following console message:

```
%LDP-5-NBRCHG: LDP Neighbor 6.6.6.6:0 (1) is UP
```

Let's verify the configuration:

```
On R7:

R7# show mpls interfaces

Interface              IP            Tunnel    BGP Static Operational
GigabitEthernet0/0     Yes (ldp)     No        No  No     Yes
```

Once the LSRs are configured, they will attempt to discover neighbors. This discovery uses hello messages. The hello messages are UDP packets sent to a destination multicast address of 224.0.0.2, with a source and destination port of 646. Every hello message has a hold timer; by default, the hello messages are sent every 5 seconds, and the hold timer is set to 15 seconds.

Let's view the discover messages:

```
On R1:

R1# show access-list

R1(config)# access-list 100 permit udp host 12.1.1.1 eq 646 any

R1# Debug ip packet detail 100
IP packet debugging is on (detailed)

IP: s=12.1.1.1 (local), d=224.0.0.2 (Serial1/2), len 62, sending broad/multicast UDP
    src=646, dst=646
```

> **Note** The output of the preceding **debug** command reveals that the hello messages are sent to a destination address of 224.0.0.2 using UDP port 646 as the source and destination.

Let's disable the debug:

```
On R1:

R1# undebug all

R1# show mpls ldp neighbor

    Peer LDP Ident: 2.2.2.2:0; Local LDP Ident 1.1.1.1:0
        TCP connection: 2.2.2.2. 47638 - 1.1.1.1.646
        State: Oper; Msgs sent/rcvd: 60/62; Downstream
        Up time: 00:39:04
        LDP discovery sources:
          Serial1/2, Src IP addr: 12.1.1.2
        Addresses bound to peer LDP Ident:
          23.1.1.2        12.1.1.2        2.2.2.2        22.2.2.2
```

The **Peer LDP Ident** section identifies the LDP ID of the peer. In this case, the peer's LDP ID is 2.2.2.2:0, and the 2-byte value of :0 identifies the label space. This can be a platform-wide or per-interface label space. If the value is zero, it's platform-wide, and anything other than zero is per-interface. In a per-interface label space, the packets are forwarded based on both the incoming interface and the label. In a platform-wide label space, the LSR generates a label for a given destination and advertises that same label to all of its peers, and the packets are forwarded purely based on the actual label. In frame-mode MPLS, the label space will always be platform-wide with a value of 0.

In the second line, the TCP connection information is revealed. You can see that the remote router uses a high port value of 47638 and connects to R1 (1.1.1.1) port 646. Note that the high TCP port can be a different value on your router. The router with a numerically higher LDP RID will always be the TCP client; in this case, you can see that R2's LDP RID is higher than R1's LDP RID and based on the TCP port numbers. R2 will be the TCP client and R1 the TCP server.

The third and the fourth lines display the number of messages sent and received and the amount of time that the two LSRs have been up.

The fifth and the sixth lines (**LDP discovery sources**) display the interface through which the neighbor was found, and they include the IP address of the neighbor.

The last line (**Addresses bound to peer LDP Ident**) displays the IP addresses that are directly connected to the neighboring LSR.

Let's verify neighbor 1.1.1.1 on R2:

```
On R2:


R2# show mpls ldp neighbor 1.1.1.1

    Peer LDP Ident: 1.1.1.1:0; Local LDP Ident 2.2.2.2:0
        TCP connection: 1.1.1.1.646 - 2.2.2.2. 47638
        State: Oper; Msgs sent/rcvd: 69/67; Downstream
        Up time: 00:45:17
        LDP discovery sources:
          Serial1/1, Src IP addr: 12.1.1.1
        Addresses bound to peer LDP Ident:
          12.1.1.1          1.1.1.1          11.1.1.1

On R3:


R3# show mpls ldp neighbor

    Peer LDP Ident: 2.2.2.2:0; Local LDP Ident 3.3.3.3:0
        TCP connection: 2.2.2.2.646 - 3.3.3.3. 24198
        State: Oper; Msgs sent/rcvd: 45/45; Downstream
        Up time: 00:24:47
        LDP discovery sources:
          FastEthernet0/0, Src IP addr: 23.1.1.2
        Addresses bound to peer LDP Ident:
          23.1.1.2         12.1.1.2         2.2.2.2         22.2.2.2
```

```
    Peer LDP Ident: 4.4.4.4:0; Local LDP Ident 3.3.3.3:0
        TCP connection: 4.4.4.4. 60179 - 3.3.3.3.646
        State: Oper; Msgs sent/rcvd: 38/39; Downstream
        Up time: 00:19:00
        LDP discovery sources:
          FastEthernet0/1, Src IP addr: 34.1.1.4
        Addresses bound to peer LDP Ident:
          45.1.1.4        34.1.1.4        4.4.4.4        44.4.4.4

On R4:


R4# show mpls ldp neighbor


    Peer LDP Ident: 3.3.3.3:0; Local LDP Ident 4.4.4.4:0
        TCP connection: 3.3.3.3.646 - 4.4.4.4. 60179
        State: Oper; Msgs sent/rcvd: 51/51; Downstream
        Up time: 00:30:10
        LDP discovery sources:
          Serial1/3, Src IP addr: 34.1.1.3
        Addresses bound to peer LDP Ident:
          23.1.1.3        34.1.1.3        3.3.3.3        33.3.3.3
    Peer LDP Ident: 5.5.5.5:0; Local LDP Ident 4.4.4.4:0
        TCP connection: 5.5.5.5. 20637 - 4.4.4.4.646
        State: Oper; Msgs sent/rcvd: 45/46; Downstream
        Up time: 00:25:21
        LDP discovery sources:
          Serial1/5, Src IP addr: 45.1.1.5
        Addresses bound to peer LDP Ident:
          56.1.1.5        45.1.1.5        5.5.5.5        55.5.5.5
On R5:


R5# show mpls ldp neighbor


    Peer LDP Ident: 4.4.4.4:0; Local LDP Ident 5.5.5.5:0
        TCP connection: 4.4.4.4.646 - 5.5.5.5. 20637
        State: Oper; Msgs sent/rcvd: 48/47; Downstream
        Up time: 00:26:32
        LDP discovery sources:
          Serial1/4, Src IP addr: 45.1.1.4
        Addresses bound to peer LDP Ident:
          34.1.1.4        45.1.1.4        4.4.4.4        44.4.4.4
    Peer LDP Ident: 6.6.6.6:0; Local LDP Ident 5.5.5.5:0
        TCP connection: 6.6.6.6. 19720 - 5.5.5.5.646
        State: Oper; Msgs sent/rcvd: 45/45; Downstream
```

```
    Up time: 00:25:10
    LDP discovery sources:
        FastEthernet0/1, Src IP addr: 56.1.1.6
    Addresses bound to peer LDP Ident:
        67.1.1.6          56.1.1.6          6.6.6.6          66.6.6.6
```

On R6:

R6# **show mpls ldp neighbor**

```
    Peer LDP Ident: 5.5.5.5:0; Local LDP Ident 6.6.6.6:0
        TCP connection: 5.5.5.5.646 - 6.6.6.6. 19720
        State: Oper; Msgs sent/rcvd: 45/46; Downstream
        Up time: 00:25:51
        LDP discovery sources:
            FastEthernet0/1, Src IP addr: 56.1.1.5
        Addresses bound to peer LDP Ident:
            56.1.1.5          45.1.1.5          5.5.5.5          55.5.5.5
    Peer LDP Ident: 7.7.7.7:0; Local LDP Ident 6.6.6.6:0
        TCP connection: 7.7.7.7. 53376 - 6.6.6.6.646
        State: Oper; Msgs sent/rcvd: 45/45; Downstream
        Up time: 00:24:55
        LDP discovery sources:
            FastEthernet0/0, Src IP addr: 67.1.1.7
        Addresses bound to peer LDP Ident:
            67.1.1.7          7.7.7.7          77.7.7.7
```
On R7:

R7# **show mpls ldp neighbor**

```
    Peer LDP Ident: 6.6.6.6:0; Local LDP Ident 7.7.7.7:0
        TCP connection: 6.6.6.6.646 - 7.7.7.7. 53376
        State: Oper; Msgs sent/rcvd: 46/46; Downstream
        Up time: 00:25:50
        LDP discovery sources:
            GigabitEthernet0/0, Src IP addr: 67.1.1.6
        Addresses bound to peer LDP Ident:
            67.1.1.6          56.1.1.6          6.6.6.6          66.6.6.6
```

```
To see the LDP-RID of the local router:

R7# show mpls ldp discovery

Local LDP Identifier:
    7.7.7.7:0
    Discovery Sources:
    Interfaces:
        GigabitEthernet0/0 (ldp): xmit/recv
            LDP Id: 6.6.6.6:0
```

Task 4

Configure the interval of discovery hellos to be 15 seconds, with a hold timer of 45 seconds on all LSRs.

Note   There are two types of discovery:

■ **Basic:** This type is used to discover directly connected LDP LSRs. These messages are sent to all routers on this subnet out of each interface that has LDP enabled.

■ **Extended:** This type is used between nondirectly connected LDP LSRs. For this, an LSR sends targeted hello messages to a specified IP address.

Once the LSRs discover one another, they attempt to establish an LDP session between them. This session is based on TCP and uses port 646. LSRs will send discovery hellos every 5 seconds with a holdtime of 15 seconds; these are sent to all routers on local subnets using UDP port 646.

The following shows the different ways to see the default parameters:

```
On R7:

R7# show mpls ldp discovery detail | inc Hello|Hold

            Hello interval: 5000 ms; Transport IP addr: 7.7.7.7
                Hold time: 15 sec; Proposed local/peer: 15/15 sec

R7# show mpls ldp parameters | include Discovery hello

Discovery hello: holdtime: 15 sec; interval: 5 sec
```

In the output of the **show mpls ldp discovery** command, the **Hello interval** is displayed in milliseconds (ms), whereas the **Hold time** is displayed in seconds.

Let's change the timers based on the requirements of this task:

```
On R7:


R7(config)# mpls ldp discovery hello holdtime 45
R7(config)# mpls ldp discovery hello interval 15
```

The output of the following **show** command reveals that the local timers are set to 15/45:

```
On R7:


R7# show mpls ldp parameters | include Discovery hello

Discovery hello: holdtime: 45 sec; interval: 15 sec

On R6:


R6(config)# mpls ldp discovery hello interval 15
R6(config)# mpls ldp discovery hello holdtime 45
```

Let's verify the configuration:

```
On R6:


R6# show mpls ldp discovery detail | include Hello|Hold

        Hello interval: 5000 ms; Transport IP addr: 6.6.6.6
          Hold time: 45 sec; Proposed local/peer: 45/45 sec
        Hello interval: 5000 ms; Transport IP addr: 6.6.6.6
          Hold time: 15 sec; Proposed local/peer: 45/15 sec

On R7:


R7# show mpls ldp discovery detail | include Hello|Hold

        Hello interval: 5000 ms; Transport IP addr: 7.7.7.7
          Hold time: 15 sec; Proposed local/peer: 45/45 sec

On All routers:


Rx(config)# mpls ldp discovery hello interval 15
Rx(config)# mpls ldp discovery hello holdtime 45
```

Task 5

Configure the session keepalives and hold timers of all routers to 30 and 90 seconds, respectively.

Let's see the default values:

```
On R7:

R7# show mpls ldp parameters | include Session

Session hold time: 180 sec; keep alive interval: 60 sec
```

Let's change the keepalives to 30 seconds and the hold timer to 90 seconds:

```
R7(config)# mpls ldp holdtime 90
```

You should see the following console message stating that the new sessions will be affected with the new parameters but the existing sessions might not:

```
%Previously established sessions may not use the new holdtime.
```

Let's verify the configuration:

```
On R7:

R7# show mpls ldp parameters  | include Session

Session hold time: 90 sec; keep alive interval: 30 sec
```

Note   Once the hold time is changed, the keepalives are set to roughly 1/3 of the hold timer:

```
On All Routers:

Rx(config)# mpls ldp holdtime 90
```

Task 6

Configure the LDP's router ID of R1 to be its loopback1 interface. You should not reload the router to accomplish this task.

The LDP's router ID can be found using the following **show** commands:

```
On R1:


R1# show mpls ldp discovery


Local LDP Identifier:
    1.1.1.1:0
    Discovery Sources:
    Interfaces:
        Serial1/2 (ldp): xmit/recv
          LDP Id: 2.2.2.2:0

On R2:

R2# show mpls ldp discovery


Local LDP Identifier:
    2.2.2.2:0
    Discovery Sources:
    Interfaces:
        FastEthernet0/0 (ldp): xmit/recv
            LDP Id: 3.3.3.3:0
        Serial1/1 (ldp): xmit/recv
            LDP Id: 1.1.1.1:0 → R1's LDP router-id
```

The following **show** command reveals R1's directly connected interfaces:

```
R2# show mpls ldp neighbor 1.1.1.1


    Peer LDP Ident: 1.1.1.1:0; Local LDP Ident 2.2.2.2:0
        TCP connection: 1.1.1.1.646 - 2.2.2.2.63282
        State: Oper; Msgs sent/rcvd: 135/136; Downstream
        Up time: 01:31:42
        LDP discovery sources:
          Serial1/1, Src IP addr: 12.1.1.1
        Addresses bound to peer LDP Ident:
          12.1.1.1        11.1.1.1        1.1.1.1
```

Based on the output of the preceding **show** command, you can see that R1's directly
connected interfaces are 12.1.1.1 (the link between R1 and R2), 1.1.1.1 (the existing LDP's
router ID), and 11.1.1.1. Therefore, 11.1.1.1 must be R1's Lo1 interface. Let's verify:

```
On R1:


R1# show ip interface brief | exclude unass


Interface      IP-Address      OK? Method Status          Protocol
Serial1/2      12.1.1.1        YES manual up              up
Loopback0      1.1.1.1         YES manual up              up
Loopback1      11.1.1.1        YES manual up              up
```

The LDP's router ID can be changed using the **mpls ldp router-id** global configuration
command. If LDP's router ID is changed, the router must be reloaded so that the new
LDP router ID is implemented, unless the **force** keyword is used with the command:

```
On R1:

R1(config)# mpls ldp router-id loopback 1 force
```

The keyword **force** resets the TCP session and uses the new router ID. You should see the
following console message:

```
%LDP-5-NBRCHG: LDP Neighbor 2.2.2.2:0 (1) is DOWN (LDP Router ID changed)
```

The console message states that the LDP neighbor 2.2.2.2:0 is down—but when will it
come up?

Let's check:

```
On R1:

R1# show mpls ldp neighbor
```

R1 does *not* have any neighbors:

```
R1# show mpls ldp discovery

Local LDP Identifier:
    11.1.1.1:0
    Discovery Sources:
    Interfaces:
        Serial1/2 (ldp): xmit/recv
            LDP Id: 2.2.2.2:0
```

If R1 does not see R2 as a neighbor, then how does it see 2.2.2.2:0 in this output?

The preceding **show** command only indicates the router that the local router is exchanging LDP discovery hello messages with. The hello messages are sent to 224.0.0.2, and as long as R2 is up, it should process the messages. However, the TCP port 646 is used to establish an LDP session, and R2 *must* have reachability to the neighbor's transport address (in this case, R1's LDP router ID).

Let's check the routing table of R2:

```
On R2:

R2# show ip route 11.1.1.0
% Network not in table
```

You can see that the local router (R2) does not have a route to R1's LDP router ID. Let's advertise the loopback1 interface of R1 in OSPF:

```
On R1:

R1(config)# router ospf 1
R1(config-router)# network 11.1.1.1 0.0.0.0 area 0
```

Note   Once the loopback1 interface of R1 is advertised, the LDP neighbor is established, and the following console message is displayed:

```
%LDP-5-NBRCHG: LDP Neighbor 2.2.2.2:0 (1) is UP

R1# show mpls ldp neighbor

    Peer LDP Ident: 2.2.2.2:0; Local LDP Ident 11.1.1.1:0
        TCP connection: 2.2.2.2.646 - 11.1.1.1. 13674
        State: Oper; Msgs sent/rcvd: 17/18; Downstream
        Up time: 00:00:14
        LDP discovery sources:
          Serial1/2, Src IP addr: 12.1.1.2
        Addresses bound to peer LDP Ident:
          23.1.1.2        12.1.1.2        2.2.2.2        22.2.2.2
```

```
On R2:

R2#show mpls ldp neighbor 11.1.1.1

    Peer LDP Ident: 11.1.1.1:0; Local LDP Ident 2.2.2.2:0
        TCP connection: 11.1.1.1. 29824 - 2.2.2.2.646
        State: Oper; Msgs sent/rcvd: 19/18; Downstream
        Up time: 00:01:03
        LDP discovery sources:
          Serial1/1, Src IP addr: 12.1.1.1
        Addresses bound to peer LDP Ident:
          12.1.1.1          11.1.1.1          1.1.1.1
```

Task 7

The label space of the routers is platform dependent. By default, the routers begin numbering the labels with 16 up to 100000. Change the label space such that the routers use the labels shown in Table 15-1.

Table 15-1   *Labels for Task 6*

Router	Label Range
R1	100–199
R2	200–299
R3	300–399
R4	400–499
R5	500–599
R6	600–699
R7	700–799

By default, on low-end routers the minimum value within the label range is 16 and the maximum value within the range is 100000. Therefore, the LSR will start assigning labels starting from 16 and will go up to 100000, which means that the LSR can assign up to 99,985 labels (100,000 − 16 + 1 = 99,985). This range can be extended to the maximum allowable range using the **MPLS label range 16 1048575** command.

```
On R1:

R1# show mpls label range

Downstream Generic label region: Min/Max label: 16/100000
```

You would not normally change a label range after MPLS is fully deployed. The planning of labels should be performed during the initial phase of implementation. However, if they must be changed, a reload is required for the new range to take effect.

Note You would never do this in the production network, unless the range is changed to its maximum allowable value. In this task we will change the default range to include all possible 20 bits, just to demonstrate that we can.

```
On R1:

R1(config)# mpls label range 16 ?
  <16-1048575>  Maximum label value for dynamic label range
```

The following changes the label range based on the task's requirement:

```
R1(config)# mpls label range 100 199
```

Let's verify the configuration:

```
On R1:

R1# show mpls label range

Downstream Generic label region: Min/Max label: 16/199
[Configured range for next reload: Min/Max label: 100/199]
```

Note The preceding **show** command states that the label range should be from 100 to 199 after a reload; this is why the configured range is between brackets.

Let's verify the configuration:

```
On R1:

R1# wr

R1# reload
```

Here's what happens when the router comes up:

```
R1# show mpls label range

Downstream label generic region: min label: 100; max label: 199

On R2:

R2(config)# mpls label range 200 299

On R3:

R3(config)# mpls label range 300 399

On R4:

R4(config)# mpls label range 400 499

On R5:

R5(config)# mpls label range 500 599

On R6:

R6(config)# mpls label range 600 699

On R7:

R7(config)# mpls label range 700 799
```

Note   You may get the following console message on some of the routers; this is not an error message because we don't have 100 routes in the routing table of any of the routers in this topology. You should save and reload the router; the number of labels stated in the following console message may vary:

```
On All Routers :

Rx# write

Rx# reload
```

The label range change will cause 12 labels in the old dynamic range (16–100000) to go out of range.

Let's look at the new label range:

```
On R1:

R1# show mpls label range

Downstream Generic label region: Min/Max label: 100/199

R1# show ip route ospf | begin Gate
Gateway of last resort is not set

      2.0.0.0/32 is subnetted, 1 subnets
O        2.2.2.2 [110/782] via 12.1.1.2, 00:09:04, Serial1/2
      3.0.0.0/32 is subnetted, 1 subnets
O        3.3.3.3 [110/783] via 12.1.1.2, 00:08:14, Serial1/2
      4.0.0.0/32 is subnetted, 1 subnets
O        4.4.4.4 [110/784] via 12.1.1.2, 00:07:41, Serial1/2
      5.0.0.0/32 is subnetted, 1 subnets
O        5.5.5.5 [110/785] via 12.1.1.2, 00:07:41, Serial1/2
      6.0.0.0/32 is subnetted, 1 subnets
O        6.6.6.6 [110/786] via 12.1.1.2, 00:07:41, Serial1/2
      7.0.0.0/32 is subnetted, 1 subnets
O        7.7.7.7 [110/787] via 12.1.1.2, 00:07:41, Serial1/2
      23.0.0.0/24 is subnetted, 1 subnets
O        23.1.1.0 [110/782] via 12.1.1.2, 00:08:24, Serial1/2
      34.0.0.0/24 is subnetted, 1 subnets
O        34.1.1.0 [110/783] via 12.1.1.2, 00:07:51, Serial1/2
      45.0.0.0/24 is subnetted, 1 subnets
O        45.1.1.0 [110/784] via 12.1.1.2, 00:07:41, Serial1/2
      56.0.0.0/24 is subnetted, 1 subnets
O        56.1.1.0 [110/785] via 12.1.1.2, 00:07:41, Serial1/2
      67.0.0.0/24 is subnetted, 1 subnets
O        67.1.1.0 [110/786] via 12.1.1.2, 00:07:41, Serial1/2
```

Task 8

Examine and describe the control plane for the 7.7.7.0/24 prefix.

Let's examine the control plane for the 7.7.7.0/24 prefix advertised by R7. We are going to check if the interface is directly connected to R7 and if the interface is in up state:

```
On R7:

R7# show ip interface brief | exclude unass

Interface              IP-Address      OK? Method Status                Protocol
GigabitEthernet0/0     67.1.1.7        YES NVRAM  up                    up
Loopback0              7.7.7.7         YES NVRAM  up                    up
Loopback1              77.7.7.7        YES NVRAM  up                    up
```

Let's look at the routing protocol that is running on this router:

```
R7# show ip protocol | include Routing Protocol

Routing Protocol is "application"
Routing Protocol is "ospf 1"
```

Let's see if OSPF is running on the lo0 interface:

```
R7# show ip ospf interface brief

Interface  PID  Area     IP Address/Mask    Cost  State Nbrs F/C
Lo0        1    0        7.7.7.7/24         1     P2P   0/0
Gi0/0      1    0        67.1.1.7/24        1     DR    1/1
```

The output of the following **show** command reveals that the local router has assigned **imp-null**, or label number 3, instructing the neighboring LSR (R6) to pop the label:

```
R7# show mpls ldp binding 7.7.7.0 24

  lib entry: 7.7.7.0/24, rev 4
        local binding:  label: imp-null
        remote binding: lsr: 6.6.6.6:0, label: 600
```

The entry that is not highlighted will not be used; this is the result of liberal label retention. LSRs generate a label for each route they see in the routing table, and they advertise the routes to their neighboring router. Even though R7 was the LSR that originated the 7.7.7.0/24 prefix, R6 will still advertise a label for that prefix back to R7, but R7 will not use that label at all.

We can see that the local LSR has assigned label 600 to the 7.7.7.0/24 prefix; therefore, it will advertise this label for the 7.7.7.0/24 prefix to R5.

```
On R6:

R6# show mpls ldp binding 7.7.7.0 24

  lib entry: 7.7.7.0/24, rev 31
        local binding:  label: 600 → Locally originated label for 7.7.7.0
        remote binding: lsr: 7.7.7.7:0, label: imp-null → received from R7
        remote binding: lsr: 5.5.5.5:0, label: 510
```

The entry that is not highlighted will not be used; this is the result of liberal label retention.

R5 has assigned label number 510, and it will advertise this label for the 7.7.7.0/24 prefix to the upstream LSR (in this case, R4).

```
On R5:

R5# show mpls ldp bindings 7.7.7.0 24

  lib entry: 7.7.7.0/24, rev 32
        local binding:  label: 501 → Locally originated label for 7.7.7.0
        remote binding: lsr: 6.6.6.6:0, label: 600 → received from R6
        remote binding: lsr: 4.4.4.4:0, label: 407
```

The entry that is not highlighted will not be used; this is the result of liberal label retention.

R4 has assigned label number 410, and it will advertise this label for the 7.7.7.0/24 prefix to its upstream LSR (R3).

```
On R4:

R4# show mpls ldp binding 7.7.7.0 24

  lib entry: 7.7.7.0/24, rev 32
        local binding:  label: 407 → Locally originated for 7.7.7.0
        remote binding: lsr: 5.5.5.5:0, label: 501 → received from R5
        remote binding: lsr: 3.3.3.3:0, label: 308
```

The entry that is not highlighted will not be used; this is the result of liberal label retention.

R3 has assigned label 308, and it will advertise this label for 7.7.7.0/24 to its upstream LSR (R2).

```
On R3:

R3# show mpls ldp binding 7.7.7.0 24

  lib entry: 7.7.7.0/24, rev 32
        local binding:  label: 308 → Locally originated for 7.7.7.0
        remote binding: lsr: 4.4.4.4:0, label: 407 → received from R4
        remote binding: lsr: 2.2.2.2:0, label: 208
```

The entry that is not highlighted will not be used; this is the result of liberal label retention.

R2 has assigned label 210, and it will advertise this label for 7.7.7.0/24 to its upstream LSR (R1).

```
On R2:

R2# show mpls ldp binding 7.7.7.0 24

  lib entry: 7.7.7.0/24, rev 31
        local binding:  label: 208 → Locally originated for 7.7.7.0
        remote binding: lsr: 3.3.3.3:0, label: 308 → received from R3
        remote binding: lsr: 11.1.1.1:0, label: 107
```

The entry that is not highlighted will not be used; this is the result of liberal label retention.

Even though R1 doesn't have any upstream LDP neighbor, it still generates a label for the 7.7.7.0/24 prefix.

```
On R1:

R1# show mpls ldp bindings 7.7.7.0 24

  lib entry: 7.7.7.0/24, rev 29
        local binding:  label: 107 → Locally originated
        remote binding: lsr: 2.2.2.2:0, label: 208 → received from R2
```

Task 9

Examine and describe the data plane for the 7.7.7.0/24 prefix.

Let's examine the data plane for the 7.7.7.0/24 prefix; in this case, we need to start from R1:

```
On R1:

R1# show ip cef 7.7.7.0/24 detail

7.7.7.0/24, epoch 0
  local label info: global/107
  nexthop 12.1.1.2 Serial1/2 label 208
```

You can see that if the local router receives an IP packet destined to 7.7.7.0/24, it will impose label 210 and will exit out of S1/2 and go to the 12.1.1.2 IP address as the labeled packet.

Here's another way to display the data plane information (LFIB) for 7.7.7.0/24:

```
R1# show mpls ip binding 7.7.7.0 24

  7.7.7.0/24
      in label:     107 → This is locally generated label and it's ignored
      out label:    208       lsr: 2.2.2.2:0           inuse
```

You can see that the local router (R1) uses label 208 to forward the traffic toward the 7.7.7.0/24 prefix. Let's verify this information by looking in the LFIB:

```
R1# show mpls forwarding-table 7.7.7.0 24

Local    Outgoing    Prefix        Bytes Label    Outgoing    Next Hop
Label    Label       or Tunnel Id  Switched       interface
107      208         7.7.7.0/24    0              Se1/2       point2point
```

Note   R1 is the ingress LSR for the 7.7.7.0/24 prefix, so when it receives an IP packet, it will impose label 208 and forward the packet as a labeled packet out of its S1/2 interface toward 7.7.7.0/24.

When R2 receives a labeled packet with the top label of 208, it will swap it with label 308 and then forward the packet out of its f0/0 interface to the 23.1.1.3 IP address toward the 7.7.7.0/24 prefix:

```
On R2:

R2# show mpls forwarding-table 7.7.7.0 24

Local       Outgoing    Prefix          Bytes Label    Outgoing     Next Hop
Label       Label       or Tunnel Id    Switched       interface
208         308         7.7.7.0/24      0              Fa0/0        23.1.1.3
```

When R3 receives a labeled packet with the top label of 308, it will swap that label with label 407 and it'll forward the packet out of its S1/4 interface toward the 7.7.7.0/24 prefix:

```
On R3:

R3# show mpls for 7.7.7.0 24

Local       Outgoing    Prefix          Bytes Label    Outgoing     Next Hop
Label       Label       or Tunnel Id    Switched       interface
308         407         7.7.7.0/24      0              Se1/4        point2point
```

Note   Because the connection between R3 and R4 is a serial back-to-back connection, the next hop shows up as P2P, whereas on Ethernet links the IP address of the next hop is displayed.

When R4 receives a labeled packet with the top label of 407, it will swap that label with label 501 and will forward the packet out of its S1/5 interface toward the 7.7.7.0/24 prefix:

```
On R4:

R4# show mpls forwarding-table 7.7.7.0 24

Local       Outgoing    Prefix          Bytes Label    Outgoing     Next Hop
Label       Label       or Tunnel Id    Switched       interface
407         501         7.7.7.0/24      0              Se1/5        point2point
```

When R5 receives a labeled packet with the top label of 501, it will swap that label with label 600 and will forward the packet out of its F0/1 interface toward the 7.7.7.7/32 prefix:

```
On R5:

R5# show mpls forwarding-table 7.7.7.0 24
Local       Outgoing    Prefix         Bytes Label   Outgoing    Next Hop
Label       Label       or Tunnel Id   Switched      interface
501         600         7.7.7.0/24     0             Fa0/1       56.1.1.6
```

When R6, the second-last-hop router (the *penultimate* router) receives a labeled packet with the top label of 600, it will pop that label and forward the packet out of its F0/0 interface toward the 7.7.7.0/24 prefix:

```
On R6:

R6# show mpls forwarding-table 7.7.7.0 24

Local       Outgoing    Prefix         Bytes Label   Outgoing    Next Hop
Label       Label       or Tunnel Id   Switched      interface
600         Pop Label   7.7.7.0/24     0             Fa0/0       67.1.1.7
```

Since R7 receives an IP packet and *not* a labeled packet, it checks its FIB:

```
On R7:

R7# Show ip cef 7.7.7.0/24

7.7.7.0/24
   receive for Loopback0

R7# show mpls forwarding-table 7.7.7.0 24

Local   Outgoing   Prefix         Bytes Label   Outgoing    Next Hop
Label   Label      or Tunnel Id   Switched      interface
None    No Label   7.7.7.0/24     0             drop
```

Note   The IP packet is received by the local router, and there is no outgoing label.

Task 10

Configure LDP conditional label advertising to exclude the links that interconnect the routers in this topology.

Configure R1 to stop advertising labels:

```
On R1:

R1(config)# no mpls ldp advertise-labels
```

Let's verify the configuration:

```
On R2:

R2# show mpls ldp binding neighbor 11.1.1.1
```

> **Note** The output of the preceding **show** command reveals that R2 is no longer receiving any labels from R1.

Configure an access list to deny the networks assigned to the links that interconnect the LSRs and allow everything else; this access list will be referenced by the **FOR** keyword of the **mpls ldp advertise-labels** command:

```
On R1:

R1(config)# access-list 1 deny 12.1.1.0 0.0.0.255
R1(config)# access-list 1 deny 23.1.1.0 0.0.0.255
R1(config)# access-list 1 deny 34.1.1.0 0.0.0.255
R1(config)# access-list 1 deny 45.1.1.0 0.0.0.255
R1(config)# access-list 1 deny 56.1.1.0 0.0.0.255
R1(config)# access-list 1 deny 67.1.1.0 0.0.0.255
R1(config)# access-list 1 permit any
```

Configure an access list to identify the peer(s) that the labels will be advertised to; this access list will be referenced by the **TO** keyword of the **mpls ldp advertise-labels** command:

```
R1(config)# access-list 2 permit any
```

Configure the **mpls ldp advertise-labels** command to reference the two access lists:

```
R1(config)# mpls ldp advertise-labels for 1 to 2
```

Now let's verify the configuration:

```
On R2:


R2# show mpls ldp binding neighbor 11.1.1.1

  lib entry: 1.1.1.1/32, rev 12
       remote binding: lsr: 11.1.1.1:0, label: imp-null
  lib entry: 2.2.2.2/32, rev 6
       remote binding: lsr: 11.1.1.1:0, label: 100
  lib entry: 3.3.3.3/32, rev 18
       remote binding: lsr: 11.1.1.1:0, label: 104
  lib entry: 4.4.4.4/32, rev 16
       remote binding: lsr: 11.1.1.1:0, label: 103
  lib entry: 5.5.5.5/32, rev 14
       remote binding: lsr: 11.1.1.1:0, label: 102
  lib entry: 6.6.6.6/32, rev 28
       remote binding: lsr: 11.1.1.1:0, label: 108
  lib entry: 7.7.7.0/24, rev 31
       remote binding: lsr: 11.1.1.1:0, label: 110
  lib entry: 11.1.1.1/32, rev 10
       remote binding: lsr: 11.1.1.1:0, label: imp-null
```

Note   R1 (11.1.1.1) is no longer advertising the links to this neighbor. R1 will assign labels to the links that interconnect the LSRs, but it won't advertise them to its neighboring LSR(s). Let's take a look:

```
On R1:


R1# Show mpls ldp bindings local

  lib entry: 1.1.1.1/32, rev 45
       local binding:  label: imp-null
  lib entry: 2.2.2.2/32, rev 46
       local binding:  label: 100
  lib entry: 3.3.3.3/32, rev 47
       local binding:  label: 104
  lib entry: 4.4.4.4/32, rev 48
       local binding:  label: 103
```

```
 lib entry: 5.5.5.5/32, rev 49
      local binding:  label: 102
 lib entry: 6.6.6.6/32, rev 50
      local binding:  label: 108
 lib entry: 7.7.7.0/24, rev 51
      local binding:  label: 110
 lib entry: 11.1.1.1/32, rev 52
      local binding:  label: imp-null
 lib entry: 12.1.1.0/24, rev 38
      local binding:  label: imp-null
 lib entry: 23.1.1.0/24, rev 40
      local binding:  label: 101
 lib entry: 34.1.1.0/24, rev 41
      local binding:  label: 107
 lib entry: 45.1.1.0/24, rev 42
      local binding:  label: 106
 lib entry: 56.1.1.0/24, rev 43
      local binding:  label: 105
 lib entry: 67.1.1.0/24, rev 44
      local binding:  label: 109


On All Routers:

Rx(config)# no mpls ldp advertise-labels

Rx(config)# access-list 1 deny 12.1.1.0 0.0.0.255
Rx(config)# access-list 1 deny 23.1.1.0 0.0.0.255
Rx(config)# access-list 1 deny 34.1.1.0 0.0.0.255
Rx(config)# access-list 1 deny 45.1.1.0 0.0.0.255
Rx(config)# access-list 1 deny 56.1.1.0 0.0.0.255
Rx(config)# access-list 1 deny 67.1.1.0 0.0.0.255
Rx(config)# access-list 1 permit any

Rx(config)# access-list 2 permit any

Rx(config)# mpls ldp advertise-labels for 1 to 2
```

Now let's verify the configuration:

```
On R7:


R7# show mpls ldp binding neighbor 6.6.6.6

  lib entry: 1.1.1.1/32, rev 42
      remote binding: lsr: 6.6.6.6:0, label: 605
  lib entry: 2.2.2.2/32, rev 43
      remote binding: lsr: 6.6.6.6:0, label: 604
  lib entry: 3.3.3.3/32, rev 44
      remote binding: lsr: 6.6.6.6:0, label: 603
  lib entry: 4.4.4.4/32, rev 45
      remote binding: lsr: 6.6.6.6:0, label: 602
  lib entry: 5.5.5.5/32, rev 46
      remote binding: lsr: 6.6.6.6:0, label: 601
  lib entry: 6.6.6.0/24, rev 47
      remote binding: lsr: 6.6.6.6:0, label: imp-null
  lib entry: 7.7.7.0/24, rev 48
      remote binding: lsr: 6.6.6.6:0, label: 610
  lib entry: 11.1.1.1/32, rev 49
      remote binding: lsr: 6.6.6.6:0, label: 600
  lib entry: 66.6.6.0/24, rev 55
      remote binding: lsr: 6.6.6.6:0, label: imp-null


On R6:


R6# show mpls ldp binding neighbor 5.5.5.5

  lib entry: 1.1.1.1/32, rev 50
      remote binding: lsr: 5.5.5.5:0, label: 506
  lib entry: 2.2.2.2/32, rev 51
      remote binding: lsr: 5.5.5.5:0, label: 505
  lib entry: 3.3.3.3/32, rev 52
      remote binding: lsr: 5.5.5.5:0, label: 501
  lib entry: 4.4.4.4/32, rev 53
      remote binding: lsr: 5.5.5.5:0, label: 500
  lib entry: 5.5.5.0/24, rev 54
      remote binding: lsr: 5.5.5.5:0, label: imp-null
  lib entry: 6.6.6.6/32, rev 55
      remote binding: lsr: 5.5.5.5:0, label: 508
  lib entry: 7.7.7.0/24, rev 56
      remote binding: lsr: 5.5.5.5:0, label: 510
  lib entry: 11.1.1.1/32, rev 57
      remote binding: lsr: 5.5.5.5:0, label: 504
```

```
  lib entry: 55.5.5.0/24, rev 58
        remote binding: lsr: 5.5.5.5:0, label: imp-null


On R5:


R5# show mpls ldp binding neighbor 4.4.4.4

  lib entry: 1.1.1.1/32, rev 50
        remote binding: lsr: 4.4.4.4:0, label: 406
  lib entry: 2.2.2.2/32, rev 51


        remote binding: lsr: 4.4.4.4:0, label: 405
  lib entry: 3.3.3.3/32, rev 52
        remote binding: lsr: 4.4.4.4:0, label: 400
  lib entry: 4.4.4.0/24, rev 53
        remote binding: lsr: 4.4.4.4:0, label: imp-null
  lib entry: 5.5.5.5/32, rev 54
        remote binding: lsr: 4.4.4.4:0, label: 402
  lib entry: 6.6.6.6/32, rev 55
        remote binding: lsr: 4.4.4.4:0, label: 408
  lib entry: 7.7.7.0/24, rev 56
        remote binding: lsr: 4.4.4.4:0, label: 410
  lib entry: 11.1.1.1/32, rev 57
        remote binding: lsr: 4.4.4.4:0, label: 404
  lib entry: 44.4.4.0/24, rev 58
        remote binding: lsr: 4.4.4.4:0, label: imp-null


On R4:


R4# show mpls ldp binding neighbor 3.3.3.3

  lib entry: 1.1.1.1/32, rev 50
        remote binding: lsr: 3.3.3.3:0, label: 306
  lib entry: 2.2.2.2/32, rev 51
        remote binding: lsr: 3.3.3.3:0, label: 305
  lib entry: 3.3.3.0/24, rev 52
        remote binding: lsr: 3.3.3.3:0, label: imp-null
  lib entry: 4.4.4.4/32, rev 53
        remote binding: lsr: 3.3.3.3:0, label: 300
  lib entry: 5.5.5.5/32, rev 54
        remote binding: lsr: 3.3.3.3:0, label: 302
  lib entry: 6.6.6.6/32, rev 55
        remote binding: lsr: 3.3.3.3:0, label: 308
  lib entry: 7.7.7.0/24, rev 56
        remote binding: lsr: 3.3.3.3:0, label: 310
```

```
   lib entry: 11.1.1.1/32, rev 57
         remote binding: lsr: 3.3.3.3:0, label: 304
   lib entry: 33.3.3.0/24, rev 58
         remote binding: lsr: 3.3.3.3:0, label: imp-null


On R3:


R3# show mpls ldp binding neighbor 2.2.2.2

   lib entry: 1.1.1.1/32, rev 50


         remote binding: lsr: 2.2.2.2:0, label: 201
   lib entry: 2.2.2.0/24, rev 51
         remote binding: lsr: 2.2.2.2:0, label: imp-null
   lib entry: 3.3.3.3/32, rev 52
         remote binding: lsr: 2.2.2.2:0, label: 204
   lib entry: 4.4.4.4/32, rev 53
         remote binding: lsr: 2.2.2.2:0, label: 203
   lib entry: 5.5.5.5/32, rev 54
         remote binding: lsr: 2.2.2.2:0, label: 202
   lib entry: 6.6.6.6/32, rev 55
         remote binding: lsr: 2.2.2.2:0, label: 208
   lib entry: 7.7.7.0/24, rev 56
         remote binding: lsr: 2.2.2.2:0, label: 210
   lib entry: 11.1.1.1/32, rev 57
         remote binding: lsr: 2.2.2.2:0, label: 200
   lib entry: 22.2.2.0/24, rev 58
         remote binding: lsr: 2.2.2.2:0, label: imp-null


On R2:


R2# show mpls ldp binding neighbor 11.1.1.1

   lib entry: 1.1.1.0/24, rev 48
         remote binding: lsr: 11.1.1.1:0, label: imp-null
   lib entry: 2.2.2.2/32, rev 49
         remote binding: lsr: 11.1.1.1:0, label: 100
   lib entry: 3.3.3.3/32, rev 50
         remote binding: lsr: 11.1.1.1:0, label: 104
   lib entry: 4.4.4.4/32, rev 51
         remote binding: lsr: 11.1.1.1:0, label: 103
   lib entry: 5.5.5.5/32, rev 52
         remote binding: lsr: 11.1.1.1:0, label: 102
```

```
lib entry: 6.6.6.6/32, rev 53
      remote binding: lsr: 11.1.1.1:0, label: 108
lib entry: 7.7.7.0/24, rev 54
      remote binding: lsr: 11.1.1.1:0, label: 110
lib entry: 11.1.1.0/24, rev 55
      remote binding: lsr: 11.1.1.1:0, label: imp-null
```

Task 11

In this task, the effects of TTL propagation will be tested.

Remove the **mpls ip** command from the F0/0 interface of R6, the G0/0 interface of R7, and the serial interfaces of R1 and R2 that connect the two LSRs. R1 and R7 will pose as customer routers that do not have MPLS enabled. From R7, test the connection to 1.1.1.1 using traceroute.

```
On R1:

R1(config)# interface Serial1/2
R1(config-if)# no mpls ip


On R2:

R2(config)# interface Serial1/1
R2(config-if)# no mpls ip


On R7:

R7(config)# interface GigabitEthernet0/0
R7(config-if)# no mpls ip


On R6:

R6(config)# interface FastEthernet0/0
R6(config-if)# no mpls ip
```

Let's test the configuration:

```
On R7:

R7# traceroute 1.1.1.1 numeric

Type escape sequence to abort.
Tracing the route to 1.1.1.1
```

```
VRF info: (vrf in name/id, vrf out name/id)
 1 67.1.1.6 0 msec 4 msec 0 msec
 2 56.1.1.5 [MPLS: Label 507 Exp 0] 140 msec 136 msec 140 msec
 3 45.1.1.4 [MPLS: Label 405 Exp 0] 120 msec 124 msec 124 msec
 4 34.1.1.3 [MPLS: Label 303 Exp 0] 108 msec 108 msec 116 msec
 5 23.1.1.2 [MPLS: Label 201 Exp 0] 64 msec 60 msec 64 msec
 6 12.1.1.1 48 msec *  48 msec
```

The traceroute exposes all the links and labels within the provider's network.

Task 12

Reconfigure the appropriate router(s) such that a traceroute from R7 to 1.1.1.1 or R1 to 7.7.7.7 will not display the links from the provider's network.

The following command has two optional keywords that can be used:

- **forwarded:** Propagates IP TTL for forwarded traffic. This option will hide the MPLS structure from the customers.

- **local:** Propagates IP TTL for locally originated traffic. This option will hide the MPLS structure from the LSRs.

```
On R2 to R6:


Rx(config)# no mpls ip propagate-ttl forwarded
```

Let's verify the configuration:

```
On R7:



R7# traceroute 1.1.1.1 numeric

Type escape sequence to abort.
Tracing the route to 1.1.1.1
VRF info: (vrf in name/id, vrf out name/id)
 1 67.1.1.6 0 msec 4 msec 0 msec
 2 23.1.1.2 [MPLS: Label 201 Exp 0] 64 msec 60 msec 64 msec
 3 12.1.1.1 48 msec *  48 msec
```

Note   The MPLS structure is hidden from the customer's perspective. The only internal hop and label exposed is the last-hop LSR (23.1.1.2), but the following traceroute reveals that the LSRs within the cloud will see the structure of the cloud:

```
On R2:


R2# traceroute 7.7.7.7 numeric

Type escape sequence to abort.
Tracing the route to 7.7.7.7
VRF info: (vrf in name/id, vrf out name/id)
  1 23.1.1.3 [MPLS: Label 308 Exp 0] 92 msec 96 msec 92 msec
  2 34.1.1.4 [MPLS: Label 407 Exp 0] 76 msec 76 msec 76 msec
  3 45.1.1.5 [MPLS: Label 501 Exp 0] 60 msec 64 msec 60 msec
  4 56.1.1.6 [MPLS: Label 600 Exp 0] 64 msec 60 msec 64 msec
  5 67.1.1.7 32 msec *  32 msec
```

Let's test the second option (local). The following command will override the previous one:

```
On R2 to R6:

Rx(config)# no mpls ip propagate-ttl local
```

Let's verify the configuration:

```
On R1:

R1# traceroute 7.7.7.7 numeric

Type escape sequence to abort.
Tracing the route to 7.7.7.7
VRF info: (vrf in name/id, vrf out name/id)
  1 12.1.1.2 16 msec 12 msec 16 msec
  2 23.1.1.3 [MPLS: Label 308 Exp 0] 124 msec 120 msec 120 msec
  3 34.1.1.4 [MPLS: Label 407 Exp 0] 108 msec 104 msec 108 msec
  4 45.1.1.5 [MPLS: Label 501 Exp 0] 88 msec 92 msec 88 msec
  5 56.1.1.6 [MPLS: Label 600 Exp 0] 88 msec 88 msec 88 msec
  6 67.1.1.7 48 msec *  44 msec
```

This reveals that the **no mpls ip propagate-ttl local** command does not affect the customers.

Note   As you can see here, the **no mpls ip propagate-ttl local** command only affected the LSRs within the cloud:

```
On R2:


R2# traceroute 7.7.7.7 numeric


Type escape sequence to abort.
Tracing the route to 7.7.7.7
VRF info: (vrf in name/id, vrf out name/id)
  1 56.1.1.6 [MPLS: Label 600 Exp 0] 60 msec 64 msec 60 msec
  2 67.1.1.7 36 msec *  32 msec
```

Task 13

Remove the **mpls ip** command from all interfaces and verify the configuration:

```
On R2:


R2(config)# interface FastEthernet0/0
R2(config-if)# no mpls ip


R2# show mpls interface


Interface               IP           Tunnel    BGP Static Operational

On R3:


R3(config)# interface FastEthernet0/0
R3(config-if)# no mpls ip


R3(config)# interface Serial1/4
R3(config-if)# no mpls ip


R3# show mpls interface


Interface               IP           Tunnel    BGP Static Operational

On R4:


R4(config)# interface Serial1/3
R4(config-if)# no mpls ip


R4(config)# interface Serial1/5
R4(config-if)# no mpls ip


R4# show mpls interface
```

```
Interface              IP           Tunnel   BGP Static Operational


On R5:


R5(config)# interface FastEthernet0/1
R5(config-if)# no mpls ip


R5(config)# interface Serial1/4
R5(config-if)# no mpls ip


R5# show mpls interface


Interface              IP           Tunnel   BGP Static Operational


On R6:


R6(config)# interface FastEthernet0/1
R6(config-if)# no mpls ip


R2# show mpls interface


Interface              IP           Tunnel   BGP Static Operational
```

Task 14

Enable LDP on all the links connecting the routers to each other. This should include
R1 and R7. Do not use the **mpls ip** interface configuration mode command or a global
configuration command to accomplish this task.

LDP is enabled by configuring **mpls ip** in the interface configuration mode; typically,
some type of IGP will need to run on that given interface. To minimize the configuration
and errors (forgetting to enable LDP on a given interface), LDP autoconfiguration can
be used. When this feature is enabled, LDP is automatically enabled on every interface
of that LSR. However, if LDP must be disabled for a given interface, you can use the **no
mpls ldp igp autoconfig** interface configuration mode. In this case, because OSPF is
running as the IGP within the MPLS cloud, LDP autoconfiguration is enabled for all interfaces within Area 0.

```
On R7:


R7(config)# router ospf 1
R7(config-router)# mpls ldp autoconfig area 0
```

Let's verify the configuration on R7:

```
On R7:


R7# show mpls interfaces

Interface              IP           Tunnel   BGP Static Operational
GigabitEthernet0/0     Yes (ldp)    No       No  No     Yes


On R6:


R6(config)# router ospf 1
R6(config-router)# mpls ldp autoconfig area 0
```

Let's verify the configuration on R6:

```
On R6:


R6# show mpls interfaces

Interface              IP           Tunnel   BGP Static Operational
FastEthernet0/0        Yes (ldp)    No       No  No     Yes
FastEthernet0/1        Yes (ldp)    No       No  No     Yes
```

You should see the following console message:

```
%LDP-5-NBRCHG: LDP Neighbor 7.7.7.7:0 (1) is UP

On R5:


R5(config)# router ospf 1
R5(config-router)# mpls ldp autoconfig area 0
```

Let's verify the configuration on R5:

```
On R5:


R5# show mpls interfaces

Interface              IP           Tunnel   BGP Static Operational
Serial1/4              Yes (ldp)    No       No  No     Yes
FastEthernet0/1        Yes (ldp)    No       No  No     Yes
```

You should see the following console message:

```
%LDP-5-NBRCHG: LDP Neighbor 6.6.6.6:0 (1) is UP


On R4:


R4(config)# router ospf 1
R4(config-router)# mpls ldp autoconfig area 0
```

Let's verify the configuration on R4:

```
On R4:


R4# show mpls interfaces


Interface          IP           Tunnel   BGP Static Operational
Serial1/3          Yes (ldp)    No       No  No     Yes
Serial1/5          Yes (ldp)    No       No  No     Yes
```

You should see the following console message:

```
%LDP-5-NBRCHG: LDP Neighbor 5.5.5.5:0 (1) is UP


On R3:


R3(config)# router ospf 1
R3(config-router)# mpls ldp autoconfig area 0
```

Let's verify the configuration on R3:

```
On R3:


R3# show mpls interfaces


Interface          IP           Tunnel   BGP Static Operational
FastEthernet0/0    Yes (ldp)    No       No  No     Yes
Serial1/4          Yes (ldp)    No       No  No     Yes
```

You should see the following console message:

```
%LDP-5-NBRCHG: LDP Neighbor 4.4.4.4:0 (1) is UP
%LDP-5-NBRCHG: LDP Neighbor 2.2.2.2:0 (2) is UP


On R2:


R2(config)# router ospf 1
R2(config-router)# mpls ldp autoconfig area 0
```

Let's verify the configuration on R2:

```
On R2:


R2# show mpls interfaces


Interface            IP            Tunnel   BGP Static Operational
FastEthernet0/0      Yes (ldp)     No       No  No     Yes
Serial1/1            Yes (ldp)     No       No  No     Yes
```

You should see the following console message:

```
%LDP-5-NBRCHG: LDP Neighbor 3.3.3.3:0 (1) is UP


On R1:


R1(config)# router ospf 1
R1(config-router)# mpls ldp autoconfig area 0
```

Let's verify the configuration on R1:

```
On R1:


R1# show mpls interfaces


Interface            IP            Tunnel   BGP Static Operational
Serial1/2            Yes (ldp)     No       No  No     Yes
```

You should see the following console message:

```
%LDP-5-NBRCHG: LDP Neighbor 2.2.2.2:0 (1) is UP
```

Task 15

Configure a serial connection between R3 and R5 using the following parameters and policy:

R3: S1/5, 35.1.1.3/24, bandwidth 1544

R5: S1/3, 35.1.1.5/24, bandwidth 1544

This link should be included in OSPF Area 0:

```
On R3:

R3(config)# interface Serial1/5
R3(config-if)# ip address 35.1.1.3 255.255.255.0
R3(config-if)# clock rate 64000
R3(config-if)# bandwidth 1544
R3(config-if)# no shutdown

R3(config)# router ospf 1
R3(config-router)# network 35.1.1.3 0.0.0.0 area 0

On R5:

R5(config)# interface Serial1/3
R5(config-if)# ip address 35.1.1.5 255.255.255.0
R5(config-if)# bandwidth 1544
R5(config-if)# no shutdown

R5(config)# router ospf 1
R5(config-router)# network 35.1.1.5 0.0.0.0 area 0
```

You should see the following console messages stating that OSPF and an LDP session have been established between the two LSRs. The LDP session is established between the two LSRs because of the **mpls ldp autoconfig area 0** command from the previous task.

```
%OSPF-5-ADJCHG: Process 1, Nbr 0.0.0.3 on Serial1/3 from LOADING to FULL, Loading
  Done

%LDP-5-NBRCHG: LDP Neighbor 3.3.3.3:0 (3) is UP
```

Let's verify the configuration:

```
On R3:


R3# show mpls ldp neighbor 5.5.5.5

        Peer LDP Ident: 5.5.5.5:0; Local LDP Ident 3.3.3.3:0
        TCP connection: 5.5.5.5.16346 - 3.3.3.3.646
        State: Oper; Msgs sent/rcvd: 15/15; Downstream
        Up time: 00:01:07
        LDP discovery sources:
          Serial1/5, Src IP addr: 35.1.1.5
        Addresses bound to peer LDP Ident:
          56.1.1.5          5.5.5.5           55.5.5.5          45.1.1.5
          35.1.1.5
```

Task 16

Configure the appropriate router(s) such that a failure in one of the links between R3 and R5 does not tear down the LDP session between the two LSRs. Do not configure a GRE or an IPnIP tunnel to accomplish this task.

When a link between two LSRs goes down, the two LSRs that share the link will tear down the LDP session. When the link comes back up, the two LSRs have to reestablish their session and populate the Label Information Base (LIB) and the Label Forwarding Information Base (LFIB). This behavior can be changed by protecting the LDP session using a feature called *LDP session protection*.

With LDP session protection, a targeted LDP session is built between the routers that have this feature configured. When the directly connected link goes down, the targeted LDP session remains up as long as a redundant link exists between the two LSRs.

This feature can be enabled using the **mpls ldp session protection** global configuration command.

There are two ways to configure LDP session protection:

- Configure the feature on all routers.

- Configure the feature on one router and then configure the other router to accept the targeted LDP hellos. This can be accomplished using the **mpls ldp discovery targeted-hello accept** global configuration command.

In this case, the MPLS LDP session protection must be configured on R3, R4, and R5 because they have redundant links between them.

```
On R3:

R3# show mpls ldp neighbor | include Peer LDP

    Peer LDP Ident: 5.5.5.5:0; Local LDP Ident 3.3.3.3:0
    Peer LDP Ident: 2.2.2.2:0; Local LDP Ident 3.3.3.3:0
    Peer LDP Ident: 4.4.4.4:0; Local LDP Ident 3.3.3.3:0
```

Let's shut down the s1/4 interface to emulate a link failure and see the result:

```
R3(config)# interface Serial1/4
R3(config-if)# shutdown
```

You should see the following console messages:

```
%OSPF-5-ADJCHG: Process 1, Nbr 0.0.0.4 on Serial1/4 from FULL to DOWN, Neighbor
  Down: Interface down or detached

%LDP-5-NBRCHG: LDP Neighbor 4.4.4.4:0 (1) is DOWN (Interface not operational)

%LINK-5-CHANGED: Interface Serial1/4, changed state to administratively down

%LINEPROTO-5-UPDOWN: Line protocol on Interface Serial1/4, changed state to down
```

Note   Because the link that R3 and R4 share is down, the LDP session is torn down as well.

Let's look at the existing LDP sessions:

```
R3# show mpls ldp neigh | include Peer LDP

    Peer LDP Ident: 2.2.2.2:0; Local LDP Ident 3.3.3.3:0
    Peer LDP Ident: 5.5.5.5:0; Local LDP Ident 3.3.3.3:0
```

You can see that R3 has two LDP sessions: one with R2 and another with R5.

Let's bring the s1/4 interface back up and configure the LDP session protection feature:

```
On R3:


R3(config)# interface Serial1/4
R3(config-if)# no shutdown
```

You should see the following console messages:

```
%LINK-3-UPDOWN: Interface Serial1/4, changed state to up


%LDP-5-NBRCHG: LDP Neighbor 4.4.4.4:0 (1) is UP


%LINEPROTO-5-UPDOWN: Line protocol on Interface Serial1/4, changed state to up


%OSPF-5-ADJCHG: Process 1, Nbr 0.0.0.4 on Serial1/4 from LOADING to FULL, Loading
  Done
```

We will now need to verify the MPLS neighbors directly. We will start on R3.

```
On R3:


R3# show mpls ldp neighbor | include Peer LDP


    Peer LDP Ident: 5.5.5.5:0; Local LDP Ident 3.3.3.3:0
    Peer LDP Ident: 2.2.2.2:0; Local LDP Ident 3.3.3.3:0
    Peer LDP Ident: 4.4.4.4:0; Local LDP Ident 3.3.3.3:0


On R3, R4, and R5:


Rx(config)# mpls ldp session protection
```

We will also want to look at the specific discovery mechanisms used to form these neighbors.

```
On R3:


R3# show mpls ldp discovery


Local LDP Identifier:
    3.3.3.3:0
    Discovery Sources:
    Interfaces:
        FastEthernet0/0 (ldp): xmit/recv
            LDP Id: 2.2.2.2:0
```

```
     Serial1/4 (ldp): xmit/recv
         LDP Id: 4.4.4.4:0
     Serial1/5 (ldp): xmit/recv
         LDP Id: 5.5.5.5:0
  Targeted Hellos:
     3.3.3.3 -> 2.2.2.2 (ldp): active, xmit

     3.3.3.3 -> 5.5.5.5 (ldp): active/passive, xmit/recv
         LDP Id: 5.5.5.5:0
     3.3.3.3 -> 4.4.4.4 (ldp): active/passive, xmit/recv
         LDP Id: 4.4.4.4:0
```

You can see the targeted hellos in full mesh.

Let's test the configuration:

```
On R3:

R3# debug mpls ldp session protection
LDP session protection events debugging is on

R3(config)# interface Serial1/4
R3(config-if)# shutdown
```

You should see the following debug output which indicates clearly that the OSPF adjacency is torn down:

```
%OSPF-5-ADJCHG: Process 1, Nbr 0.0.0.4 on Serial1/4 from FULL to DOWN,
Neighbor Down: Interface down or detached
```

The primary LDP adjacency is lost, the holddown timer has started counting down, and the LDP session has transitioned from ready to protecting. The holddown timer is typically one hour:

```
LDP SP: 4.4.4.4:0: last primary adj lost; starting session protection holdup timer

LDP SP: 4.4.4.4:0: LDP session protection holdup timer started, 86400 seconds
LDP SP: 4.4.4.4:0: state change (Ready -> Protecting)
%LDP-5-SP: 4.4.4.4:0: session hold up initiated

%LDP-5-SP: 4.4.4.4:0: session hold up initiated
```

```
%OSPF-5-ADJCHG: Process 1, Nbr 0.0.0.4 on Serial1/4 from FULL to DOWN, Neighbor
  Down: Interface down or detached

%LINK-5-CHANGED: Interface Serial1/4, changed state to administratively down

%LINEPROTO-5-UPDOWN: Line protocol on Interface Serial1/4, changed state to down
```

Let's verify the configuration:

```
On R3:

R3# show mpls ldp neighbor | include Peer LDP

    Peer LDP Ident: 2.2.2.2:0; Local LDP Ident 3.3.3.3:0
    Peer LDP Ident: 5.5.5.5:0; Local LDP Ident 3.3.3.3:0
    Peer LDP Ident: 4.4.4.4:0; Local LDP Ident 3.3.3.3:0
```

Let's bring up the link and observe the debug and console output:

```
R3(config)# interface Serial1/4
R3(config-if)# no shutdown
```

You should see the following console messages and debug output:

```
%LINK-3-UPDOWN: Interface Serial1/4, changed state to up
LDP SP: 4.4.4.4:0: primary adj restored; stopping session protection holdup timer
LDP SP: 4.4.4.4:0: state change (Protecting -> Ready)
%LDP-5-SP: 4.4.4.4:0: session recovery succeeded
%LINEPROTO-5-UPDOWN: Line protocol on Interface Serial1/4, changed state to up

%OSPF-5-ADJCHG: Process 1, Nbr 0.0.0.4 on Serial1/4 from LOADING to FULL, Loading
  Done
```

Erase the startup configuration of the routers and reload them before proceeding to the next lab.

Lab 15-2: RIPv2 Routing in a VPN

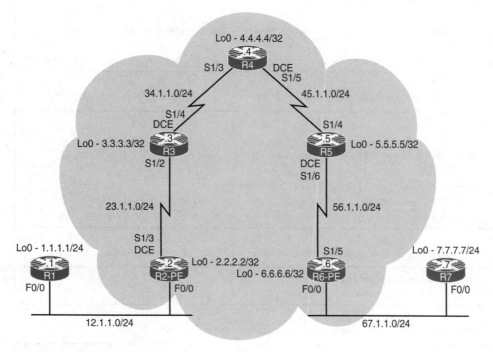

Figure 15-2 *Configuring RIPv2 Routing in a VPN*

RIPv2 as a PE-CE routing protocol is used by service providers for customers who use RIPv2 as their IGP routing protocol and, hence, prefer to use RIPv2 to exchange routing information between the customer sites across an MPLS VPN backbone. In an MPLS VPN environment, to achieve this, the original RIPv2 metrics must be carried inside Multi-Protocol-BGP (MP-BGP) updates. This is achieved by using BGP extended community attributes to carry and preserve RIPv2 metrics when crossing the MultiProtocol-interiorBGP (MP-iBGP) domain. These communities define the native characteristics associated with RIPv2.

Route propagation in MPLS VPN networks using RIPv2 PE-CE routing is based on the RIPv2 domain configured on the PE routers:

Step 1.   Enable the global RIPv2 routing process.

Step 2.   Define per VRF (Virtual Routing and Forwarding) the EIGRP routing context and parameters.

Step 3.   Configure the MP-BGP VPNv4 backbone.

Step 4.   Redistribute BGP VPNv4 routes in RIPv2.

Step 5.   Redistribute Routing Information Protocol (RIP) routes in BGP.

Task 1

Configure the topology shown in Figure 15-2. Do not configure any routing protocol. Use a VLAN ID of your choice.

```
On SW1:

SW1(config)# interface range FastEthernet0/1-2
SW1(config-if-range)# switchport mode access
SW1(config-if-range)# switchport access vlan 12
% Access VLAN does not exist. Creating vlan 12
SW1(config-if-range)# no shutdown

SW1(config)# interface range FastEthernet0/6-7
SW1(config-if-range)# switchport mode access
SW1(config-if-range)# switchport access vlan 67
% Access VLAN does not exist. Creating vlan 67
SW1(config-if-range)# no shutdown


On R1:

R1(config)# interface loopback0
R1(config-if)# ip address 1.1.1.1 255.255.255.0

R1(config)# interface FastEthernet0/0
R1(config-if)# ip address 12.1.1.1 255.255.255.0
R1(config-if)# no shutdown


On R2:

R2(config)# interface loopback0
R2(config-if)# ip address 2.2.2.2 255.255.255.255

R2(config)# interface FastEthernet0/0
R2(config-if)# ip address 12.1.1.2 255.255.255.0
R2(config-if)# no shutdown

R2(config-if)# interface Serial1/3
R2(config-if)# clock rate 64000
R2(config-if)# ip address 23.1.1.2 255.255.255.0
R2(config-if)# no shutdown


On R3:

R3(config)# interface loopback0
R3(config-if)# ip address 3.3.3.3 255.255.255.255
```

```
R3(config)# interface Serial1/2
R3(config-if)# ip address 23.1.1.3 255.255.255.0
R3(config-if)# no shutdown


R3(config)# interface Serial1/4
R3(config-if)# clock rate 64000
R3(config-if)# ip address 34.1.1.3 255.255.255.0
R3(config-if)# no shutdown


On R4:

R4(config)# interface loopback0
R4(config-if)# ip address 4.4.4.4 255.255.255.255


R4(config)# interface Serial1/3
R4(config-if)# ip address 34.1.1.4 255.255.255.0
R4(config-if)# no shutdown


R4(config)# interface Serial1/5
R4(config-if)# clock rate 64000
R4(config-if)# ip address 45.1.1.4 255.255.255.0
R4(config-if)# no shutdown


On R5:

R5(config)# interface loopback0
R5(config-if)# ip address 5.5.5.5 255.255.255.255


R5(config)# interface Serial1/4
R5(config-if)# ip address 45.1.1.5 255.255.255.0
R5(config-if)# no shutdown


R5(config)# interface Serial1/6
R5(config-if)# clock rate 64000
R5(config-if)# ip address 56.1.1.5 255.255.255.0
R5(config-if)# no shutdown


On R6:

R6(config)# interface loopback0
R6(config-if)# ip address 6.6.6.6 255.255.255.255


R6(config)# interface Serial1/5
R6(config-if)# ip address 56.1.1.6 255.255.255.0
R6(config-if)# no shutdown
```

```
R6(config)# interface FastEthernet0/0
R6(config-if)# ip address 67.1.1.6 255.255.255.0
R6(config-if)# no shutdown


On R7:


R7(config)# interface loopback0
R7(config-if)# ip address 7.7.7.7 255.255.255.0


R7(config)# interface GigabitEthernet0/0
R7(config-if)# ip address 67.1.1.7 255.255.255.0
R7(config-if)# no shutdown
```

Task 2

Configure OSPF on the core MPLS routers (R2 to R6). You should run OSPF Area 0 on the Lo0 interfaces and the links that connect these routers to each other. The router IDs of R2, R3, R4, R5, and R6 should be configured as 0.0.0.2, 0.0.0.3, 0.0.0.4, 0.0.0.5, and 0.0.0.6 respectively. Do *not* configure OSPF between R1 and R2 and between R6 and R7.

```
On R2:


R2(config)# router ospf 1
R3(config-router)# router-id 0.0.0.2
R2(config-router)# network 2.2.2.2 0.0.0.0 area 0
R2(config-router)# network 23.1.1.2 0.0.0.0 area 0


On R3:


R3(config)# router ospf 1
R2(config-router)# router-id 0.0.0.3
R3(config-router)# network 3.3.3.3 0.0.0.0 area 0
R3(config-router)# network 23.1.1.3 0.0.0.0 area 0
R3(config-router)# network 34.1.1.3 0.0.0.0 area 0
```

OSPF adjacency change messages will appear on the console as we proceed through this configuration.

```
%OSPF-5-ADJCHG: Process 1, Nbr 0.0.0.2 on Serial1/2 from LOADING to FULL, Loading
   Done


On R4:


R4(config)# router ospf 1
R4(config-router)# router-id 0.0.0.4
R4(config-router)# network 4.4.4.4 0.0.0.0 area 0
R4(config-router)# network 34.1.1.4 0.0.0.0 area 0
R4(config-router)# network 45.1.1.4 0.0.0.0 area 0
```

The console lets us know that we have formed a neighbor relationship with R3.

```
%OSPF-5-ADJCHG: Process 1, Nbr 0.0.0.3 on Serial1/3 from LOADING to FULL, Loading
   Done


On R5:


R5(config)# router ospf 1
R5(config-router)# router-id 0.0.0.5
R5(config-router)# network 5.5.5.5 0.0.0.0 area 0
R5(config-router)# network 45.1.1.5 0.0.0.0 area 0
R5(config-router)# network 56.1.1.5 0.0.0.0 area 0
```

We can see that Neighbor 0.0.0.4 will form an OSPF peering relationship.

```
%OSPF-5-ADJCHG: Process 1, Nbr 0.0.0.4 on Serial1/4 from LOADING to FULL, Loading
   Done


On R6:


R6(config)# router ospf 1
R6(config-router)# router-id 0.0.0.6
R6(config-router)# network 6.6.6.6 0.0.0.0 area 0
R6(config-router)# network 56.1.1.6 0.0.0.0 area 0
```

Lastly, R5 will join the OSPF domain.

```
%OSPF-5-ADJCHG: Process 1, Nbr 0.0.0.5 on Serial1/5 from LOADING to FULL,
Loading Done
```

Let's verify the configuration:

```
On R2:


R2# show ip route ospf | begin Gate
Gateway of last resort is not set


      3.0.0.0/32 is subnetted, 1 subnets
O        3.3.3.3 [110/782] via 23.1.1.3, 00:01:22, Serial1/3
      4.0.0.0/32 is subnetted, 1 subnets
O        4.4.4.4 [110/1563] via 23.1.1.3, 00:01:11, Serial1/3
      5.0.0.0/32 is subnetted, 1 subnets
O        5.5.5.5 [110/2344] via 23.1.1.3, 00:00:59, Serial1/3
      6.0.0.0/32 is subnetted, 1 subnets
O        6.6.6.6 [110/3125] via 23.1.1.3, 00:00:43, Serial1/3
      34.0.0.0/24 is subnetted, 1 subnets
O        34.1.1.0 [110/1562] via 23.1.1.3, 00:01:11, Serial1/3
      45.0.0.0/24 is subnetted, 1 subnets
O        45.1.1.0 [110/2343] via 23.1.1.3, 00:00:59, Serial1/3
      56.0.0.0/24 is subnetted, 1 subnets
O        56.1.1.0 [110/3124] via 23.1.1.3, 00:00:43, Serial1/3


On R6:


R6# show ip route ospf | begin Gate
Gateway of last resort is not set


      2.0.0.0/32 is subnetted, 1 subnets
O        2.2.2.2 [110/3125] via 56.1.1.5, 00:02:43, Serial1/5
      3.0.0.0/32 is subnetted, 1 subnets
O        3.3.3.3 [110/2344] via 56.1.1.5, 00:02:43, Serial1/5
      4.0.0.0/32 is subnetted, 1 subnets
O        4.4.4.4 [110/1563] via 56.1.1.5, 00:02:43, Serial1/5
      5.0.0.0/32 is subnetted, 1 subnets
O        5.5.5.5 [110/782] via 56.1.1.5, 00:02:43, Serial1/5
      23.0.0.0/24 is subnetted, 1 subnets
O        23.1.1.0 [110/3124] via 56.1.1.5, 00:02:43, Serial1/5
      34.0.0.0/24 is subnetted, 1 subnets
O        34.1.1.0 [110/2343] via 56.1.1.5, 00:02:43, Serial1/5
      45.0.0.0/24 is subnetted, 1 subnets
O        45.1.1.0 [110/1562] via 56.1.1.5, 00:02:43, Serial1/5
```

Task 3

Configure LDP between the core routers. These routers should use their loopback0 inter-faces as their LDP router ID; the core MPLS routers (R2, R3, R4, R5, and R6) should use the following label range:

R2: 200–299

R3: 300–399

R4: 400–499

R5: 500–599

R6: 600 –699

Let's set up the usable range of labels on R2:

```
On R2:
R2(config)# mpls label range 200 299
```

The following command configures LDP as the label protocol:

```
R2(config)# mpls label protocol ldp
```

The following command configures the Lo0 interfaces as the router IDs. The **force** key-word at the end of the command forces the lo0 interface to be the LDP RID:

```
R2(config)# mpls ldp router-id lo0 force
```

MPLS forwarding of IPv4 packets along normally routed paths is enabled on the local router's interface facing R3:

```
R2(config)# interface Serial1/3
R2(config-if)# mpls ip

On R3:

R3(config)# mpls label protocol ldp
R3(config)# mpls ldp router-id lo0
R3(config)# mpls label range 300 399

R3(config)# interface Serial1/2
R3(config-if)# mpls ip

R3(config-if)# interface Serial1/4
R3(config-if)# mpls ip
```

We will move to R4 and continue the configuration.

```
%LDP-5-NBRCHG: LDP Neighbor 2.2.2.2:0 (1) is UP


On R4:


R4(config)# mpls label protocol ldp
R4(config)# mpls ldp router-id lo0
R4(config)# mpls label range 400 499


R4(config)# interface Serial1/3
R4(config-if)# mpls ip


R4(config)# interface Serial1/5
R4(config-if)# mpls ip
```

R5 will need MPLS enabled on its Serial interfaces.

```
%LDP-5-NBRCHG: LDP Neighbor 3.3.3.3:0 (1) is UP


On R5:


R5(config)# mpls label protocol ldp
R5(config)# mpls ldp router-id lo0
R5(config)# mpls label range 500 599


R5(config)# interface Serial1/4
R5(config-if)# mpls ip


R5(config)# interface Serial1/6
R5(config-if)# mpls ip
```

R6 is the last device we need to configure.

```
%LDP-5-NBRCHG: LDP Neighbor 4.4.4.4:0 (1) is UP


On R6:


R6(config)# mpls label protocol ldp
R6(config)# mpls ldp router-id lo0
R6(config)# mpls label range 600 699


R6(config)# interface Serial1/5
R6(config-if)# mpls ip
```

You should see the following console message:

```
%LDP-5-NBRCHG: LDP Neighbor 5.5.5.5:0 (1) is UP
```

To see all the interfaces that are configured for label switching:

```
On R2:

R2# show mpls interfaces

Interface              IP           Tunnel   BGP Static Operational
Serial1/3              Yes (ldp)    No       No  No     Yes
```

Let's look at the neighboring LDP LSRs:

```
R2# show mpls ldp neighbor

    Peer LDP Ident: 3.3.3.3:0; Local LDP Ident 2.2.2.2:0
        TCP connection: 3.3.3.3.45826 - 2.2.2.2.646
        State: Oper; Msgs sent/rcvd: 15/14; Downstream
        Up time: 00:02:26
        LDP discovery sources:
          Serial1/3, Src IP addr: 23.1.1.3
        Addresses bound to peer LDP Ident:
          23.1.1.3        34.1.1.3        3.3.3.3
```

Note Because the LDP RID of R3 is higher than the local router, R3 will initiate the LDP session using a high port:

```
R2# show mpls ldp discovery all

Local LDP Identifier:
    2.2.2.2:0
    Discovery Sources:
    Interfaces:
        Serial1/3 (ldp): xmit/recv
            LDP Id: 3.3.3.3:0

R2# show mpls label range

Downstream Generic label region: Min/Max label: 200/299
```

The default range for the labels is 16 to 100000 on this platform. The default range can be changed using the **mpls label range** global configuration command:

```
R2(config)# mpls label range ?
  <16-1048575>  Minimum label value for dynamic label range

R2(config)# mpls label range 16 ?
  <16-1048575>  Maximum label value for dynamic label range


On R4:


R4# show mpls interfaces

Interface            IP           Tunnel   BGP Static Operational
Serial1/3            Yes (ldp)    No       No  No     Yes
Serial1/5            Yes (ldp)    No       No  No     Yes


R4# show mpls ldp neighbor

    Peer LDP Ident: 3.3.3.3:0; Local LDP Ident 4.4.4.4:0
        TCP connection: 3.3.3.3.646 - 4.4.4.4.25499
        State: Oper; Msgs sent/rcvd: 14/14; Downstream
        Up time: 00:02:13
        LDP discovery sources:
          Serial1/3, Src IP addr: 34.1.1.3
        Addresses bound to peer LDP Ident:
          23.1.1.3        34.1.1.3        3.3.3.3
    Peer LDP Ident: 5.5.5.5:0; Local LDP Ident 4.4.4.4:0
        TCP connection: 5.5.5.5.34768 - 4.4.4.4.646
        State: Oper; Msgs sent/rcvd: 14/14; Downstream
        Up time: 00:02:02
        LDP discovery sources:
          Serial1/5, Src IP addr: 45.1.1.5
        Addresses bound to peer LDP Ident:
          45.1.1.5        56.1.1.5        5.5.5.5


R4# show mpls ldp discovery all

Local LDP Identifier:
    4.4.4.4:0
    Discovery Sources:
    Interfaces:
        Serial1/3 (ldp): xmit/recv
            LDP Id: 3.3.3.3:0
        Serial1/5 (ldp): xmit/recv
            LDP Id: 5.5.5.5:0
```

```
R4# show mpls label range

Downstream Generic label region: Min/Max label: 400/499

On R6:

R6# show mpls interface

Interface              IP              Tunnel   BGP Static Operational
Serial1/5              Yes (ldp)       No       No  No     Yes

R6# show mpls ldp neighbor

    Peer LDP Ident: 5.5.5.5:0; Local LDP Ident 6.6.6.6:0
        TCP connection: 5.5.5.5.646 - 6.6.6.6.33139
        State: Oper; Msgs sent/rcvd: 14/14; Downstream
        Up time: 00:01:51
        LDP discovery sources:
          Serial1/5, Src IP addr: 56.1.1.5
        Addresses bound to peer LDP Ident:
          45.1.1.5        56.1.1.5        5.5.5.5

R6# show mpls ldp neighbor | include Peer

    Peer LDP Ident: 5.5.5.5:0; Local LDP Ident 6.6.6.6:0

R6# show mpls ldp discovery all

 Local LDP Identifier:
    6.6.6.6:0
    Discovery Sources:
    Interfaces:
        Serial1/5 (ldp): xmit/recv
            LDP Id: 5.5.5.5:0
```

Task 4

Configure MP-BGP AS 100 between R2 and R6, which represent the provider edge routers in this topology. You should configure their loopback0 interfaces as the source for
the updates. Do not allow the BGP peers to share IPv4 routing information by default.
The only BGP peering should be VPNv4.

```
On R2:

R2(config)# router bgp 100
R2(config-router)# no bgp default ipv4-unicast

R2(config-router)# neighbor 6.6.6.6 remote-as 100
R2(config-router)# neighbor 6.6.6.6 update-source lo0
```

Note   The exchange of IPv4 routes between BGP neighbors is enabled by default, which means the configured neighbors not only will establish a BGP session but they will also receive the advertised prefixes. Because the **no bgp default ipv4-unicast** command is configured, the local router will *not* establish a BGP peer session with any neighbor unless that neighbor is activated under the address family.

```
On R6:

R6(config)# router bgp 100
R6(config-router)# no bgp default ipv4-unicast

R6(config-router)# neighbor 2.2.2.2 remote-as 100
R6(config-router)# neighbor 2.2.2.2 update-source lo0
```

Let's verify the configuration:

```
On R2:

R2# show ip bgp

R2# show ip bgp summary
```

Note   There is no IPv4 neighbor adjacency established between the two routers. Because the task states that these two BGP speakers should *only* establish a VPNv4 peer session, the neighbors *must* be activated in the VPNv4 address family.

```
On R2:

R2(config)# router bgp 100
R2(config-router)# address-family vpnv4 unicast
R2(config-router-af)# neighbor 6.6.6.6 activate

On R6:

R6(config)# router bgp 100
R6(config-router)# address-family vpnv4 unicast
R6(config-router-af)# neighbor 2.2.2.2 activate
```

You should see the following console message:

```
%BGP-5-ADJCHANGE: neighbor 2.2.2.2 Up
```

Let's verify the configuration:

```
On R2:

R2# show bgp vpnv4 unicast all summary | begin Neighbor

Neighbor        V    AS MsgRcvd MsgSent    TblVer  InQ OutQ Up/Down   State/PfxRcd
6.6.6.6         4   100       4       4         1    0    0 00:01:29           0
```

The **show ip bgp vpnv4 all summary | b Neighbor** command can also be used. The result will be the same. Let's verify this:

```
R2# show ip bgp vpnv4 all summary | begin Neighbor

Neighbor        V    AS MsgRcvd MsgSent    TblVer  InQ OutQ Up/Down   State/PfxRcd
6.6.6.6         4   100       4       4         1    0    0 00:01:29           0
```

As you can see, the preceding two commands show the same output:

```
On R6:

R6# show ip bgp vpnv4 all summary | begin Neighbor

Neighbor        V    AS MsgRcvd MsgSent    TblVer  InQ OutQ Up/Down   State/PfxRcd
2.2.2.2         4   100       7       8         1    0    0 00:04:23           0
```

Task 5

Configure the VRFs, route distinguishers (RDs), and route targets (RTs) based on Table 15-2.

Table 15-2 *Parameters for Configuring Task 5*

Router	VRF Name	RD	Route Target
R2	CA	1:10	1:100
R6	CB	1:20	1:100

The **IP vrf** and **VRF definition** commands can be used to create a new VRF and enter the global configuration mode for the configured VRF. The name of the VRF is locally significant and is case sensitive. In MPLS L3/VPNs, the VRF is not operational unless the RD is defined.

VRFs are locally significant, and you need to advertise CA's prefixes over the cloud to CB. If VRFs are locally significant, then how do we distinguish CA's prefixes from CB's prefixes once they get on the cloud?

Well, we have route distinguishers (RDs) for that purpose. What are route distinguishers?

An RD is a 64-bit value that is concatenated to the customer routes to keep the customer routes unique when MP-BGP carries them from one PE to another.

The format of an RD is "32 bits: 32 bits." Typically the first 32 bits identify the AS number of the customer, but there is no standard.

Let's configure the VRFs and the RDs:

```
On R2:


R2(config)# vrf definition CA
R2(config-vrf)# rd 1:10


On R6:


R6(config)# vrf definition CB
R6(config-vrf)# rd 1:20
```

VRFs are locally significant, and the RDs will keep the CE routes unique within the cloud. Once the PE router receives the VPNv4 routes, it strips off the 64-bit RD value. The question is, how does the receiving PE router know which VRF it should inject the routes into? The answer is, the *route target*.

Route targets, or RTs, are extended BGP communities that indicate which routes should be exported from the VRF into the MP-BGP and which routes should be imported from the MP-BGP into a given VRF. RTs are attached to the VPNv4 routes.

You need to remember that when BGP communities are involved, you need to manually configure the communities to be sent; otherwise, they will not be sent.

The **route-target export** command specifies an RT that is to be attached to every route exported from the local VRF into the MP-BGP. By contrast, the **route-target import** command specifies an RT to be used as an import filter; only routes matching the RT are imported into the VRF.

This implementation allows a route to have many imported or exported RTs, all to be attached to every imported or exported route.

The following configuration attaches an RT of 1:100 to all exported routes, and the **import** command instructs the PE router to import any VPNv4 route that carries an RT of 1:100:

```
On R2:

R2(config)# vrf definition CA
R2(config-vrf)# address-family ipv4
R2(config-vrf-af)# route-target export 1:100
R2(config-vrf-af)# route-target import 1:100
```

In the following configuration, the **both** keyword is used to replace both the **import** and **export** keywords:

```
On R6:

R6(config)# vrf definition CB
R6(config-vrf)# address-family ipv4
R6(config-vrf-af)# route-target both 1:100
```

The route targets are BGP extended communities that are attached to the VPNv4 addresses. Remember that communities are not sent unless they are configured to be sent. Let's configure the PE routers to send the extended communities:

```
On R2:

R2(config)# router bgp 100
R2(config-router)# address-family vpnv4 unicast
R2(config-router-af)# neighbor 6.6.6.6 send-community extended

On R6:

R6(config)# router bgp 100
R6(config-router)# address-family vpnv4 unicast
R6(config-router-af)# neighbor 2.2.2.2 send-community extended
```

Note   In some IOS versions, the **neighbor** *x.x.x.x* **send-community extended** command may be automatically configured, but it is a good practice to make a point to configure it, just in case your IOS version in the lab does *not* auto-configure this command for you, or the command was removed for troubleshooting purposes.

Let's verify the VRF configuration:

```
On R2:

R2# show vrf
  Name                     Default RD          Protocols   Interfaces
  CA                       1:10                ipv4
```

Think of VRFs as VLANs; once a VLAN is configured, the appropriate interfaces are assigned to that VLAN. The same philosophy applies to VRFs, which are Layer 3 VLANs. In this case, the VRFs are configured, and now the appropriate interfaces need to be assigned to that VRF. The following commands associate the f0/0 interface facing the customer to the VRF CA:

```
On R2:

R2(config)# interface FastEthernet0/0
R2(config-if)# vrf forwarding CA
```

The preceding command associates an interface with the specified VRF. When this command is applied to a given interface, the IP address of that interface is removed and it should be reconfigured.

You should see the following console message:

```
% Interface FastEthernet0/0 IPv4 disabled and address(es) removed due to enabling
  VRF CA

R2(config-if)# ip address 12.1.1.2 255.255.255.0

On R6:

R6(config)# interface FastEthernet0/0
R6(config-if)# vrf forwarding CB
R6(config-if)# ip address 67.1.1.6 255.255.255.0
```

Let's verify the configuration:

```
On R2:


R2# show vrf detail


VRF CA (VRF Id = 1); default RD 1:10; default VPNID <not set>
  Interfaces:
    Fa0/0
Address family ipv4 (Table ID = 1 (0x1)):
  Export VPN route-target communities
    RT:1:100
  Import VPN route-target communities
    RT:1:100
  No import route-map
  No export route-map
  VRF label distribution protocol: not configured
  VRF label allocation mode: per-prefix
Address family ipv6 not active
```

The preceding output begins with the name of the VRF, the configured route distinguisher value, and the VPNID, which is normally not set by default. The VPNID is an extension used to further identify the VPN by using the customer *OUI* and *VPN index*, which can be keyed in as a hexadecimal- or decimal-formatted number.

The interfaces that have the VRF CA applied will be listed under the Interfaces column. It is a good practice to have at least one route target that the router will both export and import.

```
On R6:

R6# show ip vrf CB


Name                        Default RD          Interfaces
CB                          1:20                Fa0/0


R6# show ip vrf interfaces


Interface           IP-Address      VRF                         Protocol
Fa0/0               67.1.1.6        CB                          up
```

The following command will give you the same information:

```
R6# show vrf ipv4 interfaces

Interface            VRF                        Protocol   Address
Fa0/0                CB                         up         67.1.1.6
```

Let's verify the connectivity between the PEs and CEs:

```
On R2:

R2# ping 12.1.1.1

Type escape sequence to abort.
Sending 5, 100-byte ICMP Echos to 12.1.1.1, timeout is 2 seconds:
.....
Success rate is 0 percent (0/5)
```

A regular ping will no longer work. A **ping** command with no other keywords will default to using the global routing table. The 12.1.1.0/24 prefix is not accessible in the global routing table anymore. The ping must be added with the proper VRF keyword. Remember the IP address is in the VRF and not the global routing table.

```
R2# ping vrf CA 12.1.1.1

Type escape sequence to abort.
Sending 5, 100-byte ICMP Echos to 12.1.1.1, timeout is 2 seconds:
.!!!!
Success rate is 80 percent (4/5), round-trip min/avg/max = 1/1/1 ms

On R6:

R6# ping vrf CB 67.1.1.7

Type escape sequence to abort.
Sending 5, 100-byte ICMP Echos to 67.1.1.7, timeout is 2 seconds:
.!!!!
Success rate is 80 percent (4/5), round-trip min/avg/max = 1/1/4 ms
```

Task 6

Configure RIPv2 between R1 and PE-2 and between R7 and PE-6. The customer routers (R1 and R7) should advertise their lo0 interfaces in this routing domain. Disable auto-summary. If this configuration is performed successfully, the CE routers (R1 and R7) should have reachability to each other's routes.

```
On R1:

R1(config)# router rip
R1(config-router)# no auto-summary
R1(config-router)# version 2
R1(config-router)# network 1.0.0.0
R1(config-router)# network 12.0.0.0

On RE-2:

R2(config)# router rip
R2(config-router)# no auto-summary
R2(config-router)# version 2
R2(config-router)# address-family ipv4 vrf CA
R2(config-router-af)# network 12.0.0.0
```

Let's verify the configuration:

```
On PE-2:

R2# show ip route vrf CA rip | begin Gate
Gateway of last resort is not set

     1.0.0.0/24 is subnetted, 1 subnets
R       1.1.1.0 [120/1] via 12.1.1.1, 00:00:18, FastEthernet0/0
```

Let's configure PE-6 and R7:

```
On R7:

R7(config)# router rip
R7(config-router)# no auto-summary
R7(config-router)# version 2
R7(config-router)# network 7.0.0.0
R7(config-router)# network 67.0.0.0
```

```
On PE-6:

R6(config)# router rip
R6(config-router)# no auto-summary
R6(config-router)# version 2
R6(config-router)# address-family ipv4 vrf CB
R6(config-router-af)# network 67.0.0.0
```

Let's verify the configuration:

```
On PE-6:

R6# show ip route vrf CB rip | begin Gate
Gateway of last resort is not set

      7.0.0.0/24 is subnetted, 1 subnets
R        7.7.7.0 [120/1] via 67.1.1.7, 00:00:13, FastEthernet0/0
```

In the last step of this task, the RIP routes should be redistributed into BGP so the neighboring PE router can see the routes in its BGP table. This redistribution should be done under another address family called "IPv4 unicast" in BGP. In some IOS releases, this address family is created automatically when the VRF, RD, and RTs are configured. But once again, you should never depend on the defaults.

Once you get to this final step, you should perform redistribution in one direction and verify each step of the way and then do the redistribution in the opposite direction. Let's start with PE-2:

```
On PE-2:

R2(config)# router bgp 100
R2(config-router)# address-family ipv4 vrf CA
R2(config-router-af)# redistribute rip
```

Let's verify the configuration:

```
R2# show bgp vpnv4 unicast all | begin Network

   Network          Next Hop          Metric LocPrf Weight Path
Route Distinguisher: 1:10 (default for vrf CA)
*> 1.1.1.0/24       12.1.1.1              1        32768 ?
*> 12.1.1.0/24      0.0.0.0               0        32768 ?
```

Because the prefixes are in BGP as VPNv4 prefixes, PE-6 should also see these routes. Let's verify:

```
On PE-6:


R6# show bgp vpnv4 unicast all | begin Network

   Network          Next Hop         Metric LocPrf Weight Path
Route Distinguisher: 1:10
*>i1.1.1.0/24       2.2.2.2               1    100      0 ?
*>i12.1.1.0/24      2.2.2.2               0    100      0 ?
Route Distinguisher: 1:20 (default for vrf CB)
*>i1.1.1.0/24       2.2.2.2               1    100      0 ?
*>i12.1.1.0/24      2.2.2.2               0    100      0 ?
```

You can see the routes advertised by R1 on PE-6, so let's redistribute these routes into RIP and verify:

```
R6(config)# router rip
R6(config-router)# address-family ipv4 vrf CB
R6(config-router-af)# redistribute bgp 100 metric 1
```

Let's verify the configuration on R7, the customer router:

```
On R7:


R7# show ip route rip | begin Gate
Gateway of last resort is not set

      1.0.0.0/24 is subnetted, 1 subnets
R        1.1.1.0 [120/1] via 67.1.1.6, 00:00:02, GigabitEthernet0/0
      12.0.0.0/24 is subnetted, 1 subnets
R        12.1.1.0 [120/1] via 67.1.1.6, 00:00:02, GigabitEthernet0/0
```

To test this configuration, you need to enable **debug ip icmp** on R1 and generate a ping to 1.1.1.1 from R7. If this configuration is done correctly, you should see the ICMP-ECHO packets on R1.

Note   The ping on R7 will fail because the redistribution is performed in one direction only, meaning that R1 doesn't have a return route.

```
On R1:


R1# debug ip icmp
ICMP packet debugging is on


On R7:


R7# ping 1.1.1.1 repeat 2


Type escape sequence to abort.
Sending 2, 100-byte ICMP Echos to 1.1.1.1, timeout is 2 seconds:
..
Success rate is 0 percent (0/2)
```

Let's see if R1 can see the ICMP echos generated by R7:

```
On R1:


ICMP: echo reply sent, src 1.1.1.1, dst 67.1.1.7, topology BASE, dscp 0 topoid 0


ICMP: echo reply sent, src 1.1.1.1, dst 67.1.1.7, topology BASE, dscp 0 topoid 0
```

Now you know the redistribution is working in one direction. You should configure the redistribution in the opposite direction:

```
On PE-6:


R6(config)# router bgp 100
R6(config-router)# address-family ipv4 vrf CB
R6(config-router-af)# redistribute rip
```

Let's verify the configuration:

```
R6# show bgp vpnv4 unicast all | begin Network


   Network            Next Hop            Metric LocPrf Weight Path
Route Distinguisher: 1:10
*>i1.1.1.0/24        2.2.2.2                  1     100      0 ?
*>i12.1.1.0/24       2.2.2.2                  0     100      0 ?
Route Distinguisher: 1:20 (default for vrf CB)
*>i1.1.1.0/24        2.2.2.2                  1     100      0 ?
*> 7.7.7.0/24        67.1.1.7                 1          32768 ?
*>i12.1.1.0/24       2.2.2.2                  0     100      0 ?
*> 67.1.1.0/24       0.0.0.0                  0          32768 ?
```

One of the reasons to use different route distinguishers for all VRFs in the network is clarity, especially when trying to figure out which VPN a route belongs to and where it originated. As you can see, the 1:20 RD is local, but the 1.1.1.0/24 network is present in both RDs, which means that the 1.1.1.0/24 network is participating in the same *VPN*.

You should see the prefixes on PE-2:

```
On PE-2:


R2# show bgp vpnv4 unicast all | begin Network


   Network          Next Hop         Metric LocPrf Weight Path
Route Distinguisher: 1:10 (default for vrf CA)
*>  1.1.1.0/24       12.1.1.1             1          32768 ?
*>i7.7.7.0/24        6.6.6.6              1    100       0 ?
*>  12.1.1.0/24      0.0.0.0              0          32768 ?
*>i67.1.1.0/24       6.6.6.6              0    100       0 ?
Route Distinguisher: 1:20
*>i7.7.7.0/24        6.6.6.6              1    100       0 ?
*>i67.1.1.0/24       6.6.6.6              0    100       0 ?
```

Sure enough, you can see the routes. Now you must redistribute BGP into RIP so R1 can see R7's prefixes:

```
R2(config)# router rip
R2(config-router)# address-family ipv4 vrf CA
R2(config-router-af)# redistribute bgp 100 metric 1
```

Let's verify the configuration:

```
On R1:


R1# show ip route rip | begin Gate
Gateway of last resort is not set


     7.0.0.0/24 is subnetted, 1 subnets
R       7.7.7.0 [120/1] via 12.1.1.2, 00:00:20, FastEthernet0/0
     67.0.0.0/24 is subnetted, 1 subnets
R       67.1.1.0 [120/1] via 12.1.1.2, 00:00:20, FastEthernet0/0
```

Now let's test and verify the configuration:

```
On R1:


R1# ping 7.7.7.7


Type escape sequence to abort.
Sending 5, 100-byte ICMP Echos to 7.7.7.7, timeout is 2 seconds:
!!!!!
Success rate is 100 percent (5/5), round-trip min/avg/max = 120/122/124 ms


R6# show bgp vpnv4 unicast vrf CB 1.1.1.0


BGP routing table entry for 1:20:1.1.1.0/24, version 4
Paths: (1 available, best # 1, table CB)          VPNv4 address
  Not advertised to any peer
  Local, imported path from 1:10:1.1.1.0/24
    2.2.2.2 (metric 3125) from 2.2.2.2 (2.2.2.2)
      Origin incomplete, metric 1, localpref 100, valid, internal, best
      Extended Community: RT:1:100
      mpls labels in/out nolabel/207
```

In the output of the preceding **show** command, you can see that the route was imported with a VPNv4 address of 1:10:1.1.1.0/24 and an extended community of RT:1:100. If the local router receives an unlabeled packet destined for network 1.1.1.0/24, the local LSR will impose label 207, which is the VPN label, and send it to 2.2.2.2.

Let's see the LFIB for this network:

```
R6# show mpls forwarding-table vrf CB 1.1.1.0


Local      Outgoing    Prefix         Bytes Label    Outgoing    Next Hop
Label      Label       or Tunnel Id   Switched       interface
None       207         1.1.1.0/24[V]  0              Se1/5       point2point
```

The output of the preceding **show** command reveals that when a packet comes in with no label, it will go out with label 207, and the outgoing interface is S1/5.

The output of the following command shows that the next hop to reach network 1.1.1.0/24 is 2.2.2.2. You can also see that the route was redistributed correctly with an RD of 1:10 to 1:20:

```
R6# show bgp vpnv4 unicast all | begin Network

   Network          Next Hop          Metric LocPrf Weight Path
Route Distinguisher: 1:10
*>i1.1.1.0/24       2.2.2.2               1    100      0 ?
*>i12.1.1.0/24      2.2.2.2               0    100      0 ?
Route Distinguisher: 1:20 (default for vrf CB)
*>i1.1.1.0/24       2.2.2.2               1    100      0 ?
*> 7.7.7.0/24       67.1.1.7              1         32768 ?
*>i12.1.1.0/24      2.2.2.2               0    100      0 ?
*> 67.1.1.0/24      0.0.0.0               0         32768 ?
```

Let's see how the local router reaches 2.2.2.2:

```
R6# show mpls forwarding-table 2.2.2.2

Local      Outgoing    Prefix         Bytes Label   Outgoing    Next Hop
Label      Label       or Tunnel Id   Switched      interface
600        500         2.2.2.2/32     0             Se1/5       point2point
```

You can see that PE-6 (the PE router) will assign label 500, and it'll send it out of its S1/5 interface. This label is *not* the VPN label; it is the IPv4 label or the top label, and the top label will be swapped from one "P" LSR to another "P" LSR. Therefore, R6 will assign a bottom label of 207 (the VPN label) and a top label of 502 (the IPv4 label). Let's verify this on R6's CEF table:

```
R6# show ip cef vrf CB 1.1.1.0
1.1.1.0/24
  nexthop 56.1.1.5 Serial1/5 label 500 207
```

Sure enough, the top label that gets swapped from one LSR to another is label 500; this label was advertised to the local router by R5. The second label, or the bottommost label, is label 207, and this label was imposed by PE-2—to be more specific, by the MP-BGP process running on PE-2. This is called the VPN label. Let's move a little closer.

If the local LSR receives a labeled packet with the top label of 500, it will swap that label with 400 and send it out of its S1/4 interface toward R4:

```
On R5:


R5# show mpls for 2.2.2.2 32


Local       Outgoing    Prefix          Bytes Label    Outgoing    Next Hop
Label       Label       or Tunnel Id    Switched       interface
500         400         2.2.2.2/32      88737          Se1/4       point2point
```

If the local LSR receives a labeled packet with the top label of 400, it will swap that label with 300 and send it out of its S1/3 interface toward R3:

```
On R4:


R4# show mpls for 2.2.2.2 32


Local       Outgoing    Prefix          Bytes Label    Outgoing    Next Hop
Label       Label       or Tunnel Id    Switched       interface
400         300         2.2.2.2/32      88919          Se1/3       point2point
```

If the local LSR (R3) receives a labeled packet with the top label of 300, it will pop that label and send it out of its S1/2 interface toward R2:

```
On R3:


R3# show mpls for 2.2.2.2 32


Local       Outgoing    Prefix          Bytes Label    Outgoing    Next Hop
Label       Label       or Tunnel Id    Switched       interface
300         Pop Label   2.2.2.2/32      82942          Se1/2       point2point
```

R2 receives the packet with *only* one label—that's label 207, or the VPN label. Let's see what action this LSR takes when it receives the labeled packet:

```
On R2:


R2# show mpls for 2.2.2.2 32


Local       Outgoing    Prefix          Bytes Label    Outgoing    Next Hop
Label       Label       or Tunnel Id    Switched       interface
None        No Label    2.2.2.2/32      0              aggr-punt
```

```
R2# show ip cef vrf CA 1.1.1.0

1.1.1.0/24
  nexthop 12.1.1.1 FastEthernet0/0

R2# show ip route vrf CA 1.1.1.0

Routing Table: CA
Routing entry for 1.1.1.0/24
  Known via "rip", distance 120, metric 1
  Redistributing via bgp 100, rip
  Advertised by bgp 100
  Last update from 12.1.1.1 on FastEthernet0/0, 00:00:22 ago
  Routing Descriptor Blocks:
  * 12.1.1.1, from 12.1.1.1, 00:00:22 ago, via FastEthernet0/0
      Route metric is 1, traffic share count is 1
```

The output of the following **show** command reveals what the local router does before it sends the packet to R1. If R2 sees label 207 coming in, it will send the packet out with no labels whatsoever and send it to 12.1.1.1:

```
R2# show bgp vpnv4 unicast vrf CA labels

  Network          Next Hop        In label/Out label
Route Distinguisher: 1:10 (CA)
  1.1.1.0/24       12.1.1.1         207/nolabel
  7.7.7.0/24       6.6.6.6          nolabel/607
  12.1.1.0/24      0.0.0.0          208/nolabel(CA)
  67.1.1.0/24      6.6.6.6          nolabel/608
```

Let's see how the labels are imposed, swapped, and popped:

```
On R7:

R7# traceroute 1.1.1.1 numeric

Type escape sequence to abort.
Tracing the route to 1.1.1.1
VRF info: (vrf in name/id, vrf out name/id)
  1 67.1.1.6 0 msec 0 msec 4 msec
  2 56.1.1.5 [MPLS: Labels 500/207 Exp 0] 176 msec 180 msec 184 msec
  3 45.1.1.4 [MPLS: Labels 400/207 Exp 0] 160 msec 164 msec 160 msec
  4 34.1.1.3 [MPLS: Labels 300/207 Exp 0] 148 msec 144 msec 144 msec
  5 12.1.1.2 [MPLS: Label 207 Exp 0] 128 msec 128 msec 128 msec
  6 12.1.1.1 76 msec *  72 msec
```

- **First line:** The packet is sent to the next-hop router with an IP address of 67.1.1.6; this is router R6.

- **Second line:** When PE-6 receives the packet destined to 1.1.1.1, it looks up its LFIB and assigns label 207, which is the VPN label. Then it realizes that the next hop is 2.2.2.2, its peer neighbor—but the question is, what label should it assign that will forward the packet toward 2.2.2.2? The answer is 500. Therefore, R6 assigns the second label, or the IPv4 label of 500, and sends it to R5 (56.1.1.5).

- **Third line:** R5 swaps the top label with 400 and sends it to R4 with an IP address of 45.1.1.4.

- **Fourth line:** R4 swaps the top label with 300 and sends it to R3 with an IP address of 34.1.1.3.

- **Fifth line:** Because R3 is the penultimate hop popper (PHP), it pops the top label (300) and forwards the packet as a labeled packet with a VPN label of 207 and sends the labeled packet to R2.

- **Sixth line:** R2 pops the VPN label and sends the packet with no labels to R1 with an IP address of 12.1.1.1.

We need to take a closer look at the control plane process happening here.

Table 15-3 shows how each LSR will assign a label for R2's 2.2.2.2 locally.

Table 15-3 *LSR Label Assignments for R2*

R2	R3	R4	R5	R6
Local – Imp-null	Local – 300	Local – 400	Local – 500	Local – 600

Once the labels are assigned locally, they are advertised to their neighboring LDP peer, as shown in Table 15-4.

Table 15-4 *Advertising Labels to the Neighboring LDP Peer*

R2	R3	R4	R5	R6
Local – Imp-null	Local – 300	Local – 400	Local – 500	Local – 600
	Remote – Imp-null	Remote – 300	Remote – 400	Remote – 500

Therefore, if R6 needs to connect to 2.2.2.2, it has to impose label 500 and send it to R5:

- R5 swaps label 500 with 400 and sends it to R4.

- R4 swaps label 400 with 300 and sends it to R3.

- R3 pops label 300, and the packet is sent to R2.

When R2 receives a routing update from R1 (customer router), it assigns label 207, an RD and an RT, and sends them to R6, as outlined in Table 15-5.

Table 15-5 *Packet Label Assignment*

R2	R3	R4	R5	R6
Local – Imp-null	Local – 300	Local – 400	Local – 500	Local – 600
	Remote – Imp-null	Remote – 300	Remote – 400	Remote – 500
207, RD, RT	207, RD, RT	207, RD, RT	207, RD, RT	207, RD, RT

- Now R6 knows which label (207 in this case) it has to assign to reach 1.1.1.0/24.

- R7 (the customer) pings R1 and sends the IP packet to the next-hop IP address of 67.1.1.6 or R6.

- R6 receives the unlabeled packet destined to 1.1.1.1 with a next-hop IP address of 2.2.2.2.

- R6 assigns label 207 (the VPN label that R6 received from R2), an RD, and an RT and then realizes that this needs to be sent to 2.2.2.2 (R2). R6 assigns label 207 to reach 1.1.1.0/24.

- R6 assigns the second label of 500 (the IPv4 label to reach 2.2.2.2) and sends the labeled packet to R5.

- R5 *only* looks at the top label and swaps the top label of 500 with 400 and sends it to R4.

- R4 receives a labeled packet. It swaps label 400 with 300 and sends it to R3.

- R3 receives label 300. It pops the label and sends the labeled packet to R2.

- R2 receives a labeled packet. It removes the RD and then checks its BGP configuration to see which VRF is importing that particular RT. Once it finds this, it pops the RT and label 207 and sends the IP packet to the customer.

It is very important to have a process that you can follow. The following outlines the process:

1. **Configure and verify the topology:** This is where you ping the directly connected router and verify the IP addresses and the loopback interfaces, as well as verify that CEF is running.

2. **Configure OSPF in the core:** This provides reachability within the core. I recommend agreeing on a process identifier (I use PID 1) when configuring OSPF on the core routers. What if the IGP between the CE and the PE routers is also OSPF? In that case, a PID of 2 is what I use for that purpose. In this step, you should run OSPF on *only* the links and the loopback interfaces within the core.

3. **Configure LDP and verify neighbor adjacency:** Label distribution protocol is one way that you can exchange information regarding label assignment. In this lab, we will rely on it to translate all relevant label information between MPLS-enabled devices.

4. **Configure BGP:** In this step, you should pay close attention to the task. If the task states that *only* VPNv4 routes should be exchanged, which loopback interface should be used as the source of BGP updates?

5. **Configure VRFs:** The VRFs, RD, and RTs are configured. Ensure that the RTs match on both PEs; otherwise, the customers will not see each other's routes. Assign the interface that connects the PE to the CE in the VRF. Names are always case sensitive. You must go back to BGP and activate the neighboring PE in the address family for VPNv4.

6. **Configure routing between the CE and the PE routers:** Ordinarily, organizations run static routing between their sites and the service provider, but routing protocols can also be used. We will explore all the routing options mentioned in the blueprint.

7. **Redistribution:** Always redistribute in one direction and verify before redistributing in the opposite direction.

The preceding list is *not* detailed, and you should create your own process in a detailed manner. Once you come up with your own process, you should configure MPLS/L3VPNs using that process for both implemetation and troubleshooting.

Erase the startup configuration of these routers and reload them before proceeding to the next lab.

Lab 15-3: EIGRP Routing in a VPN

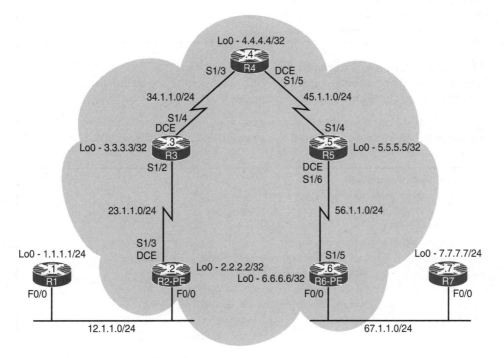

Figure 15-3 *Configuring RIPv2 Routing in a VPN*

Figure 15-3 illustrates the topology that will be used in the following tasks.

Task 1 through Task 5 of RIPv2 routing in Lab 15-2 are identical to the first five tasks in this lab. Therefore, repeat Tasks 1 through 5 before proceeding to the next task.

Task 6

Configure EIGRP between R1 and PE-2 and between R7 and PE-6. The customer routers (R1 and R7) should also run EIGRP on their lo0 interfaces. If this configuration is performed successfully, the CE routers (R1 and R7) should have reachability to each other's routes. You should use EIGRP named mode when configuring EIGRP on R1 and R7. Use any AS number on the PE routers.

Let's configure R1 and R2:

```
On R1:


R1(config)# router eigrp AS100
R1(config-router)# address-family ipv4 unicast as 100
R1(config-router-af)# network 1.1.1.1 0.0.0.0
R1(config-router-af)# network 12.1.1.1 0.0.0.0


On PE-2:


R2(config)# router eigrp 100
R2(config-router)# address-family ipv4 vrf CA
R2(config-router-af)# network 12.1.1.2 0.0.0.0
```

The **autonomous-system** command is mandatory and it *must* be configured, because the VRF configured under **router eigrp 100** will not inherit the AS number from the global EIGRP process. Therefore, there are two options.

In IOS release 12 or earlier, the AS number was configured under the address family using the **autonomous-system** command. This command is hidden in Cisco's IOS 15 code. Let's verify:

```
R2(config)# router eigrp 100
R2(config-router)# address-family ipv4 vrf CA
R2(config-router-af)# network 12.1.1.2 0.0.0.0
R2(config-router-af)# ?
Address Family configuration commands:
  auto-summary         Enable automatic network number summarization
  bfd                  BFD configuration commands
  default              Set a command to its defaults
  default-information  Control distribution of default information
  default-metric       Set metric of redistributed routes
  distance             Define an administrative distance
```

```
distribute-list     Filter entries in eigrp updates
eigrp               EIGRP specific commands
exit-address-family Exit Address Family configuration mode
help                Description of the interactive help system
maximum-paths       Forward packets over multiple paths
maximum-prefix      Maximum number of prefixes acceptable in aggregate
metric              Modify metrics and parameters for advertisement
neighbor            Specify a neighbor router
network             Enable routing on an IP network
no                  Negate a command or set its defaults
offset-list         Add or subtract offset from EIGRP metrics
passive-interface   Suppress routing updates on an interface
redistribute        Redistribute IPv4 routes from another routing protocol
shutdown            Shutdown address family
summary-metric      Specify summary to apply metric/filtering
timers              Adjust routing timers
traffic-share       How to compute traffic share over alternate paths
variance            Control load balancing variance
```

Even though the command is hidden, it can be configured; the Tab key cannot be used to complete the command, but you don't have to configure every letter. Let's verify:

```
R2(config-router-af)# autonomous-system 100
```

You should see the following console message:

```
DUAL-5-NBRCHANGE: EIGRP-IPv4 100: Neighbor 12.1.1.1 (FastEthernet0/0) is up:
new adjacency
```

The AS number can also be configured as part of the **address-family** command. Let's configure and verify. But first, let's remove EIGRP and reconfigure it:

```
R2(config)# no router eigrp 100


R2(config)# router eigrp 100
R2(config-router)# address-family ipv4 vrf CA ?
  autonomous-system  Specify Address-Family Autonomous System Number

R2(config-router)# address-family ipv4 vrf CA autonomous-system 100
R2(config-router-af)# network 12.1.1.2 0.0.0.0
```

You should get the following console message:

```
%DUAL-5-NBRCHANGE: EIGRP-IPv4 100: Neighbor 12.1.1.1 (FastEthernet0/0) is up:
new adjacency
```

Let's verify the configuration:

```
On PE-2:

R2# show ip route vrf CA eigrp | begin Gate
Gateway of last resort is not set

      1.0.0.0/24 is subnetted, 1 subnets
D        1.1.1.0 [90/156160] via 12.1.1.1, 00:02:35, FastEthernet0/0
```

Let's configure PE-6 and R7:

```
R6(config)# router eigrp 100
R6(config-router)# address-family ipv4 vrf CB autonomous-system 100
R6(config-router-af)# network 67.1.1.6 0.0.0.0

On R7:

R7(config)# router eigrp AS100
R7(config-router)# address-family ipv4 unicast autonomous-system 100
R7(config-router-af)# network 7.7.7.7 0.0.0.0
R7(config-router-af)# network 67.1.1.7 0.0.0.0
```

You should see the following console message:

```
%DUAL-5-NBRCHANGE: EIGRP-IPv4 100: Neighbor 67.1.1.7 (FastEthernet0/0) is up:
new adjacency
```

Let's verify the configuration:

```
On PE-6:

R6# show ip route vrf CB eigrp | begin Gate
Gateway of last resort is not set

      7.0.0.0/24 is subnetted, 1 subnets
D        7.7.7.0 [90/28192] via 67.1.1.7, 00:00:52, FastEthernet0/0
```

The final step is to perform the route redistribution:

```
On PE-2:


R2(config)# router bgp 100
R2(config-router)# address-family ipv4 vrf CA
R2(config-router-af)# redistribute eigrp 100
```

Let's verify the configuration:

```
R2# show bgp vpnv4 unicast all | begin Network

   Network            Next Hop          Metric LocPrf Weight Path
Route Distinguisher: 1:10 (default for vrf CA)
*> 1.1.1.0/24         12.1.1.1          156160        32768 ?
*> 12.1.1.0/24        0.0.0.0                0        32768 ?
```

Let's verify this configuration on PE-6:

```
On PE-6:


R6# show bgp vpnv4 unicast all | begin Network

   Network            Next Hop          Metric LocPrf Weight Path
Route Distinguisher: 1:10
*>i1.1.1.0/24         2.2.2.2           156160    100     0 ?
*>i12.1.1.0/24        2.2.2.2                0    100     0 ?
Route Distinguisher: 1:20 (default for vrf CB)
*>i1.1.1.0/24         2.2.2.2           156160    100     0 ?
*>i12.1.1.0/24        2.2.2.2                0    100     0 ?
```

Now you need to redistribute BGP into EIGRP so that R7 (the customer router) can see the routes from R1:

```
R6(config)# router eigrp 100
R6(config-router)# address-family ipv4 vrf CB
R6(config-router-af)# redistribute bgp 100 metric 1 1 1 1 1
```

Let's verify the configuration:

```
On R7:


R7# show ip route eigrp | begin Gate
Gateway of last resort is not set
```

```
        1.0.0.0/24 is subnetted, 1 subnets
D          1.1.1.0 [90/2713600] via 67.1.1.6, 00:00:34, GigabitEthernet0/0
        12.0.0.0/24 is subnetted, 1 subnets
D          12.1.1.0 [90/153600] via 67.1.1.6, 00:00:34, GigabitEthernet0/0
```

Now you need to perform redistribution going in the opposite direction:

```
On PE-6:

R6(config)# router bgp 100
R6(config-router)# address-family ipv4 vrf CB
R6(config-router-af)# redistribute eigrp 100
```

Now we will make the necessary configuration on R2 which is acting as a Provider Edge device.

```
On PE-2:

R2(config)# router eigrp 100
R2(config-router)# address-family ipv4 vrf CA
R2(config-router-af)# redistribute bgp 100 metric 1 1 1 1 1
```

We need to confirm that we have formed EIGRP adjacencies.

```
On R1:

R1# show ip route eigrp | begin Gate
Gateway of last resort is not set

     7.0.0.0/24 is subnetted, 1 subnets
D       7.7.7.0 [90/30752] via 12.1.1.2, 00:00:28, FastEthernet0/0
     67.0.0.0/24 is subnetted, 1 subnets
D       67.1.1.0 [90/30720] via 12.1.1.2, 00:00:28, FastEthernet0/0
```

Let's test the configuration:

```
On R1:

R1# ping 7.7.7.7
Type escape sequence to abort.
Sending 5, 100-byte ICMP Echos to 7.7.7.7, timeout is 2 seconds:
!!!!!
Success rate is 100 percent (5/5), round-trip min/avg/max = 120/121/124 ms
```

```
R1# ping 7.7.7.7 source loopback0
Type escape sequence to abort.
Sending 5, 100-byte ICMP Echos to 7.7.7.7, timeout is 2 seconds:
Packet sent with a source address of 1.1.1.1
!!!!!
Success rate is 100 percent (5/5), round-trip min/avg/max = 120/121/124 ms
```

Erase the startup configuration of these routers and reload them before proceeding to the next lab.

Lab 15-4: OSPF Routing in a VPN

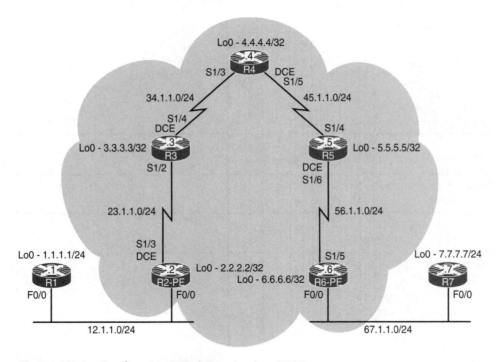

Figure 15-4 *Configuring RIPv2 Routing in a VPN*

Figure 15-4 illustrates the topology that will be used in the following tasks.

Task 1 through Task 5 of Lab 15-2 are identical to the first five tasks in this lab. Therefore, repeat Tasks 1 through 5 before proceeding to the next task.

Task 6

Configure the CEs (R1 and R7) with a VRF service that incorporates OSPF as the routing protocol. PE-2 should use an OSPF process ID of 2, whereas PE-6 should use a PID of 6 to accomplish this task.

- R1 should use an OSPF RID of 0.0.0.1, and R7 should use an OSPF RID of 0.0.0.7.

- R1 and R7 should be configured in Area 0 on all their directly connected interfaces, and they should see each other's routes as intra-area OSPF routes. The loopback interfaces of R1 and R7 should be advertised with their correct mask.

Let's start by configuring OSPF on R1 and PE-2:

```
On R1:

R1(config)# interface loopback0
R1(config-if)# ip ospf network point-to-point

R1(config)# router ospf 1
R1(config-router)# router-id 0.0.0.1
R1(config-router)# network 1.1.1.1 0.0.0.0 area 1
R1(config-router)# network 12.1.1.1 0.0.0.0 area 1

On PE-2:

R2(config)# router ospf 2 vrf CA
R2(config-router)# network 12.1.1.2 0.0.0.0 area 0
```

You should see the following console message:

```
%OSPF-5-ADJCHG: Process 2, Nbr 0.0.0.1 on FastEthernet0/0 from LOADING to FULL,
Loading Done
```

Let's verify the configuration:

```
On PE-2:

R2# show ip route vrf CA ospf | begin Gate
Gateway of last resort is not set

      1.0.0.0/24 is subnetted, 1 subnets
O        1.1.1.0 [110/2] via 12.1.1.1, 00:01:43, FastEthernet0/0
```

Let's configure OSPF on PE-6 and R7:

```
On R7:

R7(config)# interface loopback0
R7(config-if)# ip ospf network point-to-point
```

```
R7(config)# router ospf 1
R7(config-router)# router-id 0.0.0.7
R7(config-router)# network 7.7.7.7 0.0.0.0 area 0
R7(config-router)# network 67.1.1.7 0.0.0.0 area 0


On PE-6:


R7(config)# router ospf 6 vrf CB
R7(config-router)# network 67.1.1.6 0.0.0.0 area 0
```

You should see the following console message:

```
%OSPF-5-ADJCHG: Process 6, Nbr 0.0.0.7 on FastEthernet0/0 from LOADING to FULL,
Loading Done
```

Let's verify the configuration:

```
On PE-6:


R6# show ip route vrf CB ospf | begin Gate
Gateway of last resort is not set


     7.0.0.0/24 is subnetted, 1 subnets
O        7.7.7.0 [110/2] via 67.1.1.7, 00:01:34, FastEthernet0/0
```

So far you can see that the CE and PE routers are successfully exchanging routes. The next step is to perform the redistribution. You should do this in one direction first and then perform redistribution in the opposite direction. Let's start with PE-2:

```
On PE-2:


R2(config)# router bgp 100
R2(config-router)# address-family ipv4 vrf CA
R2(config-router-af)# redistribute ospf 2
```

Let's verify the configuration:

```
R2# show bgp vpnv4 unicast all | begin Network


   Network          Next Hop            Metric LocPrf Weight Path
Route Distinguisher: 1:10 (default for vrf CA)
*> 1.1.1.0/24       12.1.1.1                 2          32768 ?
*> 12.1.1.0/24      0.0.0.0                  0          32768 ?
```

This means that PE-6 should also have these prefixes in its BGP table. Let's verify:

```
On PE-6:


R6# show bgp vpnv4 unicast all | begin Network


   Network          Next Hop           Metric LocPrf Weight Path
Route Distinguisher: 1:10
*>i1.1.1.0/24       2.2.2.2                 2    100      0 ?
*>i12.1.1.0/24      2.2.2.2                 0    100      0 ?
Route Distinguisher: 1:20 (default for vrf CB)
*>i1.1.1.0/24       2.2.2.2                 2    100      0 ?
*>i12.1.1.0/24      2.2.2.2                 0    100      0 ?
```

To be more specific, you can also use the following **show** command:

```
R6# show bgp vpnv4 unicast vrf CB | begin Network


   Network          Next Hop           Metric LocPrf Weight Path
Route Distinguisher: 1:20 (default for vrf CB)
*>i1.1.1.0/24       2.2.2.2                 2    100      0 ?
*>i12.1.1.0/24      2.2.2.2                 0    100      0 ?
```

Let's redistribute the VPNv4 routes into OSPF so that R7 can see them:

```
R6(config)# router ospf 6 vrf CB
R6(config-router)# redistribute bgp 100 subnets
```

R7 should have these routes in its routing table. Let's verify:

```
On R7:


R7# show ip route ospf | begin Gate
Gateway of last resort is not set


      1.0.0.0/24 is subnetted, 1 subnets
O E2     1.1.1.0 [110/2] via 67.1.1.6, 00:00:15, GigabitEthernet0/0
      12.0.0.0/24 is subnetted, 1 subnets
O E2     12.1.1.0 [110/1] via 67.1.1.6, 00:00:15, GigabitEthernet0/0
```

Well, this is good and bad news. The good news is that the redistribution has worked. The bad news is that the routes are showing up in the routing table of R7 as external type-2, or E2. Let's perform the redistribution in the opposite direction and then find out why the routes are showing up as E2.

```
On PE-6:

R6(config)# router bgp 100
R6(config-router)# address-family ipv4 vrf CB
R6(config-router-af)# redistribute ospf 6
```

Let's verify the configuration:

```
R6# show bgp vpnv4 unicast vrf CB | begin Network

   Network          Next Hop          Metric LocPrf Weight Path
Route Distinguisher: 1:20 (default for vrf CB)
*>i1.1.1.0/24       2.2.2.2               2    100     0 ?
*> 7.7.7.0/24       67.1.1.7              2          32768 ?
*>i12.1.1.0/24      2.2.2.2               0    100     0 ?
*> 67.1.1.0/24      0.0.0.0               0          32768 ?
```

This means that PE-2 should have these prefixes in its BGP table:

```
On PE-2:

R2# show bgp vpnv4 unicast all | begin Network

   Network          Next Hop          Metric LocPrf Weight Path
Route Distinguisher: 1:10 (default for vrf CA)
*> 1.1.1.0/24       12.1.1.1              2          32768 ?
*>i7.7.7.0/24       6.6.6.6               2    100     0 ?
*> 12.1.1.0/24      0.0.0.0               0          32768 ?
*>i67.1.1.0/24      6.6.6.6               0    100     0 ?
Route Distinguisher: 1:20
*>i7.7.7.0/24       6.6.6.6               2    100     0 ?
*>i67.1.1.0/24      6.6.6.6               0    100     0 ?
```

The output of the preceding **show** command reveals that 7.7.7.0/24 and 67.1.1.0/24 are in the BGP table of PE-2. Let's redistribute BGP into OSPF so that R1 can see the routes advertised by R7:

```
R2(config)# router ospf 2 vrf CA
R2(config-router)# redistribute bgp 100 subnets
```

Let's verify the configuration:

```
On R1:


R1# show ip route ospf | begin Gate
Gateway of last resort is not set


      7.0.0.0/24 is subnetted, 1 subnets
O E2     7.7.7.0 [110/2] via 12.1.1.2, 00:00:21, FastEthernet0/0
      67.0.0.0/24 is subnetted, 1 subnets
O E2     67.1.1.0 [110/1] via 12.1.1.2, 00:00:21, FastEthernet0/0
```

Sure enough, R1 can see the routes, but once again they are showing up as E2. Let's test this configuration:

```
R1# ping 7.7.7.7

Type escape sequence to abort.
Sending 5, 100-byte ICMP Echos to 7.7.7.7, timeout is 2 seconds:
!!!!!
Success rate is 100 percent (5/5), round-trip min/avg/max = 120/120/124 ms


R1# ping 7.7.7.7 source loopback0

Type escape sequence to abort.
Sending 5, 100-byte ICMP Echos to 7.7.7.7, timeout is 2 seconds:
Packet sent with a source address of 1.1.1.1
!!!!!
Success rate is 100 percent (5/5), round-trip min/avg/max = 120/121/124 ms
```

Note   All OSPF routes are showing up as external type-2. Was this because of the redistribution?

Although redistribution results in this behavior under normal circumstances, this does not follow classic OSPF default behavior. Let's look at the reason behind the behavior:

```
On PE-2:

R2# show bgp vpnv4 unicast vrf CA 7.7.7.0 | include OSPF DOMAIN

      Extended Community: RT:1:100 OSPF DOMAIN ID:0x0005:0x000000060200
```

Every domain ID on Cisco routers will begin with 0005, 0105, or 0205, which identifies the type of format used. With the 0005 value used, the next four octets are viewed as the global administrator field, and it's used as part of the domain ID (in this case, 0x00000006). This value is highlighted in the preceding output.

The last two octets would be used as a local administrator field, which is ignored. This is the 0200 at the end of this domain ID. Let's repeat the same **show** command on PE-6 for prefix 1.1.1.0/24:

```
On PE-6:

R6# show bgp vpnv4 unicast vrf CB 1.1.1.0 | include OSPF DOMAIN

        Extended Community: RT:1:100 OSPF DOMAIN ID:0x0005:0x000000020200
```

As you can see, the domain IDs don't match at all. Under normal OSPF design rules, the process ID of an OSPF router doesn't need to match any other peer's process ID. However, with MPLS, the router uses the OSPF process as a portion of the domain ID. Therefore, you must manually change the process ID to match on all sides of the cloud or statically configure a *domain ID* that matches on all routers.

Routers that do not share the same domain ID are considered external to OSPF. If the domain IDs match, the routes are considered type-3 LSAs.

Manually configuring the domain ID is preferred because this does not change the classic understanding of the process ID in OSPF. A clearing of BGP with **clear ip bgp * in** and **clear ip bgp * out** can be used to enforce the change faster.

Let's change the domain IDs:

```
On PE-2:

R2(config)# router ospf 2 vrf CA
R2(config-router)# domain-id 0.0.0.1

On PE-6:

R6(config)# router ospf 6 vrf CB
R6(config-router)# domain-id 0.0.0.1

On PE-2 and PE-6:

Rx# clear ip bgp * in
Rx# clear ip bgp * out
```

Let's verify the configuration:

```
On R1:


R1# show ip route ospf | begin Gate
Gateway of last resort is not set


      7.0.0.0/24 is subnetted, 1 subnets
O IA      7.7.7.0 [110/3] via 12.1.1.2, 00:02:05, FastEthernet0/0
      67.0.0.0/24 is subnetted, 1 subnets
O IA      67.1.1.0 [110/2] via 12.1.1.2, 00:02:05, FastEthernet0/0


On R7:


R7# show ip route ospf | begin Gate
Gateway of last resort is not set


      1.0.0.0/24 is subnetted, 1 subnets
O IA      1.1.1.0 [110/3] via 67.1.1.6, 00:03:12, GigabitEthernet0/0
      12.0.0.0/24 is subnetted, 1 subnets
O IA      12.1.1.0 [110/2] via 67.1.1.6, 00:03:12, GigabitEthernet0/0
```

This looks a little better, but why are the prefixes showing up as inter-area?

In an MPLS environment, the cloud is known as the *MPLS VPN Backbone* area or the *Super Backbone* area, and the PE routers are known as the *ABRs*. Therefore, the prefixes from one CE traversed through the Super Backbone into Backbone area, and this is the reason they are seen as inter-area routes on the other CE. Let's look at the Super Backbone area:

```
On PE-2:


R2# show ip ospf 2 | include Super
 Connected to MPLS VPN Superbackbone, VRF CA
```

There are two solutions to this problem:

- **Solution 1:** In this solution, a **sham-link** is configured, which is the preferred method. It's the native solution to this problem. We will configure **sham-link** in the next lab.

- **Solution 2:** In this solution, a GRE tunnel is configured.

In this lab, we configure a GRE tunnel. When a GRE tunnel is configured, you must remember the following two important points:

- The tunnel interface must be advertised in the area that the customer routes are configured in.

■ The tunnel interface must be configured in the customer's VRF using the **vrf forwarding** or **ip vrf forwarding** command.

We are going to use the loopback0 interface of PE-2 as the source and the loopback0 interface of PE-6 as the destination of the tunnel. Remember that if the **vrf forwarding** command is entered after the IP address is configured, the IP address will be removed and it must be reconfigured.

```
R2(config)# interface tunnel 26
R2(config-if)# vrf forwarding CA
R2(config-if)# ip address 26.1.1.2 255.255.255.0
R2(config-if)# tunnel source loopback0
R2(config-if)# tunnel destination 6.6.6.6

R2(config)# router ospf 2 vrf CA
R2(config-router)# network 26.1.1.2 0.0.0.0 area 0

On PE-6:

R6(config)# interface tunnel 62
R6(config-if)# vrf forwarding CB
R6(config-if)# ip address 26.1.1.6 255.255.255.0
R6(config-if)# tunnel source loopback0
R6(config-if)# tunnel destination 2.2.2.2

R6(config)# router ospf 5 vrf CB
R6(config-router)# network 26.1.1.6 0.0.0.0 area 0
```

You should see the following console message:

```
%OSPF-5-ADJCHG: Process 6, Nbr 12.1.1.2 on Tunnel62 from LOADING to FULL,
Loading Done
```

Let's verify the configuration:

```
On R1:

R1# show ip route ospf | begin Gate
Gateway of last resort is not set

     7.0.0.0/24 is subnetted, 1 subnets
O       7.7.7.0 [110/1003] via 12.1.1.2, 00:04:15, FastEthernet0/0
     26.0.0.0/24 is subnetted, 1 subnets
O       26.1.1.0 [110/1001] via 12.1.1.2, 00:05:52, FastEthernet0/0
     67.0.0.0/24 is subnetted, 1 subnets
O       67.1.1.0 [110/1002] via 12.1.1.2, 00:04:15, FastEthernet0/0
```

You can see that R1's cost to reach 7.7.7.0/24 is 1003. Let's see why. To do this, add the cost of all the links from R1 to R7's loopback0 interface. You can see that the cost of the F0/0 interface of R1 is 1:

```
On R1:


R1# show ip ospf interface FastEthernet0/0 | include Cost

 Process ID 1, Router ID 0.0.0.1, Network Type BROADCAST, Cost: 1
 Topology-MTID    Cost    Disabled    Shutdown    Topology Name
```

Let's see the cost of the tunnel interface on PE-2:

```
On PE-2:


R2# show ip ospf interface tunnel 26 | include Cost

 Process ID 2, Router ID 12.1.1.2, Network Type POINT_TO_POINT, Cost: 1000
 Topology-MTID    Cost    Disabled    Shutdown    Topology Name
```

Let's see the cost of the F0/0 interface of PE-6:

```
On PE-6:


R6# show ip ospf interface FastEthernet0/0 | include Cost

 Process ID 6, Router ID 67.1.1.6, Network Type BROADCAST, Cost: 1
 Topology-MTID    Cost    Disabled    Shutdown    Topology Name
```

Let's check the cost of the loopback0 interface of R7:

```
On R7:


R7# show ip ospf interface loopback0 | include Cost

 Process ID 1, Router ID 0.0.0.7, Network Type POINT_TO_POINT, Cost: 1
 Topology-MTID    Cost    Disabled    Shutdown    Topology Name
```

Note The cost from R1 to R7's Lo0 interface is 1003.

Erase the startup configuration of the routers and reload them before proceeding to the next lab.

Lab 15-5: Backdoor Links and OSPF

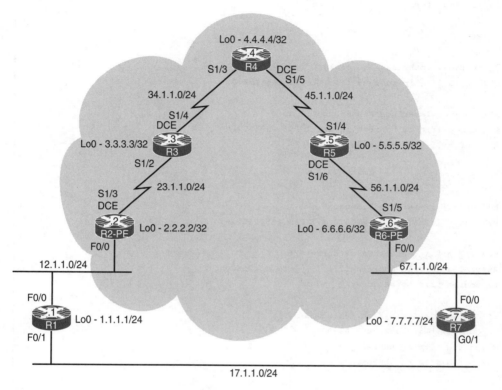

Figure 15-5 *Configuring RIPv2 Routing in a VPN*

Task 1

Configure the topology shown in Figure 15-5. Do not configure any routing protocol, or the F0/1 interface of R1 and the G0/1 interface of R7. Use a VLAN ID of your choice.

```
On SW1:

SW1(config)# interface range FastEthernet0/1-2
SW1(config-if-range)# switchport mode access
SW1(config-if-range)# switchport access vlan 12
% Access VLAN does not exist. Creating vlan 12
SW1(config-if-range)# no shutdown

SW1(config)# interface range FastEthernet0/6-7
SW1(config-if-range)# switchport mode access
SW1(config-if-range)# switchport access vlan 67
```

```
% Access VLAN does not exist. Creating vlan 67
SW1(config-if-range)# no shutdown


On R1:

R1(config)# interface loopback0
R1(config-if)# ip address 1.1.1.1 255.255.255.0

R1(config)# interface FastEthernet0/0
R1(config-if)# ip address 12.1.1.1 255.255.255.0
R1(config-if)# no shutdown


On R2:

R2(config)# interface loopback0
R2(config-if)# ip address 2.2.2.2 255.255.255.255

R2(config)# interface FastEthernet0/0
R2(config-if)# ip address 12.1.1.2 255.255.255.0
R2(config-if)# no shutdown

R2(config-if)# interface Serial1/3
R2(config-if)# clock rate 64000
R2(config-if)# ip address 23.1.1.2 255.255.255.0
R2(config-if)# no shutdown


On R3:

R3(config)# interface loopback0
R3(config-if)# ip address 3.3.3.3 255.255.255.255

R3(config)# interface Serial1/2
R3(config-if)# ip address 23.1.1.3 255.255.255.0
R3(config-if)# no shutdown

R3(config)# interface Serial1/4
R3(config-if)# clock rate 64000
R3(config-if)# ip address 34.1.1.3 255.255.255.0
R3(config-if)# no shutdown


On R4:

R4(config)# interface loopback0
R4(config-if)# ip address 4.4.4.4 255.255.255.255
```

```
R4(config)# interface Serial1/3
R4(config-if)# ip address 34.1.1.4 255.255.255.0
R4(config-if)# no shutdown


R4(config)# interface Serial1/5
R4(config-if)# clock rate 64000
R4(config-if)# ip address 45.1.1.4 255.255.255.0
R4(config-if)# no shutdown


On R5:

R5(config)# interface loopback0
R5(config-if)# ip address 5.5.5.5 255.255.255.255


R5(config)# interface Serial1/4
R5(config-if)# ip address 45.1.1.5 255.255.255.0
R5(config-if)# no shutdown


R5(config)# interface Serial1/6
R5(config-if)# clock rate 64000
R5(config-if)# ip address 56.1.1.5 255.255.255.0
R5(config-if)# no shutdown


On R6:

R6(config)# interface loopback0
R6(config-if)# ip address 6.6.6.6 255.255.255.255


R6(config)# interface Serial1/5
R6(config-if)# ip address 56.1.1.6 255.255.255.0
R6(config-if)# no shutdown


R6(config)# interface FastEthernet0/0
R6(config-if)# ip address 67.1.1.6 255.255.255.0
R6(config-if)# no shutdown


On R7:

R7(config)# interface loopback0
R7(config-if)# ip address 7.7.7.7 255.255.255.0


R7(config)# interface GigabitEthernet0/0
R7(config-if)# ip address 67.1.1.7 255.255.255.0
R7(config-if)# no shutdown
```

Task 2

Configure OSPF on the core MPLS routers (R2 to R6). You should run OSPF Area 0 on the Lo0 interfaces and the links that connect these routers to each other. The router IDs of R2, R3, R4, R5, and R6 should be configured as 0.0.0.2, 0.0.0.3, 0.0.0.4, 0.0.0.5, and 0.0.0.6 respectively. Do *not* configure OSPF between R1 and R2 and between R6 and R7.

```
On R2:

R2(config)# router ospf 1
R3(config-router)# router-id 0.0.0.2
R2(config-router)# network 2.2.2.2 0.0.0.0 area 0
R2(config-router)# network 23.1.1.2 0.0.0.0 area 0


On R3:

R3(config)# router ospf 1
R2(config-router)# router-id 0.0.0.3
R3(config-router)# network 3.3.3.3 0.0.0.0 area 0
R3(config-router)# network 23.1.1.3 0.0.0.0 area 0
R3(config-router)# network 34.1.1.3 0.0.0.0 area 0
```

You should see the following console message:

```
%OSPF-5-ADJCHG: Process 1, Nbr 0.0.0.2 on Serial1/2 from LOADING to FULL,
Loading Done
```

```
On R4:

R4(config)# router ospf 1
R4(config-router)# router-id 0.0.0.4
R4(config-router)# network 4.4.4.4 0.0.0.0 area 0
R4(config-router)# network 34.1.1.4 0.0.0.0 area 0
R4(config-router)# network 45.1.1.4 0.0.0.0 area 0
```

Now we will transition to R5 and setup OSPF there as specified in the task.

```
%OSPF-5-ADJCHG: Process 1, Nbr 0.0.0.3 on Serial1/3 from LOADING to FULL,
Loading Done


On R5:

R5(config)# router ospf 1
R5(config-router)# router-id 0.0.0.5
```

```
R5(config-router)# network 5.5.5.5 0.0.0.0 area 0
R5(config-router)# network 45.1.1.5 0.0.0.0 area 0
R5(config-router)# network 56.1.1.5 0.0.0.0 area 0
```

R6 also needs to be added to the OSPF Domain.

```
%OSPF-5-ADJCHG: Process 1, Nbr 0.0.0.4 on Serial1/4 from LOADING to FULL,
Loading Done


On R6:


R6(config)# router ospf 1
R6(config-router)# router-id 0.0.0.6
R6(config-router)# network 6.6.6.6 0.0.0.0 area 0
R6(config-router)# network 56.1.1.6 0.0.0.0 area 0
```

Once R6 is configured you should see the following console message:

```
%OSPF-5-ADJCHG: Process 1, Nbr 0.0.0.5 on Serial1/5 from LOADING to FULL,
Loading Done
```

Let's verify the configuration:

```
On R2:


R2# show ip route ospf | begin Gate
Gateway of last resort is not set

      3.0.0.0/32 is subnetted, 1 subnets
O        3.3.3.3 [110/782] via 23.1.1.3, 00:01:22, Serial1/3
      4.0.0.0/32 is subnetted, 1 subnets
O        4.4.4.4 [110/1563] via 23.1.1.3, 00:01:11, Serial1/3
      5.0.0.0/32 is subnetted, 1 subnets
O        5.5.5.5 [110/2344] via 23.1.1.3, 00:00:59, Serial1/3
      6.0.0.0/32 is subnetted, 1 subnets
O        6.6.6.6 [110/3125] via 23.1.1.3, 00:00:43, Serial1/3
      34.0.0.0/24 is subnetted, 1 subnets
O        34.1.1.0 [110/1562] via 23.1.1.3, 00:01:11, Serial1/3
      45.0.0.0/24 is subnetted, 1 subnets
O        45.1.1.0 [110/2343] via 23.1.1.3, 00:00:59, Serial1/3
      56.0.0.0/24 is subnetted, 1 subnets
O        56.1.1.0 [110/3124] via 23.1.1.3, 00:00:43, Serial1/3
```

```
On R6:

R6# show ip route ospf | begin Gate
Gateway of last resort is not set


      2.0.0.0/32 is subnetted, 1 subnets
O        2.2.2.2 [110/3125] via 56.1.1.5, 00:02:43, Serial1/5
      3.0.0.0/32 is subnetted, 1 subnets
O        3.3.3.3 [110/2344] via 56.1.1.5, 00:02:43, Serial1/5
      4.0.0.0/32 is subnetted, 1 subnets
O        4.4.4.4 [110/1563] via 56.1.1.5, 00:02:43, Serial1/5
      5.0.0.0/32 is subnetted, 1 subnets
O        5.5.5.5 [110/782] via 56.1.1.5, 00:02:43, Serial1/5
      23.0.0.0/24 is subnetted, 1 subnets
O        23.1.1.0 [110/3124] via 56.1.1.5, 00:02:43, Serial1/5
      34.0.0.0/24 is subnetted, 1 subnets
O        34.1.1.0 [110/2343] via 56.1.1.5, 00:02:43, Serial1/5
      45.0.0.0/24 is subnetted, 1 subnets
O        45.1.1.0 [110/1562] via 56.1.1.5, 00:02:43, Serial1/5
```

Task 3

Configure LDP between the core routers. These routers should use their loopback0 interfaces as their LDP router ID; the core MPLS routers (R2, R3, R4, R5, and R6) should use the following label range:

> **R2:** 200–299
>
> **R3:** 300–399
>
> **R4:** 400–499
>
> **R5:** 500–599
>
> **R6:** 600–699

```
On R2:

R2(config)# mpls label range 200 299
R2(config)# mpls label protocol ldp
R2(config)# mpls ldp router-id lo0 force

R2(config)# interface Serial1/3
R2(config-if)# mpls ip
```

```
On R3:

R3(config)# mpls label protocol ldp
R3(config)# mpls ldp router-id lo0
R3(config)# mpls label range 300 399


R3(config)# interface Serial1/2
R3(config-if)# mpls ip


R3(config-if)# interface Serial1/4
R3(config-if)# mpls ip
```

Once R3 is configured we will move to R4 and set up the MPLS parameters and enable the interfaces.

```
%LDP-5-NBRCHG: LDP Neighbor 2.2.2.2:0 (1) is UP

On R4:

R4(config)# mpls label protocol ldp
R4(config)# mpls ldp router-id lo0
R4(config)# mpls label range 400 499

R4(config)# interface Serial1/3
R4(config-if)# mpls ip

R4(config)# interface Serial1/5
R4(config-if)# mpls ip
```

You should see the following console message; once you do you can move to R5.

```
%LDP-5-NBRCHG: LDP Neighbor 3.3.3.3:0 (1) is UP

On R5:

R5(config)# mpls label protocol ldp
R5(config)# mpls ldp router-id lo0
R5(config)# mpls label range 500 599

R5(config)# interface Serial1/4
R5(config-if)# mpls ip

R5(config)# interface Serial1/6
R5(config-if)# mpls ip
```

Lastly, R6 will be configured.

```
%LDP-5-NBRCHG: LDP Neighbor 4.4.4.4:0 (1) is UP

On R6:

R6(config)# mpls label protocol ldp
R6(config)# mpls ldp router-id lo0
R6(config)# mpls label range 600 699

R6(config)# interface Serial1/5
R6(config-if)# mpls ip
```

An adjacency should form with R5 as evidenced by the console message that should appear.

```
%LDP-5-NBRCHG: LDP Neighbor 5.5.5.5:0 (1) is UP
```

Let's look at all the interfaces configured for label switching:

```
On R2:

R2# show mpls interfaces

Interface            IP          Tunnel    BGP Static Operational
Serial1/3            Yes (ldp)   No        No  No     Yes
```

Let's see the neighboring LDP LSRs:

```
R2# show mpls ldp neighbor

    Peer LDP Ident: 3.3.3.3:0; Local LDP Ident 2.2.2.2:0
        TCP connection: 3.3.3.3.45826 - 2.2.2.2.646
        State: Oper; Msgs sent/rcvd: 15/14; Downstream
        Up time: 00:02:26
        LDP discovery sources:
          Serial1/3, Src IP addr: 23.1.1.3
        Addresses bound to peer LDP Ident:
          23.1.1.3        34.1.1.3        3.3.3.3
```

Note Because the LDP RID of R3 is higher than the local router, R3 will initiate the LDP session using a high port.

```
R2# show mpls ldp discovery all

Local LDP Identifier:
    2.2.2.2:0
    Discovery Sources:
    Interfaces:
        Serial1/3 (ldp): xmit/recv
            LDP Id: 3.3.3.3:0

R2# show mpls label range

Downstream Generic label region: Min/Max label: 200/299

On R4:

R4# show mpls interfaces

Interface            IP            Tunnel   BGP Static Operational
Serial1/3            Yes (ldp)     No       No  No     Yes
Serial1/5            Yes (ldp)     No       No  No     Yes

R4# show mpls ldp neighbor

    Peer LDP Ident: 3.3.3.3:0; Local LDP Ident 4.4.4.4:0
        TCP connection: 3.3.3.3.646 - 4.4.4.4.25499
        State: Oper; Msgs sent/rcvd: 14/14; Downstream
        Up time: 00:02:13
        LDP discovery sources:
          Serial1/3, Src IP addr: 34.1.1.3
        Addresses bound to peer LDP Ident:
          23.1.1.3        34.1.1.3        3.3.3.3
    Peer LDP Ident: 5.5.5.5:0; Local LDP Ident 4.4.4.4:0
        TCP connection: 5.5.5.5.34768 - 4.4.4.4.646
        State: Oper; Msgs sent/rcvd: 14/14; Downstream
        Up time: 00:02:02
        LDP discovery sources:
          Serial1/5, Src IP addr: 45.1.1.5
        Addresses bound to peer LDP Ident:
          45.1.1.5        56.1.1.5        5.5.5.5

R4# show mpls ldp discovery all

Local LDP Identifier:
    4.4.4.4:0
    Discovery Sources:
```

```
        Interfaces:
            Serial1/3 (ldp): xmit/recv
                LDP Id: 3.3.3.3:0
            Serial1/5 (ldp): xmit/recv
                LDP Id: 5.5.5.5:0


R4# show mpls label range

Downstream Generic label region: Min/Max label: 400/499


On R6:


R6# show mpls interface
Interface              IP           Tunnel    BGP Static Operational
Serial1/5              Yes (ldp)    No        No  No     Yes

R6# show mpls ldp neighbor

    Peer LDP Ident: 5.5.5.5:0; Local LDP Ident 6.6.6.6:0
        TCP connection: 5.5.5.5.646 - 6.6.6.6.33139
        State: Oper; Msgs sent/rcvd: 14/14; Downstream
        Up time: 00:01:51
        LDP discovery sources:
          Serial1/5, Src IP addr: 56.1.1.5
        Addresses bound to peer LDP Ident:
          45.1.1.5        56.1.1.5        5.5.5.5


R6# show mpls ldp neighbor | include Peer

    Peer LDP Ident: 5.5.5.5:0; Local LDP Ident 6.6.6.6:0

R6# show mpls ldp discovery all

  Local LDP Identifier:
    6.6.6.6:0
    Discovery Sources:
    Interfaces:
        Serial1/5 (ldp): xmit/recv
            LDP Id: 5.5.5.5:0
```

Task 4

Configure MP-BGP AS 100 between R2 and R6 because they represent the provider edge routers in this topology. You should configure their loopback0 interface as the source for the updates. Do not allow the BGP peers to share IPv4 routing information by default. The only BGP peering should be VPNv4.

```
On R2:


R2(config)# router bgp 100
R2(config-router)# no bgp default ipv4-unicast
R2(config-router)# neighbor 6.6.6.6 remote-as 100
R2(config-router)# neighbor 6.6.6.6 update-source lo0
R2(config-router)# address-family vpnv4 unicast
R2(config-router-af)# neighbor 6.6.6.6 activate


On R6:


R6(config)# router bgp 100
R6(config-router)# no bgp default ipv4-unicast
R6(config-router)# neighbor 2.2.2.2 remote-as 100
R6(config-router)# neighbor 2.2.2.2 update-source lo0
R6(config-router)# address-family vpnv4 unicast
R6(config-router-af)# neighbor 2.2.2.2 activate
```

You should see the following console message:

```
%BGP-5-ADJCHANGE: neighbor 2.2.2.2 Up
```

Let's verify the configuration:

```
On R2:


R2# show bgp vpnv4 unicast all summary | begin Neighbor


Neighbor       V    AS MsgRcvd MsgSent   TblVer  InQ OutQ Up/Down   State/PfxRcd
6.6.6.6        4   100       4       4        1    0    0 00:01:29            0
```

As you can see, the two commands show the same output:

```
On R6:


R6# show ip bgp vpnv4 all summary | begin Neighbor


Neighbor       V    AS MsgRcvd MsgSent   TblVer  InQ OutQ Up/Down   State/PfxRcd
2.2.2.2        4   100       7       8        1    0    0 00:04:23            0
```

Task 5

Configure VRFs, RDs, and RTs based on Table 15-6.

Table 15-6   *Configuration Parameters for Task 5*

Router	VRF Name	RD	Route Target
PE-2	CA	1:10	1:100
PE-6	CB	1:20	1:100

```
On R2:

R2(config)# vrf definition CA
R2(config-vrf)# rd 1:10
R2(config-vrf)# address-family ipv4
R2(config-vrf-af)# route-target both 1:100

On R6:

R6(config)# vrf definition CB
R6(config-vrf)# rd 1:20
R6(config-vrf)# address-family ipv4
R6(config-vrf-af)# route-target both 1:100

On R2:

R2(config)# router bgp 100
R2(config-router)# address-family vpnv4 unicast
R2(config-router-af)# neighbor 6.6.6.6 send-community extended

On R6:

R6(config)# router bgp 100
R6(config-router)# address-family vpnv4 unicast
R6(config-router-af)# neighbor 2.2.2.2 send-community extended
```

Let's verify the VRF configuration:

```
On R2:

R2# show vrf
  Name                     Default RD        Protocols   Interfaces
  CA                       1:10              ipv4
```

Let's assign the VRF to the interfaces:

```
On R2:


R2(config)# interface FastEthernet0/0
R2(config-if)# vrf forwarding CA


R2(config-if)# ip address 12.1.1.2 255.255.255.0
On R6:


R6(config)# interface FastEthernet0/0
R6(config-if)# vrf forwarding CB
R6(config-if)# ip address 67.1.1.6 255.255.255.0
```

Let's verify the configuration:

```
On R2:


R2# show vrf detail


VRF CA (VRF Id = 1); default RD 1:10; default VPNID <not set>
  Interfaces:
    Fa0/0
Address family ipv4 (Table ID = 1 (0x1)):
  Export VPN route-target communities
    RT:1:100
  Import VPN route-target communities
    RT:1:100
  No import route-map
  No export route-map
  VRF label distribution protocol: not configured
  VRF label allocation mode: per-prefix
Address family ipv6 not active


On R6:


R6# show ip vrf CB


Name                            Default RD          Interfaces
CB                              1:20                Fa0/0


R6# show ip vrf interfaces


Interface            IP-Address       VRF                                     Protocol
Fa0/0                67.1.1.6         CB                                      up
```

Let's verify the connectivity between the PEs and CEs:

```
On R2:


R2# ping vrf CA 12.1.1.1


Type escape sequence to abort.
Sending 5, 100-byte ICMP Echos to 12.1.1.1, timeout is 2 seconds:
.!!!!
Success rate is 80 percent (4/5), round-trip min/avg/max = 1/1/1 ms


On R6:


R6# ping vrf CB 67.1.1.7


Type escape sequence to abort.
Sending 5, 100-byte ICMP Echos to 67.1.1.7, timeout is 2 seconds:
.!!!!
Success rate is 80 percent (4/5), round-trip min/avg/max = 1/1/4 ms
```

Task 6

Configure the CEs (R1 and R7) with a VRF service that incorporates OSPF as the routing protocol. R1 should use an OSPF RID of 0.0.0.1, and R7 should use an OSPF RID of 0.0.0.7. R1 and R7 should have OSPF Area 0 configured on their Lo0 and F0/0 interfaces. The loopback interfaces of R1 and R7 should be advertised with their correct mask.

Let's start by configuring OSPF on R1 and PE-2:

```
On R1:


R1(config)# interface loopback0
R1(config-if)# ip ospf network point-to-point


R1(config)# router ospf 1
R1(config-router)# router-id 0.0.0.1
R1(config-router)# network 1.1.1.1 0.0.0.0 area 1
R1(config-router)# network 12.1.1.1 0.0.0.0 area 1


On PE-2:


R2(config)# router ospf 2 vrf CA
R2(config-router)# network 12.1.1.2 0.0.0.0 area 0
```

You should see the following console message:

```
%OSPF-5-ADJCHG: Process 2, Nbr 0.0.0.1 on FastEthernet0/0 from LOADING to FULL,
  Loading Done
```

Let's verify the configuration:

```
On PE-2:

R2# show ip route vrf CA ospf | begin Gate
Gateway of last resort is not set

     1.0.0.0/24 is subnetted, 1 subnets
O       1.1.1.0 [110/2] via 12.1.1.1, 00:01:43, FastEthernet0/0
```

Let's configure OSPF on PE-6 and R7:

```
On R7:

R7(config)# interface loopback0
R7(config-if)# ip ospf network point-to-point

R7(config)# router ospf 1
R7(config-router)# router-id 0.0.0.7
R7(config-router)# network 7.7.7.7 0.0.0.0 area 0
R7(config-router)# network 67.1.1.7 0.0.0.0 area 0

On PE-6:

R7(config)# router ospf 2 vrf CB
R7(config-router)# network 67.1.1.6 0.0.0.0 area 0
```

You should see the following console message:

```
%OSPF-5-ADJCHG: Process 6, Nbr 0.0.0.7 on FastEthernet0/0 from LOADING to FULL,
Loading Done
```

Let's verify the configuration:

```
On PE-6:

R6# show ip route vrf CB ospf | begin Gate
Gateway of last resort is not set

     7.0.0.0/24 is subnetted, 1 subnets
O       7.7.7.0 [110/2] via 67.1.1.7, 00:01:34, FastEthernet0/0
```

So far you can see that the CE and PE routers are successfully exchanging routes. The next step is to perform the redistribution. You should do this in one direction first and then perform redistribution in the opposite direction. Let's start with PE-2:

```
On PE-2:


R2(config)# router bgp 100
R2(config-router)# address-family ipv4 vrf CA
R2(config-router-af)# redistribute ospf 2
```

Let's verify the configuration:

```
R2# show bgp vpnv4 unicast all | begin Network


   Network          Next Hop          Metric LocPrf Weight Path
Route Distinguisher: 1:10 (default for vrf CA)
*> 1.1.1.0/24       12.1.1.1               2           32768 ?
*> 12.1.1.0/24      0.0.0.0                0           32768 ?
```

This means that PE-6 should also have these prefixes in its BGP table. Let's verify:

```
On PE-6:


R6# show bgp vpnv4 unicast all | begin Network


   Network          Next Hop          Metric LocPrf Weight Path
Route Distinguisher: 1:10
*>i1.1.1.0/24       2.2.2.2                2    100      0 ?
*>i12.1.1.0/24      2.2.2.2                0    100      0 ?
Route Distinguisher: 1:20 (default for vrf CB)
*>i1.1.1.0/24       2.2.2.2                2    100      0 ?
*>i12.1.1.0/24      2.2.2.2                0    100      0 ?
```

To be more specific, you can also use the following **show** command:

```
R6# show bgp vpnv4 unicast vrf CB | begin Network


   Network          Next Hop          Metric LocPrf Weight Path
Route Distinguisher: 1:20 (default for vrf CB)
*>i1.1.1.0/24       2.2.2.2                2    100      0 ?
*>i12.1.1.0/24      2.2.2.2                0    100      0 ?
```

Let's redistribute the VPNv4 routes into OSPF so that R7 can see them:

```
R6(config)# router ospf 2 vrf CB
R6(config-router)# redistribute bgp 100 subnets
```

R7 should have these routes in its routing table. Let's verify:

```
On R7:

R7# show ip route ospf | begin Gate
Gateway of last resort is not set

      1.0.0.0/24 is subnetted, 1 subnets
O IA     1.1.1.0 [110/3] via 67.1.1.6, 00:00:15, GigabitEthernet0/0
      12.0.0.0/24 is subnetted, 1 subnets
O IA     12.1.1.0 [110/2] via 67.1.1.6, 00:00:15, GigabitEthernet0/0
```

R7 can see the routes advertised by R1. Let's perform the redistribution in the opposite direction:

```
On PE-6:

R6(config)# router bgp 100
R6(config-router)# address-family ipv4 vrf CB
R6(config-router-af)# redistribute ospf 2
```

Let's verify the configuration:

```
R6# show bgp vpnv4 unicast vrf CB | begin Network

   Network          Next Hop         Metric LocPrf Weight Path
Route Distinguisher: 1:20 (default for vrf CB)
*>i1.1.1.0/24       2.2.2.2               2    100      0 ?
*>  7.7.7.0/24      67.1.1.7              2         32768 ?
*>i12.1.1.0/24      2.2.2.2               0    100      0 ?
*>  67.1.1.0/24     0.0.0.0               0         32768 ?
```

This means that PE-2 should have these prefixes in its BGP table:

```
On PE-2:


R2# show bgp vpnv4 unicast all | begin Network


   Network          Next Hop          Metric LocPrf Weight Path
Route Distinguisher: 1:10 (default for vrf CA)
*> 1.1.1.0/24       12.1.1.1              2           32768 ?
*>i7.7.7.0/24       6.6.6.6               2     100       0 ?
*> 12.1.1.0/24      0.0.0.0               0           32768 ?
*>i67.1.1.0/24      6.6.6.6               0     100       0 ?
Route Distinguisher: 1:20
*>i7.7.7.0/24       6.6.6.6               2     100       0 ?
*>i67.1.1.0/24      6.6.6.6               0     100       0 ?
```

The output of the preceding **show** command reveals that 7.7.7.0/24 and 67.1.1.0/24 are in the BGP table of PE-2. Let's redistribute BGP into OSPF so R1 can see the routes advertised by R7:

```
R2(config)# router ospf 2 vrf CA
R2(config-router)# redistribute bgp 100 subnets
```

Let's verify the configuration:

```
On R1:


R1# show ip route ospf | begin Gate
Gateway of last resort is not set

     7.0.0.0/24 is subnetted, 1 subnets
O IA    7.7.7.0 [110/3] via 12.1.1.2, 00:00:07, FastEthernet0/0
     67.0.0.0/24 is subnetted, 1 subnets
O IA    67.1.1.0 [110/2] via 12.1.1.2, 00:00:07, FastEthernet0/0
```

Sure enough, R1 can see the routes, but once again they are showing up as **E2**. Let's test this configuration:

```
R1# ping 7.7.7.7

Type escape sequence to abort.
Sending 5, 100-byte ICMP Echos to 7.7.7.7, timeout is 2 seconds:
!!!!!
Success rate is 100 percent (5/5), round-trip min/avg/max = 120/120/124 ms


R1# ping 7.7.7.7 source loopback0

Type escape sequence to abort.
Sending 5, 100-byte ICMP Echos to 7.7.7.7, timeout is 2 seconds:
Packet sent with a source address of 1.1.1.1
!!!!!
Success rate is 100 percent (5/5), round-trip min/avg/max = 120/121/124 ms
```

Task 7

Configure the F0/1 interface of R1 and the G0/1 interface of R7 in OSPF Area 0. This link should be used as a backup link to the MPLS cloud. The CE routers (R1 and R7) should see each other's routes as intra-area. You *must* use **sham-link** to accomplish this task. Use a VLAN ID of your choice.

```
On SW2:

SW2(config)# interface range FastEthernet0/1,FastEthernet0/7
SW2(config-if-range)# switchport mode access
SW2(config-if-range)# switchport access vlan 17
% Access VLAN does not exist. Creating vlan 17
SW2(config-if-range)# no shutdown


On R1:

R1(config)# interface FastEthernet0/1
R1(config-if)# ip address 17.1.1.1 255.255.255.0
R1(config-if)# no shutdown


On R7:

R7(config)# interface GigabitEthernet0/1
R7(config-if)# ip address 17.1.1.7 255.255.255.0
R7(config-if)# no shutdown
```

Let's verify the configuration:

```
R7# ping 17.1.1.1

Type escape sequence to abort.
Sending 5, 100-byte ICMP Echos to 17.1.1.1, timeout is 2 seconds:
.!!!!
Success rate is 80 percent (4/5), round-trip min/avg/max = 1/1/4 ms
```

Let's run OSPF Area 0 on this link:

```
On R1:

R1(config)# router ospf 1
R1(config-router)# network 17.1.1.1 0.0.0.0 area 0

On R7:

R7(config)# router ospf 1
R7(config-router)# network 17.1.1.7 0.0.0.0 area 0
```

You should see the following console message:

```
%OSPF-5-ADJCHG: Process 1, Nbr 0.0.0.7 on FastEthernet0/1 from LOADING to FULL,
Loading Done
```

Let's verify the configuration:

```
On R1:

R1# show ip route ospf | begin Gate
Gateway of last resort is not set

     7.0.0.0/24 is subnetted, 1 subnets
O       7.7.7.0 [110/2] via 17.1.1.7, 00:00:25, FastEthernet0/1
     67.0.0.0/24 is subnetted, 1 subnets
O       67.1.1.0 [110/2] via 17.1.1.7, 00:00:25, FastEthernet0/1
```

Note   The routes are reachable via the backup link. Manipulating the OSPF cost will not change the routing table because *intra*-area routes are always preferred over *inter*-area routes. One way to fix this problem is to configure a sham link.

A sham link was created to resolve this problem by extending OSPF Area 0 from one customer to the other, making Area 0 contiguous. Sham link is an OSPF intra-area link configured between the two PE routers. A sham link is included in the SPF calculation, just like any other link in OSPF.

Follow these steps to configure a sham link:

1. Configure a loopback interface on R2 and another one on R6, and then assign an IP address with a prefix length of 32.

2. Enable VRF forwarding on the loopback interfaces (in this case, **vrf forwarding CA** on R2 and **vrf forwarding CB** on R6).

3. Advertise the loopback interfaces configured in step 1 in BGP. These loopback interfaces should be advertised under **address-family ipv4 vrf CA** on R2 and **address-family ipv4 vrf CB** on R6.

4. Configure the sham link under OSPF. This should be done under **router ospf 2 vrf CA** on R2 and **router ospf 2 vrf CB** on R7.

Step 1.   Configure the loopback with a prefix length of 32:

```
On R2:

R2(config-router)# interface loopback26
R2(config-if)# ip address 26.1.1.2 255.255.255.255

On R6:

R6(config)# interface loopback62
R6(config-if)# ip address 26.1.1.6 255.255.255.255
```

Step 2.   Configure VRF forwarding on the loopback interface:

```
On R2:

R2(config)# interface loopback26
R2(config-if)# vrf forwarding CA
R2(config-if)# ip addr 24.1.1.2 255.255.255.255

On R6:

R6(config)# interface loopback62
R6(config-if)# vrf forwarding CB
R6(config-if)# ip address 24.1.1.4 255.255.255.255
```

Step 3.   Advertise the IP address of the loopback interfaces in MP-BGP:

```
On R2:


R2(config)# router bgp 100
R2(config-router)# address-family ipv4 vrf CA
R2(config-router-af)# network 26.1.1.2 mask 255.255.255.255


On R6:


R6(config-if)# router bgp 100
R6(config-router)# address-family ipv4 vrf CB
R6(config-router-af)# network 26.1.1.6 mask 255.255.255.255
```

Step 4.   Configure the sham link:

```
On R2:


R2(config)# router ospf 2 vrf CA
R2(config-router)# area 0 Sham-link 26.1.1.2 26.1.1.6 cost 1


On R6:


R6(config)# router ospf 2 vrf CB
R6(config-router)# area 0 Sham-link 26.1.1.6 26.1.1.2 cost 1
```

You should see the following console message:

```
%OSPF-5-ADJCHG: Process 2, Nbr 12.1.1.2 on OSPF_SL0 from LOADING to FULL,
Loading Done
```

Let's verify the configuration:

```
On R2:


R2# show ip ospf sham-links


Sham Link OSPF_SL0 to address 26.1.1.6 is up
Area 0 source address 26.1.1.2
  Run as demand circuit
  DoNotAge LSA allowed. Cost of using 1 State POINT_TO_POINT,
  Timer intervals configured, Hello 10, Dead 40, Wait 40,
    Hello due in 00:00:08
    Adjacency State FULL (Hello suppressed)
```

```
Index 2/2, retransmission queue length 0, number of retransmission 0
First 0x0(0)/0x0(0) Next 0x0(0)/0x0(0)
Last retransmission scan length is 0, maximum is 0
Last retransmission scan time is 0 msec, maximum is 0 msec
```

Area 0 is the source for the sham link. This will commonly match the area that has been configured between the PE and the CE. This connection is considered up and operational at this time.

As you can see, this connection will run as a point-to-point demand circuit with a cost of 1. The remaining timers reflect normal OSPF peering.

```
On R2:


R2# show ip ospf neighbor

Neighbor ID     Pri   State          Dead Time   Address         Interface
0.0.0.3          0    FULL/  -       00:00:31    23.1.1.3        Serial1/3
67.1.1.6         0    FULL/  -          -        26.1.1.6        OSPF_SL0
0.0.0.1          1    FULL/DR        00:00:34    12.1.1.1        FastEthernet0/0


On R1:


R1# show ip route ospf | begin Gate
Gateway of last resort is not set

     7.0.0.0/24 is subnetted, 1 subnets
O       7.7.7.0 [110/2] via 17.1.1.7, 00:32:07, FastEthernet0/1
     26.0.0.0/32 is subnetted, 2 subnets
O E2    26.1.1.2 [110/1] via 12.1.1.2, 00:08:57, FastEthernet0/0
O E2    26.1.1.6 [110/1] via 12.1.1.2, 00:07:44, FastEthernet0/0
     67.0.0.0/24 is subnetted, 1 subnets
O       67.1.1.0 [110/2] via 17.1.1.7, 00:32:07, FastEthernet0/1
```

Note   The routers still prefer the backup link because of the OSPF cost. You can see that the routes are no longer inter-area routes and they have preserved their true route type.

The routers see the routes through the provider and the backup link as intra-area routes; therefore, the cost can be manipulated such that the routers will take the provider as their primary, and the backup link will be used only if the primary link is down.

Let's see the actual cost through the provider by shutting down the backup link:

```
On R1:


R1(config)# interface FastEthernet0/1
R1(config-if)# shutdown
```

The following **show** command reveals the OSPF cost through the provider:

```
R1# show ip route ospf | begin Gate
Gateway of last resort is not set


     7.0.0.0/24 is subnetted, 1 subnets
O       7.7.7.0 [110/4] via 12.1.1.2, 00:00:18, FastEthernet0/0
     17.0.0.0/24 is subnetted, 1 subnets
O       17.1.1.0 [110/8] via 12.1.1.2, 00:00:18, FastEthernet0/0
     26.0.0.0/32 is subnetted, 2 subnets
O E2    26.1.1.2 [110/1] via 12.1.1.2, 00:06:14, FastEthernet0/0
O E2    26.1.1.6 [110/1] via 12.1.1.2, 00:06:14, FastEthernet0/0
     67.0.0.0/24 is subnetted, 1 subnets
O       67.1.1.0 [110/3] via 12.1.1.2, 00:00:18, FastEthernet0/0
```

In order to force the provider link to be used as the primary and the f0/1 link as the backup, a cost of 5 is assigned to the backup link:

```
On R1:


R1(config)# interface FastEthernet0/0
R1(config-if)# no shutdown


R1(config)# interface FastEthernet0/1
R1(config-if)# ip ospf cost 5
R1(config-if)# no shutdown
```

Let's verify the configuration:

```
On R1:


R1# show ip route ospf | begin Gate
Gateway of last resort is not set


      7.0.0.0/24 is subnetted, 1 subnets
O        7.7.7.0 [110/4] via 12.1.1.2, 00:01:12, FastEthernet0/0
      26.0.0.0/32 is subnetted, 2 subnets
O E2    26.1.1.2 [110/1] via 12.1.1.2, 00:01:12, FastEthernet0/0
O E2    26.1.1.6 [110/1] via 12.1.1.2, 00:01:12, FastEthernet0/0
      67.0.0.0/24 is subnetted, 1 subnets
O        67.1.1.0 [110/3] via 12.1.1.2, 00:01:12, FastEthernet0/0


On R7:


R7(config)# interface GigabitEthernet0/1
R7(config-if)# ip ospf cost 5


R7# show ip route ospf | begin Gate
Gateway of last resort is not set


      1.0.0.0/24 is subnetted, 1 subnets
O        1.1.1.0 [110/4] via 67.1.1.6, 00:00:14, GigabitEthernet0/0
      12.0.0.0/24 is subnetted, 1 subnets
O        12.1.1.0 [110/3] via 67.1.1.6, 00:00:14, GigabitEthernet0/0
      26.0.0.0/32 is subnetted, 2 subnets
O E2    26.1.1.2 [110/1] via 67.1.1.6, 00:19:06, GigabitEthernet0/0
O E2    26.1.1.6 [110/1] via 67.1.1.6, 00:17:53, GigabitEthernet0/0
```

Erase the startup configuration of the routers and reload them before proceeding to the next lab.

Lab 15-6: BGP Routing in a VPN

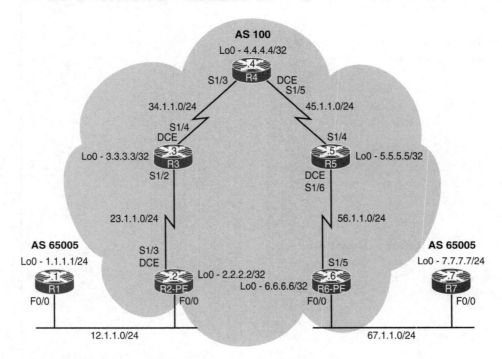

Figure 15-6   *Configuring RIPv2 Routing in a VPN*

Figure 15-6 illustrates the topology that will be used in the following tasks.

Task 1 through Task 5 of Lab 15-2 are identical to the first five tasks in this lab. Therefore, repeat Tasks 1 through 5 before proceeding to the next task.

Task 6

Configure BGP as the MPLS routing context between the CEs (R1 and R7) and their respective PEs (R2 and R6). The customer AS of 65005 should be assigned to both customer sites, whereas the provider should use AS 100.

Let's configure the CE routers:

```
On R1:

R1(config)# router bgp 65005
R1(config-router)# no auto-summary
R1(config-router)# neighbor 12.1.1.2 remote 100
R1(config-router)# network 1.1.1.0 mask 255.255.255.0
```

```
On R7:

R7(config)# router bgp 65005
R7(config-router)# no auto-summary
R7(config-router)# neighbor 67.1.1.6 remote 100
R7(config-router)# network 7.7.7.0 mask 255.255.255.0
```

Let's configure the PE routers to establish a peer session with the CE routers:

Note   No redistribution is necessary for MP-BGP. The peering is identical to that of normal BGP, except it is in the VPN instead. However, normal BGP rules apply within the VPN.

```
On R2:

R2(config)# router bgp 100
R2(config-router)# address-family ipv4 vrf CA
R2(config-router-af)# neighbor 12.1.1.1 remote 65005
```

You should see the following console messages before moving on:

```
%BGP-5-ADJCHANGE: neighbor 12.1.1.1 vpn vrf CA Up
```

Let's verify the configuration:

```
R2# show bgp vpnv4 unicast vrf CA | begin Network

   Network          Next Hop            Metric LocPrf Weight Path
Route Distinguisher: 1:10 (default for vrf CA)
*> 1.1.1.0/24       12.1.1.1                 0          0 65005 i

On R6:

R6(config)# router bgp 100
R6(config-router)# address-family ipv4 vrf CB
R6(config-router-af)# neighbor 67.1.1.7 remote 65005
```

You should see the following console messages before moving on:

```
%BGP-5-ADJCHANGE: neighbor 67.1.1.7 vpn vrf CB Up
```

Let's verify the configuration:

```
On R6:


R6# show bgp vpnv4 unicast vrf CB | begin Network


   Network          Next Hop          Metric LocPrf Weight Path
Route Distinguisher: 1:20 (default for vrf CB)
*>i1.1.1.0/24       2.2.2.2                0    100      0 65005 i
*> 7.7.7.0/24       67.1.1.7               0             0 65005 i
```

It is not enough to verify the configuration on R6; we also need to verify on both R1 and R7.

```
On R1:


R1# show ip bgp | begin Net


   Network          Next Hop          Metric LocPrf Weight Path
*> 1.1.1.0/24       0.0.0.0                0         32768 i

On R7:


R7# show ip bgp | begin Network


    Network         Next Hop          Metric LocPrf Weight Path
*>  7.7.7.0/24      0.0.0.0                0         32768 i
```

Although the routes were verified to have been received via MP-BGP and redistribution is not a problem that can exist here, the routes are not learned by the CE routers. This is a result of the normal BGP process of loop prevention; the AS numbers of both customers match. There are two ways to resolve this matter:

1. Configuring the CE solution using **allowas-in**.

2. Configuring the PE solution using **as-override**.

Let's configure the CE solution and verify:

```
On R1:


R1(config)# router bgp 65005
R1(config-router)# neighbor 12.1.1.2 allowas-in
```

This feature can be used as an alternative if the service provider controls the CE router(s).

When network 7.7.7.0/24 is advertised by R7, the AS number is prepended (65005), which is used as a loop-prevention mechanism in BGP. The prefix is received by the provider and then advertised to R1, which is also in AS 65005 (same as R7's AS). When R1 receives the route, it sees its own AS number in the **AS-Path** attribute and it discards the route as a loop-avoidance mechanism. The **allowas-in** command allows the local router to receive routes even if the local router sees its own AS in the **AS-Path** attribute.

Let's verify the configuration:

```
On R1:


R1# show ip bgp | begin Network


   Network          Next Hop          Metric LocPrf Weight Path
*> 1.1.1.0/24       0.0.0.0                0        32768 i
*> 7.7.7.0/24       12.1.1.2                          0 100 65005 i
```

The same feature must be configured on R7:

```
On R7:


R7(config)# router bgp 65005
R7(config-router)# neighbor 67.1.1.6 allowas-in
```

Let's verify the configuration:

```
On R7:


R7# show ip bgp | begin Network


     Network          Next Hop          Metric LocPrf Weight Path
 *>  1.1.1.0/24       67.1.1.6                          0 100 65005 i
 *>  7.7.7.0/24       0.0.0.0                0        32768 i
```

Let's test the configuration:

```
R7# ping 1.1.1.1

Type escape sequence to abort.
Sending 5, 100-byte ICMP Echos to 1.1.1.1, timeout is 2 seconds:
.....
Success rate is 0 percent (0/5)
```

As you can see, the ping failed—but why?

The ping was sourced from the f0/0 interface of R7, and because the IP address of this interface is not advertised to R1, the return traffic fails.

To test this condition, **debug ip icmp** is enabled on R1 and a ping is generated by R7 with a **repeat** count of 2:

```
On R1:


R1# debug ip icmp
ICMP packet debugging is on


On R7:


R7# ping 1.1.1.1 repeat 2


Type escape sequence to abort.
Sending 2, 100-byte ICMP Echos to 1.1.1.1, timeout is 2 seconds:
..
Success rate is 0 percent (0/2)
```

Let's verify the console messages on R1:

```
On R1:


ICMP: echo reply sent, src 1.1.1.1, dst 67.1.1.7, topology BASE, dscp 0 topoid 0


ICMP: echo reply sent, src 1.1.1.1, dst 67.1.1.7, topology BASE, dscp 0 topoid 0
```

This proves that R1 is receiving the ICMP-Echo messages, but it does not have a route back to 67.1.1.7 (R7's f0/0 interface's IP address). Let's fix this problem:

```
On R2:


R2(config)# router bgp 100
R2(config-router)# address-family ipv4 vrf CA
R2(config-router-af)# redistribute connected


On R7:


R6(config)# router bgp 100
R6(config-router)# address-family ipv4 vrf CB
R6(config-router-af)# redistribute connected
```

Let's verify the configuration:

```
On R7:


R7# ping 1.1.1.1


Type escape sequence to abort.

Sending 5, 100-byte ICMP Echos to 1.1.1.1, timeout is 2 seconds:

!!!!!

Success rate is 100 percent (5/5), round-trip min/avg/max = 120/122/124 ms
```

Now let's configure the PE routers to resolve the problem. Before the PE solution is used, let's remove the **neighbor allowas-in** command from the CE routers:

```
On R1:


R1(config)# router bgp 65005

R1(config-router)# no neighbor 12.1.1.2 allowas-in


On R7:


R7(config)# router bgp 65005

R7(config-router)# no neighbor 67.1.1.6 allowas-in
```

Let's configure the PE solution:

```
On R2:


R2(config)# router bgp 100

R2(config-router)# address-family ipv4 vrf CA

R2(config-router-af)# neighbor 12.1.1.1 as-override


On PE-6:


R6(config)# router bgp 100

R6(config-router)# address-family ipv4 vrf CB

R6(config-router-af)# neighbor 67.1.1.7 as-override
```

Let's verify the configuration:

```
On R1:


R1# show ip bgp | begin Network

   Network          Next Hop          Metric LocPrf Weight Path
*> 1.1.1.0/24       0.0.0.0                0         32768 i
*> 7.7.7.0/24       12.1.1.2                            0 100 100 i
r  12.1.1.0/24      12.1.1.2               0             0 100 ?
*> 67.1.1.0/24      12.1.1.2                             0 100 ?
```

Note   The AS number of the provider is prepended.

```
On R7:


R5# show ip bgp | begin Network

    Network          Next Hop          Metric LocPrf Weight Path
*>  1.1.1.0/24       67.1.1.6                            0 100 100 i
*>  7.7.7.0/24       0.0.0.0                0      32768 i
*>  12.1.1.0/24      67.1.1.6                            0 100 ?
r>  67.1.1.0/24      67.1.1.6               0            0 100 ?
```

Unlike with the previous solution, where the AS number was ignored, using this feature the provider replaces the customer's AS number with its own. The customers must allow prepended AS numbers; otherwise, they will not receive the BGP routes, because from the customers' perspective, it looks like the provider has prepended its own AS number an additional time.

Erase the startup configuration of the routers and reload them before proceeding to the next lab.

Index

Numbers

A

D

I

M

S

W-X-Y-Z